McGraw-Hill's

NATIONAL ELECTRICAL CODE® HANDBOOK,

Sixteenth Edition

Based on the Current 1978 National Electrical Code®

J. F. McPartland, Editor
Editorial Director, McGraw-Hill Electrical Construction Communications Center, New York, New York

J. F. McPartland III, Assistant Editor
Northeast Manager, Emerson Electric Company, Industrial Controls Division, New York, New York

"NATIONAL ELECTRICAL CODE® is a registered trademark of National Fire Protection Association, Inc., Boston, Massachusetts, for a triennial electrical copyrighted publication of such corporation. The term NATIONAL ELECTRICAL CODE as used herein means the publication constituting the NATIONAL ELECTRICAL CODE and is used with permission of National Fire Protection Association, Inc. This book does not emanate from and is not sponsored nor authorized by the National Fire Protection Association, Inc."

McGRAW-HILL BOOK COMPANY
New York   St. Louis   San Francisco   Auckland   Bogotá
Düsseldorf   Johannesburg   Singapore   Madrid   Mexico   Montreal
New Delhi   Panama   Paris   São Paulo
London   Sydney   Tokyo   Toronto

1234567890   MUBP   7865432109

Although every effort has been made to make the explanation
of the **Code** accurate, neither the Publisher nor the Author
assumes any liability for damages that may result from the
use of the Handbook.

*The editors for this book were Harold B. Crawford and Lester Strong
and the production supervisor was Teresa Leaden. It was set in Baskerville
by University Graphics. It was printed by The Murray Printing Company
and bound by The Book Press.*

Contents

Article   *Page*

Chapter 3 _____

Chapter 4 _____

Preface

This is a reference book of commentary, discussion, and analysis on the most commonly encountered rules of the 1978 **National Electrical Code**. Designed to be used in conjunction with the 1978 **NE Code** book published by the National Fire Protection Association, this handbook presents thousands of illustrations—diagrams and photos—to supplement the detailed text in explaining and clarifying **NEC** regulations. Description of the background and rationale of specific **Code** rules is aimed at affording a broader, deeper, and readily developed understanding of the meaning and application of those rules. The style of presentation is conversational and intended to facilitate a quick, practical grasp of the ideas and concepts that are couched in the necessarily terse, stiff, quasilegal language of the **NEC** document itself.

This handbook follows the order of "articles" as presented in the **NE Code** book, starting with "Article 90" and proceeding through "Article 820" and "Chapter 9—Tables and Examples." The **Code** rules are referenced by "section" numbers (e.g., "250-45.   Equipment Connected by Cord and Plug"). This format assures quick and easy correlation between **NEC** sections and the discussions and explanations of the rules involved. This companion reference to the **NEC** book expands on the rules and presents common interpretations that have been put on the many difficult and controversial **Code** requirements. A user of this handbook should refer to the **NEC** book for the precise wording of a rule and then refer to the corresponding section number in this handbook for a practical evaluation of the details.

Because many **NEC** rules do not present difficulty in understanding or interpretation, not all sections are referenced. But the vast majority of sections are covered, especially all sections that have proved troublesome or controversial. And particular emphasis is given to changes and additions that have been made in **Code** rules over recent editions of the **NEC**. Although this new edition of the handbook does not contain the complete wording of the **NE Code** book, it does contain much greater analysis and interpretation than any other version of the handbook has ever contained, and it is more thoroughly illustrated than any previous edition.

Today, the universal importance of the **NE Code** has been established by the federal government (OSHA and other safety-related departments), by state and local inspection agencies, and by all kinds of private companies and organizations. To meet the great need for information on the **NEC**, the McGraw-Hill Book Company has been publishing a handbook on the **National Electrical Code** since 1932. Originally developed by Arthur L. Abbott in that year, the handbook has been carried on in successive editions for each revision of the **National Electrical Code**. This edition of the Handbook of the **National Electrical Code** replaces the edition published in 1975 by the McGraw-Hill Book Company.

One final point—words such as "workmanlike" are taken directly from the **Code** and are intended in a purely generic sense. Their use is in no way meant to deny the role women already play in the electrical industries or their importance to the field.

Joseph F. McPartland

Introduction to the National Electrical Code®

This *Handbook of the National Electrical Code* is based on the 1978 Edition of the **National Electrical Code** as developed by the National Electrical Code Committee of the American National Standards Institute (ANSI), sponsored by the National Fire Protection Association (NFPA). The **National Electrical Code** is identified by the designation NFPA No. 70-1978. The NFPA adopted this 1978 **Code** at the NFPA Annual Meeting held in Washington, D.C., May 16–19, 1977.

The **National Electrical Code**, as its name implies, is a nationally accepted guide to the safe installation of electrical wiring and equipment. The committee sponsoring its development includes all parties of interest having technical competence in the field, working together with the sole objective of safeguarding the public in its utilization of electricity. The procedures under which the **Code** is prepared provide for the orderly introduction of new developments and improvements in the art, with particular emphasis on safety from the standpoint of its end use. The rules of procedure under which the **National Electrical Code** Committee operates are published in each official edition of the **Code** and in separate pamphlet form so that all concerned may have full information and free access to the operating procedures of the sponsoring committee. The **Code** has been a big factor in the growth and wide acceptance of the use of electrical energy for light and power and for heat, radio, television, signaling, and other purposes from the date of its first appearance (1897) to the present.

The **National Electrical Code** is primarily designed for use by trained electrical people and is necessarily terse in its wording.

The sponsoring National Electrical Code Committee is composed of a Correlating Committee and 23 Code-Making Panels, each responsible for one or more Articles in the **Code**. Each Panel is composed of experienced men representing balanced interests of all segments of the industry and the public concerned with the subject matter. The present Chairman of the National Electrical Code Committee is Richard L. Lloyd, Assistant to the President, Codes and Standards of the Underwriters' Laboratories, Inc. Wilford Summers has been the Secretary of the National Electrical Code Committee and Electrical Field Specialist of the NFPA since April 1974. The internal operations of the sponsoring committee are guided by a *Manual of Procedure for Code-Making Panels*. This Manual is published in pamphlet form, and copies are available from the NFPA, 470 Atlantic Avenue, Boston, Massachusetts 02210.

The National Fire Protection Association also has organized an Electrical Section to provide the opportunity for NFPA members interested in electrical safety to become better informed and to contribute to the development of NFPA electrical standards. This new Handbook reflects the fact that the **National Electrical Code** was revised for the 1978 edition, requiring an updating of the previous Handbook which was based on the 1975 Edition of the **Code**. The established schedule of the National Electrical Code Committee contemplates a new edition of the **National Electrical Code** every three years. Provision is made under the rules of procedure for handling urgent emergency matters through a Tentative Interim Amendment Procedure. The Committee also has established rules for rendering Official Interpretations. Two general forms of findings for such Interpretations are recognized: (1) those making an interpretation of literal text and (2) those making an interpretation of the intent of the **National Electrical Code** when a particular rule was adopted. All Tentative Interim Amendments and Official Interpretations are published by the NFPA as they are issued, and notices are sent to all interested trade papers in the electrical industry.

The **National Electrical Code** is purely advisory as far as the National Fire Protection Association is concerned but is very widely used as the basis of law and for legal regulatory purposes. The **Code** is administered by various local inspection agencies, whose decisions govern the actual application of the **National Electrical Code** to individual installations. Local inspectors are largely members of the International Association of Electrical Inspectors, 802 Busse Highway, Park Ridge, Illinois 60068. This organization, the National Electrical Manufacturers Association, the National Electrical Contractors Association, the Edison Electric Institute, the Underwriters' Laboratories, Inc., the International Brotherhood of Electrical Workers, governmental groups, and independent experts all contribute to the development and application of the **National Electrical Code**.

Brief History of the
National Electrical Code®

The **National Electrical Code** was originally drawn in 1897 as a result of the united efforts of various insurance, electrical, architectural, and allied interests. The original **Code** was prepared by the National Conference on Standard Electrical Rules, composed of delegates from various interested national associations. Prior to this, acting on an 1881 resolution of the National Association of Fire Engineers' meeting in Richmond, Virginia, a basis for the first **Code** was suggested to cover such items as identification of the white wire, the use of single disconnect devices, and the use of insulated conduit.

In 1911, the National Conference of Standard Electrical Rules was disbanded, and since that year, the National Fire Protection Association (NFPA) has acted as sponsor of the **National Electrical Code**. Beginning with the 1920 edition, the **National Electrical Code** has been under the further auspices of the American National Standards Institute (and its predecessor organizations, United States of America Standards Institute, and the American Standards Association), with the NFPA continuing in its role as Administrative Sponsor. Since that date, the Committee has been identified as "ANSI Standards Committee C1" (formerly "USAS C1" or "ASA C1").

Major milestones in the continued updating of successive issues of the **National Electrical Code** since 1911 appeared in 1923, when the **Code** was rearranged and rewritten; in 1937, when it was editorially revised so that all the general rules would appear in the first chapters followed by supplementary rules in the following chapters; and in 1959, when it was editorially revised to incorporate a new numbering system under which each Section of each Article is identified by the Article Number preceding the Section Number.

For many years the **National Electrical Code** was published by the National Board of Fire Underwriters (now American Insurance Association), and this public service of the National Board helped immensely in bringing about the wide public acceptance which the **Code** now enjoys. It is recognized as the most widely adopted **Code** of standard practices in the U.S.A. The National Fire Protection Association first printed the document in pamphlet form in 1951 and has, since that year, supplied the **Code** for distribution to the public through its own office and through the American National Standards Institute. The **National Electrical Code** also appears in Volume 6 of the National Fire Codes, issued annually by the National Fire Protection Association.

About the 1978 NE Code®

The 1978 edition of the **National Electrical Code** contains detailed and comprehensive revisions in a very wide range of specific **NE Code** regulations. The new edition contains completely new articles on equipment never covered by the **Code** before and has dozens of radically new regulations and changes in old regulations covering the widest range of everyday electrical details involved in the basic wiring of all buildings.

Electrical people everywhere have a vital, immediate, and awesome task before them. The **NE Code** is today more important than it has ever been. The Occupational Safety and Health Administration (OSHA) has made it a mandatory federal standard, binding under force of legal sanctions. OSHA's application of the **NE Code** to all new electrical construction and to modernization and expansion of existing systems has been deeply and widely felt throughout the nation over recent years. This new **Code** will deepen and intensify the government's insistence on maximum safety and effectiveness in electrical work.

At the state and local levels, electrical inspection agencies everywhere are tightening their control over electrical work and are exercising stricter enforcement. "Listing" and "labeling" of products by nationally recognized testing labs is a must with inspectors and engineers. And now the **NE Code** has many rules that virtually insist on the use of certified equipment and materials.

A runaway rate of growth in the use of electric energy for light, power, heat, control, signaling, and communications is still another factor that is promoting greater attention to the **Code**. As the electrical percentage of the construction dollar moves ever upward, the visibility and universality of electrical usage demand closer, more penetrating concern for safety in electrical work. In today's sealed buildings, with entire interior environments totally dependent on effective electrical usage, the critical role of electrical systems demands not only concern for eliminating fire and shock hazards, but also concern for continuity and reliability of electrical usage as essential to safety of people and property.

Another factor that emphasizes the importance of the **NE Code** is the highly competitive nature of construction work. With a booming electrical market and the universal concern for energy conservation, forces in the industry are promoting maximum economy in such a way as to jeopardize full attention to safety. The **NE Code** is an effective, commendable barrier against any compromises with basic electrical safety.

In this handbook, the discussion delves into the letter and intent of **Code** rules. Read and study the material carefully. Talk it over with your associates; engage in as much discussion as possible. In particular, check out any questions or problems with your local inspection authorities. It is true that only time and discussion provide final answers on how some of the rules are to be interpreted. But now is the time to start. Do not delay. Use this handbook to begin a regular, continuous, and enthusiastic program of updating yourself on this big new **Code**.

This handbook's illustrated analysis of the 1978 **NE Code** is most effectively used by having your copy of the new **Code** book at hand and referring to each section as it is discussed. The commentary given here is intended to supplement and clarify the actual wording of the **Code** rules as given in the **Code** book itself.

ARTICLE 90. INTRODUCTION

90-1. Purpose. (a). This section clearly and simply describes the function of the **NE Code** in relation to electrical design and installation work. But it is important to understand that the **NE Code** is intended only to assure that electrical work is done safely—that is, to provide a system that is "essentially free from hazard."

The **NE Code** is recognized as a legal criterion of safe electrical design and installation. It is used in court litigation and by insurance companies as a basis for insuring buildings. Because the **Code** is such an important instrument of safe design, it must be thoroughly understood by all electrical designers. They must be familiar with all sections of the **Code** and should know the accepted interpretations which have been placed on many specific rulings of the **Code**. They should keep abreast of official interpretations which are issued by the **NE Code** committee. They should know the intent of **Code** requirements—i.e., the spirit as well as the letter of each provision. They should keep informed on interim amendments to the **Code**. And, most important, they should keep this **Code** handbook handy and study it often.

(b). As stated, compliance with the provisions of the **National Electrical Code** can effectively minimize fire and accident hazards in any electrical design. The **Code** (throughout this manual, the word "**Code**" refers to the **National Electrical Code**) sets forth requirements, recommendations, and suggestions and constitutes a minimum standard for the framework of electrical design. As stated in its own introduction, the **Code** is concerned with the "practical safeguarding of persons and property from hazards arising from the use of electricity" for light, heat, power, radio, signaling, and other purposes.

Although the **Code** assures minimum safety provisions, actual design work must constantly consider safety as required by special types or conditions of electrical application. For example, effective provision of automatic protective devices and selection of control equipment for particular applications involve engineering skill of the designer, above routine adherence to **Code** requirements. Then, too, designers must know the physical characteristics—application advantages and limitations—of the many materials they use for enclosing, supporting, insulating, isolating, and, in general, protecting electrical equipment. The task of safe application based on skill and experience is particularly important in hazardous locations. Safety is not automatically made a characteristic of a system by simply observing codes. Safety must be designed into a system.

(c). The **National Electrical Code** contains provisions considered necessary for safety, but does not provide information of a design nature, other than for safety purposes, and should not be used to ensure adequate or efficient forms of installation. These features should be obtained from design manuals or through the services of a competent consulting engineer or electrical contractor.

90-2. Scope. (a). The **Code** applies to all electrical work—indoors and outdoors—other than that work excluded by the rules of part **(b)** in this section.

(b). The rules of the **Code** do not apply to the electrical work described in **(1)** through **(5).** The most common controversy that arises concerns exclusion of electrical work done by electric utilities (power companies).

It should be carefully noted that not all electrical systems and equipment belonging to utilities are exempted from **Code** compliance. Those circuits and equipment that are related to "generation, control, transformation, transmission, and distribution of electric energy" are considered as being safe because of the competence of the utility engineers and electricians who design and install such work. **Code** rules do not apply to such circuits and equipment—nor to any "communication" "metering" installations of an electric utility. But, any conventional electrical systems for power, lighting, heating, and other applications within buildings or on structures belonging to utilities *must* comply with **Code** rules because such systems are not "used exclusively by utilities" for the supply of electric power to the utilities' customers.

An example of the kind of utility-owned electrical circuits and equipment *covered* by **Code** rules would be the electrical installations in, say, an office building of the utility or even an office area in a generating station. But in the generating station, **Code** rules would not apply to the circuits and equipment used for generation and supply of electric power to the utility's transmission and distribution system.

90-4. Enforcement.   This is one of the most basic and most important of **Code** rules because it establishes the necessary conditions for use of the **Code**.

Fig. 90-1. CIRCUITS AND EQUIPMENT of any utility company are exempt from the rules of the **NEC** when the particular installation is part of the utility's system for transmitting and distributing power to the utility's customers—*provided* that such an installation is accessible only to the utility's personnel and access is denied to others. Outdoor, fenced-in utility-controlled substations, transformer mat installations, utility pad-mount enclosures, and equipment isolated by elevation are typical utility areas to which the **NEC** does not apply. The same is also true of indoor, locked transformer vaults or electric rooms. (Sec. 90-2.)

The **NE Code** stipulates that, when questions arise about the meaning or intent of any **Code** rule as it applies to a particular electrical installation, the electrical inspector having jurisdiction over the installation is the only one authorized by the **NE Code** to make interpretations of the rules. The wording of Sec. 90-4 reserves that power to the local inspection authority along with the authority to approve equipment and materials and to grant the special permission for methods and techniques that might be considered alternatives to those **Code** rules that specifically mention such "special permission" [for instance, Sec. 250-57(c)].

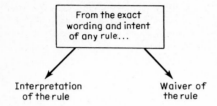

Fig. 90-2. INSPECTOR'S AUTHORITY may be exercised either by enforcement of that individual's interpretation of a code rule or by waiver of the code rule when the inspector is satisfied that a specific non-code-conforming method or technique satisfies the safety intent of the Code. (Sec. 90-4.)

Up until the 1975 **NE Code**, Sec. 90-4 aimed only at giving the inspector the right to "interpret" **Code** rules. But the 1975 **NE Code**, for the first time, specifically gave the inspector the authority to "waive" specific requirements—that is, to disregard the wording and meaning of individual **Code** rules. However, use of this authority by the inspector was allowed (1) only in "industrial establishments and research and testing facilities" and (2) only where the inspector is satisfied that the safety objectives sought by the **Code** rule are achieved by the particular design and/or installation techniques that are used as alternatives to the specifics of the **Code** rule. The 1975 **NE Code** referred to the necessity for "establishing and maintaining effective safety and maintenance procedures" whenever a rule was "waived" or whenever "alternative methods" were accepted.

Now the 1978 **NE Code** permits the electrical inspector to "waive specific requirements" or "permit alternate methods" in *any* type of electrical installation. The new wording of the last sentence of Sec. 90-4 no longer limits waiver of **Code** rules to industrial establishments and research and testing facilities. In residential, commercial, and institutional electrical systems—as well as in industrial—inspectors may now accept design and/or installation methods that do not conform to a specific **Code** rule, provided they are satisfied that the safety objectives of the **Code** rule are achieved.

It should be noted that permission for any such variations from normal **NE Code** practice is granted only to the authority having jurisdiction in enforcing the **Code**. This permission is given to the electrical inspectors to permit them to recognize practices at variance with the **Code**, provided such practices are carefully controlled and under rigorously maintained conditions. In addition, such practices must be based on sound engineering principles and techniques which otherwise assure the safety of personnel and freedom from shock and fire hazard that the NE Code itself seeks to provide.

This recognition of practices at variance with the Code is provided only for special conditions and must not be interpreted as a general permission to engage in non-Code methods, techniques, or design procedures. In fact, it is likely that inspectors will exercise this authority only with reluctance and then with great care, because of the great responsibility this places on the inspector.

90-5. Formal Interpretations. Official interpretations of the National Electrical Code are based on specific sections of specific editions of the Code. In most cases, such official interpretations apply to the stated conditions on given installations. Accordingly, they would not necessarily apply to other situations that vary slightly from the statement on which the official interpretation was issued.

As official interpretations of each edition of the Code are issued, they are published in the NFPA Fire News and press releases are sent to interested trade papers.

All official interpretations issued on a specific Code edition are reviewed by the appropriate Code-making panel during the period when the specific Code edition is being revised. In reviewing an interpretation, a Code panel may agree with the interpretation findings and clarify the Code text to avoid further misunderstanding of intent, or the panel may reject the findings of the interpretation and alter the Code text to clarify the Code panel's intent. On the other hand, the Code panel may not recommend any change in the Code text because of the special conditions described in the official interpretation. For these reasons, the NFPA does not catalog official interpretations issued on previous editions of the Code. And in reviewing all previous interpretations, it can be stated that practically none of them would apply to the present edition of the Code because of revised Code wording that materially changes the intent.

If anyone feels that a past interpretation applies to the present text, they should submit it in the form of a proposed Code change when revisions for the next edition of the Code are being considered.

With the wide adoption of the Code throughout the country, the authority having jurisdiction has the prime responsibility of interpreting Code rules in its area and disagreements on the intent of particular Code rules in its area; and disagreements on the intent of particular Code rules should be resolved at the local level if at all possible. There is no guarantee that the authority having jurisdiction will accept the findings of an official interpretation.

90-6. Examination of Equipment for Safety. It is not the intent of the National Electrical Code to include the detailed requirements for internal wiring of electrical equipment. Such information is usually contained in individual standards for the equipment concerned.

The last sentence does not intend to take away the authority of the local inspector to examine and approve equipment, but rather to indicate that the requirements of the **National Electrical Code** do not generally apply to the internal construction of devices which have been listed by a nationally recognized electrical testing laboratory.

Although the specifics of **Code** rules on examination of equipment for safety are presented in Sec. 110-2 and Sec. 110-3, the general **Code** statement on this matter is made here in Sec. 90-6. Although the **Code** does not place emphasis on the need for third-party certification of equipment by independent testing laboratories, it does not make a flat rule to that effect. However, the rules of OSHA are very rigid in insisting on product certification.

The clear effect of OSHA regulations is to *require* "listed," "labeled," "accepted," and/or "certified" equipment be used whenever available. If any electrical system component is "of a kind" that *any* nationally recognized testing lab "accepts, certifies, lists, labels, or determines to be safe," then *that* component *must* be so designated in order to be acceptable for use under OSHA regulations. For instance, because liquidtight flexible metal conduit is a product that is listed and labeled by Underwriters Laboratories Inc. (UL), it is clearly and certainly a violation of the OSHA rule to use any nonlisted, nonlabeled *version* of liquidtight flexible metal conduit. A nonlisted, nonlabeled, noncertified component may be used *only* if it is "of a kind" that *no* nationally recognized lab covers. And even then, the nonrecognized component must be inspected or tested by another federal agency or by a state, municipal, or other local authority responsible for enforcing occupational safety provisions of the **NE Code**.

Every electrical designer and installer must exercise great care in evaluating any and all equipment and products used in electrical work to assure compliance with OSHA rules on certification by a nationally recognized testing lab. In many cases, "listed" components are combined to make up an assembled piece of equipment, but the entire assembly is not listed or labeled as an assembly and may constitute an assembly that is not safe for use. For instance, a listed circuit breaker and a listed magnetic starter may be combined in a listed electric cabinet, but that does not of itself constitute a listed "circuit-breaker combination motor starter." A listed "combination motor control unit" is an entire assembly that has been tested as an assembly and is labeled as such. It is critically important to be fully aware of the meaning and extent of the "listing" or "label" for every product. This is particularly true of combination products and custom-made equipment.

Codes and standards must be carefully interrelated and followed with care and precision. Modern work that fulfills these demands should be the objective of all electrical construction people.

Chapter One

ARTICLE 100. DEFINITIONS

Accessible: "(As applied to wiring methods.)"

Accessible: "(As applied to Equipment.)"

Note that the first definition for "accessible" makes reference to "concealed" and "exposed." Because these words are critically important to applications of wiring methods and equipment, their definitions must be carefully studied and cross referenced with each other, as well as related to Code rules using these words. Since discussions involving the definitions can become complex and murky, it should be noted that Sec. 90-4 gives the local inspector the authority to make the binding interpretation.

Note that there are definitions for words that apply to wiring methods and definitions that apply to equipment. Wiring methods are any of the NE Code -recognized techniques for running circuits between equipment. These include conductors in EMT, (electric metallic tubing) rigid metal or nonmetallic conduit; wireway; cable tray; underfloor raceways; all the cable assemblies covered in Arts. 330 to 340; busway; and the other hookup methods covered in Chap. 3. "Equipment" covers all the products that are connected or hooked by any of these recognized wiring methods.

For electrical applications above suspended ceilings with lift-out panels, it is necessary to distinguish between "equipment" and "wiring methods."

It also is necessary to distinguish between ceiling spaces used for air handling and those not used as air-handling plenum spaces. Typical applications of **Code** rules to both those categories are as follows for nonair-handling ceilings.

1. Wiring methods above lift-out ceiling panels are considered to be "exposed" because the definition of that word includes reference to "behind panels designed to allow access." A typical application of this definition is where wireways are installed in a hung ceiling. Section 362-2 says that wireways are permitted only for exposed work. Therefore, wireway may be installed in the open and visible *or* it may be installed above lift-out panels of a suspended ceiling.

   Any wiring methods above a ceiling made up of lift-out ceiling elements are, therefore, accessible, as shown in Fig. 100-1.

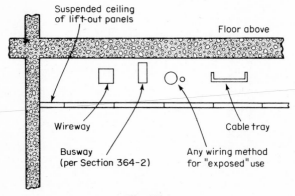

Suspended ceiling
of lift-out panels

Floor above

Wireway

Cable tray

Busway
(per Section 364-2)

Any wiring method
for "exposed" use

Fig. 100-1

2. The rules on installation of busway used to be worded the same as that quoted above for wireway. But now, Sec. 364-4(a) permits busway above panels, if means of access are provided. It further limits such use to totally enclosed, nonventilated busway, without plug-in switches or CBs on the busway and only in ceiling space that is not used for air handling.

3. Section 318-5(h) requires cable trays to be exposed and accessible. Note that the two words "exposed" and "accessible" must be taken "as applied to wiring methods." Cable tray may be used above a suspended, nonair-handling ceiling; and, if used with a wiring method permitted by Sec. 300-22(c), it may be used also above an air-handling ceiling.

4. In many of the articles on cables it is noted, under "Uses Permitted," that the cable may be used for both "exposed" and "concealed" work. Such cables may, therefore, be used above suspended ceilings.

5. Fuses and circuit breakers that provide overcurrent protection required by the **NE Code** are generally required by Sec. 240-24 to be "readily accessible"—that is, they must be capable of being reached quickly. Note that the definition for "readily accessible" applies to equipment rather than wiring methods and is a different concept from that of the word 'accessible." Fuses and/or CBs in a distribution panel or switchboard or motor control center are *not* readily accessible, for instance, if a bunch of crates piled on the floor block access and present an obstacle in getting to the fuses or CBs. They also are not readily accessible if it is necessary to get a portable ladder or stand on a chair or table to get at them.

Equipment is not "readily accessible" if conditions shown in Fig. 100-2 obtain.

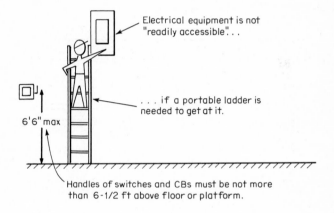

Electrical equipment is not "readily accessible"...

... if a portable ladder is needed to get at it.

6'6" max

Handles of switches and CBs must be not more than 6-1/2 ft above floor or platform.

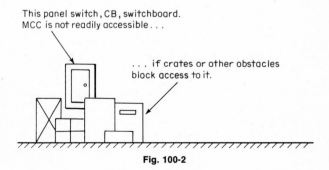

This panel switch, CB, switchboard. MCC is not readily accessible . . .

... if crates or other obstacles block access to it.

Fig. 100-2

Exception No. 2 in Sec. 240-24 permits overcurrent devices to be used high up on a busway where access to them could require use of a ladder, but not on busway above a suspended ceiling (Sec. 364-2).

Supplementary overcurrent devices—over and above those required by the **NE Code** and which the **Code** defines as supplementary protection [Sec. 424-22(d) covering fuses or CBs permitted above a suspended ceiling for protection of electric duct heaters]—do not have to be readily accessible (Sec. 240-10) and may be installed above a suspended ceiling. A CB- or fusible-type panelboard may be used in the ceiling space to satisfy Sec. 424-22.

In general, aside from the cases noted above, fuses and CBs must *not* be used above a suspended ceiling because they would be not readily accessible. But equipment that is not required by a **Code** rule to be "accessible" or to be "readily accessible" may be mounted above a suspended ceiling, as indicated in Fig. 100-3.

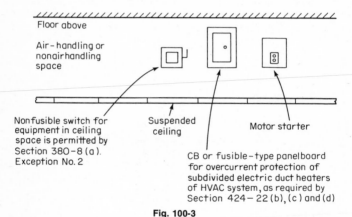

Floor above

Air-handling or nonairhandling space

Nonfusible switch for equipment in ceiling space is permitted by Section 380-8 (a). Exception No. 2

Suspended ceiling

Motor starter

CB or fusible-type panelboard for overcurrent protection of subdivided electric duct heaters of HVAC system, as required by Section 424—22 (b), (c) and (d)

Fig. 100-3

Approved:

The electrical inspector having jurisdiction on any specific installation is the person who will decide what conductors and/or equipment are "approved." Although inspectors are not required to use "listing" or "labeling" by a national testing lab as the deciding factor in their approval of products, they invariably base their acceptance of products on listings by testing labs. Certainly the 1975 **NE Code** almost makes the same insistence as OSHA does that, whenever possible, acceptability must be based on some kind of listing or certification of a national lab. But on this matter, the OSHA law takes precedence— a "listed," "labeled," or otherwise "certified" product must *always* be used in preference to the same "kind" of product that is not recognized by a national testing lab.

Approved for the Purpose:

Because this phrase is used frequently in the NE Code and has raised
questions about the need for third-party certification (such as UL listing),
an explanatory note was added in the 1978 NE Code.

The definition is the same as it was:

Approved for a specific purpose, environment, or application described in a
particular Code requirement.

But, now, the note answers the question: "Approved by whom?" Such
approval of equipment or materials for a specific purpose may be given
by "a nationally recognized testing laboratory" (such as UL, Factory
Mutual, ETL). Or an "inspection agency" may determine that a piece of
equipment or a certain material is "approved for the purpose." Or any
other organization concerned with product evaluation may designate
approval for a specific purpose.

Because the note to the definition includes reference to the words
"Labeled" and "Listed," heavy emphasis is placed on UL listing or similar
certification (Fig. 100-4). It is reasonable to assume that electrical inspectors will base their approval on "listing" and/or "labeling" by national test

Fig. 100-4

labs whenever possible. For those cases where no test-lab certification
covers approval of a product that a Code rule requires to be approved for
a specific purpose, it will be up to the electrical inspector to rule on
acceptability of the product.

Bonding:

This defintion covers a general concept that metal parts are conductively
connected by a cable, wire, bolt, screw, or some other metallic connection
of negligible impedance. The term is used frequently throughout the
Code to imply that metal parts that are "bonded" together have no
potential difference between them. Two common "bonding" techniques
are bonding of switchboards and bonding of panelboards. When bond-

ing is done by a short length of bare or insulated conductor, the conductor is referred to as a "bonding jumper." Examples of bonding are given in Figs. 100-5 and 100-6.

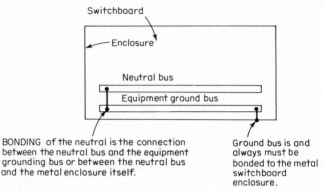

BONDING of the neutral is the connection between the neutral bus and the equipment grounding bus or between the neutral bus and the metal enclosure itself.

Ground bus is and always must be bonded to the metal switchboard enclosure.

Fig. 100-5

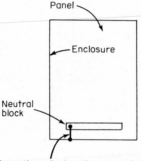

BONDING is the insertion of a bonding screw into the panel neutral block to connect the block to the panel enclosure, or it is use of a bonding jumper from the neutral block to an equipment grounding block that is connected to the enclosure.

NOTE: Bonding – the connection of the neutral terminal to the enclosure or to the ground terminal that is, itself, connected to the enclosure – might also be done in an individual switch or CB enclosure.

Fig. 100-6

Bonding Jumper:

This is any bare or insulated conductor used to provide bonding between metal parts in a system—such as between a metal switchboard enclosure and metal service conduits that stub-up under a service switchboard. The bonding jumper or jumpers provide for making an electrically conductive connection between the metal switchboard enclosure and the metal conduits—as required by **NEC** Sec. 250-71(a) and (b). An example is shown in Fig. 100-7.

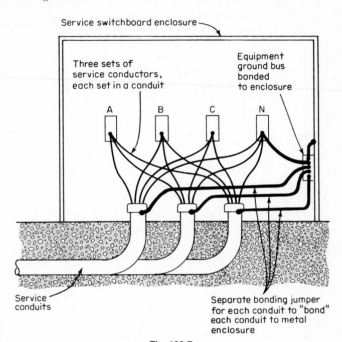

Fig. 100-7

Branch Circuit:

A branch circuit is that part of a wiring system extending beyond the final automatic overload protective device which is approved for use as branch-circuit protection. Thermal cutouts or motor overload devices are not branch-circuit protection. Neither are fuses in luminaires or in plug connections, where used for ballast protection or individual fixture protection. Such supplementary overcurrent protection is not a substitute for branch-circuit protection and does not establish the point of origin of the branch circuit. The extent of a branch circuit is illustrated in Fig. 100-8.

In its simplest form, a branch circuit consists of two wires which carry current at a particular voltage from protective device to utilization device.

The branch circuit represents the last step in the transfer of power from the service or source of energy to utilization devices. First, the loads are circuited. Then the circuits are lumped on the feeders. Finally, the distribution system is connected to one or more sources of power.

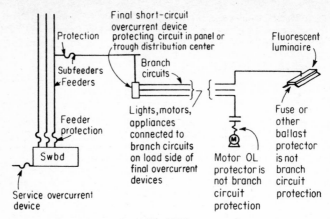

Fig. 100-8

Branch Circuit, General Purpose:

Refer to Fig. 100-9.

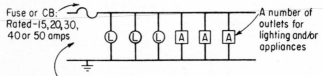

Circuit voltage shall not exceed 150 volts to ground
for circuits supplying lampholders, fixtures or receptacles
of standard 15-amp rating. For fluorescent, incandescent or
mercury lighting under certain conditions, voltage to
ground may be as high as 300 volts. In certain cases, voltage
for electric discharge lighting may be up to 500 volts ungrounded.

Fig. 100-9

Branch Circuit, Appliance:

Refer to Fig. 100-10.

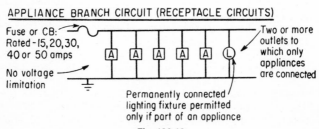

Fig. 100-10

Branch Circuit, Individual:

Refer to Fig. 100-11.

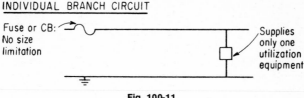

Fig. 100-11

Branch Circuit, Multiwire:

A multiwire branch circuit must be made up of a neutral conductor (grounded) and at least two ungrounded or "hot" conductors. The most common multiwire circuits are shown in Fig. 100-12.

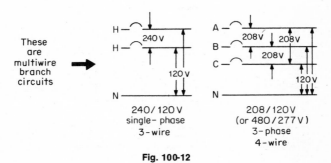

Fig. 100-12

A 3-wire, 3-phase circuit (without a neutral) is not a "multiwire branch circuit," even though it does consist of "multi" wires, as shown in Fig. 100-13.

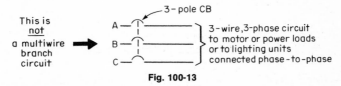

Fig. 100-13

Building:

Most areas have building codes to establish the requirements for buildings, and such codes should be used as a basis for deciding the use of the definition given in the **National Electrical Code**. The use of the term "fire walls" in this definition has resulted in differences of opinion among electrical inspectors and others. Since the definition of a fire wall may differ in each jurisdiction, the processing of an interpretation of a "fire wall" has been studiously avoided in the **National Electrical Code** because this is a function of building codes and not a responsibility of the **National Electrical Code**.

Cabinet:

The door of a cabinet is hinged to a trim covering wiring space, or gutter. The door of a cutout box is hinged directly to the side of the box. Cabinets usually contain panelboards; cutout boxes contain cutouts, switches, or miscellaneous apparatus.

Concealed:

Any electrical equipment that is closed-in by structural surfaces is considered to be "concealed" as shown in Fig. 100-14.

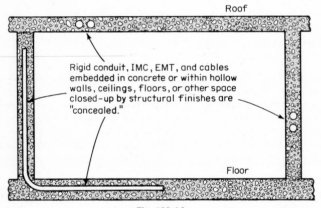

Fig. 100-14

Circuits run in an unfinished basement or an accessible attic are not "rendered inaccessible by the structure of finish of the building," and are therefore considered as exposed work rather a concealed type of wiring.

Conduit Body:

An added sentence notes that FS and FD boxes—as well as larger cast or sheet metal boxes—are not considered to be "conduit bodies," as far as the **NE Code** is concerned. Although some manufacturers' literature refers to FS and FD boxes as conduit fittings, care must be used to distinguish between "conduit bodies" and "boxes" in specific **Code** rules.

For instance, the last sentence of Sec. 370-6(c) prohibits splicing and use of devices in conduit bodies with less than three conduit hubs (although a provision is made for splicing in conduit bodies under certain conditions). However, FS and FD boxes are not conduit bodies and may contain splices and/or house devices. Table 370-6(a) lists FS and FD boxes as boxes." See Fig. 100-15.

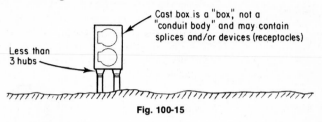

Cast box is a "box," not a "conduit body" and may contain splices and/or devices (receptacles)

Less than 3 hubs

Fig. 100-15

Continuous Load:

Any condition in which the maximum load current in a circuit flows without interruption for a period of not less than 3 hr.

Demand Factor:

Two terms constantly used in electrical design are "demand factor" and "diversity factor." Because there is a very fine difference between the meanings for the words, the terms are often confused.

Demand factor is the ratio of the maximum demand of a system, or part of a system, to the total connected load on the system, or part of the system, under consideration. This factor is always less than unity.

Diversity factor is the ratio of the sum of the individual maximum demands of the various subdivisions of a system, or part of a system, to the maximum demand of the whole system, or part of the system, under consideration. This factor generally varies between 1.00 and 2.00.

Demand factors and diversity factors are used in design. For instance, the sum of the connected loads supplied by a feeder is multiplied by the demand factor to determine the load which the feed must be sized to serve. This load is termed the maximum demand of the feeder. The sum of the maximum demand loads for a number of subfeeders divided by the diversity factor for the subfeeders will give the maximum demand load to be supplied by the feeder from which the subfeeders are derived.

It is common and preferred practice in modern design to take unity as the diversity factor in main feeders to loadcenter substations to provide a measure of spare capacity. Main secondary feeders are also commonly sized on the full value of the sum of the demand loads of the subfeeders supplied.

From power distribution practice, however, basic diversity factors have been developed. These provide general indication of the way in which main feeders can be reduced in capacity below the sum of the demands of the subfeeders they supply. On a radial feeder system, diversity of demands made by a number of transformers reduces the maximum load which the feeder must supply to some value less than the sum of the transformer loads. Typical application of demand and diversity factors for main feeders is shown in Fig. 100-16.

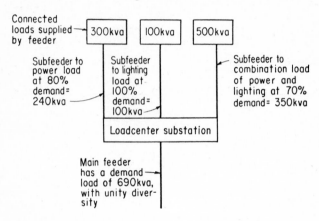

1. Sum of individual demands = 240 + 100 + 350 = 690 kva.
2. Sizing the substation at unity diversity, the required

$$\text{kva} = \frac{690}{1.00} = 690 \text{ kva.}$$

3. To meet this load, use a 750-kva substation.
4. If analysis dictates the use of a diversity factor of 1.4 , the

$$\text{required kva} = \frac{690}{1.40} = 492 \text{ kva.}$$

5. To meet this load, use a 500-kva substation.
6. Primary feeder to unit substation must have capacity to match the substation load.

Fig. 100-16

Device:

Switches, fuses, circuit breakers, controllers, receptacles, and lampholders are "devices."

Dwelling:

Dwelling unit.   Because so many **Code** rules involve the words "dwelling" and "residential," there have been problems applying **Code** rules to the various types of "dwellings"—one-family houses, two-family houses, apartment houses, condominium units, dormitories, hotels, motels, etc.

The 1978 **NE Code** includes changes in terminology to eliminate such problems and uses new definitions of "dwelling" coordinated with changes in the words used in specific **Code** rules.

A "dwelling unit" is now defined as "one or more rooms" used "as a housekeeping unit" and *must* contain space or areas specifically dedicated to "eating, living, and sleeping" and *must* have "permanent provisions for cooking and sanitation." A one-family house is a "dwelling unit." So is an apartment in an apartment house or a condominium unit. But, a guest room in a hotel or motel or a dormitory room or unit is not a "dwelling unit" if it does not contain "permanent provisions for cooking"—which must mean a built-in range or counter-mounted cooking unit (with or without an oven). As a result, the rule of, say, Sec. 210-8, which requires GFCI (ground-fault circuit interrupter) protection of receptacles in bathrooms of "dwelling units," does not apply to bathroom receptacles in standard hotel or motel units or dormitory units, because such units do not contain "permanent provisions for cooking."

Any "dwelling unit" must include all the required elements shown in Fig. 100-17.

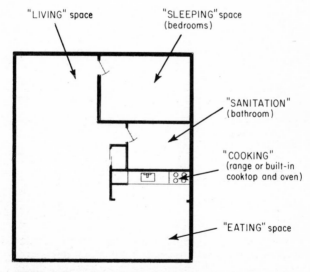

"LIVING" space

"SLEEPING" space
(bedrooms)

"SANITATION"
(bathroom)

"COOKING"
(range or built-in
cooktop and oven)

"EATING" space

NOTE: Eating, living, and sleeping space could be one individual area, as in an efficiency apartment. But the unit must contain a "bathroom," defined in Section 210-8(a) as "an area including a basin with one or more of the following: a toilet, a tub, or a shower." And the unit must contain permanent cooking equipment.

Fig. 100-17

Exposed: "(As applied to wiring methods.)"

Wiring methods and equipment that are not permanently closed-in by building surfaces or finishes are considered to be "exposed." See Fig. 100-18.

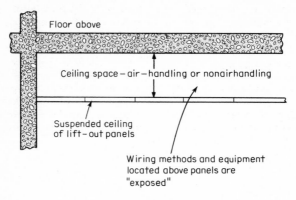

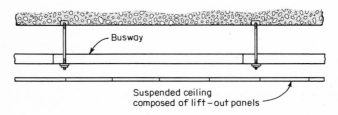

BUSWAY above this suspended ceiling is considered "exposed" as required by Section 364-2.

Fig. 100-18

Feeder:

A "feeder" is a set of conductors which carry electric power from the service equipment (or generator switchboard where power is generated on the premises) to the overcurrent protective devices for branch circuits supplying the various loads.

A feeder may originate at a main distribution center and feed one or more subdistribution centers, one or more branch-circuit distribution centers, one or more branch circuits (as in the case of plug-in busway or motor circuit taps to a feeder), or a combination of these. It may be a primary or secondary voltage circuit, but its function is always to deliver a block of power from one point to another point at which the power capacity is apportioned among a number of other circuits. In some systems, feeders may be carried from a main distribution switchboard to subdistribution switchboards or panelboards from which subfeeders originate to feed branch-circuit panels or motor branch circuits. In still other systems, either or both of the two foregoing feeder layouts may be incorporated with transformer substations to step the distribution voltage to utilization levels.

Grounded Conductor:

This is the conductor of an electrical system which is intentionally connected to a grounding electrode at the service of a premises, at a transformer secondary, or at a generator or other source of electric power. See Fig. 100-19. It is most commonly a neutral conductor of a

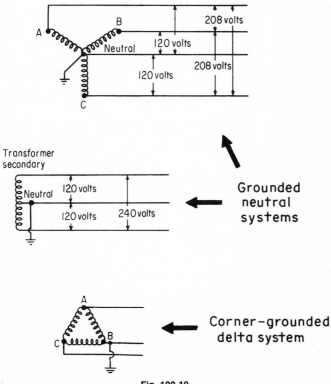

Fig. 100-19

system, but may be one of the phase legs—as in the case of a corner-grounded delta system.

Grounding one of the wires of the electrical system is done to limit the voltage upon the circuit which might otherwise occur through exposure to lightning or other voltages higher than that for which the circuit is designed. Another purpose in grounding one of the wires of the system is to limit the maximum voltage to ground under normal operating conditions. Also, a system which operates with one of its conductors intentionally grounded will provide for automatic opening of the circuit if an accidental or fault ground occurs on one of its ungrounded conductors.

Selection of the wiring system conductor to be grounded depends upon the type of system. In 3-wire, single-phase systems, the midpoint of the transformer winding—the point from which the system neutral is derived—is grounded. For grounded 3-phase wiring systems, the neutral point of the wye-connected transformer(s) or generator is usually the point connected to ground. In delta-connected transformer hookups, grounding of the system can be effected by grounding one of the three phase legs, by grounding a center-tap point on one of the transformer windings (as in the 3-phase, 4-wire "red-leg" delta system), or by using a special grounding transformer which establishes a neutral point of a wye connection which is grounded.

Grounding Conductor, Equipment:

The phase "equipment grounding conductor" is used to describe any of the electrically conductive paths that tie together the noncurrent-carrying metal enclosures of electrical equipment in an electrical system. The term "equipment grounding conductor" includes bare or insulated conductors, metal raceways (rigid metal conduit, intermediate metal conduit, EMT), and metal cable jackets where the Code permits such metal raceways and cable enclosures to be used for equipment grounding—which is a basic Code-required concept as follows:

Equipment grounding is the grounding of all metal enclosures that contain electrical wires or equipment when an insulation failure in such enclosures might place a potential on the enclosures and constitute a shock or fire hazard. It is a permanent and continuous bonding together (i.e., connecting together) of all noncurrent-carrying metal enclosures and frames of electrical equipment—conduit, boxes, cabinets, housings of lighting fixtures and machines, frames of motors, etc.—and connection of this interconnected system of enclosures to the system grounding electrode. The interconnection of all metal enclosures must be made to provide a low-impedance path for fault-current flow along the enclosures in the event that one of the energized conductors within a metal enclosure should make contact with the enclosure and thereby energize it. This fault-current flow assures operation of overcurrent devices which will open a circuit in the event of a fault. By opening a faulted circuit, the system prevents dangerous voltages from being present on equipment enclosures which could be touched by personnel, with consequent electric shock to such personnel.

Simply stated, grounding of all metal enclosures of electric wires and equipment prevents any potential-above-ground on the enclosures. Such bonding together and grounding of all metal enclosures are required for both grounded electrical systems (those systems in which one of the circuit conductors is intentionally grounded) and ungrounded electrical systems (systems with none of the circuit wires intentionally grounded).

As shown in the sketch of Fig. 100-20, metal enclosures, metal raceways, and metal cable armors may serve as the "equipment grounding

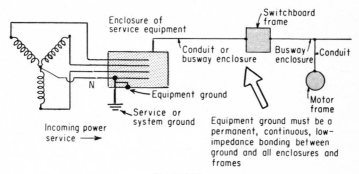

Fig. 100-20

conductor." When nonmetallic raceways or cables are used, a bare or insulated conductor must be used within the raceway or cable to provide the interconnection of all metal enclosures. And the overall equipment grounding system must be connected to a grounding electrode at the service or power source (local transformer or a generator) and must also be connected at the service or source to the system-grounded conductor (such as a grounded neutral) if a grounded conductor is used.

Effective equipment grounding depends upon sure connection of all equipment grounding conductors of adequate ampacity. Equipment grounding is extremely important for grounded electrical systems to provide the automatic fault clearing, which is one of the important advantages of grounded electrical systems. A low-impedance path for fault current is necessary to permit enough current to flow to operate the fuses or circuit breakers protecting the circuit.

In a grounded electrical system with a high-impedance equipment ground return path (equipment grounding conductor path), if one of the phase conductors of the system (i.e., one of the ungrounded conductors of the wiring system) should accidentally come in contact with one of the metal enclosures in which the wires are run, not enough fault current would flow to operate the overcurrent devices. In such a case, the faulted circuit would not automatically open and a dangerous voltage would be present on the conduit and other metal enclosures.

Grounding Electrode Conductor:

The conductor that runs from the bonded neutral block or busbar in service equipment to the system grounding electrode is clearly and specifically identified as the "grounding electrode conductor." See Fig. 100-21. It is also the conductor used to ground the bonded neutral of a transformer secondary or a generator.

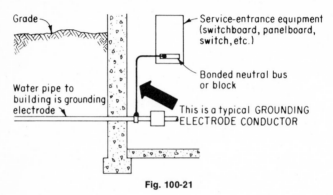

Fig. 100-21

Labeled:

The label of a nationally recognized testing laboratory on a piece of electrical equipment is a sure and ready way to be assured that the equipment is properly made and will function safely when used in accordance with the application data and limitations established by the testing organization. Each label used on an electrical product gives the exact name of the type of equipment as it appears in the listing book of the testing organization.

Typical labels are shown in Fig. 100-22.

Underwriters Laboratories Inc., the largest nationally recognized testing laboratory covering the electrical field, describes its "Identification of Listed Products" as shown in Fig. 100-23.

Listed:

As a result of broader, more intensive and vigorous enforcement of third-party certification of electrical system equipment and components, OSHA and the **NE Code** have made it necessary that all electrical

Fig. 100-22

construction people be fully aware of and informed about "nationally recognized testing laboratories." The following organizations are widely known and recognized by governmental agencies for their independent product testing and certification activities. Each should be contacted directly for full information on available product listings and other data on standards and testing.

Underwriters Laboratories Inc.
207 E. Ohio St.
Chicago, Ill. 60611

Other UL offices and testing stations:

33 Pfingsten Rd.
Northbrook, Ill. 60062

1285 Walt Whitman Rd.
Melville, N.Y. 11746

The Listing Mark may appear in various forms as authorized by Underwriters Laboratories Inc. Typical forms which may be authorized are shown below:

Listing Marks include one of the forms illustrated above, the word "Listed", and a control number assigned by UL. The product name as indicated in this Directory under each of the product categories is generally included as part of the Listing Mark text, but may be omitted when in UL's opinion, the use of the name is superfluous and the Listing Mark is directly and permanently applied to the product by stamping, molding, ink-stamping, silk screening or similar processes.

Separable Listing Marks (not part of a name plate and in the form of decals, stickers or labels) will always include the four elements: UL's name and/or symbol, the word "Listed", the product or category name, and a control number.

Fig. 100-23

1655 Scott Blvd.
  Santa Clara, Calif. 95050

UL Marine Department
  2602 Tampa East Blvd.
  Tampa, Fla. 33619

Factory Mutal Engineering Corp.
  1151 Boston-Providence Turnpike
  Norwood, Mass. 02062

Electrical Testing Laboratories, Inc.
  2 East End Ave.
  New York, N.Y. 10021

Note: Although the OSHA law specifically mentions Underwriters Labs and Factory Mutual as "nationally recognized" independent testing laboratories, OSHA recognition is "not limited to" (the actual expression used in the law) the two testing organizations named as typical.

Typical publications of nationally recognized testing laboratories are shown in Fig. 100-24 and may be obtained by writing to the various test labs at the above addresses.

Fig. 100-24. A complete library of listing publications is a *must* for every electrician—
to check on listed and labeled products recognized by national testing laboratories.

Raceway:

Whenever this term is used in the Code, it must be understood that the
meaning includes all the many enclosures used for running conductors
between cabinets and housings of electrical distribution components—
like panels, switches, motor starters, etc.—and housings of utilization
equipment—like lighting fixtures, motors, heaters, etc. When the Code
refers to "conduit" it means only those raceways containing the word
"conduit" in their title. But "EMT" is not conduit. Table 1 of Chap. 9 in
the back of the Code book refers to "Conduit and Tubing." The Code,
thus, distinguishes between the two. "EMT" is tubing.

Readily Accessible:

If it is necessary to use a portable (but not a fixed) ladder to get to a switch
or CB or transformer or other piece of equipment, then the equipment is
not "readily accessible." See the more complete description of the concept
under the comments on "accessible."

The term "readily accessible" implies a need for performing promptly
an indicated act, for example, to reach quickly a disconnecting switch or
circuit breaker without the use of ladders, chairs, etc. The installation of
such a switch or circuit breaker at a height above 6½ ft from a standing
level is not considered "readily accessible."

Receptacle:

Each place where a plug-cap may be inserted is a "receptacle," as shown in Fig. 100-25.

Only a single receptacle can be served by an individual branch circuit. See Secs. 210-21(b) and 555-3.

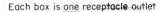

Each box is one receptacle outlet

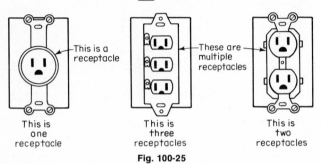

This is a receptacle

These are multiple receptacles

This is one receptacle

This is three receptacles

This is two receptacles

Fig. 100-25

Receptacle Outlet:

The "outlet" is the outlet box. But this definition must be carefully related to Sec. 220-2(c) (4) for calculating receptacle loads in other than dwelling occupancies. A "receptacle outlet"—for purposes of calculating load—is taken as each mounting strap (or bracket) and 180 VA must be counted for each strap, whether it supports one, two, or three receptacles.

Remote-Control Circuit:

The circuit that supplies energy to the operating coil of a relay, a magnetic contactor, or a magnetic motor starter is a "remote-control circuit" because that circuit controls the circuit that feeds through the contacts of the relay, contactor, or starter as shown in Fig. 100-26.

A control circuit as shown is any circuit which has as its load device the operating coil of a magnetic motor starter, a magnetic contactor, or a relay. Strictly speaking, it is a circuit which exercises control over one or more other circuits. And these other circuits controlled by the control circuit may themselves be control circuits or they may be "load" circuits—carrying utilization current to a lighting, heating, power, or signal device. The sketch clarifies the distinction between control circuits and load circuits.

The elements of a control circuit include all the equipment and devices concerned with the function of the circuit: conductors, raceway, contactor operating coil, source of energy supply to the circuit, overcurrent

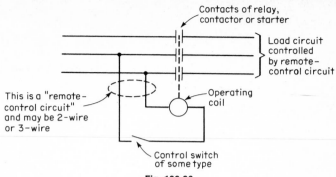

Fig. 100-26

protective devices, and all switching devices which govern energization of the operating coil.

The **NE Code** covers application of remote-control circuits in Art. 725 and in Secs. 240-3 and 430-71 through 430-74.

Service:

The word "service" includes *all* the materials and equipment involved with the transfer of electric power from the utility distribution line to the electrical wiring system of the premises being supplied. Although service layouts vary widely, depending upon the voltage and amp rating, the type of premises being served, and the type of equipment selected to do the job, every service generally consists of "service-drop" conductors (for overhead service from a utility pole line) or "service-lateral" conductors (for an underground service from either an overhead or underground utility system)—plus metering equipment, some type of switch or circuit-breaker control, overcurrent protection, and related enclosures and hardware. A typical layout of "service" for a one-family house breaks down as in Fig. 100-27.

That part of the electrical system which directly connects to the utility supply line is referred to as the "service entrance." Depending upon the type of utility line serving the house, there are two basic types of service entrances—an overhead and an underground service.

The **overhead service** has been the most commonly used type of service. In a typical example of this type, the utility supply line is run on wood poles along the street property line or back-lot line of the building, and a cable connection is made high overhead from the utility line to a bracket installed somewhere high up on the building. This wood pole line also carries the telephone lines, and the poles are generally called "telephone poles."

The aerial cable that runs from the overhead utility lines to the bracket

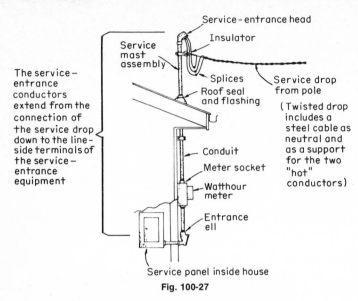

The service–
entrance
conductors
extend from the
connection of
the service drop
down to the line–
side terminals of
the service –
entrance
equipment

Service mast assembly

Service-entrance head

Insulator

Splices

Roof seal and flashing

Service drop from pole

(Twisted drop includes a steel cable as neutral and as a support for the two "hot" conductors)

Conduit

Meter socket

Watthour meter

Entrance ell

Service panel inside house

Fig. 100-27

on the outside wall of the building is called the "service drop." This cable is installed by the utility line worker. At the bracket which terminates the service drop, conductors are then spliced to the drop cable conductors to carry power down to the electric meter and into the building.

The **underground service** is one in which the conductors that run from the utility line to the building are carried underground. Such an underground run to a building may be tapped from either an overhead utility pole line or an underground utility distribution system. Although underground utility services tapped from a pole line at the property line have been used for many years to eliminate the unsightliness of overhead wires coming to a building, the use of underground service tapped from an underground utility system has only started to gain widespread usage in residential areas over recent years. This latter technique is called "URD"—which stands for *U*nderground *R*esidential *D*istribution.

As noted above, when a building is supplied by an overhead drop, an installation of conductors must be made on the outside of the building to pick up power from the drop conductors and carry it into the meter enclosure and service-entrance equipment (switch, CB, panelboard, or switchboard) for the building. On underground services, the supply conductors are also brought into the meter enclosure on the building and then are run into the service equipment installed, usually, within the building.

Service Conductors:

This is a general term that covers all the conductors used to connect the utility supply circuit or transformer to the service equipment of the premises served. This term includes "service-drop" conductors, "service-lateral" (underground service) conductors, and "service-entrance" conductors. In an overhead distribution system, the service conductors begin at the line pole where connection is made. If a primary line is extended to transformers installed outdoors on private property, the service conductors to the building proper begin at the secondary terminals of the transformers. See Sec. 230-200.

Where the supply is from an underground distribution system, the service conductors begin at the point of connection to the underground street mains.

In every case the service conductors terminate at the service equipment.

Service Drop:

As the name implies, these are the conductors that "drop" from the overhead utility line and connect to the service-entrance conductors at their upper end on the building or structure supplied. See Fig. 100-28.

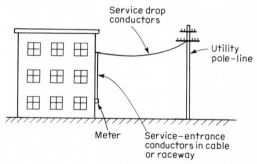

Fig. 100-28

Service Lateral:

This is the name given to a set of underground service conductors. A service lateral serves a function similar to that of a service drop as shown in Fig. 100-29.

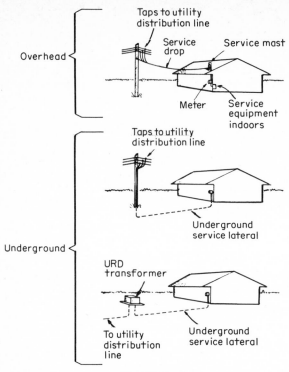

Overhead — Taps to utility distribution line, Service drop, Service mast, Meter, Service equipment indoors

Underground — Taps to utility distribution line, Underground service lateral, URD transformer, To utility distribution line, Underground service lateral

Fig. 100-29

Special Permission:

It *must* be carefully noted that any **Code** reference to "special permission" as a basis for accepting any electrical design or installation technique *requires* that such "permission" be in *written form*. Whenever the inspection authority gives "special permission" for an electrical condition that is at variance with **Code** rules or not covered fully by the rules, the authorization must be "written" and not simply verbal permission.

Voltage to Ground:

For a grounded electrical system, voltage to ground is the voltage that exists from any ungrounded circuit conductor to either the grounded circuit conductor (if one is used) or the grounded metal enclosures (conduit, boxes, panelboard cabinets, etc.) or other grounded metal, such as building steel. Examples are given in Fig. 100-30.

Single - phase, 3 – wire system

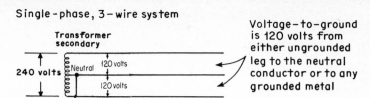

Voltage – to – ground
is 120 volts from
either ungrounded
leg to the neutral
conductor or to any
grounded metal

3 – Phase, 4 – wire wye system

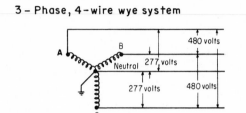

Voltage – to – ground
is the voltage from
any phase leg to the
grounded neutral –
277 volts, in this
case

3 – Phase, 4 – wire delta system

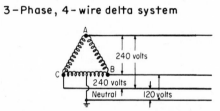

Voltage – to – ground
is 208 volts from
phase A conductor
and 120 volts from
phase B or C to the
grounded neutral

Fig. 100-30

For an ungrounded electrical system, voltage to ground is *taken to be* equal to the maximum voltage that exists between any two conductors of the system. This is based on the reality that an accidental ground fault on one of the ungrounded conductors of the system places the other system conductors at a voltage aboveground that is equal to the value of the voltage between conductors. Under such a ground-fault condition, the voltage to ground is the phase-to-phase voltage between the accidentally grounded conductor and any other phase leg of the system. On, say, a 480-V, 3-phase, 3-wire ungrounded delta system voltage to ground is, therefore, 480 V, as shown in Fig. 100-31.

In many **Code** rules, it is critically necessary to distinguish between references to "voltage" and to "voltage to ground." The **Code** also refers to "voltage between conductors," as in Sec. 210-6(b), to make very clear how rules must be observed.

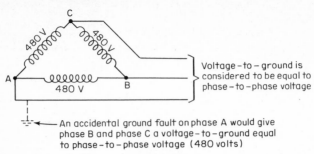

Ungrounded delta system at 480 volts

Voltage–to–ground is
considered to be equal to
phase–to–phase voltage

An accidental ground fault on phase A would give
phase B and phase C a voltage–to–ground equal
to phase–to–phase voltage (480 volts)

Fig. 100-31

ARTICLE 110. REQUIREMENTS FOR
ELECTRICAL INSTALLATIONS

110-1. Mandatory Rules and Explanatory Material. Although the NE
Code consists essentially of specific regulations on details of electrical
design and installation, there is much explanatory material in the form of
notes to rules. Compliance with the Code consists in satisfying all requirements and conditions that are stated by use of the word "shall." That
word, anywhere in the Code, designates a mandatory rule. Failure to
comply with any mandatory Code rule constitutes a "Code violation."

110-2. Approval. This section of the NE Code regulates the use of
electrical products and equipment in a rule similar to the OSHA regulation on acceptability of equipment. OSHA regulations on electrical installations contain strong insistence on third-party certification of the essential safety of the equipment and component products used to assemble an
electrical installation.

The use of custom-made equipment is also covered in OSHA rules.
Every manufacturer of custom equipment must provide documentary
safety-test data to the owner on whose work premises the custom equipment is installed. And it seems to be a reasonable conclusion from the
whole rule itself that custom-equipment assemblies must make maximum
use of "listed," "labeled," or "certified" components.

The word "approved," as used in this rule, must be taken to have the
meaning given in the NE Code definition for that word. "Approved" is
"acceptable to the authority having jurisdiction." The electrical inspector
having jurisdiction on any specific installation is the final judge of what
conductors and/or equipment are "approved." Although inspectors are
not *required* to use "listing" or "labeling" by a national testing lab as the
deciding factor in their approval of products, they invariably base their
acceptance of products on listings by testing labs. The note in this section

almost makes the same insistence as OSHA does that, whenever possible, acceptability must be based on some kind of listing or certification of a national lab.

110-3. Examination, Installation and Use of Equipment.   This section presents general rules on "Examination, Installation and Use of Equipment." Part **(a)** lists eight factors that must be evaluated in determining acceptability of equipment for Code-recognized use. The 1978 NE Code has added a new factor in item **(3)**. This new consideration for electrical inspectors to include in their examination to determine suitability of equipment for safe and effective use is listed as "wire-bending and connection space." See Fig. 110-1. This new factor was added because of

Fig. 110-1. Equipment must be evaluated for adequate gutter space to assure safe and effective bending of conductors at terminals. [Sec. 110-3(a)(3).]

increasing concern over inadequate gutter space at conductor terminal locations in enclosures for switches, CBs, and other control and protection equipment. This general mention of the need for sufficient conductor bending space is aimed at avoiding poor terminations and conductor damage that can result from excessively sharp conductor bends required by tight gutter spaces at terminals. Specific rules that cover this consideration are given in Sec. 373-6 on "Deflection of Conductors" at terminals or where entering or leaving cabinets or cutout boxes—covering gutter widths and wire-bending spaces.

Part **(b)** of this section is a critically important **Code** rule because it incorporates, as part of the **NE Code** itself, all the application regulations and limitations published by product-testing organizations, such as UL, Factory-Mutual, ETL, etc. That rule clearly and certainly says, for instance, that any and every product listed in the UL *Electrical Construction Materials List* (green book) must be used exactly as described in the application data given with the listing in the book. Because the *Electrical Construction Materials List* and the other UL books of product listings, such as the *Hazardous Location Equipment List* (red book) and the *Electrical Appliance and Utilization Equipment List* (orange book), contain massive amounts of installation and application instruction, all those specific bits of application data become mandatory **NE Code** regulations as a result of the rule in Sec. 110-3(b). The data given in the UL listing books supplement and expand upon rules given in the **NE Code**. In fact, effective compliance with **NE Code** regulations can only be assured by careful study and observance of the limitations and conditions spelled out in the application instructions given in the UL listings books or similar instructions provided by other national testing labs. A sample of such application data from the UL green book is shown in Fig. 110-2.

In the preface to its *Electrical Construction Materials List* (the green book), UL points out certain basic conditions that apply to products listed.

1. In general, equipment listed is intended for use in ordinary locations, which may be dry, damp, or wet locations, as defined in the **NE Code**. All limitations on use specified in the **NE Code** and in the general information preceding the section on listing in the green book must be carefully observed. Equipment and products for use in hazardous locations are covered in the UL red book, *Hazardous Location Equipment List*.

2. Listed equipment has been investigated only for use indoors in dry locations, unless outdoor use is specifically permitted by **NE Code** rules, is indicated in the UL listing information, or is obvious from the designation of the equipment in the listing (such as "Swimming Pool Fixtures").

3. The amperage or wattage marking on power-consuming equipment is valid only when the equipment is supplied at its marked rated voltage. In general, current input to resistive loads increases in direct proportion to input voltage increase. Current input to an induction motor with a fixed load increases in direct proportion to decrease in input voltage. When calculating branch-circuit conductor sizes, overcurrent protection, disconnect requirements, etc., the actual input voltage rather than rated voltage should be used, except as noted in **NE Code** Sec. 430-6.

CIRCUIT BREAKERS, MOLDED-CASE, AND CIRCUIT BREAKER ENCLOSURES (DIVQ)

This listing covers circuit breakers specifically designed to provide service-entrance, feeder or branch circuit protection and also covers circuit-breaker enclosures. They are covered by the classifications indicated by the label designations as follows:

"Circuit Breaker"—without enclosure, and with noninterchangeable trip units.

"Circuit-Breaker Frame"—frame only of circuit breaker with provision for interchangeable trip units. A labeled "Circuit Breaker Frame" is listed for use only with labeled "Circuit Breaker Trip Unit."

"Circuit-Breaker Trip Unit"—trip unit only of circuit breaker having provision for interchangeable trip units.

"Circuit-Breaker Enclosure"—enclosure only for individual 1-, 2-, or 3-pole circuit breaker or for two single-pole breakers not interconnected.

Listed circuit breakers are intended for use in listed enclosures, or as part of other listed equipment, or without enclosures where acceptable.

Listed circuit breakers are rated 600 v or less.

Class CTL circuit breakers may be identified by the words "Class CTL" or "CTL" on the circuit breaker as part of the marking.

Class CTL circuit breakers have physical size, configuration or other means which, in conjunction with the physical means provided in a Class CTL assembly, are designed to prevent the installation of more circuit breaker poles than the number for which the assembly is designed and rated.

Circuit breakers marked "SWD" are suitable for switching 120 volt fluorescent lighting on a regular basis.

Single pole circuit breakers rated 120 volts ac are suitable for use in a single phase multiwire circuit where the neutral is connected to the load.

Single pole circuit breakers rated 125 volts or 125 volts dc are suitable for use in a single phase and a dc multiwire circuit where the neutral is connected to the load.

Single pole circuit breakers rated 120/240 volts ac are suitable for use in a single phase multiwire circuit with or without the neutral connected to the load.

Single pole circuit breakers rated 125/250 volts or 125/250 volts dc are suitable for use in a single phase and a dc multiwire circuit with or without the neutral connected to the load.

Circuit breakers that are capable of correct operation where the temperature of the ambient air within the enclosure housing the circuit breaker attains 40 degrees C, are marked "40 C."

Unless otherwise marked, circuit breakers should not be loaded to exceed 80 percent of their current rating, where in normal operation the load will continue for 3 hours or more.

Circuit breakers ... n interrupt... ratin... ...er than 5000 amperes a...
...rked to indicat... ...8). ...r...
...n interrupt...
...utoma...

Fig. 110-2. Product application rules contained in UL Green Book and other test-lab literature are, in effect, mandatory NEC requirements. [Sec. 110-3(b).]

4. All permanently connected equipment and appliances provided with terminals are intended for use with *copper* supply conductors. Terminals that are suitable for *either* copper or aluminum conductors are marked to indicate that. Such marking must be independent of any marking on terminal connectors and must be on a wiring diagram or other readily visible location. Permanently connected equipment and appliances with pigtail leads are intended for use with copper supply conductors. But aluminum supply wires may be used if they are spliced to the pigtails by splicing devices that are suitable for joining copper to aluminum.

5. A very important qualification is indicated for the temperature ratings of terminations. Although application data on minimum required temperature ratings of conductors connected to equipment terminals are not given in the NE Code, it nevertheless becomes part of the mandatory regulations of the Code because of Sec. 110-3(b).

A basic rule in the preface of the listing of "Equipment for Use in Ordinary Locations" in the UL *Electrical Construction Materials List* states that, in general,

... the termination provisions on equipment are based on the use of 60°C conductors in circuits rated 100 amperes or less and the use of 75°C conductors in higher rated circuits.

If the termination provisions on equipment are based on the use of other conductors, the equipment is either marked with both the size and temperature rating of the conductors to be used or with only the temperature rating of the conductors to be used. If the equipment is marked with only the temperature rating of the conductors to be used, that temperature rating is required for the ambient temperature in the equipment and the 60°C ampacity (100-ampere or less circuits) or 75°C ampacity (over 100-ampere circuits) should be used to determine the size of the conductors.

Higher-temperature-rated conductors may be used, though not required, if the size of the conductors is determined on the basis of the 60°C ampacity (100-ampere or less circuits) or 75°C ampacity (over 100-ampere circuits).

Application of these data to various types of equipment is repeated in many sections of the *Electrical Construction Materials List*. And, as the UL wording says, this temperature limitation on terminals applies to the terminals on all equipment—circuit breakers, switches, motor starters, contactors, etc.—except where some other specific condition is recognized in the general information preceding the product category. This is a vitally important matter, which has been widely disregarded in general practice.

When terminals are tested for suitability at 60° or 75°C, the use of 90°C conductors operating at their higher current ratings poses definite threat of damage to terminals on switches, breakers, etc. Many termination failures experienced in electrical equipment suggest overheating even where the load current did not exceed the current rating of the breaker or switch or other equipment.

When a 60°C-rated terminal is fed by a conductor operating at 90°C, there will be substantial heat conducted from the 90°C conductor metal to the 60°C-rated terminal; and, over a period of time, that can damage the termination—even though the load current does not exceed the equipment current rating and does not exceed the ampacity of the 90°C conductor. Whenever two metallic parts at different operating temperatures are tightly connected together, the higher-temperature part (say 75° or 90°C wire) will give heat to the lower-temperature part (the 60°C terminal) and thereby raise its temperature over 60°C.

The basic UL limitation on termination temperature rating is shown in Fig. 110-3.

For any given size of conductor, the greater ampacity of a higher-temperature conductor is established by the ability of the conductor insulation to withstand the I^2R heat produced by the higher current flowing through the conductor. But it must not be assumed that the equipment to which that conductor is connected is also capable of with-

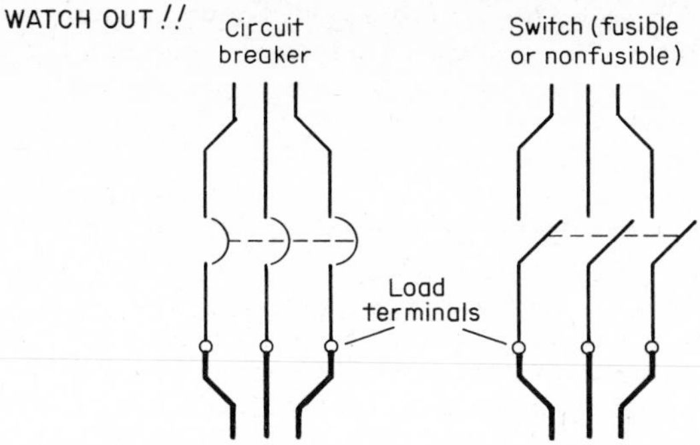

WATCH OUT !!

Fig. 110-3. [Sec. 110-3(b), Example.]

Unless a circuit breaker or switch is marked otherwise, circuit conductors connected to the terminals must not operate at more than a 60°C ampacity for a breaker or switch rated 100 amps or less and must not operate at more than a 75°C ampacity for a breaker or switch rated over 100 amps [refer to Tables 310-16 through -19]. That means:

FOR CBs, SWITCHES, CONTACTORS, ETC. RATED 100 AMPS OR LESS — Use TW wire (or use THW, THHN, RHH, XHHW, or other higher-temperature wire at the ampacity of the corresponding size of TW wire).

FOR CBs, SWITCHES, CONTACTORS, ETC. RATED OVER 100 AMPS — Use TW, THW, THWN or XHHW wire at their ampacities permitted up to 75°C (or use RHH, THHN, or other higher-temperature wire at the ampacity of the corresponding size of 75°C wire).

standing the heat that will be thermally conducted from the metal of the conductor into the metal of the terminal to which the conductor is tightly connected.

Although this limitation on the operating temperature of terminals in equipment does reduce the advantage that higher-temperature conductors have over temperature conductors, there are still many advantages to using the higher-temperature conductors because of their reduced cross-section areas that permit more economical raceway fills—either smaller conduit for a given number of conductors or more conductors in a given size of conduit. However, where higher-temperature conductors are used, they must be applied at the ampacities of corresponding sizes of 60 or 75°C conductors—as required.

In conductor sizes No. 14, No. 12, and No. 10, with their 15-, 20-, and 30-A ratings, there is no difference in load rating between the same size conductors of different temperature rating. A No. 12 TW copper conductor, for instance, has a 20-A basic rating in **NE Code** Table 310-16; and a No. 12 THW (75°C), a No. 12 RHH (90°C), a No. 12 XHHW (75°C in wet or dry locations or 90°C in dry locations only), and a No. 12 THHN (90°C) are all rated at a basic loading value of 20 A. Even though the different types of conductors in sizes No. 14, No. 12, and No. 10 have the same current ratings, there is still an advantage in using the thin-wall-insulated, higher-temperature wires because they permit greater conduit fill.

In those conductor sizes where there are differences in ampacity between conductors of different temperature ratings (conductors No. 8 and larger), careful consideration must be given to a number of factors involved in selection of the correct and most effective conductor for any specific circuit application. Attention must certainly be paid to the above described temperature limitation at equipment terminals. Selection of circuit conductors must also be based on load limitation required by **NE Code** Sec. 210-22(c), 220-2(a), and 220-10(b) for "continuous load"—that is, any case "where the maximum current is expected to continue for three hours or more," such as branch circuits and feeders for commercial and industrial lighting or similar loads that are left on all day or for periods over 3 hr. And the greater conduit fill of thin-wall-insulated, high-temperature conductors (offering use of smaller conduits) must also be factored into conductor selection, along with the impact of conductor ampacity de-rating due to conduit fills over three current-carrying conductors. All these considerations are interrelated, and the most effective and most economical circuit makeup for any case can be determined only by thorough study and careful calculation. For typical details of this kind of analysis to relate all the applicable **NE Code** and UL rules, see Sec. 310-15 on ampacity of conductors.

110-4. Voltages.   In all electrical systems there is a normal, predictable spread of voltage values over the impedances of the system equipment. It has been common practice to assign these basic levels to each nominal system voltage. The highest value of voltage is that at the service entrance or transformer secondary, such as 480Y/277 V. Then considering voltage drop due to impedance in the circuit conductors and equipment, a "nominal" midsystem voltage designation would be 460Y/265, and finally a "load" or "outlet" voltage is given as 440Y/254. Variations in "nominal" voltages have come about because of (1) differences in utility supply voltages throughout the country, (2) varying transformer secondary voltages produced by different and often uncontrolled voltage drops in primary feeders, and (3) preferences of different engineers and other design authorities.

110-6. Conductor Sizes.   In this country, the American Wire Gage (AWG) is the standard for copper wire and for aluminum wire used for electrical conductors. The American Wire Gage is the same as the Brown & Sharpe (B & S) gage. The largest gage size is No. 0000; above this size the sizes of wires and cables are stated in circular mils.

The circular mil is a unit used for measuring the cross-sectional area of the conductor, or the area of the end of a wire which has been cut square across. One circular mil (commonly abbreviated CM or cmil) is the area of a circle $\frac{1}{1,000}$ in. in diameter. The area of a circle 1 in. in diameter is 1,000,000 CM; also, the area of a circle of this size is 0.7854 sq in.

To convert square inches to circular mils, multiply the square inches by 1,273,200.

To convert circular mils to square inches, divide the circular mils by 1,273,200 or multiply the circular mils by 0.7854 and divide by 1,000,000.

In interior wiring the gage sizes 14, 12, and 10 are usually solid wire; No. 8 and larger conductors in raceways are required to be stranded. (See Sec. 310-3.)

A cable (if not larger than 1,000,000 CM) will have one of the following numbers of strands: 7, 19, 37, or 61. In order to make a cable of any standard size, in nearly every case the individual strands cannot be any regular gage number but must be some special odd size. For example, a No. 00 cable must have a total cross-sectional area of 133,100 CM and is usually made up of 19 strands. No. 12 has an area of 6,530 CM and No. 11, an area of 8,234 CM; therefore each strand must be a special size between Nos. 12 and 11.

110-7. Insulation Integrity.   Previous editions of the Code contained *recommended* values for testing insulation resistance. It was found that those values were incomplete and not sufficiently accurate for use in modern installations, and the recommendation was deleted from the Code. However, basic knowledge of insulation-resistance testing is important.

Measurements of insulation resistance can best be made with a megohmmeter insulation tester. As measured with such an instrument, insulation resistance is the resistance to the flow of direct current (usually at 500 or 1,000 V for systems of 600 V or less) through or over the surface of the insulation in electrical equipment. The results are in ohms or megohms, but insulation readings will be in the megohm range.

The insulation-resistance test is nondestructive, quite different from a high-voltage or *breakdown* test. It is made with direct current rather than alternating current, and is not a measure of dielectric strength as such. However, insulation-resistance tests assist greatly in determining when and where not to apply high voltage.

In general, insulation resistance decreases with increased size of a machine or length of cable, because there is more insulating material in contact with conductors and frame, ground, or sheath. Insulation resistance usually increases with higher voltage rating of apparatus because of increased thickness of insulating material. Insulation-resistance readings are not only *quantitative,* but are *relative* or *comparative* as well; and since they are influenced by moisture, dirt, and deterioration, they are reliable indicators of the presence of those conditions.

Cable and conductor installations present a wide variation of conditions from the point of view of the resistance of the insulation. These conditions result from the many kinds of insulating materials used, the voltage rating or insulation thickness, and the length of the circuit involved in the measurement. Furthermore, such circuits usually extend over great distances and may be subject to wide variations in temperature, which will have an effect on the insulation-resistance values obtained. The terminals of cables and conductors will also have an effect on the test values unless they are clean and dry, or guarded.

It is important to understand the correct use of insulation testers. The use of an insulation tester is not complicated. However, temperature correction, humidity, temporary dampness during construction, types of conductor insulation, lengths of runs, and the proper *interpretation* of readings are major factors that must be considered. The important thing is to make an insulation test and to record the results for immediate and future attention.

Excellent manuals on this subject are available from instrument manufacturers and thorough knowledge in the use of insulation testers is essential if the test results are to be meaningful.

110-8. Wiring Methods.   All Code-recognized wiring methods are covered in Chap. 3 of the NE Code—Arts. 300 through 384.

110-9. Interrupting Rating.   Interrupting rating of electrical equipment is divided into two categories: current at fault levels and current at operating levels.

Equipment intended to clear fault currents must have interrupting rating equal to the maximum fault current that the circuit is capable of delivering at the line (not the load) terminals of the equipment. See Fig. 110-4. The internal impedance of the equipment itself may not be factored in to use the equipment at a point where the available fault current on its line side is greater than the rated, marked interrupting capacity of the equipment.

All short-circuit protective devices. . .

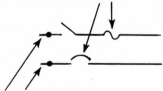

. . . must have an interrupting rating at least equal to the maximum fault current that the circuit could deliver into a short circuit on the *line side* of the device.

NOTE: That means that the fault current "available" at the line terminals of all fuses and circuit breakers *must be known* in order to assure that the device has a rating sufficient for the level of fault current.

Fig. 110-4. (Sec. 110-9.)

If overcurrent devices with a specific IC (interrupting capacity) rating are inserted at a point on a wiring system where the available short-circuit current exceeds the IC rating of the device, a resultant downstream solid short circuit between conductors or between one ungrounded conductor and ground (in grounded systems) could cause serious damage to life and property.

Since each electrical installation is different, the selection of overcurrent devices with proper IC ratings is not always a simple task. To begin with, the amount of available short-circuit current at the service equipment must be known. Such short-circuit current depends upon the capacity rating of the utility primary supply to the building, transformer impedances, and service conductor impedances. Most utilities will provide this information.

Downstream from the service equipment IC ratings of overcurrent devices may be reduced to lower than those at the service, depending on lengths and sizes of feeders, line impedances, and other factors. However, large motors and capacitors, while in operation, will feed additional current into a fault, and this must be considered when calculating short-circuit currents.

Manufacturers of overcurrent devices have excellent literature on figuring short-circuit currents, including graphs, charts, and one-line-diagram layout sheets to simplify the selection of proper overcurrent devices.

Equipment intended only for control of load or operating currents, such as contactors and unfused switches, must be rated for the current to be interrupted but does not have to be rated for interrupting available fault level, as shown in Fig. 110-5.

All switches, contactors, starters, relays. . .

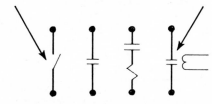

. . . must have an interrupting rating at least equal to "the current that must be interrupted" — which could be full-load current or, in the case of isolating or disconnect switches, some lesser value of operating current (such as transformer magnetizing current).

Fig. 110-5. (Sec. 110-9.)

110-10. Circuit Impedance and Other Characteristics. This section requires that all equipment be rated to withstand the level of fault current that is let through by the circuit protective device in the time it takes to operate—without "extensive damage" to any of the electrical components of the circuit as illustrated in Fig. 110-6.

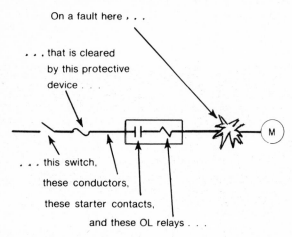

On a fault here , . .

. . . that is cleared
by this protective
device . . .

. . . this switch,

these conductors,

these starter contacts,

and these OL relays . . .

M

. . . must all be rated to safely withstand the energy of the
fault let-through current

Fig. 110-6. (Sec. 110-10.)

The phrase "the component short-circuit withstand ratings" has been added to this rule. The intent of this addition is to require all circuit components that are subjected to ground faults or short-circuit faults to be capable of withstanding the thermal and magnetic stresses produced within them from the time a fault occurs until the circuit protective device (fuse or CB) opens to clear the fault, without extensive damage to the components.

110-12. Mechanical Execution of Work This statement has been the source of many conflicts because opinions differ as to what is a "neat and workmanlike manner."

The **Code** places the responsibility for determining what is acceptable on the authority having jurisdiction and how it is applied in the particular jurisdiction. This basis in most areas is the result of:

1. Competent knowledge and experience of installation methods
2. What has been the established practice by the qualified journeyman in the particular area
3. What has been taught in the trade schools having certified electrical training courses for apprentices and journeyman

There should be an understanding that individual inspectors will not make an arbitrary ruling of their own but will apply in a uniform manner the practice established by the organization having responsibility for enforcement of electrical requirements.

Examples which generally would not be considered as "neat and workmanlike" include nonmetallic cables installed with kinks or twists; unsightly exposed runs; wiring improperly trained in enclosures; slack in cables between supports; flattened conduit bends; or improvised fittings, straps, or supports. See Fig. 110-7.

Fig. 110-7. Stapling of BX to bottoms of joists and ragged drilling of joists add up to an unsightly installation that does not appear "workmanlike." (Sec. 110-12.)

110-14. Electrical Connections. Proper electrical connections at terminals and splices are absolutely essential to ensure a safe installation. Improper connections are the cause of most failures of wiring devices, equipment burndowns, and electrically oriented fires.

Many years ago soldered splices and lugs were widely used in the electrical industry, but in modern practice such methods have been replaced with solderless-type lugs, terminals, and splicing devices. These modern solderless devices have overcome most of the flaws inherent in soldered splices and lugs. However, solderless devices are only as good as they are selected and used, and misapplications of poor quality work account for many failures.

Proper connections for all types of solderless devices can be assured if suitable wire combinations, types of conductor material (copper, copper-clad aluminum, or aluminum), and proper torque-tightening of screws are used with specific devices. In general, approved pressure-type wire splicing lugs or connectors bear no marking if approved for only copper wire. If approved for copper, copper-clad aluminum, and/or aluminum they are marked "AL-CU"; and if approved for aluminum only they are marked "AL." Devices listed by Underwriters Laboratories Inc, indicate the range or combination of wire sizes for which such devices have been listed.

Reports have been made of field failures where aluminum conductors have been connected to the screw terminals of wiring devices. These failures have been largely due to poor quality work and the use of minimum-quality wiring devices.

Terminals of 15- and 20-A receptacles not marked "CO/ALR" are for use with copper and copper-clad aluminum conductors only. Terminals marked "CO/ALR" are for use with aluminum, copper, and copper-clad aluminum conductors.

Screwless pressure terminal connectors of the conductor push-in type are for use only with copper and copper-clad aluminum conductors.

Terminals of receptacles rated 30 A and above not marked "AL-CU" are for use with copper and copper-clad aluminum conductors only. Terminals of receptacles rated 30 A and above marked "AL-CU" are for use with aluminum, copper, and copper-clad aluminum conductors.

The vast majority of distribution equipment has always come from the manufacturer with mechanical set-screw-type lugs for connecting circuit conductors to the equipment terminals. Lugs on such equipment are commonly marked "AL-CU" or "CU-AL," indicating that the set-screw terminal is suitable for use with *either* copper or aluminum conductors. But, such marking on the lug itself is not sufficient evidence of suitability for use with aluminum conductors. UL requires that equipment with terminals that are found to be suitable for use with *either* copper or aluminum conductors must be marked to indicate such use on the label or wiring diagram of the equipment—completely independent of a marking like "AL-CU," on the lugs themselves. A typical safety switch, for instance, would have lugs marked "AL-CU" *but also must have* a notation on the label or nameplate of the switch that reads like this: "Lugs suitable for copper or aluminum conductors."

Although equipment of the type described above may satisfy UL regulations and NE Code rules [Sec. 110-14(a)] with aluminum conductors terminated directly in mechanical set-screw lugs, many design engineers specify and many installers insist upon use of only "compression-type" lugs for termination of aluminum conductors at all equipment terminals. Because skillful technique and application of correct torque in the tightening of such terminations are critical to eliminating the adverse effects of the "creep" and "cold-flow" characteristics of aluminum, many electrical construction people simply avoid such set-screw terminations.

There are two possible ways to go when using aluminum conductors with distribution equipment that comes with mechanical set-screw terminals:

1. A termination device or copper pigtail may be put on the end of each aluminum conductor to provide an "end" that is suitable, tested, and proven for effective use in a set-screw-type lug. A number of manufacturers make "adapters" which are readily crimped onto the end of an aluminum conductor to "convert" the end to copper or an alloy that will not exhibit the creep and cold-flow disadvantages of aluminum in a set-screw termination. This is shown in Fig. 110-8.

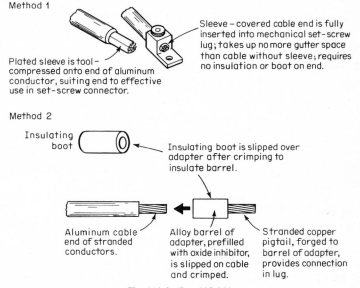

Method 1

Plated sleeve is tool-compressed onto end of aluminum conductor, suiting end to effective use in set-screw connector.

Sleeve – covered cable end is fully inserted into mechanical set-screw lug; takes up no more gutter space than cable without sleeve; requires no insulation or boot on end.

Method 2

Insulating boot

Insulating boot is slipped over adapter after crimping to insulate barrel.

Aluminum cable end of stranded conductors.

Alloy barrel of adapter, prefilled with oxide inhibitor, is slipped on cable and crimped.

Stranded copper pigtail, forged to barrel of adapter, provides connection in lug.

Fig. 110-8. (Sec. 110-14.)

2. Another way to attack the problem is to remove the set-screw lug from the switch or breaker or panel and replace the set-screw lug with a crimp-type lug designed to accept an aluminum conductor which is crimped in the barrel of the lug.

UL-listed equipment must be used in the condition as supplied by the manufacturer—in accordance with **NE Code** rules and any instructions covered in the UL listing in the *Electrical Construction Materials List* (the UL green book)—as required by **NE Code** Sec. 110-3(b). Unauthorized alteration or modification of equipment in the field voids the UL listing and can lead to very dangerous conditions. For this reason, any arbitrary or unspecified changing of terminal lugs on equipment is *not acceptable unless such field modification is recognized by UL* and spelled out very carefully in the manufacturers' literature and on the label of the equipment itself.

For instance, UL-listed authorization for field changing of terminals on a safety switch is described in manufacturers' catalog data and on the switch label itself. It is obvious that field replacement of set-screw lugs with compression-type lugs can be a risky matter if great care is not taken to assure that the size, mounting holes, bolts, and other characteristics of the compression lug line up with and are fully compatible for replacement of the lug that is removed. Careless or makeshift changing of lugs in the field has produced overheating, burning, and failures. To prevent junk-box assembly of replacement lugs, UL requires that any authorized field replacement data *must* indicate the specific lug to be used and *also must* indicate the tool to be used in making the crimps. Any crimp connection of a lug should always be done with the tool specified by the lug manufacturer. Otherwise, there is no assurance that the type of crimp produces a sound connection of the lug to the conductor.

For connecting aluminum branch-circuit conductors to wiring devices, a number of rules and recommendations have been widely publicized:

1. For direct connection use only 15-A and 20-A receptacles and switches marked "CO/ALR" and connected as described below under "Installation Method."

   The "CO/ALR" marking is on the device mounting strap. The "CO/ALR" marking means the devices have been tested to stringent heat-cycling requirements to determine their suitability for use with UL-labeled aluminum, copper, or copper-clad aluminum wire.

   Note: Pigtailing, either field or factory-wired, is recognized by the NEC.

2. Use solid aluminum wire, No. 12 or 10 AWG marked with the Underwriters Laboratories new aluminum insulated wire label, as shown in Fig. 110-9. Follow the installation instructions packaged

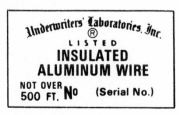

Fig. 110-9. (Sec. 110-14.)

with the wire. Conductor bearing this UL label is judged under the requirements for the chemistry, physical properties, and processing of the conductor.

Installation Method

1. Wrap the freshly stripped end of the wire ⅔ to ¾ of the distance around the wire binding screw post, as shown in Fig. 110-10.

Correct method of terminating aluminum wire at wire-binding-screw terminals of receptacles and snap switches

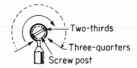

Two-thirds
Three-quarters
Screw post

Step A: Strip and wrap wire

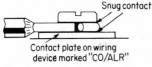

Snug contact

Contact plate on wiring device marked "CO/ALR"

Step B: Tighten screw to full contact

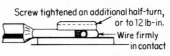

Screw tightened an additional half-turn, or to 12 lb-in.
Wire firmly in contact

Step C: Complete connection

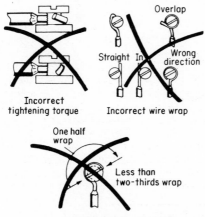

Incorrect tightening torque

Straight In

Overlap

Wrong direction

Incorrect wire wrap

One half wrap

Less than two-thirds wrap

Fig. 110-10. (Sec. 110-14.)

The loop is made so that rotation of the screw in tightening will tend to wrap the wire around the post rather than unwrap it.

2. Tighten the screw until the wire is snugly in contact with the underside of the screw head, and with the contact plate on the wiring device.

3. Tighten the screw an additional ½ turn, thereby providing a firm connection. Where torque screwdrivers are used, tighten to 12 pound-inches.

4. Position the wires behind the wiring device so as to decrease the likelihood of the terminal screws loosening when the device is positioned into the outlet box.

Section 110-14(a), last sentence, prohibits use of more than one conductor in a terminal (see Fig. 110-11) *unless the terminal is approved for the purpose* (meaning, approved for use with two or more conductors in the terminal).

WATCH OUT!

Fig. 110-11. [Sec. 110-14(a).]

Section 110-14(b) covers splice connectors and similar devices used to connect fixture wires to branch-circuit conductors and to splice circuit wires in junction boxes and other enclosures (Fig. 110-12). Much valuable application information on such devices is given in the UL *Electrical*

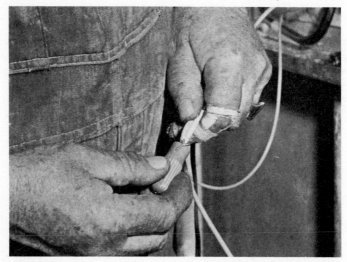

Fig. 110-12. UL data must be observed in using twist-on-type splice devices. [Sec. 110-14(b).]

Construction Materials Directory, under the heading of "Wire Connectors and Soldering Lugs." Details are given about the following factors involved in selecting connectors:

1. Wire connectors for use with aluminum conductors are marked to indicate such use.
2. Except where otherwise indicated, connectors for use with aluminum or copper-clad aluminum conductors are limited to use with insulation rated not more than 75°C.
3. Cartons containing insulated connectors or insulating caps or covers are specifically marked to show the maximum permissible operating temperature, which must be related to conductor-insulation temperature ratings.
4. Where connectors are made to be attached to wire by use of a special tool, that tool and only that tool is acceptable for use. Tools and shipping cartons are marked to facilitate correct usage.

Application of connectors and terminating devices must, of course, conform to the design of the particular device and its intended use. Wire connectors are designed for specific sizes and/or combinations of copper, aluminum, or copper-clad aluminum conductors. Wire connectors are generally classified as either pressure or thermal types. The pressure type, which is most commonly used, includes bolted-pressure connectors, compression-type connectors, and twist-on connectors.

Bolted-pressure connectors include those for making pigtail, straight, tee, or terminal connections. Such connectors depend on the applied force of bolts or screws to produce the clamping and contact pressures between the conductors and the connector.

For making pigtail connections in wire combinations up to No. 10, set-screw connectors with a separate insulated cap that threads onto the connector after securing the wires are readily available. These connectors are used in branch-circuit wiring, fixture hanging, and equipment hookups. The only tool required is a screwdriver, and the connectors can be reused.

Many forms of bolted connectors are designed for making branch connections from main conductors. In such instances, minimum and maximum wire sizes for both main and branch (tap) conductors are usually marked on the connector. For satisfactory connections, only conductors within the range permitted should be used. Split-bolt, clamp-type, gutter-tap, and parallel cable-tap connectors are a few of the common types used. In most instances, these connectors are taped after the wires have been connected. However, some cable-tap connectors feature snap-on or bolt-on plastic covers that fit over the connector and cover uninsulated parts. This eliminates the time required for taping and makes it possible to remove the connector quickly.

Bolted-type lugs secure wires by one or more bolts, depending on design and ampere ratings. Two- or four-barrel lugs are used to terminate multiple conductors.

Tap-in insulated connectors are time-saving devices designed for fast makeup of taps and pigtails by eliminating the need for stripping conductors. The connector consists of a plastic body furnished with a metallic splice bar with teeth that pierce the conductor insulation providing a quick, easy connection of two or more conductors. The plastic body consists of two hinged halves that can be latched together to form a permanent, insulated splice. Inside one half are grooves that align the conductors to be spliced with the "bridging" splice bar, or yoke, mounted in the other half. The insulated conductors are simply placed in the grooves, and the cover is closed and squeezed together with pump pliers. These connectors are designed for conductors sized from No. 10 to No. 12 Cu or No. 10 Al and are rated at 600 V.

Compression-type connectors and lugs include those in which hand, pneumatic, or hydraulic tools indent or circumferentially crimp tubelike sleeves that hold the one or more conductors. The crimping action changes the size and shape of the connector, and a properly crimped joint deforms the conductor strands enough to provide good electrical conductivity and mechanical strength.

Twist-on connectors consist of insulated caps made of phenolic plastics, porcelain, or nylon and an internal threaded core with or without a metallic coil spring. Such connectors require no hand tools and are simply twisted onto appropriate combinations of bared conductors. Connector types consisting of metallic spring coils (copper-coated or steel) are listed by UL as pressure cable connectors, which means they can also be used for connecting branch-circuit conductors No. 14 and larger according to listed sizes and combinations. Connectors without metallic coil springs are regarded as fixture-type splicing connectors for joining fixture wires or branch-circuit wires to fixture wires in a combination of sizes from No. 18 to No. 10 within the listed capacities of the conductor. They are not acceptable for general use in branch-circuit wiring.

Maximum voltage ratings for twist-on connectors are 600 V (or 1,000 V inside a fixture or sign), although some types cannot be used on circuits over 300 V. Also, temperature ratings will vary according to the type of insulating cap. Data for voltage and temperature ratings of the various connectors can be obtained from the individual manufacturer's catalog.

Thermal connectors include those in which heat is applied to form soldered, brazed, or welded joints and terminals. Thermal connections are still permitted but in most applications are rarely used because of the dependability and installation ease of modern solderless pressure connectors.

One technique that uses a thermal connection is called exothermic welding, or sometimes mold-type welding. This method is highly recommended for joining bare copper conductors together or to reinforcing rods, ground rods, or steel surfaces. This process consists of a mold and starting and mixing powder. After conductors, sleeves, and/or lugs are placed in the mold, a flint gun is used to ignite the starting powder. This forms liquid copper, which fuses conductors into a solid mass and results in a permanent electrical connection. The mold-type welding process can be performed easily without special training.

110-16. Working Space About Electric Equipment (600 Volts or Less, Nominal). The intent of the second sentence of Sec. 110-16(a), which calls for a work space at least 30 in. wide in front of electrical equipment, is to provide sufficient "elbow room" in front of such equipment as column-type panelboards and single enclosed switches (e.g., 12 in. wide) to permit the equipment to be operated or maintained under safer conditions.

It should be noted that the next sentence requires distances to be measured *from the live parts* if exposed or from the enclosure containing live parts. It is assumed that the width measurement is to be made *parallel with* the face of the equipment, and *not from* the live parts. This interpretation is shown in Fig. 110-13.

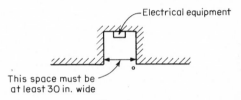

Fig. 110-13. Working space required in front of electrical equipment for side-to-side clearance. [Sec. 110-16(a).]

In Code Table 110-16(a), some of the dimensions of working space in the direction of access to live electrical parts operating at 600 V or less have been increased in the 1978 NEC. All minimum clearances of 2½ ft have been increased to 3 ft. Section 110-16(d) has required a working space at least 3 ft deep in front of switchboards or motor control centers that have live parts normally exposed on their front. The minimum of 3 ft was adopted for Code Table 110-16(a) to make all electrical equipment—panelboards, switches, breakers, starters, etc.—subject to the same 3-ft minimum to increase the level of safety and assure consistent, uniform spacing where anyone might be exposed to the hazard of working on any kind of live equipment. Application of Code Table 110-16(a) to the three "conditions" described in Sec. 110-16(a) is shown in the sketches making up this handbook's Table 110-1. Figure 110-14 shows a typical example of Condition 3.

As an added safety measure, to prevent the case where personnel might be trapped in the working space around burning or arcing electrical equipment, the rule of Sec. 110-16(c) requires *two* "entrances" or directions of access to the working space around switchboards and control panels rated 1,200 A or more and over 6 ft wide. At each end of the

Table 110-1. Clearance Needed in Direction of Access to Live Parts in Enclosures for Switchboards, Panelboards, Switches, CBs, or Other Electrical Equipment—Plan Views. [Sec. 110-16(a).]

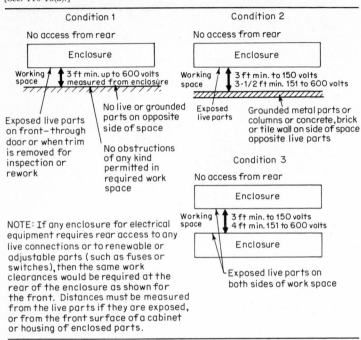

Condition 1
No access from rear

Enclosure

Working space — 3 ft min. up to 600 volts measured from enclosure

Exposed live parts on front—through door or when trim is removed for inspection or rework

No live or grounded parts on opposite side of space

No obstructions of any kind permitted in required work space

Condition 2
No access from rear

Enclosure

Working space — 3 ft min. to 150 volts / 3-1/2 ft min. 151 to 600 volts

Exposed live parts

Grounded metal parts or columns or concrete, brick or tile wall on side of space opposite live parts

Condition 3
No access from rear

Enclosure

Working space — 3 ft min. to 150 volts / 4 ft min. 151 to 600 volts

Enclosure

Exposed live parts on both sides of work space

NOTE: If any enclosure for electrical equipment requires rear access to any live connections or to renewable or adjustable parts (such as fuses or switches), then the same work clearances would be required at the rear of the enclosure as shown for the front. Distances must be measured from the live parts if they are exposed, or from the front surface of a cabinet or housing of enclosed parts.

working space at such equipment, an entranceway or access route at least 24 in. wide must be provided "where reasonably practicable." That last phrase in the rule is undefined and leaves final decision up to the inspector. Because personnel have been trapped in work space by fire between them and the only route of exit from the space, rigid enforcement of this rule is likely. Certainly, design engineers should make two paths of exit a standard requirement in their drawings and specs. Although the rule does not *require* two doors into an electrical equipment room, it may be necessary to use two doors in order to obtain the required two entrances to the required work space—especially where the switchboard or control panel is in tight quarters and does not afford a 24-in. wide path of exit at each end of the work space.

In Fig. 110-15, sketch "A" shows compliance with the **Code** rule—providing two areas for entering or leaving the defined work space. In that sketch, placing the switchboard with its front to the larger area of the room and/or other layouts would also satisfy the intent of the new rule. It

Fig. 110-14. Condition 3 in Code Table 110-16(a) for the rule covered by Sec. 110-16(a) applies to the case of face-to-face enclosures, as shown here where two switchboards face each other. The distance indicated must be at least 3 or 4 ft depending on the voltage of enclosed parts. [Sec. 110-16(a).]

is only necessary to have an assured means of exit from the defined work space. If the space in front of the equipment is deeper than the required depth of work space, then a person could simply move back out of the work space at any point along the length of the equipment.

Sketch "B" in Fig. 110-16(c) shows the layout that must be avoided. With sufficient space available in the room, layout of any switchboard or control center rated 1,200 A or more with only one exit route from the required work space would most likely be a clear violation of the new rule because compliance with the rule would be "reasonably practicable." As shown in sketch "B," a door at the right end of the work space would eliminate the violation.

Prior to the 1978 **NEC**, the rule of Sec. 110-16(e) required lighting of all work spaces at "switchboards and motor control centers." Because the **NE Code** gives clear, specific definitions of those two types of equipment, the wording of the rule made work-space lighting necessary only for those types of equipment. Lighting was not required for work spaces at panelboards or at individually enclosed switches, circuit breakers, motor starters, and other equipment that fell outside the narrow, limited meanings of the two assemblies mentioned. In fact, a group of combination motor starters nippled out of an auxiliary gutter would not technically require lighting of the work space in front of them—even though such a layout is functionally identical to a motor control center.

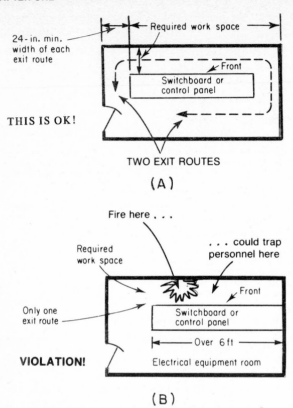

Fig. 110-15. There must be *two* paths out of the work space required in front of switchboards rated 1200 A or more and over 6 ft wide. [Sec. 110-16(c).]

In the 1978 **NEC**, Sec. 110-16(e) requires lighting of work space at "service equipment, switchboards, panelboards, or motor control centers installed indoors." The basic rule and its exception are shown in Fig. 110-16.

The important Exception to this rule excludes "service equipment or panelboards, in dwelling units, that do not exceed 200 amperes" from the need to have lighting installed at their locations. But note that the Exception applies only to such equipment in "dwelling units"—which means in a one-family house or in an apartment within an apartment house. The narrow definition of "dwelling unit" does not make this Exception applicable to service equipment or panelboards that are in an apartment building but are located outside any of the "dwelling units"—such as in hallways, electric closets, and basements.

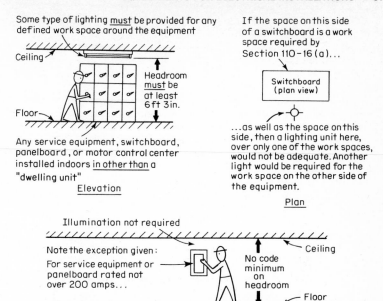

Some type of lighting <u>must</u> be provided for any defined work space around the equipment

Ceiling

Headroom <u>must</u> be at least 6 ft 3 in.

Floor

Any service equipment, switchboard, panelboard, or motor control center installed indoors <u>in other than a</u> "dwelling unit"

Elevation

If the space on this side of a switchboard is a work space required by Section 110–16 (a)...

Switchboard (plan view)

...as well as the space on this side, then a lighting unit here, over only one of the work spaces, would not be adequate. Another light would be required for the work space on the other side of the equipment.

Plan

Illumination not required

Note the exception given:

For service equipment or panelboard rated not over 200 amps...

No code minimum on headroom

Ceiling

Floor

... BUT only in a one-family house, an apartment unit of an apartment house or other "dwelling unit."

Fig. 110-16. Electrical equipment requires lighting and 6¼ ft headroom at *all* work spaces around equipment. [Secs. 110-16(e) and (f).]

It should be noted that although lighting is required for safety of personnel in work spaces, nothing specific is said about the kind of lighting (incandescent, fluorescent, mercury-vapor), no minimum foot-candle level is set, and such details as the position and mounting of lighting equipment are omitted. All of that is left to the designer and/or installer, with the inspector the final judge of acceptability.

In Sec. 110-16(f) of the 1978 **NEC**, there is no change on the required minimum headroom of 6¼ ft in working spaces required around electrical equipment; but, as in Sec. 110-16(e), the change is in the type of equipment to which the requirement applies. Where the 1975 **NE Code** applied the rule to "switchboards or motor control centers," the 1978 rule applies to "service equipment, switchboards, panelboards, or motor control centers." The same Exception as in Sec. 110-16(e) is added that permits "service equipment or panelboards, in dwelling units, that do not exceed 200 amperes" to be installed with less than 6¼ ft of headroom—such as in crawl spaces under single-family houses. But the permission for reduced headroom of the equipment described in the Exception applies only in "dwelling units" that meet the new definition of that phrase. In any space other than a dwelling unit, all indoor service equipment, switchboards, panelboards, or control centers must have 6¼-ft headroom in any space around the equipment that is work space required by Sec. 110-16(a).

Details on lighting and headroom are shown in Fig. 110-16(e) and (f). But, in that sketch, it should be noted that the 6-ft 3-in. headroom must be available for the entire length of the work space. It must be clearance from the floor up to the light fixture or to any other overhead obstruction—and not simply to the ceiling or bottom of the joists.

110-17. Guarding of Live Parts (600 volts or less, nominal). After the 1968 NEC, old Sec. 110-17(a)(3) accepting guard rails as suitable for guarding live parts was deleted. It was felt that a guard rail is not proper or adequate protection in areas accessible to other than qualified persons.

Live parts of equipment should in general be protected from accidental contact by complete enclosure; i.e., the equipment should be "dead-front." Such construction is not practicable in some large control panels, and in such cases the apparatus should be isolated or guarded as required by these rules.

110-18. Arcing Parts. The same considerations apply here as in the case covered in Sec. 110-17. Full enclosure is preferable, but where this is not practicable, all combustible material must be kept well away from the equipment.

110-21. Marking. The marking required in Sec. 110-21 should be done in a manner which will allow inspectors to examine such marking without removing the equipment from a permanently installed position. It should be noted that the last sentence in Sec. 110-21 requires electrical equipment to have a marking durable enough to withstand the environment involved (such as equipment designed for wet or corrosive locations).

110-22. Identification of Disconnecting Means. As shown in Fig. 110-17, it is a mandatory Code rule that all disconnect devices (switches or CBs)

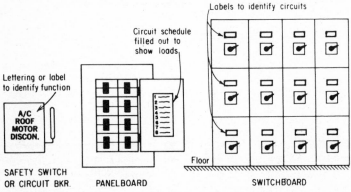

Fig. 110-17. All circuits and disconnects must be identified. OSHA regulations make NE Code Sec. 110-22 mandatory and retroactive for existing installations and for all new, expanded or modernized systems—applying to switches as well as circuit breakers. (Sec. 110-22.)

for load devices and for circuits be clearly and permanently marked to show the purposes of the disconnects. This is a "must" and, under OSHA, it applies to all existing electrical systems, no matter how old, and also to all new, modernized, expanded, or altered electrical systems. This requirement for marking has been widely neglected in electrical systems in the past. Panelboard circuit directories must be fully and clearly filled out. And all such marking on equipment must be in painted lettering or other substantial identification.

Effective identification of all disconnect devices is a critically important safety matter. When a switch or CB has to be opened to de-energize a circuit quickly—as when a threat of injury to personnel dictates—it is absolutely necessary to identify quickly and positively the disconnect for the circuit or equipment that constitutes the hazard to a person or property. Painted labeling or embossed identification plates affixed to enclosures would comply with the requirement that disconnects be "legibly marked" and that the "marking shall be of sufficient durability." Paste-on paper labels or marking with crayon or chalk could be rejected as not complying with the intent of this rule. Ideally, marking should tell exactly what piece of equipment is controlled by a disconnect (switch or CB) and should tell where the controlled equipment is located and how *it* may be identified. Figure 110-18 shows a case of this kind of identification as used in an industrial facility where all equipment is marked in two languages because personnel speak different languages. And that is an

Fig. 110-18. Identification of disconnect switch and pushbutton stations is "legibly marked" in both English and French—and is of "sufficient durability to withstand the environment"—as required by the Code rule. (Sec. 110-22.)

old installation, attesting to the long-standing recognition of this safety feature.

110-30. General. Figure 110-19 notes that high-voltage switches and circuit breakers must be marked to indicate the circuit or equipment controlled. This requirement arises because Sec. 110-30 says that high-voltage equipment must comply with preceding sections of Art. 110.

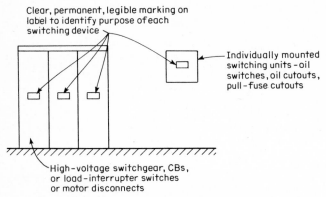

Clear, permanent, legible marking on label to identify purpose of each switching device

Individually mounted switching units - oil switches, oil cutouts, pull - fuse cutouts

High-voltage switchgear, CBs, or load-interrupter switches or motor disconnects

Fig. 110-19. High-voltage switches and breakers must be properly marked to indicate their function. (Sec. 110-30.)

Therefore, the rule of Sec. 110-22 calling for marking of all disconnecting means must be observed for high-voltage equipment as well as for equipment rated up to 600 V.

110-31. Enclosure for Electrical Installations. Figure 110-20 illustrates the rules which cover installation of high-voltage equipment indoors in places accessible to unqualified persons. Installation must be in a locked vault or locked area, or equipment must be metal-enclosed.

Section 110-31(b) specifies that outdoor installations *with exposed live parts* must *not* provide access to unqualified persons. Elevation may be used to prevent access [Sec. 110-34(e)], or equipment may be enclosed by a wall, screen, or fence under lock and key, as shown in Fig. 110-21. Outdoor installations that are open to unqualified persons must comply with Art. 225, "Outside Branch Circuits and Feeders."

For any equipment, rooms, or enclosures where the voltage exceeds 600 V, permanent and conspicuous warning signs reading WARNING— HIGH VOLTAGE, KEEP OUT should always be provided. Although this is not required by the Code, it is a safety measure that alerts unfamiliar or unqualified persons who may for some reason gain access to a locked, high-voltage area.

Where high-voltage equipment is installed in places accessible only to qualified persons, the rules of Sec. 110-34, 710-32, and 710-33 apply. In

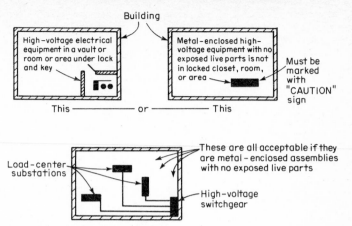

Fig. 110-20. NE Code rules on high-voltage equipment installations in buildings accessible to electrically unqualified persons. [Sec. 110-31(a).]

Fig. 110-21. High-voltage equipment enclosed by a wall, screen, or fence at least 8 ft high with a lockable door or gate—is considered as accessible only to qualified persons. [Sec. 110-31(b).]

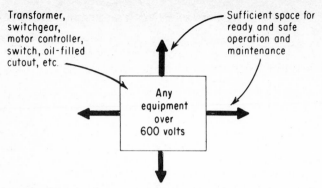

Fig. 110-22. This is the general rule for work space around any high-voltage equipment. (Sec. 110-32.)

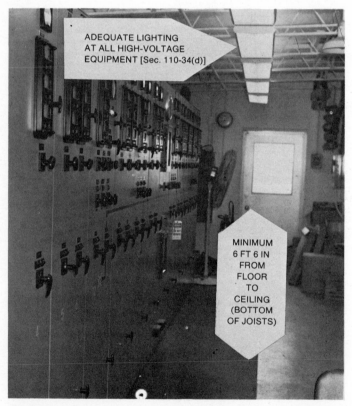

Fig. 110-23. Sufficient headroom and adequate lighting are essential to safe operation, maintenance, and repair of high-voltage equipment. (Sec. 110-32.)

such areas, circuit conductors may be installed in conduit, in duct systems, in metal-clad cable, as bare wire, cable, and busbars, or as nonmetallic-sheathed cables or conductors as permitted by **NE Code** Secs. 710-3 through 710-6.

110-32. Workspace About Equipment. Figure 110-22 points out the basic **Code** rule of Sec. 110-32 relating to working space around electrical equipment.

Figure 110-23 shows the rules on adequate headroom and necessary illumination for safely working on high-voltage electrical equipment.

Figure 110-24 shows required side-to-side working space for adequate elbow room in front of high-voltage equipment.

110-33. Entrance and Access to Workspace. Entrances and access to workspace around high-voltage equipment must comply with the rules shown in Fig. 110-25.

Fig. 110-24. Working space in front of equipment must be at least 3 ft wide measured parallel to front surface of the enclosure. (Sec. 110-32.)

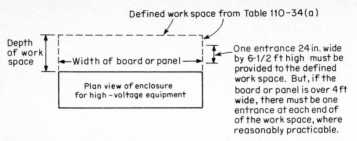

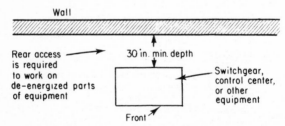

Fig. 110-25. Access to required work space around high-voltage equipment must be assured. (Sec. 110-33.)

110-34. Work Space and Guarding.   Application of Code Table 110-34(a) to work space around high-voltage equipment is made in the same way as shown for Code Table 110-16(a)—except that the depths are greater to provide more room because of the higher voltages.

As shown in Fig. 110-26, a 30-in.-deep work space is required behind

Fig. 110-26. Space for safe work on de-energized parts. [Sec. 110-34(a).]

enclosed high-voltage equipment that requires rear access to "de-energized" parts. The Exception to Sec. 110-34(a)(3) has been expanded in the 1978 NEC. As in the 1975 NEC, this Exception notes that working space is not required behind dead-front equipment when there are no fuses, switches, other parts, or connections requiring rear access. But the rule now adds that if rear access is necessary to permit work on "de-energized" parts of the enclosed assembly, the work space must be at least 30 in. deep. This was added to prohibit cases where switchgear requiring rear access is installed too close to a wall behind it, and personnel have to work in cramped quarters to reach taps, splices, and terminations. However, it must be noted that this applies only where "de-energized" parts are accessible from the back of the equipment. If energized parts are accessible, then Condition 2 of Sec. 110-34(a) would exist, and the depth of working space would have to be anywhere from 4 to 10 ft, depending upon the voltage [see Table 110-34(a)].

Fig. 110-27 Elevation may be used to isolate unguarded live parts from unqualified persons. [Sec. 110-34(e).]

Section 110-34(c) requires that the entrances to all buildings, rooms, or enclosures containing live parts or exposed conductors operating in excess of 600 V shall be kept locked, except where such entrances are under the observation of a qualified attendant at all times.

The rule of Sec. 110-34(d) on lighting of high-voltage work space is shown in Fig. 110-23. Note that the rule calls for "adequate illumination" but does not specify a footcandle level or any other characteristics.

Figure 110-27 shows how "elevation" may be used to protect high-voltage live parts from unauthorized persons.

Chapter Two

ARTICLE 200. USE AND IDENTIFICATION OF GROUNDED CONDUCTORS

200-2. General. As indicated, some circuits and systems may be operated without an intentionally grounded conductor—that is, without a grounded neutral or a grounded phase leg. Sections 250-7, 503-13(a), and 517-104(b) *require* use of *ungrounded* circuits.

Ungrounded circuits are required in anesthetizing locations—which include hospital operating rooms, delivery rooms, emergency rooms, and any place where anesthetics are administered. (See Sec. 517-104.)

200-6. Means of Identifying Grounded Conductors. The basic rule in part **(a)** requires that any grounded neutral conductor or other circuit conductor that is operated intentionally grounded must have a white or natural gray outer finish for *the entire length* of the conductor *if* the conductor is No. 6 size or smaller. See Fig. 200-1.

Exception No. 2 to the basic rule that requires use of continuous white or natural gray color along the entire length of any insulated grounded conductor (such as grounded neutral) in sizes No. 6 or smaller permits use of a conductor of other colors (black, purple, yellow, etc.) for a grounded conductor in a *multiconductor cable* under certain conditions (see Fig. 200-2):

    1. That such a conductor is used only where qualified persons supervise and do service or maintenance on the cable—such as in industrial and mining applications.

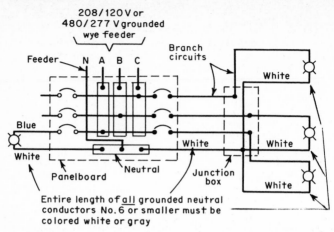

Fig. 200-1. Generally any grounded circuit conductor that is No. 6 size or smaller must have a continuous white or natural gray outer finish. [Sec. 200-6(a).]

2. That every grounded conductor of color other than white or gray will be effectively and permanently identified at all terminations by distinctive white marking or other effective means applied at the time of installation.

This permission for such use of grounded conductors in multiconductor cable was added to allow the practice in those industrial facilities

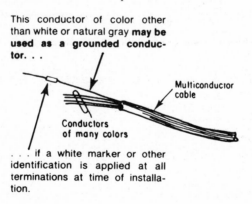

NOTE: This permission applies to No. 6 and smaller conductors —as well as to conductors larger than No. 6.

Fig. 200-2. [Sec. 200-6(a), Exception No. 2.]

where multiconductor cables are commonly used—although the rule does not limit the use to industrial occupancies.

An Exception identical to the one described above under Sec. 200-6(a) has been added to the rule of Sec. 200-6(b) that requires any grounded conductor larger than No. 6 to be either white or gray color for its whole length or to be marked with white identification (like white tape) at all terminations at time of installation.

For conductors installed in raceways or in general-use cable assemblies like NM cable or BX cable (NEC Type (AC), continuous white or gray marking along the entire lengths of grounded conductors is not required for conductors larger than No. 6. Such grounded conductors may be of color other than white or gray provided that a "distinctive white marking"—such as white tape or paint—is applied to the conductor surface at all points of splice or termination to readily designate that it *is* a grounded conductor. See Fig. 200-3.

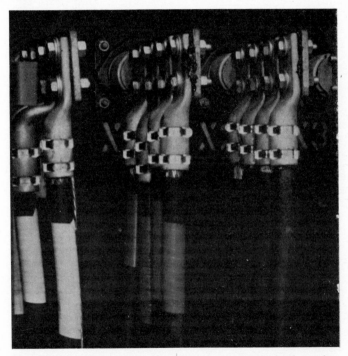

Fig. 200-3. Conductors of colors other than white or gray—in sizes larger than No. 6—may be used as grounded neutrals or grounded phase legs if marked white at all terminations—such as by white tape on the grounded feeder neutrals, at left. [Other color tapes are used on other circuit conductors to identify the three phases as A, B, and C—as required by Sec. 384-3(f).] [Sec. 200-6(b).]

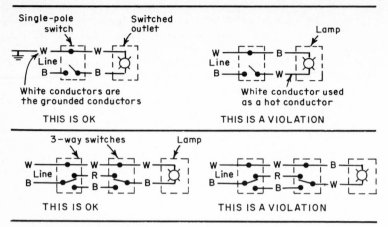

Fig. 200-4. A white or gray-colored conductor must normally be used *only* as a grounded conductor (the grounded circuit neutral or grounded phase leg of a delta system.). (Sec. 200-7.)

200-7. Use of White or Natural Gray Color. Although the basic rule here limits conductors with white or gray outer covering to use only as grounded conductors (that is, as grounded neutral or grounded phase conductors (see Fig. 200-4), a number of exceptions to the rule are noted:

Figure 200-5 shows a white-colored conductor used for an ungrounded phase conductor of a feeder to a panelboard. As shown in

Fig. 200-5. White conductor in lower left of panel gutter is used as an ungrounded phase conductor of a feeder, with black tape wrapped around the conductor end to "reidentify" the conductor as *not* a grounded conductor. (Sec. 200-7, Exception No. 1.)

the left side of the panel bottom gutter, the white conductor has black tape wrapped around its end for a length of a few inches. This almost satisfies Exception No. 1 of Sec. 200-7, which permits a white conductor to be used for an ungrounded (a hot phase leg) conductor if the white is "permanently reidentified"—such as by wrapping with black or other color tape—to indicate clearly and effectively that the conductor is ungrounded. The wording of the Exception, however, might be interpreted to require that the black or other color tape be wrapped over the entire visible length of the conduit bushing.

Exception No. 2 indicates conditions under which a white conductor in

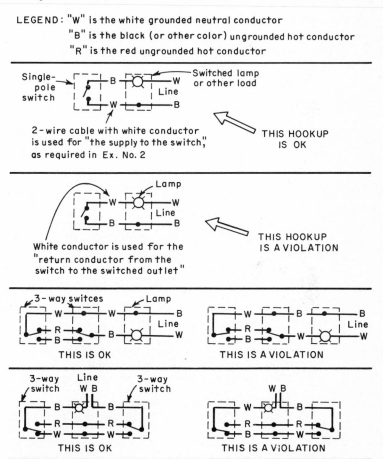

Fig. 200-6. For switch loops from load outlets with hot supply to the load outlet, white conductor in cable must be the "supply to the switch." (Sec. 200-7, Exception No. 2.)

a cable (such as BX or nonmetallic-sheathed cable) may be used for an ungrounded (hot-leg) conductor—*without need* for "reidentification" (such as painting or taping). When used as described, the white conductor is acceptable even though it is not a grounded conductor. Figure 200-6 shows examples of correct and incorrect hookups of switch loops where hot supply is run first to the switched outlet then to switches.

Exception No. 3 covers flexible cords for connecting appliances to a receptacle outlet. Exception No. 4 applies to circuits derived from the secondary side of transformers that step down to less than 50 V. Such circuits may use a white conductor.

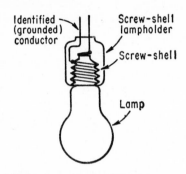

SCREW-SHELL LAMPHOLDERS are wired so that ungrounded conductor is connected to center terminal to reduce shock hazard. The identified (grounded) conductor is connected to the screw-shell.

Fig. 200-7. Screw-shell sockets must have the grounded wire (the neutral) connected to the screw-shell part. [Sec. 200-10(c).]

ARTICLE 210.   BRANCH CIRCUITS

210-3. Classifications.   A branch circuit is rated according to the setting or rating of the overcurrent device used to protect the circuit. Any branch circuit with more than one outlet *must* be rated at 15, 20, 30, 40, or 50 A (Fig. 210-1). That is, the protective device must have one of those ratings for multioutlet circuits, and the conductors must meet the other size requirements of Art. 210. Under the definition for "receptacle" in NE Code Art. 100, it is indicated that a duplex convenience outlet (a duplex receptacle) is two receptacles and not one—even though there is only one box. Thus, a circuit that supplies only one duplex receptacle has "more than one outlet," that is, more than one point at which current is taken from the current to supply utilization equipment.

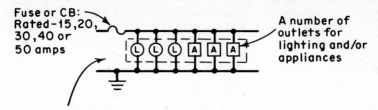

Fuse or CB:
Rated-15,20,
30,40 or
50 amps
A number of
outlets for
lighting and/or
appliances
Circuit voltage shall not exceed 150 volts to ground for circuits supplying lampholders, fixtures or receptacles of standard 15-amp rating. For incandescent or electric-discharge lighting under certain conditions, voltage to ground may be as high as 300 volts. In certain cases, voltage for electric discharge lighting may be up to 500 volts "between conductors" and may be an ungrounded circuit.

Fig. 210-1. Any multioutlet branch circuit must have a rating (of its overcurrent protective device) at one of the five values set by Sec. 210.3. (Sec. 210-3.)

It is important to note that it is the size of the overcurrent device which determines the rating of any circuit covered by Art. 210, even when the conductors used for the branch circuit have an ampere rating higher than that of the protective device. In a typical case, for example, a 20-A circuit breaker in a panelboard might be used to protect a branch circuit in which No. 10 conductors are used as the circuit wires. Although the load on the circuit does not exceed 20 A and No. 12 conductors would have sufficient current-carrying capacity to be used in the circuit, the No. 10 conductors with their rating of 30 A were selected to reduce the voltage drop in a long home-run. The rating of the circuit is 20 A because that is the size of the overcurrent device. The current rating of the wire does not enter into the ampere classification of the circuit.

Although multioutlet branch circuits are limited in rating to 15, 20, 30, 40, or 50 A, a branch circuit to a single-load outlet (for instance, a branch circuit to one machine or to one receptacle outlet) may have any ampere rating (Fig. 210-2). For instance, there could be a 200-A branch circuit to a special receptacle outlet or a 300-A branch circuit to a single machine.

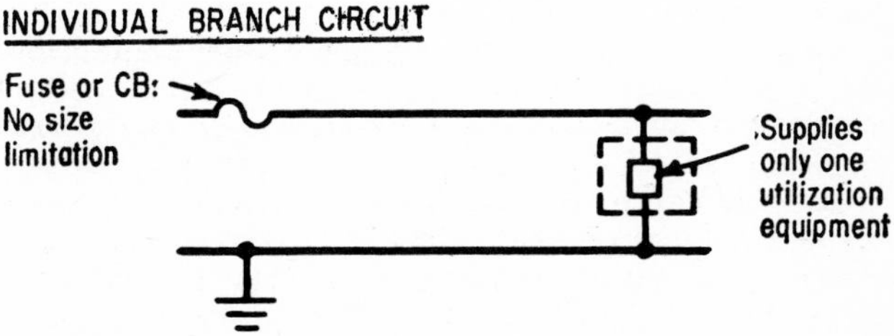

INDIVIDUAL BRANCH CIRCUIT
Fuse or CB:
No size
limitation
Supplies
only one
utilization
equipment

Fig. 210-2. A circuit to a single load device or equipment may have any rating. (Sec. 210-3.)

210-4. Multiwire Branch Circuits. A "branch circuit" as covered by Art. 210 may be a 2-wire circuit or may be a "multiwire" branch circuit. A "multiwire" branch circuit consists of two or more ungrounded conductors having a potential difference between them and an identified grounded conductor having equal potential difference between it and each of the ungrounded conductors and which is connected to the neutral conductor of the system. Thus, a 3-wire circuit consisting of two opposite-polarity ungrounded conductors and a neutral derived from a 3-wire, single-phase system or a 4-wire circuit consisting of three different phase conductors and a neutral of a 3-phase, 4-wire system is a *single* multiwire branch circuit. This is only one circuit, even though it involves two or three single-pole protective devices in the panelboard (Fig. 210-3).

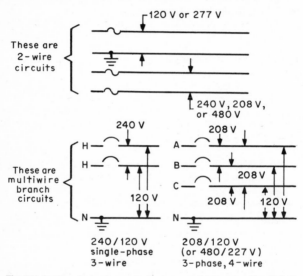

Fig. 210-3. Branch circuits may be 2-wire or multiwire type. (Sec. 210-4.)

This is important, because other sections of the Code refer to conditions involving "one branch circuit" or "the single branch circuit." (See Secs. 250-24 and 410-31.)

The basic rule of the second sentence of this section states that multiwire branch circuits (such as 240/120-V, 3-wire, single-phase and 3-phase, 4-wire circuits at 280/120 V or 480/277 V) may be used only with loads connected from a hot or phase leg to the neutral conductor (Fig. 210-4). The two exceptions to that rule are shown in Fig. 210-5.

Exception No. 1 permits use of single-pole protective devices for an individual circuit to "only one utilization equipment"—in which load may be connected line-to-line as well as line-to-neutral. "Utilization equipment," as defined in Art. 100, is "equipment which utilizes electric energy

When using single-pole devices
for branch-circuit protection
(fuses or single-pole CBs). . .

**THIS IS
THE
BASIC
RULE**

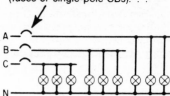

. . . multiwire branch circuits shall supply only line-to-
neutral connected loads.

Fig. 210-4. With single-pole protection only line-to-neutral loads may
be fed. (Sec. 210-4.)

for mechanical, chemical, heating, lighting, or similar purposes." The
definition of "appliance," in Art. 100, notes that an appliance is "*utilization equipment,* generally other than industrial, normally built in standard-
ized sizes or types . . . such as clothes washing, air conditioning, food
mixing, deep frying, etc." Because of those definitions, the wording of
Exception No. 1 opens its application to commercial and industrial
equipment as well as residential.

Ex. No. 1 A multiwire branch circuit may supply a single utilization equipment with line-to-line and line-to-neutral voltage
using single-pole switching devices in branch-circuit protection.

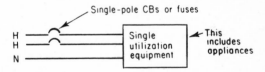

Ex. No. 2 If a multipole CB is used, loads may be connected line-
to-line and/or line-to-neutral.

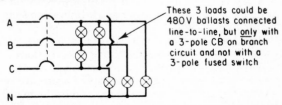

Fig. 210-5. Line-to-line loads may only be connected on multiwire circuits that
conform to the Exceptions given. (Sec. 210-4.)

Exception No. 2 permits a circuit to supply line-to-line connected loads only when it is protected by a multipole circuit breaker. The intent of Exception No. 2 is that line-to-line connected loads may be used (other than in Exception No. 1) *only* where the poles of the *circuit protective device* operate together, or simultaneously. A multipole CB satisfies the rule, but a fused multipole switch would not comply because the hot circuit conductors are *not* "opened simultaneously by the branch-circuit over-current device." This rule requiring a multipole CB for any circuit that supplies line-to-line connected loads as well as line-to-neutral loads was put in the Code to prevent equipment loss under the conditions shown in Fig. 210-6. However, some electrical inspectors have applied an interpretation to the basic rule of Sec. 210-4 and its Exception No. 2 to require a

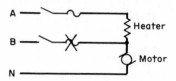

Should fuse B open, the heater and motor would be
in series on 115 volts, and the motor could burn out
if not properly protected.

Fig. 210-6. Single-pole protection can expose equipment to damage. (Sec. 210-4.)

multipole CB on multiwire circuits with line-to-line loads to provide safety to maintenance personnel or any persons working on or replacing lighting fixtures or receptacle outlets connected line-to-line in existing systems. This has been a widely discussed and very controversial problem in Code interpretation over recent years. Shock hazard may exist in replacing or maintaining any piece of electrical equipment where *only one* of *two* hot supply conductors has been opened. If only one of the two single-pole CBs protecting a 240-V circuit or a 240/120-V 3-wire circuit is shut off, the load will be de-energized and electrical workers may presume that they will not contact any hot terminals of equipment supplied and then be surprised by electric shock from the other hot leg.

The problem arises when, say, a receptacle or lighting fixture is fed by more than one hot wire. If a person attempts to work on the receptacle after shutting off only one of the branch-circuit breakers or switching devices in the branch-circuit panelboard, the other leg to the receptacle is still hot and poses a shock hazard to the person, who thinks the circuit has been killed. The same is true of lighting fixtures connected phase-to-phase at 240 V, 208 V or 480 V.

Because any such condition is a real hazard and is as likely (if not *more* likely) to occur at a receptacle outlet as at an outlet to a 240- or 208-V lighting or heating load, some inspectors believe the Code rule requires a

2-pole CB in any case where the branch circuit supplies a line-to-line connected load, including a split-wired receptacle, and enforce that understanding of the rule of Sec. 210-4 (Fig. 210-7). A split-wired receptacle with each receptacle feeding two plugged-in loads of the same current has no neutral current; and the circuit, at that point, *is* supplying strictly line-to-line connected load. In any case, use of a 2-pole CB for such appliances is better practice and certainly does not violate the Code.

WATCH OUT FOR THIS!

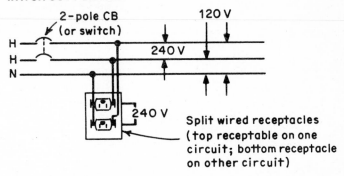

Because a line-to-line connection is made on one side of the duplex receptacle, some inspectors consider that to be a line-to-line load and require that a 2-pole CB be used as the branch-circuit overcurrent device to satisfy Sec. 210-4 in accordance with Exception No. 2.

Fig. 210-7. A split-wired receptacle may be ruled a line-to-line load. (Sec. 210-4.)

The Code is not clear about the meaning of "line-to-neutral load" and "line-to-line load." The Code has no definition of the word "load"; and the definition of "continuous load" indicates that "load" is "current." In general electrical vocabulary, it is and always has been common practice to use the word "load" to describe a condition of current flow. We speak of "service load," "feeder load," "branch-circuit load," "transformer load," etc. To a utility, even a whole building is a "load." As noted above, if a split-wired receptacle supplies, say, two 1,200-W, 120-V resistive appliances, the duplex receptacle is *only* a "line-to-line" load—that is, it is drawing 10 A at 240 V, with no neutral current flowing through the receptacle. In long-time industry usage, current flow only on two line conductors, with the neutral connected, is a "line-to-line load," whether in a branch circuit, at a transformer in an appliance, or at a *receptacle.* To consider a receptacle as a "load" is supported by the Code. Section 220-2(c) specifies "the minimum *load* for each outlet for general-use receptacles." Part **(4)** designates that each single or multiple receptacle be taken as a *load* of 180 VA—even when nothing is connected to the receptacles.

Section 220-13 and Table 220-13 are headed "Receptacle Loads." Given the fact that the Code itself refers to receptacles as "loads," the interests of safety are best served by using the word "load" in its usual broad sense. And it should be noted that the threat of motor burnout shown in the diagram of Fig. 210-6 can exist just as readily where the 230-V resistance device and the 115-V motor are fed from a dual-voltage (240-V, 120-V) duplex receptacle as where loads are fixed-wired.

It is not clear that the Code rule requires a 2-pole circuit breaker or switch as the branch-circuit protective device for any circuit supplying a split-wired receptacle. It seems, however, that certain local inspectors who have insisted that any split-wired receptacles be supplied by a branch circuit with a 2-pole switching device will use this Code rule as basis for their contention that it is safer to use a 2-pole device on a branch circuit as opposed to a split-wired receptacle to assure against shock hazard to unsuspecting personnel.

But, as shown in Fig. 210-8, the rule of Sec. 210-4 does clearly call for a 2-pole CB (and not single-pole CBs or fuses) for a circuit supplying a dual-voltage receptacle. In such a case, a line-to-line load and a line-to-neutral load could be connected and subjected to the condition shown in Fig. 210-6.

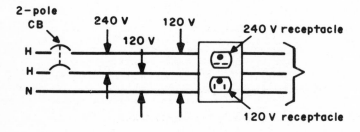

If any load on a multiwire circuit supplying more than one outlet is connected line-to-line (such as a 240-volt load on the receptacle above), a multipole CB must be used.

Fig. 210-8. A dual-voltage receptacle requires a 2-pole CB on its circuit. (Sec. 210-4.)

210-5. Color Code for Branch Circuits. Code rules on color coding of conductors (Sec. 210-5) apply only to branch-circuit conductors and do not directly require color coding of feeder conductors. However, NE Code Sec. 384-3(f) does require identification of phase legs of feeders to panelboards, switchboards, etc.—and that requires some technique for marking the phase legs. Many design engineers do insist on color coding of feeder conductors to afford effective balancing of loads on the different phase legs.

Fig. 210-9. (Sec. 210-5.)

Color coding of branch-circuit conductors is divided into three categories:

Grounded conductor: The grounded conductor of a branch circuit (the neutral of a wye system or a grounded phase of a delta) must be identified by a continuous white or natural gray color, for the entire length of conductors No. 6 or smaller. Where wires of different systems (such as 120/208 and 480/277) are installed in the same raceway, box, or other enclosure, the neutral or grounded wire of one system must be white; and the neutral of the other system must be gray or white with a color stripe. If there are three or more systems in the same raceway or enclosure, the additional neutrals must be white with colored tracers other than green. The point is that neutrals of different systems must be distinguished from each other when they are in the same enclosure [Code Sec. 210-5(a) and Fig. 210-10].

WHEN THERE IS ONLY ONE SYSTEM VOLTAGE:

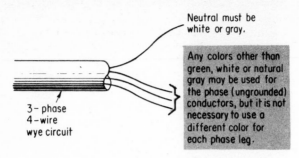

Neutral must be
white or gray.

Any colors other than
green, white or natural
gray may be used for
the phase (ungrounded)
conductors, but it is not
necessary to use a
different color for
each phase leg.

3-phase
4-wire
wye circuit

BUT, Neutrals of different systems must be distinguished

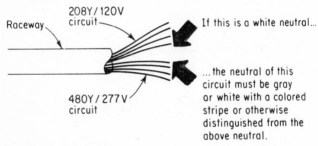

Raceway

208Y/120V
circuit

If this is a white neutral...

...the neutral of this
circuit must be gray
or white with a colored
stripe or otherwise
distinguished from the
above neutral.

480Y/277V
circuit

Fig. 210-10. Grounded circuit conductors (neutrals) must have color identification. [Sec. 210-5(a).]

As already noted, Exceptions to Sec. 200-6 modify the basic rule that requires use of continuous white or natural gray color along the entire length of any insulated grounded conductor (such as a grounded neutral) in sizes No. 6 or smaller. Likewise, Exception No. 2 to Sec. 210-5(a) also permits use of a conductor of other colors (black, purple, yellow, etc.) for a grounded conductor in a *multiconductor* cable under the following conditions:

1. That such a conductor is used only where qualified persons supervise and do service or maintenance on the cable—such as in industrial and mining applications.
2. That every grounded conductor of color other than white or gray will be effectively and permanently identified at all terminations by distinctive white marking or other effective means applied at the time of installation.

This permission for such use of grounded conductors in multiconductor cable allows the practice in commercial and industrial facilities where multiconductor cables are commonly used.

Hot conductors: The NE Code no longer requires that individual hot conductors of a multiwire circuit be identified. It is no longer necessary, for instance, to use black, red, and blue for phase conductors of a circuit, with a white conductor as the neutral. Absence of a specific Code rule on required color for phase (or hot) legs of branch circuits permits all phase conductors (hot legs) of a circuit to be the same color. That is, all circuit conductors could be black, or blue, or red, or any other color (Fig. 210-11).

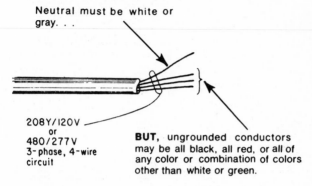

Neutral must be white or gray. . .

208Y/120V
or
480/277V
3-phase, 4-wire
circuit

BUT, ungrounded conductors may be all black, all red, or all of any color or combination of colors other than white or green.

IF THERE ARE TWO SYSTEM VOLTAGES:

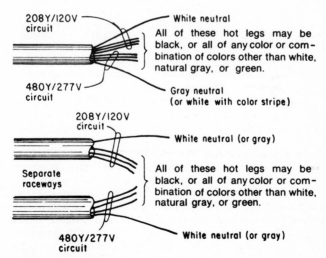

208Y/120V
circuit

White neutral

All of these hot legs may be black, or all of any color or combination of colors other than white, natural gray, or green.

480Y/277V
circuit

Gray neutral
(or white with color stripe)

208Y/120V
circuit

White neutral (or gray)

Separate
raceways

All of these hot legs may be black, or all of any color or combination of colors other than white, natural gray, or green.

480Y/277V
circuit

White neutral (or gray)

Fig. 210-11. Color coding is no longer required for ungrounded (hot) conductors of multiwire branch circuits (Sec. 210-5.)

Grounding conductor: An equipment grounding conductor of a branch circuit (if one is used) must be color-coded green or green with one or more yellow stripes—or the conductor may be bare [Sec. 210-5(b)].

However, Exception No. 1 refers to Sec. 250-57(b), which says that an equipment grounding conductor larger than No. 6 may be other than a green-insulated conductor or a green-with-yellow-stripe conductor. Section 250-57 permits an equipment grounding conductor with insulation that is black, blue, or any other color—provided that one of the three techniques specified in Sec. 250-57 is used to identify this conductor as an equipment grounding conductor.

The first technique consists of stripping the insulation from the insulated conductor for the entire length of the conductor appearing within a junction box, panel enclosure, switch enclosure, or any other enclosure. With the insulation stripped from the conductor, the conductor then appears as a bare conductor, which is recognized by the **Code** for grounding purposes. A second technique which is acceptable is to paint the exposed insulation green for its entire length within the enclosure. If, say, a black insulated conductor is used in a conduit coming into a panelboard, the length of the black conductor within the panelboard can be painted green to identify this as an equipment grounding conductor.

The third acceptable method is to mark the exposed insulation with green-colored tape or green-colored adhesive labels. Figure 210-12 summarizes the rules on identification of equipment grounding conductors. Green-colored conductors must not be used for any purpose other than equipment grounding.

Color coding of circuit conductors (or some other method of identifying them) is a wiring consideration that deserves the close, careful, complete attention of all electrical people. By providing ready identification of the two or three phase legs and neutrals in wiring systems, color coding is the easiest and surest way of balancing loads among the phase legs, thereby providing full, safe, effective use of total circuit capacities. In circuits where color coding is missing or not effectively applied, loads or phases get unbalanced, many conductors are either badly underloaded or excessively loaded, and breakers or fuses often are increased in size to eliminate tripping due to overload on only one phase leg. Modern electrical usage—for reasons of safety and energy conservation, as well as full, economic application of system equipment and materials—demands the many real benefits that color coding can provide.

For the greater period of its existence, the **NE Code** required a very clear, rigid color coding of branch circuits for good and obvious safety reasons. Color coding of hot legs to provide load balancing is a safety matter. Section 220-3(d) requires balancing of loads from branch-circuit hot legs to neutral. Section 220-22 bases sizing of feeder neutrals on clear knowledge of load balance in order to determine "maximum unbalance." And mandatory differentiation of voltage levels is in the safety interests

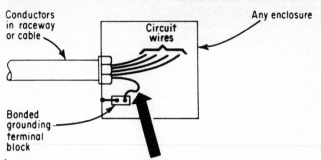

Conductors in raceway or cable

Circuit wires

Any enclosure

Bonded grounding terminal block

Equipment grounding conductor may be bare, or covered to show a green color or green with one or more yellow stripes.

Exception No. 1
But, for a grounding conductor larger than No. 6, an insulated conductor of other than green color or green with yellow stripes may be used provided *one* of the following steps is taken:

1. Stripping the insulation from an insulated conductor of another color (say, black) for the entire length that is exposed in the box or other enclosure— so that the conductor appears as a bare conductor.

2. Painting the exposed insulation green for its entire length within the enclosure.

3. Wrapping the entire length of exposed insulation with green-colored tape or green-colored adhesive labels.

Fig. 210-12. Equipment grounding conductor for branch circuit. [Sec. 210-5(b).]

of electricians and others maintaining or working on electrical circuits, to warn of different levels of hazard.

Because 99 percent of electrical systems involve no more than two voltage configurations for circuits up to 600 V, and because there has been great standardization in circuit voltage levels, there should be industrywide standardization on circuit conductor identifications. A clear, simple set of rules could cover the preponderant majority of installations, with exceptions made for the relatively small number of cases where unusual conditions exist and the local inspector may authorize other techniques. Color coding should follow some basic pattern— such as the following:

- 120-V, 2-wire circuit: grounded neutral—white; ungrounded leg— black.

- 240/120-V, 3-wire, single-phase circuit: grounded neutral—white; one hot leg—black; the other hot leg—red.
- 208Y/120-V, 3-phase, 4-wire; grounded neutral—white; one hot leg—black; one hot leg—red; one hot leg—blue.
- 240-V, delta, 3-phase, 3-wire: one hot leg—black; one hot leg—red; one hot leg—blue.
- 240/120-V, 3-phase, 4-wire, high-leg delta: grounded neutral—white; high leg (208-V to neutral)—orange; one hot leg—black; one hot leg—blue.
- 480Y/277-V, 3-phase, 4-wire: grounded neutral—gray; one hot leg—brown; one hot leg—orange; one hot leg—yellow.
- 480-V, delta, 3-phase, 3-wire: one hot leg—brown; one hot leg—orange; one hot leg—yellow.

By making color coding a set of simple, specific color designations, standardization will assure all the safety and operating advantages of color coding to all electrical systems. Particularly today, with all electrical systems being subjected to an unprecedented amount of alterations and additions because of continuing development and expansion in electrical usage, conductor identification is a regular safety need over the entire life of the system.

A second step in clarification and expansion of color coding would require color coding for all circuits—multiwire branch circuits, branch circuits without a neutral or other grounded conductor, feeders, and even for service conductors. As now indicated in Sec. 384-3(f) of the **NE Code**, correct, effective loading of all circuits—to get full capacity of all phases and to prevent unknown unbalances with the attendant chance of oversizing of protection and overloading of conductors—depends upon ready identification of all conductors at all points in a system.

Of course, there are alternatives to "color" identification throughout the length of conductors. Color differentiation is almost worthless for color-blind electricians. And it can be argued that color identification of conductors poses problems because electrical work is commonly done in darkened areas where color perception is reduced even for those with good eyesight. The **NE Code** already recognizes white tape or paint over the conductor insulation-end at terminals to identify neutrals where conductors are larger than No. 6 (Sec. 200-6). Number markings spaced along the length of a conductor on the insulation (1, 2, 3, etc.)—particularly, say, white numerals on black insulation—might prove very effective for identifying and differentiating conductors. Or the letters "A," "B," and "C" could be used to designate specific phases. Or a combination of color and markings could be used. But some kind of conductor identification is essential to safe, effective hookup of the ever-expanding array of conductors used throughout buildings and systems today.

210-6. Maximum Voltage. Voltage limitations for branch circuits are presented in Sec. 210-6. In general, branch circuits serving lampholders, fixtures, or receptacles of the standard 15-A or less rating are limited to operation at a maximum voltage rating of 150 V to ground. Exceptions to this rule are given in this basic Code rule of Sec. 210-6(a).

Exception No. 1. *In industrial occupancies* where the conditions of maintenance and supervision assure that only qualified individuals will service the lighting fixtures, branch circuits supplying only lighting fixtures with mogul-base, screw-shell lampholders or other approved types of lampholders may be operated above 150 V to ground, but not above 300 V to ground. That means that fluorescent, mercury-vapor, metal-halide, high-pressure sodium, low-pressure sodium, and/or incandescent fixtures may be supplied by 480/277-V, grounded-wye circuits—with loads connected phase-to-neutral and/or phase-to-phase. Such circuits operate at 277 V to ground—that is, *not* over 300 V to ground—even, say, when 480-V ballasts are connected phase-to-phase on such circuits. Or lighting could be supplied by 240-V delta systems—either ungrounded or with one of the phase legs grounded, because such systems operate at not more than 300 V to ground.

Use of incandescent lighting at over 150 V to ground is accepted by the NE Code for industrial plants, but incandescent fixtures must be mounted at least 8 ft above the floor—if sufficient mounting height is available. If 8-ft mounting height is not available—such as in pipe tunnels or other low-overhead industrial passages or areas—277-V incandescent units may be mounted lower than 8 ft. (See Fig. 210-13.)

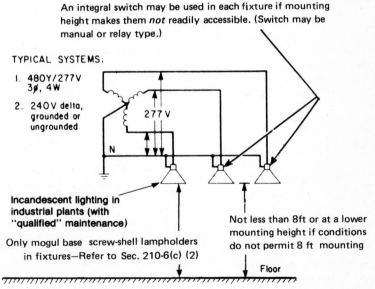

Fig. 210-13. Incandescent lighting at over 150 volts to ground is permitted *only* in industrial locations. [Sec. 210-6(a), Ex. No. 1.]

It should be noted that Exception No. 1 to Sec. 210-6(a) applies only to "industrial establishments." And there is *no requirement* that electric-discharge fixtures with mogul-base screw-shell lampholders must be mounted 8 ft above the floor.

Although 277-V incandescent lamps are available with medium screw bases, and fixtures for them are available with medium screw-shell lampholders, use of such equipment violates the NE Code rule in Sec. 210-6(a) Exception No. 1(b). And Sec. 210-6(c) (2) limits medium base, screw-shell lampholders to use only where connected to circuit wires with not more than 150 V between the wires—such as 2-wire 120-V circuits.

Exception No. 2. *In commercial and institutional occupancies,* branch circuits serving only ballasts for electric-discharge lighting may be rated over 150 V to ground, but not above 300 V to ground, provided the ballasts are in permanently installed fixtures. Note that *incandescent* fixtures are not recognized for supply by 277-V circuits in these nonindustrial type occupancies. Only fluorescent, mercury-vapor, metal-halide, high-pressure sodium, and low-pressure sodium are the common lamps permitted on 280/277-V circuits in stores, health care facilities, office buildings, schools, public and commercial areas of hotels, transportation terminals, etc. And when any of those electric-discharge lamps are used with *screw-shell* lampholders, the fixtures must be installed not less than 8 ft above the floor.

Both of the Exceptions to Sec. 210-6(a) permit installations on 480/277-V, 3-phase, 4-wire wye systems—with equipment connected from phase-to-phase (480-volt circuits) or connected phase-to-neutral (277-V circuits). In either case, the voltage to ground is only 277 V and therefore does not exceed the 300-V maximum. Figure 210-14 covers the use of electric-discharge lighting on such circuits in the various types of occupancies. In any such application, it is important that the neutral point of the 480/277-V wye be grounded to limit the voltage aboveground to 277 V. If the neutral were not grounded and the system operated ungrounded, the voltage to ground, according to the Code, would be 480 V (see definition "voltage to ground," Art. 100), and lighting equipment could be used on such circuits only for outdoor applications as specified under Sec. 210-6(b) (discussed later).

On a neutral-grounded 480/277-V system, incandescent, fluorescent, mercury-vapor, metal-halide, high-pressure sodium, and low-pressure sodium equipment can be connected from phase-to-neutral on the 277-V circuits. If fluorescent or mercury-vapor fixtures are to be connected phase-to-phase, some Code authorities contend that autotransformer-type ballasts cannot be used when these ballasts raise the voltage to more than 300 V, because, they contend, the NE Code calls for connection to a circuit made up of a grounded wire and a hot wire. (See Sec. 410-78.) On phase-to-phase connection these ballasts would require use of 2-winding, electrically isolating ballast transformers. The wording of Sec. 410-78 does, however, lend itself to interpretation that it is only necessary for the

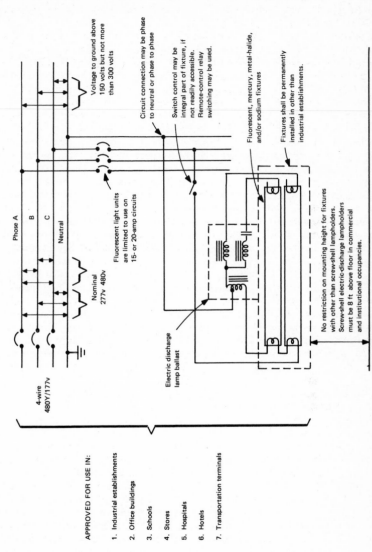

Fig. 210-14. Electric-discharge lighting on 480/277-volt grounded wye circuits must satisfy varying rules. [Sec. 210-6(a).]

supply system to the ballast to *be grounded*—thus permitting the two hot legs of a 480-V circuit to supply an autotransformer because the hot legs are derived from a neutral-grounded "system." But Sec. 210-9 can become a complicating factor. Use of a 2-winding (isolating) ballast is clearly acceptable and avoids all confusion.

Section 210-6 permits use of an integral switch in a 277-V or 480-V lighting fixture, provided the switch is not readily accessible. That means that a manual or relay switch is OK in the fixture if the fixture is mounted up out of reach of persons not qualified in electrical work and access to the fixture by qualified maintenance personnel would require use of a ladder or some type of lift or platform. Remote control is accepted, with the relay as a switch in the fixture and control exercised at low voltage by another switch (manual or automatic) away from the fixture. Use of multilevel ballasts for different light outputs from lamps can be facilitated by integral switches in the fixture or the box supplying the fixture. And energy conservation is served by the integral switches, which permit turning off certain lights or groups of lights when not needed for changing work patterns or desk layouts.

SECTION 210-6(b) of the **NE Code** permits fluorescent and/or mercury-vapor units to be installed on circuits rated up to 500 V between conductors—but only where the lamps are mounted in permanently installed fixtures on poles or similar structures for the illumination of areas such as highways, bridges, athletic fields, parking lots, at a height not less than 22 ft, or on other structures such as tunnels at a height not less than 18 ft. (See Fig. 210-15.)

This permission for use of fluorescent and mercury units under the conditions described is based on phase-to-phase voltage rather than on phase-to-ground voltage. This rule has the effect of permitting the use of 240-V or 480-V ungrounded circuits for the lighting applications

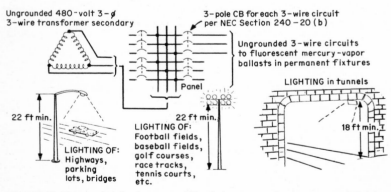

Fig. 210-15. Ungrounded circuits, at up to 500 volts between conductors, may supply lighting only as shown. [Sec. 210-6(b).]

described. But as described above, autotransformer-type ballasts may not be permitted on an ungrounded system if they raise the voltage to more than 300 V [Sec. 410-78]. In such cases, ballasts with 2-winding transformation would have to be used.

Certain electric railway applications utilize higher circuit voltages. Infrared lamp industrial heating applications may be used on higher circuit voltages as allowed in Sec. 422-15(c) of the Code.

SECTION 210-6(c) (1) applies to "dwelling unit(s) and guest rooms in hotels, motels, and similar occupancies." Note that the wording differentiates between "dwelling unit(s)" and rooms in hotels, motels, and other living or sleeping units that do not satisfy the new definition in Art. 100 on "dwelling unit." This is an important clarification that arises in a number of other Code rules. Note that a hotel or motel room or a room in a dormitory is *not* a "dwelling unit" and is not subject to those rules that apply only to "dwelling unit(s)."

The rule of part **(1)** of Sec. 210-6(c) prohibits use of circuits with over 150 V between conductors to supply screw-shell lampholders, receptacles, or appliances in dwelling units and the other specified rooms, except for permanently connected appliances and cord-and-plug-connected appliances rated over 1,380 W or ¼ or more hp. The rule limits incandescent lighting to a 120-V rating at all lighting outlets in those places. But this rule has caused considerable discussion and controversy in the past when applied to split-wired receptacles and duplex receptacles of two voltage levels.

It has been argued that split-wired general-purpose duplex receptacles are not acceptable in dwelling units and in hotel and motel guest rooms because they are supplied by conductors with *more* than 150 V between them—i.e., 240 V on the 3-wire, single-phase, 120/240-V circuit so commonly used in residences. The two hot legs connect to the brass-colored terminals on the receptacle, with the shorting tab broken off, and the voltage between those conductors *does* exceed 150 V. The same condition applies when a 120/240-V duplex receptacle is used—the 240-V receptacle is fed by conductors with more than 150 V between them. Use of split-wired receptacles and 120/240-V duplex receptacles must be evaluated against the rules of Sec. 210-6(c) (1) and its two Exceptions to determine if they are acceptable in dwelling-type occupancies as noted in the rule, as discussed in Fig. 210-16.

Split-wired receptacles on the two or more 20-A small-appliance circuits required by Sec. 220-3(b) for the kitchen, dining room, and family room of dwellings might be justified as complying with Exception No. 2 of Sec. 210-6(c) because such receptacles supply electric toasters, broilers, fry pans, and other high-wattage devices. But general-purpose, split-wired receptacles in other areas of the type of dwelling places specified have been objectionable to some inspectors. And where a 120/240-V receptacle is installed in such dwelling areas, it must be provided for a specific cord-connected load of adequate rating, as noted in the rule.

WATCH THIS!

Because a line-to-line connection is made on one side of the duplex receptacle, some inspectors consider that to be a line-to-line load and require that a 2-pole CB or switch be used as the branch-circuit overcurrent device to satisfy Sec. 210-4 in accordance with Exception No. 2.

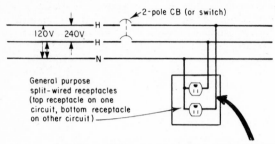

... BUT, two of the conductors supplying the receptacle have more than 150 volts between them, and such a hookup has been considered by some inspectors to be a violation of Sec. 210-6(c) (1) in dwelling units and in hotel and motel guest rooms.

AND THIS!

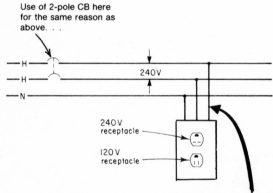

... and 240 volts between these conductors supplying the receptacle would limit such use to nondwelling occupancies — except if the 240-volt receptacle supplies an appliance or load rated over 1380 watts or rated ¼ hp or more.

Fig. 210-16. Rule requires careful application of split-wired receptacles and two-voltage receptacles in "dwelling units" and hotel/motel rooms. [Sec. 210-6(c).]

Objection to split-wired receptacles in dwelling units has a sound basis: Two appliances connected by 2-wire cords to a split-wired receptacle in a kitchen do present real potential hazard. With, say, a coffee maker and a toaster plugged into a split-wired duplex, if the hot wire in each appliance should contact the metal enclosure of the appliance, there would be 240 V between the two appliance enclosures. The user would be exposed to the extremely dangerous chance of touching each appliance with a different hand—putting 240 V across the person, from hand-to-hand, through the heart path (Fig. 210-17). Use of nonsplit-wired receptacles on the usual spacing of up to 12 ft does tend to separate appliances on different hot legs.

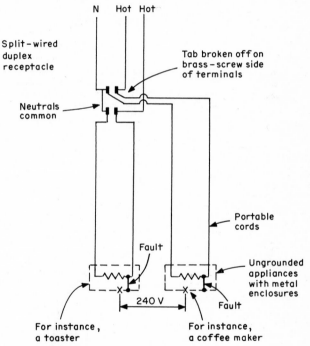

Fig. 210-17. This can be dangerous. [Sec. 210-6(c) (1).]

Use of split-wired receptacles and other receptacles with more than 150 V between terminals is, of course, not ruled out by Sec. 210-6(c) (1) in any commercial, institutional, or industrial location. Of course, it is perfectly acceptable at any time to use a split-wired receptacle for switch control of one plug-in point leaving the other hot all the time (Fig. 210-18).

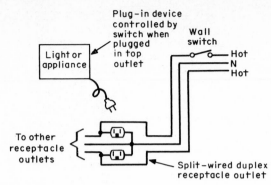

Fig. 210-18. Split-wiring of receptacles to control one of the receptacles is acceptable. (Sec. 210-6.)

SECTION 210-6(c) (2) is worded in such a way as to make use of 277-V lamps acceptable only when such lamps have mogul-bases. Any medium base lamp may be used only on a circuit that does not have more than 150 V between conductors. Use of medium base 277-V incandescent lamps is clearly prohibited by that rule as well as the rule of Sec. 210-6(a), Exception No. 1—as noted in Fig. 210-13.

210-7. Receptacles and Cord Connectors. Section 210-7 states that "receptacles installed on 15- and 20-A branch circuits shall be of the grounding type." This requires that on all new installations a grounding-type device must be used (Fig. 210-19). This rule came into effect in 1968. Prior to that, ungrounded devices were permitted on branch circuits. If a residence or office is equipped with these older devices, it is not necessary to replace them as long as they are serviceable.

In all cases where a grounding-type receptacle is installed, it shall be grounded. For nonmetallic-sheathed cable the grounding conductor is run with the branch-circuit conductors. The armor of Type AC metal-clad cable, the sheath of ALS cable, and certain metallic raceways are acceptable as grounding means (Fig. 210-20).

The purpose here is to make certain that grounding-type receptacles are used and grounded where a ground is available, and nongrounding-type receptacles are used where grounding is impractical so that no one will be deceived as to the availability of a grounding means for appliances.

The rule of Sec. 210-7(b), requiring grounding of the ground terminal of receptacles and cord connectors, has an important Exception. It permits receptacles mounted on portable or vehicle-mounted generators, in accordance with Sec. 250-6, to have their ground terminals left ungrounded, when the generator frame itself is not grounded (Fig. 210-21). But where such receptacles are mounted on portable or vehicle-mounted generators, the grounding terminal of the receptacle *must* be bonded to the generator frame [Sec. 250-6(a) (2)].

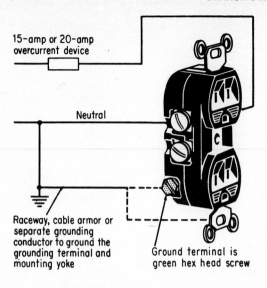

15-amp or 20-amp
overcurrent device

Neutral

Raceway, cable armor or
separate grounding
conductor to ground the
grounding terminal and
mounting yoke

Ground terminal is
green hex head screw

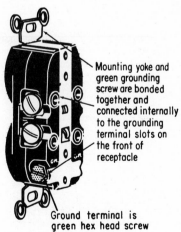

Mounting yoke and
green grounding
screw are bonded
together and
connected internally
to the grounding
terminal slots on
the front of
receptacle

Ground terminal is
green hex head screw

Fig. 210-19. Any receptacle on a 15- or 20-amp branch
circuit must be a grounding type. (Sec. 210-7.)

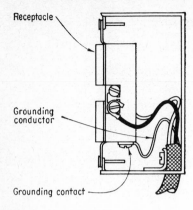

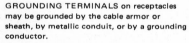

GROUNDING TERMINALS on receptacles may be grounded by the cable armor or sheath, by metallic conduit, or by a grounding conductor.

SELF—GROUNDING RECEPTACLE includes mounting screw equipped with pressure clip to assure tight contact between screws and device yoke, eliminating the need for a grounding jumper from green hex-head screw to metal box.

Fig. 210-20. The grounded terminal must be grounded in an approved manner. [Sec. 210-7(c).]

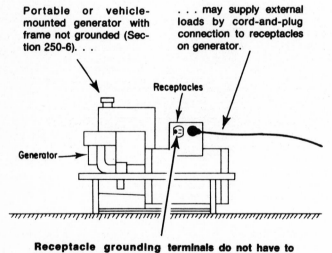

Portable or vehicle-mounted generator with frame not grounded (Section 250-6). . .

. . . may supply external loads by cord-and-plug connection to receptacles on generator.

Receptacles

Generator

Receptacle grounding terminals do not have to be grounded but *must* be bonded to generator frame.

Fig. 210-21. Grounding is not required for generator-mounted receptacles. [Sec. 210-7(b).]

For correlation purposes, a note after Sec. 210-7(c) refers to the use of "quiet grounding" for electrical noise reduction for sensitive equipment, as covered in Sec. 250-74, Exception No. 4.

Very important!

On replacement of receptacles that become defective in an already existing installation, the Exception to Sec. 210-7(d) clarifies the rule. Although the basic rule is that grounding-type receptacles be used as replacements for existing nongrounding types, the Exception *requires* that a *nongrounding*-type receptacle be used as the replacement in any case where the box or other enclosure of the existing receptacle is *not* grounded and *does not* contain an equipment grounding conductor—as with older installations of nonmetallic-sheathed cable without a ground wire or knob-and-tube wiring (Fig. 210-22).

Fig. 210-22. A non-grounding-type receptacle must always be used when replacing a nongrounding receptacle in any case where the box does not contain an equipment grounding conductor. [Sec. 210-7(d).]

A new paragraph has been added to this section; 210-7(g) requires that when aluminum conductors are connected directly to the terminals of any receptacle rated 20 A or less, the device must be "approved for the purpose" *and* must be marked "CO/ALR" (Fig. 210-23).

210-8. Ground-Fault Circuit Protection.   Part **(a)** of Section 210-8 of the NE Code is headed "Dwelling Units." The very clear and detailed defini-

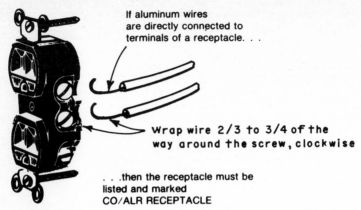

If aluminum wires
are directly connected to
terminals of a receptacle. . .

Wrap wire 2/3 to 3/4 of the
way around the screw, clockwise

. . .then the receptacle must be
listed and marked
CO/ALR RECEPTACLE

Fig. 210-23. Only CO/ALR receptacles for aluminum wire. [Sec. 210-7(g).]

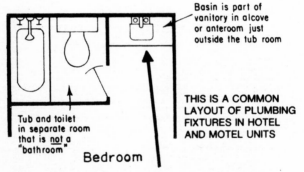

Basin is part of
vanitory in alcove
or anteroom just
outside the tub room

Tub and toilet
in separate room
that is not a
"bathroom"
Bedroom

THIS IS A COMMON
LAYOUT OF PLUMBING
FIXTURES IN HOTEL
AND MOTEL UNITS

Guest rooms in hotels and motels are required by Section
210-25(c) to have the same receptacle outlets required by
Section 210-25(b) for "dwelling units." The requirement for
a wall receptacle outlet at the "basin location" applies to
bathrooms; and the anteroom area with only a basin is, by
definition and intent, part of the "bathroom." A
receptacle at the basin would, therefore, be required.
But, Section 210-8(a) which applies only to bathrooms in
"dwelling units," does not apply in hotels and motels—and
GFCI protection is not required for this receptacle.

Fig. 210-24. GFCI not needed in hotel and motel "guest rooms" that
do not include "permanent" cooking provisions. (Sec. 210-8.)

tion of those words, as given in Art. 100 of the NE Code, indicates that all of the ground-fault circuit interruption rules apply to:

- **all one-family houses**
- **each dwelling unit in a two-family house**
- **each apartment in an apartment house**
- **each dwelling unit in a condominum**

GFCI protection is required for all 120-V, single-phase, 15- and 20-A receptacles installed in **bathrooms** and **garages** of dwelling units only (Fig. 210-25). The requirement for GFCI protection in "garages" is included because home owners do use outdoor appliances (lawnmowers, hedge trimmers, etc.) plugged into garage receptacles. Such receptacles require GFCI protection for the same reason as "outdoor" receptacles. In either place, GFCI protection may be provided by a GFCI circuit breaker that protects the whole circuit and any receptacles connected to it or the receptacle may be a GFCI-type that incorporates the components that give it the necessary tripping capability on low-level ground faults.

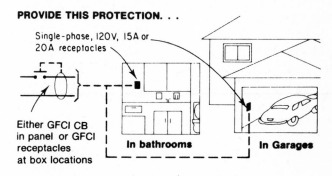

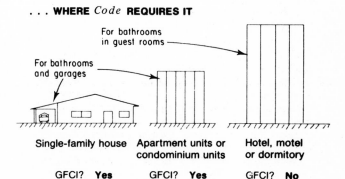

Fig. 210-25. GFCI protection is required for receptacles in garages as well as in bathrooms [Sec. 210-8(a) (1).]

A lot of the controversy that was generated by the question "What is a bathroom?" is eliminated because a definition of the word "bathroom" is added to the section. A "bathroom" is "an area" (which means it could be a room or a room plus another area) that contains first a "basin" (sometimes called a "sink"), and then at least one more plumbing fixture—a toilet, a tub, and/or a shower. A small room with only a "basin" (a washroom) is not a "bathroom." Neither is a room that contains only a toilet and/or a tub or shower (Fig. 210-26).

But, the definition makes clear that GFCI protection required by Sec. 210-8(a) is not required in bathrooms of hotel or motel rooms or dormitory rooms or any other residential occupancy that does not conform to the definition of "dwelling unit" (Fig. 210-24).

The rule requiring GFCI protection in garages applies to both attached garages and detached (or separate) garages associated with "dwelling units"—such as one-family houses or multifamily houses where each unit has its own garage. But, Sec. 210-25(b) requires at least one receptacle only for "attached" garages. A receptacle is not required in a detached garage; but if one is used in such a garage, it must have GFCI protection.

Part **(a) (2)** of Sec. 210-8, on outdoor receptacles, required GFCI protection of "all 120-V, single-phase, 15- and 20-A receptacles installed outdoors" at dwelling units. The rule specifies that such protection of outdoor receptacles is required only "where there is direct grade level access to the dwelling unit and to the receptacles . . ." (Fig. 210-27). The phrase "direct grade level access" is not defined and does lend itself to many varied interpretations. Because there is no "grade level access" to apartment units constructed above ground level, there would be no need for GFCI protection of receptacles installed outdoors on balconies for such apartments or condominium units. Likewise, GFCI protection would not be required for any outdoor receptacle installed on a porch or other raised part of even a one-family house provided that there was not grade level access to the receptacle, as in the examples of Fig. 210-27.

In any case of an outdoor receptacle at a dwelling unit. GFCI protection is not required if there is no access to the receptacle from the grade level of ground around the building. This important change in the rule on GFCI protection of outdoor outlets was made to reflect the Code-making panel's conviction that such protection is not needed where the receptacle cannot readily be used by someone plugging in a tool or appliance and making contact with earth of any masonry walk or other surface or grade.

SECTION 210-8(b) introduces major changes in the rules that concern GFCI protection for all "120-V, single-phase, 15- and 20-A receptacle outlets" on construction sites. (Note that there are no requirements for GFCI protection of 240-V receptacles, 3-phase receptacles, or receptacles rated *over* 20 A.)

The basic rule of this section says that ground-fault circuit interrupters (either GFCI circuit breakers or GFCI receptacles) must be used to

TYPICAL BEDROOM SUITE IN ONE-FAMILY HOUSE OR APARTMENT UNIT

Bedroom

Receptacle not required in this room

Tub

Toilet

Basin in vanitory outside room with tub and toilet

Alcove

Although this area with basin is outside room with tub and toilet, the intent of Section 210-25(b) requires a receptacle at basin; and Section 210-8(a) requires that it be GFCI-protected.

NOTE: It is important to understand that the *Code* meaning of "bathroom" refers to the total "area" made up of the basin in the alcove *plus* the "room" that contains the tub and toilet. Although a receptacle is *not* required in the "room" with the tub and toilet, if one is installed in that room, it must be GFCI-protected because such a receptacle is technically "in the bathroom," just as the one at the basin location is "in the bathroom."

THIS IS HOW A "BATHROOM" IS DEFINED

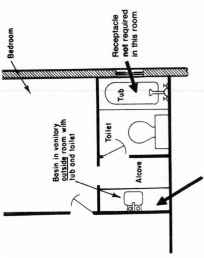

Toilet and sink

A BATHROOM!

Sink plus tub and/or shower

A BATHROOM!

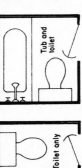

Toilet only

NOT A BATHROOM!

Tub and toilet

NOT A BATHROOM!

Sink only

NOT A BATHROOM!

NOTE: If a room is not a bathroom according to the definition of Section 210-8(a), then the requirement of Section 210-25(b) for "at least one wall receptacle outlet . . . adjacent to the basin location" does not apply. If, however, a receptacle is installed in a room that is *not* a "bathroom"— such as the one above containing a basin *only*—GFCI protection is not required for the receptacle because it is not a bathroom receptacle.

Fig. 210-26. For GFCI use, a bathroom may be a "room" or an area that includes one or more "rooms." [Sec. 210-8(a).]

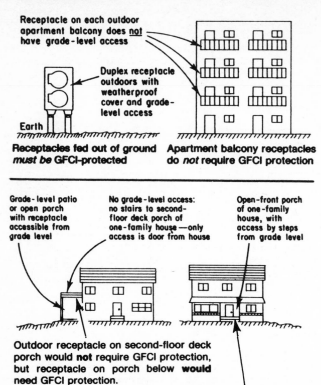

Receptacle on each outdoor
apartment balcony does **not**
have grade-level access

Duplex receptacle
outdoors with
weatherproof
cover and grade-
level access

Earth

**Receptacles fed out of ground
must be GFCI-protected**

**Apartment balcony receptacles
do not require GFCI protection**

Grade-level patio
or open porch
with receptacle
accessible from
grade level

No grade-level access:
no stairs to second-
floor deck porch of
one-family house —only
access is door from house

Open-front porch
of one-family
house, with
access by steps
from grade level

Outdoor receptacle on second-floor deck
porch would **not** require GFCI protection,
but receptacle on porch below **would**
need GFCI protection.

Outdoor receptacle on this porch might
likely be used to connect appliance used
on ground, and GFCI protection **would**
seem to be required.

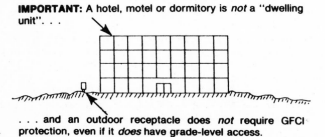

IMPORTANT: A hotel, motel or dormitory is *not* a "dwelling
unit". . .

. . . and an outdoor receptacle does *not* require GFCI
protection, even if it *does* have grade-level access.

Fig. 210-27. For dwelling units, only outdoor receptacles with "direct grade
level access" require GFCI protection. [Sec. 210-8(a) (2).]

provide personnel protection for all receptacles of the designated rating—that "are *not* part of the permanent wiring of the building or
structure" (Fig. 210-28). That phrase was in the 1975 **NE Code** and
excludes from the need for GFCI protection all receptacle outlets that are
intended to serve the occupants of the building after construction is

BASIC RULE

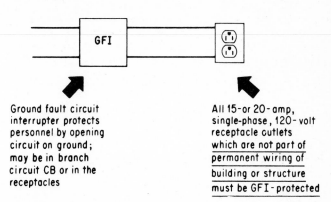

Ground fault circuit
interrupter protects
personnel by opening
circuit on ground;
may be in branch
circuit CB or in the
receptacles

All 15-or 20-amp,
single-phase, 120-volt
receptacle outlets
which are not part of
permanent wiring of
building or structure
must be GFI-protected

Fig. 210-28. GFCI protection on construction sites for receptacles in use. [Sec.
210-8(b).]

completed and are not simply installed as temporary outlets intended
only for use by construction workers during the course of construction
activities. Figure 210-29 shows two ways to satisfy the basic rule on GFCI
for receptacles on construction sites.

But the first big change in that rule in the 1978 **NE Code** is the addition
of a phrase that significantly qualifies the *need* for GFCI protection of the
designated receptacle outlets:

GFCI PROTECTION IS REQUIRED *ONLY* FOR THOSE RECEP-
TACLES THAT "ARE *IN USE* BY EMPLOYEES."

That phrase clearly limits required GFCI protection to receptacles that
are actually being used at any particular time. Receptacles *not* in use do
not have to be GFCI protected. This change means that *portable* GFCI
protectors may be used at only those outlets being used (Fig. 210-30).
There is no need to use GFCI breakers in the panel to protect *"all"*
receptacles or to use all GFCI-type receptacles—as the situation was
under the rule in the 1975 **NE Code**. This change seems to seriously
confuse the task of electrical inspection: If all cord-connected tools and
appliances are unplugged from receptacles when the inspector comes on
the job, then *none* of the receptacles is "in use" and none of them has to
have GFCI protection and there is no **Code** violation. Just how this new

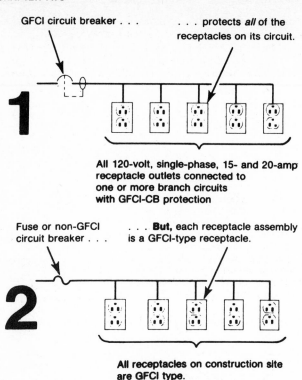

GFCI circuit breaker . . .   . . . protects *all* of the
                                              receptacles on its circuit.

1

All 120-volt, single-phase, 15- and 20-amp
receptacle outlets connected to
one or more branch circuits
with GFCI-CB protection

Fuse or non-GFCI   . . . **But,** each receptacle assembly
circuit breaker . . .   is a GFCI-type receptacle.

2

All receptacles on construction site
are GFCI type.

Fig. 210-29. Two ways to satisfy the basic rule on personnel shock
protection at *temporary* receptacles on construction sites. [Sec. 210-8(b).]

rule will be applied is up to each user on the job site, but the rule itself
radically reduces the extent of application of GFCI protection on construction sites and virtually makes evasion of the rule an easy matter.

Still another option for avoiding use of GFCI protection on construction sites is given in a new Exception No. 2 to Sec. 210-8(b). As explained
in the Exception, GFCI protection of receptacles *may be omitted* totally if a
"written procedure" is established to assure testing and maintenance of
"equipment grounding conductors" for receptacles, cord sets, and cord-
and-plug-connected tools and appliances used on the construction site
(Fig. 210-31). In effect, the **NE Code** accepts such an equipment grounding conductor program as a measure that provides safety that is equivalent to the safety afforded by GFCI protection. GFCI protection is not
required if all the following conditions are satisfied:

  1. The inspection authority having jurisdiction over a construction site
     must approve a written procedure for an equipment grounding
     program.

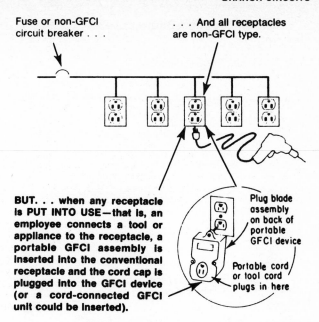

Fuse or non-GFCI circuit breaker . . .

. . . And all receptacles are non-GFCI type.

BUT. . . when any receptacle is PUT INTO USE—that is, an employee connects a tool or appliance to the receptacle, a portable GFCI assembly is inserted into the conventional receptacle and the cord cap is plugged into the GFCI device (or a cord-connected GFCI unit could be inserted).

Plug blade assembly on back of portable GFCI device

Portable cord or tool cord plugs in here

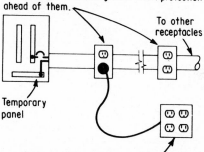

These 15A receptacles are fed by a temporary branch circuit without ground-fault protection ahead of them.

To other receptacles

Temporary panel

Wherever personnel are using cord-connected tools they plug in this portable ground-fault circuit interrupter having protected receptacles on its face for connection of the tools.

Fig. 210-30. Portable GFCI devices may be used to satisfy GFCI rule. [Sec. 210-8(b).]

A written procedure must cover testing of...

. . . all cord-connected tools
and equipment

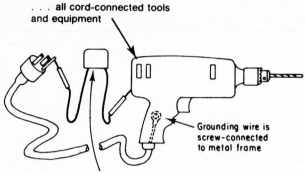

Grounding wire is
screw-connected
to metal frame

Continuity tester to assure connection
of equipment grounding conductor

. . . and all receptacles, cord
sets, and extension cords.

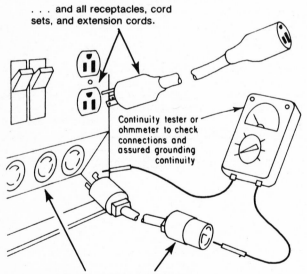

Continuity tester or
ohmmeter to check
connections and
assured grounding
continuity

15- and 20-amp locking plugs and
receptacles are also covered under the
assured grounding program.

Fig. 210-31. Assured grounding program of Exception No. 2 eliminates the need for GFCI. [Sec. 210-8(b).]

2. The program must be enforced by a single designated person at the construction site.

3. "Electrical continuity" tests must be conducted on all equipment grounding conductors and their connections. The requirements on making such tests are vague, but they do call for:

   a. Testing of fixed receptacles where there is any evidence of damage.

   b. Testing of extension cords before they are first used and again where there is evidence of damage or after repairs have been made on such cords.

   c. Testing of all tools, appliances, and other equipment that connects by cord and plug before they are first used on a construction site, again any time there is any evidence of damage, after any repair, and at least every 3 months (Fig. 210-32).

Obviously, those rules are very general and could be satisfied in either a rigorous, detailed manner or in a fast, simple way that barely meets the qualitative criteria. How an assured equipment grounding program can be fully and realistically enforced by electrical inspectors will only become clear as field experience develops. It does seem clear that the electrical contractor who has responsibility for the temporary wiring on any job site is the one to develop, write, and supervise the assured equipment grounding program, where that option is chosen as an alternative to use of GFCI protection. This whole NE Code approach to use of either GFCI or an "assured equipment grounding program" directly parallels the new OSHA approach to the matter of receptacle protection on construction sites.

210-9. Circuits Derived from Autotransformers. Figure 210-33 shows how a 110-V system for lighting may be derived from a 220-V system by means of an autotransformer. The 220-V system either may be single phase or may be one leg of a 3-phase system. Note that the hookup complies with Exception No. 1. In the case illustrated the "supplied" system has a grounded wire solidly connected to a grounded wire of the "supplying" system: 220-V single-phase system with one conductor grounded.

Autotransformers are commonly used to supply reduced voltage for starting induction motors.

Exception No. 2 permits the use of an autotransformer in existing installations for an individual branch circuit without connection to a similar identified grounded conductor where transforming from 208 to 240 V or vice versa (see Fig. 210-34). Typical applications are with cooking equipment, heaters, motors, and air-conditioning equipment. For such applications transformers are commonly used. This has been long-established practice in the field of voltage ranges where a hazard is not considered to exist.

Buck or boost transformers are designed for use on single- or 3-phase circuits to supply $^{12}/_{24}$- or $^{16}/_{32}$-V secondaries with a $^{120}/_{240}$-V primary.

A designated person on construction site must assure these details:

A. Install wiring according to *NE Code* requirements with a continuous grounding conductor maintained throughout and carried back to grounding bus at service panel.

B. Make visual inspection of cord (and harnesses) before each day's use.

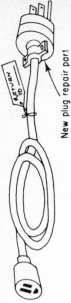

Loose or missing screws?

Loose or broken blades?

C. Perform periodic electrical tests for continuity using appropriate testing devices.

(1) When cord set is first used

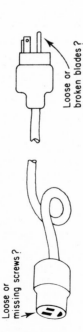

SO/3   25 ft

(2) Following repair of set

RETURN to

New plug repair part

(3) After an incident that could cause damage to set.

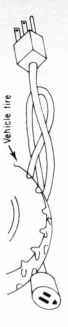

Vehicle tire

In addition, cord-connected equipment must be tested at continuous 3-month intervals.

Date of first use test or return to service test

Testing due date

APRIL   MAY   JUNE   JULY

D. Maintain the necessary test verification records by . . . written log or physical tagging.

Fig. 210-32. Requirements of assured grounding program. [Sec. 210-8(b), Ex. No. 2.]

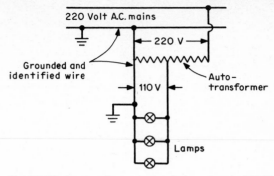

Fig. 210-33. Autotransformer used to derive a two-wire 110-V system for lighting from a 220-V power system. (Sec. 210-9, Ex. No. 1.)

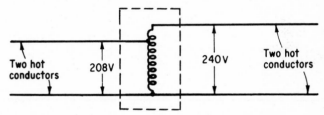

Fig. 210-34. Autotransformers without grounded conductors are recognized. (Sec. 210-9, Ex. No. 2.)

When connected as autotransformers the kVA load they will handle is large in comparison with their physical size and relative cost.

210-10. Ungrounded Conductors Tapped from Grounded Systems. This section permits use of 2-wire branch circuits tapped from the outside conductors of systems, where the neutral is grounded on 3-wire DC or single-phase, 4-wire, 3-phase, and 5-wire 2-phase systems.

Figure 210-35 illustrates the use of unidentified 2-wire branch circuits

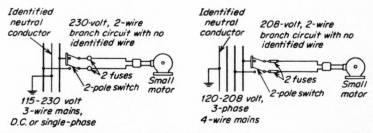

Fig. 210-35. Tapping circuits of ungrounded conductors from the hot legs of grounded systems. (Sec. 210-10.)

to supply small motors, the circuits being tapped from the outside conductors of a 3-wire DC or single-phase system and a 4-wire 3-phase wye system.

All poles of the disconnecting means used for branch circuits supplying permanently connected appliances must be operated at the same time. This requirement applies where the circuit is supplied by either circuit breakers or switches.

In the case of fuses and switches, when a fuse blows in one pole, the other pole may not necessarily open and the requirement to "manually switch together" involves only the manual operation of the switch. Similarly, when a pair of circuit breakers is connected with handle ties, an overload on one of the conductors with the return circuit through the neutral may open only one of the circuit breakers; but the manual operation of the pair when used as a disconnecting means will open both poles. The words "manually switch together" should be considered as "operating at the same time," i.e., during the same operating interval, and apply to the equipment used as a disconnecting means and not as an overcurrent protective device.

Circuit breakers with handle ties are, therefore, considered as providing the disconnection required by this section. The requirement to "manually switch together" can be achieved by a "master handle" or "handle tie" since the operation is intended to be effected by manual operation. The intent was not to require a common trip for the switching device but to require that it have the ability to disconnect ungrounded conductors by one movement of the hand. For service disconnecting means see Sec. 230-71.

210-19. Conductors—Minimum Ampacity and Size.   The basic rule of Sec. 210-19(a) requires branch-circuit conductors to have "an ampacity of not less than the rating of the branch circuit." Because Sec. 210-3 clearly notes that the amp rating of a multioutlet circuit (typical lighting and appliance branch circuits) is determined (established) by the rating of the circuit protective device, the idea behind Sec. 210-19(a) can be expanded as follows:

For a multioutlet branch circuit, the conductors of the circuit must have an ampacity of not less than the rating of the fuses on circuit-breaker poles that protect them. AND IT SHOULD BE NOTED THAT THERE ARE NO EXCEPTIONS GIVEN FOR THAT REQUIRE-MENT (Fig. 210-36).

In part (b), the rule also calls for the same approach to sizing conductors for branch circuits to household electric ranges, wall-mounted ovens, counter-mounted cooking units, and other household cooking appliances (Fig. 210-37).

The maximum demand for a range of 12 kW rating or less is sized from NEC Table 220-19 as a load of 8 kW. 8,000 W divided by 230 V is approximately 35 A. Therefore, No. 8 conductors with an ampacity of 40 A may be used for the range branch circuit.

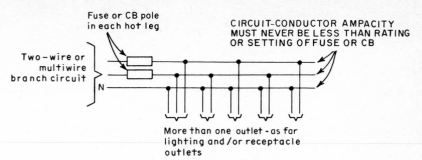

Fig. 210-36. No exception is given to basic rule on sizing branch-circuit wires. [Sec. 210-19(a).]

On modern ranges the heating elements of surface units are controlled by five-heat unit switches. The surface-unit heating elements will not draw current from the neutral unless the unit switch is in one of the low-heating positions. This is also true to a greater degree as far as the oven-heating elements are concerned, so that the maximum current in the neutral of the range circuit seldom exceeds 20 A. Because of that condition, Exception No. 1 permits a smaller-size neutral than the ungrounded conductors, but not smaller than No. 10. Exception No. 2 permits taps from electric cooking circuits (Fig. 210-38).

This would permit a 50-A branch circuit to be run to counter-mounted electric cooking units and wall-mounted electric ovens. The tap to each unit must be as short as possible and should be made in a junction box immediately adjacent to each unit. The words "no longer than necessary for servicing the appliance" mean that it should be necessary only to move the unit to one side in order that the splices in the junction box be accessible.

SECTION 210-19(c) sets No. 14 as the smallest size of general-purpose circuit conductors. But tap conductors of smaller sizes are permitted

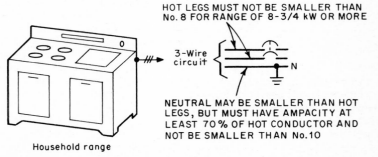

Fig. 210-37. Sizing circuit conductors for household electric range. [Sec. 210-19(b).]

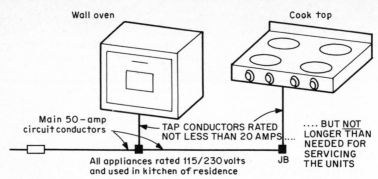

Fig. 210-38. Tap conductors may be smaller than wires of cooking circuit. [Sec. 210-19(b), Ex. No. 2.]

as explained in Exceptions No. 1 and No. 2 (Fig. 210-39). No. 14 wire, not longer than 18 in., may be used to supply an outlet unless the circuit is a 40- or 50-A branch circuit, in which event the minimum size of the tap conductor must be No. 12.

210-20. Overcurrent Protection.   According to the basic Code rule of this section, the rating or setting of an overcurrent device in any branch

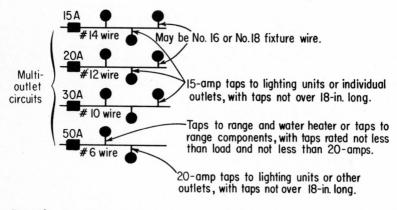

Fig. 210-39. Tap conductors may be smaller than circuit wires. [Sec. 210-19(c), Ex. Nos. 1 and 2.]

circuit must not exceed the current-carrying capacity of the circuit conductor. Figure 210-40 shows the basic rules that apply to use of overcurrent protection for branch circuits. (Section 240-2 designates other **Code** articles that present data and regulations on overcurrent protection for branch circuits to specific types of equipment.)

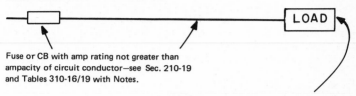

Branch circuit for other than motor load

Fuse or CB with amp rating not greater than
ampacity of circuit conductor—see Sec. 210-19
and Tables 310-16/19 with Notes.

If load on circuit operates for any period of 3 or
more hours, load current must not exceed 80%
of fuse or CB rating.

NOTE: Sec. 210-22 (c), Exception No. 2, and Sec. 220-2 (a), Exception No.1, both
permit loading of the above circuit to 100% of its rating if the conductors of the
circuit have had their ampacity derated in accordance with Note 8 to Tables 310-16/19
because there are more than 3 current-carrying conductors in a raceway or
bunch of cables.

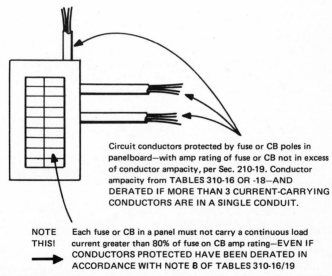

Circuit conductors protected by fuse or CB poles in
panelboard—with amp rating of fuse or CB not in excess
of conductor ampacity, per Sec. 210-19. Conductor
ampacity from TABLES 310-16 OR -18—AND
DERATED IF MORE THAN 3 CURRENT-CARRYING
CONDUCTORS ARE IN A SINGLE CONDUIT.

NOTE
THIS!

Each fuse or CB in a panel must not carry a continuous load
current greater than 80% of fuse on CB amp rating—EVEN IF
CONDUCTORS PROTECTED HAVE BEEN DERATED IN
ACCORDANCE WITH NOTE 8 OF TABLES 310-16/19

Fig. 210-40. Branch-circuit protection involves a number of rules. (Sec. 210-20.)

Branch-circuit taps—as covered in Secs. 210-19 and 210-20—are considered protected by the branch-circuit overcurrent devices, even where the rating or setting of the protective device is greater than the amp rating of the tap conductors, fixture wires, or cords.

When only three No. 12 TW or THW conductors of a branch circuit are in a conduit, each has an ampacity of 20 A and may be protected by a fuse or CB rated not over 20 A. This satisfies Sec. 210-19, which requires branch-circuit conductors to have an ampacity not less than the rating of the branch circuit—and Sec. 210-3 notes that the rating of a branch circuit is established by the rating of the protective device. It also satisfies Sec. 210-20, which says:

Branch-circuit conductors . . . shall be protected by overcurrent protective devices having a rating or setting . . . *not exceeding that specified in Section 240-3* for conductors. . . .

Note that the reference in Sec. 210-20 is a general reference to Sec. 240-3 and not a reference to Exception No. 1 of Sec. 240-3, which permits higher rated protection in certain cases.

The basic rule of Section 240-3 says:

Conductors . . . shall be protected against overcurrent *in accordance with their ampacities* as specified in Tables 310-16 through 310-19 and all applicable notes to these tables.

That rule says that conductors may be required to be protected at a current value less than their table ampacities if indicated by the table notes, such as Note 8.

If, after de-rating, 16 A becomes the new ampacity of four No. 12 conductors in a conduit, the three rules mentioned above—Secs. 210-19, 210-20, and 240-3—require that the overcurrent-device rating must not exceed 16 A. Because there are no standard 16-A fuses or CBs, we must protect the circuit with a 15-A fuse or CB.

Using a 20-A CB or fuse to protect each of the above described No. 12s would produce a condition where the branch-circuit conductors, with their ampacity of 16 A, would have an ampacity less than the rating of the branch circuit and would be a violation of the clear wording of Sec. 210-19(a), for which no exception is given. A 20-A-rated fuse or CB on conductors that are not rated for loads over 16 A and that will represent a fire hazard at higher current cannot satisfy the **Code** and has no economic or operating justification. Because branch circuits are those parts of an electrical system most easily overloaded by users who might (and usually do) add load in excess of an initial limit of 16 A, use of 20-A-rated protection too easily (and almost certainly presents opportunity for widespread overheating, with attendant deterioration of conductor insulation, thermal damage to protective devices, and nuisance opening of the fuse of CB—all of which lead to oversized replacement of protective devices and aggravated fire potential.

210-21. Outlet Devices.   Specific limitations are placed on outlet devices for branch circuits: Lampholders must not have a rating lower than the load to be served; and lampholders connected to circuits rated over 20A must be heavy-duty type (that is, rated at least 660 W if it is an "admedium" type and at least 750 W for other types). Because fluorescent lampholders are not of the heavy-duty type, this excludes the use of fluorescent luminaires on 30, 40, and 50-A circuits. The intent is to limit the rating of lighting branch circuits supplying fluorescent fixtures to 20 A. The ballast is connected to the branch circuit rather than the lamp, but by controlling the lampholder rating, a 20-A limit is established for the ballast circuit. Most lampholders manufactured and intended for use with electric-discharge lighting for illumination purposes are rated less than 750 W, and are not classified as heavy-duty lampholders. If the luminaires are individually protected, such as by a fuse in the cord plug of a luminaire cord connected to, say, a 50-A trolley or plug-in busway, some inspectors have permitted use of fluorescent luminaires on 30, 40, and 50-A circuits. But such protection in the cord plug or in the luminaire is supplementary (Sec. 240-10) and branch-circuit protection of 30, 40, or 50-A rating would still exclude use of fluorescent fixtures according to Sec. 210-21(a).

Section 210-21(b) contains two paragraphs of importance. A new second paragraph reads: "A *single* receptacle installed on an individual branch circuit shall have an ampere rating of not less than that of the branch circuit." Since the branch-circuit overcurrent device determines the branch-circuit rating (or classification), a single receptacle (not a duplex receptacle) supplied by an individual branch circuit cannot have a rating *less than* the branch-circuit overcurrent device, as shown in Fig. 210-41.

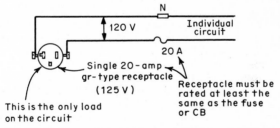

Fig. 210-41. Receptacle amp rating must *not* be less than circuit protection rating for an individual circuit. [Sec. 210-21(b).]

Receptacles must have ratings at least equal to the load. On circuits having two or more outlets, receptacles shall be rated as follows:

- On 15-A circuits—not over 15-A rating
- On 20-A circuits—15- or 20-A rating
- On 30-A circuits—30-A rating
- On 40-A circuits—40- or 50-A rating
- On 50-A circuits—50-A rating

210-22. Maximum Loads.   Section 210-22(c) says that, for loads other than motor loads, the total load on a branch circuit must not exceed 80 percent of the circuit rating when the load will constitute a continuous load—such as store lighting and similar loads (Fig. 210-42).

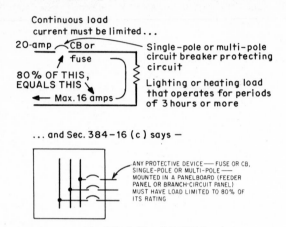

Continuous load
current must be limited...

20-amp CB or fuse

80% OF THIS,
EQUALS THIS

◄— Max. 16 amps

Single-pole or multi-pole
circuit breaker protecting
circuit

Lighting or heating load
that operates for periods
of 3 hours or more

... and Sec. 384-16 (c) says —

ANY PROTECTIVE DEVICE — FUSE OR CB,
SINGLE-POLE OR MULTI-POLE —
MOUNTED IN A PANELBOARD (FEEDER
PANEL OR BRANCH-CIRCUIT PANEL)
MUST HAVE LOAD LIMITED TO 80% OF
ITS RATING

Fig. 210-42. [Sec. 210-22(c).]

Because branch circuits for multioutlet circuits, such as lighting circuits, are rated in accordance with the rating or setting of the overcurrent device, the maximum permitted load is

Load = 80 percent × rating of protective device

Although the above limitation applies only to loads other than motor loads, Sec. 384-16(c) says that, "the total load on *any* overcurrent device located in a panelboard shall not exceed 80 percent of its rating where in normal operation the load will continue for 3 hours or more."

NOTE: In both of the above cases, the 80 percent load limitation does not apply "where the assembly including the overcurrent device is approved for continuous duty at 100 percent of its rating."

Exception No. 2 to Sec. 210-22(c) and Exception No. 1 to Section 220-2(a) eliminate the requirement for 80 percent limitation on continuous load for a branch circuit in cases "where branch-circuit conductors have been derated" because of the number of conductors in a raceway (Note 8 to Tables 310-16 through 19). *But* Sec. 384-16(c) requires any CB or fuse *in a panelboard* to have its load limited to 80 percent, and only one exception, the same as Exception No. 3 of Sec. 210-22(c), is made for such protective devices in a panel—a continuous load of 100 percent is permitted *only* when the protective device assembly (fuse in switch or CB) is approved for 100 percent continuous duty. (And there are no such devices rated less than 600 A. UL has a hard and fast rule that *any* breaker *not* marked for continuous load must have its load limited to 80 percent of its rating.) For panelboard applications, use of conductors that have been derated because more than three are in a raceway (Note 8 to Tables 310-16 through 19) does not eliminate the requirement for 80 percent limit on continuous load.

210-23. Permissible Loads. A single branch circuit to one outlet or load may serve any load and is unrestricted as to amp rating. Circuits with more than one outlet are subject to **NE Code** limitations on the use of branch circuits with two or more outlets, as follows:

1. Branch circuits rated 15 and 20 A may serve lighting units and/or appliances. The rating of any one cord- and plus-connected appliance shall not exceed 80 percent of the branch-circuit rating. Appliances fastened in place may be connected to a circuit serving lighting units and/or plug-connected appliances, provided the total rating of the fixed appliances fastened in place does not exceed 50 percent of the circuit rating (Fig. 210-43). *Example:* 50 percent of a 15-A branch circuit = 7.5 A. A room-air-conditioning unit fastened in place, with a rating not in excess of 7.5 A may be installed on a 15-A circuit having two or more outlets. Such units may not be installed on one of the small appliance branch circuits required in Sec. 220-3(b).

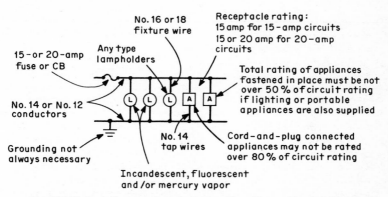

Fig. 210-43. General-purpose branch circuits—15 or 20 amp. [Sec. 210-23(a).]

However, modern design provides separate circuits for individual fixed appliances. In commercial and industrial buildings, separate circuits should be provided for lighting and separate circuits for receptacles.

2. Branch circuits rated 30 A may serve fixed lighting units (with heavy-duty type lampholders) in other than dwelling units or appliances in any occupancy. Any individual cord- and plug-connected

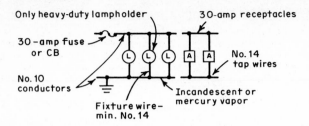

Note: Lighting or appliances, not both

Fig. 210-44. Multioutlet 30-amp circuits. [Sec. 210-23(b).]

appliance which draws more than 24 A may not be connected to this type of circuit (Fig. 210-44).

3. Branch circuits rated 40 and 50 A may serve fixed lighting units (with heavy-duty lampholders) or infrared heating units in other than dwelling units or cooking appliances in any occupancy (Fig. 210-45). It should be noted that a 40-A or 50-A circuit may be used to supply any kind of load equipment—such as a dryer or a water heater—where the circuit is an individual circuit to a single appliance. The conditions shown in that figure apply only where more than one outlet is supplied by the circuit. Figure 210-46 shows the combination of loads.

Except as permitted in Sec. 660-4 for portable, mobile, and transportable medical x-ray equipment, branch circuits having two or more outlets may supply only the loads specified in each of the above categories. It should be noted that any other circuit is not permitted to have more than one outlet and would be an individual branch circuit.

Application of those rules—and other **Code** rules that refer to "dwelling unit"—must take into consideration the **NE Code** definition for that phrase. A "dwelling unit" is defined as "one or more rooms" used "as a housekeeping unit" and must contain space or areas specifically dedicated to "eating, living, and sleeping" and must have "permanent provisions for cooking and sanitation." A one-family house is a "dwelling unit." So is an apartment in an apartment house or a condominium unit. But, a guest room in a hotel or motel or a dormitory room or unit is not a "dwelling unit" if it does not contain "permanent provisions for cooking"—which must mean a built-in range or counter-mounted cooking unit (with or without an oven).

It should be noted that the requirement calling for heavy-duty type lampholders for lighting units on 30-, 40-, and 40-A multioutlet branch circuits excludes the use of fluorescent lighting on these circuits because lampholders are not rated "heavy-duty" in accordance with Sec. 210-21(a) (Fig. 210-47). Mercury-vapor units with mogul lampholders may be used on these circuits provided tap conductor requirements are satisfied.

Multioutlet 40-amp circuits

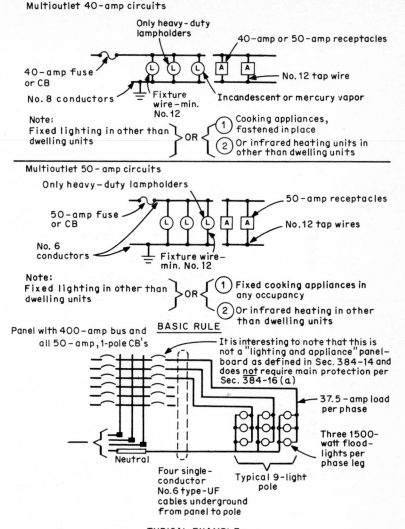

Note:
Fixed lighting in other than } OR { ① Cooking appliances, fastened in place
dwelling units   ② Or infrared heating units in other than dwelling units

Multioutlet 50-amp circuits

Only heavy-duty lampholders

Note:
Fixed lighting in other than } OR { ① Fixed cooking appliances in any occupancy
dwelling units   ② Or infrared heating in other than dwelling units

BASIC RULE

Panel with 400-amp bus and all 50-amp, 1-pole CB's

It is interesting to note that this is not a "lighting and appliance" panel-board as defined in Sec. 384-14 and does not require main protection per Sec. 384-16(a)

37.5-amp load per phase

Three 1500-watt flood-lights per phase leg

Neutral

Four single-conductor No.6 type-UF cables underground from panel to pole

Typical 9-light pole

TYPICAL EXAMPLE

50-amp, 3-phase, 4-wire circuits to supply incandescent floodlights on pole for lighting of a baseball field.

Fig. 210-45. Larger circuits. [Sec. 210-23(c).]

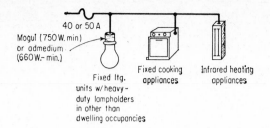

Mogul (750 W. min)
or admedium
(660 W.- min.)

40 or 50 A

Fixed ltg.
units w/ heavy-
duty lampholders
in other than
dwelling occupancies

Fixed cooking
appliances

Infrared heating
appliances

NOTE: Usually, all outlets on the circuit would supply
the same type of load — i.e., all lamps or all
cooking units, etc.

Fig. 210-46. Only specified loads may be used for multioutlet circuit. [Sec. 210-23(c).]

As indicated, multioutlet branch circuits for lighting are limited to a maximum loading of 50 A. Individual branch circuits may supply any loads. Excepting motors, this means that an individual piece of equipment may be supplied by a branch circuit which has sufficient carrying capacity in its conductors, is protected against current in excess of the capacity of the conductors, and supplies only the single outlet for the load device.

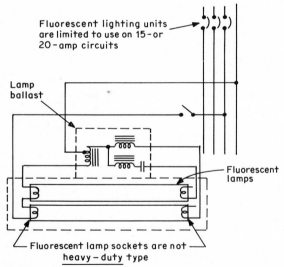

Fluorescent lighting units
are limited to use on 15- or
20-amp circuits

Lamp
ballast

Fluorescent
lamps

Fluorescent lamp sockets are not
heavy-duty type

Fig. 210-47. Watch out for this limitation on fluorescent equipment. (Sec. 210-23.)

Fixed outdoor electric snow-melting and de-icing installations may be supplied by any of the above described branch circuits provided the circuit supplies no other load. (See Sec. 426-3 in Art. 426, "Fixed Outdoor Electric De-Icing and Snow-Melting Equipment.")

210-24. Branch-Circuit Requirements—Summary.   Table 210-24 summarizes the requirements for the size of conductors where two or more outlets are supplied. The asterisk note also indicates that these ampacities are for copper conductors where derating is not required. Where more than three conductors are contained in a raceway or a cable, Note 8 to Tables 310-16 through 310-19 specifies the derating factors to apply for the number of conductors involved. A 20-A branch circuit is required to have conductors which have an ampacity of 20 A after derating and also must have the overcurrent protection rated 20 A where the branch circuit supplies two or more outlets. If four of these branch-circuit conductors are placed in conduit, they would need to have an ampacity of 20 A after derating. Thus, four No. 10 AWG Type TW copper conductors derated to 80 percent would have a rating of 24 A and be acceptable for the 20-A multioutlet branch circuit.

Where an individual branch circuit supplies only one load, the conductors can be selected on the basis that the maximum allowable load current of each conductor could not exceed 16 A. If the maximum load was 16 A or less, it would then be permissible to use No. 12 AWG Type TW with a 20-A overcurrent device.

210-25. Receptacle Outlets Required.   Part **(a)** simply requires that wherever it is known that cord- and plug-connected equipment is going to be used, receptacle outlets must be installed. That is a general rule that applies to any electrical system in any type of occupancy or premises.

Part **(b)** of this section sets forth a whole list of rules requiring specific installations of receptacle outlets in all "dwelling units"—i.e., one-family houses, apartments in apartment houses, and other places that conform to the definition of "dwelling unit." As indicated, receptacle outlets on fixed spacing must be installed in every room of a dwelling unit except the bathroom. The Code rule lists the specific rooms that are covered by the rule requiring receptacles spaced no greater than 12 ft apart in any continuous length of wall. As shown in Fig. 210-48, general-purpose convenience receptacles, usually of the duplex type, must be laid out around the perimeters of living room, bedrooms, and all the other rooms. Spacing of receptacle outlets should be such that no point along the floor line of an unbroken wall is more than 6 ft from a receptacle outlet. Care should be taken to provide receptacle outlets in smaller sections of wall space segregated by doors, fireplaces, bookcases, or windows. Although not required by the Code in hallways, good design practice dictates that convenience receptacles should be spaced to provide at least one for each 20 ft of wall length.

In determining the location of a receptacle outlet, the measurement is

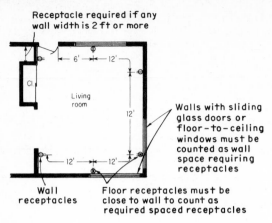

Fig. 210-48. From any point along wall, at floor line, a receptacle must be not more than 6 ft away. [Sec. 210-25(b).]

to be made along the floor line of the wall and is to continue around corners of the room, but is not to extend across doorways, archways, fireplaces, passageways, or other space unsuitable for having a flexible cord extended across it. The location of outlets for special appliances within 6 ft of the appliance does not affect the spacing of general-use convenience outlets but merely adds a requirement for special-use outlets.

Figure 210-49 shows two wall sections 9 ft and 3 ft wide extending from the same corner of the room. The receptacle shown located in the

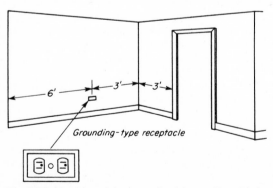

Fig. 210-49. Location of the receptacle as shown will permit the plugging in of a lamp or appliance located 6 ft on either side of the receptacle. [Sec. 210-25(b).]

wider section of the wall will permit the plugging in of a lamp or appliance located within 6 ft of either side of the receptacle. The same rule would apply to the other wall shown.

Receptacle outlets shall be provided for all wall space within the room except individual isolated sections which are less than 2 ft in width. For example, a wall space 23 in. wide and located between two doors would not need a receptacle outlet. Sliding panels in exterior walls are counted the same as regular wall space, and a floor-type receptacle can be used to meet the required spacing. It is considered more desirable and safer to have an outlet at these locations than to run extension cords which may in many instances have to cross a passageway used in connection with the sliding glass door or panel.

The last sentence of the first paragraph of part **(b)** requires fixed room dividers to be considered in spacing receptacles. This is illustrated by the sketch of Fig. 210-50. In effect, the two side faces of the room divider

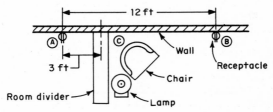

Fig. 210-50. Fixed room dividers must be counted as wall space requiring receptacles. [Sec. 210-25(b).]

provide additional wall space, and a table lamp placed as shown would be more than 6 ft from both receptacles A and B. Also, even though no place on the wall is more than 6 ft from either A or B, a lamp or other appliance placed at a point such as C would be more than 6 ft from B and out of reach of from A because of the divider. This rule would ensure placement of a receptacle in the wall on both sides of the divider or in the divider itself if its construction so permitted.

The second paragraph requires a receptacle outlet in kitchens and dining rooms at each counter space wider than 12 in., defines counter spaces, and disqualifies as "required outlets" any receptacles rendered inaccessible by the installation of appliances that are either fastened in place or are positioned in a space that is "dedicated"—i.e., assigned for permanent positioning of an appliance. Refrigerators and freezers would be typical of appliances "occupying dedicated space" (Fig. 210-51).

The fourth paragraph requires the installation of at least one wall receptacle outlet adjacent to the wash basin location in bathrooms of dwelling units—and part **(c)** requires the same receptacle in bathrooms of hotel and motel guest rooms (Fig. 210-52).

Receptacle required at each counter space wider than 12 in.

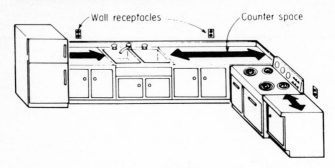

COUNTER SPACES in kitchen and dining rooms such as shown by arrows (above) must be supplied with receptacles if they are over 12 in. wide. Appliances are frequently used even on narrow counter widths; this requirement is designed to remove the dangerous practice of stretching cords across sinks, behind ranges, etc., to feed such appliances.

Inaccessible receptacles.

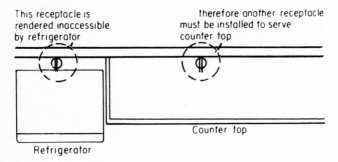

RECEPTACLE LOCATED behind an appliance, making the receptacle inaccessible, does not count as one of the required "counter-top" receptacles. (Neither does it count as one of the appliance-circuit receptacles required to be located every 12 ft.)

Fig. 210-51. Counter-top receptacles are needed and must be accessible. [Sec. 210-25(b).]

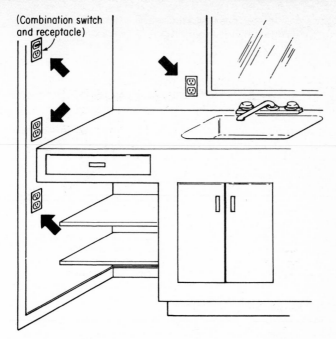

(Combination switch
and receptacle)

LOCATION of receptacle will vary, depending upon available wall
space. Arrows show several possibilities. A receptacle in a medicine
cabinet or in the bathroom lighting fixture does not satisfy this rule.

Fig. 210-52. Receptacle required adjacent to wash basin in residence. [Sec.
210-25(b).]

At least one outdoor receptacle must be installed for each one-family
dwelling. The definition of "one-family" dwelling (Art. 100) makes clear
that an outdoor receptacle is not required for apartment units, motels,
hotels, or other units in multioccupancy buildings.

Figure 210-53 notes the following:

At least one receptacle outlet must be installed in the basement of a
one-family dwelling. The requirement applies to basements of all one-
family houses but not to apartment houses, hotels, motels, dormitories,
and the like.

Any one-family dwelling having an attached garage also must have at
least one receptacle outlet in the garage. A receptacle is not required in a
detached garage; but if one is installed there, it must be GFCI protected
just as one in an attached garage. Section 210-8(a) refers to "garages"—
attached or detached.

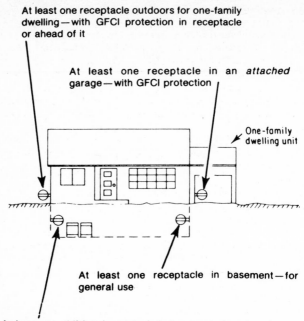

At least one receptacle outdoors for one-family
dwelling—with GFCI protection in receptacle
or ahead of it

At least one receptacle in an *attached*
garage—with GFCI protection

One-family
dwelling unit

At least one receptacle in basement—for
general use

At least one additional receptacle in basement—for a laundry area
that might be located there. And a receptacle is required at the
laundry no matter where it is located in any dwelling unit.

Fig. 210-53. These specific receptacles are required for "one-family dwelling"—that is, a one-family house. [Sec. 210-25(b).]

At least one receptacle—single or duplex or triplex—must be installed
for the laundry of a dwelling unit. Such a receptacle and any other
receptacles for special appliances must be placed within 6 ft of the
intended location of the appliance. The Code rule requires a receptacle
outlet in a basement in addition to any receptacle outlet(s) that may be
provided as the required receptacle(s) to serve a laundry area in the
basement. This point was not clear in previous NE Code , which left the
possibility that one receptacle in the basement at the laundry area located
there could satisfy as *both* the required "laundry" receptacle and the
required "basement" receptacle. Now, a separate receptacle has to be
provided for each requirement to satisfy the Code rule.

As noted in the next-to-last paragraph of Sec. 210-25(b), any receptacle
that is an integral part of a lighting fixture or an appliance or a cabinet
may not be used to satisfy the specific receptacle requirements of the
section. For instance, a receptacle in a medicine cabinet or lighting fixture
may not serve as the required bathroom receptacle. And a receptacle in a

post-light may not serve as the required outdoor receptacle for a one-family dwelling.

In spacing receptacle outlets so that no floor point along the wall space of the rooms designated by Sec. 210-25(b) is more than 6 ft from a receptacle, a receptacle that is part of an appliance must not generally be counted as one of the required spaced receptacles. However, the Exception at the end of part **(b)** states that a receptacle that is "factory installed" in a "permanently installed electric baseboard heater" (not a portable heater) may be counted as one of the required spaced receptacles for the wall space occupied by the heater. Or a receptacle "provided as a separate assembly by the manufacturer" may also be counted as a required spaced receptacle. But, such receptacles must not be connected to the circuit that supplies the electric heater. Such a receptacle must be connected to another circuit.

Because of the increasing popularity of low-density electric baseboard heaters, their lengths are frequently so long (up to 14 ft) that required maximum spacing of receptacles places receptacles above heaters and produces the undesirable and dangerous condition where cord sets to lamps, radios, TVs, etc., will droop over the heater and might droop into the heated-air outlet. And UL rules prohibit use of receptacles above electric baseboard heaters for that reason. Receptacles in heaters can afford the required spaced receptacle units without mounting any above heater units. They satisfy the UL concern and also the preceding note near the end of Sec. 210-25(b) that calls for the need "to minimize the use of cords across doorways, fireplaces, and similar openings"—and the heated-air outlet along a baseboard heater is a "similar opening" that must be guarded (Fig. 210-54).

The Exception to Sec. 210-25(c) permits receptacles in hotel and motel rooms to be conveniently located to suit the permanent furniture layout adopted. In such cases, the spacing requirements of not more than 12 ft between receptacles, etc., do not have to be observed.

Part **(d)** of this section calls for one receptacle in show windows for each 12 ft of length (measured horizontally) to accommodate portable window signs and other electrified displays (Fig. 210-55).

210-26. Lighting Outlets Required.   The basic rule requires "at least one wall switch controlled lighting outlet" in rooms, halls, stairways, attached garages, and at outdoor entrances. The word "bathrooms" is added in the basic rule because various building codes do not include bathrooms under their definition of "habitable rooms." So the word "bathroom" was needed to assure that the rule covered bathrooms. The rule does not stipulate that these must be ceiling lighting outlets; they also may be wall-mounted lighting outlets (Fig. 210-56).

A note clarifies that "a vehicle door in an attached garage is *not* considered as an outdoor entrance." This makes it clear that the Code does not require such a light outlet at any garage door that is provided as a vehicle entrance because the lights of the car provide adequate illumi-

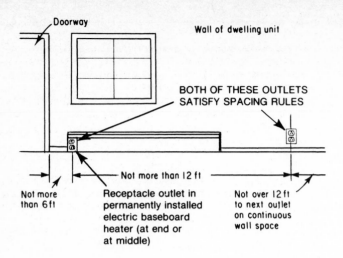

Doorway

Wall of dwelling unit

BOTH OF THESE OUTLETS
SATISFY SPACING RULES

— Not more than 12 ft

Not more
than 6 ft

Receptacle outlet in
permanently installed
electric baseboard
heater (at end or
at middle)

Not over 12 ft
to next outlet
on continuous
wall space

BUT WATCH THIS!
Separate circuiting required for heater and receptacle.

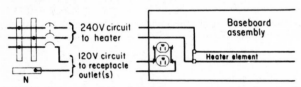

240V circuit
to heater

120V circuit
to receptacle
outlet(s)

N

Baseboard
assembly

Heater element

Fig. 210-54. Receptacles in baseboard heaters may serve as "required" receptacles. [Sec. 210-25(b).]

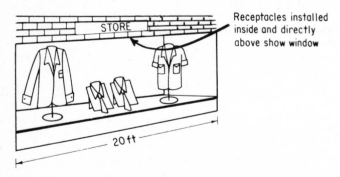

STORE

Receptacles installed
inside and directly
above show window

20 ft

For a 20-ft-long store show window,

a minimum of two receptacles must be installed, one for
each 12 linear ft or major fraction thereof of show window
length.

Fig. 210-55. Receptacles are required for show windows in stores or other buildings. [Sec. 210-25(d).]

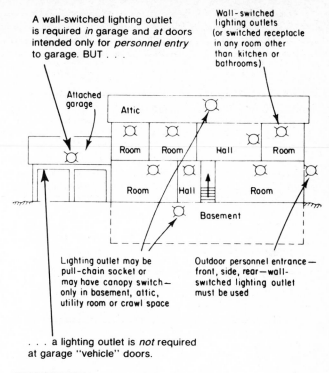

A wall-switched lighting outlet is required *in* garage and *at* doors intended only for *personnel entry* to garage. BUT . . .

Wall-switched lighting outlets (or switched receptacle in any room other than kitchen or bathrooms)

Attached garage

Attic

Room   Room   Hall   Room

Room   Hall   Room

Basement

Lighting outlet may be pull-chain socket or may have canopy switch— only in basement, attic, utility room or crawl space

Outdoor personnel entrance— front, side, rear—wall- switched lighting outlet must be used

. . . a lighting outlet is *not* required at garage "vehicle" doors.

EXCEPTION:

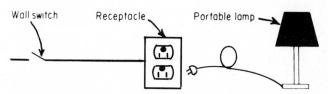

Wall switch   Receptacle   Portable lamp

Wall-switched receptacle(s) may be used instead of a lighting outlet in habitable rooms other than kitchens and bathrooms.

Fig. 210-56. Lighting outlets required in dwelling units. (Sec. 210-26.)

nation when such a door is being used during darkness. But the wording of this note does suggest that a rear or side door that is provided for personnel entry to an attached garage would be "considered as an outdoor entrance" because the note excludes only "vehicle" doors. Such personnel entrances from outdoors to the garage would seem to require a wall-switched lighting outlet.

In addition, at least one lighting outlet must be installed in every attic, underfloor space, utility room, and basement if it is used for storage or if it contains equipment requiring servicing. In these latter cases, the lighting outlet does not have to be controlled by a wall switch, although it may be. A lamp socket controlled by a pull chain or a canopy switch could be used.

Two exceptions are given to the basic requirements. Exception No. 1 notes that in rooms other than kitchens or bathrooms a wall switch controlled receptacle outlet may be used instead of a wall switch controlled lighting outlet. The receptacle outlet can serve to supply a portable lamp, which would give the necessary lighting for the room. Exception No. 2 states that "in hallways, stairways, and at outdoor entrances remote, central, or automatic control of lighting shall be permitted." This latter recognition appears to accept remote, central, or automatic control as an alternative to the wall switch control mentioned in the basic rules.

But note carefully that every kitchen and every bathroom must have at least one wall switch controlled lighting outlet (Fig. 210-57).

Kitchen and all bathrooms—
Each must have at least one lighting outlet that is **wall-switch-controlled** (not pullchain or switch in fixture or canopy)

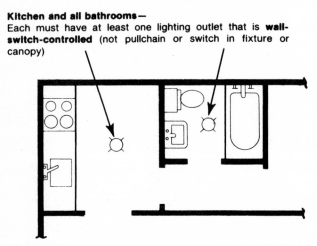

Fig. 210-57. Switch-controlled lighting outlet in kitchen and bathroom. [Sec. 210-26(a).]

Section 210-26(b) notes that "at least one wall switch controlled lighting outlet or wall switch controlled receptacle shall be installed in guest rooms in hotels, motels, or similar occupancies."

ARTICLE 215. FEEDERS

215-1. Scope. "Feeders" are the conductors which carry electric power from the service equipment (or generator switchboard, where power is generated on the premises) to the overcurrent protective devices for branch circuits supplying the various loads. "Subfeeders" originate at a distribution center other than the service equipment or generator switchboard and supply one or more other distribution panelboards, branch-circuit panelboards, or branch circuits. Code rules on feeders apply also to all subfeeders (Fig. 215-1).

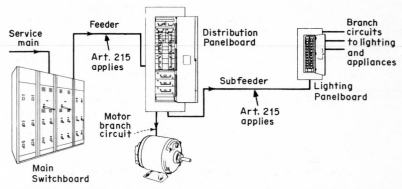

Fig. 215-1. Article 215 applies only to those circuits that conform to the NEC definition of "feeder." (Sec. 215-1.)

For the given circuit voltage, feeders and subfeeders must be capable of carrying the amount of current required by the load, plus any current which may be required in the future. Selection of the size of a feeder depends upon the size and nature of the known load computed from branch-circuit data, the anticipated future load requirements, and voltage drop.

Article 215 deals with the determination of the minimum sizes of feeder conductors necessary for safety. Overloading of conductors may result in insulation breakdowns due to overheating; overheating of switches, busbars, and terminals; the blowing of fuses and consequent overfusing; excessive voltage drop and excessive copper losses. Thus the overloading will in many cases create a fire risk and is sure to result in very unsatisfactory service.

The actual maximum load on a feeder depends upon the total load connected to the feeder and the demand factor. If at certain times the entire connected load is in operation, the demand factor is 100 percent; i.e., the maximum load, or maximum demand, is equal to the total connected load. If the heaviest load ever carried is only one-half the total connected load, the demand factor is 50 percent.

215-2. Minimum Rating and Size.   There are two steps in the process of predetermining the maximum load that a feeder will be required to carry: first, a reasonable estimate must be made of the probable connected load; and, second, a reasonable value for the demand factor must be assumed. From a survey of a large number of buildings, the average connected loads and demand factors have been ascertained for lighting and small appliance loads in buildings of the more common classes of occupancy, and these data are presented in Sec. 220-2 and Part **B** of Art. 220 as minimum requirements.

The load is specified in terms of watts per square foot for certain occupancies. These loads are here referred to as standard loads, because they are minimum standards established by the **Code** in order to assure that the feeders and branch circuits will have sufficient carrying capacity for safety.

In this section, the last two sentences of the first paragraph note that it is never necessary for feeder conductors to be larger than the service-entrance conductors (assuming use of the same conductor material and the same insulation). In particular, this is aimed at those cases where the size of service-entrance conductors for a dwelling unit is selected in accordance with the higher-than-normal ampacities permitted by Note 3 to **Code** Table 310-16 for services to residential occupancies. If the service conductors are brought in to a single service disconnect (a single fused switch or circuit breaker) and load-side feeder conductors carry the entire service load to a switchboard or panelboard some distance away, diversity on the feeder conductors does give them the same reduced heat-loading that enables the service conductors to be assigned the higher ampacity. This new rule simply extends the permission of Note 3 to those feeders that carry the whole service load and is applicable for any such feeder in a one-family dwelling or for mobile home feed (Fig. 215-2).

Part **(a)** specifies that the feeder wires must never be smaller than No. 10 when the feeder supplies at least the number of circuits as shown in Fig. 215-3.

As shown in Fig. 215-4, the rule of part **(b)** of this section requires that the ampacity of feeder conductors must be at least equal to that of the service conductors where the total service current is carried by the feeder conductors. In the case shown, No. 4 TW aluminum is taken as equivalent to No. 6 TW copper and has the same ampacity.

A note at the end of Sec. 215-2 comments on voltage drop in feeders. It should be carefully noted that the **NEC** does not establish any mandatory rules on voltage drop for either branch circuits or feeders. The references to 3 and 5 percent voltage drops are purely advisory—i.e., recommended maximum values of voltage drop. The **Code** does not consider excessive voltage drop to be unsafe.

The voltage drop note suggests not more than 3 percent for feeders supplying power, heating, or lighting loads. It also provides for a maximum drop of 5 percent for the conductors between the service-entrance equipment and the connected load. If the feeders have an actual voltage drop of 3 percent, then only 2 percent is left for the branch circuits. If a lower voltage drop is obtained in the feeder, then the branch circuit has more voltage drop available, provided that the total drop does not exceed

If Note 3 of Table 310-16 is used to assign higher ampacity to the service entrance conductors . . .

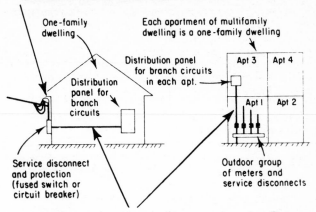

. . . then feeder conductors that carry the total current supplied by the service may also be assigned the higher ampacities of Note 3 (for instance, No. 2/0 copper THW is rated at 200 amps instead of 175 amps). (They do not have to be larger than the service conductors.)

Or, a multifamily dwelling might be fed like this —

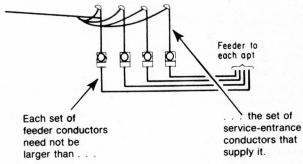

Fig. 215-2. Feeder conductors need not be larger than service-entrance conductors when higher ampacity of Note 3, Table 310-16, is used. (Sec. 215-2.)

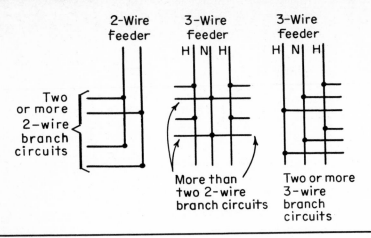

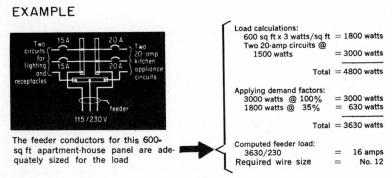

EXAMPLE

The feeder conductors for this 600-sq ft apartment-house panel are adequately sized for the load

Load calculations:
600 sq ft x 3 watts/sq ft = 1800 watts
Two 20-amp circuits @
1500 watts   = 3000 watts
                                 _____
                        Total = 4800 watts

Applying demand factors:
3000 watts @ 100%   = 3000 watts
1800 watts @ 35%   = 630 watts
                                 _____
                        Total = 3630 watts

Computed feeder load:
3630/230   =   16 amps
Required wire size   =   No. 12

BUT, THE FEEDER CONDUCTORS MUST **NOT** BE SMALLER THAN No. 10 FROM SEC. 215–2 (a) (3).

Fig. 215-3. Feeder must be minimum of No. 10 wire in these cases. [Sec. 215-2(a).]

5 percent. For any one load, the total voltage drop is made up of the voltage drop in the one or more feeders plus the voltage drop in the branch circuit supplying that load.

Again, however, values stated in Sec. 215-2(c) are recommended values and are not intended to be enforced as a requirement.

Voltage drop must always be carefully considered in sizing feeder conductors, and calculations should be made for peak load conditions. For maximum efficiency, the size of feeder conductors should be such that voltage drop up to the branch-circuit panelboards or point of branch-circuit origin is not more than 1 percent for lighting loads or

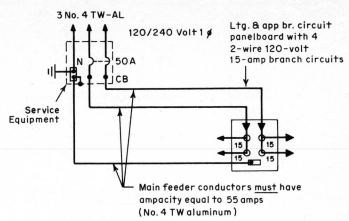

Fig. 215-4. Feeder conductors must not have ampacity less than service conductors. [Sec. 215-2(b).]

combined lighting, heating, and power loads and not more than 2 percent for power or heating loads. Local codes may impose lower limits of voltage drop. Voltage-drop limitations are shown in Fig. 215-5 for NEC levels and better levels of drop, as follows:

1. For combinations of lighting and power loads on feeders and branch circuits, use the voltage-drop percentages for lighting load (at left in Fig. 215-5).

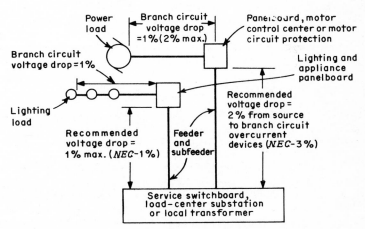

Fig. 215-5. Recommended basic limitations on voltage drop. [Sec. 215-2(c).]

2. The word *feeder* here refers to the overall run of conductors carrying power from the source to the point of final branch-circuit distribution, including feeders, subfeeders, sub-subfeeders, etc.
3. The voltage-drop percentages are based on nominal circuit voltage at the source of each voltage level. Indicated limitations should be observed for each voltage level in the distribution system.

There are many cases in which the above-mentioned limits of voltage drop (1 percent for lighting feeders, etc.) should be relaxed in the interests of reducing the prohibitive costs of conductors and conduits required by such low drops. In many installations 5 percent drop in feeders is not critical or unsafe—such as in apartment houses.

Voltage-drop tables and slide calculators are available from a good number of electrical equipment manufacturers. Voltage-drop calculations will vary according to the actual circuit parameters, e.g., AC or DC, single- or multiphase, power factor, circuit impedance, line reactance, types of enclosures (nonmetallic or metallic), length and size of conductors, and conductor material (copper, copper-clad aluminum, or aluminum).

Calculations of voltage drop in any set of feeders can be made in accordance with the formulas given in electrical design literature, such as those shown in Fig. 215-6. From this calculation, it can be determined if the conductor size initially selected to handle the load will be adequate to maintain voltage drop within given limits. If it is not, the size of the conductors must be increased (or other steps taken where conductor reactance is not negligible) until the voltage drop is within prescribed limits. Many such graphs and tabulated data on voltage drop are available in handbooks and from manufacturers. Figure 215-7 shows an example of excessive voltage drop—over 10 percent in the feeder.

215-4. Feeders with Common Neutral.   A frequently discussed Code requirement is that of Sec. 215-4, covering the use of a common neutral with more than one set of feeders. This section says that a common neutral feeder may be used for two or three sets of 3-wire feeders, or two sets of 4-wire feeders. It further requires that all conductors of feeder circuits employing a common neutral feeder must be within the same enclosure when the enclosure or raceway containing them is metal.

A common neutral is a single neutral conductor used as the neutral for more than one set of feeder conductors. It must have current-carrying capacity equal to the sum of the neutral conductor capacities if an individual neutral conductor were used with each feeder set. Figure 215-8 shows a typical example of a common neutral, used for three-feeder circuits. A common neutral may be used only with feeders. It may never be used with branch circuits. A single neutral of a multiwire branch circuit is not a "common neutral." It is the neutral of only a single circuit even though the circuit may consist of 3 or 4 wires. A feeder common neutral is used with more than one feeder circuit.

Two-wire, single-phase circuits (inductance negligible)

$$V = \frac{2k \times L \times I}{d^2} = 2R \times L \times I$$

$$d^2 = \frac{2k \times L \times I}{V}$$

V = drop in circuit voltage (volts)
R = resistance per ft of conductor (ohms/ft)
I = current in conductor (amperes)

Three-wire, single-phase circuits (inductance negligible)

$$V = \frac{2k \times L \times I}{d^2}$$

V = drop between outside conductors (volts)
I = current in more-heavily loaded outside conductor (amps)

Three-wire, three-phase circuits (inductance negligible)

$$V = \frac{2k \times L \times I}{d^2} \times 0.866$$

V = voltage drop of 3-phase circuit

Four-wire, three-phase balanced circuits (inductance negligible)

Lighting loads

Voltage drop between one outside conductor and neutral equals one-half of drop calculated by formula above for 2-wire circuits.

Motor loads

Voltage drop between any two outside conductors equals 0.866 times the drop determined by formula above for two-wire circuits.

In the above formulas:

L = one-way length of circuit (ft)
d^2 = cross-section area of conductor (circular mils)
k = resistivity of conductor metal (cir mil-ohms/ft)
   = 12 for circuits loaded to more than 50% of allowable circuit capacity
   = 11 for circuits loaded less than 50%
   = 18 for aluminum or copper-clad aluminum conductors

Example: 230-V two-wire heating circuit. Load is 24 A. Circuit size is No. 10 AWG copper, and the one-way circuit length is 200 ft.

$$VD = \frac{24 \times 200 \times 24}{10,380} = \frac{115,200}{10,380} = 11$$

An 11-V drop on a 230-V circuit is about a 5 percent drop (11/230 = 0.0478). No. 8 AWG copper conductors would be needed to reduce the voltage drop to 3 percent on the branch circuit and allow 2 percent more on the feeder.

Fig. 215-6. Calculating voltage drop in feeder circuits. [Sec. 215-2(c).]

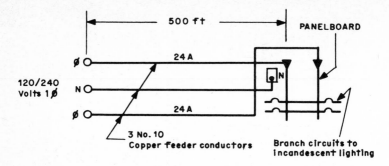

1. No. 10 copper conductor has a resistance of 1.018 ohms per 1000 ft (Table 8, Chapter 9).
2. The two 500-ft lengths of circuit conductors total 1000 ft and have a resistance of 1.018 ohms.
3. Voltage Drop = load current x conductor resistance
   = 24 amps x 1.018 ohms = **24.43 volts**
4. $\frac{24.43}{240}$ = 10.2% VOLTAGE DROP—*NEC* SUGGESTS MAX. 3%

Fig. 215-7. Feeder voltage drop should be checked. [Sec. 215-2(c).]

215-7. Ungrounded Conductors Tapped from Grounded Systems. Refer to Sec. 210-10 for a discussion that applies as well to feeder circuits as to branch circuits.

215-8. Means of Identifying Conductor with the Higher Voltage to Ground. The wording of this section recognizes orange as the preferred color of the high leg of a 4-wire delta supply without disturbing current practices in various local areas where other colors (such as red, yellow, or blue) or other means of identification are required by electric utility regulations or by local code (Fig. 215-9).

Note that identification of the phase leg with 208 V to ground is required only at those points in the system where the neutral is present—such as in panelboards, motor-control centers, and other enclosures where circuits are connected. The purpose of this is to warn that 208 V, not 120 V, exist from the high leg to the neutral. Such indication minimizes the chance that a 208-V circuit might be accidentally or unwittingly connected to 120-V loads, such as lamps or appliances of 120-V operating coils in motor starters. Such connection would burn out 120-V equipment and presents a hazard to personnel.

215-9. Ground-Fault Personnel Protection. A ground-fault circuit-interrupter may be located in the feeder and protect all branch circuits connected to that feeder. In such cases, the provisions of Sec. 210-8 will be satisfied and additional *downstream* ground-fault protection on the individual branch circuits would not be required. It should be mentioned, however, that downstream ground-fault protection is more desirable

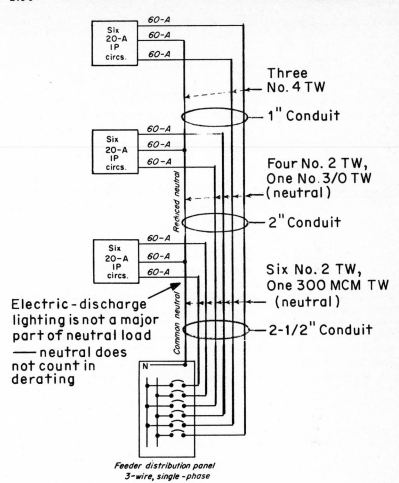

Three
No. 4 TW

1" Conduit

Four No. 2 TW,
One No. 3/0 TW
(neutral)

2" Conduit

Six No. 2 TW,
One 300 MCM TW
(neutral)

2-1/2" Conduit

Electric-discharge
lighting is not a major
part of neutral load
— neutral does
not count in
derating

*Feeder distribution panel
3-wire, single-phase*

*Note: Conductor sizes conform to
reduced carrying capacities
for more than three conductors
in conduit.*

Fig. 215-8. Example of three feeder circuits using a single, "common neutral"—with neutral size reduced as permitted. (Sec. 215-4.)

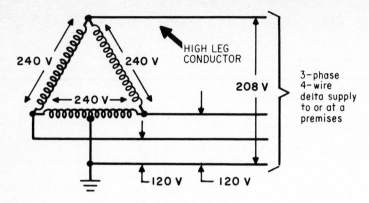

HIGH LEG CONDUCTOR

240 V   240 V

240 V

208 V

120 V   120 V

3-phase
4-wire
delta supply
to or at a
premises

HIGH-LEG CONDUCTOR may be orange in color or may be some other color—such as red or yellow—as long as the color or tagging or other identification clearly distinguishes this as the one with higher voltage to ground at any connection point where the neutral is present.

Fig. 215-9. Identifying the high-leg of 4-wire delta circuits. (Sec. 215-8.)

than ground-fault protection in the feeder because less equipment will be de-energized when the ground-fault circuit-interrupter opens the supply in response to a line-to-ground fault.

As shown in Fig. 215-10, if a ground-fault protector is installed in the feeder to a panel for branch circuits to outdoor residential receptacles, this protector may provide the ground-fault protection required by Sec. 210-8 for such outdoor receptacles.

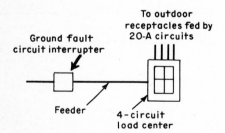

To outdoor
receptacles fed by
20-A circuits

Ground fault
circuit interrupter

Feeder

4-circuit
load center

Fig. 215-10. GFCI in feeder does satisfy as protection for branch circuits (Sec. 215-9.)

ARTICLE 220. BRANCH-CIRCUIT AND FEEDER CALCULATIONS

All the calculations and design procedures covered by Art. 220 involve mathematical manipulation of units of voltage, current, resistance, and other measures of electrical conditions or characteristics.

NE Code references to voltages vary considerably. The Code contains references to 120 V, 125 V, 115/230 V, 120/240 V, 120/208 V. Such variety of references—particularly when Code sections are referring to the same "nominal" system voltage, such as "115/230" in Sec. 220-30 and then "120/240" in Sec. 250-60—can be an annoying inconsistency. But the designer or installer using the Code has to make the necessary distinction between significant voltage differences and discrepancies in nominal values.

In all electrical systems there is a normal, predictable spread of voltage values over the impedances of the system equipment. It has been common practice to assign these basic levels to each nominal system voltage. The highest value of voltage is that at the service entrance or transformer secondary, such as 480Y/277 V. Then considering voltage drop due to impedance in the circuit conductors and equipment, a "nominal" midsystem voltage designation would be 460Y/254 (Fig. 220-1). Variations in

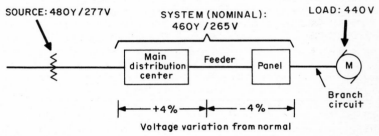

Fig. 220-1. Designation of source, system, and load voltages. (Art. 220.)

"nominal" voltages have come about because of (1) differences in utility supply voltages throughout the country, (2) varying transformer secondary voltages produced by different and often uncontrolled voltage drops in primary feeders, and (3) preferences of different engineers and other design authorities.

Because the NE Code is produced by contributors from all over the nation and of varying technical experiences, it is understandable that diversity of designations would creep in. As with many other things, we just have to live with problems until we solve them.

To standardize calculations, however, Part **B** of Chap. 9 specifies that nominal voltages of 230 and 115 V are to be used in computing the ampere load on a conductor. [Dividing these voltages into the watts load will produce higher current values than would 240 and 120 V, thus resulting in larger (safer) conductor sizes.] That rule clearly requires that *all* branch-circuit, feeder, and service conductor calculations must be made at those basic voltage levels. It can be assumed that calculations at higher voltages must be made at the proper multiples of those voltages.

It seems clear that the NE Code adopts 115 V as the basic operating voltage of equipment designed for operation at 110 to 125 V. That is indicated in Table 430-12(b) and Tables 430-148 to 430-151. References are made to "rated motor voltages" of 115, 230, 460, 575, and 2,300—all values over 115 are integral multiples of 115. The last note in Tables 430-149 and 430-150 indicates that motors of those voltage ratings are applicable on systems rated 110–120, 220–240, 440–480, and 550–600 V. Although the motors can operate satisfactorily within those ranges, it is better to design circuits to deliver rated voltage. These Code voltage designations for motors are consistent with the trend over recent years for manufacturers to rate equipment for corresponding values of voltage.

Where calculations result in values involving a fraction of an ampere, the fraction may be dropped if it is 0.5 or less. A value such as 20.7 A should be continued to be used as 20.7 or rounded off as the next higher whole number, in this case 21 A. Again, this is on the safe side. There are occasions, however, when current values must be added together. In such cases, it is on the safe side to retain fractions less than 0.5, since several fractions added together can result in the next whole ampere.

220-2. Computation of Branch Circuits.   Part **(a)** is essentially the same as the requirement of Sec. 210-22(c). (Refer to that discussion.)

The task of calculating a branch-circuit load and then determining the size of circuit conductors required to feed that load is common to all electrical system calculations. Although it may seem to be a simple matter (and it usually is), there are many conditions which make the problem confusing (and sometimes controversial) because of the NE Code rules that must be observed.

The requirements for loading and sizing of branch circuits are covered in Art. 210 and in Sec. 220-2. In general, the following basic points must be considered.

- The ampacity of branch-circuit conductors must not be less than the maximum load to be served [Sec. 210-19(a)].
- The ampacity of branch-circuit conductors must not be less than the rating of the branch circuit. Section 210-19(a) requires that the conductors of a branch circuit must have an ampacity not less than the rating of the branch circuit, which rating is determined by the rating or setting of the overcurrent device protecting the circuit, and gives no exceptions to that rule.
- The rating of a branch circuit is established by the rating or setting of its OC (overcurrent) protective device (Sec. 210-3).
- The normal, maximum, continuous ampacities of conductors in cables or raceways are given in Table 310-16 for both copper and aluminum.
- These normal ampacities may have to be reduced (derated) where there are more than three conductors in a cable or raceway (Note 8 to Tables 310-16 through 310-19).

- The current permitted to be carried by the branch-circuit conductors may have to be reduced if the load is continuous [Sec. 210-22(c) and Sec. 220-2(a)].

Section 210-20 says that the rating or setting of the branch-circuit overcurrent protective device is not to exceed that specified in Sec. 240-3 for conductors. Section 240-3 says that conductors shall be protected against overcurrent in accordance with their ampacities; but Exception No. 1 to that rule allows that where the ampacity of the conductor does not correspond with the standard ampere rating of a fuse or a circuit breaker, the next higher standard device rating shall be permitted if this rating does not exceed 800 A. However, in selecting the size of the branch-circuit overcurrent device, the rule of *both* Secs. 210-19(a) and 210-20 must be satisfied, because *all* **Code** rules bearing on a particular detail must always be observed.

Because Sec. 210-19(a) is more restrictive than Sec. 210-20 and does not recognize *any* case where branch-circuit conductors would have an ampacity of less than the ampere rating of the circuit protective device, Sec. 210-19(a) actually negates the permission given in Exception No. 1 to Sec. 240-3 to use a protective device of "the next higher standard rating" on branch circuits. That conclusion is supported by the fact that Sec. 210-20(a) refers to "Section 240-3" and not to the Exception No. 1.

Section 220-2(a) must be evaluated against all that background data from Art. 210. Although determination of ampacities from Tables 310-16 through 310-19 yields the maximum allowable *continuous* current ratings of conductors, there are **Code** rules that limit the load that may be carried continuously (3 hr or more) to no more than 80 percent of the rated current value. Section 210-22(c) says that a continuous load on a branch circuit must not exceed 80 percent of the "rating of the branch circuit." Although the rating of the branch circuit is set by the ampere rating or setting of the overcurrent device protecting the circuit, the conductors of a branch circuit may not have a rated ampacity of less than the rating of the protective device [Section 210-19(a)]. Thus, limiting the load to 80 percent of the circuit rating does make it "not more than 80 percent" of the circuit conductors. Section 220-2(a) repeats the limitation of continuous load to no more than 80 percent of the rating of the branch circuit (the rating of its fuse or CB) and no more than 80 percent of the conductor rating.

Section 220-10(b) also has the effect of limiting a continuous load to not more than 80 percent of the ampacity of the circuit conductors. In that case, they are feeder conductors that must not be loaded over 80 percent of their capacity.

The limitation to 80 percent maximum loading, as set forth in those **NE Code** sections, is not established because the conductors cannot carry 100 percent of their rated current continuously. The conductors still have the same ampacity—the same maximum allowable continuous current rating. Likewise, a fused switch or circuit breaker can, itself, withstand the heat produced within it by 100 percent of its current rating. The 80 percent limit is set because of the following:

1. Conductors of any circuit must connect to the terminals of the fusible switch or circuit breaker that provides disconnect and protection for a branch circuit or feeder.
2. Current flow through a circuit produces heating in the fusible switch or circuit breaker as well as in the conductors.
3. The heat produced in the switch or CB does not generally harm the switch or CB itself, but that heat is readily conducted into the end lengths of conductors that are attached to the terminals.
4. Although the conductors can take the heat input from 100 percent of their own current rating, the extra heat conducted into the conductor from the switch or CB adds to the heat load on the conductors adjacent to the terminations.
5. For a continuous load, excessive heat will be produced in the conductor insulation if the conductor is already carrying its full rated current; and that can cause damage to the conductor insulation.

Exception No. 2 to Sec. 210-22(c) and Exception No. 1 to Sec. 220-2(a) eliminate the requirement for 80 percent limitation on continuous load for a branch circuit in cases "where branch-circuit conductors have been derated" because of the number of conductors in a raceway (Note 8 to Tables 310-16 through 19). *But* Sec. 384-16(c) requires any CB or fuse *in a panelboard* to have its load limited to 80 percent, and only one exception is made for such protective devices in a panel—a continuous load of 100 percent is permitted *only* when the protective device assembly (fuse in switch or CB) is approved for 100 percent continuous duty. (And there are no such devices rated less than 600 A, so the exceptions referring to 100 percent rated devices do not apply to any branch circuits of less than 600 A. UL has a hard and fast rule that *any* breaker *not* marked for continuous load must have its load limited to 80 percent of its rating.) For panelboard applications, use of conductors that have been derated because more than three are in a raceway (Note 8 to Tables 310-16 through 19) does not eliminate the requirement for 80 percent limit on continuous load.

It should also be carefully noted that one **Code** rule *may never be taken* as an exception to another **Code** rule unless an exception is given. For example, Sec. 384-16(c) says that a protective device in a panelboard may not be loaded continuously (3 hr or more) in excess of 80 percent of the rating of the device, with the single exception where the overcurrent device is specifically "approved" for continuous operation at 100 percent of its rating. Exception No. 1 to Sec. 220-2(a) permits a continuous load at 100 percent of the rating of a branch-circuit protective device that is *not* approved for continuous operation at 100 percent of its rating, provided that the circuit conductors have been derated for conduit fill. But Exception No. 1 of Sec. 220-2(a) is *not* given in Sec. 384-16(c) and may not be used as such. *Every* CB or fuse in a panelboard, if it is not approved for 100 percent continuous loading, must be loaded to not over 80 percent of the device rating for a continuous load—even if the circuit conductors to the fuse or CB *have been derated* for conduit fill.

This all leads to a fundamental principle in the application of **NE Code** rules: *Each and every rule must be satisfied under all conditions if no exception is given.*

Code Table 220-2(b) lists certain occupancies (types of buildings) for which a minimum general lighting load is specified in watts per square foot. In each type of building, there must be adequate branch-circuit capacity to handle the total load that is represented by the product of watts per square foot times the square-foot area of the building. For instance, if one floor of an office building is 40,000 sq ft in area, that floor must have a total branch-circuit capacity of 40,000 times 5 W per sq ft [**Code** Table 220-2(b)] for general lighting. Note that the total load to be used in calculating required circuit capacity must never be taken at less than the indicated watts per square foot times square foot for those occupancies listed. Of course, if branch-circuit load for lighting is determined from a lighting layout of specific fixtures of known voltamp rating, the load value must meet the previous watts-per-square-foot minimum; and if the load from a known lighting layout is greater, then the greater watts or voltamp value must be taken as the required branch-circuit capacity.

As indicated in Sec. 220-2(b), when load is determined on a watts-per-square-foot basis, open porches, garages, unfinished basements, and unused areas are not counted as part of the area. Area calculation is made using the *outside* dimensions of the "building, apartment, or other area involved."

When fluorescent or mercury-vapor lighting is used on branch circuits, the presence of the inductive effect of the ballast or transformer creates a power factor consideration. Determination of the load in such cases must be based on the total of the voltampere rating of the units and not on the wattage of the lamps.

Part **(c)** covers rules on providing branch-circuit capacity for loads other than lighting and designates specific amounts of load that must be allowed for each outlet.

Receptacle Outlets

Section 220-2(c) (4) requires that every general-purpose, single or duplex or triplex convenience receptacle outlet in nonresidential occupancies be taken as a load of 180 VA, and that amount of circuit capacity must be provided for each such outlet (Fig. 220-2). **Code** intent is that each individual device strap—whether it holds one, two, or three receptacles—is a load of 180 VA.

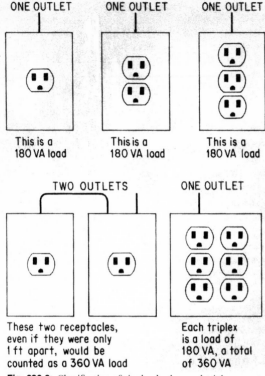

Fig. 220-2. Classification of single, duplex, and triplex receptacles. (Sec. 220-2.)

If a 51-A, 115-V circuit is used to supply *only* receptacle outlets, then the maximum number of general-purpose receptacle outlets that may be fed by that circuit is

$$15 \text{ A} \times 115 \text{ V} \div 180 \text{ VA or 9 receptacle outlets}$$

For a 20-A, 115-V circuit, the maximum number of general-purpose receptacle outlets is

$$20 \text{ A} \times 115 \text{ V} \div 180 \text{ VA or 12 receptacle outlets}$$

See Fig. 220-3.

NOTE: In these calculations, the actual results work out to be 9.58 receptacles on a 15-A circuit and 12.77 on a 20-A circuit. Some inspectors round off these values to the nearest integral numbers and permit 10 receptacle outlets on a 15-A circuit and 13 on a 20-A circuit.

15A, 115V CIRCUIT—Maximum of 9 receptacle outlets

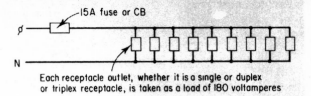

Each receptacle outlet, whether it is a single or duplex
or triplex receptacle, is taken as a load of 180 voltamperes

20A, 115V CIRCUIT—Maximum of 12 receptacle outlets

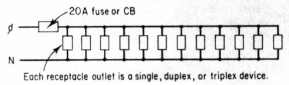

Each receptacle outlet is a single, duplex, or triplex device.

Fig. 220-3. Number of receptacles per circuit, nonresidential occupancy. [Sec. 220-2(c) (4).]

Although the **Code** gives the above-described data on maximum permitted number of receptacle outlets in commercial, industrial, institutional, and other nonresidential installations, there are no such limitations on the number of receptacle outlets on residential branch circuits. There are reasons for this approach.

In Sec. 210-25, the **Code** specifies where and when receptacle outlets are required on branch circuits. Note that there are no specific requirements for receptacle outlets in commercial, industrial, and institutional installations other than for store show windows in Sec. 210-25(d). There is the general rule that receptacles do have to be installed where flexible cords are used. In nonresidential buildings, if flexible cords are not used, there is no *requirement* for receptacle outlets. They have to be installed only where they are needed, and the number and spacing of receptacles is completely up to the designer. But because the **Code** takes the position that receptacles in nonresidential buildings only have to be installed where needed for connection of specific flexible cords and caps, it demands that where such receptacles are installed, each must be taken as a load of 180 VA.

A different approach is used for receptacles in dwelling-type occupancies. The **Code** simply assumes that cord-connected appliances will always be used in all residential buildings and requires general-purpose receptacle outlets of the number and spacing indicated in Sec. 210-25(b) and (c). These rules cover one-family houses, apartments in multifamily houses, guest rooms in hotels and motels, living quarters in dormitories, etc. But because so many receptacle outlets are required in such occupancies and because use of plug-connected loads is intermittent and has great diversity of load values and operating cycles, the Code notes at the bottom of Table 220-2(b) that the loads connected to such receptacles are adequately served by the branch-circuit capacity required by Sec. 220-3, and no additional load calculations are required for such outlets.

In dwelling occupancies, it is first necessary to calculate the total "general lighting load" from Sec. 220-2(b) and Table 220-2(b) (at 3 W per sq ft for dwellings or 2 W per sq ft for hotels and motels, including apartment houses without provisions for cooking by tenants) and then provide the minimum required number and rating of 15-A and/or 20-A general-purpose branch circuits to handle that load as covered in Sec. 200-3(a). As long as that basic circuit capacity is provided, any number of lighting outlets may be connected to any general-purpose branch circuit, up to the rating of the branch circuit if loads are known. The lighting outlets should be evenly distributed among all the circuits. Although residential lamp wattages cannot be anticipated, the Code method covers fairly heavy loading.

When the above Code rules on circuits and outlets for general lighting in dwelling units, guest rooms of hotels and motels, and similar occupancies are satisfied, general-purpose convenience receptacle outlets may be connected on circuits supplying lighting outlets; or receptacles only may be connected on one or more of the required branch circuits; or additional circuits (over and above those required by Code) may be used to supply the receptacles. But no matter how general-purpose receptacle outlets are circuited, *any number of* general-purpose receptacle outlets may be connected on a residential branch circuit—with or without lighting outlets on the same circuit.

And when small appliance branch circuits are provided in accordance with the requirements of Sec. 220-3(b), *any number* of small appliance receptacle outlets may be connected on the 20-A small appliance circuits—*but only* receptacle outlets may be connected to these circuits and only in the specified rooms.

Section 210-25(b) applies to spacing of receptacles connected on the 20-A small appliance circuits, as well as spacing of general-purpose receptacle outlets. That section, therefore, establishes the *minimum* number of receptacles that must be installed for greater convenience of use.

Exception No. 1 to Sec. 220-2(c) requires branch-circuit capacity to be calculated for multioutlet assemblies (prewired surface metal raceway with plug outlets spaced along its length). Exception No. 1 says that each 1-ft length of such strip must be taken as a load of $1\frac{1}{2}$ A when the strip is used where a number of appliances are likely to be used simultaneously. For instance, in the case of industrial applications on assembly lines involving frequent, simultaneous use of plugged-in tools, the loading of $1\frac{1}{2}$ A per ft must be used. (A loading of $1\frac{1}{2}$ A for each 5-ft section may be

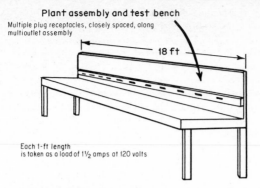

Plant assembly and test bench

Multiple plug receptacles, closely spaced, along
multioutlet assembly

18 ft

Each 1-ft length
is taken as a load of 1½ amps at 120 volts

Load allowed for this bench = 18 × 1½ = **27 A**
At 120 volts, this represents a load of **3240 VA**

THEREFORE, 3240 VOLTAMPERES OF CIRCUIT
CAPACITY MUST BE PROVIDED IN THIS EXAMPLE

Fig. 220-4. Calculating required branch-circuit capacity for
multioutlet assembly. (Sec. 220-2, Ex. No. 1.)

used in commercial or institutional applications of multioutlet assemblies
when use of plug-in tools or appliances is not heavy.) Figure 220-4 shows
an example of such load calculation.

Exception No. 3 permits branch-circuit capacity for the outlets
required by Sec. 210-25(d) to be calculated as shown in Fig. 220-5—
instead of using the load-per-outlet value from part **(c)**.

220-3. Branch Circuits Required.   After following the rules of Sec. 220-2
to assure that adequate branch-circuit capacity is available for the various
types of load that might be connected to such circuits, Sec. 220-3(a)
requires that the minimum required number of branch circuits be deter-

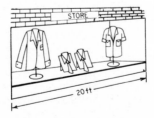

STORE

20 ft

Required branch-
circuit capacity   } = 200 watts X 20 linear ft
for show window   = 4000 watts

Fig. 220-5. Alternate method for calculating show-window circuit capacity. (Sec. 220-2, Ex. No. 3.)

mined from the total computed load, as computed from Sec. 220-2, and from the load rating of the branch circuits used.

For example, a 15-A, 115-V, 2-wire branch circuit has a load rating of 15 A times 115 V, or 1,725 VA. If the load is resistive, like incandescent lighting or electric heaters, that capacity is 1,725 W. If the total load of lighting, say, that was computed from Sec. 220-2 was 3,450 W, then exactly two 15-A, 115-V, 2-wire branch circuits would be adequate to handle the load, provided that the load on the circuit is not a "continuous" load (one that operates steadily for 3 hr or more). Because Sec. 220-2(a) requires that branch circuits supplying a continuous load be loaded to not more than 80 percent of the branch-circuit rating, if the above load of 3,450 W was a continuous load, it could not be supplied by *two* 15-A, 115-V circuits loaded to full capacity. A continuous load of 3,450 W could be fed by *three* 15-A, 115-V circuits—divided among the three circuits in such a way that no circuit has a load of over 15 A times 115 V times 80 percent, or 1,380 VA. If 20-A, 115-V circuits are used, because each such circuit has a continuous load rating of 20 times 115 times 80 percent, or 1,840 VA, the total load of 3,450 W can be divided between two 20-A, 115-V circuits—but not more than 1,840 W on any one circuit.

example   Given the required unit load of 3 W per sq ft for dwelling units [Table 220-2(b)], the **Code**-minimum number of 20-A, 120-V branch circuits required to supply general lighting and general-purpose receptacles (not small appliance receptacles in kitchen, dining room, etc.) in a 2,200 sq ft one-family house is _____ circuits. Each such 20-A circuit has a capacity of 2,400 W. The required total circuit capacity is 2,200 times 3 W per sq ft or 6,600 W. Then dividing 6,600 by 2,400 equals 2.75. Thus, at least three such circuits would be needed.

example   In Sec. 220-2(b), the **NE Code** requires a minimum unit load of 3 W per sq ft for general lighting in a school, as shown in Table 220-2(b). For the school in this example, *minimum capacity for general lighting* would be

$$1,500 \text{ sq ft} \times 3 \text{ W/sq ft or } 4,500 \text{ W}$$

Using 115-V circuits, when the total load capacity of branch circuits for general lighting is known, it is a simple matter to determine how many lighting circuits are needed. By dividing the total load by 115 V, the total current capacity of circuits is determined:

$$\frac{4,500 \text{ W}}{115 \text{ V}} = 39.1 \text{ A}$$

But, because the circuits will be supplying continuous lighting loads (over 3 hr), it is necessary to multiply that value by 1.25 in order to keep the load on any circuit to not more than 80 percent of the circuit rating. Then, using either 15-A or 20-A, 2-wire, 115-V circuits (and dropping the fraction of an ampere):

$$\frac{1.25 \times 39 \text{ A}}{15 \text{ A}} = 3.25$$

which means four 15-A circuits or:

$$\frac{1.25 \times 39 \text{ A}}{20 \text{ A}} = 2.43$$

which means three 20-A circuits. And then each circuit must be loaded without exceeding the 80 percent maximum on any circuit.

Part **(b)** of Sec. 220-3 requires that two or more 20-A branch circuits be provided to supply all the receptacle outlets in the kitchen, pantry, family room, dining room, and breakfast room of any dwelling occupancy— one-family houses, apartment houses, and motel and hotel suites with cooking facilities or serving pantries. That means that at least one 3-wire, 20-A, 240/120- or 208/120-V circuit shall be provided to serve only receptacles for the small appliance load in the kitchen, pantry, dining room, family room, and breakfast room of dwelling occupancies. Of course, two 2-wire, 20-A, 120-V circuits are equivalent to the 3-wire circuit and could be used.

If a 3-wire, 240/120-V circuit is used to provide the required two-circuit capacity for small appliances, the 3-wire circuit can be split-wired to receptacle outlets in these areas provided that the local inspection author- ity does not interpret Sec. 210-6(c) (1) as prohibiting split-wired recepta- cles because the circuit to the duplex receptacle has more than "150 volts between conductors." That is discussed under Sec. 210-6(c) (1).

The two or more small appliance circuits serving the kitchen and other specified rooms must not have outlets in any other rooms (Fig. 220-6). Section 220-3(b) (2) requires that at least two such circuits must supply receptacle outlets in the kitchen itself. The two circuits feeding outlets in the kitchen may also feed outlets in the other areas above (family room, pantry, etc.). What the **Code** prohibits is, say, one circuit feeding the kitchen outlets and the other circuit or circuits feeding the outlets in the other prescribed areas. At least two circuits must have outlets in the kitchen (Fig. 220-7).

It should be noted that the wording of Sec. 220-3(b) (1) requires that the "two or *more*" small appliance circuits must supply the receptacle outlets for any "refrigeration equipment" in the designated rooms. Therefore, receptacles for refrigerators and freezers in those rooms must be connected on the 20-A small appliance circuits. Because such appli- ances are often high-amperage appliances, some inspectors require a single (not duplex) receptacle fed by an individual 20-A branch circuit. And in such cases, the inspector usually requires that there must be two 20-A small appliance circuits, in addition to the separate circuit for the refrigerator or freezer, to supply the general purpose receptacle outlets spaced around the kitchen and other designated rooms. Such require- ments are defended on the basis that the rule of the **NEC** calls for two "or more" circuits, that it is not acceptable to allow a refrigerator or freezer to consume the major capacity of one small appliance circuit when only two such circuits are provided and that it is the intent of the **Code** to require at least *two* small appliance circuits in addition to any individual appliance circuits (Fig. 220-8).

Another controversy arises over a definition of "family room," because that room requires all its receptacles to be connected only on 20-A

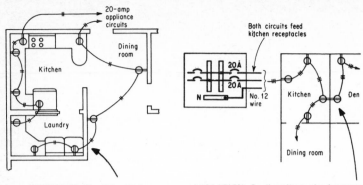

VIOLATION—Circuit for kitchen, dining room, etc., may not serve laundry

VIOLATION—Small-appliance circuits may not have any outlets in other than designated rooms

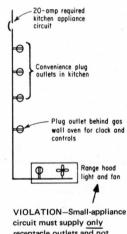

VIOLATION—Small-appliance circuit must supply only receptacle outlets and not other loads

Fig. 220-6. Small appliance circuits for eating areas must not have outlets for other rooms or uses. [Sec. 220-3(b) (1).]

appliance circuits—while a "recreation room" does not come under the rule. A common approach to the problem of determining whether a room is a "family room" or a "rec room" is to note its location in a dwelling unit. Many inspectors contend that a "family room" adjoins and is an extension of the kitchen of a dwelling unit and is an "eating location"—like the kitchen and dining room. A rec room or a den is commonly removed from the kitchen, even in the basement or on a different level from the kitchen.

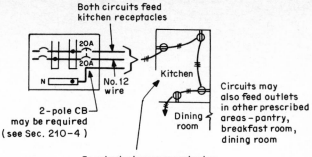

Both circuits feed
kitchen receptacles

20A

20A

N

No. 12
wire

Kitchen

2-pole CB
may be required
(see Sec. 210-4)

Circuits may
also feed outlets
in other prescribed
areas – pantry,
breakfast room,
dining room

Dining
room

In a typical case receptacles
could be split wired to 3–wire
1– Ø,120/240– v circuit

METHOD 1– A 3-wire circuit to all outlets
in prescribed areas.

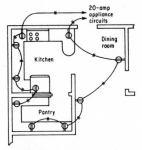

20-amp
appliance
circuits

Dining
room

Kitchen

Pantry

METHOD 2– Two 2-wire circuits, each
with at least one kitchen outlet.

Fig. 220-7. Two appliance circuits must have outlets in kitchen area. [Sec. 220-3(b) (2).]

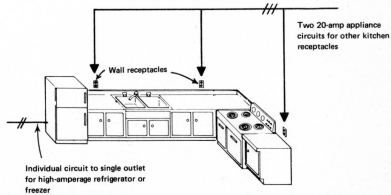

Two 20-amp appliance
circuits for other kitchen
receptacles

Wall receptacles

Individual circuit to single outlet
for high-amperage refrigerator or
freezer

Fig. 220-8. Separate circuit for large appliance is sometimes required. [Sec. 220-3(b).]

151

As noted in the Exception to part **(b) (1),** electric clock-hanger outlets and outdoor receptacle outlets may be connected on *either* a small appliance circuit *or* a general purpose circuit (Fig. 220-9). Part **(c)** of Sec. 220-3 requires that at least one 20-A branch circuit must be provided for the one or more laundry receptacles installed, as required by Sec. 210-25(b), at the laundry location in a dwelling unit. Outlets in sections of the

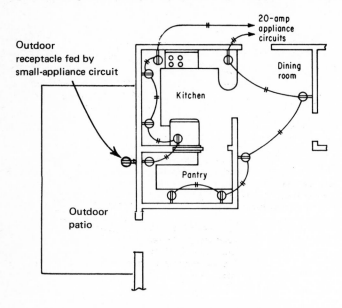

Outdoor receptacle

3-wire grounding. Outlet recessed for plug cap, allows clock to hang flush with wall. Clock hook furnished with each device.

Clock-hanger receptacle

Fig. 220-9. Certain outlets may be fed by small appliance circuit or other circuit. [Sec. 220-3(b) (1), Exception.]

dwelling for special appliances, such as laundry equipment, must be placed within 6 ft of the intended location of the appliance. This rule prohibits the use of that laundry circuit for supplying outlets that are not at the laundry area. And because laundry outlets are required by Sec. 210-25(b) to be within 6 ft of the intended location of the appliance, it would seem that any receptacle outlet more than 6 ft from laundry equipment could not be connected to the required 20-A laundry circuit (Fig. 220-10).

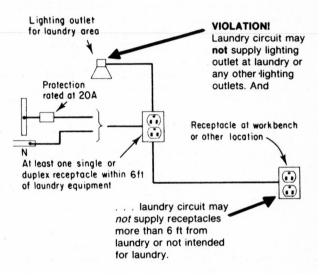

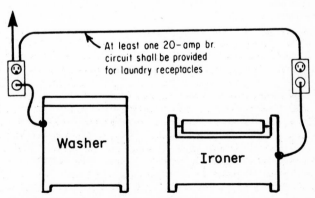

Fig. 220-10. *No* "other outlets" are permitted on 20-amp circuit required for laundry receptacle(s). [Sec. 220-3(c).]

220.10. General.

Calculating Feeder Load

The key to accurate determination of required feeder conductor capacity in amperes is effective calculation of the total load to be supplied by the feeder. Feeders and subfeeders are sized to provide sufficient power to the circuits they supply. For the given circuit voltage, they must be capable of carrying the amount of current required by the load, plus any current which may be required in the future. The size of a feeder depends upon known load, future load, and voltage drop.

The minimum load capacity which must be provided in any feeder or subfeeder can be determined by considering **NE Code** requirements on feeder load. As presented in Sec. 220-10, these rules establish the minimum load capacity to be provided for all types of loads. Of course, some feeders only supply one type of load—such as general lighting or motor circuits or electric heating. Others may supply a combination of types of loads. A step-by-step evaluation of any feeder will take into account the particular types of loads supplied by the feeder and the amount of each load. The minimum total load of any feeder can be established by adding up the loads—using those load types that apply.

It should be noted that the requirements of the **Code** cover minimum load conditions. This is particularly true of the watts-per-square-foot unit loads given in the table, which are based on 100 percent power factor. Determination of feeder size solely on the basis of **Code** requirements provides no relation to particular operating conditions in an occupancy, such as voltage stability and power losses, or any allowance for future growth in the load served by the feeder.

Although there are certain feeder applications which can be satisfactorily sized by use of the indicated **Code** method of sizing, modern feeder-design practice carefully incorporates such factors as voltage drop, power factor, detailed analysis of watts-per-square-foot loads, realistic and studied application of demand factors, and provision of substantial spare capacity as required in each case. According to the basic rule of this section, feeders are sized to carry a computed load current which is not less than the sum of all branch-circuit load currents supplied by each feeder, with certain qualifications. And, as noted in part **(b)**, when a feeder supplies continuous loads or any combination of continuous and noncontinuous loads, the rating of the feeder overcurrent device must not be less than the "noncontinuous load plus 125 percent of the continuous load" (Fig. 220-11). However, if the overcurrent protection for the feeder is an assembly approved for operation at 100 percent of its rating, the ampacity of the feeder would simply have to be at least equal to the sum of the continuous load plus the noncontinuous load. The Exception to Sec. 220-10(b) says that any overcurrent assembly that is used at 100 percent of its rating on a continuous feeder load *must* be "listed" for such

THE RULE

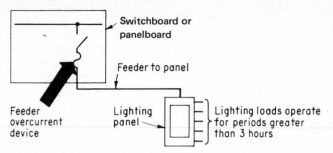

Switchboard or
panelboard

Feeder to panel

Feeder
overcurrent
device

Lighting
panel

Lighting loads operate
for periods greater
than 3 hours

FEEDER OVERCURRENT DEVICE must be rated not less than 125% of
the continuous load, *and* the feeder conductors must be sized on the
same basis to assure them effective protection in accordance with their
ampacity.

EXAMPLE

For this feeder, with conductors rated at 380 amps, the maximum load permitted for a conventional fused switch is
80% of 380 amps, or 304 amps.

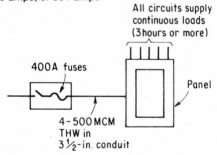

All circuits supply
continuous loads
(3 hours or more)

400A fuses

Panel

4-500MCM
THW in
3½-in. conduit

Rating of fuses and ampacity of feeder conductors are both at
least equal to 125% times the continuous load.

Fig. 220-11. Feeders must generally be loaded to no more than 80 percent for
a continuous load. [Sec. 220-10(b).]

operation. And that means "listed" by UL or some other recognized test
lab. The important factors about such equipment are as follows:

Fuses for feeder protection   The rating of a fuse is taken as 100
percent of rated nameplate current when enclosed by a switch or panel
housing. But, because of the heat generated by many fuses, the maximum continuous load permitted on a fused switch is restricted by a

number of NEMA, UL, and **NE Code** rules to 80 percent of the rating of the fuses. Limitation of circuit-load current to *no more than* 80 percent of the current rating of fuses in equipment is done to protect the switch or other piece of equipment from the heat produced in the fuse element— and also to protect attached circuit wires from excessive heating close to the terminals. The fuse itself can actually carry 100 percent of its current rating continuously without damage to itself, but its heat is conducted into the adjacent wiring and switch components.

NEMA standards require that a fused, enclosed switch be marked, as part of the electrical rating, "Continuous Load Current Not to Exceed 80 Percent of the Rating of Fuses Employed in Other Than Motor Circuits" (Fig. 220-12). That derating compensates for the extra heat produced by

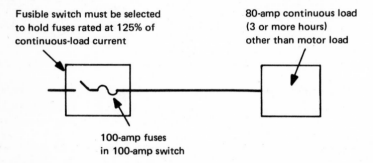

**Fusible switch must be selected
to hold fuses rated at 125% of
continuous-load current**

**80-amp continuous load
(3 or more hours)
other than motor load**

**100-amp fuses
in 100-amp switch**

**Circuit conductors must have 100-amp rating (or may be sized so 100-amp
protection is next higher standard rating of protective device above ampacity
of conductors).**

Fig. 220-12. For branch circuit or feeder, fuses in enclosed switch must be limited for continuous duty. [Sec. 220-10(b).]

continuous operation. Motor circuits are excluded from that rule, but a motor circuit is required by the **NE Code** to have conductors rated at least 125 percent of the motor full-load current—which, in effect, limits the load current to 80 percent of the conductor ampacity and limits the load on the fuses rated to protect those conductors. But, the UL *Electrical Construction Materials List* does recognize fused bolted-pressure switches and high-pressure butt-contact switches for use at 100 percent of their rating on circuits with available fault currents of 100,000, 150,000, or 200,000 rms symmetrical amps—as marked (Fig. 220-13). (See "Fused Power Circuit Devices" in that UL publication.)

Manual and electrically operated switches designed to be used with Class L current-limiting fuses rated 601 to 4,000 A, 600 V AC are listed by UL as "Fused Power Circuit Devices." This category covers bolted-pressure-contact switches and high-pressure, butt-type-contact switches

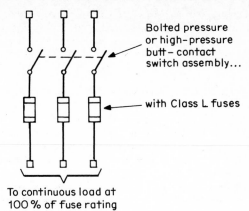

Bolted pressure
or high-pressure
butt-contact
switch assembly...

with Class L fuses

To continuous load at
100% of fuse rating

Fig. 220-13. Some fused switches may be used at 100 percent rating for continuous load. [Sec. 220-10(b).]

suitable for use as feeder devices or service switches if marked "Suitable for Use As Service Equipment." Such devices "have been investigated for use at *100 percent of their rating* on circuits having available fault currents of 100,000, 150,000 or 200,000 rms symmetrical amperes" as marked.

CB for feeder protection The nominal or theoretical continuous-current rating of a CB generally is taken to be the same as its trip setting— the value of current at which the breaker will open, either instantaneously or after some intentional time delay. But, as described above for fuses, the real continuous-current rating of a CB—the value of current that it can safely and properly carry for periods of 3 hr or more— frequently is reduced to 80 percent of the nameplate value by codes and standards rules.

The UL *Electrical Construction Materials List* contains a clear, simple rule in the instructions under "Circuit Breakers, Molded-Case." It says:

Unless otherwise marked, circuit breakers should not be loaded to exceed 80 percent of their current rating, where in normal operation the load will continue for three or more hours.

A load that continues for 3 hr or more is a *continuous* load. If a breaker is marked for *continuous* operation, it may be loaded to 100 percent of its rating and operate continuously.

There are some CBs available for continuous operation at 100 percent of their current rating, but they must be used in the mounting and enclosure arrangements established by UL for 100 percent rating. Molded-case CBs of the 100 percent continuous type are made in ratings from 600 A up. Information on use of 100 percent rated breakers is given on their nameplates.

Figure 220-14 shows two examples of CB nameplate data for two types

EXAMPLE 1

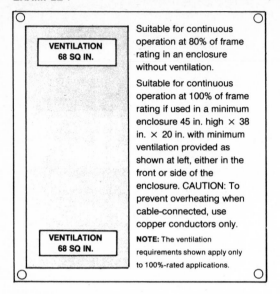

VENTILATION
68 SQ IN.

VENTILATION
68 SQ IN.

Suitable for continuous operation at 80% of frame rating in an enclosure without ventilation.

Suitable for continuous operation at 100% of frame rating if used in a minimum enclosure 45 in. high × 38 in. × 20 in. with minimum ventilation provided as shown at left, either in the front or side of the enclosure. CAUTION: To prevent overheating when cable-connected, use copper conductors only.

NOTE: The ventilation requirements shown apply only to 100%-rated applications.

EXAMPLE 2

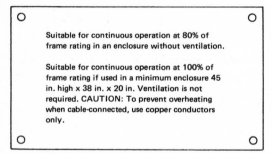

Suitable for continuous operation at 80% of frame rating in an enclosure without ventilation.

Suitable for continuous operation at 100% of frame rating if used in a minimum enclosure 45 in. high x 38 in. x 20 in. Ventilation is not required. CAUTION: To prevent overheating when cable-connected, use copper conductors only.

Fig. 220-14. Nameplates from CBs rated for 100 percent continuous loading. [Sec. 220-10(b).]

of UL-listed 2,000-A, molded-case CBs that are specifically tested and listed for continuous operation at 100 percent of their 2,000-A rating—*but* only under the conditions described on the nameplate. These two typical nameplates clearly indicate that ventilation may or may not be required. Because most switchboards have fairly large interior volumes, the "minimum enclosure" dimensions shown on these nameplates (45 by

38 by 20 in.) usually are readily achieved. *But,* special UL tests must be performed if these dimensions are *not* met. Where busbar extensions and lugs are connected to the CB within the switchboard, the caution about copper conductors does not apply, and aluminum conductors may be used.

If the ventilation pattern of a switchboard does not meet the ventilation pattern and the required enclosure size specified on the nameplate, the CB must be applied at 80 percent rating. Switchboard manufacturers have UL tests conducted with a CB installed in a specific enclosure, and the enclosure may receive a listing for 100 percent rated operation even though the ventilation pattern or overall enclosure size may not meet the specifications. In cases where the breaker nameplate specifications are not met by the switchboard, the customer would have to request a letter from the manufacturer certifying that a 100 percent rated listing has been received. Otherwise, the breaker must be applied at 80 percent.

To realize savings with devices listed by UL at 100 percent of their continuous-current rating, use must be made of a CB manufacturer's data sheet to determine the types and ampere ratings of breakers available that are 100 percent rated, along with the frame sizes, approved enclosure sizes, and the ventilation patterns required by UL, if any. According to UL Standard 489, paragraph 33.37A, "a circuit breaker having a frame size less than 600 amperes shall not be marked suitable for continuous operation at 100 percent of rating." Of course, trip units with lower ampere ratings may be installed in the 600-A frame.

It is essential to check the instructions given in the UL listing to determine **if** and under what conditions a CB (or a fuse in a switch) is rated for continuous operation at 100 percent of its current rating.

220-11. General Lighting.   For general illumination, a feeder must have capacity to carry the total load of lighting branch circuits determined as part of the lighting design and not less than a minimum branch-circuit load determined on a watts-per-square-foot basis from the table given in Sec. 220-2(b) of the Code.

Demand factor permits sizing of a feeder according to the amount of load which operates simultaneously.

Demand factor is the ratio of the maximum amount of load that will be operating at any one time on a feeder to the total connected load on the feeder under consideration. This factor is always less than one. The sum of the connected loads supplied by a feeder is multiplied by the demand factor to determine the load which the feeder must be sized to serve. This load is termed the maximum demand of the feeder:

Maximum demand load = connected load × demand factor

Tables of demand and diversity factors have been developed from experience with various types of load concentrations and various layouts of feeders and subfeeders supplying such loads. Table 220-11 of the **NE Code** presents common demand factors for feeders to general lighting loads in various types of buildings (Fig. 220-15).

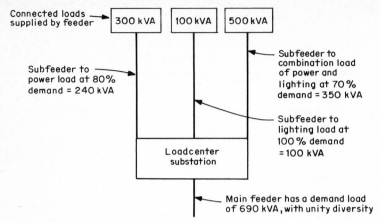

Connected loads supplied by feeder ⟶ 300 kVA | 100 kVA | 500 kVA

Subfeeder to power load at 80% demand = 240 kVA

Subfeeder to combination load of power and lighting at 70% demand = 350 kVA

Subfeeder to lighting load at 100% demand = 100 kVA

Loadcenter substation

Main feeder has a demand load of 690 kVA, with unity diversity

Fig. 220-15. How demand factors are applied to connected loads. (Sec. 220-11.)

The demand factors given in Table 220-11 may be applied to the total branch-circuit load to get required feeder capacity for lighting (but must not be used in calculating branch-circuit capacity). Note that a feeder may have capacity of less than 100 percent of the total branch-circuit load for only the types of buildings designated in Table 220-11, that is, for dwelling units, hospitals, hotels, motels, and storage warehouses. In all other types of occupancies, it is assumed that *all* general lighting will be operating at the same time, and each feeder in those occupancies must have capacity (ampacity) for 100 percent of the watts or voltamperes of branch-circuit load of general lighting that the feeder supplies.

example If a warehouse feeder fed a total branch-circuit load of 20,000 W of general lighting, the minimum capacity in that feeder to supply that load must be equal to 12,500 W plus 50 percent times (20,000−12,500) W. That works out to be 12,500 plus 0.5 × 7,500 or 16,250 W.

But, the note to Table 220-11 warns against using any value less than 100 percent of branch-circuit load for sizing any feeder that supplies loads that will all be energized at the same time.

220-12. Show-Window Lighting. If show-window lighting is supplied by a feeder, capacity must be included in the feeder to handle 200 W per linear foot of show-window length. Because that is the same loading as given in Sec. 220-2(c), Exception No. 3, it works out to be a 100 percent demand for the entire branch-circuit load of show-window lighting.

220-13. Receptacle Loads—Nondwelling Units. This rule permits two possible approaches in determining the required feeder ampacity to supply receptacle loads in "other than dwelling units." (In dwelling units and in guest rooms of hotels and motels, no feeder capacity is required for 15- or 20-A general-purpose receptacle outlets. Such load is considered sufficiently covered by the load capacity provided for general lighting.) But in other than dwelling units, where a load of 180 VA of feeder capacity must be provided for all general-purpose 15- and 20-A receptacle outlets, a *demand factor* may be applied to the total calculated receptacle load as follows.

In other than dwelling units, the branch-circuit load for receptacle outlets for which not more than 180 VA were allowed per outlet may be added to the general lighting load and may also be reduced by the demand factors in Table 220-11. That is the basic rule of Sec. 220-13 and, in effect, requires any feeder to have capacity for the total number of receptacles it feeds and requires that capacity to be equal to 180 VA (per single or multiple receptacle) times the total number of receptacles—with a reduction from 100 percent of that value permitted only for the occupancies listed in Table 220-11.

Because the demand factor of Table 220-11 is shown as 100 percent for "All Other" types of occupancies, the basic rule of Sec. 220-13 as it appeared prior to the 1978 NE Code required a feeder to have ampacity for a load equal to 180 VA times the number of general-purpose receptacle outlets that the feeder supplied. That is no longer required. Recognizing that there is great diversity in use of receptacles in office buildings, stores, schools, and all the other occupancies that come under "All Others" in Table 220-11, Sec. 220-13 contains a table to permit reduction of feeder capacity for receptacle loads on feeders. Those demand factors apply to *any* "nondwelling" occupancy. It should be noted that the total receptacle load, obtained by multiplying the total number of receptacles by 180 VA, comes out in "voltamperes." Yet, Table 220-13 refers to the "receptacle load" in "wattage." It msut be assumed that the "voltampere" load is taken as unity power factor so that the load then becomes the same value as "watts."

The amount of feeder capacity for a typical case where a feeder, say, supplies two or more panelboards with a total of 500 receptacles fed from them is shown in Fig. 220-15.

Although the calculation of Fig. 220-16 cannot always be taken as realistically related to usage of receptacles, it is realistic relief from the 100 percent demand factor, which presumed that all receptacles were supplying 180 VA loads simultaneously.

220-14. Motors.   Any feeder that supplies a motor load or a combination load (motors plus lighting and/or other electrical loads) must satisfy the indicated NEC sections of Art. 430. Feeder capacity for motor loads is usually taken at 125 percent of the full-load current rating of the largest motor supplied, plus the sum of the full-load currents of the other motors supplied.

220-15. Fixed Electric Space Heating.   Capacity required in a feeder to supply fixed electrical space heating equipment is determined on the basis of a load equal to the total connected load of heaters on all branch

Take the total number of general-purpose receptacle outlets
fed by a given feeder. . .

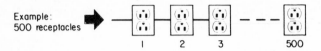

Example:
500 receptacles

1   2   3   500

. . . multiply the total by 180 voltamperes
[required load of Section 220-2(c) (4) for each recepta-
cle]. . .

500 × 180 VA = 90,000 VA

. . .and take the result as a load of unity power factor. (This
is not mentioned in the code rule.)

90,000 VA = 90,000 watts

Then apply the demand factors from Table 220-13:

First 10 kw or less @ 100% demand   **= 10,000 watts**
Remainder over 10 kw @ 50% demand
   = (90,000 – 10,000) × 50%
   = 80,000 × 0.5   **= 40,000 watts**

Minimum demand-load total= **50,000 watts**

Therefore, the feeder must have a capacity of **50 kw** for the
total receptacle load. Required minimum ampacity for that
load is then determined from the voltage and phase-makeup
(single- or 3-phase) of the feeder.

Fig. 220-16. Table 220-13 permits demand factor in calculating feeder
demand load for general-purpose receptacles. (Sec. 220-13.)

circuits served from the feeder. Under conditions on intermittent operation or where all units cannot operate at the same time, permission may
be granted for use of less than a 100 percent demand factor in sizing the
feeder. Sections 220-30, 220-31, and 220-32 permit alternate calculations
of electric heat load for feeders or service-entrance conductors (which
constitute a service feeder) in dwelling units. But reduction of the feeder
capacity to less than 100 percent of connected load must be authorized by
the local electrical inspector.

220-16. Small Appliance and Laundry Loads—Dwelling Unit. For a
feeder or service conductors in a single-family dwelling, in an individual
apartment of a multifamily dwelling with provisions for cooking by
tenants, or in a hotel or motel suite with cooking facilities or a serving
pantry, at least 1,500 W of load must be provided for each 2-wire, 20-A
small appliance circuit (to handle the small appliance load in kitchen,

pantry, and dining areas). The total small appliance load determined in this way may be added to the general lighting load and the resulting total load may be reduced by the demand factors given in Table 220-11.

A feeder load of at least 1,500 W must be added for each 2-wire, 20-A laundry circuit installed as required by Sec. 220-3(c). And that load may also be added to the general lighting load and subjected to the demand factors in Table 220-11.

220-17. Fixed Appliance Load—Dwelling Unit(s). For fixed appliances (fastened in place) other than ranges, clothes dryers, air-conditioning equipment, and space heating equipment, feeder capacity in dwelling occupancies must be provided for the sum of these loads; but, if there are at least four such fixed appliances, the total load of four or more such appliances may be reduced by a demand factor of 75 percent (**NE Code** Sec. 220-17). Wording of this rule makes clear that a "fixed appliance" is one that is "fastened in place."

As an example of application of this **Code** provision, consider the following calculation of feeder capacity for fixed appliances in a single-family house. The calculation is made to determine how much capacity must be provided in the service-entrance conductors (the service feeder):

Water heater	2,500 W	230 V =	11.0 A
Kitchen disposal.......	½ hp	115 V = 6.5 A + 25% =	8.1 A
Furnace motor........	¼ hp	115 V =	4.6 A
Attic fan...........	¼ hp	115 V = 4.6 A	0.0 A
Water pump ...	½ hp	230 V =	3.7 A

Load in amperes on each ungrounded leg of feeder = 27.4 A

To comply with Sec. 430-24, 25 percent is added to the full-load current of the ½ hp, 115-V motor because it is the highest-rated motor in the group. Since it is assumed that the load on the 115/230-V feeder will be balanced and each of the ¼ hp motors will be connected to different ungrounded conductors, only one is counted in the above calculation. Except for the 115-V motors, all the other appliance loads are connected to both ungrounded conductors and are automatically balanced. Since there are four or more fixed appliances in addition to a range, clothes dryer, etc., a demand factor of 75 percent may be applied to the total load of these appliances. Seventy-five percent of 27.4 = 20.5 A, which is the current to be added to that computed for the lighting and other loads to determine the total current to be carried by the ungrounded (outside) service-entrance conductors.

The above demand factor may be applied to similar loads in multifamily dwellings.

220-18. Electric Clothes Dryers—Dwelling Unit(s). This rule prescribes a *minimum* demand of 5 kW for 120/240-V electric clothes dryers in determining branch-circuit and feeder sizes. Note that this rule applies only to "household" electric clothes dryers, and not to commercial applications. This rule is helpful because the ratings of electric clothes dryers are not usually known in the planning stages when feeder calculations must be determined (Fig 220-17).

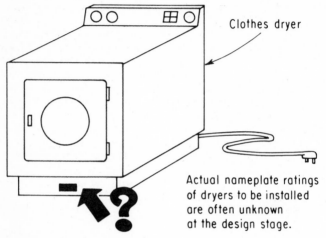

Clothes dryer

Actual nameplate ratings of dryers to be installed are often unknown at the design stage.

Fig. 220-17. Feeder load of 5 kW per dryer must be provided if actual load is not known. (Sec. 220-18.)

When sizing a feeder for one or more electric clothes dryers, a load of 5,000 W or the nameplate rating, whichever is larger, shall be included for each dryer—subject to the demand factors of Table 220-11 when the feeder supplies a number of clothes dryers, as in an apartment house.

220-19. Electric Ranges and Other Cooking Appliances—Dwelling Unit(s). Feeder capacity must be allowed for household electric cooking appliances rated over 1¾ kW, in accordance with Table 220-19 of the Code. Feeder demand loads for a number of cooking appliances on a feeder may be obtained from Table 220-19.

Section 210-19(b), Exception No. 1, refers to Table 220-19 for sizing of a branch circuit to supply a single electric range, a wall-mounted oven, or a counter-mounted cooking unit. That table is also used in sizing a feeder (or service conductors) that supplies one or more electric ranges or cooking units. Note that Sec. 220-19 and Table 220-19 apply only to such cooking appliances in a "dwelling unit" and do not cover commercial or institutional applications.

Figure 220-18 shows a typical NEC calculation of the minimum

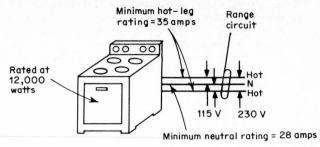

Fig. 220-18. Minimum amp-rating of branch-circuit conductors for a 12-kW range. (Sec. 220-19.)

demand load to be used in sizing the branch circuit to the range. The same value of demand load is also used in sizing a feeder (or service conductors) from which the range circuit is fed. Calculation is as follows:

A branch circuit for the 12-kW range is selected in accordance with Note 4 of Table 220-19, which says that the branch-circuit load for a range may be selected from the table itself. Under the heading "Number of Appliances," read across from "1." The maximum demand to be used in sizing the range circuit for a 12-kW range is shown under the heading "Maximum Demand" to be not less than 8 kW. The minimum rating of the range-circuit ungrounded conductors will be

$$\frac{8,000 \text{ W}}{230 \text{ V}} = 34.78 \text{ or } 35 \text{ A}$$

NE Code Table 310-16 shows that the minimum size of copper conductors that may be used is No. 8 (TW—40 A, THW—45 A, XHHW or THHN—50 A). No. 8 is also designated in Sec. 210-19(b) as the minimum size of conductor for any range rated 8¾ kW or more.

The overload protection for this circuit of No. 8 TW conductors would be *40-A fuses or a 40-A circuit breaker.* If THW, THHN, or XHHW wires are used for the circuit, they must be taken as having an ampacity of not more than 40 A and protected at that value. That requirement follows from the UL rule that a CB or fuse rated up to 100 A is recognized for use with wire rated at 60°C—the rating of TW wire.

Although the two hot legs of the 230/155-V, 3-wire circuit must be not smaller than No. 8, Exception No. 1 of Sec. 210-19(b) permits the neutral conductor to be smaller, but it specifies that it must have an ampacity not less than 70 percent of the ampacity of the hot (ungrounded) legs and may never be smaller than No. 10.

For the range circuit in this example, the neutral may be rated

$$70\% \times 40 \text{ A (if TW is used)} = 28 \text{ A}$$

This calls for a No. 10 neutral.

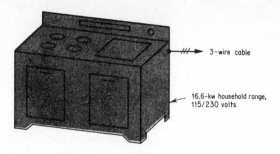

3-wire cable

16.6-kw household range,
115/230 volts

Refer to *NE Code* Table 220-19.

1. Column A applies to ranges rated not over 12 kW, but this range is rated 16.6 kW.
2. Note 1, below the Table, tells how to use the Table for ranges over 12 kW and up to 27 kW. For such ranges, the maximum demand in Column A must be increased by 5% for each additional kW of rating (or major fraction) above 12 kW.
3. This 16.6-kW range exceeds 12 kW by 4.6 kW.
4. 5% of the demand in Column A for a single range is 400 watts (8000 watts x 0.05).
5. The maximum demand for this 16.6-kW range must be increased above 8 kW by 2000 watts:

   400 watts (5% of Column A) X 5 (4 kW + 1 for the remaining 0.6 kW)
6. The required branch circuit must be sized, therefore, for a total demand load of

   8000 watts + 2000 watts = 10,000 watts
7. Required size of branch circuit—

$$\text{amp rating} = \frac{10,000 \text{ w}}{230 \text{ v}} = 43 \text{ amps}$$

USING 60C CONDUCTORS, AS REQUIRED BY UL, THE BRANCH CIRCUIT WOULD CONSIST OF NO. 6 TW CONDUCTORS.

Fig. 220-19. Sizing a branch circuit for a household range over 12 kW. (Sec. 220-19.)

Figure 220-19 shows a more involved calculation for a range rated over 12 kW. Figure 220-20 shows two units that total 12 kW and are taken at a demand load of 8 kW, as if they were a single range. Figure 220-21 shows another calculation for separate cooking units on one circuit. And a feeder that would be used to supply any of the cooking installations shown in Figs. 220-18 through 220-21 would have to include capacity equal to the demand load used in sizing the branch circuit.

A feeder supplying more than one range (rated not over 12 kW) must have ampacity sufficient for the maximum demand load given in Table 220-19 for the number of ranges fed. For instance, a feeder to 10 such ranges would have to have ampacity for a load of 25 kW.

Other Calculations on Electric Cooking Appliances

The following "roundup" points out step-by-step methods of wiring the various types of household electric cooking equipment (ranges, counter-mounted cooking units, and wall-mounted ovens) according to the NEC.

Tap Conductors

Section 210-19(b), Exception No. 1, gives permission to reduce the size of the neutral conductor of a 3-wire range branch circuit to 70 percent of the current-carrying capacity of the ungrounded conductors. However, this rule does not apply to smaller taps connected to a 50-A circuit—where the smaller taps (none less than 20-A ratings) must all be the same size. Further, it does not apply when individual branch circuits supply each wall- or counter-mounted cooking unit, and all circuit conductors are of the same size and less than No. 10.

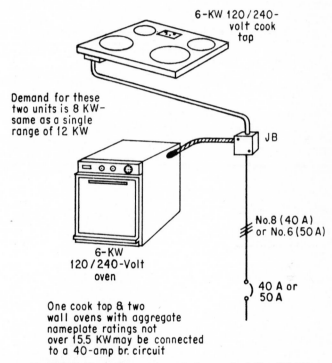

6-KW 120/240-volt cook top

Demand for these two units is 8 KW—same as a single range of 12 KW

JB

No.8 (40 A) or No.6 (50 A)

6-KW 120/240-Volt oven

40 A or 50 A

One cook top & two wall ovens with aggregate nameplate ratings not over 15.5 KW may be connected to a 40-amp br. circuit

Fig. 220-20. Two units treated as a single-range load. (Sec. 220-19.)

Section 210-19(b), Exception No. 2, permits tap conductors, rated not less than 20 A, to be connected to 50-A branch circuits that supply ranges, wall-mounted ovens, and counter-mounted cooking units. These taps cannot be any longer than necessary for servicing. Figures 220-22 and 220-23 illustrate the application of this rule.

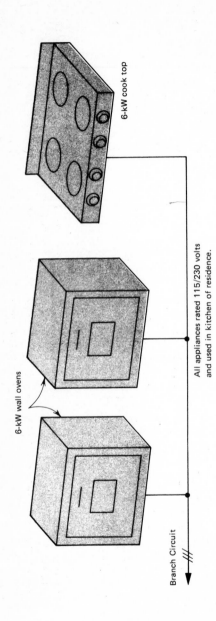

6-kW wall ovens

6-kW cook top

Branch Circuit

All appliances rated 115/230 volts and used in kitchen of residence.

1. Note 4 of Table 220-19 says that the branch-circuit load for a counter-mounted cooking unit and not more than two wall-mounted ovens, all supplied from a single branch circuit and located in the same room, shall be computed by adding the nameplate ratings of the individual appliances and treating this total as a single range.

2. Therefore, the three appliances shown may be considered to be a single range of 18-kW rating (6 kW + 6 kW + 6 kW).

3. From Note 1 of Table 220-19, such a range exceeds 12 kW by 6 kW and the 8-kW demand of Column A must be increased by 400 watts (5% of 8000 watts) for each of the 6 additional kilowatts above 12 kW.

4. Thus, the branch-circuit demand load is—

8000 WATTS + (6×400 WATTS) = 10,400 WATTS

A 50-AMP CIRCUIT IS REQUIRED.

Fig. 220-21. Determining branch-circuit load for separate cooking appliances on a single circuit. (Sec. 220-19.)

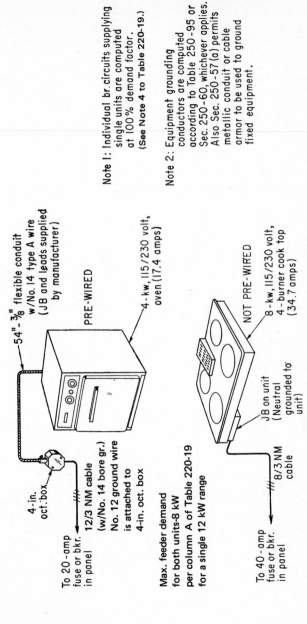

Note 1: Individual br. circuits supplying single units are computed at 100% demand factor. (See Note 4 to Table **220-19**.)

Note 2: Equipment grounding conductors are computed according to Table 250-95 or Sec. 250-60, whichever applies. Also Sec. 250-57 (a) permits metallic conduit or cable armor to be used to ground fixed equipment.

54"- $\frac{3}{8}$" flexible conduit w/No. 14 type A wire (JB and leads supplied by manufacturer)

PRE-WIRED

4 - kw, 115 /230 volt, oven (17.4 amps)

NOT PRE-WIRED

8 - kw, 115/230 volt, 4 - burner cook top (34.7 amps)

JB on unit (Neutral grounded to unit)

8/3 NM cable

To 40 - amp fuse or bkr. in panel

4 - in. oct. box.

To 20 - amp fuse or bkr. in panel

12/3 NM cable (w/No. 14 bore gr.) No. 12 ground wire is attached to 4-in. oct. box

Max. feeder demand for both units-8 kW per column A of Table 220-19 for a single 12 kW range

An 8-kW cook top is supplied by an individual No. 8 (40-amp) branch circuit, and a No. 12 (20-amp) branch circuit supplies a 4-kW oven. Such circuits are calculated on the basis of the nameplate rating of the appliance. In most instances individual branch circuits cost less than 50-amp, multi-outlet circuits for cooking and oven units.

Fig. 220-22. Separate branch circuit to cooking units. (Sec. 220-19.)

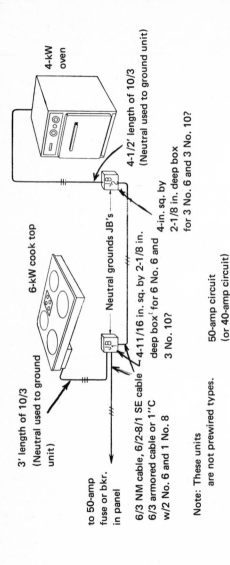

4-kW oven

6-kW cook top

4-1/2' length of 10/3
(Neutral used to ground unit)

3' length of 10/3
(Neutral used to ground unit)

Neutral grounds JB's

4-in. sq. by
2-1/8 in. deep box
for 3 No. 6 and 3 No. 10?

4-11/16 in. sq. by 2-1/8 in.
deep box for 6 No. 6 and
3 No. 10?

to 50-amp
fuse or bkr.
in panel

6/3 NM cable, 6/2-8/1 SE cable
6/3 armored cable or 1"C
w/2 No. 6 and 1 No. 8

50-amp circuit
(or 40-amp circuit)

Note: These units
are not prewired types.

NEC rules permit a 50-amp circuit to supply cook tops and ovens. Typical arrangement shows such a circuit. Junction box sizes are computed from Table 370-6(a) and Table 370-6(b) for No. 6 conductor combinations. Taps to each unit are No. 10 to permit the use of the neutral as an equipment ground. Using the neutral to ground the junction boxes is permitted by Sec. 250-60.

Fig. 220-23. One branch circuit to cooking units. (Sec. 220-19.)

In Sec. 210-19(b), Exception No. 2, the wording "no longer than necessary for servicing" encourages the location of circuit junction boxes as close as possible to each cooking and oven unit connected to 50-A circuits. A number of counter-mounted cooking units have integral supply leads about 36 in. long and some ovens come with supply conduit and wire in lengths of 48 to 54 in. Therefore, a box should be installed close enough to connect these leads.

Feeder and Circuit Calculations

Section 220-19 refers to the feeder calculation of ranges and other cooking appliances. It permits the use of Table 220-19 for calculating the feeder load for ranges and other cooking appliances that are individually rated more than $1\frac{3}{4}$ kW.

Note 4 of the table reads: "The branch-circuit load for one wall-mounted oven or one counter-mounted cooking unit shall be the name-plate rating of the appliance." Common sense dictates that there is no difference in demand factor between a single range of 12 kW and a wall-mounted oven and surface-mounted cooking unit totaling 12 kW. This is explained in the last sentence of Note 4 of Table 220-19. The mere division of a complete range into two or more units doesn't change the demand factor. Therefore, the most direct and accurate method of computing the branch-circuit and feeder calculations for wall-mounted ovens and surface-mounted cooking units within each occupancy is to total the kilowatt ratings of these appliances and treat this total kilowatt rating as a single range of the same rating. For example, a particular dwelling has an 8-kW, 4-burner, surface-mounted cooking unit and a 4-kW wall-mounted oven. This is a total of 12 kW and the maximum permissible demand given in Column A of Table 220-19 for a single 12-kw range is 8 kw.

Similarly, it follows that if the ratings of a 2-burner, counter-mounted cooking unit and a wall-mounted oven are each 3.5 kw, the total of the two would be 7 kW—the same total as a small 7-kW range. Because the 7-kW load is less than $8\frac{3}{4}$ kW, note 3 of Table 220-19 permits Column C of Table 220-19 to be used in lieu of Column A. The demand load is 5.6 kW (7 kW times 0.80). Range or total cooking and oven unit ratings less than $8\frac{3}{4}$ kW are more likely to be found in small apartment units of multifamily dwellings than in single-family dwellings.

Because the demand loads in Column A of Table 220-19 apply to ranges not exceeding 12 kW, they also apply to wall-mounted ovens and counter-mounted cooking units within each individual occupancy by totaling their aggregate nameplate kilowatt ratings. Then if the total rating exceeds 12 kW, Note 1 to the table should be used as if the units were a single range of equal rating. For example, assume that the total rating of a counter-mounted cooking unit and two wall-mounted ovens is 16 kW in a dwelling unit. The maximum demand for a single 12-kW range is given as 8 kW in Column A. Note 1 requires that the maximum demand in Column A be increased 5 percent for each additional kilowatt or major fraction thereof that exceeds 12 kW. In this case 16 kW exceeds 12 kW by 4 kW. Therefore, 5 percent times four equals 20 percent, and 20 percent of 8 kW is 1.6 kW. The maximum feeder and branch-circuit demand is then 9.6 kW (8 kW plus 1.6 kW). A 9,600-W load would draw over 40 A at 230 V, thereby requiring a circuit rated over 40 A.

For the range or cooking unit demand factors in a multifamily dwelling, say a 12-unit apartment building, a specific calculation must be made, as follows:

1. Each apartment has a 6-kW counter-mounted cooking unit and a 4-kW wall-mounted oven. And each apartment is served by a separate feeder from a main switchboard. The maximum cooking demand in each apartment feeder should be computed in the same manner as previously described for single-family dwellings. As the total rating of cooking and oven units in each apartment is 10 kW (6 kW plus 4 kW), Column A of Table 220-19 for one appliance should apply. Thus, the maximum cooking demand load on each feeder is 8 kW.

2. In figuring the size of the main service feeder, Column A should be used for 12 appliances. Thus, the demand would be 27 kW.

As an alternate calculation, assume that each of the 12 apartments has a 4-kW counter-mounted cooking unit and 4-kW wall-mounted oven. This would total 8 kW per apartment. In this case Column C of Table 220-19 can be used to determine the cooking load in each separate feeder. Applying Column C on the basis of a single 8-kW range, the maximum demand is 6.4 kW (8 kW times 0.80). Therefore, 6.4 kW is the cooking load to be included in the calculation of each feeder. Notice that this is 1.6 kW less than the previous example where cooking and oven units, totaling 10 kW, had a demand load of 8 kW. And this is logical, because smaller units should produce a smaller total kilowatt demand.

On the other hand, it is better to use Column A instead of Column C, for computing the main service feeder capacity for twelve 8-kW cooking loads. The reason for this is that Column C is inaccurate where more than five 8-kW ranges (or combinations) and more than twelve 7-kW ranges (or combinations) are to be used. In these instances, calculations made on the basis of Column C result in a demand load greater than that of Column A for the same number of ranges. As an example, twelve 8-kW ranges have a demand load of 30.72 kW (12 times 8 kW times 0.32) in applying Column C, but only a demand load of 27 kW in Column A. And in Column A the 27 kW is based on twelve 12-kW ranges. This discrepancy dictates use of Column C only on the limited basis previously outlined.

Branch-Circuit Wiring

Where individual branch circuits supply each counter-mounted cooking unit and wall-mounted oven, there appears to be no particular problem. Figure 220-22 gives the details for wiring units on individual branch circuits.

Figure 220-23 shows an example of how typical counter-mounted cooking units and wall-mounted ovens are connected to a 50-A branch circuit.

Several manufacturers of cooking units provide an attached flexible metal conduit with supply leads and a floating 4-in. octagon box as a part of each unit. These units are commonly called "prewired types." With this arrangement, an electrician does not have to make any supply connections in the appliance. Where such units are connected to a 50-A circuit, the 4-in. octagon box is removed, and the flexible conduit is connected to a larger circuit junction box, which contains the No. 6 circuit conductors.

On the other hand, some manufacturers do not furnish supply leads with their cooking units. As a result, the electrical contractor must supply the tap conductors to these units from the 50-A circuit junction box. See Fig. 200-23. In this case, connections must be made in the appliance as well as in the junction box.

Figure 220-24 shows a single branch circuit supplying the same units as shown in Fig. 220-23.

40-A Circuits

The **NEC** does recognize a 40-A circuit for two or more outlets, as noted in Sec. 210-23(c). Because a No. 8 (40-A) circuit can supply a single range rated not over 15.4 kW, it can also supply counter- and wall-mounted units not exceeding the same total of 15.4 kW. The rating of 15.4 kW is determined as the maximum rating of equipment that may be supplied by a 40-A branch circuit, which has a capacity of 9,200 W (40 A × 230 V). From Note 1 to Table 220-19, a 15.4-kW load would require a demand capacity equal to 8,000 W plus [(15.4 − 12) × 0.05 × 8,000] = 8,000 W plus 3 × 0.05 × 8,000 = 8,000 plus 1,200 = 9,200 W.

Figure 220-25 shows an arrangement of a No. 8 (40-A) branch circuit supplying one 7.5-kW cooking unit and one 4-kW oven. Or individual branch circuits may be run to the units.

220-20. Kitchen Equipment—Other Than Dwelling Unit(s). Commercial electric cooking loads must comply with Sec. 220-20 and its table of feeder demand factors for *commercial* electric cooking equipment— including dishwasher booster heaters, water heaters, and other kitchen equipment.

At one time, the **Code** did not recognize demand factors for such equipment. **Code** Table 220-20 is the result of extensive research on the

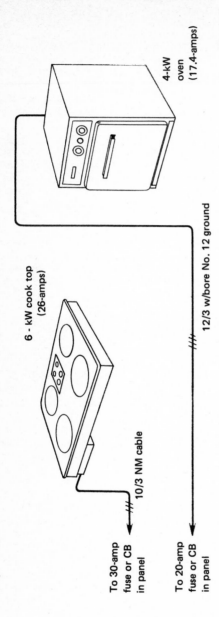

6 - kW cook top
(26-amps)

4-kW
oven
(17.4-amps)

To 30-amp
fuse or CB
in panel

10/3 NM cable

To 20-amp
fuse or CB
in panel

12/3 w/bare No. 12 ground

Same size and type of units as in Fig. 220-23,
but wired on individual circuits

Individual branch circuits supply the same units that appear in Fig. 220-23. With this arrangement, smaller branch circuits supply each unit with no JBs required. Although two additional fuse or CB poles are required in a panelboard, overall labor/material costs are less than the 50-amp circuit shown in Fig. 220-23. However, one disadvantage to individual circuits is that smaller size circuits will not handle larger units, which may be installed at a later date.

Fig. 220-24. Separate circuits have advantages. (Sec. 220-19.)

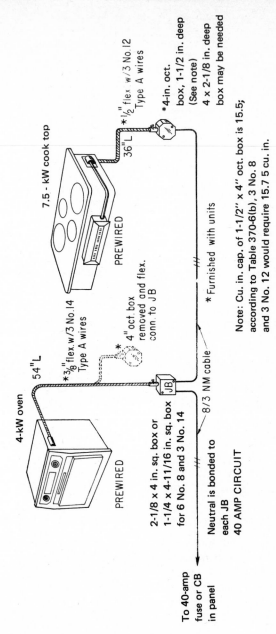

Fig. 220-25. A single 40-amp circuit may supply units. (Sec. 220-19.)

The *NEC* permits 40-amp circuits in lieu of 50-amp circuits where the aggregate nameplate rating of cook tops and ovens is less than 15.5 kW. Most ranges are less than 15.5 kW and so are most combinations of cook tops and ovens.

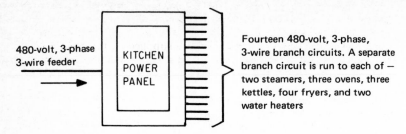

Fourteen 480-volt, 3-phase, 3-wire branch circuits. A separate branch circuit is run to each of — two steamers, three ovens, three kettles, four fryers, and two water heaters

Kitchen panel supplies fourteen 480-volt, 3-phase, 3-wire branch circuits.
A separate branch circuit is run to each of—
    Two steamers,
    Three ovens,
    Three kettles,
    Four fryers, and
    Two water heaters
The 14 appliances make up a total connected load of 303.3 kVA

QUESTION:
Is a full-capacity feeder (303.3 kVA/480 X 1.73 = 366 amps) required here? Or can a demand factor be applied?

ANSWER:
Although it is possible that all of the appliances might operate simultaneously, it is not expected that they will all be operating at full connected load. Table 220-20 of the *NE Code* does permit use of a demand factor on a feeder for commercial electric cooking equipment (including dishwasher, booster heaters, water heaters and other kitchen equipment). As shown in the Table, for six or more units, a demand factor of 65% can be applied to the feeder sizing:

366 amps × 0.65 = 238 amps

The feeder must have at least that much capacity, and that much capacity must be included in the building service entrance conductors for this load.

Fig. 220-26. Demand factor for commercial-kitchen feeder. (Sec. 220-20.)

part of electric utilities. Figure 220-26 shows an example of reduced sizing for a feeder to such kitchen appliances.

220-21. Noncoincident Loads. When dissimilar loads (such as space heating and air cooling in a building) are supplied by the same feeder, the smaller of the two loads may be omitted from the total capacity required for the feeder if it is unlikely that the two loads will operate at the same time.

220-22. Feeder Neutral Load. This section covers requirements for sizing the neutral conductor in a feeder, that is, determining the required amp rating of the neutral conductor. It states that "the feeder neutral load shall be the maximum unbalance" of the feeder load.

"The maximum unbalanced load shall be the maximum connected load between the neutral and any one ungrounded conductor. . . ." In a 3-wire, 120/240-V, single-phase feeder, the neutral must have a current-carrying capacity at least equal to the current drawn by the total 120-V load connected between the more heavily loaded hot leg and the neutral. As shown in Fig. 220-27, under unbalanced conditions, with one hot leg fully loaded to 60 A and the other leg open, the neutral would carry 60 A and must have the same rating as the loaded hot leg. Thus No. 6 THW hot legs would require No. 6 THW neutral (copper).

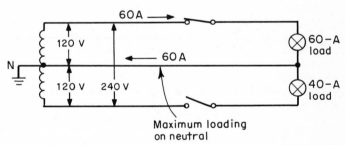

Fig. 220-27. Neutral must be sized the same as hot leg with heavier load. (Sec. 220-22.)

It should be noted that straight 240-V loads, connected between the two hot legs, do not place any load on the neutral. As a result, the neutral conductor of such a feeder must be sized to make up a 2-wire, 120-V circuit with the more heavily loaded hot leg. Actually, the 120-V circuit loads on such a feeder would be considered as balanced on both sides of the neutral. The neutral, then, would be the same size as each of the hot legs if only 120-V loads were supplied by the feeder. If 240-V loads also were supplied, the hot legs would be sized for the total load; but the neutral would be sized for only the total 120-V load connected between one hot leg and the neutral, as shown in Fig. 220-28.

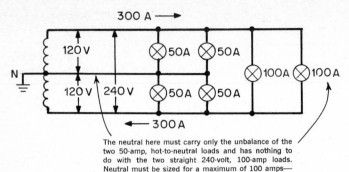

300 A
120 V
120 V
240 V
N
50A
50A
50A
50A
100A
100 A
300 A
The neutral here must carry only the unbalance of the two 50-amp, hot-to-neutral loads and has nothing to do with the two straight 240-volt, 100-amp loads. Neutral must be sized for a maximum of 100 amps—the maximum unbalance from hot to neutral.

Fig. 220-28. Neutral sizing is not related to phase-to-phase loads. (Sec. 220-22.)

But, there are qualifications on the basic rule of Sec. 220-22, as follows:

1. When a feeder supplies household electric ranges, wall-mounted ovens, and/or counter-mounted cooking units, the neutral conductor may be smaller than the hot conductors but must have a carrying capacity at least equal to 70 percent of the current capacity required in the ungrounded conductors to handle the load (i.e., 70 percent of the load on the ungrounded conductors). Table 220-19 gives the demand loads to be used in sizing feeders which supply electric ranges and other cooking appliances. The 70 percent demand factor may be applied to the minimum required size of a feeder phase (or hot) leg in order to determine the minimum permitted size of neutral, as shown in Fig. 220-29.

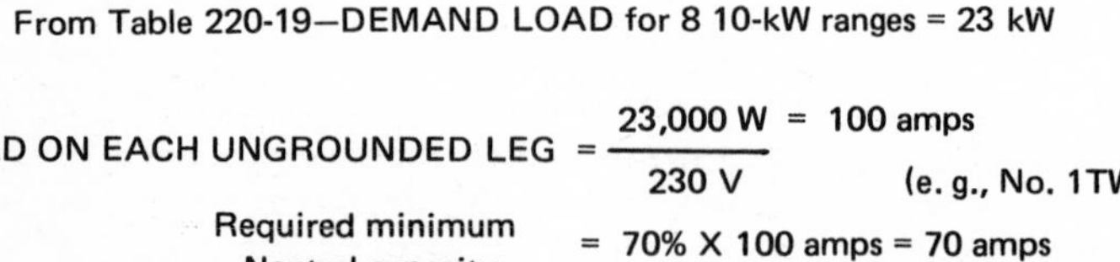

H
115/230-v feeder
N
H
To 8 electric ranges rated 10 kW each

From Table 220-19—DEMAND LOAD for 8 10-kW ranges = 23 kW

LOAD ON EACH UNGROUNDED LEG $= \frac{23{,}000 \text{ W}}{230 \text{ V}} = 100$ amps (e. g., No. 1TW)

Required minimum Neutral capacity = 70% X 100 amps = 70 amps (e.g., No. 4TW)

Fig. 220-29. Sizing the neutral of a feeder to electric ranges. (Sec. 220-22.)

2. For feeders of three or more conductors—3-wire, DC; 3-wire, single-phase; and 4-wire, 3-phase—a further demand factor of 70 percent may be applied to that portion of the unbalanced load in excess of 200 A. That is, in a feeder supplying only 120-V loads evenly divided between each ungrounded conductor and the neutral, the neutral conductor must be the same size as each ungrounded conductor up to 200-A capacity, but may be reduced from the size of the ungrounded conductors for loads above 200 A by adding to the 200 A only 70 percent of the amount of load current above 200 A in computing the size of the neutral. It should be noted that this 70 percent demand factor is applicable to the unbalanced load in excess of 200 A and not simply to the total load, which in many cases may include 240-V loads on 120/240-V, 3-wire, single-phase feeders or 3-phase loads or phase-to-phase connected loads on 3-phase feeders. Figure 220-30 shows an example of neutral reduction as permitted by Sec. 220-22.

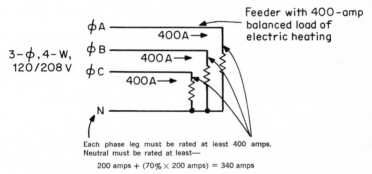

Fig. 220-30. Neutral may be smaller than hot-leg conductors on feeders over 200 amps. (Sec. 220-22.)

WATCH OUT!

The foregoing reduction of the neutral to 200 A plus 70 percent of the current over 200 A does not apply to electric-discharge lighting. In a feeder supplying ballasts for electric-discharge lamps, there must not be a reduction of the neutral capacity for that part of the load which consists of discharge light sources, such as fluorescent mercury-vapor or other HID lamps. For feeders supplying only electric-discharge lighting, the neutral conductor must be the same size as the phase conductors no matter how big the total load may be (Fig. 220-31). Full-sizing of the neutral of such feeders is required because, in a balanced circuit supplying ballasts, neutral current approximating the phase current is produced by third (and other odd-order) harmonics developed by the

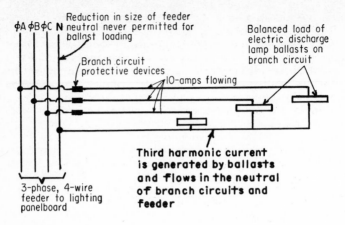

φA φB φC **N**   Reduction in size of feeder
              neutral never permitted for
              ballast loading

Balanced load of
electric discharge
lamp ballasts on
branch circuit

Branch circuit
protective devices

10-amps flowing

**Third harmonic current
is generated by ballasts
and flows in the neutral
of branch circuits and
feeder**

3-phase, 4-wire
feeder to lighting
panelboard

EXAMPLE:

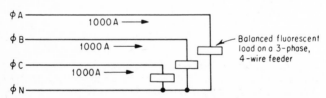

φ A

1000 A →

φ B

1000 A →

φ C

1000 A →

φ N

Balanced fluorescent
load on a 3-phase,
4-wire feeder

**There must be no reduction in amp rating of this neutral.
It must have 1000-amp rating like the phase conductors.**

Fig. 220-31. Full-size neutral for feeders to ballast loads. (Sec. 220-22.)

ballasts. For large electric-discharge lighting loads, this factor affects sizing of neutrals all the way back to the service. It also affects rating of conductors in conduit because such a feeder circuit consists of *four* current-carrying wires, which required application of an 80 percent reduction factor. [See Note 8 and Note 10(c) of the "Notes to Tables 310-16 through 310-19" in the **NE Code**.]

In the case of a feeder supplying, say, 200 A of fluorescent lighting and 200 A of incandescent, there can be no reduction of the neutral below the required 400-A capacity of the phase legs, because the 200 A of fluorescent lighting load cannot be used in any way to take advantage of the 70 percent demand factor on that part of the load in excess of 200 A.

It should be noted that the **Code** wording in Sec. 220-22 prohibits reduction in the size of the neutral when electric-discharge lighting is used, even if the feeder supplying the electric-discharge lighting load over 200 A happens to be a 120/240-V, 3-wire, single-phase feeder. In such a feeder, however, the third harmonic currents in the hot legs are 180° out of phase with each other and, therefore, would not be additive in the neutral as they are in a 3-phase, 4-wire circuit. In the 3-phase, 4-wire circuit, the third harmonic components of the phase currents are in phase with each other and add together in the neutral instead of canceling out. Figure 220-32 shows a 120/240-V circuit.

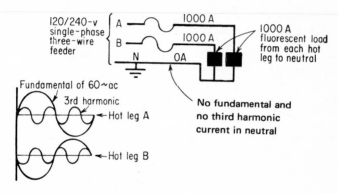

As shown, both the fundamental and harmonic currents are 180° out of phase and both cancel in the neutral. Under balanced conditions, the neutral current is zero. But the literal wording of Sec. 220-22 says there can be no reduction in neutral capacity when fluorescent lighting is supplied. As a result, there should be no use of the 70% factor for current over 200 amps as there would be for incandescent loading. Neutral here must be rated for 1000 amps.

Fig. 220-32. No reduction of neutral capacity even with zero neutral current? (Sec. 220-22.)

Figure 220-33 shows a number of circuit conditions involving the rules on sizing a feeder neutral.

220-30. Optional Calculation—Dwelling Unit. This section sets forth an optional method of calculating service demand load for a residence. This method may be used instead of the standard method under the following conditions:

1. Only for a one-family residence or an apartment in a multifamily dwelling, or other "dwelling unit"
2. Served by a 115/230-V, or 120/208-V 3-wire, 100-A or larger service
3. Where the total load is supplied by one set of service-entrance conductors

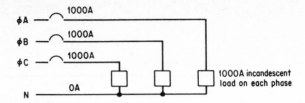

1. Incandescent lighting only

Serving an incandescent load, each phase conductor must be rated for 1000 amps. But neutral only has to be rated for 200 amps plus (70% x 800 amps) or 200 + 560 = 760 amps.

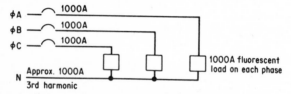

2. Electric discharge lighting only

Because load is electric discharge lighting, there can be no reduction in the size of the neutral. Neutral must be rated for 1000 amps, the same as the phase conductors, because the third harmonic currents of the phase legs add together in the neutral. This applies also when the load is mercury-vapor or other metallic-vapor lighting.

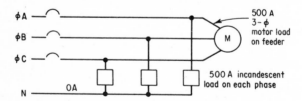

3. Incandescent plus motor load

Although 1000 amps flow on each phase leg, only 500 amps is related to the neutral. Neutral, then, is sized for 200 amps plus (70% x 300 amps) or 200 + 210 = 410 amps. The amount of current taken for 3-phase motors cannot be "unbalanced load" and no capacity has to be provided for this in the neutral.

Fig. 220-33. Sizing the feeder neutral for different conditions of loading. (Sec. 220-22.)

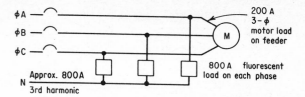

4. Electric discharge lighting plus motor load

Here, again, the only possible load that could flow on the neutral is the 800 amps flowing over each phase to the fluorescent lighting. But because it is fluorescent lighting there can be no reduction of neutral capacity below the 800-amp value on each phase. The 70% factor for that current above 200 amps DOES NOT APPLY in such cases.

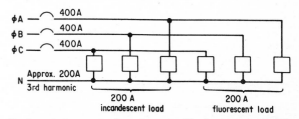

5. Incandescent plus electric discharge lighting

Each phase leg carries a total of 400 amps to supply the incandescent load plus the fluorescent load. But because there can be no reduction of neutral capacity for the fluorescent and because the incandescent load is not over 200 amps, the neutral must be sized for the maximum possible unbalance, which is 400 amps.

Fig. 220-33. (*Continued*)

This method recognizes the greater diversity attainable in large capacity installations. It therefore permits a smaller size of service-entrance conductors for such installations than would be permitted by using the load calculations of Sec. 220-10 through Sec. 220-22.

example   A typical application of the data and table of Sec. 220-30, in calculating the minimum required size of service conductors, is as follows:

A 1,500 sq ft house (excluding unoccupied basement, unfinished attic, and open porches) contains the following specific electric applicances:

12-kW range
2.5-kW water heater
1.2-kW dishwasher
9 kW of electric heat (in five rooms)
5-kW clothes dryer
6-A, 230-V AC unit

When using the optional method, if a house has air conditioning as well as electric heating, there is recognition in Sec. 220-21 that if "it is unlikely that two dissimilar loads will be in use simultaneously," it is permissible to omit the smaller of the two in calculating required capacity in feeder or in service-entrance conductors. In Sec. 220-30, that concept is spelled out to require adding only the larger of either an air-conditioning load *or* the connected load of *four or more* separately controlled electric space heating units. For the residence considered here, these loads would be as follows:

$$\text{Air conditioning} = 6 \text{ A} \times 230 \text{ V} = 1.38 \text{ kW}$$
$$\text{Heating (five separate units)} = 9.00 \text{ kW}$$

It is permissible, therefore, to disregard the air-conditioning load.

The heating and other loads (except the air conditioning) must be totaled up in accordance with Sec. 220-30:

		Watts
1.	1,500 W for each of two small appliance circuits (2-wire, 20-A) required by Sec. 220-3(b) (1)	3,000
	Laundry branch circuit (3-wire, 20-A)	1,500
2.	3 W per sq ft of floor area for general lighting and general-use receptacles (3 × 1,500 sq ft)	4,500
3.	Nameplate rating of fixed appliances:	
	Range	12,000
	"4 or more" separately controlled heating units	9,000
	Water heater	2,500
	Dishwasher	1,200
	Clothes dryer	5,000
	Total	38,700

Referring to Table 220-30, the first three load categories given are not applicable here. "Air conditioning" has already been excluded as a load because the heating load is greater. There is no "central" electric space heating; and there are *not* "less than four" separately controlled electric space heating units.

The total load of 38,700 W as summed up above, is classified as "all other load," as referred to on line 6 of **Code** Table 220-30. The last two references in Table 220-30 constitute all the "optional" calculation in this example:

		Watts
1.	Take 10 kW of "all other load" at 100% demand	10,000
2.	Take the "remainder of other load" at 40% demand factor: (38,700 − 10,000) × 40% = 28,700 × 0.4	11,480
	Total demand	21,480

At 230 V, single phase, the *minimum ampacity of each service hot leg would then have to be:*

$$\frac{21,480 \text{ W}}{230 \text{ V}} = 93.39 \text{ or } 93 \text{ A}$$

But, Sec. 230-41(b) (2) requires a minimum conductor rating when demand load is 10 kW or more:

Minimum service conductor required = 100 A

Then the neutral service-entrance conductor is calculated in accordance with Sec. 220-22, based on Sec. 220-10. All 230-V loads have no relation to required neutral capacity. The water heater, clothes dryer, and electric space heating units operate at 230 V, 2-wire and have no neutrals. Considering only those loads served by a circuit with a neutral conductor and determining their maximum unbalance, the minimum required size of neutral conductor can be determined.

When a 3-wire, 230/115-V circuit serves a total load that is balanced from each hot leg to neutral—that is, half the total load is connected from one hot leg to neutral and the other half of total load from the other hot leg to neutral—the condition of maximum unbalance occurs when all the load fed by one hot leg is operating and all the load fed by the other hot leg is off. Under that condition, the neutral-current and hot-leg current are equal to half the total load watts divided by 115 V (half the volts between hot legs). But that current is exactly the same as the current that results from dividing the *total* load (connected hot leg to hot leg) by 230 V (which is twice the voltage from hot leg to neutral). Because of this relationship, it is easy to determine neutral-current load by simply calculating hot-leg current load—total load from hot leg to hot leg divided by 230 V.

In the example here, the neutral-current load is determined from the following steps that sum up the components of the neutral load:

		Watts
1.	Take 1,500 sq ft at 3 W per sq ft	4,500
2.	Add three small appliance circuits	
	(two kitchen, one laundry) at 1,500 W each	4,500
	Total lighting and small appliance load	9,000
3.	Take 3,000 W of that value	
	at 100% demand factor	3,000
4.	Take the balance of the load	
	(9,000 − 3,000) at 35% demand factor:	
	6,000 W × 0.35	2,100
	Total of 3 and 4	5,100

Assuming an even balance of this load on the two hot legs, the neutral load under maximum unbalance will be the same as the total load (5,100 W) divided by 230 V (Fig. 220-34):

$$\frac{5,100 \text{ W}}{230 \text{ V}} = 22.17 \text{ A}$$

And the neutral unbalanced current for the range load can be taken as equal to

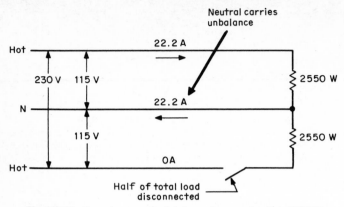

Fig. 220-34. Neutral current for lighting and receptacles. (Sec. 220-30.)

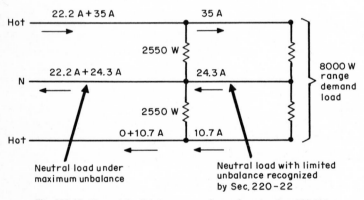

Fig. 220-35. Neutral for lighting, receptacles, and range. (Sec. 220-30.)

the 8,000-W range demand load multiplied by the 70 percent demand factor permitted by Sec. 220-22 and then divided by 230 V (Fig. 220-35):

$$\frac{8,000 \times 0.7}{230} = \frac{5,600}{230} = 24.34 \text{ A}$$

Then, the neutral-current load that is added by the 115-V, 1,200-W dishwasher must be added:

$$\frac{1,200 \text{ W}}{115 \text{ V}} = 10.43 \text{ A}$$

The minimum required neutral capacity is, therefore,

22.17 A

24.34 A

10.43 A

Total: 56.94 A (Fig. 220-36)

Adding the 0.94 A as 1 A, the required capacity becomes **57 A.**
From Code Table 310-16, the neutral minimum is

No. 4 copper TW, THW, THHN or XHHW

No. 3 aluminum TW, THW, THHN or XHHW

And the 75 or 90°C conductors must be used at the ampacity of 60°C conductors, as required by UL instructions in the UL's *Electrical Construction Materials Directory.*

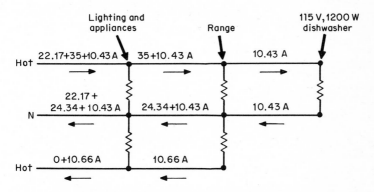

Neutral load = 22.17 + 24.34 + 10.43 = 56.94 amps

Fig. 220-36. Neutral current for total load. (Sec. 220-30.)

Note: The above calculation of the minimum required capacity of the neutral conductor differs from the calculation and results shown in Example No. 1(b) in Chap. 9 in the NE Code book. In the book, the 1,200-W dishwasher load is added as a 230-V load to the range load and general lighting and receptacle load. To include a 115-V load as a 230-V load (and then divide the total by 230 V, as shown) does not accurately represent the neutral load that the 115-V, 1,200-W dishwasher will produce. In fact, it yields exactly half the neutral load that the dishwasher represents. The optional calculation method of Sec. 220-30 does indicate in part **(3)** that fixed appliances be added at nameplate load and does not differentiate between 115-V devices and 230-V devices. It simply totals all load and then applies the 100 percent and 40 percent demand factors as indicated. That method clearly is based on well-founded data about diversity of loads and is aimed at determining a reasonable size of the service hot legs. But, calculation of the feeder neutral in accordance with Sec. 220-22 is aimed at determining the *maximum unbalanced current* to which the service neutral might be subjected.

Although the difference is small between the NE Code book value of 51.7 A and the value of 56.9 A determined here, precise calculation should be made to assure real adequacy in conductor ampacities. The difference of 5.2 A actually changes the required minimum size of neutral conductor from No. 6 up to No. 4 for copper, and from No. 4 up to No. 3 for aluminum. A load like a dishwasher, which draws current for a considerable period of time and is not just a few-minute device like a toaster, should be factored into the calculation with an eye toward adequate capacity of conductors.

220-31. Optional Calculation for Additional Loads in Existing Dwelling Unit. This covers an optional calculation for additional loads in an existing single-family occupancy which contains an existing 230/115-V or 208/120-V, 3-wire, 60-A service. The method of calculation is similar to that shown in Table 220-30.

The purpose of this section is to permit the *maximum load* to be applied to an *existing 60-A* service without the necessity of increasing the size of the service. The calculations are based on numerous load surveys and tests made by local utilities throughout the country. This optional method would seem to be particularly advantageous when smaller loads such as window air conditioners or bathroom heaters are to be installed in a dwelling with an existing 60-A service.

If there is an existing electric range, say, 12 kW (and no electric water heater), it would not be possible to add any load of substantial rating. Based on the formula 13,800 W (230 V × 60 A) = 8,000 + 0.4 (X − 8,000), the total "gross load" that can be connected to an existing 115/230 V, 60-A service would be X = 22,500 W.

example Thus, an existing 1,000 sq ft dwelling with a 12-kW electric range, two 20-A appliance circuits, a 750-W furnace circuit, and a 60-A service would have a gross load of:

	Watts
1,000 sq ft × 3 W per sq ft	3,000
Two 20-A appliance circuits @ 1,500 W each	3,000
One electric range @	12,000
Furnace circuit @	750
Gross watts	18,750

Since the *maximum* permitted gross load is 22,500 W, an appliance not exceeding *3,750 W* could be added to this existing 60-A service. However, the tabulation at the end of this section lists air-conditioning equipment, central space heating, and less than four separately controlled space heating units at 100 percent demands; and if the appliance to be added is one of these, then it would be limited to *1,500 W:*

From the 18,750-W gross load we have 8,000 W @ 100 percent demand + [10,750 W (18,750 − 8,000) × 0.40] or 12,300 W. Then, 13,800 W (60 A × 320 V) − 12,300 W = 1,500 W for an appliance listed at *100 percent demand.*

220-33. Optional Calculation—Two Dwelling Units. This is a new section that provides an optional calculation for sizing a feeder to "two dwelling units." It notes that if calculation of such a feeder according to the basic long method of calculating given in part **B** of Art. 220 exceeds the minimum load ampacity permitted by Sec. 220-32 for three identical dwelling units, then the *lesser* of the two loads may be used. This rule was added to eliminate the obvious illogic of requiring a greater feeder ampacity for two dwelling units than for the three units of the same load makeup. Now optional calculations provide for a feeder to one dwelling unit, two dwelling units, or three or more dwelling units.

220-34. Optional Method—Schools. The optional calculation for feeders and service-entrance conductors for a school has been clarified. Feeders "within the building or structure" must be calculated in accordance with the standard long calculation procedure established by part **B** of Art. 220, **But** the ampacity of any individual feeder does not have to be greater than the minimum required ampacity for the whole building, regardless of the calculation result from part **B**.

ARTICLE 225. OUTSIDE BRANCH CIRCUITS AND FEEDERS

225-4. Conductor Covering. The wiring method known as "open wiring" is recognized in Art. 225 as suitable for overhead use outdoors— "run between buildings, other structures or poles" (Fig. 225-1). This is derived from Secs. 225-1, 225-4, 225-14, 225-18, and 225-19. Section 225-4 requires open wiring to be insulated *or* covered if it comes within 10 ft of any building or other structure, which it must do if it attaches to

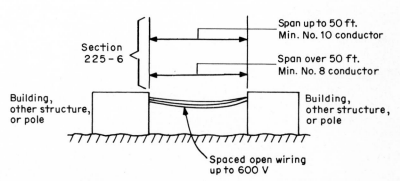

Fig. 225-1. Open wiring is OK for overhead circuits. (Sec. 225-4.)

the building or structure. Insulated conductors have a dielectric covering that prevents conductive contact with the conductor when it is energized. Covered conductors—such as braided, weatherproof conductors (sometimes referred to as TBWP)—have a certain mechanical protection for the conductor but are not rated as having insulation, and thus there is no protection against conductive contact with the energized conductor.

Because Sec. 225-4 says that conductors in *"cables"* (except Type MI) must be of the rubber or thermoplastic type, a number of questions arise.

1. What kind of *"cable"* does the Code recognize for overhead spans between buildings, structures, and/or poles?

2. May an overhead circuit from one building to another or from lighting fixture to lighting fixture on poles use service-entrance cable, UF cable, or Type NM or NMC nonmetallic-sheathed cable?

Although the Code covers specific types of cables in turn (Arts. 330 through 340), it does not refer to use for outdoor overhead applications. And no other mention is made in the Code of cable suitable for overhead, outdoor spans.

The closest the Code comes to overhead cable assemblies is that of Art. 342, "Nonmetallic Extensions." This includes a nonmetallic cable assembly with an integral supporting messenger cable (within the assembly) for "aerial" applications. But this aerial cable is suitable only for limited use indoors, in industrial plants that are dry locations. This cable assembly is listed as an "aerial cable" by UL, but it is the *only* aerial cable listed by UL. Such aerial cable is also the only aerial cable recognized by the NE Code But again, *it may not be used outdoors.*

Use of service-entrance cable between buildings, structures, and/or poles is not supported by Art. 338. No mention is made of overhead use; and Sec. 338-4(b) requires that "unarmored" SE cable be supported as required by Sec. 336-5, which says that the cable must be "secured in place at intervals not exceeding 4½ feet." No exceptions are given. It could be argued that such support could be made to a messenger cable to which the SE cable is secured, but this is not common practice.

Where Sec. 338-3(b) refers to SE cable as "a feeder to supply other buildings," it clearly refers only to "type SE" cable with a bare neutral and an overall outer jacket. (Type USE cable is recognized by UL and the Code for use as a feeder or branch circuit underground where all conductors are insulated.) The UL listing on type SE cable recognizes it only for aboveground installation. That certainly means on building surfaces or in raceway, but there is no mention of aerial or overhead use.

Use of NM, NMC, or UF cable for outdoor, overhead circuits is likewise not at all supported by any data in the articles covering these cables (Arts. 336 and 339). There are no exceptions given to the support requirements in Sec. 336-5 that would let NM or NMC be used aerially, and UF aboveground must be supported the same as NM and NMC. [See Sec. 339-3(a) (4).]

Service-Drop Cable

Although the NE Code has no article covering the use of "service-drop" cable and the UL has no listing for or reference to such cable, the NE Code does make reference to it; and its use for aerial circuits between buildings, structures, and/or poles is particularly dictated (Fig. 225-2).

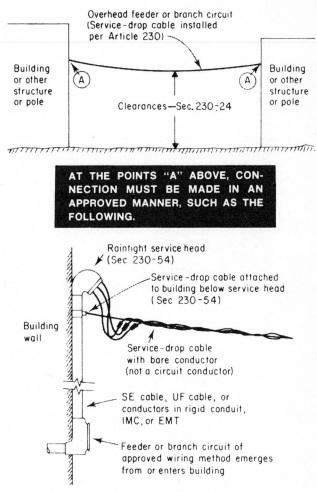

Fig. 225-2. Aerial cable for overhead circuits. (Sec. 225-4.)

Experience with this cable is very extensive and highly satisfactory. It is an engineered product specifically designed and used for outdoor, overhead circuiting.

NE Code Secs. 230-21 through 230-29 cover use of service-drop cable for overhead service conductors. Because the general rules of Art. 225 on outside branch circuits and feeders do make frequent references to other sections of Art. 230, it is logical to equate cables for overhead branch circuits and feeders to cables for overhead services. In the absence of clear, definitive, detailed Code regulations on the use of cables for outdoor circuits, use of service-drop cable is the best choice—because such cable is covered by the application rules of Secs. 230-21 through 230-29. Other types of available aerial cable assemblies, although not listed by UL or mentioned in the NE Code, might satisfy some inspection agencies. But, in these times of OSHA emphasis on codes and standards, use of service-drop cable has the strongest sanction.

One important consideration in the use of service-drop cable as a branch circuit or feeder is the general Code prohibition against use of bare circuit conductors. Section 310-2 requires conductors to be insulated. An exception notes that bare conductors may be used where "specifically permitted." Bare *equipment grounding conductors* are permitted in Sec. 250-91(b). Bare neutrals for SE cable are permitted in Sec. 338-3(b). Bare neutrals are permitted for service-entrance conductors in Sec. 230-40, for underground service-entrance (service lateral) conductors in Sec. 230-30, and for *service-drop conductors* in Sec. 230-22(a) *when used as service conductors.* When service-drop cable is used as a feeder or branch circuit, however, there is no permission for use of a bare circuit conductor—although it may be acceptable to use the bare conductor of the service-drop cable as an equipment grounding conductor. (If service-drop cable is used as a feeder to another building and the bare conductor is *not* used as an equipment grounding conductor, then a grounding electrode *must* be installed at the other building in accordance with Sec. 250-24.)

When service-drop cable is used between buildings, the method for leaving one building and entering another *must* satisfy Secs. 230-43, 230-52, and 230-54. This is required in Sec. 225-11.

Because the matter of outdoor, overhead circuiting is complex, check with local inspection agencies on required methods. As NE Code Sec. 90-4 says, the local inspector has the responsibility for making interpretations of the rules.

225-6. Minimum Size of Conductor.   Open wiring must be of the minimum sizes indicated in Sec. 225-6 for the various lengths of spans indicated.

Section 225-6 gives a definition of *festoon lighting* as "a string of outdoor lights suspended between two points more than 15 feet apart" (Fig. 225-3). Such lighting is used at carnivals, displays, used-car lots, etc. Such

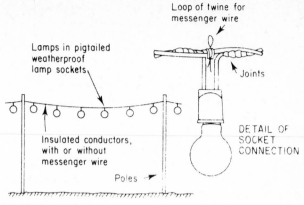

Fig. 225-3. Festoon lighting is permitted outdoors. (Sec. 225-6.)

application of lighting is limited because it has a generally poor appearance and does not enhance commercial activities.

Overhead conductors for festoon lighting must not be smaller than No. 12; and where any span is over 40 ft, the conductors must be supported by a messenger wire, which itself must be properly secured to strain insulators. But the rules on festoon lighting do not apply to overhead circuits between buildings, structures, and/or poles.

225-7. Lighting Equipment on Poles or Other Structures.   Part **(b)** permits a common neutral for outdoor branch circuits—something not permitted for indoor circuits (a neutral of a 3-phase, 4-wire circuit is *not* a common neutral). For a 120/208-V multiwire circuit consisting of six ungrounded conductors and one neutral feeding a bank of floodlights on a pole, if the maximum calculated load on any one circuit is 12 A and the maximum calculated load on any one phase is 24 A, the ungrounded circuit conductors may be No. 14 and the neutral may be No. 10.

225-14. Open-Conductor Spacings.   Open wiring runs must have a minimum spacing between individual conductors (as noted in Sec. 225-14) in accordance with Table 230-51(c), which gives the spacing of the insulator supports on a building surface and the clearance between individual conductors on the building or run in spans (Fig. 225-4).

It should be noted that Sec. 225-14 and Table 230-51(c) require that the *minimum spacing* between individual conductors in spans run overhead be 3 in. for circuits up to 300 V (such as 120 V, 120/240 V, 120/208 V, 240 V). For circuits up to 600 V, such as 40 V and 480/277 V, the *minimum spacing* between individual conductors must be at least 6 in.

225-18. Clearance from Ground.   Open conductors must be protected from contact by persons by keeping them high enough aboveground or

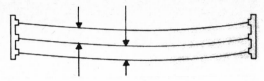

Minimum clearance distance between
conductors is given in Table 230-51 (c)

Fig. 225-4. Spacing of open-wiring conductors. (Sec. 225-14.)

above other positions where people might be standing. And they must not present an obstruction to vehicle passage or other activities below the lines (Fig. 225-5).

225-19. Clearance from Buildings for Conductors of Not Over 600 Volts. This section gives minimum mounting heights above roofs and for other mountings (Fig. 225-6).

225-22. Raceways on Exterior Surfaces of Buildings. Condensation of moisture is very likely to take place in conduit or tubing located outdoors. The conduit or tubing should be considered suitably drained when it is

Open conductors are strung from one building to another:

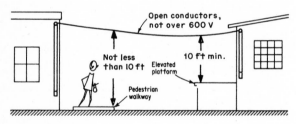

Individual open conductors supported by poles pass over both a residential driveway and a road bearing truck traffic:

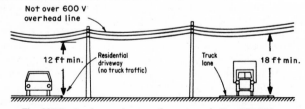

Fig. 225-5. Conductor clearance from ground. (Sec. 225-18.)

Open conductors feeding a flood-light pass over a shed:

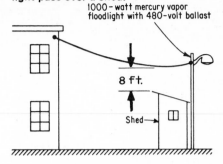

NOTE: If luminaire operated at not over 300 volts, exception No. 1 to Sec. 225-19(a) might apply.

Fig. 225-6. Clearance from roof. (Sec. 225-19.)

installed so that any moisture condensing inside the raceway or entering from the outside cannot accumulate in the raceway or fittings. This requires that the raceway shall be installed without "pockets," that long runs shall not be truly horizontal but shall always be pitched, and that fittings at low points be provided with drainage openings.

In order to be raintight, all conduit fittings must be made up wrench-tight. Couplings and connectors used with electrical metallic tubing shall be of the raintight type. See See Sec. 348-8.

225-24. Outdoor Lampholders. This section applies particularly to lampholders used in festoons. Where "pigtail" lampholders are used, the splices should be staggered (made a distance apart) in order to avoid the possibility of short circuits, in case the taping for any reason should become ineffective.

According to the UL Standard for Edison-Base Lampholders, "pin-type" terminals shall be employed only in lampholders for temporary lighting or decorations, signs, or specifically approved applications.

225-25. Location of Outdoor Lamps. In some types of outdoor lighting it would be difficult to keep all electrical equipment above the lamps and hence a disconnecting means may be required. A disconnecting means should be provided for the equipment on each individual pole, tower, or other structure if the conditions are such that lamp replacements may be necessary while the lighting system is in use. It may be assumed that grounded metal conduit or tubing extending below the lamps would not constitute a condition requiring that a disconnecting means must be provided.

ARTICLE 230. SERVICES

230-2. Number of Services.   For any building, the service consists of the conductors and equipment used to deliver electric energy from the utility supply lines to the interior distribution system. Service may be made to a building either overhead or underground, from a utility pole line or from an underground transformer vault.

The basic rule of this section requires that a building or other structure be fed by only one service drop (overhead service) or by only one set of service lateral conductors (underground service). As shown in Fig. 230-1,

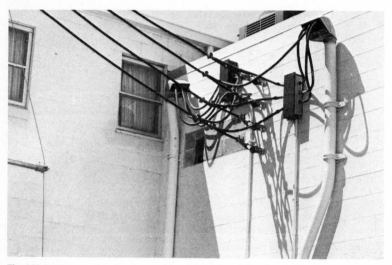

Fig. 230-1. One set of service-drop conductors supply building from utility line (coming from upper left) and two sets of SE conductors are tapped through separate metering CTs. (Sec. 230-2.)

a building with only one service drop to it satisfies the basic rule even when more than one set of service-entrance conductors are tapped from the single drop (or from a single lateral circuit). The seven Exceptions to that basic rule cover cases where two or more service drops or laterals may supply a single building or structure.

Exceptions No. 1 and No. 2 permit a separate drop or lateral for supply to a fire pump and/or to emergency electrical systems, like emergency lighting or exit lights.

In the case of apartment houses, shopping centers, and other multiple-occupancy buildings, Exception No. 3b permits two or more sets of service-entrance conductors to be tapped from a single set of service drop or lateral conductors or two or more sub-sets of service-entrance conductors may be tapped from a single set of main service-entrance conductors (Fig. 230-2). This permission is also explained in **NE Code** Sec. 230-45 and must always be coordinated with the rules on disconnect and protection in Secs. 230-72(d) and 230-90(a). Refer to Sec. 230-45.

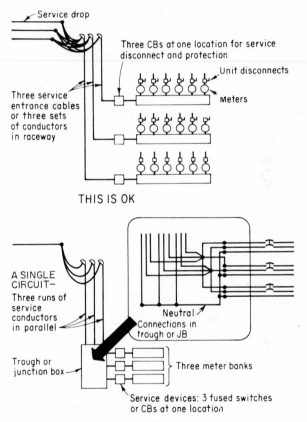

Fig. 230-2. Tapping SE conductors from one service drop for multiple-occupancy buildings. (Sec. 230-2.)

Two or more services to one building are permitted when the total demand load of all the feeders is more than 3,000 A, up to 600 V, where a single-phase service needs more than one drop, or by special permis-

Ex. No. 4

1. . . .when the total demand load of all feeders is greater than 3000 amps (up to 600 volts), or

2. . . .when the load demand of a single-phase installation is higher than the utility's normal maximum for a single service, or

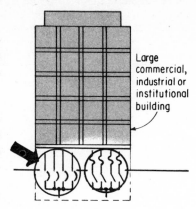

Large commercial, industrial or institutional building

3. . . .when special permission is obtained from the inspection authority.

NOTE: "Two or more services" means two or more service drops or service laterals—not sets of service-entrance conductors tapped from one drop or lateral.

Ex. No. 6

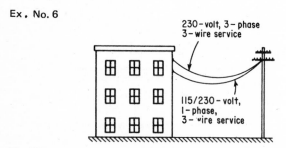

230 – volt, 3 – phase
3 – wire service

115/230 – volt,
1 – phase,
3 – wire service

Fig. 230-3. Exceptions to Sec. 230-2 permits two or more services under certain conditions. (Sec. 230-2.)

sion (Fig. 230-3). Exception No. 4 relates capacity to permitted services. Where requirements exceed 3,000 A, two or more sets of service conductors may be installed. Below this value, special permission is required to install more than one set. The term "capacity requirements" appears to apply to the total calculated load for sizing service-entrance conductors and service equipment for a given installation.

Cases of separate light and power services to a single building and separate services to water heaters for purposes of different rate schedules are also exceptions to the general rule of single service. And if a single building is so large that one service cannot handle the load, special permission can be given for additional services.

Exception No. 5 requires special permission to install more than one service to buildings of large area. Examples of large-area buildings are high-rise buildings, shopping centers, and major industrial plants. In granting special permission the authority having jurisdiction must examine the availability of utility supplies for a given building, load concentrations within the building, and the ability of the utility to supply more than one service. Any of the special permission clauses in the exceptions in Sec. 230-2 require close cooperation and consultation between the authority having jurisdiction and the serving utility.

Exception No. 6 is illustrated at the bottom of Fig. 230-3.

Exception No. 7 to the basic rule requiring that any "building or other structure" must be supplied by "only one set of service drop or service lateral conductors" adds an important qualification of that rule as it applies only to Sec. 230-45 covering service-entrance layouts where two to six service disconnects are to be fed from one drop or lateral and are installed in separate individual enclosures at one location, with each disconnect supplying a separate load. As described in Sec. 230-45, such a service equipment layout may have a separate set of service-entrance conductors run to *"each or several"* of the two to six enclosures. Exception No. 7 notes that where a separate set of underground conductors of size 1/0 or larger is run to each or several of the two to six service disconnects, the several sets of underground conductors are considered to be one service lateral, even though they are run as separate circuits, that is, connected together at their supply end (at the transformer on the pole or in the pad-mount enclosure or vault) *but not* connected together at their load ends. The several sets of conductors are taken to be "one service lateral" in the meaning of Sec. 230-2, although they actually function as separate circuits (Fig. 230-4).

Although Sec. 230-45 applies to "service-entrance conductors" and service equipment layouts fed by *either* a "service drop" (overhead service) or a "service lateral" (underground service), Exception No. 7 is addressed specifically and only to service "lateral" conductors because of the need for clarification based on the **Code** definitions of "service drop," "service lateral," "service-entrance conductors, overhead system," and "service-entrance conductors, underground system." (Refer to these definitions in the **Code** book to clearly understand the intent of Exception No. 7 and its relation to Sec. 230-45).

The matter involves these separate but related considerations:

1. Because a "service lateral" may (and usually does) run directly from a transformer on a pole or in a pad-mount enclosure to gutter taps where short tap conductors feed the terminals of the service discon-

The 1975 *NE Code* **had this limitation on service laterals** (and this is still acceptable)—

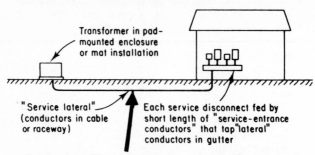

Transformer in pad-
mounted enclosure
or mat installation

"Service lateral"
(conductors in cable
or raceway)

Each service disconnect fed by
short length of "service-entrance
conductors" that tap "lateral"
conductors in gutter

"Service lateral" conductors are **not** "service entrance" conductors and were, therefore, not applicable to the subdivision permission of Section 230-45. The requirement of Section 230-2 for "one set of service lateral conductors" demanded **one circuit** of single-conductor **or** parallel-conductor makeup.

Now, Exception No. 7 considers this type of hookup to be "one set of service lateral conductors"—

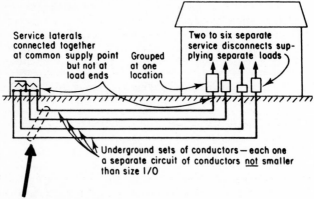

Service laterals
connected together
at common supply point
but not at
load ends

Grouped
at one
location

Two to six separate
service disconnects sup-
plying separate loads

Underground sets of conductors—each one
a separate circuit of conductors <u>not</u> smaller
than size 1/0

This is **one** service lateral, in the meaning of the basic rule of Section 230-2.

Fig. 230-4. "One" service lateral may be made up of several circuits. (Sec. 230-2.)

nects, most layouts of that type literally do not have any "service-entrance conductors" that would be subject to the application permitted by Sec. 230-45—other than the short lengths of tap conductors in the gutter or box where splices are made to the lateral conductors.

2. Because Sec. 230-45 refers only to sets of "service-entrance conductors" as being acceptable for individual supply circuits tapped from *one* drop or lateral to feed the separate service disconnects, that rule clearly does not apply to "service lateral" conductors which by definition are not "service-entrance conductors." So there is no permission in Sec. 230-45 to split up "service lateral" capacity. And the basic rule of Sec. 230-2 has the clear, direct requirement that a building or structure be supplied through only *one* lateral for any underground service. That is, a service lateral must be either a single circuit of one set of conductors or, if circuit capacity requires multiple conductors per phase leg, the lateral must be made up of sets of conductors in parallel—connected together at *both* the supply and load ends—in order to constitute a single circuit (that is, one lateral).

3. Exception No. 7 permits "laterals" to be subdivided into separate, nonparallel sets of conductors in the way that Sec. 230-45 permits such use for "service-entrance conductors"—*but only* for conductors of 1/0 and larger and *only* where each separate set of lateral conductors (each separate lateral circuit) supplies *one* or *several* of the two to six service disconnects.

Exception No. 7 recognizes the importance of subdividing the total service capacity among a number of sets of smaller conductors rather than a single parallel circuit (that is, a number of sets of conductors connected together at *both* their *supply and load* ends). The single parallel circuit would have much lower impedance and would, therefore, require a higher short-circuit interrupting rating in the service equipment. The higher impedance of each separate set of lateral conductors (not connected together at their load ends) would limit short-circuit current and reduce short-circuit duty at the service equipment, permitting lower IC (interrupting capacity)-rated equipment and reducing the destructive capability of any faults at the service equipment.

230-3. One Building or Other Structure Not to Be Supplied through Another.   The service conductors supplying each building or structure shall not *pass through the inside* of another building, unless these buildings are under single occupancy or management (Fig. 230-5). Section 230-44 points out that conductors in raceway enclosed within 2 in. of concrete or masonry are considered to be "outside" the building even when they are run within the building.

A building as defined in Art. 100 is a "structure which stands alone or is cut off from adjoining structures by fire walls with all openings therein

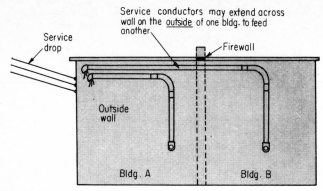

Fig. 230-5. This is not a violation of the basic rule of Sec. 230-3. (Sec. 230-3.)

protected by approved fire doors." A building divided into four units by such fire walls may be supplied by four separate service drops, but a similar building without the fire walls may be supplied by only one service drop, except as permitted in Sec. 230-2.

A commercial building may be a single building but may be occupied by two or more tenants whose quarters are separate, in which case it might be undesirable to supply the building through one service drop. Under these conditions special permission may be given to install more than one service drop.

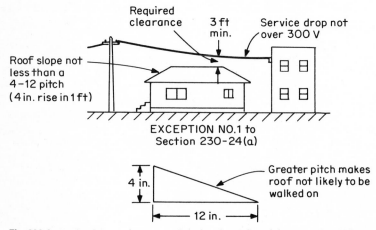

Fig. 230-6. Service-drop conductors may have less than 8-ft roof clearance. (Sec. 230-24.)

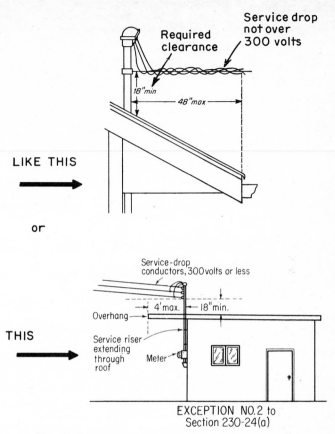

Fig. 230-7. Reduced clearance for service drop. (Sec. 230-24.)

230-4. Insulation of Service Conductors. It is not necessary to insulate the neutral conductor, because it is solidly tied to the service conduit, tubing, or cable armor at the service equipment enclosure.

230-24. Clearances. There are two exceptions to the basic rule of part **(a)** that service-drop conductors must have at least an 8-ft clearance from the highest point of roofs over which they pass.

The intent of Exception No. 1 is that where the roof has a slope greater than 4 in. in 12 in. it is considered difficult to walk upon, and the height of conductors could then be less than 8 ft from the highest point over which they pass but in no case less than 3 ft except as permitted in Exception No. 2. Figure 230-6 shows the rule. Figure 230-7 shows the conditions permitted by Exception No. 2.

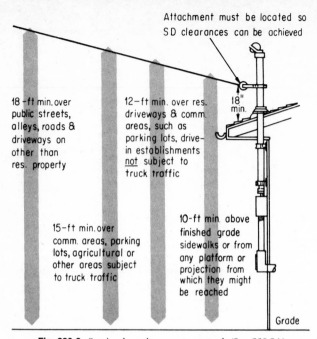

Attachment must be located so SD clearances can be achieved

18" min.

18–ft min. over public streets, alleys, roads & driveways on other than res. property

12–ft min. over res. driveways & comm. areas, such as parking lots, drive-in establishments not subject to truck traffic

15–ft min. over comm. areas, parking lots, agricultural or other areas subject to truck traffic

10-ft min. above finished grade sidewalks or from any platform or projection from which they might be reached

Grade

Fig. 230-8. Service-drop clearance to ground. (Sec. 230-24.)

Part **(b)** covers service-drop clearance to ground, as shown in Fig. 230-8. Where mast-type service risers are provided, the new clearances in Sec. 230-24(b) will have to be considered by the installer.

Part **(c)** is intended to provide the clearance specified, to prevent mechanical damage to and accidental contact with service conductors (Figs. 230-9 and 230-10). The clearances required in Secs. 230-24, 230-26, and 230-29 are based on safety-to-life considerations in that wires are required to be kept a reasonable distance from people who stand, reach, walk, or drive under service-drop conductors.

230-28. Service Masts as Supports. Figure 230-11 illustrates this rule.

230-30. Insulation. The exceptions to Secs. 230-30 and 230-40(a) clarify the use of aluminum, copper-clad aluminum, and bare copper conductors used as grounded conductors inservice laterals and service-entrance conductors (Fig. 230-12).

For service lateral conductors (underground service), an individual grounded conductor (such as a grounded neutral) of aluminum or copper-clad aluminum without insulation or covering may *not* be used in raceway underground. A bare copper neutral may be used—in raceway, in a cable assembly, or even directly buried in soil where local experience establishes that soil conditions do not attack copper.

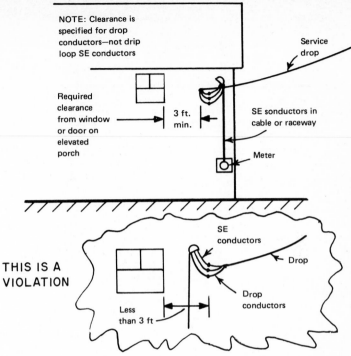

NOTE: Clearance is specified for drop conductors—not drip loop SE conductors

Service drop

Required clearance from window or door on elevated porch

3 ft. min.

SE sonductors in cable or raceway

Meter

THIS IS A VIOLATION

SE conductors

Drop

Drop conductors

Less than 3 ft

Fig. 230-9. Drop conductors must have clearance from building openings. (Sec. 230-24.)

The way this rule was worded in the 1975 **NE Code**, an individual *bare* aluminum neutral (along with individual insulated aluminum phase legs) of an underground service lateral appeared to be permitted if the circuit was installed in conduit or other raceway, and that interpretation was common. The wording of part **(d)** of the Exception permits an aluminum

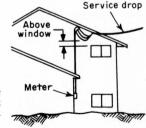

Fig. 230-10. Drop conductors above top level of a window or door do not require 3-ft horizontal clearance. (Sec. 230-24.)

Service drop

Above window

Meter

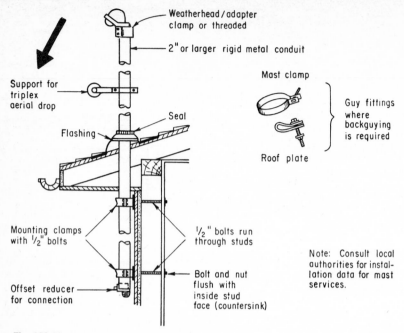

Weatherhead/adapter
clamp or threaded

2" or larger rigid metal conduit

Mast clamp

Support for
triplex
aerial drop

Guy fittings
where
backguying
is required

Seal

Flashing

Roof plate

Mounting clamps
with 1/2" bolts

1/2" bolts run
through studs

Note: Consult local
authorities for instal-
lation data for mast
services.

Bolt and nut
flush with
inside stud
face (countersink)

Offset reducer
for connection

Fig. 230-11. Service mast must provide adequate support for connecting drop conductors.
(Sec. 230-28.)

grounded conductor of an underground service lateral to be without
individual insulation or covering "when part of a cable assembly
approved for the purpose" where the cable is directly buried or run in a
raceway. Of course, a lateral made up of individual insulated phase legs
and an *insulated* neutral is acceptable in underground conduit or raceway
(Fig. 230-13).

230-40. Insulation of Service-Entrance Conductors.   The same change in
wording has been made in part **d** of the Exception in Sec. 230-40(a) as
described above for Sec. 230-30. In this section, the reference is to
"service-entrance conductors" instead of "service lateral conductors."
But, again, a bare *individual* aluminum or copper-clad aluminum
grounded conductor (grounded neutral or grounded phase leg) may not
be used in raceway or for direct burial. Any such bare conductor is
acceptable *only* when enclosed in an approved, jacketed cable assembly—
whether installed as a direct burial cable or in a raceway.

230-41. Size and Rating.   Sizing of service-entrance conductors involves
the same type of step-by-step procedure as set forth for sizing feeders
covered in Art. 220. A set of service-entrance conductors is sized just as if
it were a feeder. In general, the service-entrance conductors must have a

Ground

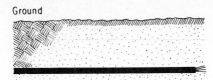

INSULATED PHASE CONDUCTORS and a bare copper neutral for an underground service lateral in buried raceway. Note: A bare aluminum or copper-clad aluminum neutral could be used here when part of a moisture- and fungus-resistant cable.

Ground

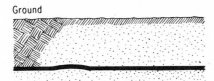

BARE COPPER NEUTRAL in a direct-buried cable assembly with moisture- and fungus-resistant outer covering. Note: A bare aluminum or copper-clad aluminum could be used like this, but it must be within the same type of cable assembly.

Ground

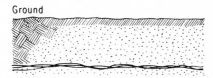

TYPE USE PHASE CONDUCTORS and a bare copper neutral directly buried where soil conditions are suitable for the bare copper.

Fig. 230-12. Sections 230-30 and 230-40(a) permit neutrals for service conductors. (Secs. 230-30 and 230-40.)

minimum current-carrying capacity sufficient to handle the total lighting and power load served. Where the Code gives demand factors to use or allows the use of acceptable demand factors based on sound engineering determination of less than 100 percent demand requirement, the lighting and power loads may be modified.

From the analysis and calculations given in the feeder circuit section, a total power and lighting load can be developed to use in sizing service-entrance conductors. Of course, where separate power and lighting services are used, the sizing procedure should be divided into two separate procedures.

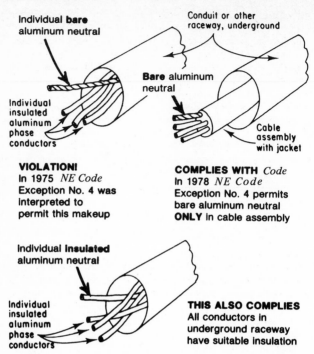

Fig. 230-13. Underground bare aluminum grounded leg must always be in a cable assembly. (Sec. 230-30.)

When a total load has been established for the service-entrance conductors, the required current-carrying capacity is easily determined by dividing the total load in kilovoltamperes (or killowatts with proper correction for power factor or the load) by the voltage of the service.

From the required current rating of conductors, the required size of conductors is determined. Sizing of the service neutral is the same as for feeders. Although suitably insulated conductors must be used for the phase conductors of service-entrance feeders, the NE Code does permit use of bare grounded conductors (such as neutrals) under the conditions covered in Secs. 230-30 and 230-40(a).

An extremely important element of service design is that of fault consideration. Service busway and other service conductor arrangements must be sized and designed to assure safe application with the service disconnect and protection. That is, service conductors must be capable of withstanding the let-through thermal and magnetic stresses on a fault.

After calculating the required circuits for all the loads in the electrical system, the next step is to determine the minimum required size of service-entrance conductors to supply the entire connected load. The NE

Code procedure for sizing SE conductors is the same as sizing feeder conductors for the entire load—as set forth in Sec. 220-10. Basically, the service "feeder" capacity must be not less than the sum of the loads on the branch circuits for the different applications.

The *general lighting load* is subject to demand factors from Table 220-11, which takes into account the fact that simultaneous operation of all branch-circuit loads, or even a large part of them, is highly unlikely. Thus, feeder capacity does not have to equal the connected load. The other provisions of Art. 220 are then factored in.

Part **(b)** of Sec. 230-41 makes a 100-A service conductor ampacity a mandatory minimum if the system supplied is a one-family dwelling with more than five 2-wire branch circuits (or the equivalent of that for multiwire circuits) or if a one-family dwelling has an initial computed load of 10,000 W. Now that three 20-A small appliance branch circuits are required in a single-family dwelling, the average new home will need a 100-A, 3-wire service, because, even without *electric* cooking, heating, drying, or water heating appliances more than five 2-wire branch circuits will be installed.

230-43. Wiring Methods for 600 Volts or Less. The list of acceptable wiring methods for running service-entrance conductors does not include flexible metallic conduit (Greenfield) or liquidtight flexible metal-lic conduit. Although such raceways were permitted under previous NEC editions if a bonding jumper was used to assure ground continuity between the ends of the flex, those raceways are no longer permitted to enclose service-entrance conductors, such as to provide flexible routing around a pipe or other obstruction—as shown in Fig. 230-14.

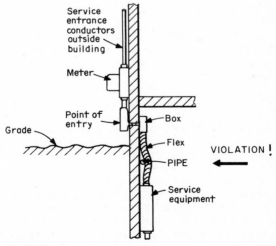

Fig. 230-14. Flex may not be used as a service raceway. (Sec. 230-43.)

230-44. Conductors Considered Outside of Building.   Conductors in conduit or duct enclosed by concrete or brick not less than 2 in. thick are considered to be outside the building, even through they are actually run within the building. Figure 230-15 shows how a service conduit was encased within a building so that the conductors are considered as entering the building right at the service protection and disconnect where the conductors emerge from the concrete, to satisfy the rule of Sec. 230-72(c), which requires the service disconnect to be as close as possible to the point where the SE conductors enter the building. Figure 230-16 shows an actual case of this application, where forms were hung around the service conduit and then filled with concrete to form the required case.

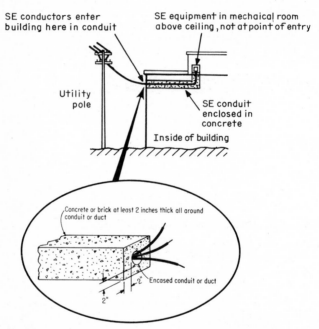

Fig. 230-15. Encasement of service raceway can serve to satisfy Sec. 230-72(c). (Sec. 230-44.)

230-45. Separate Enclosures.   This section permits two to six disconnecting means to be supplied from a single service drop or lateral where each disconnect supplies a separate load (Fig. 230-17). Section 230-2, Exception No. 3 recognizes the use of, say, six 400-A, individually metered sets of service-entrance conductors to a multiple-occupancy

Fig. 230-16. Top photo shows service conduit carried above suspended ceiling, without the SE disconnect located at the point of entry. When conduit was concrete-encased, the service conductors then "enter" the building at the SE disconnect—where they emerge from the concrete. Service conduit enters building at lower left and turns up into SE disconnect (right) in roof electrical room.

FOR SINGLE-OCCUPANCY BUILDINGS
SUCH AS FACTORIES, SCHOOLS AND STORES
OR FOR MULTIPLE-OCCUPANCY BUILDINGS

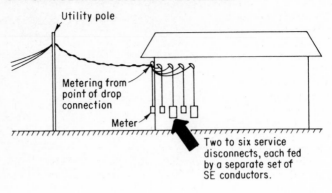

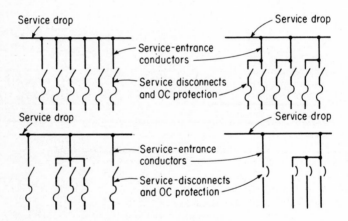

From two to six separate sets of service-entrance conductors
may be supplied by a single service drop for either single- or multiple-occupancy buildings. Disconnects can be of same or different ratings, and each set of service-entrance conductors can be
installed using any approved wiring method. This sketch shows

Fig. 230-17. Tapping sets of service-entrance conductors from one drop (or
lateral). (Sec. 230-45.)

building in lieu of a single main 2,500-A service. Section 230-45 recognizes the use of up to six subdivided loads extending from a single drop or lateral in a *single-occupancy* as well as multi-occupancy building. Where single metering is required, doughnut-type CTs could be installed at the service drop.

The real importance of this rule is to eliminate the need for "paralleling" conductors of large-capacity services, as widely required by inspection authorities to satisfy old Sec. 230-2 of previous editions of the NEC. Refer to Sec 230-2.

This same approach could be used in subdividing services into smaller load blocks to avoid the use of the equipment ground-fault circuit protection required by Sec. 230-95.

This rule can also facilitate expansion of an existing service. Where less than six sets of service-entrance conductors were used initially, one or more additional sets can be installed subsequently without completely replacing the original service. Of course, metering considerations will affect the layout.

It should be noted that this NE Code permission to use up to six sets of service-entrance conductors applies to single-occupancy buildings as well as multiple-occupancy buildings.

230-46. Unspliced Conductors.   For Exception No. 3, an underground service conduit usually terminates at the inside of the building wall unless the building has no basement. A metal conduit or a service cable may terminate at this point or may be run directly to the service equipment. From the terminal box, the conductors are run to the service equipment in rigid metal conduit or electrical metallic tubing or in an auxiliary gutter, and may terminate at any suitable point behind the switchboard.

Figure 230-18 shows the conditions of Exception No. 3 and Exception No. 4. The sketch on the right shows a form of construction sometimes employed where the inside meter of an existing installation is removed and an outdoor meter is installed. New service-entrance conductors are connected to the service drop and are carried down to a meter fitting in raceway or cable. From the meter, the outside service conductors return in the raceway or cable and are spliced to the old service-entrance conductors. These splices are permitted by Exception No. 4.

230-47. Other Conductors in Raceway or Cable.   Although the basic rule permits only service-entrance conductors to be used in a service raceway, exceptions do recognize the use of grounding conductors in service raceway and also permit conductors for a time switch if overcurrent protection is provided for the conductors, as shown in Fig. 230-19.

230-48. Raceway Seal.   Figure 230-20 indicates that Sec. 300-5(g) may apply to underground service conduits.

230-49. Protection Against Damage—Underground.   Service conductors—whether directly buried cables, conductors in metal conduit, conductors in nonmetallic conduit, or conductors in EMT—must comply with Sec. 300-5 for protection against physical damage (Fig. 230-21).

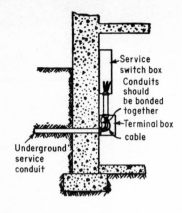

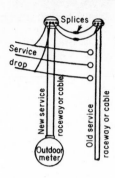

Exception No. 3 Terminal box used at the end of an underground service conduit.

Exception No. 4 Splices in service-entrance conductors where an outdoor meter is installed in place of an indoor meter for an existing installation.

Fig. 230-18. Permitted splices in service-entrance conductors. (Sec. 230-46.)

230-53. Raceways to Drain.   Service-entrance conductors in EMT or rigid conduit must be made raintight, using raintight raceway fittings, and must be equipped with a drain hole in the service ell at the bottom of the run or must be otherwise provided with a means of draining off condensation (Fig. 230-22).

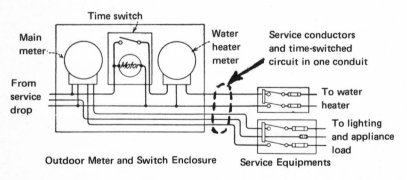

NOTE: Time-switch conductors may be hooked up so they are in same conduit as service conductors but the time-switch conductors must be supplied with over current protection.

Fig. 230-19. A time switch with its control circuit connected on the supply side of the service equipment. (Sec. 230-47.)

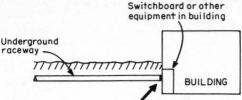

Service raceways must be sealed or plugged at either or both
ends if moisture could contact live parts

Fig. 230-20. Service raceways may have to be sealed. (Sec. 230-48.)

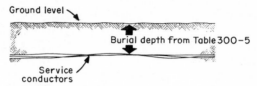

Fig. 230-21. Protecting underground service conductors.
(Sec. 230-49.)

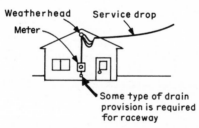

Fig. 230-22. Outdoor service raceway must be
raintight *and* drained. (Sec. 230-53.)

230-54. Connections at Service Head.

When rigid metal conduit, IMC, or EMT are used for a service, the raceway must be provided with a service head (or weather head). Figure 230-23 shows details of service-head installation.

Part **(c)** of this section requires that service heads be located above the service-drop attachment. Although this arrangement alone will not always prevent water from entering service raceways and equipment, such an arrangement will solve most of the water-entrance problems. An exception to this rule permits a service head to be located not more than 24 in. from the service-drop termination where it is found that it is impractical for the service head to be located above the service-drop

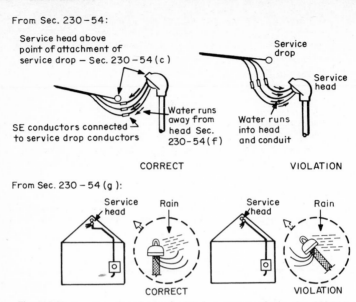

From Sec. 230–54:

Service head above
point of attachment of
service drop – Sec. 230–54(c)

SE conductors connected
to service drop conductors

Water runs
away from
head Sec.
230-54(f)

Service
drop

Service
head

Water runs
into head
and conduit

CORRECT   VIOLATION

From Sec. 230 – 54 (g):

Service
head   Rain

Service
head   Rain

CORRECT   VIOLATION

Fig. 230-23. Location of service head minimizes entrance of rain. (Sec. 230-54.)

termination. In such cases a *mechanical connector* is required at the lowest point in the drip loop to prevent siphoning. This Exception will permit the Code-enforcing authority to handle hardship cases that may occur.

The intent of part **(g)** is to require use of connections of conductor arrangements, both at the pole and at the service, so that water will not enter connections and siphon under head pressure into service raceways or equipment.

Where no service head is used at the upper end of a service cable, the cable should be bent over so that the individual conductors leaving the cable will extend in a downward direction and the end of the cable should be carefully taped and painted to exclude moisture.

A sketch in Fig. 230-23 shows a service cable terminating in a gooseneck above the service drop. The connections to the conductors of the service drop tend to hold the gooseneck in shape.

Where the pole connection is higher than the connection of the service-entrance conductors at the service head, the connections at the pole should be made in such a manner that moisture will not enter the conductor. In many cases the connection at the utility pole is higher than the connection at the building. Any stranded service-drop conductors act as a hose and the moisture is forced up through the service-entrance conductors by this head pressure and down into the meter or service equipment.

230-70. General. Switches used for service-entrance disconnecting means must be approved for use as service equipment. This rule is meant to require that the switch be listed and labeled by the UL as suitable for service entrance. Check manufacturers' catalogs on this.

230-71. Maximum Number of Disconnects. Service-entrance conductors must be equipped with a readily accessible means of disconnecting the conductors from their source of supply.

The disconnect means for the SE conductors may consist of not more than six switches or six circuit breakers, in a common enclosure or individual enclosures, located either inside or outside the building wall as close as possible to the point at which the conductors enter the building (Fig. 230-24).

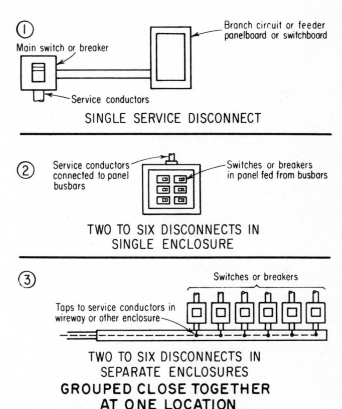

Fig. 230-24. The three basic ways to provide service disconnect means. (Sec. 230-71.)

The intent of this section is to limit to six operations of the hand the disconnection of all conductors of the service. The limitation is applicable to all the service disconnecting means located in one place or "grouped" as required in Sec. 230-72. It does not include the "separate" services for fire pumps, emergency lighting, etc., which are recognized in Sec. 230-2 as being separate services for specific purposes.

For other than residential application, a power panel (not a lighting and appliance panel, as described in Sec. 384-14) containing up to six

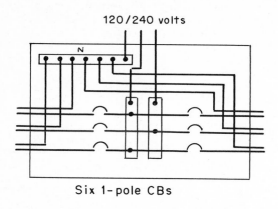

120/240 volts

Six 1-pole CBs

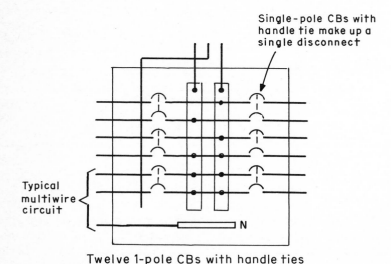

Single-pole CBs with handle tie make up a single disconnect

Typical multiwire circuit

Twelve 1-pole CBs with handle ties

Fig. 230-25. Both of these arrangements constitute six disconnects. (Sec. 230-71.)

switches or circuit breakers may be used as service disconnect. A lighting
and appliance panel used as service equipment in individual residential
occupancies may have up to six main breakers or fused switches. However, a lighting and appliance panel used as service equipment for
commercial or industrial buildings (i.e., any nonresidential use) must
have not more than two main devices—with the sum of their ratings not
greater than the panel bus rating.

Part **(b)** notes that single-pole switches or circuit breakers equipped
with handle ties may be used in groups as single disconnects for multiwire
circuits, simultaneously providing overcurrent protection for the service
(Fig. 230-25). Multipole switches and circuit breakers may also be used as
single disconnects. The requirements of the **Code** are satisfied if all the
service-entrance conductors can be disconnected with no more than six
operations of the hand—regardless of whether each hand motion operates a single-pole unit, a multipole unit, or a group of single-pole units
with "handle ties" or a "master handle" controlled by a single hand
motion. Of course, a single main device for service disconnect and
overcurrent protection—such as a main CB or fused switch—gives better
protection to the service conductors.

It is important to note that from one to six switches (or circuit breakers)
may serve as the service disconnecting means for each class of service for
a building. For example, if a *single-occupancy* building has a 3-phase
service and a separate single-phase service, each such service may have
up to six disconnects (Fig. 230-26)

AS PERMITTED BY EXCEPTIONS TO SEC. 230-2

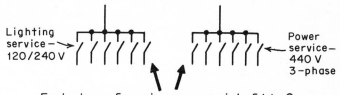

Lighting
service—
120/240 V

Power
service—
440 V
3-phase

Each class of service may consist of 1 to 6
fused switches or CBs in a common enclosure,
or a group of separate enclosures, grouped
together at a common location

Fig. 230-26. Each separate service may have up to six disconnect devices. (Sec.
230-71.)

The footnote to this section refers to Sec. 384-16(a), which requires a
higher degree of overcurrent protection for *lighting and appliance* branch-
circuit panelboards. Each such panelboard must be individually protected on the supply side by not more than two main circuit breakers or
two sets of fuses having a combined rating not greater than that of the

panelboard. Exception No. 2 to Sec. 384-16(a) eliminates the need for individual protection for a lighting and appliance branch-circuit panelboard where such panelboards are used as service-entrance equipment in an *individual residential occupancy*. Examples of these provisions are shown in illustrations in Sec. 384-16. It should be noted that these rules concern only a lighting and appliance branch-circuit panelboard, which is defined in Sec. 384-14 as a panelboard having more than 10 percent of its overcurrent devices rated 30 A or less, for which neutral connections are provided. Panelboards other than that type which are used as service equipment can still follow the basic six-switch rule.

230-72. Grouping of Disconnects.   The basic rule of part **(a)** requires that for a service disconnect arrangement of more than one disconnect—such as where two to six disconnect switches or CBs are used, as permitted by Sec. 230-71(a)—all the disconnects must be grouped together and not spread out at different locations. The basic idea is that anyone operating the two to six disconnects must be able to do it while standing at one location. Service conductors must be able to be readily disconnected from all loads at one place. And each of the individual disconnects must have lettering or a sign to tell what load it supplies (Fig. 230-27).

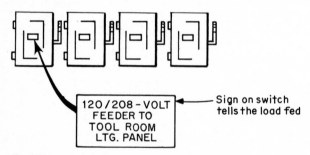

Fig. 230-27. Two to six disconnect switches or CBs must be grouped and *identified*. (Sec. 230-72.)

It should be noted that the disconnects for each service, as permitted by Sec. 230-2, have to be grouped. But all the groups for two or more services do not have to be installed at the same location.

The special or emergency service equipments permitted by Sec. 230-2 do not have to be grouped with the regular service equipment. It should also be noted that Sec. 700-6(c) requires emergency services to be widely separated from the other services, to prevent failure of both due to a single fault.

Exception No. 2 *permits* (note: it permits, it does *not require*) one of the two to six service disconnects to be located remote from the other disconnecting means that are grouped in accordance with the basic rule—PROVIDED THAT *the remote disconnect is used only to supply a water pump that is also intended to provide fire protection.* In a residence or other building that gets its water supply from a well, a spring, or a lake, the use of a remote disconnect for the water pump will afford improved reliability of the water supply for fire suppression in the event that fire or other faults disable the normal service equipment. And it will distinguish the water-pump disconnect from the other normal service disconnects, minimizing the chance that firefighters will unknowingly open the pump circuit when they routinely open service disconnects during a fire. This Exception ties into the rule of Sec. 230-72(b), which *requires* (not simply permits) remote installation of a fire-pump disconnect switch that is permitted to be tapped ahead of the one to six switches or CBs that constitute the normal service disconnecting means (see Sec. 230-82, Exception No. 5). The Exception provides remote installation of a *normal service disconnect* when it is used for the same purpose (water pump used for fire fighting) as the *emergency service disconnect* (fire pump) covered in Sec. 230-72(b). In both cases, remote installation of the pump disconnect isolates the critically important pump circuit from interruption or shutdown due to fire, arcing-fault burndown, or any other fault that might knock out the main (normal) service disconnects.

A wide variety of layouts can be made to satisfy the Code *permission* for remote installation of a disconnect switch or CB service as a *normal* service disconnect (one of a maximum of six) supplying a water pump. Figure 230-28 shows three typical arrangements that would basically provide the isolated fire-pump disconnect.

Part **(b)**, as noted above, makes it mandatory to install emergency disconnect devices where they would not be disabled or affected by any fault or violent electrical failure in the normal service equipment (Fig. 230-29). Figure 230-30 shows a service disconnect for emergency and exit lighting installed very close to the normal service switchboard. An equipment burndown or fire near the main switchboard might knock out the emergency circuit. And the tap for the switch, which is made in the switchboard ahead of the service main, is particularly susceptible to being opened by *an arcing failure in the board.* The switch should be 10 or 15 ft away from the board. And because the switchboard is fed from an outdoor transformer-mat layout directly outside the building, the tap to the safety switch would have greater reliability if it was made from the transformer secondary terminals rather than from the switchboard service terminals. Although the rule sets no specific distance of separation, remote locating of emergency disconnects is a mandatory Code rule.

Part **(c)** covers the place of installation of a service disconnect. The disconnecting means required for every set of service-entrance conductors must be located at a readily accessible point nearest to the point at which the service conductors enter the building, either on the inside or the outside of the building (Fig. 230-31). The service disconnect switch (or circuit breaker) is generally placed on the inside of the building as near as possible to the point at which the conductors come in.

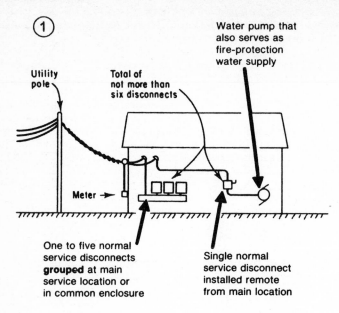

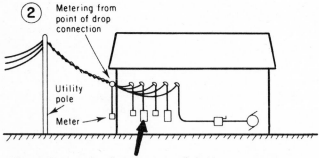

Fig. 230-28. Rule *permits* remote installation of one of two-to-six service disconnects to protect fire-pump circuits (typical layouts). (Sec. 230-72.)

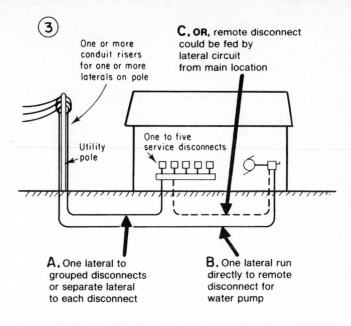

③

One or more
conduit risers
for one or more
laterals on pole

C. OR, remote disconnect
could be fed by
lateral circuit
from main location

One to five
service disconnects

Utility
pole

A. One lateral to
grouped disconnects
or separate lateral
to each disconnect

B. One lateral run
directly to remote
disconnect for
water pump

Fig. 230-28. (*Continued*)

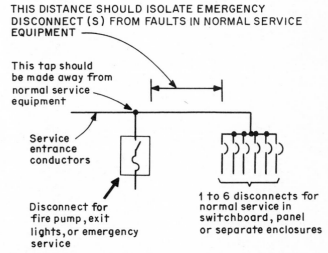

THIS DISTANCE SHOULD ISOLATE EMERGENCY
DISCONNECT (S) FROM FAULTS IN NORMAL SERVICE
EQUIPMENT

This tap should
be made away from
normal service
equipment

Service
entrance
conductors

Disconnect for
fire pump, exit
lights, or emergency
service

1 to 6 disconnects for
normal service in
switchboard, panel
or separate enclosures

Fig. 230-29. Emergency service disconnects must be isolated from faults in
normal SE equipment. (Sec. 230-72.)

Fig. 230-30. Emergency disconnect close to service switchboard and fed by tap from it could readily be disabled by fault in board. (Sec. 230-72.)

Although the Code does not set any maximum distance from the point of conductor entry to the service disconnect, various inspection agencies set maximum limits on this distance. For instance, service cable may not run within the building more than 18 in. from its point of entry to the point at which it enters the disconnect. Or service conductors in conduit must enter the disconnect within 10 ft of the point of entry. Or, as one agency requires, the disconnect must be within 10 ft of the point of entry, but overcurrent protection must be provided for the conductors right at the point at which they emerge from the wall into the building. The concern is to minimize the very real and proven potential hazard of having unprotected service conductors within the building. Faults in such unprotected service conductors must burn themselves clear and such application has caused fires and fatalities.

Part **(d)** applies to two specific applications of service disconnect for multiple-occupancy buildings—such as apartment houses, condominiums, town houses, office buildings, and shopping centers.

Multiple-occupancy buildings having individual occupancy above the

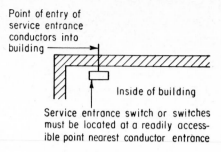

Point of entry of
service entrance
conductors into
building

Inside of building

Service entrance switch or switches
must be located at a readily accessible point nearest conductor entrance

GENERAL CONCEPT

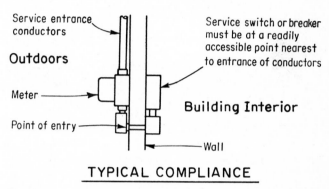

Service entrance
conductors

Outdoors

Service switch or breaker
must be at a readily
accessible point nearest
to entrance of conductors

Meter

Point of entry

Building Interior

Wall

TYPICAL COMPLIANCE

Fig. 230-31. Service disconnect must open current for any conductors within building. (Sec. 230-72.)

second floor shall have service equipment grouped in a common accessible place, and the disconnect means may consist of not more than six switches (or six CBs), as in Fig. 230-32.

Multiple-occupancy buildings that do not have individual occupancy above the second floor may have service conductors run to each occupancy. The service disconnecting means in each occupancy may then consist of not more than six switches (or six CBs) as shown in Fig. 230-33. Example B in that illustration could be a hotel with stores on the lower two floors. The hotel owner would represent an "occupant" who has occupancy on the lower floors and is the only occupant of the upper floors. Such a building would not have "individual" occupancy above the second floor.

The phrase "individual occupancy" means any space such as an office or apartment that is independent of any other occupancy in the building.

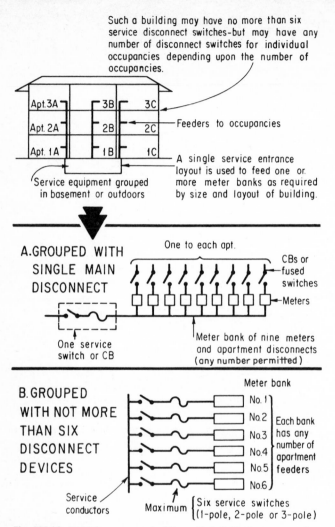

Such a building may have no more than six service disconnect switches-but may have any number of disconnect switches for individual occupancies depending upon the number of occupancies.

Apt. 3A   3B   3C
Apt. 2A   2B   2C   ── Feeders to occupancies
Apt. 1A   1B   1C   ── A single service entrance

Service equipment grouped in basement or outdoors

layout is used to feed one or more meter banks as required by size and layout of building.

A. GROUPED WITH SINGLE MAIN DISCONNECT

One to each apt.

CBs or fused switches

Meters

One service switch or CB

Meter bank of nine meters and apartment disconnects (any number permitted)

B. GROUPED WITH NOT MORE THAN SIX DISCONNECT DEVICES

Meter bank

No. 1
No. 2   Each bank
No. 3   has any
No. 4   number of
No. 5   apartment
No. 6   feeders

Service conductors

Maximum Six service switches (1-pole, 2-pole or 3-pole)

Fig. 230-32. Multiple-occupancy building with individual occupancy above the second floor. (Sec. 230-72.)

Generally each such space is supplied through a separate meter. Each apartment intended for use as living quarters by one family is an individual occupancy. Each apartment might be supplied through a separate meter, or all might be supplied through one meter.

It should be noted that the access for each occupant as required by the

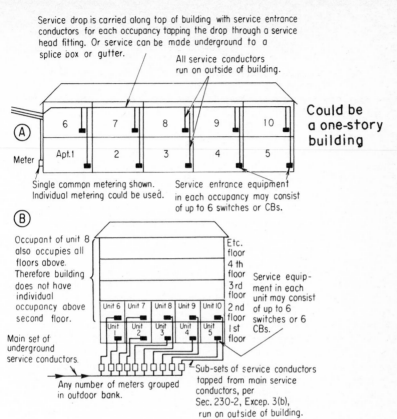

Service drop is carried along top of building with service entrance
conductors for each occupancy tapping the drop through a service
head fitting. Or service can be made underground to a
splice box or gutter.

All service conductors
run on outside of building.

Could be
a one-story
building

Single common metering shown.
Individual metering could be used.

Service entrance equipment
in each occupancy may consist
of up to 6 switches or CBs.

Occupant of unit 8
also occupies all
floors above.
Therefore building
does not have
individual
occupancy above
second floor.

Etc.
floor
4 th
floor
3rd
floor
2 nd
floor
I st
floor

Service equip-
ment in each
unit may consist
of up to 6
switches or 6
CBs.

Main set of
underground
service conductors.

Any number of meters grouped
in outdoor bank.

Sub-sets of service conductors
tapped from main service
conductors, per
Sec. 230-2, Excep. 3(b),
run on outside of building.

Fig. 230-33. Service to buildings without individual occupancy above second floor. (Sec.
230-72.)

first sentence of paragraph **(d)** would not apply where the building was
under the management of a building superintendent or the equivalent
and where electrical service and maintenance were furnished. See Sec.
240-24(b), Exception.

Where there *is* individual occupancy above the second floor, the
disconnecting means must be located in a commonly accessible place, and
must not consist of more than six normal service disconnects.

In order to comply with Sec. 230-72(c), the conductors should either be
run on the outside of the building to each occupancy or, if run inside the
building, be encased in 2 in. of concrete or masonry in accordance with
Sec. 230-44. In either case the service equipment should be located
"nearest to the entrance of the conductors inside the building," and each
occupant would have "access to his disconnecting means."

Any desired number of sets of service-entrance conductors may be tapped from the service drop or lateral, or two or more subsets of service-entrance conductors may be tapped from a single set of main service conductors.

230-75. Disconnection of Grounded Conductor.   In this section the other means for disconnecting the grounded conductor from the interior wiring may be a screw or bolted lug on the neutral terminal block. The grounded conductor must not be run straight through the service equipment enclosure with no means of disconnection.

230-76. Manually or Power Operable.   Any switch or CB used for service disconnect must be manually operable. In addition to manual operation, the switch may have provision for electrical operation—such as for remote control of the switch, provided it can be manually operated to the open or "OFF" position.

Code wording clearly indicates that an electrically operated breaker with a mechanical trip button which will open the breaker even if the supply power is dead is suitable for use as a service disconnect. The manually operated trip button assures that the breaker "can be opened by hand." To provide manual closing of electrically operated circuit breakers, manufacturers provide emergency manual handles as standard accessories. Thus such breaker mechanisms can be both closed and opened manually if operating power is not available.

Local requirements on the use of electrically operated service disconnects should be considered in selecting such devices.

230-78. Externally Operable.   If a switch can be opened and closed without exposing the operator to contact with live parts, it is an externally operable switch, even through access to the switch handle requires opening the door of a cabinet. The Exception pertains to electrically operated switches and circuit breakers, and it explains that such switches or CBs are required to be externally operable only to the *open* position, and not necessarily to the *closed* position (Fig. 230-34).

230-79. Rating of Disconnect.   Aside from the limited conditions covered in parts **(a)** and **(b)**, this section requires that service equipment (in general) shall have a rating not less than 60 A, applicable to both fusible and CB equipment. Part **(c)** requires 100-A minimum rating of a single switch or CB used in the service disconnect for any "one-family dwelling" with an *initial* load of 10 kW or more or where the *initial* installation contains more than *five 2-wire* branch circuits. It should be noted that the rule applies to one-family houses only, because of the definition of "one-family dwelling" as given in Art. 100. It does not apply to apartments or similar dwelling units that are in two-family or multifamily dwellings.

If the demand on a total connected load, as calculated from Sec. 220-10 through Sec. 220-21, is 10 kW or more, a 100-A service disconnect, as well as 100-A rated service-entrance conductors [Sec. 230-41(b) (2)], must be used. Any one-family house with an electric range rated 8¾ kW must always have a 100-A rated disconnect (or service equipment) because

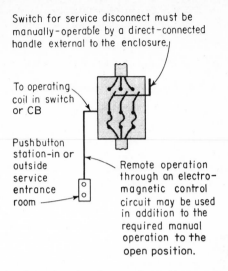

Switch for service disconnect must be
manually-operable by a direct-connected
handle external to the enclosure.

To operating
coil in switch
or CB

Pushbutton
station-in or
outside
service
entrance
room

Remote operation
through an electro-
magnetic control
circuit may be used
in addition to the
required manual
operation to the
open position.

Note: Some local codes require both manual and
electrical means of operation.

Fig. 230-34. Manual operation of any service switch is required. (Sec. 230-78.)

such a range is a demand load of 8 kW and the two required 20-A kitchen appliance circuits come to a demand load of 3,000 W [Sec. 220-16(a)] at 100 percent from Table 220-11—and the 8 kW plus 3 kW exceeds the 10-kW level at which a minimum 100-A rated service is required.

If a 100-A service is used, the demand load may be as high as 23 kW. By using the optional service calculations of Table 220-30, a 23-kW demand load is obtained from a connected load of 42.5 kW. This shows the effect of diversity on large-capacity installations.

230-80. Combined Rating of Disconnects.   Figure 230-35 shows an application of this rule, based on determining what rating of a single disconnect would be required *if* a single disconnect were used instead of multiple ones. It should be noted that the sum of ratings above 400 A does comply with the rule of this section and with Exception No. 3 of Sec. 230-90(a) even though the 400-A service-entrance conductors could be heavily overloaded. Exception No. 3 exempts this type of layout from the need to protect the conductors at their rated ampacity, as required in the basic rule of Sec. 230-90. The Code assumes that the 400-A rating of the service-entrance conductors was carefully calculated from Art. 220 to be adequate for the maximum sum of the demand loads fed by the five disconnects shown in the layout.

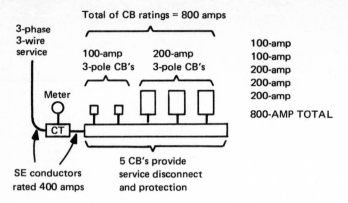

Total of CB ratings = 800 amps

3-phase
3-wire
service

100-amp   200-amp
3-pole CB's   3-pole CB's

Meter

CT

SE conductors
rated 400 amps

5 CB's provide
service disconnect
and protection

100-amp
100-amp
200-amp
200-amp
200-amp

800-AMP TOTAL

From Art. 220 (Secs. 220-10 through 220-21), calculation of demand load
indicated that a single disconnect for this service must be rated at least 400 amps.
The rating of multiple disconnects must total at least that value.

Fig. 230-35. Multiple disconnects must have their sum of ratings at least equal to the
minimum rating of a single disconnect. (Sec. 230-80.)

230-82. Equipment Connected to the Supply Side of Service Disconnect.   Service fuses, high-impedance shunt circuits (such as potential
coils of meters, etc.), supply conductors for time switches, surge-protective capacitors, instrument transformers, lightning arresters and circuits
for emergency systems, fire pump equipment, and fire and sprinkler
alarms may be connected on the supply side of the disconnecting means.
Emergency-lighting circuits, surge-protective capacitors, and fire alarm
and other protective signaling circuits, when placed ahead of the regular
service disconnecting means, must have separate disconnects and overcurrent protection.

Meters can be connected on the supply side of the service disconnecting means and overcurrent protective devices if the meters are connected
to service not in excess of 600 V where the grounded conductor bonds
the meter cases and enclosures to the grounding electrode (Fig. 230-36).

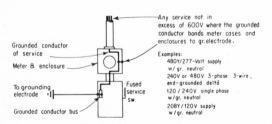

Grounded conductor
of service

Meter & enclosure

To grounding
electrode

Grounded conductor bus

Fused
service
sw.

Any service not in
excess of 600V where the grounded
conductor bonds meter cases and
enclosures to gr. electrode.

Examples:
    480Y/277-Volt supply
    w/gr. neutral
    240V or 480V 3-phase 3-wire,
    end-grounded delta
    120/240V single phase
    w/gr. neutral
    208Y/120V supply
    w/gr. neutral

Fig. 230-36. (Sec. 230-82.)

230-84. More Than One Building or Other Structure. For a group of buildings under single management, disconnect means must be provided for each building, as in Fig. 230-37. This rule requires that the conductors supplying each building in the group be provided with a means for disconnecting all ungrounded conductors from the supply. Because this is covered under Art. 230, it is usually interpreted to permit the disconnect for each building or structure to be the same kind as permitted for a service disconnect—that is, up to six switches or CBs, as covered in Sec. 230-71.

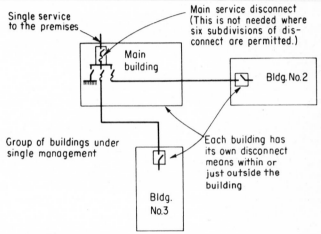

Fig. 230-37. Each building must have its own disconnect means. (Sec. 230-84.)

The wording of this rule has often caused confusion in applying the rule. Some authorities permit the use of the feeder switch in the main building as the only disconnect for each feeder to the outlying buildings, provided the switches in the main building are accessible to the occupants of the outlying buildings. There is nothing in the present wording of this rule to clearly require that the disconnect for any outbuilding be located within or adjacent to the building itself. However, many inspection and engineering authorities prefer a readily accessible feeder disconnect within each outlying building, as shown regardless of distance from main building.

Part **(b)** requires that the disconnect for each building of a multibuilding layout must be recognized for service use—usually that means that the disconnect means for each building must be listed by UL, or another national test lab, as suitable for service equipment. The Exception waives that requirement for wiring device switches (snap switches) used for on–off control of lighting or other loads under the conditions noted.

230-90. (Overcurrent Protection) Where Required. The intent in paragraph **(a)** is to assure that the overcurrent protection required in the service-entrance equipment protects the service-entrance conductors from "overload." It is obvious that these overcurrent devices cannot provide "fault" protection for the service-entrance conductors if the fault occurs in the service-entrance conductors, but can protect them from overload where so selected as to have proper rating. Conductors on the load side of the service equipment are considered as feeders or branch circuits and are required by the Code to be protected as described in Arts. 210, 215, and 240.

Each ungrounded service-entrance conductor must be protected by an overcurrent device in series with the conductor (Fig. 230-38). The overcurrent device must have a rating or setting not higher than the allowable current capacity of the conductor, with the Exceptions noted.

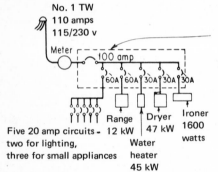

No. 1 TW
110 amps
115/230 v
Meter
100 amp
60A 60A 30A 30A 30A
Range   Dryer   Ironer
Five 20 amp circuits - 12 kW | 47 kW | 1600
two for lighting,   Water   watts
three for small appliances heater
                            45 kW

Service equipment with one overall 100-amp main disconnect and fuse. Current through service conductors limited to 100 amperes. Without a main disconnect and overcurrent device, current is not limited and current over 110 amps could flow. Sum of protective devices is 210 amps per hot leg.

NOTE: Service-entrance conductors must be selected with adequate ampacity for the calculated service demand load, from Secs. 220-10 through 220-21.

Fig. 230-38. Single main service protection must not exceed conductor ampacity (or may be next higher rated device above conductor ampacity). (Sec. 230-90.)

Exception No. 1. If the service supplies one motor in addition to other load (such as lighting and heating), the overcurrent device may be rated or set in accordance with the required protection for a branch circuit supplying the one motor (Sec. 430-52) plus the other load, as shown in Fig. 230-39. Use of 175-A fuses where the calculation calls for 170 A conforms to Exception No. 2 of Sec. 230-90—next higher standard rating of fuse (Sec. 240-6). For motor branch circuits and feeders, Arts. 220 and 430 permit the use of overcurrent devices having ratings or settings higher than the capacities of the conductors. Article 230 makes similar provisions for services where the service supplies a motor load or a combination load of both motors and other loads.

If the service supplies two or more motors as well as other load, then

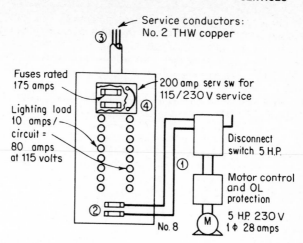

Service conductors:
No. 2 THW copper

Fuses rated
175 amps

200 amp serv sw for
115/230 V service

Lighting load
10 amps /
circuit =
80 amps
at 115 volts

Disconnect
switch 5 H.P.

Motor control
and OL
protection

5 H.P. 230 V
1 φ 28 amps

No. 8

1. Size of motor branch circuit conductors: 125% x 28 amps equals 35 amps. This requires No. 8's.

2. Size of motor branch circuit fuses: 300% x 28 amps equals 84 amps. This requires maximum fuse size of 90 amps. Smaller fuses, such as time-delay type, may be used.

3. Size of service entrance conductors must be adequate for a load of 125% x 28 amps plus 80 amps (lighting load) or 115 amps.

4. Size of main fuses: 90 amps (from 2 above) plus 80 amps equals 170 amps. This requires maximum fuse size of 175 amps. Again, smaller fuses may and should be used where possible to improve the overload protection on the circuit conductors.

Fig. 230-39. Service protection for lighting plus motor load. (Sec. 230-90.)

the overcurrent protection must be rated in accordance with the required protection for a feeder supplying several motors plus the other load (Sec. 430-63). Or if the service supplies only a multimotor load (with no other load fed), then Sec. 430-62 sets the maximum permitted rating of overcurrent protection.

Exception No. 3. Not more than six CBs or six sets of fuses may serve as overcurrent protection for the service-entrance conductors even though the sum of the ratings of the overcurrent devices is in excess of the ampacity of the service conductors supplying the devices—as illustrated in Fig. 230-40. The grouping of single-pole CBs as multipole devices, as permitted for disconnect means, may also apply to overcurrent protection. And a set of fuses is all the fuses required to protect the ungrounded service-entrance conductors.

This Exception ties into Sec. 230-80. Service conductors are sized for the *total* maximum demand load—applying permitted demand factors

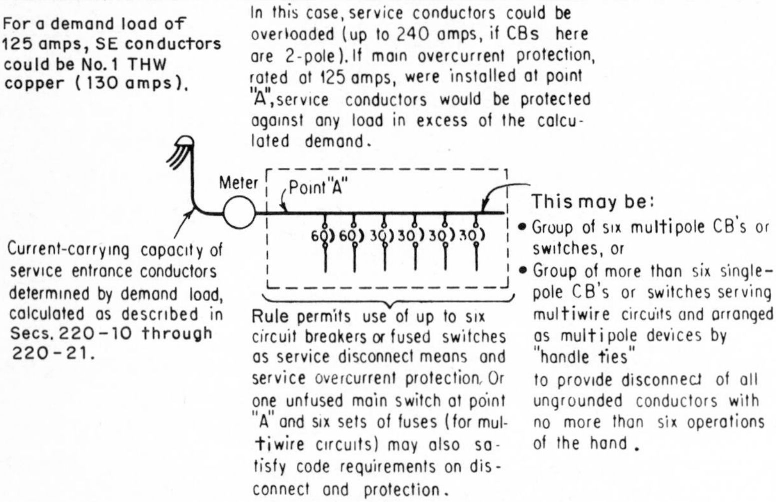

For a demand load of 125 amps, SE conductors could be No. 1 THW copper (130 amps).

In this case, service conductors could be overloaded (up to 240 amps, if CBs here are 2-pole). If main overcurrent protection, rated at 125 amps, were installed at point "A", service conductors would be protected against any load in excess of the calculated demand.

Meter   Point "A"

Current-carrying capacity of service entrance conductors determined by demand load, calculated as described in Secs. 220-10 through 220-21.

Rule permits use of up to six circuit breakers or fused switches as service disconnect means and service overcurrent protection. Or one unfused main switch at point "A" and six sets of fuses (for multiwire circuits) may also satisfy code requirements on disconnect and protection.

This may be:
• Group of six multipole CB's or switches, or
• Group of more than six single-pole CB's or switches serving multiwire circuits and arranged as multipole devices by "handle ties" to provide disconnect of all ungrounded conductors with no more than six operations of the hand.

Fig. 230-40. With six subdivisions of protection, conductors could be overloaded. (Sec. 230-90.)

from Table 220-11. Then each of the two to six feeders fed by the SE conductors is also sized from Art. 220 based on the load fed by each feeder. When those feeders are given overcurrent protection in accordance with their ampacities, it is frequently found that the sum of those overcurrent devices is greater than the ampacity of the SE conductors which were sized by applying the applicable demand factors to the total connected load of all the feeders. Exception No. 3 recognizes that possibility as acceptable even though it departs from the rule in the first sentence of Sec. 230-90(a). The assumption is that if calculation of demand load for the SE conductors is correctly made, there will be no overloading of those conductors because the diversity of feeder loads (some loads "on," some "off") will be adequate to limit load on the SE conductors.

Assume that the load of a building computed in accordance with Art. 220 is 255 A. Under Sec. 240-3, Exception No. 1, 300-A fuses or a 300-A CB may be considered as the proper-size overcurrent protection for service conductors rated between 255 and 300 A if a single service disconnect is used.

If the load is separated in such a manner that six 70-A CBs could be used instead of a single service disconnect means, total rating of the CBs would be greater than the ampacity of the service-entrance conductors. And that would be acceptable.

Exception No. 4 must be correlated to Sec. 230-72(d). Exception No. 5 is shown in Fig. 230-41 and is intended to prevent opening of the fire pump circuit on any overload up to and including stalling or even seizing of the pump motor. Because the conductors are "outside the building,"

If the service conductors to the fire-pump
room enter the fire-pump service equipment
directly from the outside or if they are
encased in 2-in.-thick concrete . . .

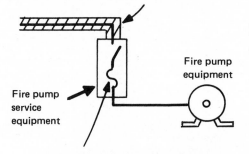

Fire pump
equipment

. . . they are judged to be
"outside of the building,"
and . . .

Fire pump
service
equipment

. . . the overcurrent protective device (fuses
or CB) must be rated or set to carry the
motor locked-rotor current indefinitely.

Fig. 230-41. (Sec. 230-90.)

operating overload is no hazard; and, under fire conditions, the pump must have no prohibition on its operation. It is better to lose the motor than attempt to protect it against overload when it is needed.

Part **(c)** permits overcurrent protection for a feeder from one building to another to be at the supply end of the circuit in the building where the circuit originates (Fig. 230-42).

230-95. Ground-Fault Protection of Equipment.   Fuses and CBs applied as described in the previous section on "Overcurrent Protection," are sized to protect conductors in accordance with their current-carrying capacities. The function of a fuse or CB is to open the circuit if current exceeds the rating of the protective device. This excessive current might be caused by operating overload, by a ground fault, or by a short circuit. Thus, a 1,000-A fuse will blow if current in excess of that value flows over the circuit. It will blow early on heavy overcurrent and later on low overcurrents. But it will blow, and the circuit and equipment will be protected against the damage of the overcurrent. But, there is another type of fault condition which is very common in grounded systems and will not be cleared by conventional overcurrent devices. That is the

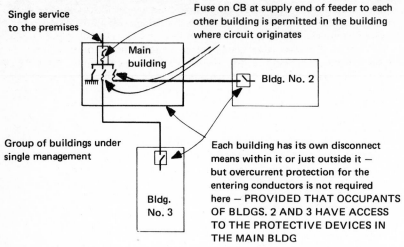

Single service
to the premises

Fuse on CB at supply end of feeder to each
other building is permitted in the building
where circuit originates

Main
building

Bldg. No. 2

Group of buildings under
single management

Bldg.
No. 3

Each building has its own disconnect
means within it or just outside it —
but overcurrent protection for the
entering conductors is not required
here — PROVIDED THAT OCCUPANTS
OF BLDGS. 2 AND 3 HAVE ACCESS
TO THE PROTECTIVE DEVICES IN
THE MAIN BLDG

Fig. 230-42. Overcurrent protection for multibuilding layout. (Sec. 230-90.)

phase-to-ground fault (usually arcing) which has a current value less than
the rating of the overcurrent device.

On any high-capacity feeder, a line-to-ground fault (i.e., a fault from a
phase conductor to a conduit, to a junction box, or to some other metallic
equipment enclosure) can and frequently does draw current of a value
less than the rating or setting of the circuit protective device. For
instance, a 500-A ground fault on a 2,000-A protective device which has
only a 1,200-A load will not be cleared by the device. If such a fault is a
"bolted" line-to-ground fault, a highly unlikely fault, there will be a
certain amount of heat generated by the I^2R effect of the current; but
this will usually not be dangerous, and such fault current will merely
register as additional operating load, with wasted energy (wattage) in the
system. But, bolted phase-to-ground faults are very rare. The usual
phase-to-ground fault exists as an intermittent or arcing fault, and an
arcing fault of the same current rating as the essentially harmless bolted
fault can be fantastically destructive because of the intense heat of the arc.

Of course, any ground-fault current (bolted or arcing) above the rating
or setting of the circuit protective device will normally be cleared by the
device. In such cases, bolted-fault currents will be eliminated. But, even
where the protective device eventually operates, in the case of a heavy
ground-fault current which adds to the normal circuit load current to
produce a total current in excess of the rating of the normal circuit
protective device (fuse or CB), the time delay of the device may be
minutes or even hours—more than enough time for the arcing-fault
current to burn out conduit and enclosures, acting just like a torch, and
even propagating flame to create a fire hazard.

In spite of the growth of effective and skilled application of conventional overcurrent protective devices, the problem of ground faults continues to persist and even grows with expanding electrical usage. In the interests of safety, definitive engineering design must account for protection against such faults. Phase overcurrent protective devices are normally limited in their effectiveness because (1) they must have a time delay and a setting somewhat higher than full load to ride through normal inrushes, and (2) they are unable to distinguish between normal currents and low-magnitude fault currents which may be less than full-load currents.

Dangerous temperatures and magnetic forces are proportional to current for overloads and short circuits; therefore, overcurrent protective devices usually are adequate to protect against such faults. However, the temperatures of arcing faults are, generally, independent of current magnitude; and arcs of great and extensive destructive capability can be sustained by currents not exceeding the overcurrent device settings. Other means of protection are therefore necessary. A ground-detection device which "sees" only ground-fault current can be coupled to an automatic switching device to open all three phases when a line-to-ground fault exists on the circuit.

Section 230-95 requires ground-fault protection equipment to be provided for each service *disconnecting means* rated 1,000 A or more in a solidly grounded wye electrical service that operates with its ungrounded legs at more than 150 V to ground. Note that this applies to the rating of the disconnect, not to the rating of the overcurrent devices nor to the capacity of the service-entrance conductors.

The wording of the first sentence of this section makes clear that service GFP (ground-fault protection) is required under specific conditions: only for grounded wye systems that have voltage over 150 V to ground. In effect, that means the rule applies only to 480/277-V grounded wye and *not* to 120/208-V systems or any other commonly used systems (Fig. 230-43). And GFP is *not* required on any systems operating over 600 V.

In a typical GFP hookup as shown in Fig. 230-44, part **(a)** of the section specifies that a ground-fault current of 1,200 A or more must cause the disconnect to open all ungrounded conductors. Thus the maximum GF pick-up setting permitted is 1,200 A, although it may be set lower.

With a GFP system, at the service entrance a ground fault anywhere in the system is immediately sensed in the ground-relay system, but its action to open the circuit usually is delayed to allow some normal overcurrent device near the point of fault to open if it can. As a practical procedure, such time delay is designed to be only a few cycles or seconds, depending on the voltage of the circuit, the time-current characteristics of the overcurrent devices in the system, and the location of the ground-fault relay in the distribution system. Should any of the conventional short-circuit overcurrent protective devices fail to operate in the time predetermined to clear the circuit, and if the fault continues, the ground-

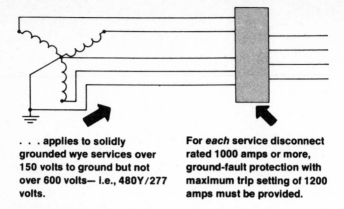

. . . applies to solidly
grounded wye services over
150 volts to ground but not
over 600 volts— i.e., 480Y/277
volts.

For *each* service disconnect
rated 1000 amps or more,
ground-fault protection with
maximum trip setting of 1200
amps must be provided.

GFP IS NOT MANDATORY FOR

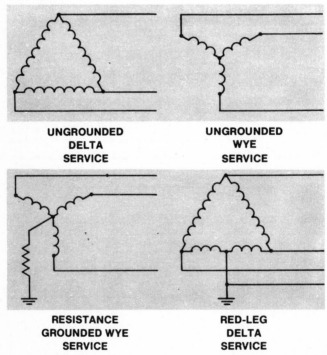

UNGROUNDED
DELTA
SERVICE

UNGROUNDED
WYE
SERVICE

RESISTANCE
GROUNDED WYE
SERVICE

RED-LEG
DELTA
SERVICE

Fig. 230-43. Service ground-fault protection is mandatory. (Sec. 230-95.)

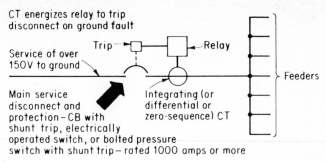

Fig. 230-44. GFP is required for each disconnect rated 1,000 amps or more. (Sec. 230-95.)

fault protective relays will open the circuit. This provides added overcurrent protection not available by any other means.

In the 1978 **NE Code**, the rule requiring GFP for any service disconnect rated 1,000 A or more (on 480/277-V services) specifies a maximum *time delay of 2 sec for ground-fault currents of 3,000 A or more* (Fig. 230-45). Previously, the **NE Code** did not mention "time delay."

The maximum permitted setting of a service GFP hookup is 1,200 A, but the time-current trip characteristic of the relay must assure opening of the disconnect in not more than 1 sec for any ground-fault current of 3,000 A or more. This change in the **Code** was made to establish a specific level of protection in GFP equipment by setting a maximum limit on $i^2 t$ of fault energy.

The reasoning behind this change was explained as follows:

The amount of damage done by an arcing fault is directly proportional to the time it is allowed to burn. Commercially available GFP systems can easily meet the 1-sec limit. Some users are requesting time delays up to 60 sec so all downstream overcurrent devices can have plenty of time to trip thermally before the GFP on the main disconnect trips. However, an arcing fault lasting 60 sec can virtually destroy a service equipment installation. Coordination with downstream overcurrent devices can and should be achieved by adding GFP on feeder circuits where needed. The **Code** should require a reasonable time limit for GFP. 3,000 A is 250 percent of 1,200 A. 250 percent of setting is a calibrating point specified in ANSI 37.17. Specifying a maximum time delay starting at this current value will allow either flat or inverse time-delay characteristics for ground-fault relays with approximately the same level of protection.

Selective coordination between GFP and conventional protective devices (fuses and CBs) on service and feeder circuits is now a very clear and specific task as a result of rewording of Sec. 230-95(a) that calls for a maximum time delay of 1 sec at any ground-fault current value of 3,000 A or more.

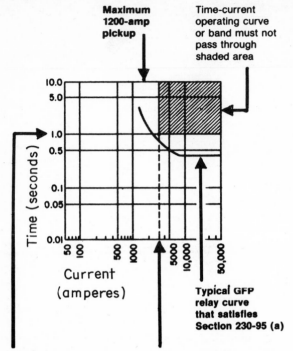

Maximum 1200-amp pickup

Time-current operating curve or band must not pass through shaded area

Typical GFP relay curve that satisfies Section 230-95 (a)

Time-delay setting of GFP relay must *not* exceed 1 second at 3000 amps.

Fig. 230-45. The rule specifies maximum energy let-through for GFP operation. [Sec. 230-95(a).]

For applying the rule of Sec. 230-95, the rating of any service disconnect means shall be determined as shown in Fig. 230-46.

Because the rule on required service GFP applies to the rating of each service disconnect, there are many instances where GFP would be required if a single service main disconnect is used but *not* if the service subdivision option of Sec. 230-71(a) is taken, as shown in Fig. 230-47.

By the Exception to part **(a)**, continuous industrial process operations are exempted from the GFP rules of Sec. 230-95(a) where the electrical system is under the supervision of qualified persons who will effect orderly shutdown of the system and thereby avoid hazards, greater than ground fault itself, that would result from the nonorderly, automatic interruption that GFP would produce in the supply to such critical continuous operations. The Exception excludes GFP requirements where a nonorderly shutdown will introduce additional or increased hazards. The idea behind that is to provide maximum protection against

FUSED SWITCH (bolted pressure switch, service protector, etc.)

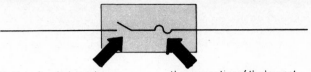

Rating of switch is taken as...   ...the amp rating of the largest fuse that can be installed in the switch fuseholders.

EXAMPLE

If 900-amp fuses are used in this service switch, ground-fault protection would be required, because the switch can take fuses rated 1200 amps—which is above the 1000-amp level at which GFP becomes mandatory.

CIRCUIT BREAKER

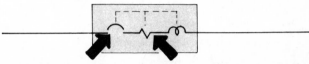

Rating of breaker   ... the maximum continuous current rating
is taken as...   (pickup of long time-delay) for which the
                           trip device in the breaker is set or can
                           be adjusted.

Example: GFP would be required for a service CB with, say, an 800-amp trip setting if the CB had a trip device that can be adjusted to 1000 amps or more.

Fig. 230-46. Determining rating of service disconnect for GFP rule. (Sec. 230-95.)

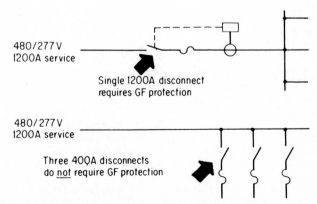

480/277 V
1200A service

Single 1200A disconnect requires GF protection

480/277 V
1200A service

Three 400A disconnects do <u>not</u> require GF protection

Fig. 230-47. Subdivision option on disconnects affects GFP rule. (Sec. 230-95.)

241

service outage for such industrial processes. With highly trained personnel at such locations, design and maintenance of the electrical system can often accomplish safety objectives more readily without GFP on the service. Electrical design can account for any danger to personnel resulting from loss of process power versus damage to electrical equipment.

Important considerations are given in fine-print notes in this section. Obviously, the selection of ground-fault equipment for a given installation merits a detailed study. The option of subdividing services discussed under *six service entrances from one drop* (Sec. 230-2, Exception No. 7) should be evaluated. A 4,000-A service, for example, could be divided using five 800-A disconnecting means, and in such cases GFP would not be required.

One very important note in Sec. 230-95(b) warns about potential desensitizing of ground-fault sensing hookups when an emergency gen-

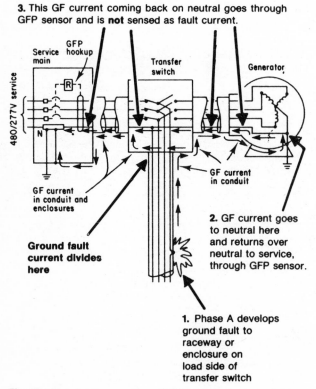

Fig. 230-48. Improper operation of GFP equipment can result from emergency system transfer switch. (Sec. 230-95.)

erator and transfer switch are provided in conjunction with the normal service to a building. The note applies to those cases where a solid neutral connection from the normal service is made to the neutral of the generator through a 3-pole transfer switch. With the neutral grounded at the normal service and the neutral bonded to the generator frame, ground-fault current on the load side of the transfer switch can return over two paths, one of which will escape detection by the GFP sensor, as shown in Fig. 230-48. Such a hookup can also cause nuisance tripping of the GFP due to normal neutral current. Under normal (nonfaulted) conditions, neutral current due to normal load unbalance on the phase legs can divide at common neutral connection in transfer switch, with some current flowing toward the generator and returning to the service main on the conduit—indicating falsely that a ground fault exists and causing nuisance tripping of GFP. The note points out that "means or devices" (such as a 4-pole, neutral-switched transfer switch) "may be needed" to assure proper, effective operation of the GFP hookup (Fig. 230-49).

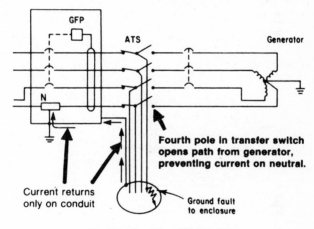

Refer to Fig. 230-48

Fig. 230-49. Four-pole transfer switch is one way to avoid desensitizing GFP. (Sec. 230-95.)

VERY IMPORTANT!

Because of so many reports of improper and/or unsafe operation (or failure to operate) of ground-fault protective hookups, a part **(c)** of Sec. 230-95 *requires* (a mandatory rule) that *every* GFP hookup be "performance tested when first installed." This rule requires that such testing be done according to "approved instructions . . . provided with the equipment." A written record must be made of the test and must be available to the inspection authority.

GROUND–STRAP SENSING

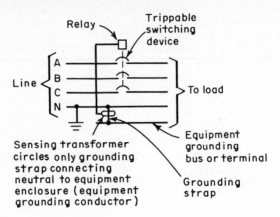

Sensing transformer
circles only grounding
strap connecting
neutral to equipment
enclosure (equipment
grounding conductor)

ZERO–SEQUENCE SENSING

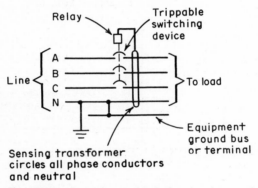

Sensing transformer
circles all phase conductors
and neutral

Fig. 230-50. Types of ground-fault detection that may be selected for use at services. (Sec. 230-95.)

Figure 230-50 shows two basic types of GFP hookup used at service entrances.

230-200. General (Services over 600 Volts). A definition at the end of this section is intended to clarify the basic rule on high-voltage services that the provisions of Art. 230 apply only to equipment on the load side of the "service-point." Because there has been so much controversy over identifying what is and what is not "service" equipment in the many complicated layouts of outdoor high-voltage circuits and transformers, the definition defines "service-point." All equipment on the load side of that point is subject to **NE Code** rules. Any equipment on the line side is the concern of the power company and is not regulated by the **Code**. In any particular installation, identification of that point can be made by the utility company and design personnel. The new definition was added to clarify that the property line is not the determinant as to where **NE Code** rules must begin to be applied. This is particularly important in cases of multibuilding industrial complexes where the utility has distribution circuits on the property (Fig. 230-51).

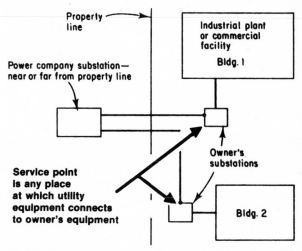

Fig. 230-51. NE Code rules apply on load side of "SERVICE POINT"—not from property line. (Sec. 230-200.)

230-201. Classification of Service Conductors.   One of the most persistent and perplexing controversies about **NE Code** rules revolves around **NE Code** Sec. 230-201. This is where the **Code** attempts to identify the "service entrance" for systems fed at more than 600 V. After noting in Sec. 230-200 that "service conductors and equipment used on circuits exceeding 600 volts" must comply with *all* the rules in Art. 230 (including any "applicable provisions" that cover services up to 600 V), the **NE Code** then proceeds to say that in many cases where the utility feeder is operating above 600 V, the "service" must be taken to be located on the secondary side of transformers, where the voltage may be either above or under 600 V (Fig. 230-52). Design engineers, contractors, plant people, and electrical inspectors find difficulty in determining where the service entrance exists on premises served by high-voltage (over 600 V) utility lines—especially on multibuilding properties with both outdoor and indoor transformers and/or with two outdoor voltage transformations.

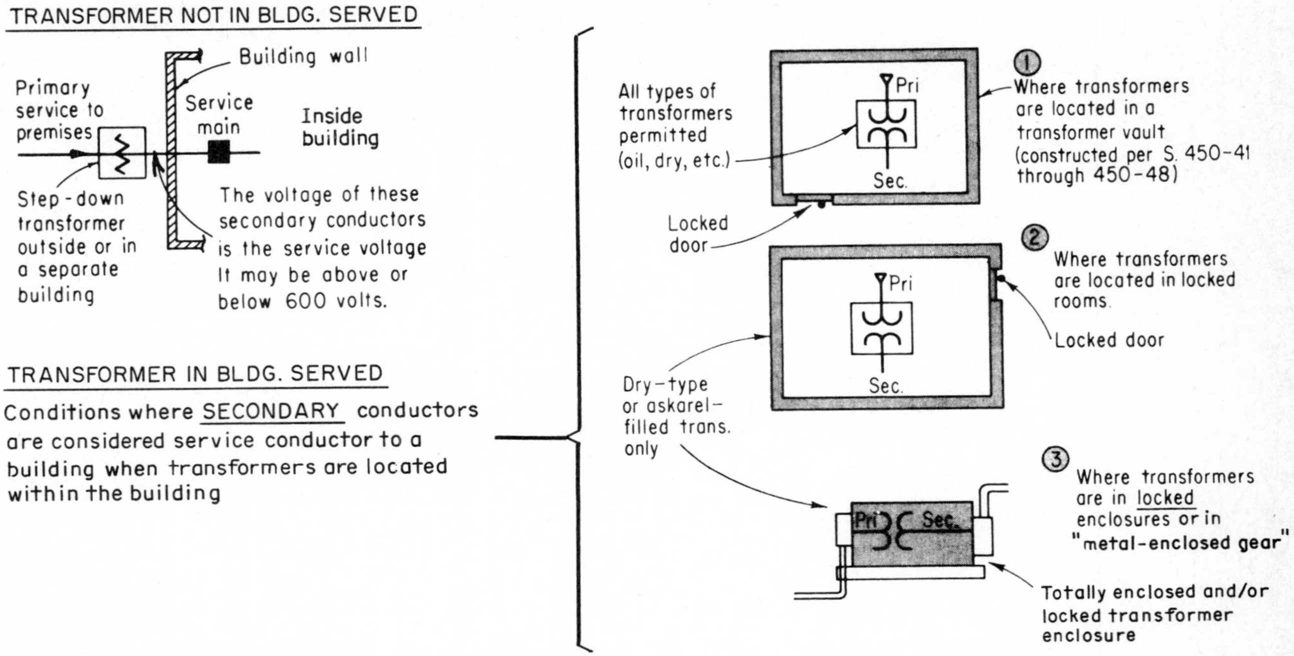

TRANSFORMER NOT IN BLDG. SERVED

Building wall — Inside building

Primary service to premises

Service main

The voltage of these secondary conductors is the service voltage It may be above or below 600 volts.

Step-down transformer outside or in a separate building

TRANSFORMER IN BLDG. SERVED

Conditions where SECONDARY conductors are considered service conductor to a building when transformers are located within the building

① Where transformers are located in a transformer vault (constructed per S. 450-41 through 450-48)

All types of transformers permitted (oil, dry, etc.)

Locked door

② Where transformers are located in locked rooms

Locked door

Dry-type or askarel-filled trans. only

③ Where transformers are in locked enclosures or in "metal-enclosed gear"

Totally enclosed and/or locked transformer enclosure

Pri Sec.

Fig. 230-52. Secondary conductors are the service conductors to the building or structure. (Sec. 230-201.)

246

The circuit that crosses the property line of the premises, connecting the utility system off the premises to the customer's system *on* the premises, is the "service" for premises fed at voltages up to 600 V. But when we get into high-voltage utility supplies, the "service" starts sliding around on the plot plan and pinning it down is commonly like trying to finger quicksilver.

Design and layout of any "service" is critically related to safety, adequacy, economics, and effective use of the whole system. It is absolutely essential that we know clearly and surely what circuits and equipment of any electrical system constitute the "service" and what parts of the system are not involved in the "service." For instance, in a system with utility feed at 13.2 kV and step-down to 480/277 V, the mandatory application of Sec. 230-95 requiring GFP hinges on establishing whether the "service" is on the primary or secondary side of the transformers. If the secondary is the service, we may have a mandatory need for GFP and none of the Code rules on service would apply to any of the 13.2-kV circuits— regardless of their length or location. If the primary is the service, Sec. 230-95 does not require GFP on services over 600 V, all the primary circuit and equipment must comply with all Art. 230, and the secondary circuits and devices do not have to comply with any of the service regulations.

The whole problem involved here is complex and requires careful, individual study to see clearly the many interrelated considerations. Let's look at a few important things to note about Code definitions as given in Art. 100:

1. "Service conductors" run to the *service equipment* of the *premises* supplied. Note that they run to "premises" and are not required to run to a "building." The Code does not define the word *premises,* but a typical dictionary definition is "a tract of land, including its buildings." But for many years, the Code rule of Sec. 230-201 did refer to "service conductors to the building." Although that phrase no longer is used in the rule, the wording does clearly aim at establishing the service conductors to the "building or other structure served."

2. "Service equipment" *usually* consists of "a circuit breaker or switch and fuses, and their accessories, located near the point of entrance of *supply* conductors to a building or other structure, or an otherwise defined area." Note that the service equipment is the means of cutoff of the supply, for the service conductors may enter "a building" or "other structure" or a "defined area." But, again, a service does not necessarily have to be to "a building." It could be to such a "structure" as an outdoor switchgear or unit substation enclosure.

The wording of Sec. 230-201 bases identification of "service conductors" on location of "step-down transformers." Assuming the rule is talking about *any* "step-down transformers" *on* the premises (whether the transformers belong to the power company or the property owner), application of the concept to modern high-voltage systems on multibuilding properties is, at best, extremely difficult. Exactly what "step-down transformers" *is* the **Code** rule talking about? Today's commercial and industrial systems commonly have step-down transformers *both* outdoors *and* indoors. And there are many systems with two voltage transformations made outdoors—say from 34 kV to 4,160 V and then to 480 V. Which secondary circuit constitutes the service conductors—the 4,160-V circuit or the 480-V circuit? The 4,160-V level is the secondary for one outdoor transformer and primary level for another.

Or take the case where, say, outdoor transformers step 34 kV down to 4,160 V and each of six different buildings is fed by a separate 4,160-V circuit to a load center unit sub stepping down to 480 V in a locked room in each building. To which circuits must the rules on services be applied?

1. Clearly, Sec. 230-201 eliminates as service conductors the 34-kV utility circuit that crosses the property line—even though that *is* the circuit for "delivering energy from the electricity supply system to the wiring system of the premises supplied" (**Code** definition of "service"). The 34-kV line becomes simply a feeder requiring only short-circuit (not overload) protection (Secs. 240-100 and 710-20) and no requirement exists on disconnecting means. Pull-fuse cutouts on a pole crossarm would satisfy the rules. Surely, that is an undesirable arrangement.

2. If we conclude that the 4,160-V side of the 34-kV transformers is the service, then all **Code** rules on services apply there. And the 480-V secondary of each 4,160-V step-down transformer is not a service.

3. If we conclude that the 480-V side of each unit sub is a service (and that is the correct identification from the wording of Sec. 230-201), then service rules apply there and the 4,160-V circuits (along with the 34-kV circuits) are feeders with only the need for short-circuit protection and isolation as covered in **Code** rules on high-voltage feeders.

Code rules do not resolve the issues and decisions must be made carefully.

Condition No. 5 of Sec. 230-201(a) will clarify many common situations involving use of load-center unit subs located indoors, fed by a high-voltage utility line from outdoors, and operating at not over 600 V on the secondary. Condition No. 5 says that, if the transformer serving the facility is located "inside the building or other structure" and is "in metal-enclosed gear," then the secondary conductors *from* the transformer—not the primary conductors *to* the transformer—*are* the service conductors to the building. As this was covered by condition No. 4 in the 1975 **Code**, the secondary conductors were the service conductors when the serving transformer was "inside the building or other structure served where *in a locked room or other locked enclosure and accessible to qualified persons only.*"

Under the wording of condition No. 4, if a load-center unit substation that handles the electrical load for a building was in a locked room or locked enclosure (accessible only to qualified persons) in the building and was fed, say, by an underground high-voltage (over 600 Volts) utility line from outdoors, then the secondary conductors from the transformer of the unit sub were the "service conductors" to the building. *And* the switching and control devices (up to six CBs on fused switches) in the secondary section of the unit sub constituted the "service equipment" for the building. Under such a condition, if any of the secondary section "service disconnects" were rated 1,000 A or more, at 480/277 V grounded wye, they had to comply with Sec. 230-95, requiring GFP for the service disconnects.

However, under the wording of condition No. 4, if the same unit sub was inside the building but *not* in a locked enclosure or locked room, then the primary conductors would be the service conductors; and the primary switch or CB would be the "service disconnect." In that case, no GFP would be needed on the "service disconnect" because Sec. 230-95 applies only up to 600 V, and there is no requirement for GFP on high-voltage services. Also, in that case, there would be no need for GFP on the secondary section disconnects, because they would not be "service disconnects"—and those are the same disconnects that would be subject to Sec. 230-95 if the unit sub was in a locked room.

Condition No. 5 adapts the concept of condition No. 4 to "metal-enclosed gear," which covers load-center subs and any other assembly in which the *transformer* is actually in metal-enclosed gear. Under condition No. 5, any load-center sub inside a building and used for service to the building would always have the secondary conductors from the transformer section as the "service conductors," and the secondary control and protection section must satisfy all Code rules on service equipment—including any service GFP as required by Sec. 230-95 (Fig. 230-53).

In applying Sec. 230-201, care must be taken to distinguish between "secondary conductors" that are not over 600 V (such as a 480/277-V unit sub secondary) and "secondary conductors" that *are* over 600 V (such as 34 kV stepped down to 4,160/2,400 V). In the latter case, all of part K of Art. 230 applies to the secondary.

230-202. Service-Entrance Conductors.   This section specifies the wiring methods that are acceptable for use as service-entrance conductors where it has been established that primary conductors (over 600 V) are the service conductors or where the secondary conductors are the service conductors and operate at more than 600 V.

Paragraph **(b)** points out that *cable tray* systems are also acceptable for high-voltage services, provided that the cables used in the tray are "approved for use as service-entrance conductors." Section 318-2(a) recognizes "*multiconductor* service-entrance cable" for use in tray, for cables rated up to 600 V. High-voltage (over 600 V) service-entrance cables may be used if the cables are "approved"—which, in today's strict

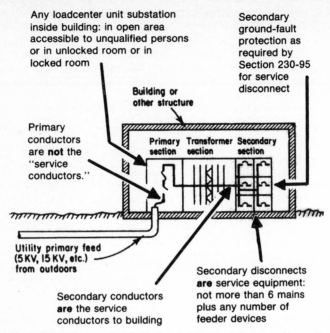

Any loadcenter unit substation inside building: in open area accessible to unqualified persons or in unlocked room or in locked room

Secondary ground-fault protection as required by Section 230-95 for service disconnect

Building or other structure

Primary conductors are **not** the "service conductors."

Primary section   Transformer section   Secondary section

Utility primary feed (5 KV, 15 KV, etc.) from outdoors

Secondary conductors **are** the service conductors to building

Secondary disconnects **are** service equipment: not more than 6 mains plus any number of feeder devices

Fig. 230-53. The secondary is the "service" for *any* indoor transformer "in metal-enclosed gear" and fed by utility line. (Sec. 230-201.)

usage, virtually means that such cable must be listed by a nationally recognized test lab (UL, etc.) as suitable for the purpose. Article 338 on "Service-Entrance Cable" does not refer to any high-voltage cable for service-entrance use. Details of this section are shown in Fig. 230-54.

230-204. Isolating Switches.   An air-break isolating switch must be used between an oil switch or an air or oil CB and the supply conductors, unless removable truck panels or metal-enclosed units are used providing disconnect of all live parts in the removed position. This line-side disconnect assures safety to personnel in maintenance (Fig. 230-55). Part **(d)** requires a grounding connection for an isolating switch, as in Fig. 230-56.

230-205. Disconnecting Means.   This rule covering the electrical fault characteristics requires that the service disconnect be *capable of closing,* safely and effectively, on a fault equal to or greater than the maximum short-circuit current that is available at the line terminals of the disconnect. The last sentence notes that where fuses are used within the disconnect or in conjunction with it, the fuse characteristics may contribute to fault-closing rating of the disconnect. The idea behind this rule is to assure that the disconnect switch may be safely closed on a level of fault that can be safely interrupted by the fuse.

(a) HIGH-VOLTAGE SERVICE CONDUCTORS FOR LOCATIONS ACCESSIBLE TO OTHER THAN QUALIFIED PERSONS

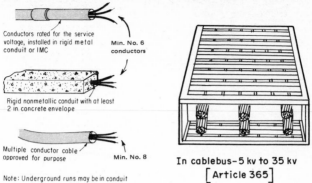

Conductors rated for the service voltage, installed in rigid metal conduit or IMC

Min. No. 6 conductors

Rigid nonmetallic conduit with at least 2 in. concrete envelope

Multiple conductor cable approved for purpose

Min. No. 8

Note: Underground runs may be in conduit or duct or approved cable assemblies and must conform to Sec. 710-3(b)

In cablebus—5 kv to 35 kv
[Article 365]

(h) SERVICE CONDUCTORS OPERATING AT MORE THAN 15 KV

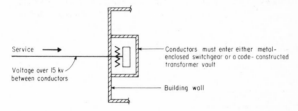

Service →

Voltage over 15 kv between conductors

Conductors must enter either metal-enclosed switchgear or a code-constructed transformer vault

Building wall

(f) POTHEAD ON SERVICE CONDUCTORS

(i) CONDUCTORS ENCLOSED IN MASONRY ARE CONSIDERED AS INSTALLED OUTSIDE THE BUILDING

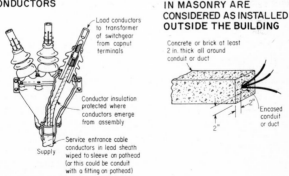

Load conductors to transformer of switchgear from capnut terminals

Conductor insulation protected where conductors emerge from assembly

Supply

Service entrance cable conductors in lead sheath wiped to sleeve on pothead (or this could be conduit with a fitting on pothead)

Concrete or brick at least 2 in. thick all around conduit or duct

Encased conduit or duct

Fig. 230-54. Provisions for service conductors rated over 600 volts (refer to sub-part letter identification of rules). (Sec. 230-202.)

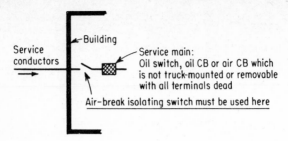

Service conductors →

←Building

Service main:
Oil switch, oil CB or air CB which
is not truck-mounted or removable
with all terminals dead

Air-break isolating switch must be used here

EXAMPLE:

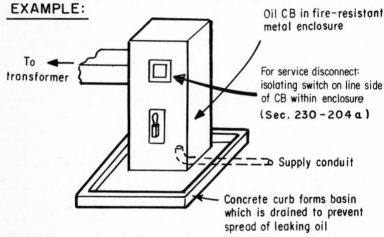

To transformer →

Oil CB in fire-resistant
metal enclosure

For service disconnect:
isolating switch on line side
of CB within enclosure
(Sec. 230-204a)

⊃ Supply conduit

Concrete curb forms basin
which is drained to prevent
spread of leaking oil

Fig. 230-55. Isolating switch may be needed to kill line terminals of service disconnect. (Sec. 230-204.)

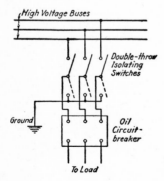

High Voltage Buses

Double-throw
Isolating
Switches

Ground

Oil
Circuit-
breaker

To Load

Fig. 230-56. One method for grounding the load-side of an open isolating switch. (Sec. 230-204.)

230-208. Overcurrent Protection Requirements. Service conductors operating at voltages over 600 V must have a short-circuit (not overload) device in each ungrounded conductor, installed either (1) on load side of service disconnect, of (2) as an integral part of the service disconnect.

All devices must be able to detect and interrupt all values of current in excess of their rating or trip setting, which must be as shown in Fig. 230-57.

FUSED LOAD INTERRUPTER SWITCH

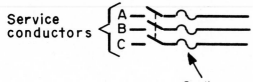

Continuous current rating of each fuse **not over** 300% (3 times) the ampacity of the **service** conductors

AIR, OIL, OR VACUUM CB

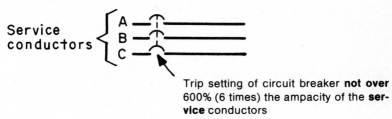

Trip setting of circuit breaker **not over** 600% (6 times) the ampacity of the **service** conductors

TYPES OF DEVICES PERMITTED

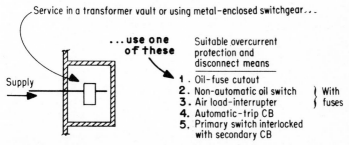

Fig. 230-57. Maximum permitted rating or setting of high-voltage overcurrent protection for service. (Sec. 230-208.)

The difference between 300 percent for fuses and 600 percent for CBs is explained as follows:

The American National Standards Institute (ANSI) publishes standards for power fuses. The continuous current ratings of power fuses are given with the letter "E" following the number of continuous amps—for instance, 65E or 200E or 400E. The letter "E" indicates that the fuse has a melting time-current characteristic in accordance with the standard for E-rated fuses:

The melting time-current characteristics of fuse units, refill units, and links for power fuses shall be as follows:

(1) The current-responsive element with ratings 100 amperes or below shall melt in 300 seconds at an rms current within the range of 200 or 240 percent of the continuous current rating of the fuse unit, refill unit, or fuse link.

(2) The current-responsive element with ratings above 100 amperes shall melt in 600 seconds at an rms current within the range of 220 to 264 percent of the continuous current rating of the fuse unit, refill unit, or fuse link.

(3) The melting time-current characteristic of a power fuse at any current higher than the 200 to 240 or 264 percent specified in (1) or (2) above shall be shown by each manufacturer's published time current curves, since the current-responsive element is a distinctive feature of each manufacturer.

(4) For any given melting time, the maximum steady-state rms current shall not exceed the minimum by more than 20 percent.

The fact that E-rated fuses are given melting times at 200 percent or more of their continuous current rating explains why **NE Code** Secs. 230-208 and 240-100 set 300 percent of conductor ampacity as the maximum fuse rating but permit CBs up to 600 percent. In effect, the 300 percent for fuses times 2 (200 percent) becomes 600 percent—the same as for CBs.

Part **(e)** of this section permits overcurrent protection for services over 600 V to be loaded up to 100 percent of its rating even on continuous loads (operating for periods of 3 hr or more).

ARTICLE 240. OVERCURRENT PROTECTION

240-1. Scope. For any electrical system, required current-carrying capacities are determined for the various circuits—feeders, subfeeders, and branch circuits. Then these required capacities are converted into standard circuit conductors which have sufficient current-carrying capacities based on: the size of the conductors, the type of insulation on the conductors, the ambient temperature at the place of installation, the number of conductors in each conduit, the type and continuity of load, and judicious determination of spare capacity to meet future load growth. Or if busway, armored cable, or other cable assemblies are to be used, similar considerations go into selection of conductors with required current-carrying capacities. In any case, then, the next step is to provide overcurrent protection for each and every circuit:

The overcurrent device for conductors or equipment must automatically open the circuit it protects if the current flowing in that circuit reaches a value which will cause an excessive or dangerous temperature in the conductor or conductor installation.

Overcurrent protection for conductors must also be rated for safe operation at the level of fault current obtainable at the point of their application. Every fuse and circuit breaker for short-circuit protection must be applied in such a way that the fault current produced by a bolted short circuit on its load terminals will not damage or destroy the device. Specifically this requires that a short-circuit overcurrent device have a proven interrupting capacity at least equal to the current which the electrical system can deliver into a short on its load terminals.

But safe application of a protective device does not stop with adequate interrupting capacity for its own use at the point of installation in the system. The speed of operation of the device must then be analyzed in relation to the thermal and magnetic energy which the device permits to flow in the faulted circuit. A very important consideration is the provision of conductor size to meet the potential heating load of short-circuit currents in cables. With expanded use of circuit-breaker overcurrent protection, coordination of protection from loads back to the source has introduced time delays in operation of overcurrent devices. Cables in such systems must be able to withstand any impressed short-circuit currents for the durations of overcurrent delay. For example, a motor circuit to a 100-hp motor might be required to carry as much as 15,000 A for a number of seconds. To limit damage to the cable due to heating effect, a much larger size conductor than necessary for the load current alone may be required.

A device may be able to break a given short-circuit current without damaging itself in the operation; but in the time it takes to open the faulted circuit, enough energy may get through to damage or destroy other equipment in series with the fault. This other equipment might be cable or busway or a switch or motor controller—any circuit component which simply cannot withstand the few cycles of short-circuit current which flows in the period of time between initiation of the fault and interruption of the current flow.

A strict interpretation of **NE Code** Sec. 240-2 often raises questions about the approved use of conductors and overcurrent protection to withstand faults.

example   Assume a panelboard with 20-A breakers rated 10,000 A IC (interrupting capacity) and No. 12 copper branch-circuit wiring. Available fault current at the point of breaker application is 8,000 A. The short-circuit withstand capability of a No. 12 copper conductor with plastic or polyethylene insulation rated 60°C would be approximately 3,000 A of fault or short-circuit current for one cycle.

Question: Assuming that the CB (circuit breaker) will take at least one cycle to operate, would use of the conductor where exposed to 8,000 A violate Sec. 240-2? This section states that overcurrent protection for conductors and equipment is provided for the purpose of opening the electrical circuit if the current reaches a value which will cause an excessive or dangerous temperature in the conductor or conductor insulation. The 8,000-A available fault current would seem to call for use of conductors with that rating of short-circuit withstand. This could mean that branch-circuit wiring from all 20-A CBs in this panelboard must be *No. 6 copper* (the next larger size suitable for an 8,000-A fault current).

Answer: As noted in UL Standard 489, a CB is required to operate safely in a circuit where the available fault current is up to the short-circuit current value for which the breaker is rated. The CB must clear the fault without damage to the insulation of conductors of proper size for the rating of the CB. A UL-listed, 20-A breaker is, therefore, tested and rated to be used with 20-A rated wire (say, No. 12 THW) and will protect the wire in accordance with Sec. 240-2 when applied at a point in a circuit where the short-circuit current available does not exceed the value for which the breaker is rated. This is also true of a 15-A breaker on No. 14 (15-A) wire, for a 30-amp breaker on No. 10 (30-A) wire and all wire sizes.

UL 489 states:

A circuit breaker shall be capable of performing successfully when operated under short-circuit conditions as described in paragraphs 193–209. There shall be no electrical or mechanical failure of the device; cotton or cloth placed in contact with the enclosure at any hole, slot, or other opening as described in the following paragraphs shall not be ignited; *there shall be no damage to the insulation of conductors, of proper size for the rating of the breaker, used to wire the device;* and after the final operation, the breaker shall be capable of making and breaking 200 percent of its rated current when manually operated.

240-3. Protection of Conductors—Other Than Flexible Cords and Fixture Wires.   Aside from general-purpose lighting and appliance branch circuits [which are clearly and rigidly regulated on overcurrent protection as described in Secs. 210-3, 210-19(a), 210-20, 210-22(c), and 220-2(a)], conductors for all other circuits must conform to the rules and exceptions of Sec. 240-3.

Clearly, the rule wants overcurrent devices to prevent conductors from being subjected to currents in excess of values for which the conductors are rated by Tables 310-16/19 **with all notes.**

That last phrase in the first sentence of this section (about "all applicable notes to these tables") is important because it points out that when conductors are derated because of conduit fill (Note 8 to the tables) or because of elevated ambient temperature (Note 13), the conductors must be protected at the *derated* ampacities and *not* at the values given in the tables.

Specifically, the general rule is that the device must be rated to protect conductors in accordance with their safe allowable current-carrying capacities. Of course, there will be cases where standard ampere ratings and settings of overcurrent devices will not correspond with conductor capacities. In such cases, the next larger standard size of overcurrent device may be used where the rating of the protective device is 800 A or less. Therefore, a basic guide to effective selection of the amp rating of overcurrent devices for any feeder or service application is given in the exceptions.

For example, if a circuit conductor of, say, 500 MCM THW copper (not more than three in a conduit at not over 86°F ambient) satisfies design requirements and NE Code rules for a particular load current not in excess of the conductor's Table ampacity of 380 A, then the conductor *may* be protected by a 400-A rated fuse or CB.

Section 240-6, which gives the "Standard Ampere Ratings" of protective devices to correspond to the word "standard" in Exception No. 1, shows devices rated at 350 A and 400 A, but none at 380 A. In such a case, the NE Code accepts a 400-A rated device as "the next higher standard device rating" above the conductor ampacity of 380 A.

But, such a 400-A device would permit load increase above the 380 A that is the safe maximum limit for the conductor. It would be more effective practice to use 350-A rated protection and prevent such overload.

For application of fuses and CBs, Exception No. 1 has this effect:

1. If the allowable current-carrying capacity of a conductor does not correspond to the rating of a standard-size fuse, the next *larger* rating of fuse may be used only where the rating is 800 A or less. Over 800 A, the next *smaller* fuse must be used.

2. A nonadjustable-trip breaker (one without overload trip adjustment above its rating—although it may have adjustable short-circuit trip) must be rated in accordance with the current-carrying capacity of the conductors they protect—except that a higher-rated CB may be used if the carrying capacity of the conductor does not correspond to a standard unit rating. In such a case, the next higher standard setting may be used only where the rating is 800 A or less. An example of such application is shown in Fig. 240-1, where a nonadjustable CB with a rating of 1,200 A is used to protect the conduc-

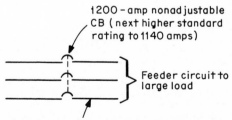

Fig. 240-1. This would violate the 800-A condition of Exception No. 1. (Sec. 240-3.)

tors of a feeder circuit which are rated at 1,140 A. As shown there, use of that size CB to protect a circuit rated at 1,140 A (3 × 380 A = 1,140 A) clearly violates Exception No. 1 because the CB is the next higher rating above the ampacity of the conductors—on a circuit rated over 800 A. With a feeder circuit as shown (three 500 MCM THW, each rated at 380 A), the CB must *not* be rated over 1,140 A. A standard 1,000-A CB would satisfy the Code rule—being the *next lower* rated protective device from Sec. 240-6. Of course, if 500 MCM THHN or XHHW conductors are used instead of THW conductors, then each 500 is rated at 405 A and three per phase would give the circuit an ampacity of 1,215 A (3 × 405), and the 1,200-A CB would satisfy the basic rule in the first sentence of Sec. 240-3 and Exception No. 1 would not be involved.

Exception No. 3 refers the matter of protecting motor-control circuits to Art. 430 on motors.

Exception No. 4 covers protection of the remote-control circuit that energizes the operating coil of a magnetic contactor, as distinguished from a magnetic motor starter (Fig. 240-2). Although it is true that a

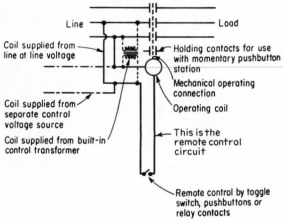

Fig. 240-2. Coil-circuit wires of magnetic contactor must be protected. (Sec. 240-3.)

magnetic starter is a magnetic contactor with the addition of running overload relays, Exception No. 4 covers only the coil circuit of any magnetic contactor but does not apply to protection of the coil circuit of a magnetic starter. Exception No. 4 states that remote-control conductors other than those for motor-control circuits can be satisfactorily protected by overcurrent devices which are rated at not more than 300 percent of the carrying capacity of the control-circuit conductors. That applies to control wires for magnetic contactors used for control of lighting or heating loads, but not motor loads. Section 430-72 covers that requirement for motor-control circuits. In Fig. 240-3, the remote-control conductors may be considered property protected by the branch-circuit overcurrent devices (A) if these devices are rated or set at not more than 300 percent of (3 times) the current rating of the control conductors. If

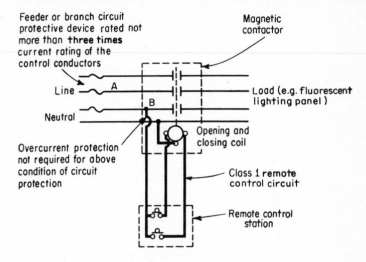

For instance, 30-amp fuses at A would be adequate protection if No. 14 wire, rated at 15 amps, is used for the remote-control circuit because 30 amps is <u>less</u> than 3 X 15 amps. If fuses at A were over 45 amps, then 15-amp protection would be required at B for No. 14 wire.

Fig. 240-3. Protecting a remote-control circuit. (Sec. 240-3.)

the branch-circuit overcurrent devices were rated or set at more than 300 percent of the rating of the control conductors, the control conductors would have to be protected by separate protective devices located at the point (B) where the conductor to be protected receives its supply. It should be noted that the overcurrent protection is required for the control conductors and not for the operating coil. Because of this, the size of control conductors can be selected to allow application without separate overcurrent protection.

As shown in Fig. 240-3, separate protection of the control conductors is not required under the given conditions. If the stated requirements were not satisfied, a fuse or CB would have to be inserted in the control circuit tapped to the operating coil from the hot-line conductor. And if the control circuit were energized from two hot conductors, some inspectors require that both taps be protected. Control circuit could have been derived from a separate source instead of the line side of the remote-control switch.

Exception No. 5 permits the secondary circuit from a transformer to be protected by means of fuses or a CB in the primary circuit to the transformer—*if* the transformer has no more than a 2-wire primary circuit *and* a 2-wire secondary. As shown in Fig. 240-4, using the 2-to-1 primary-to-secondary turns ratio of the transformer, 20-A primary protection will protect against any secondary current in excess of 40 A—

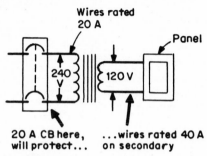

Fig. 240-4. Primary fuses or CB may protect secondary circuit for 2-wire to 2-wire transformer. (Sec. 240-3.)

thereby protecting, say, secondary No. 8 TW wires rated at 40 A. As the wording of the Exception states, the protection on the primary (20 A) must not exceed the value of the secondary conductor ampacity (40 A) multiplied by the secondary-to-primary transformer voltage ratio (120 ÷ 240 = 0.5). Thus, 40 A × 0.5 = 20 A. But it should be carefully noted that the rating of the primary protection must comply with the rules of Sec. 450-3(a) (1) or (b) (1).

A sentence at the end of Exception No. 5 clearly and emphatically states that the secondary conductors from a transformer may *not* be protected by overcurrent protection on the primary side of the transformer—**except** for a transformer with a *2-wire* secondary. That has long been the intent of the Code, but much discussion and controversy have regularly concentrated on this matter because the Code has not previously had the simple prohibition against secondary protection by a primary CB or set of fuses. The whole issue of transformers and overcurrent protection is now firmly established as follows:

The basic way to provide overcurrent protection for a dry-type transformer rated 600 V or less is to use fuses or CBs rated at not more than 125 percent of the transformer primary full-load current (TPFLC) to protect *both* the transformer and the circuit conductors that supply the transformer primary. [This is presented in Sec. 450-3(b).] These circuit conductors must have an ampacity of not less than the rating of the overcurrent protection or must have an ampacity such that the overcurrent protective device is "the next higher standard device rating" above the conductor ampacity, as described in Exception No. 1 of Sec. 240-3. *But the primary circuit protection is not acceptable as suitable protection for the secondary conductors of a transformer with more than 2 wires on its secondary—* even if the secondary conductors have an ampacity equal to the ampacity of the primary conductors times the primary-to-secondary voltage ratio. Figure 240-5 covers these points.

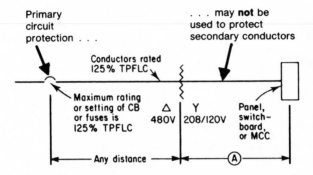

Distance "A" from transformer to first protection on the secondary side is limited to 10 or 25 ft, subject to the requirements of Exceptions 2, 3 and 8 of Section 240-21. If overcurrent protection is placed at the transformer secondary connection to protect secondary conductors, the circuit can run any distance to the panel.

Fig. 240-5. Exception No. 5 *clearly* resolves long-standing controversy. (Sec. 240-3.)

When primary devices are used for protection of 3- and 4-wire transformer secondaries, it is possible that an unbalanced load may greatly exceed the secondary conductor ampacity, which was selected assuming balanced conditions. As shown in Fig. 240-6, if the primary CB is set at 20 A, it will protect the primary No. 12 wires, which are rated for 20 A. Under conditions of full load of 20 A in the primary and a balanced secondary loading (left), the secondary current is 40 A, and the primary CB will protect the secondary No. 8 TW wires at their 40-A rating. But unbalance (right) can permit overloading of the secondary conductors without an increase in the primary current. Thus, the primary CB will not clear a 100 percent overload on the secondary wires.

However, Exception No. 5 recognizes such primary protection of the secondary conductors of single-phase, 2-wire to 2-wire transformers if the primary OC protection complies with Sec. 450-3 (e.g., not over 125 percent of rated primary current) and does not exceed the value deter-

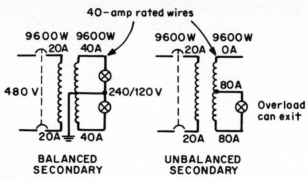

Fig. 240-6. Why primary protection may not do the job for 3-wire or 4-wire secondary 40-A rated wires. (Sec. 240-3.)

mined by multiplying the secondary conductor ampacity by the secondary-to-primary transformer voltage ratio. In such applications, the lengths of the primary or secondary conductors are not limited.

Exception No. 8 to the basic rule represents a basic concept in Code application. When conductors supply a load to which loss of power would create a hazard, this Exception states it is not necessary to provide "overload protection" for such conductors, **but** "short-circuit protection" *must* be provided. By "overload protection," this Exception means "protection at the conductors' ampacity"—i.e., protection that would *prevent* overload (Fig. 240-7).

Several points should be noted about this Exception.

1. Use of this Exception is reserved only to applications where circuit opening on "overload" would be more objectionable than the overload itself, "such as in a material handling magnet circuit." In that example mentioned in the Exception, loss of power to such a

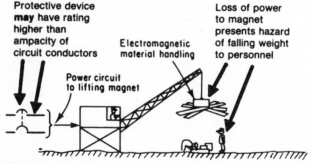

Fig. 240-7. If "overload protection" creates a hazard, it *may* be eliminated. (Sec. 240-3.)

magnet while it is lifting a heavy load of steel would cause the steel to fall and would certainly be a serious hazard to personnel working below or near the lifting magnet. To minimize the hazard created by such power loss, the circuit to it *need not* be protected at the conductor ampacity. A higher value of protection may be used—letting the circuit sustain an overload rather than opening on it and dropping the steel. Because such lifting operations are usually short-time, intermittent tasks, occasional overload is far less a safety concern than the dropping of the magnet's load.

2. The permission to eliminate *only* "overload protection" is not limited to a lifting magnet circuit, which is mentioned simply as an example. Other electrical applications that present a similar concern for "hazard" would be equally open to use of this Exception.

3. Although the Exception *permits* elimination of overload protection and requires short-circuit protection, it gives no guidance on selecting the actual rating of protection that must be used. For such circuits, fuses or a CB rated, say, 200 to 400 percent of the full-load operating current would give freedom from overload opening. Of course, the protective device ought to be selected with as low a rating as would be compatible with the operating characteristics of the electrical load. And it must have sufficient interrupting capacity for the circuit's available short-circuit current.

4. Finally, this Exception is *not* a mandatory rule but a *permissible* application. It says " . . . overload protection *shall not be required* . . ."; it does *not* say that overload protection "shall *not be used.*" Overload protection *may be used,* or it *may be eliminated.* Obviously, careful study should always go into use of this Exception.

240-4. Protection of Fixture Wires and Cords.   The basic rule says that No. 16 or No. 18 fixture wire or cord is adequately protected by the protective device of the branch circuit it is connected to when such a device is rated at 15 or 20 A. Figure 240-8 shows such application for recessed fixtures where higher temperature wire is required by Sec. 410-67(c), where, for instance, a fixture calls for 150°C wire to its hot terminal box. Of course, use of fixture wire must also satisfy all other Code rules that apply—as in Art. 400 on cords, Art. 402 on fixture wires, and Sec. 725-16 on fixture wires for control circuits.

A tabulation is given to show the minimum sizes of flexible cords that may be used on circuits rated at 20, 30, 40, and 50 A. A similar tabulation is given for fixture wire. This eliminates cross-referencing Sec. 240-4 to amp ratings of tap conductors given in Exception No. 1 of Sec. 210-19(c).

240-6. Standard Ampere Ratings.   This is a listing of the "standard ampere ratings" of fuses and CBs for purposes of Code application. Although other ratings of devices are available in between the values given here, the Code relates its rules on protection to those "standard" ratings. But an exception designates "additional standard ratings" of *fuses* at 1, 3, 6, 10, and 601 A. These values apply *only* to fuses and *not* to CBs.

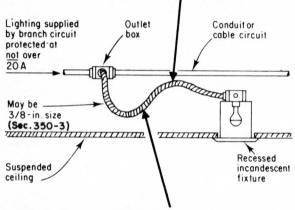

Typical use of fixture wire:
4-to-6-ft length of flex for
fixture whip in ceiling, containing
two No. 18 Type AF wires (for 6-amp
fixture load, see Section 402-5)
or two No. 16 Type AF wires (for
8-amp fixture load). Section 240-4
permits No. 16 and No. 18 fixture
wire to be protected at 20 amps.

Lighting supplied
by branch circuit
protected at
not over
20 A

Outlet
box

Conduit or
cable circuit

May be
3/8-in. size
(Sec. 350-3)

Suspended
ceiling

Recessed
incandescent
fixture

**IMPORTANT!! Flex is equipment grounding
conductor** because AF wires in flex are tapped
from circuit protected at not over 20 amps, as permitted
in Section 250-91(b), Exception No. 1.

Fig. 240-8. No. 16 or No. 18 fixture wire is OK on a 20-A circuit. (Sec.
240-4.)

The 601-A rating gives Code recognition to use of Class L fuses rated
less than 700 A. The reasoning of the Code panel on this was as follows:

An examination of fuse manufacturers' catalogs will show that 601 amperes is a
commonly listed current rating for the Class L nontime-delay fuse. Section 430-52
(Exception f) also lists this current rating as a break point in application rules.

Without a 601 ampere rating, the smallest standard fuse which can be used in
Class L fuse clips is rated 700 amperes. Since the intent of Table 430-152 and
Section 430-52 is to encourage closer short-circuit protection, it seems prudent to
encourage availability and use of 601-ampere fuses in combination motor controllers having Class L fuse clips.

Because ratings of inverse time circuit breakers are not related to fuse clip size, a
distinction between 600 and 601 amperes in circuit breakers would serve no useful
purpose. Hence, inverse-time circuit breaker ratings are listed separately. Such
separation also facilitates recognition of other fuse ratings as standard.

The smaller sizes of fuses (1, 3, 6, and 10 A) listed as "standard ratings" provide more effective short-circuit and ground-fault protection for motor circuits—in accordance with Sec. 430-52, Sec. 430-40, and UL requirements for protecting the overload relays in controllers for very small motors. The Code panel reasoning was as follows:

Fuses rated less than 15 amperes are often required to provide short circuit and ground-fault protection for motor branch circuits in accordance with Section 430-52.

Tests indicate that fuses rated 1, 3, 6 and 10 amperes can provide the intended protection in motor branch circuits for motors having full load currents less than 3.75 amperes (3.75 × 400% = 15). These ratings are also those most commonly shown on control manufacturers overload relay tables. Overload relay elements for very small full load motor currents have such a high resistance that a bolted fault at the controller load terminals produces a short-circuit current of less than 15 amperes, regardless of the available current at the line terminals. An overcurrent protective device rated or set for 15 amperes is unable to offer the short circuit or ground fault protection required by Section 110-10 in such circuits.

An examination of fuse manufacturer's catalogs will show that fuses with these ratings are commercially available. Having these ampere ratings established as standard should improve product availability at the user level and result in better overcurrent protection.

Since inverse time circuit breakers are not readily available in the sizes added, it seems appropriate to list them separately.

Listing of those smaller fuse ratings has a significant effect on use of several small motors (fractional and small-integral-horsepower sizes) on a single branch circuit as described under Sec. 430-53(b).

240-8. Fuses or Circuit Breakers in Parallel.   The basic rule *prohibits* the use of parallel fuses, which at one time was acceptable when fused switches had ratings above 600 A. However, fused switches and *single fuses* (such as Class L) are now readily available in sizes up to 6,000 A. Moreover, this rule prohibits the use of CBs in parallel unless they are tested and approved as a single unit. At one time, this Code rule did not mention CBs. However, it is acceptable to factory-assemble CBs or fuses in parallel and have them tested and approved as a unit.

240-10. Supplementary Overcurrent Protection.   Supplementary overcurrent protection is commonly used in lighting fixtures, heating circuits, appliances, or other utilization equipment to provide individual protection for specific components within the equipment itself. Such protection is not branch-circuit protection and *the* NE Code *does not require supplemental overcurrent protective devices to be readily accessible.* Typical applications of supplemental overcurrent protection are fuses installed in fluorescent fixtures, cooking or heating equipment where the devices are sized to provide lower overcurrent protection than that of the branch circuit supplying such equipment. This is discussed under Sec. 424-19 and Sec. 424-22 on electric space heating equipment.

240-12. Electrical System Coordination.   This rule is aimed at "industrial locations" where hazard to personnel would result from disorderly shutdown of electrical equipment under fault conditions. The purpose of this rule is to permit elimination of "overload" protection—i.e., protection of conductors at their ampacities—and to eliminate unknown or random relation between operating time of overcurrent devices connected in series.

The new section recognizes two requirements, both of which must be fulfilled to perform the task of "orderly shutdown."

One is selective coordination of the time-current characteristics of the short-circuit protective devices in series from the service to any load—so that, automatically, any fault will actuate only the short-circuit protective device closest to the fault on the line side of the fault, thereby minimizing the extent of electrical outage due to a fault.

The other technique that must also be included if *overload* protection is eliminated is "overload indication based on monitoring systems or

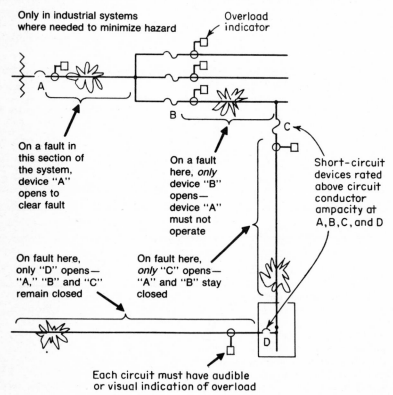

Fig. 240-9. Short-circuit protection *must* be selectively coordinated and "overload" must be monitored. (Sec. 240-12.)

devices." A note to this new section gives brief descriptions of both requirements and establishes only a generalized understanding of "overload indication." Effective application of this rule will depend upon careful design and coordination with inspection authorities.

It should be noted, however, that it says that the technique of eliminating overload protection to afford orderly shutdown "shall be permitted"—but does *not require* such application. Although it could be argued that the wording implies a mandatory rule, consultation with electrical inspection authorities on this matter is advisable because of the safety implications in nonorderly shutdown due to overload (Fig. 240-9).

240-20. Ungrounded Conductors.   Figure 240-10 shows the basic types of protective devices required by part **(a)**. And such a device must be placed in each ungrounded circuit conductor—as shown in Fig. 240-11.

PROTECTIVE DEVICE IN SERIES

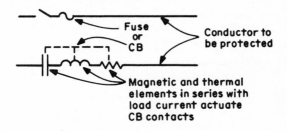

CT–RELAY RESPONDS TO LOAD CURRENT

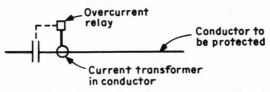

Fig. 240-10. Each ungrounded conductor must have one of these devices. (Sec. 240-20.)

Although part **(b)** basically requires a CB to open all ungrounded conductors of a circuit simultaneously, the Exception covers acceptable uses of a number of single-pole CBs instead of multipole CBs.

The basic rule on use of single-pole versus multipole CBs is covered in this section.

Circuit breakers must open simultaneously all ungrounded conductors of circuits they protect; i.e., they must be multipole CB units, except that

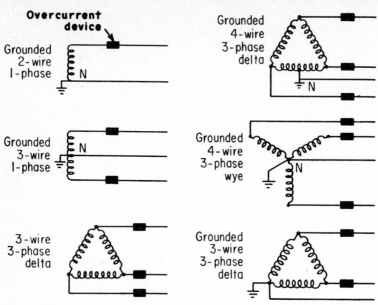

Fig. 240-11. What conductors require an overcurrent device? (Sec. 240-20.)

individual single-pole CBs may be used for protection of each ungrounded conductor of certain types of circuits, including ungrounded 2-wire circuits, 3-wire single-phase circuits, or lighting or appliance branch circuits connected to 4-wire, 3-phase systems provided that such lighting or appliance circuits are supplied from a grounded-neutral system and the loads are connected line-to-neutral. Figure 240-12 covers the rules.

Although 1-pole CBs may be used, as noted, for some 2-wire and 3-wire circuits, it is better practice to use multipole CBs for circuits to individual load devices which are supplied by two or more ungrounded conductors.

Refer also to Sec. 210-4 for limitation on use of single-pole protective devices with line-to-neutral loads. And Sec. 110-3(b) requires that use of single-pole CBs be related to UL rules as described in Fig. 240-13.

240-21. Location in Circuit.   The basic rule of this section and Exception No. 1 is shown in Fig. 240-14.

Although basic Code requirements dictate the use of an overcurrent device at the point at which a conductor receives its supply, exceptions to this rule are made in the case of taps to feeders. That is, to meet the practical demands of field application, certain lengths of unprotected conductors may be used to tap energy from protected feeder conductors.

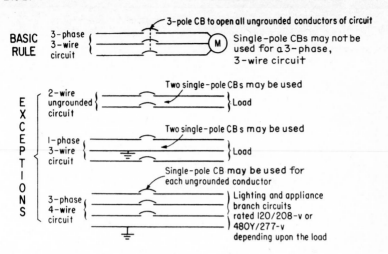

BASIC RULE

3-phase 3-wire circuit { 3-pole CB to open all ungrounded conductors of circuit — Single-pole CBs may not be used for a 3-phase, 3-wire circuit

EXCEPTIONS

2-wire ungrounded circuit { Two single-pole CBs may be used } Load

1-phase 3-wire circuit { Two single-pole CBs may be used } Load

3-phase 4-wire circuit { Single-pole CB may be used for each ungrounded conductor — Lighting and appliance branch circuits rated 120/208-v or 480Y/277-v depending upon the load

EXAMPLES:

Two 1-pole CBs may be used for a 240-volt or 208-volt circuit to an electric heating unit or air-conditioning unit if the CBs are not intended to provide the disconnect means required by Secs. 424-19(b)(1), 440-63, 426-20, 422-21(b), 430-85, or 430-103.

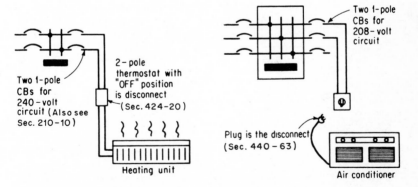

Two 1-pole CBs for 240-volt circuit (Also see Sec. 210-10)

2-pole thermostat with "OFF" position is disconnect (Sec. 424-20)

Heating unit

Two 1-pole CBs for 208-volt circuit

Plug is the disconnect (Sec. 440-63)

Air conditioner

NOTE: If multipole breakers are used instead of the single-pole units shown, the breakers could serve as disconnect means because they would satisfy Section 210-10 requiring poles of a disconnect to switch together.

NOTE: A 3-pole CB must always be used for a 3-phase, 3-wire circuit supplying phase-to-phase loads fed from an ungrounded delta system, such as 480-volt outdoor lighting for a parking lot, etc., as permitted by Section 210-6(b).

Fig. 240-12. Single-pole vs. multipole breakers. (Sec. 240-20.)

1. "Single-pole CBs rated 120 volts ac are suitable for use in a single-phase multiwire circuit where the neutral is connected to the load."

Single-pole 120V ac CB units

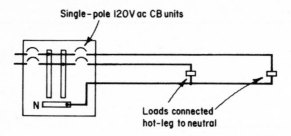

Loads connected
hot-leg to neutral

2. "Single-pole circuit breakers rated 120/240 volts ac are suitable for use in a single-phase multiwire circuit *with or without* the neutral connected to the load."

Single-pole 120/240V ac CB units

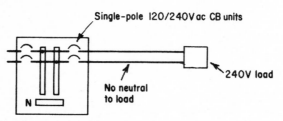

No neutral
to load

240V load

Fig. 240-13. NE Code rules must be correlated with the following UL requirements. (Sec. 240-20.)

Exceptions to the rule for protecting conductors at their points of supply are made in the case of 10-ft and 25-ft taps from a feeder, as described in Sec. 240-21, Exceptions No. 2 and No. 3. Application of the tap exceptions should be made carefully to effectively minimize any sacrifice in safety. The two tap exceptions are permitted without overcurrent protective devices at the point of supply.

Unprotected taps not over 10 ft long (Fig. 240-15) may be made from feeders or transformer secondaries provided:

1. The smaller conductors have a current rating that is not less than the combined computed loads of the circuits supplied by the tap conductors and must have ampacity of—

   Not less than the rating of the "device" supplied by the tap conductors,

   or

BASIC RULE

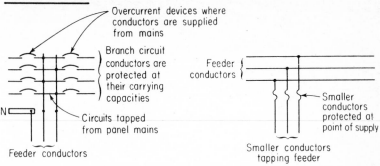

Overcurrent devices where conductors are supplied from mains

Branch circuit conductors are protected at their carrying capacities

Circuits tapped from panel mains

N

Feeder conductors

Feeder conductors

Smaller conductors protected at point of supply

Smaller conductors tapping feeder

EXCEPTION No. 1

PROTECTING TWO SIZES OF CONDUCTORS

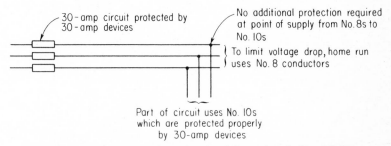

30-amp circuit protected by 30-amp devices

No additional protection required at point of supply from No. 8s to No. 10s

To limit voltage drop, home run uses No. 8 conductors

Part of circuit uses No. 10s which are protected properly by 30-amp devices

Fig. 240-14. Conductors must be protected at their supply ends. (Sec. 240-21.)

Not less than the rating of the overcurrent device (fuses or CB) that might be installed at the termination of the tap conductors.

2. The tap does not extend beyond the switchboard, panelboard, or control device which it supplies.

3. The tap conductors are enclosed in conduit, EMT, metal gutter, or other approved raceway when not a part of the switchboard or panelboard.

Exception No. 2 specifically recognizes that a 10-ft tap may be made from a transformer secondary in the same way it has always been permitted from a feeder. In either case, the tap conductors must not be over 10 ft long and must have ampacity not less than the amp rating of the switchboard, panelboard, or control device—or the tap conductors may be terminated in an overcurrent protective device rated not more than the ampacity of the tap conductors.

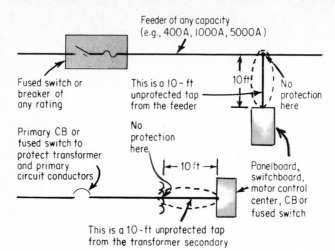

Fig. 240-15. Ten-ft taps may be made from a feeder or a transformer secondary. (Sec. 240-21.)

Although such 10-ft taps have been made since the 1971 **NE Code** ruled against protecting transformer secondary conductors by means of the primary circuit overcurrent device, there was some controversy about making unprotected 10-ft taps from transformer secondaries. The wording of the Code rule now clearly covers this practice.

Taps not over 25 ft long (Fig. 240-16) may be made from feeders, as noted in Exception No. 3, provided:

1. The smaller conductors have a current rating at least one-third that of the conductors from which they are tapped.

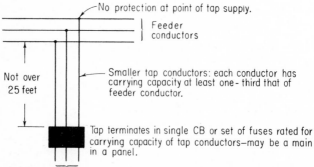

Fig. 240-16. Sizing feeder taps not over 25 ft long. (Sec. 240-21.)

2. The tap conductors are suitably protected from mechanical damage.
3. The tape is terminated in a single CB or set of fuses which will limit the load on the tap to its allowable current-carrying capacity.

Examples of Taps

Figure 240-17 shows use of a 10-ft feeder tap to supply a single motor branch circuit. The conduit feeder may be a horizontal run or a vertical run, such as a riser. If the tap conductors are of such size that they have a

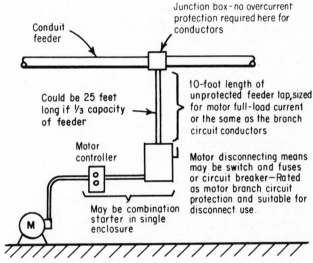

Fig. 240-17. A 10-ft tap for a single motor circuit. (Sec. 240-21.)

current rating at least one-third that of the feeder conductors from which they are tapped, they could be run a distance of 25 ft without protection at the point of tap-off from the feeder or busway because they would comply with the rules of Exception No. 3 which permit a 25-ft tap if the conductors terminate in a single protective device rated not more than the conductor ampacity. Because Sec. 364-11 requires that any busway used as a feeder must have overcurrent protection on the busway for any subfeeder or branch circuit tapped from the busway, the use of a cable tap box on busway without overcurrent protection (as shown in the conduit installation of Fig. 240-17) would be a violation. Refer to Secs. 240-24 and 364-11.

A common application of the 10-ft tap exception is the supply of panelboards from conduit feeders or busways, as shown in Fig. 240-18.

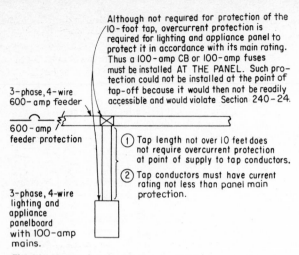

Although not required for protection of the 10-foot tap, overcurrent protection is required for lighting and appliance panel to protect it in accordance with its main rating. Thus a 100-amp CB or 100-amp fuses must be installed AT THE PANEL. Such protection could not be installed at the point of tap-off because it would then not be readily accessible and would violate Section 240-24.

3-phase, 4-wire 600-amp feeder

600-amp feeder protection

① Tap length not over 10 feet does not require overcurrent protection at point of supply to tap conductors.

② Tap conductors must have current rating not less than panel main protection.

3-phase, 4-wire lighting and appliance panelboard with 100-amp mains.

Fig. 240-18. Ten-ft tap to lighting panel with unprotected conductors. (Sec. 240-21.)

The case shows an interesting requirement that arises from Sec. 384-16, which requires that lighting and appliance panelboards be protected on their supply side by overcurrent protection rated not more than the rating of the panelboard busbars. If the feeder is busway, the protection must be placed (a requirement of Sec. 364-11) at the point of tap on the busway. In that case a 100-A CB or fused switch on the busway would provide the required protection of the panel, and the panel would not require a main in it. But, if the feeder circuit is in conduit, the 100-A panel protection would have to be in the panel or just ahead of it. It could not be at the junction box on the conduit because that would make it not readily accessible and therefore a violation of Sec. 240-24. With a conduit feeder, a fused-switch or CB main in the panelboard could be rated up to the 100-A main rating.

For transformer applications, typical 10-ft and 25-ft tap considerations are shown in Fig. 240-19.

Figure 240-20 shows application of Exception No. 8 of Sec. 240-21 in conjunction with the rule of Sec. 450-3(b) (2), covering transformer protection. As shown in Example 1, the 100-A main protection in the panel is sufficient protection for the transformer and the primary and secondary conductors when these conditions are met:

1. Tap conductors have ampacity at least one-third that of the 125-A feeder conductors.
2. Secondary conductors are rated at least one-third the ampacity of the 125-A feeder conductors, based on the primary-to-secondary transformer ratio.

10-FT TAP

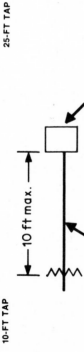

1. A 10-ft tap may be made from transformer secondary to a panel, switchboard, MCC, etc.

2. If this is a lighting panel that requires main protection, a fused switch or CB must be installed as a main protective device in the panel or just ahead of it, at the end of the 10-ft tap.

3. If the panel is *not* a lighting panel (such as a panel with 240-volt or 480-volt heating circuits or other makeup that does not make it a lighting panel as specified in Section 384-14), then main protection is not required at all, and the 10-ft tap conductors terminate in main lugs of the panel switchboard, or other equipment.

25-FT TAP

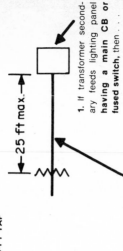

|← 25 ft max. →|

1. If transformer secondary feeds lighting panel **having a main CB or fused switch,** then . . .

2. . . . secondary tap conductors from transformer may be 25 ft long, as permitted by Section 240-21, Exception No. 3, but *only* where the tap terminates in a single CB or set of fuses.

3. Or, a 25-ft tap may be made from a transformer to a CB or fused switch in an individual enclosure or serving as a main in a switchboard or MCC.

NOTE: From a single transformer secondary of adequate capacity, more than one set of 10-ft tap conductors may be run to more than one panel or other distribution equipment.

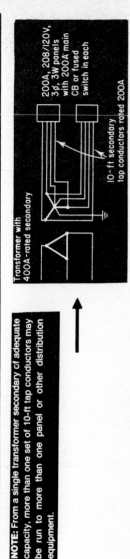

Fig. 240-19. Taps from transformer secondaries. (Sec. 240-21.)

275

EXAMPLE 1:

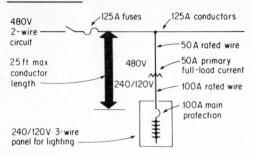

240/120V 3-wire
panel for lighting

EXAMPLE 2:

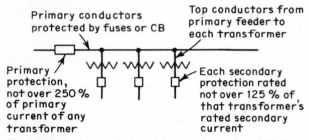

Fig. 240-20. Feeder tap of primary-plus-secondary not over 25 ft long.
(Sec. 240-21.)

3. Total tap is not over 25 ft, primary plus secondary.
4. All conductors are in conduit.
5. Secondary conductors terminate in the 100-A main protection that
   limits secondary load to the ampacity of the secondary conductor,
   and simultaneously provides the protection required by the lighting
   panel and is not rated over 125 percent of transformer secondary
   current.
6. Primary feeder protection is not over 250 percent of transformer
   rated primary current.

In Example 2, each set of tap conductors from the primary feeder to
each transformer may be same size as primary feeder conductors **or** may
be smaller than primary conductors if sized in accordance with Sec. 240-
21, Exception No. 8—which permits a 25-ft tap from a primary feeder to
be made up of both primary and secondary tap conductors. The 25-ft tap
may have any part of its length on the primary or secondary but must not
be longer than 25 ft and must terminate in a single CB or set of fuses.

Figure 240-21 shows another example of Exception No. 8 and Sec.
450-3(b) (2). Because the primary wires tapped to each transformer from
the main 100-A feeder are also rated 100 A and are therefore protected

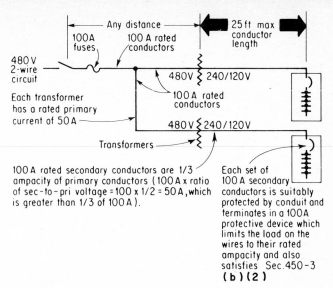

Fig. 240-21. Sizing a 25-ft tap and transformer protection. (Sec. 240-21.)

by the 100-A feeder protection, all the primary circuit to each transformer is excluded from the allowable 25 ft of tap to the secondary main protective device. The 100-A protection in each panel is not over 125 percent of the rated transformer secondary current. It, therefore, provides the transformer protection required by Sec. 450-3(b) (2). The same device also protects each panel at its main busbar rating of 100 A.

Figure 240-22 compares the two different 25-ft tap techniques covered by Exception No. 3 and Exception No. 8.

240-22. Grounded Conductors. The basic rule prohibits use of a fuse or CB in any conductor that is intentionally grounded—such as a grounded neutral or a grounded phase leg of a delta system. Figure 240-23 shows the two exceptions to that rule and a clear violation of the basic rule.

240-23. Change in Size of Grounded Conductor. In effect, this recognizes the fact that if the neutral is the same size as the ungrounded conductor, it will be protected wherever the ungrounded conductor is protected. One of the most obvious places this is encountered is in a distribution center where a small grounded conductor may be connected directly to a large grounded feeder conductor.

240-24. Location in or on Premises. According to part **(a)**, overcurrent devices must be readily accessible. And in accordance with the definition of "readily accessible" in Art. 100, they must be "capable of being reached quickly for operation, renewal, or inspections, without requiring those to whom ready access is requisite to climb over or remove obstacles or to resort to portable ladders, chairs, etc." (Fig. 240-24).

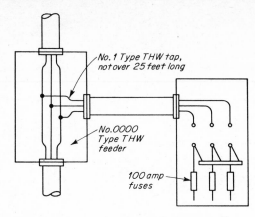

25-ft tap — EXCEPTION No. 3

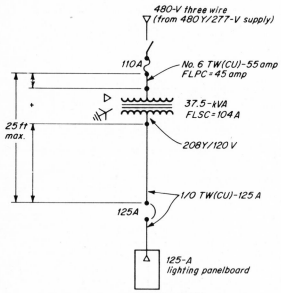

Taps protected from physical damage.
Secondary-to-primary voltage ratio = 208:480 = 1:2.3

25-ft tap—EXCEPTION No. 8

Fig. 240-22. Examples show difference between the two types of
25-ft taps. (Sec. 240-21.)

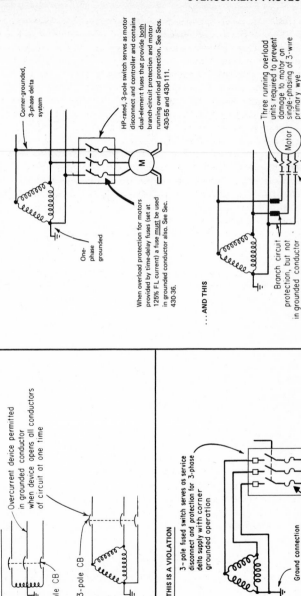

EXCEPTION NO. 2 RECOGNIZES THIS...

Corner-grounded, 3-phase delta system

HP-rated, 3-pole switch serves as motor disconnect and controller and contains dual-element fuses that provide both branch-circuit protection and motor running overload protection. See Secs. 430-55 and 430-111.

One-phase grounded

When overload protection for motors provided by time-delay fuses (set at 125% FL current) a fuse must be used in grounded conductor also. See Sec. 430-36.

...AND THIS

Three running overload units required to prevent damage to motor on single-phasing of 3-wire primary wye

Motor

Third unit in grounded conductor **(See Sec. 430-37)**

Branch circuit protection, but not in grounded conductor

Controller

EXCEPTION NO. 1 PERMITS THIS

Overcurrent device permitted in grounded conductor when device opens all conductors of circuit at one time

Grounded 3-wire 1-phase

3-pole CB

3-pole CB

Grounded 3-wire 3-phase delta

THIS IS A VIOLATION

3-pole fused switch serves as service disconnect and protection for 3-phase delta supply with corner grounded operation

Ground connection made at transformer

Overcurrent device not permitted in grounded conductor

Fig. 240-23. Overcurrent protection in grounded conductor. (Sec. 240-22.)

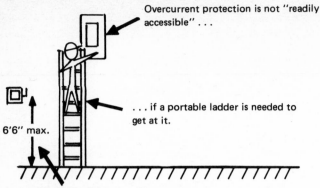

Overcurrent protection is not "readily accessible" . . .

. . . if a portable ladder is needed to get at it.

6'6" max.

Handles of switches and CBs must be not more than 6½ ft above floor or platform (Sec. 380-8).

Overcurrent device in a panel, switch, CB, switchboard, MCC is not readily accessible . . .

. . . if crates or other obstacles block access to it.

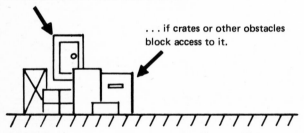

Fig. 240-24. Overcurrent devices must be "readily accessible." (Sec. 240-24.)

Although the Code gives no maximum heights at which overcurrent protective devices are considered readily accessible, some guidance can be obtained from Sec. 380-8, which provides detailed requirements for location of switches and CBs. This section states that switches and CBs shall be so installed that the center of the grip of the operating handle, when in its highest position, will not be more than 6½ ft above the floor or working platform.

Exception No. 1 to this rule is made in the case of service overcurrent protection when it is installed at the outer end of the service (such as at the service head or on a pole) or when the service overcurrent protection is locked or sealed. Exception No. 2 covers any case where an overcurrent device is used in a busway plug-in unit to tap a branch circuit from the busway. Section 364-12 requires that such devices consist of an externally operable CB or an externally operable fusible switch. These devices must be capable of being operated from the floor by means of ropes, chains, or sticks. Exception No. 3 refers to Sec. 240-10, which states that where supplementary overcurrent protection is used, such as for lighting fixtures, appliances, or for internal circuits or components of equipment, this supplementary protection is not required to be readily accessible. An example of this would be an overcurrent device mounted in the cord plug of a fixed or semi-fixed luminaire supplied from trolley busway or mounted on a luminaire that is plugged directly into a busway (Fig. 240-25).

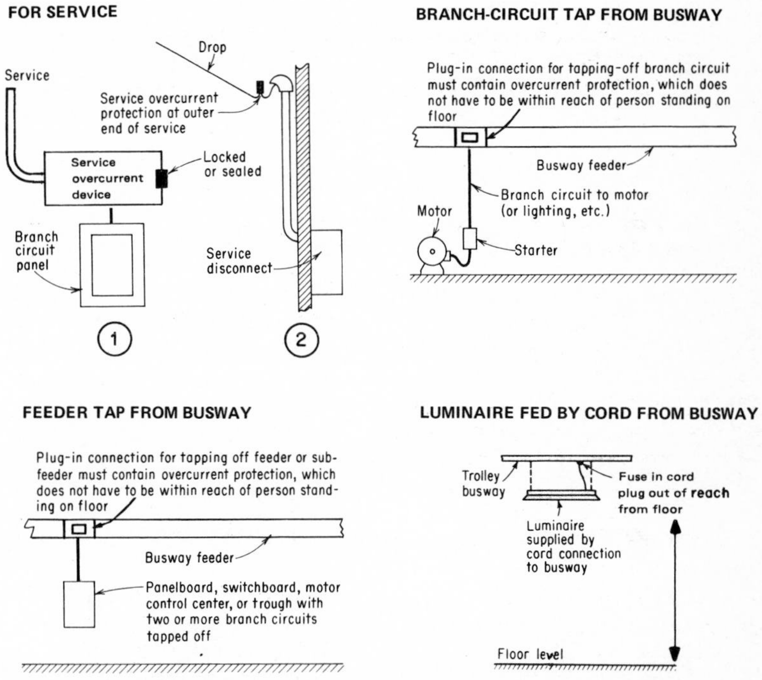

FOR SERVICE

Service

Drop

Service overcurrent protection at outer end of service

Locked or sealed

Service overcurrent device

Branch circuit panel

Service disconnect

① ②

BRANCH-CIRCUIT TAP FROM BUSWAY

Plug-in connection for tapping-off branch circuit must contain overcurrent protection, which does not have to be within reach of person standing on floor

Busway feeder

Branch circuit to motor (or lighting, etc.)

Motor

Starter

FEEDER TAP FROM BUSWAY

Plug-in connection for tapping off feeder or sub-feeder must contain overcurrent protection, which does not have to be within reach of person standing on floor

Busway feeder

Panelboard, switchboard, motor control center, or trough with two or more branch circuits tapped off

LUMINAIRE FED BY CORD FROM BUSWAY

Trolley busway

Fuse in cord plug out of **reach** from floor

Luminaire supplied by cord connection to busway

Floor level

Fig. 240-25. Fuses and CBs may be used in these ways. (Sec. 240-24.)

Section 240-24 clarifies the use of plug-in overcurrent protective devices on busway for protection of circuits tapped from busway. After making the general rule that overcurrent protective devices must be readily accessible (capable of being reached without stepping on a chair or table or resorting to a portable ladder), the Exception notes that it is not only *permissible* to use busway protective devices up on the busway—it is *required* by Sec. 364-12. Such devices on high-mounted busway are not "readily accessible" (not within reach of a person standing on the floor). The wording of Sec. 364-12 makes clear that this requirement for overcurrent protection in the device on the busway applies to subfeeders tapped from the busway as well as branch circuits tapped from the busway. The rules of NE Code Sec. 240-24, 364-12, and 380-8 must be correlated with each other to assure effective Code compliance.

Figure 24-26 shows the intent of part **(b)** of this section.

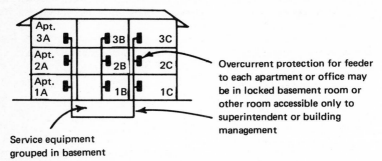

Service equipment
grouped in basement

Fig. 240-26. Other fuses or CBs that are permitted to be *not* readily accessible. (Sec. 240-24.)

In addition, it is important to note that Sec. 240-24 requires that overcurrent devices be located where they will not be exposed to physical damage or in the vicinity of easily ignitible material.

240-30. General (Enclosures).

240-32. Damp or Wet Locations.

240-33. Vertical Position.   Figure 240-27 shows the basic requirements of Secs. 240-30, 240-32, and 240-33.

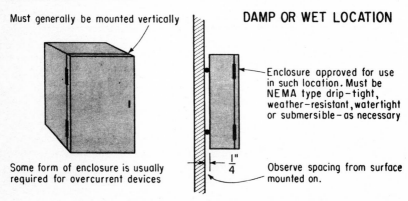

Fig. 240-27. Enclosures for overcurrent protection. (Sec. 240-30.)

240-40. Disconnecting Means for Fuses and Thermal Cutouts. The basic rules are shown in Fig. 240-28. Exception No. 2 is illustrated in Fig. 240-29.

240-50. General (Plug Fuses). Plug fuses must not be used in circuits of more than 125 V between conductors, but they may be used in grounded-neutral systems where the circuits have more than 125 V between ungrounded conductors but not more than 150 V between any ungrounded conductor and ground (Fig. 240-30). And the screw-shell of plug fuseholders must be connected to the load side of the circuit.

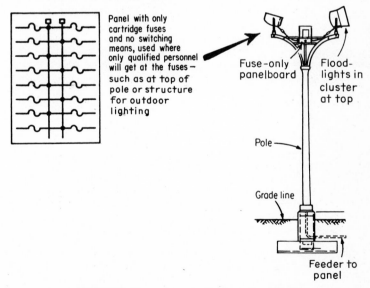

Fig. 240-28. Disconnect means for fuses. (Sec. 240-40.)

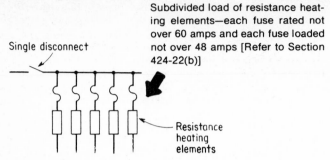

Fig. 240-29. Single disconnect for one set of fuses is permitted for electric space heating with subdivided resistance-type heating elements. (Sec. 240-40.)

240-51. Edison-Base Fuses.
240-52. Edison-Base Fuseholders.
240-53. Type S Fuses.
240-54. Type S Fuses, Adapters, and Fuseholders.   Rated up to 30 A, plug fuses are Edison-base or Type S. Section 240-51(b) limits the use of Edison-base fuses to replacements of existing fuses of this type. Type S plug fuses are required by Sec. 240-53 for all new plug-fuse installations. Type S plug fuses must be used in Type S fuseholders or in Edison-base fuseholders with a Type S adapter inserted, so that a Type S fuse of one ampere classification cannot be replaced with a higher-amp rated fuse (Fig. 240-31). Type S fuses, fuseholders, and adapters are rated for three classifications based on amp rating and are noninterchangeable from one classification to another. The classifications are 0–15, 16–20, and 21–30 A. The 0 to 15-A fuseholders or adapters must not be able to take any fuse rated over 20 A. The purpose of this rule is to prevent overfusing of 15- and 20-A circuits.

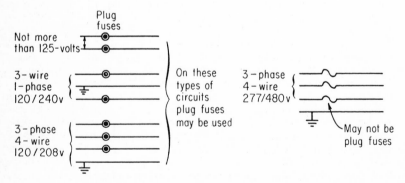

Fig. 240-30. Using plug fuses. (Sec. 240-50.)

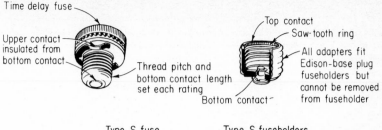

Fig. 240-31. Type S plug fuse. (Sec. 240-53.)

240-60. General (Cartridge Fuses).   The last sentence of part **(b)** must always be carefully observed. It is concerned with an extremely important matter:

The installation of current-limiting fuses demands extreme care in the selection of the fuse clips to be used. Because current-limiting fuses have an additional protective feature (that of current limitation, i.e., extremely fast operation to prevent the flow of the extremely high currents which many modern circuits can produce into a ground fault or short circuit) as compared to noncurrent-limiting fuses, some condition of the mounting arrangement for current-limiting fuses must prevent replacement of the current-limiting fuses by noncurrent-limiting. This is necessary to maintain safety in applications where, for example, the busbars of a switchboard or motor control center are braced in accordance with the maximum let-through current of current-limiting fuses which protect the busbars, but would be exposed to a much higher potential value of fault let-through current if noncurrent-limiting fuses were used to replace the current-limiting fuses. The possibility of higher current flow than that for which the busbars are braced is created by the lack of current limitation in the noncurrent-limiting fuses.

Section 240-60(b) takes the above matter into consideration when it rules that "fuseholders for current-limiting fuses shall not permit insertion of fuses that are not current limiting." To afford compliance with the Code and to obtain the necessary safety of installation, fuse manufacturers provide current-limiting fuses with special ferrules or knife blades for insertion only in special fuse clips. Such special ferrules and blades do permit the insertion of current-limiting fuses into standard NEC fuse clips, to cover those cases where current-limiting fuses (with their higher type of protection) might be used to replace noncurrent-limiting fuses. But the special rejection-type fuseholders will not accept noncurrent-limiting fuses—thereby assuring replacement only with current-limiting fuses.

The very real problem of Code compliance and safety is created by the fact that many fuses with standard ferrules and knife-blade terminals are current-limiting type and are made in the same construction and dimensions as corresponding sizes of noncurrent-limiting fuses, for use in standard fuseholders. Such current-limiting fuses are not marked "current limiting" but may be used to obtain limitation of energy let-through. Replacement of them by standard nonlimiting fuses could be hazardous.

Class J and L fuses   Both the Class J (0–600 A, 600 V AC) and L (601–6,000 A, 600 V AC) fuses are current-limiting, high-interrupting-capacity types. The interrupting ratings are 100,000 or 200,000 rms symmetrical amperes, and the designated rating is marked on the label of each Class J or L fuse. Class J and L fuses are also marked "Current Limiting," as required in part **(c)** of Sec. 240-60.

Class J fuse dimensions are different from those for standard Class H cartridge fuses of the same voltage rating and ampere classification. As such, they will require special fuseholders that will not accept noncurrent-limiting fuses. This arrangement complies with the last sentence of NEC Sec. 240-60(b).

Class K fuses   These are subdivided into Class K-1, K-5, and K-9. Class K fuses have the same dimensions as Class H (Standard NE Code) fuses and are interchangeable with them. Class K-1, K-5, and K-9 fuses have different degrees of current limitation but are not permitted to be labeled "current limiting" because physical characteristics permit these fuses to be interchanged with noncurrent-limiting types. Use of these fuses, for instance, to protect equipment busbars that are braced to withstand 40,000 A of fault current at a point where, say, 60,000 A of current would be available if noncurrent-limiting fuses were used is a clear violation of the last sentence of part **(b)**. As shown in Fig. 240-32,

Fuseholders in main switch of motor
control center require Class K–1 fuses
for current limitation to protect busbars.
Fuseholders furnished permit replacement of K–1
fuses with non–current–limiting type.

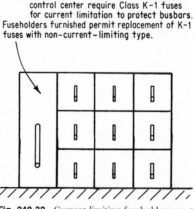

Fig. 240-32. Current-limiting fuseholders must be rejection type. (Sec. 240-60.)

because such fuses can be replaced with nonlimiting fuses, the equipment bus structure would be exposed to dangerous failure. Classes R and T have been developed to provide current limitation and prevent interchangeability with noncurrent-limiting types.

Class R fuses　These fuses are made in two designations: RK1 and RK5. UL data are as follows:

Fuses marked "Class RK1" or "Class RK5" are high-interrupting-capacity types and *are* marked "Current Limiting." Although these fuses will fit into standard fuseholders that take Class H and Class K fuses, special rejection-type fuseholders designed for Class RK1 and RK5 fuses will not accept Class H and Class K fuses. In that way, circuits and equipment protected in accordance with the characteristics of RK1 or RK5 fuses cannot have that protection reduced by the insertion of other fuses of a lower protective level.

Other UL application data that affect selection of various types of fuses are as follows:

Fuses designated as Class CC (0–20 A, 600 V AC) are high-interrupting-capacity types and are marked "Current Limiting." They are not interchangeable with fuses of higher voltage or interrupting rating or lower current rating.

Class G fuses (0–60 A, 300 V AC) are high-interrupting-capacity types and are marked "Current Limiting." They are not interchangeable with other fuses mentioned above and below.

Fuses designated as Class T (0–600 A, 250 and 600 V AC) are high-interrupting-capacity types and are marked "Current Limiting." They are not interchangeable with other fuses mentioned above.

Part **(c)** requires use of fuses to conform to the marking on them. Fuses that are intended to be used for current limitation must be marked "Current Limiting."

Class K-1, K-5, and K-9 fuses are marked, in addition to their regular voltage and current ratings, with an interrupting rating of 200,000, 100,000, or 50,000 A (rms symmetrical).

Class CC, RK1, RK5, J, L, and T fuses are marked, in addition to their regular voltage and current ratings, with an interrupting rating of 200,000 A (rms symmetrical).

Class CC, RK1, RK5, J, L, and T fuses are marked, in addition to their regular voltage and current ratings, with an interrupting rating of 200,000 A (rms symmetrical).

Although it is not required by the Code, manufcturers are in a position to provide fuses that are advertised and marked indicating they have "time-delay" characteristics. In the case of Class CC, Class G, Class H, Class K, and Class RK fuses, time-delay characteristics of fuses (minimum blowing time) have been investigated. Class G or CC fuses, which can carry 200 percent of rated current for 12 sec or more, and Class H, Class K, or Class RK fuses, which can carry 500 percent of rated current for 10 sec or more, may be marked with "D," "Time Delay," or some equivalent designation. Class L fuses are permitted to be marked "Time Delay" but

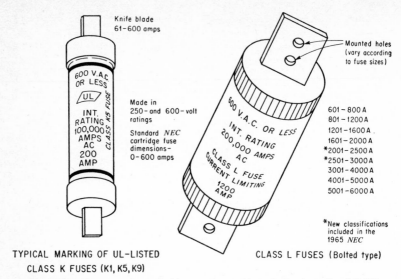

Knife blade
61–600 amps

Mounted holes
(vary according
to fuse sizes)

600 V.A.C.
OR LESS

UL

INT.
RATING
100,000
AMPS
AC
200
AMP

CLASS K5 FUSE

Made in
250- and 600-volt
ratings

Standard *NEC*
cartridge fuse
dimensions–
0–600 amps

600 V.A.C. OR LESS
INT. RATING
200,000 AMPS
AC
CLASS L FUSE
CURRENT LIMITING
1200
AMP

601 – 800 A
801 – 1200 A
1201 – 1600 A
1601 – 2000 A
*2001 – 2500 A
*2501 – 3000 A
3001 – 4000 A
4001 – 5000 A
5001 – 6000 A

*New classifications
included in the
1965 *NEC*

TYPICAL MARKING OF UL–LISTED
CLASS K FUSES (K1, K5, K9)

CLASS L FUSES (Bolted type)

Fig. 240-33. Fuses must be applied in accordance with marked ratings. (Sec. 240-60.)

have not been evaluated for such performance. Class J and T fuses are not permitted to be marked "Time Delay."

240-61. Classification.   A sentence was added to this section noting that any fuse may be used at its voltage rating or at any voltage below its voltage rating. The two exceptions of this section recognize fuses larger than 6,000 A when "approved for the purpose" and fuses of voltage other than those designated.

240-80. Method of Operation (Circuit Breakers).   This rule ties in with that in Sec. 230-76, although this rule requires manual operation to *both* the closed and open position of the CB (Fig. 240-34).

240-81. Indicating.   This rule requires the up position of CBs on switchboards to be the "on" position. This applies only to breakers that have vertically (rather than horizontally or rotationally) operated handles.

Electrically operated power CB
for service disconnect may be
tripped manually and provides
for manual closing of its contacts by
opening cover to get at handle inside.

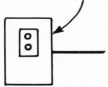

Fig. 240-34. Every CB must be manually operable. (Sec. 240-80.)

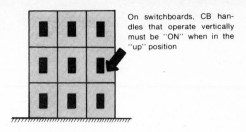

On switchboards, CB handles that operate vertically must be "ON" when in the "up" position

THIS IS REQUIRED

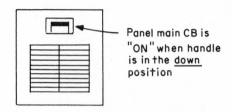

Panel main CB is "ON" when handle is in the <u>down</u> position

THIS IS NOT A VIOLATION

Fig. 240-35. Handle position of CBs on switchboards. (Sec. 240-81.)

Note that the requirement applies only to CBs in switchboards—but not in panelboards or individual enclosures (Fig. 240-35).

240-83. Marking. Part **(d)** of this section requires that any CB used to switch 120-V fluorescent lighting be "approved for the purpose" and be marked "SWD" (Fig. 240-36).

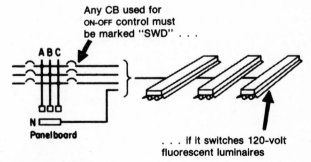

Any CB used for ON-OFF control must be marked "SWD" . . .

A B C

N

Panelboard

. . . if it switches 120-volt fluorescent luminaires

Fig. 240-36. Circuit breakers used for switching lights must be "SWD" type. [Sec. 240-83(d).]

In commercial and industrial electrical systems, ON-OFF control of lighting is commonly done by the breakers in the lighting panel, eliminating any local wiring-device switches. UL states that "circuit breakers marked SWD are suitable for switching 120-volt fluorescent lighting on a regular basis." Such listing indicates that any CB used for regular switching of 120-V fluorescents must be marked SWD and that breakers *not* so marked are *not* suitable for panel switching of lighting. There is, however, no indication in UL listing data that suggests that breakers are suitable for ON-OFF control of lighting on a regular basis at any other voltage. Although 277-V CBs are not required to be designated as suitable for regular or frequent switching of lighting of any kind, such CBs are available with the "SWD" marking and are suitable for switching duty because they are more ruggedly constructed than the usual 120-V CBs.

Under this rule, only those 120-V breakers bearing the designation "SWD" (switching duty) may be used as snap switches for lighting control. Type "SWD" breakers have been tested and found suitable for the greater frequency of ON-OFF operations required for switching duty than for strictly overcurrent protection, in which the breaker is used only for generally infrequent disconnect for circuit repair or maintenance.

240-100. Feeders (Over 600 V). This section presents rules on overcurrent protection for high-voltage (over 600 V) feeder conductors. It requires short-circuit protection of adequate interrupting capacity for its point of use. Although the rule calls for "short-circuit" protection, it does *not* require that conductors be protected in accordance with their rated ampacities. Refer to Sec. 230-208, which is referenced in this section (Fig. 240-37).

A high-voltage feeder:

1. *Must* have a "short-circuit protective device in *each* ungrounded conductor." OR—
2. It may be protected by a CB equipped with overcurrent relays and current transformers in *only two phases* and arranged as described in Sec. 230-208(d) (2) or (d) (3), which covers overcurrent protection of high-voltage service conductors.

The requirement on maximum value of high-voltage overcurrent protection is as follows:

A FUSE must be rated in continuous amps at *not* more than THREE TIMES the ampacity of the circuit conductor.

A CIRCUIT BREAKER must have a long-time trip element rated *not* more than SIX TIMES the ampacity of the feeder conductor.

As explained under Sec. 230-208, E-rated fuses used for circuits over 600 V can carry 200 percent of their rated current continuously. Therefore, THREE TIMES the current rating of such a fuse is the *same value* of protection as SIX TIMES the current rating of a CB of the same amp rating as the fuse. For instance, three times the 100-A rating of an E-rated fuse is actually three times 200 A or 600 A—which is the same as six times the 100-A rating of a CB.

TYPE OF DEVICE

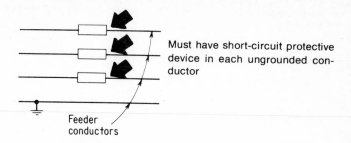

Must have short-circuit protective device in each ungrounded conductor

Feeder conductors

REQUIRED MINIMUM RATING

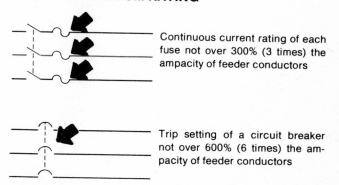

Continuous current rating of each fuse not over 300% (3 times) the ampacity of feeder conductors

Trip setting of a circuit breaker not over 600% (6 times) the ampacity of feeder conductors

Fig. 240-37. Overcurrent protection of high-voltage (over 600 V) feeder conductors. (Sec. 240-100.)

240-101. Branch Circuits. This applies to high-voltage branch circuits, which are invariably branch circuits for high-voltage motors and as such must also satisfy Sec. 430-125 covering overload and fault-current protection for high-voltage motor circuits. A high-voltage branch circuit must be protected by a short-circuit protective device in *each* ungrounded conductor **or** it may be protected by a CB with relays in *only two* phase legs, as described in Sec. 230-208(d) (2) or (d) (3).

ARTICLE 250. GROUNDING

250-1. Scope. One of the most important, but least understood, considerations in design of electrical systems is that of grounding. The word "grounding" comes from the fact that the technique itself involves making a low-resistance connection to the earth or to ground. For any given piece of equipment or circuit, this connection may be a direct wire connection to the grounding electrode which is buried in the earth; or it may be a connection to some other conductive metallic element (such as conduit or switchboard enclosure) which is connected to a grounding electrode.

The purpose of grounding is to provide protection of personnel, equipment, and circuits by eliminating the possibility of dangerous or excessive voltages.

There are two distinct considerations in grounding for electrical systems: grounding of one of the conductors of the wiring system, and grounding of all metal enclosures which contain electrical wires or equipment when an insulation failure in such enclosures might place a potential on the enclosures and constitute a shock or fire hazard. The types of grounding are:

1. *Wiring system ground.* This consists of grounding one of the wires of the electrical system, such as the neutral, to limit the voltage upon the circuit which might otherwise occur through exposure to lightning or other voltages higher than that for which the circuit is designed. Another purpose in grounding one of the wires of the system is to limit the maximum voltage to ground under normal operating conditions. Also, a system which operates with one of its conductors intentionally grounded will provide for automatic opening of the circuit if an accidental or fault ground occurs on one of its ungrounded conductors (Fig. 250-1).

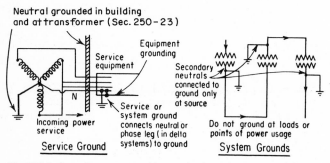

Fig. 250-1. Operating a system with one circuit conductor grounded. (Sec. 250-1.)

2. *Equipment ground.* This is a permanent and continuous bonding together (i.e., connecting together) of all noncurrent-carrying metal parts of equipment enclosures—conduit, boxes, cabinets, housings, frames of motors, and lighting fixtures—and connection of this interconnected system of enclosures to the system grounding electrode (Fig. 250-2). The interconnection of all metal enclosures must

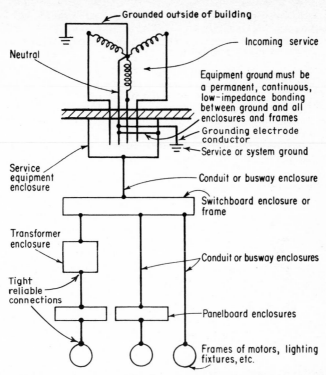

Fig. 250-2. Equipment grounding is interconnection of metal enclosures of equipment and their connection to ground. (Sec. 250-1.)

be made to provide a low-impedance path for fault-current flow along the enclosures to assure operation of overcurrent devices which will open a circuit in the event of a fault. By opening a faulted circuit, the system prevents dangerous voltages from being present on equipment enclosures which could be touched by personnel, with consequent electric shock to such personnel.

Simply stated, grounding of all metal enclosures of electric wires and equipment prevents any potential-above-ground on the enclosures. Such bonding together and grounding of all metal enclosures are required for both grounded electrical systems (those systems in which one of the circuit conductors is intentionally grounded) and ungrounded electrical systems (systems with none of the circuit wires intentionally grounded).

But effective equipment grounding is extremely important for grounded electrical systems to provide the automatic fault clearing which is one of the important advantages of grounded electrical systems. A low-impedance path for fault current is necessary to permit enough current to flow to operate the fuses or CB protecting the circuit.

In a grounded electrical system with a high-impedance equipment ground-return path, if one of the phase conductors of the system (i.e., one of the ungrounded conductors of the wiring system) should accidentally come in contact with one of the metal enclosures in which the wires are run, it might produce a condition where not enough fault current would flow to operate the overcurrent devices. In such a case, the faulted circuit would not automatically open, and a dangerous voltage would be present on the conduit and other metal enclosures. This voltage presents a shock hazard and a fire hazard due to possible arcing or sparking from the energized conduit to some grounded pipe or other piece of grounded metal.

In a grounded system with a high-impedance equipment ground-return system, a ground fault will not open the circuit, and a phase-to-phase fault must develop to operate the overcurrent device, with all the attendant hazards of such conditions.

One of the most consistently troublesome and controversial areas of modern electrical construction is application of National Electrical Code rules and OSHA regulations concerned with system grounding. For both new electrical systems and exsting systems, many questions are raised about the need to operate with the neutral or one of the phase legs intentionally grounded at the service or transformer secondary. When *must* one of the circuit conductors be a *grounded* conductor? (Note that this is a matter of *system* grounding and is a separate consideration from *equipment* grounding—which is the effective tieing together and grounding of equipment enclosures, housings, and similar noncurrent-carrying exposed metal parts of electrical equipment.)

There are several NE Code sections that relate to this very important subject:

- Section 210-6(a) regulates use of lampholders, lighting fixtures, and receptacles on circuits of different voltages to ground. Although such load devices are basically limited to use on circuits rated not over 150 V to ground (240/120-V, 3-wire, single-phase and 208/120-V, 3-phase, 4-wire systems), incandescent and electric-discharge lighting may be used on circuits rated up to 300 V to ground in industrial, commercial, and institutional occupancies under the conditions given. "Voltage to ground" is the maximum voltage between any ungrounded circuit conductor and an intentionally grounded conductor (such as a grounded neutral or phase leg). For an ungrounded system, the NE Code specifies "voltage to ground" is the maximum voltage between any two of the circuit conductors (which would occur if one of the circuit conductors became accidentally grounded).

- Section 210-6(b) permits electric-discharge lighting units on circuits of not more than 500 V "between conductors"—*but only* for outdoor use or in tunnels.

■ Section 410-78 requires that *only a grounded* system (one circuit conductor intentionally grounded) may be used to supply lighting equipment that contains an autotransformer-type ballast that raises the voltage to more than 300 V.

■ Section 250-(b) specifies when electrical systems must be operated with one of the circuit conductors grounded.

OSHA requires that all the rules of Sec. 210-6, 410-78, and 250-5(b) apply to new electrical installations in any "place of employment." **But in addition,** OSHA has made Sec. 250-5 retroactive so that all existing installations that do not conform to Sec. 250-5(b) *must* be altered to comply with those rules. Note, however, that OSHA did *not* make Sec. 210-6 and 410-78 retroactive. Existing systems that do not comply with those rules are not required to be brought into compliance.

The effect of the foregoing rules on various types and voltages of electrical systems are as follows:

1. Any new or existing circuits rated 120 V must have one conductor grounded. And this applies to the secondary of even the smallest lighting transformer that might be used for a light at a machine or other local application. Exceptions permitting ungrounded 120-V circuits are made in Sec. 250-5(b), Exception No. 3 for control circuits and in Sec. 517-104 for circuits in anesthetizing locations in hospitals and health-care facilities. Any new or existing 240/120-V, 3-wire, single-phase system or a 208/120-V, 3-phase, 4-wire system *must* have the neutral grounded.

   For instance, a 120-V, 3-wire, ungrounded delta system violates Sec. 250-5(b) (1) and must be converted to a corner-grounded delta or grounded wye (by a zig-zag grounding autotransformer—see NE Code Sec. 450-4).

2. Any new *or* existing 480/277-V wye system must have the neutral point of the wye grounded if a neutral conductor is derived from that point and used as a circuit conductor to supply any kind of loads. **But** if a 480/277-V transformer secondary is used to supply only 480-V loads and no neutral conductor is used, the neutral point of the wye does *not* have to be grounded to satisfy the NE Code. Utility company rules, however, may require grounding of the wye, and such rules must be checked.

3. A 480-V ungrounded delta system may not be used to supply *indoor* lighting of any kind for a *new* system. In such a system, the voltage to ground is taken as 480 V and would be a violation of Sec. 210-6(a), Exception No. 1 and Exception No. 2. A 480-V ungrounded delta system may be used for outdoor and tunnel lighting as permitted by Sec. 210-6(b), *but* in such cases only 2-winding transformer ballasts (not autotransformer type) must be used to satisfy Sec. 410-78.

4. Existing 480-V ungrounded delta systems that supply 480-V indoor lighting fixtures (of either 2-winding or autotransformer-type ballasts) are not in violation of retroactive Sec. 250-5(b) and therefore

do not have to be converted to grounded operation. Such hookups are, however, contrary to the rules of Sec. 210-6(a) and may violate Sec. 410-78 if autotransformer ballasts are used. But OSHA does *not* require retroactive application of **NE Code** Sec. 210-6(a) and 410-78. Of course, it is always good practice to update existing systems and bring them into compliance, even if it is not required.

5. Existing 480-V, 3-phase, 3-wire ungrounded systems derived from a 480/277-V wye transformer secondary and supplying 480-V indoor lighting connected phase-to-phase are *not* in violation of retroactive Sec. 250-5(b) and do not have to have the neutral point grounded. Again, such hookup could not be used without the neutral grounded for new indoor lighting because it violates Sec. 210-6(a). But it could be used for new outdoor and/or tunnel lighting as in Sec. 210-6(b). And, again, Sec. 410-78 must be observed for new installations.

6. New *or* existing 240-V, 3-phase, 3-wire ungrounded systems may supply incandescent or electric-discharge lighting in accordance with Sec. 210-6(a). In such a system, the voltage to ground is 240 V—which does not exceed the 300-V maximum in Exception No. 1 and Exception No. 2 of Sec. 210-6(a). And a 240-V ungrounded delta system is not in violation of the retroactive rules of Sec. 250-5(b). But use of an ungrounded system to supply autotransformer ballasts that raise the voltage to more than 300 V violates Sec. 410-78.

In all design and installation work today, it is imperative to observe *all* applicable regulations and carefully relate the rules to each other.

250-3. Direct-Current Systems. Direct-current systems—both 2-wire and 3-wire—must also be grounded if the voltage to ground will not exceed 300 V. A 2-wire DC system, with no more than 300 V between conductors, must be grounded unless it is used for supplying industrial equipment in limited areas and is equipped with a ground detector. In a 3-wire DC system, the neutral conductor must be grounded.

250-5. Alternating-Current Circuits and Systems to Be Grounded.   Part (a) does recognize use of ungrounded circuits or systems when operating at less than 50 V. But grounding of circuits under 50 V is required, as shown in Fig. 250-3.

According to part (b) of this rule, all alternating-current wiring systems from 50 to 1,000 V *must* be grounded if they can be so grounded that the maximum voltage to ground does not exceed 150 V. This rule makes it *mandatory* that the following systems or circuits operate with one conductor grounded:

1. 120-V, 2-wire systems or circuits must have one of their wires grounded.
2. 240/120-V, 3-wire, single-phase systems or circuits must have their neutral conductor grounded.
3. 208/120-V, 3-phase, 4-wire, wye-connected systems or circuits must be operated with the neutral conductor grounded.

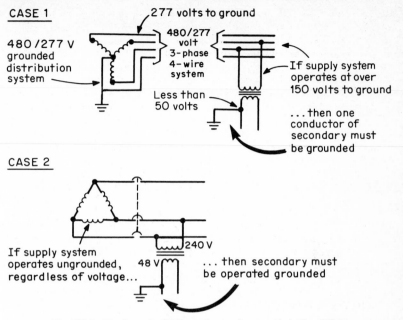

Fig. 250-3. Circuits under 50 V may have to be grounded. (Sec. 250-5.)

In all the foregoing systems or circuits, the neutrals must be grounded because **the maximum voltage to ground does not exceed 150 V** from any other conductor of the system when the neutral conductor is grounded.

Section 250-5(b) requires that the neutral conductor of a 240/120-V, 3-phase, 4-wire system (with the neutral taken from the midpoint of one phase) must be grounded. It is also mandatory that 480Y/277-V, 3-phase, 4-wire interior wiring systems have the neutral grounded if the neutral is to be used as a circuit conductor—such as for 277-V lighting. And if 480-V autotransformer-type fluorescent or mercury-vapor ballasts are to be supplied from 480/277-V systems, then the neutral conductor will have to be grounded at the voltage source to conform to Sec. 410-78, even though the neutral is not used as a circuit conductor. Of course, it should be noted that 480/277-V systems are usually operated with the neutral grounded to obtain automatic fault-clearing of a grounded system (Fig. 250-4).

Any AC system of 1,000 V or more must be grounded if it supplies portable equipment. Otherwise, such systems do not have to be grounded, although they *may* be grounded.

Although the NE Code does not require grounding of electrical systems in which the voltage to ground would exceed 150 V, it does

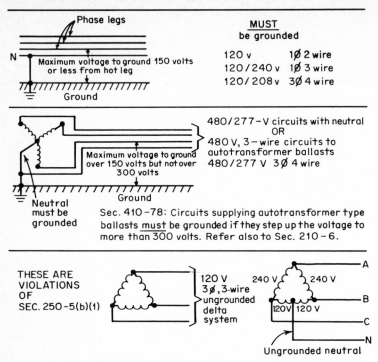

Fig. 250-4. Some systems or circuits must be grounded. (Sec. 250-5.)

recommend that ground-fault detectors be used with ungrounded systems which operate at more than 150 V and less than 1,000 V. Such detectors indicate when an accidental ground fault develops on one of the phase legs of ungrounded systems. Then the indicated ground fault can be removed during downtime of the industrial operation—i.e., when the production machinery is not running.

Many industrial plants prefer to use an ungrounded system with ground-fault detectors instead of a grounded system. With a grounded system, the occurrence of a ground fault is supposed to draw enough current to operate the overcurrent device protecting the circuit. But such fault-clearing opens the circuit—which may be a branch circuit supplying a motor or other power load or may be a feeder which supplies a number of power loads; and many industrial plants object to the loss of production caused by downtime. They would rather use the ungrounded system and have the system kept operative with a single ground fault and clear the fault when the production machinery is not in use. In some plants, the cost of downtime of production machines can run to thousands of

dollars per minute. In other plants, interruption of critical process is
extremely costly.

The difference between a grounded and ungrounded system is that a
single ground fault will automatically cause opening of the circuit in a
grounded system, but will not interrupt operations in an ungrounded
system. However, the presence of a single ground fault on an
ungrounded system exposes the system to the very destructive possibilities of a phase-to-phase short if another ground fault should simultaneously develop on a different phase leg of the system (Fig. 250-5).

UNGROUNDED SYSTEMS

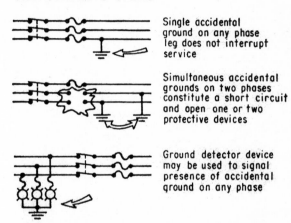

Single accidental
ground on any phase
leg does not interrupt
service

Simultaneous accidental
grounds on two phases
constitute a short circuit
and open one or two
protective devices

Ground detector device
may be used to signal
presence of accidental
ground on any phase

Fig. 250-5. Characteristics of ungrounded systems. (Sec. 250-5.)

Grounded neutral systems are generally recommended for high-voltage (over 600) distribution. Although ungrounded systems do not
undergo a power outage with only one-phase ground faults, the time and
money spent in tracing faults indicated by ground detectors and other
disadvantages of ungrounded systems have favored use of grounded
neutral systems. Grounded systems are more economical in operation
and maintenance. In such a system, if a fault occurs, it is isolated
immediately and automatically.

Grounded neutral systems have many other advantages. The elimination of multiple faults caused by undetected restriking grounds greatly
increases service reliability. The lower voltage to ground which results
from grounding the neutral offers greater safety for personnel and
requires lower equipment voltage ratings. And on high-voltage (above
600) systems, residual relays can be used to detect ground faults before
they become phase-to-phase faults which have substantial destructive
ability.

Exception No. 3 to the basic rule requiring grounding of one conductor of AC electrical systems recognizes use of *ungrounded* control circuits derived from transformers.

According to the rules of part **(b)** of this section, any 120-V, 2-wire circuit *must* normally have one of its conductors grounded, the neutral conductor of any 240/120-V, 3-wire, single-phase circuit *must* be grounded, and the neutral of a 208/120-V, 3-phase, 4-wire circuit *must* be grounded. Those requirements have often caused difficulty when applied to control circuits derived from the secondary of a control transformer that supplies power to the operating coils of motor starters, contactors, and relays. For instance, there are cases where a ground fault on the hot leg of a grounded control circuit can cause a hazard to personnel by actuating the control circuit fuse or CB and shutting down an industrial process in a sudden, unexpected, nonorderly way. A metal-casting facility is an example of an installation where sudden shutdown due to a ground fault in the hot leg of a grounded control circuit could be objectionable. Because designers often wish to operate such 120-V control circuits ungrounded, Exception No. 3 of Sec. 250-5(b) permits ungrounded control circuits under certain specified conditions.

A 120-V control circuit may be operated ungrounded when all the following exist:

1. The circuit is derived from a transformer that has a primary rating less than 1,000 V.
2. Whether in a commercial, institutional, or industrial facility, supervision will assure that only persons qualified in electrical work will maintain and service the control circuits.
3. There is a need for preventing circuit opening on a ground fault— i.e., continuity of power is required for safety or for operating reliability.
4. Some type of ground detectors are used on the ungrounded system to alert personnel to the presence of any ground fault, enabling them to clear the ground fault in normal downtime of the system (Fig. 250-6).

Although no mention is made of secondary voltage in this Code rule, this Exception permitting ungrounded control circuits is primarily significant only for 120-V control circuits. The NE Code has long permitted 240-V and 480-V control circuits to be operated ungrounded. Application of this Exception can be made for any 120-V control circuit derived from a control transformer in an individual motor starter or for a separate control transformer that supplies control power for a number of motor starters or magnetic contactors. Of course, the Exception could also be used to permit ungrounded 277-V control circuits under the same conditions.

Part **(d)** of Sec. 250-5 has special meaning on grounding requirements for emergency generators used in electrical sytems. It is best studied in steps:

1. The wording here presents the basic rule that covers grounding of "separately derived systems"—which has always been understood to refer to generator output circuits and transformer secondary circuits because such systems are "derived" separate from other wiring systems and have no conductor connected to the other systems.

2. For a separately derived system, if the voltage and hookup requires grounding as specified in Sec. 250-5(b), then such systems have to be grounded and bonded as described in Sec. 250-26.

3. With respect to 2-winding transformers (i.e., single-phase or polyphase transformers that are *not* autotransformers and have *only* magnetic coupling from the primary to the secondary), there is no question that the secondary circuits are "separately derived," and grounding must always be done as required by Secs. 250-5(b) and 250-26.

4. But, when the rule of Sec. 250-5(d), as worded in the 1975 **NE Code**, was applied to 208/120-V or 480/277-V generators used for emergency power in the event of an outage of the normal electric utility service, difficulties arose. The 1975 **NE Code** wording of that rule required such an emergency generator to have its neutral bonded to the generator housing and to be connected to a grounding electrode—both as spelled out in Sec. 250-26. Such generators were tied into the automatic transfer switch that is also fed from the

FOR SEPARATE OR BUILT-IN TRANSFORMER—

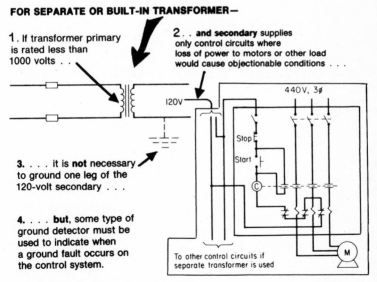

1. If transformer primary is rated less than 1000 volts . . .

2. . . **and secondary** supplies only control circuits where loss of power to motors or other load would cause objectionable conditions . . .

120V

440V, 3∅

Stop

Start

C

3. . . . . it is **not** necessary to ground one leg of the 120-volt secondary . . .

4. . . . . **but,** some type of ground detector must be used to indicate when a ground fault occurs on the control system.

To other control circuits if separate transformer is used

M

Fig. 250-6. Ungrounded 120-V circuits may be used for controls. (Sec. 250-5.)

normal service equipment—with a solidly connected neutral conductor running from the service equipment, through the transfer switch, to the generator neutral terminal; and the neutral is bonded and grounded at both the normal service and at the generator.

5. Section 250-21 prohibits grounding connections that produce objectionable flow of current over grounding conductors or grounding paths. But the two grounding connections—at the service and at the generator, as described in 4 can produce objectionable current flow under both normal and fault conditions:

 Under normal conditions, neutral current of the connected load in the building has two paths of current flow from the common neutral point in the transfer switch back to the service neutral terminal. One path, of course, is over the neutral conductor from the transfer switch to the service equipment. The other path is over the neutral conductor from the transfer switch to the generator, at which point the current can flow back to the service equipment over the grounding conductor (the conduit and enclosure interconnections) that runs between the service equipment and the generator.

 Under ground-fault conditions, a similar double path for current flow can cause desensitizing of ground-fault protective equipment—as discussed and shown under Sec. 230-95, when a 3-pole transfer switch is used.

6. Prior to the 1978 NE Code, elimination of the desensitizing of service GF protection could be accomplished by the use of a 4-pole transfer switch that prevented a solid neutral connection from the service equipment to the generator.

7. **Now,** in the 1978 NE Code, the grounding requirements of Sec. 250-5(d) apply to a generator *only* where the generator "has no direct electrical connection, including a solidly grounded circuit conductor" to the normal service. The rule would apply to a generator that fed its load without any tie-in through a transfer switch to *any* other system. If a generator *does have* a solidly connected neutral from it to the service through a 3-pole, solid-neutral transfer switch, then that generator is *not* a separately derived system and Sec. 250-26 does not apply (Fig. 250-7). The Code, in such a case, *does not* require the generator neutral to be bonded to the frame or to be grounded to a grounding electrode.

The effect of the rule of Sec. 250-5(d) on transfer switches is as follows:

3-pole transfer switch   If a solid neutral connection is made from the service neutral, through the transfer switch, to the generator neutral, then bonding and grounding of the neutral at the generator are *not* required because the neutral is already bonded and grounded at the service equipment. And if bonding and grounding were done at the generator, it could be considered a violation of Sec. 250-21(a) and would have to be corrected by Sec. 250-21(b).

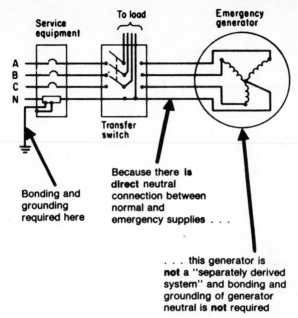

Fig. 250-7. With 3-pole transfer, generator neutral need not be bonded. (Sec. 250-5.)

4-pole transfer switch   Because there is no direct electrical connection of either the hot legs or the neutral between the service and the generator, the generator in such a hookup is a "separately derived system" and must be grounded and bonded to the generator case at the generator (Fig. 250-8).

It should be noted that the 4-pole transfer switch and other neutral-switching techniques came into use to eliminate problems of GFP desensitizing that were caused by use of a 3-pole transfer switch **when the neutral of the generator was bonded to the generator housing.** By eliminating that bonding requirement for emergency generators in Sec. 250-5(d) it was the Code intent to make possible use of 3-pole transfer switches without disruption of service GFP. But that has not resulted and the neutral-switching concept has prevailed.

Although the 1978 NE Code altered the rule in Sec. 250-5(d) to permit use of an ungrounded and nonbonded generator neutral in conjunction with a 3-pole transfer switch, such application has been found to produce other conditions of undesirable current flow, resulting in other forms of desensitizing of service GFP. As a result, the use of a 4-pole transfer

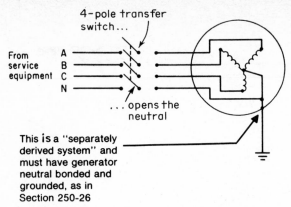

Fig. 250-8. Generator neutral *must* be bonded when neutral is opened. (Sec. 250-5.)

switch or some other technique that opens the neutral is the only effective way to avoid GFP desensitizing. Ground-fault protection is not compatible with a solid neutral tie between the service and an emergency generator—with or without its neutral bonded.

250-6. Portable and Vehicle Mounted Generators.   Part **(a)** rules that the frame of a portable generator does not have to be grounded if the generator supplies only equipment mounted on the generator and/or plug-connected equipment through receptacles mounted on the generator, provided that the noncurrent-carrying metal parts of equipment and the equipment grounding conductor terminals are bonded to the generator frame. See Fig. 250-9.

A clarification in part **(a)** points out that, where a portable generator is used with its frame *not* grounded, the frame is permitted to act as the grounding electrode for any cord-connected tools or appliances plugged into the generator's receptacles (Fig. 250-10). This assures that tools and appliances that are required by Sec. 250-45 to be grounded do satisfy the Code when plugged into a receptacle on the ungrounded frame of a portable generator. It should also be noted that part **(c)** of this section requires the neutral conductor of the generator output to be bonded to the frame of the generator when it is not used as an emergency source connected to a transfer switch.

Part **(b)** notes that the frame of a vehicle mounted generator may be bonded to the vehicle frame, which then serves as the grounding electrode—but only when the generator supplies only equipment mounted on the vehicle and/or cord- and plug-connected equipment through receptacles on the vehicle or generator. When the frame of a vehicle is used as the grounding electrode for a generator mounted on the vehicle,

1. . . . the generator supplies equipment mounted on generator and/or cord-and-plug-connected equipment through receptacles on the generator, and

2. metal parts of equipment and equipment grounding terminals of receptacles are bonded to generator frame.

Fig. 250-9. Grounding of portable generator frame is *not* required if these conditions exist. (Sec. 250-6.)

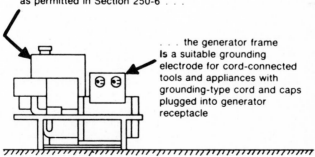

When frame of portable generator is left ungrounded as permitted in Section 250-6 . . .

. . . the generator frame is a suitable grounding electrode for cord-connected tools and appliances with grounding-type cord and caps plugged into generator receptacle

Fig. 250-10. "Ungrounded" generator frame is acceptable grounding electrode. (Sec. 250-6.)

Portable or vehicle generator as sole source or separately derived

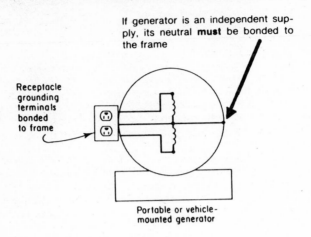

If generator is an independent supply, its neutral **must** be bonded to the frame

Receptacle grounding terminals bonded to frame

Portable or vehicle-mounted generator

Portable generator supplying premises wiring

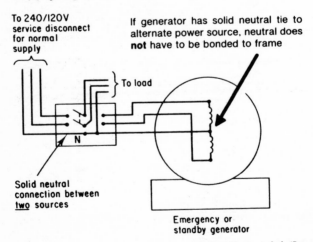

To 240/120V service disconnect for normal supply

If generator has solid neutral tie to alternate power source, neutral does **not** have to be bonded to frame

To load

N

Solid neutral connection between **two** sources

Emergency or standby generator

Fig. 250-11. Generator neutral may be required to be grounded. (Sec. 250-6.)

grounding terminals of receptacles on the generator must be bonded to the generator frame, which must be bonded to the vehicle frame.

If either a portable or vehicle mounted generator supplies a fixed wiring system external to the generator assembly, it must then be grounded as required for any separately derived system (as, for instance, a transformer secondary), as covered in Sec. 250-26.

The wording of part **(c)** brings application of portable and vehicle mounted generators into compliance with the concept described above in Sec. 250-5(d) on grounding and bonding of the generator neutral conductor. A generator neutral *must be* bonded to the generator frame when the generator is a truly separately derived source, such as the sole source of power to the loads it feeds, and is *not* tied into a transfe switch as part of a **normal emergency** hookup for feeding the load normally from the utility service and from the generator on an emergency or standby basis (Fig. 250-11). A note to this section refers to Sec. 250-5(d) and makes that rule applicable to grounding and bonding of portable generators that supply a fixed wiring system on a premises. In such a case, bonding of the neutral to the generator frame is not required if there is a solid neutral connection from the utility service, through a transfer switch to the generator, as shown in the bottom sketch of Fig. 250-11.

250-22. Point of Connection for Direct-Current Systems. On a 3-wire DC distribution system, the neutral is shown grounded at the supply station only as shown in Fig. 250-12. On a 2-wire DC system, grounding would be accomplished in the same manner.

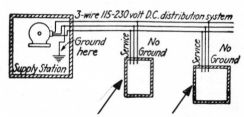

Grounding connections of the grounded conductor at each service entrance are prohibited.

Fig. 250-12. Required grounding of DC systems. (Sec. 250-22.)

250-23. Grounding Connections for Alternating-Current Systems. As noted in part **(a)**, when an electrical system is to be operated with one conductor grounded—either because it is required by the Code (e.g., 240/120-V, single phase) or because it is desired by the system designer (e.g., 240-V, 3-phase, corner grounded)—a connection to the grounding electrode must be made at the service entrance (Fig. 250-13). That is, the

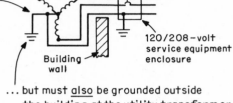

System "grounded" conductor must be connected
to electrode (S) at service entrance . . .

Outside

For instance, utility
transformer on pole,
with connection to a
ground rod

120/208 – volt
service equipment
enclosure

Building
wall

. . . but must also be grounded outside
the building at the utility transformer
or customer's transformer.

Fig. 250-13. Grounded interior systems must have *two* grounding points (Sec. 250-23.)

neutral conductor or other conductor to be grounded must be connected at the service equipment to a conductor which runs to a grounding electrode. The conductor that runs to the grounding electrode is called the "grounding electrode conductor"—an official definition in the NE Code.

The Code says that the connection of the grounding electrode conductor to the system conductor which is to be grounded must be made "on the supply side of the service disconnecting means." This means that the grounding electrode conductor (which runs to building steel and/or water pipe or driven ground rod) must be connected to the system neutral or other system wire to be grounded either in the enclosure for the service disconnect or in some enclosure on the supply side of the service disconnect. Such connection may be made, for instance, in the main service switch or CB or in a service panelboard or switchboard. Or, the grounding electrode conductor may be connected to the system grounded conductor in a gutter, CT cabinet, or meter housing on the supply side of the service disconnect (Fig. 250-14). The utility company should be checked on grounding connections in meter sockets or other metering equipment.

In addition to the grounding connection for the grounded system conductor at the point of service entrance to the premises, it is further required that another grounding connection be made to the same grounded conductor at the transformer which supplies the system. This means, for example, that a grounded service to a building must have the grounded neutral connected to a grounding electrode at the utility transformer on the pole, away from the building, as well as having the neutral grounded to a water pipe and/or other suitable electrode at the building, as shown at the lower part of Fig. 250-13. And in the case of a

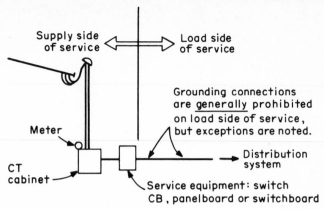

Fig. 250-14. Grounding connection must be made in SE equipment or on its line side. (Sec. 250-23.)

building served from an outdoor transformer pad or mat installation, the conductor which is grounded in the building must also be grounded at the transformer pad or mat, per Sec. 250-23(a).

One of the most important and widely discussed regulations of the entire Code revolves around this matter of making a grounding connection to the system grounded neutral or grounded phase wire. The Code says, "Grounding connections shall not be made on the load side of the service disconnecting means." Once a neutral or other circuit conductor is connected to a grounding electrode at the service equipment, the general rule is that the neutral or other grounded leg must be insulated from all equipment enclosures or any other grounded parts on the load side of the service. That is, bonding of subpanels (or any other connection between the neutral or other grounded conductor and equipment enclosures) is prohibited by the NE Code.

There are some exceptions to that rule, but they are few and are very specific:

1. In a system, even though it is on the load side of the service, when voltage is stepped down by a transformer, a grounding connection *must* be made to the secondary neutral to satisfy Sec. 250-5(b) and Sec. 250-26.

2. When a circuit is run from one building to another, it may be necessary or simply permissible to connect the system "grounded" conductor to a grounding electrode at the other building—as covered by Sec. 250-24.

3. Section 250-61 permits frames of ranges, wall ovens, counter-top cook units, and clothes dryers to be "grounded" by connection to the grounded neutral of their supply circuit (Sec. 250-60).

The **Code** makes it a violation to bond the neutral block in a panelboard to the panel enclosure in other than a service panel. In a panelboard used as service equipment, the neutral block (terminal block) is bonded to the panel cabinet by the bonding screw provided. And such bonding is required to tie the grounded conductor to the interconnected system of metal enclosures for the system (i.e., service equipment enclosures, conduits, busway, boxes, panel cabinets, etc.). It is this connection which provides for flow of fault current and operation of the overcurrent device (fuse or breaker) when a ground fault occurs. But, there must not be any connection between the grounded system conductor and the grounded metal enclosure system at any point on the load side of the service equipment, because such connection would constitute connection of the grounded system conductor to a grounding electrode (through the enclosure and raceway system to the water pipe or driven ground rod). Such connections, like bonding of subpanels, can be dangerous, as shown in Fig. 250-15.

This rule on not connecting the grounded system wire to a grounding electrode on the load side of the service disconnect must not be confused with the rule of Sec. 250-60 which permits the grounded system conductor to be used for grounding the frames of electric ranges, wall ovens, counter-mounted cooking units, and electric clothes dryers. The connection referred to in Sec. 250-60 is that of an ungrounded metal enclosure to the grounded conductor for the purpose of grounding the enclosure.

A very important qualification in the next-to-last sentence of part **(a)** of this rule on grounding connections for AC systems eliminates confusion and controversy about connection of the grounding electrode conductor when a building is fed by service conductors from a meter on a yard pole.

The basic rule of this section says that the grounding electrode conductor required for grounding both the grounded service conductor (usually a grounded neutral) and the metal enclosure of the service equipment *must be* connected to the grounded service conductor *within* or on the *supply side* of the service disconnect. But the rule further requires that the connection of the grounding electrode conductor **must be connected at the load end of the service drop or lateral.**

As a result of that requirement, if a service is fed to a building from a meter enclosure on a pole or other structure some distance away, as commonly done on farm properties, and an overhead or underground run of service conductors is made to the service disconnect in the building, the grounding electrode conductor will not satisfy the **Code** if it is connected to the neutral in the meter enclosure but must be connected at the *load end* of the underground or overhead service conductors. And, as the rule states, the connection should "preferably" be made "*within*" the service disconnect enclosure.

This rule on grounding connection is shown in Fig. 250-16. If, instead of an underground lateral, an overhead run was made to the building from the pole, the overhead line would be a "service drop." The rule of

1. THIS CONDITION WILL EXIST....AND...

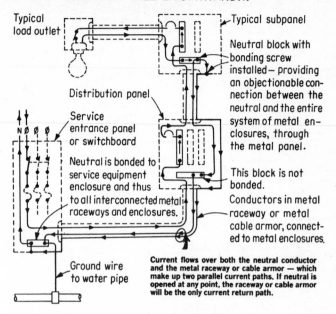

Typical
load outlet

Typical subpanel

Neutral block with
bonding screw
installed — providing
an objectionable con-
nection between the
neutral and the entire
system of metal en-
closures, through
the metal panel.

Distribution panel

Service
entrance panel
or switchboard

Neutral is bonded to
service equipment
enclosure and thus
to all interconnected metal
raceways and enclosures.

This block is not
bonded.

Conductors in metal
raceway or metal
cable armor, connect-
ed to metal enclosures.

Ground wire
to water pipe

**Current flows over both the neutral conductor
and the metal raceway or cable armor — which
make up two parallel current paths. If neutral is
opened at any point, the raceway or cable armor
will be the only current return path.**

2. THIS HAZARD COULD DEVELOP

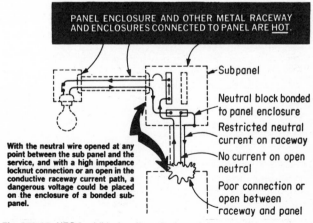

PANEL ENCLOSURE AND OTHER METAL RACEWAY
AND ENCLOSURES CONNECTED TO PANEL ARE <u>HOT</u>.

Subpanel

Neutral block bonded
to panel enclosure

Restricted neutral
current on raceway

No current on open
neutral

Poor connection or
open between
raceway and panel

**With the neutral wire opened at any
point between the sub panel and the
service, and with a high impedance
locknut connection or an open in the
conductive raceway current path, a
dangerous voltage could be placed
on the enclosure of a bonded subpanel.**

Fig. 250-15. NEC prohibits bonding of subpanels because of these reasons.
(Sec. 250-23.)

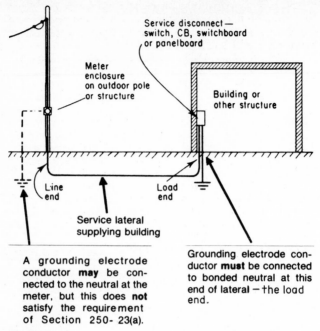

Service disconnect—
switch, CB, switchboard
or panelboard

Meter
enclosure
on outdoor pole
or structure

Building or
other structure

Line
end

Load
end

Service lateral
supplying building

A grounding electrode conductor **may** be connected to the neutral at the meter, but this does **not** satisfy the requirement of Section 250- 23(a).

Grounding electrode conductor **must** be connected to bonded neutral at this end of lateral — the load end.

Fig. 250-16. Connection to grounded conductor at load end of lateral or drop. (Sec. 250-23.)

Sec. 250-23(a) would likewise require the grounding connection at the load end of the service drop. If a fused switch or CB is installed as service disconnect and protection at the load side of the meter on the pole, then that would establish the service at that point, and the grounding electrode connection to the bonded neutral terminal would be required at that point. The circuit from that point to the building would be a feeder and not service conductors. But, electrical safety and effective operation would require that an equipment grounding conductor be run with the feeder circuit conductors for grounding the interconnected system of conduits and metal equipment enclosures along with metal piping systems and building steel within the building. Or, if an equipment grounding conductor is not in the circuit from the pole to the building, the neutral could be bonded to the main disconnect enclosure in the building and a grounding electrode connection made at that point also. Either technique complies with the concepts of Sec. 50-24(a) and Exception b.

There is an important Exception to the rule that each and every service for a grounded AC system have a grounding electrode conductor connected to the grounded system conductor anywhere on the supply side of the service disconnecting means (preferably within the service equipment enclosure) and that the grounding electrode conductor be run to a grounding electrode at the service. Because controversy has arisen in the past about how many grounding electrode conductors have to be run for a dual-feed (double-ended) service with a secondary tie, Exception No. 4 recognizes the use of a single grounding electrode conductor connection for such dual services. It says that the single grounding electrode connection may be made to the "tie point of the grounded circuit conductors from each power source." The explanation on this **Code** permission was made by NEMA, the sponsor of the rule, as follows:

Unless center neutral point grounding and the omission of all other secondary grounding is permitted, the selective ground-fault protection schemes now available for dual power source systems with secondary ties will not work. Dual power source systems are utilized for maximum service continuity. Without selectivity, both sources would be shut down by any ground fault. This proposal permits selectivity so that one source can remain operative for half the load, after a ground fault on the other half of the system.

Figure 250-17 shows two cases involving the concept of single grounding point on a dual-fed service:

In Case 1, if the double-ended unit substation is in a locked room in a building it serves or consists of metal-enclosed gear or a locked enclosure for each transformer, the secondary circuit from each transformer is a "service" to the building. The question then arises, "Does there have to be a separate grounding electrode conductor run from each secondary service to a grounding electrode?"

In Case 2, if each of the two transformers is located outdoors, in a separate building from the one they serve, in a transformer vault in the building they serve, or in a locked room or enclosure and accessible to qualified persons only or in metal-enclosed gear—then the secondary circuit from each transformer constitutes a service to the building. Again, is a separate grounding connection required for each service?

In both cases, a single grounding electrode connection may serve both services, as shown at the bottom of Fig. 250-17.

The **Code** rule in Exception No. 4 refers to "services that are dual fed (double ended) in a *common enclosure or grouped together.*" The phrase "common enclosure" can readily cover use of a double-ended load-center unit substation in a single, common enclosure. But the phrase "grouped together" can lend itself to many interpretations and has caused difficulties. For instance, if each of two separate services was a single-ended unit sub, do both the unit subs have to be in the same room or within the same fenced area outdoors? How far apart may they be and still be considered "grouped together"? As shown in Case 2 of Fig. 250-17, if separate transformers and switchboards are used instead of unit subs, may one of the transformers and its switchboard be installed at the opposite end of the building from the other one? The **Code** does not answer those questions, but it seems clear that the wording does suggest that both of

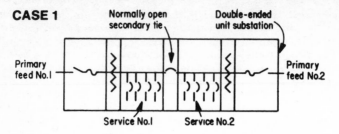

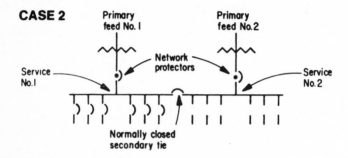

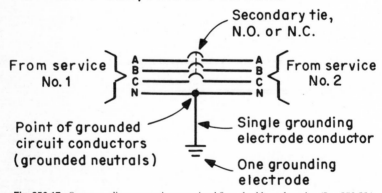

Fig. 250-17. *One* grounding connection permitted for a double-end service. (Sec. 250-23.)

the services must be physically close and at least in the same room or vault or fenced area. That understanding has always been applied to other Code rules calling for "grouping"—such as for switches and CBs in Sec. 380-8 and for service disconnects in Sec. 230-72(a).

Part **(b)** requires that whenever a service is derived from a grounded neutral system, the grounded neutral conductor must be brought into the service-entrance equipment, even if the grounded conductor is not needed for the load supplied by the service. This is required to provide a low-impedance ground-fault current return path to the neutral to assure operation of the overcurrent device, for safety to personnel and property. See Fig. 250-18 and **NE Code** Sec. 250-23(b). In such cases, the

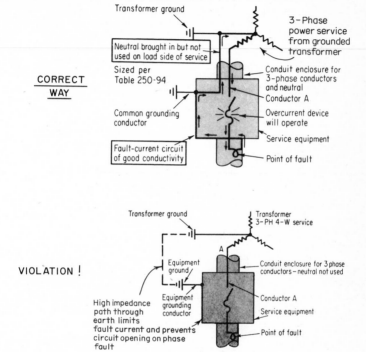

Fig. 250-18. Neutral brought in and bonded to SE enclosure, for fault clearing. (Sec. 250-23.)

neutral functions strictly as an equipment grounding conductor, to provide a closed circuit back to the transformer for automatic circuit opening in the event of a phase-to-ground fault anywhere on the load side of the service equipment. Only one phase leg is shown in these diagrams to simplify the concept. The other two phase legs have the same relation to the neutral.

The same requirements apply to installation of separate power and light services derived from a common 3-phase, 4-wire, grounded "red-leg" delta system. The neutral from the center-tapped transformer winding must be brought into the 3-phase power service equipment as well as

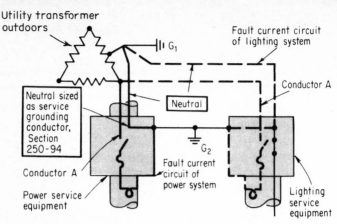

Fig. 250-19. Neutral must be brought in to each service equipment and bonded to enclosure. (Sec. 250-23.)

into the lighting service, even though the neutral will not be used for power loads. This is shown in Fig. 250-19 and is also required by Sec. 250-23(b), which states that such an unused neutral must be at least equal to the required minimum size of grounding electrode conductor specified in Table 250-94 for the size of phase conductors. In addition, if the phase legs associated with that neutral are larger than 1,100 MCM, the grounded neutral must not be smaller than 12½ percent of the area of the largest phase conductor. An example of this is shown in Fig. 250-20.

The minimum required size for the grounded neutral conductor run from the supply transformer to the service is based on the size of the service phase conductors. In this case, the overall size of the service phase conductors is 4 × 500 MCM per phase leg or 2,000 MCM. Because that is larger than 1,100 MCM, it is not permitted to simply use Table 250-94 in sizing the neutral. Instead, 2,000 MCM must be multiplied by 12½ percent. Then 2,000 MCM × 0.125 equals 250 MCM—which is the minimum permitted size of the neutral conductor run from the transformer to the service equipment.

250-24. Two or More Buildings Supplied from Single Service Equipment. In Sec. 250-23(a), bonding of a panel neutral block to the enclosure is required in service equipment. Exception No. 2 of that section permits bonding of the neutral conductor on the load side of the service equipment in those cases where a panelboard is used to supply circuits in a building and the panel is fed from another building. This is covered in Sec. 250-24 which says that, where two or more buildings are supplied from a single service equipment, a grounding electrode at each building shall be connected to the AC system grounded conductor on the supply side of the building disconnecting means of a grounded system as shown in Fig. 250-21 or connected to the metal enclosure of the building

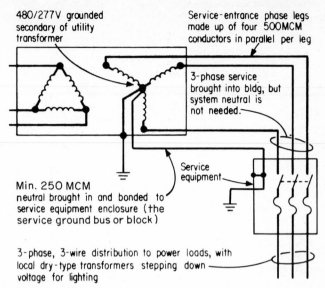

Fig. 250-20. Grounded service conductor must *always* be brought in. (Sec. 250-23.)

disconnecting means of an ungrounded system. That is the basic rule of the section. *But* the Exception notes that a grounding electrode at a separate building supplied by a feeder or branch circuit is not required where either of the following conditions are met: (1) Only one branch circuit is supplied and there is no noncurrent-carrying equipment in the building that required grounding. An example would be a small residential garage with a single lighting outlet or switch with no *metal* boxes, faceplates, or lighting fixtures within 8 ft vertically or 5 ft horizontally from a grounded condition. (2) An equipment grounding conductor is run with the circuit conductors for grounding any noncurrent-carrying equipment, water piping, or building metal frames in the separate building and no livestock is housed in the building as shown in Fig. 250-22. And, as shown at the bottom of that illustration, the need for a grounding electrode at the outbuilding is eliminated because the words "equipment grounding conductor" as used in Exception b of Sec. 250-24 are understood to include "conduit" as indicated by Sec. 250-91(b), which recognizes an "equipment grounding conductor . . . enclosing the circuit conductors." If the separate building has an approved grounding electrode and/or interior metallic piping system, the equipment grounding conductor shall be bonded to the electrode and/or piping system.

A subpanel in a building fed from another building must have its neutral block bonded and must have connection to a grounding electrode

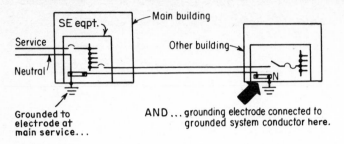

Grounded to
electrode at
main service...

AND ... grounding electrode connected to
grounded system conductor here.

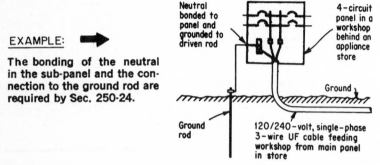

EXAMPLE: ➡

The bonding of the neutral
in the sub-panel and the connection to the ground rod are
required by Sec. 250-24.

Neutral
bonded to
panel and
grounded to
driven rod

4-circuit
panel in a
workshop
behind an
appliance
store

Ground

Ground
rod

120/240-volt, single-phase
3-wire UF cable feeding
workshop from main panel
in store

Fig. 250-21. Grounded conductor (e.g., a neutral) must be grounded at each building.
(Sec. 250-24.)

if livestock is housed in the building. The necessity for bonding the
neutral block in such a subpanel is based on Sec. 250-24 and Sec. 250-54.
The latter section says, "Where an AC system is connected to a grounding
electrode in or at a building as specified in Sections 250-23 and 250-24,
the same electrode shall be used to ground conductor enclosures and
equipment in or on that building." Although the Code permits and even
requires bonding at both ends, if the feeder circuit is in conduit, neutral
current flows on the conduit because it is electrically in parallel with the
neutral conductor, being bonded to it at both ends.

Figure 250-23 shows another condition in which a grounding electrode
connection must be made at the *other* building, as specified in the basic
rule of Sec. 250-24(b). In the sketch shown, if the 3-phase, 3-wire,
ungrounded feeder circuit to the outbuilding had been run with a
separate equipment grounding conductor which effectively connected
the metal enclosure of the disconnect in the outbuilding to the grounding
electrode conductor in the SE equipment of the main building, a connection to a grounding electrode would be required at the outbuilding only
if the outbuilding had any grounding electrode, such as a water service

THE EXCEPTION STATES THIS...

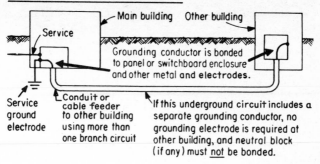

Main building   Other building

Service

Grounding conductor is bonded
to panel or switchboard enclosure
and other metal and electrodes.

Service
ground
electrode

Conduit or
cable feeder
to other building
using more than
one branch circuit

If this underground circuit includes a
separate grounding conductor, no
grounding electrode is required at
other building, and neutral block
(if any) must <u>not</u> be bonded.

... AND THIS IS RECOGNIZED

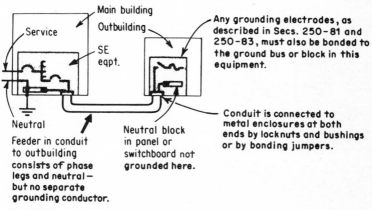

Main building
Outbuilding

Service

SE
eqpt.

Any grounding electrodes, as
described in Secs. 250-81 and
250-83, must also be bonded to
the ground bus or block in this
equipment.

Conduit is connected to
metal enclosures at both
ends by locknuts and bushings
or by bonding jumpers.

Neutral

Feeder in conduit
to outbuilding
consists of phase
legs and neutral —
but no separate
grounding conductor.

Neutral block
in panel or
switchboard not
grounded here.

Fig. 250-22. Grounding connection at outbuildings may be eliminated. (Sec. 250-24.)

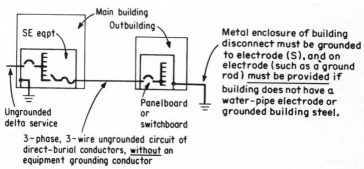

Main building
Outbuilding

SE eqpt.

Metal enclosure of building
disconnect must be grounded
to electrode (S), and on
electrode (such as a ground
rod) must be provided if
building does not have a
water-pipe electrode or
grounded building steel.

Ungrounded
delta service

Panelboard
or
switchboard

3-phase, 3-wire ungrounded circuit of
direct-burial conductors, <u>without</u> an
equipment grounding conductor

Fig. 250-23. Grounding connection for an ungrounded supply to outbuilding. (Sec. 250-24.)

pipe. All grounding electrodes that *exist* at the outbuilding must be bonded to the ground bus or terminal in the disconnect at the outbuilding, whether or not an equipment grounding conductor is run with the circuit conductors from the main building. If, as shown in the sketch, an equipment grounding conductor is *not* run to the outbuilding, then a grounding electrode conductor must be run from the ground bus or terminal in the outbuilding disconnect to a suitable grounding electrode which *must be provided* as specified in Secs. 250-81 and 250-83. But, if an equipment grounding conductor *is* run to the outbuilding and connected to the enclosure of the building disconnect, there is no need to provide a grounding electrode if none *exists* at the outbuilding. Watch that word "exist," as used in the last line of the Exception.

Figure 250-24 applies these rules to overhead feed from one building to another.

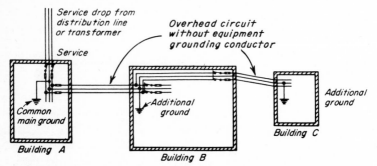

Three buildings served by a single service. The additional grounds are required in most cases under the conditions described.

Fig. 250-24. Overhead feeds require grounding electrode connection at each building. (Sec. 250-24.)

250-25. Conductor to Be Grounded—Alternating-Current Systems.
Selection of the wiring system conductor to be grounded depends upon the type of system. In 3-wire, single-phase systems, the midpoint of the transformer winding—the point from which the system neutral is derived—is grounded. For grounded 3-phase wiring systems, the neutral point of the wye-connected transformer(s) or generator is the point connected to ground. In delta-connected transformer hookups, grounding of the system can be effected by grounding one of the three phase legs, by grounding a center-tap point on one of the transformer windings (as in the 3-phase, 4-wire "red-leg" delta system), or by using a special grounding transformer which establishes a neutral point of a wye connection which is grounded.

250-26. Grounding Separately Derived Alternating-Current Systems. A
separately derived AC wiring system is a source derived from an on-site

generator (emergency or standby), a battery-inverter, or the secondary supply of a transformer. Any such AC supplies required to be grounded by Sec. 250-5 must comply with Sec. 250-26:

1. Any system which operates at over 50 V but not more than 150 V to ground must be grounded [Sec. 250-5(b)].

2. This requires the grounding of generator windings and secondaries of transformers serving 208/120-V, 3-phase or 240/120-V, single-phase circuits for lighting and appliance outlets and receptacles, at loadcenters throughout a building, as shown for the very common application of dry-type transformers in Fig. 250-25.

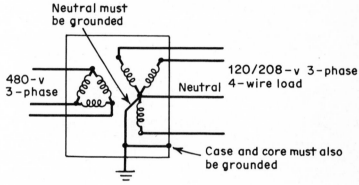

Fig. 250-25. Grounding is required for "separately derived" systems. (Sec. 250-26.)

3. All Code rules applying to both system and equipment grounding must be satisfied in such installations.

Referring to Fig. 250-26, the steps involved in satisfying the Code rules are as follows:

Step 1—Sec. 250-26(a)

A bonding jumper must be installed between the transformer secondary neutral terminal and the metal case of the transformer. The size of this bonding conductor is based on Sec. 250-79(c) and is selected from Table 250-94 of the Code—based on the size of the transformer secondary phase conductors and selected to be the same size as a required grounding electrode conductor. For cases where the transformer secondary circuit is larger than 1,100 MCM copper or 1,750 MCM aluminum per phase leg, the bonding jumper must be not less than 12½ percent of the cross-section area of the secondary phase leg.

example   Assume this is a 75-kVA transformer with a 120/208-V, 3-phase, 4-wire secondary. Such a unit would have a full-load secondary current of

$$75{,}000 \div (208 \times 1.732) \text{ or } 209 \text{ A}$$

STEP 1 — BONDING JUMPER

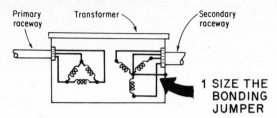

1 SIZE THE
BONDING
JUMPER

STEP 2 — GROUNDING ELECTRODE CONDUCTOR

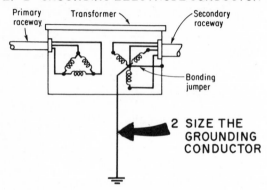

2 SIZE THE
GROUNDING
CONDUCTOR

STEP 3 — GROUNDING ELECTRODE

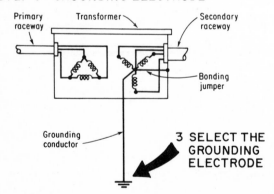

3 SELECT THE
GROUNDING
ELECTRODE

Fig. 250-26. Grounding a transformer secondary. (Sec. 250-26.)

If we use No. 4/0 THW copper conductors for the secondary phase legs (with a 230-A rating), we would then select the size of the required bonding jumper from Table 250-94 as if we had 4/0 service conductors. The table shows that 4/0 copper service conductors require a minimum of No. 2 copper or No. 1/0 aluminum for a grounding electrode conductor. And the bonding jumper would have to be either of those two sizes.

If the transformer was a 500-kVA unit with a 120/208-V secondary, its rated secondary current would be

$$\frac{500 \times 1,000}{1.732 \times 208} = 1,388 \text{ A}$$

Using, say, THW aluminum conductors, the size of each secondary phase leg would be four 700 MCM aluminum conductors in parallel (each 700 MCM THW aluminum is rated at 375 A, four are 4 × 375 or 1,500 A, which suits the 1,388-A load).

Then, because 4 × 700 MCM equals 2,800 MCM per phase leg and is in excess of 1,750 MCM, Sec. 250-79(c) requires the bonding jumper from the case to the neutral terminal to be at least equal to 12½ percent × 2,800 MCM (0.125 × 2,800) or 350 MCM aluminum.

Step 2—Sec. 250-26(b)

A grounding electrode conductor must be installed from the transformer secondary neutral terminal to a suitable grounding electrode. This grounding conductor is sized the same as the required bonding jumper in Step 1. That is, this grounding electrode conductor is sized from Table 250-94 as if it is a grounding electrode conductor for a service with service-entrance conductors equal in size to the phase conductors used on the transformer secondary side. But, this grounding electrode conductor does *not* have to be larger than 3/0 copper or 250 MCM aluminum when the transformer secondary circuit is over 1,100 MCM copper or 1,750 MCM aluminum.

example   For the 75-kVA transformer in Step 1, the grounding electrode con-ductor must be not smaller than the required minimum size shown in Table 250-94 for 4/0 phase legs, which makes the same size as the bonding jumper—i.e., No. 2 copper or No. 1/0 aluminum. But, for the 500-kVA transformer, the grounding electrode conductor is sized directly from Table 250-94—which requires a 3/0 copper or 250 MCM aluminum where the phase legs are over 1,100 MCM copper or 1,750 MCM aluminum.

It should be noted that this rule calls for bonding and grounding of a transformer secondary neutral "*at* the source of the separately derived system"—which seems to insist that the bonding jumper and the connection of a grounding electrode conductor be made *right at* the transformer and not within the enclosure for the disconnecting means immediately fed by the transformer secondary circuit (Fig. 250-27). The latter point of connection was permitted by some inspectors on the basis that such connection was "*ahead* of any system dsconnecting means." The wording may call for the inspector's interpretation.

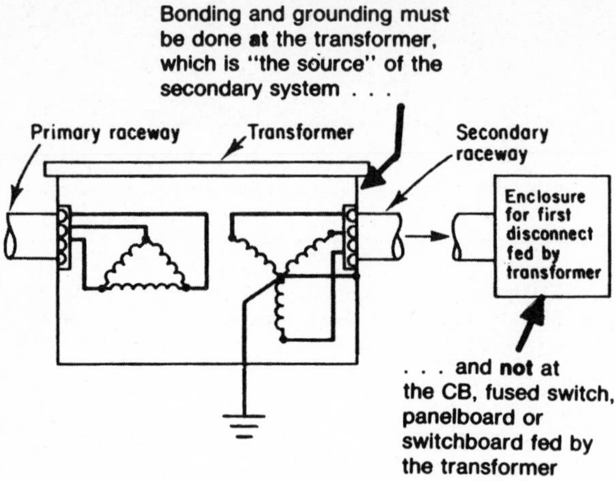

Bonding and grounding must
be done at the transformer,
which is "the source" of the
secondary system . . .

Primary raceway   Transformer   Secondary
                                         raceway

Enclosure
for first
disconnect
fed by
transformer

. . . and not at
the CB, fused switch,
panelboard or
switchboard fed by
the transformer

Fig. 250-27. Transformer secondary bonding and grounding must be
"at the source." (Sec. 250-26.)

Step 3—Sec. 250-26(c)

The grounding electrode conductor, installed and sized as in Step 2,
must be properly connected to a grounding electrode which must be "as
near as practicable to and preferably in the same area as the grounding
conduction connection to the system." That is, the grounding electrode
must be as near as possible to the transformer itself. In order of preference, the grounding electrode must be:
1. The nearest available structural steel of the building provided it is
   established that such building steel is effectively grounded.
2. The nearest available metal water pipe, provided it is effectively
   grounded. Section 250-112 clarifies the term "effectively grounded"
   by noting that the grounding connection to a grounding electrode
   must "assure a permanent and effective ground" (Fig. 250-28).

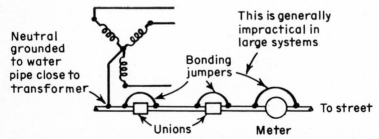

Neutral
grounded
to water
pipe close to
transformer

This is generally
impractical in
large systems

Bonding
jumpers

To street

Unions   Meter

Fig. 250-28. Sec. 250-112 defines "effectively grounded" water pipe electrode. (Sec. 250-
26.)

Thus, when a nearby cold water pipe is used as a grounding electrode, it would appear to be necessary to always bond around any unions or valves that might be opened and thereby break the piping connection to outside earth. And Sec. 250-81(a) requires a bonding jumper to be used around all indoor water meters to assure continuity to earth or through the interior water piping system. The size of such bonding jumpers must be at least the same size as the grounding conductor from the transformer to the water pipe and other electrodes. Of course, the water piping system must satisfy Sec. 250-80. There must be at least 10 ft of the metal water piping buried in earth outside the building for the waer pipe system to qualify as a grounding electrode. There must always be a connection between an interior metal water piping system and the service-entrance grounded conductor (the neutral of the system which feeds the primary of any transformers in the building). That grounding connection for the neutral or other system grounded conductor must be made at the service. And where a metallic water piping system in a building is fed from a nonmetallic underground water system or has less than 10 ft of metal pipe underground, the service neutral or other service grounded conductor must have a connection to a ground rod or other electrode in addition to the connection to the interior metal water piping system. Refer to Secs. 250-80 and 250-81. Where building steel or a metal water pipe are not available for grounding of local dry-type units, other electrodes may be used, based on Secs. 250-81 or 250-83.

Figure 250-29 shows techniques of transformer grounding that have been used in the past but are no longer acceptable to the rules of Sec. 250-26. The hookup of grounding and bonding, as shown, has been made a mandatory and retroactive requirement by the Occupational Safety and Health Act. OSHA now lists **NE Code** Sec. 250-5 as applicable to all electrical systems—existing installations as well as new ones. And Sec. 250-5(a) requires that Sec. 250-26 be fully satisfied in transformer installations, along with Secs. 250-79, 250-83, and 250-94.

250-33. Other Conductor Enclosures. Exception No. 1 permits the installation of short runs as extensions from existing open wiring, knob-and-tube work, or nonmetallic-sheathed cable without grounding where there is little likelihood of an accidental connection to ground or of a person touching both the conduit, raceway, or armor and any grounded metal or other grounded surface at the same time.

250-42. Equipment Fastened in Place or Connected by Permanent Wiring Methods (Fixed). The word "fixed" as applied to equipment requiring grounding now applies to "equipment fastened in place or connected by permament wiring," as shown in Fig. 250-30. And that usage is consistently followed in other Code sections.

250-45. Equipment Connected by Cord and Plug. Figure 250-31 shows cord-connected loads that must either be operated grounded or be double-insulated. Except when supplied through an isolating trans-

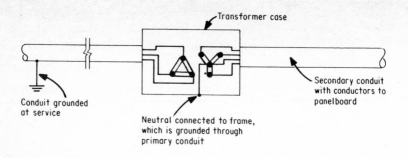

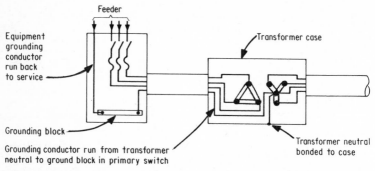

Fig. 250-29. These are *not* acceptable ways to ground a transformer secondary. (Sec. 250-26.)

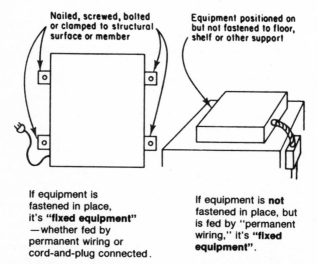

If equipment is fastened in place, it's **"fixed equipment"** —whether fed by permanent wiring or cord-and-plug connected.

If equipment is **not** fastened in place, but is fed by "permanent wiring," it's **"fixed equipment"**.

Fig. 250-30. "Fixed" equipment is now clearly and readily identified for grounding rules. (Sec. 250-42.)

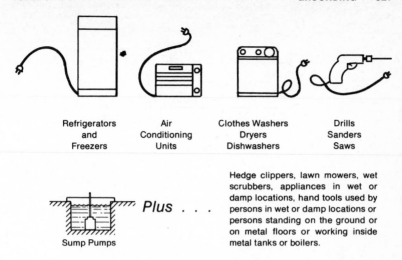

| Refrigerators and Freezers | Air Conditioning Units | Clothes Washers Dryers Dishwashers | Drills Sanders Saws |

Sump Pumps   *Plus . . .*   Hedge clippers, lawn mowers, wet scrubbers, appliances in wet or damp locations, hand tools used by persons in wet or damp locations or persons standing on the ground or on metal floors or working inside metal tanks or boilers.

NOTE: USE OF DOUBLE INSULATION ON TOOLS OR APPLIANCES ELIMINATES NEED FOR GROUNDING.

Fig. 250-31. Grounding cord and plug-cap are required for shock protection. (Sec. 250-45.)

former as permitted in paragraph (**d**) of this section, the frames of portable tools should be grounded by means of an equipment grounding conductor in the cord or cable through which the motor is supplied. Portable hand lamps used inside boilers or metal tanks should preferably be supplied through isolating transformers having a secondary voltage of 50 V or less, with the secondary ungrounded. Code-recognized double-insulated tools and appliances may be used in all types of occupancies other than hazardous locations, in lieu of required grounding.

OSHA regulations have made NE Code Sec. 250-45 retroactive, requiring grounded operation of cord- and plug-connected appliances in all existing as well as new installations. Check on local ruling on that matter.

250-46. Spacing From Lightning Rods. Lightning discharges with their steep wave fronts build up tremendous voltages to metal near the lightning rods, so the 6-ft separation or bonding is to prevent flashover with its attendant hazard.

250-50. Equipment Grounding Conductor Connections. Part (**a**) requires that the equipment grounding conductor at a service—such as the ground bus or terminal in the service-equipment enclosure, or the enclosure itself—must be connected to the system *grounded* conductor (the neutral or grounded phase leg). The equipment ground and the neutral or other grounded leg must be bonded together and it must be done on the supply side of the service disconnecting means—which means either *within* or *ahead of* the enclosure for the service equipment (Fig. 250-32).

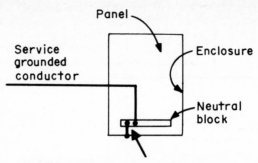

Bonding is the insertion of a bonding screw into the panel neutral block to connect the block to the panel enclosure, or it is use of a bonding jumper from the neutral block to an equipment grounding block that is connected to the enclosure.

NOTE: Bonding—the connection of the neutral terminal to the enclosure or to the ground terminal that is, itself, connected to the enclosure—might also be done in an individual switch or CB enclosure.

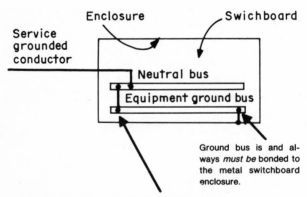

Ground bus is and always *must be* bonded to the metal switchboard enclosure.

Bonding of the neutral is the connection between the neutral bus and the equipment grounding bus or between the neutral bus and the metal enclosure itself.

Fig. 250-32. Equipment ground must be "bonded" to grounded conductor at the service equipment. (Sec. 250-50.)

Part **(b)** requires the ground bus or the enclosure to be simply bonded to the grounding electrode conductor within or ahead of the service disconnect for an ungrounded system.

As shown in Fig. 250-33, some switchboard sections or interiors include neutral busbars factory-bonded to the switchboard enclosure and are marked "suitable for use only as service equipment." They may not be used as subdistribution switchboards—i.e., they may not be used on the load side of the service except where used, with the inspector's permission, as the first disconnecting means fed by a transformer secondary or a generator and where the bonded neutral satisfies Sec. 250-26(a) for a separately derived system.

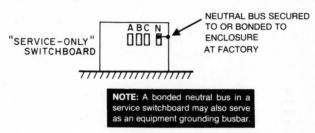

Fig. 250-33. This is the "bonding" required by Sec. 250-50. (Sec. 250-50.)

250-51. Effective Grounding Path.   This section sets forth basic rules on the effectiveness of grounding. In effect, this rule defines the phrase "effective grounding path" and establishes *mandatory* requirements on the quality and quantity of conditions in any and every grounding circuit. The three parts of the section "shall" be satisfied.

Because each of the three required characteristics of grounding paths set forth in **(a)**, **(b)**, and **(c)** is a real and important factor of safety, it is logical and desirable that compliance with the **Code** hinges on carefully establishing each separate condition:

(a).   That every ground path is "permanent and continuous" can be established by the installer by proper mounting, coupling, and terminating of the conductor or raceway intended to serve as the grounding conductor [as permitted by Sec. 250-91(a) and (b)]. And the condition can be visually checked by the electrical inspector, the design engineer and/or any other authority concerned. There is nothing in the wording of that part **(a)** or in other **Code** rules to demand that any kind of actual test be made to verify the condition. However, an inspector could insist that the word "continuous" refers to a path of current and that only a continuity test with a meter or light or bell could positively assure that the path is "continuous."

(b).   That every grounding conductor has "capacity to conduct safely any fault current likely to be imposed on it" can be established by falling back on those other **Code** rules [Secs. 250-93, 250-94, 250-95, 250-23(b),

250-26, 250-79, 680-25(a)(d)(e), etc.] that specifically establish a minimum required size of grounding conductor. Certainly, it is reasonable to conclude that adequate sizing of grounding conductors in accordance with those rules provides adequate "capacity to conduct safely . . . etc."

(c). But when we come to part (c) of Sec. 250-51, questions arise as to the intent of the rule; and much logic supports the argument that testing is essential to Code compliance. Certainly, on a grounded system, when a phase-to-ground fault occurs, the impedance of the fault current path over the raceways or equipment grounding conductors must be low enough to cause enough current to flow to operate the fuse or CB nearest the fault on its line side (Fig. 250-34). To *know* for sure that impedance of

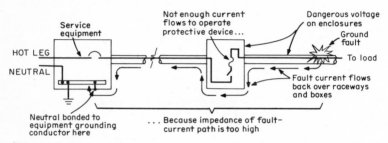

Fig. 250-34. This is a violation of the basic concept of effective grounding. (Sec. 250-51.)

any and every grounding conductor is "sufficiently low to limit . . . etc." requires that the actual value of impedance be measured; and such measurement not only involves use of testing equipment but also demands a broad and deep knowledge of the often sophisticated technology of testing in circuits operating on alternating current where inductance and capacitance are operative factors. In short, what is "sufficiently low impedance" and what does "facilitate the operation of the circuit protective devices" mean? And if testing *is* done, is it necessary to test "every" equipment grounding conductor? Are all these possible interpretations of the intent of the Code rule unrealistic? Is all of this beyond the capability of personnel and out of the economic reach of customers who have to pay for it? It all comes down to the hard question: *Just how much is safety worth?*

After all these questions and speculations, we are still left with the fact that Sec. 250-51(c) *is* a mandatory rule that can be fully satisfied only by testing. It is unreasonable to assume that the Code-making panel never intended this rule to be enforced. And the concept behind the rule as well as the logic of testing being essential to compliance are theoretical ideals with which every electrical person would agree.

It comes down to this: Safety is the objective of the rule in Sec. 250-51(c), and although the rule does not spell out the means for accomplishing the result, it is the responsibility of electrical construction people to come to grips with this issue and advise effective means to satisfy the rule in a manner consistent with the proprofessional, ethical, technically proficient, and safety-conscious attitude that should motivate everyone in the industry.

250-53. Grounding Path to Grounding Electrode. Section 250-53(a) requires all the bonded components—the service-equipment enclosure, the grounded neutral or grounded phase leg, and any equipment grounding conductors that come into the service enclosure—to be connected to a *common* grounding electrode (Sec. 250-54) by the single grounding electrode conductor. A common grounding electrode conductor shall be run from the common point so obtained to the grounding electrode as required by Code Secs. 250-53 and 250-54 (Fig. 250-35). Connection of the system neutral to the switchboard frame or ground bus within the switchboard provides the lowest impedance for the equipment ground return to the neutral. The main bonding jumper that bonds the service enclosure and equipment grounding conductors [which may be either conductors or conduit, EMT, etc., as permitted by Sec. 250-91(b)] to the grounded conductor of the system is required by part **(b)** of this section to be installed within the service equipment or within a service conductor enclosure on the line side of the service. This is the bonding connection required by Sec. 250-50(a) (Fig. 250-36). And it should be noted that in a service panel, equipment grounding conductors for load-side circuits may be connected to the neutral block and there is no need for an equipment grounding terminal bar or block.

If a grounding conductor was used to ground the neutral to the water pipe or other grounding electrode and a separate grounding conductor was used to ground the switchboard frame and housing to the water pipe or other electrode, without the neutral and the frame being connected together in the switchboard, the length and impedance of the ground path would be increased. The proven hazard is that the impedance of the fault current path can limit fault current to a level too low to operate the overcurrent devices "protecting" the faulted circuit.

Note that a number of grounding electrodes that are bonded together, as required by Sec. 250-81, are considered to be *one* grounding electrode.

250-54. Common Grounding Electrode. The same electrode(s) that is used to ground the neutral or other grounded conductor of an AC system must also be used for grounding the entire system of interconnected raceways, boxes, and enclosures. The single, common grounding electrode conductor required by Sec. 250-53 connects to the single grounding electrode and thereby grounds the bonded point of the system and equipment grounds.

In any building housing livestock, all piping systems, metal stanchions, drinking troughs, and other metalwork with which animals might come in contact should be bonded together and to the grounding electrode used to ground the wiring system in the building. See Sec. 250-81.

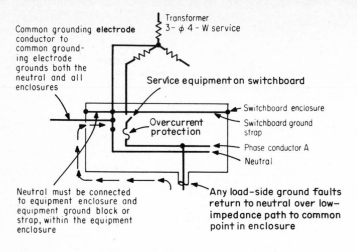

Common grounding **electrode**
conductor to
common ground-
ing electrode
grounds both the
neutral and all
enclosures

Transformer
3- φ 4 - W service

Service equipment on switchboard

Overcurrent
protection

Switchboard enclosure

Switchboard ground
strap

Phase conductor A

Neutral

Neutral must be connected
to equipment enclosure and
equipment ground block or
strap, within the equipment
enclosure

Any load-side ground faults
return to neutral over low-
impedance path to common
point in enclosure

PROPER CONNECTIONS:

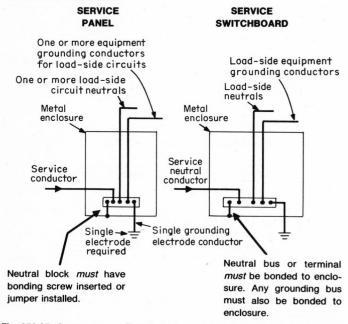

**SERVICE
PANEL**

One or more equipment
grounding conductors
for load-side circuits

One or more load-side
circuit neutrals

Metal
enclosure

Service
conductor

Single ─ ⊥
electrode
required

Neutral block *must* have
bonding screw inserted or
jumper installed.

**SERVICE
SWITCHBOARD**

Load-side equipment
grounding conductors

Load-side
neutrals

Metal
enclosure

Service
neutral
conductor

Single grounding
electrode conductor

Neutral bus or terminal
must be bonded to enclosure. Any grounding bus
must also be bonded to
enclosure.

Fig. 250-35. Common grounding electrode conductor for service and equipment
ground. (Sec. 250-53.)

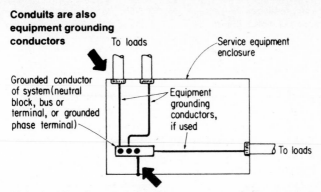

Main bonding jumper (wire, bus, screw or similar conductor) must be _within_ service equipment or service conductor enclosure

Fig. 250-36. Main bonding jumper must be within SE enclosure. (Sec. 250-53.)

250-56. Short Sections of Raceway. Where grounding is required, bonding jumpers connected to grounded runs of conduit, raceway, or armor, if available, should be used.

250-57. Equipment Fastened in Place or Connected by Permanent Wiring Methods (Fixed)—Gounding. This section requires that metal equipment enclosures, boxes, and cabinets to be grounded must be grounded by metal cable armor or by the metal raceway that supplies such enclosures (rigid metal conduit, intermediate metal conduit, EMT, flex or liquidtight flex as permitted by Sec. 350-5 or 351-7), _or_ by an equipment grounding conductor, such as where the equipment is fed by rigid nonmetallic conduit. Refer to Sec. 250-91(b). _But_ in Sec. 250-57(b), the rule explicitly requires that _when_ a separate equipment grounding conductor (i.e., other than the metal raceway or metal cable armor) is used for alternating-current circuits it _must_ be contained _within_ the same raceway, cable, or cord or otherwise run with the circuit conductors (Fig. 250-37). External grounding of equipment enclosures or frames or housings is a violation for AC equipment. It is not acceptable, for instance, to feed an AC motor with a nonmetallic conduit or cable, without a grounding conductor in the conduit or cable, and then provide grounding of the metal frame by a grounding conductor connected to the metal frame and run to building steel or to a grounding-grid conductor. An equipment grounding conductor _must always_ be run with the circuit conductors.

The rule in Sec. 250-57(b) which insists on keeping an equipment grunding conductor physically close to AC circuit supply conductors is a logical follow-up to the rules of Sec. 250-51 which call for minimum

If equipment grounding conductor (other than raceway) is used to ground motor, it must be run in raceway with circuit wires

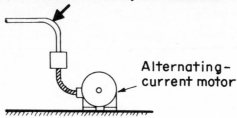

Alternating–
current motor

Fig. 250-37. Equipment grounding conductor must be in raceway or cable with circuit conductors for AC equipment. (Sec. 250-57.)

impedance in grounding current paths to provide most effective clearing of ground faults. When an equipment grounding conductor is kept physically close to any circuit conductor that would be supplying the fault current (that is, the grounding conductor is in the "same raceway, cable, or cord or otherwise run with the circuit conductors"), the impedance of the fault circuit has minimum inductive reactance and minimum AC resistance because of mutual cancellation of the magnetic fields around the conductors and the reduced skin effect. Under such condition of "sufficiently low impedance," the meaning of Sec. 250-51(c) is best fulfilled—voltage to ground is limited to the greatest extent, the fault current is higher because of minimized impedance, the circuit overcurrent device will operate at a faster point in its time-current characteristic to assure maximum fault-clearing speed, and the entire effect will be to "facilitate the operation of the circuit protective devices in the circuit."

That this effect is clearly the intent of the wording of Sec. 250-57(b) is verified by Exception No. 2 of Sec. 250-57(b), which *excludes* DC circuits from the need to keep the grounding conductor close to the circuit conductors. Because there are no alternating magnetic fields around DC conductors, there is no inductive reactance or skin effect in DC circuits. The only impedance to current flow in a DC circuit is resistance—which will be the same for a DC ground-fault path whether or not the equipment grounding conductor is placed physically close to the circuit conductors which would supply the fault current in the event of a ground fault. External equipment grounding—by connection to grounded building steel or to an external ground grid—is, therefore, OK for DC equipment, provided the external grounding path is effectively tied back to the grounded conductor of the DC system.

The arrangement shown in Fig. 250-38 violates the basic rule of Sec. 250-57(b) because the lighting fixture, which must be grounded to satisfy Sec. 250-42, is not grounded in accordance with Secs. 250-57 and 250-91(b) or by an equipment grounding conductor contained within the cord, as noted in Sec. 250-57(b).

EXTERNAL EQUIPMENT GROUNDING IS A VIOLATION!

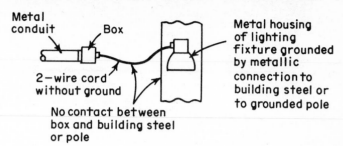

Fig. 250-38. Supply to AC equipment must include equipment grounding conductor. (Sec. 250-57.)

Note that Sec. 250-91(b) refers very clearly to an "equipment grounding condutor run with or enclosing the circuit conductors." Except for DC circuits [Sec. 250-57(b), Exception No. 2] and for isolated, ungrounded power sources [Sec. 517-88], an equipment grounding conductor of any type must not be run separately from the circuit conductors. The engineering reason for keeping the ground return path and the phase legs in close proximity (that is, in the same raceway) is to minimize the impedance of the fault circuit by placing conductors so their magnetic fields mutually cancel each other, keeping inductive reactance down, and allowing sufficient current to flow to "facilitate the operation of the circuit protective devices," as required by Sec. 250-51.

The hookup in Fig. 250-38 also violates the rule of the last sentence in Sec. 250-58(a), which prohibits use of building steel as the equipment grounding conductor for AC equipment. And the rules of Sec. 250-58 often have to be considered in relation to the rules of Sec. 250-57.

Note: CARE MUST BE TAKEN TO DISTINGUISH BETWEEN AN "EQUIPMENT *GROUNDING CONDUCTOR*" AS COVERED BY SEC. 250-57 AND AN "EQUIPMENT *BONDING JUMPER*" AS COVERED BY SEC. 250-79(e). A *"BONDING JUMPER"* MAY BE USED EXTERNAL TO EQUIPMENT BUT IT MUST NOT BE OVER 6 FT LONG.

Exception No. 1 recognizes conductors of colors other than green for use as equipment grounding conductors if the conductor is stripped for its exposed length within an enclosure, so it appears bare, or if green coloring, green tape, or green label is used on the conductor at the termination. As shown in Fig. 250-39, the phase legs may be any color other than white, gray, or green. The neutral may be white or gray or any other color other than green if it is larger than No. 6 and if white tape, marking, or paint is applied to the neutral near its terminations. The grounding conductor may be green or may be any insulated conductor if all insulation is stripped off for the exposed length. Alternatives to

EXAMPLE

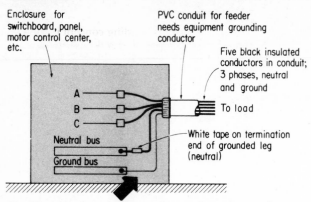

Enclosure for
switchboard, panel,
motor control center,
etc.

PVC conduit for feeder
needs equipment grounding
conductor

Five black insulated
conductors in conduit;
3 phases, neutral
and ground

To load

White tape on termination
end of grounded leg
(neutral)

Neutral bus

Ground bus

**Black insulated conductor used as equipment grounding
conductor has all insulation stripped from entire length exposed
in enclosure**

Fig. 250-39. Equipment grounding conductor larger than No. 6 may be a stripped conductor of any color covering. (Sec. 250-57.)

stripping the black insulated conductor used for equipment ground include (1) coloring the exposed insulation green or (2) marking the exposed insulation with green tape or green adhesive labels.

Exeption No. 3 permits specific on-the-job identification of an insulated conductor used as an equipment grounding conductor in a multiconductor cable. Such a conductor, regardless of size, may be identified in the same manner permitted by Exception No. 1 of that section for conductors larger than No. 6 used in raceway. The conductor may be stripped bare or colored green to indicate that it is a grounding conductor. But such usage is recognized only for industrial-type systems under the conditions given in the first two lines of the Exception.

250-58. Equipment Considered Effectively Grounded. This rule clarifies the way in which structural metal may be used as an equipment grounding conductor, consistent with the rule of Sec. 250-57(b) requiring a grounding conductor to be kept physically close to the conductors of any AC circuit for which the grounding conductor provides the fault return path.

Part **(a)** notes that if a piece of electrical equipment is attached and electrically conductive to a metal rack or structure supporting the equipment, the metal enclosure of the equipment is considered suitably grounded by connection to the metal rack PROVIDED THAT the metal rack itself is effectively grounded by metal raceway enclosing the circuit conductors supplying the equipment or by an equipment grounding conductor run with the circuit supplying the equipment. An example of such application is shown in Fig. 250-40. Although this example shows grounding of lighting fixtures to a rack, the Code rule recognizes any "electric equipment" when this basic grounding concept is observed. It is important to note that if a ground fault developed in equipment so grounded (as at point A), the fault current takes the path indicated by the small arrows. In such case, although the fault-current path through the steel rack is not close to the hot conductor in the flexible cord that is feeding the fault—as normally required by Sec. 250-57(b)—the distance of the external ground path is not great, from the fixture to the panel

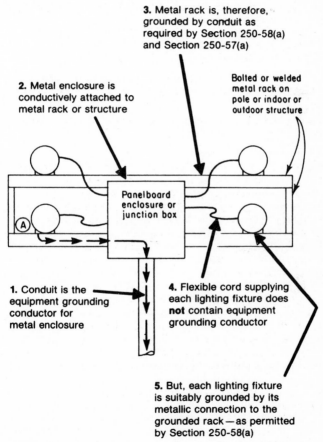

3. Metal rack is, therefore, grounded by conduit as required by Section 250-58(a) and Section 250-57(a)

2. Metal enclosure is conductively attached to metal rack or structure

Bolted or welded metal rack on pole or indoor or outdoor structure

Panelboard enclosure or junction box

1. Conduit is the equipment grounding conductor for metal enclosure

4. Flexible cord supplying each lighting fixture does **not** contain equipment grounding conductor

5. But, each lighting fixture is suitably grounded by its metallic connection to the grounded rack—as permitted by Section 250-58(a)

Fig. 250-40. This use of metal rack as equipment ground is permitted. (Sec. 250-58.)

enclosure or box. Because such a short external ground path produces only a relatively slight increase in ground path impedance, Sec. 250-58(a) permits it. The permission for external bonding of flexible metal conduit and liquidtight flex in Sec. 250-79(e) is based on the same acceptance of only slight increase of overall impedance of the ground path.

The second sentence of Sec. 250-58(a) clearly prohibits using structural building steel as an equipment grounding conductor for equipment mounted on or fastened to the building steel—IF THE SUPPLY CIRCUIT TO THE EQUIPMENT OPERATES ON ALTERNATING CURRENT. BUT, structural building steel that is effectively grounded and bonded to the grounded circuit conductor of a DC supply system may be used as the equipment grounding conductor for the metal enclosure of DC operated equipment that is conductively attached to the building steel.

It is important to understand the basis for the Code rules of Sec. 250-57(b) and Sec. 250-91(b) and their relation to the new concept of Sec. 250-58(a):

Note that Sec. 250-91(b) refers very clearly to an "equipment grounding conductor run with or enclosing the circuit conductors." Except for DC circuits [Sec. 250-57(b), Exception No. 2] and for isolated, ungrounded power sources [Sec. 517-86], an equipment grounding conductor of any type must not be run separately from the circuit conductors. The engineering reason for keeping the ground return path and the phase legs in close proximity (that is, in the same raceway) is to minimize the impedance of the fault circuit by placing conductors so their magnetic fields mutually cancel each other, keeping inductive reactance down, and allowing sufficient current to flow to "facilitate the operation of the circuit protective devices," as required by Sec. 250-51.

The second sentence of Sec. 250-58(a) applies the above concept of ground-fault impedance to the metal frame of a building and prohibits its use as an equipment grounding conductor for AC equipment enclosures. As shown in Fig. 250-41, use of building steel as a grounding conductor provides a long fault return path ov very high impedance because the path is separated from the feeder circuit hot legs—thereby violating Sec. 250-51(c). Ground-fault current returning over building steel to the point where the building steel is bonded to the AC system neutral (or other grounded) conductor is separated from the circuit conductor that is providing the fault current. Impedance is, therefore, elevated and the optimum conditions required by Sec. 250-51 are not present, so that the grounding cannot be counted on to "facilitate the operation" of the fuse or CB protecting the faulted circuit. The current may not be high enough to provide fast and certain clearing of the fault.

The first sentence of Sec. 250-58(a) accepts a limited variation from the basic concept of keeping circuit hot legs and equipment grounding conductors physically close to each other. When equipment is grounded by connection to a "metal rack or structure" that is specifically provided to

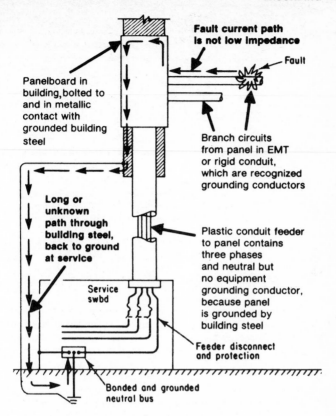

Fault current path is not low impedance

Fault

Panelboard in building, bolted to and in metallic contact with grounded building steel

Branch circuits from panel in EMT or rigid conduit, which are recognized grounding conductors

Long or unknown path through building steel, back to ground at service

Plastic conduit feeder to panel contains three phases and neutral but no equipment grounding conductor, because panel is grounded by building steel

Service swbd

Feeder disconnect and protection

Bonded and grounded neutral bus

THIS LAYOUT IS A VIOLATION !

Fig. 250-41. Building metal frame is not an acceptable grounding conductor for AC equipment. (Sec. 250-58.)

support the equipment and *is* grounded, the separation between the circuit hot legs and the rack, which serves as the equipment grounding conductor exists only for a very short length that will not significantly raise the overall impedance of the ground-fault path. Figure 250-42 shows another application of that type, similar to the one shown in Fig. 250-40. Although this shows a 2-wire cord as being acceptable, use of a 2-wire cord (two circuit wires and an equipment grounding wire) is better practice, at very slight cost increase.

Aside from the limited applications shown in Figs. 250-40 and 250-42, *required* equipment grounding must always keep the equipment grounding conductor alongside the circuit conductor for grounded AC systems.

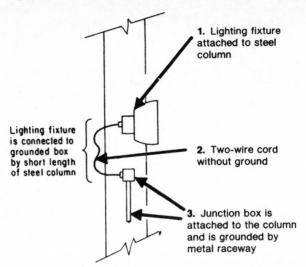

1. Lighting fixture attached to steel column

Lighting fixture is connected to grounded box by short length of steel column

2. Two-wire cord without ground

3. Junction box is attached to the column and is grounded by metal raceway

Fig. 250-42. This satisfies basic rule of Sec. 250-58(a). [Sec. 250-58(a).]

Of course, as long as required grounding techniques are observed, there is no objection to additional connection of equipment frames and housings to building steel or to grounding grids to provide potentials to ground. But the external grounding path is not suitable for clearing AC equipment ground faults.

250-59. Cord- and Plug-Connected Equipment.   The proper method of grounding portable equipment is through an extra conductor in the supply cord. Then if the attachment plug and receptacle comply with the requirements of Sec. 250-59, the grounding connection will be completed when the plug is inserted in the receptacle.

A grounding-type receptacle and an attachment plug should be used where it is desired to provide for grounding the frames of small portable appliances. The receptacle will receive standard two-pole attachment plugs, so grounding is optional with the user. The grounding contacts in the receptacle are electrically connected to the supporting yoke so that when the box is surface-mounted the connection to ground is provided by a direct metal-to-metal contact between the device yoke and the box. For a recessed box a grounding jumper must be used on the receptacle or a self-grounding receptacle must be used. See Secs. 250-74 and 250-114.

Figure 250-43 shows a grounding-type attachment plug with a movable, self-restoring grounding member—as covered in the exceptions of this section.

250-60. Frames of Ranges and Clothes Dryers.   Under the conditions stated, the frame of an electric range, wall-mounted oven, or counter-

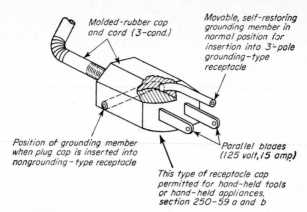

Molded-rubber cap
and cord (3-cond.)

Movable, self-restoring
grounding member in
normal position for
insertion into 3-pole
grounding-type
receptacle

Position of grounding member
when plug cap is inserted into
nongrounding-type receptacle

Parallel blades
(125 volt, 15 amp.)

This type of receptacle cap
permitted for hand-held tools
or hand-held appliances.
section 250-59 a and b

Fig. 250-43. This type of plug-cap is permitted on cords for tools and
appliances. (Sec. 250-59.)

mounted cooking unit may be grounded by direct connection to the
grounded circuit conductor (the grounded neutral) and thus may be
supplied by a 3-wire cord-set and range receptacle irrespective of
whether or not the conductor to the receptacle contains a separate
grounding conductor.

The reason for permitting these appliances to be grounded by connecting them to the circuit neutral is that the circuit is usually short and the
grounded neutral conductor is large enough to provide against its being
broken. On such equipment if the neutral were broken, the equipment
would usually become inoperative and it would be necessary to have
repairs made before operation could be resumed.

Parts **(a)** and **(b)** clarify the use of a No. 10 or larger grounded neutral
conductor of a *120/208-V* circuit for grounding the fames of electric
ranges, wall-mounted ovens, counter-mounted units, or clothes dryers.
This method is acceptable whether the 3-wire supply is 120/208 V or 120/
240 V. However, a provision, applicable to both 3-wire supply voltages,
does require that when using service-entrance cable having an uninsulated neutral conductor the branch circuit must originate at the service-
entrance equipment. The purpose of this provision is to prevent the
uninsulated neutral from coming in contact with a panelboard supplied
by a feeder and a separate grounding conductor (in the case of nonmetallic-sheathed cable). This would place the neutral in parallel with the
grounding conductor, or with feeder *metal* raceways or cables if they are
used. Insulated nuetrals in such situations will prevent this (Fig. 250-44).

Wording of the rule that permits frames of ranges and clothes dryers
to be grounded by connection to the grounded neutral conductor of their
supply circuits also permits the same method of grounding of "outlet or
junction boxes" serving such appliances. The rule permits grounding of

Conditions when grounded neutral
conductor (No. 10 or larger) may be used to
ground metal frames of specified appliances.

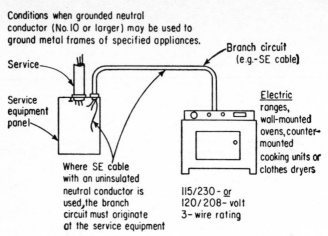

Fig. 250-44. Ranges and dryers may be grounded to the circuit neutral. (Sec. 250-60.)

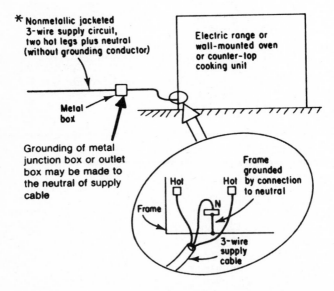

✱ **Service cable or NM or NMC cable. But NM or NMC cable must have an insulated neutral.**

Fig. 250-45. Neutral may be used to ground boxes as well as appliances. (Sec. 250-60.)

an outlet or junction box, as well as cooking unit or dryer, by the circuit grounded neutral (Fig. 250-45). That practice has been common for many years but has raised questions about the suitability of the neutral for such grounding. Now, the revised rule makes clear that such grounding of the box is acceptable. Figure 250-46 shows other details of such application. Without this permission to ground the metal box to the

FIXED CONNECTION

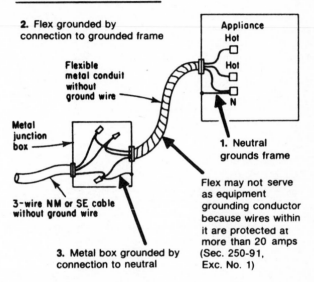

2. Flex grounded by connection to grounded frame

Appliance
Hot
Hot
N

Flexible metal conduit without ground wire

Metal junction box

1. Neutral grounds frame

3-wire NM or SE cable without ground wire

Flex may not serve as equipment grounding conductor because wires within it are protected at more than 20 amps (Sec. 250-91, Exc. No. 1)

3. Metal box grounded by connection to neutral

CORD CONNECTION

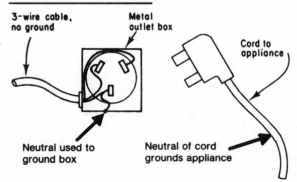

3-wire cable, no ground

Metal outlet box

Cord to appliance

Neutral used to ground box

Neutral of cord grounds appliance

Fig. 250-46. These techniques may be used to ground boxes in circuit. (Sec. 250-60.)

grounded neutral, it would be necessary to run a 4-wire supply cable to the box, with one of the wires serving as an equipment grounding conductor sized from Table 250-95.

Important: As shown in the asterisk note under Fig. 250-45, if a nonmetallic-sheathed cable is used, say, to supply a wall oven or cook-top, such cable is required by part **(c)** of Sec. 250-60 to have an *insulated* neutral. It would be a violation, for instance, to use a 10/2 NM cable with a bare No. 10 grounding conductor to supply a cooking appliance—connecting the two insulated No. 10 wires to the hot terminals and using the bare No. 10 as a neutral conductor to ground the appliance. An uninsulated grounded neutral may be used only when part of a service-entrance cable.

250-47. Use of Grounded Circuit Conductor for Grounding Equipment. Part **(a)** permits connection between a grounded neutral (or grounded phase leg) and equipment enclosures, for the purpose of grounding the enclosures to the grounded circuit conductor—but limits such general permission to the supply side of service equipment and on the supply side of a main disconnect for a separate building or for a

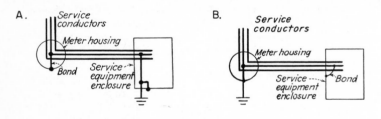

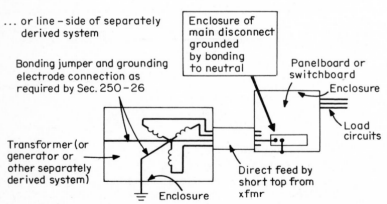

Fig. 250-47. Using grounded circuit conductor to ground equipment housings on line-side of service. (Sec. 250-61.)

separately derived system—such as a transformer secondary. Figure 250-47 shows such applications. At A, the grounded service neutral is bonded to the meter housing by means of the bonded neutral terminal lug in the socket—and the housing is thereby grounded by this connection to the grounded neutral, which itself is grounded at the service equipment as well as at the utility transformer secondary supplying the service. At B, the service equipment enclosure is grounded by connection (bonding) to the grounded neutral—which itself is grounded at the meter socket and at the supply transformer. These same types of grounding connections may be made for CT cabinets, auxiliary gutters, and other enclosures on the line side of the service-entrance disconnect means, including the enclosure for the service disconnect. In some areas, the utilities and inspection departments will not permit the arrangement shown in Fig. 250-47 because the connecting lug in the meter housing is not always accessible for inspection and testing purposes.

Aside from the permission given in the three exceptions to the rule of part **(b)** of this section, the wording of part **(b)** prohibits connection between a grounded neutral and equipment enclosures on the load side of the service. The wording supports the prohibition in Sec. 250-23 of grounding connections. So aside from the few specific exceptions mentioned, bonding between any system grounded conductor, neutral or phase leg, and equipment enclosures is prohibited on the load side of the service (Fig. 250-48). The use of a neutral to ground panelboard or other

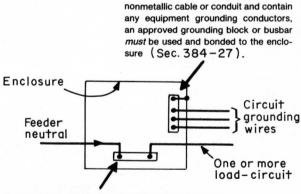

Fig. 250-48. Panel, switchboard, CB, and switch on load side of service within a single building. (Sec. 250-61.)

equipment (other than specified in the exceptions) on the load side of service equipment would be extremely hazardous if the neutral became loosened or disconnected. In such cases any line-to-neutral load would energize all metal components connected to the neutral, creating a dangerous potential aboveground. Hence, the prohibition of such a practice. This is fully described in Fig. 250-15.

Although this rule of the Code prohibits neutral bonding on the load side of the service, Secs. 250-50(a) and 250-53(b) clearly require such bonding at the service entrance. And the exceptions to prohibiting load-side neutral bonding to enclosures are few and very specific:

▪ In a system, even though it is on the load side of the service, when voltage is stepped down by a transformer, a grounding connection *must* be made to the secondary neutral to satisfy Sec. 250-5(b) and Sec. 250-26.

▪ When a circuit is run from one building to another, it may be necessary or simply permissible to connect the system "grounded" conductor to a grounding electrode at the other building—as covered by Sec. 250-24 and Exception No. 2 of Sec. 250-61(b).

▪ Exception No. 1 of Sec. 250-61(b) permits frames of ranges, wall ovens, counter-top cook units, and clothes dryers to be "grounded" by connection to the grounded neutral of their supply circuit (Sec. 250-60).

▪ Exception No. 3 to Sec. 250-61(b) permits grounding of meter enclosures to the grounded circuit conductor (generally, the grounded neutral) on the *load side* of the service disconnect if the meter enclosures are located near the service disconnect and the service is not equipped with ground-fault protection. There is no definition for the word "near," but it can be taken to mean in the same room or general area. This rule applies, of course, to multioccupancy buildings (apartments, office buildings, etc.) with individual tenant metering (Fig. 250-49).

If a meter bank is on the upper floor of a building, as in a high-rise apartment house, or otherwise away from service disconnect, such meter enclosures would not meet the rule that they must be "near" the service disconnect. In such cases, the enclosures must not be grounded to the neutral. And if the service has ground-fault protection, meter enclosures on the load side must not be connected to the neutral, even if they are "near" the service disconnect.

250-70. General (Bonding). One of the most interesting and controversial phases of electrical work involves the grounding and bonding of secondary-voltage service-entrance equipment. Modern practice in such work varies according to local interpretations of Code requirements and specifications of design engineers. In all cases, however, the basic intent is to provide an installation which is essentially in compliance with National Electrical Code rules on the subject, using practical methods for achieving objectives.

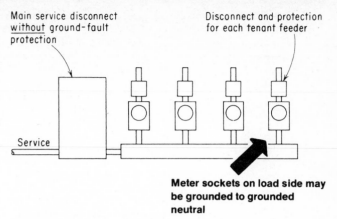

Main service disconnect without ground-fault protection

Disconnect and protection for each tenant feeder

Service

Meter sockets on load side may be grounded to grounded neutral

Fig. 250-49. Grounding meter enclosures to grounded conductor on *load side* of service disconnect. (Sec. 250-61.)

In order to ensure electrical continuity of the grounding circuit, bonding (special precautions to ensure a permanent, low-resistance connection) is required at all conduit connections in the service equipment and where any nonconductive coating exists which might impair such continuity. This includes bonding at connections between service raceways, service cable armor, all service-equipment enclosures containing service-entrance conductors, including meter fittings, boxes, and the like.

The need for effective grounding and bonding of service equipment arises from the electrical characteristics of utility-supply circuits. In the common arrangement, service conductors are run to a building and the service overcurrent protection is placed near the point of entry of the conductors into the building, at the load end of the conductors. With such a layout, the service conductors are not properly protected against ground faults or shorts occurring on the supply side of the service overcurrent protection. Generally, the only protection for the service conductors is on the primary side of the utility's distribution transformer. By providing "bonded" connections (connecting with special care to reliable conductivity), any short circuit in the service-drop or service-entrance conductors is given the greatest chance of burning itself clear—because there is not effective overcurrent protection ahead of those conductors to provide opening of the circuit on such heavy fault currents. And for any contact between an energized service conductor and grounded service raceway, fittings, or enclosures, bonding provides discharge of the fault current to the system grounding electrode—and again burning the fault clear. This condition of services is shown in Fig. 250-50.

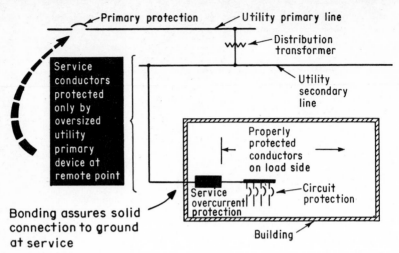

Fig. 250-50. Service bonding must assure burn-clear on shorts and grounds in service conductors. (Sec. 250-70.)

250-71. Bonding Service Equipment.   Because of the requirement set forth in Sec. 250-70, all enclosures for service conductors must be grounded to prevent a potential aboveground on the enclosures as a result of fault—which would be a very definite hazard—and to facilitate operation of overcurrent devices anywhere on the supply side of the service conductors. However, because of the distant location of the protection and the normal impedance of supply cables, it is important that any fault to an enclosure of a hot service conductor of a grounded electrical system find a firm, continuous, low-impedance path to ground to assure sufficient current flow to operate the primary protective device or to burn the fault clear quickly. This means that all enclosures containing the service conductors—service raceway, cable armor, boxes, fittings, cabinets—must be effectively bonded together; that is, they must have low impedance through themselves and must be securely connected to each other to assure a continuous path of sufficient conductivity to the conductor which makes the connection to ground (Fig. 250-51).

The spirit of the Code and good engineering practice have long recognized that the conductivity of any equipment ground path should be at least equivalent to 25 percent of the conductivity of any phase conductor with which the ground path will act as a circuit conductor on a ground fault. Or, to put it another way, making the relationship without reference to insulation or temperature rise, the impedance of the ground path must not be greater than four times the impedance of any phase conductor with which it is associated. This figure should always be used as

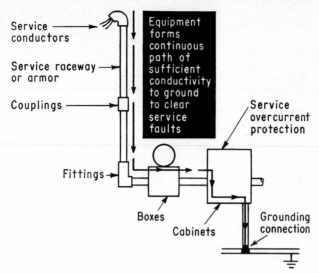

Fig. 250-51. Bonding assures low-impedance path through all service conductor enclosures. (Sec. 250-71.)

a specific guide when evaluating the suitability of raceways or conductors as a grounding path.

In ungrounded electrical systems, the same careful attention should be paid to the matter of bonding together the noncurrent-carrying metal parts of all enclosures containing service conductors. Such a low-impedance ground path will quickly and surely ground any hot conductor which might accidentally become common with the enclosure system.

Specific **NE Code** requirements on grounding and bonding are as follows:

1. Section 230-63 requires that service raceways, metal sheath of service cables, metering enclosures, and cabinets for service disconnect and protection be grounded. An exception to this rule is made in the case of certain lead-sheathed cable services as covered in Sec. 250-55. And, at one time, the **Code** required that flexible metal conduit used in a run of service raceway must be bonded around. But, the **NEC** no longer permits use of flexible metal conduit or liquidtight flex (Fig. 250-52). Section 230-43 lists the *only* types of raceway that may enclose service-entrance conductors.

2. Section 250-32 also requires that service raceways and service cable sheaths or armoring—when of metal—be grounded.

3. Section 250-71 sets forth the service equipment which must be bonded—that is, the equipment for which the continuity of the

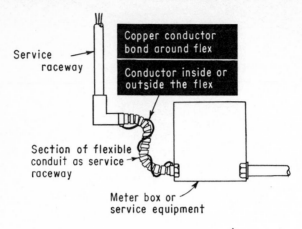

Service raceway

Copper conductor bond around flex

Conductor inside or outside the flex

Section of flexible conduit as service raceway

Meter box or service equipment

THIS IS NOW A VIOLATION !

Fig. 250-52. Flex may not be used as a service raceway, even with a jumper. (Sec. 250-71.)

grounding path must be specifically assured by using specific connecting devices or techniques. As indicated in Fig. 250-53, this equipment includes: (a) service raceway, cable trays, cable sheath, and cable armor; (b) all service equipment enclosures containing service-entrance conductors, including meter fittings, boxes, etc., interposed in the service raceway or armor; and (c) any conduit or armor that encloses a grounding electrode conductor that runs to and is connected to the grounding electrode or "system" of electrodes, as described under Sec. 250-81.

Part **(c)** of the rule on "bonded connections" for all interconnected service equipment makes *clear* that bonded terminations must be used at ends of conduit (rigid metal conduit, IMC or EMT) or cable armor that encloses a grounding electrode conductor. That means that connection of conduit or cable armor must be made using a bonding locknut or bonding bushing (with a bonding jumper around unpunched concentric or eccentric rings left in any sheet metal knockout) or must be connected to a threaded hub or boss. Such connections must comply with the techniques covered in Sec. 250-72.

Section 250-92(a), first sentence of second paragraph, bears on the same matter and requires a metal enclosure for a grounding electrode conductor to be electrically in parallel with the grounding electrode conductor. As a result, a metal conduit or EMT enclosing a grounding electrode conductor—whether or not such conduit or EMT is mechanical protection required by Sec. 250-92(a)—forms *part* of the grounding

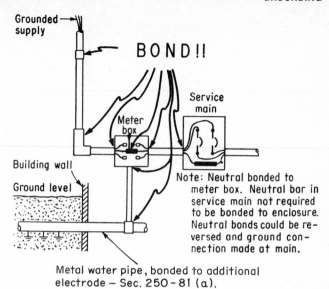

Grounded supply

BOND!!

Service main

Meter box

Building wall

Ground level

Note: Neutral bonded to meter box. Neutral bar in service main not required to be bonded to enclosure. Neutral bonds could be reversed and ground connection made at main.

Metal water pipe, bonded to additional electrode – Sec. 250 – 81 (a).

Fig. 250-53. "Bonding" consists of using prescribed fittings and/or methods for connecting components enclosing SE conductors. (Sec. 250-71.)

electrode conductor. In fact, such conduit or EMT has a much lower impedance than its enclosed grounding electrode conductor (due to the relation of magnetic fields) and is, therefore, even more important than the enclosed conductor in providing an effective path for current to the grounding electrode.

Assuring the continuity of raceway or armor for a grounding conductor does reduce the impedance of the ground path compared with what the impedance would be if the raceway or armor had poor connections or even opens. Effective bonding of the raceway or armor minimizes the DC resistance of the ground path and reduces the overall impedance which includes the choke action due to presence of magnetic material (steel conduit or armor), the increased inductive reactance of the circuit. Because of that, Sec. 250-71(c) requires "bonding" connection of such raceway to any service enclosure, as shown in Fig. 250-54. Refer to Sec. 250-92(a).

250-72. Method of Bonding Service Equipment. Section 250-71 is very specific in listing the many types of equipment that require bonding connections but the actual "how to" is often hazy. For virtually every individual situation where a bonding connection must be made, there is available a variety of products on the market which present the installer with a choice of different methods.

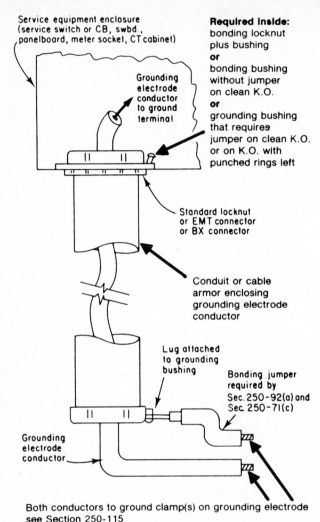

Service equipment enclosure
(service switch or CB, swbd.,
panelboard, meter socket, CT cabinet)

Required Inside:
bonding locknut
plus bushing
or
bonding bushing
without jumper
on clean K.O.
or
grounding bushing
that requires
jumper on clean K.O.
or on K.O. with
punched rings left

Grounding
electrode
conductor
to ground
terminal

Standard locknut
or EMT connector
or BX connector

Conduit or cable
armor enclosing
grounding electrode
conductor

Lug attached
to grounding
bushing

Bonding jumper
required by
Sec. 250-92(a) and
Sec. 250-71(c)

Grounding
electrode
conductor

Both conductors to ground clamp(s) on grounding electrode
see Section 250-115

Fig. 250-54. Grounding-conductor enclosure must be "bonded" at both
ends. (Sec. 250-71.)

This section sets forth the specific means which may be used to connect service conductor enclosures together to satisfy the bonding requirements of Sec. 250-71. These means include:

a. Bonding equipment to the grounded service conductor by means of suitable lugs, pressure connectors, clamps, or other approved means—except that soldered connections must not be used. Section 250-61 permits grounding of meter housings and service equipment to the grounded service conductor on the supply side of the service disconnecting means.

b. Threaded couplings in rigid metal conduit or IMC (Intermediate Metal Conduit) runs and threaded bosses on enclosures to which rigid metal conduit or IMC connects.

c. Threadless couplings made up tight for rigid metal conduit, IMC, or electrical metallic tubing.

d. Bonding jumpers to securely connected metallic parts. Bonding jumpers must be used around concentric or eccentric knockouts which are punched or otherwise formed in such a manner that would impair the electrical current flow through the reduced cross-section of metal that bridges between the enclosure wall and punched ring of the KO (knockout). And the bonding jumpers must be sized from Sec. 250-79(c).

e. Other devices (not standard locknuts and bushings) approved for the purpose.

Based on those briefly worded Code requirements, modern practice follows more or less standard methods.

Where rigid conduit is the service raceway, threaded or threadless couplings are used to couple sections of conduit together. Conduit connection to a meter socket may be made: by connecting a threaded conduit end to a threaded hub or boss on the socket housing, where the housing is so constructed; by a locknut and bonding bushing; by a locknut outside with a bonding wedge or bonding locknut and a standard metal or completely insulating bushing inside; or sometimes by a locknut and standard bushing where the socket enclosure is bonded to the grounded service conductor. Conduit connections to KOs in sheet metal enclosures can be made with a bonding locknut (Fig. 250-55), a bonding wedge, or a bonding bushing where no KO rings remain around the opening through which the conduit enters. Where a KO ring does remain around the conduit entry hole, a bonding bushing or wedge with a jumper wire must be used to assure a path of continuity from the conduit to the enclosure. Figure 250-56 summarizes the various acceptable techniques. It should be noted that the use of the common locknut and bushing type of connection is not allowed. Neither is the use of double locknuts—one inside, one outside—and a bushing, although that is permitted on the load side of the service equipment. The special methods set forth in Sec. 250-72 are designed to prevent poor connections or loosening of connec-

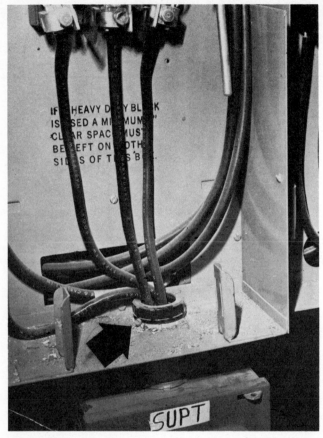

Fig. 250-55. Bonding locknut is a recognized method for bonding a service conduit nipple to a meter socket, when the KO is clean (no rings left in enclosure wall) or is cut on the job. With plastic bushing permitted, this is the most economical of the several methods for making a bonded conduit termination. (Sec. 250-72.)

tions due to vibration. This minimizes the possibility of arcing and consequent damage which might result when a service conductor faults to the grounded equipment.

Similar provisions are used to assure continuity of the ground path when EMT is the service raceway or when armored cable is used. EMT is coupled by threadless devices—compression-type, indenter-type, or set-

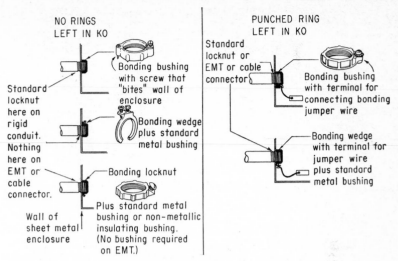

Fig. 250-56. Methods for "bonding" wiring methods to sheet-metal enclosures. (Sec. 250-72.)

screw-type, using raintight couplings outdoors. Standard connectors are used to connect EMT to enclosures. Bonding between the EMT fittings and the enclosures is accomplished in the same way as with rigid conduit. And fittings used with service cable armor must assure the same degree of continuity of ground path.

It should be noted that Sec. 250-72 makes no specific mention of connectors for rigid conduit or EMT, except for the use of threaded bosses with rigid conduit. The use of bonding bushings, bonding wedges, and bonding locknuts is recognized without reference to types of raceways or types of connectors used with the raceways or cable armor. As a result, common sense and experience have molded modern field practice in making raceway and armored service cable connection to service cabinets. The top of Fig. 250-57 shows how a bonding wedge is used on existing connections at services or for raceway connections on the load side of the service—such as required by Sec. 501-16(b) for Class I hazardous locations. A bonding bushing, with provision for connecting a bonding jumper, is the common method for new service installations where some of the concentric or eccentric "doughnuts" (knockout rings) are left in the wall of the enclosure, therefore requiring a bonding jumper. Great care must be taken to assure that each and every type of bushing, locknut, or other fitting is used in the way for which it is intended to best perform the bonding function.

Figure 250-58 shows detailed application of the above rules to typical

FOR EXISTING INSTALLATION

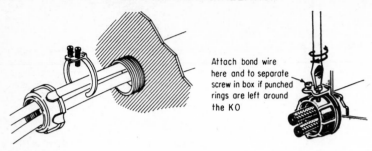

Attach bond wire
here and to separate
screw in box if punched
rings are left around
the KO

FOR NEW WIRING

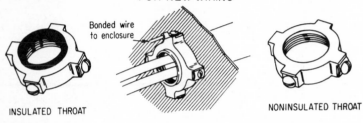

Bonded wire
to enclosure

INSULATED THROAT

NONINSULATED THROAT

ALWAYS
NEEDS JUMPER

NO JUMPER
ON CLEAN KO

Screw here
bonds to wall
on clean KO

Bonding bushing with lug
for jumper wire – may be
used with jumper for clean
KO or with rings left in
wall of enclosure

Bonding bushing with screw
that "bites" into enclosure
wall may be used without a
jumper on a clean KO or
with a jumper when KO
rings are left in wall

Fig.250-57. Bonding bushings and similar fittings must be used in their intended manners. (Sec. 250-72.)

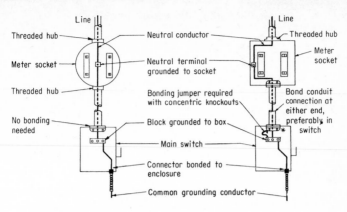

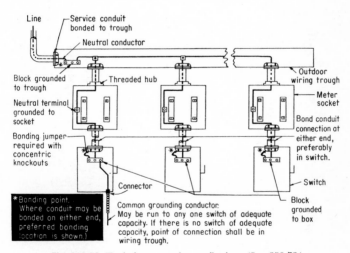

Fig. 250-58. Typical meter socket applications. (Sec. 250-72.)

meter-socket installations. Meter-enclosure bonding techniques are shown in Fig. 250-59. Bonding details for current-transformer installations are shown in Fig. 250-60. Those illustrations are intended to portray typical field practice aimed at satisfying the various Code rules.

250-74. Connection Receptacle Grounding Terminal to Box.   The first paragraph requires that a jumper be used when the outlet box is installed in the wall (Fig. 250-61). Because boxes installed in walls are very seldom found to be perfectly flush with the wall, direct contact between device

TROUGH INSTALLATION – MORE THAN 6 METERS

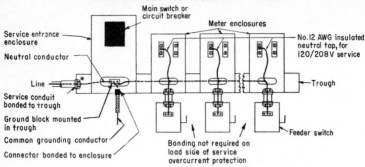

TROUGH INSTALLATION – UP TO 6 METERS

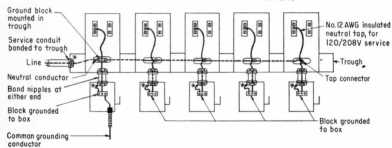

METER ENCLOSURES NIPPLED TOGETHER

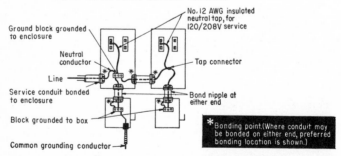

Fig. 250-59. Typical meter enclosure installations (120/208-V or 120/240-V services). (Sec. 250-72.)

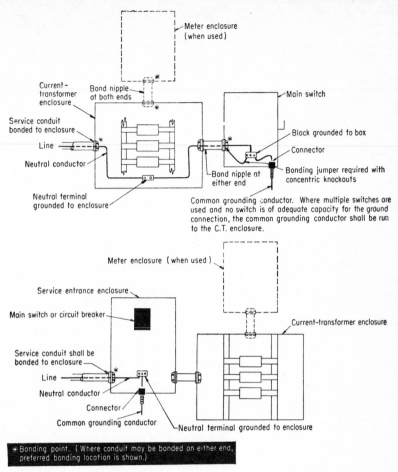

Fig. 250-60. Bonding at CT cabinets. (Sec. 250-72.)

yokes and boxes is seldom achieved. Screws and yokes and boxes is seldom achieved. Screws and yokes currently in use were designed solely for the support of devices rather than as part of the grounding circuit.

Although the general rule states that a flush-type box, installed in a wall for a receptacle outlet, does require a bonding jumper from a grounded box to the receptacle grounding terminal, Exception No. 1 pertains to surface-mounted boxes and eliminates the need for a separate bonding jumper between a surface-mounted box and the receptacle grounding terminal (Fig. 250-62).

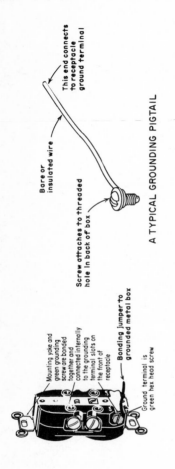

Mounting yoke and green grounding screw are bonded together and connected internally to the grounding terminal slots on the front of receptacle

Bonding jumper to grounded metal box

Ground terminal is green hex head screw

Bare or insulated wire

This end connects to receptacle ground terminal

Screw attaches to threaded hole in back of box

A TYPICAL GROUNDING PIGTAIL

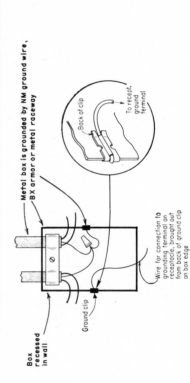

Metal box is grounded by NM ground wire, BX armor or metal raceway

Back of clip

To recept. ground terminal

Wire for connection to grounding terminal on receptacle, brought out from back of ground clip on box edge

Box recessed in wall

Ground clip

Fig. 250-61. Bonding jumper connects receptacle ground to grounded box. (Sec. 250-74.)

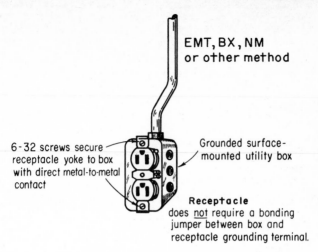

EMT, BX, NM
or other method

6-32 screws secure
receptacle yoke to box
with direct metal-to-metal
contact

Grounded surface-
mounted utility box

Receptacle
does not require a bonding
jumper between box and
receptacle grounding terminal.

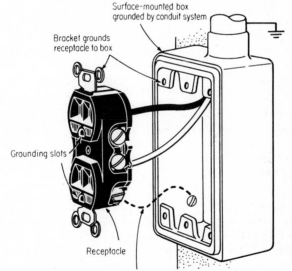

Surface-mounted box
grounded by conduit system

Bracket grounds
receptacle to box

Grounding slots

Receptacle

A jumper wire to connect the grounding-screw terminal to the grounded box
is not required with a surface-mounted box, but is required when receptacle
is used in a recessed box

Fig. 250-62. Typical applications where surface box does not need
receptacle bonding jumper. (Sec. 250-74.

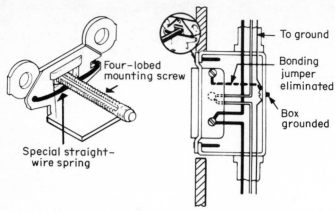

Fig. 250-63. Self-grounding screws ground receptacle in recessed box without bonding jumper. (Sec. 250-74.)

Figure 250-63 illustrates a grounding device which is intended to provide the electrical grounding continuity between the receptacle yoke and the box on which it is mounted and serves the dual purpose of both a mounting screw and a means of providing electrical grounding continuity in lieu of the required bonding jumper. As shown in the sketch, special wire springs and four-lobed machine screws are part of a receptacle design for use without a bonding jumper to box. This complies with Sec. 250-74, Exception No. 2.

Exception No. 3 permits nonself-grounding receptacles without an equipment grounding jumper to be used in floor boxes which are designed for and listed as providing proper continuity between the box and the receptacle mounting yoke.

Exception No. 4 allows the use of a receptacle with an isolated grounding terminal (no connection between the receptacle grounding terminal and the yoke). Sensitive electronic equipment that is grounded normally through the building ground is often adversely affected by pickup of transient signals which cause an imbalance in the delicate circuits. This is particularly true with highly intricate medical and communications equipment, which often pick up unwanted currents, even of very low magnitude.

The use of an isolated grounding receptacle allows a "pure" path to be established back to the system grounding terminal, in the service disconnecting means, without terminating in any other intervening panelboard. In Fig. 250-64, a cutaway of an isolated grounding receptacle shows the insulation between the grounding screw and the yoke.

See comments that follow Sec. 384-27, Exception.

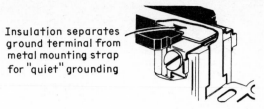

Insulation separates
ground terminal from
metal mounting strap
for "quiet" grounding

Fig. 250-64. Receptacles with isolated ground terminal are used with "clean" or "quiet" ground. (Sec. 250-74.)

250-75. Bonding Other Enclosures. Figure 250-65 shows a composite illustration of a whole range of grounding and bonding techniques used for various raceways and cables throughout an electrical system.

250-76. Bonding for Over 250 V. Single locknut-and-bushing terminations are permitted for 120/240-V systems and 120/208-V systems. Any

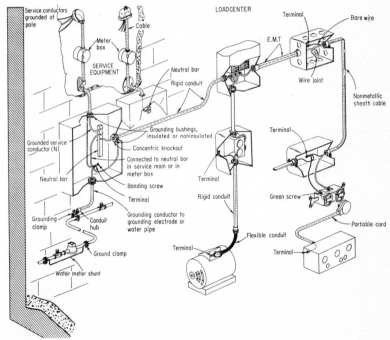

Fig. 250-65. Grounding and bonding techniques apply to all points in any electrical system. (Sec. 250-75.)

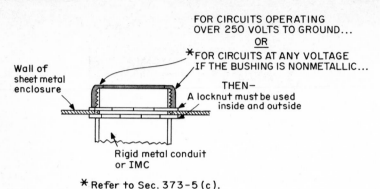

FOR CIRCUITS OPERATING
OVER 250 VOLTS TO GROUND...

OR

*FOR CIRCUITS AT ANY VOLTAGE
IF THE BUSHING IS NONMETALLIC...

THEN—
A locknut must be used
inside and outside

Wall of
sheet metal
enclosure

Rigid metal conduit
or IMC

* Refer to Sec. 373-5 (c).

Fig. 250-66. Double-locknut conduit terminals are required under either condition. (Sec. 250-76.)

480/277-V grounded system, 480-V ungrounded system, or higher must use double locknut-and-bushing terminals on rigid metal conduit and IMC (Fig. 250-66).

Where good electrical continuity is desired on installations of rigid metal conduit or IMC, two locknuts are always specified so that the metal of the box can be solidly clamped between the locknuts, one being on the outside and one on the inside. The reason for not relying on the bushing in place of the inside locknut is that both conduit and box may be secured in place and if the conduit is placed so that it extends into the box to a greater distance than the thickness of the bushing, the bushing will not make contact with the inside surface of the box. But that possible weakness in the single-locknut termination does not exclude it from use on systems up to 250 V to ground.

250-77. Bonding Loosely Jointed Metal Raceways.   Provision must be made for possible expansion and contraction in concrete slabs due to temperature changes by installing expansion joints in long runs of raceways run through slabs. See Sec. 300-7(b). Because such expansion joints are loosely jointed to permit back-and-forth movement to handle changes in gap between batting slabs, bonding jumpers must be used for equipment grounding continuity (Fig. 250-67). Expansion fittings may be selected as vibration dampers and deflection mediums as well as to provide for movement between building sections or for expansion and contraction due to temperature changes in long conduit runs. The fitting diagrammed in Fig. 250-67 provides for movement from the normal in all directions plus 30° deflection, is available up to 4 in. diameter, and may be installed in concrete.

250-78. Bonding in Hazardous Locations.   All raceway terminations in hazardous locations must be made by one of the techniques shown in Fig. 250-56 for service raceways. And as required by Sec. 501-16(b) such

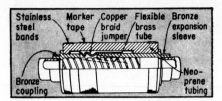

Fig. 250-67. Conduit expansion fitting includes bonding jumper for ground continuity. (Sec. 250-77.)

---

bonding techniques must be used in "all intervening raceways, fittings, boxes, enclosures, etc., between hazardous areas and the point of grounding for service equipment." Refer to Secs. 501-16(b), 502-16(b), and 503-16 (Fig. 250-68).

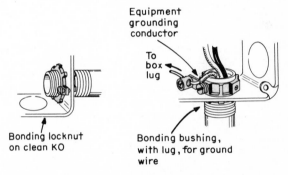

NOTE: Connection of threaded rigid metal conduit or IMC to a threaded boss or hub is considered to be a bonded conduit termination.

Fig. 250-68. Bonded raceway terminations must be used at sheet-metal KOs in hazardous areas. (Sec. 250-78.)

250-79. Main and Equipment Bonding Jumpers. Part **(a)** calls for use of copper or other "corrosion-resistant" conductor material—which does include aluminum and copper-clad aluminum. Part **(b)** demands use of connectors, lugs, and other fittings that have been designed, tested, and listed for the particular application.

Part **(c)** covers sizing of any bonding jumper within the service equipment enclosure or on the line or supply side of that enclosure. Refer to the definition of "Bonding Jumper, Main" in Art. 100.

Figure 250-69 shows examples of sizing bonding jumpers in accordance with the first sentence of part **(c)** of this section.

A.

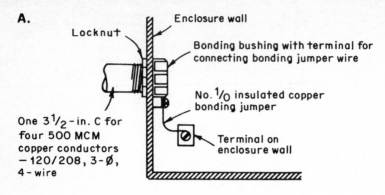

One 3½-in. C for four 500 MCM copper conductors — 120/208, 3-∅, 4-wire

Locknut

Enclosure wall

Bonding bushing with terminal for connecting bonding jumper wire

No. ¹/₀ insulated copper bonding jumper

Terminal on enclosure wall

B.

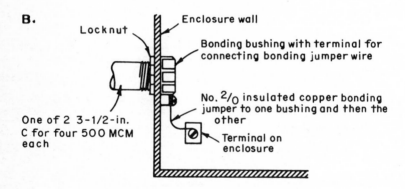

One of 2 3-1/2-in. C for four 500 MCM each

Locknut

Enclosure wall

Bonding bushing with terminal for connecting bonding jumper wire

No. ²/₀ insulated copper bonding jumper to one bushing and then the other

Terminal on enclosure

NOTE: Bushing with jumper is acceptable bonding for a clean KO or one with punched rings still in place.

Fig. 250-69. Examples of the basic sizing of service bonding jumpers. (Sec. 250-79.)

At A, the bonding bushing and jumper are used to comply with part **(d)** of Sec. 250-72. Referring to Table 250-94, with 500 MCM copper as the "largest service-entrance conductor," the minimum permitted size of grounding electrode conductor is No. 1/0 copper (or No. 3/0 aluminum). That therefore is the minimum permitted size of the required bonding jumper.

At B, with each service phase leg made up of two 500 MCM copper conductors in parallel, the left-hand column heading in Table 250-94 refers to the "equivalent for parallel conductors." As a result, the phase leg is taken at 2 × 500 or 1,000 MCM, which is the physical equivalent of the makeup. Then Table 250-94 requires a minimum bonding jumper of No. 2/0 copper (or No. 4/0 aluminum).

Figure 250-70 shows an example of sizing a service bonding jumper in accordance with the second sentence of part **(c)** of this section. In this

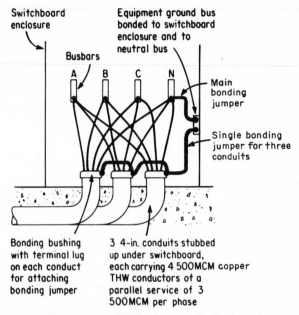

Fig. 250-70. Sizing main bonding jumper and other jumpers at service equipment. (Sec. 250-79.)

sketch, the jumper between the neutral bus and the equipment ground bus is defined by the NE Code as a "main bonding jumper" and the minimum required size of this jumper for this installation is determined by calculating the size of one service phase leg. With three 500 MGM per phase, that works out to 1,500 MCM copper per phase. Because that value is in excess of 1,100 MCM copper, as noted in the Code rule, the minimum size of the main bonding jumper must equal at least 12½ percent of the phase leg cross-section area. Then—

$$12\frac{1}{2}\% \times 1{,}500 \text{ MCM} =$$
$$0.125 \times 1{,}500 = 187.5 \text{ MCM}$$

Referring to Table 8 in Chap. 9 in the back of the Code book, the smallest conductor with at least that cross-section area (csa) is No. 4/0 with a csa of 211,600 CM or 211.6 MCM. Note that a No. 3/0 has a csa of only

167.8 MCM. Thus No. 4/0 copper with any type of insulation would satisfy the Code.

The jumper shown in Fig. 250-70 running from one conduit bushing to the other and then to the equipment ground bus is defined by the NE Code as an "equipment bonding jumper." It is sized the same as a main bonding jumper (above). In this case, therefore, the equipment bonding jumper would have to be not smaller than No. 4/0 copper. And with the calculation that uses the 12½ percent value, if the jumper conductor is to be aluminum instead of copper, a calculation must be made as described below.

In the sketch of Fig. 250-70, if each of the three 4-in. conduits had a separate bonding jumper connecting each one individually to the equipment ground bus, the last sentence of part (c) may be applied to an individual bonding jumper for each separate conduit (Fig. 250-71). The

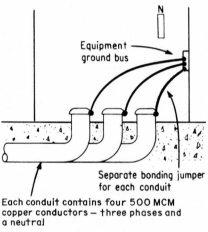

Each conduit contains four 500 MCM
copper conductors — three phases and
a neutral

Fig. 250-71. An individual bonding jumper may be used for each conduit. (Sec. 250-79.)

size of a separate bonding jumper for each conduit in a parallel service must be not less than the size of the grounding electrode conductor for a service of the size of the phase conductor used in each conduit. Referring to Table 250-94, a 500 MCM copper service calls for at least a No. 1/0 grounding electrode conductor. Therefore, the bonding jumper run from the bushing lug on each conduit to the ground bus must be at least a No. 1/0 copper (or 3/0 aluminum).

It is argued that the last sentence of part (c) *requires* separate bonding jumpers when the service is made up of multiple conduits and that a single bonding jumper, as shown in Fig. 250-70, is not acceptable. But, the wording does not make separate jumpers mandatory.

The second sentence of part **(c)** sets minimum sizes of copper *and* aluminum service-entrance conductors above which a service bonding jumper must have a cross-section area "not less than 12½ percent of the area of the largest phase conductor." And the rule states that if the service conductors and the bonding jumper are of different material (i.e., service conductors are copper, say, and the jumper is aluminum), the minimum size of the jumper shall be based on the assumed use of phase conductors of the same material as the jumper and with an ampacity equivalent to that of the installed phase conductors.

example If an aluminum bonding jumper is used at a service fed by copper service-entrance conductors in conduit and if the service feeder is made up of, say, four sets of conductors in four conduits, with four 500 MCM THW copper conductors per phase, then the size of the aluminum bonding jumper must be selected as if the service were made up using aluminum instead of copper, and the assumed size of the aluminum phase conductors must be such that they have an ampacity not less than 380 A per conductor (the ampacity of each 500 MCM THW copper phase leg). From Table 310-16 an aluminum THW conductor with ampacity at least equal to 380 A is 750 MCM size (385 A). Four 750 MCM conductors per phase is a total of 4 × 750 MCM = 3,000 MCM of cross-section for each phase leg of the service. Because that is larger than 1,750 MCM aluminum, as noted in the rule of Sec. 250-79(c), the bonding jumper must have a minimum cross-section area of not less than 12½ percent times 3,000 MCM. The result of the calculation is 0.125 × 3,000 = 375 MCM, minimum size of the aluminum bonding jumper.

Figure 250-72 shows a sample calculation for the opposite combination of conductor materials—aluminum service conductors and a copper bonding jumper. The calculation is clear and similar, following the steps of the Code rule, as follows:

1. Each 750 MCM THW aluminum has ampacity of 385 A.
2. The smallest copper conductor of at least that ampacity is 600 MCM THW copper (420 A). (It might be considered reasonable to use 500 MCM THW copper because its ampacity of 380 A is so close to 385 A.)
3. Three 600 MCM THW copper provides a per-phase cross-section area of 3 × 600 = 1,800 MCM.
4. Because that value is in excess of 1,100 MCM copper, Sec. 250-79(c) requires the copper bonding jumper to have a cross-section area not less than 12½ percent of 1,800 MCM.
5. 0.125 × 1,800 = 225 MCM (250 is the next standard size).

Therefore a copper bonding jumper must be at least 250 MCM size.

Part **(d)** requires a bonding jumper on the load side of the service to be sized as if it were an equipment grounding conductor for the largest circuit with which it is used. And sizing would have to be done from Table 250-95, as follows.

Figure 250-73 shows a floor trench in the switchboard room of a large hotel. The conductors are feeder conductors carried from circuit breakers in the main switchboard (just visible in upper right corner of photo) to feeder conduits going out at left, through the concrete wall of the trench, and under the slab floor to the various distribution panels throughout the building. Because the conduits themselves are not metallically connected

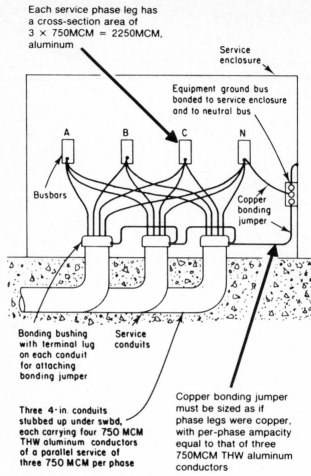

Each service phase leg has
a cross-section area of
3 × 750MCM = 2250MCM,
aluminum

Service
enclosure

Equipment ground bus
bonded to service enclosure
and to neutral bus

A   B   C   N

Busbars

Copper
bonding
jumper

Bonding bushing   Service
with terminal lug   conduits
on each conduit
for attaching
bonding jumper

Three 4-in. conduits
stubbed up under swbd,
each carrying four 750 MCM
THW aluminum conductors
of a parallel service of
three 750 MCM per phase

Copper bonding jumper
must be sized as if
phase legs were copper,
with per-phase ampacity
equal to that of three
750MCM THW aluminum
conductors

Fig. 250-72. Sizing a copper bonding jumper for aluminum service conductors. (Sec. 250-79.)

to the metal switchboard enclosure, bonding jumpers must be run from the conduits to the switchboard ground bus to assure electrical continuity and conductivity as required by NE Code Secs. 250-33, 250-42(e), 250-51, and 250-57.

   1. The bonding conductor from each conduit to the switchboard must be sized in accordance with NE Code Table 250-95.

   2. If one of these conduits is a 3-in. conduit carrying three 500 MCM conductors from a 400-A CB in the switchboard to a motor control

Fig. 250-73. Conduits in trench carry feeder conductors from switchboard at right (arrow) out to various panels and control centers. Grounding bushings on conduit ends have lugs for bonding jumpers to the ground bus in the switchboard. (Sec. 250-79.)

center, the minimum acceptable size of bonding jumper from a grounding bushing on the conduit end of the switchboard ground bus would be No. 3 copper or No. 1 aluminum or copper-clad aluminum, as shown opposite the value of 400 A in the left column of Table 250-95.

Another two of the 3-in. conduits are used for a feeder consisting of two parallel sets of three 500 MCM conductors (each set of three 500 MCMs in a separate conduit) for a circuit protected at 800 A. A single bonding jumper is used, run from one grounding bushing to the other grounding bushing and then to the switchboard ground bus. This single bonding jumper would have to be a minimum of No. 1/0 copper, from NE Code Table 250-95 on the basis of the 800-A rating of the feeder overcurrent protective device.

Because part **(d)** of Sec. 250-79 refers to Table 250-95, that is sometimes interpreted to require that any bonding jumper on the load side of the service be subject to the rules of Sec. 250-95; that is, use of a bonding jumper must conform to the requirements for equipment grounding conductors. As a result, bonding of conduits for a parallel circuit makeup would have to comply with the second sentence in Sec. 250-95, which requires equipment grounding conductors to be run in parallel "where conductors are run in parallel in multiple raceways. . . ." That would then be taken to require that bonding jumpers *also* must be run in parallel for multiple-conduit circuits. And that concept is supported by the last sentence of part **(c)** of Sec. 250-79. In the case of the 800-A circuit above, instead of a single No. 1/0 copper jumper from one bushing-lug to the other bushing-lug and then to the ground bus, it would be necessary to use a separate No. 1/0 copper from each bushing to the ground bus, so the jumpers are run in parallel—as required for equipment grounding conductors. Figure 250-74 shows the two possible arrangements. The

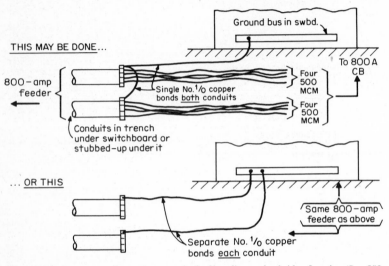

Fig. 250-74. Controversy does exist on method of bonding on load side of service. (Sec. 250-79.)

wording of Secs. 250-79(d) and 250-95 can be used to support either method. Bonding jumpers on the load side of service equipment are sized and routed the same as equipment grounding conductors because such bonding jumpers and equipment grounding conductors serve identical functions. And note that Sec. 250-95 requires the equipment grounding conductor for each of the conduits for a parallel circuit to be the full size determined from the circuit rating. In the case here, a No. 1/0 copper for each conduit is required, based on the 800-A rating of the feeder protective device.

Part **(e)** of Sec. 250-79 follows the thinking that was described in Sec. 250-58(a) for external grounding of equipment attached to a properly grounded metal rack or structure. A short length of flexible metal conduit, liquidtight flex, or any other raceway may, if the raceway itself is not acceptable as a grounding conductor, be provided with grounding by a "bonding jumper" (note *not* an "equipment grounding conductor") run *either* inside or *outside* the raceway or enclosure PROVIDED THAT the *length* of the *equipment bonding Jumper* is *not more* than 6 ft and the jumper is routed with the raceway or enclosure.

Note that this application has limited use for the conditions specified and is a special variation from the concept of Sec. 250-57(b), which requires grounding conductors run inside raceways. Its big application is for external bonding of short lengths of liquidtight or standard flex, under those conditions where the particular type of flex itself is not suitable for providing the grounding continuity required by Sec. 350-5 and Sec. 351-9. Refer also to Sec. 250-91(b), Example Nos. 1 and 2.

Figure 250-75 shows how an external bonding jumper may be used with standard flexible metallic conduit (so-called "Greenfield"). If the

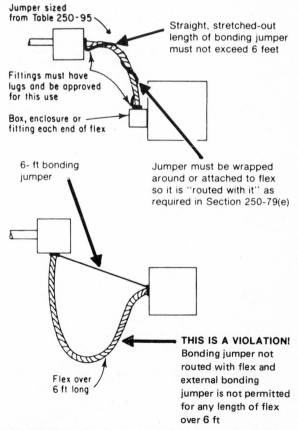

Fig. 250-75. Bonding jumper required for flex may be outside the flex. (Sec. 250-79.)

length of the flex is not over 6 ft, but the conductors run within the flex are protected at more than 20 A, a bonding jumper *must* be used either inside or outside the flex. An outside jumper must comply as shown in Fig. 250-75. For a length of flex not over 6 ft and containing conductors that are protected at not more than 20 A, a bonding jumper is *not* required—as covered in Sec. 250-91(b), Example No. 1

Figure 250-76 shows use of an external bonding jumper with liquid-tight flexible metallic conduit. If liquidtight flex is not over 6 ft long *but* is

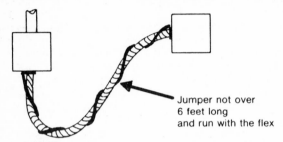

Jumper not over
6 feet long
and run with the flex

Fig. 250-76. Liquidtight flex larger than 1¼-in. size must have bonding jumper—inside or outside—in any length up to 6 ft. (Sec. 250-79.)

larger than 1¼-in. trade size, a bonding jumper must be used, installed *either* inside or outside the liquidtight. An outside jumper must comply as shown. If a length of liquidtight flex larger than 1¼-in. is short enough to permit an external bonding jumper that is not more than 6 ft long between external grounding-type connectors at the ends of the flex, an external bonding jumper may be used. BUT WATCH OUT! The rule says the *jumper,* not the flex, must not exceed 6 ft in length *AND* the jumper "shall be routed with the raceway"—that is, run along the flex surface and not separated from the flex.

250-80. Bonding of Piping Systems.   This section on bonding of piping systems in buildings is divided into two parts—metal *water* piping and *other* metal piping. This section is a rather elaborate sequence of phrases that may be understood in several ways. Of course, the basic concept is to ground any metal pipes that would present a hazard if energized by an electrical circuit.

Part **(a)** requires any "interior metal water piping system" to be bonded to the service equipment enclosure, the grounded conductor (usually, a neutral) at the service, the grounding electrode conductor, *OR* the one or more grounding electrodes used. This rule applies where the metal water piping system does not have 10 ft of metal pipe buried in the earth and is, therefore, not a grounding electrode. In such cases, though, this rule makes clear that the water piping system must be bonded to the service grounding arrangement. And the bonding jumper used to connect the interior water piping to, say, the grounded neutral bus or terminal (or to the ground bus or terminal) must be sized from Table 250-94 based on the size of the service conductors. The jumper is sized from that table because that is the table that would have been used *if* the water piping has 10 ft buried under the ground, making it suitable as a grounding electrode. Note that the "bonding jumper" is sized from Table 250-94 [and not from Sec. 250-79(c)], which means it never has to be larger than 3/0 copper or 250 MCM aluminum. But the "bonding jumper" referred to in Sec. 250-81 is sized from Sec. 250-79(c), which means it may have to be larger. Refer to the illustrations for Sec. 250-81, which also cover bonding of water piping.

Part **(b)** requires a bonding connection from "other" (than water) metal piping systems—such as process liquids or fluids—that "may become energized" to the grounded neutral, the service ground terminal, the grounding electrode conductor, or the grounding electrodes. BUT, for these *other* piping systems the bonding jumper is sized from Table 250-95, using the rating of the overcurrent device of the circuit that *may* energize the piping.

Understanding and application of part **(b)** of Sec. 250-80 hinges on the reference to metal piping "which may become energized." What does that phrase mean? Is it not true that any metal piping "may" become energized? Or does the rule mean to apply only to metal piping that conductively connects to metal enclosures of electrical equipment—such as pump motors, solenoid valves, pressure switches, etc.—in which electrical insulation failure would put a potential on the metal piping system? It does seem that the latter case is what the Code rule means. And that concept is supported by the second paragraph of part **(b)**, which notes that where a particular circuit poses the threat of energization to a piping system, the equipment grounding conductor for that circuit (which could be the conduit or other raceway enclosing the circuit) may be used as the means of bonding the piping back to the service ground point. That has the effect of saying, for instance, that the equipment grounding conductor for a circuit to a solenoid valve in a pipe may also ground the piping (Fig. 250-77).

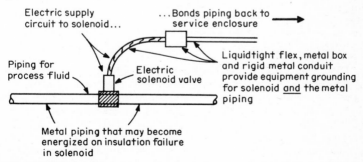

Fig. 250-77. Grounding conductor for circuit that *may* energize piping bonds it to service ground. (Sec. 250-80.)

250-81. Grounding Electrode System. The rules in this section cover the grounding electrode arrangement required at the service entrance of a premise or in a building or other structure fed from a service in another building or other structure, as covered in Sec. 250-24. But, the rules do not apply to grounding of a separately derived system, such as a local step-down transformer, which is covered by part **(c)** of Sec. 250-26 (Fig. 250-78).

Section 250-81 calls for a "grounding electrode system" instead of simply a "grounding electrode" as required by all previous NE Code editions. There are several considerations involved with this radical change.

Up to the 1978 NEC, the "water-pipe"electrode was the premier electrode for service grounding and "other electrodes" or "made electrodes" were acceptable *only* "where a water system (electrode) . . . is not available." If a metal water pipe to a building had at least 10 ft of its length buried in the ground, that *had* to be used as the grounding electrode and no other electrode was required. The underground water pipe was the preferred electrode, the *best* electrode.

In the 1978 NEC, of all the electrodes previously and still recognized by the NEC, the water pipe is the least acceptable electrode and is the only one that may never be used by itself as the *sole* electrode. It must always be supplemented by at least one "additional" grounding electrode (Fig. 250-79). Any one of the other grounding electrodes recognized by the NEC *is* acceptable as the *sole* grounding electrode, by itself.

Take a typical water supply of 12-in. diameter metal pipe running, say, 400 ft underground to a building with a 4,000-A service. From Sec. 250-81(a), that water pipe, connected by a 3/0 copper conductor to the bonded service equipment neutral, *must* be used as a grounding electrode but may *not* serve as the only grounding electrode. It must be supplemented by one of the other electrodes from Secs. 250-81 or 250-83. So the installation can be made acceptable by, say, running a No. 6 copper grounding electrode conductor from the bonded service neutral to an 8-ft, ½-in. diameter ground rod. Although that seems like using a mouse to help an elephant pull a load, it is the literal requirement of Sec. 250-81. And if the same building did not have 10 ft of metal water pipe in the ground, the 8-ft ground rod would be entirely acceptable as the *only* electrode.

The basic rule of Sec. 250-81 requires that all or any of the electrodes specified in **(a)**, **(b)**, **(c)**, and **(d)**, if they are available on the premises, must be bonded together to form a "grounding electrode system."

(a) If there is at least a 10-ft length of underground metal water pipe, connection of a grounding electrode conductor must be made to the water pipe.

(b) If, in addition, the building has a metal frame that is "effectively grounded" (although that phrase is not defined or explained), the frame must be bonded to the water pipe—or vice versa, because

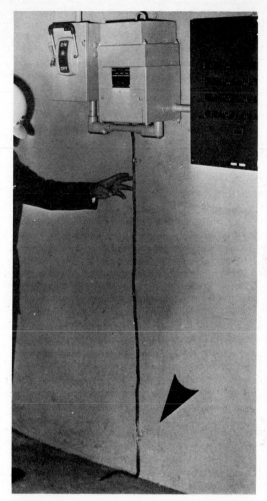

Fig. 250-78. Grounding electrode conductor from the bonded secondary neutral of this local transformer was connected to grounded building steel before concrete floor was poured. This installation is not covered by the rules of Sec. 250-81, but is covered by Sec. 250-26 and complies with those rules. (Sec. 250-81.)

Fig. 250-79. Connection to an underground metal water-supply pipe is never adequate grounding for electric service equipment. (Sec. 250-81.)

the rules do not spell out where actual connections are to be made for grounding electrode conductors and bonding jumpers.

(c) Then, if there is at least a total of 20 ft of one or more ½-in. diameter steel reinforcing bars or rods embedded in the concrete footing or foundation, a bonding connection must be made from one of the other electrodes to one of the rebars—and obviously that has to be done before concrete is poured for the footing or foundation.

Bonding between each pair of electrodes is sized from Sec. 250-79(c)—which means the jumper must not be smaller than the required size of grounding electrode conductor selected from Table 250-94, based on the size of the service-entrance conductors, and not less than 12½ percent of the cross-section area of the service phase leg where the phase leg is over 1,100 MCM copper, or 1,750 MCM aluminum. And it seems clear that the grounding electrode conductor, run from the bonded service neutral in service equipment, may be connected to any one of the two or more electrodes that are bonded together. The rule of Sec. 250-81 is performance oriented and not an equipment spec.

In parts (c) and (d) of Sec. 250-81, the "20 feet of bare copper conductor" referred to is going to be "available" at a building only if either 20-ft arrangement has been specified by the electrical designer, because they are clearly and only grounding electrodes; whereas the other electrodes in parts **(a)**, **(b)**, and the rebars in **(c)** are specified by other than the electrical designer and may be "available."

If a building has all or some of the electrodes described, the above applications are mandatory. If it has none, then any *one* of the electrodes described in Sec. 250-83 may be used for service grounding.

Part **(a)** calls for a bonding jumper around any water meter within a building and any place where piping on both sides of the meter is required to be grounded.

The several requirements set by this revised section and the conditions established for application of the new rules can be best understood by considering a step-by-step approach in making the necessary provisions for typical installations. Restating the above general description of Sec. 250-81:

First, take the case of a building fed by an underground water piping system with at least a 10-ft length of *metal* water pipe buried in the earth ahead of the point at which the metal pipe enters the building. Such buried pipe *is* a grounding electrode, and connection must be made to the underground pipe by a grounding electrode conductor sized from Table 250-94 and run from the grounding point in the service equipment. But now, a number of other factors must be accounted for, as follows:

1. EVEN THOUGH THE WATER PIPE *IS* A SUITABLE GROUNDING ELECTRODE, SEC. 250-81(a) REQUIRES THAT AT LEAST ONE MORE GROUNDING ELECTRODE MUST BE PROVIDED AND MUST BE BONDED TO THE WATER-PIPE ELECTRODE. A water pipe, by itself, is not an adequate grounding electrode and must be supplemented by at least one other electrode to provide a "grounding electrode system."

2. The additional electrode may be:
   ▪ The metal frame of the building provided the frame is effectively grounded (embedded in earth and/or in buried concrete). Figure 250-80 shows an example of the metal frame electrode supplementing the water pipe.
   ▪ OR, a concrete-encased electrode within and near the bottom of a concrete foundation or footing in direct contact with earth. The electrode must consist of at least 20 ft of one or more steel reinforcing bars or rods of not less than ½-in. diameter, or it must consist of at least 20 ft of bare solid copper conductor not smaller than No. 4 AWG. If the building footing or foundation shown in Fig. 250-80 did contain such steel reinforcing, connection of a bonding conductor would have to be made to the steel and the conductor would have to be brought out for connection to the water pipe, the building steel, or the bonded service neutral.

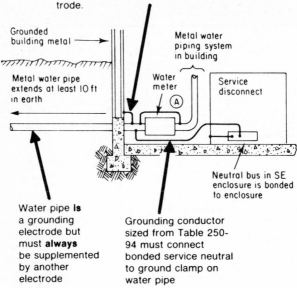

Section 250-81 requires building metal frame to be bonded to water pipe electrode by jumper sized from Section 250-79(c) and metal frame may serve as the additional required grounding electrode.

Grounded building metal

Metal water piping system in building

Metal water pipe extends at least 10 ft in earth

Water meter

Service disconnect

A

Neutral bus in SE enclosure is bonded to enclosure

Water pipe **is** a grounding electrode but must **always** be supplemented by another electrode

Grounding conductor sized from Table 250-94 must connect bonded service neutral to ground clamp on water pipe

Note: At point "A," a bonding jumper **must** be used around the water meter and must be sized from Section 250-79(c).

Fig. 250-80. Metal building frame *must* be used as an electrode if present. (Sec. 250-81.)

- OR, a "ground ring encircling the building or structure," buried directly in the earth at least 2½ ft down. The ground ring must be "at least 20 feet" of bare No. 2 or larger copper conductor. (In most cases, the conductor will have to be considerably longer than 20 ft in order to "encircle" the building or structure.)
- OR, underground bare metal gas piping or other metal underground piping or tanks. Figure 250-81 shows such piping as the "additional electrode" in a building without a metal frame and without rebars in the footing or foundation.
- OR, a buried 8-ft ground rod or pipe or a plate electrode.

Sections 250-81 and 250-83 list the acceptable electrodes and describe installation requirements.

3. As worded in Sec. 250-81, any of the four types of grounding electrodes mentioned there [**(a)**, **(b)**, **(c)**, and **(d)**] must be bonded

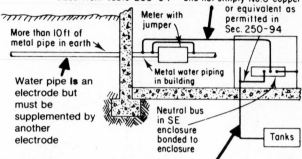

Grounding electrode conductor sized from Table 250-94 must connect bonded service neutral to clamp on water-pipe electrode.

Because the underground tanks are not a "made" electrode, this grounding electrode conductor must be sized from Table 250-94 — and not simply No.6 copper or equivalent as permitted in Sec. 250-94

More than 10 ft of metal pipe in earth

Meter with jumper

Water pipe **is** an electrode but must be supplemented by another electrode

Metal water piping in building

Neutral bus in SE enclosure bonded to enclosure

Tanks

Because building does not have grounded metal frame or either of the electrodes described in Section 250-81(c) and (d), the last sentence of Section 250-81(a) requires that one of the electrodes of Section 250-83 be used to supplement the water pipe electrode—such as metal piping to underground metal tanks.

NOTE: A No. 6 copper to an 8 ft. ground rod could be used instead of the underground piping, as a supplement to the water pipe electrode.

Fig. 250-81. Supplementing water-pipe electrode in building without metal frame. (Sec. 250-81.)

together IF THEY ARE PRESENT. Note that the rule does not state that any of those electrodes must be provided. But if any or all of them are present, they must be bonded together to form a "grounding electrode system," sizing such bonding jumpers from Sec. 250-79(c). And where a water-pipe electrode, as described, is present any one of the three electrodes in Sec. 250-81 may be used as the required "additional electrode."

In the case of a building fed by a nonmetallic underground piping system or one where there is *not* 10 ft of metal pipe underground, the water piping system is *not* a grounding electrode—HOWEVER, THE INTERIOR METAL WATER PIPING SYSTEM MUST BE BONDED TO THE SERVICE GROUNDING, as described above under Sec. 250-80(a). But when the water pipe is not a grounding electrode, another type of electrode must be provided to accomplish the service grounding. Any

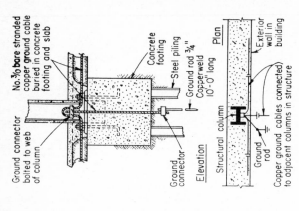

No.3/0 bare stranded copper ground cable buried in concrete footing and slab

Concrete footing

Steel piling

Ground connector bolted to web of column

Ground rod 3/4" Copperweld 10'-0" long

Ground connector

Elevation

Structural column

Exterior wall in building

Plan

Ground rod

Copper ground cables connected to adjacent columns in structure

ONE METHOD of grounding building structural members to ground cable system.

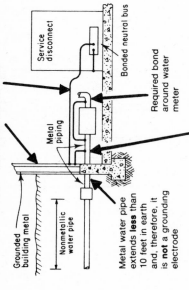

Section 250-81(b) recognizes the grounded metal building frame as a suitable grounding electrode by itself, connected to bonded service neutral by conductor sized from Table 250-94.

Service disconnect

Bonded neutral bus

Required bond around water meter

Metal piping

Grounded building metal

Nonmetallic water pipe

Metal water pipe extends **less** than 10 feet in earth and, therefore, it is **not** a grounding electrode

Section 250-80(a) requires interior metal water piping to be bonded to service grounding, such as by bonding to the grounding electrode (the building frame in this case), with jumper sized from Table 250-94.

NOTE: Rebars in foundation could also serve as the only electrode if building did not have metal frame.

Fig. 250-82. Building metal frame may be sole grounding electrode. (Sec. 250-81.)

one of the other three electrodes of Sec. 250-81 [(b), (c), or (d)] may be used as the required grounding electrode. For instance, if the metal frame of the building is effectively grounded, a grounding electrode conductor, sized from Table 250-94, and run from the bonded service neutral or ground terminal to the building frame, may satisfy the Code, as shown in Fig. 250-82. Where none of the four electrodes described in Sec. 250-81 is present, *one* of the electrodes from Sec. 250-83 MUST BE USED, such as a ground rod as shown in Fig. 250-83. Note that any type of electrode other than a water-pipe electrode MAY BE USED BY ITSELF AS THE SOLE ELECTRODE.

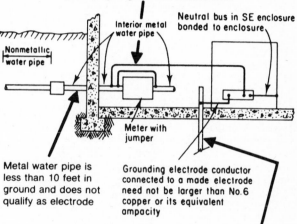

Section 250-80(a) requires interior metal water piping to be bonded to service grounding, such as by bonding to grounded neutral bus.

Interior metal water pipe

Neutral bus in SE enclosure bonded to enclosure

Nonmetallic water pipe

Meter with jumper

Metal water pipe is less than 10 feet in ground and does not qualify as electrode

Grounding electrode conductor connected to a made electrode need not be larger than No. 6 copper or its equivalent ampacity

Because building does not have a grounded metal frame or either of the electrodes described in Section 250-81(c) and (d), Section 250-83 requires that at least one of the electrodes described in that Section be used — such as a ground rod.

Fig. 250-83. Ground rod may be only electrode in building without any of the electrodes in Sec. 250-81. (Sec. 250-81.)

The four illustrations shown for this section are only typical examples of the many specific ways in which the new rules on grounding electrodes may be applied.

A very important sentence of Sec. 250-81(a) says that "continuity of the grounding path or the bonding connection to interior piping shall not rely on water meters." The intent of that rule is that a bonding jumper always MUST BE USED around a water meter. This has been added because of the chance of loss of grounding if the water meter is removed or replaced with a nonmetallic water meter. The bonding jumper around a meter must be sized in accordance with Sec. 250-79(c)—which is based on Table 250-94, but may call for a conductor even larger than the grounding electrode conductor run to the grounding electrode (i.e., 12½ percent of service phase leg cross-section area).

The concrete-encased electrode that is described in part **(c)** of Sec. 250-81, known as the "Ufer system," has particular merit in new construction where the bare copper conductor or steel reinforcing bar or rod can be readily installed in a foundation or footing form before concrete is poured. Installations of this type using a bare copper conductor have been installed as far back as 1940, and tests have proved this system to be highly effective.

The intent of "bottom of a concrete foundation" is to completely encase the electrode within the concrete, in the footing near the bottom. The footing shall be in direct contact with the earth, which means that dry gravel or polyethylene sheets between the footing and the earth are not permitted (Fig. 250-84).

It may be advisable to provide additional corrosion protection in the form of plastic tubing or sheath at the point where the grounding electrode leaves the concrete foundation.

For concrete-encased steel reinforcing bar or rod systems used as a grounding electrode in underground footings or foundations, welded-type connections (metal-fusing methods) may be used for connections that are encased in concrete. Compression or other type mechanical connectors may also be used.

250-83. Made and Other Electrodes.   This section covers grounding electrodes that may be used if none of the electrodes of Sec. 250-81 is available. Or one of the electrodes of Sec. 250-83 may be used as the "additional electrode" required by Sec. 250-81(a) to supplement a water-pipe electrode. Figure 250-81 shows use of a local metal underground piping system as a supplement to a water-pipe electrode.

As a general rule, if a water piping system or other approved electrode is not available, a driven rod or pipe is used as the electrode (Fig. 250-85). A rod or pipe driven in the ground does not always provide as low a ground resistance as is desirable, particularly where the soil becomes very dry. In some cases where several buildings are supplied, grounding at each building reduces the ground resistance. (See Sec. 250-24.)

Where it is necessary to bury more than one pipe or rod in order to lower the resistance to ground, they should be placed at least 6 ft apart. If they are placed closer together there would be little improvement.

Where two driven or buried electrodes are used for grounding two different systems that should be kept entirely separate from one another, such as a grounding electrode of a wiring system for light and power and a grounding electrode for a lightning rod, care must be taken to guard against the conditions of low resistance between the two electrodes and

BARE COPPER CONDUCTOR... OR

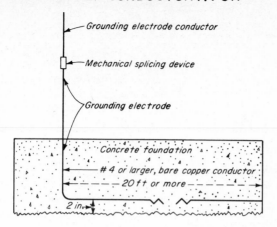

... 1/2 IN. DIAMETER REBARS OR RODS

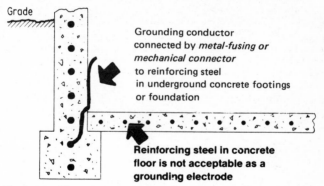

Fig. 250-84. The "Ufer" grounding electrode is concrete-encased. (Sec. 250-81.)

high resistance from each electrode to ground. If two driven rods or pipes are located 6 ft apart, the resistance between the two is sufficiently high and cannot be greatly increased by increasing the spacing. The rule of this section requires at least 6 ft of spacing between electrodes serving different systems.

In addition to ground rods, plate electrodes are another form of "made" (manufactured) electrodes (Fig. 250-86). Such electrodes are listed in the UL *Electrical Construction Materials Directory* under the heading "Grounding and Bonding Equipment"—which also covers bonding

Fig. 250-85. A driven ground rod must have at least 8 ft of its length buried in the ground, although the buried length may be less than that, but not less than 4 ft, where rock bottom is hit. If underground rock prevents driving the rod at least 4 ft, the rod may then be laid horizontally in a trench, with its 8-ft length completely buried. (Sec. 250-83.)

devices, ground clamps, grounding and bonding bushings, ground rods, armored grounding wire, protector grounding wire, grounding wedges, ground clips for securing the ground wire to an outlet box, water-meter shunts, and similar equipment. Only listed devices are acceptable for use. And listed equipment is suitable only for use with copper, unless it is marked "AL" and "CU."

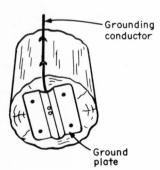

Fig. 250-86. Ground plates for pole-bottom mounting are made in copper and galvanized steel. (Sec. 250-83.)

250-84. Resistance of Made Electrodes.

This section on the resistance to earth of made electrodes clarifies Code intent and eliminates a cause of frequent controversy. The rule says that if a single made electrode (rod, pipe, or plate) shows a resistance to ground of over 25 ohms, *one* addition made electrode must be used in parallel, but there is then no need to make any measurement or add more electrodes or be further concerned about the resistance to ground. In previous Code editions, wording of this rule implied that additional electrodes had to be used in parallel with the first one until a resistance of 25 ohms or less was obtained. Now, as soon as the second electrode is added, it does not matter what the resistance to ground reads, and there is no need for more electrodes (Fig. 250-87).

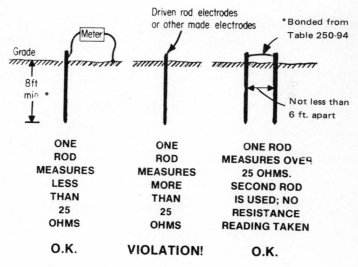

*4 ft. min. if rod contacts rack bottom

Fig. 250-87. Earth resistance of ground rod must be considered. (Sec. 250-84.)

Insofar as made electrodes are concerned, there is a wide variation of resistance to be expected, and the present requirements of the National Electrical Code concerning the use of such electrodes do not provide for a system that is in any way comparable to that which can be expected where a good underground metallic piping can be utilized.

It is recognized that some types of soil may create a high rate of corrosion and will result in a need for periodic replacement of grounding electrodes. It should also be noted that the intimate contact of two dissimilar metals, such as iron and copper, when subjected to wet conditions can result in electrolytic corrosion.

Under abnormal conditions, when a cross occurs between a high-tension conductor and one of the conductors of the low-tension secondaries, the electrode may be called upon to conduct a heavy current into the earth. The voltage drop in the ground connection, including the conductor leading to the electrode and the earth immediately around the electrode, will be equal to the current multiplied by the resistance. This results in a difference of potential between the grounded conductor of the wiring system and the ground. It is therefore important that the resistance be as low as practicable.

Where made electrodes are used for grounding interior wiring systems, resistance tests should be conducted on a sufficient number of electrodes to determine the conditions prevailing in each locality. The

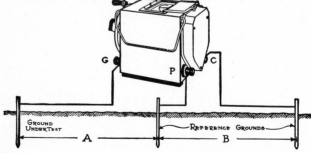

Fig. 250-88. Ground-resistance testing must be done with the proper instrument and in strict accordance with the manufacturer's instructions. (Sec. 250-84.)

tests should be repeated several times a year to determine whether the conditions have changed because of corrosion of the electrodes or drying out of the soil.

Figure 250-88 shows a ground tester being used for measuring the ground resistance of a driven electrode. Two auxiliary rod or pipe electrodes are driven to a depth of 1 or 2 ft, the distances A and B in the figure being 50 ft or more. Connections are made as shown between the tester and the electrodes; then the crank is turned to generate the necessary current, and the pointer on the instrument indicates the resistance to earth of the electrode being tested. In place of the two driven electrodes, a water piping system, if available, may be used as the reference ground, in which case terminals P and C are to be connected to the water pipe.

But, as noted above, where two made electrodes are used, it is not necessary to take a resistance reading, which is required in the case of fulfilling the requirement of 25 ohms to ground for one made electrode.

250-86. Use of Lightning Rods. This rule requires an individual "grounding electrode system" for grounding of the grounded circuit conductor (e.g., the neutral) and the equipment enclosures of electrical systems, and prohibits use of the lightning ground electrode system for grounding the electrical system. Although the rule does *not* generally prohibit or require bonding between different grounding electrode systems (such as for lightning and for electric systems), it does note that such bonding is sometimes required by rules in the sections listed. And the note calls attention to the advantage of such bonding. There have been cases where fires and shocks have been caused by a potential difference between separate ground electrodes and the neutral of AC electrical circuits.

250-91. Material (Grounding Conductors). Figure 250-89 shows the typical use of copper, aluminum, or copper-clad aluminum conductor to connect the bonded neutral and equipment ground terminal of service

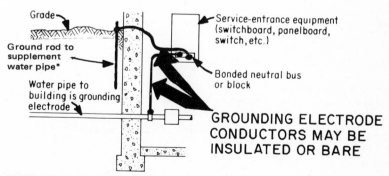

Fig. 250-89. An insulated grounding electrode conductor may be any color other than white, natural gray, or green. (Sec. 250-91.)

equipment to each of the one or more grounding electrodes used at a service. Controversy has been common on the permitted color of an insulated (or covered) grounding electrode conductor. Section 200-7 prohibits use of white or natural gray color for any conductor other than a "grounded conductor"—such as the grounded neutral or phase leg, as described in the definition of "grounded conductor." Green color is reserved for equipment grounding conductors, although there is no **Code** rule clearly prohibiting a green grounding electrode conductor. Refer to Sec. 310-10.

Exception No. 2 of Sec. 250-91(a) covers the installation of the grounding electrode conductor for a service layout consisting of two to six service disconnects in separate enclosures with a separate set of service-entrance conductors run down to each disconnect. Such an arrangement is covered in Sec. 230-45. Previous **Code** editions required either that a separate grounding electrode conductor be run from each enclosure to the grounding electrode or that a single, unspliced conductor be looped from enclosure to enclosure. A single grounding electrode conductor used to ground all the service disconnects had to be without splice [the last line in Sec. 250-91(a)]—run from one enclosure to the other and then to the water pipe or other grounding electrode. In the present **Code**, Exception No. 2 says that splices may be made in the grounding electrode conductor to tap into each of the service disconnect enclosures, as shown in Fig. 250-90.

Exception No. 2 also covers the sizing of a main grounding electrode conductor and taps from it to provide system grounding in each separate service enclosure where two to six service disconnects are used in separate enclosures. Wording of the Exception requires the main grounding electrode conductor to be sized from Table 250-94 but does not tell on what basis that table is used. The main grounding electrode conductor might be sized for the sum of the cross-section areas of the total number of conductors connected to one hot leg of the service drop. Or, the main grounding electrode conductor eould be sized from Table 250-94 on the basis of the size of one hot leg of a service of sufficient size to handle the demand load fed by the two to six service disconnects.

The wording of the rule does, however, make clear that the size of the grounding electrode tap to each separate enclosure may be determined from Table 250-94 on the basis of the largest service hot leg serving each enclosure, as shown in Fig. 250-91. Although that illustration shows an overhead service to the layout, the two to six service disconnects could be fed by individual sets of underground conductors, making up a "single" service lateral as permitted by Exception No. 7 to Sec. 230-2.

Part **(b)** describes the various types of conductors and metallic cables or raceways that are considered suitable for use as equipment grounding conductors. And the **Code** recognizes cable tray as an equipment grounding conductor as permitted by Art. 318.

Exception No. 1 recognizes flexible metal conduit or flexible metallic

WHERE THE LAYOUT IS LIKE THIS . . .

Metering from point of drop connection or individual metering

Commercial or industrial building with one or more tenants or occupancies

Utility pole

Two to six service disconnects, each fed by a separate set of SE conductors (Sec. 230-45)

. . . THE BASIC RULE CALLS FOR THIS, BUT . . .

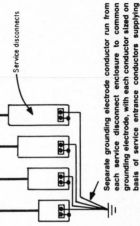

Bonded neutral in each disconnect

A difficult, costly method

Single, unspliced grounding electrode conductor, sized according to the size of a single set of SE conductors that would handle demand load on the four disconnects, run or looped from enclosure to enclosure to grounding electrode

GROUNDING MAY BE DONE LIKE THIS . . .

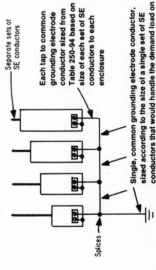

Separate sets of SE conductors

Each tap to common grounding electrode conductor sized from Table 250-94 based on size of each set of SE conductors to each enclosure

Single, common grounding electrode conductor, sized according to the size of a single set of SE conductors that would handle the demand load on the four disconnects

Splices

. . . OR LIKE THIS

Service disconnects

Separate grounding electrode conductor run from each service disconnect enclosure to common grounding electrode, with each conductor sized on basis of service entrance conductors supplying each enclosure

Fig. 250-90. Grounding electrode conductor may be spliced for multiple service disconnects. (Sec. 250-91.)

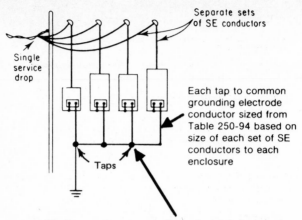

Separate sets of SE conductors

Single service drop

Each tap to common grounding electrode conductor sized from Table 250-94 based on size of each set of SE conductors to each enclosure

Taps

Single, common grounding electrode conductor, sized according to the size of a single set of SE conductors that would handle the demand load on the four disconnects or sized for the sum of the cross-sections of the total number of conductors fed by one hot leg of the drop

Fig. 250-91. Rule covers sizing main and taps of grounding electrode conductor at multiple-disconnect services. (Sec. 250-91.)

tubing (See Art. 349) with termination fittings "approved for the purpose" as a grounding means (without a separate equipment grounding wire) if the length of the flex is not over 6 ft and the contained circuit conductors are protected by overcurrent devices rated at 20 A or less.

Standard flexible metal conduit (also known as "Greenfield") is not listed by UL as suitable for grounding in itself. However, Sec. 350-5 of the **NE Code** as well as Exception No. 1 in part **(b)** permits flex to be used without any supplemental grounding conductor when any length of flex in a ground return path is not over 6 ft and the conductors contained in the flex are protected by overcurrent devices rated not over 20 A (Fig. 250-92). Use of standard flex with the permission given in Sec. 250-79(e) for either internal or external bonding must be as follows:

1. When conductors within a length of flex up to 6 ft are protected at more than 20 A, equipment grounding may not be provided by the flex, but a separate conductor must be used for grounding. If a length of flex is short enough to permit a bonding jumper not over 6 ft long to be run between external grounding-type connectors at the flex ends, while keeping the jumper *along* the flex, such an external jumper may be used where equipment grounding is required—as for a short length of flex with circuit conductors in it protected at more than 20 A. Of course, such short lengths of flex

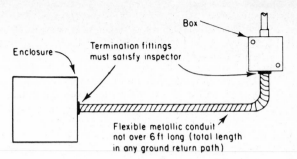

Flex not over 6 ft long is suitable as a grounding means (without a separate ground wire) if the conductors in it are protected by OC devices rated not more than 20 amps.

Fig. 250-92. Standard flex is limited in use without an equipment ground wire. (Sec. 250-91.)

may also be "bonded" by a bonding jumper inside the flex, instead of external. Refer to Sec. 250-79(e).

2. Any length of standard flex that would require a bonding jumper longer than 6 ft may not use an external jumper. In the Code sense, when the length of such a grounding conductor exceeds 6 ft, it is *not* a BONDING JUMPER BUT *IS* AN EQUIPMENT GROUND-ING CONDUCTOR AND MUST BE RUN ONLY *INSIDE* THE FLEX, AS REQUIRED BY SEC. 250-57(b). Combining UL data with the rule of Sec. 250-79(e) and the Exception to Sec. 350-5, *every* length of flex that is over 6 ft must contain an equipment grounding conductor run *only* inside the flex (Fig. 250-93).

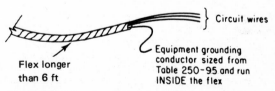

Fig. 250-93. Internal equipment grounding is required for any flex over 6 ft long. (Sec. 250-91.)

In part **a** of Exception No. 1 it should be noted that exemption from the need for an equipment grounding conductor applies only to flex where there is not over 6 ft of "total length in any ground return path." That means that from any branch-circuit load device—lighting fixture, motor, etc.—all the way back to the service ground, the total permitted length of flex without a ground wire is 6 ft. In the total circuit run from the service to any outlet, there could be one 6-ft length of flex, or two 3-ft lengths, or three 2-ft lengths, or a 4-ft and a 2-ft length—where the flex lengths are in series as equipment ground return paths. In any circuit run—feeder to subfeeder to branch circuit—any length of flex that would make the total series length over 6 ft would have to use an internal or external bonding jumper, regardless of any other factors.

In all cases, sizing of bonding jumpers for all flex applications is made according to Sec. 250-79(d), which requires the same minimum size for bonding jumpers as is required for equipment grounding conductors. In either case, the size of the conductor is selected from Table 250-95, based on the maximum rating of the overcurrent devices protecting the circuit conductors that are within the flex.

In part **c** of Exception No. 1, the term "approved for the purpose," as applied to termination fittings, will require the authority having jurisdiction to evaluate the grounding capabilities of fittings used with these short conduit lengths. See also Secs. 350-5 and 351-7.

Exception No. 2 presents conditions under which *liquidtight* flexible metal conduit may be used without need for a separate equipment grounding conductor.

1. Both Exception No. 2 and the UL's *Electrical Construction Materials Directory* (the green book) note that any listed liquidtight flex in 1¼-in. and smaller trade size, in a length not over 6 ft, is satisfactory as a grounding means through the metal core of the flex and does *not* require a bonding jumper (or equipment grounding conductor) either internal or external (Fig. 250-94). Liquidtight flex in 1¼-in.

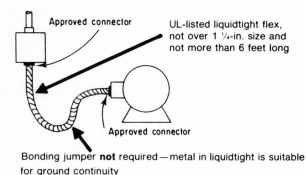

Bonding jumper **not** required — metal in liquidtight is suitable for ground continuity

Fig. 250-94. Liquidtight flex may be used with a separate ground wire. (Sec. 250-91.)

and smaller trade size may be used without a bonding jumper inside *or* outside provided that the "total length" of that flex "in any ground return path" is not over 6 ft. Thus, two or more separate 6-ft lengths installed in a raceway run would not be acceptable with the bonding jumper omitted from all of them. In such cases, one 6-ft length or more than one length that does not total over 6 ft may be used with a bonding jumper, but any additional lengths 6 ft or less in the same raceway run must have an internal or external bonding jumper sized from Table 250-95.

Although UL gives the same grounding recognition to their "listed" liquidtight flex, this **Code** rule covers liquidtight that the UL does not list, such as high-temperature type.

2. For liquidtight flex over 1¼ in., UL does not list any as suitable for equipment grounding, thereby requiring use of a separate equipment grounding conductor installed in *any* length of the flex, as required by **Code**. If a length of liquidtight flex larger than 1¼ in. is short enough to permit an external bonding jumper not more than 6 ft long between external grounding-type connectors at the ends of the flex, an external bonding jumper may be used. BUT WATCH OUT! The rule says the *jumper*, not the flex, must not exceed 6 ft in length AND the jumper "shall be routed with the raceway"—that is, run along the flex surface and not separated from the flex.

3. If any length of flex is *over 6 ft*, then the flex is not a suitable grounding conductor, regardless of the trade size of the flex, whether it is larger or smaller than 1¼ in. In such cases, an *equipment grounding conductor* (not a "bonding jumper"—the phrase reserved for short lengths) must be used to provide grounding continuity and IT MUST BE RUN *INSIDE* THE FLEX, NOT EXTERNAL TO IT, IN ACCORDANCE WITH SEC. 250-57(b).

There is a conflict between Sec. 250-91(b) and Sec. 351-9. In its nine listed types of equipment grounding conductors, Sec. 250-91(b), for instance, recognizes standard flexible metal conduit for grounding if "approved for the purpose," but standard flex is not recognized in the UL listing as suitable for grounding. Section 250-91(b) does not give the same recognition to liquidtight flex that is "approved for the purpose," even though there is such liquidtight flex listed by UL. The only recognition of liquidtight flex for grounding is that given in Sec. 250-91(b), Exception No. 2, which is at odds with Sec. 351-9. Refer to Sec. 351-9.

Exception No. 3 of this section covers the same point described under Sec. 250-57 for DC circuits.

Part **(c)** of Sec. 250-91 is an extremely important rule that has particular impact on the use of electrical equipment outdoors. The first part of the rule accepts the use of "supplementary grounding electrodes"—such as a ground rod—to "augment" the equipment grounding conductor; *BUT* an equipment grounding conductor must always be used where needed and the connection of outdoor metal electrical enclosures to a ground rod is never a satisfactory alternative to the use of an equipment grounding conductor because use of just ground-rod grounding would have the earth as "the sole equipment grounding conductor" and that is expressly prohibited by the last clause of part **(c)**.

This whole matter of earth ground usually comes up as follows:

Question: When direct-burial or nonmetallic-conduit circuits are run underground to supply lighting fixtures or other equipment mounted on metal standards or poles or fed by metal conduit run up a pole or building wall, is it necessary to run an equipment grounding conductor to ground the metal standard or pole or conduit if a ground rod has been driven for the same purpose?

Answer: Yes. An equipment grounding conductor is necessary to provide low impedance for ground-fault current return to assure fast, effective operation of the circuit protective device when the circuit is derived from a grounded electrical system (such as 240/120 V, single-phase or 208Y/120V or 480Y/277 V, 3-phase). Low impedance of a grounding path "to facilitate the operation of the circuit protective devices in the circuit" is clearly and specifically required by NE Code Sec. 250-51. When a ground rod is used to ground an outdoor metal standard or pole or outdoor metal conduit and no other grounding connection is used, ground-fault current must attempt to return to the grounded system neutral by flowing through the earth. Such an earth return path has impedance that is too high, limiting the current to such a low value that the circuit protective device does not operate. In that case, a conductor that has fault d (made conductive contact) to a metal standard, pole, or conduit will put a dangerous voltage on the metal—exposing persons to shock or electrocution hazard as long as the fault exists. The basic concept of this problem—and Code violation—is revealed in Fig. 250-95.

The same undesirable condition would exist where a direct-burial or nonmetallic-conduit circuit feeds up through a metal conduit outdoors. As shown in Fig. 250-96, fault current would have to return through the high impedance of the earth.

The hazard of arrangements using only a ground rod as shown arises from the chance that a person might make contact with the energized metal standard or conduit and have a high enough voltage across the person to produce a dangerous current flow through the person's body. The actual current flow through the body will depend upon the contact resistances and the body resistance in conjunction with the voltage gradient (potential difference) imposed across the body. As shown in Fig. 250-97, a person contacting an energized metal pole can complete a circuit to earth or to some other pipe or metal that is grounded back to the system neutral.

It is important to note that part (c) of Sec. 250-91 applies to these situations where outside metal standards or conduits are grounded by means of a ground rod at the standard or conduit. The installations shown in Figs. 250-95, 250-96, and 250-97 are in violation of the last clause of Sec. 250-91(c) as well as Sec. 250-51(c). Figure 250-98 is another example of a violation of the rule.

Compliance with the letter and spirit of those Code sections—and other sections on equipment grounding—will result from use of an

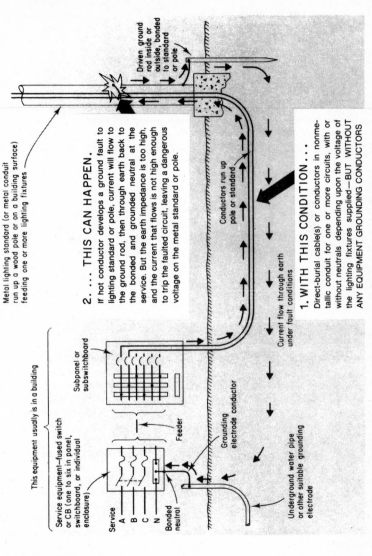

Fig. 250-95. This Code violation produces a dangerous condition at a metal standard. (Sec. 250-91.)

This equipment usually is in a building

Service equipment—fused switch or CB (one to six in panel, switchboard, or individual enclosure)

Service
A
B
C
N
Bonded neutral

Subpanel or subswitchboard

Feeder

Grounding electrode conductor

Underground water pipe or other suitable grounding electrode

Metal lighting standard (or metal conduit run up a wood pole or on a building surface) feeding one or more lighting fixtures

2. ... THIS CAN HAPPEN.

If hot conductor develops a ground fault to lighting standard or pole, current will flow to the ground rod, then through earth back to the bonded and grounded neutral at the service. But the earth impedance is too high, and the current that flows is not high enough to trip the faulted circuit, leaving a dangerous voltage on the metal standard or pole.

Driven ground rod inside or outside, bonded to standard or pole

Conductors run up pole or standard

Current flow through earth under fault conditions

1. WITH THIS CONDITION...

Direct-burial cable(s) or conductors in nonmetallic conduit for one or more circuits, with or without neutrals depending upon the voltage of the lighting fixtures supplied—BUT WITHOUT ANY EQUIPMENT GROUNDING CONDUCTORS

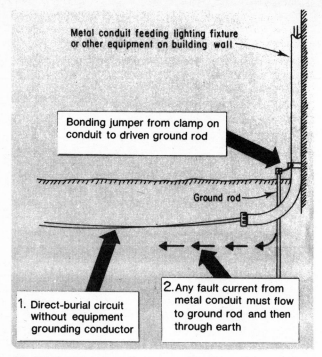

Metal conduit feeding lighting fixture
or other equipment on building wall

Bonding jumper from clamp on
conduit to driven ground rod

Ground rod

1. Direct-burial circuit
without equipment
grounding conductor

2. Any fault current from
metal conduit must flow
to ground rod and then
through earth

Fig. 250-96. This is also a dangerous condition for conduit up a pole or
building. (Sec. 250-91.)

equipment grounding conductor run with the circuit conductors—either
closely placed in the same trench with direct-burial conducts (Type UF or
Type USE) or pulled into nonmetallic conduit with the circuit conductors. Such arrangement is also dictated by Sec. 250-57(b), which requires
that an equipment grounding conductor *must* be within the same raceway, cable, or cord or otherwise run with the circuit conductors.

Effective grounding methods that are in accordance with **NE Code**
rules are shown in Figs. 250-99 and 250-100.

[Although **NE Code** Art. 338 on "Service-Entrance Cable" does not say
that Type USE cable may be used as a feeder or branch circuit (on the
load side of service equipment), the UL listing on Type USE cable says it
"is suitable for all of the underground uses for which Type UF cable is
permitted by the **National Electrical Code**."]

If an underground circuit to a metal standard or pole is run in metal
conduit, a separate equipment grounding conductor is not needed in the

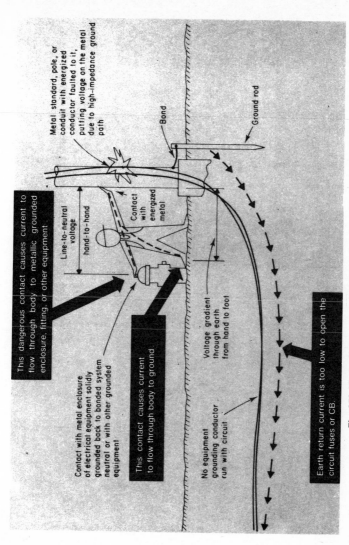

This dangerous contact causes current to flow through body to metallic grounded enclosure, fitting, or other equipment.

Metal standard, pole, or conduit with energized conductor faulted to it, putting voltage on the metal due to high-impedance ground path

Bond

Ground rod

Line-to-neutral voltage

hand-to-hand

Contact with energized metal

Contact with metal enclosure of electrical equipment solidly grounded back to bonded system neutral or with other grounded equipment

This contact causes current to flow through body to ground.

Voltage gradient through earth from hand to foot

No equipment grounding conductor run with circuit

Earth return current is too low to open the circuit fuses or CB.

Fig. 250-97. Ineffective grounding creates shock hazards. (Sec. 250-91.)

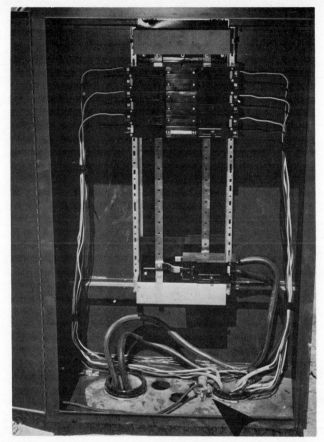

Fig. 250-98. Driven ground rod (arrow) has conductor run to it from a large lug at the left rear of the enclosure. All of the equipment grounding conductors from UF 480-V circuits to pole lights are connected to that lug. But the ground rod and earth path are the sole return path for fault currents. The two larger conductors make up a 480-V underground USE circuit, without the neutral or an equipment grounding conductor brought to the panel. [Sec. 250-91(c).]

conduit if the conduit end within the standard is bonded to the standard by a bonding jumper (Fig. 250-101). Section 250-91(b) recognizes metal conduits as suitable equipment grounding conductors in themselves.

250-92. Installation.   Part **(a)**, in its first paragraph, covers physical protection for a grounding electrode conductor, as shown in Fig. 250-102.

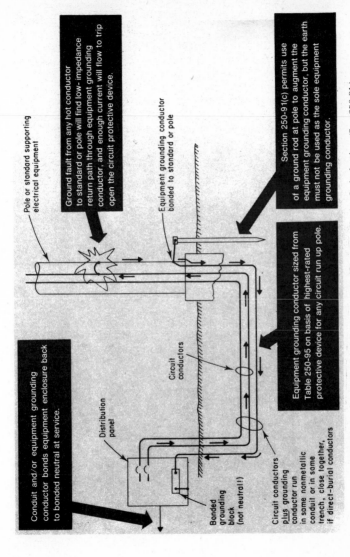

Pole or standard supporting electrical equipment

Ground fault from any hot conductor to standard or pole will find low-impedance return path through equipment grounding conductor, and enough current will flow to trip open the circuit protective device.

Section 250-91(c) permits use of a ground rod at pole to augment the equipment grounding conductor, but the earth must not be used as the sole equipment grounding conductor.

Equipment grounding conductor bonded to standard or pole

Conduit and/or equipment grounding conductor bonds equipment enclosure back to bonded neutral at service.

Equipment grounding conductor sized from Table 250-95 on basis of highest-rated protective device for any circuit run up pole.

Circuit conductors

Distribution panel

Bonded grounding block (not neutral)

Circuit conductors plus grounding conductor run in some nonmetallic conduit or in some trench, close together, if direct-burial conductors

Fig. 250-99. Equipment grounding conductor assures effective fault clearing. (Sec. 250-91.)

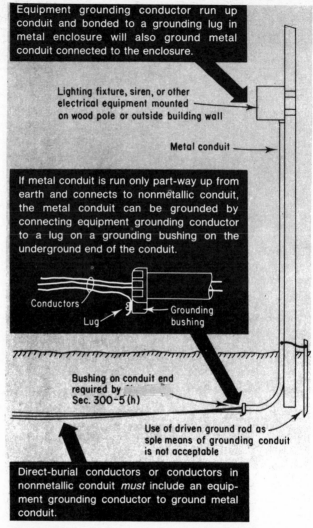

Equipment grounding conductor run up conduit and bonded to a grounding lug in metal enclosure will also ground metal conduit connected to the enclosure.

Lighting fixture, siren, or other electrical equipment mounted on wood pole or outside building wall

Metal conduit

If metal conduit is run only part-way up from earth and connects to nonmetallic conduit, the metal conduit can be grounded by connecting equipment grounding conductor to a lug on a grounding bushing on the underground end of the conduit.

Conductors

Lug

Grounding bushing

Bushing on conduit end required by Sec. 300-5 (h)

Use of driven ground rod as sole means of grounding conduit is not acceptable

Direct-burial conductors or conductors in nonmetallic conduit *must* include an equipment grounding conductor to ground metal conduit.

Fig. 250-100. Watch out for grounding details like these! (Sec. 250-91.)

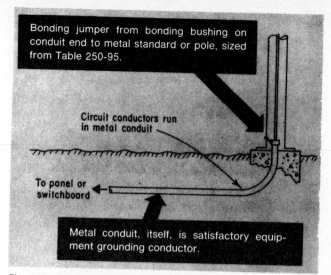

Bonding jumper from bonding bushing on conduit end to metal standard or pole, sized from Table 250-95.

Circuit conductors run in metal conduit

To panel or switchboard

Metal conduit, itself, is satisfactory equipment grounding conductor.

Fig. 250-101. Underground metal conduit to metal standard provides Code-acceptable ground-fault return path. (Sec. 250-91.)

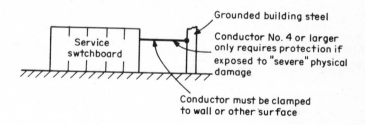

Grounded building steel

Conductor No. 4 or larger only requires protection if exposed to "severe" physical damage

Service swtchboard

Conductor must be clamped to wall or other surface

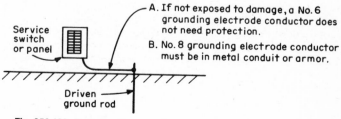

A. If not exposed to damage, a No. 6 grounding electrode conductor does not need protection.

B. No. 8 grounding electrode conductor must be in metal conduit or armor.

Service switch or panel

Driven ground rod

Fig. 250-102. Protection for grounding electrode conductor. (Sec. 250-92.)

A common technique for protecting bare or insulated grounding conductors (one which grounds the wiring system and equipment cases) makes use of a metal conduit sleeve, run open or installed in concrete. In all such cases, the second paragraph of part **(a)** covers details on the use of "metal enclosures" for grounding electrode conductors. The grounding conductor must be connected to its protective conduit at both ends so that any current which might flow over the conductor will also have the conduit as a parallel path. The regulation presented is actually a performance description of the rule of Sec. 250-71(c) which specifically and simply requires that any conduit or armor enclosing a grounding electrode conductor be bonded to a service enclosure at one end and to the grounding electrode at the other end. The concept involved is to assure that any metal raceway (or other enclosure) containing a grounding electrode conductor is electrically in parallel with the conductor, as shown in Fig. 250-103. Bonded connection at both ends of an enclosing raceway

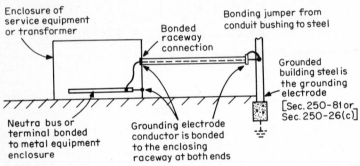

Enclosure of service equipment or transformer

Bonded raceway connection

Bonding jumper from conduit bushing to steel

Grounded building steel is the grounding electrode
[Sec. 250-81 or Sec. 250-26(c)]

Neutral bus or terminal bonded to metal equipment enclosure

Grounding electrode conductor is bonded to the enclosing raceway at both ends

Fig. 250-103. Grounding electrode conductor must be electrically in parallel with enclosing raceway and other enclosures. (Sec. 250-92.)

must be used for any grounding electrode arrangement at a service and for grounding of a separately derived system, such as a generator or transformer secondary, as shown in Fig. 250-104. And in that illustration, where the transformer secondary phase leg is larger than 1,100 MCM copper or 1,750 MCM aluminum, the bonding jumper from the conduit bushing to the case will, invariably, have to be larger than the grounding electrode conductor. Table 250-94 shows that a grounding electrode conductor never has to be larger than No. 3/0 copper or 250 MCM aluminum, whereas Sec. 250-79(c) requires a bonding jumper to have a cross-section area of at least 12½ percent of the cross-section area of the largest one of the transformer secondary phase legs (or service-entrance phase legs). (Usually, all the phase legs are the same size, so the rule can be read as "12½ percent of *one* of the phase legs.") Refer to Sec. 250-79(c).

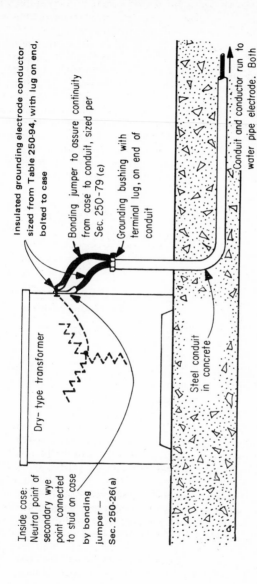

Insulated grounding electrode conductor sized from Table 250-94, with lug on end, bolted to case

Bonding jumper to assure continuity from case to conduit, sized per Sec. 250-79 (c)

Grounding bushing with terminal lug, on end of conduit

Conduit and conductor run to water pipe electrode. Both conduit and conductor are connected to electrode.

Inside case:
Neutral point of secondary wye point connected to stud on case by bonding jumper — Sec. 250-26(a)

Dry-type transformer

Steel conduit in concrete

Fig. 250-104. Protective metal conduit on grounding conductor must always be electrically in parallel with conductor. (Sec. 250-92.)

The necessity for making a grounding electrode conductor electrically in parallel with its protective conduit applies to all applications of such conductors. If the protective conduit in any such case was arranged so that the conductor and conduit were not acting as parallel conductors—such as the conduit would be in Fig. 250-104 if there were no bonding jumper from the conduit bushing to the conductor lug—the presence of magnetic metal conduit (steel) would serve to greatly increase the inductive reactance of the grounding conductor to limit any flow of current to ground. The steel conduit would act as the core of a "choke" to restrict current flow. Figure 250-105 shows the "skin effect" of current flow over a conduit in parallel with a conductor run through it, resulting in a condition which makes it critically necessary to keep the conduit connected electrically in parallel with an enclosed grounding electrode conductor. The condition is as follows.

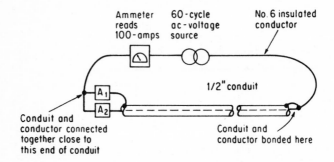

Ammeter A₁ (indicates amount of current in conduit) = 97 amps

Ammeter A₂ (indicates amount of current in conductor) = 3 amps

Fig. 250-105. Enclosing conduit is more important than the enclosed grounding electrode conductor. (Sec. 250-92.)

The presence of the steel conduit acts as an iron core to greatly increase the inductive reactance of the conductor. This choke action raises the impedance of the conductor to such a level that only 3 A flow through the conductor and the balance of 97 A flows through the conduit. This division of current between the conduit and the conductor points up the importance of assuring tight couplings and connectors throughout every conduit system and for every metal raceway system and metal cable jacketing. In particular, this stresses the need for bonding both ends of any raceway used to protect a grounding conductor run to a water pipe or other grounding electrode. Such conduit protection must be securely connected to the ground electrode and to the equipment enclosure in which the grounding conductor originates. If such conduit is left open, lightning and other electric discharges to earth through the grounding conductor will find a high-impedance path. The importance of high conductivity in the conduit system is also important for effective equipment grounding, even when a specific equipment grounding conductor is used in the conduit.

Figure 250-105 clearly shows the conduit itself to be a more important conductor than the actual conductor. Figure 250-106 is a clear example of a violation of this rule. Figure 250-107 shows two other examples of

Fig. 250-106. Grounding electrode conductors are run in conduit from their connections to an equipment grounding bus in an electrical room to the point where they connect to the grounding electrodes. Without a bonding jumper from each conduit to the ground bus, this is a clear VIOLATION of the second paragraph rule of Sec. 250-92(a). Sec. 250-92.)

violations. Of course, nonmagnetic conduit—such as aluminum—would have a different effect, but it should also be in parallel because it would not be a low-reluctance core for the magnetic field around the enclosed conductor. The inductive reactance of the conductor would not be elevated and the magnetic choking would be minimized. However, the **Code** rules on bonding [Sec. 250-71(c)] and parallel connection of conduit containing a grounding electrode conductor apply to *all metal* raceways. Aluminum conduit must, therefore, be connected the same as steel conduit or EMT.

Fig. 250-107. Two examples of very clear violations of the rule that requires enclosing metal raceways (rigid metal conduit at top and flex at right) to be bonded at both ends to a grounding electrode conductor within the raceway. [Secs. 250-71(c) and 250-92(a).]

The third paragraph of Sec. 250-92(a) requires special care for aluminum grounding electrode conductors. If such a conductor is to be run, say, along a concrete wall, it would have to be clamped to a wooden "running board" that is nailed to the wall—to keep it from "direct contact with masonry." And outdoors, such a conductor must be kept at least 18 in. above the ground. But, there has been controversy about these rules. Although the wording of this paragraph literally requires those installation methods for *all* aluminum and copper-clad aluminum grounding electrode conductors—whether bare or insulated, installed within or without raceway—some inspectors have taken the rules as applying only to *bare* conductors (Fig. 250-108). Because Sec. 230-30 and the **NEC**, in

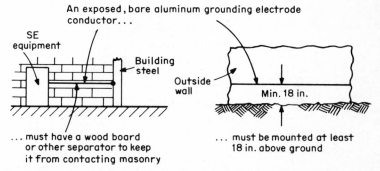

NOTE: An insulated aluminum conductor or a bare conductor installed in conduit may not be subject to these limitations, depending upon the inspector's interpretation.

Fig. 250-108. Does this controversial rule apply only to *bare* aluminum conductor? (Sec. 250-92.)

general, recognize insulated aluminum conductors in conduit underground and directly buried in soil, it is argued that *insulated* aluminum conductor may be run in direct contact with masonry and within 18 in. of earth—even directly buried in the soil if it is Type UF or USE, or within conduit or other raceway underground (Fig. 250-109). Of course, all such application must not have exposed (bare) aluminum, even short lengths, such as at terminations, that would violate the above rules. That means that terminations must be made at least 18 in. aboveground.

Part **(b)** of Sec. 250-92 covers installation of "equipment grounding conductors" as distinguished from "grounding electrode conductors." (Refer to "Definitions," Art. 100.) Where the equipment grounding conductor is a bare or insulated conductor (a cable) that is run by itself, instead of a metal raceway or armor, all the rules of part **(a)**, as described above, must be satisfied. A separately run equipment ground wire is a basic exception to the normal **Code** practice of keeping the ground wire

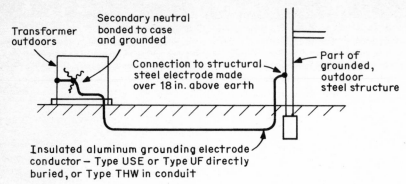

Transformer outdoors

Secondary neutral bonded to case and grounded

Connection to structural steel electrode made over 18 in. above earth

Part of grounded, outdoor steel structure

Insulated aluminum grounding electrode conductor — Type USE or Type UF directly buried, or Type THW in conduit

Fig. 250-109. This has been accepted but does violate literal Code wording. (Sec. 250-92.)

and circuit wires close together. When so run, it must follow the rules for a grounding electrode conductor, which is normally run by itself, either exposed or in raceway. If a steel conduit or tubing is used for mechanical protection of the grounding conductor, it needs to be bonded to the grounding conductor where it enters and where it leaves the protecting steel conduit in order to keep the impedance of the grounding circuit at an acceptable level, as described in part **(a)** above.

250-93. Size of Direct-Current System Grounding Conductor. Figure 250-110 is a diagram of a balancer set used with a 2-wire 230-V generator to supply a 3-wire system as referred to in part **(a)** of this section.

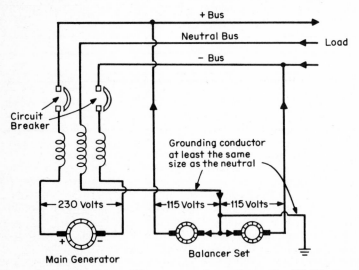

+ Bus

Neutral Bus

Load

− Bus

Circuit Breaker

Grounding conductor at least the same size as the neutral

230 Volts

115 Volts

115 Volts

+ −

Main Generator

Balancer Set

Fig. 250-110. Sizing a DC system grounding conductor. (Sec. 250-93.)

250-94. Size of Alternating-Current Grounding Electrode Conductor. For copper wire, a minimum size of No. 8 is specified in order to provide sufficient carrying capacity to ensure an effective ground and sufficient mechanical strength to be permanent. Where one of the service conductors is a grounded conductor, the same grounding electrode conductor is used for grounding both the system and the equipment. Where the service is from an ungrounded 3-phase power system, a grounding electrode conductor of the size given in Table 250-94 is required at the service.

If the sizes of service-entrance conductors for an AC system are known, the minimum acceptable size of grounding electrode conductor can be determined from **NE Code** Table 250-94. Where the service consists of only one conductor for each hot leg or phase, selection of the minimum permitted size of grounding electrode conductor is a relatively simple, straightforward task. If the largest phase leg is, say, a 500 MCM copper THW, Table 250-94 shows No. 1/0 copper or No. 3/0 aluminum (reading across from "Over 350 MCM thru 600 MCM") as the minimum size of a grounding electrode conductor.

But, use of the table for services with multiple conductors per phase leg (e.g., four 500 MCM for each of three phase legs of a service), is more involved.

The heading over the left-hand columns of this table is "Size of Largest Service-Entrance Conductor or Equivalent for Parallel Conductors." To make proper use of this table, the meaning of the word "equivalent" must be clearly understood. "Equivalent" means that parallel conductors per phase are to be converted to a single conductor per phase that has a cross-section area of its conductor material at least equal to the sum of the cross-section areas of the conductor materials of the two or more parallel conductors per phase. (The cross-section area of the insulation must be excluded.)

For instance, two parallel 500 MCM copper RHH conductors in separate conduits would be equivalent to a single conductor with a cross-section area of 500 + 500 or 1,000 MCM. From Table 250-94, the minimum size of grounding electrode conductor required is shown to be No. 2/0 copper or No. 4/0 aluminum—opposite the left column entry, "Over 600 MCM thru 1100 MCM." Note that use of this table is based solely on the size of the conductor material itself, regardless of the type of insulation. No reference is made at all to the kind of insulation.

Figure 250-111 shows a typical case where a grounding electrode conductor must be sized for a multiple-conductor service. A 208/120-V, 3-phase, 4-wire service is made up of two sets of parallel copper conductors of the sizes shown in the sketch. The minimum size of grounding electrode conductor which may be used with these service-entrance conductors is determined by first adding together the physical size of the two No. 2/0 conductors which make up each phase leg of the service:

1. From **NE Code** Table 8 in Chap. 9 in the back of the **Code** book, which gives physical dimensions of the conductor material itself

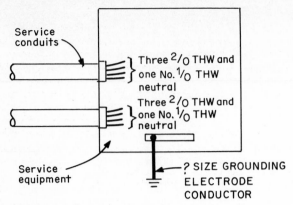

Fig. 250-111. Typical task of sizing the conductor to the grounding electrode. (Sec. 250-94.)

(excluding insulation cross-section area), each of the phase conductors has a cross-section area (csa) of 133,100 MCM. Two such conductors per phase have a total csa of 266,200 MCM.

2. The same table shows that the single conductor which has a csa at least equal to the total csa of the two conductors per phase is a 300 MCM size of conductor. That conductor size is then located in the left-hand column of Table 250-94 to determine the minimum size of grounding electrode conductor, which turns out to be No. 2 copper or No. 1/0 aluminum or copper-clad aluminum.

Figure 250-112 shows another example of conductor sizing, as follows:

1. The grounding electrode conductor A connects to the street side of the water meter of a metallic water supply to a building. The metallic pipe extends 30 ft underground outside the building.

2. Because the underground metallic water piping is at least 10 ft long, the underground piping system is a grounding electrode and must be used as such.

3. Based on the size of the service-entrance conductors (5 × 500 MCM = 2,500 MCM per phase leg), the minimum size of grounding electrode conductor to the water pipe is No. 3/0 copper or 250 MCM aluminum or copper-clad aluminum.

4. The connection to the ground rod at B satisfies the rules of Sec. 250-81 on grounding.

5. But, the minimum size of grounding electrode conductor B required between the neutral bus and the made electrode is No. 6 copper or its equivalent in ampacity, as covered by the two exceptions to the basic rule of Sec. 250-94. Although the **Code** does not require the conductor to a made electrode to be larger than No. 6, regardless of the ampacity of the service phases, a larger size

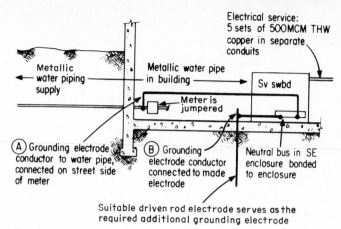

Fig. 250-112. Two different sizes of grounding electrode conductors are required for installations like this. (Sec. 250-94.)

conductor is commonly used for mechanical strength, to protect it against breaking or damage.

250-95. Size of Equipment Grounding Conductors.   When an individual equipment grounding conductor is used in a raceway—either in a non-metallic raceway, as required by Sec. 347-4, or in a metal raceway where such a conductor is used for grounding reliability even though Sec. 250-91(b) accepts metal raceways as a suitable grounding conductor—the grounding conductor must have a minimum size as shown in Table 250-95. The minimum acceptable size of an equipment grounding conductor is based on the rating of the overcurrent device (fuse or CB) protecting the circuit, run in the same raceway, for which the equipment grounding conductor is intended to provide a path of ground-fault current return (Fig. 250-113). Each size of grounding conductor in the table is adequate to carry enough current to blow the fuse or trip the CB of the rating indicated beside it in the left-hand column. In Fig. 250-113, if the fuses are rated at 60 A, Table 250-95 shows that the grounding electrode conductor used with that circuit must be at least a No. 10 copper or a No. 8 aluminum or copper-clad aluminum.

Whenever an equipment grounding conductor is used for a circuit that consists of only one conductor for each hot leg (or phase leg), the grounding conductor is sized simply and directly from Table 250-95, as described. When a circuit is made up of parallel conductors per phase, say an 800-A circuit with two conductors per phase, an equipment grounding conductor is also sized in the same way and would, in that case, have to be at least a No. 1/0 copper or No. 3/0 aluminum. *But,* if such a circuit is made up using two conduits—that is, three phase legs

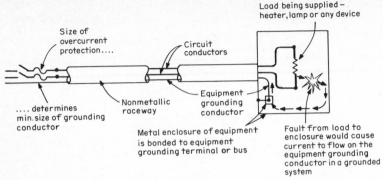

Fig. 250-113. Size of grounding conductor must carry enough current to operate circuit overcurrent device. (Sec. 250-95.)

and a neutral in each conduit—Sec. 250-95 requires that an individual grounding conductor be run in each of the conduits *and* each of the two grounding conductors must be at least No. 1/0 copper or No. 3/0 aluminum (Fig. 250-114). Another example is shown in Fig. 250-115, where a 1,200-A protective device on a parallel circuit calls for No. 3/0 copper or 250 MCM aluminum grounding conductor.

[Note in that example that each 500 MCM XHHW circuit conductor has an ampacity of 405 A (Table 310-16) and three per phase gives a circuit ampacity of $3 \times 405 = 1,215$ A. Use of a 1,200-A protective device satisfies the basic rule of Sec. 240-3, protecting each phase leg within its ampacity. Because the load on the circuit is continuous (over 3 hr), the

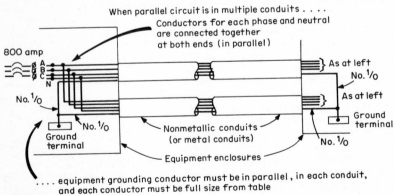

Fig. 250-114. Grounding conductor must be used in each conduit for parallel-conductor circuits. (Sec. 250-95.)

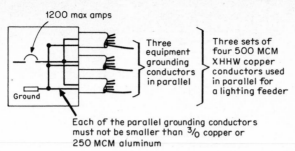

Fig. 250-115. Using equipment grounding conductors in parallel. (Sec. 250-95.)

circuit is loaded to just under 972 A—satisfying Sec. 220-10(b), which required a continuous load to be limited to no more than 80 percent of the circuit conductor ampacity and no more than 80 percent of the protection rating. Each circuit conductor is actually made up of three 500 MCM XHHW, with a total-per-phase ampacity of 3 × 405 = 1,215 A. But load is limited to 0.8 × 1,215 = 972 A per phase. Each 500 MCM is then carrying 972 ÷ 3 = 324 A. Because that value is less than 380 A, which is the ampacity of a 500 MCM THW copper, the use of XHHW conductors *does* comply with the UL requirement that, for equipment rated over 100 A, conductors connected to the equipment be rated at not over 75°C (such as THW) or, if 90°C conductors are used (such as XHHW), they must be used at no more than the ampacity of 75°C conductors of the same size. However, some authorities object to that usage on the grounds that the use of 1,200-A protection would not be acceptable to Sec. 240-3, Exception No. 1 if 75°C (THW) conductors were used. Therefore, they note, the XHHW conductors are not actually being used as 75°C conductors; the load current could later be increased above the 75°C ampacity; and the application does violate the letter and intent of the UL rule, thereby violating Sec. 110-3(b) of the NEC.]

Exception No. 2 states that the equipment grounding conductor *need not* be larger than the circuit conductors. The main application for this Exception is for motor circuits where short-circuit protective devices are usually considerably larger than the motor branch-circuit-conductor ampactiy, as permitted in Sec. 430-52 (up to 400 percent) to permit starting of a motor without opening on inrush current. In such cases, literal use of Table 250-95 could result in grounding conductors larger than the circuit conductors.

Exception No. 3 points out that metal raceways and cable armor are recognized as equipment grounding conductors and Table 250-95 does not apply to them.

Figure 250-116 shows details of a controversy that often arises about Sec. 250-95 and Sec. 250-57(a). When two or more circuits are used in the

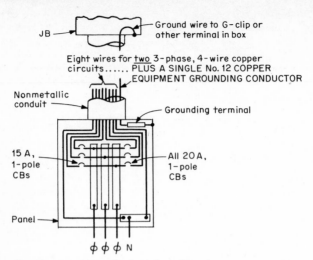

Fig. 250-116. This application is logical but does create controversy.
(Sec. 250-95.)

same conduit, it is logical to conclude that a single equipment grounding
conductor within the conduit may serve as the required grounding
conductor for each circuit if it satisfies Table 250-95 for the circuit with
the highest rated overcurrent protection. The common contention is that
if a single metal conduit is adequate as the equipment grounding conductor for all the contained circuits, a single grounding conductor can serve
the same purpose when installed in a nonmetallic conduit that connects
two metal enclosures (such as a panel and a home-run junction box)
where both circuits are within both enclosures. As shown, a No. 12
copper conductor satisfies Table 250-95 as an equipment grounding
conductor for the circuit protected at 20 A. The same No. 12 also may
serve for the circuit protected at 15 A, for which a grounding conductor
must not be smaller than No. 14 copper.

250-112. To Grounding Electrode.   The rule requires that the connection
of a grounding electrode conductor to the grounding electrode "shall be
accessible" (Fig. 250-117). Inspectors want to be able to see and/or be able
to get at any connection to a grounding electrode. But because there are
electrodes permitted in Sec. 250-81 and Sec. 250-83 that would require
underground or concrete-encased connections, an Exception was added
to the basic rule to permit inaccessible connections in such cases (Fig. 250-
118). This section now places the burden on the installer to make such
connections accessible wherever possible.

The second sentence of this section requires assured connection to a
metal piping system electrode, as shown in Fig. 250-119. In a typical case

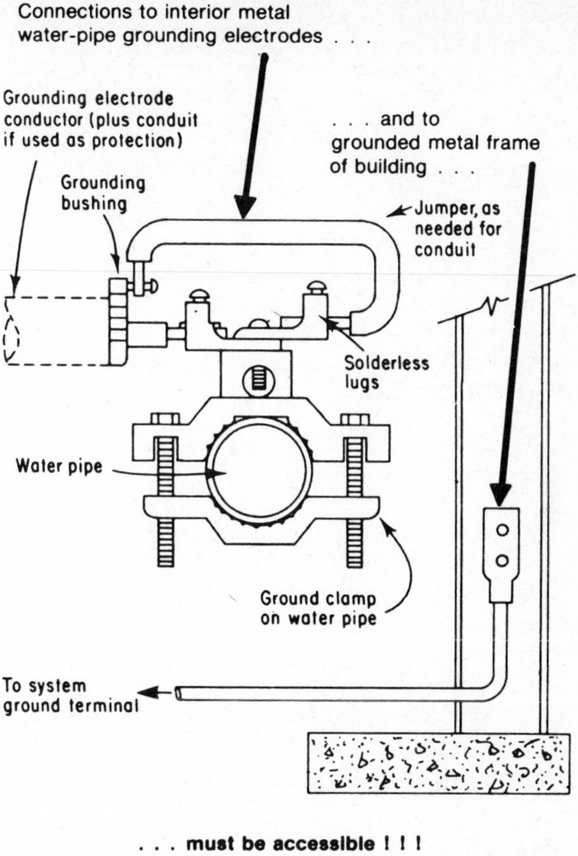

Connections to interior metal
water-pipe grounding electrodes . . .

Grounding electrode
conductor (plus conduit
if used as protection)

Grounding
bushing

. . . and to
grounded metal frame
of building . . .

Jumper, as
needed for
conduit

Solderless
lugs

Water pipe

Ground clamp
on water pipe

To system
ground terminal

. . . must be accessible ! ! !

Fig. 250-117. Whenever possible, connections to grounding electrodes must be "accessible." (Sec. 250-112.)

of grounding for a local transformer within a building, Sec. 250-26(b)
notes that grounding of the secondary neutral may be made to the
nearest water pipe anywhere in the building; but Sec. 250-112 actually
requires that bonding jumpers be used to assure continuity of the ground
path back to the underground pipe, wherever the piping may contain
insulating sections or is liable to become disconnected, as at meters,
valves, and service unions. The bonding shown in the sketch may or may
not be required by individual inspectors. The NE Code does not specifically clarify this point, although literal wording appears to require
bonding.

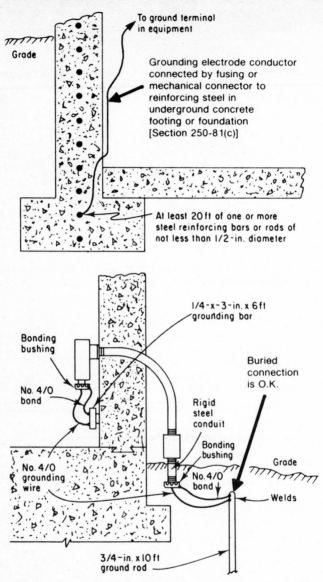

To ground terminal
in equipment

Grounding electrode conductor
connected by fusing or
mechanical connector to
reinforcing steel in
underground concrete
footing or foundation
[Section 250-81(c)]

At least 20 ft of one or more
steel reinforcing bars or rods of
not less than 1/2-in. diameter

Grade

Bonding
bushing

No. 4/0
bond

No. 4/0
grounding
wire

1/4-x-3-in. x 6 ft
grounding bar

Rigid
steel
conduit

Bonding
bushing

No. 4/0
bond

Buried
connection
is O.K.

Grade

Welds

3/4-in. x 10 ft
ground rod

Fig. 250-118. Encased and buried electrode connections are permitted by
Exception to basic rule. (Sec. 250-112.)

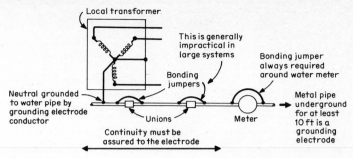

Fig. 250-119. Although required, bonding of metal piping can pose problems. (Sec. 250-112.)

250-113. To Conductors and Equipment. There are many grounding and bonding fittings on the market which can be used to properly attach the grounding conductors. The one selected should satisfy the following principles:

1. It must be UL listed.
2. It should be rugged, strong, and well plated so that it will fasten and stay tight.
3. It must fasten mechanically.
4. It must have capacity for a large enough ground wire.
5. It must be compatible with the metals used in the system. For example: Aluminum conductors should not be connected with copper connectors. Compatible aluminum connectors are available for such requirements.

250-114. Continuity and Attachment of Branch-Circuit Equipment Grounding Conductors to Boxes. The basic rule requires all ground wires in boxes to be solidly connected together. Then part **(a)** states that where a grounding conductor enters a metal outlet box it must be connected to the box by means of a grounding screw (used for no other purpose) or by an approved grounding device (such as the popular spring-steel grounding clip). Where several grounding conductors enter the same box they must be properly joined together and a final connection made to the grounding screw or grounding clip. In part **(b)**, covering nonmetallic boxes, grounding conductors must be attached to any metal fitting or wiring device required to be grounded.

From this rule, grounding conductors in any metal box must be connected to each other and to the box itself. Figure 250-120 shows a method of connecting ground wires in a box to satisfy the letter of Sec. 250-114. Note that the two ground wires are solidly connected to each other by means of a crimped-on spade tongue terminal, with one of the ground wires (arrow) cut long enough so that it is bent back out of the crimp lug to provide connection to the green hex-head screw on a recep-

Fig. 250-120. Both ground wires are solidly bonded together in the crimped barrel of the spade lug, which is screwed to back of metal box. (Sec. 250-114.)

tacle outlet (if required by Sec. 250-74). The spade lug is secured firmly under a screw head, bonding the lug to the box. Of course, the specific connections could be made in other ways. For instance, the ground wires could be connected to each other by twist-on splicing devices; and connection of the ground wires to the box could be made by simply wrapping a single wire under the screw head or by connecting a wire from the splice connector to an approved grounding clip on the edge of the box (Fig. 250-121).

In all the sketches here, connection to the box is made either by use of a screw in a threaded hole in the side or back of the box or by an approved ground clip device which tightly wedges a ground wire to the edge of the box wall, as shown in Fig. 250-122. Preassembled pigtail wires with attached screws are available for connecting either a receptacle or the system ground wire to the box.

Figure 250-123 shows connection of two cable ground wires by means of two grounding clips on the box edges (arrow). Such use has been disallowed by some inspection authorities because the ground wires are not actually connected to each other—as required by the rule—but are connected only through the box.

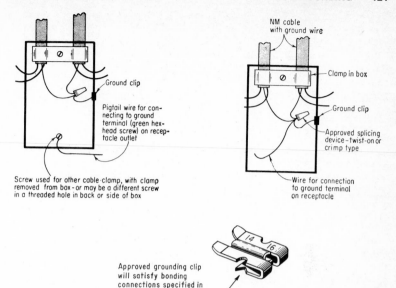

Ground clip

Pigtail wire for con-
necting to ground
terminal (green hex-
head screw) on recep-
tacle outlet

Screw used for other cable-clamp, with clamp
removed from box - or may be a different screw
in a threaded hole in back or side of box

NM cable
with ground wire

Clamp in box

Ground clip

Approved splicing
device-twist-on or
crimp type

Wire for connection
to ground terminal
on receptacle

Approved grounding clip
will satisfy bonding
connections specified in
S. 250-74 and S.250-114

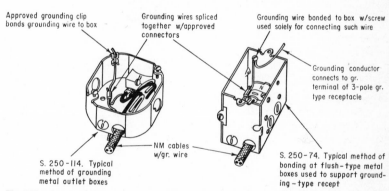

Approved grounding clip
bonds grounding wire to box

Grounding wires spliced
together w/approved
connectors

Grounding wire bonded to box w/screw
used solely for connecting such wire

Grounding conductor
connects to gr.
terminal of 3-pole gr.
type receptacle

NM cables
w/gr. wire

S. 250-114. Typical
method of grounding
metal outlet boxes

S. 250-74. Typical method of
bonding at flush-type metal
boxes used to support grounding-type recept

Fig. 250-121. All these techniques bond the ground wires together and to the box. (Sec. 250-114.)

Figure 250-124 shows another objectionable method. That has been objected to as clear violation of **NE Code** Sec. 250-114(a) which requires that a screw used for connection of grounding conductors to a box "shall be used for no other purpose." Use of this screw, simultaneously, to hold the clamp is for "other purpose" than grounding. Objection is not generally made to use of the clamp screw for ground connection when, in

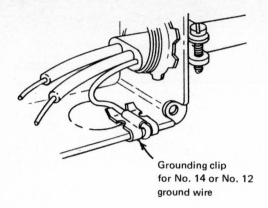

Grounding clip
for No. 14 or No. 12
ground wire

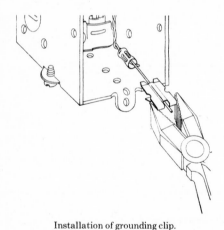

Installation of grounding clip.

Fig. 250-122. Ground clip is "an approved grounding device" of Sec. 250-114(a). (Sec. 250-114.)

cases where the clamp is not in use, the clamp is removed and the screw serves only the one purpose—to ground the grounding wires.

250-131. Services of Less Than 1,000 Volts.   Figure 250-125 shows the three methods of grounding the ground terminals of lightning arresters at service entrances. At left, the arrester is connected to the service neutral. At center, it is connected to the grounding electrode conductor of a grounded system. And at right, the arrester is connected for an ungrounded system.

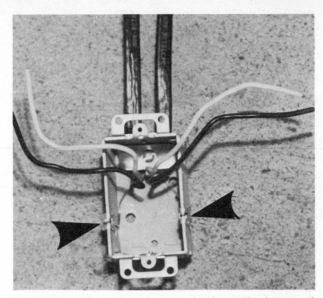

Fig. 250-123. Each ground wire is connected to the metal box by a ground clip (one on each side at arrows). This has been rejected because the two ground wires are *not* "in good electrical contact with each other." (Sec. 250-114.)

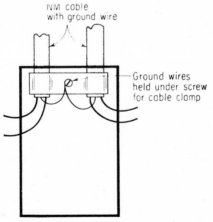

Fig. 250-124. This clearly violates Sec. 250-114(a). (Sec. 250-114.)

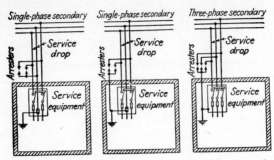

Fig. 250-125. Lightning arrester grounding conductor must be connected in one of these ways. (Sec. 250-131.)

250-152. Solidly Grounded Neutral Systems.   Figure 250-126 shows the details of this set of rules. This section does permit a neutral conductor of a solidly grounded "Y" system to have insulation rated at only 600 V, instead of requiring insulation rated at only 600 V, instead of requiring insulation rated for the high voltage (over 1,000 V). It also points out that a bare copper neutral may be used in such systems for service-entrance conductors or for direct buried feeders, and bare copper or copper-clad aluminum may be used for overhead sections of outdoor circuits.

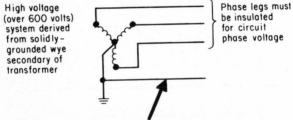

Solidly grounded neutral conductor must have insulation rated for at least 600 volts, although a bare copper neutral may be used for SE conductors or for direct-buried feeders, and bare copper or aluminum may be used for overhead parts of outdoor circuits.

Fig. 250-126. Neutral of high-voltage system generally must be insulated for 600 V. (Sec. 250-152.)

ARTICLE 280.   LIGHTNING ARRESTERS

280-10. Where Required.   This basic requirement notes that lightning arresters are mandatory only "where thunderstorms are frequent"—but they are *not* needed if some other type of lightning protection is provided. And the mandatory need applies only to "industrial stations," which is a well-defined facility. The term *station* means either a generating station or a substation. An *industrial station* is a generating station or substation serving principally a single industrial plant or factory, as distinguished from a station serving several customers of a public utility power company (Fig. 280-1). There are, however, cases where an inspection authority might consider other application of lightning arresters to be necessary where the facility might be a variation on the definition of "industrial station." Figure 280-2 shows a lightning arrester used on one of several high-voltage circuits serving the heavy electrical needs of a modern sports stadium.

Fig. 280-1. Lightning arresters are required by the NEC only in an electric substation serving an industrial plant, in an area where lightning is a problem. (Sec. 280-10.)

280-11. Number Required.   A double-throw switch which disconnects the outside circuits from the station generator and connects these circuits to ground would satisfy the condition for a single set of arresters for a station bus, as covered in the Exception.

280-32. Arrester Conductors—Size and Material.   Part **(3)** of this rule is particularly important because bends and turns enormously increase the impedance to lighting discharges and therefore tend to nullify the effectiveness of a grounding conductor.

Fig. 280-2. Lightning arrester (arrow) may be required for applications *like* "industrial stations" when lightning storms are severe in an area. (Sec. 280-10.)

280-33. Insulation. Figure 280-3 shows the position of a choke coil where it is used as a lightning-protection accessory to an arrester.

280-34. Switch for Isolating Arrester. Switches used to disconnect lightning arresters should be so mounted that when they are open, a lightning discharge will go to ground rather than jump to another switch or another part of the conductor system.

280-35. Grounding. This section refers to Secs. 250-131 and 250-132, which cover connection of lightning arresters. The second sentence covers the need to keep grounding conductors electrically in parallel with their enclosing metal raceway—as discussed under Sec. 250-71(c) and Sec. 250-92(a).

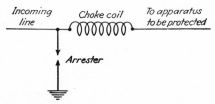

Fig. 280-3. Using a choke coil as an accessory to an arrester. (Sec. 280-33.)

For instance, assume that a lightning arrester is installed at the service head on a conduit service riser, with the grounding conductor run inside the service conduit, bonded to the meter socket at the grounding lug, then run through a hole in the meter socket to the grounding electrode without a metal enclosure from the drilled hole to the electrode. In such a hookup, this rule requires the grounding conductor to be bonded to the conduit at the service head (Fig. 280-4). Ordinarily the meter enclosure

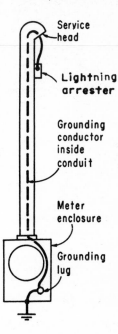

Service head

Lightning arrester

Grounding conductor inside conduit

Meter enclosure

Grounding lug

Fig. 280-4. Arrester grounding conductor must be bonded to both ends of enclosing metal raceway (or other enclosure). (Sec. 280-35.)

has a threaded hub, which would mean the conduit would be in good electrical contact with the meter enclosure and would be bonded at the meter socket end. However, Sec. 280-35 requires that the grounding conductor, if in a metallic enclosure, be bonded at both ends. Therefore, bonding at the service head is necessary.

The reason given for putting that rule in the **NEC** was explained as follows:

When conducting lightning currents, the impedance of a lightning arrester grounding conductor is materially increased if run through a metallic enclosure, especially if of magentic material. The voltage drop in this impedance may be sufficient to cause arcing to the enclosure, and in any event it reduces the effectiveness of the lightning arrester. Bonding of the conductor to both ends of the enclosure is necessary to eliminate this detrimental effect where metallic enclosures are used.

Chapter Three

ARTICLE 300. WIRING METHODS

300-1. Scope. The exceptions in this section indicate clearly that not all the general requirements in Art. 300 apply to remote-control circuits, to signal circuits, to low-energy circuits, to fire protective signaling circuits, and to communications systems. Only those sections of Art. 300 that are referenced in Art. 725, in Art. 760, and in Art. 800 apply to the types of circuits covered by those articles. In effect, not all the regulations on wiring for general-purpose power and light circuits apply to the specialized circuits covered by Arts. 725, 760, and 800.

300-3. Conductors of Different Systems. This section expresses the intent of the **Code** on applications where circuits of different voltage are installed in common enclosures.

In part **(a)**, the words "cable or raceway" after the words "wiring enclosure" clearly indicate that it is the intent of the **Code** that circuits of different voltage up to 600 V may occupy the same wiring enclosure (cabinet, box, housing), cable, or raceway provided all the conductors are insulated for the maximum voltage of any circuit in the enclosure, cable, or raceway. It is the intent of the **Code** panel to indicate clearly that, for instance, motor power conductors and motor control conductors be permitted in the same conduit. In the past, there has been a long-standing controversy about the use of control-circuit conductors in the same conduit with power leads to motors.

For a long time it was argued that Sec. 300-3(e) in the 1975 **Code** required a separate raceway for each motor when the control conductors were run in the raceway with the power conductors (Fig. 300-1). This was supported by Sec. 725-15, which also indicated that Class 1 control conductors were permitted to be run *only in the raceway* for the power conductors which the control conductors actually control.

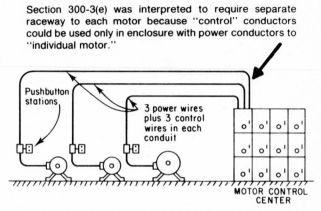

Section 300-3(e) was interpreted to require separate raceway to each motor because "control" conductors could be used only in enclosure with power conductors to "individual motor."

Pushbutton stations

3 power wires plus 3 control wires in each conduit

MOTOR CONTROL CENTER

Fig. 300-1. The 1975 NE Code limited mixing of control and power wires in raceways. (Sec. 300-3.)

The wording of Sec. 300-3(a) recognizes the use of power and control wires in a single raceway to supply more than one motor, but such usage must be made to conform to the last sentence of Sec. 725-15. The two NE Code rules of Sec. 300-3(a) and Sec. 725-15 must be put together carefully.

A common raceway, as shown in Fig. 300-2, may be used *only* where the two or more motors are required to be operated together in order to serve their load function. Many industrial and commercial installations have machines, manufacturing operations, or processes which are based on use of a number of motors driving various parts or stages of the task. In such cases, either all motors operate or none do. Use of all control wires and power wires in the same raceway does not produce a situation where a fault in one motor circuit could disable another circuit to a motor that might otherwise be kept operating.

But when a common raceway is used for power and control wires to separate, independent motors, a fault in one circuit could knock out all the others that do not have to shut down when one goes out. With motor circuits so closely associated with vital, important functions like elevators, fans, pumps, etc., in modern buildings, it is a safety matter to separate such circuits and minimize outage due to any fault in a single circuit. For safety's sake, the Code, in effect, says "Do not put all your eggs in one basket." But the objectionable loss of more than one motor on a single

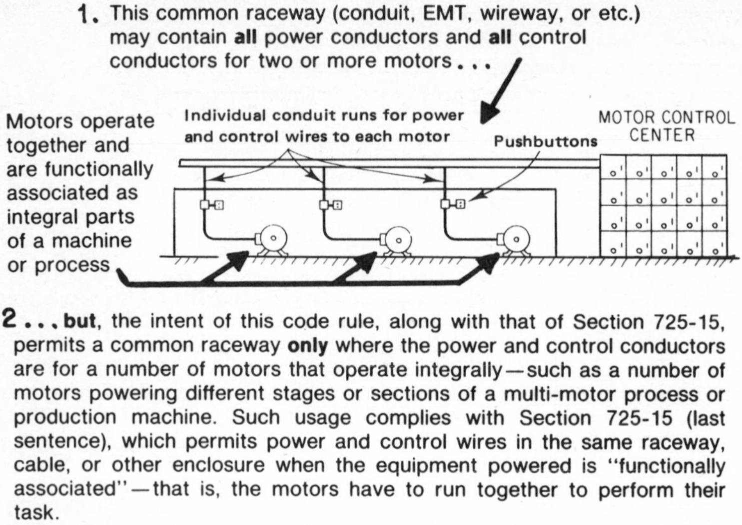

1. This common raceway (conduit, EMT, wireway, or etc.) may contain **all** power conductors and **all** control conductors for two or more motors . . .

Motors operate together and are functionally associated as integral parts of a machine or process

Individual conduit runs for power and control wires to each motor

Pushbuttons

MOTOR CONTROL CENTER

2 . . . **but**, the intent of this code rule, along with that of Section 725-15, permits a common raceway **only** where the power and control conductors are for a number of motors that operate integrally—such as a number of motors powering different stages or sections of a multi-motor process or production machine. Such usage complies with Section 725-15 (last sentence), which permits power and control wires in the same raceway, cable, or other enclosure when the equipment powered is "functionally associated"—that is, the motors have to run together to perform their task.

Fig. 300-2. Mixing of power and control wires in common raceway is still limited. (Sec. 300-3.)

fault does not apply where all motors must be shut down when any one is stopped—as in multimotor machines and processes.

For those cases where each motor is serving a separate, independent load—with no interconnection of their control circuits and no mechanical interlocking of their driven loads, the use of a separate raceway for each motor is required by the last sentence of Sec. 725-15—**but only** when control wires are carried in the raceways (Fig. 300-3). For the three motors shown, it would be acceptable to run the power conductors for all the motors in a single raceway and all the control circuit wires in another raceway. Such hookup would not violate Sec. 725-15, although deratings would have to be made and there is the definite chance of loss of more than one motor on a fault in only one of the circuits in either the power raceway or the control raceway.

Part **(b)** of Sec. 300-3 states that conductors operating at more than 600 V *must not* occupy the same equipment wiring enclosure, cable, or raceway with conductors of 600 V or less. But, the rule lists three exceptions to paragraph **(b)** [not to paragraph **(a)**]. Exception No. 3 is intended to apply to enclosures, not raceways, such as used for high-voltage motor starters, permitting the high voltage conductors operating at over 600 V to occupy the same controller housing as the control conductors operating at less than 600 V (Fig. 300-4). In addition, Exception No. 1 of Sec. 300-32 specifically recognizes use of high-voltage and low-voltage conductors in the same enclosure of "motors, switchgear and control assemblies, and similar equipment."

Separate conduit or raceway is required
for power and control wires to each motor . . .

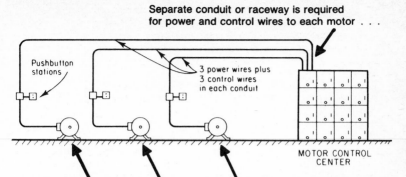

. . . When these are individual motors that do not operate together as
parts of a machine or process—that is, each motor has a separate,
independent load that may operate by itself.

Fig. 300-3. Section 725-15 prohibits intermixing of power and starter coil-circuit wires when
motors are not "functionally associated." (Sec. 300-3.)

SECTION 300-3(b) PROHIBITS THIS—

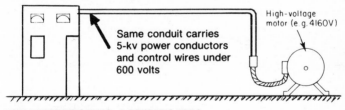

BUT, EXCEPTION NO. 3 PERMITS THIS—

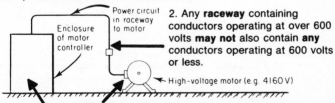

1. For any **individual** motor or starter—excitation, control, relay and/or
ammeter conductors operating at 600 volts or less **may** occupy the same
starter or motor enclosure as the conductors operating at over 600
volts.

Fig. 300-4. Control wires for high-voltage starters may be used in the starter enclosure,
but not in *raceway* with power conductors. (Sec. 300-3.)

If BX, NM cable, or raceway wiring (rigid conduit, EMT, etc.) is used through holes bored in joists, rafters or similar wood members. . .

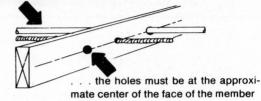

. . . the holes must be at the approximate center of the face of the member

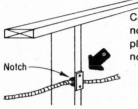

Cable (BX, NM, etc.) may be run in notch in wood member, but a steel plate 1/16 in. thick must be used over notch to protect cable from nails, etc.

Notch

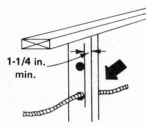

1-1/4 in. min.

Cable wiring (BX, NM, etc.) through holes bored in studs must be at center of face and edge of bored cable hole must be not less than 1-1/4 in. from nearest edge of stud

. . .OR . . .

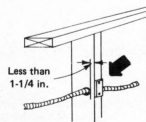

Less than 1-1/4 in.

If hole is less than 1¼ in. from nearest edge, a steel plate 1/16 in. thick must be used to protect cable against driven nails or screws.

Fig. 300-5. Holes in wood framing must not weaken structure or expose cable to nail puncture. (Sec. 300-4.)

Fig. 300-6. Drilled holes at the center of the face of a joist do not reduce the structural strength of the joist. (Sec. 300-4.)

Fig. 300-7. Signal and alarm wiring is run through the same stud holes as the NM cables. The NEC does not prohibit use of more than one cable through a single hole. (Sec. 300-4.)

300-4. Protection Against Physical Damage.   Part **(a)** gives the rules on protection required for cables run through wood framing members, as shown in Fig. 300-5. Figure 300-6 shows cable holes drilled at the approximate center of the face of structural wood members.

Clearance must be provided from the edge of a hole in a wood member to the edge of the wood member. Where the 1975 NE Code required a minimum of 1½ in. from the edge of a cable hole in a stud to the edge of the stud, the 1978 NE Code now requires only 1¼ in. This permits realistic compliance when drilling holes in studs that are 3½ in. deep. It also was taken into consideration that the nails commonly used to attach wall surfaces to studs were of such length that the 1¼-in. clearance to the edge of the cable hole afforded entirely adequate protection against possible penetration of the cable by the nail.

Fig. 300-8. Excessive drilling of structural wood members can result in dangerous notching (arrow) that weakens the structure, violating Sec. 300-4(a) (2). (Sec. 300-4.)

Figure 300-7 shows typical application of cable through drilled studs, with holes at centers and adequate clearance to edge of stud. Figure 300-8 shows an objectionable example of drilled hole, violating the rule of this section, which warns against "weakening the building structure." Figure 300-9 shows an acceptable way of protecting cables run through holes in wood members.

Fig. 300-9. Steel plates are attached to wood structure member to protect cable from penetration by nail or screw driven into finished wall, where the edge of the cable hole is less than 1¼ in. from the edge of the wooden member. (Sec. 300-4.)

300-5. Underground Installations.   This section is a comprehensive set of rules on installation of underground circuits. The table establishes *minimum* burial depths and the exceptions given in part **(a)** reduce or alter the depth requirements for specific conditions of use. Figure 300-10 shows the basic depth requirements for the various wiring methods.

Because Table 300-5 does not specifically mention electrical metallic tubing (EMT), it could be taken to indicate that the NEC does not recognize EMT for underground use. But Sec. 348-1 (in condition No. 3) does recognize EMT for direct earth burial, and so does UL, with this stipulation: "In general, electrical metallic tubing in contact with soil requires supplementary corrosion protection." Note that such protection is not always mandatory. The UL note means to indicate that EMT may

DIRECT-BURIED CABLES

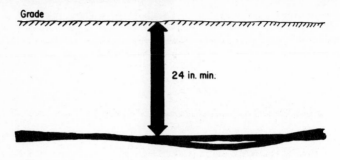

RIGID METAL CONDUIT

INTERMEDIATE METAL CONDUIT

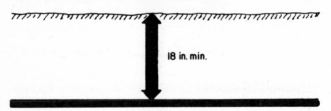

Fig. 300-10. These are the *basic* burial depths. **but** exceptions are given for certain conditions. (Sec. 300-5.)

be buried without a protective coating (like asphalt paint) where local experience verifies that soil conditions do not attack and corrode the EMT.

Figure 300-11 shows Exception No. 1. If a 2-in.-thick or thicker concrete pad is used over any underground circuit, the burial depth in Table 300-5 may be reduced by 6 in. But note that the concrete pad must

ELECTRICAL METALLIC TUBING (EMT)

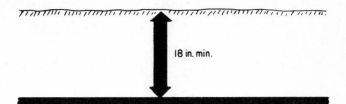

18 in. min.

RIGID NONMETALLIC CONDUIT

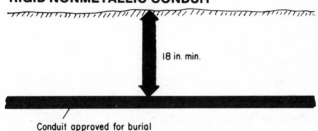

18 in. min.

Conduit approved for burial
without concrete encasement

RIGID NONMETALLIC CONDUIT (ENCASED)

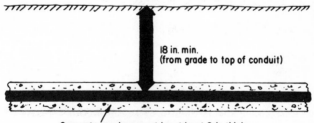

18 in. min.
(from grade to top of conduit)

Concrete envelope must be at least 2 in. thick
around conduit approved for burial
only when encased

be "in the trench," right over the cable or raceway. It may not be a walk or other concrete at grade level. And the burial depth may not be reduced by more than 6 in. no matter how thick the concrete pad is. This rule is at odds with the rule of Sec. 710-3(b) where burial depth for high-voltage circuits may be reduced "6 inches for each 2 inches of concrete" and the concrete, in that case, does not have to be in the trench but simply has to

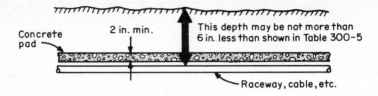

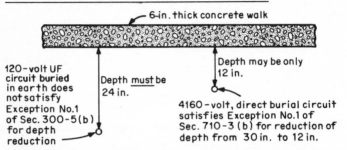

Fig. 300-11. Concrete pad "in trench" permits only a 6-in. reduction of burial depth. (Sec. 300-5.)

be "above the conductors." Thus, a 4-in. sidewalk above a high-voltage circuit would permit the burial depth of the particular wiring method to be reduced by 2 × 6 in., or 12 in. Yet a circuit up to 600 V under that same sidewalk would not be permitted at a depth less than Table 300-5 because the concrete is not "in the trench." Compliance with Exception No. 1 of Sec. 300-5 is a tricky matter. And it can be seen by comparing the rule of that section with the rule and Exception No. 1 of Sec. 710-3(b), that, say, a 120-V circuit in one trench might have to be buried deeper than a 4,160-V circuit in an adjacent trench. As shown at the bottom of Fig. 300-11, the 4,160-V circuit, which has a basic depth requirement of 30 in. from Table 710-3(b), may have the depth reduced by 6 in. for each 2 in. of concrete above it. A 6-in. walk permits a burial-depth reduction of 3 × 6, or 18 in. Then 30−18 equals 12 in.

As shown in Fig. 300-12, Exception No. 2 recognizes that raceways run under concrete slabs or under buildings have sufficient protection against digging and are not required to be subject to the burial-depth requirements given in Table 300-5. Where raceways are so installed, the rule requires that the slab or building extend at least 6 in. beyond the underground raceway. This Exception applies only to "conduits or other raceways" but not to direct buried cables:

    1. Any direct burial cable run under a building must be installed in raceway, as required by Sec. 300-5(c), and the raceway may be

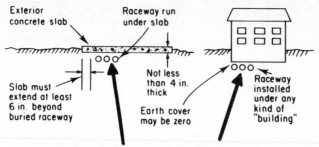

Burial-depth requirements of Table 300-5 do not apply
to raceways installed like this.

Fig. 300-12. Exception No. 2 eliminates burial-depth requirements for
direct buried "raceways" under specified conditions. (Sec. 300-5.)

installed in the earth, immediately under the bottom of the building—without any earth cover.
2. Any direct buried cable under a slab is subject to the 24-in. minimum burial-depth requirement of Table 300-5, but burial depth
   may be reduced as permitted by Exceptions No. 4, 5, 6, and 8.
   Application of Exception No. 1 to reduce cable burial depth under
   a grade-level slab is questionable, as noted above, because that
   Exception calls for "concrete pad" protection to be "in the trench
   over the underground installation."
Figure 300-13 shows Exception No. 3, which supersedes the depths

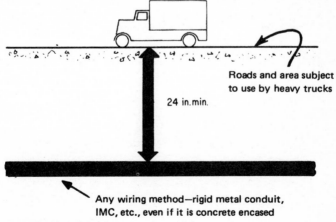

Fig. 300-13. All wiring methods must be at least 2 ft under "heavy vehicular
traffic." (Sec. 300-5.)

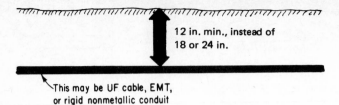

12 in. min., instead of
18 or 24 in.

This may be UF cable, EMT,
or rigid nonmetallic conduit

Fig. 300-14. This is OK only for a residential branch circuit rated not over 30 A. (Sec. 300-5.)

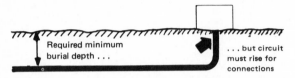

Required minimum
burial depth . . .

. . . but circuit
must rise for
connections

No. 5 Of course, lesser depths than shown in Table 300-5 are permitted where cable or conductors in raceway come up to terminations or splices in boxes or equipment.

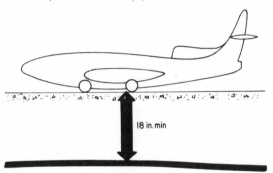

18 in. min

No. 6 Cable, without raceway or concrete encasement, may be buried 18 in. deep under airport runways and adjacent defined areas where trespass is prohibited.

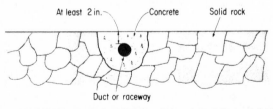

At least 2 in.   Concrete   Solid rock

Duct or raceway

No. 7 Duct and raceway installed in solid rock may be buried at lesser depths than shown in Table 300-5 if concrete at least 2 in. thick covers the raceway and extends down to the rock surface.

Fig. 300-15. These applications are also exempted from the table burial depths. (Sec. 30-5.)

given in Table 300-5 for *any* wiring methods buried under public or private roads, parking lots, or other areas subject to car and truck traffic. Driveways and parking areas of private residences are excluded from this stiff requirement.

Any circuit—direct burial cable or any approved raceway with conductors—must always be down at least 24 in. under areas subject to *heavy* vehicular traffic, such as public roads, commercial parking areas, gas stations, etc. And it is not acceptable to apply Exceptions No. 1 or No. 2 or any other Exceptions to reduce the 24-in. depth.

Exception No. 4 gives limited use of lesser burial depth for the residential circuits described, as shown in Fig. 300-14. Any residential *"branch circuit"* not over 300 V and protected at 30 A or less may be buried only 12 in. below grade, instead of, say, 24 in. as required for Type UF cable for any nonresidential use or for a residential "feeder."

Figure 300-15 shows three other exceptions on burial depth.

Exception No. 8 recognizes reduced burial depth for low-voltage landscape lighting circuits and supply circuits to lawn sprinkler and irrigation valves, as shown in Fig. 300-16. This Exception recognizes the reduced hazards and safety considerations for circuits operating at not more than 300 V.

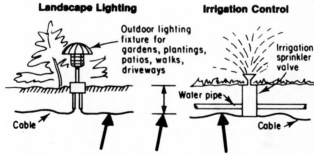

Fig. 300-16. Reduced burial depth for low-voltage landscape lighting and lawn-sprinkler controls. (Sec. 300-5.)

Part **(b)** of Sec. 300-5 says that metal conduit and metal sheath or electrostatic shielding must be effectively grounded at all terminations by connection to grounded metal enclosure, by bonding jumper, etc., to limit voltage to ground and facilitate operation of overcurrent protective devices, as shown in Fig. 300-17.

Figure 300-18 shows the rule of part **(c)**.

As shown at the top of Fig. 300-19, conductors coming up a pole from underground installation must be protected as required by part **(d)** of

Bonding jumper or other connection
to grounded equipment enclosure

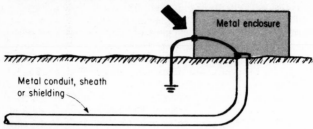

Fig. 300-17. Metal of wiring system must be grounded at *all* terminations.
(Sec. 300-5.)

this section. Raceways on poles must be rigid conduit, IMC, PVC Schedule 80, or equivalent, and the raceway or other enclosure for underground conductors must extend from below the ground line up to 8 ft above finished grade. The bottom sketch covers the case where the circuit comes up to a building.

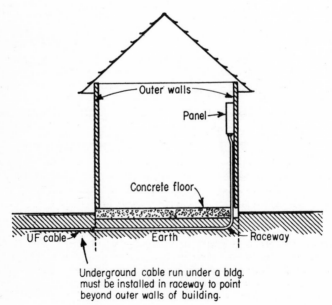

Underground cable run under a bldg.
must be installed in raceway to point
beyond outer walls of building.

Fig. 300-18. Burial of cable in earth is not permitted under a building. (Sec. 300-5.)

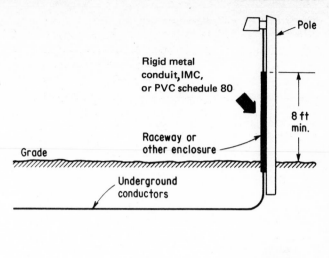

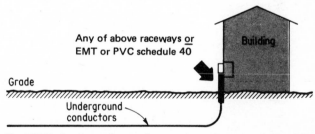

Fig. 300-19. Conductors from underground must be protected. (Sec. 300-5.)

Figures 300-20 and 300-21 show other rules of Sec. 300-5. Note that part **(f)** specifically requires that backfilled trenches must contain any necessary protection for raceways or cables buried in the trench. It specifies that sand or suitable running boards of wood or concrete or other protection must be afforded in those cases where backfill consists of heavy stones or sharp objects that otherwise would present the possibility of damage to the cable or raceway.

Part **(i)** of this section requires that an underground circuit made up of single conductor cables for direct burial must have all conductors of the circuit run in the same trench. That rule has raised the question: When an underground direct burial circuit is made up of conductors in multiple, must all the conductors be installed in the same trench? And if they are, is derating required for more than three conductors in a trench, just as it would be for three conductors in a single raceway?

Part (e)

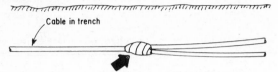

Cable in trench

Splices or taps are permitted in trench without a box—but only if approved methods and materials are used.

Part (f)

Backfill of heavy rocks or sharp or corrosive materials must not be used if it may cause damage or prevent adaquate compaction of ground.

Underground circuit of approved cable or raceway

Part (g)

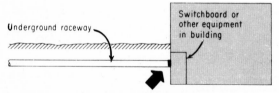

Underground raceway

Switchboard or other equipment in building

Conduits or other raceways must be sealed or plugged at either or both ends if moisture could contact live parts

Part (h)

Bushing must be used on any conduit end where direct-burial cables leave conduit. Or, a seal that gives the same protection may be used instead of a bushing.

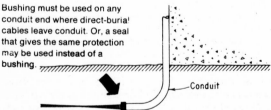

Conduit

Fig. 300-20. Underground wiring must satisfy these requirements. (Sec. 300-5.)

Fig. 300-21. For direct burial underground conductors, a box must be
used at splice points, with conductors brought up in sweep ells and the
box properly grounded—*unless approved* materials are used to make
directly buried splices in the conductors. (Sec. 300-5.)

The wording of the rule in part **(i)** clearly indicates that *all* the
conductors making up a direct burial circuit of single conductors in
parallel must be run in the same trench and *must* be "in close proximity."
It is interesting that the wording of Sec. 300-5(i) also requires that all
conductors of a circuit made up of conductors in parallel be run in the
same raceway if raceway is used (with building wire suitable for wet
locations, such as THW).

Then, when the multiple-conductor makeup of the circuit is installed
with all the parallel circuit conductors in the same trench, it becomes
necessary to observe the rule of the second paragraph of Note 8 to Tables
310-16/19 of the NE Code. It says:

Where single conductors . . . are stacked or bundled without maintaining spacing and are not installed in raceways, the maximum allowable load current of each
conductor *shall* be reduced as shown in the above table.

That means that the same deratings must be made as when more than
three conductors are used in a single conduit—as explained in Note 8.
Certainly, direct burial single conductors are covered by that requirement because Table 310-16 specifically covers direct burial conductors.

Those Code rules often make for tricky and troublesome applications.
For instance, as shown in Fig. 300-22, an underground circuit of Type
USE insulated aluminum conductors might be used for a 3-wire, single-
phase service to a multifamily dwelling. Because that is a residential

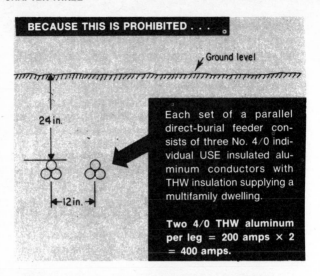

BECAUSE THIS IS PROHIBITED . . .

Ground level

24 in.

Each set of a parallel direct-burial feeder consists of three No. 4/0 individual USE insulated aluminum conductors with THW insulation supplying a multifamily dwelling.

Two 4/0 THW aluminum per leg = 200 amps × 2 = 400 amps.

12 in.

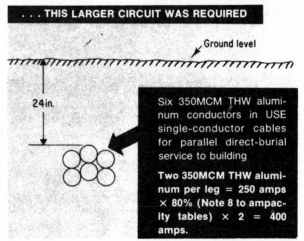

. . . THIS LARGER CIRCUIT WAS REQUIRED

Ground level

24 in.

Six 350MCM THW aluminum conductors in USE single-conductor cables for parallel direct-burial service to building

Two 350MCM THW aluminum per leg = 250 amps × 80% (Note 8 to ampacity tables) × 2 = 400 amps.

Fig. 300-22. Literal application of Code rules often imposes stiff requirements. (Sec. 300-5)

service, Note 3 to Tables 310-16/19 may be observed to gain a higher-than-normal ampacity for the conductors.

Assuming that a 400-A conductor ampacity is indicated by the calculated demand load from Art. 220, each phase leg of the service feeder must have an ampactiy of 400 A. Referring to Note 3 of the ampacity tables, a No. 4/0 THW aluminum has an ampacity of 200 A. Two such conductors per hot leg and two for the neutral would give the required 400-A capacity for the service.

But how should the parallel circuit be run?

All the circuit conductors *must* be run in close proximity in the same trench, as required by Sec. 300-5(i). That means all six USE conductors are in the same trench; and because the neutrals do not count as current-carrying conductors, the derating of these "bundled" conductors must be to 80 percent of the 200-A ampacity—as required for four conductors in the table of Note 8. With each 4/0 THW aluminum now derated to 160 A (0.8 × 200), the ampacity of each hot leg is only 320 A (2 × 160).

The rule requiring all conductors to be in the same trench makes the circuit of two 4/0 THW aluminum per leg inadequate. Referring to Table 310-16, it now becomes necessary to pick a larger size of THW aluminum—such that, derated to 80 percent, two of them will provide the required 400-A rating. A 350 MCM THW aluminum has a normal rating of 250 A. Derated to 80 percent (250 × 0.8), it has the needed ampacity of 200 A, so that two of them in parallel per hot leg and neutral will have the ampacity of 400 A.

If the two parallel sets of conductors could have been run in separate trenches, the 4/0 THW aluminum conductors would have met the need.

300-6. Protection Against Corrosion. These are general regulations that are repeated in more detail in the various articles covering raceways and enclosures. The last sentence in part **(a)** allows organic coatings to be applied to metallic boxes or cabinets to prevent corrosion when used outdoors, in lieu of the standard "4-dip" zinc galvanizing method.

Part **(b)** is a general rule that is best understood when related to the specific recommendations given in the UL green book for the various types of raceways. See Arts. 345, 346, and 348 for such data.

Figure 300-23 shows the *right* and *wrong* ways of installing equipment in indoor wet locations—as covered in part **(c)** of this section.

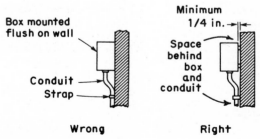

Fig. 300-23. Water or moisture must not be trapped in contact with metal. (Sec. 300-6.)

300-7. Raceways Exposed to Different Temperatures.   Part **(a)** requires protection against moisture accumulation. If air is allowed to circulate from the warmer to the colder section of the raceway, moisture in the warm air will condense in the cold section of the raceway. This can usually be eliminated by sealing·the raceway just outside the cold rooms so as to prevent the circulation of air. Sealing may be accomplished by stuffing a suitable compound in the end of the pipe (Fig. 300-24).

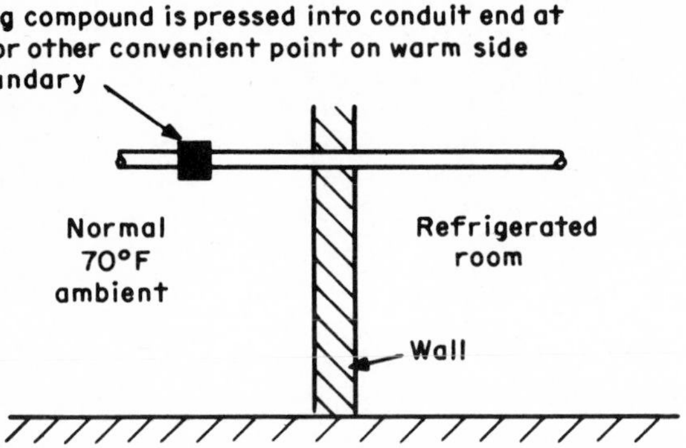

Sealing compound is pressed into conduit end at a box or other convenient point on warm side of boundary

Fig. 300-24. Sealing protects against moisture accumulation in raceway. (Sec. 300-7.)

300-10. Electrical Continuity of Metal Raceways and Enclosures.   This is the basic rule requiring a permanent and continuous bonding together (i.e., connecting together) of all noncurrent-carrying metal parts of equipment enclosures—conduit, boxes, cabinets, enclosures, housings, frame of motors and lighting fixtures—and connection of this interconnected system of enclosures to the system grounding electrode at the service or transformer (Fig. 300-25). The interconnection of all metal enclosures must be made to connect all metal to the grounding electrode and to provide a low-impedance path for fault-current flow along the enclosures to assure operation of overcurrent devices which will open a circuit in the event of a fault. By opening a faulted circuit, the system prevents dangerous voltages from being present on equipment enclosures which could be touched by personnel, with consequent electric shock to such personnel.

Simply stated, this interconnection of all metal enclosures of electric wires and equipment prevents any potential-above-ground on the enclosures. Such bonding together and grounding of all metal enclosures are required for both grounded electrical systems (those systems in which one of the circuit conductors is intentionally grounded) and ungrounded electrical systems (systems with none of the circuit wires intentionally grounded).

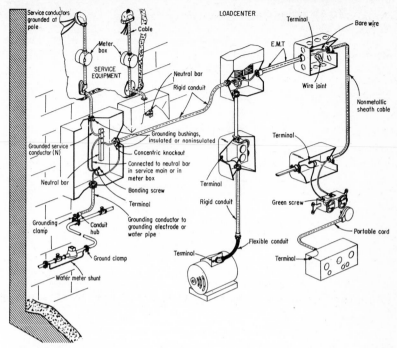

Fig. 300-25. All metal enclosures must be interconnected to form "a continuous electric conductor." (Sec. 300-10.)

But effective equipment interconnection and grounding is extremely important for grounded electrical systems to provide the automatic fault clearing which is one of the important advantages of grounded electrical systems. A low-impedance path for fault current is necessary to permit enough current to flow to operate the fuses or CB protecting the circuit.

300-13. Mechanical and Electrical Continuity—Conductors.   Part **(b)** prohibits dependency upon device terminals (such as internally connected screw terminals of duplex receptacles) for the splicing of neutral conductors in multiwire (3-wire or 4-wire) circuits. **Grounded neutral wires** must not depend on device connection (such as the break-off tab between duplex receptacle screw terminals) for continuity. White wires can be spliced together with a pigtail to neutral terminal on receptacle. If receptacle is removed, neutral will not be opened (Fig. 300-26).

This rule is to prevent the establishment of unbalanced voltages should a neutral conductor be opened *first* when replacing a receptacle or similar device on energized circuits. In such cases, the line-to-neutral connections downstream from this point (farther from the point of supply)

Do it this way...

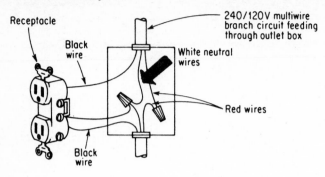

Receptacle

Black wire

240/120V multiwire branch circuit feeding through outlet box

White neutral wires

Red wires

Black wire

... or this way

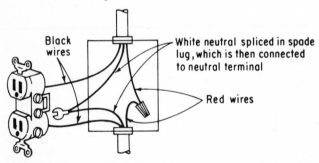

Black wires

White neutral spliced in spade lug, which is then connected to neutral terminal

Red wires

Fig. 300-26. Neutrals of multiwire circuit must *not* be spliced at receptacle terminals. (Sec. 300-13.)

could result in a considerably higher-than-normal voltage on one part of a multiwire circuit and damage equipment, because of the "open" neutral, if the downstream line-to-neutral loads are appreciably unbalanced.

Note that this paragraph does not apply to 2-wire circuits or circuits which do not have a grounded conductor. This rule applies only where multiwire circuits feed receptacles or lampholders. This would most commonly be a 3-wire 240/120-V or a 3- or 4-wire 208/120-V, or even a 480/277-V branch circuit.

The reason for the pigtailing requirement is to prevent the neutral conductor from being broken and creating downstream hazards. The problem lies in the inclination of electricians to work on hot circuits. Assume that a duplex receptacle on a 240/120-V 3-wire circuit becomes defective, and the first thing the electrician does, working hot, is to disconnect the neutral wires from the receptacle. Downstream, 2.4- and 12-A loads have been operating (plugged into additional receptacles on the multiwire circuit), each connected to a different hot leg. When the neutral is broken by the electrician upstream, normal operation of the loads reverts to the condition shown in Fig. 300-27. The two loads are now in series across 240 V. As shown, load A now has 200 V impressed across it. It could run extremely hot and burn out. Load B now has only 40 V across it; if it is a motor-operated device, the low voltage could cause the motor to burn up. Both could cause injuries.

Also, in disconnecting the neutral, the electrician could get a 120-V shock if both the disconnected neutral conductor going downstream and the box were touched—not unlikely, since the neutral is usually considered to be dead—that is, at ground potential.

An open neutral like this...

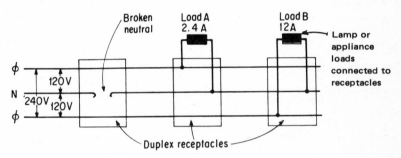

... puts 200 volts across a 120-volt load

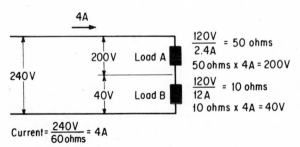

Fig. 300-27. Splicing neutrals on receptacle screws causes "open" in neutral if receptacle is removed. (Sec. 300-13.)

300-14. Length of Free Conductors at Outlets and Switch Points. The rule here applies only to the length of the conductor at its end. The Exception covers wires running through the box. Wires looping through the box and intended for connection to outlets at the box need have only sufficient slack so that any connections can be made easily.

300-15. Boxes or Fittings—Where Required. Part **(a)** permits *either* a "box" or a "fitting" to be used at splice points or connection points in *raceway* systems. The word "fitting" as used here refers to "conduit bodies"—even though the definition of "fitting" in Art. 100 suggests that only locknuts and bushings are fittings. Type T or Type L fittings (conduit bodies) actually become a part of the conduit or tubing and should not contain more conductors than permitted for the raceway. Conduit bodies must not contain splices, taps, or devices unless they comply with the rules of Sec. 370-6(c). For conductors No. 4 or larger see Sec. 370-18(a). Use of boxes and fittings for splicing, for connections to switches or outlet wiring devices, or for pulling must conform ro the many detailed rules of Art. 370. Refer to those rules for further discussion.

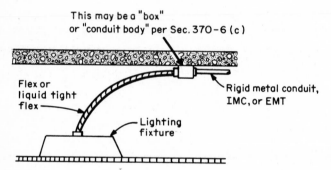

But with type AC cable (BX) Type NM cable, or any other cable, a "box" must be used at all splice and outlet points, and even where cable connects to raceway

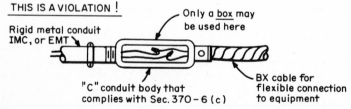

Fig. 300-28. "Raceways" may use boxes or conduit bodies at conductor splice points. (Sec. 300-15.)

Exception No. 2 permits splices to be made within lighting fixture wiring compartments where the branch-circuit wires are spliced to fixture or ballast wires.

Part **(b)** accepts *only* a box for splices and connections to devices when the wiring system is *"cable"* instead of raceway (Fig. 300-28).

Exception No. 5 of this section recognizes use of wiring devices that have "integral enclosures." These are the so-called boxless devices made and acceptable for use in nonmetallic-sheathed cable systems (Type NM). Such listed devices do not require a separate box at each outlet because the construction of the device forms an integral box in itself.

300-16. Raceway or Cable to Open or Concealed Wiring. Where the wires are run in conduit, tubing, metal raceway, or armored cable, and are brought out for connection to open wiring or concealed knob-and-tube work, a fitting such as is shown in Fig. 300-29 may be used.

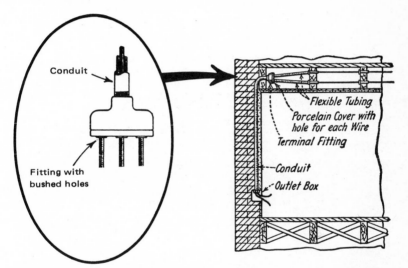

Fig. 300-29. A terminal fitting satisfies the rule on transition from raceway to knob-and-tube. (Sec. 300-16.)

Where the terminal fitting is an accessible outlet box, the installation may be made as shown in Fig. 300-30.

300-18. Inserting Conductors in Raceways. Part **(a)** requires all raceways, boxes, enclosures, and their associated fittings to be completely installed as a total wiring enclosure system *before* conductors are pulled in. Pulling conductors into a partially completed raceway system—such as where boxes, enclosures, and/or additional raceway is to be installed—is a violation of this rule. Figure 300-31 shows an example of such a condi-

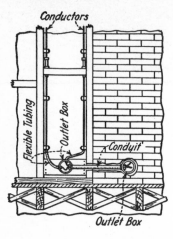

Conductors

Flexible Tubing

Outlet Box

Conduit

Outlet Box

Fig. 300-30. An outlet box may be used where raceway connects to open wiring or concealed knob-and-tube. (Sec. 300-16.)

tion. Another common violation of this rule occurs on very long underground circuits where friction of conductors inside the conduit will not permit pulling the circuit for the whole length of the conduit run, even though the conduit fill complies with Tables 3A, 3B, or 3C in Chap. 9 of the Code. For instance, Table 3A permits four No. 10 THW conductors

Fig. 300-31. Conductors shown here have been pulled into the conduit before boxes and continuation of the raceway system was installed to supply underground circuits to outdoor building lighting. This violates Sec. 300-18(a). (Sec. 300-18.)

in a ½-in. conduit, but those conductors cannot be pulled into a 200-ft length of ½-in. conduit without damaging or breaking the conductors. In such cases, three or four lengths of conduit are made up at the edge of the trench and the conductors pulled through. Then that section of raceway is dropped in the trench and the conductors pulled through another section of several lengths, which is dropped into the trench and coupled to the first section. And that is repeated to make up the 200-ft run. Technically, that is a Code violation. The correct way would be to make up a 200-ft length of conduit larger than ½ in.—a size in which the friction would not impede the long pull.

300-19. Supporting Conductors in Vertical Raceways.   Long vertical runs of conductors should not be supported by the terminal to which they are connected. Supports as shown in Fig. 300-32 may be used to comply with Sec. 300-19(a).

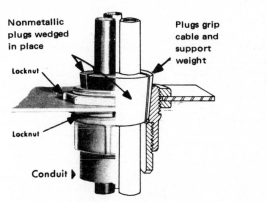
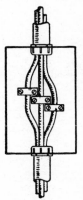

Conductor-support bush-
ing screwed on end of conduit at a
cabinet, pull box, or conductor-
support box. (*Russell & Stoll.*)

Conductor-support box
with single-wire cleats to clamp conductors.

Fig. 300-32. Some type of support must carry the weight of conductors in long risers. (Sec. 300-19.)

example   A vertical raceway contains 4/0 copper conductors. One cable support—at or near the top of the run—would be required if the vertical run is from
20 to 80 ft. If the vertical run in this example is less than 20 ft, no cable support
would be required, because Exception No. 1 excludes need for a support at or near
the top when the total vertical length of a riser is less than 25 percent of the spacing
shown for No. 4/0 copper in Table 300-19(a). Figure 300-33 shows another
permitted variation from the basic rule, using a technique detailed in Fig. 300-34.

300-20. Induced Currents in Metal Enclosures or Metal Raceways.   By
keeping all conductors of an AC circuit close together—in raceway, or a
box, or other enclosure—the magnetic fields around the conductos tend

Fig. 300-33. Bore-hole cable, with steel wire armor, is permitted by Exception No. 2 to be supported only at the top of very high risers because the steel armor supports the length of the cable when the steel wires are properly clamped in the support ring of the type of fitting shown here. (Sec. 300-19.)

to oppose or cancel each other, thereby minimizing the inductive react-ance of the circuit and also minimizing the amount of magnetic flux that can cause heat due to hysteresis loss (magnetic friction) in steel or iron and due to the I^2R losses of currents that are induced in adjacent metal. The rule of this section calls for always running a neutral conductor with the phase legs of an AC circuit to minimize such induction heating. The equipment grounding conductor must also be run close to the circuit conductors to achieve the reduction in inductive reactance and minimize

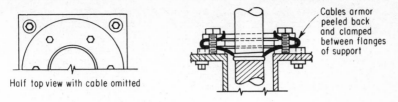

Half top view with cable omitted

Cables armor
peeled back
and clamped
between flanges
of support

TYPE FS CABLE SUPPORTS

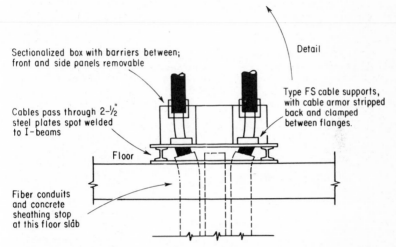

Detail

Sectionalized box with barriers between;
front and side panels removable

Cables pass through 2-½"
steel plates spot welded
to I-beams

Type FS cable supports,
with cable armor stripped
back and clamped
between flanges.

Floor

Fiber conduits
and concrete
sheathing stop
at this floor slab

Fig. 300-34. Separate strands of cable armor are snubbed between flanges of support fitting at top of run. Partitioned enclosure protects unarmored sections of cable. (Sec. 300-19.)

the impedance of the fault-current return path when a fault does occur—thereby assuring the fastest possible operation of the protective device (fuse or CB) in the circuit (Fig. 300-35).

When an AC circuit is arranged in such a way that the individual conductors are not physically close for mutual cancellation of their field flux, it is particularly important to take precautions where a single conductor passes through a hole in any magnetic material—like a steel enclosure surface. The presence of the magnetic material forms a closed (circular) magnetic core that raises the flux density of the magnetic field around the conductor (that is, it greatly strengthens the magnetic field). Under such conditions, there can be substantial heating in the enclosure due to hysteresis (friction produced by the alternating reversals of the magnetic domains in the steel) and due to currents induced in the steel by the strong magnetic field. To minimize those effects, the second paragraph of Sec. 300-20 requires special treatment, such as that shown in Fig. 300-36.

In a typical 3 – phase circuit —

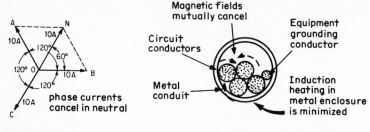

the magnetic fields around the conductors have the phase displacements of the currents . . .

. . . therefore, the magnetic fields tend to cancel each other (like the neutral current becomes zero under balanced loading) if the conductors are close together

Fig. 300-35. Close placement of AC conductors minimizes magnetic fields and induction. (Sec. 300-20.)

300-21. Prevention of Fire Spread.   Application of this section to all kinds of building constructions is a very broad and expanding controversy in modern electrical work, in particular because of the phrase "substantially increased." The rule here requires that electrical installations shall be made to substantially protect the integrity of rated fire walls, fire-resistant or fire-stopped walls, partitions, ceilings, and floors. Electrical installations must be so made that the possible spread of fire through hollow

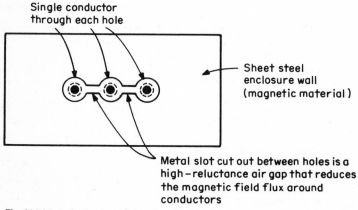

Fig. 300-36. Induction heating is reduced by opening the magnetic core. (Sec. 300-20.)

spaces, vertical shafts, and ventilating or air-handling ducts will be reduced to a minimum. These rules require close cooperation with building officials to avoid destruction of fire ratings when electrical installations extend through such areas.

Floor Penetrations

Certainly, the electrical industry has come to agree that poke-through wiring—that technique in which floor outlets in commercial buildings are wired through holes in concrete slab floors—is an acceptable wiring method if use is made of UL-listed poke-through fittings that have been tested and found to preserve the fire rating of the concrete floor. Throughout the country, the use of poke-through wiring continues to be a popular and very effective method of wiring floor outlets in office areas and other commercial and industrial locations. Holes are cut or drilled in concrete floors at the desired locations of floor outlets, and floor box assemblies are installed and wired from the ceiling space of the floor below. The method permits installation of each and every floor box at the precise location that best serves the layout of desks and other office equipment.

But a very serious question is posed about how the use of the poke-through wiring technique can be properly reconciled with Sec. 300-21.

The wiring of each floor outlet at a poke-through location may be done basically in either of two ways—by some job-fabricated assembly of pipe nipples and boxes (as shown in Fig. 300-37) *or* by means of a manufactured through-floor assembly (Fig. 300-38) made expressly for the purpose and tested and listed by a nationally recognized testing lab, such as UL. Job-assembled parts for poke-through wiring to floor outlets provide for telephone or 120-V wiring, but not both. But there is no third-party certification of the safety or effectiveness of these methods (Fig. 300-39).

May either of the methods be used? A clear regulation of the Occupational Safety and Health Administration appears to rule decisively on this question. In the *Occupational Safety and Health Standards,* Subpart S—Electrical, paragraph 1910.308(d)(2) clearly and flatly *demands* that an installation or equipment determined to be safe by a nationally recognized testing lab must *always* be used in preference to any equipment *not* certified by a testing lab.

For example, because there are UL-listed panelboards, it is totally unacceptable to use a nonlisted assembly that is constructed like and functions like a panelboard. If a product is of a "kind" that UL lists, then only a listed one may be used.

Thus, if a UL-listed poke-through fitting is available, then the use of any nonlisted, homemade assembly—which has not been determined to be safe—appears to be clearly not acceptable to OSHA and could be construed as a violation of **NE Code** Sec. 110-2, which calls for all equipment to be "approved."

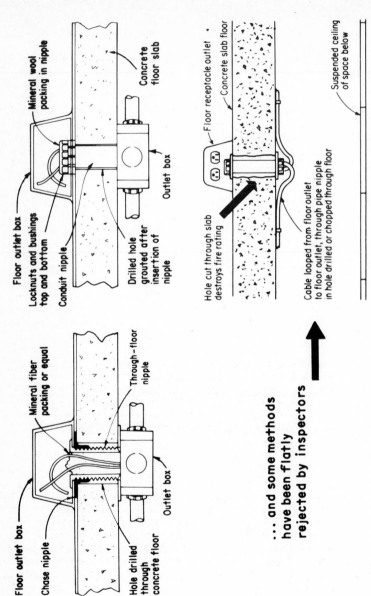

Fig. 300-37. Field-fabricated techniques for poke-through floor outlets are not third-party certified. (Sec. 300-21.)

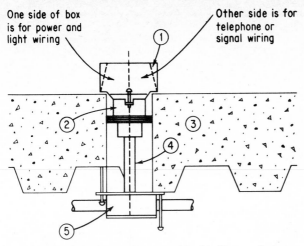

One side of box is for power and light wiring

Other side is for telephone or signal wiring

Numbered components include (1) combination floor service box, (2) fire-rated center coupling, (3) concrete slab, (4) barriered extension, and (5) barriered junction box.

Fig. 300-38. UL-listed assembly is fire-rated for thickest concrete slab. (Sec. 300-21.)

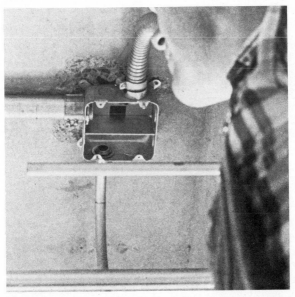

Fig. 300-39. Bottom end of UL-listed poke-through fitting consists of a partitioned box for 120-V circuit and telephone circuit run through vertical channels of fitting into dual-service floor outlet box on top of slab. (Sec. 300-21.)

As a result of OSHA's inclusion of the NE Code as its own standard, the wording of NE Code Sec. 110-2 and 110-3 (which covers examination, installation, and use of equipment) certainly reinforces the wording of OSHA 1910.308(d)(2). Designers, installers, and inspectors must give careful consideration to the liabilities incurred by less-than-strict compliance with the letter and intent of NE Code and OSHA regulations. In the nature of today's electrical work—with much broader, more intensified enforcement of national codes and standards—the use of new types of products, such as fire-rated floor outlets, must be thoroughly evaluated. This also applies to cable and/or conduit penetrations of fire-rated walls, floors, or ceilings without altering the fire rating of the structural surface (Figs. 300-40 and 300-41).

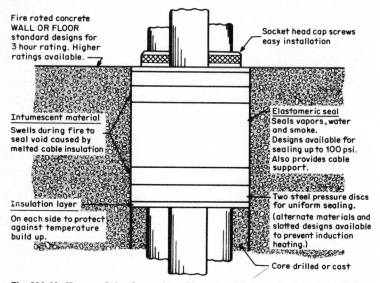

Fig. 300-40. Fire-stop fitting for passing cables or conduit through a fire-rated wall, floor slab, or similar concrete surface, without altering the fire rating of the surface. (Sec. 300-21.)

Ceiling Penetrations

Another similar concern covered by this section is the installation of lay-in lighting fixtures in a fire-rated suspended ceiling. Suspended ceilings are usually evaluated only for their esthetic and acoustic value, but they also serve as fire-protective membranes for the floor above. Although concrete floor structures have various fire-resistance ratings by themselves (depending on the concrete thickness and aggregate used), some assemblies require some type of protective cover. When this is the case,

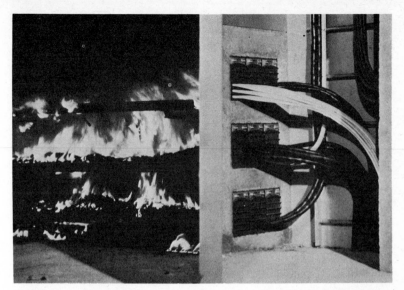

Fig. 300-41. Another type of device to provide for passing cable and/or conduit through fire-rated building surfaces without altering the conditions of fire resistance. (Sec. 300-21.)

the ceiling is tested in combination with the floor-slab structure for which the rating is desired.

Such a ceiling properly serves its function of fire protection until an installer cuts holes in it, such as for recessed lighting fixtures or for air diffusers or grilles. Because of that, the acceptability of the overall ceiling system must be carefully determined.

First, check the Underwriters Laboratories' *Electrical Construction Materials Directory* (commonly called the UL green book), which notes that recessed fixtures that have been shown to provide a degree of fire resistance with the floor, roof, or ceiling assemblies with *which they have been tested* are labeled as follows: "Recessed-type electric fixture classified for fire resistance; fire-resistance classification floor and ceiling Design No. ——."

Next, find the design referred to in the UL *Fire Resistance Index*. This booklet follows the format of the *Electrical Construction Materials List*. Refer to a design of the required fire rating and be sure that the fixtures are listed for use with that design.

Designers must specify the particular UL design that suits their requirement, note this in the specifications, and be certain that the lighting fixtures are fire-rated in accordance. But it is advisable for the electrical contractor to investigate the ceiling design for possible fire rating in all cases and to receive from the designer written confirmation of the exact nature and value of the rating, if one exists.

In the UL *Building Materials Directory,* various fire-rated assemblies are listed by "design number" and by "rating time." A companion publication, the *Fire Resistance Index,* contains detailed cross-section drawings of the assemblies, with all critical dimensions shown. Each pertinent element is usually flagged with an identifying number. Keyed to the number are clarifying statements listing additional critical limitations (such as the size and number of penetrations in the ceiling).

The top installation in Fig. 300-42 was tested and given a 1½-hr rating.

Recessed fixture without protective covering (1½-hr rating)

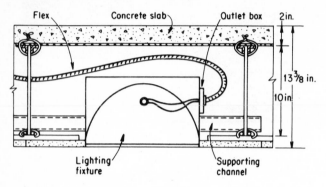

Recessed fixture with box board shell (2-hr rating)

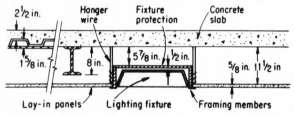

Fig. 300-42. The complete assembly of concrete slab plus fixture and ceiling gets a fire rating. (Sec. 300-21.)

No protective material was used between the fixture and the floor slab above. A somewhat better rating could have been obtained had protection been provided over the fixture.

At the bottom of Fig. 300-42 is a fixture with protection. When this construction was tested, failure occurred after 2 hr and 48 min and it received a 2-hr time rating. Even with this type of protection, the UL listing will limit the area occupied by fixtures to 25 percent of the total ceiling area. (But a coffered ceiling may contain 100 percent lighted vaulted modules.)

Figure 300-43 shows various fire-resistive shells commonly used over fixtures. Fire-resistive shell design cannot be selected independently of

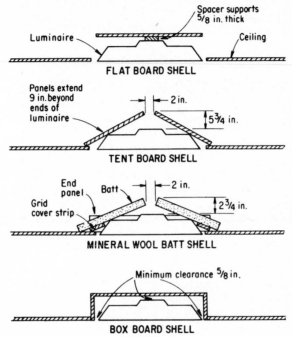

Fig. 300-43. Typical fire-resistive shells that may be used with a 2 by 4 ft grid ceiling. (Sec. 300-21.)

the floor/ceiling assembly, because fire-protection ratings are available only for a specific combination of assembly components including the specific types of fire-resistive shells over luminaires. But variation in the type of shell used can, to a certain extent, be based on study of floor/ceiling-assembly fire tests that yield similar time ratings but utilize various forms of shell design. And any penetrations for air ducts, louvers, etc., must also be part of the overall floor/ceiling assembly tested.

Use of these fire-resistive shell designs does have an effect upon ballast temperature and light output of fluorescent fixtures in such ceilings. In general, the tent-type shell permits the ballast to remain almost at the same temperature as with no fire-resistive protection. Figure 300-44 shows published data on the effect of protective shells on Class P ballast temperature and on light output.

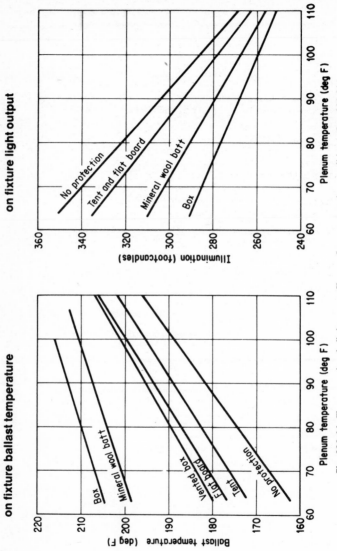

Fig. 300-44. Fire-protective shells have an effect on fixture operating conditions. (Sec. 300-21.)

Other published data on suspended-ceiling systems used for air-handling purposes make the following points:

1. Use of return-air fixtures and return-air plenums can provide cooler operating plenums.
2. Assemblies with air-supply plenums can be considered as having fire resistances at least equal to those of assemblies with static plenums.
3. Code inspection authorities have ruled that assemblies with return air should be fire-rated on specific-use testing basis. Studies have shown that supply air serves to *increase* fire resistance of the assembly, assuming that operation will continue during a fire.
4. Return air, on the other hand, acts to reduce the fire resistance of a floor/ceiling assembly.
5. The most conservative approach for *supply* air is to assume that the system would *not* be in operation during a fire; thus, the system would then revert back to a static one—a tested condition.
6. The most conservative approach for *return* air is to assume *continued operation*. Under such conditions, a 20 percent reduction should be made for the tested fire rating under typical conditions. A 2-hr design listing resulting from a test that actually went over 2½ hr before failure occurred could be interpreted as still retaining a 2-hr rating (20 percent of 2½ hr is ½ hr).

Other Penetrations

Application of Sec. 300-21 to other building surfaces has proved consistently difficult. Section 300-21 is a very broad rule that can easily lend itself to many varied interpretations, depending upon the specific details of any given installation. But the concern that is expressed there for making sure that electrical work does not create fire hazards is one that all electrical people share. Certainly, with the great extent of electrification in modern buildings and with the future bringing even broader and more detailed electrical application in all buildings, electrical people must be diligent and thorough in supporting and complying with regulations that aim to minimize fire hazards. In particular, they must be involved in developing interpretations of the Code rule of Sec. 300-21. And installations in plasterboard walls pose some problems.

Plasterboard (gypsum board) panels used so commonly for interior wall construction in modern buildings is fire-rated. UL and other labs make tests and assign fire ratings (in hours) to wall assemblies or constructions that make use of plasterboard. For instance, a wall made up of wood or metal studs with a single course of ⅝-in. plasterboard on each side of the studs would be assigned a 1-hr fire rating. A wall with two courses of ½-in. or ⅝-in. plasterboard on each side of the studs would be a 2-hr wall (Fig. 300-45). The assigned fire ratings are based on the thickness and number of courses of plasterboard. And the fire rating is for the wall assembly *without any penetrations into the wall*.

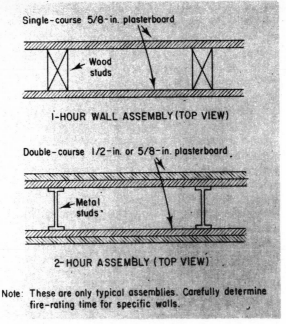

Fig. 300-45. Wall assemblies using plasterboard are fire-rated by UL and others. (Sec. 300-21.)

Because of the fire rating assigned to the assembly, any wall so constructed is fire-rated. The wall may be between rooms or between a room and a corridor or stairwell. And no distinction is made between an interior wall of an apartment, say, and a wall that separates one apartment from another. All wall assemblies using plasterboard are fire-rated and immediately raise concern 'over violation of Sec. 300-21 if any electrical equipment is recessed in the wall.

The prevailing practice on use of electrical equipment in plasterboard walls has been regulated by building inspectors and fire marshals—and not primarily by electrical inspectors. Today, however, Sec. 300-21 does make this a matter for the electrical inspector to consider.

When any electrical equipment is installed as a penetration of a wall, there is the immediate question, Does this substantially increase the possible spread of fire or the spread of products of combustion (smoke and/or heated air)? Building inspectors and electrical inspectors have generally permitted installation of wall switches, thermostats, dimmers, and receptacles in boxes recessed in plasterboard walls. In single-family houses, the entire interior is not considered to be compartmented. It is assumed that individual rooms or areas are not normally closed off from each other and that fire or smoke spread would not at all be affected by those penetrations. The consensus has been that such small openings cut in the plasterboard do not violate the letter or intent of Sec. 300-21, although there is no specific Code rule that exempts any wall from the concern of Sec. 300-21 (Fig. 300-46).

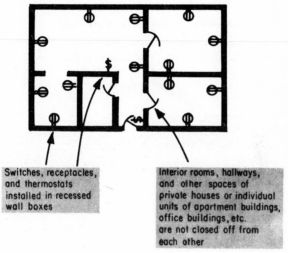

Fig. 300-46. Electrical penetrations of interior walls most likely do not violate Sec. 300-21. (Sec. 300-21.)

In apartment houses, office buildings, and other multioccupancy buildings, however, inspectors could logically question use of wiring devices installed in common walls between apartments or between an apartment and a corridor or stairwell. Such walls are assumed to be between interior spaces that are normally closed off from each other by the main doors to the individual apartments. Fire and/or smoke spread, which is normally restricted by the closed doors, might be considered *substantially increased* by any penetrations of those fire-rated walls (Fig. 300-47). Although switch and receptacle boxes are usually accepted, use of a panelboard in a common wall has been rejected.

For larger electrical equipment, such as panelboards, the same general analysis would apply as described above. For interior walls of private houses or individual unit occupancies in apartment houses, hotels, dormitories, office buildings, and the like, a panel installed in a wall between two rooms or spaces that are normally *not* closed off from each other cannot "substantially" contribute to greater fire and/or smoke spread. *But,* panelboards and similar large equipment should normally not be

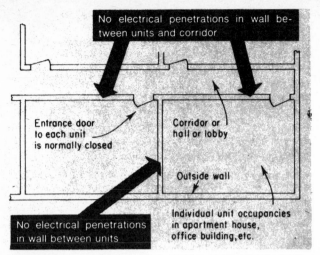

Fig. 300-47. Walls separating closed-off spaces must have maintained fire rating. (Sec. 300-21.)

installed in fire-rated walls between spaces that *are* closed off from each other by doors that are normally closed.

When it is necessary to install a panelboard or other large equipment in a wall between areas that are normally closed off from each other, a boxed recess in the wall should be constructed of the fire-rated plasterboard to maintain the fire rating of the wall (Fig. 300-48). This is also common practice for installing recessed enclosures for fire extinguishers in corridor walls and medicine cabinets mounted in walls between apartment units. In addition to requiring plasterboard boxing of such recessed equipment for fire integrity of the wall, local codes also specify sound-absorbent material in the wall space for acoustical isolation between different occupancies.

Another technique that has been used to maintain fire rating where a panelboard is installed in a wall between individual apartments is to glue pieces of plasterboard to the top, bottom, sides, and back of the recessed panel. In one particular job, this was done as a corrective measure where panelboards had first been installed in such walls without attention to maintaining the fire rating of the wall. But the use of plasterboard directly affixed to the panelboard surfaces could be considered an unauthorized modification of the panel that voids UL listing because of improper application.

Each and every electrical penetration—for all equipment in all kinds of walls, floors and/or ceilings—must be scrutinized carefully and correlated to all applicable NE Code rules and listing data from the testing lab that lists the equipment.

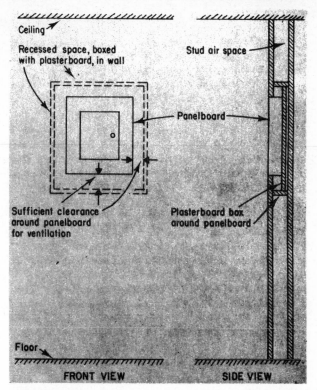

Fig. 300-48. Boxing of large-area penetrations has been required in fire walls. (Sec. 300-21.)

300-22. Wiring in Ducts, Plenums, and Other Air Handling Spaces. Part **(a)** of this section applies only to wiring in the types of ducts described.

Part **(b)** covers use of wiring methods and equipment within "ducts or plenums"—which are channels or chambers intended and used only for supply or return of conditioned air. Such "ducts or plenums" are sheet metal or other types of enclosures which are provided expressly for air handling and must be distinguished from "Other Space Used for Environmental Air"—such as the space between a suspended ceiling and the floor slab above it or the space between a raised floor (Fig. 300-49, as used for data process wiring) and the slab below the raised floor, which may or may not be intended and used for air handling. Space of that type is covered by part **(c)** of this section, although a raised floor used for data processing circuits must also comply with Sec. 645-2(c). NFPA Standard 90A defines a duct system as "a continuous passageway for the transmission of air which, in addition to ducts, may include duct fittings, dampers,

Fig. 300-49. Space under a raised floor is commonly used for circuits to data processing equipment and provides for passage of conditioned air to the room and to the equipment. (Sec. 300-22.)

plenums, fans, and accessory air handling equipment." The word "duct" is not defined, but a plenum is defined as "an air compartment or chamber to which one or more ducts are connected and which forms part of an air distribution system."

Parts **(b)** and **(c)** of this section clearly limit acceptable wiring methods to the ones described. Under the wording of the 1975 NEC a strict interpretation of the text of both parts required the Code administering authority to permit use of materials named in the paragraph. There was, however, no restriction whatsoever placed on the use of materials not named, a situation erroneously reflecting intent of the text.

To eliminate the possible misunderstanding, both parts were reworded to tighten up Code rules on the use of wiring methods in air handling space in "ducts and plenums" as well as above suspended-ceiling tiles. In listing the wiring methods permissible, the word "only" was inserted in the first sentence of both parts **(b)** and **(c)** to make clear that *only* the indicated wiring methods may be used. Previous wording accepted a number of wiring methods but did not clearly exclude wiring methods not mentioned.

Figure 300-50 shows wiring methods for use in an air handling ceiling space.

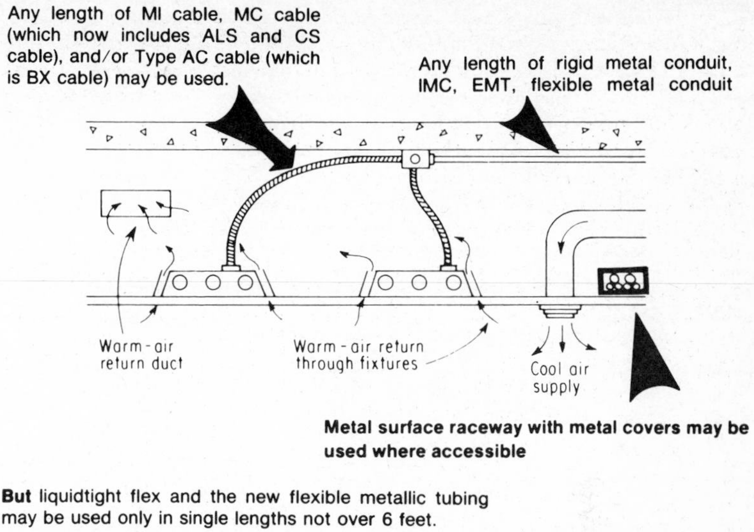

Any length of MI cable, MC cable
(which now includes ALS and CS
cable), and/or Type AC cable (which
is BX cable) may be used.

Any length of rigid metal conduit,
IMC, EMT, flexible metal conduit

Warm-air
return duct

Warm-air return
through fixtures

Cool air
supply

**Metal surface raceway with metal covers may be
used where accessible**

But liquidtight flex and the new flexible metallic tubing
may be used only in single lengths not over 6 feet.

Fig. 300-50. Any wiring method other than these is a violation in air handling space. (Sec. 300-22.)

The listing of raceway methods acceptable includes flexible metallic tubing, which is a raceway recognized by the NE Code and covered in Art. 349. But flexible metallic tubing may be used in air handling ceilings only in single lengths not over 6 ft long. The same length limitation applies to liquidtight flexible metal conduit used in air handling ceilings.

As a result of proposed changes for the 1978 NEC, the Code panel made clear that they generally oppose nonmetallic wiring methods in ducts and plenums and in air handling ceilings. It is also the intent of the Code that cables with an outer nonmetallic jacket should not be permitted in ducts or plenums. Although the jacket material, usually PVC, would not propagate a fire, it would contribute to the smoke and provide additional flammable material in the air duct.

It is the effect of the rules in parts **(a)** and **(b)** to exclude from use in all air handling spaces any wiring that is not metal jacketed or metal enclosed, to minimize the creation of toxic fumes due to burning plastic under fire conditions. Section 800-3(d) basically requires telephone, intercom, and other communications circuits to be wired with one of the metal-type wiring methods covered in Sec. 300-22 when such circuits are used in ducts or plenums or air handling ceilings. However, the Exception to that rule does recognize nonmetallic communication cables (without raceway) for use in such air handling spaces *provided* that such conductors are "listed" (by UL or some other test lab) as having "adequate fire-resistant and low-smoke producing characteristics." *Only* that type of cable is permitted for use without metal raceway or jacketing.

The whole subject of use of wiring methods and equipment above suspended ceilings is broad and detailed. Although the rules of Sec. 300-22(c) apply only to air handling spaces above suspended ceiling, such spaces are also subject to the general rules that apply to nonair handling spaces. For a thorough understanding of this complex and interrelated matter refer to these definitions in Art. 100: "accessible," "concealed," "exposed," and "readily accessible."

Because all those words or phrases are used in the Code and are critically important to applications of wiring methods and equipment, their definitions must be carefully studied and cross-referenced with each other, as well as related to Code rules using those words or phrases. Many common controversies about Code rules revolve around those words and phrases and interpretation of the definitions. Refer to the discussion on "suspended ceilings" given under the definition for "accessible" in Art. 100 of this handbook. In addition to that information, other rules relate to use above a suspended ceiling as follows:

1. All switches and CBs must be located so they may be operated from a readily accessible place, and the distance from the floor or platform up to the center of the handle in its highest position must not be over 6 ft 6 in. (Sec. 380-8). Exception No. 2 of that rule does permit switches to be installed at high locations that are not readily accessible, even above suspended ceilings, **but only unfused switches**, because use of a fused switch would violate Sec. 240-24 on ready accessibility of overcurrent devices (the fuses in the switch). However, Sec. 430-102 requires a motor disconnect switch to be in sight from the motor controller location. And Sec. 430-107 says one disconnecting means shall be readily accessible. That means *not* above a suspended ceiling, where it would *not* be readily accessible.

2. Section 430-86 permits a motor to be out of sight from the location of its controller, and there is no rule requiring that motor controllers be readily accessible. Motor controllers may be installed above suspended ceilings.

3. Section 450-2 requires transformers to be installed so they *are* readily accessible, but certain exceptions are made. Exception No. 1 permits dry-type transformers rated 600 V or less to be located "in the *open* on walls, columns, or structures"—without the need to be readily accessible. And Exception No. 2 permits dry-type transformers up to 600 V, 50 kVA, to be installed in "fire-resistant hollow spaces of buildings not permanently closed in by structure," provided the transformer is designed to have adequate ventilation for such installation. Refer to Sec. 450-2.

Air Handling Ceilings

All the foregoing rules also apply to wiring and equipment installed above suspended ceilings in space used for air-conditioning purposes.

But, in addition to those rules, the broad and detailed rules of Sec. 300-22(c) cover electrical installations in spaces above suspended ceilings when the space is used to handle environmental air. This section makes two basic determinations:

1. It lists all the wiring methods that are permitted in air handling ceilings (which also may be used in nonair handling ceiling spaces) and gives conditions and limitations for such use. This is a straightforward materials list which needs little or no interpretation (Fig. 300-50).

2. Section 300-22(c) further comments on "other electric equipment" that is permitted in such spaces. That means "other than wiring methods" and refers to switches, starters, motors, etc. The basic condition that must be satisfied is that the wiring materials and other construction of the equipment are suitable for the expected ambient temperature to which they will be subjected. It is clear that this is not a list of approved equipment as for wiring methods in (1) above.

Application of that **Code** permission on use of "equipment" calls for substantial interpretation. The designer and/or installer must check carefully with equipment manufacturers and with inspection agencies to determine what is acceptable in air handling space above a suspended ceiling. Practice in the field varies widely on this rule, and **Code** interpretation has proved difficult. The expected ambient of the air handling space must be determined. Equipment ratings must be related to ambient temperature. Manufacturers should be consulted on equipment temperature maximums, recommended deratings, limitations due to humidity, and similar related physical considerations.

Exception No. 2 of this section recognizes the installation of motors and control equipment in air handling ducts where such equipment has been specifically approved for the purpose. Equipment of this type is listed by Underwriters Laboratories Inc. and may be found in the *Electrical Appliance and Utilization Equipment List* under the heading "Heating and Ventilating Equipment."

Exception No. 3 is intended to exclude from the requirements those areas which may be occupied by people. Hallways and habitable rooms are being used today as portions of air-return systems, and while having air of a heating or cooling system passing through them, the prime purpose of these spaces is obviously not air handling.

ARTICLE 305. TEMPORARY WIRING

305-1. Scope. Although a temporary electrical system does not have to be made up with the detail and relative permanence that characterizes a so-called *permanent* wiring system, the specific rules of this article cover the only permissible ways in which a temporary wiring system may differ from a permanent system. Aside from the given permissions for variation from rules on permanent wiring, all temporary systems are required to comply in all other respects with Code rules covering permanent wiring (Fig. 305-1).

Fig. 305-1. Temporary wiring is not an "anything goes" condition and must comply with standard Code rules to prevent a rat-nest condition which can pose hazard to life and property. (Sec. 305-1.)

In part **(a)**, the words "maintenance" and "repair" indicate that the less rigorous methods of temporary wiring may be used and that all rules on temporary wiring must be observed wherever maintenance or repair work is in process. This expands the applicability of temporary wiring beyond new construction or remodeling work.

Part **(b)** recognizes use of temporary wiring for seasonal or holiday displays and decorations, as shown in Fig. 305-2.

Fig. 305-2. Temporary wiring techniques are permitted for 90 days for such "experimental" work as energy demand analysis. (Sec. 305-1.)

305-2. General. Although part **(a)** requires a temporary *service* to satisfy all the rules of Art. 230, part **(b)** recognizes use of temporary *feeders* that are open wiring (Fig. 305-3) multiconductor cord or cable of the type covered by Art. 400, "Flexible Cords and Cables"—which are not acceptable for use as feeder or branch-circuit conductors of permanent wiring systems. Section 400-8 specifically prohibits use of such cords and cables "as a substitute for the fixed wiring of a structure." As shown in Fig. 305-4, prewired portable cables with plug and socket assemblies are available for power risers in conjunction with GFCI-protected branch-circuit centers, or cable can be run horizontally on a single floor to suit needs. GFCI breakers may be used in temporary panelboards interconnected with cable and feeding standard receptacles in portable boxes, as shown in Fig. 305-5.

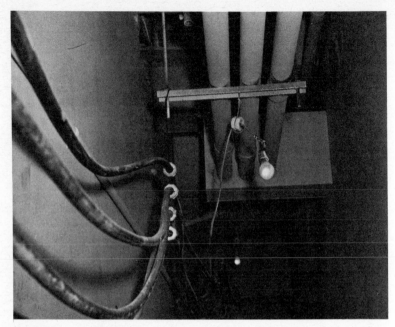

Fig. 305-3. Temporary feeders may be run as open conductors supported by insulators spaced not over 10 ft apart. (Sec. 305-2.)

Section 305-2(c) permits temporary branch circuits to originate in a panelboard *or* "an approved power outlet," which is one of the manufactured assemblies made for jobsite temporary wiring. As shown in Fig. 305-6, the temporary branch circuits for receptacle outlets may be part of a manufactured temporary system, which consists of cable harnesses and power centers (or outlets). Several variations of protection may be provided by such portable receptacle boxes, as shown in Fig. 305-6. Box 1 may have GFCI protection for its own receptacles without providing downstream protection. Box 2 may have the same protection as box 1 and in addition have GFCI protection for its 50-A outlet, thus providing protection for box 3. With this arrangement, box 1 will sense the ground fault from the worker at upper left and will trip, allowing boxes 2 and 3 to continue to provide power. Or, all three boxes could receive GFCI protection from a permanently mounted loadcenter feeding the 50-A receptacle outlet at upper left. In this case, the ground fault shown would interrupt the power to all boxes.

Section 210-8(b) of the NEC makes it clear that only receptacles used under temporary job conditions require GFCI protection. The implication is that the nonmetallic-sheathed cable runs and pigtail connections

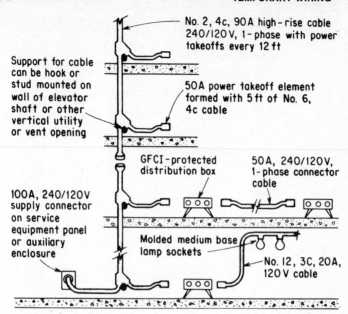

Fig. 305-4. Temporary feeders may be cord assemblies made especially for such use. (Sec. 305-2.)

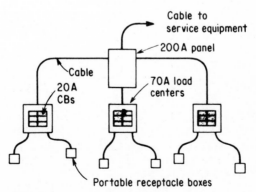

Fig. 305-5. Distribution for temporary power may utilize cable or raceway feeders. (Sec. 305-2.)

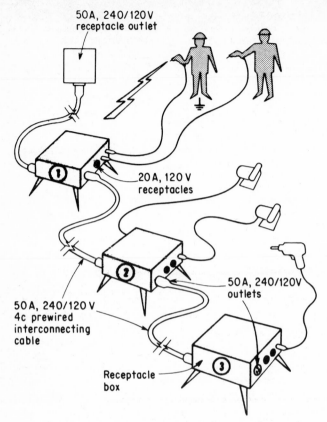

Fig. 305-6. Temporary branch circuits may be part of a manufactured system. (Sec. 305-2.)

traditionally associated with temporary power on the jobsite would not win awards for neatness and safety, but that once the permanent feeders and panelboards are in place and energized, the shock hazard is considerably reduced.

However, as long as portable tools are being used in damp locations in close proximity with grounded building steel and other conductive surfaces, the possibility of shock exists from faulty equipment whether it is energized from temporary or permanent circuits.

Standard panelboards used for temporary power on the jobsite may be fitted with GFCI circuit breakers for the protection of entire circuits, in accordance with the rules of Sec. 210-8. However, the many varieties of portable power distribution centers and modules have been developed with integral GFCI breakers protecting single-phase, 15- and 20-A, 120-V circuits. Other circuits (higher amperage, higher voltage, and 3-phase) are not required by the NE Code to have GFCI protection, and these usually are protected by standard overcurrent devices. A variety of cord sets are also available for use with GFCI-protected plug-in units to supply temporary lighting and receptacle outlets.

While manufactured systems of cable harnesses and power outlet centers cost more than nonmetallic-sheathed cable runs and pigtail sockets, it is completely recoverable; and its cost can be written off over several jobs. From then on, with the exception of costs for setup and removal, storage, and transportation, much of the temporary power charges included in bids could be profit.

Part **(g)** requires lamps for general lighting on temporary wiring tems to be "protected from accidental contact or breakage." Protection may be provided by mounting the lamps at least 7 ft above normal working surface or by a suitable fixture or lampholder with a guard (Fig. 305-7). Note that these rules differ slightly from OSHA rules, which do not recognize elevation as a safeguard but do require use of a suitable

Fig. 305-7. A lampholder with a guard is proper protection for a lamp at any height in a temporary wiring system (above). Unguarded lamps at less than 7-ft mounting height constitute a Code violation (right). (Sec. 305-2.)

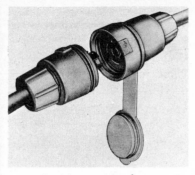

Special watertight plugs
and connectors provide insurance
against nuisance tripping caused by
weather conditions on construction
sites.

Fig. 305-8. Temporary lighting strings of cable and sockets are available from manufacturers. (Sec. 305-2.)

metal or plastic guard on each lamp. As shown in Fig. 305-8, commercial lighting strings provide illumination where required. Splice enclosure is equipped with integral support means, and a variety of lamp-guard styles provide protection for lamp bulbs.

In part **(h)**, splices or tap-offs are permitted to be made in temporary wiring circuits of cord or cable without the use of a junction box or other enclosure at the point of splice or tap (Fig. 305-9). But this new permis-

Temporary wiring for new construction or
modernization or repair of existing buildings

Box not required at splices
and taps in multiconductor cords
or cables or in open wiring

OSHA requires a guard on the lamp even though the *NEC* accepts
a 7 ft mounting height as adequate protection without a guard.

Fig. 305-9. Splices may be used without boxes for cord and cable runs on construction sites. (Sec. 305-2.)

sion applies only to nonmetallic cords and cables. A box must be used when a change is made from a cord or cable circuit to a raceway system or to a metal-clad or metal-sheathed cable.

New regulations in part **(i)** require protection of flexible cords and cables from damage due to pinching, abrasion, cutting, or other abuse.

ARTICLE 310. CONDUCTORS FOR GENERAL WIRING

310-2. Conductors to Be Insulated. Although conductors are generally required by this rule to be insulated for the phase-to-phase voltage between any pair of conductors, bare conductors may be used for equipment grounding conductors, for bonding jumpers, for grounding electrode conductors, and for grounded neutral conductors—as covered by Secs. 230-22, 230-30, 230-40, 250-57, 250-60, 250-91, and 338-3.

The application shown in Fig. 310-1 is a commonly encountered violation of Sec. 310-2 because it involves an unauthorized use of a bare conductor. The bare No. 10 conductor is an equipment grounding conductor.

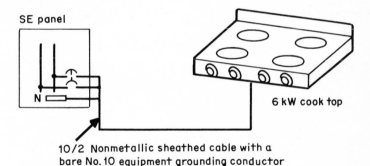

Fig. 310-1. This is a controversial application that violates Secs. 310-2 and 336-2. (Sec. 310-2.)

Section 310-2 states that "conductors shall be insulated," except when covered or bare conductors (see definition in Art. 100) are specifically approved in this Code. As noted above, several sections in Art. 250 state that grounding conductors may be insulated or bare. Article 230 cites several instances when a grounded conductor may be uninsulated or bare.

Section 338-3(b) permits use of *Type* SE cable without individual insulation on the grounded circuit conductor to be used as a branch circuit for a range, a wall oven, a cook-top, or a clothes dryer if such a cable originates at the service equipment panel.

Nonmetallic-sheathed cable, Types NM and NMC are covered in Art. 336, and do not enjoy the same status as Type SE cable does in Sec. 338-3(b). To the contrary, Sec. 336-2 states: "In addition to the insulated conductors, the [NM or NMC] cable may have an approved size of insulated or bare conductor for equipment grounding purposes *only*." Use of the bare conductor as a neutral in addition to a grounding conductor would be a violation of Sec. 336-2.

The same evaluation would apply to UF cable, because Sec. 339-3(a) (4) requires UF cable to comply with the provisions of Art. 336 when used for interior wiring as a nonmetallic-sheathed cable. The bare grounding conductor in a Type NM, NMC, or UF cable cannot be used as a neutral conductor under any condition.

Although the basic rule of this section requires conductors to be insulated, a note has been added to refer to Sec. 250-152 on the use of solidly grounded neutral conductors in high-voltage systems. As an exception to the general rule that conductors must be insulated, Sec. 250-152 does permit a neutral conductor of a solidly grounded "Y" system to have insulation rated at only 600 V (Fig. 310-2). It also points out that a bare copper neutral may be used for service-entrance conductors or for direct buried feeders, and bare copper or copper-clad aluminum may be used for overhead sections of outdoor circuits.

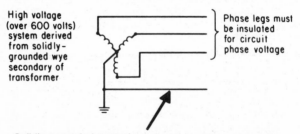

Solidly grounded neutral conductor must have insulation rated for at least 600 volts, although a bare copper neutral may be used for SE conductors or for direct-buried feeders, and bare copper or aluminum may be used for overhead parts of outdoor circuits.

Fig. 310-2. A note refers to neutral conductors of solidly grounded high-voltage systems (Sec. 250-152). (Sec. 310-2.)

Of course, for such high-voltage systems, the phase legs—the ungrounded conductors—must be insulated for the circuit phase voltage. It is interesting, however, that there is no specific Code rule that requires insulation of any circuit to be rated for phase-to-phase voltage.

Code rules do not distinguish between phase-to-phase voltage or phase-to-neutral voltage on grounded systems, with respect to insulation. Thus, the use of circuit conductors with insulation rated only for phase-to-neutral voltage would not constitute a violation of any specific Code rule, and such practice is used on high-voltage systems.

310-3. Stranded Conductors. Although No. 8 and larger conductors must be stranded when they are installed in conduit, EMT, or any other "raceway," the use of solid conductor No. 8 is permitted for the equipment bonding conductor required by Secs. 680-20(b) (1) and 680-22(b) at swimming pools for bonding together noncurrent-carrying metal parts of pool equipment—metal ladder, diving board stands, pump motor frame, lighting fixtures in wet niches, etc.

310-4. Conductors in Parallel. The requirements of Sec. 310-4 for conductors in parallel recognize copper, copper-clad aluminum, and aluminum conductors in sizes 1/0 and larger. Also, this section makes it clear that the rules for paralleling conductors apply to grounding conductors (except for sizing) when they are used with conductors in multiple.

This section recognizes the use of conductors in sizes 1/0 and larger for use in parallel under the conditions which are stated (Fig. 310-3). This

Fig. 310-3. Multiple conductors (two in parallel for each phase leg) are used for Normal and Emergency feeder through this automatic transfer switch. (Sec. 310-4.)

provision is intended to allow a practical means of installing large-capacity feeders and services. Paralleling of conductors relies on a number of factors to ensure equal division of current, and thus all these factors must be satisfied in order to ensure that none of the individual conductors will become overloaded. As shown in Fig. 310-4, six conductors are used per phase and neutral to obtain 2,000-A capacity per phase,

Fig. 310-4. Six conductors in parallel make up each phase leg and the neutral of this feeder. Fusible limiter lug on each conductor, although not required by Code on other than transformer tie circuits, is sized for the conductor to protect against division of current among the six conductors that would put excessive current on any conductor. (Sec. 310-4.)

which simply could not be done without parallel conductors per phase leg. Note that a fusible limiter lug is used to terminate each individual conductor. Although limiter lugs are required by the NEC only as used in Sec. 450-5(a) (3), they may be used to protect each conductor of any parallel circuit against current in excess of the ampacity of the particular size of conductor. The CB or fuses on such circuits are rated much higher than the ampacity of each conductor. There does not appear to be any practical need to parallel conductors in sizes smaller than 1/0, and such a practice would not be recognized under the requirements of the National Electrical Code.

Where large currents are involved, it is particularly important that the separate phase conductors be located close together to avoid excessive voltage drop and ensure equal division of current. It is also essential that each phase and the neutral, and grounding wires, if any, be run in each conduit even where the conduit is of nonmetallic material.

The reason for the last sentence of the first paragraph is to provide for the same type of raceway or enclosure for conductors in parallel in separate enclosures. The impedance of the circuit in a nonferrous raceway will be different from the same circuit in a ferrous raceway or enclosure. See Sec. 300-20.

From the Code tables of current-carrying capacities of various sizes of conductors, it can be seen that small conductor sizes carry more current per circular mil of cross section than do large conductors. This results from rating conductor capacity according to temperature rise. The larger a cable, the less is the radiating surface per circular mil of cross section. Loss due to "skin effect" (apparent higher resistance of conductors to alternating current than to direct current) is also higher in the larger conductor sizes. And larger conductors cost more per ampere than smaller conductors.

All the foregoing factors point to the advisability of using a number of smaller conductors in multiple to get a particular carrying capacity, rather than using a single conductor of that capacity. In many cases, multiple conductors for feeders provide distinct operating advantages and are more economical than the equivalent-capacity single-conductor makeup of a feeder. But, it should be noted, the reduced overall cross section of conductor resulting from multiple conductors instead of a single conductor per leg produces higher resistance and greater voltage drop than the same length as a single conductor per leg. Voltage drop may be a limitation.

Figure 310-5 shows a typical application of copper conductors in multiple, with the advantages of such use. The following four circuit makeups show:

1. Without derating for conduit occupancy, circuit 2 would be equivalent to circuit 1.
2. A circuit of six 400 MCMs can be made equivalent in current-carrying capacity to a circuit of three 2,000 MCMs by dividing the 400s between two conduits (3 conductors/3-in. conduit). If three different phases are used in each of two 3-in. conduits for this circuit, the multiple circuit would not require derating and its 670-A rating would not exceed the 665-A rating of circuit 1.
3. Circuit 2 is almost equivalent to circuit 3 in current rating.
4. Circuit 4 is equivalent to circuit 1 in current rating, but uses less conductor copper and a smaller conduit. And the advantages are obtained even with the occupancy derating.

Except where the conductor size is governed by conditions of voltage drop, it is seldom economical to use conductors of sizes larger than 1,000 MCM, because above this size the increase in ampacity is very small in

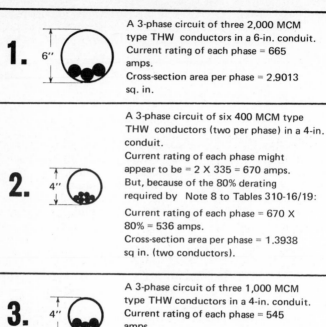

1. 6″

A 3-phase circuit of three 2,000 MCM type THW conductors in a 6-in. conduit.
Current rating of each phase = 665 amps.
Cross-section area per phase = 2.9013 sq. in.

2. 4″

A 3-phase circuit of six 400 MCM type THW conductors (two per phase) in a 4-in. conduit.
Current rating of each phase might appear to be = 2 X 335 = 670 amps.
But, because of the 80% derating required by Note 8 to Tables 310-16/19:
Current rating of each phase = 670 X 80% = 536 amps.
Cross-section area per phase = 1.3938 sq in. (two conductors).

3. 4″

A 3-phase circuit of three 1,000 MCM type THW conductors in a 4-in. conduit.
Current rating of each phase = 545 amps.
Cross-section area per phase = 1.5482 sq in.

4. 4-1/2″

A 3-phase circuit of six 600 MCM type THW conductors in a 5-in. conduit
Current rating of each phase might appear to be = 2 X 420 = 840 amps.
But 80% derating must be applied because of the number of conductors in the conduit:
Current rating of each phase = 840 X 80% = 672 amps.
Cross-section area per phase = 2.0522 sq in. (two conductors).

Fig. 310-5. The following circuit makeups represent typical considerations in the application of multiple conductor circuits. (Sec. 310-4.)

proportion to the increase in the size of the conductor. Thus, for a 50 percent increase in the conductor size, i.e., from 1,000,000 to 1,500,000 CM, the ampacity of a Type THW conductor increases only 80 A or less than 15 percent, and for an increase in size from 1,000,000 to 2,000,000 CM, a 100 percent increase, the ampacity increases only 120 A or about

20 percent. In any case where single conductors larger than 500,000 CM would be required, it is worthwhile to compute the total installation cost using single conductors and the cost using two (or more) conductors in parallel.

The last paragraph of Sec. 310-4 warns that when multiple conductors are used per circuit phase leg they may require more space at equipment terminals to bend and install the conductors. Refer to Sec. 373-6.

Figure 310-6 shows an interesting application of parallel conductors. A

Fig. 310-6. A 1,200-A circuit of three sets of four 500 MCM conductors (top) is tapped by a single set of 500 MCMs to a 400-A CB (bottom) that feeds an adjacent meter center in an apartment house. This was ruled a violation because the tap must be made from all the conductors of the 1,200-A circuit. (*Note:* The conduits feeding the splice box at top are behind the CB enclosure at bottom.) (Sec. 310-4.)

1,200-A riser is made up of three conduits, each carrying three phases and a neutral. At the basement switchboard, the 1,200-A circuit of three conductors per phase plus three conductors for the neutral originates in a bolted-pressure switch with a 1,200-A fuse in each of the three phase poles. Because the total of 12 conductors make up a *single* 3-phase, 4-wire circuit, a 400-A 3-phase, 4-wire tap-off must tap all the conductors in the junction box at top. That is, the three phase A legs (one from each conduit) must be skinned and bugged together and then the phase A tap made from that common point to one of the lugs on the 400-A CB. Phase B and phase C must be treated the same way—as well as the neutral. The method shown in the photo was selected by the installer on the basis that the conductors in the right-hand conduit are tapped on this floor, the center-conduit conductors tapped to a 400-A CB on the floor above, and the left-conduit conductors tapped to a 400-A CB on the floor above that. But such a hookup can produce excessive current on some of the 500 MCMs. Because it does not have the parallel conductors of equal length at points of load-tap, the currents will not divide equally and is a violation of the second sentence of Sec. 310-4.

A new exception was added after the first paragraph of this section to clearly indicate long-time **Code** acceptance of paralleling conductors smaller than No. 1/0 for use in traveling cables of elevators, dumbwaiters, and similar equipment. This permitted use is not new in the **Code** but was never specifically indicated in Sec. 310-4 as an exception to the basic minimum size of conductor for parallel circuit makeup.

310-6. Underground Conductors. This section says any cable for direct earth burial must be "approved for the purpose and use." Section 110-2 appears to equate that with UL listing for the purpose. A note to Sec. 310-6 refers to Sec. 339-3, which makes UF cable OK for direct earth burial. Although Sec. 338-1(b) says USE cable is OK for "underground use," it does not say it is OK for direct burial. But the UL *Electrical Construction Materials Directory* (the green book) notes that listed USE cable is recognized for "burial directly in the earth" (Fig. 310-7).

Besides UF and USE, then, what other cables can be directly buried? Section 334-3(5) does recognize MC cable for direct burial. Sections 330-3(5) and (9) recognize MI cable for direct burial. Note that Sec. 330-3(5) permits MI in "fill" below grade.

Other than UF and USE, must any other cable used for direct burial be UL-listed for such application? Sections 310-6 and 110-2 and 110-3(b) seem to say so. And watch out for Sec. 110-3(b) with respect to all electrical equipment and materials. That section very clearly makes it a mandatory **Code** rule to observe the instructions given in all the UL listing books (green book, orange book, red book, etc.). UL application rules are given the status of mandatory **NE Code** rules.

Section 710-3(b) now notes that *only shielded* high-voltage cables may be directly buried.

For burial-depth requirements on directly buried cables, refer to Sec.

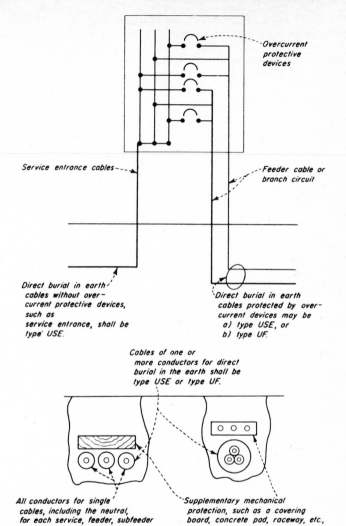

Overcurrent protective devices

Service entrance cables

Feeder cable or branch circuit

Direct burial in earth cables without over-current protective devices, such as service entrance, shall be type USE.

Direct burial in earth cables protected by over-current devices may be
a) type USE, or
b) type UF.

Cables of one or more conductors for direct burial in the earth shall be type USE or type UF.

All conductors for single cables, including the neutral, for each service, feeder, subfeeder or branch circuit shall be run continuously in the same trench or raceway.

Supplementary mechanical protection, such as a covering board, concrete pad, raceway, etc., may be required by the authority enforcing the code.

Fig. 310-7. Types USE and UF cables are designated by the letter "U" for underground use. (Sec. 310-6.)

300-5, Table 300-5, and part **(i)** of that section. Cables approved for direct earth burial must be installed a minimum of 24 in. below grade, subject to the exceptions of Sec. 300-5(a), or at least 30 in. below grade for high-voltage cables as covered in Table 710-3(b), with its exceptions.

Direct burial conductors should be trench-laid without crossovers; slightly "snaked" to allow for possible earth settlement, movement or heaving due to frost action; and have cushions and covers of sand or screened fill to protect conductors against sharp objects in trenches or backfill. Figure 310-8 shows some recommended details on installing direct burial cables. Moreover, when conductors are routed beneath

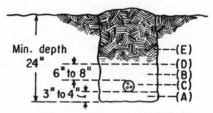

Min. depth
24"
6" to 8"
3" to 4"

A—Soft bed of sand or screened fill.

B—Blanket of sand or screened fill 6 in. to 8 in. above top of cable.

C—Cable "snaked" slightly in trench for slack when earth settles. Keep single-conductor cables uniformly apart about 6 in. in trench. Avoid cable crossovers. Keep cable below frost line.

D—Add protective slab (creosoted plank, etc.) on sand fill in areas where future digging might occur. Enclose cable in pipe or conduit under highways or rail tracks.

E—Normal backfill.

Fig. 310-8. This satisfies the intent of the second paragraph of Sec. 310-6. (Sec. 310-6.)

roadways or railroads, they should be additionally protected by conduits. And, to guard against damage which might occur during future digging, conductors in soft fill should be covered by concrete slabs or treated planks.

Where prewired cable-in-conduit is being buried, it also should be slightly snaked, although it is unnecessary to provide sand beds or screen the backfill. Inasmuch as these complete conductor-raceway assemblies can be delivered on reels in specified factory-cut lengths, installation is simplified and expedited.

310-7. Wet Locations.   Any conductor used in a "wet location" (refer to the definition under "location" in Art. 100) *must* be one of the designated types—each of which has the letter "W" in its marking to indicate suitability to **wet** locations. Any conduit run underground is assumed to be subject to water infiltration and is, therefore, a *wet location*, requiring use of only the listed conductor types within the raceway.

Figure 310-9 shows a clear violation of the last sentence of Sec. 310-7 and is related to the rule of Sec. 310-6. In the photo, conductors marked

Fig. 310-9. Bundle of conductors (arrow) are Type RHW individual building conductors that would be suitable for installation in conduit underground but are not marked "USE"; and their use here, run directly buried to outdoor lighting poles, constitutes a violation of the last sentence of Sec. 310-7. (Sec. 310-7.)

RHW are run, from the junction box below the magnetic contactor, directly buried in the ground. Although Type RHW is suitable for wet locations, it is not approved for direct burial. If, however, the conductors were of the type that is marked "RHW-USE"—that is, it is listed and recognized as *both* a single-conductor RHW or as a single-conductor Type USE (Underground Service Entrance) cable—then such conductors would satisfy Secs. 310-6 and 338-1(b). The reference to Sec. 339-3, at the end of Sec. 310-6, has the effect of tieing the rules of Sec. 339-3 to all the types of cables covered by Sec. 310-6. That is, the rules of Sec. 339-3 are made applicable to Type USE as well as Type UF cable—and even to any other cables that are recognized for direct earth burial.

310-8. Corrosive Conditions. Figure 310-10 shows how conductors are marked to indicate that they are gasoline- and oil-resistant, such as Type THHN-THWN, for use in gasoline stations and similar places.

TYPE THHN 600 V OIL AND GASOLINE RESISTANT

Fig. 310-10. Typical marking indicates suitability of conductors for use under unusual environmental conditions. (Sec. 310-8.)

310-9. Temperature Limitation of Conductors. This requirement is extremely important and is the basis of safe operation of insulated conductors. As shown in Table 310-13, conductors have various ratings—60°C, 75°C, 90°C, etc.

Since Tables 310-16 through 310-19 are based on an assumed ambient (surrounding) temperature of 30°C (86°F), conductor ampacities are based on the ambient temperature plus the heat (I^2R) produced by the conductor (wire) while carrying current. Therefore, the type of insulation used on the conductor determines the maximum permitted conductor ampacity.

example A No. 3/0 THW copper conductor for use in a raceway has an ampacity of 200 according to Table 310-16. In a 30°C ambient the conductor is subjected to this temperature when it carries *no* current. Since a THW-insulated conductor is rated at 75°C, this leaves 45°C (75 minus 30) for increased temperature due to current flow. If the ambient temperature exceeds 30°C, the conductor ampacity must be reduced proportionally (see "Correction Factors" at the bottom of Tables 310-16 through 310-19) so that the total temperature (ambient plus conductor temperature rise due to current flow) will not exceed the temperature rating of the conductor insulation (60°C, 75°C, etc.). For the same reason, conductor ampacities are derated where more than three conductors are contained in a raceway or cable (see Note 8 to Tables 310-16 through 310-19).

While it can be shown that smaller conducors, such as Nos. 14 and 12 60°C-insulated conductors, will not reach 60°C at their assigned ampacities (Table 310-16) in a 30°C ambient, ampacities beyond those listed in Tables 310-16 through 310-19 would create excessive voltage drop (*IR* drop) and would not be compatible with most termination devices.

Although conductor ampacities increase with the rating of conductor insulation, it should be noted that most terminations are designed only for 60°C or 75°C maximum temperatures (ambient plus current). Accordingly, the higher rated ampacities for conductors of 90°C, 110°C, etc., cannot be utilized unless the terminations have comparable ratings, or where derating of such higher-amp conductors brings load current down to the allowable ampacities for 60°C or 75°C conductors of the same size.

To find the temperature in degrees Fahrenheit (F) where the temperature is given in degrees Celsius (C), apply the formula

$$\text{Degrees F} = \tfrac{9}{5} \times \text{degrees C} + 32$$

Thus, the maximum operating temperature for Type T insulation is 60°C, $\tfrac{9}{5} \times 60° = 108°$. $108° + 32° = 140°$, which is the same temperature on the Fahrenheit scale as 60 degrees on the Celsius scale.

Reversing the process, where the temperature is given in degrees F:

$$\text{Degrees C} = (\text{degrees F} - 32) \times \tfrac{5}{9}$$

The maximum operating temperature for Type THW insulation is 167°F.

$$167° - 32° = 135°$$

$135° \times \tfrac{5}{9} = 75°$, the corresponding temperature in degrees C.

Watch out when conductors are used in locations with elevated ambient temperatures—in boiler rooms, near furnaces, etc. All load ratings are based on a given ambient—such as 30°C, 86°F for conductors covered by **NE Code** Tables 310-16/19. It is up to the designer and/or installer to make the necessary deratings *required* by the "Correction Factors" given with those tables. Equipment deterioration and ultimate thermal failure is the price of carelessness. Moisture or excessive dampness that may degrade aluminum terminations can also result in high-resistance terminations with resultant heating that damages or destroys equipment and conductors.

310-10. Conductor Identification. For part **(a)**, refer to the discussion given for Secs. 200-6 and 200-7. For part **(b)** refer to Exception Nos. 1 and 3 in Sec. 250-57(b). Section 310-10(a), Exception No. 5, now recognizes the use in multiconductor cables of a *grounded* conductor that is not white throughout its entire length provided that only qualified persons will service the installation. The rule requires that such grounded conductors be identified by white marking at their termination at the time of installation.

Similarly, a *grounding* conductor in a multiconductor cable may be identified at each end and at every point where the conductor is accessible by stripping the insulation from the entire exposed length or by coloring the exposed insulation green or by marking with green tape or green adhesive labels [Sec. 310-10(b), Exception No. 2].

310-11. Marking. A new cable, power-limited tray cable (PLTC), has been added to the list in Sec. 310-11(b) of the conductors and cables required to have surface marking. This cable, intended for use in power-limited circuits, is referenced in other articles of the **Code** covering use of such cable.

310-13. Conductor Construction. Table 310-13 presents application and construction data on the wide range of 600-V insulated, individual conductors recognized by the **NE Code**, with the appropriate letter designation used to identify each type of insulated conductor. Figure 310-11 shows a typical detail on application, as covered for Type THW conductor in Table 310-13. Type THW wire has a special application provision for electric-discharge lighting, which makes THW the answer for installers needing a 90°C conductor for wiring end-to-end fixtures in compliance with Sec. 410-31.

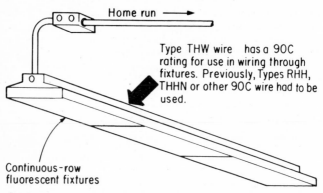

Home run →

Type THW wire has a 90C rating for use in wiring through fixtures. Previously, Types RHH, THHN or other 90C wire had to be used.

Continuous-row fluorescent fixtures

Fig. 310-11. THW wire has the 90°C rating required of conductors within 3 in. of a ballast (Sec. 410-31). (Sec. 310-13.)

Conductors intended for general wiring under the requirements of the **National Electrical Code** are required to be one of the recognized types listed in **Code** Table 310-13 and not smaller than No. 14 AWG. The National Electrical Code does not contain detailed requirements for insulated conductors as these are covered in separate standards such as those of Underwriters Laboratories Inc.

"Dry locations" in this case would mean for "general use" in dry locations. It should be noted that "dry locations only" following "Asbestos A" permits such wire to be used in raceways only for leads to or within apparatus.

Table 310-13 permits maximum operating temperatures of 90°C (194°F) in dry locations for Types FEP, FEPB, RHH, XHHW, and THHN wire; but the ampacities for Nos. 14, 12, and 10 copper conductors and Nos. 12 and 10 aluminum conductors are limited to those permitted for 75°C (167°F) insulated conductors. See footnote to Table 310-16. The reason is that the wiring devices which are commonly connected by these sizes of conductors are not suitable for conditions encountered in the 90°C application.

Terminals of 15- and 20-A receptacles not marked "CO/ALR" are for use with copper and copper-clad aluminum conductors only. Terminals marked "CO/ALR" are for use with aluminum, copper, and copper-clad aluminum conductors. Screwless pressure terminal connectors of the conductor push-in type are for use only with copper and copper-clad aluminum conductors.

Terminals of receptacles rated 30 A and above not marked "AL-CU" are for use with copper and copper-clad aluminum conductors only. Terminals of receptacles rated 30 A and above marked "AL-CU" are for use with aluminum, copper, and copper-clad aluminum conductors.

The newest conductor material being used is copper-clad aluminum. This material is made from a metallurgical materials system—using a core of aluminum with a bonded outer skin of copper. There is 10 percent copper by volume (the outer skin) and 26.8 percent by weight. Terminations for copper-clad aluminum conductors should be marked "AL-CU" except where listings by Underwriters Laboratories indicate otherwise.

310-15. Ampacity.   The rules of this section are presented in Tables 310-16 through 310-19 and the notes to those tables.

Tables 310-16 through 310-19 and accompanying Notes 1 through 12 cover the maximum continuous ampacities for copper, aluminum, and copper-clad aluminum conductors. The tables have been altered in format from previous Code editions. For instance, Table 310-16 now covers both copper conductors and aluminum or copper-clad aluminum conductors, with insulation temperature ratings from 60°C up to 90°C, rated up to 2,000 V where not more than three conductors are installed in a raceway or cable or are directly buried in the earth—based on an ambient temperature of 30°C.

Table 310-17 covers both copper conductors and aluminum or copper-clad aluminum conductors up to 2,000 V where conductors are used as single conductors in free air based on an ambient of 30°C.

Tables 310-18 and 319-19 now apply to conductors rated 110°C to 250°C, used either in raceway or cable or as single conductors in free air. Care must be taken in using these tables and in noting references to them throughout the Code.

Using the Ampacity Tables

An important step in design of circuits is selection of the type of conductor to be used—TW, THW, THWN, RHH, THHN, XHHW, etc. The various types of conductors are covered in Art. 310 of the NE Code, and the ampacities of conductors with the different insulations and temperature ratings are given in Tables 310-16 through 310-19 for the varying conditions of use—in raceway, in open air, at normal or higher-than-normal ambient temperatures. Conductors must be used in accordance with all the data in those tables and in the detailed notes given with them.

In selecting the type and temperature rating of wire for circuits, consideration must be given to a very important UL qualification indicated for the temperature ratings of equipment terminations. Although application data on minimum required temperature ratings of conductors connected to equipment terminals is not given in the **NE Code**, it nevertheless becomes part of the mandatory regulations of the **Code** because of **Code** Sec. 110-3(b). This section incorporates the instructions in UL and other listing books as part of the **Code** itself. It reads as follows:

Listed or labeled equipment shall be used or installed in accordance with any instructions included in the listing or labeling.

A basic rule in the UL *Electrical Construction Materials Directory* states that, in general:

. . . the termination provisions on equipment are based on the use of 60C conductors in circuits rated 100 amperes or less and the use of 75C conductors in higher rated circuits.

If the termination provisions on equipment are based on the use of other conductors, the equipment is either marked with both the size and temperature rating of the conductors to be used or with only the temperature rating of the conductors to be used. If the equipment is marked with only the temperature rating of the conductors to be used, that temperature rating is required for the ambient temperature in the equipment and the 60C ampacity (100-ampere or less circuits) or 75C ampacity (over 100-ampere circuits) should be used to determine the size of the conductors.

Higher-temperature-related conductors may be used, though not required, if the size of the conductors is determined on the basis of the 60C ampacity (100-ampere or less circuits) or 75C ampacity (over 100-ampere circuits).

This temperature limitation on terminals applies to the terminals on all equipment—circuit breakers, switches, motor starters, contactors, etc.—except where some other specific condition is recognized in the general information preceding the product category. Figure 310-12 illustrates this vitally important matter, which has been widely disregarded in general practice. When terminals are tested for suitability at 60°C or 75°C, the use of 90°C conductors operating at their higher current ratings poses definite threat of heat damage to switches, breakers, etc. Many termination failures in equipment suggest overheating even where the load current did not exceed the current rating of the breaker, switch, or other equipment.

When a 60°C-rated terminal is fed by a conductor operating at 90°C, there will be substantial heat conducted from the 90°C conductor metal to the 60°C-rated terminal; and, over a period of time, that can damage the termination—even though the load current does not exceed the equipment current rating and does not exceed the ampacity of the 90°C conductor. Whenever two metallic parts at different operating temperatures are tightly connected together, the higher-temperature part (say 75°C or 90°C wire) will give heat to the lower-temperature part (the 60°C terminal) and thereby raise its temperature over 60°C.

For any given size of conductor, the greater ampacity of a higher-temperature conductor is established by the ability of the conductor

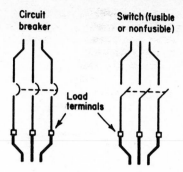

Unless a circuit breaker or switch is marked otherwise, circuit conductors connected to the terminals must not operate at more than a 60C ampacity for a breaker or switch rated 100 amps or less and must not operate at more than a 75C ampacity for a breaker or switch rated over 100 amps [refer to NE Code Tables 310-16 through -19]. That means:

FOR CBs, SWITCHES, CONTACTORS, ETC. RATED 100 AMPS OR LESS—Use TW wire (or use THW, THHN, RHH, XHHW or other higher-temperature wire at the ampacity of the corresponding size of TW wire).

FOR CBs, SWITCHES, CONTACTORS, ETC. RATED OVER 100 AMPS—Use TW, THW, THWN or XHHW wire at their ampacities permitted up to 75C (or use RHH, THHN or other higher-temperature wire at the ampacity of the corresponding size of 75C wire).

Fig. 310-12. UL specifies maximum temperature rating for conductors connecting to equipment terminals. (Sec. 310-15.)

insulation to withstand the I^2R heat produced by the higher current flowing through the conductor. But it must not be assumed that the equipment to which that conductor is connected also is capable of withstanding the heat that will be thermally conducted from the metal of the conductor into the metal of the terminal to which the conductor is tightly connected.

Although this limitation on the operating temperature of terminals in equipment does somewhat reduce the advantage that higher-temperature conductors have over lower-temperature conductors, there are still many advantages to using the higher-temperature wires.

In conductor sizes No. 14, 12, and 10, Table 310-16 clearly indicates that 90°C-rated conductors do, in fact, have higher ampacities than those given for the corresponding sizes of 60°C and 75°C conductors. As shown in Fig. 310-13, No. 12 TW and No. 12 THW copper conductors are both assigned an ampacity of 20 A under the basic application conditions of the table. *But,* a No. 12 THHN, RHH, or XHHW (dry location) has an

Size	Temperature Rating of Conductor.			
	60°C (140°F)	75°C (167°F)	90°C (194°F)	
AWG MCM	TYPES RUW, T, TW, UF	TYPES FEPW, RH, RHW, RUH, THW, THWN, XHHW, USE, ZW	TYPES TA, TBS, SA, AVB, SIS, †FEP, †FEPB, †RHH, †THHN, †XHHW*	
	COPPER			C
18	....	....	....	21	.
16	....	....	22	22	.
14	15	15	25	25	.
12	20	20	30	30	
10	30	30	40	40	
8	40	45	50	50	

1978 Edition Table 310-16.

Fig. 310-13. NE Code table shows higher "usable" ampacities for 90°C branch-circuit wires (Nos. 14, 12, and 10). (Sec. 310-15.)

ampacity of *30* A. Although that information was shown exactly the same in **NE Code** editions prior to the 1978 **NE Code**, a note at the bottom of Table 310-16 used to state that the *ampacities* of No. 14, 12, and 10 90°C conductors were *the same* as the ampacities of the corresponding sizes of 60°C and 75°C wires. That is, for instance, a No. 12 THHN had an "ampacity" of only *20* A. That note from the 1975 **NE Code** is shown in Fig. 310-14, along with the significantly reworded note as it now appears in the 1978 **NE Code**. As shown, the 1978 note no longer indicates that the 90°C ampacities are not allowed. Instead, the 1978 note simply requires that "load rating" and "overcurrent protection" for 90°C wires in

1978 Edition

†The load current rating and the overcurrent protection for these conductors shall not exceed 15 amperes for 14 AWG, 20 amperes for 12 AWG, and 30 amperes for 10 AWG copper; or 15 amperes for 12 AWG and 25 amperes for 10 AWG aluminum and copper-clad aluminum.

1975 Edition

†The ampacities for Types FEP, FEPB, RHH, THHN, and XHHW conductors for sizes 14, 12, and 10 shall be the same as designated for 75°C conductors in this Table.

Fig. 310-14. Major change in note below Table 310-16 radically alters conductor applications for Nos. 14, 12, and 10. (Sec. 310-15.)

those sizes be taken at 15, 20, and 30 A. When applied to selection of branch-circuit wires in cases where conductor ampacity derating is required by Note 8 of Tables 310-16 through 310-19 for conduit fill (over three wires in a raceway), the revised approach of the 1978 **NE Code** affords much broader and advantageous use of the 90°C wires for branch-circuit makeup. Under previous **Code** editions, when, say, a No. 12 THHN had to be derated, the derating had to be applied to its "ampacity" of 20 A. *Now,* the derating factor may be applied to its "ampacity" of 30 A and application simply has to keep the load and overcurrent device within the 20-A maximum set by the note. The sequence of factors involved in such usage must be evaluated carefully as follows.

When not more than three conductors are used in a conduit, copper and aluminum conductors have the ampacities given in **NE Code** Table 310-16 for the various sizes and insulation of conductors with temperature rating up to 90°C. These ampacities apply when the ambient temperature does not exceed 30°C (86°F). If higher ambients exist, derating must be done in accordance with the table of "Correction Factors," given at the bottom of Table 310-16.

A true neutral conductor (a neutral carrying current only under conditions of unbalanced loading on the phase conductors) is not counted as a current-carrying conductor. If a 208Y/120-V circuit or a 480Y/277-V circuit is made up of three phase legs and a true neutral in a conduit, the circuit is counted as only three conductors in the conduit, and derating for conduit fill, as described in Note 8 of Tables 310-16/19, is not necessary. But neutrals for circuits with these voltage ratings must be counted as current-carrying conductors if the major portion of the load consists of electric-discharge lighting [Note 10(c) of the tables]. Thus, if the circuit supplies fluorescent, mercury, or metal-halide lamps, the neutral is counted as the fourth current-carrying conductor because it carries third harmonic current, which approximates the phase-leg current, under balanced loading. Any such 4-wire circuit must have its conductors derated to 80 percent of the ampacity given in Table 310-16, as required by Note 8 to those tables (page 136, **NE Code**).

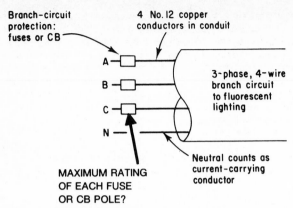

Fig. 310-15. Loading and protection of branch-circuit wires must also account for derating of wire "ampacity." (Sec. 310-15.)

Let's look at an example. Refer to Fig. 310-15.

If a 3-phase, 4-wire circuit to fluorescent lighting is made up of four No. 12 TW or THW copper conductors in a conduit, the ampacity of each No. 12 is no longer 20 A as indicated in Table 310-16. Because there are four conductors in the conduit (the neutral counts here), each No. 12 then has an ampacity of only 80 percent of the table value. This derating is required by Note 8 to Tables 310-16/19, which says that "the maximum allowable *load current* of each conductor shall be reduced" to 0.8 × 20 A or 16 A. (In the 1971 **NE Code**, Note 8 said the "allowable *ampacity* shall be reduced." From that it was taken to mean that the "ampacity" of the conductors was reduced from the table value.)

The *new* ampacity of 16 A for each conductor when four of them are in a conduit has the same status as the ampacity of 20 A has when not more than three conductors are in a conduit. In either case, 16 A or 20 A is the most current the conductor can carry under the conditions given without reaching the point at which the I^2R heat produced by the current flow would damage the insulation. Because of the reduced ventilation around the conductors when more than three are in a conduit, a current of 20 A would overheat the conductor and damage the insulation. Establishing 16 A as the new ampacity, when four conductors are used, keeps the I^2R heat at a safe level.

With an ampacity (maximum allowable current rating) of 16 A, the question then arises, What is the proper rating of overcurrent devices to protect these conductors?

When only three No. 12s are in a conduit, each has an ampacity of 20 A and may be protected by a fuse or CB rated not over 20 A. This satisfies Sec. 210-19, which requires branch-circuit conductors to have an ampacity not less than the rating of the branch circuit—and Sec. 210-3 notes that the rating of a branch circuit is established by the rating of the protective device. It also satisfies Sec. 210-20, which says:

Branch-circuit conductors . . . shall be protected by overcurrent protective devices having a rating or setting . . . not exceeding that specified in Section 240-3 for conductors. . . .

Note that the reference in Sec. 210-20 is a general reference to Sec. 240-3 and not a reference to Exception No. 1 of Sec. 240-3.

The basic rule of Sec. 240-3 says:

Conductors . . . shall be protected against overcurrent in accordance with their ampacities as specified in Tables 310-16 through 310-19 and *all applicable notes to these tables.*

That rule says that conductors may be required to be protected at a current value less than their table ampacities by the table notes, such as Note 8.

If, after derating, 16 A becomes the new ampacity of four No. 12 conductors in a conduit, the three rules mentioned above—Secs. 210-19, 210-20, and 240—require that the overcurrent-device rating must not exceed 16 A. Because there are no standard 16-A fuses or CBs, we must protect the circuit with a 15-A fuse or CB.

Using a 20-A CB or fuse to protect each of the above-described No. 12s would produce a condition where the branch-circuit conductors, with their ampacity of 16 A, would have an ampacity less than the rating of the branch circuit and would be a violation of the clear wording of Sec. 210-19(a), for which no exception is given. A 20-A-rated fuse or CB on conductors that are not rated for loads over 16 A and that will represent a fire hazard at higher current cannot satisfy the Code and has no economic or operating justification. Because branch circuits are those parts of an electrical system most easily overloaded by users who might (and usually do) add load in excess of an initial limit of 16 A, use of 20-A-rated protection too easily (and almost certainly) presents opportunity for widespread overheating, with attendant deterioration of conductor insulation, thermal damage to protective devices, and nuisance opening of the fuse or CB—all of which lead to oversized replacement of protective devices and aggravated fire potential.

In the case discussed here, use of 15-A-rated fuses or CBs on the 16-A-rated conductors fully satisfies *both* Sec. 210-19(a) and Sec. 210-20 and positively prevents overloading. Such circuits supplying noncontinuous loads (less than 3 hr continuously) may be loaded to 14 or 15 A. For continuous loading (3 hr or more), Sec. 384-16(c) would limit the load on fuses or CBs in panels to not more than 12 A (15 × 80 percent).

Note that this analysis, thus far, applies to branch circuits as regulated by Art. 210. The situation is entirely different with feeders, because they have much greater load diversity, they are not so easily overloaded after initial installation, and modern practice dictates the wisdom and long-term economy of providing adequate feeder spare capacity for load growth. But, although feeders are not subject to the same considerations as branch circuits, and although there is no Code rule that says "feeder conductors shall have an ampacity not less than the rating of the feeder protection," it is always good practice *to protect conductors in accordance with their ampacities—feeders as well as branch circuits.*

Advantage of 90°C Wires

If the four circuit wires in Fig. 310-15 are 90°C-rated conductors—such as THHN, RHH, or XHHW—the loading and protection of the circuit must be related to required derating as shown in Fig. 310-16. The application is based on these considerations:

1. As described in Figs. 310-13 and 310-14, each No. 12 THHN has an ampacity of 30 A from Table 310-16, but the footnote to that table limits the load and overcurrent protection on any No. 12 THHN to not more than 20 A.

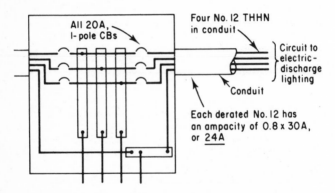

NOTE: TW or THW wires would have to be derated from 20 amps to 16 amps.

Fig. 310-16. Derating of 90°C branch-circuit wires (Nos. 14, 12, and 10) is based on higher ampacities. (Sec. 310-15.)

2. Because the neutral of the 3-phase, 4-wire circuit must be counted as a current-carrying wire, there are four conductors in the conduit—thereby requiring that each conductor be derated to 80 percent of its table-value ampacity, as required by Note 8 of Tables 310-16/19. Each No. 12 then has a *new,* derated ampacity of 0.8 × 30 or 24 A.

3. Using a 20-A, single-pole protective device (fuse, single-pole CB, or one pole of a 3-pole CB), which is the maximum protection permitted by the Table 310-16 footnote, each No. 12 THHN easily complies with the Sec. 210-19 requirement that the branch-circuit wire have an ampacity "not less than" the *circuit rating* of 20 A.

4. If the lighting load on the circuit is noncontinuous—that is, does *not* operate for any period of 3 hr or more—the circuit may be loaded up to its 20-A maximum rating.

5. If the load fed is continuous—full-load current flow for 3 hr or more—the load on the circuit must be limited to 80 percent of rating of each 20-A fuse or CB pole, as required by Sec. 384-16(c). Then 16 A is the maximum load. [Although Exception No. 2 of Sec. 210-22(c) dispenses with the 80 percent load limitation on conductors for continuous circuit operation if conductors are derated in accordance with Note 8, a protective device in a *panelboard* must comply with Sec. 384-16(c), which does require the 80 percent load limitation in any case where the protective device is not recognized (by UL) for continuous operation at 100 percent load. UL rules state that "unless otherwise marked, circuit breakers should not be loaded to exceed 80% of their current rating, where in normal operation the load will continue for 3 hours or more."]

Figure 310-17 shows the use of two 3-phase, 4-wire circuits of THHN conductors in a single conduit. The 90°C wires offer distinct advantages (substantial economies) over use of either 60°C (TW) or 75°C (THW) wires for the same application, as follows.

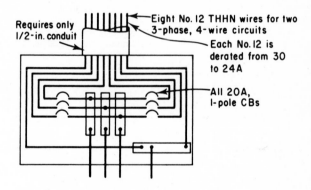

Requires only 1/2-in. conduit

Eight No. 12 THHN wires for two 3-phase, 4-wire circuits

Each No. 12 is derated from 30 to 24A

All 20A, 1-pole CBs

NOTE: TW or THW wires would have to be derated from 20 amps to 16 amps.

Fig. 310-17. 90°C conductors can take derating without need to increase size. (Sec. 310-15.)

Resistive load   If the circuit shown feeds only incandescent lighting or other resistive loads (or electric-discharge lighting does not make up "a major portion of the load"), then Note 10(c) of Tables 310-16/19 does not require the neutral conductor to be counted as a current-carrying conductor. In such cases, circuit makeup and loading could follow these considerations:

1. With the six phase legs as current-carrying wires in the conduit, Note 8 requires that the ampacity of each No. 12 be derated from its basic table value of 30 A to 80 percent of that value—or 24 A.
2. Then each No. 12 is properly protected by a 20-A CB or fuse—satisfying Sec. 210-19 and the footnote to Table 310-16.
3. If the circuit load is not continuous, each phase leg may be loaded to 20 A.
4. If the load is continuous, a maximum of 16 A (80 percent) must be observed to satisfy Sec. 384-16(c).

Electric-discharge Load   If the two circuits of Fig. 310-17 supplied electric-discharge lighting (fluorescent, mercury-vapor, metal-halide, high-pressure sodium or low-pressure sodium), makeup and loading would have to be as shown in Fig. 310-18. Each 21-A-rated No. 12 is properly protected by a 20-A CB pole or fuse. And the *continuous* load

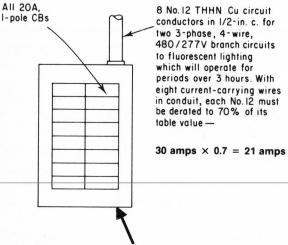

All 20A,
1-pole CBs

8 No. 12 THHN Cu circuit conductors in 1/2-in. c. for two 3-phase, 4-wire, 480/277V branch circuits to fluorescent lighting which will operate for periods over 3 hours. With eight current-carrying wires in conduit, each No.12 must be derated to 70% of its table value —

30 amps × 0.7 = 21 amps

Panelboard with two 3-phase, 4-wire circuits run in one conduit to supply fluorescent or other electric-discharge lighting. Neutrals must be counted as current-carrying wires as required by Note 10(c) to *NE Code* Tables 310-16 through -19.

Maximum permitted load per pole = 0.8 × 20 = 16 amps [from Section 384-16(c)].

Fig. 310-18. Circuit application with conduit-fill derating, continuous-load limitation, and 90°C conductors—plus current-carrying neutral. (Sec. 310-15.)

must be limited to 16 A per pole. For the same circuits supplying noncontinuous load, the circuit could supply up to 20 A per pole.

Although THHN is shown as the 90°C conductor in Figs. 310-16, 310-17, and 310-18, it would be acceptable of course to use other 90°C conductors—such as RHH or XHHW (for dry locations only). Figure 310-19 shows that the only difference between such circuit makeups and the ones using THHN is the need for ¾ in. conduit instead of ½-conduit because of the larger cross-section area of RHH and XHHW (see Tables 3A and 3B, Chap. 9, **NE Code**).

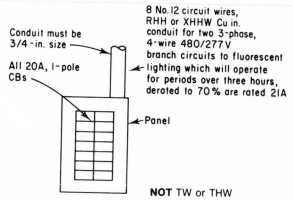

Fig. 310-19. RHH or XHHW wires call for larger conduit size but offer same advantage as THHN. (Sec. 310-15.)

Feeder Applications

Applying the UL temperature limitation to selection of feeder conductors is generally similar to the procedure described above for selection of branch-circuit conductors.

Refer to Fig. 310-20:

1. Because the load on the feeder is continuous, the 100-A, 3-pole CB must have its load current limited to 80 A [80 percent of its rating, per **NE Code** Sec. 220-10(b)]. The 76-A load is, therefore, OK.

2. The CB load terminals are recognized by UL for use with 60°C conductors or higher-temperature conductors loaded not over the 60°C ampacity of the given size of conductor.

3. The feeder phase conductors must have an ampacity of not less than 125 percent × the continuous load of 76 A, which means not less than 95 A, to satisfy Sec. 220-10(b). The feeder neutral is not subject to this limitation because the netural does not connect to the terminal of a switch, CB, starter, etc.—the devices for which heating would be a problem under continuous load.

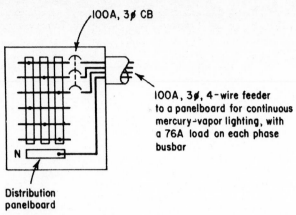

IOOA, 3∅ CB

IOOA, 3∅, 4-wire feeder
to a panelboard for continuous
mercury-vapor lighting, with
a 76A load on each phase
busbar

N

Distribution
panelboard

Fig. 310-20. Feeder conductors for up to 100-A equipment must use 60°C ampacity. (Sec. 310-15.)

4. If 60°C copper conductors are used for this feeder, reference must be made to the second column of Table 310-16. Because this feeder supplies electric-discharge lighting, Note 10(c) of the tables requires that the feeder neutral be counted as a current-carrying conductor because of the harmonic currents present in the neutral. Then, because there are four current-carrying conductors in the conduit, the ampacity of each conductor must be derated to 80 percent of its value in column 2 of Table 310-16. After the conductor is derated to 80 percent, it must have an ampacity of at least 95 A, as required by Sec. 220-10(b). From Table 310-16, a No. 1/0 TW conductor is rated at 125 A when not more than three conductors are used in a conduit. With four conductors in a conduit, the 125-A rating is reduced to 80 percent (0.8 × 125 A), or 100 A.

Note that this derating of ampacity to 80 percent, based on Note 8 of Tables 310-16/19, is in addition to the 80 percent load limitation (not a conductor derating) of Sec. 220-10(b). This is, in effect, a "double derating." Both Secs. 210-22(c) and 220-2(a) contain exceptions that make such a double derating unnecessary for *branch circuits.* **But,** Sec. 220-10(b)—which was written by the same Code-making panel that wrote Sec. 210-22(c) and 220-2(a)—does *not* contain an exception that eliminates the need for double derating of *feeder* conductors. It is certainly true that such a double derating provides a valuable and important amount of reserve capacity that is needed in feeder circuits to effectively minimize damage due to careless and/or "temporary" overloading during the operating life of the system. It should be noted that Exception No. 2 to Note 8 of

Tables 310-16/19 contains a reference to Sec. 220-10(b) that is not consistent with the difference pointed out above between Secs. 210-22(c) and 220-2(a) on one hand and Sec. 220-10(b) on the other.

The feeder circuit of four No. 1/0 TW conductors, rated at 100 A, would require a minimum of 2-in. conduit. [*Note:* A reduced size of neutral could be used, because Sec. 220-10(b) does not apply to the neutral.]

5. If 75°C conductors are used for this feeder circuit instead of 60°C conductors, the calculations would be different. Using THW copper conductors, Table 310-16 shows that No. 1 conductors, rated at 130 A for not more than three current-carrying conductors in a conduit, would have an ampacity of 0.8 × 130 or 104 A when four are used in the conduit and derated. Because 125 percent × 76 A equals 95 A, the 104-A conductor ampacity would satisfy Sec. 220-10(b) on the ampacity of the feeder conductors for a continuous load.

Although UL listing and testing of the CB is based on the use of 60°C conductors, the use of No. 1 75°C THW conductors is acceptable because the terminals of the breaker in this case would not be loaded to more than the amp rating of a 60°C conductor of the same size. A No. 1 60°C TW conductor is rated at 110 A when not more than three current-carrying conductors are used in a conduit. When four conductors are in one conduit, the 60°C No. 1 wires are derated to 80 percent of 110 A, or 88 A. Because that value is greater than the load of 76 A on each CB terminal, the CB terminals are not loaded in excess of the 88-A allowable ampacity of 60°C No. 1 conductors, and the UL limitation is satisfied.

Four No. 1 THW conductors, rated at 104 A, would require a minimum of 1½-in. conduit. Or, four No. 1 XHHW conductors could be used in 1½-in. conduit.

6. If 90°C THHN conductors are used for this feeder (in a dry location), No. 2 copper conductors could be used. From Table 310-16, No. 2 THHN with a basic ampacity of 120 A would be derated to 80 percent × 120, or 96 A—which satisfies Sec. 220-10(b) as in point 3 above. The ampacity of a 60°C No. 2 conductor is 95 A normally and derated to 80 percent is 0.8 × 95 or 76 A—which gives the conductors the same rating as the load. Under such a condition the load current is not in excess of the 76-A allowable ampacity of a 60°C No. 2 conductor, and the UL limitation is satisfied.

Four No. 2 THHN conductors, rated exactly at the required minimum rating of 96 A, would require a minimum of 1¼-in. conduit; or four No. 2 XHHW could be used in 1¼-in. conduit (in dry locations only).

Note: Of course, voltage drop in the feeder will vary with the different size conductors and must be accounted for.

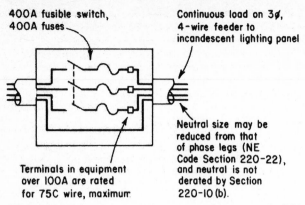

400A fusible switch, 400A fuses

Continuous load on 3∅, 4-wire feeder to incandescent lighting panel

Terminals in equipment over l00A are rated for 75C wire, maximum

Neutral size may be reduced from that of phase legs (NE Code Section 220-22), and neutral is not derated by Section 220-10 (b).

Fig. 310-21. Equipment over 100 A may use conductors up to the 75°C ampacity. (Sec. 310-15.)

Figure 310-21 shows an example where feeder conductors could be used at up to the 75°C ampacity, as follows:

1. Because the load on this feeder is continuous, Sec. 220-10(b) limits the load current to not more than 80 percent of the rating of the fuses *and* not more than 80 percent of the ampacity of the conductors. Immediately, we know that the feeder load may not exceed 80 percent of the 400-A fuse rating: 0.8 × 400 = 320 A.

2. If 75°C conductors are used, because they are permitted by UL test conditions, Table 310-16 shows that 700 MCM THW aluminum conductors rated at 375 A could be used and suitably protected by the 400-A fuses in accordance with Sec. 240-3, Exception No. 1, because 400 A is the next higher standard fuse rating (from Sec. 240-6) above the 375-A rating of the conductors. In that case the maximum continuous feeder load could be no more than 375 × 80 percent or 300 A, as required by Sec. 220-10(b).

3. If the maximum capacity of the fusible switch is desired using 75°C conductors, 800 MCM THW aluminum conductors rated at 395 A could be used and loaded up to 80 percent × 395 or 316 A. If 900 MCM THW aluminum is used, 80 percent × 425 A is 340 A; but the load may not exceed 80 percent of the 400-A fuse rating—that is, 320 A.

4. If 90°C conductors are used, they must be used at no more than the ampacity of a 75°C conductor of the same size as the 90°C conductor. Table 310-16 shows that 600 MCM XHHW aluminum conductors (in a dry location) have a 370-A rating, and the 400-A fuses constitute acceptable protection for those conductors in accordance with Sec. 240-3, Exception No. 1. The load on the feeder phase legs would have to be limited to 80 percent × 370, or 296 A. Checking

the suitability of the 90°C conductors, the ampere rating of a 75°C 600 MCM aluminum conductor is given in Table 310-16 as 340 A. Because the load of 296 A is not in excess of the 340-A rating of a 75°C conductor, the UL limitation on maximum rating of conductor termination is satisfied.

5. The smaller conduit size required for the reduced size of higher-temperature conductors is a labor and material advantage.

Notes to Tables 310-16 through 310-19

Note 3. Because electrical loads in residential occupancies are not continuous loads, in general, and there is great diversity in use of connected load devices that minimizes heat loading on service conductors and feeders, the **NEC** permits use of the designated conductors at the amp ratings shown. Refer to Sec. 215-2 of the **Code** and the example discussed under Sec. 300-5(i) in this handbook.

In Note 3, it is clearly indicated that the higher allowable ampacities for residential occupancies using 3-wire, single-phase services also may be applied to 3-wire, single-phase feeders in those cases where the feeder conductors from the service equipment to a subpanel or other distribution point carry the total current supplied by the service conductors. This permission was added to logically permit the feeder conductors to have the same elevated ampacities as are allowed for service conductors in those cases where the service conductors and the feeder conductors are carrying the identical load.

Note 5. This note provides that, if an uninsulated conductor is used with insulated conductors in a raceway or cable, its size shall be the size that would be required for a conductor having the same insulation as the insulated conductors and having the required ampacity (Fig. 310-22).

Bare conductor has the capacity of a
conductor of its size that has...

... the same insulation as used
on the insulated conductors
run with the bare conductor.

Fig. 310-22. How to figure ampacity of a bare conductor, where permitted. (Sec. 310-15.)

example Two No. 6 Type THW conductors and one bare No. 6 conductor in a raceway or cable. The ampacity of the bare conductor would be 65 A.

If the insulated conductor were Type TW, the ampacity of the bare conductor would be 55 A.

Note 8. *Where more than three conductors* are used in a raceway or cable, their current-carrying capacities must be reduced to compensate for proximity heating effect and reduced heat dissipation due to reduced ventilation of the individual conductors that are bunched or form an enclosed group of closely placed conductors. Where the number of conductors in a raceway or cable exceeds three, the allowable current-carrying capacity of each conductor shall be reduced as indicated in the table of Note 8.

Figure 310-23 shows a condition of bunched or bundled Type NM cables where they come together at a panelboard location. The paragraph following the table of Note 8 requires conductors in bundled cables to be derated as noted in the table.

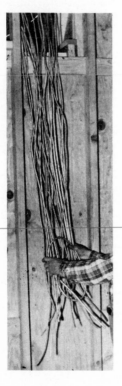

Fig. 310-23. If a large number of multiconductor cables are bundled together in a stud space, derating of the conductor ampacities would be required. If the individual cables are spaced apart and stapled, then derating would not be needed. (Sec. 310-15.)

Note 8 does not apply to conductors in wireways and auxiliary gutters, as covered in Secs. 362-5 and 374-5. Wireways or auxiliary gutters may contain up to 30 conductors at any cross section (excluding signal circuits and control conductors used for starting duty only between a motor and its starter). The total cross-sectional area of the group of conductors must not be greater than 20 percent of the interior cross-sectional area of the wireway or gutter. And derating factors for more than three conductors do not apply to wireway the way they do to wires in conduit. However, if the derating factors from Note 8 of the **NE Code** Tables 310-16 through 310-19 are used, there is no limit to the number of wires permitted in a wireway or auxiliary gutter. But, the sum of the cross-section areas of all contained conductors at any cross section of the wireway must not exceed 20 percent of the cross-section area of the wireway or auxiliary gutter. More than 30 conductors may be used under those conditions.

Note 10. In the determination of conduit size, neutral conductors must be included in the total number of conductors because they occupy space as well as phase conductors. A completely separate consideration, however, is the relation of neutral conductors to the number of conductors which determines whether a derating factor must be applied to conductors in a conduit, as follows.

Neutral conductors which carry only unbalanced current from phase conductors (as in the case of normally balanced 3-wire, single-phase or 4-wire, 3-phase circuits) are not counted when determining the current derating of conductors on the basis of the number in a conduit, as described. Of course, a neutral conductor used with two phase legs of a 4-wire, 3-phase system to make up a 3-wire feeder is not a true neutral in the sense of carrying only current unbalance. Such a neutral carries the same current as the other two conductors under balanced load conditions and must be counted as a phase conductor when derating more than three conductors in conduit.

Because the neutral of a 3-phase, 4-wire wye feeder to a load of fluorescent or mercury ballasts will carry harmonic current even under balanced loading on the phases (refer to Sec. 220-22), such a neutral is not a true noncurrent-carrying conductor and must be counted as a phase wire when determining the number of conductors to arrive at a derating factor for more than three conductors in a conduit. As a result, all the conductors of a 3-phase, 4-wire feeder to a fluorescent load would be derated to 80 percent of their nominal allowable current-carrying capacities from Tables 310-16 or 310-18. And because this is a derating of the conductor current capacity, the conductors must be protected in accordance with their new derated capacity.

Figure 310-24 shows four basic conditions of neutral loading and the need for counting the neutral conductor when derating a circuit to fluorescent or mercury ballasts, as follows:

CASE 1—With balanced loads of equal power factor, there is no neutral current, and consequently no heating contributed by the neutral conductor. For purposes of heat derating according to the **Code**, this circuit produces the heating effect of only three conductors.

CASE 2—With two phases loaded and the third unloaded, the neutral carries the same as the phases, but there is still the heating effect of only three conductors.

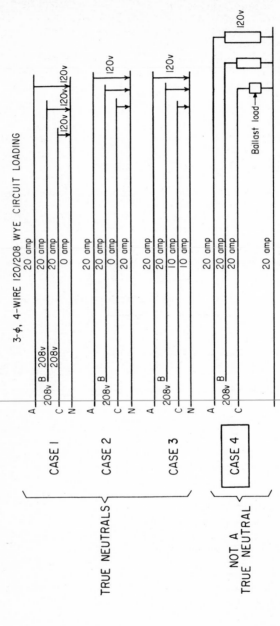

Fig. 310-24. All neutrals count for conduit fill, but only "true neutrals" do not count for ampacity derating. (Sec. 310-15.)

CASE 3—With two phases fully loaded and the third phase partially loaded, the neutral carries the difference in current between the full phase value and the partial phase value, so that again there is the heating effect of only three full-load phases.

CASE 4—With a balanced load of fluorescent ballasts, third harmonic current generation causes a neutral current approximating phase current and there will be the heating effect of four conductors. Such a neutral conductor must be counted with the phase conductors when determining conductor derating due to conduit occupancy, as required in part (**b**) of Note 10.

Although Note 10 exempts only neutral conductors from those conductors which must be counted in determining derating factors for more than three conductors in a raceway or cable (per Note 8), similar exemption should be allowed for one of the "travelers" in a 3-way (or 3-way and 4-way) switch circuit. As shown in Fig. 310-25, only one of the two conductors is a current-carrying conductor at any one time; therefore, the other should not be counted for derating where such switch legs are run in conduit or EMT along with other circuit conductors.

FOR DERATING PURPOSES —

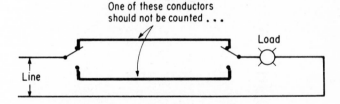

One of these conductors
should not be counted . . .

Load

Line

... **where these wires are in conduit
or EMT with other wires.**

Fig. 310-25. 3-wire run in conduit between 3-way switches contains only two current-carrying conductors. (Sec. 310-15.)

Note 11. This note makes it clear that an equipment grounding conductor, which under normal conditions is carrying no current, does not have to be counted when determining ampacities of conductors when more than three conductors are used in a raceway or cable. As a result, equipment grounding conductors do not have to be factored into the calculation of required derating of ampacities specified in Note 8.

310-38. Ampacity (Of Conductors Over 600 V, Nominal).   Since the 1975 edition, the **NEC** has added a vast amount of new information and data in part C of Art. 310. For instance, Tables 310-19 through 310-54 give maximum continuous ampacities for copper and aluminum solid dielectric insulated conductors rated from 2,001 to 35,000 V. These tables cover single conductors and multiconductor cables in air, in conduit, in underground ducts, and under various conditions of use. Care should be exercised in using these tables and relating this data to selection of high-voltage cables under the application conditions given at the head of each of the tables.

310-61. Shielding. The effect of this Code rule is to require all conductors operating over 2 kV to be shielded, *unless* the conductor is UL-listed for operation unshielded at voltages above 2 kV. Because 2,300-V delta (which is over 2 kV) is the lowest general-purpose, high-voltage circuit in use today, unlisted conductors *must* be shielded for such circuits and any other voltages above that—such as 4,160/2,300-V, 3-phase, 4-wire wye (grounded or ungrounded neutral). *But note this*—UL does list 5-kV unshielded conductors for use in accordance with Sec. 310-61, Table 310-33, and other Code rules (Fig. 310-26).

Fig. 310-26. A nonshielded conductor (arrow) is permitted for use on a 2,300-V circuit (phase-to-neutral), as shown here, *only* if the conductor is listed by UL or another national test lab and approved for use without electrostatic shielding. (Sec. 310-61.)

UL also lists shielded polyethylene insulated conductors up to 35 kV. And, in accordance with NE Code Table 310-34, UL has been listing Type RHH insulated conductors (rubber or cross-linked polyethylene insulation) with electrostatic shielding for operation up to 5 kV.

In addition to applicable **NE Code**, Insulated Power Cable Engineers Association (IPCEA), and UL data on use of cable shielding, manufacturers' data should be consulted to determine the need for shielding on the various types and constructions of available cables.

Shielding of high-voltage cables protects the conductor assembly against surface discharge or burning (due to corona discharge in ionized air) which can be destructive to the insulation and jacketing. It does this by distributing stress in the insulation and eliminating charging current drain to intermittent grounds. It also prevents ionization of any tiny air spaces at the surface of the insulation by confining electrical stress to the insulation. Shielding, when effectively grounded, increases safety to human life by eliminating the shock hazard presented by the external surface of unshielded cables. By preventing electrical discharges from cable surfaces to ground, shielding also reduces fire or explosive hazards and minimizes any radio interference high-voltage circuits might cause.

Electrostatic shielding of cables makes use of both nonmetallic and metallic materials. As shown in accompanying sketches of typical cable assemblies, semiconductive tapes or extruded coverings of semiconductive materials are combined with metal shielding to perform the shielding function. Metallic shielding may be done with:

1. A copper shielding tape wrapped over a semiconducting shielding of nonmetallic tape that is applied over the conductor insulation (Fig. 310-27)

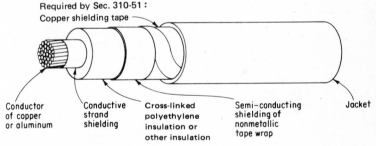

Fig. 310-27. A flat copper tape spiraled over the insulation is an electrostatic shield. (Sec. 310-61.)

2. A concentric wrapping of bare wires over a semiconducting, non-metallic jacket over the conductor insulation (Fig. 310-28)
3. Bare wires embedded in the semiconducting, nonmetallic jacket that is applied over the insulation (Fig. 310-29)
4. A metal sheath over the conductor insulation, as with lead-jacketed cable

For many years, high-voltage shielded power cables for indoor distribution circuits rated from 5 kV to 15 kV were of the type using copper

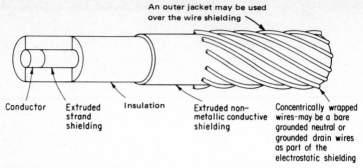

An outer jacket may be used
over the wire shielding

Conductor

Extruded
strand
shielding

Insulation

Extruded non-
metallic conductive
shielding

Concentrically wrapped
wires-may be a bare
grounded neutral or
grounded drain wires
as part of the
electrostatic shielding

Fig. 310-28. Wires, instead of metal tape, are also used for electrostatic shielding (URD and UD type). (Sec. 310-61.)

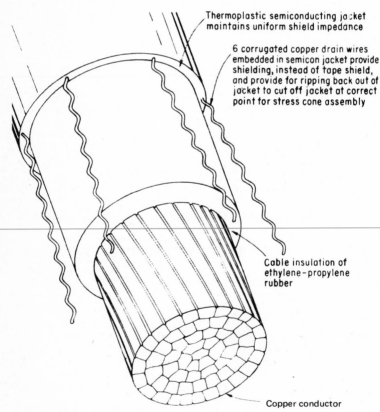

Thermoplastic semiconducting jacket
maintains uniform shield impedance

6 corrugated copper drain wires
embedded in semicon jacket provide
shielding, instead of tape shield,
and provide for ripping back out of
jacket to cut off jacket at correct
point for stress cone assembly

Cable insulation of
ethylene-propylene
rubber

Copper conductor

Fig. 310-29. Wires embedded in semiconducting jacket form another type of shielding. (Sec. 310-61.)

518

tape shielding and an outer overall jacket. But in recent years, cables shielded by concentric-wrapped bare wires have also come into widespread use—particularly for underground outdoor systems up to 15 kV. These latter cables are the ones commonly used for underground residential distribution (called "URD"). Such a conductor is shown in Fig. 310-28.

In addition to use for URD (directly buried with the concentric-wire-shield serving as the neutral or second conductor of the circuit), concentric-wire-shielded cables are also available for indoor power circuits, such as in conduit, with a nonmetallic outer jacket over the concentric wires. Such cable assemblies are commonly called "drain-wire-shielded" cable rather than "concentric-neutral" cable because the bare wires are used only as part of the electrostatic shielding and not also as a neutral. Smaller gauge wires are used where they serve only for shielding and not as a neutral.

Figure 310-29 shows drain-wire-shielded high-voltage cable with electrostatic shielding by means of drain wires *embedded* in a semiconducting jacket over the conductor insulation. This type of drain-wire-shielded conductor is designed to be used for high-voltage circuits in conduit or duct for commercial and industrial distribution as an alternative to tape-shielded cables. For the same conductor size, this type of embedded drain-wire-shielded cable has a smaller outside diameter and lighter weight than a conventional tape-shielded cable. For the drain-wire cable the assembly difference reduces installation labor, permits reduced bending radius for tight conditions and easier pulling in conduit, and affords faster terminations (with stress cones) and splices. An extremely important result of the smaller overall cross-section area (csa) of the drain-wire-shielded cable is the chance to use smaller conduits—with lower material and labor costs—when filling conduit to 40 percent of its csa based on the actual cable csa, as covered by Note 4 to the tables in Chap. 9 of the NE Code.

Another consideration in conductor assemblies is that of strand shielding. As shown in Fig. 310-30, a semiconducting material is tape-wrapped

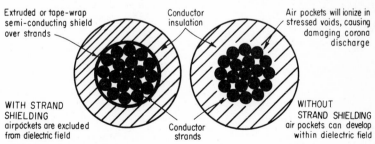

Extruded or tape-wrap semi-conducting shield over strands

Conductor insulation

Air pockets will ionize in stressed voids, causing damaging corona discharge

WITH STRAND SHIELDING airpockets are excluded from dielectric field

Conductor strands

WITHOUT STRAND SHIELDING air pockets can develop within dielectric field

Fig. 310-30. Strand shielding is part of the overall electrostatic shielding system on the conductor. (Sec. 310-61.)

or extruded onto the conductor strands and prevents voids between the insulation and the strands, thereby reducing possibilities of corona cutting on the inside of the insulation.

Refer to Sec. 710-6 on terminating and grounding shielded conductors.

ARTICLE 318. CABLE TRAYS

318-1. Scope. Cable trays are open, raceway-like support assemblies made of metal or suitable nonmetallic material and are widely used for supporting and routing circuits in many types of buildings. Troughs of metal mesh construction provide a sturdy, flexible system for supporting feeder cables, particularly where routing of the runs is devious or where provision for change or modification in circuiting is important. Ladder-type cable trays are used for supporting interlocked-armor cable feeders in many installations (Fig. 318-1). Where past Code editions treated cable tray simply as a support system for cables, in the same category as a clamp

Through-type (or expanded - metal-type) tray

Ladder-type tray

Fig. 318-1. Two basic types of cable tray. (Sec. 318-1.)

or hanger, the Code today recognizes cable tray as a type of raceway, under prescribed conditions, and an integral part of a Code-approved wiring method. However, cable tray is not listed under the Code definition of "raceway" in Art. 100 (Fig. 318-2).

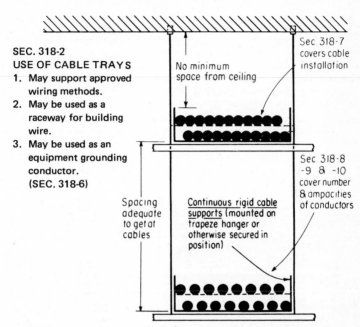

SEC. 318-2
USE OF CABLE TRAYS
1. May support approved wiring methods.
2. May be used as a raceway for building wire.
3. May be used as an equipment grounding conductor. (SEC. 318-6)

No minimum space from ceiling

Sec 318-7 covers cable installation

Spacing adequate to get at cables

Continuous rigid cable supports (mounted on trapeze hanger or otherwise secured in position)

Sec 318-8 -9 & -10 cover number & ampacities of conductors

Fig. 318-2. Cable-tray use is subject to many specific rules in Art. 318. (Sec. 318-1.)

318-2. Uses Permitted.   The NEC still recognizes cable tray as a support for wiring methods that may be used without a tray (metal-clad cable, conductors in EMT, IMC, or rigid conduit, etc.). Where cables are available in both single-conductor and multiconductor types—such as SE (service entrance) cable and UF cable—only the multiconductor type may be used in tray. However, Sec. 318-2(b) permits use of single-conductor building wires in tray in sizes 250 MCM and larger, Types RHH and RHW without outer braids, Types MV, USE, THW and other types that are specifically approved for use in cable trays. This rule states that such use of building wire is permitted in industrial establishments only, where conditions of maintenance and supervision assure that only competent individuals will service the installed cable tray system. This applies to ladder-type tray, ventilated trough, or 4-in. ventilated channel-type cable tray.

Section 318-2(d) specifically uses the word "only" when referring to cable types that are permitted to be used in cable trays in hazardous locations. In previous Code editions, wording was more open-ended and permitted specific cables without limiting use to only such cables.

318-5. Installation.   Part **(a)** makes clear that cable tray *must* be used as a complete system—that is, straight sections, angle sections, offsets, saddles, etc.—to form a cable support system that is continuous and grounded as required by Sec. 318-6(a). Cable tray must not be installed with separate, unconnected sections used at spaced positions to support the cable. Manufactured fittings or field-bent sections of tray may be used for changes in direction or elevation.

In the 1971 NEC, part **(c)** of Sec. 318-4 on Installation (now Sec. 318-5) read as follows:

(c) Continuous rigid cable supports shall be mechanically connected to any enclosure or raceway into which the cables contained in the continuous rigid cable support extend or terminate.

That wording clearly made a violation of the kind of hookup shown in Fig. 318-3, where the tray does not connect to the transformer enclo-

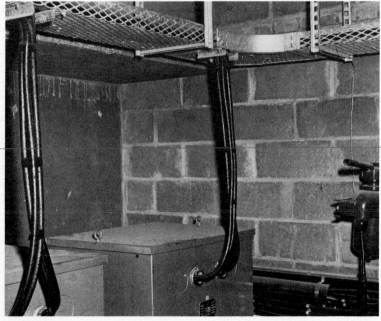

Fig. 318-3. This was clearly a violation of Sec. 318-4(c) in the 1971 NEC because the tray does not connect to the transformer enclosures. The tray continuity required by Sec. 318-5(a) of the present NEC does seem to be violated by lack of connection to the enclosures. (Sec. 318-5.)

sures—and is not bonded by jumpers to those enclosures. Although that rule from the 1971 **NEC** has been deleted, it seems clear that the same intent is conveyed by the wording of part **(a)** described above. Whether the tray must come down and connect to the transformer enclosure or whether the continuity may be provided by a bonding jumper from the tray to each enclosure is a matter of local interpretation. Refer also to Sec. 318-6

Section 318-5(e) notes that any multiconductor cables rated 600 V or less may be used in the same cable tray. Section 318-5(f) points out that although cables rated over 600 V must not be installed in the same cable tray with cables rated 600 V or less, there are two exceptions to that rule. High-voltage cables and low-voltage cables may be used in the same tray if a solid, noncombustible, fixed barrier is installed in the tray to separate high-voltage cables from low-voltage cables. Where cables are Type MC, it is not necessary to have a barrier in the cable tray, and MC cables operating above 600 V may be used in the same tray with MC cables operating less than 600 V. But for cables other than Type MC, a barrier must be used in the tray to separate high-voltage from low-voltage cables (Fig. 318-4).

Figure 318-5 shows the rule of part **(i)**.

318-6. Grounding. Part **(a)** requires cable tray to be grounded, just as conduit or other metal enclosures for conductors must be grounded.

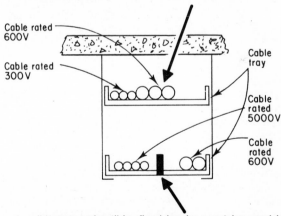

Multiconductor cables rated up to 600 volts may be used in the same tray, even when voltage ratings differ.

Cable rated 600V

Cable rated 300V

Cable tray

Cable rated 5000V

Cable rated 600V

A solid, noncombustible, fixed barrier must be used in tray to separate high-voltage and low-voltage cables with nonmetallic jackets—**but** barrier is not needed in tray if **all** of the cables are Type MC.

Fig. 318-4. Cables of different voltage ratings may be used in the same tray. (Sec. 318-5.)

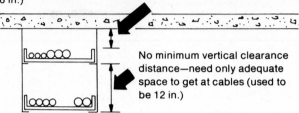

No minimum vertical clearance distance from tray top to ceiling, beam or other obstruction (used to be 6 in.)

No minimum vertical clearance distance—need only adequate space to get at cables (used to be 12 in.)

Fig. 318-5. Tray spacing must simply be adequate for cable installation and maintenance. (Sec. 318-5.)

That rule combined with part **(a)** of Sec. 318-5—which requires cable tray to be installed as a continuous, interconnected system—makes cable tray comply with the **Code** concept that metal raceways constitute an equipment grounding conductor to carry fault currents back to the bonded neutral at a service, at a transformer secondary, or at a generator. Part **(b)** of Sec. 318-6 combines with the above described Sec. 318-2(b) (1) to make cable tray a raceway and a wiring method. The **Code** permits steel or aluminum cable tray to serve as an equipment grounding conductor for the circuits in the tray in much the same way as conduit or EMT may serve as the equipment grounding conductor—a return path for fault current—for the circuit conductors they contain, under the conditions specified in part **(b)**.

Note that paragraph **(4)** under part **(b)** requires all tray system components to be bonded together—either by the bolting means provided with the tray sections or fittings or by bonding jumpers, as shown in Fig. 318-6.

318-7. Cable Installation.   Although splices are generally limited to use in conductor enclosures with covers, and are prohibited in the various conduits, part **(a)** permits splicing of conductors in cable tray.

Part **(c)** permits cables to drop out of tray in conduits that have protective bushings and are clamped to the tray side rail by cable-tray conduit clamps.

Figure 318-7 shows how single-conductor cables must be grouped to satisfy part **(d)** of this section for a 1,200-A circuit made up of three 500 MCM copper XHHW conductors per phase and three for the neutral. By distributing the phases and neutral among three groups of four, and alternating positions, more effective cancellation of magnetic fluxes results from the more symmetrical placement—thereby tending to balance current by balancing inductive reactance of the overall 1,200-A circuit.

Fig. 318-6. Bare equipment bonding jumpers tie all tray runs together, with jumpers carried up to the equipment grounding bus in the switchboard above. (Sec. 318-6.)

318-8. Number of Multiconductor Cables, Rated 2,000 Volts or Less, in Cable Trays.   These rules apply to multiconductor cables rated 2,000 V or less. For cables rated 2,001 V or higher, the number permitted in a cable tray is now covered in Sec. 318-11.

Section 318-8 is broken down into parts **(a)**, **(b)**, **(c)**, and **(d)**, each part covering a different condition of use. Section 318-8(a) applies to ladder

Each group of four conductors
is bound in circuit groups of
phases A, B, C and neutral

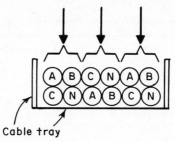

Cable tray

Fig. 318-7. A parallel 1,200-A circuit must have
conductors grouped for reduced reactance and
effective current balance. (Sec. 318-7.)

or ventilated trough cable trays containing multiconductor power or
lighting cables or any mixture of multiconductor power, lighting, control,
and signal cables.

Section 318-8(a) has three subdivisions:

1. Where all the multiconductor cables are made up of conductors No.

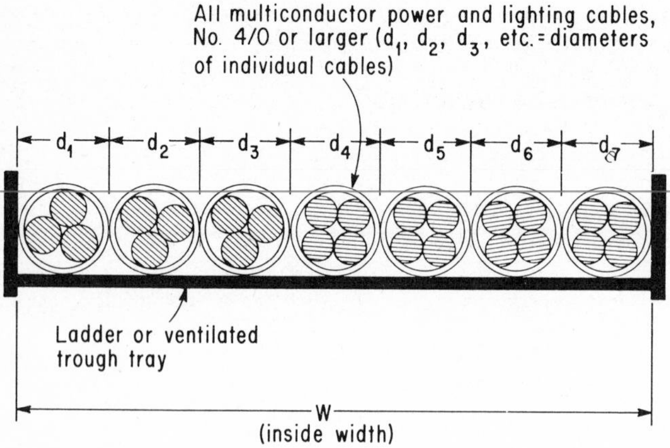

All multiconductor power and lighting cables,
No. 4/0 or larger (d_1, d_2, d_3, etc. = diameters
of individual cables)

Ladder or ventilated
trough tray

W
(inside width)

1. Cable-tray width (W) = at least
   $d_1 + d_2 + d_3 + d_4 + d_5 + d_6 + d_7$ in.
2. All cables *must* lie flat, side by side,
   in one layer.

Fig. 318-8. No. 4/0 and larger multiconductor cables *must* be in a *single* layer.
(Sec. 318-8.)

4/0 or larger, the sum of the outside diameters of all the multiconductor cables in the tray must not be greater than the cable tray width: and the cables *must* be placed side by side in the tray in a single layer as shown in Fig. 318-8.

2. Where all the multiconductor cables in the tray are made up of conductors smaller than No. 4/0, the sum of the cross-sectional areas of all cables *must not exceed* the maximum allowable cable fill area in column 1 of Table 318-8 for the particular width of cable tray being used. The table shows, for instance, that if an 18-in.-wide ladder or ventilated trough cable tray is used with multiconductor cables smaller than No. 4/0, column 1 sets 21 sq in. as the maximum value for the sum of the overall cross-section areas of all the cables permitted in that tray, as in Fig. 318-9.

3. Where a tray contains one or more multiconductor cables No. 4/0 or larger along with one or more multiconductor cables smaller than

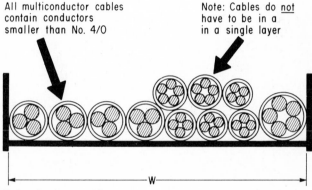

All multiconductor cables contain conductors smaller than No. 4/0

Note: Cables do <u>not</u> have to be in a in a single layer

Sum of cross-section areas
of all cables in cable tray
   = not less than cable fill in sq in. given in column 1 of Table 318-8 for the particular cable-tray width involved.

Note: Cross-section area (in sq in.) of each cable can be obtained from cable manufacturers' catalogs or spec sheets. If, in the case shown here, the sum of the cross-section areas of the 10 cables in the tray came to, say, 26 sq in., the smallest permissible width of cable tray would be 24 in., as shown in column 1 of Table 318-8. An 18-in.-wide cable tray would be good only for a sum of cable areas up to 21 sq in.

Fig. 318-9. Smaller than No. 4/0 cables may be stacked in tray. (Sec. 318-8.)

No. 4/0, there are two steps in determining the maximum fill of the tray.

First, the sum of the outside cross-section areas of all the cables smaller than No. 4/0 must not be greater than the maximum permitted fill area resulting from the computation in column 2 of Table 318-8 for the particular cable tray width. Then, the multiconductor cables that are No. 4/0 or larger must be installed in a single layer, and no other cables may be placed on top of them (Fig. 318-10). Note that the available cross-section area of a tray which can properly accommodate cables smaller than No. 4/0 installed in a tray along with No. 4/0 or larger cables is, in effect, equal to the allowable fill area from column 1 for each width of tray minus 1.2 times the sum of the outside diameters of the No. 4/0 or larger cables.

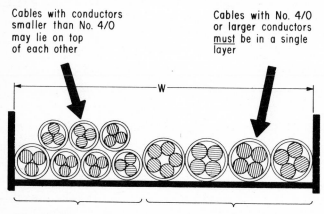

Cables with conductors smaller than No. 4/0 may lie on top of each other

Cables with No. 4/0 or larger conductors <u>must</u> be in a single layer

W

These cables contain conductors smaller than No. 4/0

These cables contain No. 4/0 or larger conductors

Inside width (W) of tray must not be less than that required by Table 318-8, based on the calculation indicated in column 2 of the table.

Fig. 318-10. Large and small cables have a more complex tray-fill formula. (Sec. 318-8.)

Another way to look at this is to consider that, for any cable tray, the sum of the cross-section areas of cables smaller than No. 4/0, when added to 1.2 times the sum of the diameters of cables No. 4/0 or larger, must not exceed the value given in column 1 of Table 318-8 for a particular cable tray width.

For the installation shown in Fig. 318-10, assume that the sum of the cross-section areas of the seven cables smaller than No. 4/0 is 16 sq in., and assume that the diameters of the four No. 4/0 or larger cables are 3 in., 3.5 in., 4 in., and 4 in. The abbreviation "Sd" in column 2 of Table 318-8 represents "sum of the diameters" of No. 4/0 and larger cables installed in the same tray with cables smaller than No. 4/0. In the example here, then, Sd is equal to 3 + 3.5 + 4 + 4 = 14.5, and 1.2 × 14.5 = 17.4. Then we add the 16-sq-in. total of the cables smaller than No. 4/0 to the 17.4 and get (17.4 + 16) = 33.4. Note that this sum is over the limit of 28 sq in., which is the maximum permitted fill given in column 1 for a 24-in.-wide cable tray. And column 1 shows that a 30-in.-wide tray (with 35-sq-in. fill capacity) would be required for the 33.4 sq in. determined from the calculation of column 2, Table 318-8.

Section 318-8(b) covers use of multiconductor control and/or signal cables (not power and/or lighting cables) in ladder or ventilated trough with a usable inside depth of 6 in. or less. For such cables in ladder or ventilated trough cable tray, the sum of the cross-section areas of all cables at any cross-section of the tray *must not* exceed 50 percent of the interior cross-section area of the cable tray. And it's important to note that a depth of 6 in. must be used in computing the allowable interior cross-section area of any tray that has a usable inside depth of more than 6 in. (Fig. 318-11).

Section 318-8(c) applies to solid bottom cable trays with multiconductor power or lighting cables or mixtures of power, lighting, control, and signal cables. The maximum number of cables must be observed, as noted.

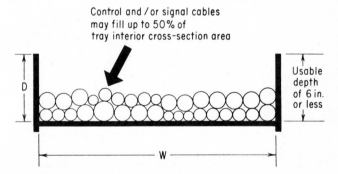

Permissible fill:

If the usable depth (D) in the above drawing is 6 in. or less, the sum of the cross-section areas of all contained cables must be not more than ½ × D × W. If the tray has a depth of more than 6 in., the value of (D) must be taken as 6 in. for computing tray fill.

Fig. 318-11. Tray fill for multiconductor control and/or signal cables is readily determined. (Sec. 318-8.)

318-9. Number of Single Conductor Cables, Rated 2,000 Volts or Less, in Cable Trays.

This section covers the maximum permitted number of single-conductor cables in cable tray and stipulates that the conductors must be evenly distributed on the cable tray. This section differentiates between (a) ladder or ventilated trough tray and (b) 4-in.-wide ventilated channel-type cable trays.

In Ladder or Ventilated Trough Tray

1. Where all cables are 1,000 MCM or larger, the sum of the diameters of all single-conductor cables must not be greater than the cable tray width, as shown in Fig. 318-12. That means the cable tray width must be at least equal to the sum of the diameters of the individual cables.

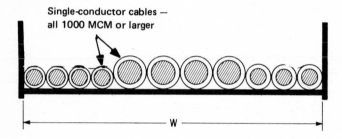

Single-conductor cables — all 1000 MCM or larger

W

Tray must be wide enough to hold all cables side-by-side, as shown.

Fig. 318-12. For large cables, tray width must at least equal sum of cable diameters. (Sec. 318-9.)

2. Where all cables are smaller than 1,000 MCM, the sum of the cross-section areas of all cables must not be greater than the maximum allowable cable fill areas in square inches, as shown in column 1 of Table 318-9 for the particular cable tray width.

example 1   Assume a number of cables, all smaller than 1,000 MCM, have a total csa of 11 sq in. Column 1 of Table 318-9 shows that a fill of 11 sq in. is greater than that allowed for 6-in.-wide tray (6.5 sq in.) but less than the maximum fill of 13 sq in. permitted for 12-in.-wide tray. Thus, 12-in.-wide tray would be acceptable.

example 2   Assume four 4-wire sets of single-conductor, 500 MCM RHH cables are used as power feeder conductors in cable tray. Table 5 in Chap. 9 of the NE Code shows that the overall csa of each 500 MCM RHH conductor (without outer covering) is 0.8316 sq in. The total area of 16 such conductors would be 16 × 0.8316 or 13.3 sq in. From Table 318-9, column 1, 13.3 sq in. is just over the maximum permissible fill for 12-in.-wide tray, but it is well below the maximum fill of 19.5 sq in. permitted for 18-in.-wide tray. Thus, 18-in.-wide tray is acceptable.

3. Where 1,000 MCM or larger single-conductor cables are installed in the same tray with single-conductor cables smaller than 1,000 MCM, the fill must not exceed the maximum fill determined by the calculation indicated in column 2 of Table 318-9—in a manner similar to the calculations indicated above for multiconductor cables.

example   If nine 750 MCM THW conductors are in a tray with six 1,000 MCM THW conductors, the required minimum width (W) of the tray would be determined as follows:

1. The sum of the csa of the nine 750 MCM conductors (those smaller than 1,000 MCM) is equal to 9 × 1.2252 sq in. (from column 5, Table 5, Chap. 9, **NE Code**) or 11.03 sq in.
2. Each 1,000 MCM THW conductor has an outside diameter of 1.404 in. The sum of the diameters of the 1,000 MCM conductors is, then, 6 × 1.404 or 8.424 in.
3. Column 2 of Table 318-9 says, in effect, that to determine the minimum required width of cable tray it is necessary to add 11.03 sq in. (from 1 above) to 1.1 × 8.424 (from 2 above) and use the total to check against column 1 of Table 318-9 to get the tray width:

$$11.03 + (1.1 \times 8.424) = 11.03 + 9.27 = 20.3 \text{ sq in.}$$

From column 1, Table 318-9, the fill of 20.3 sq in. is greater than the 19.5 sq in. permitted for 18-in.-wide tray. But, this fill is within the permitted fill of 26 sq in. for 24-in.-wide tray. The 24-in.-wide tray is, therefore, the minimum size tray that is acceptable.

In 4-in.-Wide Channel-Type Tray

Where single-conductor cables are installed in 4-in.-wide, ventilated channel-type trays, the sum of the diameters of all single conductors must not exceed the inside width of the channel.

318-10. Ampacity of Cables Rated 2,000 Volts or Less in Cable Trays.   Cables in cable tray are not subject to the ampacity derating factors given in Note 8 of Tables 310-16/19 for more than three conductors in a raceway.

Multiconductor Cables

When cable assemblies of more than one conductor are installed as required by Sec. 318-8, each conductor in any of the cables will have an ampacity as given in Table 310-16 or Table 310-18. Those are the standard tables of ampacities for cables with not more than three current-carrying conductors within the cable (excluding neutral conductors that carry current only during load unbalance on the phases). The ampacity of any conductor in a cable is based on the size of the conductor and the type of insulation on the conductor, as shown in Tables 310-16 and 310-18. For cables not installed in cable tray, if a cable contains more than three current-carrying conductors, derating of the conductor ampacities must be made in accordance with Note 8 to Tables 310-16 through 310-19. But the first sentence of Sec. 318-10 flatly exempts cables in tray from Note 8.

An exception to the above determination of conductor ampacities is made in the case of any cable tray with more than 6 ft of continuous, solid, unventilated covers. In such cases, the conductors in the cable have an ampacity of not more than 95 percent of the ampacities given in Table 310-16 or Table 310-18.

Single-Conductor Cables

The ampacity of any single-conductor cable or single conductors twisted together is determined as follows:

600 MCM and larger—Where installed in accordance with Sec. 318-9, the ampacity of any 600 MCM or larger single-conductor cable in uncovered tray is *not more* than 75 percent of the ampacity given for the size and insulation of conductor in Table 310-17 or for the size and insulation of conductor in Table 310-19. Note that this means 75 percent of the free-air ampacity of the conductor. And if more than 6 ft of the tray is continuously covered with a solid, unventilated cover, the ampacities for 600 MCM and larger conductors must not exceed 70 percent of the ampacity value in Tables 310-17 and 310-19.

250 MCM through 500 MCM—For any single-conductor cable in this range, installed in accordance with Sec. 318-9 in uncovered tray, its ampacity is not more than 65 percent of the ampacity value shown in

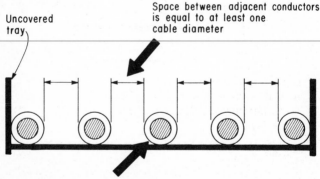

500 MCM THW single-conductor copper cables may be used at their 620 amp rating, from Table 310-17

Fig. 318-13. With spacing, cables in tray may operate at free-air ampacity. (Sec. 318-10.)

Table 310-17 or Table 310-19. And if any such cables in this range are used in tray that is continuously covered for more than 6 ft with a solid, unventilated cover, the ampacities must not exceed 60 percent of the ampacity values in Tables 310-17 and 310-19.

Where 250 MCM and larger single-conductor cables are installed in a single layer in uncovered cable tray with a maintained spacing of not less than one cable diameter between individual conductors, the ampacities of such conductors are equal to the free-air ampacities given in Tables 310-17 and 310-19, as shown in Fig. 318-13.

318-11. Number of Type MV and Type MC Cables (2,001 Volts or Over) in Cable Trays.   This section applies only to high-voltage circuits in tray. Type MV cable is a high-voltage cable now covered by new Árt. 326. Type MC cable is the metal-clad cable operating above 2,000 V—a cable assembly long known as interlocked armor cable. [Type MC or other armored cable (e.g., ALS or CS) operating at voltages up to 2,000 V must conform to Secs. 318-8 and 318-9 on number and ampacities of cables when used in tray.]

Type MV and Type MC high-voltage cables must conform to the tray fill shown in Fig. 318-14.

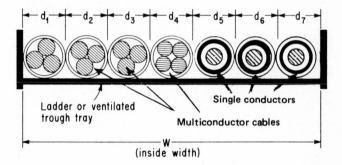

1. Cable-tray width (W) = at least
   $d_1 + d_2 + d_3 + d_4 + d_5 + d_6 + d_7$ in.
2. All cables *must* lie flat, side by side,
   in one layer.

Fig. 318-14. Tray must be wide enough for all high-voltage cables in a single layer. (Sec. 318-11.)

318-12. Ampacity of Type MV and Type MC Cables (2,001 Volts or Over) in Cable Trays.   This is a new section, covering the ampacities of MV and MC cables operating above 2,000 V in cable trays—both single-conductor and multiconductor.

ARTICLE 320. OPEN WIRING ON INSULATORS

320-1. Definition.   Conductors for open wiring may be any of the general-use types listed in Table 310-13 for "dry" locations and "dry and wet" locations such as THW, XHHW, THHN, etc.

The conductors are secured to and supported by insulators, of porcelain, glass, or other composition materials. In modern wiring practice open wiring is used for high-tension work in transformer vaults and substations. It is very commonly used for temporary work and is used for runs of heavy conductors for feeders and power circuits, as in manholes and trenches under or adjacent to switchboards, to facilitate the routing of large numbers of circuits fed into conduits.

320-3. Uses Permitted.   This section limits open wiring on insulators to industrial or agricultural establishments, up to 600 V. Section 320-15 spells out such installations in unfinished attics and roof spaces.

320-6. Conductor Supports.   Methods of dead-ending open cable runs are shown in Fig. 320-1.

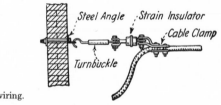

Method of dead-ending
heavy conductors used in open wiring.

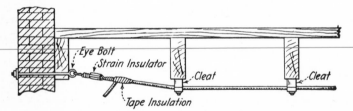

Method of dead-ending heavy conductors used in open wiring.

Fig. 320-1. Proven methods must be used for dead-ending open wiring. (Sec. 320-6.)

Where heavy AC feeders are run as open wiring, the reactance of the circuit is reduced and hence the voltage drop is reduced by using a small spacing between the conductors. Up to a distance of 15 ft between supports the 2½-in. spacing may be used if spacers are clamped to the conductors at intervals not exceeding 4½ ft. A spacer consists of the three porcelain pieces of the same form as used in the support, with a metal clamping ring.

In Exception No. 2, reference to "mill construction" is generally understood to mean the type of building in which the floors are supported on wooden beams spaced about 14 to 16 ft apart. Wires not smaller than No. 8 may safely span such a distance where the ceilings are high and the space is free from obstructions.

320-7. Mounting of Conductor Supports. Figure 320-2 illustrates mounting of knobs and cleats for the support of No. 14, No. 12, and No. 10 conductors. For conductors of larger size, solid knobs with tie wires or single-wire cleats should be used.

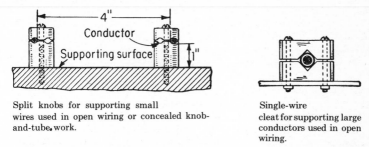

Split knobs for supporting small wires used in open wiring or concealed knob-and-tube work.

Single-wire cleat for supporting large conductors used in open wiring.

Fig. 320-2. Proper wiring support devices must be correctly mounted. (Sec. 320-7.)

320-12. Clearance from Piping, Exposed Conductors, Etc. The additional insulation on the wire, referred to in this rule, is to prevent the wire from coming in contact with the adjacent pipe or other metal.

ARTICLE 324. CONCEALED KNOB-AND-TUBE WIRING

324-3. Uses Permitted. Note that this wiring method is restricted to use only for extensions of existing installations and is not **Code** acceptable as a general-purpose wiring method for new electrical work. Under the conditions specified in **(1)** and **(2)**, concealed knob-and-tube wiring may be used only if special permission is granted by the local inspection authority having jurisdiction as noted in the second sentence of Sec. 90-4.

324-5. Conductors. Conductors for concealed knob-and-tube work may be any of the general-use types listed in Table 310-13 for "dry" locations and "dry and wet" locations such as TW, THW, XHHW, RHH, etc.

324-11. Unfinished Attics and Roof Spaces. Where wires are run on knobs or through tubes in a closed-in and inaccessible attic or roof space, the wiring is concealed knob-and-tube work; but if the attic or roof space is accessible, the wiring must conform to Art. 320 as open wiring on insulators. Both cases are covered by the foregoing rules.

Where the wiring is installed at any time after the building is completed, in a roof space having less than 3 ft headroom at any point, the wires may be run on knobs across the faces of the joists, studs, or rafters or through or on the sides of the joists, studs, or rafters. Such a space would not be used for storage purposes and the wiring may be considered as concealed knob-and-tube work.

An attic or roof space is considered accessible if it can be reached by means of a stairway or a permanent ladder. In any such attic or roof space wires run through the floor joists where there is no floor must be protected by a running board and wires run through the studs or rafters must be protected by a running board if within 7 ft from the floor or floor joists. These two cases are shown in Fig. 324-1.

ARTICLE 326. MEDIUM VOLTAGE CABLE

326-1. Definition.   This is a very limited definition of a relatively new Code designation—Type MV. The description of this cable type is amplified in the *Electrical Construction Materials Directory* of the Underwriters Laboratories, as follows:

Medium voltage cables are rated 2001 to 35,000 volts.

They are single or multi-conductor, aluminum or copper, with solid extruded dielectric insulation and may have an extruded jacket, metallic covering or combination of both over the single conductors or over the assembled conductors in a multi-conductor power cable.

All insulated conductors 8001 volts and higher have electrostatic shielding. Cables rated 2001 to 8000 volts may be shielded or nonshielded.

Nonshielded cables are intended for use where conditions of maintenance and supervision ensure that only competent individuals service and have access to the installation.

Cables marked MV-75, MV-85 or MV-90 are suitable for use in wet or dry locations at 75°C, 85°C or 90°C, respectively.

Cables which are suitable for use in dry locations only are so marked. Cables marked "oil resistant I" or "oil resistant II" are suitable for exposure to mineral oil at 60°C or 75°C, respectively.

Cables marked "sunlight resistant" may be exposed to the direct rays of the sun.

Cables intended for installation in cable trays in accordance with Article 381 of the National Electrical Code are marked "for CT Use" or "for use in cable trays."

Cables with aluminum conductors are marked with the word "aluminum" or the letters "AL."

Cables are marked with their conductor size, voltage rating and insulation level (100 percent or 133 percent).

The Listing Mark of Underwriters Laboratories Inc. on the product is the only method provided by UL to identify products manufactured under its Listing and Follow-Up Service.

326-3. Uses Permitted.   Because the Code now has an article and cable designation (Type MV) for cables operating above 2,000 V up to 35,000

V, it may be expected that electrical inspection authorities will insist that all cables in that voltage range must be Type MV to satisfy the NE Code.

Great care should be exercised in determining the attitude of local inspection authorities toward the meaning of this article. In particular, the relationship of Sec. 110-8 to Art. 326 should be determined. Section 110-8 states that "only wiring methods recognized as suitable are included in this Code." The question to be answered is: Will electrical inspection agencies require all high-voltage conductors to be Type MV? Or will inspection agencies accept high-voltage conductors not specifically designated Type MV? In other words, because the Code now has an accepted type of high-voltage cable, will it be permissible to use high-voltage cables that are not of this accepted type? For circuits in common use up to 600 V, Sec. 110-8 has consistently been interpreted to require that *any* conductor or cable must be one of the types specifically designated in the Code—Table 310-13 or elsewhere in Arts. 300 to 365. That is, conductors must be Type TW, THW, or one of the other designated types, and cable must be Type AC, NM, MI, MC, or other designated cable. It would be a Code violation to use any non-Code-designated wire or cable for systems up to 2,000 V. It would, therefore, seem to be similarly contrary to Code to use a non-Code-designated cable for higher-voltage circuits inasmuch as there is a Code-designated type (Type MV) for such applications.

Refer to Table 310-31 on Type MV conductors and to Sec. 318-12(b) for use of Type MV cables in tray.

ARTICLE 328. FLAT CONDUCTOR CABLE (Type FCC)

328-1 Scope.   This article covers design and installation regulations on a branch circuit wiring system that supplies floor outlets in office areas and other commercial and institutional interiors. The method may be used for new buildings or for modernization or expansion in existing interiors. The great flexibility and ease of installation of this surface-mounted flat-cable wiring system meets the need that arises from the fact that the average floor power outlet in an office area is relocated every two years.

Undercarpet wiring to floor outlets eliminates any need for core drilling of concrete floors—avoiding noise, water dripping, falling debris, and disruption of normal activities in an office area. Alterations or additions to Type FCC circuit runs is neat, clean, and simple and may be done during office working hours—not requiring the overtime labor rates incurred by floor drilling, which must be done at nights or on weekends. The FCC method eliminates use of conduit or cable, along with the need to fish conductors.

Type FCC wiring offers versatile supply to floor outlets for power and communication—at any locations on the floor. The flat cable is inconspicuous under the carpet squares. Elimination of floor penetrations maintains the fire integrity of the floor, as required by Sec. 300-21.

ARTICLE 330. MINERAL-INSULATED METAL-
SHEATHED CABLE

330-1. Definition.   The data from the UL green book expands on the definition (Fig. 330-1) and covers application notes as follows.

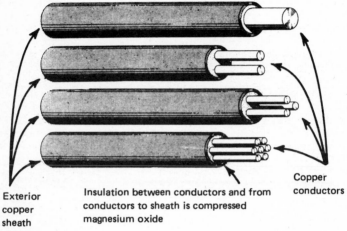

Exterior
copper
sheath

Insulation between conductors and from
conductors to sheath is compressed
magnesium oxide

Copper
conductors

Fig. 330-1. Type MI is a single or multiconductor cable that requires special termination. (Sec. 330-1.)

Mineral-insulated metal-sheathed cable is labeled in a single-conductor construction from No. 16 AWG through No. 4/0 AWG, two- and three-conductor from No. 16 AWG through No. 4 AWG, four-conductor from No. 16 AWG through No. 6 AWG, and seven-conductor Nos. 16, 14, 12, and 10 AWG.

The standard length in which any size is furnished depends on the final diameter of the cable. The smallest cable, 1/C No. 16 AWG, has a diameter of 0.216 in. and can be furnished in lengths of approximately 1,900 ft. Cables of larger diameter have proportionally shorter lengths. The cable is shipped in paper-wrapped coils ranging in diameter from 3 to 5 ft.

The original intent behind development of this cable was to provide a wiring material which would be completely noncombustible, thus eliminating the fire hazards resulting from faults or excessive overloads on electrical circuits. To accomplish this, it is constructed entirely of inorganic materials. The conductors, sheath, and protective armor are of metal. The insulation is highly compressed magnesium oxide, which is extremely stable at high temperatures (fusion temperature of 2,800°C).

330-3. Uses Permitted.   This section describes the general use of mineral-insulated metal-sheathed cable, designated Type MI. Briefly, it includes, basically, general use as services, feeders, and branch circuits in exposed and concealed work, in dry and wet locations, for underplaster extensions and embedded in plaster, masonry, concrete, or fill, for underground runs, or where exposed to weather, continuous moisture, oil, or other conditons not having a deteriorating effect on the metallic sheath (Fig. 330-2). The maximum permissible operating temperature for general use is 85°C (determined by present standard terminations).

Fig. 330-2. Type MI is recognized for an extremely broad range of applications—for any kind of circuit, indoors or outdoors, wet or dry, and even in hazardous locations, as where MI motor branch circuits supply pumps in areas subject to flammable gases or vapors. (Sec. 330-3.)

The cable itself, however, is recognized for 250°C in special applications. Permissible current ratings will be those given in Table 310-16. Type MI cable in its many sizes and constructions is suitable for all power and control circuits up to 600 V.

There is no question that MI cable can be used "in underground runs" as indicated in Sec. 330-3(9). But there is a question as to the meaning of "in underground runs." This question arises because of the wording in Sec. 310-6. Section 310-6 states that cable suitable for direct burial in the earth must be of a type specifically approved for the purpose. That would require that the local inspector is satisfied with direct burial of MI cable and that UL listing recognized such use.

Although the copper sheath of MI cable has good resistance to corrosion, acid soils may be harmful to the copper sheath. Direct earth burial in alkaline and neutral soils would generally be expected to create no problems, but in any direct burial application MI cable with an outer plastic or neoprene jacket would assure effective application and provide compliance with the phrase "protected against physical damage and corrosive conditions" in part **(9)** of Sec. 330-3. Such jacketed MI cables are available, and have been successfully used in direct burial applications.

The fact remains, however, that the Code is not clear on this subject, and local rulings may vary on this subject.

330-14. Fittings.   Connections of Type MI cable must be carefully made in accordance with UL and manufacturers' application data to assure effective operation (Fig. 330-3).

Fig. 330-3. Termination fitting for Type MI cable must be an approved connector, with its component parts assembled in proper sequence. (Sec. 330-14.)

330-15. Terminal Seals.   This rule is applied in conjunction with that of Sec. 330-14 to assure *both* sealing of the cable end and means for connecting to enclosures (Fig. 330-4).

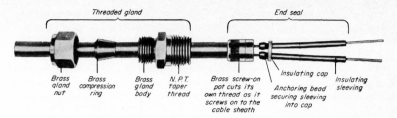

Threaded gland · End seal

| Brass gland nut | Brass compression ring | Brass gland body | N.P.T. taper thread | Brass screw-on pot cuts its own thread as it screws on to the cable sheath | Insulating cap · Anchoring bead securing sleeving into cap | Insulating sleeving |

This typical fitting is approved for MI termination in hazardous locations, in accordance with Sec. 501-4.

Fig. 330-4. MI cable termination must provide end sealing and connection means. (Sec. 330-15.)

ARTICLE 333. ARMORED CABLE

333-1. Definition. This section identifies Type AC cable, which is the cable assembly long used and known as BX cable. All the regulations on use of Type AC cable are given in the balance of the sections of this **Code** article. The rules on armored cable were contained in Art. 334 on metal-clad cable in the 1975 **NE Code** and earlier Codes. Now Type AC armored cable, the commonly used BX cable, is covered by an article of its own and is separated on application and **Code** enforcement from the use of metal-clad cables, which are now covered in Art. 334.

Type AC cable (BX) is listed and labeled by UL as "Armored Cable" in the *Electrical Construction Materials Directory*. The assembly contains the conductors within a jacket made of a spiral-wrap of steel with interlocking of the edges of the strip (Fig. 333-1).

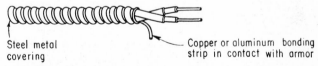

Steel metal covering ——— Copper or aluminum bonding strip in contact with armor

Fig. 333-1. Type AC cable contains insulated conductors plus bonding conductor under the armor. (Sec. 333-1.)

Armored cable assemblies of 2, 3, or 4 conductors in sizes No. 14 AWG to No. 1 AWG conform to the standards of the Underwriters Laboratories. These standards cover multiple-conductor armored cables for use in accordance with the **National Electrical Code**, in wiring systems of 600 V or less, at temperatures of 60°C or 75°C depending upon conductor insulation.

Armored cables of other types which do not come under these UL standards are listed by UL as "Metal-Clad Cable, Type MC" and are covered by Art. 334. One type of MC cable is commonly called "interlocked armor cable."

333-4. Construction. Note that Type AC cable is recognized for branch circuits and feeders, **but not** for service-entrance conductors, which *must* be one of the cables or wiring methods specified in Sec. 230-43. Type MC (metal-clad) cable, such as interlocked armor cable or the other cables covered in Art. 334, is recognized by Sec. 230-43 for use as service-entrance conductors.

Because the armor of Type AC cable is recognized as an equipment grounding conductor by Sec. 250-91(b) (6), its effectiveness must be assured by using an "internal bonding strip," or conductor, under the armor and shorting the turns of the steel jacket. The ohmic resistance of finished armor, including the bonding conductor that is required to be furnished as a part of all except lead-covered armored cable, must be within values specified by UL and checked during manufacturing. The bonding conductor run within the armor of the cable assembly is required by the UL standard.

Because the function of the bonding conductor in Type AC cable is simply to short adjacent turns of the spiral-wrapped armor, there is no need to make any connection of the bonding conductor at cable ends in enclosures or equipment. The conductor may simply be cut off at the armor end.

Construction of armored cable must permit ready insertion of an insulating bushing or equivalent protection between the conductors and the armor at each termination of the armor—such as the so-called "red head."

333-5. Conductors. UL data on conductors used within Type AC cables refer to the marking on the cable as follows:

ACT—indicates an armored cable employing conductors having thermoplastic (Type T) insulation.

AC—indicates an armored cable employing conductors having rubber insulation of the code grade.

ACH—indicates an armored cable employing conductors having rubber insulation of the heat-resistant (75 C) grade.

ACHH—indicates an armored cable employing conductors having rubber insulation of the heat-resistant (90 C) grade.

ACU—indicates an armored cable employing conductors having rubber insulation of the latex grade.

L—used as a suffix indicates that a lead covering has been applied over the conductor assembly.

333-6. Use. Type AC armored cable is familiarly used in all types of electrical systems for power and light branch circuits and feeders. Figure 333-2 shows use of three runs of 12/2 BX for the supply and two switch legs to a combination light-heat-fan unit in a bathroom. One 12/2 is the supply and the other cables control the appliance as shown in the wiring

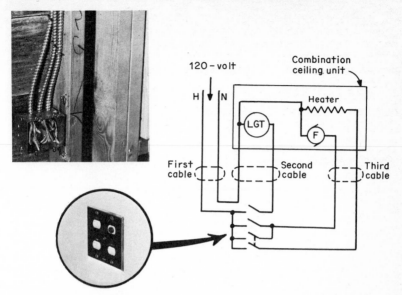

Fig. 333-2. Cable runs of 12/2 BX are used at junction box (above) which was then equipped with switches and pilot light (right) for light-heat-fan unit. Use of two 12/2 cables, with neutral in only one cable, is a violation of the concept covered in Sec. 300-20. A 12/4 cable could serve for all switch legs and satisfy the Code rule. (Sec. 333-6.)

diagram. But the use of two 12/2 cables for the switch legs violates Sec. 300-20 because the neutral is not kept with all the conductors it serves. As a result, induction heating could be produced.

Type AC is also used for signal and control circuit work. It is particularly effective for running loudspeaker circuits in public address systems and other sound systems where the flexibility of the cable lends itself to ready installation on new construction or rewiring jobs and the armor provides much needed mechanical protection. Armored cable is also especially effective for wiring Class 2 control circuits—such as low-voltage relay switching circuits—where mechanical protection for the conductors and flexibility of installation are required.

For use where Type AC cable is exposed to weather or continuous moisture, for underground runs in raceways and embedded in masonry, concrete, or fill in buildings in course of construction or where exposed to oil, gasoline, or other deteriorating agents, the conductor assembly within the armor must be protected by a lead covering—that is, the cable must be Type ACL. BUT NOTE that the last sentence of this section PROHIBITS use of *any* Type AC cable, even Type ACL, directly buried in the earth.

The Exception in this section covers use of Type AC cable in hazardous locations. Type AC cable may be used for wiring of intrinsically safe equipment, such as instruments or signals in which the electric circuit is not capable of releasing enough energy under any fault condition to cause ignition of the hazardous atmosphere (Fig. 333-3). This same

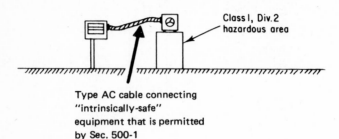

Fig. 333-3. Exception recognizes BX cable for limited use in hazardous locations. (Sec. 333-6.)

permission is also given for Type NM cable, Type NMC cable, Type UF cable, rigid nonmetallic conduit, surface raceways, multioutlet assembly, underfloor raceways, cellular metal floor raceways, and wireways in their respective articles.

333-7. Supports. Armored cable must be secured by approved staples, straps, or similar fittings, as shown in Fig. 333-4.

In exposed work, both as a precaution against physical damage and to ensure a workmanlike appearance, fastenings should be spaced not more than 24 to 30 in. apart. In concealed work in new buildings, the cable must be supported at intervals of not over 4½ ft for Type AC to keep it out of the way of possible injury by mechanics of other trades. In either exposed work or concealed work, the cable should be securely fastened in place within 1 ft of each outlet box or fitting so that there will be no tendency for the cable to pull away from the box connector.

Although Sec. 410-67(c) and Sec. 350-4, Exception No. 3, recognize a 4 to 6 ft length of flexible metal conduit to be used without any clamp or staple where a recessed lighting fixture is fed from a circuit outlet box, Exception No. 2 of Sec. 333-7 limits Type AC cable to not over a 2-ft unclamped length for flexibility where such a cable feeds a lighting fixture or connects to any enclosure or equipment. Section 350-4, Exception No. 2, and Sec. 351-8, Exception No. 2, recognize flexible metal conduit and liquidtight flexible metal conduit for an unsecured length of up to 3 ft at any termination where flexibility is needed. But that does not apply to Type AC (BX) cable (Fig. 333-5). Refer to Secs. 350-4 and 351-8.

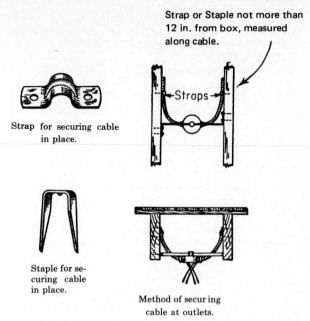

Strap or Staple not more than
12 in. from box, measured
along cable.

←Straps→

Strap for securing cable
in place.

Staple for se-
curing cable
in place.

Method of securing
cable at outlets.

Fig. 333-4. BX must be clamped every 4½ ft and within 12 in. of terminations. (Sec. 333-7.)

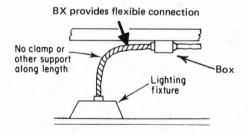

BX provides flexible connection

No clamp or
other support
along length

Box

Lighting
fixture

NOTE: Greenfield could be up to 6 ft
without clamps and liquid tight could
be up to 3 ft without clamps

Fig. 333-5. Unsecured length of BX is limited to 2 ft at terminals. (Sec. 333-7.)

Fig. 333-6. Connectors for BX entering a panelboard cabinet or other enclosure must use approved fittings—some type of single connector or duplex type (as shown, with two cables terminated at each connector through a single KO). (Sec. 333-9.)

Note that the requirements on clamping or securing of BX and flexible metal conduits must be observed for applications in suspended ceiling spaces, whether for air handling, as covered in Sec. 300-22(c), or nonair handling.

333-9. Boxes and Fittings.   Note that a termination fitting—that is, a box connector—must be used at every end of Type AC cable entering an enclosure or a box (Fig. 333-6) unless the box has an approved built-in clamp to hold the cable armor, provide for the bonding of the armor to the metal box, and protect the wires in the cable from abrasion.

A standard type of box connector for securing the cable to knockouts or other openings in outlet boxes and cabinets is shown in Fig. 333-7. A fiber bushing, as shown, must be inserted between the armor and the conductors. The fiber bushing, which can be seen through slots in the connector after installation, prevents the sharp edges of the armor from cutting into the insulation on the conductors and so grounding the copper wire.

The box shown in Fig. 333-8 is equipped with clamps to secure Type AC cables, making it unnecessary to use separate box connectors. The

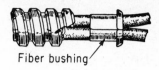

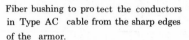

Fiber bushing

Fiber bushing to protect the conductors   Box connector for Type
in Type AC cable from the sharp edges   AC cable.
of the armor.

Fig. 333-7. Every BX termination must be equipped with a protective
bushing and a box connector or clamp built into the box. (Sec. 333-9.)

other box shown is similar but has the cable clamps outside, thus permitting one more conductor in the box. See Sec. 370-6(a) (1).

Note that a box—not a fitting, such as a "C" conduit body—must be
used where Type AC cable is connected to another wiring method.
Figure 333-9 shows a typical violation of this requirement.

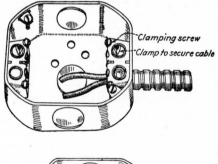

Clamping screw
Clamp to secure cable

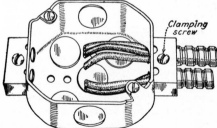

Clamping
screw

Fig. 333-8. A box connector fitting is not required if
box includes cable clamps for Type AC cable. (Sec.
333-9.)

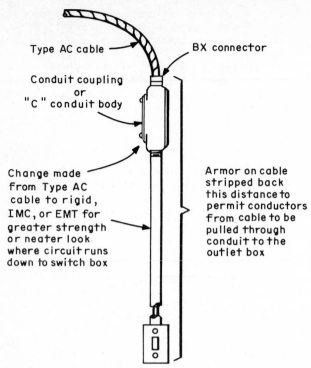

Type AC cable

BX connector

Conduit coupling
or
"C" conduit body

Change made
from Type AC
cable to rigid,
IMC, or EMT for
greater strength
or neater look
where circuit runs
down to switch box

Armor on cable
stripped back
this distance to
permit conductors
from cable to be
pulled through
conduit to the
outlet box

Fig. 333-9. This is a violation because there is no box at the required junction point. (Sec. 333-9.)

333-11. Exposed Work. ~~Exception No. 1 refers to a length not over 24~~ in. to a lighting fixture, a motor, or a range where some flexibility is necessary, as noted in Sec. 333-7.

ARTICLE 334. METAL-CLAD CABLE

334-1. Definition. This article covers "Metal-Clad Cable," as listed by UL under that heading in the *Electrical Construction Materials Directory* (the green book). This section defines this type of cable assemblies covered by this article (Fig. 334-1). The definition for metal-clad cable—"a factory assembly of one or more conductors, each individually insulated and enclosed in a metallic sheath of interlocking tape, or a smooth or corrugated tube"—also covers Type ALS and Type CS cables. Both of these cables had articles of their own in the 1975 Code, but now all metal-clad

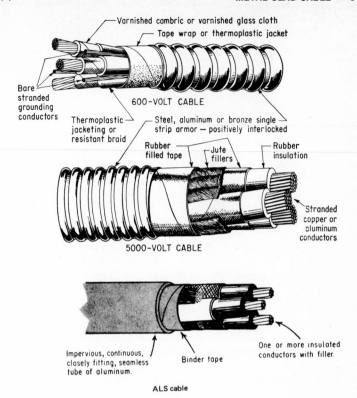

Fig. 334-1. These are some of the constructions in which Type MC cable is available. (Sec. 334-1.)

cables—Type MC, Type ALS, and Type CS—are covered in the single Art. 334.

Aluminum-sheathed (ALS) cable has insulated conductors with color-coded coverings, cable fillers, and overall wrap of mylar tape—all in an impervious, continuous, closely fitting, seamless tube of aluminum. It may be used for both exposed and concealed work in dry or wet locations, with approved fittings. CS cable is very similar with a copper exterior sheath, instead of aluminum.

Because the rules of these three cable types have been compiled into a single article, use of any one of the Type MC cables must be evaluated against the specific rules that now generally apply to all such cables. The Code no longer contains the designations Type ALS and Type CS. They are included now along with interlocked armored cable as Type MC cables.

One type of Type MC cable that has been used for many years under the name "interlocked-armor cable" is the heavy-duty, industrial feeder type of armored cable that is similar in appearance to but really different from standard BX armored cable, as covered in Art. 333. MC cable is a different, heavier-duty assembly than BX (Type AC), and great care must be taken to carefully distinguish between the design and installation regulations that apply to each of the cable types. This is particularly important now that the NE Code recognizes Type MC cable in the size range from No. 14 and larger. Now, because both cable assemblies are available in sizes No. 14 up to No. 1, armored cable must be carefully distinguished as either Type AC or Type MC. As clearly shown in NE Code Art. 334, Code rules are different for the two types of cable. And so are UL regulations as indicated in the green book. Always check the label on the cable.

Type MC is rated by UL for use up to 5,000 V, although cable for use up to 15,000 V has been available and used for many years. Type MC cable is recognized in three basic armor designs: (1) interlocked metal tape, (2) corrugated tube, and (3) smooth metallic sheath.

334-3. Uses Permitted.   Although this section clearly lists all the permitted applications of any of the various forms of Type MC cable, care must be taken to distinguish between the different constructions, based on the Code rules (Fig. 334-2). For a long time, the interlocked-armor Type MC and the corrugated sheath Type MC have been designated by UL as "intended for aboveground use." But part (5) of this section recognizes Type MC cable as suitable for direct burial in the earth. From the 1975 and previous NEC editions, the ALS (aluminum-sheathed cable) form of Type MC was recognized for direct burial "where protected by materials suitable for the condition." Now, a similar phrase is used for the Exception to Sec. 334-4, which warns against direct burial of Type MC cable. The fine distinction between acceptable and unacceptable use of directly buried Type MC cable will generally require discussion with local inspection authorities to assure clear understanding of the contrasting phrases in Sec. 334-3 and Sec. 334-4.

334-4. Uses Not Permitted.   Aluminum-sheathed cable (Type ALS) and the other Type MC cables are permitted by Sec. 334-3 to be used exposed or concealed in dry or wet locations. But such cable must not be subjected to destructive, corrosive conditions—such as direct burial in the earth, in concrete, or exposed to cinder fills, strong chlorides, caustic alkalis, or vapors of chlorine or of hydrochloric acids, unless protected by materials suitable for the condition. But the Exception to this section says that Type MC cable may be used for underground runs where suitably protected against physical damage and corrosive conditions. The UL listing for ALS cable presents related data on use of the cable, indicating that listed PVC jacketed-type ALS cable is inherently resistant to certain corrosive atmospheres and will withstand vapors or mist of caustic pickling acids,

Fig. 334-2. ALS (aluminum sheathed) Type MC cable was used for extensive power and light wiring in refrigerated rooms and storage areas of a store. The ALS was surface-mounted (exposed) on clamps in this damp location. Because the cable assembly is a tight grouping of conductors within the sheath, there would be no passage of warm air from adjacent nonrefrigerated areas through the cable which crosses the boundaries between the areas. It was therefore not necessary to seal the cables to satisfy Sec. 300-7(a). (Sec. 334-3.)

plating baths, and hydrofluoric and chromic acids. Unless indicated otherwise in an individual cable listing, PVC jacketed ALS cable has not been investigated for embedment or direct burial in concrete. One of the ALS cables listed in the green book carries the note: "When an overall PVC sheath is employed, the cable may be embedded directly in concrete."

334-10. Installation.   Figure 334-3 shows the maximum permitted spacing of supports for any Type MC cable. The interlocked-armor Type MC has commonly been used on cable tray, as permitted in part **(b)** of this section (Fig. 334-4).

334-11. Bending Radius.   Figure 334-5 shows the bending radius rules for ALS or CS cable, the "smooth sheath" Type MC cables.

334-12. Fittings.   Only approved, UL-listed connectors and fittings are permitted to be used with any Type MC cable. Figure 334-6 shows a connector for terminating ALS cable to connect to a box or enclosure.

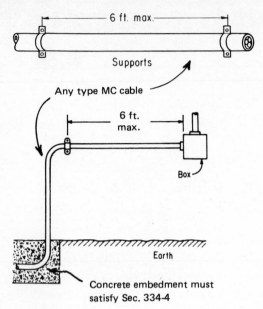

Fig. 334-3. Surface mounting of Type MC cable must be secured. (Sec. 334-10.)

Such fittings are listed in the UL green book under "Metal-Clad Cable Connectors." Figure 334-7 shows typical approved connectors for inter-locked-armor Type MC cable. As shown at left, 600-V terminations for interlocked-armor cable to switchgear or other enclosures in dry locations can be made with connectors, a locknut, and a bushing in the typical basic assembly shown. In damp locations, compound-filled or other protective terminations may be desired. High-voltage connectors (5 and 15 kV) are generally filled with sealing compound and individual conductors termi-nated in a suitable manner, depending upon whether the conductors are shielded or not. Or the IA cable may terminate in a pothead for positively sealed and insulated terminations indoors or outdoors.

ARTICLE 336. NONMETALLIC-SHEATHED
CABLE

Refer to Sec. 310-2 of this handbook for a discussion on the use of only insulated conductors as circuit conductors and the prohibition on using the bare grounding conductor in NM cable as both a neutral and

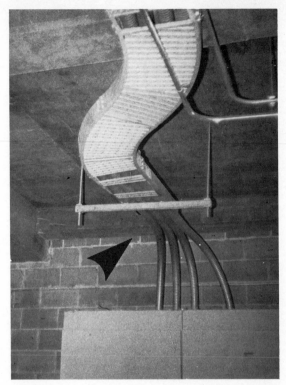

Fig. 334-4. Any Type MC cable is recognized for use in cable tray, and the interlocked-armor version has been widely used in tray, as shown here. But the tray *must* be connected to the enclosure in which the cables terminate. See Sec. 318-5 and 318-6. (Sec. 334-10.)

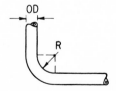

Bends: Radius (R) shall not be
         less than:
(a) 10 times O D for cables
      with O D ¾ in. or less.
(b) 12 times O D for cables
      with O D over ¾ in but
      not over 1½ in.
(c) 15 times O D for cables
      with O D over 1½ in.

Fig. 334-5. Minimum radius values prevent excessively sharp, destructive bending of ALS or CS cable. (Sec. 334-11.)

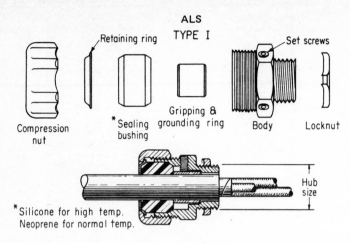

ALS
TYPE I

Retaining ring

Set screws

Compression nut

*Sealing bushing

Gripping & grounding ring

Body

Locknut

Hub size

*Silicone for high temp.
Neoprene for normal temp.

All parts aluminum except bushing & stainless steel set screws

ALS
TYPE II

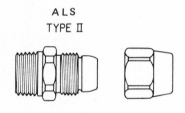

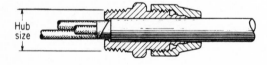

Hub size

Material: aluminum

Fig. 334-6. ALS cable and other Type MC cables must be used with approved fittings. (Sec. 334-12.)

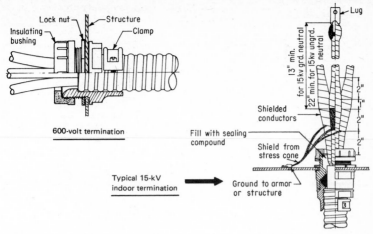

Fig. 334-7. Terminations for interlocked-armor cables must be approved devices, correctly installed. (Sec. 334-12.)

equipment grounding conductor for a circuit to a cooking appliance (Sec. 250-60).

336-1. Definition. Nonmetallic-sheathed cable is one of the most widely used cables for branch circuits and feeders in residential and commercial systems (Fig. 336-1). Such cable is commonly and generally called "Romex" by electrical construction people, even though the word *Romex* is a registered trade name of the General Cable Corp. Industry usage has made the trade name a generic title so that nonmetallic-sheathed cable made by any manufacturer might be called Romex. This generic usage of a trade name also applies to the term *BX*, which is commonly used to describe any standard armored cable, made by any manufacturer—even though the term *BX* is a registered trade name of General Electric Co. Type NM cable has an overall covering of fibrous or plastic material which is flame-retardant and moisture-resistant. Type NMC is similar but the overall covering is also fungus-resistant and corrosion-resistant. The letter "C" indicates that it is corrosion-resistant.

This type of wiring may be used either for exposed or for concealed wiring (Fig. 336-2). It may be regarded as a substitute for concealed knob-and-tube work and open wiring on insulators, and has the advantages that continuous protection is provided over the entire length of the conductor in addition to the insulation applied to ordinary rubber-covered or thermoplastic wire, and, as in the case of armored cable, no insulating supports are required and only one hole need be bored where the cable passes through a timber. Insulating bushings or grommets must

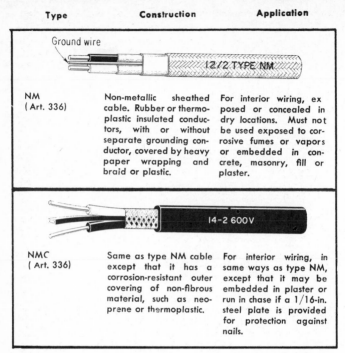

Type	Construction	Application

NM
(Art. 336)

Non-metallic sheathed cable. Rubber or thermoplastic insulated conductors, with or without separate grounding conductor, covered by heavy paper wrapping and braid or plastic.

For interior wiring, exposed or concealed in dry locations. Must not be used exposed to corrosive fumes or vapors or embedded in concrete, masonry, fill or plaster.

NMC
(Art. 336)

Same as type NM cable except that it has a corrosion-resistant outer covering of non-fibrous material, such as neoprene or thermoplastic.

For interior wiring, in same ways as type NM, except that it may be embedded in plaster or run in chase if a 1/16-in. steel plate is provided for protection against nails.

Fig. 336-1. There are two separate types of nonmetallic-sheathed cable. (Sec. 336-1.)

be used where the cable passes through holes in metal studs or similar members.

336-2. Construction. The second paragraph requires that NM and NMC cables must always have their conductors applied at the ampacity of Type TW wire—that is, the 60°C ampacity from Table 310-16.

336-3. Uses Permitted or Not Permitted. The first sentence of this section limits use of Type NM and Type NMC cables to any building that does not have more than three floors above grade (Fig. 336-3).

Because the Code rule limiting use of Types NM and NMC cables to buildings not exceeding three floors above grade produced difficulties in interpretation, a clarification on this matter was added. The problem arises when buildings are built on hillsides or sloping grades, where the building will have three floors above grade on the uphill side and four floors above grade on the downhill side. The question then is: Is this a three-story building or a four-story building, and is use of Type NM cable permitted?

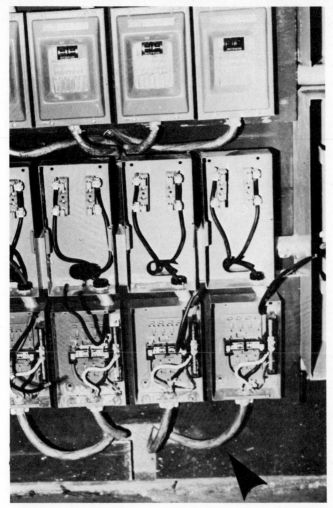

Fig. 336-2. Although NM cable is most widely used for branch circuits, the larger sizes (No. 8 and up) are commonly used for feeders, as run here from apartment disconnects to tenant panelboards. (Sec. 336-1.)

In an effort to clarify the issue, Sec. 336-3 defines the first floor of a building and attempts to establish a basis for applying the Code rule. Whether or not a particular building will be considered as a three-story building or a four-story building when installed on sloping grade depends upon the definition given for the first floor of a building. The

Type NM or type NMC may be used in any building with not more than 3 floors above grade.

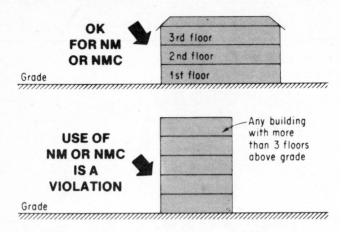

OK FOR NM OR NMC

Grade

3rd floor
2nd floor
1st floor

USE OF NM OR NMC IS A VIOLATION

Any building with more than 3 floors above grade

Grade

Note: NM or NMC may not be used at all in this building — not even on the first three floors.

Fig. 336-3. Nonmetallic-sheathed cable is limited in application. (Sec. 336-3.)

Code spells out that the first floor shall be "that floor designed for human habitation which is level with or above finished grade of the exterior wall line of 50 percent or more of its perimeter." As shown in Fig. 336-4, this determination can readily be made based on the actual ground conditions as the grade changes alongside the building.

As shown, if the bottom floor has anything over 50 percent of its floor line level with or above adjacent finished grade, then the bottom floor is the first floor. If that bottom floor is the first floor in a building with four stories or four floors, then the building is a four-story building and use of Type NM or Type NMC cable is prohibited. But as can be seen in Fig. 336-5, a bulldozer or backhoe could be used to alter the actual steepness of the grade to create the required conditions that would exclude the bottom floor as the first floor of the building and would thereby permit use of nonmetallic-sheathed cable. Application of this rule in the field remains for determination by local electrical inspectors.

Where NM cable is limited to use in "normally dry locations," NMC— the corrosion-resistant type—is permitted in "dry, damp, moist, or corrosive locations." Because it has been widely used in barns and other animals' quarters where the atmosphere is damp and corrosive (due to animal vapors), NMC cable is sometimes referred to as "barn wiring."

Where temperatures of 0°F or below are frequently experienced during the winter, the ordinary types of nonmetallic-sheathed cable, where

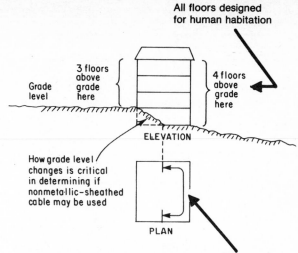

All floors designed
for human habitation

Grade
level

3 floors
above
grade
here

ELEVATION

4 floors
above
grade
here

How grade level
changes is critical
in determining if
nonmetallic-sheathed
cable may be used

PLAN

More than 50% of the perimeter of bottom floor of
building is level with or above adjacent finished grade—
THEREFORE
the **bottom** floor is the "first floor" and the building has
more than "three floors above grade."

**CONCLUSION: Both Type NM cable and Type NMC cable
are excluded from use in this building.**

Fig. 336-4. Definition of "first floor" clarifies use of NM cable in
buildings "not exceeding three floors above grade." (Sec. 336-3.)

BUT, if the grade change is like this . . .

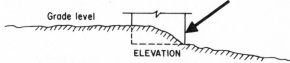

Grade level

ELEVATION

. . .**Less than 50%** of the bottom floor perimeter is level
with finished grade; and the bottom floor is, by definition, not
the first floor. The building, then, has only **three** floors above
grade. Therefore, Type NM cable and/or Type NMC cable
are acceptable for use in this building.

Fig. 336-5. Contour of grade can be altered to permit use of NM
cable. (Sec. 336-3.)

installed in dairy barns and similar farm buildings, have in some cases deteriorated rapidly, because of the growth of fungus or mold. Type NMC cable has proved very helpful in these locations.

NM cable may not be embedded in masonry as noted. In the second paragraph of Sec. 336-3(a), the word "adobe" was added to prohibit the use of nonmetallic-sheathed cable embedded in the chases in adobe brick, a material commonly used in the southwest part of the United States. Adobe is a sun-dried brick material used for building construction. Because it is brittle and because boxes embedded in it tend to become loose, the use of nonmetallic-sheathed cable offers no support for such boxes. As a result, this prohibits the cable from being run in the adobe or in the chases between the adobe bricks.

Although the second paragraph of part **(a)** prohibits NM cable embedded in plaster or other construction materials and prohibits it run in chases between bricks, stones, etc., part **(b)** of this section does *not* prohibit use of NMC cable for plaster embedment or in chases. The 1971 **NEC** had another sentence to the rule shown in part **(b)** and it allowed use of NMC as follows:

> Where embedded in plaster or run in a shallow chase in masonry walls and covered with plaster within 2 inches of the finished surface, it [NMC cable] shall be protected against damage from nails by a cover of corrosion-resistant coated steel at least ¹⁄₁₆ inch in thickness and ¾ inch wide in the chase or under the final surface finish.

That sentence permitted use of NMC (but not NM) under plaster, as shown in Fig. 336-6; however it was removed from Sec. 336-3(b) in the 1975 **NEC** and does not appear in the 1978 **NEC**. Omission of that sentence raises the question: Is NMC permitted to be embedded in plaster as covered by the old rule described?

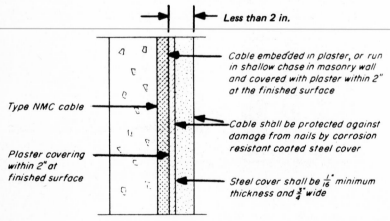

Fig. 336-6. This was permitted by previous Codes and may still be acceptable. (Sec. 335-3.)

There is no definite answer to that question and the matter must be decided by the local inspector having jurisdiction. No data were made available to explain deletion of the old Code rule described. Because the present NEC rule prohibits NM embedded in plaster, but does not prohibit NMC in plaster, it can be argued that such use of NMC is Code-acceptable. But it would be necessary to protect the cable against the possibility of being damaged by driven nails—such as nails used to hang pictures or add construction elements on the wall. Sufficient protection against nail puncture of the cable is provided by a cover of corrosion-resistant coated steel of at least $^1/_{16}$ in. thickness and $^3/_4$ in. width. Such metal protection must be run for the entire length of the cable where it is less than 2 in. below the finished surface. The metal strip protection may be run in the chase or under the plaster finish. But, it must be carefully noted that both NM and NMC are prohibited by Sec. 336-3(c)(8) from embedment in cement, concrete, or aggregate—which is distinguished from plaster.

336-5. Supports.   Figure 336-7 shows support requirements for NM or NMC cable. Figure 336-8 shows a violation. In concealed work the cable should if possible be so installed that it will be out of reach of nails. Care should be taken to avoid wherever possible the parts of a wall where the trim will be nailed in place, e.g., door and window casings, baseboards, and picture moldings. See Sec. 300-4.

Fig. 336-7. NM or NMC cables must be stapled every 4½ ft where attached to the surfaces of studs, joints, and other wood structrual members. It is not necessary to use staples or straps on runs that are supported by the drilled holes through which the cable is pulled. But there must be a staple within 12 in. of every box or enclosure in which the cable terminates. (Sec. 336-5.)

Fig. 336-8. Absence of stapling of the NM cables within 12 in. of entry into the panelboards is a clear violation of Sec. 336-5. (Sec. 336-5.)

Connectors listed for use with Type NM or NMC cable (nonmetallic-sheathed cable) are also suitable for use with flexible cord or service-entrance cable *if* such additional use is indicated on the device or carton. Connectors listed under the classifications "Armored Cable Connectors" and "Conduit Fittings" may be used with nonmetallic-sheathed cable when that is specifically indicated on the device or carton. Connectors for NM or NMC cable are also suitable for use on Type UF cable (underground feeder and branch-circuit cable— NE Code Art. 339) in dry locations, unless otherwise indicated on the carton. Each connector covered in the listing is recognized for connecting only one cable or cord— unless it is a duplex connector for connecting two cables or if the carton is marked to indicate use with more than one cable or cord.

336-6. Exposed Work—General. Figure 336-9 shows the details described in parts **(a)** and **(b)** of this section. The rules of this section tie

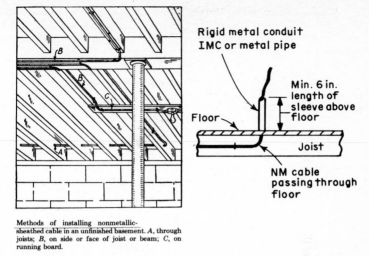

Rigid metal conduit
IMC or metal pipe

Min. 6 in.
length of
sleeve above
floor

Floor

Joist

NM cable
passing through
floor

Methods of installing nonmetallic-sheathed cable in an unfinished basement. *A*, through joists; *B*, on side or face of joist or beam; *C*, on running board.

Fig. 336-9. This applies to unfinished basements and other exposed applications. (Sec. 336-6.)

into the rules of Sec. 336-8, covering use in unfinished basements, which are really places of "exposed work."

336-8. In Unfinished Basements. Cables containing No. 14, No. 12, or No. 10 conductors must be run through holes drilled through joists. When running parallel to joists, any cable must be stapled to the wide, vertical face of a joist and never to the bottom edge. But, as shown in Fig. 336-10, larger cables may be attached to the bottom of joists when run at an angle to the joists.

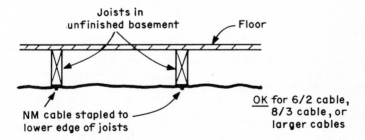

Joists in
unfinished basement

Floor

NM cable stapled to
lower edge of joists

OK for 6/2 cable,
8/3 cable, or
larger cables

Note: Method shown is a VIOLATION for cables
containing Nos. 14, 12, or 10 conductors

Fig. 336-10. Only large cables may be stapled to bottom edge of floor joists. (Sec. 336-8.)

336-11. Devices of Insulating Material.   Note this use of switch and outlet devices without boxes is limited to exposed cable systems and for rewiring in existing buildings. This reference must not be confused with that of Exception No. 2 in Sec. 336-5, which refers to approved wiring devices that incorporate their own wiring boxes, so they are devices "without a *separate* outlet box" and not devices "without boxes."

336-12. Boxes of Insulating Material.   By using nonmetallic outlet and switch boxes a completely "nonmetallic" wiring system is provided. Such a system has economic advantage and other advantages in locations where corrosive vapors are present. See Sec. 370-5.

ARTICLE 337. SHIELDED NONMETALLIC-SHEATHED CABLE

337-1. Definition.   This article recognizes shielded nonmetallic-sheathed cable as a wiring method, basically intended for use in continuous rigid cable supports, or in raceways, in Class I, Division 2 and Class II, Division 2 hazardous locations. Type SNM cable features an overlapping spiral metal tape and wire shield with an outer nonmetallic jacket. Figure 337-1 shows a cutaway view of a typical Type SNM cable.

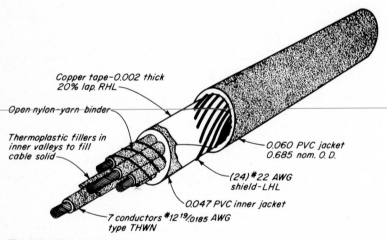

Copper tape—0.002 thick 20% lap. RHL

Open nylon-yarn binder

Thermoplastic fillers in inner valleys to fill cable solid

0.060 PVC jacket 0.685 nom. O. D.

(24) #22 AWG shield—LHL

0.047 PVC inner jacket

7 conductors #12 ¹⁹/.0185 AWG type THWN

Fig. 337-1. Type SNM cable is rugged assembly for industrial-type branch circuits and feeders. (Sec. 337-1.)

337-6. Fittings.   Only fittings approved for use with Type SNM cable may be used. Figure 337-2 shows an approved fitting for use where Type SNM cable enters ¾-in. rigid-metal conduit in Classes I and II, Division 2 hazardous locations.

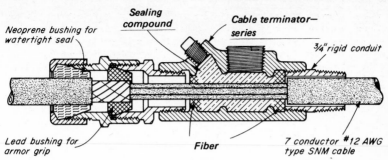

Fig. 337-2. Design of fitting assures effective application of SNM cable with conduit in hazardous areas. (Sec. 337-6.)

ARTICLE 338. SERVICE-ENTRANCE CABLE

338-1. Definition.   The Code contains no specifications for the construction of this cable; it is left to Underwriters Laboratories Inc., to determine what types of cable should be approved for this purpose. The types listed by the Laboratories at the present time conform to the following data:

Service Entrance Cable is labeled in sizes No. 12 AWG and larger for copper, and No. 10 AWG and larger for aluminum or copper-clad aluminum, with Types RH, RHW, RHH or XHHW conductors. If the type designation for the conductors is marked on the outside surface of the cable, the temperature rating of the cable corresponds to the rating of the individual conductors. When this marking does not appear, the temperature rating of the cable is 75°C.

The cables are classified as follows:

Type SE—Cable for aboveground installation.

Type USE—Cable for underground installation including burial directly in the earth. Cable in sizes No. 4/0 AWG and smaller and having all conductors insulated is suitable for all of the underground uses for which Type UF cable is permitted by the NEC.

Many single-conductor cables are dual-rated (Type USE or RHW or RHH) and may be used in raceways, for either service conductors or for feeders and branch circuits.

Cable having rubber insulation on each conductor is designed for use on circuits having a maximum voltage of 600. Cable having one uninsulated conductor is designed for use on circuits having a maximum voltage to ground of 300.

Based upon tests which have been made involving the maximum heating that can be produced, an uninsulated conductor employed in a service cable assembly is considered to have the same current-carrying capacity as the insulated conductors even though it may be smaller in size.

Figure 338-1 shows two basic styles of service-entrance cable for aboveground use. The one without an armor over the conductors is referred to as "Type SE Style U"—the letter "U" standing for "unarmored." That cable is sometimes designated as "Type SEU." The cable assembly with

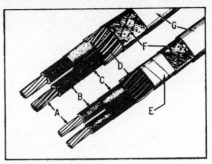

SERVICE ENTRANCE cables may consist of either copper or aluminum phase conductors (A) covered by heat resistant insulation (B) and moisture-resistant braid or tape (C) color coded for circuit identification, while basic assembly is enclosed by concentric neutral (D). Unarmored Type SE Style U is covered by variety of tapes (F) and outer braid (G) such as glass and cotton impregnated with moisture resistant and flame retardant finish labelled with pertinent data. Armored Style A additionally contains flat steel armor (E) as protection against physical abuse.

Fig. 338-1. Two types of aboveground SE cable. (Sec. 338-1.)

the armor is designated "Type ASE" cable, with the "A" standing for "armored."

Figure 338-2 shows another type of SE cable, known as "Style SER"— the letter "R" standing for "round." In a typical assembly of that cable, three conductors insulated with Type XHHW cross link polyethylene are cabled together with fillers and one bare ground conductor with a tape over them and gray PVC overall jacket. For use aboveground in build-

Each phase leg is an insulated conductor

Neutral is a bare stranded conductor

Fig. 338-2. Style SER cable contains individual conductors and no concentric neutral. (Sec. 338-1.)

ings, it is suitable for operation at 90°C in dry locations or 75°C in wet locations.

The three insulated conductors—a black, a red, and a blue—are used as the phase legs of the service and the bare conductor is used as the neutral.

Figure 338-3 shows Type USE cable for underground (including direct earth burial) applications of service or other circuits. Type USE

Fig. 338-3. Type USE cable may be multiconductor or single conductor cable. (Sec. 338-1.)

may consist of one, two, or three conductors, Type RHW insulated wire with neoprene jacket suitable for operation in wet or dry locations at a maximum temperature of 75°C. It is for underground service entrance for direct earth burial, conduit, duct, or aerial applications.

Depending upon whether USE cable is used for service entrance, for a feeder, or for a branch circuit, burial depth must conform to Sec. 300-5 and its many specific rules on direct burial cable.

338-3. Uses Permitted as Branch Circuits or Feeders. Part (a) recognizes use of service-entrance cable for branch circuits and feeders within buildings or structures provided that all circuit conductors, including the neutral of the circuit, are insulated. Such use must conform to Art. 336 on installation methods—the same as those for Type NM cable. See Sec. 338-4(b).

Part (b) covers permitted uses of service-entrance cable that contains a bare conductor for the neutral but limits such application to 120/240-V or 120/208-V systems. When a SE cable has an outer nonmetallic covering over the enclosed bare neutral, this Code rule permits the use of SE cable for circuits supplying ranges, wall-mounted ovens, and counter-mounted cooking units (Fig. 338-4). And in such cases, the bare conductor may be used as the neutral of the branch circuit as well as the equipment grounding conductor (see Sec. 250-60). However, price differences between SE cable and NM cable generally determine that SE cable will probably be used only where part of a circuit run is outdoors, or where 75°C supply conductors must be used to connect appliances. SE cables, in sizes 8/3 and smaller, generally cost more than corresponding sizes of NM cables. And even though 6/2, 8/1 SE cable costs slightly less than 6/3 NM cable, additional labor costs usually more than offset the total installation cost in favor of the 6/3 NM cable.

SE cable is also permitted to be used as a feeder from one building to another building, with the bare conductor used as a grounded neutral.

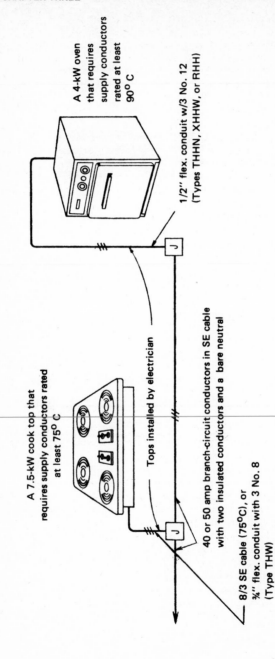

A 4-kW oven that requires supply conductors rated at least 90° C

1/2″ flex. conduit w/3 No. 12 (Types THHN, XHHW, or RHH)

A 7.5-kW cook top that requires supply conductors rated at least 75° C

Tops installed by electrician

40 or 50 amp branch-circuit conductors in SE cable with two insulated conductors and a bare neutral

8/3 SE cable (75°C), or ¾″ flex. conduit with 3 No. 8 (Type THW)

Fig. 338-4. SE Cable with bare neutral may be used for branch circuit to range or other cooking units. (Sec. 338-3.)

Or an SE cable with a bare neutral may be used as a feeder within a building, if the bare neutral is used *only* as the equipment grounding conductor and one of the insulated conductors within the cable is used as the neutral of the feeder. See Fig. 338-5.

Part **(c)** requires that SE cable used to supply appliances not be subject to conductor temperatures in excess of the temperature specified for the insulation involved. The insulated conductors of SE cables are either 60°C or 75°C, and if they are rated at 75°C, such marking will appear on the outer sheath. A cooking unit or oven that requires 75°C supply conductors would be an application for the use of SE cables, rated at 75°C. However, a review of UL listings for cooking units and ovens indicates that the vast majority of such units do not require supply conductor ratings to exceed 60°C. The details in Fig. 338-4 show a method of connecting cooking units where the supply conductors are required to be 75 or 90°C.

338-4. Installation Methods. Part **(b)** requires the "installation" of unarmored SE cable (which is the usual type of SE cable) to satisfy the "applicable provisions" of Art. 336 on nonmetallic-sheathed cable (Type NM). If the phrase "applicable provisions" is understood to mean those provisions "applicable" to installation, then Secs. 336-5, 336-6, 336-7, 336-8, 336-9, and 336-10—all of which cover *how* cable is "installed"— must be satisfied. But the wording of part **(b)** in this section has caused difficulty.

Because SE cable must be installed in accordance with Art. 336, the relation between Sec. 338-4(b) and Sec. 336-3 raises the question:

Does the 1975 NE Code permit the use of SER (Service Entrance, Round) cable for feeders in a structure more than three floors above grade?

Some inspectors have ruled that Sec. 338-4(b) ("installed in accordance with the applicable provisions of Article 336") would bring SE cable under the provision of Sec. 336-3 limiting the use of Type SER cable to structures not over three floors above grade. Others are of the opinion that Sec. 336-3 was not an applicable provision with regard to SE cable, in which case you *could* install it as a feeder in a structure with more than three floors above grade.

It does appear that Sec. 338-4(b) clearly intends to limit only the "Installation Methods" (which is the heading of that section), and requires that service cable be "installed" with supports and other installation details similar to Type NM. Section 336-3 regulates *where* nonmetallic-sheathed cables may and may not be installed and does not relate to installation methods. Because Sec. 338-3 specifically permits use of service cable for branch circuits and feeders under the limited conditions given—without any reference to Sec. 336-3 (which is the corresponding section in Art. 336 that covers "Uses Permitted or Not Permitted")—the Code clearly differentiates where each type of cable may be used. After giving permission for the uses of service cable as covered in Sec. 338-3(b)

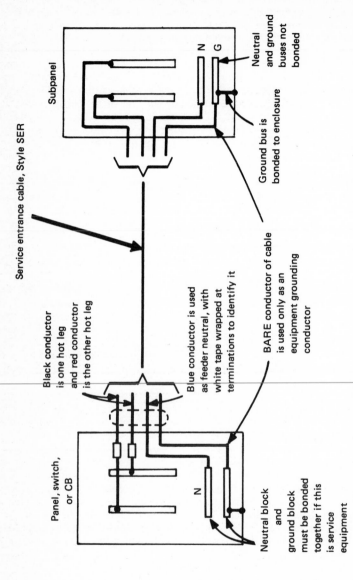

Fig. 338-5. Typical application of SE cable with a bare neutral for use as a feeder within a building. (Sec. 338-5.)

and without equating such "use" of service cable to "use" of NM and NMC, Sec. 338-4 seems simply to require the same "Installation Methods" as set forth in Secs. 336-5, 336-6, 336-7, 336-8, etc. That logic would conclude that there is no restriction on the use of Type SE cable in buildings with more than three floors above grade.

ARTICLE 339. UNDERGROUND FEEDER AND BRANCH-CIRCUIT CABLE

339-1. Description and Marking.   Figure 339-1 shows a violation of the Code rule that a bare conductor in a UF cable is for grounding purposes only.

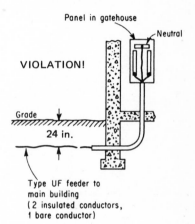

Fig. 339-1. Bare conductor in UF cable may not be used as a neutral. (Sec. 339-1.)

339-2. Other Articles.   Figures 339-2 and 339-3 show details on compliance of UF cable with Sec. 300-5. Where UF comes up out of the ground, it must be protected for 8 ft up on a pole and as described in Sec. 300-5(d).

339-3. Use.   The rules of part **(a)** are shown in Fig. 339-4 and must be correlated to the rules of Sec. 300-5 on direct burial cables. The rule of **(2)** in part **(a)** corresponds to that of Sec. 300-5(i). If multiple conductors are used per phase and neutral to make up a high current circuit, this rule requires all conductors to be run in the same trench or raceway and therefore subject to the derating factors of Note 8 to Tables 310-16/19. Refer to the paragraph right after the table in Note 8, in the NEC. Also see discussion under Sec. 300-5(i).

UF cable may be used underground, including direct burial in the earth, as feeder or branch-circuit cable when provided with overcurrent

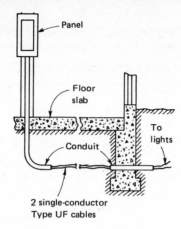

VIOLATION for cable to run under any
building if not totally in raceway
[Sec. 300-5 (c)]

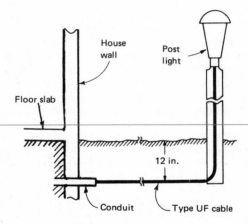

ACCEPTABLE for burial at only 12-in. depth when
used for residential branch-circuit
[Sec. 300-5(a), Ex. No. 4]

Fig. 339-2. UF cable must conform to Sec. 300-5 on
direct-burial cables. (Sec. 339-2.)

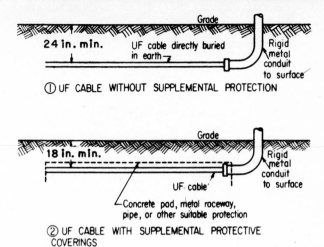

Fig. 339-3. Exception No. 1 of Sec. 300-5(a) permits a 6-in. reduction of UF burial depth. (Sec. 339-2.)

protection not in excess of the rated ampacity of the individual conductors. If single-conductor cables are installed, all cables of the feeder circuit, sub-feeder, or branch circuit, including the neutral cable, must be run together in close proximity in the same trench or raceway. It may be necessary in some installations to provide additional mechanical protection, such as a covering board, concrete pad, raceway, etc., when required by the authority enforcing the Code. Multiple-conductor Type UF cable (but not single-conductor Type UF cables) may also be used for interior wiring when used in the same way as Type NM cable, complying with the provisions of Art. 336 of the Code. And UF may be used in wet locations.

Single-conductor Type UF cable embedded in poured cement, concrete, or aggregate may be used for nonheating leads of fixed electric space heating cables, as covered in Secs. 424-43 and 426-25.

Application data of the UL are as follows:

Cables suitable for exposure to direct rays of the sun are indicated by tag marking and marking on the surface of the cable with the designation "Sunlight Resistant."

This cable may be terminated by using nonmetallic sheathed cable connectors (See Nonmetallic Sheathed Cable Connectors).

If single conductor Type UF cable is terminated with a fitting not specifically recognized for use with single conductor cable, special care should be taken to assure it is properly secured and not subject to damage.

Only multiconductor Type UF cable may be used in cable tray, in accordance with Art. 318.

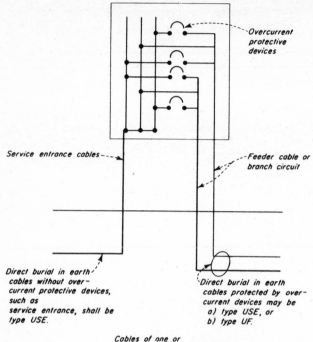

Service entrance cables

Overcurrent protective devices

Feeder cable or branch circuit

Direct burial in earth cables without over-current protective devices, such as service entrance, shall be type USE.

Direct burial in earth cables protected by over-current devices may be
a) type USE, or
b) type UF.

Cables of one or more conductors for direct burial in the earth may be type USE or type UF.

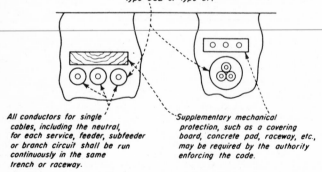

All conductors for single cables, including the neutral, for each service, feeder, subfeeder or branch circuit shall be run continuously in the same trench or raceway.

Supplementary mechanical protection, such as a covering board, concrete pad, raceway, etc., may be required by the authority enforcing the code.

Fig. 339-4. UF cable may be used only as feeders or branch circuits. (Sec. 339-3.)

ARTICLE 340. POWER AND CONTROL TRAY CABLE

340-1. Definition. This article covers the use of a nonmetallic-sheathed power and control cable, designated Type TC cable (T and C are the initials for "Tray Cable"), which may be used in cable trays, in raceways, or where supported by a messenger wire outdoors (Fig. 340-1).

Fig. 340-1. This typical 3-conductor tray cable contains bare equipment grounding conductors. (Sec. 340-1.)

340-4. Use Permitted. Type TC tray cable is limited to use in industrial establishments where maintenance and supervision assure that only competent individuals will work on the cables.

NE Code Sec. 318-2 recognizes the use of Type TC power and control tray cable installed in cable tray. Although specs on the construction and application of Type TC cable are covered in NE Code Secs. 340-1 through 340-7, great care must be used in relating those Code rules and the rules of NE Code Art. 337 to the "Power and Control Cable" listed under the heading, "Wires, Thermoplastic," in the UL green book. Type TC cable is recognized under Sec. 318-2(a) (9). The other "Power and Control Cable" is recognized under Sec. 318-2(a) (10).

UL data on "Power and Control Tray Cable" include the following:

Type TC Power and Control Tray Cable is intended for use in accordance with Article 340 of the National Electrical Code. The cable consists of two or more insulated conductors twisted together, with or without associated bare or fully insulated grounding conductors and covered with nonmetallic jacket. The cables are rated 600 volts.

Type TC cable is suitable for use in Class I, Division 2, hazardous locations, as indicated in Sec. 501-4(b) of the Natonal Electrical Code.

The cable is Listed in conductor sizes No. 18 AWG to 2,000 MCM copper or No. 12 AWG to 2,000 MCM aluminum or copper-clad aluminum.

If the type designation of the conductors is marked on the outside surface of the cable, the temperature rating of the cable corresponds to the rating of the individual conductors. When this marking does not appear, the temperature rating of the cable is 60 C unless otherwise marked on the surface of the cable.

Fittings for use with these cables are Listed by Underwriters Laboratories Inc. under the Outlet Bushings, Nonmetallic-Sheathed Cable Connectors, or Service Entrance Cable Fittings classifications.

Cables which have been investigated for use where exposed to direct rays of the sun are marked "sunlight resistant."

Cables' surface marked "Oil Resistant I" or "Oil Res I" are suitable for exposure to mineral oil at 60°C. Cables suitable for exposure to mineral oil at 75°C are surface marked "Oil Resistant II" or "Oil Res II."

UL data on the "Power and Control Cable" (covered under "Wires, Thermoplastic") include this:

Power and Control Cable—Indicates a multi-conductor cable in which the individuals are either Type TFN, TFFN, THHN or THWN conductors. The cable having two conductors is flat, or round, and the cable having three or more conductors is round. The conductors in a cable may be in any combination of sizes from 18 AWG through 500MCM inclusive, copper, and from 12 AWG through 500MCM aluminum or copper-clad aluminum. An extruded thermoplastic sheath provides the overall covering. A protective metal shield and extruded thermoplastic sheath may be applied over the covering. The cable is intended for installation in continuous rigid cable supports in accordance with Article 318 of the Natonal Electrical Code.

Note that this latter cable appears to be for cable tray only, but Type TC is recognized by Sec. 340-1 for use in raceway or with messenger support, in addition to use in tray.

340-5. Uses Not Permitted.   Although **(4)** of this section has the effect of prohibiting the use of Type TC tray cable directly buried in the earth, the rule is modified by the phrase "unless approved for the purpose." The result of this wording is to permit Type TC cable directly buried in the earth where the cable is approved for the purpose by the local electrical inspector. This permission for direct burial was added because the cable assembly was designed to withstand such application and because Type TC cable has been successfully and effectively used directly for years in many installations (Fig. 340-2 with burial conforming to Sec. 300-5).

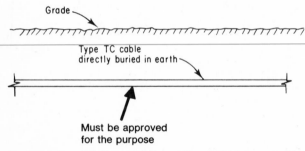

Fig. 340-2. Type TC (Power and Control Tray Cable) is recognized for direct earth burial. (Sec. 340-5.)

The proposal adding this change to the 1978 **Code** argued that such cable had been listed for direct earth burial by UL, and that the performance record has been excellent.

ARTICLE 342. NONMETALLIC EXTENSIONS

A nonmetallic extension is an assembly of two conductors without a metallic envelope, designed specially for a 15- or 20-A branch circuit as an extension from an existing outlet. Surface extensions are limited to residences and offices. Aerial extensions are limited to industrial purposes where it has been determined that the nature of the occupancy would require such wiring for connecting equipment.

ARTICLE 344. UNDERPLASTER EXTENSIONS

344-1. Use.   Such extensions are permitted in order to provide a suitable means of extending from existing outlets to new outlets without excessive expense, where there are no open spaces in walls or floors that will permit fishing from one outlet to another. In installing this work, the plaster is channeled and the conduit, cable, raceway, or tubing is secured to the concrete or tile and then plastered over.

344-2. Materials.   Note that Type NM or NMC cable is *not* one of the listed methods for making underplaster extensions. Only metal-clad wiring methods are permitted. Refer to Sec. 336-3(b), which, prior to the 1975 **NEC**, did permit Type NMC nonmetallic-sheathed cable to be used under plaster, provided it had a continuous protection of sheet steel covering if the cable was less than 2 in. behind the finish surface of the plaster.

344-5. Extension to Another Floor.   Such wiring is an expedient permitted for the purpose of avoiding an excessive amount of channeling and drilling of walls and floors. It is an expensive method, and from the standpoint of permanence, safety, and reliability the standard types of wiring are much to be preferred. For these reasons, underplaster extensions are limited to the floor within which they originate. In practice, the use of this method generally is, and should be, limited to short runs feeding not more than two or three additional outlets from one existing outlet.

ARTICLE 345. INTERMEDIATE METAL CONDUIT

This article covers a relatively new type of raceway—a conduit with wall thickness less than rigid metal conduit but greater than that of EMT. Called "IMC," this intermediate metal conduit uses the same threading method and standard fittings for rigid metal conduit and has the same general application rules as rigid metal conduit. Intermediate metal conduit actually is a lightweight rigid steel conduit which requires about 25 percent less steel than heavy-wall rigid conduit. Acceptance into the Code was based on a UL fact-finding report which showed through research and comparative tests that IMC performs as well as rigid steel conduit in many cases and surpasses rigid aluminum and EMT in most cases.

IMC may be used in any application for which rigid metal conduit is recognized by the NEC, including use in all classes and divisions of hazardous locations as covered in Secs. 501-4, 502-4, and 503-3. Its thinner wall makes it lighter and less expensive than standard rigid metal conduit, but it has physical properties that give it outstanding strength. The lighter weight facilitates handling and installation at lower labor units than rigid metal conduit. Because it has the same outside diameter as rigid metal conduit of the same trade size, it has greater interior cross-section area (Fig. 345-1). Although this extra space is not recognized by the NEC to permit the use of more conductors than can be used in the same size of rigid metal conduit, it does make wire-pulling easier.

3/4" TRADE SIZES

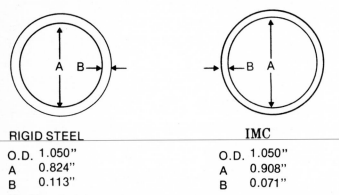

RIGID STEEL	IMC
O.D. 1.050"	O.D. 1.050"
A 0.824"	A 0.908"
B 0.113"	B 0.071"

Fig. 345-1. Typical comparison between rigid and IMC shows interior space difference. (Sec. 345-1.)

345-3. Uses Permitted. The data of the UL supplement the requirements of part **(a)** on use of IMC, as follows:

Listing of Intermediate Ferrous Metal Conduit includes standard 10 ft. lengths of straight conduit, with a coupling, special length either shorter or longer, with or without a coupling for specific applications or uses, elbows, bends, and nipples in trade sizes ½ to 4 in. incl. for installation in accordance with Article 345 of the National Electrical Code.

IMC-Type I and IMC-Type II differ only in dimensions. For threaded applications, they are interchangeable.

Fittings for use with unthreaded intermediate ferrous metal conduit are listed under conduit fittings (Guide DWTT) and are suitable only for the type of conduit indicated by the marking on the carton.

Galvanized intermediate steel conduit installed in concrete does not require supplementary corrosion protection.

Galvanized intermediate steel conduit installed in contact with soil does not generally require supplementary corrosion protection.

In the absence of specific local experience, soils producing severe corrosive effects are generally characterized by low resistivity less than 2000 ohm-centimeters.

Wherever ferrous metal conduit runs directly from concrete encasement to soil burial, severe corrosive effects are likely to occur on the metal in contact with the soil.

Although the UL refers to Type I and Type II IMC because of slight differences in dimensions due to manufacturing methods, the **NEC** considers IMC to be a single type of product and the rules of Art. 345 apply to all IMC.

Note that the wording in the UL data above includes the word "generally" in stating that IMC does not need additional protective material applied to the conduit when used in soil. That is intended to indicate that local soil conditions (acid versus alkaline) may require protection of the conduit against corrosion. And the UL note about corrosion of conduit running from concrete to soil must be observed. Refer to comments under Sec. 346-1, covering these conditions.

In part **(a)**, wording of the rule is significantly modified by the Exception, which specifically permits use of aluminum fittings and enclosures with steel intermediate metal conduit (Fig. 345-2). This same exception is

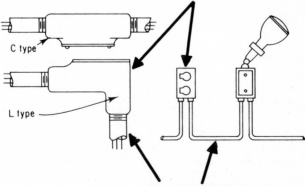

Aluminum fittings, conduit bodies, boxes . . .

C type

L type

. . . are permitted to be used with steel raceways—rigid steel conduit, IMC and EMT.

Fig. 345-2. NEC warning against use of dissimilar metals does not apply to this. (Sec. 345-3.)

also given in Art. 346 on rigid metal conduit and Art. 348 on electrical metallic tubing. Tests have established that aluminum fittings and enclosures create no difficulty when used with steel raceways. The Exception was added in the Code to counteract the implication of that phrase that cautions against use of dissimilar metals in a raceway system to guard against galvanic action. This section prohibits the use of dissimilar metals, "where practicable." This phrase is used frequently in the Code; in effect, it is saying, "You *shall* do it, if you can, or if the inspector thinks you can." By using this phrase, the Code recognizes that the contractor may not always be able to comply.

In part **(b)**, wording of the rule intends to make clear that the galvanizing or zinc coating on the IMC does give it the measure of protection required when used in concrete or when directly buried in the earth. The last phrase, "judged suitable for the condition," refers to the need to comply with UL regulations such as those contained in UL's *Electrical Construction Materials Directory,* advising how and when steel raceways and other metal raceways may be used in concrete or directly buried in earth.

The UL data point out that there are soils where some difficulties may be encountered, and there are other soil conditions that present no problem to the use of steel or other metal raceways. The phrase "judged suitable for the condition" implies that a correlation was made between the soil conditions or the concrete conditions at the place of installation and the particular raceway to be used. This means that it is up to the designers and/or installers to satisfy themselves as to the suitability of any raceway for use in concrete or for use in particular soil conditions at a given geographic location. Of course, all such determinations would have to be cleared with the electrical inspection authority to be consistent with the meaning of Code enforcement.

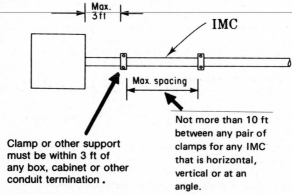

Fig. 345-3. All runs of IMC must be clamped in this way. (Sec. 345-12.)

For use of IMC in or under cinder fill, part **(c)** gives the limiting conditions. See Sec. 346-3.

345-7. Number of Conductors in Conduit. The rules on conduit fill are the same for IMC, rigid metal conduit, EMT, flexible metal conduit, flexible metallic tubing, and liquidtight flexible metallic tubing—for conduits ½ in. size and larger. Refer to Sec. 346-6.

345-12. Supports. The rule on clamping IMC is simple and straightforward (Fig. 345-3), compared with the more involved rules covered in Sec. 346-12 for rigid metal conduit.

ARTICLE 346. RIGID METAL CONDUIT

346-1. Use. UL data on rigid metal conduit are similar to that on IMC and supplement the rules of this section, as follows:

Galvanized rigid steel conduit installed in concrete does not require supplementary corrosion protection.

Galvanized rigid steel conduit installed in contact with soil does not generally require supplementary corrosion protection.

In the absence of specific local experience, soils producing severe corrosive effects are generally characterized by low resistivity less than 2000 ohm-centimeters.

Wherever ferrous metal conduit runs directly from concrete encasement to soil burial, severe corrosive effects are likely to occur on the metal in contact with the soil.

Supplementary nonmetallic coatings presently used have not been investigated for resistance to corrosion.

Supplementary nonmetallic coatings of greater than 0.010-in. thickness applied over the metallic protective coatings are investigated with respect to flame propagation and detrimental effects to the basic corrosion protection provided by the protective coatings.

For rigid aluminum conduit, the UL application notes state:

Aluminum conduit used in concrete or in contact with soil requires supplementary corrosion protection.

Supplementary nonmetallic coatings presently used have not been recognized for resistance to corrosion.

For direct earth burial of rigid conduit and IMC, the UL notes must be carefully studied and observed:

1. Galvanized rigid steel conduit and galvanized intermediate steel conduit directly buried in soil do not *generally* require supplementary corrosion protection. The use of the word "generally" in the UL instructions indicated that it is still the responsibility of the designer and/or installer to use supplementary protection where certain soils are known to produce corrosion of such conduits. Where corrosion of underground galvanized conduit is known to be a problem, a protective jacketing or a field-applied coating of asphalt paint or equivalent material must be used on the conduit.

But, UL notes on "Supplementary nonmetallic coatings" must be observed for resistance to corrosion.

2. Aluminum conduit used directly buried in soil requires supplementary corrosion protection. But again, it is completely the task and responsibility of the designer and/or installer to select an effective protection coating for the aluminum conduit, because UL says "supplementary nonmetallic coatings presently used have not been *recognized* for resistance to corrosion." That could also be interpreted as a direct prohibition on the use of aluminum conduit directly buried.

The UL notes must also be observed in all use of metal conduits in concrete, as follows:

1. Galvanized rigid steel conduit and galvanized intermediate steel conduit installed in concrete *do not require* supplementary corrosion protection. See Sec. 348-1 on EMT.

2. Aluminum conduit installed in concrete *definitely requires* supplementary corrosion protection, but the supplementary protective coatings presently used "have not been recognized for resistance to corrosion."

3. *Watch out for this!* UL warns, "Wherever ferrous metal conduit runs directly from concrete encasement to soil burial, severe corrosive effects are likely to occur on the metal in contact with the soil." Supplementary protective coating on conduit at the crossing line can eliminate the conditions shown in Fig. 346-1.

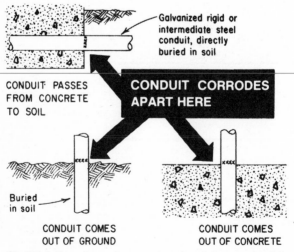

Fig. 346-1. Protective coating on section of conduit can prevent this corrosion problem. (Sec. 346-1.)

346-3. Cinder Fill.   Cinders usually contain sulfur, and if there is much moisture sulfuric acid is formed, which attacks steel conduit. A cinder fill outdoors should be considered as "subject to permanent moisture." In such a place conduit runs should be protected as described or buried in the ground at least 18 in. below the fill. This would not apply if cinders were not present.

346-6. Number of Conductors in Conduit.   The basic NE Code rule on the maximum number of conductors which may be pulled into rigid metal conduit, rigid nonmetallic conduit, intermediate metal conduit, electrical metallic tubing, flexible metal conduit, and liquidtight flexible metal conduit is contained in the single sentence of this section.

The number of conductors permitted in a particular size of conduit or tubing is covered in Chap. 9 of the Code in Tables 1 and 3 for conductors all of the same size used for either new work or rewiring. Tables 4 to 8 cover combinations of conductors of different sizes when used for new work or rewiring. For nonlead-covered conductors, three or more to a conduit, the sum of the cross-sectional areas of the individual conductors must not exceed 40 percent of the interior cross-section area (csa) of the conduit or tubing for new work or for rewiring existing conduit or tubing (Fig. 346-2). Note 3 preceding all the tables in Chap. 9, in the back of the Code book, permits a 60 percent fill of conduit nipples not over 24 in. long and no derating of ampacities is needed.

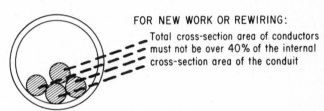

FOR NEW WORK OR REWIRING:

Total cross-section area of conductors must not be over 40% of the internal cross-section area of the conduit

Example:
   From Table 3B, with the 90C conductors used at the ampacity of 75 C 500 MCM conductors, unless equipment is marked to permit connection of 90C conductors

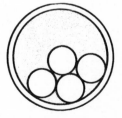

4 No. 500MCM THHN or XHHW in 3-in. conduit

Fig. 346-2. For three or more conductors the sum of their areas must not exceed 40 percent of the conduit area. (Sec. 346-6.)

When all conductors in a conduit or tubing are the same size, Tables 3A, 3B, and 3C, Chap. 9, give the maximum allowable fill for conductors up to 750 MCM, for ½- to 6-in. conduit.

Question: What is the minimum size of conduit required for six No. 10 THHN wires?

Answer: Table 3B, Chap. 9, shows that six No. 10 THHN wires may be pulled into a ½-in. conduit.

Question: What size conduit is the minimum for use with four No. 6 RHH conductors with outer covering?

Answer: Table 3C, Chap. 9, shows that a 1¼-in. minimum conduit size must be used for three to five No. 6 RHH conductors.

Question: What is the minimum size conduit required for four No. 500 MCM XHHW conductors?

Answer: Table 3B shows that 3-in. conduit may contain four 500 MCM XHHW (or THHN) conductors.

When all the conductors in a conduit or tubing are not the same size, the minimum required size of conduit or tubing must be calculated. Table 1, Chap. 9, says that conduit containing three or more conductors of any type except lead-covered, for new work or rewiring, may be filled to 40 percent of the conduit csa. Note 2 to this table refers to Tables 4 through 8, Chap. 9, for dimensions of conductors, conduit, and tubing to be used in calculating conduit fill for combinations of conductors of different sizes.

example   What size conduit is the minimum required for enclosing six No. 10 THHN, three No. 4 RHH (without outer covering), and two No. 12 TW conductors (Fig. 346-3)?

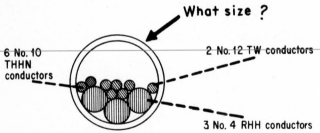

Fig. 346-3. Minimum permitted conduit size must be calculated when conductors are not all the same size. (Sec. 346-6.)

Cross-section areas of conductors:
From Table 5, Chap. 9:
    No. 10 THHN .... 0.0184 sq in.
    No. 4 RHH .... 0.1087 sq in.
    No. 12 TW .... 0.0172 sq in.
Note: RHH without outer covering has same dimensions as THW.

Total area occupied by conductors:

6 No. 10 THHN	6 × 0.0184 =	0.1104 sq in.
3 No. 4 RHH	3 × 0.1087 =	0.3261 sq in.
2 No. 12 TW	2 × 0.0172 =	0.0344 sq in.

Total area occupied by conductors .... 0.4709 sq in.

Referring to Table 4, Chap. 9:

The fifth column from the left gives the amount of square inch area that is 40 percent of the csa of the sizes of conduit given in the first column at left. The 40 percent column shows that 0.34 sq in. is 40 percent fill of a 1-in. conduit, and 0.60 sq in. is 40 percent fill of a 1¼-in. conduit. Therefore, a 1-in. conduit would be too small and—

A 1¼-in. conduit is the smallest that may be used for the 11 conductors.

Example: What is the minimum size of conduit for four No. 4/0 TW and four No. 4/0 XHHW conductors?

From Table 5, a No. 4/0 TW has a csa of 0.3904 sq in. Four of these come to 4 × 0.3904 or 1.5616 sq in.

From columns 7 and 11 of Table 5 we find that No. 4/0 XHHW has a csa of 1.3112 sq in.

$$1.5616 + 1.3112 = 2.8728 \text{ sq in.}$$

From Table 4, the csa of 3-in. conduit is 2.9500 sq in. A 2½-in. conduit would be too small.

Therefore—

A 3-in. conduit must be used.

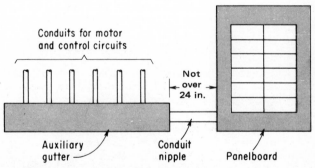

Fig. 346-4. Conduit nipples may be filled to 60 percent of csa and no derating is required. (Sec. 346-6.)

Figure 346-4 shows how a conduit nipple is excluded from the normal 40 percent limitation on conduit fill. In this typical example, the nipple between a panelboard and an auxiliary gutter contains 12 No. 10 TW wires, 6 No. 14 THHN wires, 3 No. 8 THW wires, and 2 No. 2 RHH wires (without outer covering). The minimum trade size of nipple that can be used in this case is 1¼ in. [Nipple may be filled to 60 percent of its csa if it is not over 24 in. long. Area of conductors = 12 × 0.0224 sq in. (csa of each No. 10 TW) plus 6 × 0.0087 sq in. (each No. 14 THHN) plus 3 × 0.0526 sq in. (each No. 8 THW) plus 2 × 0.1473, or a total of 0.7734 sq in., which is 60 percent of 1.2890 sq in. **NE Code** Table 4, Chap. 9, shows that a 1¼-in. nipple is the smallest that can be used. Sixty percent of the csa of 1¼-in. nipple = 0.6 × 1.50 or 0.900 sq in.; 60 percent of the csa of 1-in. nipple = 0.6 × 0.86 or 0.516 sq in.] And the conductors do *not* have to be derated in accordance with Note 8 of Tables 310-16 through 310-19. If the nipple had been 25 in. long, calculation at 40 percent fill would have called for a 1½-in. size and all conductors would have had to be derated per Note 8.

THWN and THHN are the smallest-diameter building wires. The greatly reduced insulation wall on Type THWN or THHN gives these thin-insulated conductors greater conduit fill than TW, THW, or RHH for new work and rewiring. Type XHHW wire has the same conduit fills from No. 4 through 500 MCM. And the nylon jacket on THWN and THHN has an extremely low coefficient of friction. THWN is a 75°C rated wire for general circuit use in dry or wet locations. THHN is a 90°C rated wire for dry locations only.

To fill conduit to the **Code** maximum allowance is frequently difficult or impossible from the mechanical standpoint of pulling the conductors

Fig. 346-5. Conduit terminations, other than threaded connections to threaded fittings or enclosure hubs, must be provided with bushings for protection of the conductors. (Sec. 346-8.)

into the conduit, because of twisting and bending of the conductors within the conduit. Bigger-than-minimum conduit should generally be used to provide some measure of spare capacity for load growth; and in many cases, the conduit to be used should be upsized considerably to allow future installation of some larger anticipated size of conductors.

346-8. Bushings.   As with IMC, rigid metal conduit always requires a bushing on the conduit end using locknuts and bushing for connection to knockouts in sheet-metal enclosures (Fig. 346-5). But simply because a conduit can be secured to a sheet-metal KO with two locknuts [one inside and one outside—as required by Sec. 250-76(b)], it does not mean the bushing may be eliminated. Of course, no bushing is needed where the conduit threads into a hub or boss on a fitting or enclosure.

346-9. Couplings and Connectors.   Figure 346-6 shows a threadless connection of rigid metal conduit to the hub on a fitting. It is effective both mechanically and electrically if any nonconducting coating is removed from the conduit.

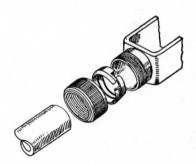

Fig.   346-6. Threadless   connectors may be used on unthreaded end of conduit. (Sec. 346-9.)

A running thread is considered mechanically weak and has poor electrical conductivity.

Where two lengths of conduit must be coupled together but it is impossible to screw both lengths into an ordinary coupling, the Erickson coupling or a swivel-coupling may be used. They make a rigid joint which is both mechanically and electrically effective. Also, bolted split couplings are available (Fig. 346-7).

It is not intended that conduit threads be treated with paint or other materials in order to assure water tightness. It is assumed that the conductors are approved for the locations and that the prime purpose of the conduit is for protection from physical damage and easy withdrawal of conductors for replacement. There are available pipe-joint compounds that seal against water without interrupting electrical conductivity.

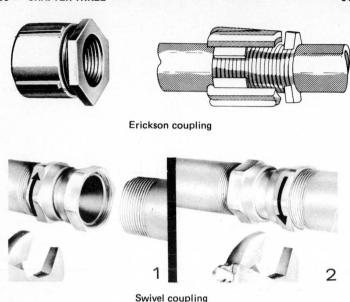

Erickson coupling

1   2

Swivel coupling

Fig. 346-7. Fittings provide for coupling conduits where conduits cannot be rotated (turned). (Sec. 346-9.)

346-10. Bends—How Made. *Field bends* means any bend made by workers during the installation of the conduit.

Table 346-10 gives minimum bending radii for field bends in rigid metal conduit, IMC, or EMT using any approved bending equipment and methods. (See Fig. 346-8.) However, the Exception to this rule permits sharper bends (i.e., smaller bending radii) if a one-shot bending machine is used in making a bend for which the machine and its accessories are designed. The minimum radii for one-shot bends are given in Table 346-10 Exception. All bending radii apply to any amount of bend—i.e., 45°, 90°, etc.

346-11. Bends—Number in One Run. Conduit runs should be so installed that the conductors can be pulled in without injuring the insulation or stretching small wires, and so that the conductors can be withdrawn easily (Fig. 346-9).

346-12. Supports. The basic rule for clamping rigid within 3 ft of connection to an enclosure or fitting and then at least every 10 ft is the same as shown in Fig. 345-3 for IMC. But the two Exceptions given in Sec. 346-12 permit wider spacing of clamps for rigid metal conduit runs that use "threaded couplings" under the conditions described.

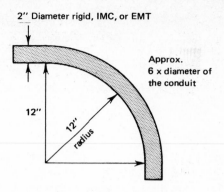

2" Diameter rigid, IMC, or EMT

Approx.
6 x diameter of
the conduit

12"

12"
radius

For conduit containing conductors without
lead sheath

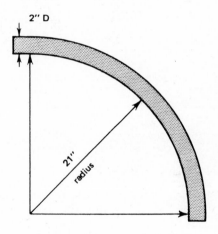

2" D

21"
radius

For conduit containing lead-sheathed conductors

NOTE: From Table 346-10 Exception, a bending radius of not less 9½ in. may
be used for a one-shot bend on 2-in. rigid, IMC, or EMT if the
conductors to be installed do not have a lead sheath.

Fig. 346-8. Minimum bending radii are specified to protect conductors from
damage during pull-in. (Sec. 346-10.)

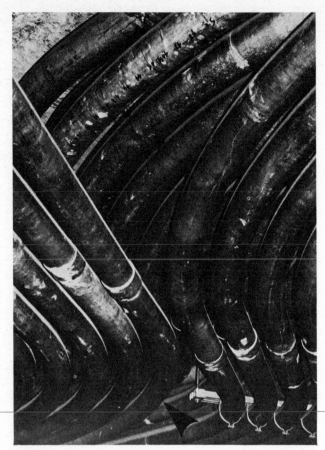

Fig. 346-9. All conduit bends must have large enough radius to satisfy Sec. 346-10, with not more than a total of 360° of bend in any conduit run. In addition, the neat workmanship required by Sec. 110-12 will require larger than minimum bending radii for the outside conduits when bends are made side-by-side (arrow). (Sec. 346-11.)

ARTICLE 347. RIGID NONMETALLIC CONDUIT

347-1. Description.   Nonmetallic conduit wiring systems include a wide assortment of products (Fig. 347-1).

All approved rigid nonmetallic conduits are suitable for underground installations. Some types are approved for direct burial in the earth while other types must be encased in concrete for underground applications.

Fig. 347-1. Rigid nonmetallic conduit systems are made up of a wide variety of components—conduit, fittings, elbows, nipples, couplings, boxes, straps. (Sec. 347-1.)

The nonmetallic conduits include fiber conduit, asbestos-cement conduit, soapstone, rigid polyvinyl chloride conduit, polyethylene conduit, and styrene conduit. Of these, medium-density polyethylene conduit and styrene conduit are not UL-listed. High-density polyethylene conduit and the others *are* UL-listed. The listed and labeled conduits differ widely in weight, cost, and physical characteristics, but each has certain application advantages.

The only nonmetallic conduit approved for use aboveground at the present time is rigid polyvinyl chloride (PVC Schedule 40, or Schedule 80) (Fig. 347-2). Since not all PVC conduits are suitable for use aboveground, the UL label in each conduit length will indicate if the conduit is suitable for such use. For use of Schedule 80, see Fig. 347-3 and Secs. 300-5(d) and 710-3(b) (1).

UL application data are detailed and divide "Rigid Nonmetallic Conduit" into three categories with specific instructions on each category, as follows:

"Plastic"

Unless marked for a higher temperature nonmetallic conduit (Schedule 40 and Schedule 80) in this category is intended for use with wires rated 75 C or less (1)

Fig. 347-2. PVC conduit is the only rigid nonmetallic conduit that may be used above ground. And when enclosing conductors run up a pole (shown here feeding a floodlight at top), the PVC conduit must be Schedule 80 and not Schedule 40. See Sec. 300-5(d). (Sec. 34-7-1.)

For conductor fill to 40% of the cross-section area, refer to data on wire-fill capacity marked on conduit surface.

Fig. 347-3. Extra-heavy-wall PVC conduit must have conductor-fill limited to its reduced csa. (Sec. 347-1.)

aboveground, (2) for direct burial underground, (3) where encased in concrete within buildings, and (4) where ambient temperature is 50 C or less. When encased in concrete in trenches outside of buildings it is suitable for use with wires rated 90 C or less.

Conduit installed aboveground is suitable for cables rated over 600 volts when encased in not less than 2 inches of concrete.

Direct buried conduit is suitable for cables rated over 600 volts when it is buried to a depth in accordance with Table 710-3(b) of the **National Electrical Code**.

Nonmetallic plastic conduit is listed in sizes ½ to 6 in. incl. Listing includes straight conduit, elbows, and bends. One coupling, integral or separable, is furnished with each length of conduit: if separable the coupling shall be attached.

For additional listings of Rigid Nonmetallic Conduit suitable for underground use, see the classifications of Conduit-Rigid Nonmetallic-Underground. Other Than Plastic, and Conduit-Rigid Nonmetallic-Underground Plastic.

Extra heavy wall conduit (Schedule 80) has a reduced cross-sectional area available for wiring space. The actual cross-sectional area and the need for reference to **National Electrical Code** Chapter 9 Table 1 for wire fill capacity are prominently marked on the conduit surface.

Listed PVC conduit is inherently resistant to atmosphere containing common industrial corrosive agents and will also· withstand vapors or mist of caustic, pickling acids, plating baths and hydrofluoric and chromic acids.

PVC conduit, elbows and bends (including couplings) which have been investigated for direct exposure to other reagents, may be identified by the designation "Reagent Resistant" printed on the surface of the product. Such special uses are described as follows:

PVC conduit, elbows and bends. Where exposed to the following reagents at 60 C or less: Acetic, nitric (25 C only) acids in concentrations not exceeding ½ normal; hydrochloric acid in concentrations not exceeding 30 percent; sulfuric acid in concentrations not exceeding 10 normal; sulfuric acid in concentrations not exceeding 80 percent (25 C only); concentrated or dilute ammonium hydroxide; sodium hyroxide solutions in concentrations not exceeding 50 percent; saturated or dilute sodium chloride solutions; cottonseed oil, or ASTM No. 3 petroleum oil.

PVC conduit is designed for connection to couplings, fittings and boxes by the use of a suitable solvent-type cement. Instructions supplied by the manufacturer describe the method of assembly and precautions to be followed.

"Other Than Plastic, Underground"

This listing covers nonmetallic conduit, for use only when installed underground as raceway for the installation of wires and cables in accordance with the **National**

Electrical Code. For plastic types of underground conduit, see Plastic Underground.

The conduit is designed for use in underground work under the following conditions:

Fiber conduit and fittings for use in underground work when laid with its entire length in concrete, identified as "Type I."

Fiber conduit and fittings for use in underground work without being encased in concrete, identified as "Type II."

Type I conduit is suitable for cables rated over 600 volts when encased in not less than 2 inches of concrete and buried in earth in accordance with Table 710-3(b) of the **National Electrical Code.**

Type II conduit is suitable for cables rated over 600 volts when buried in earth in accordance with Table 710-3(b) of the **National Electrical Code** (concrete encasement not required).

Where conduits emerge from underground installation the wiring method should be of a type recognized by the **Natonal Electrical Code.**

This listing includes straight conduit in lengths up to 10 ft (not for field bends) sizes ½- to 6-in. incl., for use with factory made elbows, couplings, reducers, and other terminal fittings.

"Plastic Underground"

This listing covers plastic types of nonmetallic conduit, for use only when installed underground as raceway for the installation of wires and cables in accordance with the **National Electrical Code.** For underground conduit of other than the plastic type, see Other Than Plastic, Underground.

The conduit is designed for use in underground work under the following conditions, as indicated on the Listing Mark, (1) when laid with its entire length in concrete (Type A), (2) when laid with its entire length in concrete in outdoor trenches (Type EB) and (3) direct burial without being encased in concrete (Schedule 40). The conduit is intended for use in ambient temperatures of 50 C or less, and unless marked otherwise. Type A and Schedule 40 conduit are intended for use with wires rated 75 C or less. Type EB conduit, Type A conduit, and Schedule 40 conduit, encased in concrete in trenches outside of buildings, may be used with wires rated 90 C or less.

Types A and EB conduit are suitable for cables rated over 600 volts when encased in concrete and buried in earth in accordance with Table 710-3(b) of the **National Electrical Code.**

Schedule 40 conduit is suitable for cables rated over 600 volts when buried in earth in accordance with Table 710-3(b) of the **National Electrical Code** (concrete encasement not required).

Where conduits emerge from underground installation the wiring method should be of a type recognized by the **Natonal Electrical Code** for the purpose.

Plastic underground conduit is listed in sizes ½- to 6-in. incl. Listing includes straight conduit, elbows and bends unless otherwise noted. Except for unthreaded high density PE (polyethylene) conduit, one coupling, integral or separable, is furnished with each length of conduit; if separable the coupling shall be attached.

PVC (polyvinyl chloride) conduit is designed for joining with PVC couplings by the use of a suitable solvent-type cement. High density PE (polyethylene) conduit is designed for joining by threaded couplings, drive-on couplings, or a butt fusing process. Instructions supplied by the manufacturer describes the method of assembly and precautions to be followed.

The Listing Mark of Underwriters Laboratories Inc. on the product is the only method provided by UL to identify products manufactured under its Listing and Follow-Up Service. The Listing Mark for these products includes the name and/or symbol of Underwriters Laboratories Inc. (as illustrated in the Introduction of this Directory) together with the word "Listed," a control number, and one of the following product names as appropriate: "Rigid Nonmetallic Conduit Underground (Schedule 40)"; "Rigid Nonmetallic Conduit Underground For Concrete Encasement in Outdoor Trenches Only. Not For Use in Ceilings, Floors, Or Walls. (Type ER)". Red printing on a white background is used as an identifying means for the Listing Mark for Schedule 40 conduit; green printing on a white background is used as an identifying means for the Listing Mark for Type A and Type EB conduit.

Note: As a result of the wording and intent of **NEC** Sec. 110-3(b), all the above application data constitute mandatory rules of the **NEC** itself—subject to the same enforcement as any other **NEC** rules.

347-2. Uses Permitted.   Part **(a)** applies to use of the conduit aboveground for circuits operating up to 600 V. The rules make rigid nonmetallic conduit a general-use raceway for interior wiring, concealed or exposed in wood or masonry construction—under the conditions stated. Only PVC is acceptable for in-building use (aboveground).

Part **(b)** applies to aboveground applications of rigid nonmetallic conduit when it contains high-voltage circuits (over 600 V). Any such conduit must be Schedule 40 or Schedule 80 PVC conduit—which is the only nonmetallic conduit listed for use aboveground—and it must be encased by concrete at least 2 in. thick on all sides.

Part **(c)** covers underground applications of all the types of rigid nonmetallic conduit—for circuits up to 600 V, as regulated by Sec. 300-5; and for circuits over 600 V, as covered by Sec. 710-3(b) (Fig. 347-4). Directly buried nonmetallic conduit carrying high-voltage conductors does not have to be concrete-encased if it is a type approved for use without concrete encasement. If concrete encasement is required, it will be indicated on the UL label and in the listing.

Figure 347-5 shows both underground and aboveground application. Referring to the circled numbers: (1) The burial depth must be at least 18 in. for any circuit up to 600 V. The buried conduit may be Schedule 40 or Schedule 80 (either without concrete encasement) or Type A or Type EB (both require concrete encasement). Refer to Sec. 347-1 and Sec. 300-5. (2) The concrete encasement where the conduit comes up from its 18-in. depth was required at one time by the **NEC**, but is no longer required. [See Sec. 300-5(a) Exception No. 5.] (3) The radius of the bend must comply with Table 346-10 (minimum 18 in.). The conduit aboveground on a pole must be Schedule 80; Sec. 300-5(d) prohibits Schedule 40 here.

In many cases where nonmetallic conduit is used to enclose conductors suitable for direct burial in the earth, inspectors and engineering authorities have accepted use of any type of conduit—PVC, polyethylene, styrene, etc.—without concrete encasement and without considering application of **Code** rules to the conduit. The reasoning is that because the cables are suitable for direct burial in the earth, the conduit itself is

Fig. 347-4. All UL-listed rigid nonmetallic conduits are acceptable for use underground. PVC Schedule 40 and Schedule 80 and Type II fiber conduits do not require concrete encasement. Other types must observe UL and NEC rules on concrete encasement. (Sec. 347-2.)

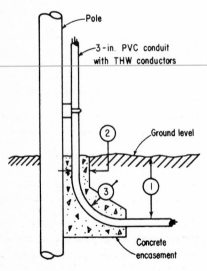

Numbers in circles refer to text.

Fig. 347-5. Schedule 80 PVC conduit may run up pole from earth to above-ground use. (Sec. 347-2.)

not required at all and its use is above and beyond Code rules. But temperature considerations are real and related to effective, long-time operation of an installation. Temperature effects must not be disregarded in any conduit-conductor application.

347-3. Uses Not Permitted.   It should be noted that nonmetallic conduit is not permitted in ducts, plenums, and other air handling spaces. See Sec. 300-21 and the comments following Sec. 300-22.

Figure 347-6 shows a difference in application rules between rigid nonmetallic conduit and metal conduit with respect to supporting equipment.

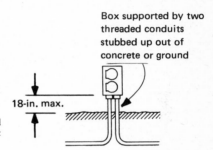

Box supported by two threaded conduits stubbed up out of concrete or ground

18-in. max.

Fig. 347-6. This is O.K. for rigid metal conduit but not for rigid nonmetallic conduit. (Sec. 347-3.)

Parts **(d)** and **(e)** require care in use of the conduits so that they are not exposed to damaging temperatures. In using nonmetallic conduits care must be taken to assure temperature compatibility between the conduit and the conductors used in it. For instance, a conduit that has a 75°C temperature rating at which it might melt and/or deform must not be used with conductors which have a 90°C temperature rating and which will be loaded so they are operating at their top temperature limit. There is available PVC rigid conduit listed by UL and marked to indicate its suitability for use with all 90°C-rated conductors, thereby suiting the conduit to use with 90°C-rated conductors. The UL data described in Sec. 347-1 give the acceptable ambient temperatures and conductor temperature ratings that correlate to these NEC rules. Conductors with 90°C insulation may be used at the higher ampacities of that temperature rating only when the conduit is concrete encased (Fig. 347-7).

347-4. Other Articles.   When equipment grounding is required for metal enclosures of equipment used with rigid nonmetallic conduit, an equipment grounding conductor must be provided. Such a conductor *must* be installed in the conduit along with the circuit conductors (Fig. 347-8). Refer to Secs. 250-57, 250-58, and 250-45.

347-5. Trimming.   See Fig. 347-9.

347-8. Supports.   In this section, Table 347-8, giving the maximum distance between supports for rigid nonmetallic conduit, permits greater spacing than previous NEC editions. For each size of rigid nonmetallic conduit, a single maximum spacing between supports, in feet, is given for

Grade

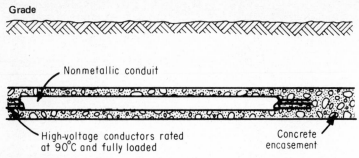

Fig. 347-7. UL data assure that this does not violate Sec. 347-3(e). (Sec. 347-3.)

all temperature ratings of conductors used in rigid nonmetallic conduit raceways (Fig. 347-10).

347-9. Expansion Joints.   Where conduits are subject to constantly changing temperatures and the runs are long, expansion and contraction of PVC conduit must be considered. In such instances an expansion coupling should be installed near the fixed end of the run to take up any expansion or contraction that may occur. Available expansion couplings have a normal expansion range of 6 in. The coefficient of linear expansion of PVC conduit can be obtained from manufacturers' data.

Expansion couplings are normally used where conduits are exposed. In underground or slab applications such couplings are seldom used because expansion and contraction can be controlled by *bowing* the conduit slightly or by immediate burial. After the conduit is buried, expansion and contraction are not a problem. Conduits left exposed for

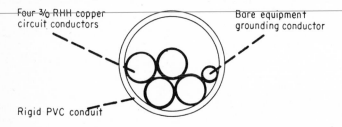

Equipment grounding conductor is sized from Table 250-95, based on the rating of the fuses or CB protecting the circuit conductor in the conduit. With 200-amp protection for the 3/0 conductors here, the equipment grounding conductor must be at least a No. 6 copper or No. 4 aluminum.

Fig. 347-8. Equipment grounding conductor must be used "within" the rigid nonmetallic conduit. (Sec. 347-4.)

Fig. 347-9. PVC conduit is designed for connection to couplings and enclosures by an approved cement, but leaving rough edges in the conduit end is a clear violation of Sec. 347-5. (Sec. 347-5.)

an extended period of time during widely variable temperature conditions should be examined to see if contraction has occurred.

347-11. Number of Conductors.   See discussion under Sec. 346-6.

347-13. Bends—How Made.   Refer to Sec. 346-10.

347-14. Bends—Number in One Run.   Refer to Sec. 346-11.

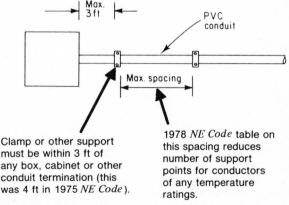

Max.
3 ft

PVC
conduit

Max. spacing

Clamp or other support
must be within 3 ft of
any box, cabinet or other
conduit termination (this
was 4 ft in 1975 *NE Code*).

1978 *NE Code* table on
this spacing reduces
number of support
points for conductors
of any temperature
ratings.

Fig. 347-10. Support rules on nonmetallic conduit are simple and direct. (Sec. 347-8.)

ARTICLE 348. ELECTRICAL METALLIC TUBING

348-1. Use. EMT is a general-purpose raceway of the same nature as rigid metal conduit and IMC. Although rigid metal conduit and IMC afford maximum protection for conductors under all installation conditions, in many instances it is permissible, feasible, and more economical to use EMT to enclose circuit wiring rated 600 V or less. Because EMT is lighter than conduit, however, and is less rugged in construction and connection details, the **NE Code** restricts its use (Art. 348) to locations (either exposed or concealed) where it will not be subjected to severe physical damage or (unless suitably protected) to corrosive agents.

EMT distribution systems are constructed by combining wide assortments or related fittings and boxes. Connection is simplified by employing threadless components that include compression, indentation, and set-screw types.

Some questions have been raised about the acceptability of EMT directly buried in soil. The last paragraph of Sec. 348-1 gives EMT exactly the same recognition for direct burial that Sec. 346-1(c) gives to rigid steel conduit. The wording of both paragraphs is identical, and it certainly seems clear that if galvanizing is enough corrosion protection for rigid steel conduit, it must provide equivalent protection for EMT in direct burial. In the UL listing on "Electrical Metallic Tubing," a note says that "galvanized steel electrical metallic tubing in a concrete slab below grade level *may* require supplementary corrosion protection." (That word "may" leaves the decision up to the designer and/or installer.) But note that the rule carefully refers to "*galvanized* steel" EMT and not just to "steel" EMT.

The next note says, "In general, *steel* electrical metallic tubing in contact with soil requires supplementary corrosion protection." That sentence certainly admits that there are locations where soil conditions are such that supplementary corrosion protection is not required. Since the word "galvanized" is not used ahead of the word "steel" as it was in the preceding paragraph it is at least a possibility that UL left the door open for galvanizing as one possible way of satisfying the requirement for supplementary corrosion protection.

Such an interpretation of UL intent would seem to be consistent with the equal approval that Secs. 345-3(b), 346-1(c), and 348-1 (last paragraph) give to direct burial of galvanized IMC rigid steel conduit and to galvanized electrical metallic tubing. The **Code** makes no distinction, where direct burial is concerned, between rigid conduit and EMT on the basis of their different wall thicknesses and structural strength differences.

It is reasonable to conclude that the phrase "judged suitable for the condition" means that past experience and local soil conditions should be considered in determining the acceptability of direct burial of EMT as well as IMC and rigid conduit, with appropriate attention given to additional protection against corrosion if necessary. Of course, the ruling of the local electrical inspector should be sought and followed.

Where corrosion protection has been provided and deemed suitable for the conditions, EMT burial depths must meet the minimum cover requirements of NE Code Sec. 300-5(a). Table 300-5 indicates that EMT would have to be at least 18 in. below grade, except that a 12-in. depth is permissible for residential branch circuits rated 300 V or less and provided with overcurrent protection of not more than 30 A (Exception No. 4).

As noted in Sec. 345-3(a), Exception, and Sec. 346-1(b), Exception, permission is given for use of aluminum fittings and enclosures with steel electrical metallic tubing.

348-5. Size.   Up to 2-in. size EMT has the same interior cross-section area as corresponding sizes of rigid metal conduit. EMT sizes of 2½ in. and larger have the *same outside diameter* as rigid metal conduits of corresponding sizes. Accordingly, the interior cross-sectional areas (square inch) are proportionally larger, and this provides more wiring space for greater ease of installation of conductors in these new sizes of EMT. Figure 348-1 illustrates some approximate dimensional comparisons between the larger EMT sizes and those for heavy-wall rigid metal conduit in corresponding sizes. It is significant that the increased internal diameters for respective sizes of EMT provide square inch cross-sectional areas from 16 percent to 22 percent greater. To prevent any misunderstanding, it should be stressed that the greater cross-sectional area of the inside of these EMT sizes, compared with rigid, *does not offer* the chance to fill such EMT runs with more conductors than could be used in corresponding sizes of rigid conduit. Number of conductors permitted in "conduit or tubing" is the same for rigid, IMC, or EMT, from Tables 1 through 8 of NE Code, Chap. 9.

348-6. Number of Conductors in Tubing.   Conductor fill for EMT is the same as described under Sec. 346-6 for rigid metal conduit.

348-7. Threads.   Here, the rules clarify Code intent. Threading of electrical metallic tubing is prohibited, but integral couplings used on EMT shall be permitted to be factory threaded. Such equipment has been used successfully in the past and has been found satisfactory. The revised Code rule recognizes such use. But it should be noted that this applies to EMT using *integral threaded fittings,* that is, fittings which are part of the EMT itself.

348-8. Couplings and Connectors.   Couplings of the raintight type are required wherever electrical metallic tubing is used on the exteriors of buildings. (See Secs. 225-22 and 230-53.)

Sec. 370-7 requires that conductors entering a box, cabinet, or fitting be protected from abrasion. The end of an EMT connector projecting inside a box, cabinet, or fitting must have smooth, well-rounded edges so that the covering of the wire will not be abraded while the wire is being pulled in. Where ungrounded conductors of size No. 4 or larger enter a

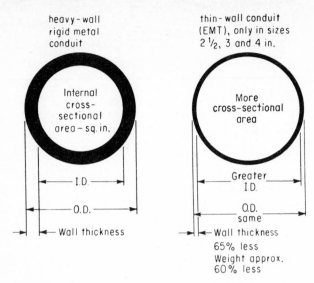

Trade size rigid and EMT	Inches outer dia. (O.D.) EMT and rigid	Wall thickness in.		Inside cross-sectional area sq. in.		More C.S.A. % for EMT
		Rigid	EMT	Rigid	EMT	
2½	2.875	0.203	0.072	4.79	5.85	22%
3	3.500	0.216	0.072	7.38	8.84	19%
4	4.500	0.237	0.083	12.72	14.75	16%

Fig. 348-1. Larger sizes of EMT have same outside diameters as rigid and IMC. (Sec. 348-5.)

raceway in a cabinet, the EMT connector must have an insulated throat (insulation set around the edge of the connector opening) to protect the conductors. See Sec. 373-6(c). For conductors smaller than No. 4, an EMT connector does *not* have to be the insulated-throat type. Using THW conductors, a circuit of No. 4 conductors (a 2-wire or 3-wire circuit) requires a 1-in. size EMT (Table 3A, Chap. 9, NEC). Therefore, for THW or TW wire, there is no requirement for insulated-throat EMT connectors in ½-in. and ¾-in. sizes. A circuit, say, of three No. 1 THW wires would call for 1¼ EMT, which would require use of insulated-throat connectors—or noninsulated-throat connector with a nonmetallic bushing on the connector end. In the larger sizes, the economics on the makeups can be significantly different. A 4-in. insulated-throat EMT

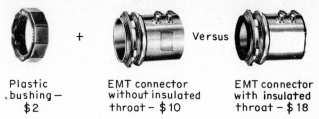

Plastic
bushing —
$2

+

EMT connector
without insulated
throat — $10

Versus

EMT connector
with insulated
throat — $18

Fig. 348-2. Different-cost makeups for 4-in. EMT satisfy code rules on EMT termination. (Sec. 348-8.)

connector might cost $18, whereas a noninsulated-throat connector in that size might cost $10 and $2 for a 4-in. plastic bushing (Figure 348-2).

When an EMT connector is used—either with or without an insulated throat to satisfy Sec. 373-6(c)—there is no requirement in Art. 348 that a bushing be used on the connector end. Note, however, that a bushing is required for rigid metal conduit and for IMC as covered in Secs. 346-8 and 345-15.

348-9. Bends—How Made.   Refer to Sec. 346-10.

348-10. Bends—Number in One Run.   Figure 348-3 shows EMT run from a panelboard to a junction box (JB) along the wall—with exactly a total of 360° of bend (from the panel: 45°, 45°, 90°, 90°, 45°, 45°).

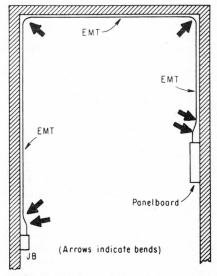

EMT

EMT

EMT

Panelboard

(Arrows indicate bends)

JB

Fig. 348-3. EMT, like other conduit runs, is limited to not over 360° of bends between raceway ends. (Sec. 348-10.)

348-12. Supports.   Figure 348-4 shows this rule applied to an EMT layout. If the word "fitting" is taken to include couplings, then a strap must be used within 3 ft of each coupling. The definition of "fitting," given in Art. 100, includes locknuts and bushings, which would logically suggest that the word also covers conduit bodies ("C," "T," etc.) and couplings.

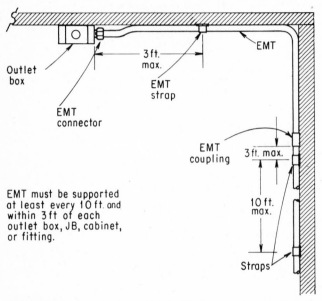

Fig. 348-4. EMT must be clamped within 3 ft of every enclosure or "fitting." (Sec. 348-12.)

ARTICLE 349.   FLEXIBLE METALLIC TUBING

349-1. Scope.   The first section of this article defines this new NE Code raceway. The rule indicates that flexible metallic tubing is intended for use where "not subject to physical damage" and gives use above suspended ceilings as an example. Although this wording does not limit its use to air-handling ceilings, it does raise some questions for electrical inspectors with respect to accepting flexible metallic tubing as a general-purpose raceway.

The meaning of the phrase, "not subject to physical damage," is not clear. When the proposal was made to add flexible metallic tubing to the Code as a suitable raceway, it was indicated that it had been designed for certain specific applications and not for general use. It was specifically intended for use as the fixture whip on recessed fixtures where high-temperature wire is run from the branch-circuit junction box to the hot wiring compartment in lighting fixtures, an application long filled by flexible metallic conduit (Fig. 349-1).

Typical use of flexible metallic
tubing: 4-to-6-ft length for
fixture whip in ceiling, containing
two No. 18 Type AF wires (for 6-amp
fixture load, see Section 402-5)
or two No. 16 Type AF wires (for
8-amp fixture load). Section 240-4
permits No. 16 and No. 18 fixture
wire to be protected at 20 amps.

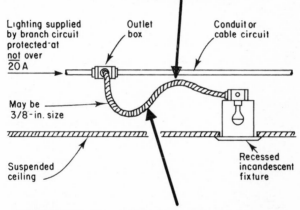

Lighting supplied
by branch circuit
protected at
not over
20 A

Outlet
box

Conduit or
cable circuit

May be
3/8-in. size

Suspended
ceiling

Recessed
incandescent
fixture

IMPORTANT!! Flex tubing is equipment grounding conductor because AF wires in flex tubing are tapped from circuit protected at not over 20 amps, as permitted in Section 250-91(b), Exception No. 1.

Fig. 349-1. New type of raceway seems limited to this application. (Sec. 349-1.)

349-3. Uses Permitted.   Although flexible metallic tubing is liquidtight without a nonmetallic jacket, part **(a)** of this section appears to limit its use to dry locations, and part **(d)** appears to limit its use to branch circuits. The problem of interpretation arises from the wording. The first sentence of Sec. 349-3 indicates where flexible metallic tubing shall be permitted to be used, but it does not say that other uses would be prohibited. For instance, it is permitted to be used in dry locations, but nowhere in the article is it prohibited from being used in wet locations—except for direct earth burial or embedding in poured concrete or aggregate (Sec. 349-4).

349-4. Uses Not Permitted. Part **(e)** limits use of flexible metallic tubing to lengths not over 6 ft long. That limitation has the effect of ruling out flexible metallic tubing as a general-purpose raceway and limiting its use to short interconnections so commonly made with flexible metal conduit or liquidtight flexible metal conduit. But it does not appear that flexible metallic tubing, in spite of its resistance to moisture or liquid penetration, is an alternative to the use of liquidtight flexible metal conduit in wet locations.

ARTICLE 350. FLEXIBLE METAL CONDUIT

350-2. Use. UL data supplement the Code data on use of standard flexible metal conduit—known also as "Greenfield" or simply "flex." The UL data note:

These listings include flexible aluminum and steel conduit in trade sizes ⁵⁄₁₆ to 4 in. incl. for installation in accordance with Article 350 of the **National Electrical Code.**

Flexible metal conduit no longer than six ft and containing circuit conductors protected by over-current devices rate at 20 amperes or less is suitable as a grounding means.

Flexible metal conduit longer than six ft has not been judged to be suitable as a grounding means.

See the classification Conduit Fittings with respect to fittings suitable as a grounding means.

To prevent possible damage to flexible aluminum conduit, care must be exercised when installing connectors employing direct bearing set screws.

Flexible aluminum conduit is marked at intervals of not more than one ft with the letters "AL."

The Listing Mark of Underwriters Laboratories Inc. on the product is the only method provided by UL to identify products manufactured under its Listing and Follow-Up Service. The Listing Mark for these products includes the name and/or symbol of Underwriters Laboratories Inc. (as illustrated in the Introduction of this Directory) together with the word "Listed," a control number, and one of the following product names as appropriate: "Flexible Aluminum Conduit" or "Flexible Steel Conduit."

Where Sec. 350-2 prohibits use of flex "in wet locations, unless conductors are of . . . type approved for the specific conditions," interpretation has raised difficulty. Any conductor with a "W" designation—such as THW or XHHW—is recognized by Sec. 310-7 for use in wet locations. From the definition of "wet location" (under "Location" in Art. 100), any indoor place subject to water spray or splashing or outdoors exposed to weather must use "W" designated wire types—such as outdoor service—entrance conductors tapped from a service drop and run in conduit down the outside of a building. The question then arises: May flex be used in such wet locations if the conductors within it are "W" type (say, THW)? It would seem that the parallel between the two applications would permit use of flex with THW wire in a wet location. However, there would still be concern for water getting inside the flex and running into enclosures or equipment. Use of liquidtight flex is the obvious answer to such application.

350-3. Minimum Size. Exception No. 3 to this rule permits ⅜-in. flexible metal conduit to be used in lengths up to 6 ft for connections to lighting fixtures. This provides correlation with Sec. 410-67(c), which includes 4 to 6 ft of metal raceway for connecting recessed fixtures (generally the nonwired types). Figure 350-1 shows such application, and it is permissible to use No. 16 or No. 18 AF wire as shown in Fig. 349-1 for flex tubing.

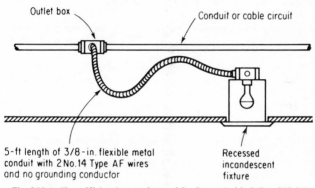

Outlet box

Conduit or cable circuit

5-ft length of 3/8-in. flexible metal conduit with 2 No.14 Type AF wires and no grounding conductor

Recessed incandescent fixture

Fig. 350-1. Flex of ⅜-in. size may be used for fixture "whip." (Sec. 350-3.)

Exception No. 3 also permits ⅜-in. flex if it is "part of an approved assembly," which assumes it is supplied as part of a UL-listed equipment.

350-4. Supports. Straps or other means of securing the conduit in place should be spaced much closer together (every 4½ ft and within 12 in. of each end) for flexible conduit than is necessary for rigid conduit. Every bend should be rigidly secured so that it will not be deformed when the wires are being pulled in, thus causing the wires to bind.

Figure 350-2 shows use of unclamped lengths of flex, as permitted by Exception No. 2. Figure 350-3 shows another example. Exception No. 3 is illustrated in Fig. 350-1.

350-5. Grounding. As shown in the UL data under Sec. 350-2, flex in any length over 6 ft is not suitable as an equipment grounding conductor and an equipment grounding conductor must be used within the flex to ground metal enclosures fed by the flex. The Exception permits flex as an equipment grounding conductor *only* under the given conditions— which would be the same as shown in Fig. 349-1 for flex tubing. Refer to Sec. 250-91(b) and to the discussion of grounding and bonding in Sec. 250-79(e).

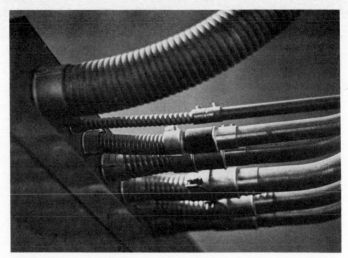

Fig. 350-2. Lengths of flex not over 3 ft long may be used without clamps or straps where the flex is used at terminals to provide flexibility for vibration isolation or for alignment of connections to knockouts. (Sec. 350-4.)

Fig. 350-3. A length of flex not over 3 ft long connects conduit to pull box in modernization job, providing the flexibility to feed from fixed conduit to box. (Sec. 350-4.)

The second sentence of this section notes that an equipment bonding jumper used with flexible metal conduit may be installed inside the conduit or outside the conduit when installed in accordance with the limitations of Sec. 250-79. The Exception to this rule makes clear that flexible metal conduit when used as an equipment grounding conductor in itself is permitted only where a length of not over 6 ft is inserted in any ground return path. The wording indicates that the total length of flex in any ground return path must not exceed 6 ft. That is, it may be a single 6-ft length. Or, it may be two 3-ft lengths, three 2-ft lengths, or any total equivalent of 6 ft. If the total length of flex in any ground return path exceeds 6 ft, the rule appears to require an equipment grounding conductor to be run within or outside any length of flex beyond the permitted 6 ft that is acceptable as a ground return path in itself.

It should be noted that the Exception of this section does not appear applicable to the use of flex in a hazardous location. The rules in Sec. 501-16(b) and Sec. 502-16(b) simply require bonding for flex, without any indication of exception (Fig. 350-4).

350-6. Bends in Concealed Work.   Figure 350-5 shows the details of this section.

Where bonding of standard or liquidtight flex is flatly required, as in Class I, Div. 2 and Class II, Div. 2 locations . . .

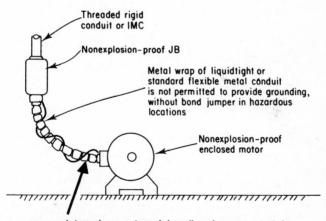

Threaded rigid conduit or IMC

Nonexplosion-proof JB

Metal wrap of liquidtight or standard flexible metal conduit is not permitted to provide grounding, without bond jumper in hazardous locations

Nonexplosion-proof enclosed motor

. . .an internal or external bonding jumper must be used at all times, for any size and any length of the flex and must conform to Section 250-79(e) as noted in Section 501-16(b) and Section 502-16(b).

Fig. 350-4. Flex must always be bonded in Class I and Class II hazardous locations. (Sec. 350-5.)

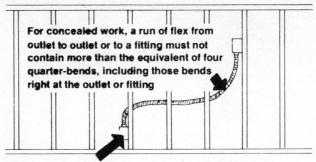

Angle connectors for flex connection to enclosures must not be used for concealed flex installations. Straight connectors are OK.

Fig. 350-5. Concealed flex must not have too many bends that could damage wires on pull-in. (Sec. 350-6.)

ARTICLE 351. LIQUIDTIGHT FLEXIBLE METAL CONDUIT

351-1. Scope. Liquidtight flex (often called "Sealtite" as a generic term in industry usage, although that word is the registered trade name of the liquidtight flex made by Anaconda Metal Hose Division) is similar in construction to the common type of flexible metal conduit, but is covered with an outer sheath of thermoplastic material (Fig. 351-1).

351-4. Use. UL data on liquidtight flex say:

These listings include liquid-tight flexible metal conduit in trade sizes ⅜ to 4 in. incl. for installation in accordance with Article 351 of the National Electrical Code.

Liquid-Tight Flexible Metal Conduit is intended for use in wet locations or where exposed to mineral oil, both at a maximum temperature of 60°C. It is not intended for use where exposed to gasoline or similar light petroleum solvents nor for use in hazardous locations unless so marked on the product.

That rule of UL has an effect on the conductors used in the flex. Because UL-listed liquidtight flexible metal conduit is intended for use at a maximum temperature of 60°C, conductors used in liquidtight flex must be 60°C-rated Type TW; or, if higher-temperature-rated conductors are used (THW, RHH, THHN, XHHW), they must be used at the 60°C ampacities of NE Code Table 310-16.

UL also lists the following:

Liquid-tight flexible metal conduit assemblies consist of a length of liquid-tight flexible metal conduit terminated at each end with a permanently attached connector.

Although UL data limit its listed liquidtight flex to use at a maximum of 60°C, there are applications requiring higher-temperature-rated flex

Fig. 351-1. Plastic jacket on liquidtight flex suits it to outdoor use exposed to rain or indoor locations where water or other liquids or vapors must be excluded from the raceway and associated enclosures. In lengths under 6 ft, UL-listed liquidtight does not require a bonding jumper. (Sec. 351-1.)

for foundries, near boilers, and in other hot places. Even though high-temperature flex is not UL-listed, it is consistent with NEC rules [Sec. 110-3(a)(5)] to use the higher-temp flex when an application would exceed the 60°C rating of UL-listed flex. High-temp flex is *not* a product listed by any test lab, and its use is, therefore, not contrary to Sec. 110-2. It would violate Secs. 351-4(b)(2) and 110-3(b) to use the listed 60°C flex in any way in which the loading on its contained conductors and the given ambient combined to produce a temperature over 60°C in the plastic jacket of the flex. Refer to temperature correction factors in Table 310-16.

351-5. Size. Refer to Sec. 350-3. Figure 351-2 satisfies Exception No. 2 of Sec. 350-3 if the No. 12 wires are stranded, as required in Sec. 430-

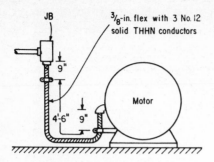

JB

³⁄₈-in. flex with 3 No. 12 solid THHN conductors

9"

Motor

4'-6" 9"

NOTE: The 6 ft length of liquid tight is suitable as an equipment grounding conductor, without bonding.

Fig. 351-2. Both standard flexible metal conduit and liquidtight may be used here. (Sec. 351-5.)

145(b). Table 350-3 accepts four No. 12 THHN in ³⁄₈-in. Greenfield of liquidtight.

351-6. Number of Conductors.   Refer to Sec. 346-6 for ½-in. to 4-in. sizes, and to Table 350-3 for ³⁄₈-in. size.

351-8. Supports.   As shown in Fig. 351-3, Exception No. 2 permits a length of liquidtight flexible metal conduit not over 3 ft long to be used at terminals where flexibility is required without any need for clamping or strapping. Previous Code wording did not contain this permission and in effect required every piece of liquidtight flexible metal conduit to be clamped within 12 in. of every outlet box or fitting. Obviously, the use of flex requires this permission for short lengths without support.

351-9. Grounding.   This means that where flexible metal conduit and fittings have not been specifically approved as a grounding means, a

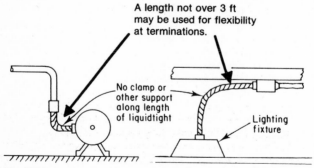

A length not over 3 ft may be used for flexibility at terminations.

No clamp or other support along length of liquidtight

Lighting fixture

Fig. 351-3. Unsupported length of liquidtight flex is O.K. at terminations. (Sec. 351-8.)

separate grounding conductor (insulated or bare) shall be run inside the conduit and bonded at each box or similar equipment to which the conduit is connected.

In regard to the Exception, see comments following Sec. 250-91(b).

The first sentence of this rule recognizes the metal in liquidtight flex as an equipment grounding conductor, as listed by UL:

Liquid-tight flexible metal conduit in the 1¼ in. and smaller trade sizes not more than six ft in length are considered suitable as a grounding means.

Liquid-tight flexible metal conduit in the 1½ in. and larger trade sizes and in all trade sizes when more than six ft in length have not been judged to be suitable as a grounding means.

When a bonding jumper is required—such as for a length of the flex that is not over 6 ft long but is over 1¼-in. size—the second sentence permits internal or external bonding of liquidtight flex as covered previously for standard flex and spelled out under Sec. 250-79. But for any size of flex run over 6 ft, *only* an internal equipment grounding conductor will satisfy this section and Sec. 250-91(b). A similar change in the wording of the Exception also focuses on a maximum total length of 6 ft in any equipment ground return path where the liquidtight flex itself is used as the equipment grounding conductor. UL applications data on the *Electrical Construction Materials Directory* (the green book) do not make that limitation to a "total length" of 6 ft. But it appears that any UL-listed liquidtight flex must also follow the "total length" concept.

351-10. Bends in Concealed Work.　Figure 351-4 shows this rule.

For concealed work, a run of liquidtight flex from outlet to outlet or to a fitting must not contain more than the equivalent of four quarter-bends, including those bends right at the outlet or fitting.

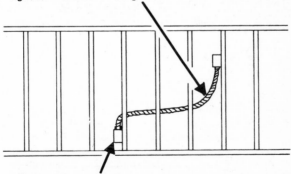

Angle connectors for flex connection to enclosures must not be used for concealed flex installations. Straight connectors are OK.

Fig. 351-4. Limitation on bends in concealed places applies to liquidtight as well as ordinary flex (Greenfield). (Sec. 351-10.)

ARTICLE 352. SURFACE RACEWAYS

352-1. Use. At one time, this article was titled "Surface *Metal* Raceways." The article now includes both metallic and *nonmetallic* surface raceways (Fig. 352-1).

Right: Typical use of small metal surface raceway for extensions from existing receptacle outlets.

Below: Shallow switch or receptacle box for surface raceway.

Fig. 352-1. Surface raceway has become popular for new works as well as for modernization. (Sec. 352-1.)

352-2. Other Articles. In every type of wiring have a metal enclosure around the conductors, it is important that the metal be mechanically continuous in order to provide protection for the conductors and that the metal form a continuous electrical conductor of low impedance from the last outlet on the run to the cabinet or cutout box. A path to ground is thus provided through the box or cabinet, in case any conductor comes in contact with the metal enclosure, an outlet box, or any other fitting. See Sec. 250-91(b).

352-3. Size of Conductors. Manufacturers of metal surface raceways provide illustrations and details on wire sizes and conductor fill for their various types of raceway. It is important to refer to their specification and application data.

352-4. Number of Conductors in Raceways. The rules of conductor fill may now be applied to surface metal raceway in very much the same way as standard wireway. This rule applies wireway conductor fill and ampacity determination to any surface metal raceway that is over 4 sq in. in cross section. As with wireway, if there are not more than 30 conductors in the raceway and they do not fill the cross-section area to more than 20 percent of its value, the conductors may be used without any ampacity derating from Note 8 of Tables 310-16 through 310-19 (Fig. 352-2).

352-6. Combination Raceways. Metal surface raceways may contain separated systems as shown in Fig. 352-3.

Ampacity derating of conductors according to Note 8 of
Tables 310^{16}/$_{19}$ is *not* needed

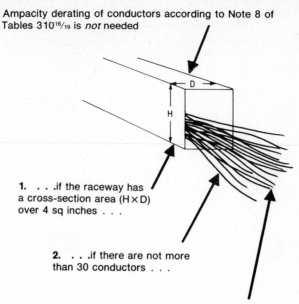

1. . . .if the raceway has
a cross-section area (H × D)
over 4 sq inches . . .

2. . . .if there are not more
than 30 conductors . . .

3. . . .and the sum of conductor
cross-section areas does not
exceed 20% of the interior
cross-section area of the raceway.

Fig. 352-2. NEC rule permits conductor fill of metal surface raceway
without ampacity derating of wires. (Sec. 352-4.)

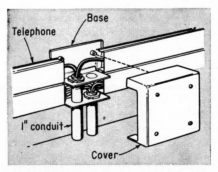

Fig. 352-3. For separating high- and low-
potential, combination raceway or tiered separate raceways may be used with barriered box
assembly. (Sec. 352-6.)

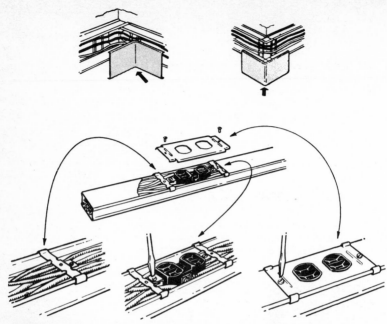

CORNER COUPLINGS enclose surface metal raceways making either internal or external right-angle turns. Raceway sections come equipped with clips for (1) holding wire in place, (2) securing raceway devices and (3) for mounting outlet covers.

Fig. 352-4. Couplings and other fittings must be designed for the specific applications. (Sec. 352-8.)

352-8. Construction.   Figure 352-4 shows details of the covers and fittings provided as standard accessories with surface raceway.

352-22. Use.   The requirements for nonmetallic surface raceways are generally similar to metal surface raceways except that nonmetallic types are limited to installations where the voltage is less than 300 V, ambient temperatures are 50°C or less, and conductor insulation temperatures are 75°C or less.

ARTICLE 353. MULTIOUTLET ASSEMBLY

353-1. Other Articles.   UL data are as follows:

This Listing covers metal raceways with factory installed conductors and attachment plug receptacles without provision for field installation of additional conductors except where the product is marked to indicate the number, type, and size of additional conductors which may be field installed. Also covered are nonmetallic raceways with factory installed conductors and attachment plug receptacles either factory installed or separately Listed as Multioutlet Assembly Fittings for field installation.

Multioutlet Assemblies are for installation in accordance with Article 353 of the National Electrical Code.

353-2. Use. These assemblies are intended for surface mounting except that the metal type may be surrounded by the building finish or recessed so long as the front is not covered. The nonmetallic type may be recessed in baseboards. In calculating the load for branch circuits supplying multioutlet assembly, see Sec. 220-2(c), Exception No. 1.

ARTICLE 354. UNDERFLOOR RACEWAYS

354-2. Use. Underfloor raceway was developed to provide a practical means of bringing conductors for lighting, power, and signaling systems to office desks and tables (Fig. 354-1). It is also used in large retail stores,

Fig. 354-1. Underfloor raceway system, with spaced grouping of three ducts (one for power, one for telephone, one for signals), is covered with concrete after installation on first slab pour. (Sec. 354-2.)

making it possible to secure connections for display-case lighting at any desired location.

This wiring method makes it possible to place a desk or table in any location where it will always be over, or very near to, a duct line. The wiring method for lighting and power between cabinets and the raceway

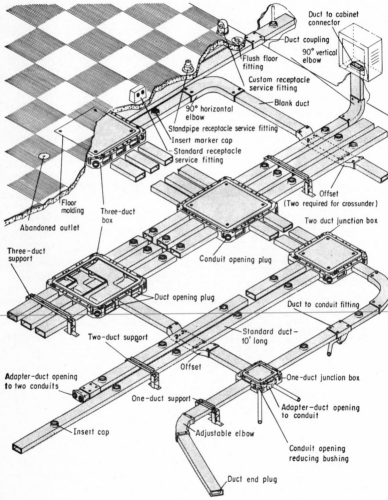

Fig. 354-2. Underfloor raceways may be installed as single- or multiple-run duct groupings, with a wide range of available accessories. (Sec. 354-2.)

junction boxes may be conduit, underfloor raceway, wall elbows, and cabinet connectors. Figure 354-2 shows a typical underfloor system.

354-3. Covering. The intent in paragraphs **(a)** and **(b)** is to provide a sufficient amount of concrete over the ducts to prevent cracks in a cement, tile, or similar floor finish. Figure 354-3 shows typical applications of coverings for various available widths of underfloor raceway.

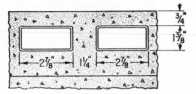

For this underfloor metal raceway, 3/4-in. wood or concerete covering is required.

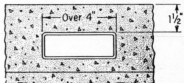

Any flat-top raceway over 4 in. wide and spaced less than 1 in. from another raceway must be covered with concrete at least 1-1/2 in. in thickness

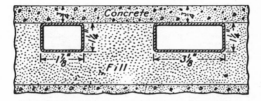

Steel metal raceway with min. 3/4 in. wood or concrete covering, except for trench-type flush raceways covered in Sec. 354-3(c). (Walker Bros.)

Fig. 354-3. Thickness of covering over underfloor raceway depends on raceway width. (Sec. 354-3.)

Figure 354-4 shows a violation. Two $1\frac{1}{2}$- by $4\frac{1}{2}$ in. underfloor raceways with 1-in.-high inserts are spaced $\frac{3}{4}$ in. apart by adjustable-height supports resting directly on a base floor-slab, as shown. After raceways are aligned, leveled, and secured, concrete fill is poured level with insert tops. But spacing between raceways must be at least 1 in.; otherwise the concrete cover must be $1\frac{1}{2}$ in. deep.

354-6. Splices and Taps. This section has a second paragraph that recognizes "loop wiring" where "unbroken" wires extend from underfloor raceways to terminals of attached receptacles, and then back into the raceway to other outlets. For purposes of this Code rule *only*, the "loop" connection method is not considered a splice or tap (Fig. 354-5).

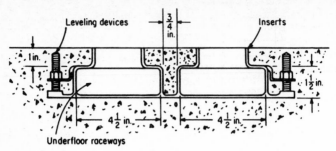

Fig. 354-4. The 1-in. cover is inadequate for raceways less than an inch apart. (Sec. 354-3.)

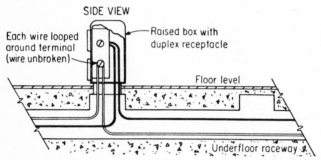

Fig. 354-5. "Loop" method permitted at outlets supplied from underfloor raceways. (Sec. 354-6.)

ARTICLE 356. CELLULAR METAL FLOOR RACEWAYS

356-1. Definitions.   This is a type of floor construction designed for use in steel-frame buildings in which the members supporting the floor between the beams consist of sheet steel rolled into shapes which are so combined as to form cells, or closed passageways, extending across the building. The cells are of various shapes and sizes, depending upon the structural strength required.

The cellular members of this type of floor construction form raceways. A cross-sectional view of one type of cellular metal floor is shown in Fig. 356-1.

356-2. Use.   Connections to the ducts are made by means of *headers* extending across the cells. A header connects only to those cells which are to be used as raceways for conductors. Two or three separate headers, connecting to different sets of cells, may be used for different systems,

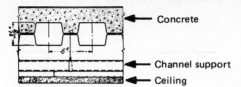

Fig. 356-1. Cross section of one type of cellular method floor construction. (Sec. 356-1.)

for example, for light and power, signaling systems, and public telephones.

Figure 356-2 shows the cells, or ducts, with header ducts in place. By means of a special elbow fitting the header is extended up to a cabinet or distribution center on a wall or column. A junction box or access fitting is

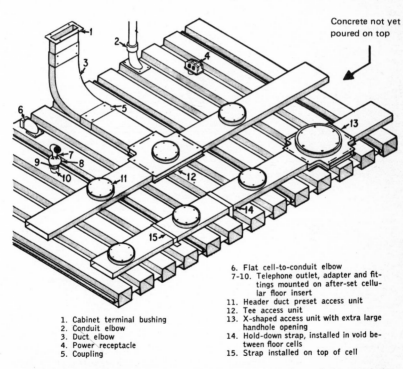

1. Cabinet terminal bushing
2. Conduit elbow
3. Duct elbow
4. Power receptacle
5. Coupling
6. Flat cell-to-conduit elbow
7-10. Telephone outlet, adapter and fittings mounted on after-set cellular floor insert
11. Header duct preset access unit
12. Tee access unit
13. X-shaped access unit with extra large handhole opening
14. Hold-down strap, installed in void between floor cells
15. Strap installed on top of cell

CELLULAR STEEL FLOOR contains unlimited number of channels for enclosing and isolating various electrical services. Wiring is routed from distribution panels to floor outlets through header ducts as shown.

Fig. 356-2. Components for electrical usage in cellular metal floor must be properly applied. (Sec. 356-2.)

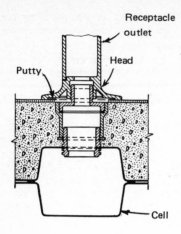

Receptacle
outlet

Head

Putty

Cell

Fig. 356-3. Typical insert for connecting from cell to floor outlet assembly. (Sec. 356-10.)

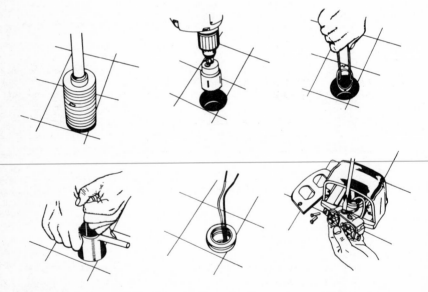

SERVICE OUTLET in cellular metal floor can be installed by using standard concrete core drill to reach top of desired raceway, then using center punch and hole saw to complete the opening. Flange and sleeve for attachment of the fittings are locked to the cell by means of a special wrench. Wires then are pulled, the service fitting positioned, wires connected to the receptacle and cover plate added.

Fig. 356-4. Debris from hole cutting must not be left in cell. (Sec. 356-10.)

provided at each point where the header crosses a cell to which it connects.

356-6. Splices and Taps.   See Sec. 354-6.

356-8. Markers.   The markers used with this system consist of special flat-head brass screws, screwed into the upper side of the cells and with their heads flush with the floor finish.

356-9. Junction Boxes.   The fittings with round covers shown in Fig. 356-2 are termed *access fittings* by the manufacturer but actually serve as junction boxes. Where additional junction boxes are needed, a similar fitting of larger size is provided which may be attached to a cell at any point.

356-10. Inserts.   The construction of an insert is shown in Fig. 356-3. A 1⅝-in.-diameter hole is cut in the top of the cell with a special tool. The lower end of the insert is provided with coarse threads of such form that the insert can be screwed into the hole in the cell, thus forming a substantial mechanical and electrical connection. Figure 356-4 shows how an outlet is derived from a floor cell.

The fitting used for connecting a threader to a cabinet is shown in Fig. 356-2. Junction boxes can be obtained with integral hubs to receive rigid conduit so that, if desired, the connections to cabinets can be made with conduit, or conduit may be run from junction boxes to wall outlets.

ARTICLE 358. CELLULAR CONCRETE FLOOR RACEWAYS

358-1. Scope.   The term *precast cellular concrete floor* refers to a type of floor construction designed for use in steel frame, concrete frame, and wall bearing construction, in which the monolithically precast reinforced concrete floor members form the structural floor and are supported by beams or bearing walls. The floor members are precast with hollow voids which form smooth round cells. The cells are of various sizes depending on the size of floor member used.

The cells form raceways which by means of suitable fittings can be adapted for use as underfloor raceways. A precast cellular concrete floor is fire resistant and requires no additional fireproofing.

358-3. Header.   Connections to the cells are made by means of *headers* secured to the precast concrete floor, extending from cabinets and across the cells. A header connects only those cells which are used as raceways for conductors. Two or three separate headers, connected to different sets of cells, may be used for different systems, for example, for light and power, signaling, and telephones.

Figure 358-1 shows three headers installed, each header connecting a cabinet with separate groups of cells. Special elbows extend the header to the cabinet.

Fig. 358-1. Headers, flush with finished concrete pour, carry wiring to cells. (Sec. 358-3.)

358-5. Junction Boxes.   Figure 358-2 shows how a JB must be arranged where a header connects to a cell.

358-6. Markers.   Markers used with this system are special flat-head brass screws which are installed level with the finished floor. One type of marker marks the location of an access point between a header and a spare cell reserved for, but not connected to, the header. A junction box can be installed at the point located by the marker if the spare cell is needed in the future. The screw for this type marker is installed in the center of a special knockout provided in the top of the header at the access point. The second type of marker is installed over the center of cells at various points on the floor to locate and identify the cells below. Screws with specially designed heads identify the type of service in the cell.

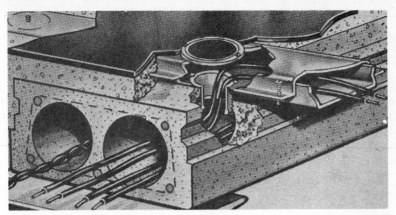

Fig. 358-2. Junction box is used to provide conductor installation from header to cell. (Sec. 358-5.)

358-7. Inserts. A 1⅞-in.-diameter hole is cut through the floor and into the center of a cell with a concrete drill bit. A plug is driven into the hole and a nipple is screwed into the plug. The nipple is designed to receive an outlet with a duplex electrical receptacle or an outlet designed for a telephone or signal system.

ARTICLE 362. WIREWAYS

362-1. Definition. Wireways are sheet-metal troughs in which conductors are laid in place after the wireway has been installed as a complete system. Wireway is available in standard lengths of 1, 2, 3, 4, 5, and 10 ft, so that runs of any exact number of feet can be made up without cutting the duct. The cover may be a hinged or removable type. Unlike auxiliary gutters, wireways represent a type of wiring, because they are used to carry conductors between points located considerable distances apart.

The purpose of a wireway is to provide a flexible system of wiring in which the circuits can be changed to meet changing conditions, and one of its principal uses is for expressed work in industrial plants. Wireways are also used to carry control wires from the control board to remotely controlled stage switchboard equipment. A wireway is approved for any voltage not exceeding 600 V between conductors or 600 V to ground. See comments following Sec. 374-1. An installation of wireway is shown in Fig. 362-1.

Fig. 362-1. Wireway in industrial plant—installed exposed, as required by Sec. 362—provides highly flexible wiring system that provides easy changes in the number, sizes, and routing of circuit conductors for machines and controls. Hinged covers swing down for ready access. Section 326-6 permits splicing and tapping in wireway. Section 362-10 covers use of conduit for taking circuits out of wireway. (Sec. 362-2.)

362-2. Use.   Figure 362-1 shows a typical Code-approved application of 4- by 4-in. wireway in an exposed location.

362-5. Number of Conductors.   Wireways may contain up to 30 "current-carrying" conductors at any cross section (signal circuits and control conductors used for starting duty only between a motor and its starter are not "current-carrying" conductors). The total cross-sectional area of the group of conductors must not be greater than 20 percent of the interior cross-sectional area of the wireway or gutter. And derating factors for more than three conductors do not apply to wireway the way they do to wires in conduit. However, if the derating factors from Note 8 of NE Code Tables 310-16 through 310-19 are used, there is no limit to the number of current-carrying wires permitted in a wireway or auxiliary gutter. But, the sum of the cross-section areas of all contained conductors at any cross section of the wireway must not exceed 20 percent of the cross-section area of the wireway or auxiliary gutter. More than 30 conductors may be used under these conditions.

Exception No. 1 says that wireway used 'for circuit conductors for an elevator or escalator may be filled with any number of wires, occupying up to 50 percent of the interior cross section of the wireway, and no derating has to be made for fill.

Exception No. 2 has the effect of saying that any number of signal and/ or motor control wires (even over 30) may be used in wireway provided the sum of their cross-section areas does not exceed 20 percent of wireway csa. And derating of conductor ampacity is not required for such conductors.

Figure 362-2 shows examples of wireway fill calculations. The example of Exception No. 2 shows a case where power and lighting wires (which *are* current-carrying wires) are mixed with signal wires. Because there are not over 30 power and light wires, no derating of conductor ampacities is

Basic rule
1. Any number of current-carrying conductors up to a maximum of 30, without derating.

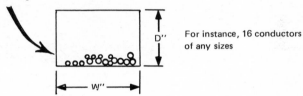

For instance, 16 conductors of any sizes

2. The sum of the cross-section areas of all the conductors (from table 5 in Chap. 9 of the *NEC*) must not be more than 20% X W″ X D″

Note: Signal and motor control wires are not considered to be current-carrying wires. Any number of such wires are permitted to fill up 20% of wireway cross-section area.

EXCEPTION No. 2

THIS IS OK !

45 conductors in wireway:
29 are current-carrying power and light wires;
16 are signal-circuit wires

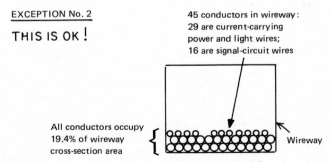

All conductors occupy 19.4% of wireway cross-section area

Wireway

Fig. 362-2. Wireway fill and need for derating must be carefully evaluated. (Sec. 362-5.)

needed. If, say, 31 power and light wires were in the wireway, then all 49 conductors would be subject to derating. If all 49 conductors were signal and/or control wires, then no derating would be required. But, in all cases, wireway fill must not be over 20 percent.

Exception No. 3 permits more than 30 power and/or lighting wires to occupy up to 20 percent of the wireway csa **but only if** the ampacity derating factors from Note 8 of Tables 310-16/19 are used (derating to 60 or 50 percent of table values, depending upon number of conductors).

362-6. Splices and Taps.   The conductors should be reasonably accessible so that any circuit can be replaced with conductors of a different size if necessary and so that taps can readily be made to supply motors or other equipment. Accessibility is ensured by limiting the number of conductors and the space they occupy as provided in Secs. 362-5 and 362-6.

362-10. Extensions from Wireways.   Knockouts are provided in wireways so that circuits can be run to motors or other apparatus at any point. Conduits connect to such knockouts, as shown in Fig. 362-1.

Sections of wireways are joined to one another by means of flanges which are bolted together, thus providing rigid mechanical connection and electrical continuity. Fittings with bolted flanges are provided for elbows, tees, and crosses, and for connections to cabinets. See Sec. 250-91(b).

ARTICLE 363. FLAT CABLE ASSEMBLIES

363-1. Definition.   Type FC cable is a flat assembly with three or four parallel No. 10 special stranded copper conductors. The assembly is installed in an approved U-channel surface metal raceway with one side open. Then tap devices can be inserted anywhere along the run. Connections from tap devices to the flat cable assembly are made by "pin-type" contacts when the tap devices are fastened in place. The pin-type contacts penetrate the insulation of the cable assembly and contact the multi-stranded conductors in a matched phase sequence (phase 1 to neutral, phase 2 to neutral, and phase 3 to neutral).

Covers are required when the installation is less than 8 ft from the floor. The maximum branch-circuit rating is 30 A.

Figure 363-1 shows the basic components of this wiring method.

363-3. Uses Permitted.   Figure 363-2 shows a Type FC installation supplying lighting fixtures. As shown in the details, one tap device provides for circuit tap-off to splice to cord wires in the junction box; and the other device is simply a fitting to support the fixture from the lips of the channel.

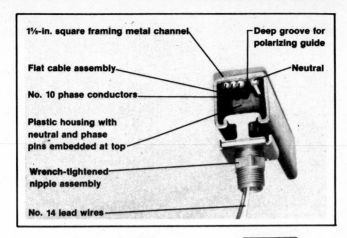

1⅝-in. square framing metal channel

Deep groove for polarizing guide

Flat cable assembly

Neutral

No. 10 phase conductors

Plastic housing with neutral and phase pins embedded at top

Wrench-tightened nipple assembly

No. 14 lead wires

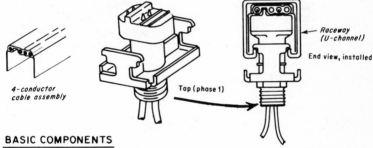

4-conductor cable assembly

Tap (phase 1)

Raceway (U-channel)

End view, installed

BASIC COMPONENTS

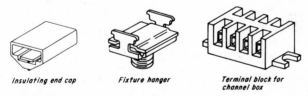

Insulating end cap

Fixture hanger

Terminal block for channel box

ACCESSORIES

Fig. 363-1. Type FC wiring system uses cable in channel, with tap devices to loads. (Sec. 363-1.)

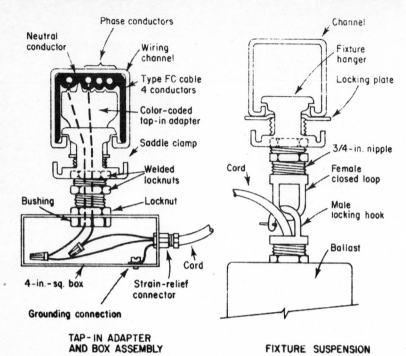

Fig. 363-2. Limited application of Type FC cable system includes use as branch-circuit wiring method to supply luminaires. (Sec. 363-3.)

363-5. Installation.   Figure 363-3 shows the basic installation procedures for Type FC cable systems.

363-6. Number of Conductors.   Figure 363-4 shows how a four-conductor cable assembly is used for a 3-phase, 4-wire, 480Y/277-V branch circuit to 277-V lighting fixtures.

ARTICLE 364. BUSWAYS

364-2. Definition.   Busways consist of metal enclosures containing insulator-supported busbars. Varieties are so extensive that possibilities for 600-V distribution purposes are practically unlimited. Busways are available for either indoor or outdoor use as point-to-point feeders or as plug-in takeoff routes for power. Progressive improvements in busway designs

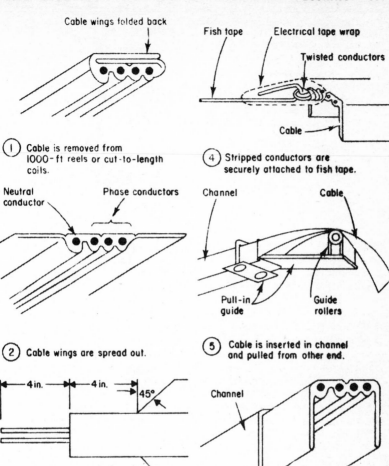

Fig. 363-3. This procedure complies with the NEC rule. (Sec. 363-5.)

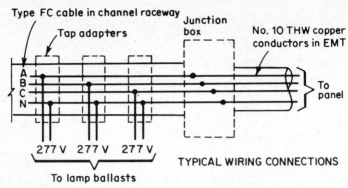

Fig. 363-4. A 4-wire Type FC system makes up a complete lighting branch circuit. (Sec. 363-6.)

have enhanced their electrical and mechanical characteristics, reduced their physical size, and simplified the methods used to connect and support them. These developments in turn have reduced installation labor to the extent that busways are most favorably considered when it is required to move large blocks of power to loadcenters (via low-imped-ance feeder busway), to distribute current to closely spaced power utiliza-tion points (via plug-in busway), or to energize rows of lighting fixtures or power tools (via trolley busway).

Busways classed as indoor low-reactance assemblies can be obtained in small incremental steps up to 6,500 A for copper busbars and 5,000 A for aluminum. Enclosed outdoor busways are similarly rated. In the plug-in category, special assemblies are available up to 5,000 A, although normal 600-V AC requirements generally are satisfied by standard busways in the 225-to-1,000-A range. Where power requirements are limited, small compact busways are available with ratings from 250 down to 20 A.

Plug-in and clamp-on devices include fused and nonfusible switches and plug-in CBs rated up to about 800 A. Other plug-in devices include ground detectors, temperature indicators, capacitors, and transformers designed to mount directly on the busway.

364-4. Use.   Figure 364-1 shows the most common way in which busway is installed—in the open.

Wiring methods above lift-out ceiling panels are considered to be "exposed"—because the definition of that word includes reference to "behind panels designed to allow access." This section calls for busway to be "located in the open and visible" but does permit busway above lift-out panels of a suspended ceiling, if means of access are provided. It limits such to totally enclosed, nonventilated busway, without plug-in switches or CBs on the busway and only in ceiling space that is not used for air handling. Figure 364-2 shows how other Code rules tie into this section.

Fig. 364-1. Ventilated-type (with open grills for ventilation) busway may be used only "in the open" and "visible." Only the totally enclosed, nonventilating type may be used above a suspended ceiling that does not form an air-handling space. (Sec. 364-4.)

For instance, fuses and CBs that provide overcurrent protection required by the **NE Code** must generally be readily accessible—that is, they must be capable of being reached quickly (Sec. 240-24). Fuses and/or CBs are not readily accessible if it is necessary to get a portable ladder or stand on a chair or table to get at them. However, Exception No. 2 in Sec. 240-24 permits overcurrent devices to be used high up on a busway where access

When busway is visible –

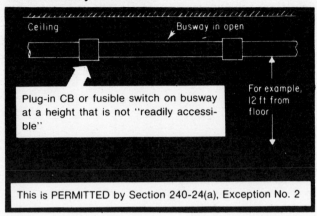

Ceiling   Busway in open

Plug-in CB or fusible switch on busway at a height that is not "readily accessible"

For example, 12 ft from floor

This is PERMITTED by Section 240-24(a), Exception No. 2

When busway is in non–air–handling ceiling space

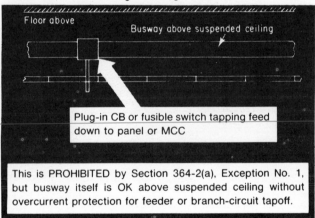

Floor above   Busway above suspended ceiling

Plug-in CB or fusible switch tapping feed down to panel or MCC

This is PROHIBITED by Section 364-2(a), Exception No. 1, but busway itself is OK above suspended ceiling without overcurrent protection for feeder or branch-circuit tapoff.

Fig. 364-2. Use of busway involves NEC rules on accessibility of overcurrent devices. (Sec. 364-4.)

to them could require use of a ladder, but Sec. 364-4(a), Exception (1), says **not on busway above a suspended ceiling**.

Other data limiting application of busway are contained in the UL regulations on listed busway—all of which information becomes mandatory Code rules because of NEC Sec. 110-3(b). Such UL data are as follows:

Busways may carry various markings to indicate the intended use for which the busway was investigated and listed. Busway intended to supply and support industrial and commercial lighting fixtures is marked "Lighting Busway." Busway with sliding or other continuously movable means for tapping-off current to load circuits is marked "Trolley Busway." And, if the same busway is also acceptable for supporting and feeding lighting fixtures, it will *also* be marked "Lighting Busway." If busway is designed to accept plug-in devices at any point along its length and is intended for general use, it is marked "Continuous Plug-in Busway." Busway marked "Lighting Busway" and protected by overcurrent devices rated in excess of 20 A is intended for use only with fixtures having heavy-duty lampholders—unless each fixture is equipped with additional overcurrent protection to protect the lampholders. This rule correlates with **NE Code** Secs. 210-23(b) and (c), which require only heavy-duty lampholders on branch circuits rated 25, 30, 40, or 50 A. A "heavy-duty lampholder" is defined in Sec. 210-21(a) as one having "a rating of not less than 660 watts if of the admedium type and not less than 750 watts if of any other type." Medium-base lampholders—the ordinary 120-V incandescent lampholder—and all fluorescent lampholders are not "heavy-duty" lampholders and are acceptable on lighting busway fed by branch-circuit fuses or breakers rated not over 20 A. But, 50-A lighting busway, for instance, may be used as a branch circuit to supply fixtures with incandescent, mercury-vapor, or other electric-discharge lamps with mogul-base, screw-shell lampholders or other lampholders rated "heavy-duty." In such applications, there is no need for additional overcurrent protection in each fixture. In such a case, the busway is used as a branch circuit in accordance with Sec. 364-12.

However, if fluorescent lighting fixtures are fed by a 50-A lighting busway and each fixture is individually fused at a few amps to protect the nonheavy-duty lampholders with the fuse in each fixture or its cord plug, that is permitted in the UL application information as well as by **NE Code** Sec. 364-12, Exception Nos. 2 or 3. In that case, the lighting busway is a feeder and each fixture tap is a "branch circuit." Note that in such a case the fuse in the plug or in the fixture is not "supplementary overcurrent protection," as described in Sec. 240-10—in spite of the conflict between Secs. 240-10 and 364-12, Exception No. 2. Figure 364-3 shows how those rules are applied. Note that the details involved are related to Sec. 210-21(a)—which prohibits fluorescent lampholders (nonheavy-duty) on circuits rated over 20 A—and Sec. 364-12, Exception No. 2—which identifies the fuse in the cord plug or in the fixture as "branch-circuit overcurrent device."

364-5. Support. As shown in Fig. 364-4, busway risers may be supported by a variety of spring-loaded hangers, wall brackets, or channel arrangements where busways pierce floor slabs or are supported on masonry walls or columns. As shown in Fig. 364-5, spring mounts for vertical busways may be located at successive floor-slab levels or, as indicated, supported by wall brackets located at intermediate elevations. Springs

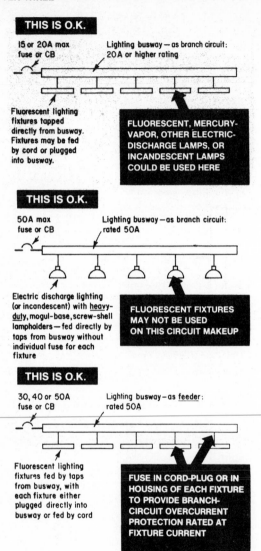

THIS IS O.K.

15 or 20A max fuse or CB

Lighting busway — as branch circuit: 20A or higher rating

Fluorescent lighting fixtures tapped directly from busway. Fixtures may be fed by cord or plugged into busway.

FLUORESCENT, MERCURY-VAPOR, OTHER ELECTRIC-DISCHARGE LAMPS, OR INCANDESCENT LAMPS COULD BE USED HERE

THIS IS O.K.

50A max fuse or CB

Lighting busway — as branch circuit: rated 50A

Electric discharge lighting (or incandescent) with heavy-duty, mogul-base, screw-shell lampholders — fed directly by taps from busway without individual fuse for each fixture

FLUORESCENT FIXTURES MAY NOT BE USED ON THIS CIRCUIT MAKEUP

THIS IS O.K.

30, 40 or 50A fuse or CB

Lighting busway — as feeder: rated 50A

Fluorescent lighting fixtures fed by taps from busway, with each fixture either plugged directly into busway or fed by cord

FUSE IN CORD-PLUG OR IN HOUSING OF EACH FIXTURE TO PROVIDE BRANCH-CIRCUIT OVERCURRENT PROTECTION RATED AT FIXTURE CURRENT

Fig. 364-3. These applications involve UL data and several Code sections. (Sec. 364-4.)

VERTICAL MOUNTING

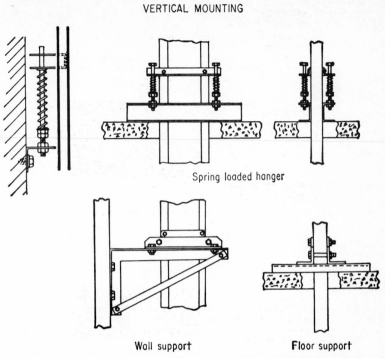

Spring loaded hanger

Wall support   Floor support

Fig. 364-4. Vertical busway runs must be supported at least every 16 ft. (Sec. 364-5.)

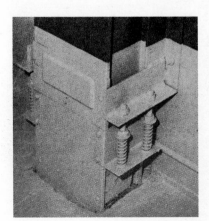

Fig. 364-5. Opening for busway riser through slab must be closed off, as required by Sec. 300-21. (Sec. 364-5.)

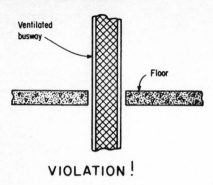

Ventilated
busway

Floor

VIOLATION !

Fig. 364-6. Ventilated busway may not be used through a floor slab and for 6 ft above the floor. (Sec. 364-6.)

provide floating cradles for absorbing transient vibrations or physical shocks. Fire-resistant material is packed into space between busway and edges of slab-piercing throat.

364-6. Through Walls and Floors.   Figure 364-6 shows a violation of this section, which requires busway to be totally enclosed within the floor slab and for 6 ft above it.

364-8. Branches from Busways.   Figure 364-7 shows feeds into and out of busway.

Fig. 364-7. Circuits fed from busway may be run in any conventional wiring method—such as EMT or rigid conduit (left) or as "suitable cord," such as "bus-drop" cable down to machines. And cable-tap-boxes may be used (arrow at right) to connect feeder conductors that supply power to busway. (Sec. 364-8.)

364-10. Rating of Overcurrent Protection—Feeders and Sub-Feeders.   The rated ampacity of a busway is fixed by the allowable temperature rise of the conductors. The ampacity can be determined in the field only by reference to the nameplate.

364-11. Reduction in Size of Busway.   Overcurrent protection—either a fused-switch or CB—is usually required in each busway sub-feeder tapping power from a busway feeder of higher ampacity, protected at the higher ampacity. This is necessary to protect the lower current-carrying capacity of the sub-feeder and should be placed at the point at which the sub-feeder connects into the feeder. However, this section provides that overcurrent protection may be omitted where busways are reduced in size, if the smaller busway does not extend more than 50 ft and has a current rating at least equal to one-third the rating or setting of the overcurrent device protecting the main busway feeder (Figs. 364-8 and 364-9).

Where the smaller busway is kept within the limits specified, the hazards involved are very slight and the additional cost of providing

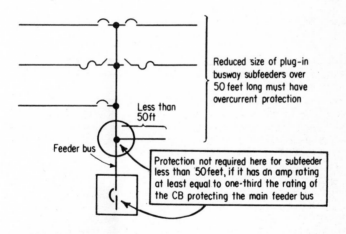

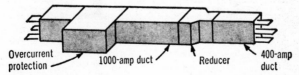

Fig. 364-8. Busway subfeeder may sometimes be used without protection. (Sec. 364-11.)

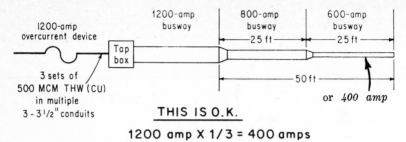

Fig. 364-9. Total length of reduced busway is not over 50 ft. (Sec. 364-11.)

overcurrent protection at the point where the size is changed is not considered as being warranted.

364-12. Sub-Feeder or Branch Circuits. The rules of this section are interrelated with those of Secs. 240-24 and 380-8. The basic rule of this section makes it clear that branch circuits or sub-feeders tapped from busway must have overcurrent protection on the busway at the point of tap. And if they are out of reach from the floor, all fused switches and CBs must be provided with some means for a person to operate the handle of the device from the floor (hookstick, chain operator, rope-pull operator, etc.).

Although no definition is given for "out of reach" from the floor, the wording of Sec. 380-8(a) can logically be taken to indicate that a switch or CB *is* "out of reach" if the center of its operating handle, when in its highest position, is more than 6½ ft above the floor or platform on which the operator would be standing. Thus, busway over 6½ ft above the floor would require some means (hookstick or etc.) to operate handles of any switches or CBs on the busway.

Figure 364-10 relates the rules of Sec. 240-24 Exception No. 2 to Sec. 364-12—with the rule of Sec. 240-24 *permitting* overcurrent devices to be "not readily accessible" when used up on high-mounted busway, and Sec. 364-12 *requiring* such protection to be mounted on the busway. To get at overcurrent protection in either case, personnel might have to use portable ladder or chair or some other climbing technique. Again, 6½ ft could be taken as the height above which the overcurrent protection is not "readily accessible"—or the height above which the **Code** considers that some type of climbing technique (ladder, chair, etc.) may be needed by some persons to reach the protective device.

Then, where the plug-in switch or CB on the busway is "out of reach" from the floor (that is, over 6½ ft above the floor), provision must be made for operating such switches or CBs from the floor, as shown in Fig. 364-11. The plug-in switch or CB unit must be able to be operated by a hookstick or chain or rope operator if the unit is mounted out of reach up on a busway. Section 380-8 says all busway switches and CBs must be operable from the floor. Refer to Sec. 380-8. Figure 364-12 shows a typical application of hookstick-operated disconnect.

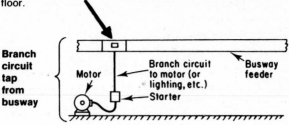

NE Code Section 364-12—Plug-in connection for tapping-off branch circuit shall contain overcurrent protection, which does not have to be within reach of person standing on floor.

Branch circuit tap from busway

Motor

Branch circuit to motor (or lighting, etc.)

Busway feeder

Starter

Plug-in connection for tapping-off a feeder or subfeeder shall contain overcurrent protection, which does not have to be within reach of person standing on floor.

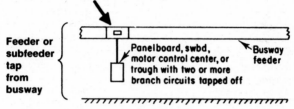

Feeder or subfeeder tap from busway

Panelboard, swbd, motor control center, or trough with two or more branch circuits tapped off

Busway feeder

Fig. 364-10. Protection must always be used on busway for these taps—regardless of busway mounting height. (Sec. 364-12.)

Figure 364-13 shows an application that has caused controversy because Sec. 364-12 says that any busway used as a feeder must have overcurrent protection on the busway for any sub-feeder or branch circuit tapped from the busway. Therefore, use of a cable tap box on busway without overcurrent protection could be ruled a Code violation. It can be argued that the installation shown—a 10- or 25-ft tap without overcurrent protection on the busway—is covered by Exception No. 1 of that section, which recognizes taps as permitted in Sec. 240-21—including 10-ft and 25-ft taps. However, wording of Sec. 240-21 refers to "busway taps" in Exception No. 7 which refers the whole matter back to Secs. 364-10 through 364-14—creating a problem in understanding how Exception No. 1 of Sec. 364-12 is to be understood. Because the phrase "feeder taps" in Sec. 240-21 clearly and certainly means "taps from feeders" and "branch-circuit taps" means "taps from branch circuits," it seems logical to conclude that "busway taps" means "taps from busways." Exception No. 7 of Sec. 240-21, therefore, appears to be applicable to all busway taps and to exclude busway taps from the other provisions of Sec. 240-21. In Fig. 364-13, if the feeder was conduit with conductors instead of busway, the installation shown would be acceptable. [It is also interesting to note that the precise wording of Sec. 240-21, Exception No. 2b,

Plug-in device must be externally operable circuit breaker or
fused switch that provides overcurrent protection for the
subfeeder or branch circuit tapped from the busway.

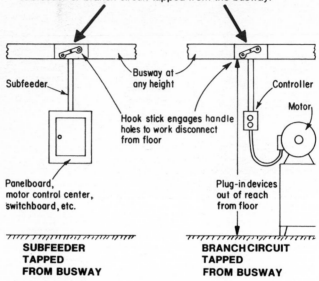

**SUBFEEDER
TAPPED
FROM BUSWAY**

**BRANCH CIRCUIT
TAPPED
FROM BUSWAY**

Fig. 364-11. Busway plug-in devices must be operable from the floor or
platform where operator stands. (Sec. 364-12.)

literally calls for the 10-ft tap conductors to have ampacity at least equal
to the rating or setting of the fuses or CB (whichever is used) at the load
end of the tap. And such protection may be rated up to four times motor
full-load current.]

364-13. Rating of Overcurrent Protection—Branch Circuits.   Refer to data
on busways on lighting branch circuits in Sec. 364-4 and Fig. 364-3.

364-14. Length of Busways Used as Branch Circuits.   A busway used as a
branch circuit is usually installed for a specific purpose, and the probable
maximum load to be supplied by the circuit can be estimated without
difficulty.

Figure 364-14 shows details of trolley busway used to supply fluorescent lighting in an industrial plant. Trolley busway runs are fed from
four 50-A CBs in lighting panel. The panel is supplied from transformer
secondary, powered from a tap to a busway feeder or subfeeder. The
lighting fixtures are suspended from the trolley busway, from beams, or
from the ceiling. The trolley busway is supported from ceiling, beams,
messenger cable, or braces supported from the beams. But because
fluorescent fixtures are fed, each fixture cord plug must be equipped
with fuse protection at not over 20 A to satisfy Sec. 210-21(a), which
permits only heavy-duty lampholders on circuits rated over 20 A.

Fig. 364-12. Disconnects mounted up on busway (top arrow) are out of reach from floor but do have hook-eye lever operators to provide operation by person standing in front of machines. Although the NEC does not literally require ready availability of a hookstick, it is certainly the intent of the code that one be handy (lower arrow). (Sec. 364-12.)

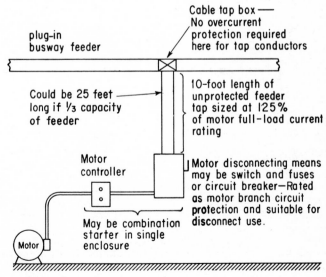

Fig. 364-13. This use of unprotected tap from busway conflicts with Sec. 364-12. (Sec. 364-12.)

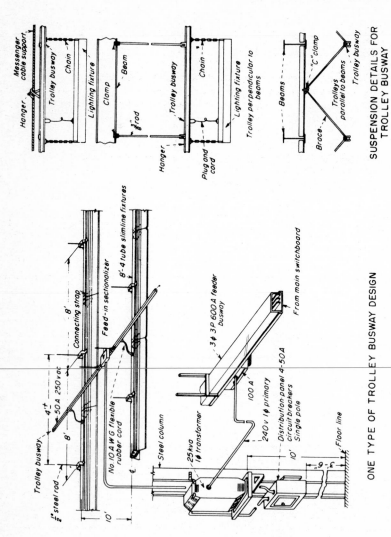

SUSPENSION DETAILS FOR TROLLEY BUSWAY

ONE TYPE OF TROLLEY BUSWAY DESIGN

Fig. 364-14. Trolley busway may serve as a feeder or as a branch circuit, depending upon circuit protection method. (Sec. 364-13.)

Because Sec. 364-12, Exception No. 2, designates the cord-plug fuse as "the branch-circuit overcurrent device," the 50-A trolley busway is a "feeder" and not a "branch circuit."

ARTICLE 365. CABLEBUS

Cablebus is an approved assembly of insulated conductors mounted in "spaced" relationship in a *ventilated* metal protective supporting structure including fittings and conductor terminations. In general, cablebus is

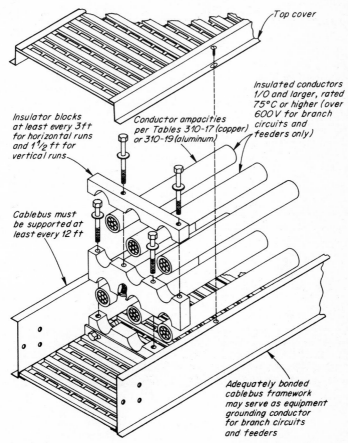

Top cover

Insulated conductors 1/0 and larger, rated 75°C or higher (over 600V for branch circuits and feeders only)

Insulator blocks at least every 3 ft for horizontal runs and 1½ ft for vertical runs

Conductor ampacities per Tables 310-17 (copper) or 310-19 (aluminum)

Cablebus must be supported at least every 12 ft

Adequately bonded cablebus framework may serve as equipment grounding conductor for branch circuits and feeders

Fig. 365-1. Cablebus systems are field assembled from manufactured components. (Sec. 365-1.)

assembled at the point of installation from components furnished by the manufacturer.

Field-assembly details are shown in Fig. 365-1. First, the cablebus framework is installed in a manner similar to continuous rigid cable support systems. Next, insulated conductors are pulled into the cablebus framework. Then the conductors are supported on special insulating blocks at specified intervals. And finally, a removable (ventilated) top is attached to the framework.

ARTICLE 366. ELECTRICAL FLOOR ASSEMBLIES

366-1. Scope.   This article covers a field-installed wiring system using laminated panels containing sheets of electrical conducting and dielectric material. The electrical floor assembly is designed to provide random access for separate, or combinations of, power and signaling/communication systems. Receptacle units are installed and removed using special tools approved for the purpose.

The features of this total system's package provide power (120 V, 20 A, 60 Hz) and signal (telephone, audio, data control) on a random basis as required. Flexibility is the biggest advantage of this system. The electrical floor assembly uses modular panels, located beneath the floor covering, to carry both power and signal. The panels contain four conductive planes: two ground planes, a neutral plane, and a phase (hot) plane,

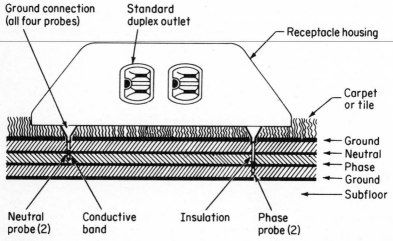

Fig. 366-1. Floor cross section shows receptacle probes contacting conducting sheets in floor panel. (Sec. 366-1.)

insulated from each other in the form of a "sandwich" (Fig. 366-1). The panels, sealed on all sides by a metallic, electrically grounded sheet, are connected to a standard 120-V, 20-A, 60-Hz branch-circuit panelboard power source, through a panel input unit located at the start of the string of panels.

Panels are electrically interconnected using screw-type terminations to form "power areas." Each power area is protected by a standard 20-A fuse or CB. The power areas typically are from 200 to 1,000 sq ft each, depending on individual needs.

ARTICLE 370. OUTLET, SWITCH AND JUNCTION BOXES, AND FITTINGS

370-1. Scope. This rule makes clear that Art. 370 regulates use of conduit bodies when they are used for splicing, tapping, or pulling conductors. And the word "fittings" in this article does refer to conduit bodies.

370-2. Round Boxes.   The purpose of this rule is to require the use of rectangular or octagonal metal boxes having, at each knockout or opening, a flat bearing surface for the locknut or bushing or connector device to seat against a flat surface. But, round outlet boxes may be used with nonmetallic-sheathed cable because the cable is brought into the box through a knockout, without the use of a box connector to secure the cable to the box. However, Sec. 370-7(c) permits only "single gang boxes" to be used without securing the NM or NMC cable to the box itself—as long as it is stapled to the stud or joist within 8 in. of the box. Because "round" boxes are *not* "single gang" boxes, it appears that all such round outlet boxes must be equipped with cable clamps to satisfy the last two sentences of Sec. 370-7(c) (Fig. 370-1). Shallow metal boxes with internal clamps for NM cable are acceptable as round boxes.

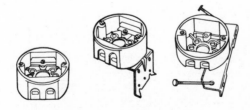

Round nonmetallic outlet boxes
may be used only with NM cable

Fig. 370-1. Round boxes may be used only for connecting cables with internal clamps—such as NM or BX cable. (Sec. 370-2.)

370-3. Nonmetallic Boxes. The second paragraph of this section recognizes the use of nonmetallic boxes with metal raceways or metal-sheathed cables. In the 1975 and previous Code editions, nonmetallic boxes were permitted to be used only with open wiring on insulators, concealed knob-and-tube wiring, nonmetallic-sheathed cable, and approved rigid nonmetallic conduit. But there was no permission to use nonmetallic boxes with metal raceways.

Growth in the application of nonmetallic boxes over past years has stimulated the addition of the new paragraph, which regulates the conditions under which nonmetallic boxes may be used with metal raceways or metal-sheathed cable. The need and popularity of these boxes developed out of industrial applications where corrosive environments dictated their use to resist the ravages of various punishing atmospheres.

In many applications it was desirable to use nonmetallic boxes along with plastic-coated metal conduits for a total corrosion-resistant system. However, the Code prohibition in Sec. 370-3 presented a serious problem. The need for such application is now recognized by the Code, although a limitation is placed requiring internal bonding means in such boxes. The permission applies only to nonmetallic boxes sufficiently large—that is, over 100 cu in. (Fig. 370-2). PVC boxes, fiberglass boxes,

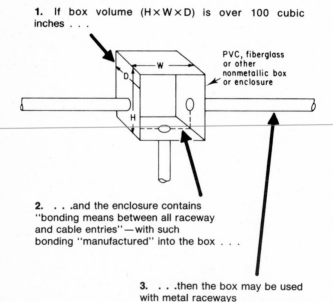

1. If box volume (H × W × D) is over 100 cubic inches . . .

PVC, fiberglass or other nonmetallic box or enclosure

2. . . .and the enclosure contains "bonding means between all raceway and cable entries"—with such bonding "manufactured" into the box . . .

3. . . .then the box may be used with metal raceways or metal-sheathed cable.

Fig. 370-2. Larger nonmetallic boxes are now recognized for use with metal raceways and metal-sheathed cable. (Sec. 370-3.)

or other nonmetallic boxes or enclosures may be used with metal raceway or metal-sheathed cable, but the bonding means between all raceway and cable entries must be manufactured into the box. That is, the grounding continuity from each raceway entry to each other raceway entry must be a part of the provisions of the box itself. That requirement was placed in the Code rule to assure the safety of effective equipment grounding where metal raceway systems are used with nonmetallic boxes. As worded, the manufacturer of the nonmetallic box must provide the necessary bonding means for all raceway and/or cable entries and such provisions "manufactured" into the box. The wording clearly seems to prohibit the use of accessory hubs with ground lugs to achieve equipment grounding continuity through such boxes.

370-4. Metal Boxes.   With a metal box in contact with metal walls or ceilings covered with metal, or with metal lath or with conductive thermal insulation, a stray current may flow to ground through an unknown path if a "hot" wire should accidentally become grounded on the box. To prevent this, the box must be effectively grounded by means of a separate grounding conductor.

370-5. Damp or Wet Locations.   "Weatherproof" is defined as meaning "so constructed or protected that exposure to the weather will not interfere with its successful operation." A box or fitting may be considered weatherproof when so made and installed that it will exclude rain and snow. Such a box or fitting need not necessarily be sealed against the entrance of moisture.

The left part of Fig. 370-3 shows a fitting which is considered as weatherproof because the openings for the conductors are so placed that

Fitting for use at the outer end of a service conduit.

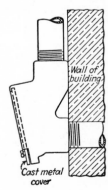

Type LB conduit fittting used where a service cc nduit passes through a building wall. See Sec. 370-18.

Fig. 370-3. Fittings must be suited to use in wet locations. (Sec. 370-5.)

rain or snow cannot enter the fitting. On the right, it shows a fitting made weatherproof by means of a metal cover that slides under flanges on the face of the fitting, and, as required by Sec. 230-53, an opening is provided through which any moisture condensing in the conduit can drain out.

See definitions of "wet locations" and "damp locations" in Art. 100.

Weatherproof boxes are for use in "wet locations" as defined by the NE Code. In "damp locations," boxes must be "located or equipped" to prevent water from entering or accumulating in the box. Boxes with threaded conduit hubs will normally prevent water from entering except for condensation within the box or connected conduit.

Caution: Extreme care must be exercised in correlating UL and NE Code rules on the use of boxes and enclosures in damp or wet locations because of uncertainties about their definitions. UL requires a weatherproof box for wet locations (such as outdoors exposed to rain). Weatherproof, in the NE Code definition, means only that it must be constructed or protected so that exposure to weather will not interfere with operation of contained equipment and does *not* mean that entry of water must be excluded. NE Code Sec. 370-5 on use of outlet boxes requires that boxes in *either damp or wet* locations must be "placed or equipped" to prevent entry of any moisture; or, if water does enter, the box must be drained so that water will not accumulate within the box. In damp locations (but not in wet locations), UL requires boxes to be "located or equipped" to prevent entry of water into the box.

From the above, it could be argued that a UL weatherproof box, which is intended for wet locations, does not satisfy NE Code Sec. 370-5 because that section requires exclusion of moisture from all boxes in wet (and damp) locations, and weatherproof boxes do not necessarily exclude moisture. It also could be contended that UL rules requiring exclusion of water from boxes in damp locations are more strict than the rule on use of weatherproof boxes in wet locations.

However, the last sentence of NE Code Sec. 370-5 says that boxes in wet locations "shall be approved for the purpose." Because UL says "weatherproof boxes are intended for use in wet locations," it seems clear that such usage is approved.

370-6. Number of Conductors in Switch, Outlet, Receptacle, Device, and Junction Boxes. Note that motor terminal housings are excluded from the rules on box conductor fill. And where any box or conduit body contains No. 4 or larger conductors, all the requirements of Sec. 370-18 on pull boxes must be satisfied. Refer to Sec. 370-18 for applications of conduit bodies as pull boxes.

Selection of any outlet or junction box for use in any electrical circuit work must take into consideration the maximum number of wires permitted in the box by Sec. 370-6. Safe electrical practice demands that wires *not* be jammed into boxes because of the possibility of nicks or other damage to insulation—posing the threat of grounds/or shorts.

As stated in part **(a)** of this section, Table 370-6(a) shows the maximum number of wires permitted in the *standard* metal boxes listed in that table. But that table applies only where all wires in a given box are all of the same size, i.e., all No. 14 or all No. 12, etc. Table 370-6(b) is provided for sizing a box where all the wires in the box are not the same size, by using so much cubic-inch space for each size of wire.

Part **(1)** of Sec. 370-6(a) describes the detailed way of counting wires in a box and reducing the permitted number of wires shown in Table 370-6(a) where cable clamps, fittings, or devices like switches or receptacles take up box space.

Important details of the wire-counting procedure of part **(1)** are as follows:

1. From the wording, it is clear that no matter how many ground wires come into a box, whether they are ground wires in NM cable or ground wires run in metal or nonmetallic raceways, a deduction of only one conductor must be made from the number of wires shown in Table 370-6(a) (Fig. 370-4). Or, as will be shown in later examples, one or more ground wires in a box must be counted as a single wire of the size of the largest ground wire in the box. Any wire running unbroken through a box counts as one wire. Each wire coming into a splice device (crimp or twist-on type) is counted as one wire. And each wire coming into the box and connecting to a wiring device terminal is *one* wire.

2. Regarding the deduction of a wire from the **Code**-given number, Table 370-6(a), for fixture studs, cable clamps, and hickeys, does this apply to the above-mentioned items collectively regardless of number and combination, or does it apply to each item individually, such as clamps—minus one, studs—minus one, etc?

   Answer: The items mentioned are treated collectively as one deduction, whether the box has one clamp, two clamps, or any combination of clamps and/or studs and/or hickeys.

3. Must unused cable clamps be removed from a box? And if clamps are not used at all in a box, must they be removed to permit removal of the one-wire reduction?

   Answer: Unused cable clamps may be removed to gain space or fill in the box, or they may be left in the box if adequate space is available without the removal of the clamp or clamps. If one clamp is left, the one-wire deduction must be made. If no clamps are used at all in a box, such as where the cable is attached to the box by box connectors, the one-wire deduction is not made.

4. Is the short jumper installed between the grounding screw on a grounding-type receptacle and the box in which the receptacle is contained officially classified as a *bonding jumper*? And is this conductor counted when the box wire count is taken?

   Answer: The jumper is classed as a *bonding jumper*. Section 250-74 uses the wording "bonding jumper" in the section pertaining to this subject. This conductor is not counted because it does not leave the box. The next to last sentence of Sec. 370-6(a) (1) covers that point.

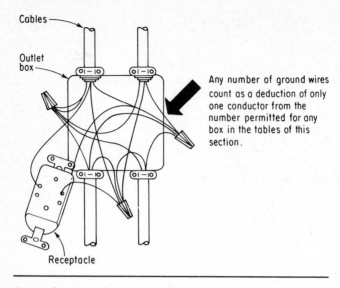

Cables

Outlet box

Any number of ground wires count as a deduction of only one conductor from the number permitted for any box in the tables of this section.

Receptacle

Any wire passing through counts as one, as follows:

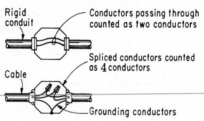

Rigid conduit

Conductors passing through counted as two conductors

Spliced conductors counted as 4 conductors

Cable

Grounding conductors

Fig. 370-4. Count all ground wires as *one* wire of the largest size of ground wire in the box. (Sec. 370-6.)

The last sentence of Sec. 370-6(a) (1) requires that ganged boxes be treated as a single box of volume equal to the sum of the volumes of the sections that are connected together to form the larger box. An example of wire counting and correct wire fill for ganged boxes is included in the following examples. *Note:* In the examples given here, the same rules apply to wires in boxes for any wiring method—conduit, EMT, BX, NM.

Examples of Box Wire-Fill

Figure 370-5 shows a nonmetallic-sheathed cable with three No. 14 copper conductors supplying a 15-A duplex receptacle (one ungrounded

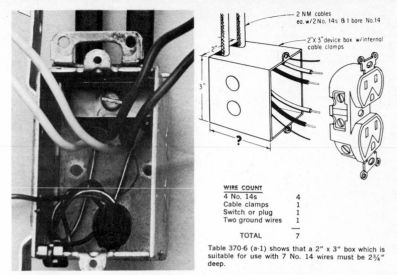

WIRE COUNT

4 No. 14s	4
Cable clamps	1
Switch or plug	1
Two ground wires	1
TOTAL	**7**

Table 370-6 (a-1) shows that a 2" x 3" box which is suitable for use with 7 No. 14 wires must be 2¾" deep.

Fig. 370-5. Correct wire count determines proper minimum size of outlet box. (Sec. 370-6.)

conductor, one grounded conductor, and one "bare" grounding conductor).

After supplying the receptacle, these conductors are extended to other outlets and the conductor count would be as follows:

Circuit conductors	4
Grounding conductors	1
For internal cable clamps	1
For receptacle	1
Total	7

The No. 14 conductor column of Table 376-6(a) indicates that a device box not less than 3 by 2 by 2¾ in. is required. Where a square box with plaster ring is used, a 4 by 1½ in. size is required. (See Sec. 370-14.)

Table 370-6(a) includes the most popular types of metal "trade-size" boxes used with wires No. 14 to No. 6. Cubic-inch capacities are listed for each box shown in the table. According to paragraph **(b)**, boxes other than those shown in Table 370-6(a) are required to be marked with the cubic inch content so wire combinations can be readily computed.

Figure 370-6 shows another example with the counting data in the caption. The wire fill in this case violates the limit set by Sec. 370-6(a).

Figure 370-7 shows an example of wire-fill calculation for a number of ganged sections of sectional boxes. The photo shows a four-gang assembly of 3-in. by 2-in. by 3½-in. box sections with six 14/2 NM cables, each with a No. 14 ground wire and one 14/3 NM cable with a No. 14 ground. The feed to the box is 14/3 cable (at right side), with its black wire

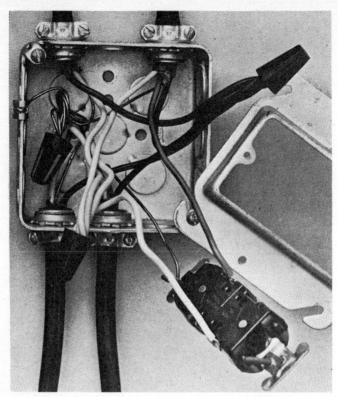

Fig. 370-6. THIS IS A CODE VIOLATION! A 4 × 4 × 1½-in. square metal box, generally referred to as a "1900" box, has four NM cables coming into it. At upper right is a 14/3 cable with No. 14 ground. The other three cables are 14/2 NM, each with a No. 14 ground. The red wire of the 14/3 cable feeds the receptacle to be installed in the one-gang plaster ring. The black wire of the 14/3 feeds the black wires of the three 14/2 cables. All the whites are spliced together, with one brought out to the receptacle, as required by Sec. 300-13(b). All the ground wires are spliced together, with one brought out to the grounding terminal on the receptacle and one brought out to the ground clip on the left side of the box. The wire count is as follows: nine No. 14 insulated wires, plus one for all of the ground wires and one for the receptacle. That is a total of 11 No. 14s. Note that box connectors are used instead of clamps and there is, therefore, no addition of one conductor for clamps. But Table 370-6(a) shows that a 4 × 1½-in. square box may contain only 10 No. 14 wires. (Sec. 370-6.)

supplying the receptacle which will be installed in the right-hand section. The red wire serves as feed to three combination devices—one in each of the other sections—each device consisting of two switches on a single strap. When finished, the four-gang box will contain a total of six switches and one duplex receptacle. Each of the 14/2 cables will feed a switched

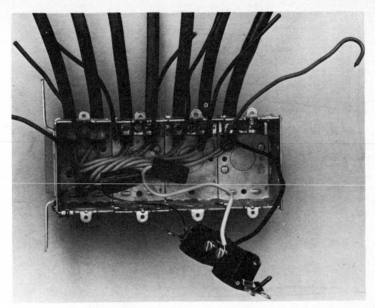

Fig. 370-7. Calculation of the proper minimum box size for the number of conductors used in gauged boxes must follow Sec. 370-6(a) (1), taking the assembly as a single box of the sum of the volumes of the ganged sections and filling it to the sum of the conductor count. (Sec. 370-6.)

load. All the white neutrals are spliced together and the seven bare No. 14 ground wires are spliced together, with one bare wire brought out to the receptacle ground terminal and one to the ground clip on the bottom of the left-hand section. The four-gang assembly is taken as a box of volume equal to four times the volume of one 3 by 2 by 3½-in. box. From Table 370-6(a), that volume is 18 cu in. for each sectional box. Then for the four-gang assembly, the volume of the resultant box is 4 × 18 or 72 cu in. Then wire fill for the four-gang assembly may be four times that permitted for the basic single gang box used in the assembly. Because a 3 by 2 by 3½-in. box is shown in Table 370-6(a) to have a permitted fill of 9 No. 14 wires, the four-gang assembly may contain 4 × 9 or 36 No. 14 wires—with deductions made as required by Sec. 370-6(a) (1).

Deduct one wire for all the clamps; deduct one No. 14 for all the bare equipment ground wires; and deduct one No. 14 for each "strap containing one or more devices," which calls for a deduction of four because there are four device "straps" (one for each of the three combination switches and one for the receptacle). The total deductions come to 1 + 1 + 4 or 6.

Deducting 6 from 36 gives a permitted fill of 30 No. 14 insulated circuit wires. In the arrangement shown, there are 6 cables with 2 insulated wires and 1 with 3 insulated wires, for a total of 15 insulated No. 14 wires. Because that is well within the maximum permitted fill of 30 No. 14 wires, such an arrangement satisfies Sec. 370-6(a) (1).

The alternative method of counting wires and determining proper box size would be as follows:

1. There are 15 No. 14 insulated circuit wires.
2. Add one wire for all the cable clamps.
3. Add one wire for all the No. 14 ground wires.
4. Add one wire for each of the four device straps.

The total of the wire count is: 15 + 1 + 1 + 4 or 21 No. 14 wires.

Then dividing that among the four box sections gives five-plus wires per section—which is taken as six No. 14 wires per section. Referring to Table 370-6(a), it will be noted that a 3 by 2 by 2½-in. box may contain 6 No. 14 wires. This calculation, therefore, establishes that the four-gang assembly could be made up of 3 by 2 by 2½ boxes instead of the 3 by 2 by 3½ boxes—although there is no Code violation in using the larger boxes.

Although the Code wire-counting method in Sec. 370-6(a) (1) does not make reference to the counting method of Sec. 370-6(a) (2)—which applies where all the wires in a box are not the same size—that part **(2)** does confirm the calculation made above. As shown in Table 370-6(b) each No. 14 wire in a box must be allowed at least 2 cu in. of free space within the box. In the alternative calculation above, with a total of 21 No. 14 wires determined as the overall count, part **(2)** of Sec. 370-6(a) would require the box to have a minimum volume of 2 × 21 or 42 cu in. Each 3 by 2 by 2½-in. box has a volume of 12.5 [Table 370-6(a)]—for a total of 4 × 12.5 or 50 cu in. volume of the four-gang assembly. That volume easily exceeds the minimum 42 cu in. volume required.

When different sizes of wires are used in a box, part **(2)** of Sec. 370-6(a) requires that Table 370-6(b) must be used in establishing adequate box size. Using the same method of counting conductors as described in Sec. 370-6(a) (1), the volume of cubic inches shown in Table 370-6(b) must be allowed for each wire depending upon its size. And where two or more ground wires of different sizes come into a box, they must all be counted as a single wire of the largest size used.

Figure 370-8 shows a calculation with different wire sizes in a box. When conduit or EMT is used, there are no internal box clamps and, therefore, no addition for clamps. In this example, the metal raceway is the equipment grounding conductor—so no addition has to be made for one or more ground wires. And the red wire is counted as one wire because it is run through the box without splice or tap. As shown in the wire count under the sketch, the logical way to account for the space taken up by the wiring devices is to take each one as a single wire of the same size as the wires connecting to it. Note that the neutral pigtail required by Sec. 300-13(b) is excluded from the wire count as it would be under Sec. 370-6(a) (1).

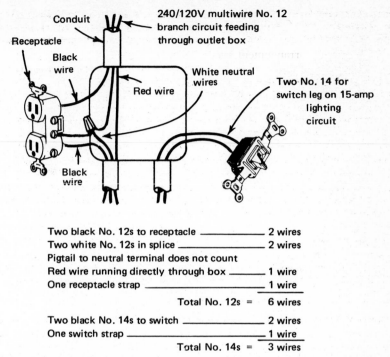

Two black No. 12s to receptacle ———————— 2 wires
Two white No. 12s in splice ————————————— 2 wires
Pigtail to neutral terminal does not count
Red wire running directly through box ———— 1 wire
One receptacle strap ——————————————————— 1 wire
Total No. 12s =   6 wires

Two black No. 14s to switch ——————————— 2 wires
One switch strap ———————————————————— 1 wire
Total No. 14s =   3 wires

Fig. 370-8. When wires are different sizes, volumes from Table 370-6(b) must be used. (Sec. 370-6.)

From Table 370-6(b) each No. 12 must be provided with 2.25 cu in.—a total of 6 × 2.25 or 13.5 cu in. for the No. 12's. Then each No. 14 is taken at 2 cu in.—a total of 2 × 2 or 4 cu in. for both. Adding the two resultant volumes—13.5 plus 4—gives a minimum required box volume of 17.5 cu in. From Table 370-6(a), a 4 by 4-in. square box of 1¼-in. depth, with 18 cu in. interior volume, would satisfy this application.

For the many kinds of tricky control and power wire hookups so commonly encountered today—such as shown in Fig. 370-9—care must be taken to count all sizes of wires and make the proper volume provisions of Table 370-6(b).

FS and FD Boxes—WATCH OUT!

Table 370-6(a) gives the maximum number of wires permitted in FS and FD boxes. But the last sentence of the first paragraph of Sec. 370-6(b) does indicate that FS and FD boxes may contain more wires if their internal volumes are marked and are greater than shown in Table 370-6(a).

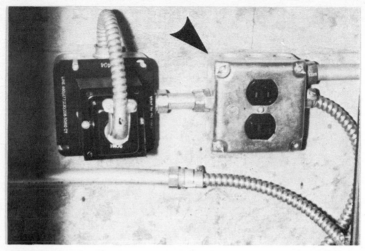

Fig. 370-9. Many boxes contain several sizes of wires—some running through, some spliced, and some connected to wiring devices. Calculation of minimum acceptable box size must be carefully made. The combination switch and receptacle here is on a single mounting strap and is taken as one wire of the size of wires connected to it. (Sec. 370-6.)

Because the volumes in the table are minimums, most manufacturers continue to mark their products with the actual volume. This in many cases is considerably greater than the volumes shown in the table. The last sentence of the first paragraph of Sec. 370-6(b) says that boxes that are marked to show a cubic inch capacity greater than the 13.5 to 24 cu in. minimums in the table may have conductor fill calculated in accordance with their actual volume, using the volume per conductor given in Table 370-6(b).

Part **(b)** of Sec. 370-6 covers boxes—metal and nonmetallic—that are not listed in Table 370-6(a) and conduit bodies with provision for more than two conduit entries (cross and T conduit bodies). And the basic way of determining correct wire fill is to count wires in accordance with the intent of Sec. 370-6(a) (1) and then calculate required volume of the box or conduit body by totaling up the volumes for the various wires from Table 370-6(b). The rules of part **(b)** can be broken down into two categories: boxes and conduit bodies.

   1. BOXES—Part **(b)** covers wire fill for metal boxes, up to 100 cu in. volume, that are not listed in Table 370-6(a) and for nonmetallic outlet and junction boxes. Although **Code** rules have long regulated the maximum number of conductors permitted in metal wiring boxes [such as given in Table 370-6(a)], there was no regulation on the use of conductors in nonmetallic device boxes up to the 1978

NEC. Now Sec. 370-6(b) requires that *both* metal boxes not listed in Table 370-6(a) and nonmetallic boxes be durably and legibly marked by their manufacturer with their cubic inch capacities to permit calculation of the maximum number of wires that the Code will permit in the box. Calculation of the conductor fill for these boxes will be based on the marked box volume and the method of counting conductors set forth in Sec. 370-6(a). The conductor volume will be taken at the values given in Table 370-6(b), and deductions of space as required for wiring devices or for clamps must be made in accordance with the rules of Sec. 370-6(a). This requirement for marking of both metal and nonmetallic boxes arises from the wording of Sec. 370-6(b), which refers to boxes other than those described in Table 370-6(a) and to nonmetallic boxes.

As shown in Fig. 370-10, a nonmetallic box for a switch has two 14/2 NM cables, each with a No. 14 ground. The wire count is: four No. 14 insulated wires, plus one for the switch to be installed, and one for the two ground wires. That is a total of six No. 14 wires. From Table 370-6(b), at least 2 cu in. of box volume must be allowed for each No. 14. This box must, therefore, be marked to

Fig. 370-10. Every nonmetallic box must be "durably and legibly marked by the manufacturer" with its cubic-inch capacity to permit calculation of number of wires permitted in the box—using Table 370-6(b) and the additions of wire space required to satisfy Sec. 370-6(a) (1). (Sec. 370-6.)

show that it has a capacity of at least 6 × 2 cu in., or 12 cu in. (As shown, the ground wires are connected by a twist-on connector, with one end of the wire brought out to connect to a ground screw on the switch mounting yoke. Such a technique is required to provide grounding of a metal switchplate that is used on an outlet within reach of water faucets or other grounded objects. Refer to Sec. 410-18.)

2. CONDUIT BODIES—Conduit bodies with provision for more than two conduit entries must be marked with their cubic inch capacity, and conductor fill is determined on the basis of Table 370-6(b). Such conduit bodies may contain splices or taps. An example of such application is shown in Fig. 370-11. Each of the eight No. 12

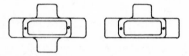

All such bodies must be durably and legibly marked by manufacturer with their cubic-inch capacities.

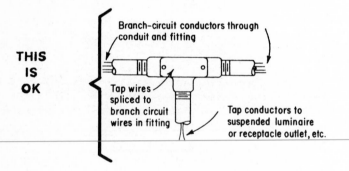

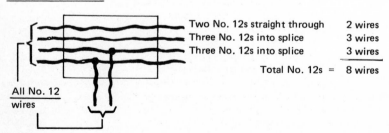

Fig. 370-11. Conduit bodies with more than *two* entries for conduit may contain splices or taps. (Sec. 370-6.)

wires that are "counted" as shown at bottom must be provided with at least 2.25 cu in., from Table 370-6(b). The T conduit body must, therefore, be marked to show a capacity of not less than 8 × 2.25 cu in. or 18 cu in.

For each No. 6 conductor used in the boxes or conduit bodies covered by Sec. 370-6(b), there must be at least 5 cu in. of box volume *and* a minimum space at least 1½ in. wide where any No. 6 is bent in a box or fitting.

Part (c) of Sec. 370-6 contains a number of provisions which must be carefully evaluated. Figure 370-12 shows the first rule. For

Cross-section area of conduit body must be . . .

Type C conduit body

. . . at least twice the cross-section area of largest conduit connected to it . . .

No. 6 or smaller conductors

Type L conduit body (LB, LR, LF, etc.)

No. 6 or smaller conductors

. . . **and the maximum number of conductors permitted in the conduit body is the number of conductors permitted in the conduit connected to the conduit body, from** *Code* **tables on conduit fill (Chapter 9).**

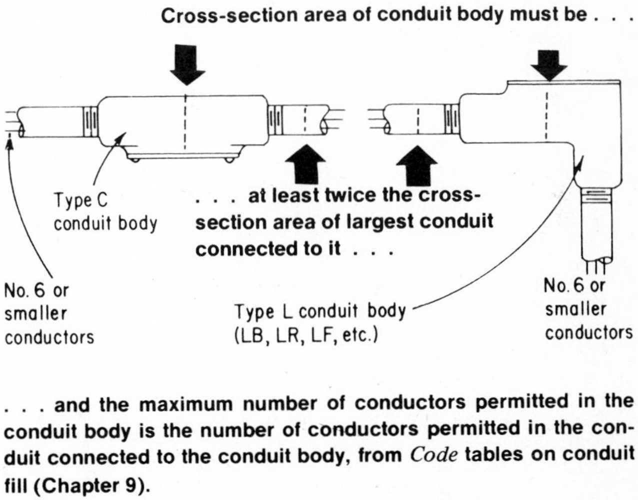

Fig. 370-12. For No. 6 and smaller conductors, conduit body must have a csa twice that of largest conduit. (Sec. 370-6.)

instance, in that sketch, if a conduit body is connected to ½-in. conduit, the conduit and the conduit body may contain seven No. 12 TW wires—as indicated in Table 3A, Chap. 9—and the conduit body must have a csa at least equal to 2 × 0.3 sq in. (the csa of ½-in. conduit), or 0.6 sq in. That is really a matter for the fitting manufacturers to observe.

The second paragraph of part (c) covers the details shown in Fig. 370-13. The rule requires that where fittings are used as shown in the sketch, they must be supported in a rigid and secure manner. Because Sec. 370-13 establishes the correct methods for supporting of boxes and fittings, it must be observed, and that section refers to support by "conduits"—which seems to exclude such use on EMT because the **NEC** distinguishes between "conduit" and "tubing" (EMT), as in the headline for Table 1 of Chap. 9 in the back of the

Although the basic rule still prohibits splicing and tapping in these fittings . . .

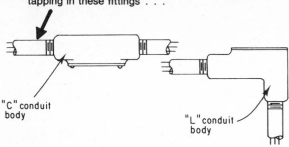

"C" conduit body

"L" conduit body

. . . .Permission is **now** given to splice in such fittings, if Section 370-6(b) is satisfied; that is, if—

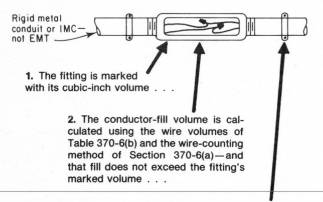

Rigid metal conduit or IMC— not EMT

1. The fitting is marked with its cubic-inch volume . . .

2. The conductor-fill volume is calculated using the wire volumes of Table 370-6(b) and the wire-counting method of Section 370-6(a)—and that fill does not exceed the fitting's marked volume . . .

3. And the fitting is "supported in a rigid and secure manner"—such as by the "conduit," if the conduit is clamped on each side of the fitting as described in the next-to-last paragraph of Section 370-13.

Fig. 370-13. Splices may be made in "C" and "L" conduit bodies—if the conditions shown in this illustration are satisfied. (Sec. 370-6.)

Code book. Figure 370-14 shows typical applications of those conduit bodies for splicing.

370-7. Conductors Entering Boxes or Fittings. Part **(b)** requires cable or raceway to be secured to *all metal* outlet boxes or fittings—such as by threaded connection, connector devices, or internal box clamps.

Part **(c)** requires that, where nonmetallic-sheathed cable is connected to nonmetallic boxes, the cable must enter through a knockout (KO) open-

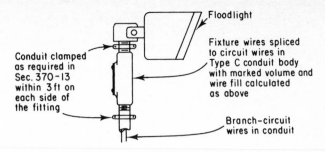

Floodlight

Conduit clamped
as required in
Sec. 370-13
within 3 ft on
each side of
the fitting

Fixture wires spliced
to circuit wires in
Type C conduit body
with marked volume and
wire fill calculated
as above

Branch-circuit
wires in conduit

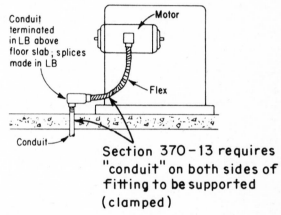

Conduit
terminated
in LB above
floor slab; splices
made in LB

Motor

Flex

Conduit

Section 370-13 requires
"conduit" on both sides of
fitting to be supported
(clamped)

Fig. 370-14. Splicing in "C" or "L" conduit bodies is common practice. (Sec. 370-6.)

ing provided for nonmetallic-sheathed cable, and not through a hole made at any point on the box. At least ¼ in. of the cable sheath must be brought inside the box.

Another very important limitation in this **Code** section applies to the need for clamping nonmetallic-sheathed cable at a KO where the cable enters anything other than a single gang box. The **Code** has always accepted the use of nonmetallic-sheathed cable without box clamps or any type of connector where the cable is stapled within 8 in. of the box. The cable is then brought into the box through a NM cable KO on the box, without any kind of a connector at the KO or any clamps in the box (Fig. 370-15). But the intention of the **Code** rule is that boxes or enclosures other than single gang boxes must be provided with a clamp or connector to secure nonmetallic-sheathed cable to such boxes (Fig. 370-16). *Only single gang nonmetallic boxes may be used without a cable clamp at the*

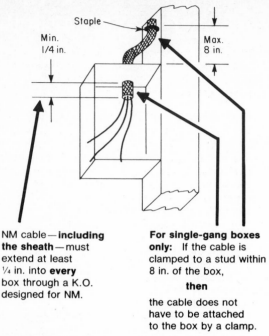

NM cable—**including the sheath**—must extend at least ¼ in. into **every** box through a K.O. designed for NM.

For single-gang boxes only: If the cable is clamped to a stud within 8 in. of the box,

then

the cable does not have to be attached to the box by a clamp.

Fig. 370-15. NM cable does not have to be clamped to single-gang boxes. (Sec. 370-7.)

box KOs. Where the Code permits elimination of a cable clamp if the cable is clamped to the stud within 8 in. of the box, the rule specifies that the 8-in. length be measured *along the cable* and not simply from the point of the cable strap to the box edge itself.

When used with open wiring on insulators, knob-and-tube work, or

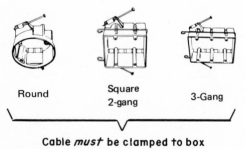

Round

Square 2-gang

3-Gang

Cable *must* be clamped to box

Fig. 370-16. NM cable must be clamped to all nonmetallic boxes that are *not* "single gang boxes." (Sec. 370-7.)

nonmetallic-sheathed cable, nonmetallic boxes have the advantage that an accidental contact between a "hot" wire and the box will not create a hazard.

370-9. Boxes Enclosing Flush Devices.   A through-the-wall box is a box which is manufactured to be installed in a partition wall so that a receptacle or switch may be attached to either side; therefore, it is not necessary to use two standard boxes one facing each side and connected by a jumper.

From the literal wording of Sec. 370-9, it could be interpreted to prohibit the use of such boxes. If a single device were used on only one side, then the other side would have to be closed by a cover of a thickness as required in Sec. 370-20(b) and 370-21—generally 14 gauge. If a device is installed on both sides and the requirements of Sec. 410-56(b) regarding faceplates are followed, the boxes could be considered to comply with the Code because the walls and backs of the boxes would be enclosed.

If the screws used for attaching the receptacles and switches to boxes were used also for the mounting of boxes, a poor mechanical job would result, since the boxes would be insecurely held whenever the devices were not installed and the screws loosened for adjustment of the device position. Hence the prohibition.

370-11. Repairing Plaster.   The purpose of Secs. 370-10 and 370-11 is to prevent openings around the edge of the box through which fire could be readily communicated to combustible material in the wall or ceiling. For this reason inspection authorities do not allow square or hexagonal boxes in ceilings, finished with sheetrock, without the use of "mud rings."

370-12. Exposed Surface Extensions.   The extension should be made as illustrated in Fig. 370-17. The extension ring is secured to the original box by two screws passing through ears attached to the box.

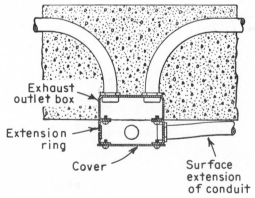

Fig. 370-17. Extension ring must be secured to box for surface extension. (Sec. 370-12.)

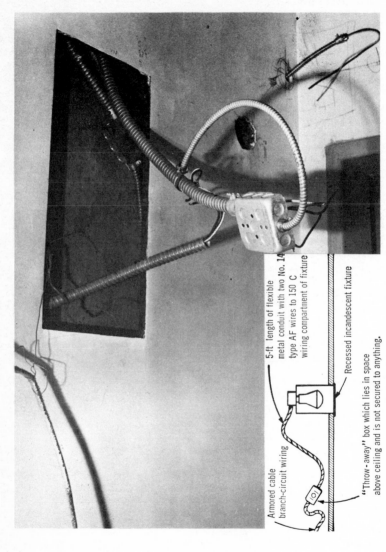

Fig. 370-18. Fixture supply flex is tapped out of junction box fed by flex or BX branch-circuit wiring in ceiling space. Box is later "thrown-away," unattached, into ceiling space. (Sec. 370-13.)

Armored cable branch-circuit wiring

5-ft length of flexible metal conduit with two No. 14 type AF wires to 150 C wiring compartment of fixture

"Throw-away" box which lies in space above ceiling and is not secured to anything.

Recessed incandescent fixture

370-13. Supports.   The Code rule strictly requires all boxes to be fastened in their installed position—and the various paragraphs of this section cover different conditions of box support for commonly encountered box applications. The one widely accepted exception to that rule—although actually not recognized by the Code—is the so-called "throwaway" box or "floating" box, which is a junction box used to connect flexible metal conduit from a recessed fixture to flex or BX branch-circuit wiring, in accordance with Sec. 410-67(c) (Fig. 370-18). In such cases, the connection of the fixture "whip" (the 4 to 6 ft of flex with high-temperature wires, e.g., 150°C Type AF) is made to the branch-circuit junction box which hangs down through the ceiling opening, and then the junction box is pushed back out of the way in the ceiling space and the fixture raised into position. But with suspended ceilings of lift-out panels, there is no need to leave such a loose box in the ceiling space, because connection can be made to a fixed box before the ceiling tiles are laid in place.

Figure 370-19 shows the rule of the second sentence of this section.

An outlet box built into a concrete ceiling, as shown in Fig. 370-20, seldom needs any special support. At such an outlet, if it is intended for a fixture of great weight to be safely hung on an ordinary ⅜-in. fixture stud, a special fixture support consisting of a threaded pipe or rod is required, such as is shown in Fig. 370-21.

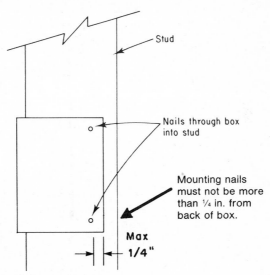

Fig. 370-19. Box-mounting nails must not obstruct box interior space. (Sec. 370-13.)

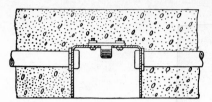

Fig. 370-20. Box in concrete is securely supported. (Sec. 370-13.)

In a tile arch floor (Fig. 370-6) a large opening must be cut through the tile to receive the conduit and outlet box.

The requirement of metal or wood supports for boxes applies to concealed work in walls and floors of wood-frame construction and other types of construction having open spaces in which the wiring is installed. In walls or floors of concrete, brick, or tile where conduit and boxes are solidly built into the wall or floor material, special box supports are not usually necessary.

In an existing building, where any type of wiring is installed either exposed or concealed, the boxes may be mounted on plaster or any other ceiling or wall finish, the only requirement being that they must be securely fastened in place. Where no structural members are available for support, boxes not over 100 cu in. in size, specifically approved for the purpose, shall be affixed with approved anchors or clamps. Figure 370-22 illustrates the intent of "specifically approved for the purpose." For

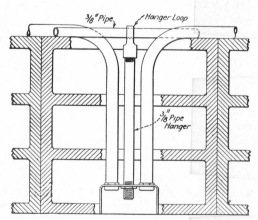

Fig. 370-21. Box in tile arch ceiling requires pipehanger support if very heavy lighting fixture is to be attached to the box stud. (Sec. 370-13.)

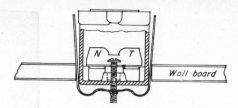

1. Inserting box and bracket through wall board.

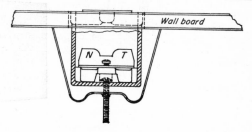

2. Box anchored to wall.

For clamping boxes to openings cut in existing walls ➡️

"MADISON HOLDITS"
STEEL

Fig. 370-22. Second paragraph of Sec. 370-13 refers to these types of clamping devices. (Sec. 370-13.)

cutting metal boxes into existing walls, "Madison Holdits" are used to clamp the box tightly in position in the opening. Actually, the local inspector can determine acceptable methods of securing "cut-in" device boxes because this provision provides appreciable latitude for such decisions.

Figure 370-23 shows box-support methods that are covered by the next-to-last paragraph of Sec. 370-13. The rule there applies to "conduit" [rigid metal conduit and IMC, but not EMT or PVC conduit, Sec. 347-3(b)] used to support boxes—as for overhead conduit runs. Where locknut and bushing connections are used, the box must be independently fastened in place. Figure 370-24 shows a violation.

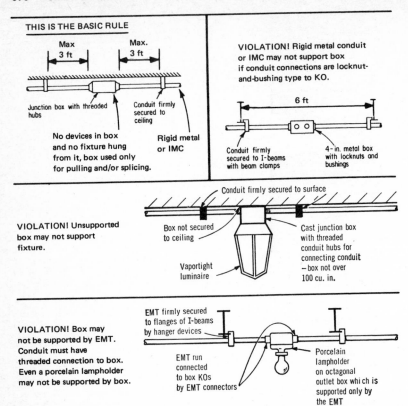

Fig. 370-23. Box may be supported by "conduit" that is clamped, but box must not contain or support anything. (Sec. 370-13.)

The rules of the last paragraph of Sec. 370-13 are shown in Fig. 370-25. The rule recognizes the support of elevated threaded-hub junction boxes by conduits emerging from a floor, or concrete, or the earth, such as those used near swimming pools, patios, or shrubbery. Support by a single conduit is not recognized. Figure 370-26 shows several installations that are in violation of these rules.

370-14. Depth of Outlet Boxes.   Sufficient space should be provided inside the box so that the wires do not have to be jammed together or against the box, and the box should provide enough of an enclosure so that in case of trouble, burning insulation cannot readily ignite flammable material outside the box.

Fig. 370-24. "T" fittings are supported by the rigid conduit that connects to their threaded hubs, but the fitting at right does not have the conduit supported on two sides of the fitting. Note angle iron brace to conduit from I-beam flange. (Sec. 370-13.)

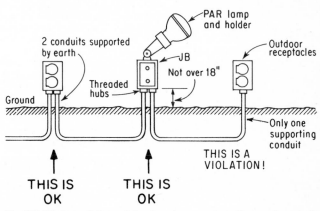

Fig. 370-25. Boxes fed out of the ground or a concrete floor, patio, or walk must observe these rules. (Sec. 370-13.)

Fig. 370-26. A *single* rigid metal conduit may not support a box, even with concrete fill in the ground (left). Box may not be supported on EMT, even with several connections used (center). Method at right is a violation on three counts: EMT, not "conduit," supports the box; only one hub on box is connected; box is more than 18 in. above ground. (Sec. 370-13.)

370-15. Covers and Canopies.
This rule requires every outlet box to be covered up—by a cover plate, a fixture canopy, or a faceplate, which has the openings for a receptacle, snap switch, or other device installed in a box.

Part **(a)** requires all metal faceplates to be grounded as required by Sec. 250-42. Because metal faceplates are *exposed* conductive parts, they must satisfy Sec. 250-42(a), which, in effect, says that ungrounded metal faceplates shall not be installed within 8 ft vertically or 5 ft horizontally of ground or grounded objects—laundry tubs, bathtubs, shower baths, plumbing fixtures, steam pipes, radiators, or other grounded surfaces—that are subject to contact by persons.

And part **(b)** of Sec. 250-42 requires metal faceplates to be grounded in wet or damp locations (which have been judged to include bathrooms)—unless the faceplates are isolated from contact.

A metal faceplate, if not grounded, may become "alive" by reason of contact of the ungrounded circuit wire with the plate or switch box, and a hazard is thus created if the plate is within reach from any conductive object. The hazard still exists, however, if a plate of insulating material is attached by means of metal screws with exposed metal heads. Insulated screws and metal screws with insulated heads are available.

When a metal faceplate is attached to a switch or receptacle in a grounded metal box, it is thereby grounded and complies with Sec. 410-21, which covers grounding of lighting fixtures and faceplates. This is true for a faceplate on a switch or a receptacle because the faceplate attaches to the metal mounting strap of the device and that strap is connected to the ears on the grounded metal box by the mounting screws and, sometimes, additionally by a bonding jumper used for grounding the receptacle ground terminal and strap. In a nonmetallic box fed by NM cable, a receptacle mounting strap is grounded by connection of the cable ground wire to the ground terminal (green hex-head screw)—thereby grounding a metal faceplate attached to the receptacle strap. But in the case of a snap switch in a nonmetallic box, the switch must be equipped with a ground terminal on its strap to permit connection of the NM cable ground wire to the strap—thereby assuring grounding of a metal faceplate attached to the strap of the switch. Figure 370-27 shows such a switch used to ensure effective grounding of metal wall plates when nonmetallic switch boxes are used.

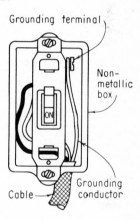

Fig. 370-27. Grounding switch must be used for metal faceplate on any non-metallic box. (Sec. 370-15.)

It should be noted that Secs. 370-15(a) and 250-42(a) combine to require grounding of metal faceplates that are "within 8 feet vertically or 5 feet horizontally . . ." etc. But, Sec. 410-18, which is referenced after Sec. 370-15(a), flatly requires grounding of *any* metal faceplate if it is attached to a wiring device in a box fed by a wiring system that contains an equipment grounding means—regardless of any distances to grounded objects. In Fig. 370-27, when a metal faceplate is to be used for a switch in a nonmetallic box, Sec. 370-15(a) requires the plate to be grounded if it is "within 8 feet . . ." etc. But, if the faceplate is *not* in a wet or damp location and is *not* "within 8 feet . . ." etc., it does *not* have to be grounded to satisfy Sec. 370-15. *However,* if NM with a ground wire is used, then Sec. 410-18(a) requires use of that type of switch to ground the metal faceplate, no matter where it is used. But, if NM cable without a ground wire is used, Sec. 410-18(b) would make it mandatory to use a faceplate of insulating material—thereby prohibiting the metal faceplate. So to use a metal faceplate on any nonmetallic box, the NM cable must have a ground wire and the type of switch shown must be used.

In part (b) of Sec. 370-15, if the ceiling or wall finish is of combustible material, the canopy and box must form a complete enclosure. The chief purpose of this rule is to require that no open space be left between the canopy and the edge of the box where the finish is wood or other combustible material. Where the wall or ceiling finish is plaster the requirement does not apply, since plaster is not classed as a combustible material; however, the plaster must be continuous up to the box, leaving no opening around the box.

370-17. Outlet Boxes.   Part (b) requires floor boxes to be completely suitable for the particular way in which they are used, as in Fig. 370-28. Adjustable floor boxes and associated service receptacles can be installed in every type of floor construction. Metal cap, shown at top, keeps assembly clean during pouring of concrete slabs. After the concrete has cured, this cap can then be removed and discarded and floor plates and service fittings added.

370-18. Pull and Junction Boxes.   As noted in Sec. 370-6, conduit bodies must be sized the same as pull boxes when they contain No. 4 or larger conductors.

For raceways of ¾-in. trade size and larger containing conductors of No. 4 or larger size, the **NE Code** specifies certain minimum dimensions for a pull or junction box installed in a raceway run. These rules also apply to pull and junction boxes in cable runs—but instead of using the cable diameter, the minimum trade size raceway required for the number and size of conductors in the cable must be used in the calculations. Basically there are two types of pulls—straight pulls and angle pulls. Figure 370-29 covers straight pulls. Figure 370-30 covers angle pulls. In all the cases shown in those illustrations, the depth of the box only has to be sufficient to permit installation of the locknuts and bushings on the largest conduit. And the spacing between adjacent conduit entries is also determined by the diameters of locknuts and bushings—to provide proper installation. Depth is the dimension not shown in the sketches.

Figure 370-31 shows a more complicated conduit and pull box arrangement, which requires more extensive calculation of the minimum permitted size. In this particular layout shown, the upper 3-in. conduits running straight through the box represent a problem separate from the 2-in. conduit angle pulls. In this case the 3-in. conduit establishes the box length in excess of that required for the 2-in. conduit. After computing the 3-in. requirements, the box size was calculated for the angle pull involving the 2-in. conduit.

Subparagraph (3) of Sec. 370-18(a) permits smaller pull or junction boxes where such boxes have been approved for and marked with the

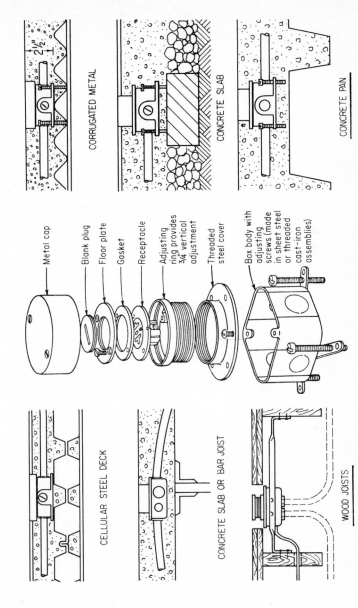

Fig. 370-28. Floor boxes for receptacles must be "especially approved" for their use. (Sec. 370-17.)

CORRUGATED METAL

CONCRETE SLAB

CONCRETE PAN
(Sec. 370-17.)

Metal cap

Blank plug

Floor plate

Gasket

Receptacle

Adjusting ring provides 3/4" vertical adjustment

Threaded steel cover

Box body with adjusting screws (made in sheet steel or threaded cast-iron assemblies)

CELLULAR STEEL DECK

CONCRETE SLAB OR BAR JOIST

WOOD JOISTS

EXAMPLES:

1.

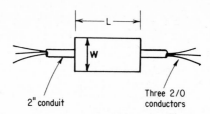

L = 8 × 2 in. = 16 in. minimum

W = Whatever width is necessary to provide proper installation of the conduit locknuts and bushings within the enclosure.

2.

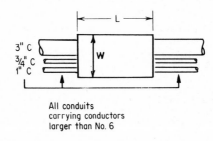

The 3-in. conduit is the largest.
Therefore—

L = 8 × 3 in. = 24 in. minimum

W = Width necessary for conduit locknuts and bushings.

Fig. 370-29. In straight pulls, the length of the box must be not less than eight times the trade diameter of the largest raceway. (Sec. 370-18.)

maximum number and size of conductors and the conduit fills are *less* than the maximum permitted in Table 1, Chap. 9. This rule provides guidelines for boxes which have been widely used for years, but which have been smaller than the sizes normally required in subparagraphs **(1)** and **(2)**. These smaller pull boxes must be listed by UL under the new rule.

EXAMPLE:

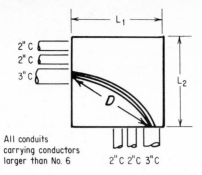

The 3-in. conduit is the largest.
Therefore—

$L_1 = 6 \times 3$ in. $+ (2$ in. $+ 2$ in.$) = 22$ in. min.
$L_2 = 6 \times 3$ in. $+ (2$ in. $+ 2$ in.$) = 22$ in. min.
$D = 6 \times 3$ in. $= 18$ in., **minimum distance between raceway entries enclosing the same conductors**

Fig. 370-30. Box size must be calculated for angle pulls. For boxes in which the conductors are pulled at an angle or in a "U," the distance between each raceway entry inside the box and the opposite wall of the box must not be less than six times the trade diameter of the largest raceway. And the distance must be increased for additional raceway entries by the amount of the sum of the diameters of all other raceway entries on the same wall of the box. The distance between raceway entries enclosing the same conductors must not be less than six times the trade diameter of the larger raceway. (Sec. 370-18.)

There are many instances where an installation is made in which raceways and conductors are not matched so as to utilize maximum conduit fill as permitted by the **Code**. An example would be a 2-in. conduit with six No. 4 THHN conductors. The **Code** would permit up to 16 conductors depending upon the type of insulation. It was felt that in such installations provisions should be made for the use of boxes or fittings which would not necessarily conform to the letter of the law as exemplified by the standards listed in subsections **(1)** and **(2)**, but would compare favorably under test with a box sized as is required for the conductor and conduit.

A pull or junction box used with 2-in. conduit and conductors No. 4 AWG or larger must be 16 in. long if straight pulls are made and must be 12 in. long if angle pulls are to be made. If we have a 2-in. conduit and we

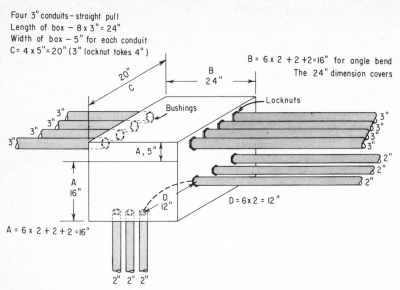

Four 3" conduits – straight pull
Length of box – 8 x 3" = 24"
Width of box – 5" for each conduit
C = 4 x 5" = 20" (3" locknut takes 4")

B = 6 x 2 + 2 + 2 = 16" for angle bend
The 24" dimension covers

20"
C

B
24"

Bushings

Locknuts

3"
3"
3"

3"
3"
3"
3"

A, 5"

2"
2"
2"

A
16"

D
12"

D = 6 x 2 = 12"

A = 6 x 2 + 2 + 2 = 16"

2" 2" 2"

Fig. 370-31. A number of calculations are involved when angle and straight pulls are made in different directions and different planes. (Sec. 370-18.)

are installing eight No. RHH conductors, all pull or junction boxes would have to conform to these measurements. If, however, we are installing five No. 4 RH conductors, a smaller box would be acceptable, provided it has been tested for and is marked with this number.

Figure 370-32 shows how the rules of Sec. 370-18(a) apply to conduit bodies. **Important:** The Exception given in Sec. 370-18(a) (2) establishes the minimum dimension of L2 for angle runs, but this Exception only applies to conduit bodies which have the removable cover opposite one of the entries, such as a Type LB body. Types LR, LL, and LF do not qualify under that Exception, and for such conduit bodies the dimension L2 would have to be at least equal to the dimension L1 (that is, six times raceway diameter).

Figure 370-33 shows the racking of cable required by part **(b)** of this section.

Figure 370-34 shows another consideration in sizing a pull box for angle conduit layouts. A pull box is to be installed to make a right-angle turn in a group of conduits consisting of two 3-in., two 2½-in., and four 2-in. conduits.

Subparagraph **(2)** of Sec. 370-18(a) gives two methods for computing the box dimensions, and both must be met.

STRAIGHT RUN

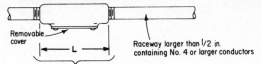

Removable cover

Raceway larger than 1/2 in. containing No. 4 or larger conductors

Type C conduit body must have length L equal to 8 times diameter of the raceway

Examples

If four No. 4 THHN are used in 1-in. conduit, conduit body must be at least 8 in. long.

If four 500MCM XHHW are used in 3-in. conduit, conduit body must be at least 24 in. long.

ANGLE RUN

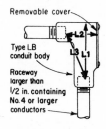

Removable cover

Type LB conduit body

Raceway larger than 1/2 in. containing No. 4 or larger conductors

From Sec. 370-18(a)(2):

L1 = at least 6 times diameter of raceway (inside dimension)

L2 = at least equal to the distance given in Table 373-6(a) for the given size of conductor, as shown in the column for *one wire per terminal*

L3 = at least 6 times diameter of raceway

Examples

If four No. 4 THW conductors are used in 1¼-in. conduit, minimum dimensions would be calculated as follows:

L1 = 6 × 1¼ in. = 7.5 in.
L2 = 2 in., from Table 373-6(a) for one No. 4 conductor per terminal
L3 = 6 × 1¼ in. = 7.5 in.

If four 500MCM THW conductors are used in 3½-in. conduit, minimum dimensions would be:

L1 = 6 × 3½ in. = 21 in.
L2 = 6 in., from Table 373-6(a)
L3 = 6 × 3½ in. = 21 in.

Fig. 370-32. Conduit bodies must be sized as pull boxes under these conditions. (Sec. 370-18.)

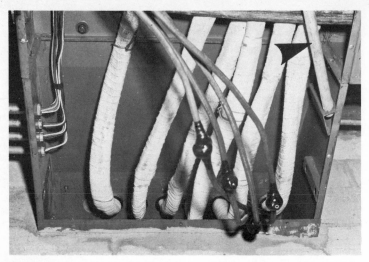

Fig. 370-33. If a pullbox has *any* dimension over 6 ft, the conductors within it must be supported by suitable racking (arrow) or cabling, as shown here for arc-proofed bundles of feeder conductors, to keep the weight of the many conductors off the sheet metal cover that attaches to the bottom of the box. (Sec. 370-18.)

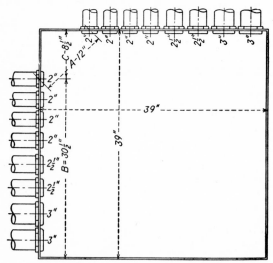

Fig. 370-34. Distance between conduits carrying same cables has great impact on overall box size. (Sec. 370-18.)

First method:

$$6 \times 3 \text{ in.} = 18 \text{ in.}$$
$$1 \times 3 \text{ in.} = 3$$
$$2 \times 2\tfrac{1}{2} \text{ in.} = 5$$
$$4 \times 2 \text{ in.} = \underline{8}$$
$$\text{Total} = 34 \text{ in.}$$

Second method:

Assuming that the conduits are to leave the box in the same order in which they enter, the arrangement is shown in Fig. 370-34 and the distance A between the ends of the two conduits must be not less than 6×2 in. = 12 in. It can be assumed that this measurement is to be made between the centers of the two conduits. By calculation, or by laying out the corner of the box, it is found that the distance C should be about $8\tfrac{1}{2}$ in.

The distance B should be not less than $30\tfrac{1}{2}$ in., approximately, as determined by applying practical data for the spacing between centers of conduits,

$$30\tfrac{1}{2} \text{ in.} + 8\tfrac{1}{2} \text{ in.} = 39 \text{ in.}$$

In this case the box dimensions are governed by the second method. The largest dimension computed by either of the two methods is of course the one to be used. Of course, if conduit positions for conduits carrying the same cables are transposed—as in Fig. 370-30—then box size can be minimized.

The most practical method of determining the proper size of a pull box is to sketch the box layout with its contained conductors on a paper.

Section 370-18 applies particularly to the pull boxes commonly placed above distribution switchboards and which are often, and with good reason, termed *tangle boxes*. In such boxes, all conductors of each circuit should be cabled together by serving them with twine so as to form a self-supporting assembly that can be formed into shape, or the conductors should be supported in an orderly manner on racks, as required by part **(b)** of Sec. 370-18. The conductors should not rest directly on any metalwork inside the box, and insulating bushings should be provided wherever required by Sec. 373-6(c).

For example, the box illustrated in Fig. 370-34 could be approximately 5 in. deep and accommodate one horizontal row of conduits. By making it twice as deep, two horizontal rows or twice the number of conduits could be installed.

Insulating racks are usually placed between conductor layers, and space must be allowed for them.

370-20. Metal Outlet, Switch and Junction Boxes, and Fittings.   This section through Sec. 370-24 covers construction of boxes. UL data on application of boxes supplement this Code data as follows:

1. Cable clamps in outlet boxes are marked to indicate the one or more types of cables that are suitable for use with that clamp.

2. Box clamps have been tested for securing only one cable per clamp, except that multiple-section clamps may secure one cable under each section of the clamp, with each cable entering the box through a separate KO.

370-51(a). Size of Pull and Junction Boxes (Over 600 V).   Figure 370-35 shows these rules.

Part **(c)** of this section covers the pull boxes regulated by Sec. 370-18. UL data on such boxes are important and must be related to the Code

STRAIGHT PULLS

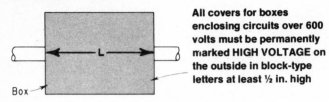

All covers for boxes enclosing circuits over 600 volts must be permanently marked HIGH VOLTAGE on the outside in block-type letters at least ½ in. high

L - not less than 48 times the outside diameter, over sheath, of the largest *conductor* or *cable* entering the box

NOTE: The box length must be 48 times the conductor or cable diameter, *not the conduit* diameter.

ANGLE PULLS

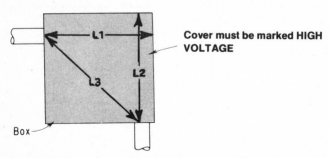

Cover must be marked HIGH VOLTAGE

L1, L2, L3—not less than 36 times the outside diameter, over sheath, of the largest *conductor* or *cable*

Fig. 370-35. Minimum dimensions are set for high-voltage pull and junction boxes. [Sec. 370-51(a).]

rules. Listed pull and junction boxes may be sheet metal, cast metal, or nonmetallic, and all of these have a volume greater than 100 cu in. Because listed boxes of this type are available, the intent of **NE Code** Sec. 110-2 and the clear regulations of OSHA on equipment acceptability demand that only listed pull and junction boxes be used. To use a pullbox or junction box that is not listed is a violation of those regulations. Boxes marked "Raintight" or "Rainproof" are tested under a condition simulating exposure to beating rain. "Raintight" means water will not enter the box. "Rainproof" means that exposure to beating rain will not interfere with proper operation of the apparatus within the enclosure. Use of a box with either designation must satisfy **NE Code** Sec. 370-5, which notes that boxes in wet locations (such as outdoors where exposed to rain or indoors where exposed to water spray) must prevent moisture from entering *or* accumulating within the box. That is, water *may* enter the box if it does not accumulate in the box, where the box is drained. A box that is raintight or rainproof may satisfy that rule. Be sure, though, that any equipment installed in a box labeled "rainproof" is mounted within the location restrictions marked in the box.

ARTICLE 373. CABINETS AND CUTOUT BOXES

373-1. Scope.   Cabinets and cutout boxes, according to the definitions in Art. 100, must have doors and are thus distinguished from large boxes with covers consisting of plates attached with screws or bolts. Article 373 applies to all boxes used to enclose operating apparatus, i.e., apparatus having moving parts or requiring inspection or attention, such as panelboards, cutouts, switches, circuit breakers, or control apparatus.

373-3. Position in Wall.   Figure 373-1 shows how the $\frac{1}{4}$-in. setback relates to cabinets installed in noncombustible walls.

373-5. Conductors Entering Cabinets or Cutout Boxes.   Part **(c)** makes clear that all cables used with cabinets or cutout boxes must be attached to the enclosure. NM cable, for instance, does not have to be connected by clamp or connector device to a single gang nonmetallic outlet box as in Sec. 370-7(c), *but must always* be connected to KOs in panelboard enclosures and other cabinets (Fig. 373-2).

373-6. Deflection of Conductors.   Parts **(a)** and **(b)** cover a basic Code rule that is referenced in a number of Code articles to assure safety and effective conductor application by providing enough space to bend conductors within enclosures. In Fig. 373-3, the three clearances shown are determined from Table 373-6(a), under the column for one wire per terminal. For multiple-conductor circuit makeups, the clearance at terminals and in side gutters has to be greater, as shown under two, three, four, etc., wires per terminal.

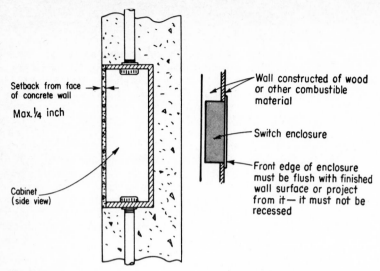

Setback from face of concrete wall

Max. ¼ inch

Cabinet (side view)

Wall constructed of wood or other combustible material

Switch enclosure

Front edge of enclosure must be flush with finished wall surface or project from it— it must not be recessed

Fig. 373-1. In masonry wall, cabinet does not have to be flush with wall surface—as it does in wood wall. (Sec. 373-3.)

Paragraph **(c)** applies to all conductors of size No. 4 or larger entering a cabinet or box from rigid metal conduit, flexible metal conduit, electrical metallic tubing, etc. To protect the conductors from cutting or abrasion a smoothly rounded insulating surface is required. While many fittings are provided with insulated sleeves or linings, it is also possible to use a separate insulating lining or sleeve to meet the requirements of the Code. Figure 373-4 shows use of a bushing with an insulated edge or a completely nonmetallic bushing to satisfy this rule. Figure 373-5 shows an

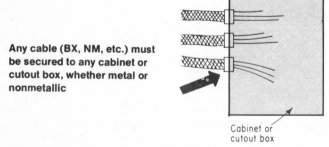

Any cable (BX, NM, etc.) must be secured to any cabinet or cutout box, whether metal or nonmetallic

Cabinet or cutout box

Fig. 373-2. All cables must be secured to all cabinets or cutout boxes. (Sec. 373-5.)

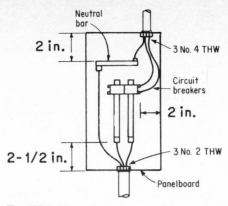

Fig. 373-3. These clearances are minimums that must be observed. (Sec. 373-6.)

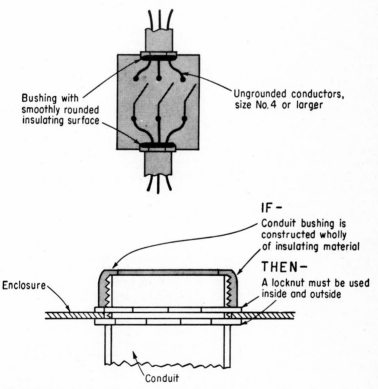

Fig. 373-4. An insulated-throat bushing or other protection must be used at enclosure openings. (Sec. 373-6.)

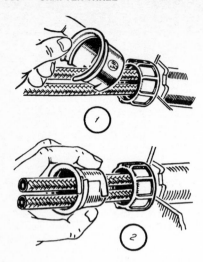

Fig.   373-5. Slip-over   nonmetallic
sleeve may be used to cover metal bushing throat. (Sec. 373-6.)

approved sleeve which may be used to separate the conductors from the
raceway fitting, which may be installed after the conductors are already
installed and connected.

   This rule of part **(c)** also requires that any insulating bushing or
insulating material used to protect conductors from abrasion must have a
temperature rating at least equal to the temperature rating of the
conductors.

373-8. Enclosures for Switches or Overcurrent Devices.   The basic rule
here is a follow-up to the rule of Sec. 373-7.

   Most enclosures for switches and/or overcurrent devices have been
designed to accommodate only those conductors intended to be connected to terminals within such enclosures. And in designing such equipment it would be virtually impossible for manufacturers to anticipate

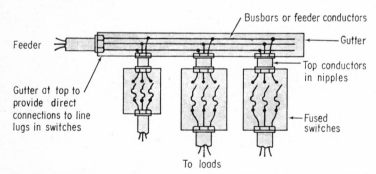

Fig. 373-6. Feeder taps in auxiliary gutter keep feeder cables and tap connectors out of
switch enclosures. (Sec. 373-8.)

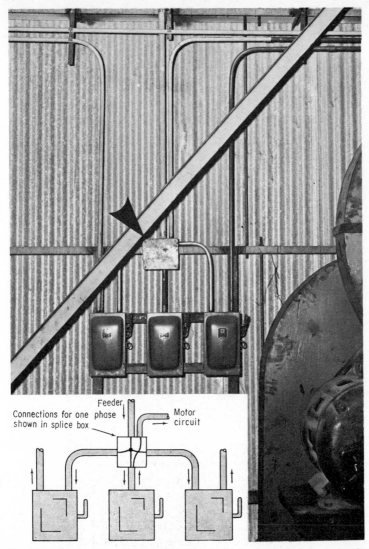

Fig. 373-7. Junction box (arrow) is used for tapping feeder conductors to supply individual motor branch circuits—as shown in inset diagram. (Sec. 373-8.)

various types of "foreign" circuits, feed-through circuits, or numerous splices or taps.

The rule here states enclosures for switches, CBs, panelboards, or other operating equipment must not be used as junction boxes, troughs, or raceways for conductors feeding through or tapping off, unless designs suitable for the purpose are employed to provide adequate space. This rule affects installations in which a number of branch circuits or subfeeder circuits are to be tapped from feeder conductors in an auxiliary gutter, using fused switches to provide disconnect and overcurrent protection for the branch or subfeeder circuits. It also applies to feeder taps in panelboard cabinets.

In general, the most satisfactory way to connect various enclosures together is through the use of properly sized auxiliary gutters (Fig. 373-6) or junction boxes. Figure 373-7 shows a hookup of three motor disconnects, using a junction box to make the feeder taps. Following this concept, enclosures for switches and/or overcurrent devices will not be overcrowded.

There are cases where large enclosures for switches and/or overcurrent devices will accommodate additional conductors and this is generally where the 40 percent (conductor space) and 75 percent (splices or taps)

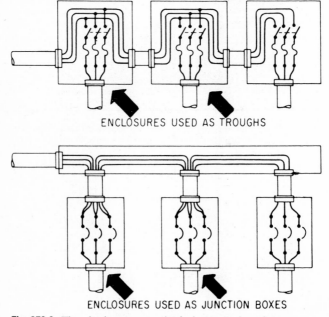

ENCLOSURES USED AS TROUGHS

ENCLOSURES USED AS JUNCTION BOXES

Fig. 373-8. These hookups are permitted where space in enclosure gutters satisfies Exception to basic rule. (Sec. 373-8.)

at one cross section would apply. An example would be control circuits tapped off or extending through 200-A or larger fusible switches or CB enclosures. The csa within such enclosures is the *free gutter wiring space* intended for conductors.

The Exception to this rule is shown in Fig. 373-8 and applied as follows:

Example: If an enclosure has a gutter space of 3 by 3 in., the csa would be 9 sq in. Thus, the total conductor fill (use Table 5, Chap. 9) at any cross section (including conductors) could not exceed 6.75 sq in. (9 × 0.75).

In the case of large conductors, a splice other than a wire-to-wire "C" or "tube" splice would not be acceptable if the conductors at the cross section are near a 40 percent fill, because this would leave only a 35 percent space for the splice. Most splices for larger conductors with split-bolt connectors or similar types are usually twice the size of the conductors being

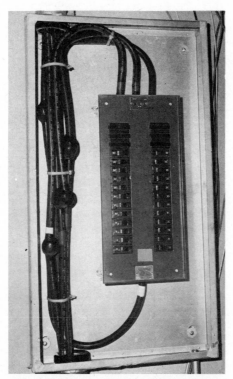

Fig. 373-9. The Exception to Sec. 373-8 permits feeding through and tapping off in cabinets for panelboards on feeder risers, where the side gutter is specially oversized for the application. (Sec. 373-8.)

spliced. Accordingly, where larger conductors are to be spliced within enclosures, the total conductor fill should not exceed *20 percent* to allow for any bulky splice at a cross section.

Figure 373-9 shows an example of feeder taps made in panelboard side gutter where the cabinet is provided with adequate space for the large feeder conductors and for the bulk of the tap devices with their insulating tape wrap.

ARTICLE 374. AUXILIARY GUTTERS

374-1. Use.   Auxiliary gutters are sheet-metal troughs in which conductors are laid in place after the gutter has been installed. Auxiliary gutters are used as parts of complete assemblies of apparatus such as switchboards, distribution centers, and control equipment, as shown in Fig. 374-1. But auxiliary gutters may not contain equipment even though it looks like surface metal raceway (Art. 352), which may contain devices and equipment (Fig. 374-2).

374-2. Extension Beyond Equipment.   Auxiliary gutters are not intended to be a type of general raceway and are not permitted to extend more than 30 ft beyond the equipment which they supplement, except in elevator work. Where an extension beyond 30 ft is necessary, Art. 362 for wireways must be complied with. The label of Underwriters Laboratories Inc. on each length of trough bears the legend "Wireways or Auxiliary Gutters," which indicates that they may be identical troughs but are distinguished one from the other only by their use. See comments following Sec. 362-1 in this handbook.

374-5. Number of Conductors.   The rules on permitted conductor fill for auxiliary gutters are basically the same as those for wireways. Refer to Sec. 362-5. Note that Exception No. 3 permits more than 30 general circuit wires; but where over 30 wires are installed, the correction factors specified in Note 8 to Tables 310-16/19 must be applied.

No limit is placed on the size of conductors that may be installed in an auxiliary gutter.

The csa of rubber-covered and thermoplastic-covered conductors given in Table 5, Chap. 9, must be used in computing the size of gutters required to contain a given combination of such conductors.

Figure 374-3 shows a typical gutter application where the conductor fill must be calculated to determine the acceptable csa of the gutter. There are several factors involved in sizing auxiliary gutters that often lead to selecting the wrong size. The two main factors are how conductors enter the gutter and the contained conductors at any cross section. The minimum required width of a gutter is determined by the csa occupied by the conductors and splices and the space necessary for bending conductors entering or leaving the gutter. The total csa occupied by the conductors

Fig. 374-1. Typical applications of auxiliary gutters provide the necessary space to make taps, splices, and other conductor connections involved where a number of switches or CBs are fed by a feeder (top) or for multiple-circuit routing, as at top of a motor control center (right) shown with a ground bus in gutter (arrow). (Sec. 374-1.)

at any cross section of the gutter must not be greater than 20 percent of the gutter interior csa at that point (Sec. 374-5). The total csa occupied by the mass of conductors and splices at any cross section of the gutter must not be greater than 75 percent of the gutter interior csa at that point [Sec. 374-8(a)].

In the gutter installation shown, assume that the staggering of the splices has been done to minimize the area taken up at any cross section—

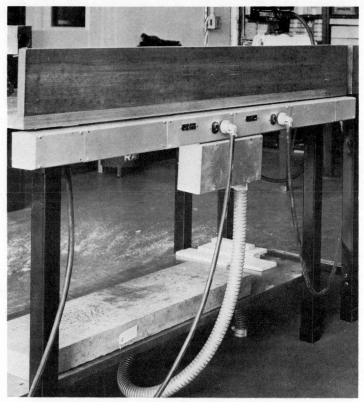

Fig. 374-2. Surface metal raceway may be used with accessory circuit breakers and/or receptacles in cover plates—but auxiliary gutters may not be used like this. (Sec. 374-1.)

to keep the mass of splices from all adding up at the same cross section. The greatest conductor concentration is therefore either at section x, where there are three 300 MCM and one 4/0 THW conductors, or at section y, where there are eight 3/0 THW conductors. To determine at which of these two cross sections the fill is greater, apply the appropriate csa's of THW conductors as given in Table 5, Chap. 9:

1. The total conductor csa at section x is 3 × 0.5581 sq in. plus 1 × 0.3904, or 2.0647 sq in.
2. The total conductor csa at section y is 8 × 0.3288 sq in. or 2.6304 sq in.

Section y is, therefore, the determining consideration. Because that fill

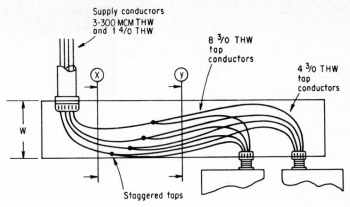

Fig. 374-3. Minimum acceptable gutter cross section and depth must be calculated. (Sec. 374-5.)

of 2.6304 sq in. can at most be 20 percent of the gutter csa, the total gutter area must be at least five times this conductor fill area, or 13.152 sq in.

Assuming the gutter has a square cross section (all sides of equal width) and the sides an integral number of inches, the nearest square value would be 16 sq in., indicating a 4 by 4-in. gutter, and that would be suitable if the 300 MCM conductors entered the end of the gutter instead of the top. But because those conductors are deflected entering and leaving the gutter, the first two columns of Table 373-6(a) must also be applied to determine whether the width of 4 in. affords sufficient space for bending the conductors. That consideration is required by Sec. 374-9(d). The worst condition (largest conductors) is where the supply conductors enter; therefore the 300 MCM cable will determine the required space.

Table 373-6(a) shows that a circuit of one 300 MCM per phase leg (or wire per terminal) requires a bending space at least 5 in. deep (in the direction of the entry of the 300 MCM conductors), calling for a standard 6 by 6-in. gutter for this application.

In Fig. 374-3, if the 300 MCM conductors entered at the left-hand end of the gutter instead of at the top, Sec. 374-9(d) would require Table 373-6(a) to be applied only to the deflection of the No. 3/0 conductors. The table shows, under one wire per terminal, a minimum depth of 4 in. is required. In that case, a 4 by 4 gutter would satisfy.

374-8. Splices and Taps.   Part **(a)** is discussed above, under Sec. 374-5.

Part **(b)** covers cases where bare busbar conductors are used in gutters. The insulation might be cut by resting on the sharp edge of the bar or the bar might become hot enough to injure the insulation. When taps are made to bare conductors in a gutter, care should be taken so as to place and form the wires in such a manner that they will remain permanently separated from the bare bars.

Part **(c)** requires that identification be provided wherever it is not clearly evident what apparatus is supplied by the tap. Thus if a single set of tap conductors are carried through a short length of conduit from a gutter to a switch and the conduit is in plain view, the tap is fully identified and needs no special marking; but if two or more sets of taps are carried in a single conduit to two or more different pieces of apparatus, each tap should be identified by some marking such as a small tag secured to each wire.

ARTICLE 380. SWITCHES

380-1. Scope.   Note that all the provisions of this article that cover switches *also* apply to circuit breakers, which are operated exactly as a switch whenever they are manually moved to the ON or OFF position.

380-2. Switch Connections.   The rule of part **(a)** is shown in Fig. 380-1. Keeping "both polarities in the same enclosure" (that is, metal raceway) minimizes inductive heating, as described under Sec. 300-20.

The rule of part **(b)** is illustrated in Fig. 380-2. The "ACCEPTABLE" three-pole switch satisfies Exception No. 1. Opening only the grounded wire of a 2-wire circuit would leave all devices that are connected to the circuit alive and at a voltage to ground equal to the voltage between wires on the mains. In case of an accidental ground on the grounded wire, the circuit would not be controlled by the single-pole switch.

In Fig. 380-3, the load consists of lamps connected between the neutral and the two outer wires and is not balanced. Opening the neutral while the other wires are connected would cause the voltages to become unbalanced and might burn out all lamps on the more lightly loaded side.

Except for Sec. 514-5, which requires a switch in a grounded neutral for a circuit to a pump at a gas station, the neutral does not need to be switched. But, where a grounded neutral or grounded phase leg is switched, it must never be by a single-pole switch.

A switch may be arranged to open the grounded conductor if it simultaneously opens all the other conductors of the circuit.

380-3. Enclosure.   Figure 380-4 shows the basic rule of this section and Sec. 380-4. This rule also requires adequate wire bending space at terminals and in side gutters of switch enclosures. In this section and in other sections applying to wiring space around other types of equipment it is a mandatory Code requirement that wire bending space and side gutter wiring space conform to the requirements of Table 373-6(a) in the Code. That table establishes minimum distance from wire terminals to

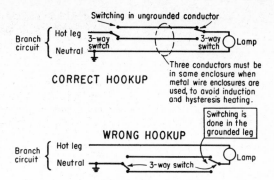

CORRECT HOOKUP

Three conductors must be
in same enclosure when
metal wire enclosures are
used, to avoid induction
and hysteresis heating.

WRONG HOOKUP

Switching is
done in the
grounded leg

... AND THE RULE APPLIES FOR ANY LAYOUT
OF SWITCH AND OUTLET BOXES

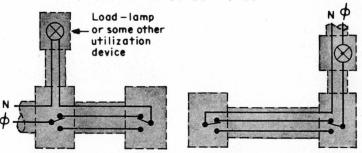

CORRECT — 3-way switches
are in the hot leg

(ungrounded leg) of the
circuit to the load.

VIOLATION! — 3-way switches
are in the grounded neutral
leg to the load.

NOTE: Wiring between switches — in the armor of BX or in metal
raceway — must have all three conductors within the
single cable or raceway.

White wire is spliced through to load

No switching
in white neutral

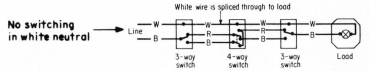

Fig. 380-1. All three-way and four-way switches must be placed in the hot conductor to
the load. (Sec. 380-2.)

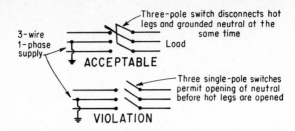

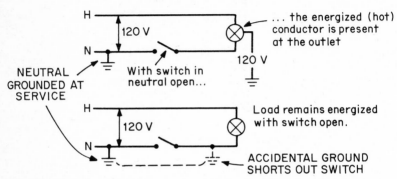

Fig. 380-2. A single-pole switch must not be used in a grounded circuit conductor. (Sec. 380-2.)

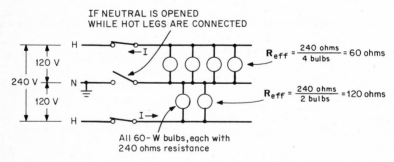

$$\text{Current} = \frac{240\,V}{60+120} = 1.33\ A$$

Voltage on top bulbs = 1.33 × 60 ohms = 80 V

Voltage on bottom bulbs = 1.33 × 120 ohms = 160 V

Fig. 380-3. A single-pole switch in neutral can cause damaging load unbalance if opened. (Sec. 380-2.)

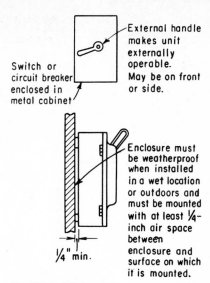

Switch or circuit breaker enclosed in metal cabinet

External handle makes unit externally operable. May be on front or side.

Enclosure must be weatherproof when installed in a wet location or outdoors and must be mounted with at least ¼-inch air space between enclosure and surface on which it is mounted.

¼" min.

Fig. 380-4. Switch and CB enclosures must be suitable. (Sec. 380-3.)

enclosure surface or from the sides of equipment to enclosure side based on the size of conductors being used, as shown in Fig. 380-5.

This whole concern for adequate wiring space in all kinds of equipment enclosures reflects a repeated theme in many Code sections as well as in Art. 110 on general installation methods. One of the most commonly heard complaints from constructors and installers in the field is the inadequacy of wiring space at equipment terminals. Section 380-3 is designed to assure sufficient space for the necessary conductors run into and through switch enclosures.

380-4. Wet Locations.   Refer to Fig. 380-4 and discussion under Sec. 373-2.

380-5. Time Switches, Flashers, and Similar Devices.   Any automatic switching device should be enclosed in a metal box unless it is a part of a switchboard or control panel which is located as required for live-front switchboards.

380-6. Position of Knife Switches.   The NE Code requires that knife switches be so mounted that gravity will tend to open them rather than close them (Fig. 380-6). But the Code recognizes use of an upside-down or reverse-mounted knife switch where provision is made on the switch to prevent gravity from actually closing the switch contacts. This permission is given in recognition of the much broader use of underground distribution, with the intent of providing a switch with its line terminals fed from

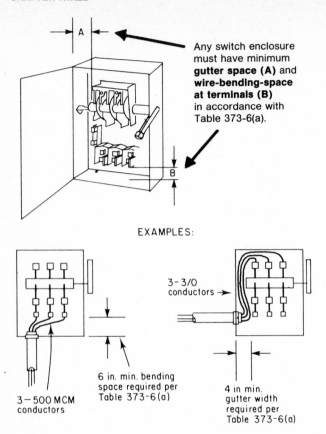

Any switch enclosure must have minimum **gutter space (A)** and **wire-bending-space at terminals (B)** in accordance with Table 373-6(a).

EXAMPLES:

3 – 3/0 conductors →

6 in. min. bending space required per Table 373-6(a)

3 – 500 MCM conductors

4 in min. gutter width required per Table 373-6(a)

Fig. 380-5. Terminating and gutter space in switch enclosures must be measured. (Sec. 380-3.)

the bottom and its load terminals connected at the top (Fig. 380-7). With such a configuration, an upside-down knife switch provides the necessary locations of such terminals, that is, "line" at bottom and "load" at top. However, use of any knife switch in the reverse or upside-down position is contingent upon the switch being approved for such use, which virtually means UL-listed for that application and also upon the switch being equipped with a locking device that will prevent gravity from closing the switch. The same type of operation is permitted for double-throw knife switches.

380-7. Connection of Knife Switches.   Figure 380-8 shows this rule.

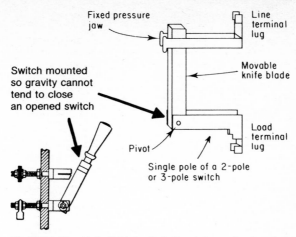

Fig. 380-6. Movable knife blade of a knife switch must be pivoted at its bottom. (Sec. 380-6.)

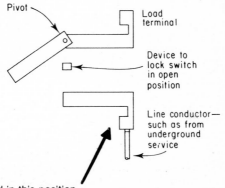

To be used in this position
where gravity tends to close
an open switch, the switch must:
1. Be approved for such use, and
2. Be equipped with a locking
device to hold switch open.

Fig. 380-7. This type of knife-switch operation is permitted. (Sec. 380-6.)

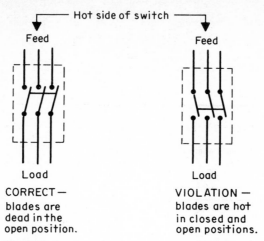

CORRECT —
blades are
dead in the
open position.

VIOLATION —
blades are hot
in closed and
open positions.

Fig. 380-8. Supply conductors must connect to "LINE" terminals of switch. (Sec. 380-7.)

380-8. Accessibility and Grouping. The rule of part **(a)** of this section, along with the exceptions, are shown in Fig. 380-9. Exception No. 1 cross-references with Sec. 364-12.

Part **(b)** of this section applies where 277-V switches, mounted in a common box (such as two- or three-ganged), control 277-V loads, with the voltage between exposed line terminals of *adjacent* switches in the common box being 480 V. If the adjacent switches have exposed live terminals, anyone changing one of the switches without disconnecting the circuit at the panel could contact 480 V, as shown in Fig. 380-10. The rule of this section requires permanent barriers between adjacent switches located in the same box where the voltage between such switches exceeds 300 V and terminals are exposed.

If screwless terminal switches (with no exposed live parts) are used, it would *not* be a violation if any number of such switches are ganged in a common box. Where screwless switches are mounted side by side in a two-gang box, it would seem to satisfy the intent (and literal text) of Sec. 380-8 because the switches would be "arranged" to prevent exposure to 480 V. Of course, the hookup shown would be acceptable if a separate single-gang box and plate are used for each switch, or a common wire from only one phase (A, B, or C) supplies all the three switches in the three-gang box.

380-9. Faceplates for Flush-Mounted Snap Switches. Figure 380-11 shows the basic rule of the first sentence of this section. Note that the recessed metal box is not grounded and that is acceptable because the box is not exposed to contact. Section 250-42 would apply to an exposed box.

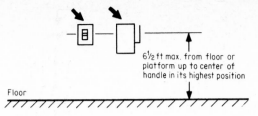

6½ ft max. from floor or
platform up to center of
handle in its highest position

Floor

EXCEPTIONS

1. Fused switch or CB may be up on
busway . . .

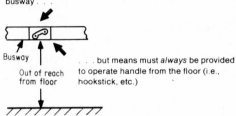

Busway

Out of reach
from floor

. . . but means must *always* be provided
to operate handle from the floor (i.e.,
hookstick, etc.)

2. Switch adjacent to motor, appliance, or other
equipment it supplies, at high mounting, but
accessible by portable ladder or similar means

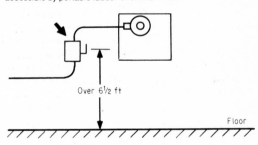

Over 6½ ft

Floor

3. Hookstick-operable isolating switches are
permitted at heights over 6½ ft

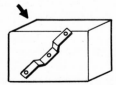

Fig. 380-9. All switches and circuit breakers used as switches
must be capable of being operated by a person from a readily
accessible place. (Sec. 380-8.)

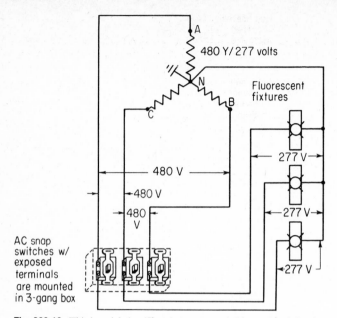

Fig. 380-10. This is a violation if barriers are not used between switches in the box. (Sec. 380-8.)

This rule conforms to the spirit of Sec. 410-18(a), which requires any metal faceplate (metal faceplates come under "exposed conductive parts of . . . equipment") to be grounded when it is attached to a box fed by a wiring system that contains an equipment grounding conductor. That is discussed also under Sec. 370-15(a).

The wording of this rule of Sec. 380-9 requires the nonmetallic faceplate on an ungrounded metal box only when the faceplate is "within reach of conducting floors," etc. But Sec. 410-18(b) is often taken as requiring a nonmetallic faceplate on every box that does not contain an equipment grounding "means" (metal raceway, metal cable armor, ground wire in NM cable)—whether or *not* it is "within reach of conducting" or grounded parts. Of course, ungrounded metal boxes are not generally encountered in new work.

The last sentence of this section requires that faceplates be installed to cover the wall opening completely to assure that the box behind the faceplate is properly covered and to prevent any openings that could afford penetration to energized parts.

380-10. Mounting of Snap Switches.   The purpose of paragraph **(b)** is to prevent "loose switches" where openings around *recessed* boxes provide no means of seating the switch mounting yoke against the box "ears"

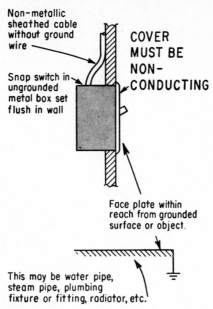

Non-metallic sheathed cable without ground wire

COVER MUST BE NON- CONDUCTING

Snap switch in ungrounded metal box set flush in wall

Face plate within reach from grounded surface or object.

This may be water pipe, steam pipe, plumbing fixture or fitting, radiator, etc.

Fig. 380-11. Nonmetallic faceplate eliminates shock hazard. (Sec. 380-9.)

properly. It also permits the maximum projection of switch handles through the installed switch plate. The cooperation of other crafts, such as dry-wall installers, will be required to satisfy this rule.

380-11. Circuit Breakers as Switches. Molded-case CBs are intended to be mounted on a vertical surface in an upright position or on their side. Use in any other position requires evaluation for such use. ON and OFF legends on CBs and switches are not intended to be mounted upside down.

380-12. Grounding of Enclosures. The wording here is a little tricky. At first reading, it sounds as if switch enclosures on 120/240-V or 120/208-V systems do not have to be grounded because the voltage is not over 150 V to ground. But Sec. 250-42 requires *all* exposed metal parts (including enclosures) of fixed equipment to be grounded under any of the conditions described. And any switch or CB enclosure that is fed by metal raceway or metal-covered cable must be grounded.

380-13. Knife Switches. UL data on ratings and application correspond to the Code data. Specific UL rules are as follows:

  1. Nonfusible switches are tested by UL up to 3,600 A, 500 hp, 600 V.

  2. UL-listed enclosed switches are rated up to 3,600 A, 500 hp, 600 V.

  3. Enclosed switches rated 800 or 1,200 A at more than 250 V are

available in two classes. One is for general use and may be used as a disconnect up to its rating; the other is for isolating use only and must be so marked. Any enclosed switch rated over 1,200 A must be marked "For Isolating Use Only—Do Not Open Under Load."

4. Enclosed switches with horsepower ratings in addition to current ratings may be used for motor circuits as well as for general-purpose circuits. Enclosed switches with ampere-only ratings are intended for general use but may also be used for motor circuits (as controllers and/or disconnects) as permitted by **NE Code** Sec. 430-83 (Exception No. 1), Sec. 430-109 (Exceptions No. 2, 3, and 4), and Sec. 430-111. See Fig. 380-12.

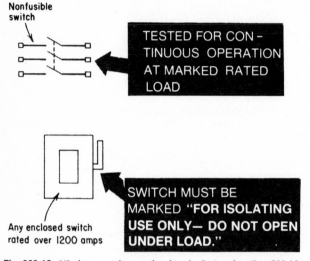

Fig. 380-12. UL data must be correlated to the Code rules. (Sec. 380-13.)

380-14. Rating and Use of Snap Switches. For a noninductive load not including any tungsten-filament lamps, a snap switch is merely required to have an ampere rating at least equal to the ampere rating of the load it controls. Electrically heated appliances are about the only common examples of such loads.

For the control of loads consisting of tungsten lamps alone, or tungsten lamps combined with any other noninductive load, snap switches should be "T" rated, or for alternating current circuits, a general-use AC snap switch should be used.

The term *snap switch* as used here and elsewhere in the Code is intended to include, in general, the common types of flush and surface-mounted switches used for the control of lighting equipment and small appliances and the switches used to control branch circuits on lighting panelboards. These switches are now usually of the tumbler or toggle type but can be the rotary-snap or pushbutton type. The term is not applied to CBs or to switches of the type that are commonly known as safety switches or *knife switches*. See definition of "switches" in Art. 100.

ARTICLE 384. SWITCHBOARDS AND PANELBOARDS

384-3. Support and Arrangement of Busbars and Conductors.   Part **(a)** notes that only those conductors intended for termination in a vertical section of a switchboard may be run within that section, other than required inner connections and/or control wiring. This rule was intended to prevent repetition of the many cases on record of damage to switchboards having been caused by termination failures in one section being transmitted to other parts of the switchboard. In order to comply with this requirement, it will be necessary in some cases to provide auxiliary gutters. The basic concept behind the rule is that any load conductors originating at the load terminals of switches or breakers in a switchboard must be carried vertically, up or down, so that they leave the switchboard from that vertical section. Such conductors may not be carried horizontally to or through any other vertical section of the switchboard (Fig. 384-1).

The last sentence of part **(a)** requires that all service switchboards have a barrier installed within the switchboard to isolate the service busbars and the service terminals from the remainder of the switchboard as shown in Fig. 384-2. Because it is commonly impossible to kill the circuit feeding a service switchboard, it has become very common practice for mechanics to work on switchboards with the service bus energized. The hazard associated with this has caused concern and is the reason for this addition to the **Code**.

Switchboard manufacturers in many parts of the country have been supplying switchboards with these barriers in place; this **Code** rule aims at making such protection for personnel a standard requirement. With a barrier of this type installed in a service switchboard mechanics working on feeder devices for other sections of the switchboard will not be exposed to accidental or surprise contact with the energized parts of the service equipment itself.

Part **(c)** requires a bonding jumper in a switchboard or panelboard used for service equipment to connect the grounded neutral or grounded phase leg to the equipment grounding conductor (the metal frame or enclosure of the equipment). UL data apply to this rule:

1. Switchboard sections or interiors are optionally intended for use either as a feeder distribution switchboard or as a service switch-

Fig. 384-1. All conductor terminals within a switchboard must be used only for connection to conductors that leave the switchboard vertically from the same switchboard section in which the terminals are located—with the conductors run out the top or out of the bottom of the switchboard. (Sec. 384-3.)

board. For service use, a switchboard must be marked "Suitable for use as service equipment."

2. Some switchboard sections or interiors include neutral busbars factory-**bonded to the switchboard enclosure. Such switchboards are marked "Suitable *only* for use as service equipment" and may *not* be used as subdistribution switchboards (Fig. 384-3). A bonded neutral bus in a service switchboard may also serve as an equipment grounding busbar.**

3. UL-listed unit substations have the secondary neutral bonded to the enclosure and have provision on the neutral for connection of a grounding conductor, as shown in Fig. 384-4. A terminal is also provided on the enclosure near the line terminals for use with an

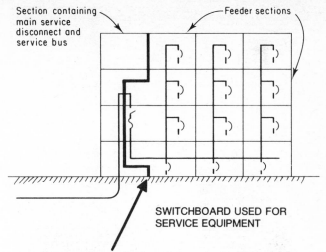

Section containing
main service
disconnect and
service bus

Feeder sections

**SWITCHBOARD USED FOR
SERVICE EQUIPMENT**

In every service switchboard, large or small, a barrier
must isolate all feeder sections from the service busbars
and terminals.

Fig. 384-2. In switchboards, service bus must be isolated from rest of
switchboard. (Sec. 384-3.)

equipment grounding conductor run from the enclosure of primary equipment feeding the unit sub to the enclosure of the unit
sub. Connection of such an equipment grounding conductor provides proper bonding together of equipment enclosures where the
primary feed to the unit sub is direct-buried underground or is run
in nonmetallic conduit without a metal conduit connection in the
primary feed.

4. Unless marked otherwise (with both the size and temperature rating of wire to be used), the termination provisions on switchboards
are for 60°C wire from No. 14 to No. 1 and 75°C for No. 1/0 and
larger wires.

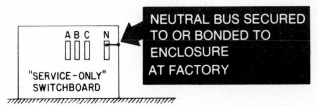

A B C   N

"SERVICE-ONLY"
SWITCHBOARD

NEUTRAL BUS SECURED
TO OR BONDED TO
ENCLOSURE
AT FACTORY

Fig. 384-3. Bonded neutral bus limits switchboard to service applications.
(Sec. 384-3.)

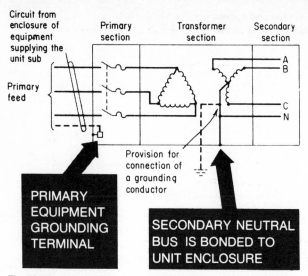

Circuit from enclosure of equipment supplying the unit sub

Primary section

Transformer section

Secondary section

Primary feed

A
B

C
N

Provision for connection of a grounding conductor

PRIMARY EQUIPMENT GROUNDING TERMINAL

SECONDARY NEUTRAL BUS IS BONDED TO UNIT ENCLOSURE

Fig. 384-4. Unit subs have bonded neutral in secondary switchboards. (Sec. 384-3.)

The rule of part **(e)** is shown in Fig. 384-5 and correlated to the rule of part **(f)**. On a 3-phase, 4-wire delta-connected system (the so-called "red-leg" delta, with the midpoint of one phase grounded), the phase busbar or conductor having the higher voltage to ground must be marked, and the higher leg to ground must be phase B, as required by part **(f)**. Without identification of the higher voltage leg, an installer connecting 120-V loads (lamps, motor starter coils, appliances) to the panelboard shown in the diagram might accidentally connect the loads from the high leg to neutral, exposing the loads to burnout with 208 V across such loads.

Part **(f)** requires a fixed arrangement (or phase sequence) of busbars in panels or switchboards. The installer must observe this sequence in hooking up such equipment and must therefore know the phase sequence (or rotation) of the feeder or service conductors. This new rule has the effect of requiring basic phase identification at the service entrance and consistent conformity to that identification and sequence throughout the whole system (Fig. 384-6).

Difficulty has been encountered with the rule of part **(f)**, requiring the high leg to be the B phase, because utility company rules may call for the high leg to be the C phase and the right-hand terminal in a meter socket—rather than the middle terminal. As shown in Fig. 384-7, the utility phase rotation can be converted to a Code phase rotation .by applying the concept that phase rotation is relative, not absolute. If the

**Bus bar and conductor with higher voltage to
ground must be marked and must be "B" phase**

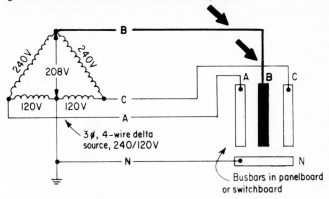

Fig. 384-5. Safety requires "high leg" identification on 4-wire delta systems.
(Sec. 384-3.)

utility C phase is designated as the NEC B phase, then the other phase
legs are identified for NEC purposes as shown. The phase rotation C-A-B
is the same as A-B-C, with voltage alternations such that wave B follows
wave A by 120 degrees, wave C follows wave B by 120 degrees, wave A
follows wave C by 120 degrees, etc. With the phase legs identified as at
the bottom of the sketch, each is carried to the appropriately designated
phase lug (A-B-C, left to right) at the panelboard shown in Fig. 384-4.

Part **(g)** refers to the need for specific clearances in top and side gutters
in both panelboards and switchboards and makes it mandatory that wire
bending space at terminals and gutter spaces must afford the room
required in Sec. 373-6. This is a repeated requirement throughout the

Three-phase buses must be arranged as A, B, C . . .

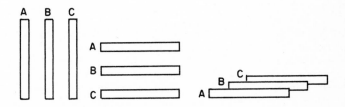

. . . as viewed from the front of the switchboard or panelboard

Fig. 384-6. Phase sequence in panelboards and switchboards must be fixed.
(Sec. 384-3.).

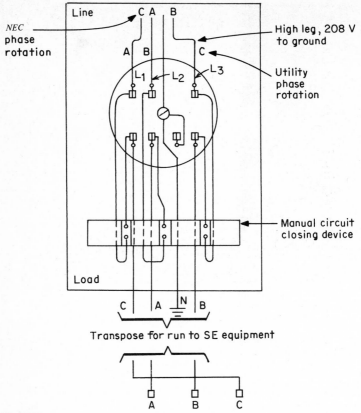

Fig. 384-7. Utility "C" phase becomes NEC "B" phase for high-leg identification. (Sec. 384-3.)

Code and is aimed at assuring safe termination of conductors as well as adequate space in the side gutters of panelboards and switchboards for installing the line and load conductors in such equipment. This concern for adequate wire bending space and gutter space is particularly important because of the very large size cables and conductors so commonly used today in panelboards and switchboards. Sharp turns to provide connection to terminal lugs does present possible damage to the conductor and does create strain and twisting force on the terminals themselves. Both of those objections can be eliminated by providing adequate wiring space.

384-4. Location of Switchboards. Live-front switchboards, as in Fig. 384-8, must always be applied with cautious regard for the conditions stated in this rule.

Fig. 384-8. A switchboard with *"any"* exposed live parts is limited to use in "permanently dry" locations, accessible only to qualified persons. (Sec. 384-4.)

384-7. Clearance from Ceiling. Although it has long been a Code rule that a clearance of at least 3 ft be provided from the top of a switchboard to a nonfireproof ceiling above, Exception No. 2 excludes totally enclosed switchboards from this rule. The original rule requiring a 3-ft clearance was based on open-type switchboards and did not envision totally enclosed switchboards. The sheet-metal top of such switchboards provides sufficient protection against heat transfer to nonfireproof ceilings. As a result of this exception, there now is no minimum clearance required above totally enclosed switchboards, as shown in Fig. 384-9.

384-8. Clearances Around Switchboards. Accessibility and working space are very necessary to avoid possible shock hazards and to provide easy access for maintenance, repair, operation, and housekeeping. It is preferable to increase the minimum space behind a switchboard where space will permit.

384-10. Clearance for Conductors Entering Bus Enclosures. Figure 384-10 shows the rules of this section which is aimed at eliminating high conduit stubups under equipment containing busbars to prevent contact or dangerous proximity between conduit stubups and the busbars. On this matter, UL says that "the acceptability of conduit stubs serving unit sections with respect to wiring space and spacing from live parts can be determined only by the local inspection authorities at the final installation."

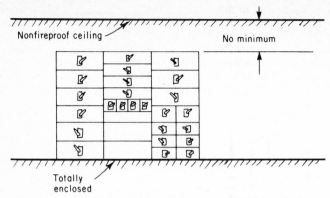

Fig. 384-9. No minimum top clearance is required to nonfireproof ceiling above enclosed switchboard. (Sec. 384-7.)

384-13. General (On Panelboards). The first sentence here establishes the minimum acceptable rating of any panelboard.

All panelboards—lighting and power—are required by this section to have a rating (the ampere capacity of the busbars) not less than the NE Code minimum feeder conductor capacity for the entire load served by the panel. That is, the panel busbars must have a nameplate ampere

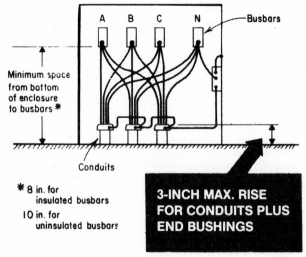

Fig. 384-10. Conduit stubups must have safe clearance from busbars. (Sec. 384-10.)

rating at least equal to the required ampere capacity of the conductors which feed the panel (Fig. 384-11). A panel may have a busbar current rating greater than the current rating of its feeder but must never have a current rating lower than that required for its feeder. [Although Sec. 220-10(b) notes that a feeder for a continuous load must be rated at least 125 percent of the load current, it is not clear that the panel busbars would have to be rated for more than 100 percent of the load current.]

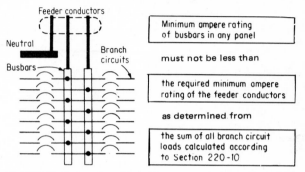

Fig. 384-11. Rating of panelboard bus must at least match required feeder ampacity. (Sec. 384-13.)

Although selection of a panelboard is based first on the number of circuits which it must serve, it must be assured that the busbars in a panelboard for any application have at least the Code-minimum circuits.

With respect to panelboards, marking may appear on the individual terminals, but terminals can often be changed in the field, and wiring space and the means of mounting the terminals may not be suitable. Therefore, panelboards should be marked independently of the marking on the terminals to identify the terminals and switch or CB units which may be used with aluminum wire. If all terminals are suitable for use with aluminum conductors as well as with copper conductors, the panelboard will be marked "use copper or aluminum wire." A panelboard marked "use copper wire only" indicates that wiring space or other factors make the panelboard unsuitable for any aluminum conductors.

384-14. Lighting and Appliance Branch-Circuit Panelboard. This definition is intended to describe the types of panelboards to which the requirements in Secs. 384-15 and 384-16(a) are applied.

Even though a panelboard may be used largely for other than lighting purposes, it is to be judged under the requirements for lighting and appliance branch-circuit panelboards if it conforms to the specific conditions stated in the definition.

Watch out for this definition! There are many panel makeups that supply no lighting and appear to be power panels or distribution panels, yet they are technically lighting and appliance panels in accordance with the above definition and must have protection for the busbars. Figure 384-12 shows an example of how it is determined whether a panelboard *is* or *is not* "a lighting and appliance branch-circuit panelboard." The determination is important because it indicates whether or not main protection is required for any particular panel, to satisfy Sec. 384-16.

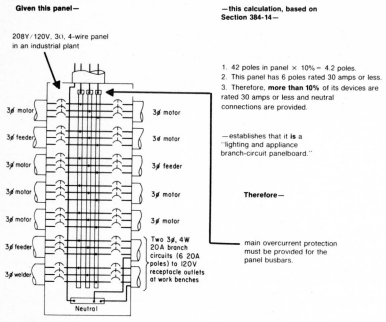

Fig. 384-12. Definition of a "lighting and appliance" panelboard hinges on a specific calculation. (Sec. 384-14.)

Figure 384-13 shows panels that do not need main protection because they are not lighting and appliance panels, which are the only type of panel required by Sec. 384-16 to have main protection. Just as it is strange to identify a panel that supplies no lighting as a lighting panel, as in Fig. 384-12, it is also strange that some panels that supply *only* lighting, as in Fig. 384-13, are technically *not* lighting panels. Because of the definition of Sec. 384-14, if the protective devices in a panel are *all* rated over 30 A **or** if there are *no* neutral connections provided in the panel, then the panel is not a lighting and appliance panel, and it does not require main overcurrent protection.

384-15. Number of Overcurrent Devices on One Panelboard. Figure 384-14 illustrates a panelboard with a 200-A main which provides for the

Example: No neutral connections provided

Example: OC devices rated over 30 amps

MAIN PROTECTION IS NOT REQUIRED

MAIN PROTECTION IS NOT REQUIRED

This is not a lighting and appliance panelboard as defined in Section 384-14

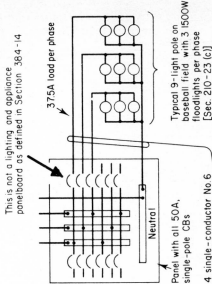

37.5A load per phase

Typical 9-light pole on baseball field with 3 1500W floodlights per phase [Sec. 210-23 (c)]

Neutral

Panel with all 50A, single-pole CBs

4 single-conductor No.6 UF cables underground from panel to pole

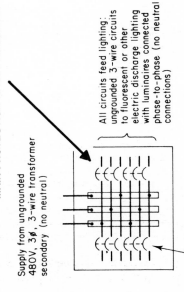

Supply from ungrounded 480V, 3∅, 3-wire transformer secondary (no neutral)

All circuits feed lighting: ungrounded 3-wire circuits to fluorescent or other electric discharge lighting with luminaires connected phase-to-phase (no neutral connections)

3-pole CB for each 3-wire circuit per Section 240-20(b) rated not over 20A for fluorescent fixtures, up to 50A for other electric discharge lighting (Sections 210-23 and 210-21(a)

NOTE: Fusible equipment is also permissible for such applications.

Fig. 384-13. Some panels that supply only lighting are technically not "lighting and appliance panels." (Sec. 384-14.)

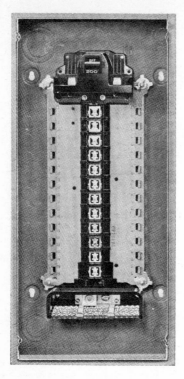

Fig. 384-14. Slots for push-in CB units have different configurations to limit the total number of poles to no more than 42. This is a CTL panelboard (or loadcenter). (Sec. 384-15.)

insertion of class CTL overcurrent devices. The top stab receivers are of an F-slot configuration. Each F slot will receive only one breaker pole. The remainder of the slots are of an E configuration which will receive two breaker poles per slot. Thus there is provision for installing not more than 42 overcurrent devices, which does not include the main CB. This panelboard may also be supplied without main overcurrent protection where overcurrent protection is supplied elsewhere, such as at the supply end of the feeder to the panel.

*Class CTL is the Underwriters Laboratories Inc. designation for the **Code** requirement for circuit limitation within a lighting and appliance branch-circuit panelboard. It means "circuit-limiting."

384-16. Overcurrent Protection.   Rules in this section of the NE Code concern the protection of "lighting and appliance branch-circuit panelboards." In general, lighting and appliance branch-circuit panels must be individually protected on the supply side by not more than two main CBs or two sets of fuses having a combined rating not greater than that of the panelboard, as shown in Fig. 384-15. Individual protection is not

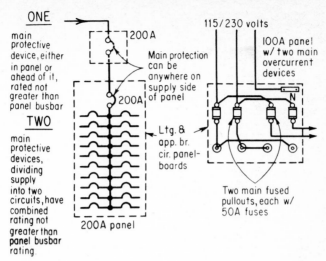

ONE

main protective device, either in panel or ahead of it, rated not greater than panel busbar

TWO

main protective devices, dividing supply into two circuits, have combined rating not greater than panel busbar rating

200 A

200A

200A panel

Main protection can be anywhere on supply side of panel

Ltg. & app. br. cir. panel-boards

115/230 volts

IOOA panel w/ two main overcurrent devices

N

Two main fused pullouts, each w/ 50A fuses

Fig. 384-15. "Main protection" may consist of one or two CBs or sets of fuses. (Sec. 384-16.)

required when a lighting and appliance branch-circuit panelboard is connected to a feeder which has overcurrent protection not greater than that of the panelboard (Case 1 in Fig. 384-16), as noted in Exception No. 1.

Because of the wording of the definition in Sec. 384-14, it is vitally important to evaluate a panel carefully to determine if main protection is required.

Where a number of panels are tapped from a single feeder protected at a current rating higher than that of the busbars in any of the panels, the main protection may be installed as a separate device just ahead of the panel or as a device within the panel feeding the busbars (Case 2 and Case 3 in Fig. 384-16). The main protection would normally be a CB or fused switch of the number of poles corresponding to the number of busbars in the panel.

Figure 384-17 shows other variations on the same protection requirements. As shown in the sketch with 400-A panels, it is often more economical to order the panels with busbar capacity higher than required for the load on the panels so the panel bus rating matches the feeder protection, thereby eliminating the need for panel main protection.

Although part **(a)** of this section does spell out those general requirements for main protection of lighting and appliance branch-circuit panelboards, Exception No. 2 of that section notes that any panel used as residential service equipment may have up to *six* main protective devices [as permitted by Sec. 230-90(a) Exception No. 3]. Such usage is limited to

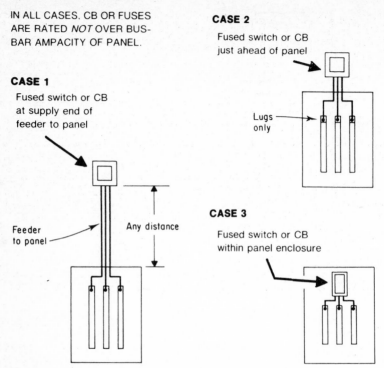

IN ALL CASES, CB OR FUSES ARE RATED *NOT* OVER BUS-BAR AMPACITY OF PANEL.

CASE 1

Fused switch or CB at supply end of feeder to panel

Feeder to panel

Any distance

CASE 2

Fused switch or CB just ahead of panel

Lugs only

CASE 3

Fused switch or CB within panel enclosure

Fig. 384-16. Main panel protection may be located at any one of these locations. (Sec. 384-16.)

"individual residential occupancy"—such as a private house or an apartment in multifamily dwellings where the panel *is* truly service equipment and not a subpanel fed from service equipment in the basement or from a meter bank on the load side of a building's service.

Exception No. 2 must be taken in conjunction with Sec. 230-71 in order to have a complete picture. In effect the intent is to permit the use of a lighting and appliance branch-circuit panelboard as the service equipment in an individual residential occupancy. That Exception No. 2 completely eliminates the need for individual overcurrent protection of lighting and appliance branch-circuit panelboards used as service equipment in supplying an individual residential occupancy. And it should be noted that the exception no longer prohibits the use of 15- and/or 20-A protective devices as main disconnects in such panels. In the 1975 and previous Codes, the rule permitted a service panel for a residential occupancy to have up to six main disconnect devices but stipulated that none of the main devices could be rated at 15 or 20 A. For any panel—a

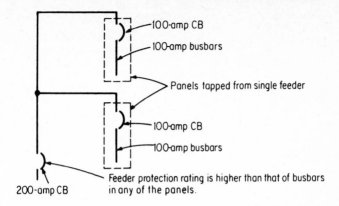

100-amp CB

100-amp busbars

Panels tapped from single feeder

100-amp CB

100-amp busbars

Feeder protection rating is higher than that of busbars in any of the panels.

200-amp CB

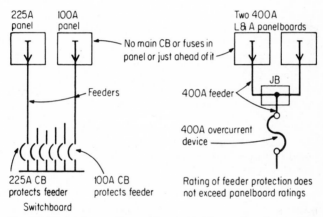

225A panel   100A panel

No main CB or fuses in panel or just ahead of it

Two 400A L & A panelboards

JB

Feeders

400A feeder

400A overcurrent device

225A CB protects feeder   100A CB protects feeder

Rating of feeder protection does not exceed panelboard ratings

Switchboard

Fig. 384-17. Panel protection may be provided in a variety of ways. (Sec. 384-16.)

standard single-section-bus panel or a split-bus-panel—previous **Codes** required that any bus supplying 15- or 20-A protective devices must be provided with a main disconnect device for the bus itself.

Now a lighting and appliance panelboard containing six single-pole breakers or six two-pole breakers (or even six three-pole breakers or fuses) of any rating may be used as residential service equipment without a main protective device ahead (Fig. 384-18). In split-bus panelboards, where it was previously permitted to use six main devices in the section fed by the service conductors, it is now permissible to use 15- and/or 20-A protective devices in that main section. Of course, 15- and/or 20-A protective devices may still be used in the bottom section of the panel,

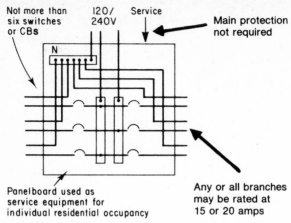

Fig. 384-18. Exception No. 2 eliminates need for main in residential service panel. (Sec. 384-16.)

which is protected by one of the mains in the top part of the panel (Fig. 384-19).

Panelboards used for service equipment are required by **NE Code** Sec. 230-70 to be marked as "suitable for use as service equipment," and panelboards are so marked.

The rule of part **(b)** of this section is covered in Fig. 384-20. Any panel, a lighting panel or a power panel, which contains snap switches (and CBs are not snap switches) rated 30 A or less must have overcurrent protection and not in excess of 200 A. Panels which are not lighting and appliance panels and do not contain snap switches rated 30 A or less do not have to be equipped with main protection and may be tapped from any size of feeder. Figure 384-21 shows these two examples of overcurrent protection requirements for panelboards.

Part **(c)** applies to *any* overcurrent device in a panel and is a similar but stricter rule than those of Sec. 210-22 or Sec. 220-2, as shown in Fig. 384-22. The only exception to the rule is for overcurrent-device assemblies that are "approved" (which means UL listed) for continuous loading at 100 percent of their current rating. Refer to Sec. 220-10(b) on feeder protection.

Part **(d)** of this section applies to a panelboard fed from a transformer. The rule requires that overcurrent protection for such a panel, as required in **(a)** and **(b)** of the same section, must be located on the secondary side of the transformer. An exception is made for a panel fed by a 2-wire, single-phase transformer secondary. Such a panel may be protected by a primary device. This concept of prohibiting use of panel protection on the primary side of a transformer feeding the panel is

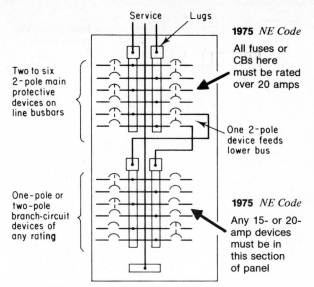

Fig. 384-19. 1978 NEC has eliminated these rules from previous codes. (Sec. 384-16.)

consistent with the rules covered under Sec. 240-3 Exception No. 5. Refer to the discussion there.

Part **(e)** is a rule prohibiting the installation of any 3-phase disconnect or 3-phase overcurrent device in a single-phase panelboard. It is now required that any three-pole disconnect or 3-phase protective device supplied by the bus within a panelboard may be used only in a 3-phase panelboard. The effect of this new rule is to outlaw the so-called delta breaker, which was a special three-pole CB with terminal layouts designed to be used in a single-phase panel fed by a 3-phase, 4-wire, 120/ 240-V delta supply where the loads served by the panel were predominantly single-phase, but where a single 3-phase motor or 3-phase feeder was needed and could readily be supplied from this type of delta breaker. The delta CB plugged into the space of three single-pole breakers, with high leg of delta feeding directly through one pole of the common-trip assembly. Unit was used to protect motor branch circuit or feeder to 3-phase panel, rated up to 100 A.

Use of delta breakers has been found hazardous. When a delta breaker is used in a single-phase panel and the main disconnect for the single-phase panel is opened, there is still the high hot leg supplying the delta breaker. This has caused confusion to personnel who were surprised to find the energized conductor and were exposed to shock hazards.

Fig. 384-20. Any panelboard containing snap switches rated 30 A or less must have main or feeder protection rated not over 200 A. (Sec. 384-16.)

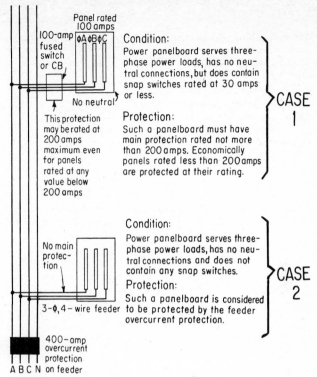

Fig. 384-21. Power panels have very limited requirement for protection. (Sec. 384-16.)

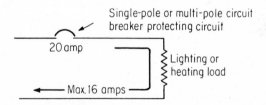

Total load on circuit must not exceed 80% of circuit rating when load is continuous (operates for 3 hours or more) – such as store lighting. CB must not be loaded over 80% of its rating.

Fig. 384-22. This applies for fuses *and* breakers protecting. (Sec. 384-16.)

384-17. Panelboards in Damp or Wet Locations.   UL data supplement the Code rules:

Enclosed panelboards marked "Raintight" will not permit entry of water when exposed to a beating rain. Enclosed panelboards marked "Rainproof" will not permit a beating rain to interfere with successful operation of the apparatus within the enclosure but may permit entry of water.

But note this carefully: NE Code Secs. 384-17 and 373-2 require that panelboard enclosures in *"damp or wet"* locations must be placed or equipped to "prevent moisture or water from *entering and accumulating* within" the enclosure, and there must be at least a $1/4$-in. air space between the enclosure and the wall or surface on which the enclosure is mounted. When installed exposed outdoors or in other wet locations, the NE Code requires that panelboard enclosures must be weatherproof. The NE Code definition of "weatherproof" is similar to the NE Code and UL definitions of "rainproof." Yet, NE Code Sec. 373-2 requires exclusion of water entry—which clearly demands a "raintight" enclosure for outdoor, exposed panelboards (and not "rainproof"). These same considerations apply to other cabinets or enclosures used outdoors.

384-18. Enclosure.   UL data cover this consideration:

1. Panelboards labeled as "Enclosed Panelboards" have been established as having adequate wiring space in the enclosure.
2. Unless a panelboard is marked otherwise, the wiring space in the assembly and the current-carrying capacity are based on use of 60°C wire in sizes No. 14 up to No. 1 or the use of 75°C wires for sizes No. 1/0 and larger. This limitation on use is covered in the general data of the UL green book. If wires of higher than 60°C or 75°C rating are used, such wires must be used at ampacities not greater than those given in NE Code Table 310-16 for wires rated 60°C or 75°C.

384-19. Relative Arrangement of Switches and Fuses.   For service equipment, switches are permitted on either the supply side or the load side of the fuses. In all other cases if the panelboards are accessible to other than qualified persons, Sec. 240-40 requires that the switches shall be on the supply side so that when replacing fuses all danger of shock or short circuit can be eliminated by opening the switch.

384-20. Panels.   The data in Secs. 384-20 to 384-27 cover requirements on construction of panelboards. UL data are also applicable. If a panelboard is not marked otherwise, it is suitable to be fed by a feeder circuit with a maximum available fault-current level at the panelboard of not more than 10,000 rms symmetrical amps if of the fusible type or not more than 5,000 rms symmetrical amps if only CBs are used.

384-27. Grounding of Panelboards.   The effect of this rule is to *require* a panelboard to be equipped with a terminal bar for connecting all equipment grounding conductors run with the circuits connected in the panel. Such a bar must be one made by the manufacturer of the panel and must be installed in the panel in the position and in the manner specified by the panel manufacturer—to assure its compliance with UL rules, as well as the NEC. The terminal bar for connecting equipment grounding conductors may be an inherent part of a panelboard, or terminal bar kits may be obtained for simple installation in any panelboard. Home-made or improvised grounding terminal bars are contrary to the intent of this Code section.

Figure 384-23 shows some details of grounding at panelboards. There

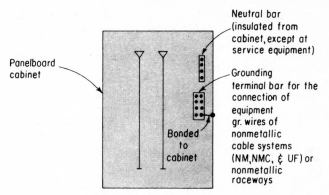

Neutral bar (insulated from cabinet, except at service equipment)

Panelboard cabinet

Grounding terminal bar for the connection of equipment gr. wires of nonmetallic cable systems (NM,NMC, & UF) or nonmetallic raceways

Bonded to cabinet

AN "APPROVED" GROUNDING BAR MUST BE USED

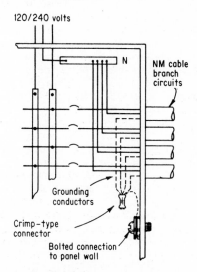

120/240 volts

N

NM cable branch circuits

Grounding conductors

Crimp-type connector

Bolted connection to panel wall

VIOLATION ! Homemade techniques are not acceptable.

Fig. 384-23. Grounding in panelboards must use listed components. (Sec. 384-27.)

have been many field problems relative to terminating grounding conductors in panelboards where nonmetallic wiring methods have been involved. The rule here requires an "equipment grounding terminal bar" in such panels so that these grounding conductors can be properly terminated and bonded to the panel.

In other than service equipment, the grounding conductor terminal bar must not be connected to the neutral bar (that is, the neutral bar must not be bonded to the panel enclosure). Refer to Secs. 250-23, 250-50, 250-53, and 250-61. In a service panel, with the neutral bonded to the enclosure, equipment grounding conductors may be connected to the bonded neutral terminal bar (or block). But the neutral bar must *not* be used for equipment grounding conductors on the load side of the service.

The Exception to this section allows an isolated ground conductor run with the circuit conductors to pass through the panelboard without being connected to the panelboard grounding terminal bar, in order to provide for the reduction of electrical noise (electromagnetic interference) on the grounding circuit as provided for in Sec. 250-74 Exception No. 4.

In order to maintain the isolation of the grounding wire necessary for a low-noise ground, the grounding wire must be connected directly to the grounding terminal bar in the service-entrance equipment. To do this it may be necessary for the grounding wires to pass through one or more panelboards. Of course, such isolated grounding conductors may be spliced together by use of a terminal block installed in the panel but

Fig. 384-24. "Quiet ground" terminal block for equipment grounding conductors provides for carrying isolated grounding conductors from circuits back to service bonded neutral, with single grounding conductor connecting terminal bar back to service. Terminal block is insulated from metal panel enclosure. Check with manufacturer to assure that isolated bar is approved. (Sec. 384-27.)

insulated from conductive contact with the metal enclosure of the panel. A "quiet ground" keeps grounding conductors apart from and independent of the metal raceways and enclosures (Fig. 384-24).

Sensitive electronic equipment utilized in hospitals, laboratories, and similar locations may malfunction because of electrical noise (electromagnetic interference) present in the electrical supply. This effect can be reduced by the proper use of an isolated grounding wire which connects directly to the service-entrance panel grounding terminal bar. Such systems are being used in increasing numbers where computers are in use.

Chapter Four

ARTICLE 400. FLEXIBLE CORDS AND CABLES

400-3. Suitability. This rule requires that any application of flexible cord or cable may require use of "hard usage" cord (such as SJ cord) or "extra hard usage" cord (such as S or SO cord) if the cord is used where it is exposed to abrasion or dragging or repetitive flexing and/or pulling, depending upon severity of use. As noted in Table 400-4, cords for portable heaters must be one of those types when used in damp places. Determination of the need for a particular cable on the basis of use severity is subjective. Table 400-4 also indicates the types of portable cable—that is, for data processing and elevator circuits—and conditions under which each type is suitable, as for hazardous or nonhazardous locations.

Other data on suitability are given in the UL green book, as follows: Jacketed cords.

Types SJ, SJO, SJT, SJTO, SO, SO, and STO cords surface-marked "Water Resistant" on the jacket are suitable for use where immersed in water.

Types SVO, SVTO, SJO, SJTO, SO and STO cords (with or without the marking "Oil-Resistant" on the jacket) are suitable for use where contact or immersion in oil is considered intermittent or occasional.

Types SVT, SVTO, SJT, SJTO, ST and STO cords surface-marked "Oil Proof" on the jacket are suitable for continuous immersion in oil.

Types SO, ST and STO cords surface-marked with the words "For mobile-home use" or "For recreational vehicle use" or "For mobile-home and recreational vehicle use" respectively, followed with the current rating in amperes, are suitable for use in mobile home or recreational vehicles.

Types SJ, SJO, SJT, SJTO, S, SO, ST and STO cords surface-marked "Outdoor" (limited to outdoor-use cord sets) or with the suffix "W-A" following the type letter designation are suitable for use outdoors.

400-5. Ampacity of Flexible Cords and Cables. A three-conductor cord set is permitted by Sec. 250-60(a) to be used with *one* conductor serving as *both* the neutral conductor *and* the equipment grounding conductor, with the frame of the range or dryer grounded by connection to the neutral. The last sentence of this rule points out that the common neutral-grounding conductor does not count as a current-carrying conductor, thereby making the 3-wire cord suitable for use at the higher ampacity shown under column B (fourth from the left) in Table 400-5—which is for cord with not more than two wires.

400-7. Uses Permitted. Figure 400-1 shows accepted uses for flexible cord. Flexible cord may be used for lighting fixtures under **(a) (2)**. Refer to Sec. 410-14 for limitations on use with electric-discharge lighting fixtures and Sec. 410-30(e) for fixtures that require aiming or adjusting after installation.

Fig. 400-1. Permitted uses for flexible cable and cord include: (left) pendant pushbutton station for crane and hoist controls, and connection of portable lamps. (Sec. 400-7).

Part **(b)** states that *if* flexible cord is used to connect portable lamps or appliances, stationary equipment to facilitate frequent interchange, or fixed or stationary appliances to facilitate removal or disconnection for maintenance or repair, the cord "shall be equipped with an *attachment plug* and shall be energized from an approved *receptacle outlet.*"

It should be noted that the cords referred to under this section are the cords attached to the appliance and not extension cords supplementing or extending the regular supply cords. The use of an extension cord would represent a conflict with the requirements of the Code in that it would serve as a substitute for a receptacle to be located near the appliance.

Extension cords are intended for temporary use with portable appliances, tools, and similar equipment which are not normally used at one specific location.

But bus-drop cable may be used to feed down to machines in factories. Such cable is UL-listed for that application in accordance with Sec. 400-7 (Fig. 400-2).

Fig. 400-2. Bus-drop power cables are flexible cables listed by UL for feeding power down from plug-in fusible switches on busway to supply machines. Cables here have connector bodies on their ends for machine cord caps to plug into. (Sec. 400-7.)

400-8. Uses Not Permitted. Although Sec. 400-7 says that flexible cord may be used for "wiring of fixtures," that is a simple, general, broad recognition that may be used by any electrical inspector to accept almost any specific assembly of cord supply to a lighting fixture. It is the kind of rule that actually requires individual inspectors to spell out their own design and installation details. And it ties into the general rule of the second sentence in Sec. 90-4 which makes the inspector the final judge of Code compliance on all questions about NE Code rules.

But Sec. 400-8(1) says that flexible cord must *not* be used "as a substitute for fixed wiring." That rule could be strictly enforced to require all lighting fixtures to be supplied by fixed wiring methods—approved, Code-recognized cables like NM or BX or by a standard raceway method (EMT, rigid, flex, etc.). The rule does create a conflict with Sec. 400-7(a) by raising the question, Is there ever a case where a lighting fixture could *not* be fed by a fixed wiring method? Certainly, any fixture that might be supplied by a cord connection from a junction box to the fixture could just as easily be fed by conductors in flexible metal conduit or in liquidtight flexible metal conduit—both of which conduit-and-wire connections are considered "fixed wiring" methods. If there are no cases where a fixture could not be fed by such a fixed wiring connection, then every use of flexible cord to supply a fixture is "a substitute for fixed wiring." The relationship between Secs. 400-7(a) (2), 400-8(1), 410-14, and 410-30(e) must be carefully evaluated to assure ready compliance with Code rules—particularly since cord connection of lighting fixtures has been used so long and so successfully for both indoor and outdoor applications.

Whether any use of flexible cord is a violation of Sec. 400-8(1) must be related to the rule of Sec. 400-7. If a use of flexible cord does not conform to one of the permitted uses in Sec. 400-7, it becomes a violation of this section.

Figure 400-3 shows one of a number of twin floodlight units that were installed outdoors for lighting of the facade of a building. The use of cord from a junction box to a stab-in-the-ground twin lampholder assem-

Fig. 400-3. This use of flexible cord to supply an outdoor lampholder assembly can readily be described as a "substitute for fixed wiring"—which is a prohibited use of cord. Here, the lampholders could have been attached to one or more threaded openings on an outlet box. (Sec. 400-8).

bly does not comply with "(2) wiring of fixtures" in Sec. 400-7 because it does not satisfy Sec. 410-14 or Sec. 410-30(e), which regulate use of cord for fixtures, as noted under Sec. 400-7 above. And the application does not comply with the other permitted uses in Sec. 400-7. Because floodlights could have been installed in lampholders that thread into hubs on a weatherproof box, use of the cord is an evasion of a fixed or permanent connection technique that would totally avoid the potential shock hazard of cord pull-out or breakage. Mounting the floodlights on the box would still allow adjustment. This use of cord is a substitute for fixed wiring and is a violation.

400-10. Pull at Joints and Terminals.   Figure 400-4 shows methods of strain relief for cords. The "Underwriters' knot" has been used for many

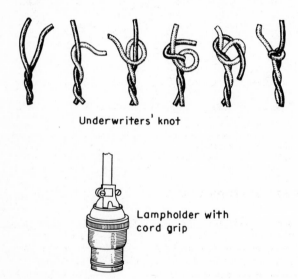

Underwriters' knot

Lampholder with cord grip

Fig. 400-4. Strain-relief must be provided at cord connections to devices. (Sec. 400-10.)

years and is a good method for taking the strain from the socket terminals where lamp cord is used for the pendant, through the hole in the lampholder or switch device. For reinforced cords and junior hard-service cords, sockets with cord grips such as shown in Fig. 400-5 provide an effective means of relieving the terminals of all strain. Figure 400-5 shows a support technique that comes under "other approved means."

400-11. In Show Windows and Show Cases.   On account of the flammable material nearly always present in show windows, great care should be taken to ensure that only approved types of cords are used and that they are maintained in good condition.

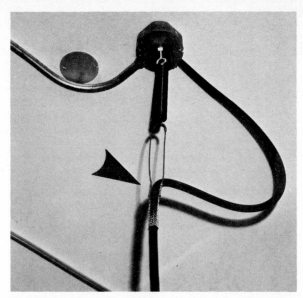

Fig. 400-5. Strain-relief for flexible cord must protect cable jacketing from damage at box connectors and protect wire terminations from pull-out. Spring-loaded come-along support supports cable against weight on bottom end of pendant and also provides up-and-down movement of cable end. (Sec. 400-10.)

ARTICLE 402. FIXTURE WIRES

402-5. Ampacity of Fixture Wires. Note that Table 402-5 gives the ampacity for each size of fixture wire **regardless of the type of insulation used on the wire.** For instance, a No. 18 Type AF fixture wire is rated for 6 A and so is No. 18 Type TFN or PF or any other type.

402-7. Number of Conductors in Conduit. The maximum number of any size and type of fixture wire permitted in a given size of conduit is selected from a different table than the ones used for determining conduit fill for building wire (THW, THHN, etc.). This must be carefully observed, especially when using fixture wires for Class 1 remote-control, signaling, or power-limited circuits, as permitted and regulated by Sec. 725-16 and Sec. 725-17.

402-10. Uses Permitted. Fixture wires may be used for internal wiring of lighting fixtures and other utilization devices. They may also be used for connecting lighting fixtures to the junction box of the branch circuit—such as by a flex whip to satisfy Sec. 410-67(c) (Fig. 402-1).

402-11. Uses Not Permitted. With the exception of their use for remote control, signaling, or power-limited circuits, fixture wires are not to be

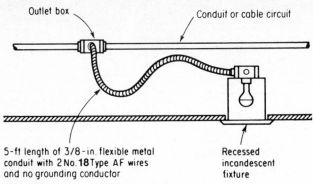

Fig. 402-1. Fixture wires may connect fixtures to branch-circuit wires. (Sec. 402-10.)

used as general-purpose branch-circuit wires. An example of the use permitted by Sec. 725-16 would be, say, No. 18 fixture wires run as remote-control wires in raceway from a motor starter to a remote push-button station, where the 6-A rating of the wire is adequate for the operating current of the coil in the starter.

402-12. Overcurrent Protection. This rule refers to Sec. 240-4, which permits No. 18 and No. 16 fixture wire of any type to be protected by a 15- or 20-A fuse or CB. That covers use of No. 18 or No. 16 in fixture "whips" on 15- or 20-A branch circuits and use for remote-control, signaling, or power-limited circuits.

ARTICLE 410. LIGHTING FIXTURES, LAMPHOLDERS, LAMPS, RECEPTACLES, AND ROSETTES

410-4. Fixtures in Specific Locations. Part **(a)** covers the kind of installations shown in Fig. 410-1. At left, the lighting fixture on the covered vehicle-loading dock is in a damp location and must be marked "SUITABLE FOR DAMP LOCATIONS" or marked "SUITABLE FOR WET LOCATIONS." At right, the lighting fixtures at a vehicle-washing area are in a wet location and must be marked "SUITABLE FOR WET LOCATIONS"—unless the fixtures are so high mounted or otherwise protected so that there is no chance of water being played on them.

An enclosed and gasketed fixture would fulfill the requirement that water shall be prevented from entering the fixture, though under some conditions water vapor might enter and a small amount of water might accumulate in the bottom of the globe.

Fixtures in the form of post lanterns, fixtures for use on service-station

 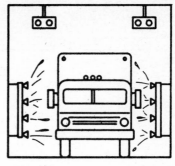

Damp location   Wet location

Fig. 410-1. Fixtures must be marked as suitable for their place of application. (Sec. 410-4.)

islands, and fixtures which are marked to indicate that they are intended for outdoor use have been investigated for outdoor installation.

An example of fixtures in "damp" locations would be those installed under canopies of stores in shopping centers where they would be protected against exposure to rain but would be subject to outside temperature variation and corresponding high humidity and condensation. Thus the internal parts of the fixture need to be of nonhygroscopic materials which will not absorb moisture and which will function under conditions of high humidity.

The UL listing of "Fixtures and Fittings" notes that—

These fixtures are incandescent-lamp and electric discharge lamp types (including show-window and showcase type) designed for installation in ordinary locations. Unless marked "Suitable for damp locations" or "Suitable for wet locations," in combination with the Listing Mark, fixtures are only suitable for dry locations.

Part **(c)** recognizes use of lighting fixtures in commercial and industrial ducts and hoods for removing smoke or grease-laden vapors from ranges and other cooking devices. The rule spells out the conditions for using fixtures and their associated wiring in all types of nonresidential cooking hoods. The requirement that such a lighting fixture be "approved for the purpose" may be taken as "listed" by UL for such use.

410-5. Fixtures Near Combustible Material. Figure 410-2 shows this rule. Much concern has been expressed by electrical inspectors because of instances where the fixture temperature has done damage to wires in outlet boxes and even to nonmetallic boxes themselves. Underwriters Laboratories tests and evaluates fixtures for such heating, with much useful data given in their *Electrical Construction Materials Directory.*

410-6. Fixtures Over Combustible Material. This refers to pendants and fixed lighting equipment, not to portable lamps. Where the lamp cannot be located out of reach, the requirement can be met by equipping the lamp with a guard.

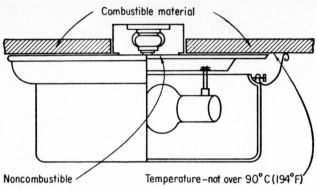

Fig. 410-2. Fixtures must not pose threat of heat to combustible materials. (Sec. 410-5.)

410-8. Fixtures in Clothes Closets. The intent is to prevent lamps from coming in contact with cartons or boxes stored on shelves and clothing hung in the closet, which would, of course, constitute a fire hazard. But, note that this rule prohibits the use of wall-mounted lighting fixtures in clothes closets, except above a closet door where proper horizontal clearances are maintained. Previously, fixtures could be mounted on other wall areas if certain clearances were observed.

It is quite obvious from the drawing in Fig. 410-3 that fixtures other than flush recessed types with solid lens cannot be located in *small* clothes closets that seem to prevail in building construction these days.

These requirements apply to incandescent and fluorescent lighting and all types of occupancies.

For small clothes closets proper lighting may be achieved by locating fixtures on the outside ceiling in front of the closet door—especially in hallways where such fixtures can serve a dual function. Flush recessed fixtures with a solid lens are considered outside of the closet because the lamp is recessed behind the wall or ceiling line.

410-9. Space for Cove Lighting. Adequate space also improves ventilation, which is equally important for such equipment.

410-11. Temperature Limit of Conductors in Outlet Boxes. Fixtures equipped with incandescent lamps may cause the temperature in the outlet boxes to become excessively high. The remedy is to use fixtures of improved design, or in some special cases to use circuit conductors having insulation that will withstand the high temperature.

The first sentence of this rule is related to the rule of Sec. 410-5. Figure 410-4 shows how a fixture may be "so installed" that the branch-circuit wires are not subjected to excessive temperature. That hookup relates to Sec. 410-67(c) for recessed fixtures, which requires a 4- to 6-ft length of

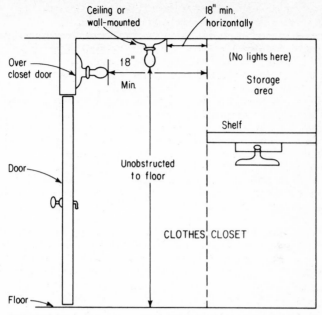

Fig. 410-3. These clearances apply to all lighting fixtures other than lensed recessed types. (Sec. 410-8.)

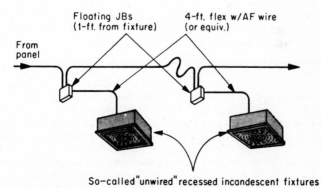

So-called "unwired" recessed incandescent fixtures

Fig. 410-4. Flex "whip" may be used to keep 60°C or 75°C wire away from 150°C terminal space in light fixtures. (Sec. 410-11.)

flex with high-temperature wire (say, Type AF) to connect hot fixture junction point (150°C) to the lower-rated branch-circuit wires.

The second sentence of this section applies to "prewired" recessed incandescent fixtures, which have been designed to permit 60°C supply conductors to be run into an outlet box attached to the fixture. Such fixtures have been listed by UL on the basis of the heat contribution by the supply conductors at *not more* than the *maximum* permitted lamp load of the fixture. Some fixtures have been investigated and listed by UL for "feed-through" circuit wiring. Accordingly, this rule requires careful use of prewired fixtures and, where necesssary, the rule calls for use of fixtures which can be connected at the *start* of the circuit as well as the *end* of a circuit without the need of "throw-away" JBs that are required for "unwired" recessed incandescent fixtures.

For quite some time this problem has created considerable controversy in the field because many inspectors have been enforcing the "feed-through" concept on the basis of an Underwriters Laboratories Inc. ruling which states:

With the exception of fluorescent-lamp fixtures, recessed fixtures are marked with the required minimum temperature rating of wiring supplying the fixture. Unless marked "Maximum of _____ No. _____ AWG branch-circuit conductors suitable for at least _____°C (_____°F) permitted in junction box," no allowance has been made for any heat contributed by branch-circuit conductors which pass through, or supply and pass through, an outlet box or other splice compartment which is part of the fixture.

The effect of that UL limitation is this: Some prewired fixtures (with attached outlet box) are suitable only for connecting the 60°C branch-circuit wires to the fixture *and* any prewired fixture for feeding the branch circuit through its outlet box must be marked to allow such use— as shown in Figure 410-5. To use a branch circuit to feed a number of prewired fixtures that are listed for only one set of 60°C supply wires, those prewired fixtures must be connected with a flex whip from each to a separate junction box, just as if they were "unwired" fixtures as shown in Fig. 410-4. The top hookup in Fig. 410-5 may be rectified by using two 60°C wires run in a 4-ft flex length to a separate outlet box mounted at least 1 ft away from the fixture.

410-12. Outlet Boxes to be Covered. This rule is similar to that of Sec. 370-15.

The canopy may serve as the box cover, but if the ceiling or wall finish is of combustible material, the canopy and box must form a complete enclosure. The chief purpose of this is to require that no open space be left between the canopy and the edge of the box where the finish is wood or fibrous or any similar material.

410-13. Covering of Combustible Material at Outlet Boxes. See comments under Sec. 370-15.

410-14. Connection of Electric-Discharge Lighting Fixtures. As Sec. 410-14 is worded, the rules presented apply to *both indoor* and *outdoor*

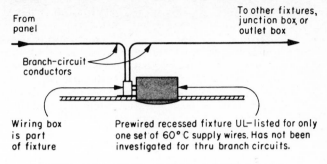

From
panel

To other fixtures,
junction box, or
outlet box

Branch-circuit
conductors

Wiring box
is part
of fixture

Prewired recessed fixture UL-listed for only
one set of 60° C supply wires. Has not been
investigated for thru branch circuits.

THIS HAS BEEN RULED A VIOLATION

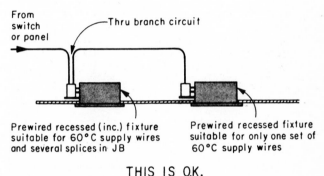

From
switch
or panel

Thru branch circuit

Prewired recessed (inc.) fixture
suitable for 60°C supply wires
and several splices in JB

Prewired recessed fixture
suitable for only one set of
60°C supply wires

THIS IS O.K.

Fig. 410-5. Care must be exercised in hooking up "prewired" *types* of fixtures. (Sec. 410-11.)

applications of electric-discharge fixtures. The rules cover general lighting in commercial and industrial interiors as well as all kinds of outdoor floodlighting and area lighting. The section covers *only* connection of electric-discharge luminaires "where . . . supported independently of the outlet box." Chain-hung fixtures, fixtures mounted on columns, poles, structures, or buildings, and any other fixture that is not "supported" by the outlet box that provides the branch-circuit conductors to feed the fixture are covered by Sec. 410-14.

The basic rule requires a fixed or permanent wiring method to be used for supply to all "electric-discharge lighting fixtures," which includes all fixtures containing mercury-vapor, fluorescent, metal-halide, high-pressure sodium, or low-pressure sodium lamps. BUT *incandescent* luminaires are *not* covered by Sec. 410-14. As a result, incandescent luminaires using cord connection are regulated only by Secs. 400-7(a) (2), 400-8(1), and 410-30(e).

The exceptions to the basic rule are noted. First, the rule permits cord-equipped fixtures to be located *directly below* the supply outlet, provided that the cord is continuously visible throughout its entire length outside the fixture (i.e., sight unobstructed by lift-out ceiling panels, etc.) and that it is terminated in a grounding-type cap or busway plug. Except for those fixtures that are UL-listed for cord-and-plug connection as part of listed modular wiring systems for use in suspended ceiling spaces, cord connection may not be used for fixtures installed in lift-out ceilings (Fig. 410-6).

The phrase "directly below the outlet box" has been ruled by inspectors to mean underneath the box and not just at a lower level. The phrase is intended to prevent cases where the fixture is connected by a cord that

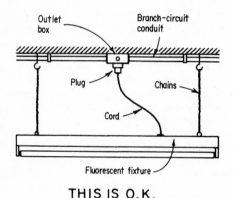

THIS IS O.K.

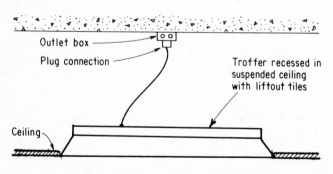

THIS IS A VIOLATION !

Fig. 410-6. Cord-and-plug fixture supply is O.K. only if cord is "continuously visible." (Sec. 410-14.)

runs horizontally as well as vertically to an outlet box that is mounted higher than the fixture but off to the side so that the box is not directly above the fixture.

That rule raises a number of questions:

- If an electric-discharge fixture is not mounted "directly below the outlet box," is it a violation to use cord connection from the box to the fixture? The answer seems to be yes.

- Is it a violation any time an electric-discharge fixture is supplied by a flexible cord with fixed cable connectors at both ends of the cord? Yes, except as permitted in Sec. 410-30(e) for fixtures that require aiming or adjustment.

- If outdoor floodlights—mounted on the ground, or on a building, or pole, or crossarms, or standards, or towers—do not comply with the precise conditions of hookup presented in the second and third sentences of Sec. 410-14, is it clearly mandatory that a "fixed wiring method" (and not flexible cord) must be used? No, as covered in Sec. 410-30(e).

But, difficulty in interpretation does arise because connection of "electric-discharge lighting fixtures" is strictly regulated and connection of incandescent fixtures is virtually ignored.

The second paragraph of this section permits electric-discharge lighting with mogul-base screw-shell lampholders (such as mercury-vapor or metal-halide units) to be supplied by branch circuits up to 50 A with the use of receptacles and caps of lesser ampere rating if such devices are rated not less than 125 percent of the fixture full-load current.

The two paragraphs at the end of this Code rule expand coverage of the use of wiring methods suitable for supplying electric-discharge lighting fixtures. The next-to-last paragraph notes that such fixtures are permitted to be supplied from busways as described in Sec. 364-12. The last paragraph provides for cord connection of a lighting fixture where the cord is equipped with a connector body at its lower end for insertion into a flanged inlet recessed in the lighting fixture housing (Fig. 410-7). This method of cord supply to electric-discharge lighting fixtures presents an alternative to the other method recognized in this section using a cord from the fixture with a plug cap on the other end of the cord for insertion into a receptacle mounted in a box directly above the fixture. The use of a connector body and flanged inlet supply affords greater ease in maintenance of the fixture, since maintenance people can disconnect the fixture at the lower end of the cord to remove it for cleaning or repair.

410-15. Supports—General. Figure 410-8 shows a 7-lb fixture shade that is 17 in. in diameter and supported by the screw-shell of the lamp and holder. On both counts that violates the rule here. Figure 410-9 shows a variety of support methods.

410-16. Means of Support. A lighting fixture may be supported by attachment to an outlet box that is securely mounted in position (see Sec.

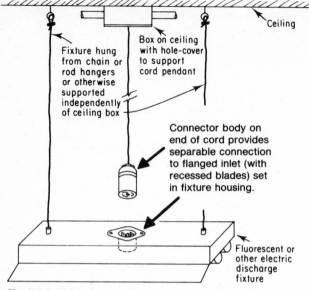

Fig. 410-7. This is the second method recognized for cord supply to lighting fixtures. (Sec. 410-14.)

370-13), or a fixture may be rigidly and securely attached or fastened to the surface on which it is mounted or it may be supported by embedment in concrete or masonry. As shown in Fig. 410-10, heavy fixtures must have better support than the outlet box.

Various techniques are used for mounting luminaires independently of the outlet box, depending somewhat on the total weight of the

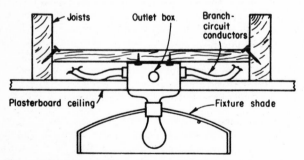

Fig. 410-8. Fixture shade assembly may be supported from a screw-shell lampholder if it is not too heavy or too big in diameter. (Sec. 410-15.)

individual luminaires. In general, pipe or rods are usually used to attach the luminaires to the building structure, and the electrical circuit is made by using flex between the luminaire and the outlet box concealed in the ceiling cavity. If provision is made for lowering the luminaire, by means of winch or otherwise, provision must also be made for disconnecting the electrical circuit.

The most common method of supporting fixtures is by means of fixture bars or straps bolted to the outlet boxes, as shown in Fig. 410-11. A fixture weighing over 50 lb can be supported on a hanger such as is shown for boxes under Sec. 370-6 for a tile-arch ceiling. Care should be taken to see that the pipe used in the construction of the hanger is of such size that the threads will have ample strength to support the weight.

Any luminaire may be attached to an outlet box where the box will provide adequate support, but, as noted in Sec. 410-15, units which weigh more than 6 lb, or exceed 16 in. in any dimension, "shall not be supported by the screw-shell of a lampholder."

A normal method of securing an outlet box in place is to use strap iron attached to back of outlet box and fastened to studs, lathing channels, steel beams, etc., nearby. Lightweight units are sometimes attached to outlet box by means of screws through luminaire canopy which thread into outlet box ears, or flanges, tapped for this purpose. For heavier luminaires, fixture studs, hickeys, tripods, or crowfeet are normally used.

410-18. Exposed Fixture Parts. The wording of this section, in referring to "lighting fixtures and equipment," does not make clear that the rules also apply to faceplates used on snap switches, receptacles, and other devices used in outlet boxes. This section went through extensive revisions and even relocation with Art. 410 since the 1968 **NEC** when, as Sec. 410-95, it referred to "ungrounded metal lighting fixtures, lampholders and face plates." But the intent of the rules was not changed.

Part **(a)** says metal faceplates must be grounded, if the box to which it is attached is fed by a wiring system with an equipment grounding means— metal raceway, metal cable armor, or a ground wire in NM cable. That applies to metal and nonmetallic boxes with a metal faceplate attached.

Part **(b)** says if the wiring system to the box does not contain a grounding means, any faceplate must be nonmetallic. That is a stricter rule than the similar rule in the first sentence of Sec. 380-9.

Other discussions on faceplates are given under Secs. 370-15 and 380-9. A note in Sec. 370-15 refers to Sec. 410-18 for faceplates.

Of course, the rules here also apply to lighting fixtures—of the metallic type in part **(a)** and nonmetallic fixtures as required by part **(b)**.

Relating Sec. 350-42(a) to the rule of Sec. 380-9, the effect is to require metal faceplates on switches and receptacles used in such places as kitchens or bathrooms to be grounded if they were within the specified distances of grounded surfaces. This rule requires covers of flush snap switches that are mounted in ungrounded metal boxes and located within reach of conducting floors or other conducting surfaces to be made of

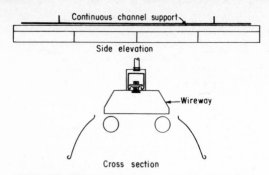

CONTINUOUS STEEL channel provides continuous line of support for industrial fluorescent luminaires, and may be supported by rod from ceiling structure at unequal spacing points.

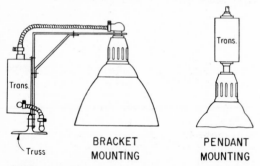

MERCURY REFLECTOR units and ncessary accessory transformers may be mounted in a variety of ways. Typical bracket and pendant mounting methods are shown here.

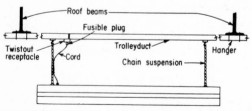

TROLLEY-DUCT attached to bottom of roof beams provides both electrical service and means of mechanical support.

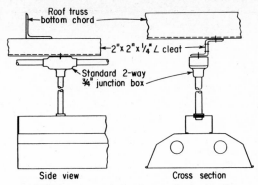

ANGLE IRON sections attached to bottom chords of roof truss provide support for conduit fittings and luminaires.

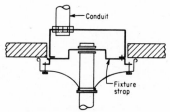

LIGHTWEIGHT LUMINAIRES may be attached to the outlet box by means of a fixture strap.

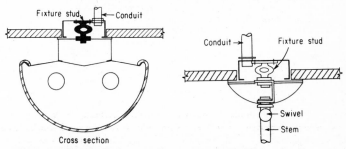

SURFACE MOUNTED fluorescent luminaire is attached to rigidly-supported outlet box by means of a fixture stud.

PENDANT MOUNTED luminaire is attached to fixture stud in outlet box, which is a typical mounting method.

Fig. 410-9. Many specific techniques may be used to satisfy the rule that fixtures "be securely supported." (Sec. 410-15.)

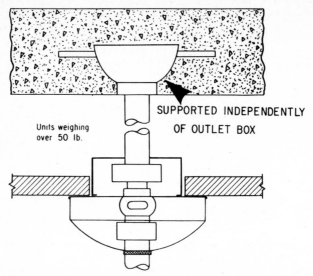

Units weighing
over 50 lb.

SUPPORTED INDEPENDENTLY
OF OUTLET BOX

Fig. 410-10. Any fixture over 50 lb must be supported from the structure or some other means other than the outlet box. (Sec. 410-16.)

nonconducting, noncombustible material. But the way the rule now stands in Sec. 410-18, it simply requires metal faceplates to be grounded if the wiring method permits it.

When a metal faceplate used on a switch mounted in a nonmetallic box has to be grounded, a simple, effective way to do it is to use a switch that has a grounding terminal (a green hex-head screw) attached to the metal mounting yoke. When the grounding conductor in the cable is connected to that screw, the mounting yoke is grounded and so is the metal faceplate that is attached by screw to the mounting yoke.

410-26. Conductors for Movable Parts. A lighting fixture fed by a conduit stem suspended from a threaded swivel-type conduit body must be supplied by stranded not solid wires run through the conduit stem—because the swivel fitting permits movement of the conductors.

410-29. Cord-Connected Showcases. Figure 410-12 shows an arrangement of cord-supplied illuminated showcases in a store. The details of this layout are lettered and involve the following rules:

   a. The first showcase is supplied by flexible cord plugged into grounding-type receptacle rated 20 A. And that is permitted.
   b. Flexible cord feeds second showcase; cord is spliced in JBs in each showcase. That is a clear violation of the requirement that in such connections, separable locking-type (twist-type) cord connectors must be used and spliced cord connections would be a violation.

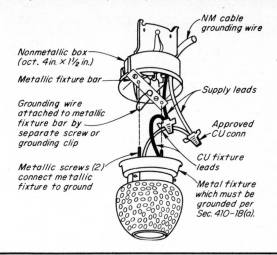

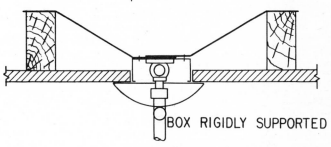

Fig. 410-11. Fixtures must be supported by approved methods. (Sec. 410-16.)

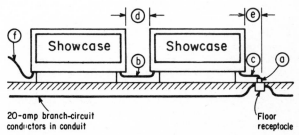

Fig. 410-12. Hookup of lighted showcases must satisfy a number of rules. (Sec. 410-29.)

c. Cord is No. 14 AWG, hard-service type. That is a violation because the cord conductors must be No. 12, the size of the branch-circuit conductors for the 20-A circuit, as required in part **(a).**

d. Showcases are separated by 2 in. That is OK but is the maximum permitted separation, as noted in part **(c).**

e. First case is 14 in. from supply receptacle. No good! The maximum permitted distance is 12 in.

f. Second showcase feeds spotlight. Violation! Part **(d)** says no other equipment may be connected to showcases.

410-30. Connections, Splices, and Taps.   Part **(e)** recognizes the use of fixed-cord connection for energy supply to lighting fixtures that require aiming or adjustment after installation (Fig. 410-13). Use of a cord supply

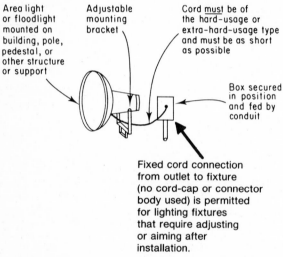

Area light or floodlight mounted on building, pole, pedestal, or other structure or support

Adjustable mounting bracket

Cord <u>must</u> be of the hard-usage or extra-hard-usage type and must be as short as possible

Box secured in position and fed by conduit

Fixed cord connection from outlet to fixture (no cord-cap or connector body used) is permitted for lighting fixtures that require adjusting or aiming after installation.

Fig. 410-13. Cord connection—either fixed cord or cord with plug cap—is permitted for adjustable fixtures. (Sec. 410-30.)

to lighting fixtures has been a recurring controversial issue, although Sec. 400-7 has permitted cord supply to lighting fixtures for a long time. Sec. 410-14 has required that electric-discharge lighting fixtures, if suitable for supply by cord, must make use of plug-and-receptacle connection of the fixture to the supply circuit. The rule here in part **(e)** permits floodlights—such as those used for outdoor and indoor areas for sporting events, for traffic control, or for area lighting—to have a fixed-cord connection from a bushed-hole cover of the branch-circuit outlet box to the wiring connection compartment in the lighting fixture itself. This rule gives adequate recognition to the type of cord connection that has long been used on floodlights, spotlights, and other fixtures used for area lighting applications.

It should be noted this rule in part **(e)** permits fixed-cord connection but does *not* prohibit use of plug connection to a receptacle or to a connector body. If plug connection is used, however, it might be required that the rules of Sec. 410-14 be satisfied—requiring the receptacle to be mounted directly above the fixture.

410-31. Fixtures as Raceways.   This Code rule has long stated basically that fixtures shall not be used as a raceway for circuit conductors (Fig. 410-14). Exceptions No. 1 and No. 2 have permitted variations from that rule.

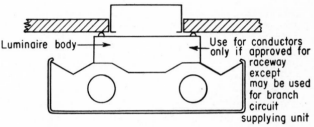

Fig. 410-14.   Use of wiring through lighting fixtures is clearly limited. (Sec. 410-31.)

Exception No. 1 permits fixtures to be used for circuit conductors if the fixtures are approved for use as a raceway (i.e., UL-listed and marked for general use as a raceway for conductors other than the circuit supplying the fixture).

Exception No. 2 permits limited use of fixture wiring compartments to carry through the circuit that supplies the fixtures, provided that the fixtures are designed for end-to-end assembly to form a continuous raceway or the fixtures are connected together by recognized wiring methods (such as rigid conduit and EMT). Most self-contained fluorescent luminaire units now available are designed for end-to-end assembly. Each luminaire contains a metal body, or housing, which serves as the structural member of the luminaire and provides a housing for the ballast, wiring, etc., which is of sufficient size to permit running the branch-circuit wiring through the unit. Each luminaire is then tied to the branch circuit by means of a single tap. When a fixture is specifically approved as a raceway, any number of branch-circuit conductors may be installed within the capacity of the raceway. When housings are approved as raceways, luminaires carry an Underwriters Laboratories label which states "Fixtures Suitable for Use as Raceway." Any type of circuit may be run through the fixture (Fig. 410-15).

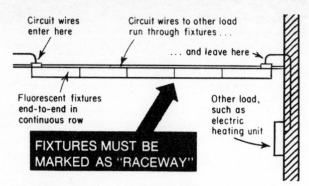

Fig. 410-15. Only fixtures approved as "Raceway" may be used for carrying-through circuit wires that supply any load other than the fixtures. (Sec. 410-31.)

It should be noted that in Exception No. 2, the permitted fixture layouts may carry only conductors of either a 2-wire or a multiwire branch circuit where the wires of the branch circuit supply only the lighting fixtures through which the circuit conductors are run. Thus, it is permissible to use a 3-phase, 4-wire branch circuit through fixtures so connected, with the total number of fixtures connected from all the phase legs to the neutral, that is, with the fixture load divided among the three phase legs. But Exception No. 2 limits such use to a single 2-wire or multiwire branch circuit.

Exception No. 3 permits one additional 2-wire branch circuit to be run through such fixtures (connected end-to-end or connected by recognized wiring methods) in addition to the 2-wire or multiwire branch circuit recognized by Exception No. 2, and this additional 2-wire branch circuit may be used only to supply one or more of the connected fixtures throughout the total fixture run supplied by the other branch circuit run through the raceway (Fig. 410-16). This was added to permit separate control of some of the fixtures fed by the additional branch circuit, providing the opportunity to turn off some of the fixtures for energy conservation during the night or other times when they are not needed.

It should be noted that UL rules tie into the above **Code** rules: Fixtures that are suitable for use as raceway—i.e., for carrying circuit wires other than the wires supplying the fixtures—must be so marked and must show the number, size, and type of conductors permitted. **NE Code** Sec. 410-31 correlates with this UL rule.

The last sentence of this section regulates use of wires run through or within fixtures where the wire would be exposed to possible contact with the ballast which has a hot-spot surface temperature of 90°C. Thus, such wires must be rated at least 90°C—which is the temperature at which the wire will operate when carrying its rated current in an ambient not over

This may now be done:

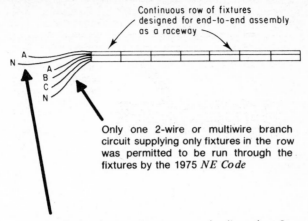

Continuous row of fixtures
designed for end-to-end assembly
as a raceway

Only one 2-wire or multiwire branch
circuit supplying only fixtures in the row
was permitted to be run through the
fixtures by the 1975 *NE Code*

Now the *Code* rule accepts one more circuit—only a **2-
wire** circuit—run through the row. But this additional
circuit **must** supply one or more of the fixtures in the row,
such as night lighting by, say, every fifth fixture, to enable
the others to be turned off for energy conservation.

And the same permission applies in this case—

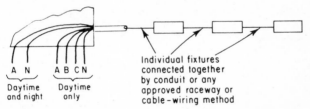

A N   A B C N

Daytime   Daytime
and night   only

Individual fixtures
connected together
by conduit or any
approved raceway or
cable-wiring method

Fig. 410-16. Expanded use of fixtures as raceways provides better control for conservation. (Sec. 410-31.)

30°C (which is 86°F). Note that Type THW wire is permitted for this use
in fixtures. Although Type THW is listed as a basic 75°C wire in Table
310-13, the table does show it as a 90°C rated wire for use in fixtures in
accordance with Sec. 410-31.

The question often arises, May Type AF (150°C) fixture wire be used
for circuiting through end-to-end connected continuous-row fluorescent
fixtures? Sec. 402-10 permits "fixture wires" to be installed "in lighting
fixtures" where they will not be subject to bending or flexing in normal

use. That would seem to approve Type AF through the fixtures connected in a row. But, Sec. 402-11 prohibits fixture wires used as branch-circuit conductors. The conductors installed in the fixture "ballast compartment" are referred to as "branch-circuit conductors" in Sec. 410-31, because they feed directly from the branch circuit and are tapped at each fixture to feed each fixture. The branch circuit extends from the point where it is protected by a CB or fuse to the last point where it feeds to the final outlet, device, apparatus, equipment, fixtures, etc. Under these conditions, it seems clear that the wiring must be that approved for branch circuits. Type AF and any other fixture wires are not approved for branch-circuit wiring.

To satisfy the last paragraph of Sec. 410-31, conductors such as Type RHH or Type THHN or Type THW must be installed. Type AF is definitely not permitted to be installed as branch-circuit conductors. But check with the local inspector if there are any doubts.

410-32. Polarization of Fixtures. This method of wiring fixtures is required in order to ensure that the screw shells of sockets will be connected to the grounded circuit wire.

410-35. Fixture Rating. This section specifically requires that any fixture be suitably marked to indicate the need for supply wires rated higher than 90°C to withstand the heat generated in the fixture. Such marking must be prominently made on the fixture itself and also on the shipping carton in which the fixture is enclosed (Fig. 410-17). And UL rules note:

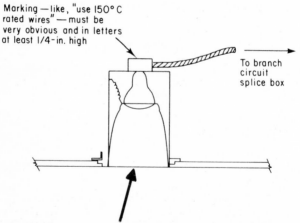

Marking — like, "use 150° C rated wires" — must be very obvious and in letters at least 1/4-in. high

To branch circuit splice box

If heat developed in fixture wiring box requires wire rated over 90C — the required temperature rating of supply wire must be marked in the fixture and on shipping carton.

Fig. 410-17. Where high-temperature wire is needed, fixture must be marked. (Sec. 410-35.)

Fixtures marked for use in commercial or industrial occupancies must *not* be used in residential occupancies, because the fixtures have maintenance features beyond the capabilities of ordinary householders or involve voltages higher than that permitted by the **NE Code** for residences.

410-42. Portable Lamps. Part **(a)** requires portable lamps (table lamps and floor lamps) to be wired with flexible cord approved for the purpose and to be equipped with polarized or grounding type attachment plugs. An exception to the rule indicates that the presently used two-prong nonpolarized attachment plugs will be permitted until January 1, 1980, but after that date, plug caps on the cords for portable lamps must be either grounding type or polarized type to permit a single orientation of the plug for insertion in the receptacle outlet. Such polarizing of the plug will provide for connecting the grounded conductor of the circuit to the screw shell of the lampholder in the lamp.

In part **(b)**, four specific rules are given on the use of portable handlamps, as shown in Fig. 410-18. The requirements of part **(a)** calling

Portable lamps

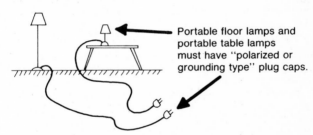

Portable floor lamps and portable table lamps must have "polarized or grounding type" plug caps.

NOTE: Nonpolarized attachment plugs will not be permitted after Jan. 1, 1980.

Portable hand lamps

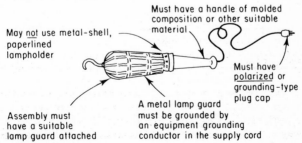

Must have a handle of molded composition or other suitable material

May <u>not</u> use metal-shell, paperlined lampholder

Must have <u>polarized</u> or grounding-type plug cap

Assembly must have a suitable lamp guard attached

A metal lamp guard must be grounded by an equipment grounding conductor in the supply cord

Fig. 410-18. NEC rules aim at greater safety in use of portable lamps and portable hand lamps. (Sec. 410-42.)

for polarized or grounding type attachment plugs also are made applicable to portable handlamps.

410-47. Screw-Shell Type (Lampholders). This warns against the previously common practice of installing screw-shell lampholders with screwplug adapters in baseboards and walls for the connecting of cord-connected appliances and lighting equipment and thereby exposing live parts to contact by persons when the adapters were moved from place to place. See Sec. 410-56(a).

410-48. Double-Pole Switched Lampholders. On a circuit having one wire grounded, the grounded wire must always be connected to the screw shell of the socket, and sockets having a single-pole switching mechanism may be used. (See Sec. 410-52). On a 2-wire circuit tapped from the outside (ungrounded) wires of a 3-wire or 4-wire system, if sockets having switching mechanisms are used, these must be double-pole so that they will disconnect both of the ungrounded wires.

410-56. Rating and Type (Receptacles, etc.). Part **(c)** is intended to prevent short circuits when attachment plugs (caps) are inserted in receptacles mounted with metal faceplates—in which case, the metal of the plate could short (or bridge) the blades of the plug cap if the faceplate is not set back from the receptacle face. The rule requires the "faces" of receptacles to project at least 0.015 in. through the faceplate opening when the faceplate is metallic. And it is necessary to assure a solid backing for receptacles so that attachment plugs can be inserted without difficulty. The requirement for receptacle faces to project at least 0.015 in. from installed metal faceplates will also prevent faults caused by countless existing attachment plugs with exposed bare terminal screws. The design requirements for attachment plugs and connectors in part **(d)** should prevent such faults at metal plates, but the problem of existing attachment plugs in this regard will be around for many years.

With receptacle faces and faceplates installed according to Sec. 410-56(c), attachment plugs can be fully inserted into receptacles and will provide a better contact. The cooperation of other crafts, such as plasterers or dry-wall applicators, will be needed to satisfy the requirements.

410-57. Receptacles in Damp or Wet Locations. The definition of "location" in Art. 100 describes places that fall into either the "wet" or "damp" category. Any receptacle used in a damp location—such as an open or screened-in porch with a roof or overhang above it—may not be equipped with a conventional receptacle cover plate. It must be provided with a cover that, although not UL-listed as "weatherproof," will make the receptacle(s) weatherproof when the cover or covers are in place. The type of cover plate that has a thread-on metal cap held captive by a short metal chain would be acceptable for damp locations but not wet locations (Fig. 410-19). And any other plate-and-cover assembly that is not listed as weatherproof and does not satisfy the conditions of part **(b)** of this section may be used in a damp location provided it covers the receptacle when not in use. The type of receptacle cover that has horizontally opening hinged flaps (doors) to cover the receptacles may be used in a damp but

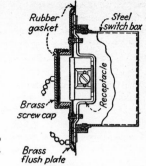

Fig. 410-19. Chain-held screw-cap cover is suitable for damp, but not wet, locations. (Sec. 410-57.)

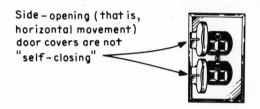

Side – opening (that is, horizontal movement) door covers are not "self - closing"

Note : If door covers were self-closing type, such a cover assembly could be used outdoors to supply a portable tool or equipment that is not left connected.

Fig. 410-20. Cover assembly with stay-open doors may be used in damp but *not* in wet locations. (Sec. 410-57.)

not wet location if the flaps are not self-closing, i.e., if the flaps can stay open (Fig. 410-20). Of course, any cover plate that is listed for weather-proof use may also be used in damp locations.

For wet locations, part **(b)** receptacles must be used with either of two types of cover assemblies:

1. For a receptacle outdoors or in any other wet location where a plug-connected load is normally left connected to the receptacle—such as for outdoor landscape lighting or for constant supply to an appliance or other load—only a fully weatherproof, listed cover plate may be used. Such an assembly maintains weatherproof protection of the receptacle at all times—either with the plug out or the plug in. Figure 410-21 shows the way in which a vertically lifting cover shields the receptacle against driving rain (coming at an angle). Such assemblies are made with one cover for a single receptacle or two covers for duplex receptacles. Other cover assemblies use a vertically lifting "canopy" that protects either a single or duplex receptacle.

2. For outdoor receptacles used solely for occasional connection of

Swing—down canopy is
self—closing

**Receptacle is kept
weatherproof with or
without plug inserted.**

Duplex cover

Fig. 410-21. UL-listed weatherproof covers protect receptacles at all times.
(Sec. 410-57.)

portable tools or appliances (lawnmowers, hedge-trimmers, etc.), it
is permissible, under the Exception, to use a cover that only provides protection against weather when the cover is closed (but not
when a plug is inserted.) But such a cover, whether installed for
vertical or horizontal movement of the cover, must have spring-
loaded *self-closing* covers or gravity-close for vertical-lift covers.

Part **(c)** pertains to flush-mounted boxes in which receptacles are
installed in wet locations, and part **(d)** requires an elevation of outdoor
receptacles to prevent accumulation of water.

**410-58. Grounding-Type Receptacles, Adapters, Cord Connectors, and
Attachment Plugs.** Paragraph **(3)** of part **(b)** requires a "rigid" terminal
for equipment grounding connection in grounding adapters for insertion into nongrounding receptacles (Fig. 410-22). Adapters with pigtail
leads are not acceptable to the rule.

Use of grounding adapters to convert a non grounding receptacle for
connection of a three-prong grounding plug cap involves a number of
NE Code and UL regulations. When a grounding receptacle connection
is required for a cord-connected appliance or tool, a nongrounding-type
receptacle should be replaced with a grounding type, as required by Sec.
210-7(d). And the branch circuit or branch-circuit raceway must include
or provide a grounding conductor to which the receptacle ground terminal must be connected.

Plug-in grounding adapters for converting nongrounding (two-slot) receptacles to grounding type are listed by UL under "Attachment Plugs" in the *Electrical Construction Materials Directory* (green book). But the NE Code makes no reference to the use of such devices. Section 410-58(b) does describe the construction of adapters and thus implies that their use is permitted.

The problem with grounding adapters having a green grounding pigtail is that such adapters used on nongrounding receptacles present the inherent risk that they will be used without assuring integrity of the grounding path. It is very easy for anyone to plug such an adapter into a nongrounding receptacle and connect the spade lug in the green pigtail under the screw that secures the faceplate on the receptacle. But experience has shown a number of conditions that might exist and prevent effective grounding of the ground terminal of the adapter. The nongrounding receptacle may be fed by NM cable without a grounding conductor (or even by 2-wire knob-and-tube wiring). If the nongrounding receptacle fed by NM cable is in a nonmetallic box, the screw that secures the faceplate is not grounded, even if the cable includes a grounding conductor.

Another potential hazard of the pigtail adapter is shown in Fig. 410-23.

NE Code **AND UL VIOLATION!** The *NE Code* prohibits use of the pigtail grounding adapters that have been available and widely used for many years. Such devices also do not satisfy UL construction standards.

THIS IS UL AND *NE Code* **RECOGNIZED.** Grounding adapter has rigid tab with spade end for connecting grounding terminal of the adapter to metal screw contacting the grounded metal yoke that mounts receptacle to the grounded metal box of the outlet (or to an equipment grounding conductor in NM cable used with a nonmetallic outlet box). Different-width blades on adapter polarize it for insertion in only one way into the polarized blade-openings on the receptacle.

Fig. 410-22. This is the NEC and UL position on grounding adapters. (Sec. 410-58.)

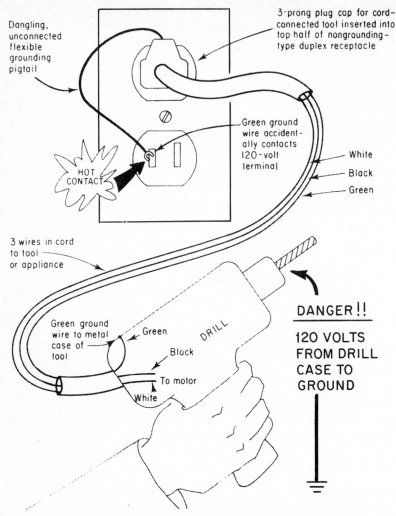

Dangling, unconnected flexible grounding pigtail

3-prong plug cap for cord-connected tool inserted into top half of nongrounding-type duplex receptacle

Green ground wire accident-ally contacts 120-volt terminal

White

Black

Green

HOT CONTACT

3 wires in cord to tool or appliance

Green ground wire to metal case of tool

Green

DRILL

Black

To motor

White

DANGER !!

120 VOLTS FROM DRILL CASE TO GROUND

Fig. 410-23. Pigtail adapter can present shock hazard to personnel. (Sec. 410-58.)

Spade lug on end of the green pigtail wire might accidentally contact a hot terminal through the blade opening of other receptacle on a duplex outlet. Or spade lug could touch the hot blade of a plug cap that is not fully inserted into lower receptacle.

410-64. General (for Flush and Recessed Fixtures).   Underwriters Laboratories rules comment on use of fixtures installed in hung ceilings, as follows:

Fixtures marked "Suitable for Use With Suspended Ceilings" have not been tested for use in ceiling spaces containing other heat sources such as steam pipes, hot-water pipes, or heating ducts.

Air-handling fixtures must be used fully in accordance with the conditions marked on the fixtures. When used in fire-rated ceilings, such fixtures must be related to the "Design Information Section" in the *Fire Resistance Index,* published by UL.

410-65. Temperature. Heat is a major problem in lighting system design, and with the trend to the use of recessed luminaires and equipment, the problem is increased. In the case of luminaires using incandescent lamps, the problem is primarily the prevention of concentrated spots of heat coming into contact with the building structure. In the case of fluorescent luminaires, the major heat problem is related to the ballast, which can build up severely high temperatures when not properly ventilated, or designed for cooler operation through adequate radiation and convection. These are problems which must be solved (1) through proper luminaire design, and (2) through proper installation methods and techniques (Fig. 410-24).

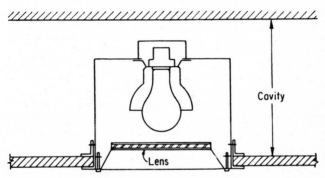

Luminaires shall not subject adjacent combustible material to a temperature in excess of 90°C (194° F).

Fig. 410-24. Recessed fixtures must not threaten combustion of building materials. (Sec. 410-65.)

410-66. Clearance. When recessed fixtures are used with thermal insulation in the recessed space, thermal insulation must have a clearance of at least 3 in. on the side of the fixture and at least 3 in. at the top of fixture and shall be so arranged that heat is not trapped in this space. Free circulation of air must be provided with this 3-in. spacing. If, however, the fixture is approved for installation with thermal insulation on closer spacing, it may be so used (Fig. 410-25).

In the past, thermal insulation has been installed in direct contact with recessed fixtures not approved for that use and caused overheating in fixtures with resulting failures and fires. Obviously, the installer of ther-

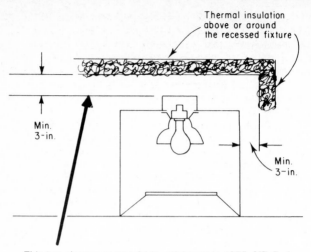

This top clearance was 24 in. minimum in 1975 *NE Code* but is only 3 inches in 1978 *NE Code*, if heat is not trapped

Fig. 410-25. Clearance of recessed fixture from thermal insulation is greatly reduced. (Sec. 410-66.)

mal insulation will have to be educated on this subject, because electrical installers have little control over how the insulation will be applied.

Figure 410-26 shows an application that involves the ½-in. clearance covered in the first sentence of this section. It shows two 40-W fluorescent strips installed in a residential kitchen ceiling. The ceiling has been furred down on all sides of the 4- by 4-ft fixture area as shown. The question arises: Is this a "recessed" installation according to the **Code**? How small or large must such an enclosed space be to be considered a recess? The **Code** does not mention "recessed installation" but refers to

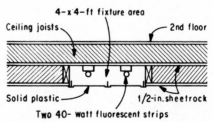

Fig. 410-26. Clearances on custom recessed lighting applications must be evaluated carefully. (Sec. 410-66.)

"recessed fixtures." The installation as shown is basically a field-fabricated recessed fixture. With only two 40-W lamps in this space, it is not likely there will be much of a heat problem. But sufficient information on the total construction of the cavity would be needed for an inspector to make an evaluation. The temperature limitations of Secs. 410-5 and 410-65 must be observed, and wiring must be in accordance with Sec. 410-67.

The next question is: Must a ½-in. clearance be maintained between the fixtures and the Sheetrock? Sheetrock is fire-rated by UL but is not fireproof. It is likely that inspectors would require the ½-in. spacing between the fixtures and the Sheetrock because the paperboard surfaces of the Sheetrock are combustible. The local inspector would have the final say on this concern.

410-67. Wiring. Supply wiring to recessed fixtures may be the branch-circuit wires, if their 60°C or 75°C or 90°C temperature rating at least matches the temperature that will exist in the fixture splice compartment under operating conditions. Typically fluorescent fixtures do not have very high operating temperatures where the branch-circuit wires splice to the fixture wires and branch-circuit conductors may be run right into the fixture. But, incandescent fixtures develop much higher localized heat because all the wattage is concentrated in a much smaller bulb, thereby requiring higher temperature wire where the branch-circuit splices to the fixture leads.

The rules of part **(b)** and part **(c)** of this section are related to the details discussed under Sec. 410-11. Figure 410-27 shows branch-circuit wires rated at 75°C coming out of ceiling boxes (left) and then connected directly to fluorescent strip units mounted over the boxes and attached to the ceiling (right). The 75°C THW branch-circuit wires are rated at 90°C for use within the fluorescent units (Sec. 410-31, last sentence).

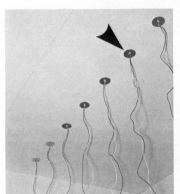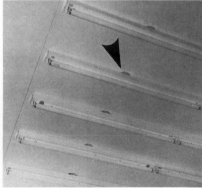

Fig. 410-27. Branch-circuit wires rated at 75°C are brought out of ceiling boxes (left) and then connected to fixture leads within the relatively cool wiring compartment of the fluorescent units. (Sec. 410-67.)

Fig. 410-28. Prewired recessed incandescent fixtures may have 60°C branch-circuit wiring run directly into their junction boxes. (Sec. 410-67.)

Figure 410-28 shows 60°C branch-circuit wiring run directly to integral junction boxes of "prewired" incandescent fixtures. The box protects the branch-circuit wires from the heat generated within the fixtures. Note these fixtures are used for supply and feed-through of the branch-circuit wires and must be UL-listed for that application (refer to Sec. 410-11).

Figure 410-29 shows an application of part **(c)** of this Code section, where a fixture wiring compartment operates so hot that the temperature exceeds that of the branch-circuit-rated value and high-temperature fixture wires must be run to the unit. The circuit outlet box supplying the high-wattage incandescent fixture must be mounted not less than 1 ft

Fig. 410-29. For fixture with circuit-connection compartment operating very hot, high-temperature wires must be run in flex (or other metal raceway) between 4 and 6 ft, from an outlet box at least 12 in. away. (Sec. 410-67.)

away from the fixture. The flex whip may be ⅜-in. flex for the number and type of fixture wires as specified in Table 350-3 (Sec. 350-3). If the branch-circuit supplying the fixture is protected at 20 A or 15 A, No. 18 fixture wires may be used for fixture load up to 6 A or No. 16 fixture wire may be used for loads up to 8 A (Sec. 402-5), and the metal flex may serve as the equipment grounding conductor [Sec. 250-91(b), Exception No. 1]. The flex may not be less than 4 ft long but not more than 6 ft long. The fixture wires could be Type AF for conditions requiring a 150°C rating or could be another type of adequate temperature rating for the fixture's marked temperature, selected from Table 402-3. For flex, refer also to Sec. 350-5.

Recessed fixtures are, in all cases, marked with the required minimum-temperature rating of wiring supplying the fixture. See Sec. 410-35(a), the last sentence. This marking does not allow for any heat contributed by a branch circuit passing through the fixture enclosure or through a splice compartment (outlet box or otherwise) that is part of the fixture construction. An insulation with a temperature rating higher than that indicated on the fixture may be required for such branch-circuit conductors. See Sec. 410-11.

The requirements in part **(c)** are special provisions that apply to recessed fixtures and take precedence over the general requirements. The tap conductors (usually in flexible conduit) connecting an unwired recessed fixture to the outlet box must be in metal raceway of at least 4 ft in length and not over 6 ft. The box is required to be at least 1 ft away from the fixture and the flexible conduit may be looped to use up the excess length (see Sec. 350-4, Exception No. 3). This rule does not apply to "prewired" fixtures designed for connection to 60°C supply wires.

The purpose of this requirement is to allow the heat to dissipate so that heat from the fixture will not cause an excessive temperature in the outlet box and thus overheat the branch-circuit conductors which could be of the general-use type limited to 60°C or 75°C temperatures.

410-73. General.   Paragraph **(e)** pertains only to fluorescent lamp ballasts used indoors. The protection called for must be a part of the ballast. Underwriters Laboratories Inc. has made an extensive investigation of various types of protective devices for use within such ballasts, and ballasts found to meet UL requirements for these applications are listed and marked as "Class P." The protective devices are thermal trip devices or thermal fuses, which are responsive to abnormal heat developed within the ballast because of a fault in components such as autotransformers, capacitors, reactors, etc.

Simple reactance-type ballasts are used with preheat-type fluorescent lamp circuits for lamps rated less than 30 W. Also, a manual (momentary-contact) or automatic-type starter is used to start the lamp. The simple reactor-type ballast supplies one lamp only, has no autotransformer or capacitor, and is exempted from the protection rule of part **(e).**

The thermal protection required for ballasts of fluorescent fixtures installed indoors must be within the ballast. Previous wording permitted the interpretation that the supplementary protection for the ballast could be in the fixture and not necessarily within the ballast.

410-75. Voltages—Dwelling Occupancies.   As required by UL, fixtures which are intended for use in other than dwelling occupancies are so marked. This usually indicates that the fixture has maintenance features which are considered to be beyond the capabilities of the ordinary householder, or involves voltages in excess of those permitted by the National Electrical Code for dwelling occupancies.

410-76. Fixture Mounting.   Underwriters Laboratories presents data which apply to part **(b)** of this section:

1. Fluorescent fixtures suitable for mounting on combustible low-density cellulose fiberboard ceilings which have been evaluated for use with thermal insulation above the ceiling and which have been investigated for mounting directly on combustible low-density cellulose fiberboard ceilings are marked "Suitable for Surface Mounting on Combustible Low-Density Cellulose Fiberboard" (Fig. 410-30).

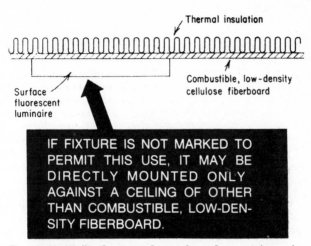

Thermal insulation

Surface fluorescent luminaire

Combustible, low-density cellulose fiberboard

IF FIXTURE IS NOT MARKED TO PERMIT THIS USE, IT MAY BE DIRECTLY MOUNTED ONLY AGAINST A CEILING OF OTHER THAN COMBUSTIBLE, LOW-DENSITY FIBERBOARD.

Fig. 410-30. UL lists fluorescent fixtures for surface mounting on low-density cellulose fiberboard ceilings with insulation above. (Sec. 410-76.)

    If a fluorescent fixture is not marked to show it is approved for surface mounting on combustible low-density cellulose fiberboard, it must be mounted with at least a 1½-in. space between it and such a ceiling.

2. Fluorescent fixtures that may not be used directly against *any* ceiling are marked "For Suspended Mounting Only. Minimum Distance From Ceiling Six Inches."

3. Surface-mounting incandescent and HID fixtures (mercury-vapor, metal-halide, etc.) are suitable for use on any ceiling including low-density fiberboard, without marking—but, except for incandescent fixtures marked "Type I.C.," such fixtures must never be used where there is thermal insulation above the ceiling over the fixture. Type I.C. (insulated ceiling) incandescent fixtures may be mounted on a ceiling with insulation above.

4. If surface-mounted or suspended fixtures require supply circuit wires rated over 60°C, they will be marked to show the required minimum temperature rating of the circuit wires. And where such

fixtures are marked to require wires rated over 60°C, the marking does not allow for any heat added by a branch circuit passing through the fixture. In such cases, it is up to the installer to determine the need for using wires of a temperature rating higher than indicated.

The note after this section describes "combustible low-density cellulose fiberboard." Material meeting these requirements is listed in Underwriters Laboratories Inc. *Building Materials Directory* and in addition to other pertinent information includes the following: "This material has been found to comply with the flame spread requirements stipulated in Sec. 410-76 of the National Electrical Code as described therein."

410-78. Autotransformers.   This rule ties in with the rules of Sec. 210-6 on voltage of branch circuits to lighting fixtures. On neutral-grounded wye systems (such as 120/208 or 277/480) incandescent, fluorescent, mercury-vapor, metal-halide, high-pressure sodium, and low-pressure sodium equipment can be connected from phase to neutral on the circuits. If fluorescent or mercury-vapor fixtures are to be connected phase to phase, some Code authorities contend that autotransformer-type ballasts cannot be used when they raise the voltage to more than 300 V, because, they contend, the reference to "a grounded system" in this rule of Sec. 410-78 calls for connection to a circuit made up of a grounded wire and a hot wire (Fig. 410-31). On phase-to-phase connection they would require use of 2-winding (electrically isolating) ballast transformers. The wording of Sec. 410-78 does, however, lend itself to interpretation that it is only necessary for the supply *system* to the ballast to *be grounded*—thus permitting the two hot legs of a 208-V or 480-V circuit to supply an autotransformer because the hot legs are derived from a neutral-grounded "system." But Sec. 210-9, which calls for a

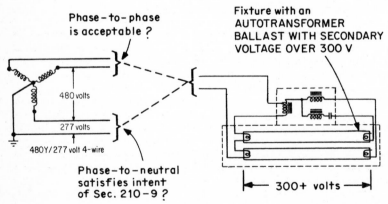

Fig. 410-31. Intent of Sec. 210-9 raises questions about connection of autotransformer ballasts. (Sec. 410-78.)

"grounded conductor" to be common to the primary and secondary of an autotransformer that supplies a branch circuit, can become a complicating factor. Use of a 2-winding (isolating) ballast is clearly acceptable and avoids all confusion.

410-80. General (Electric-Discharge Lighting—More Than 1,000 V). These sections apply to interior neon-tube lighting, lighting with long fluorescent tubes requiring more than 1,000 V, and cold-cathode fluorescent-lamp installation arranged to operate with several tubes in series.

410-81. Control. When any part of the equipment is being serviced, the primary circuit should be opened and the servicers should have assurance that the disconnecting means will not be closed without their knowledge.

410-87. Transformer Loading. See comments following Sec. 600-32.

410-88. Wiring Method—Secondary Conductors. This type of cable is not included in the table in Chap. 3 listing various types of insulated conductors, but Underwriters Laboratories Inc. have standards for such cables. The following information is an excerpt from the Underwriters Laboratories Inc. *Electrical Construction Materials Directory:*

Gas tube sign and ignition cable is classified as Type GTO-5 (5,000 volts), GTO-10 (10,000 volts), or GTO-15 (15,000 volts), and is labeled in sizes Nos. 18-10 AWG copper and Nos. 12-10 AWG aluminum and copper-clad aluminum. This material is intended for use with gas tube signs, oil burners, and inside lighting.

L-used as a suffix in combination with any of the preceding type letter designations indicates that an outer covering of lead has been applied.

The label of Underwriters' Laboratories, Inc., (illustrated above) on the product is the only method provided by Underwriters' Laboratories, Inc., to identify Gas Tube Sign and Ignition Cable which has been produced under the Label Service.

ARTICLE 422. APPLIANCES

422-1. Scope. See definition for "appliance," Art. 100. For purposes of the Code, the definition for an appliance indicates that it is utilization equipment other than industrial and generally means small equipment such as may be used in a dwelling or office (clothes washer, clothes dryer, air conditioner, food mixer, coffee maker, etc.). See also definition for "utilization equipment" in Art. 100.

422-5. Branch-Circuit Sizing. Part (a) states that the amp rating of an individual branch circuit to a single appliance must not be less than the marked ampere rating of the appliance.

422-6. Branch-Circuit Overcurrent Protection. The second sentence presents a rule based on the fact that some appliances are marked to indicate the maximum permitted rating of protective device (fuse or CB) for the branch circuit supplying that appliance.

422-8. Flexible Cords. Figure 422-1 shows application of rules on the hookup of kitchen garbage disposers. Hookup of dishwashers and trash

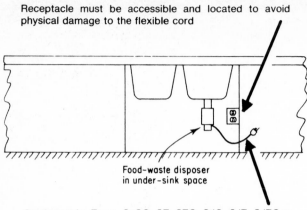

Receptacle must be accessible and located to avoid physical damage to the flexible cord

Food-waste disposer in under-sink space

Cord must be Type S, SO, ST, STO, SJO, SJT, SJTO or SPT-3—3-conductor, terminated with a grounding-type plug. Cord must be between 18 and 36 in. long.

NOTE: Double-insulated disposers do not have to be grounded.

Fig. 422-1. Code rules aim at effective grounding for kitchen garbage disposers. (Sec. 422-8.)

compactors is the same, except that the cord must be 3 to 4 ft long, instead of 1½ to 3 ft long.

422-12. Signals for Heated Appliances. The standard form of signal is a red light so connected that the lamp remains lighted as long as the appliance is connected to the circuit. No signal lamp is required if the appliance is equipped with a thermostatic switch which automatically opens the circuit after the appliance has been heated to a certain temperature.

422-14. Water Heaters. Part **(b)** ties into Sec 422-5(a) Exception No. 2 to require 120-gal water heaters or any water heater of lesser capacity to be fed by branch-circuit conductors that have an ampacity not less than 1.25 times the marked ampacity of the water heater (Fig. 422-2). Or, to put it another way, the amp rating of the water heater must not exceed 80 percent of the amp rating of the branch-circuit conductors. And that rule must be related to Sec. 422-27(e). The only case where the water-heater current may load the circuit to 100 percent is where the circuit protective device is listed for continuous operation at 100 percent of its rating. But there are not standard protective devices of that type available at the circuit ratings required for water-heater loads.

422-15. Infrared Lamp Industrial Heating Appliances. So-called "infrared" lamps are tungsten-filament incandescent lamps, similar to lamps used for lighting except that they are designed for operation with

Fig. 422-2. Any fixed storage water heater with capacity of 120 gal or less must be treated as a "continuous duty load" that does not load the circuit to more than 80 percent of its capacity. (Sec. 422-14.)

the filaments at a lower temperature, resulting, for a given wattage, in more heat radiation and less light output, and also in a much longer lamp life. In a typical infrared heating oven for industrial use, the lampholders are mounted on panels which are hinged so that the axis of each lamp is at an angle of about 45° from the surface of the panel, to ensure that all sides of an object passing through the oven will receive a uniform amount of heat radiation.

422-21. Disconnection of Permanently Connected Appliances. In part **(a)** lower-rated appliances may use the "branch-circuit overcurrent device" as their disconnect means and such a device could be a plug-fuse or a CB. Part **(b)** for higher-rated appliances does not permit use of a plug-fuse as the disconnect but requires a definite switch-action device— a switch or CB. Note that this section applies *only* to permanently connected appliances—i.e., those with fixed-wiring connection (so-called "hard wired") and not cord-and-plug connection.

In part **(a)**, the overcurrent device for the circuit to the appliance is not required to be accessible to the user. But the switch or CB in part **(b)** must be "readily accessible" to the user. See definition of "readily accessible" in Art. 100.

Section 422-26 and Sec. 422-24 relate to the rules of this section.

422-22. Disconnection of Cord- and Plug-Connected Appliances. Examples of the application of this section for disconnecting means for appliances are found in the installation of household electric ranges and clothes dryers. The purpose of these requirements is to provide that for every such appliance there will be some means for opening the circuit to the appliance when it is to be serviced or repaired or when it is to be removed.

In part **(b)**, household electric ranges may be supplied by cord-and-plug connection to a range receptacle located at the rear base of the range. The rule permits such a plug and receptacle to serve as the disconnecting means for the range if the connection is accessible from the front by removal of a drawer.

This rule refers to "electric" ranges but the concept also applies to gas ranges. For instance, there have been 115-V receptacle outlets installed behind gas ranges in mobile homes. Such a receptacle is only used as an outlet for the oven light and clock on the range and is not accessible after the range is installed. In order to disconnect the attachment plug or plugs from the receptacle, the range gas supply pipe has to be disconnected, the frame of the range disconnected from its floor fastening, and then the range moved in order to reach the receptacle outlet where the cords are plugged in (Fig. 422-3). Is such an installation in conformity with the intent of the Code? The answer seems surely to be no. The inaccessibility of the receptacle would be objectionable.

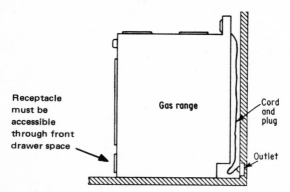

Fig. 422-3. Rule on receptacle behind "electric" ranges could be applied to gas ranges. (Sec. 422-22.)

422-24. Unit Switch(es) as Disconnecting Means. As shown in Fig. 422-4, the ON-OFF switch on an appliance, such as a cooking unit in a commercial establishment, is permitted by part **(d)** to serve as the required disconnect means if the user of the appliance has ready access to the branch-circuit switch or CB. Note that the wording does not recognize simply "the branch-circuit overcurrent device," and a plug-fuse in the circuit to the appliance would not, therefore, be acceptable as the additional means for disconnection.

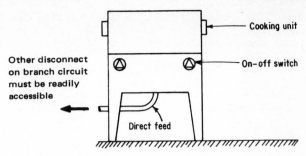

Fig. 422-4. An ON-OFF switch on an appliance must be supplemented by an additional disconnect means. (Sec. 422-24.)

422-26. Disconnecting Means for Motor-Driven Appliances. The basic rule requires that a switch or CB serving as the disconnecting means for a permanently connected motor-driven appliance of more than ⅛ hp must be within sight from the motor controller, as shown in Fig. 422-5 for the power unit of a built-in vacuum cleaner system. As permitted by Sec. 430-109 Exception No. 2, general-use AC snap switches may be used as the disconnect for motors rated up to 2 hp, not over 300 V, provided that the motor full load is not greater than 80 percent of the ampere rating of the switch.

Under the Exception to this rule, the branch-circuit switch or CB serving as the other disconnect required by Secs. 422-24(a), (b), (c), or (d) is permitted to be out of sight from the motor controller of an appliance that is equipped with a unit switch that has a marked OFF position and opens all ungrounded supply conductors to the appliance, as shown in Fig. 422-6.

422-27. Overcurrent Protection. Part **(a)** refers to part **(e)** as the basic rule on overcurrent protection for appliances. In part **(e)**, the rule specifically gives required protection to those appliances which would not be adequately protected if too large a branch-circuit protective device were used ahead of them. This rule used to apply to all appliances rated 10 A or more. Now it applies where an individual branch circuit supplies a "nonmotor-operated appliance" rated at 16.7 A or more. The value of 10 A was changed to 16.7 A because there were conflicts between the rule of Sec. 210-22 (requiring a continuous load to load a branch circuit to not more than 80 percent) and the rule that calls for the protective device to be rated no more than 150 percent of the appliance amp rating. A typical conflict was, say, for an appliance rated at 13 A. The 80 percent rule of Sec. 210-22 would require a branch circuit of 20 A for a 13-A load because 80 percent of a 15-A circuit would not permit a load over 12 A. But the maximum limit of 150 percent of 13 A would make a 20-A circuit too large. The 16.7-A and larger values eliminate the conflicts, yet preserve the appliance protection for all appliances of these ratings.

Fig. 422-5. Toggle switch in outlet box on this central vacuum cleaner serves as the disconnecting means within sight from the motor controller installed in the top of the unit. (Sec. 422-26.)

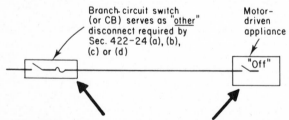

If appliance has internal unit switch with "off" position that disconnects all ungrounded conductors, then other disconnect may be "out of sight."

Fig. 422-6. Disconnect for motor-driven appliance may be "out of sight from the motor controller." (Sec. 422-26.)

Electric water heaters are typical nonmotor-operated appliances rated over 16.7 A, and, as noted in Sec. 422-14(b), all such units of 120-gal capacity or less must be taken as continuous loads.

The Exception to part **(a)** requires application of overload protection provisions of Sec. 430-32 and Sec. 430-33 to motors of motor-operated appliances. But motors that are not continuous-duty motors—and most appliances are intermittent, short-time, or varying duty types of motor loads—do not require running overload protection. The branch-circuit protective device may perform that function for such motors. See Sec. 430-33.

Part **(f)** of this section covers electric heating appliances using resistance-type heating elements. It requires that, where the elements are rated more than 48 A, the heating elements must be subdivided. Each subdivided load shall not exceed 48 A and shall be protected at not more than 60 A.

The rules of this section are generally similar to the rules contained in Sec. 424-22 for fixed electric space heating using duct heaters as part of heating, ventilating, and air-conditioning systems above suspended ceilings. But Exception No. 2 applies to commercial kitchen and cooking appliances using sheath-type heating elements. This Exception permits such heating elements to be subdivided into circuits not exceeding 120 A and protected at not more than 150 A under the conditions specified.

Exception No. 3 of this same section permits a similar subdivision into 120-A loads protected at not more than 150 A for elements of water heaters and steam boilers employing resistance-type immersion electric heating elements contained in an ASME rated and stamped vessel.

ARTICLE 424. FIXED ELECTRIC SPACE HEATING EQUIPMENT

424-3. Branch Circuits. The basic rule limits fixed electric space heating equipment to use on 15-, 20-, or 30-A circuits, **if the circuit has more than one outlet.** The Exception applies only to fixed infrared equipment on industrial and commercial premises, permitting use of 40-A and 50-A circuits for multioutlet circuits to *fixed* space heaters.

The 125 percent requirement in paragraph **(b)** means that branch circuits for electric space heating equipment cannot be loaded to more than 80 percent of the branch-circuit rating unless the branch-circuit overcurrent devices and their assemblies are approved for 100 percent load. Even though electric heating is thermostatically controlled and is a cycling load, it must be taken as a continuous load for sizing branch circuits.

Many line thermostats and contactors are approved for 100 percent load, and derating of such devices is not required.

Section 220-15 covers sizing of feeders for electric space heating loads. The computed load of a feeder supplying such equipment shall be the total connected load on all branch circuits, with an exception left up to the authority enforcing the Code which allows permission for feeder conductors to be of a capacity less than 100 percent, provided the conductors are of sufficient capacity for the load serving units operating on duty-cycle, intermittently, or from all units not operating at one time. The second exception to the rule states that Exception No. 1 does not apply if the optional method in Sec. 220-30 is the method used for calculating the load for a single-family dwelling or individual apartment of a multifamily dwelling.

424-9. General (Installation). For instance, heating cable designed for use in ceilings may not be used in concrete floors and vice versa.

This rule ties into that of Sec. 210-25(b).

In residences warmed by baseboard heaters, the question arises: How can wall receptacles be provided to satisfy the requirement of NE Code Sec. 210-25(b) that no point along the floor line be more than 6 ft from an outlet? Should the receptacles be installed in the wall above the heaters? The answer is that receptacles should not be placed above the heaters. Fires have been attributed to cords being draped across heaters. Continued exposure to heat causes the cord insulation to become brittle, leading to possible short circuits or ground faults.

Article 210 does not specifically prohibit installation of receptacles over baseboard heaters, and Art. 424 does not specifically prohibit installation of baseboard heaters under receptacles. However, Sec. 110-3(b) says:

Installation and Use. Listed or labeled equipment shall be used or installed in accordance with any instructions included in the listing or labeling.

Underwriters Laboratories now requires in Standard 1042, *Electric Baseboard Heating Equipment,* a warning that a heater is not to be located below an electrical convenience receptacle. A similar statement is included in the UL *Electrical Appliance and Utilization Equipment Directory* (orange book):

To reduce the likelihood of cords contacting the heater, the heater should not be located beneath electrical receptacles.

This instruction and the provisions of Sec. 110-3(b) make it very clear that installation of electric baseboard heaters under receptacles is a Code violation.

Receptacles can be provided in electrically heated (baseboard-type) dwelling-type occupancies as required by Sec. 210-25(b) by making use of the receptacle accessories made available by baseboard heater manufacturers. These units are designed to be mounted at the end of a baseboard section or between two sections. Refer to Sec. 210-25(b).

424-14. Grounding. Figure 424-1 shows the basic rule on grounding that applies to all electric space heating equipment.

424-19. Disconnecting Means. Extensive revision and expansion of the rules in this section have been made in the 1978 NEC. The basic rule

Fig. 424-1. The wiring method supplying any fixed electric space-heating equipment must provide a means for grounding all exposed metal parts of such equipment. That must be suitable metal raceway (rigid metal conduit, IMC, EMT) or metal cable armor (BX) or an equipment grounding conductor in NM cable or nonmetallic conduit. (Sec. 424-14.)

requires disconnecting means for the heater, motor controller(s), plus supplementary overcurrent protective devices for all fixed electric space heating equipment.

Part **(a)** of this section applies to heating equipment provided with supplementary overcurrent protection (such as fuses or CBs) to protect the subdivided resistance heaters used in duct heating, as required by Sec. 424-22. The basic rules are shown in Fig. 424-2. The disconnect in that sketch must comply with the following:

1. The disconnect must be within sight from the supplementary overcurrent panel.
2. The disconnect must also be within sight from the motor controller(s) and the heater, or may be locked in the open position.
3. The single disconnect may serve as disconnect for all equipment.

Part **(b)** applies to heating equipment *without* supplementary overcurrent protection.

Care must be taken to evaluate each of the specific requirements in this **Code** section to actual job details involved with electric heating installations.

Figure 424-3 shows two conditions that relate to the rules of part **(b)** of this section. For the two-family house, the service panel is located in a rear areaway and is accessible to both occupants. Circuit breakers in the panel constitute suitable means of disconnect for heaters in both apartments. If the house uses baseboard heaters without motors in them, the breakers would be acceptable as the disconnects in accordance with the rule of **(b) (1)**. And **(b) (3)** would also make them acceptable if the heaters had internal unit switches with an OFF position. For the four-family house

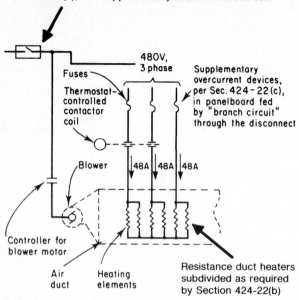

Required disconnect must disconnect heater, motor controller(s), and supplementary overcurrent devices.

480V, 3 phase

Fuses

Thermostat-controlled contactor coil

Supplementary overcurrent devices, per Sec. 424-22(c), in panelboard fed by "branch circuit" through the disconnect

Blower   48A 48A 48A

Controller for blower motor

Air duct   Heating elements

Resistance duct heaters subdivided as required by Section 424-22(b)

Fig. 424-2. Rules on disconnects for heating equipment demand careful study for HVAC systems with duct heaters and supplementary overcurrent protective devices. (Sec. 424-19.)

(a "multifamily dwelling"), the service panels accessible to all tenants are grouped in the hallway under the first-floor stairway in this four-family occupancy. Switches in the panels may constitute suitable means of disconnect for heaters in all apartments, under the rule of **(b) (1)**, as well as **(b) (3)**. But note that plug-fuses (without switches) on branch circuits to the heaters would not satisfy **(b) (1)**. In such cases, unit switches in the heaters may satisfy as disconnects under **(b) (3)**.

WATCH OUT! The rules of part **(b)** were revised in the 1978 NEC. Previous Code rules permitted "the branch-circuit overcurrent device"— which could be a plug-fuse instead of a CB—to serve as the disconnect for electric heaters up to 300 VA or ⅛ hp. Part **(b) (1)** refers only to "branch-circuit switch or circuit breaker." And it is not clear what "other means for disconnection" is meant in the rule of **(b) (3)**.

Note that **(b) (2)** requires a disconnect "within sight from" a motor controller serving a motor-operated space heater with a motor over ⅛ hp, with the limited Exception referred to part **(a) (2)**c.

424-20. Thermostatically Controlled Switching Devices. Figure 424-4 shows a hookup of duct heaters that are controlled by a magnetic

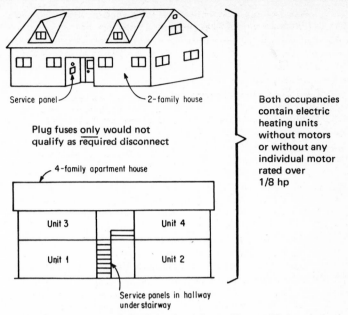

Fig. 424-3. For nonmotored electric heating units, readily accessible branch circuit switch or CB serves as disconnect. (Sec. 424-19.)

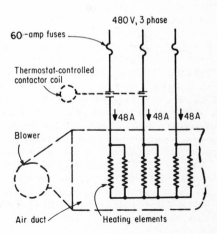

Fig. 424-4. This contactor may not serve as both controller and disconnect. (Sec. 424-20.)

contactor that responds to a thermostatic switch in its coil circuit. The subdivided heater load of 48 A per leg satisfies the rule of Sec. 424-22(b), *but* the contactor does not constitute a combination controller-and-disconnect-means because it does not open all the ungrounded conductors of the circuit. And because the heater contains the 60-A supplementary overcurrent protection, a disconnect ahead of the fuses would be required by Sec. 424-19(a) even if the contactor did open all three ungrounded conductors of the circuit.

424-22. Overcurrent Protection. Heating equipment employing resistance-type heating elements rated more than 48 A must have the heating elements subdivided, with each subdivided circuit loaded to not more than 48 A and protected at not more than 60 A. And each subdivided load must not exceed 80 percent of the rating of the protective device, to satisfy Sec. 424-3(b). Such a 60-A circuit could be classed as an individual branch circuit supplying a "single" outlet that actually consists of all the heater elements interconnected. By considering it as an "individual branch circuit" there is no conflict with Sec. 424-3(a) which sets a maximum rating of 30 A for a multioutlet circuit. The resistance-type heating elements on the market are not single heating elements in the 48-A size. They are made up of smaller wattage units into a single piece of equipment. The Code rule states that this single piece of equipment made up of smaller units must not draw more than 48 A and must be protected at not more than 60 A. Thus a heater of this type is limited to 48 A for each subdivided circuit. The subdivision is usually made by the manufacturer in the heater enclosure or housing.

Figure 424-5 shows an example of subdivision of heater elements in a heat pump with three 5-kW strip heaters in it. At 230 V, each 5-kW strip is a load of about 22 A. Two of them in parallel would be 44 A and that is not in excess of the 48-A maximum set by part **(b)** of this section. The three heaters would be a load of 66 A in parallel. There are a number of ways the total load might be supplied, but the Code rules limit the actual permitted types of hookup:

Section 424-3 states that an individual branch circuit may supply any load, but that permission is qualified by part **(b)** of this section, which requires resistance heating loads of more than 48 A to be subdivided so that no subdivided heater load will exceed 48 A, protected at not more than 60 A. As shown at A, one possible way to hook up the heaters is to use two strips on one circuit for a connected load of 2 × 22 or 44 A, and the other on one circuit with a connected load of 22 A. The two heaters would require a minimum ampacity for overcurrent protection of 44 × 1.25 or 55 A, calling for a 60-A overcurrent device. For the other circuit, 22 × 1.25 = 27.5 A, requiring a 30-A fuse or breaker. Both circuits would thus be within the limits of 48-A connected load and 60-A protection. As shown at B, it would also be acceptable to use a 30-A, 2-wire, 230-V circuit to each heater. But use of a single circuit sized at 1.25 × 66 A

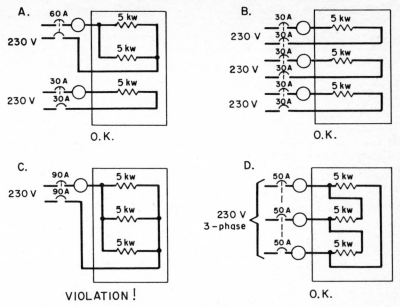

Fig. 424-5. Heater units must be limited to 48-A load with protection not over 60 A. (Sec. 424-22.)

(82.5 A) and protected by 90-A fuses or breaker would clearly violate the Code rule of 60-A maximum protection, as at C.

Another possibility which would give a better balance to the connected load would be to feed the load with a 3-phase, 3-wire, 230-V circuit, if available. For such a circuit, the loading would be:

$$\frac{15,000}{1.732 \times 230} \text{ or } 38A$$

The minimum rating would be 38 × 1.25 or 47.5 A, which calls for 50-A overcurrent protection, as at D.

It should be noted that the rule of part **(b)** in this section applies to *any type* of space heating equipment that utilizes resistance-type heating elements. The rule applies to duct heaters (as in Fig. 424-4), to the strip heaters in Fig. 424-5, and to heating elements in furnaces.

The purpose of paragraph **(c)** of this section is to require the heating manufacturer to furnish the necessary overcurrent protective devices where subdivided loads are required.

Main conductors supplying overcurrent protective devices for subdivided loads are considered as branch circuits to avoid controversies about applying the 125 percent requirement in Sec. 424-3(b) to branch circuits *only*. It is not the intent, however, to deny the use of the *feeder tap* rules in Sec. 240-21 for these *main* conductors.

Paragraph **(e)** requires that the conductors used for the subdivided electric resistance heat circuits specified in Sec. 424-22(c) must have an amp rating not less than '100 percent of the rating or setting of the overcurrent protective device protecting the subdivided circuit(s)" (Fig. 424-6). Exception is made for heaters rated 50 kW or more where under the conditions specified it is permissible for the conductors to have an ampacity not less than the load of the respective subdivided circuits, rather than 100 percent of the rating of the protective devices protecting the subdivided circuits.

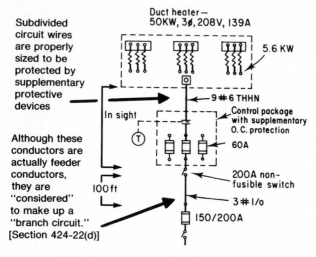

NOTE: There are exceptions for certain equipment.

Fig. 424-6. Conductors for subdivided heater circuits must fully match overcurrent device rating. (Sec. 424-22.)

424-35. Marking of Heating Cables and Panels. Note that there is a color-code for voltage identification of nonheating leads on heating cables to minimize the chance for use on a circuit of excessive voltage.

424-36. Clearances of Wiring in Ceilings. Figure 424-7 shows the details of this rule. The wire at a is OK because it is not less than 2 in. above the ceiling, but it must be treated as operating at a 50°C ambient. The same is true of the wire at c, because it is within the insulation. The Correction Factors table below Code Table 310-16 shows that TW wire (60°C-rated wire) must be derated to 58 percent (0.58) of its normal table ampacity when operating in an ambient of 41 to 50°C.

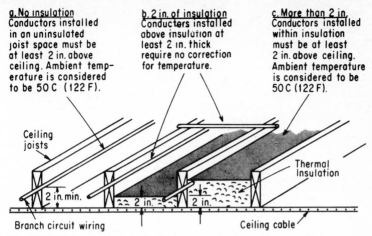

a. No insulation Conductors installed in an uninsulated joist space must be at least 2 in. above ceiling. Ambient temperature is considered to be 50 C (122 F).

b. 2 in. of insulation Conductors installed above insulation at least 2 in. thick require no correction for temperature.

c. More than 2 in. Conductors installed within insulation must be at least 2 in. above ceiling. Ambient temperature is considered to be 50 C (122 F).

Ceiling joists

Thermal Insulation

2 in. min.

2 in.

2 in.

Branch circuit wiring

Ceiling cable

Fig. 424-7. Wiring above a heated ceiling may require derating because of heat accumulation. (Sec. 424-36.)

424-37. Clearances of Branch-Circuit Wiring in Walls. When electric heating panels are mounted on interior walls of buildings, any wiring within the walls behind the heating panel is considered to be operating in an ambient of 40°C rather than the normal 30°C for which conductors are rated. Because of this, the ampacity of such conductors in wall space behind electric heating panels must be reduced in accordance with the correction factors given as part of Tables 310-16 through 310-19 [Sec. 424-37(b)] (Fig. 424-8).

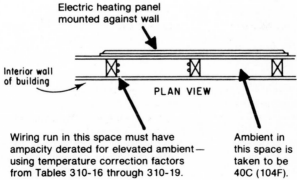

Electric heating panel mounted against wall

Interior wall of building

PLAN VIEW

Wiring run in this space must have ampacity derated for elevated ambient— using temperature correction factors from Tables 310-16 through 310-19.

Ambient in this space is taken to be 40C (104F).

Fig. 424-8. Wiring in walls behind heating panels must have ampacity corrected for more than 30°C. (Sec. 424-37.)

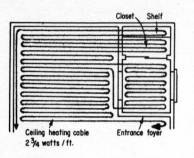

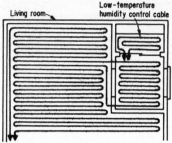

VIOLATION — cable extends beyond room and is installed in the closet. Cable in foyer is O. K.

O. K. — this cable is permitted in closet. Single cable runs that are embedded may cross partition.

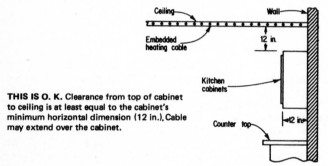

THIS IS O. K. Clearance from top of cabinet to ceiling is at least equal to the cabinet's minimum horizontal dimension (12 in.). Cable may extend over the cabinet.

Fig. 424-9. Layouts of heating cables must generally be confined to individual rooms or areas. (Sec. 424-38.)

424-38. Area Restrictions.   Figure 424-9 shows installations of heating cables and their relation to Code rules.

Heating cable shall not be installed under or over walls or partitions which extend to the ceiling except that "single runs of cable shall be permitted to pass over partitions where they are embedded." The intent here is to avoid repeated crossings of cable over (or under) partitions, since radiation from these sections would be restricted or the cable would be unnecessarily exposed to possible physical damage. While the Code specifically speaks of partitions, the same reasoning would apply to arches, exposed ceiling beams, etc.

However, there are times when a small ceiling area (such as over a dressing room or entryway) is separated from a larger room by such an arch or beam, yet it is impractical to install a separate heating cable and control. The Exception was intended as a solution to this problem. A typical floor plan of such a situation is shown in Fig. 424-10 with two

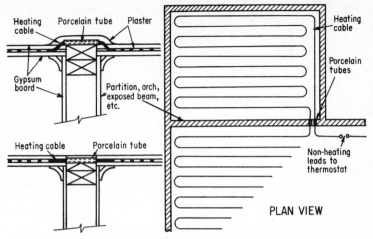

Fig. 424-10. Exception to rule permits single runs across partitions. (Sec. 424-38.)

methods of getting the heating cable past the partition or beam. In the upper sketch the cable is brought up into the attic space, through a porcelain tube, and back down through the gypsum board. Plaster is then forced into the tube and puddled over the exposed cable and tube in the attic. This should be the same plaster or joint cement that is used between the two layers of gypsum board.

In the lower sketch a hole is drilled through the top plate of the partition (or beam) and a porcelain tube pressed into the hole. Plaster is packed into the tube after the cable has been passed through. In both cases, the plaster serves to conduct heat away from the cable, avoiding hot spots and possible burnouts.

424-39. Clearance from Other Objects and Openings. Figure 424-11 shows application of the specified clearance distances for different conditions.

424-41. Installation of Heating Cables on Dry Board, in Plaster and on Concrete Ceilings. All heating cables must observe these application methods. Figure 424-12 shows the rules of paragraph **(b)** and paragraph **(f)**.

Figure 424-13 shows the rule of paragraph **(d)** and refers to the rule of Sec. 424-43(c) at the outlet box.

Heating cable installed in plaster or between two layers of gypsum board must be kept clear of ceiling fixtures and side walls. In drywall construction, cable must be embedded in mastic or plaster. Without it, dead air space between the cable runs acts as a heat reservoir, increasing the possibility of cable burnouts (Fig. 424-14). Cable movement caused by the expansion and contraction accompanying temperature changes is

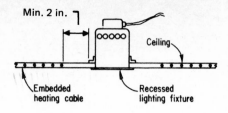

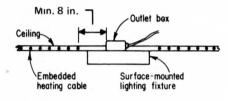

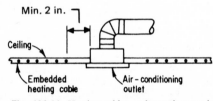

Fig. 424-11. Heating cables and panels must be kept clear of equipment. (Sec. 424-39.)

Fig. 424-12. Heating cable not over 2¾ W/ft must have at least 1½-in. spacing between adjacent conductors. (Sec. 424-41.)

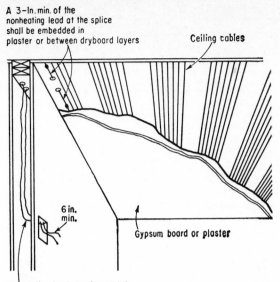

A 3-In.min. of the
nonheating lead at the splice
shall be embedded in
plaster or between dryboard layers

Ceiling cables

6 in.
min.

Gypsum board or plaster

Nonheating leads to thermostat.
Excess leads shall not be cut off,
but shall be embedded in ceiling finish.

Fig. 424-13. Ends of nonheating leads must be embedded in ceiling material. (Sec. 424-41.)

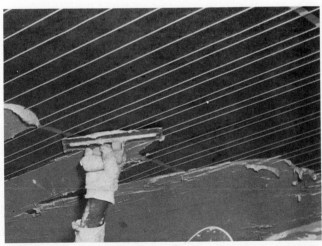

Fig. 424-14. In a drywall ceiling, the heating cable must be covered with a thermally conductive mastic before second course of gypsum board is applied to the ceiling, over the heating cable. (Sec. 424-41.)

also prevented. Laboratory tests on cable used without mastic have found properly spaced adjacent cable runs actually making contact with each other, producing a hot spot and subsequent burnout. The plaster and sand mixture normally used as a mastic is a good conductor of heat and thus accelerates the dissipation of heat from the entire circumference of the cable. In addition, it improves the conductance from the cable to the gypsum board where the cable does not make direct contact. Even in the most careful installations small irregularities in construction and material prevent perfect contact between the cable and both layers of gypsum board throughout the entire cable length. In no case should an insulating plaster be used. Thickness of the plaster coat should be just sufficient to cover the cable. Installations have been made, unfortunately, with plaster thickness as great as ¾ in. Nails are not capable of supporting the resulting excessive weight, and such ceilings have collapsed. Figure 424-15 shows various rules that apply to installation of heating cables in plaster or drywall ceilings. Figure 424-16 shows the rules of paragraph **(g)** and **(i)** of Sec. 424-41.

Where the cable is to be embedded between two layers of gypsum board ("drywall" construction), after the cable is stapled to the layer of gypsum lath, it is covered with noninsulating plaster or gypsum cement, and a finishing layer of gypsum board (Sheetrock) is nailed in place covering the cable and plaster. To make sure that nails driven to secure this gypsum board to the ceiling joists do not penetrate the cable, a clear space at least 2½ in. wide must be left between adjacent cable runs immediately beneath each joist. That is, while adjacent cable runs must in general be at least 1½ in. apart, the spacing beneath joists must be increased to at least 2½ in. This means, of course, that the cable must be run parallel to the joists, as in part **(i)**.

424-43. Installation of Nonheating Leads of Cables and Panels. Part **(c)** of this rule prohibits cutting off any of the length of nonheating leads that are provided by the manufacturers on the ends of heating cable. Any excess length of such leads must be secured to the ceiling and embedded in plaster or other approved material.

Part **(d)**, however, does permit excess nonheating leads of heating panels to be cut off (Fig. 424-17).

424-44. Installation of Panels or Cables in Concrete or Poured Masonry Floors. Details of these rules are shown in Fig. 424-18.

Paragraph **(c)** requires cables to be secured in place by nonmetallic frames or spreaders or other approved means. Metallic supports such as those commercially available for use in roadways or sidewalks are not to be used in floor space heating installations. Lumber is often used, although a more common method is to staple the cable directly to the base concrete after it has set about 4 hr. It was not the intention that this Code paragraph prohibit the use of metal staples. The object was to reduce the possibility of short circuits because of continuous metallic conducting materials spanning several adjacent cable runs.

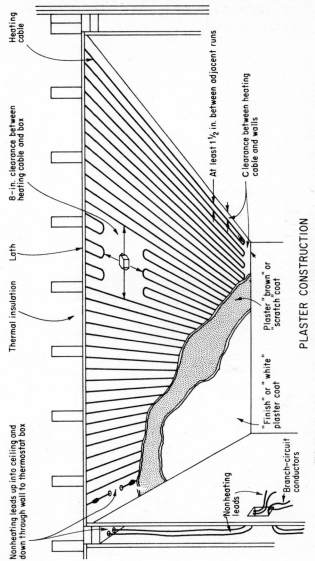

PLASTER CONSTRUCTION

Fig. 424-15. These details apply to plastered ceilings, but also to drywall ceilings. (Sec. 424-41.)

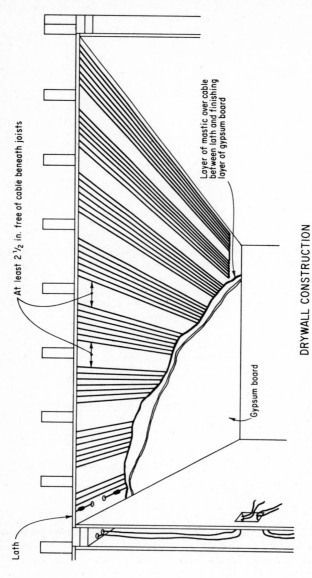

At least 2½ in. free of cable beneath joists

Layer of mastic over cable between lath and finishing layer of gypsum board

Gypsum board

Lath

DRYWALL CONSTRUCTION

Fig. 424-16. Additional rules apply only to drywall ceiling construction. (Sec. 424-41.)

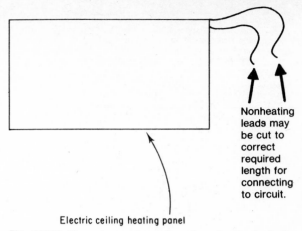

Fig. 424-17. The rule permits cutting of nonheating leads for "panels." (Sec. 424-43.)

Paragraph **(d)** requires spacing between the heating cable and other metallic bodies embedded in the floor. The intent is to reduce the possibility of contact between the cable and such conducting materials as reinforcing mesh, water pipes, and air ducts (Fig. 424-19).

Paragraph **(e)** requires leads to be protected where they leave the floor

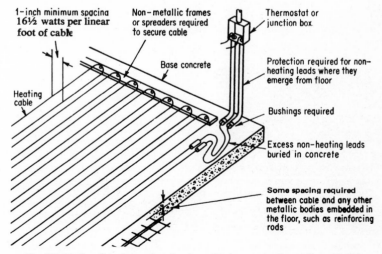

Fig. 424-18. Specific rules apply to heating cable in concrete floors. (Sec. 424-44.)

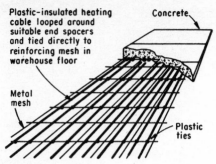

Plastic-insulated heating
cable looped around
suitable end spacers
and tied directly to
reinforcing mesh in
warehouse floor

Concrete

Metal
mesh

Plastic
ties

Fig. 424-19. This would be a violation of paragraph **(d).** (Sec. 424-44.)

and paragraph **(f)** adds that bushings shall be used where the leads
emerge in the floor slab. These provisions refer to the nonheating leads
which connect the branch circuit home-run to the heating cable. The
splices connecting the nonheating leads to the cable are always buried in
the concrete. About 6 in. of leads are left available in the junction box;
any remaining length of nonheating leads is buried in the concrete. The
conductors should not be shortened. This applies even though the
nonheating leads are Type UF cable. Section 339-3(b) (8) does prohibit
the use of UF embedded in poured cement, concrete, or aggregate;
however, an exception is noted there for nonheating leads of UF cable
because these heating cable assemblies are tested by UL and listed as
suitable for such use.

424-57. General (Duct Heaters).   The rules of part F of Art. 424 apply to
heater units that are mounted in air-duct systems, as shown in Fig. 424-
20.

Fig. 424-20. Electric heaters designed and installed to heat air flowing through the ducts of
forced-air systems are covered by Secs. 424-57 through 424-66. (Sec. 424-57.)

Fig. 424-21. Electric boilers with resistance-type heating elements are regulated by Secs. 424-70 through 424-75. (Sec. 424-70.)

424-70. Scope (Resistance-Type Boilers). In applying Code rules, care must be taken to distinguish between "resistance-type" boilers and "electrode-type" boilers (Fig. 424-21).

424-72. Overcurrent Protection. Heating elements of resistance-type electric boilers must be arranged into load groups not exceeding the values specified in paragraph **(a)** or **(b)**. Figure 424-22 shows a 360-kW electric boiler used to heat a large school.

Part **(e)** requires that the ampacity of conductors used for the subdivided heating circuits within such boilers must not be less than 100 percent of the rating or setting of the overcurrent protective devices protecting the circuit conductors from their point of application to the heating elements. Again, however, an exception is added for heaters rated 50 kW or more under certain given conditions.

ARTICLE 426. FIXED OUTDOOR ELECTRIC DE-ICING AND SNOW-MELTING EQUIPMENT

426-3. Branch-Circuit Requirements. This basic rule requires that, where more than one electric de-icing or snow-melting cable or panel (mat) is connected to a branch circuit, the rating of the branch circuit

Fig. 424-22. Electric boiler contains subdivided heating-element circuits, totalling 360 kW. Fuses protect the subdivided circuit loads. (Sec. 424-72.)

must be 15, 20, 25, 30, 40, or 50 A. However, the Exception notes that an individual branch circuit shall be permitted to supply *any* load to a *single* heating cable. That is, the rating of the branch circuit may be any value higher than 50 A—as required to adequately supply a single heating-cable assembly of any ampacity (Fig. 426-1). And because outdoor de-icing and snow-melting cables and mats must be taken as continuous loads, any circuit—whether a multioutlet circuit up to 50 A or a single-outlet circuit of any rating—must be sized at 125 percent of the load current. That is, both the circuit conductors and the overcurrent protection must be rated so the load is not over 80 percent of their amp rating.

426-10. Use. Whether used in concrete, blacktop, or other building material, this rule specifically requires that any de-icing or snow-melting cable, panel, mat, or other assembly must be properly recognized (as by UL) for installation in the particular material.

Application data from the UL's *Electrical Appliance and Utilization Equipment Directory* includes the following:

To supplement the general requirements given in the applicable Article of the National Electrical Code, the manufacturer is required to provide with the units or mats, specific installation instructions concerning any limitations of the installation and/or use of the equipment. The instructions for mats or cable units intended for burial in concrete will specifically indicate that the slab must be a double pour (poured in two parts) if that is the only acceptable means of installation. If such a limitation is not specifically mentioned, either a single or double pour may be used.

Cable units furnished with nonheating leads of single conductor UF cable, or preloomed Type TW wire, have been investigated to determine that the use of

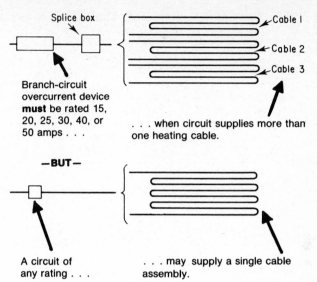

Fig. 426-1. A single heating cable may be fed by a circuit of any rating. (Sec. 426-3.)

additional flexible nonmetallic tubing is not required over the nonheating leads when the cable units are installed. The single conductor UF cable may be identified by the type designation printed at frequent intervals on the cable. Preloomed TW wire consists of Type TW wire with a fabric covering woven over the wire.

Cable units furnished with nonheating leads of Type TW wire or the equivalent shall have the nonheating leads routed through flexible nonmetallic tubing when the cable units are installed.

Radiant heating systems employing cable or other units in installations other than noted above are covered in "listings by report." The description of each system and recommended methods may be obtained upon application to the manufacturer.

426-11. Complete Units. Note that the Exception permits cutting non-heating leads provided the required marking on the leads (catalog numbers, volts, watts) is retained. That is not permitted for space heating cables, which may not be cut [Sec. 424-43(c)]. The marking on the nonheating leads of snow-melting cable must be within 3 in. of *each* end of the lead. The wording of the Exception appears to permit cutting the nonheating leads back to the marking closest to the connection to the heating cable—which would mean a length of 3 in. plus that needed for the marking is all that would be required. Or a length could be cut out between the two markings, provided that any splicing that would necessitate is made in boxes, as specified in Sec. 426-27.

426-12. Special Permission. This rule recognizes that there are frequently encountered situations where deviation from the rules may be required. But this is nothing more than the authority the inspection agency enjoys under Sec. 90-4.

426-24. Installation of Heating Cables, Units, or Panels.   The rules of Sec. 426-24 and Sec. 426-25 are shown in Fig. 426-2.

426-25. Installation of Nonheating Leads.   Applications of these rules are shown in Fig. 426-3.

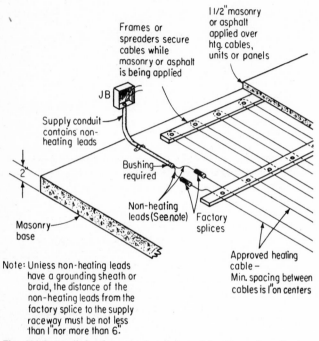

Frames or spreaders secure cables while masonry or asphalt is being applied

1 1/2" masonry or asphalt applied over htg. cables, units or panels

JB

Supply conduit contains non-heating leads

Bushing required

2"

Non-heating leads (See note)

Factory splices

Masonry base

Note: Unless non-heating leads have a grounding sheath or braid, the distance of the non-heating leads from the factory splice to the supply raceway must be not less than I" nor more than 6".

Approved heating cable – Min. spacing between cables is I" on centers

Fig. 426-2. Detailed rules cover installation of heating and nonheating conductors. (Sec. 426-24.)

ARTICLE 430. MOTORS, MOTOR CIRCUITS, AND CONTROLLERS

430-1. Motor Feeder and Branch Circuits.   Two articles in the National Electrical Code are directed specifically to motor applications:

1. Article 430 of the NE Code covers application and installation of motor circuits and motor control hookups—including conductors, short-circuit and ground-fault protection, starters, disconnects, and running overload protection.
2. Article 440, covering "Air-Conditioning and Refrigerating Equip-

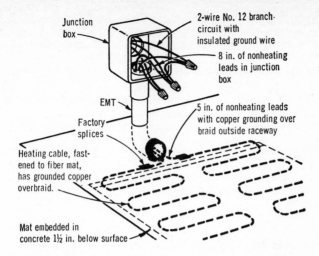

Junction box

2-wire No. 12 branch-circuit with insulated ground wire

8 in. of nonheating leads in junction box

EMT

Factory splices

5 in. of nonheating leads with copper grounding over braid outside raceway

Heating cable, fastened to fiber mat, has grounded copper overbraid.

Mat embedded in concrete 1½ in. below surface

COMPLIES WITH RULES — Nonheating leads with copper grounding braid may have any length embedded in concrete.

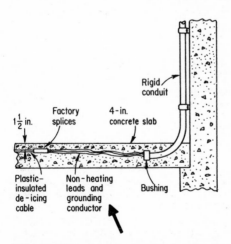

Rigid conduit

1½ in.

Factory splices

4-in. concrete slab

Plastic-insulated de-icing cable

Non-heating leads and grounding conductor

Bushing

VIOLATION — Excessive length of nonheating leads without a grounding sheath or braid.

Fig. 426-3. Installation of nonheating leads must observe all of the rules. (Sec. 426-25.)

ment," contains provisions for such motor-driven equipment and for branch circuits and controllers for the equipment, taking into account the special considerations involved with sealed (hermetic-type) motor compressors, in which the motor operates under the cooling effect of the refrigeration.

Diagram 430-1 in the NEC shows how various parts of Art. 430 cover the particular equipment categories that are involved in motor circuits. That Code diagram can be restructured, as shown in Fig. 430-1 in this handbook, to present the six basic elements which the Code requires the designer to account for in any motor circuit. Although these elements are shown separately here, there are certain cases where the Code will permit a single device to serve more than one function. For instance, in some cases, one switch can serve as both disconnecting means and controller.

In other cases, short-circuit protection and overload protection can be combined in a single CB or set of fuses.

430-2. Adjustable Speed Drive Systems.   The elements of this rule are shown in Fig. 430-2.

430-4. In Sight From.   This is an important rule that applies to the installed location of motors, their controllers, and their disconnect means, as set forth in Secs. 430-86 and 430-102. For instance, if a motor disconnect switch or CB is installed over 50 ft away from the motor starter in the same circuit, then the disconnect is *not* "in sight from" the contoller (Sec. 430-102) *even if a person standing at the controller has a clear, unobstructed view of the disconnect and can actually see it from the controller location.* "Out of sight" means "not within view" or "more than 50 ft away, even if within view."

430-6. Ampacity and Motor Rating Determination.   For general motor applications (excluding applications of torque motors and sealed hermetic-type refrigeration compressor motors), whenever the current rating of a motor is used to determine the current-carrying capacity of conductors, switches, fuses, or CBs, the values given in Tables 430-147, 430-148, 430-149, and 430-150 must be used instead of the actual motor nameplate current rating. However, selection of separate motor-running overload protection MUST be based on the actual motor nameplate current rating.

For torque motors, shaded-pole motors, permanent-split-capacitor motors, and AC adjustable voltage motors, the other rules apply.

430-7 Marking on Motors and Multimotor Equipment.   This section covers markings that manufacturers are required to put on the equipment. Code Table 430-7(b) can be used to calculate the locked-rotor current of a motor, where that value of current is related to selection of overload protection or short-circuit protection. A typical example would be selection of an instantaneous-trip CB as short-circuit protection of a motor branch circuit. The locked-rotor current of the motor represents the current value above which the breaker (and not the running overload device) must open the circuit. This is described in Sec. 430-52.

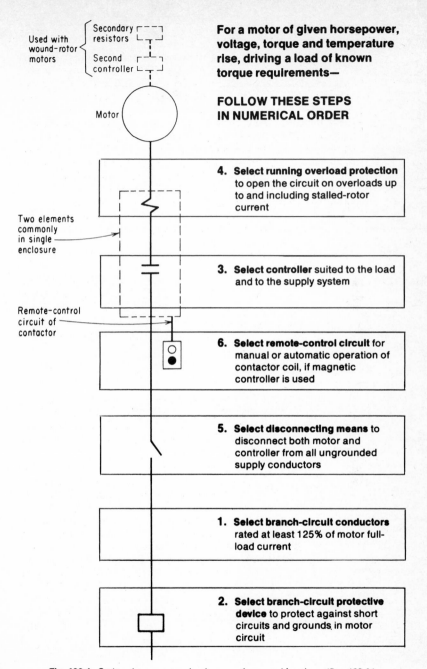

Used with wound-rotor motors
{ Secondary resistors
  Second controller }

Motor

For a motor of given horsepower, voltage, torque and temperature rise, driving a load of known torque requirements—

FOLLOW THESE STEPS IN NUMERICAL ORDER

Two elements commonly in single enclosure

Remote-control circuit of contactor

4. Select running overload protection to open the circuit on overloads up to and including stalled-rotor current

3. Select controller suited to the load and to the supply system

6. Select remote-control circuit for manual or automatic operation of contactor coil, if magnetic controller is used

5. Select disconnecting means to disconnect both motor and controller from all ungrounded supply conductors

1. Select branch-circuit conductors rated at least 125% of motor full-load current

2. Select branch-circuit protective device to protect against short circuits and grounds in motor circuit

Fig. 430-1. Code rules on motor circuits cover these considerations. (Sec. 430-1.)

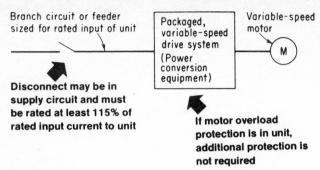

Fig. 430-2. Circuit to packaged drive systems is sized for rating of unit. (Sec. 430-2.)

430-10. Wiring Space in Enclosures. The standard types of enclosures for motor controllers provide space that is sufficient only for the branch-circuit conductors entering and leaving the enclosure and any control-circuit conductors that may be required. No additional conductors should be brought into the enclosure. For space in enclosures see Sec. 373-8. Section 430-12 provides a comprehensive set of rules and tables for motor terminal housings to solve the complaint by installers that motor terminal housings are too small to make satisfactory connections.

430-11. Protection Against Liquids. Excessive moisture, steam, dripping oil, etc., on the exposed current-carrying parts of a motor may cause an insulation breakdown which in turn may be the cause of a fire.

430-13. Bushing. Refer also to Sec. 373-6(c).

430-16. Exposure to Dust Accumulations. The conditions described in this section could make the location a Class II, Division 2 location; the types of motors required are specified in Art. 502.

430-17. Highest Rated (Largest) Motor. Note that the current rating, not the horsepower rating, determines the "highest rated" motor where Code rules refer to such. See Sec. 430-62.

430-22. Single Motor. The basic rule says that the conductors supplying a single-speed motor used for continuous duty must have a current-carrying capacity of not less than 125 percent of the motor full-load current rating, so that under full-load conditions the motor must not load the conductors to more than 80 percent of their ampacity. For a multi-speed motor, selection of branch-circuit conductors on the supply side of the controller must be based on the highest full-load current rating shown on the motor nameplate.

Figure 430-3 shows the sizing of branch-circuit conductors to four different motors fed from a panel. (Sizing is also shown for branch-circuit protection and running overload protection, as discussed in Secs. 430-34 and 430-52. Refer to Table 430-150 for motor full-load currents and Table 430-152 for maximum ratings of fuses.) Figure 430-3 is based on the following:

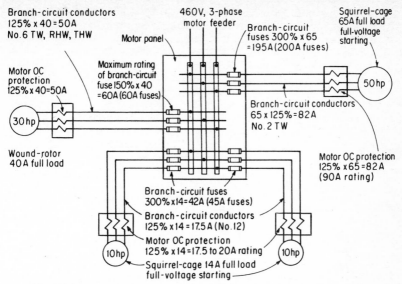

Fig. 430-3. Circuit conductors are sized at 1.25 times motor current. (Sec. 430-22.)

1. Full-load current for each motor is taken from Table 430-150.
2. Running overload protection is sized on the basis that nameplate values of motor full-load currents are the same as values from Table 430-150. If nameplate and table values are not the same, OL (overload) protection is sized according to nameplate.
3. Conductor sizes shown are for copper. Use the amp values given and Table 310-16 to select correct size of aluminum conductors.

It is important to note that this rule establishes minimum conductor ratings based on temperature rise only and does not take into account voltage drop or power loss in the conductors. Such considerations frequently require increasing the size of branch-circuit conductors.

The Exception in part **(a)** includes requirements for sizing individual branch-circuit wires serving motors used for short-time, intermittent, periodic, or other varying duty. In such cases, frequency of starting and duration of operating cycles impose varying heat loads on conductors. Figure 430-4 shows an example. Conductor sizing, therefore, varies with

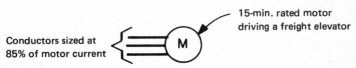

Fig. 430-4. Noncontinuous motor circuits may have lower-rated conductors. (Sec. 430-22.)

the application. But, it should be noted that the last sentence of Sec. 430-33 says any motor is considered to be for continuous duty unless the nature of the apparatus that it drives is such that the motor cannot operate continuously with load under any condition of use.

When a motor is used for one of the classes of service listed in Table 430-22(a), Exception, the necessary ampacity of the branch-circuit conductors depends upon the class of service and upon the rating of the motor. A motor having a 5-min rating is designed to deliver its rated horsepower during periods of approximately 5 min each, with cooling intervals between the operating periods. The branch-circuit conductors have the advantage of the same cooling intervals and hence can safely be smaller than for a motor of the same horsepower but having a 60-min rating.

In the case of elevator motors, the many considerations involved in determining the smallest permissible size of the branch-circuit conductors make this a complex problem, and it is always the safest plan to be guided by the recommendations of the manufacturer of the equipment. This applies also to feeders supplying two or more elevator motors and to circuits supplying noncontinuous-duty motors used for driving some other machines.

430-23. Wound-rotor Secondary.   The full-load secondary current of a wound-rotor or slip-ring motor must be obtained from the motor nameplate or from the manufacturer. The starting, or starting and speed-regulating, portion of the controller for a wound-rotor motor usually consists of two parts—a dial-type or drum controller and a resistor bank. These two parts must, in many cases, be assembled and connected by the installer, as in Fig. 430-5.

The conductors from the slip rings on the motor to the controller are

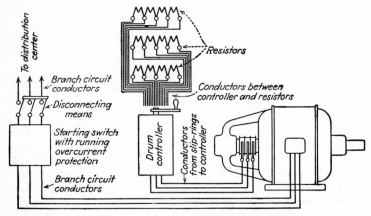

Fig. 430-5. Wound-rotor motor may be used with rotary drum switch for speed control. (Sec. 430-23.)

in circuit continuously while the motor is running and hence, for a continuous-duty motor, must be large enough to carry the secondary current of the motor continuously.

If the controller is used for starting only and is not used for regulating the speed of the motor, the conductors between the dial or drum and the resistors are in use only during the starting period and are cut out of the circuit as soon as the motor has come up to full speed. These conductors may therefore be of a smaller size than would be needed for continuous duty.

If the controller is to be used for speed regulation of the motor, some part of the resistance may be left in circuit continuously and the conductors between the dial or drum and the resistors must be large enough to carry the continuous load without overheating. In Table 430-23(c) the term *continuous duty* applies to this condition.

Conductors connecting the secondary of a wound-rotor induction motor to the controller must have a carrying capacity at least equal to 125 percent of the motor's full-load secondary current if the motor is used for continuous duty. If the motor is used for less than continuous duty, the conductors must have capacity not less than the percentage of full-load secondary nameplate current given in Table 430-22(a) Exception. Conductors from the controller of a wound-rotor induction motor to its starting resistors must have an ampacity in accordance with Table 430-23(c), as shown in Fig. 430-6 for a magnetic starter used for reduced inrush on starting but not for speed control.

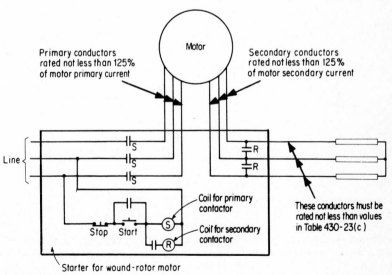

Fig. 430-6. Rules cover conductor sizing for wound-rotor motors without speed control. (Sec. 430-23.)

430-24. Conductors Supplying Several Motors.   Conductors supplying two or more motors (such as feeder conductors to a motor control center, to a panel supplying a number of motors, or to a gutter with several branch circuits tapped off) must have a current rating not less than 125 percent of the full-load current rating of the largest motor supplied plus the sum of the full-load current ratings of the other motors supplied.

Figure 430-7 shows an example of sizing feeder conductors for a load of four motors, selecting the conductors on the basis of ampacities given in Table 310-16 and using conductors with a 60°C or 75°C insulating rating—or using 90°C-rated conductors at the ampacities of 75°C. UL rules generally prohibit use of 90°C conductors at the 90°C ampacities shown in **Code** Table 310-16. (Refer to Sec. 310-15.)

For the overcurrent protection of feeder conductors of the minimum size permitted by this section, the highest permissible rating or setting of the protective device is specified in Sec. 430-62. Where a feeder protective device of higher rating or setting is used because two or more motors must be started simultaneously, the size of the feeder conductors shall be increased correspondingly.

These requirements and those of Sec. 430-62 for the overcurrent protection of power feeders are based upon the principle that a power feeder should be of such size that it will have an ampacity equal to that required for the starting current of the largest motor supplied by the feeder, plus the full-load running currents of all other motors supplied by the feeder. Except under the unusual condition where two or more motors may be started simultaneously, the heaviest load that a power feeder will ever be required to carry is the load under the condition where the largest motor is started at a time when all the other motors supplied by the feeder are running and delivering their full-rated horsepower.

430-25. Conductors Supplying Motors and Other Loads.
1. The current-carrying capacity of feeder conductors supplying a single motor plus other loads must include capacity at least equal to 125 percent of the full-load current of the motor.
2. The current-carrying capacity of feeder conductors supplying a motor load and a lighting and/or appliance load must be sufficient to handle the lighting and/or appliance load as determined from the procedure for calculating size of lighting feeders, plus the motor load as determined from the previous paragraphs.

The **Code** permits inspectors to authorize use of demand factors for motor feeders—based on reduced heating of conductors supplying motors operating intermittently or on duty-cycle or motors not operating together. Where necessary this should be checked to make sure that the authority enforcing the **Code** deems the conditions and operating characteristics suitable for reduced-capacity feeders, as noted in Sec. 430-26.

For computing the minimum allowable conductor size for a combination lighting and power feeder, the required ampacity for the lighting

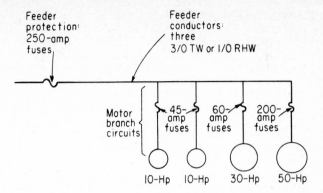

The four motors supplied by the 3-phase, 440-volt, 60-cycle feeder, which are not marked with a code letter (see Table 430-152), are as follows:

    1 50-hp squirrel-cage induction motor (full-voltage starting)

    1 30-hp wound-rotor induction motor

    2 10-hp squirrel-cage induction motors (full-voltage starting).

Step 1. Branch-circuit loads

From Table 430-150, the motors have full-load current ratings as follows:

    50-hp motor—65 amps
    30-hp motor—40 amps
    10-hp motor—14 amps

Step 2. Conductors

The feeder conductors must have a carrying capacity as follows (see Section 430-24):

$$1.25 \times 65 = 81 \, amps$$
$$81 + 40 + (2 \times 14) = 149 \, amps$$

The feeder conductors must be at least No. 3/0 TW, 1/0 THW or 1/0 RHH or THHN (copper).

Fig. 430-7. Feeder conductors are sized for the total motor load. (Sec. 430-24.)

load is to be determined according to the rules for feeders carrying lighting (or lighting and appliance) loads only. Where the motor load consists of one motor only, the required ampacity for this load is the capacity for the motor branch circuit, or 125 percent of the full-load motor current, as specified in Sec. 430-22. Where the motor load consists of two or more motors, the required ampacity for the motor load is the capacity computed according to Sec. 430-24.

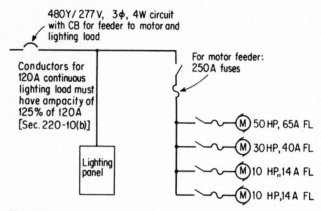

Fig. 430-8. Other load must be properly combined with motor load. (Sec. 430-25.)

Figure 430-8 shows a typical installation for which calculation of required feeder ampacity is as follows:

Step 1. Total load

Section 430-25(a) says that conductors supplying a lighting load and a motor load must have capacity for both loads, as follows:

$$\text{Motor load} = 65\text{ A} + 40\text{ A} + 14\text{ A} + 14\text{ A}$$
$$+ (0.25 \times 65\text{ A}) = 149\text{ A per phase}$$
$$\text{Lighting load} = 120\text{ A per phase} \times 1.25 = 150\text{ A}$$
$$\text{Total load} = 149 + 150 = 299\text{ A per phase leg}$$

Step 2. Conductors

Table 310-16 shows that a load of 299 A can be served by the following copper conductors:
500 MCM TW
350 MCM THW, RHH, XHHW, or THHN

Table 310-16 shows that this same load can be served by the following aluminum or copper-clad aluminum conductors:

700 MCM TW

500 MCM THW, RHH, XHHW, or THHN

430-26. Feeder Demand Factor.   A demand factor of less than 100 percent may be applied in the case of some industrial plants where the nature of the work is such that there is never a time when all the motors are operating at one time. But the inspector must be satisfied with any application of a demand factor.

Sizing of motor feeders (and mains supplying combination power and lighting loads) may be done on the basis of maximum demand current, calculated as follows:

$$\text{Running current} = (1.25 \times I_f) + (DF \times I_t)$$

where I_f = full-load current of largest motor

DF = demand factor as permitted by Sec. 430-26

I_t = sum of full-load currents of all motors except largest

But modern design dictates use of the maximum-demand starting current in sizing conductors for improved voltage stability on the feeder. This current is calculated as follows:

$$\text{Starting current} = I_s + (DF \times I_t)$$

where I_s = Average starting current of largest motor (Use the percent of motor full-load current given for fuses in Table 430-152.)

430-28. Feeder Taps.   This Code rule is an adaptation of Exceptions No. 2 and No. 3 of Sec. 240-21, covering use of 10- and 25-ft feeder taps with no overcurrent protection at the point where the smaller conductors connect to the higher-ampacity feeder conductors. The adaptation establishes that the tap conductors must have an ampacity as required by Secs. 430-22, 430-24, or 430-25.

In applying condition (1), the conductor may have an ampacity less than one-third that of the feeder conductors but must be limited to not more than 10 ft in length and be enclosed within a controller or raceway.

If conductors equal in size to the conductors of a feeder are connected to the feeder, as in condition (3), no fuses or other overcurrent protection are needed at the point where the tap is made, since the tap conductors will be protected by the fuses or CB protecting the feeder.

The more important circuit arrangement permitted by the above rule is shown in Fig. 430-9. Instead of placing the fuses or other branch-circuit protective device at the point where the connections are made to the feeder, conductors having at least one-third the ampacity of the feeder are tapped solidly to the feeder and may be run a distance not exceeding 25 ft to the branch-circuit protective device. From this point on to the motor-running protective device and thence to the motor, conductors are run having the standard ampacity, i.e., 125 percent of the full-load motor current, as specified in Sec. 430-22. If the tap conductors

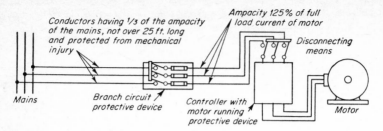

Note: Branch-circuit fuses (or CB) may be rated higher than ampacity of the tap conductors.

Fig. 430-9. Feeder tap may be sized as provided by Exception No. 3 of Sec. 240-21. (Sec. 430-28.)

shown did not have an ampacity at least equal to one-third of that of the feeder conductors, then the tap conductors must not be over 10 ft long.

Note that this rule actually modifies the requirements of Sec. 240-21 for taps to motor loads. Section 240-21 Exception No. 2b literally calls for 10-ft tap conductors to have ampacity at least equal to the rating or setting of the fuses or CB (whichever is used) at the load end of the tap. And such protection may be rated up to four times motor full-load current. But condition (1) of this **Code** section does not require such sizing of the tap conductors and simply requires that 10-ft tap conductors be the same size as the branch-circuit wires. And condition (2) does *not* require a 25-ft tap to terminate in a protective device rated to protect the conductors at their ampacity (Fig. 430-10).

example: A 15-hp 230-V 3-phase motor with autotransformer starter is to be supplied by a tap made to a 250 MCM feeder. All conductors are to be Type THW.

The feeder has an ampacity of 255 A; one-third of 255 A equals 85 A. Therefore the tap cannot be smaller than No. 4, which has an ampacity of 85 A for 75°C ratings.

The full-load current of the motor is 40 A and, according to part **D** of Art. 430, assuming that the motor is not marked with a **Code** letter, the branch-circuit fuses should be rated at not more than 300 percent of 40 A, or 120 A, which calls for 125-A fuses (Sec. 430-52) or less. With the motor-running protection set at 50 A (125 percent × 40 A), the tap conductors are well protected from overload.

The conductors tapped solidly to the feeder must never be smaller than the size of branch-circuit conductors required by Sec. 430-22.

430-31. General. Detailed requirements for the installation of fire pumps is not included in the **National Electrical Code**, but this is covered in NFPA Pamphlet No. 20.

As intended by Sec. 430-52, the motor branch-circuit protective device provides short-circuit protection for the circuit conductors. In order to carry the starting current of the motor, this device must commonly have a rating or setting so high that it cannot protect the motor against overload.

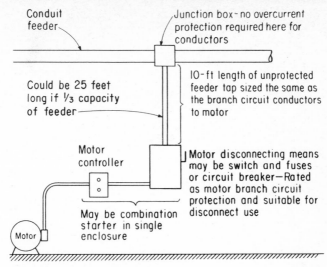

Conduit feeder

Junction box - no overcurrent protection required here for conductors

Could be 25 feet long if ⅓ capacity of feeder

10-ft length of unprotected feeder tap sized the same as the branch circuit conductors to motor

Motor controller

Motor disconnecting means may be switch and fuses or circuit breaker—Rated as motor branch circuit protection and suitable for disconnect use

May be combination starter in single enclosure

Motor

Fig. 430-10. Tap conductors may terminate in protective device rated above their ampacity. (Sec. 430-28.)

For a squirrel-cage induction motor, overload protection must be of the inverse time type with a setting of not over 20 sec at 600 percent of the motor full-load current. It is the intent that the fire-pump motor be permitted to run under any condition of loading and not be automatically disconnected by an overcurrent protection device.

Pamphlet No. 20 requires a CB instead of a fuse as the short-circuit protection for the branch circuit and also requires an unfused isolating switch ahead of the CB.

Except where time-delay fuses provide both running overload protection and short-circuit protection as described in Sec. 430-55, in practically all cases where motor-running overload protection is provided the motor controller consists of two parts: (1) a switch or contactor to control the circuit to the motor and (2) the motor-running protective device. Most of the protective devices make use of a heater coil, usually consisting of a few turns of high-resistance metal, though the heater may be of other form.

430-32. Continuous-Duty Motors. The Code makes specific requirements on motor running overload protection intended to protect the elements of the branch circuit—the motor itself, the motor control apparatus, and the branch-circuit conductors—against excessive heating due to motor overloads. Overload protection may be provided by fuses, CBs, or specific overload devices like OL relays.

Overload is considered to be operating overload up to and including stalled-rotor current. When overload persists for a sufficient length of time, it will cause damage or dangerous overheating of the apparatus. Overload does not include fault current due to shorts or grounds.

Typical overload devices include:

1. Heaters in series with line conductors acting upon thermal bimetallic overload relays.
2. Overload devices using resistance or induction heaters and operating on the solder-ratchet principle (Fig. 430-11).
3. Magnetic relays with adjustable instantaneous setting or adjustable time-delay setting.

Of course, the provisions for overload protection are integrated in the enclosure of the controller.

Overload protective devices of the straight thermal type are available with varying tripping and time-delay characteristics. In such devices, the heater coils are made in many sizes and are interchangeable to permit use of the required heater sizes to provide running protection for different motor full-load current ratings. In some units, the heater coil can be adjusted to exact current values. Individual covers are used on the heating elements in some starters to isolate the relay from possible effect on its operation because of the temperature of surrounding air.

In general, it is required that every motor shall be provided with a running protective device that will open the circuit on any current exceeding prescribed percentages of the full-load motor current, the percentage depending upon the type of motor. The running protective device is intended primarily to protect the windings of the motor; but by providing that the circuit conductors shall have an ampacity not less than 125 percent of the full-load motor current, it is obvious that these conductors are reasonably protected by the running protective device against any overcurrent caused by an overload on the motor.

Part **(a)** covers application for motors of more than 1 hp. If such a motor is used for continuous duty, running overload protection must be provided. This may be an external overcurrent device actuated by the motor running current and set to open at not more than 125 percent of the motor full-load current for motors marked with a service factor of not less than 1.15 and for motors with a temperature rise not over 40°C. See examples in Fig. 430-3. Sealed (hermetic-type) refrigeration compressor motors must be protected against overload and failure to start, as specified in Sec. 440-52. The overload device must be rated or set to trip at not more than 115 percent of the motor full-load current for all other motors, such as motors with a 1.0 service factor or a 55°C rise (Fig 430-12).

The term *rating or setting* as here used means the current at which the device will open the circuit if this current continues for a considerable length of time.

Note: Refer to Sec. 460-9, which discusses the need to correct the sizing of running overload protection when power-factor capacitors are installed on the load side of the controller.

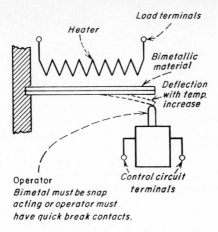

BIMETALLIC TYPE

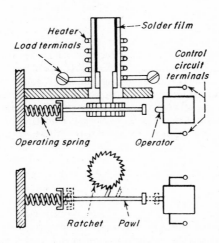

SOLDER-RATCHET TYPE

NOTE: For a manual starter, the contacts shown are the main load-current contacts of the switch—connected in series with the heater coil.

Fig. 430-11. Overload relay devices are made in various operating types. (Sec. 430-32.)

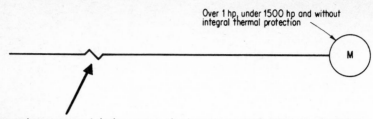

Separate overcurrent device, responsive to motor current, rated or selected to trip at no more than the following percentage of the motor full-load current rating:

Motors with marked service factor not less than 1.15.....................................125%
Motors with marked temperature rise not over 40C..125%
Sealed (hermetic type) motor compressors
  Using overload relays 140%
  Using other devices 125%
All other motors 115%

Each winding of a multispeed motor must be considered separately. This value may be modified as permitted by Section 430-34.

Fig. 430-12. Specific rules apply to continuous-duty motors rated over 1 hp. (Sec. 430-32.)

A motor having a temperature rise of 40°C when operated continuously at full load can carry a 25 percent overload for some time without injury to the motor. Other types of motors, such as enclosed types, do not have so high an overload capacity and the running protective device should therefore open the circuit on a prolonged overload which causes the motor to draw 115 percent of its rated full-load current.

Basic Code requirements are concerned with the rating or setting of overcurrent devices separate from motors. However, the Code permits the use of integral protection. Paragraph (2) of part (a) covers use of running overload protective devices within the motor assembly rather than in the motor starter. A protective device integral with the motor as used for the protection of motors is shown in Fig. 430-13. This device is placed inside the motor frame and is connected in series with the motor winding. It contains a bimetallic disk carrying two contacts, through which the circuit is normally closed. If the motor is overloaded and its temperature is raised to a certain limiting value, the disk snaps to the "open" position and opens the circuit. The device also includes a heating coil in series with the motor windings which causes the disk to become heated more rapidly in case of a sudden heavy overload.

Where the circuit-interrupting device is separate from the motor and is actuated by a device integral with the motor, the two devices must be so designed and connected that any accidental opening of the control circuit will stop the motor, otherwise the motor would be left operating without any overcurrent protection.

There is special need for running protection on an automatically

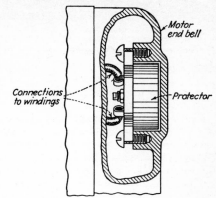

Fig. 430-13. Running overload protection may be built into the motor. (Sec. 430-32.)

started motor because, if the motor is stalled when the starter operates, the motor will probably burn out if it has no running protection.

Part **(b)** of this section applies to smaller motors. Motors of 1 hp or less which are not permanently installed and are manually started are considered protected against overload by the branch-circuit protection if the motor is within sight from the starter (Fig. 430-14). Running overload

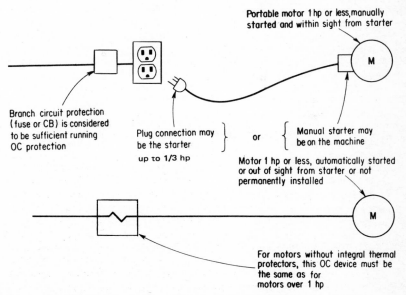

Fig. 430-14. The rules for automatic-start motors are different. (Sec. 430-32.)

devices are not required in such cases. A distance of over 50 ft is considered out of sight.

It should be noted that any motor of 1 hp or less which is not portable, is not manually started, and/or is not within sight from its starter location must have specific running overload protection. Automatically started motors of 1 hp or less must be protected against running overload in the same way as motors rated over 1 hp—as noted in part (c). That is, a separate or integral overload device must be used.

There are alternatives to the specific overload protection rules of parts (a) and (c). Under certain conditions, no specific running overload protection need be used: The motor is considered to be properly protected if it is part of an approved assembly which does not normally subject the motor to overloads and which has controls to protect against stalled rotor. Or if the impedance of the motor windings is sufficient to prevent overheating due to failure to start, the branch-circuit protection is considered adequate.

430-33. Intermittent and Similar Duty. A motor used for a condition of service which is inherently short-time, intermittent, periodic, or varying duty does not require protection by overload relays, fuses, or other devices required by Sec. 430-32, but, instead, is considered as protected against overcurrent by the branch-circuit overcurrent device (CB or fuses rated in accordance with Sec. 430-52). Motors are considered to be for continuous duty unless the motor is completely incapable of operating continuously with load under any condition of use.

430-34. Selection of Overload Relay. This rule sets the absolute maximum permitted rating of an overload relay where values are higher than the 125 or 115 percent trip ratings of Secs. 430-32(a) (1) and (c). Motors with a marked service factor not less than 1.15 and 40°C-rise motors may, if necessary to enable the motor to start or carry its load, be protected by overload relays with trip settings up to 140 percent of motor full-load current. Motors with a 1.0 service factor and motors with a temperature rise over 40°C (such as 55°C-rise motors) must have their relay trip setting at not over 130 percent of motor full-load current.

BUT WATCH OUT! The maximum settings of 140 percent or 130 percent apply only to OL relays, such as used in motor starters.

Fuses or CBs may be used for running overload protection but may not be rated or set up to the 140 or 130 percent values. Fuses and breakers must have a maximum rating as shown in Secs. 430-32(a) and (c). If the value determined as indicated there does not correspond to a standard rating of fuse or CB, the next smaller size must be used. A rating of 125 percent of full-load current is the absolute maximum for fuses or breakers.

430-35. Shunting During Starting Period. Where fuses are used as the motor-running protection, they may be cut out of the circuit during the starting period. This leaves the motor protected only by the branch-circuit fuses, but the rating of these fuses will always be well within the 400 percent limit specified in the rule. If the branch-circuit fuses are omitted, as allowed by the rule in Sec. 430-53(d), it is not permitted to use a starter that cuts out the motor fuses during the starting period unless the protection of the feeder is within the limits set by this rule. As shown in Fig. 430-15, a double-throw switch is arranged for across-the-line starting. The switch is thrown to the right to start the motor, thus cutting the running fuses out of the circuit. The switch must be so made that it cannot be left in the starting position.

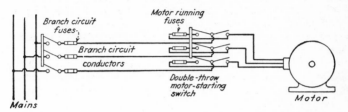

Fig. 430-15. Motor OL fuses may be shunted out for starting. (Sec. 430-35.)

430-36. Fuses—In Which Conductor.   This rule is listed in Sec. 240-22 as Exception No. 2 to the rule that prohibits use of an overcurrent device in an intentionally grounded conductor. When fuses are used for protection of service, feeder, or branch-circuit conductors, a fuse must never be used in a grounded conductor, such as the grounded leg of a 3-phase, 3-wire corner-grounded delta system. But, if fuses are used for OL protection for a 3-phase motor connected on such a system, a fuse must be used in all three phase legs—EVEN THE GROUNDED LEG. Figure 430-16 shows two conditions of such fuse application for OL protection for a motor.

430-37. Devices Other Than Fuses—In Which Conductor.   Complete data on the number and location of overcurrent devices are given in Code Table 430-37.

Table 430-37 requires three running overload devices (trip coils, relays, and thermal cutouts, etc.) for all 3-phase motors unless protected by other approved means, such as specifically designed embedded detectors with or without supplementary external protective devices.

Figure 430-17 points up this requirement.

If fuses are used as the running protective device, Sec. 430-36 requires a fuse in each ungrounded conductor. If the protective device consists of an automatically operated contactor or CB, the device must open a sufficient number of conductors to stop the current flow to the motor and must be equipped with the number of overcurrent units specified in Table 430-37.

430-42. Motors on General-Purpose Branch Circuits.   Refer to Fig. 430-19, Type 3.

Branch circuits supplying lamps are usually 115-V single-phase circuits, and on such circuits the effect of subparagraphs **(a)** and **(b)** is that

FUSES FOR OL PROTECTION ONLY

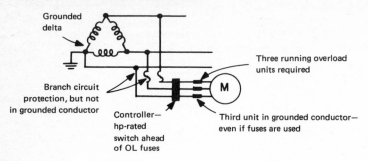

FUSES FOR BRANCH-CIRCUIT AND OL PROTECTION

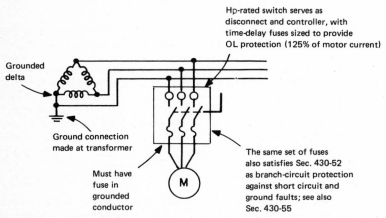

Fig. 430-16. A fuse for OL protection *must* be used in each phase leg of circuit. (Sec. 430-36.)

any motor larger than 6 A must be provided with a starter that is approved for group operation.

It is provided in Sec. 210-24 that receptacles on a 20-A branch circuit may have a rating of 20 A, and in such case subparagraph **(c)** requires that any motor or motor-driven appliance connected through a plug and receptacle must have running overcurrent protection. If the motor rating exceeds 1 hp or 6 A, the protective device must be permanently attached to the motor and subparagraph **(b)** must be complied with.

The requirements of Sec. 430-32 for the running overcurrent protec-

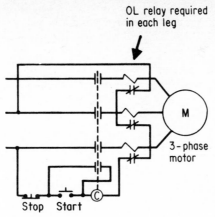

OL relay required
in each leg

Stop   Start

Fig. 430-17. Three OL units are required for 3-phase motors. (Sec. 430-37.)

tion of motors must be complied with in all cases, regardless of the type of branch circuit by which the motor is supplied and regardless of the number of motors connected to the circuit.

430-43. Automatic Restarting.   As noted in the comments to Sec. 430-32, an integral motor-running protective device may be of the type which will automatically restart, or it may be so constructed that after tripping out it must be closed by means of a reset button.

430-44. Orderly Shutdown.   Although the NE Code has all those requirements on use of running overload protection of motors, this section recognizes that there are cases when automatic opening of a motor circuit due to overload may be objectionable from a safety standpoint. In recognition of the needs of many industrial applications the rule here permits alternatives to automatic opening of a circuit in the event of overload. This permission for elimination of overload protection is similar to the permission given in Sec. 240-12 to eliminate overload protection when automatic opening of the circuit on an overload would constitute a more serious hazard than the overload itself. However, it is necessary that the circuit be provided with a motor overload sensing device conforming to the Code requirement on overload protection to indicate by means of a supervised alarm the presence of the overload (Fig. 430-18). Overload indication instead of automatic opening will alert personnel to the objectionable condition and will permit corrective action, either immediately or at some more convenient time, for an orderly shutdown to resolve the difficulty. But, as is required in Sec. 240-12, short-circuit protection on the motor branch circuit must be provided to take care of those high-level ground faults and short circuits that

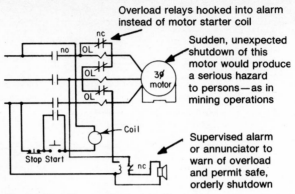

Overload relays hooked into alarm
instead of motor starter coil

Sudden, unexpected
shutdown of this
motor would produce
a serious hazard
to persons—as in
mining operations

Supervised alarm
or annunciator to
warn of overload
and permit safe,
orderly shutdown

Fig. 430-18. This type of hookup may be used to warn, but not open, an overload. (Sec. 430-44.)

would be more serious in their hazardous implications than simple overload.

Note: Section 445-4 has a new exception that permits this same use of an alarm instead of overcurrent protection where it is better to have a generator fail than stop operating.

430-51. General. This section indicates the coverage of part **D**, which requires "Motor Branch-Circuit Short-Circuit and Ground-Fault Protection." Although the phrase "ground-fault protection" is used in several of the sections of part **D**, it should be noted that it refers to the protection against ground fault that is provided by the fuses or CB that are used to provide short-circuit protection. The single CB or set of fuses is referred to as a "short-circuit and ground-fault protective device." The rule is *not* intended to require the type of ground-fault protective hookup required by Sec. 230-95 on service disconnects (such as a zero-sequence transformer and relay hookup).

Motor branch circuits are commonly laid out in a number of ways. With respect to branch-circuit protection location and type, the layouts shown in Fig. 430-19 are as follows:

Type 1

An individual branch circuit leads to each motor from a distribution center. This type of layout can be used under any conditions and is the one most commonly used.

Type 2

A feeder or subfeeder with branch circuits tapped on at convenient points. This is the same as Type 1 except that the branch-circuit overcur-

Type 1

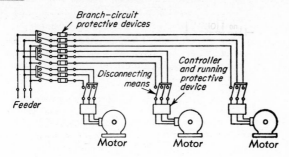

Type 2

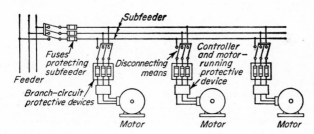

Type 3

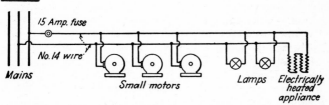

Fig. 430-19. Motor branch-circuit protection is used in various types of layouts. (Sec. 430-51.)

rent protective devices are mounted individually at the points where taps are made to the subfeeder, instead of being assembled at one location in the form of a branch-circuit distribution center. Under certain conditions, the branch-circuit protective devices may be located at any point not more than 25 ft distance from the point where the branch circuit is tapped to the feeder.

Type 3

Small motors, lamps, and appliances may be supplied by a 15- or 20-A circuit as described in Art. 210. Motors connected to these circuits must be provided with running overcurrent protective devices in most cases. See Sec. 430-42.

Figure 430-20 shows the typical elements of a motor branch circuit in

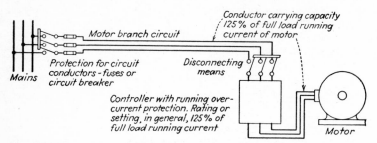

Fig. 430-20. Branch-circuit protection is on the line side of other components. (Sec. 430-51.)

their relation to branch-circuit protection, so that the protection is effective for the circuit conductors, the control and disconnect means, and the motor. Motor controllers provide protection for the motors they control against all ordinary overloads but are not intended to open short circuits. Fuses, CBs, or motor short-circuit protectors used as the branch-circuit protective device will open short circuits and therefore provide short-circuit protection for both the motor and the running protective device. Where a motor is supplied by an individual branch circuit, having branch-circuit protection, the circuit protective devices may be either fuses or a CB and the rating or setting of these devices must not exceed the values specified in Sec. 430-52. In Fig. 430-20, the fuses or CB at the panelboard must carry the starting current of the motor, and in order to carry this current the fuse rating or CB setting may be rated up to 300 or 400 percent of the running current of the motor, depending on the size and type of motor. It is evident that to install motor circuit conductors having an ampacity up to that percent of the motor full-load current would be unnecessary.

There are three possible causes of excess current in the conductors between the panelboard and the motor controller, viz., a short circuit between two of these conductors, a ground on one conductor that forms a short circuit, and an overload on the motor. A short circuit would draw so heavy a current that the fuses or breaker at the panelboard would immediately open the circuit, even though the rating or setting is in excess of the conductor ampacity. Any excess current due to an overload on the motor must pass through the protective device at the motor controller, causing this device to open the circuit. Therefore with circuit conductors having an ampacity equal to 125 percent of the motor-running current and with the motor-protective device set to operate at near the same current, the conductors are reasonably protected.

430-52. Rating or Setting for Individual Motor Circuit. The Code requires that branch-circuit protection for motor circuits must protect the circuit conductors, the control apparatus, and the motor itself against overcurrent due to short circuits or ground (Secs. 430-51 through 430-58).

The first, and obviously necessary, rule is that the branch-circuit protective device for an individual branch circuit to a motor must be capable of carrying the starting current of the motor without opening the circuit. Then the Code proceeds to place maximum values on the ratings or settings of such overcurrent devices. It says that such devices must not be rated in excess of the values given in Table 430-152.

In case the values for branch-circuit protective devices determined by Table 430-152 do not correspond to the standard sizes or ratings of fuses, nonadjustable CBs, or thermal devices, or possible settings of adjustable CBs adequate to carry the load, the next higher size, rating, or setting may be used.

Under exceptionally severe starting conditions where the nature of the load is such that an unusually long time is required for the motor to accelerate to full speed, the fuse or CB rating or setting recommended in Table 430-152 may not be high enough to allow the motor to start. It is desirable to keep the branch-circuit protection at as low a rating as possible, but in unusual cases, it is permissible to use a higher rating or setting. Where absolutely necessary in order to permit motor starting, the device may be rated at other maximum values, as follows:

1. The rating of a fuse that is *not* a dual-element time-delay fuse and is rated not over 600 A may be increased above the Code table value but must never exceed 400 percent of the full-load current.

2. The rating of a time-delay (dual-element) fuse may be increased but must never exceed 225 percent of full-load current.

3. The setting of an instantaneous trip CB (which contains only a magnetic short-circuit trip element, without time delay) may be increased but never over 1,300 percent of the motor full-load current.

4. The rating of an inverse time CB (a typical thermal-magnetic CB with a time-delay and instantaneous trip characteristic) may be increased but must not exceed 400 percent for full-load currents of 100 A or less and must not exceed 300 percent for currents over 100 A.

5. A fuse rated 601 to 6,000 A may be increased but must not exceed 300 percent of full-load current.

6. Torque motors must be protected at the motor nameplate current rating, and if a standard overcurrent device is not made in that

rating, the next higher standard rating of protective device may be used.

The rules of this section establish maximum values for branch-circuit protection, setting the limit of safe applications. However, use of smaller sizes of branch-circuit protective devices is obviously permitted by the **Code** and does offer opportunities for substantial economies in selection of CBs, fuses, and the switches used with them, panelboards, etc. In any application, it is only necessary that the branch-circuit device which is smaller than the maximum permitted rating must have sufficient time delay in its operation to permit the motor starting current to flow without opening the circuit.

But a CB for branch-circuit protection must have a continuous current rating of not less than 115 percent of the motor full-load current, as required by Sec. 430-58.

Where maximum ratings for the branch-circuit protection are shown in the manufacturer's heater table for use with a marked controller or are otherwise marked with the equipment, they must not be exceeded even though higher values are indicated in **Code** Table 430-152 and in the other rules of this section. That requirement is in the last sentence of this **Code** rule and is also specified in UL regulations which regulate the exposure of motor controllers to short-circuit currents to protect internal components, such as overload relays and contacts, from damage or destruction. Those rules state:

Motor controllers incorporating thermal cutouts, thermal overload relays, or other devices for motor-running overcurrent protection are considered to be suitably protected against overcurrent due to short circuits or grounds by motor branch circuit, short circuit and ground-fault protective devices selected in accordance with the **National Electrical Code** and any additional information marked on the product. Motor controllers may specify that protection is to be provided by fuses or by an inverse time circuit breaker. If there is no marking of protective device type, controllers are considered suitably protected by either type of device. Motor controllers may specify a maximum rating of protective device. If not marked with a rating, the controllers are considered suitably protected by a protective device of the maximum rating permitted by the **National Electrical Code**.

Unless otherwise marked, motor controllers incorporating thermal cutouts or overload relays are considered suitable for use on circuits having available fault currents not greater than [refer to Fig. 430-21]:

Horsepower rating	RMS symmetrical amperes
1 or less	1,000
1½ to 50	5,000
51 to 200	10,000
201 to 400	18,000
401 to 600	30,000
601 to 900	42,000
901 to 1600	85,000

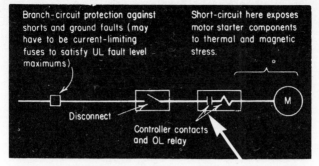

Branch-circuit protection against shorts and ground faults (may have to be current-limiting fuses to satisfy UL fault level maximums)

Short-circuit here exposes motor starter components to thermal and magnetic stress.

Disconnect

Controller contacts and OL relay

AVAILABLE SHORT-CIRCUIT CURRENT HERE MUST NOT EXCEED VALUES GIVEN BY UL OR MUST BE LIMITED TO THOSE VALUES

Fig. 430-21. UL specifies maximum short-circuit withstand ratings for controllers. (Sec. 430-52.)

Typical application of the basic rule of Sec. 430-52 on short-circuit protection for motor circuits is shown in Fig. 430-3. Overcurrent (branch-circuit) protection (from Table 430-152 and Sec. 430-52) using nontime-delay fuses is calculated as follows:

1. The 50-hp squirrel-cage motor must be protected at not more than 200 A (65 A × 300 percent).
2. The 30-hp wound-rotor motor must be protected at not more than 60 A (40 A × 150 percent).
3. Each 10-hp motor must be protected at not more than 45 A (14 × 300 percent).

As shown in Code Table 430-152, if thermal-magnetic CBs were used, instead of the fuses, for branch-circuit protection, the maximum ratings that are permitted by the basic rule are:

1. For the 50-hp motor—65 A × 250 percent or 162.5 A, with the next higher standard CB rating of 175 A permitted.
2. For the 30-hp wound-rotor motor—40 A × 150 percent or 60 A, calling for a 60-A CB.
3. For each 10-hp motor—14 A × 250 percent or 35 A, calling for a 35-A CB.

Instantaneous Trip CBs

The NE Code recognizes the use of an instantaneous trip CB (without time delay) for short-circuit protection of motor circuits. Such breakers—also called "magnetic-only" breakers—may be used only if they are adjustable and if combined with motor starters in combination assemblies. A combination motor starter using an instantaneous trip breaker must have running overload protection in each conductor and must be approved for the purpose (Fig. 430-23). Such a combination starter offers use of a smaller CB than would be possible if a standard thermal-magnetic CB were used. And the smaller CB offers faster operation for greater protection against grounds and short circuits—in addition to offering greater economy.

A combination motor starter, as shown in Fig. 430-22, is based on the

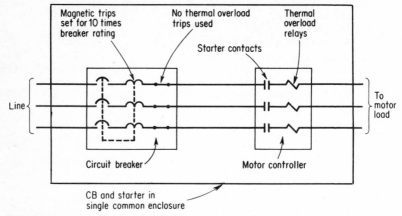

Fig. 430-22. Section 430-52 accepts use of magnetic-only circuit breakers in combination starters. (Sec. 430-22.)

characteristics of the instantaneous trip CB, which is covered by the third percent column from the left in Code Table 430-152. Molded-case CBs with only magnetic instantaneous trip elements in them are available in almost all sizes. Use of such a device requires careful accounting for the absence of overload protection in the CB, up to the short-circuit trip setting. Such a CB is designed for use as shown in Fig. 430-22. The circuit conductors are sized for at least 125 percent of motor current. The thermal overload relays in the starter protect the entire circuit and all equipment against operating overloads up to and including stalled rotor current. They are commonly set at 125 percent of motor current. In such a circuit, a CB with an adjustable magnetic trip element can be set to take over the interrupting task at currents above stalled rotor and up to the short-circuit duty of the supply system at that point of installation. The magnetic trip in a typical unit might be adjustable from 3 to 13 times the breaker current rating; i.e., a 100-A can be adjusted to trip anywhere between 300 and 1,300 A. Thus the CB serves as motor circuit disconnect and short-circuit protection.

Selection of such a CB is based on choosing a nominal CB size with a current rating at least equal to 115 percent of the motor full-load current to carry the motor current and to qualify under Secs. 430-58 and 430-110(a) as a disconnect means. Then the adjustable magnetic trip is set to provide the short-circuit protection—the value of current at which instantaneous circuit opening takes place, which should be just above the starting current of the motor involved—using a multiplier of something like 1.5 on locked-rotor current to account for asymmetry in starting current. Asymmetry can occur when the circuit to the motor is closed at that point on the alternating voltage wave where the inrush starting current is going through the negative maximum value of its alternating wave. That is the same concept as asymmetry in the initiation of a short-circuit current.

Equipment of the instantaneous CB type is available with very simple instructions by the manufacturer to make proper selection of the combination starter a quick, easy matter. The following is an example of application of an instantaneous trip CB for use in a combination starter:

Given: A 30-hp, 230-V, 3-phase, squirrel-cage motor marked with the code letter M, indicating that the motor has a locked-rotor current of 10 to 11.19 kVA per horsepower, from **Code** Table 430-7(b). A full-voltage controller is combined with the CB, with running overload protection in the controller to protect the motor within its heating damage curve on overload.

Required: Select a CB which will provide short-circuit protection and will qualify as the motor circuit disconnect means.

Solution: The motor has a full-load current of 80 A (**Code** Table 430-150). A CB suitable for use as disconnect must have a current rating at least 115 percent of 80 A. **Code** Table 430-152 will permit the use of an inverse time (the usual thermal-magnetic) CB rated not more than 250 percent of motor full-load current (although a CB could be rated as high as 400 percent of full-load current if such size were necessary to pass motor starting current without opening). Based on 2.5 × 80 or 200 A, a 225-A frame size with 200-A trip setting could be selected. The large size of this CB will generally take the starting current of the motor without tripping either the thermal element or the magnetic element in the CB. The starting current of the motor will initially be about 882 A (30 hp × 11.19 kVA per hp ÷ 220 V × 1.73). The instantaneous trip setting of the 200-A CB will be about 20 × 10 or 2,000 A. Such a CB will provide protection for grounds and shorts without interfering with motor-running overload protection.

But consider use of a 100-A CB with thermal and adjustable magnetic trips. The instantaneous trip setting at 10 times current rating would be 1,000 A, which is above the 882-A locked-rotor current. But starting current would probably trip the thermal element and open the CB. This problem can be solved by using a CB without a thermal element, leaving only the magnetic element in the CB. Then the conditions of operating overload can be cleared by the running overload devices in the motor starter, right up to stalled rotor, with the magnetic trip adjusted to open the circuit instantaneously on currents above, say, 1,300 A (882 × 1.5).

But because the value of 1,300 A is greater than 1,300 percent of the motor full-load current (80 × 13 = 1,040 A), Sec. 430-52 Exception (c) would prohibit setting the CB at 1,300 A. The maximum setting would be 1,000 A.

Because the use of a magenetic-only CB does not protect against low-level grounds and shorts in the circuit conductors on the line side of the starter running overload relays, the **NE Code** rule permits such application only where the CB and starter are installed as a combination starter in a single enclosure.

MSCPs

A motor short-circuit protector, as referred to in the second paragraph of Sec. 430-52, is a fuselike device designed for use only in its own type of fusible-switch combination motor starter. The combination offers short-circuit protection, running overload protection, disconnect means, and motor control—all with assured coordination between the short-circuit interrupter (the motor short-circuit protector) and the running OL devices. It involves the simplest method of selection of the correct MSCP for a given motor circuit. This packaged assembly is a third type of combination motor starter—added to the conventional fusible-switch and CB types.

The **NE Code** recognizes motor short-circuit protectors in Sec. 430-40 and 430-52 provided the combination is especially approved for the purpose. Practically speaking, this means a combination starter equipped with motor short-circuit protectors and listed by Underwriters Laboratories Inc. as a package called an MSCP starter.

430-53. Several Motors or Loads on One Branch Circuit.   A single branch circuit may be used to supply two or more motors as follows:

Part **(a):** Two or more motors, each rated not more than 1 hp and each drawing not over 6 A full-load current, may be used on a branch circuit protected at not more than 20 A at 125 V or less, or 15 A at 600 V or less. And the rating of the branch-circuit protective device marked on any of the controllers must not be exceeded. That is also a UL requirement.

Individual running overload protection is necessary in such circuits, unless: the motor is not permanently installed, is manually started, and is within sight from the controller location; or the motor has sufficient winding impedance to prevent overheating due to stalled rotor current; or the motor is part of an approved assembly that does not subject the motor to overloads and that incorporates protection for the motor against stalled rotor; or the motor cannot operate continuously under load.

Part **(b):** Two or more motors of any rating, each having individual running overload protection, may be connected to a branch circuit which is protected by a short-circuit protective device selected in accordance with the maximum rating or setting of a device which could protect an individual circuit to the motor of the smallest rating. This may be done only where it can be determined that the branch-circuit device so selected will not open under the most severe normal conditions of service which might be encountered.

This permission of part **(b)** offers wide application of more than one motor on a single circuit, particularly in the use of small integral-horse-power motors installed on 440-V, 3-phase systems. This application primarily concerns use of small integral-horsepower 3-phase motors as used in 208-V, 220-V, and 440-V industrial and commercial systems. Only such 3-phase motors have full-load operating currents low enough to permit more than one motor on circuits fed from 15-A protective devices.

There are a number of ways of connecting several motors on a single branch circuit, as follows:

CASE I—USING A CIRCUIT BREAKER FOR PROTECTION

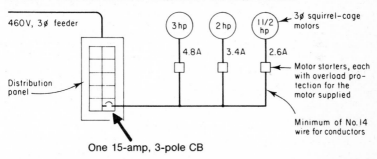

HERE IS THE KEY: A 15-amp, 3-pole CB is used, based on Section 430-52 and Table 430-152. This is the "next higher size" of standard protective device above 250% × 2.6 amps (the required rating for the smallest motor of the group). The 15-amp CB makes this application possible, because the 15-amp CB is the smallest standard rating of CB and is suitable as the branch-circuit protective device for the 1½-hp motor.

Fig. 430-23. Three integral-horsepower motors may be supplied by this circuit makeup. (Sec. 430-53.)

In Case I, Fig. 430-23, using a three-pole CB for branch-circuit protective device, application is made in accordance with part **(b)** as follows:

1. The full-load current for each motor is taken from NE Code Table 430-150 [as required by Sec. 430-6(a)].
2. Choosing to use a CB instead of fuses for branch-circuit protection, the rating of the branch-circuit protective device, 15-A, does not exceed the maximum value of short-circuit protection required by Sec. 430-52 and Table 430-152 for the smallest motor of the group—which is the 1½-hp motor. Although 15 A is greater than the maximum value of 250 percent times motor full-load current

$(2.5 \times 2.6 \text{ A} = 6.5 \text{ A})$ set by Table 430-152 (under the column "Inverse Time Breaker" opposite "polyphase squirrel-cage" motors), the 15-A breaker is the "next higher size, rating, or setting" for a standard CB—as permitted in Sec. 430-52. A 15-A CB is the smallest standard rating recognized by Sec. 240-6.

3. The total load of motor currents is:

$$4.8 \text{ A} + 3.4 \text{ A} + 2.6 \text{ A} = 10.8 \text{ A}$$

This is well within the 15-A CB rating, which has sufficient time delay in its operation to permit starting of any one of these motors with the other two already operating. Torque characteristics of the loads on starting are not high. It was therefore determined that the CB will not open under the most severe normal service.

4. Each motor is provided with individual running overload protection in its starter.

5. The branch-circuit conductors are sized in accordance with Sec. 430-24:

$$4.8 \text{ A} + 3.4 \text{ A} + 2.6 \text{ A} + (25 \text{ percent of } 4.8 \text{ A}) = 12 \text{ A}$$

Conductors must have an ampacity at least equal to 12 A. No. 14 THW, TW, RHW, RHH, THHN, or XHHW conductors will fully satisfy this application.

In Case II, Fig. 430-24, a similar hookup is used to supply three motors—also with a CB for branch-circuit protection.

1. Section 430-53(b) requires branch-circuit protection to be not higher than the maximum amps set by Sec. 430-52 for the lowest rated motor of the group.

2. From Sec. 430-52 and Table 430-152, that maximum protection rating for a CB is 250 percent × 1 A (the lowest rated motor) or 2.5 A. But, 2.5 A is not a "standard rating" of CB from Sec. 240-6; and the third paragraph of Sec. 430-52 permits use of the "next higher size, rating, or setting" of standard protective device.

3. Because 15 A is the lowest standard rating of CB, it is the "next higher" device rating above 2.5 A and satisfies Code rules on the rating of the branch-circuit protection.

The applications shown in Case I and Case II permit use of several motors up to circuit capacity, based on Secs. 430-24 and 430-53(b) and on starting torque characteristics, operating duty cycles of the motors and their loads, and the time delay of the CB. Such applications greatly reduce the number of CB poles, number of panels, and the amount of wire used in the total system. One limitation, however is placed on this practice in the last sentence of Sec. 430-52, as noted previously. Where more than one fractional- or small-integral-horsepower motor is used on a single branch circuit of 15-A rating in accordance with NE Code Sec. 430-53(a) or (b), care must be taken to observe all markings on controllers that indicate a maximum rating of short-circuit protection ahead of the controller (Fig. 430-25).

CASE II—USING A CIRCUIT BREAKER FOR PROTECTION

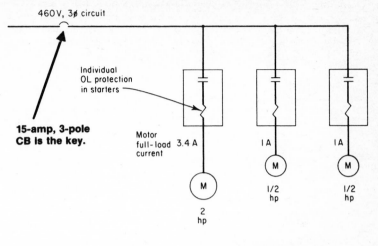

Fig. 430-24. Fractional-horsepower and integral-horsepower motors may be supplied by the same circuit. (Sec. 430-53.)

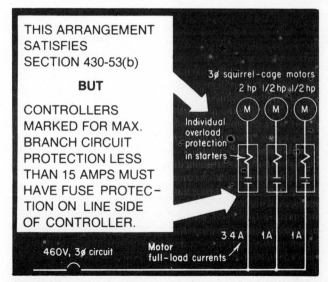

Fig. 430-25. Branch-circuit protection must not exceed marked maximum value. (Sec. 430-53.)

BUT, WATCH OUT!!!

CASE III—USING FUSES FOR CIRCUIT PROTECTION

Interpretation of *NE Code* rules of Section 430-53(b) in conjunction with the "standard" ratings of fuses in Section 240-6 may require different circuit makeup when fuses are used to protect the branch circuit to several motors.

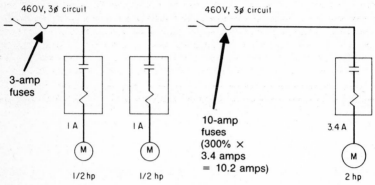

Fig. 430-26. Fuse protection may require different circuiting for several motors. (Sec. 430-53.)

In Case III, Fig. 430-26, the same three motors shown in Case II would be subject to different hookup to comply with the rules of Sec. 430-53(b) when fuses, instead of a CB, are used for branch-circuit protection, as follows:

1. To comply with Sec. 430-53(b), fuses used as branch-circuit protection must have a rating not in excess of the value permitted by Sec. 430-52 and Table 430-152 for the smallest motor of the group—one of the ½-hp motors.

2. Table 430-152 shows that the maximum permitted rating of non-time-delay type fuses is 300 percent of full-load current for 3-phase squirrel-cage motors. Applying that to one of the ½-hp motors gives a maximum fuse rating of:

$$300 \text{ percent} \times 1 \text{ A} = 3 \text{ A}$$

3. BUT, there is no permission for the fuses to be rated higher than 3 A—BECAUSE 3 A IS A "STANDARD" RATING OF FUSE (but not a standard rating of CB). Section 240-6 considers fuses rated at 1, 3, 6, and 10 A to be "standard" ratings.

4. The maximum branch-circuit fuse permitted by Sec. 430-53(b) for a ½-hp motor is 3 A.

5. The two ½-hp motors may be fed from a single branch circuit with three 3-A fuses in a three-pole switch.

6. Following the same Code rules, the 2-hp motor would require fuse protection rated not over 10 A (300 percent × 3.4 A = 10.2 A).

Note: Because the standard fuse ratings below 15 A place fuses in a different relationship to the applicable Code rules, it will require interpretation of the Code rules to resolve the question of acceptable application in Case II versus Case III. Interpretation will be necessary to determine if CBs are excluded as circuit protection in these cases where use of fuses, in accordance with the precise wording of the Code, provides lower rated protection than CBs—when applying the rule of the third paragraph of Sec. 430-52. And if the motors of Case I are fed from a circuit protected by fuses, the literal effect of the Code rules would require different circuiting for those motors.

Figure 430-27 shows one way of combining Case II and Case III to

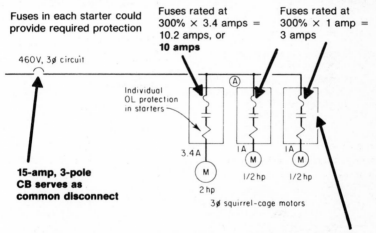

Fuses in each starter could provide required protection

Fuses rated at 300% × 3.4 amps = 10.2 amps, or **10 amps**

Fuses rated at 300% × 1 amp = 3 amps

460V, 3ø circuit

Individual OL protection in starters

Ⓐ

3.4A

1 A

1 A

15-amp, 3-pole CB serves as common disconnect

M

2 hp

M

1/2 hp

M

1/2 hp

3ø squirrel-cage motors

Fuses without individual disconnects might be acceptable under Section 240-40;or a single disconnect switch, fused at 3 amps, could be installed at point "A," eliminating the need for fuses in the two starters for the ½-hp motors.

Fig. 430-27. Multimotor circuit may be acceptable with fused starters. (Sec. 430-53.)

satisfy Sec. 430-53(b), Sec. 430-52, and Sec. 240-6; but the 15-A CB would then technically be feeder protection, because the fuses would be serving as the "branch-circuit protective devices" as required by Sec. 430-53(b). Those fuses might be acceptable in each starter, without a disconnect switch, in accordance with Sec. 240-40—which allows use of cartridge fuses at any voltage without an individual disconnect for each set of fuses, provided only qualified persons have access to the fuses. But, Sec. 430-112 would have to be satisfied to use the single CB as a disconnect for the group of motors. And part (b) of that Exception recognizes one common disconnect in accordance with Sec. 430-53(a) but not 430-53(b). Certainly, the use of a fusible-switch type combination starter for each motor would fully satisfy all rules.

Figure 430-28 shows another hookup that might be required to supply the three motors of Fig. 430-23.

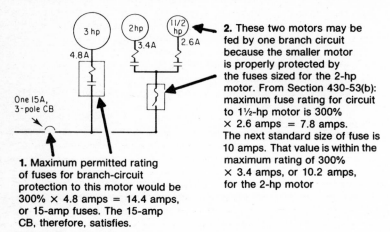

2. These two motors may be fed by one branch circuit because the smaller motor is properly protected by the fuses sized for the 2-hp motor. From Section 430-53(b): maximum fuse rating for circuit to 1½-hp motor is 300% × 2.6 amps = 7.8 amps. The next standard size of fuse is 10 amps. That value is within the maximum rating of 300% × 3.4 amps, or 10.2 amps, for the 2-hp motor

1. Maximum permitted rating of fuses for branch-circuit protection to this motor would be 300% × 4.8 amps = 14.4 amps, or 15-amp fuses. The 15-amp CB, therefore, satisfies.

Fig. 430-28. This hookup might be required to satisfy literal Code wording. (Sec. 430-53.)

Figure 430-29 shows another hookup of several motors on one branch circuit—an actual job installation which was based on application of Sec. 430-53(b). The installation was studied as follows:

Problem: A factory has 100 1½-hp, 3-phase motors, with individual motor starters incorporating overcurrent protection, rated for 460 V. Provide circuits.

Solution: Prior to 1965, the **NE Code** would not permit several integral-horsepower motors on one branch circuit fed from a three-pole CB in a

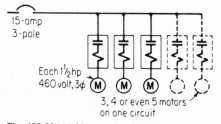

Fig. 430-29. Multimotor circuits offer economical supply to small integral-horsepower motors. (Sec. 430-53.)

panel. Each of the 100 motors would have had to have its own individual 3-phase circuit fed from a 15-A, three-pole CB in a panel. As a result, a total of 300 CB poles would have been required calling for seven panels of 42 circuits each plus a smaller panel (or special panels of greater numbers than 42 poles per panel).

Under the present Code, depending upon the starting torque characteristics and operating duty of the motors and their loads, with each motor rated for 2.6 A, three or four motors could be connected on each 3-phase, 15-A circuit—greatly reducing the number of panelboards, overcurrent devices, and the amount of wire involved, in the total system. Time delay of CB influences number of motors on each circuit.

BUT, an extremely important point that must be strictly observed is the requirement that the rating of branch-circuit protection must not exceed any maximum value that might be marked on the starters used with the motors.

Part **(c)**: Two or more motors of any rating may be connected to one branch circuit if each motor has running overload protection, if the overload devices and controllers are approved for group installation, and if the branch-circuit fuse or time-delay CB rating is in accordance with Sec. 430-52 for the largest motor plus the sum of the full-load current ratings of the other motors (Fig. 430-30). The branch-circuit fuses or CB must not be larger than the rating or setting of short-circuit protection permitted by Sec. 430-52 for the smallest motor of the group, unless the thermal device is approved for group installation with a given maximum size of fuse or time-delay CB for short-circuit protective device. (See Sec.

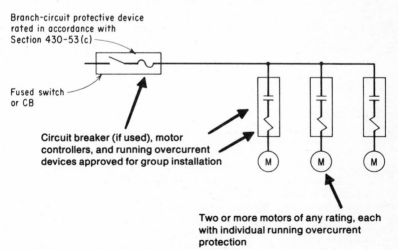

Fig. 430-30. Motors of any horsepower rating require circuit equipment for group installation. (Sec. 430-53.)

430-40.) Underwriters Laboratories notes that motor controllers for group installation are marked with a maximum rating of *fuse* required to suitably protect the controller. Section 430-53(c)(2), however, calls for a group installation controller to be marked for the rating of fuse or CB ahead of it.

Part **(d)**: For installations of groups of motors as covered in part **(c)** above, tap conductors run from the branch-circuit conductors to supply individual motors must be sized properly. Such tap conductors would, of course, be acceptable where they are the same size as the branch-circuit conductors themselves. However, tap conductors to a single motor may be smaller than the main branch-circuit conductors provided that: they have an ampacity at least ⅓ that of the branch- circuit conductors, their ampacity is not less than 125 percent of the motor full-load current, they are not over 25 ft long, and they are in raceway or are otherwise protected from physical damage (Fig. 430-31).

The principle applied here is that, since the conductors are short and protected from physical damage, it is unlikely that trouble will occur in the run between the mains and the motor protection which will cause the conductors to be overloaded, except some accident resulting in an actual short circuit. A short circuit will blow the fuses or trip the CB protecting the mains. An overload on the conductors caused by overloading the

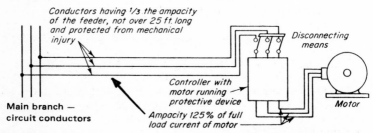

Fig. 430-31. Overcurrent protection not required for taps to single motors of a group. (Sec. 430-53.)

motor or trouble in the motor itself will cause the motor protective device
to operate and so protect the conductors.

430-55. Combined Overcurrent Protection. A CB or set of fuses may
provide both short-circuit protection and running overload protection
for a motor circuit. For instance, a CB or dual-element time-delay fuse
sized at not over 125 percent of motor full-load current (Sec. 430-32) for
a 40°C-rise continuous-duty motor would be acceptable protection for
the branch circuit and the motor against shorts, ground faults, and
operating overloads on the motor. See bottom of Fig. 430-16 for a typical
fuse application.

Figure 430-32 shows a CB used to fulfill four Code requirements

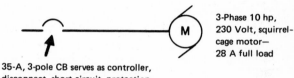

35-A, 3-pole CB serves as controller,
disconnect, short-circuit protection,
and running overload protection

3-Phase 10 hp,
230 Volt, squirrel-
cage motor—
28 A full load

Fig. 430-32. Overcurrent functions may be combined in a single CB or
set of fuses. (Sec. 430-55.)

simultaneously. For the continuous-duty, 40°C-rise motor shown, the CB
may provide running overload protection if it is rated not over 125
percent of the motor's full-load running current. Therefore, 28 A × 1.25
= 35 A, which satisfies Sec. 430-32(a). Because the rating of the thermal-
magnetic CB is not over 250 percent times the full-load current (from
Table 430-152), the 35-A CB satisfies Secs. 430-52 and 430-58 as short-
circuit and ground-fault protection. The CB may serve both those functions, as noted in Sec. 430-55. The CB may serve as the motor controller,
as permitted by Sec. 430-83 Exception No. 2. The CB also satisfies as the
required disconnect means in accordance with Sec. 430-111 and has the
rating "of at least 115 percent of the full-load current rating of the
motor," as required by Sec. 430-110(a). And because it satisfies Sec. 430-
110(a) on disconnect minimum rating, it therefore satisfies Sec. 430-58,
which sets the same minimum rating for a CB used as branch-circuit
protection.

430-56. Branch-Circuit Protective Devices—In Which Conductor. Motor
branch circuits are to be protected in the same way as other circuits with
regard to the number of fuses and the number of poles and overcurrent
units of CBs. If fuses are used, a fuse is required in each ungrounded
conductor. If a CB is used, there must be an overcurrent unit in each
ungrounded conductor.

430-57. Size of Fuseholder. The basic rule of this section covers sizing of
fuseholders for standard nontime-delay fuses used as motor branch-

circuit protection The Exception recognizes that time-delay fuses permit use of smaller switches and lower-rated fuseholders.

A fusible switch can take either standard **NE Code** fuses or time-delay fuses—up to the rating of the switch. Because a given size of time-delay fuse can hold on the starting current of a motor larger than that which could be used with a standard fuse of the same rating fusible switches are given two horsepower ratings—one for use with standard fuses, the other for use with time-delay fuses. For example, a three-pole, 30-A, 240-V fused switch has a rating of 3 hp for a 3-phase motor if standard fuses without time-delay characteristics are used. If time-delay fuses are used, the rating is raised to 7½ hp.

Consider a 7½-hp, 230-V, 3-phase motor (full-voltage starting, without code letters, or with code letters F to V), with a full-load current of 22 A. **NE Code** Table 430-152 shows that such a motor may be protected by nontime-delay fuses with a maximum rating equal to 300 percent of the full-load current (66 A), or time-delay fuses with a maximum rating equal to 175 percent of the full-load current (38.5 A).

If standard, nontime-delay fuses were used, the maximum size permitted would be 70 A (the next standard size larger than 66 A). From the table, this would require a 100-A, 15-hp switch, which would have fuseholders that could accommodate the fuses, as required by the basic rule. Or, a 60-A, 7½-hp switch might be used with standard fuses rated 60 A max. But such a switch would be required by the basic rule to have fuseholders that could accommodate 70-A fuses. Because such a fuse has knife-blade terminals instead of end ferrules and is larger than a 60-A fuse, fuseholders in the 60-A switch could be held in conflict with the **Code** rule even though the level of protection would be better with 60-A fuses in the 60-A switch. Wording of the rule is not clear. But cost, labor, and space savings would be realized using a 30-A, 7½-hp switch with 30-A time-delay fuses, with no worry about nuisance blowing of the fuses on motor starting current, and that would be acceptable under the Exception.

430-58. Rating of Circuit Breaker.   This rule sets a maximum and minimum rating for a CB as branch-circuit protection. Refer to Sec. 430-55.

In the case of a CB having an adjustable trip point, this rule refers to the capacity of the CB to carry current without overheating and has nothing to do with the setting of the breaker. The breaker most commonly used as a motor branch-circuit protective device is the nonadjustable CB (see Sec. 240-6), and any breaker of this type having a rating in conformity with the requirements of Sec. 430-52 will have an ampacity considerably in excess of 115 percent of the full-load motor current.

430-62. Rating or Setting—Motor Load.   Overcurrent protection for a feeder to several motors must have a rating or setting not greater than the largest rating or setting of the branch-circuit protective device for any motor of the group plus the sum of the full-load currents of the other motors supplied by the feeder.

The second paragraph notes that there are cases where two or more motors fed by a feeder will have the same rating of branch-circuit device. And that can happen where the motors are of the same or different horsepower ratings. It is possible for motors of different horsepower ratings to have the same rating of branch-circuit protective device, depending upon the type of motor and the type of protective device. If two or more motors in the group are of different horsepower rating but the rating or setting of the branch-circuit protective device is the same for both motors, then one of the protective devices should be considered as the largest for the calculation of feeder overcurrent protection.

And because Table 430-152 recognizes many different ratings of branch-circuit protective devices (based on use of fuses or CBs and depending upon the particular type of motor), it is possible for two motors of equal horsepower rating to have widely different ratings of branch-circuit protection. If, for instance, a 25-hp motor was protected by nontime-delay fuses, Table 430-152 gives 300 percent of full-load motor current as the maximum rating or setting of the branch-circuit device. Thus, 250-A fuses would be used for a motor that had a 78-A full-load rating. But another motor of the same horsepower and even of the same type, if protected by time-delay fuses, must use fuses rated at only 175 percent of 78 A, which would be 150-A fuses, as shown in Fig. 430-33. If the two 25-hp motors were of different types, one being a wound-

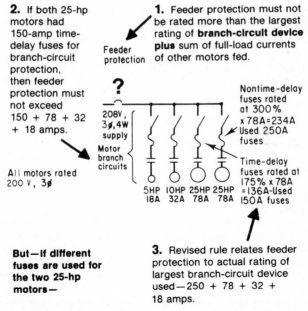

2. If both 25-hp motors had 150-amp time-delay fuses for branch-circuit protection, then feeder protection must not exceed 150 + 78 + 32 + 18 amps.

All motors rated 200 V, 3ϕ

1. Feeder protection must not be rated more than the largest rating of **branch-circuit device plus** sum of full-load currents of other motors fed.

Feeder protection

?

208V, 3ϕ,4W supply

Motor branch circuits

Nontime-delay fuses rated at 300% x 78A=234A Used 250A fuses

Time-delay fuses rated at 175% x 78A =136A-Used 150A fuses

5HP   IOHP 25HP 25HP
18A   32A   78A   78A

But—If different fuses are used for the two 25-hp motors—

3. Revised rule relates feeder protection to actual rating of largest branch-circuit device used—250 + 78 + 32 + 18 amps.

Fig. 430-33. Feeder protection is based on largest branch-circuit protection, not on motor horsepower ratings. (Sec. 430-62.)

rotor motor, it would still be necessary to base selection of the feeder protection on the largest rating or setting of a branch-circuit protective device, regardless of the horsepower rating of the motor.

Figure 430-34 shows a typical motor feeder calculation, as follows:

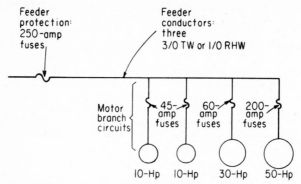

Fig. 430-34. Rating of feeder protection is based on branch protection and motor currents. (Sec. 430-62.)

The four motors supplied by the 3-phase, 440-V, 60-cycle feeder, which are not marked with a code letter (see Table 430-152), are as follows:

- 1 50-hp squirrel-cage induction motor (full-voltage starting)
- 1 30-hp wound-rotor induction motor
- 2 10-hp squirrel-cage induction motors (full-voltage starting)

Step 1. Branch-Circuit Loads

From Table 430-150, the motors have full-load current ratings as follows:
50-hp motor—65 A
30-hp motor—40 A
10-hp motor—14 A

Step 2. Conductors

The feeder conductors must have a carrying capacity as follows (see Sec. 430-24):

$$1.25 \times 65 = 81 \text{ A}$$
$$81 + 40 + (2 \times 14) = 149 \text{ A}$$

The feeder conductors must be at least No. 3/0 TW, 1/0 THW, or 1/0 RHH or THHN (copper).

Step 3. Branch-Circuit Protection

Overcurrent (branch-circuit) protection (from Table 430-152 and Sec. 430-52) using nontime-delay fuses:

1. The 50-hp motor must be protected at not more than 200 A (65 A × 300 percent).
2. The 30-hp motor must be protected at not more than 60 A (40 A × 150 percent).
3. Each 10-hp motor must be protected at not more than 45 A (14 × 300 percent).

Step 4. Feeder Protection

As covered in Sec. 430-62, the maximum rating or setting for the overcurrent device protecting such a feeder must not be greater than the largest rating or setting of branch-circuit protective device for one of the motors of the group plus the sum of the full-load currents of the other motors. From the above, then, the maximum allowable size of feeder fuses is 200 + 40 + 14 + 14 = 268 A.

This calls for a maximum standard rating of 250 A for the motor feeder fuses, which is the nearest standard fuse rating that does not exceed the maximum permitted value of 268 A.

Note: There is no provision in Sec. 430-62 which permits the use of "the next higher size, rating, or setting" of the protective device for a motor feeder when the calculated maximum rating does not correspond to a standard size of device.

According to part **(b)** of this section, in large-capacity installations where extra feeder capacity is provided for load growth or future changes, the feeder overcurrent protection may be calculated on the basis of the rated current-carrying capacity of the feeder conductors. In some cases, such as where two or more motors on a feeder may be started simultaneously, feeder conductors may have to be larger than usually required for feeders to several motors.

In selecting the size of a feeder overcurrent protective device, the **NE Code** calculation is concerned with establishing a maximum value for the fuse or CB. If a lower value of protection is suitable, it may be used.

430-63. Rating or Setting—Power and Light Loads. Protection for a feeder to both motor loads and a lighting and/or appliance load must be rated on the basis of both of these loads. The rating or setting of the overcurrent device must be sufficient to carry the lighting and/or appliance load plus the rating or setting of the motor branch-circuit protective device if only one motor is supplied, or plus the highest rating or setting of branch-circuit protective device for any one motor plus the sum of the full-load currents of the other motors, if more than one motor is supplied.

Figure 430-35 presents basic **NE Code** calculations for arriving at

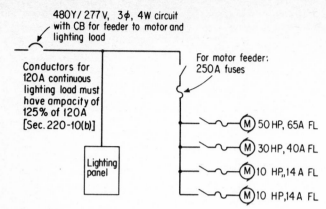

Fig. 430-35. Feeder protection for combination load must properly add both loads. (Sec. 430-63.)

minimum requirements on wire sizes and overcurrent protection for a combination power and lighting load as follows:

Step 1. Total Load

Section 430-25(a) says that conductors supplying a lighting load and a motor must have capacity for both loads, as follows:

$$\text{Motor load} = 65 \text{ A} + 40 \text{ A} + 14 \text{ A} + 14 \text{ A}$$
$$+ (0.25 \times 65 \text{ A} = 149 \text{ A per phase}$$
$$\text{Lighting load} = 120 \text{ A per phase} \times 1.25 = 150 \text{ A}$$
$$\text{Total load} = 149 + 150 = 299 \text{ A per phase leg}$$

Step 2. Conductors

Table 310-16 shows that a load of 299 A can be served by the following copper conductors:
500 MCM TW
350 MCM THW
Table 310-16 shows that this same load can be served by the following aluminum or copper-clad aluminum conductors:
700 MCM TW
500 MCM THW, RHH, or THHN

Step 3. Protective Devices

Section 430-63 says, in effect, that the protective device for a feeder supplying a combined motor load and lighting load may have a rating not

greater than the sum of the maximum rating of the motor feeder
protective device and the lighting load, as follows:

1. Motor feeder protective device = rating or setting of the largest
   branch-circuit device for any motor of the group being served plus
   the sum of the full-load currents of the other motors.

$$200 \text{ A (50-hp motor)} + 40 + 14 + 14 = 268 \text{ A max}$$

This calls for a maximum standard rating of 250 A for the motor
feeder fuses, which is the nearest standard fuse rating that does not
exceed the maximum permitted value of 268 A.

2. Lighting load = 120 A × 1.25 = 150 A

Rating of CB for combined load = 268 + 150 = 418 A max

This calls for a 400-A CB, the nearest standard rating that does
not exceed the 418-A maximum.

Again: There is no provision in Sec. 430-63 which permits the use of
"the next higher size, rating, or setting" of the protective device for a
motor feeder when the calculated maximum rating does not correspond
to a standard size of device.

Such considerations as voltage drop, I^2R loss, spare capacity, lamp
dimming on motor starting, etc., would have to be made to arrive at
actual sizes to use for the job. But, the circuiting as shown would be
safe—although maybe not efficient or effective for the particular job
requirements.

430-71. General (Motor Control Circuits). Figure 430-36 shows the
"motor control circuit" part of a motor branch circuit, as defined in part

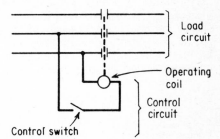

Fig. 430-36. A control circuit governs
the operating coil that switches the load
circuit. (Sec. 430-71.)

(a) of this section. A control circuit, as discussed here, is any circuit which
has as its load device the operating coil of a magnetic motor starter, a
magnetic contactor, or a relay. Strictly speaking, it is a circuit which
exercises control over one or more other circuits. And these other circuits
controlled by the control circuit may themselves be control circuits or
they may be "load" circuits—carrying utilization current to a lighting,
heating, power, or signal device.

The elements of a control circuit include all the equipment and devices concerned with the function of the circuit: conductors, raceway, contactor operating coil, source of energy supply to the circuit, overcurrent protective devices, and all switching devices which govern energization of the operating coil.

The **NE Code** covers application of control circuits in Art. 725 and in Secs. 240-3 and 430-71 through 430-74. Design and installation of control circuits are basically divided into three classes (in Art. 725) according to the energy available in the circuit. Class 2 and 3 control circuits have low energy-handling capabilities; and any circuit, to qualify as a Class 2 or 3 control circuit, must have its open-circuit voltage and overcurrent protection limited to conditions given in Sec. 725-31.

The vast majority of control circuits for magnetic starters and contactors could not qualify as Class 2 or Class 3 circuits because of the relatively high energy required for operating coils. And any control circuit rated over 150 V (such as 220- or 440-V coil circuits) can never qualify, regardless of energy.

Class 1 control circuits include all operating coil circuits for magnetic starters which do not meet the requirements for Class 2 or Class 3 circuits. Class 1 circuits must be wired in accordance with Secs. 725-11 to 725-20.

430-72. Overcurrent Protection.   Although the basic rule here calls for the conductors of a motor control circuit to be protected at the supply end by fuses or a CB rated in accordance with the conductor's ampacity, the exceptions to the rule are applied in the majority of applications.

In general, remote-control conductors must be protected against overcurrent. Section 240-3 Exception No. 4 states that remote-control conductors other than those for motor control circuits can be satisfactorily protected by overcurrent devices which are rated at not more than 300 percent of the carrying capacity of the control circuit conductors. That applies to control wires for magnetic contactors used for control of lighting or heating loads, but not motor loads. Section 430-72 modifies this requirement for motor control circuits.

Exception No. 1 indicates that the branch-circuit protective device may serve as sufficient protection for control circuit conductors where the control conductors do not actually leave the enclosure of a magnetic motor starter, such as when the START-STOP push-button station is in the cover of the starter housing. But the rule adds that this is permissible only where the branch-circuit protective device has a rating not over 400 percent of the ampacity of the control circuit wires. Obviously, this requires that the size and amp rating of control circuit wires must be known and evaluated against the rating of the branch-circuit protective device before it can be assumed that protection for the control circuit is not required within the starter. And, if such protection for the internal conrol circuit *is* required, a suitable fuse must be inserted in the controller housing. In Fig. 430-37, the conditions of Exception No. 1 are shown for those cases where the control wires do not leave the starter enclosure.

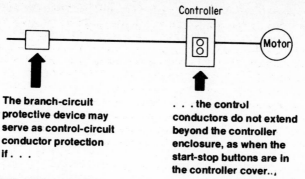

**The branch-circuit
protective device may
serve as control-circuit
conductor protection
if . . .**

**. . . the control
conductors do not extend
beyond the controller
enclosure, as when the
start-stop buttons are in
the controller cover...,**

. . . BUT, THE RATING OF THE PROTECTIVE DEVICE MUST NOT BE OVER 400% OF THE AMPACITY OF THE CONTROL WIRES WITHIN THE STARTER

NOTE: If the branch-circuit protection is in excess of 400% of the ampacity of the control conductors, then a fuse block must be used in the starter to accept fuses rated not over the conductor ampacity.

Fig. 430-37. When control wires do not leave the starter, branch-circuit protection may be adequate. (Sec. 430-72.)

For those cases where the control circuit is run from the starter to an external (remote) push-button station or other pilot control device, the rules are shown in Fig. 430-38. There, Exception No. 2 says that the remote-control conductors may be properly protected by the branch-circuit overcurrent devices (A) if these devices are rated or set at not more than 300 percent of (three times) the current rating of the control conductors. If the branch-circuit overcurrent devices were rated or set at more than 300 percent of the rating of the control conductors, the control conductors would have to be protected by separate protective devices located at the point (B) where the conductor to be protected receives its supply, such as by fuse protection in a fuse block within the starter. It should be noted that the overcurrent protection is required for the control conductors and not for the operating coil. Because of this, the size of control conductors can be selected to allow application without separate overcurrent protection.

Exception No. 4 says that the overcurrent protection for a control circuit—other than branch-circuit protection—*must* be eliminated where the opening of the control circuit would create a hazard. An example of this would be the control circuit of fire pump motors, or other cases where loss of power would be hazardous.

Exception No. 3 of part **(a)** of this section refers to the rules of part **(b)**—which covers overcurrent protection for control conductors used

Where control conductors extend
beyond the controller enclosure,
the conductors must be protected
at their ampacity by overcurrent
devices in the ungrounded legs
where they tap the main circuit
conductors, at points "B" . . .

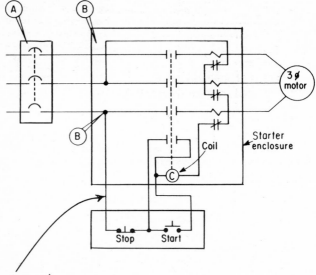

. . . BUT, protection is not
required at points "B" if motor
branch-circuit protective
device at "A" is rated not more
than 3 times (300%) the ampacity
of the control-circuit conductors.

NOTE: Regardless of the rating of the branch-circuit protective
device, protection must not be used at points "B" if opening of
the control circuit would create a hazard. For instance, no protection at points "B" would be required for the control circuit to a
fire-pump motor or similar load.

Fig. 430-38. Remote-control conductors *may* require fuse protection within starter. (Sec.
430-72.)

This is the basic rule . . .

An overcurrent device must be provided in secondary circuit of control transformer (one in each ungrounded leg). This device (or devices) must be rated or set at not more than 2 times (200%) rated transformer secondary current and not more than 2 times the ampacity of the control-circuit conductors.

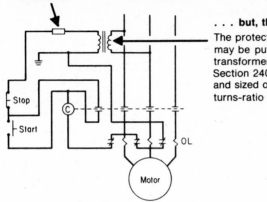

. . . but, this is an Exception:

The protection for the circuit may be put on the primary of the transformer in accordance with Section 240-3, Ex. No. 5 and sized on the basis of the turns-ratio of the transformer.

Fig. 430-39. Conductor protection may be on primary or secondary of control transformer. (Sec. 430-72.)

with a control transformer. These rules are shown in Fig. 430-39. Exception No. 1 notes that control circuit protection may be provided on the primary side of a control transformer as permitted in Sec. 240-3 Exception No. 5. This covers cases where a transformer has a 2-wire primary and a 2-wire secondary and it is permissible to protect the primary conductors, the transformer itself, and the secondary conductors all by a single overcurrent device (or set of overcurrent devices) on the primary side in accordance with the turns ratio of the transformer to afford correct protection to conductors on both sides of the transformer. This permission could apply to a control transformer installed within the starter enclosure as well as to an external control transformer fed by a separate supply from that feeding the power circuit through the motor controller. The use of secondary protection for a control transformer is suited to applications of the transformer within the starter enclosure. Primary protection, without secondary protection, is suited to use with external control transformers with 2-wire primary and 2-wire secondary.

Exception No. 4 of part **(b)** says overcurrent protection must be omitted where opening of the control circuit would create a hazard, such as when the circuit is to a fire pump motor. Other exceptions apply where the transformer supplies a Class 1 power-limited circuit or a Class 2 or Class 3 remote motor control circuit (See part C, Art. 725).

In the majority of magnetic motor controllers and contactors, the voltage of the operating coil is the voltage provided between two of the conductors supplying the load, or one conductor and the neutral. Conventional starters are factory wired with coils of the same voltage rating as the phase voltage to the motor. However, there are many cases in which it is desirable or necessary to use control circuits and devices of lower voltage rating than the motor. Such could be the case with high-voltage (over 600 V) controllers, for instance, in which it is necessary to provide a source of low voltage for practical operation of magnetic coils. And even in many cases of motor controllers and contactors for use under 600 V, safety requirements dictate the use of control circuits of lower voltage than the load circuit.

Although contactor coils and pilot devices are available and effectively used for motor controllers with up to 550-V control circuits, such practice has been prohibited in application in which atmospheric and other working conditions make it dangerous for operating personnel to use control circuits of such voltage. And certain OSHA regulations require 120-V or 240-V coil circuits for the 460-V motors. In such cases, control transformers are used to step the voltage down to permit the use of lower-voltage coil circuits.

430-73. Mechanical Protection of Conductor. The condition under which physical protection of the control circuit conductor becomes necessary is where damage to the conductors would constitute either a fire or an accident hazard. Damage to the control circuit conductors resulting in short-circuiting two or more of the conductors or breaking one of the conductors would result either in causing the device to operate or in rendering it inoperative, and in some cases either condition would constitute a hazard either to persons or to property; hence, in such cases the conductors should be installed in rigid or other metal conduit. On the other hand, damage to the conductors of the low-voltage control circuit of a domestic oil burner or automatic stoker does not constitute a hazard, because the boiler or furnace is equipped with an automatic safety control.

The second paragraph of this section focuses on the hazard of accidental starting of a motor. Figure 430-40 shows an example of a control circuit installation that should be carefully designed and is required by the second sentence of Sec. 430-73 to be observed for any control circuit which has one leg grounded. Whenever the coil is fed from a circuit made up of a hot conductor and a grounded conductor (as when the coil is fed from a panelboard or separate control transformer, instead of from the supply conductors to the motor), care must be taken to place the push-button station or other switching control device in the hot leg to the coil and not in the grounded leg to the coil. By switching in the hot leg, the starting of the motor by accidental ground fault can be effectively eliminated.

Combinations of ground faults can develop to short the pilot starting

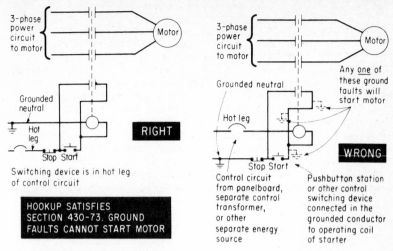

Note: OL relays are not shown in diagrams.

Fig. 430-40. Control hookup must prevent accidental starting. (Sec. 430-73.)

device—push-button, limit switch, pressure switch, etc.—accidentally starting the motor even though the pilot device is in the OFF position. And because many remote-control circuits are long, possible faults have many points at which they might occur. Insulation breakdowns, contact shorts due to accumulation of foreign matter or moisture, and grounds to conduit are common fault conditions responsible for accidental operation of motor controllers.

Although not specifically covered by **Code** rules, there are many types of ground-fault conditions that affect motor starting and should be avoided.

As shown in Fig. 430-41, any magnetic motor controller used on a 3-phase, 3-wire ungrounded system always presents the possibility of accidental starting of the motor. If, for instance, an undetected ground fault exists on one phase of the 3-phase system—even if this system ground fault is a long distance from the controller—a second ground fault in the remote-control circuit for the operating coil of the starter can start the motor.

Figure 430-42 shows the use of a control transformer to isolate the control circuit from responding to the combination of ground faults shown in Fig. 430-41. This transformer may be a one-to-one isolating transformer, with the same primary and secondary voltage, or the transformer can step the motor circuit voltage down to a lower level for the control circuit.

In the hookup shown in Fig. 430-43, a two-pole START button is used in

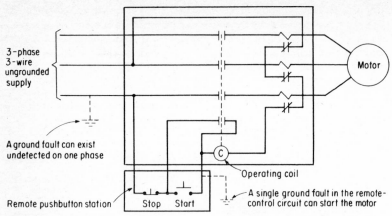

Fig. 430-41. Accidental motor starting can be hazardous and contrary to Code rule. (Sec. 430-73.)

conjunction with two sets of holding contacts in the motor starter. This hookup protects against accidental starting of the motor under the fault conditions shown in Fig. 430-41. The hookup also protects against accidental starting due to two ground faults in the control circuit simply shorting out the START button and energizing the operating coil. This could happen in the circuit of Fig. 430-41 or the circuit of Fig. 430-42.

Another type of motor control circuit fault can produce a current path through the coil of a closed contactor to hold it closed regardless of

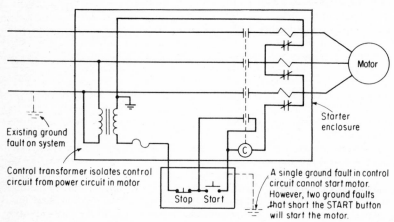

Fig. 430-42. Control transformer can isolate control circuit from accidental starting. (Sec. 430-73.)

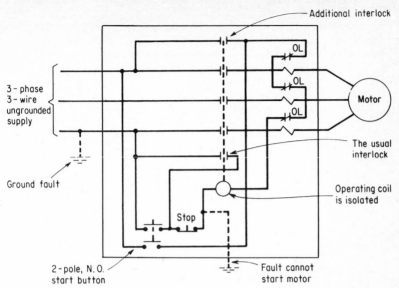

Fig. 430-43. Use of 2-pole start button can prevent accidental starting. (Sec. 430-73.)

operation of the pilot device for opening the coil circuit. Again this can be done by a combination of ground faults which short the STOP device. Failure to open can do serious damage to motors in some applications and can be a hazard to personnel. The operating characteristics of contactor coils contribute to the possible failure of a controller to respond to the opening of the STOP contacts. It takes about 85 percent of rated coil voltage to operate the armature associated with the coil; but it takes only about 50 percent of the rated value to enable the coil to hold the contactor closed once it is closed. Under such conditions, even partial grounds and shorts on control contact assemblies can produce paths for sufficient current flow to cause shorting of the stop position of pilot devices. And faults can short-out running overload relays, eliminating overcurrent protection of the motor, its associated control equipment, and conductors.

Figure 430-44 is a modification of the circuit of Fig. 430-43, using a two-pole START button and a two-pole STOP button—protecting against both accidental starting and accidental failure to stop when the STOP button is pressed. Both effects of ground faults are eliminated.

430-74. Disconnection. The control circuit of a remote-control motor controller shall always be so connected that it will be cut off when the disconnecting means is opened, unless a separate disconnecting means is provided for the control circuit.

When the control circuit of a motor starter is tapped from the line

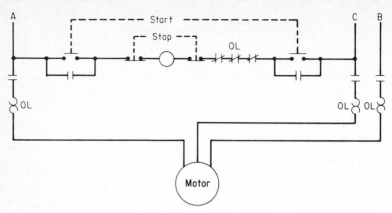

Fig. 430-44. This circuit prevents accidental starting and assures stopping. (Sec. 430-73.)

terminals of the starter—in which case it is fed at line-to-line voltage of the circuit to the motor itself—opening of the required disconnect means ahead of the starter de-energizes the control circuit from its source of supply, as shown in Fig. 430-45. But, where voltage supply to the coil circuit is derived from outside the starter enclosure (as from a panelboard or from a separate control transformer), provision must be made to assure that the control circuit is capable of being de-energized to permit safe maintenance of the starter. In such cases, the required power-circuit disconnect ahead of the starter can open the power circuit

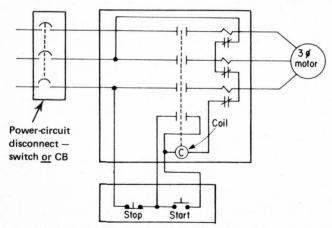

Fig. 430-45. Disconnect ahead of starter opens supply to line-voltage coil circuit. (Sec. 430-74.)

to the starter's line terminals; but, unless some provision is made to open the externally derived control circuit voltage supply, a maintenance worker could be exposed to the unexpected shock hazard of the energized control circuit within the starter.

The disconnect for control voltage supply could be an extra pole or auxiliary contact in the switch or CB used as the main power disconnect ahead of the starter, as shown in Fig. 430-46. Or the control disconnect

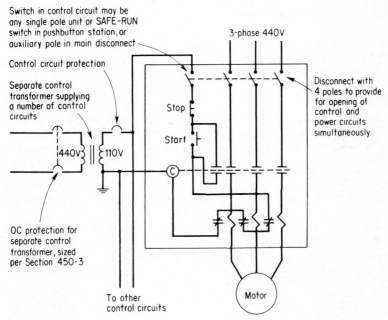

Fig. 430-46. Control disconnect means must supplement power-circuit disconnect. (Sec. 430-74.)

could be a separate switch (like a toggle switch), provided this separate switch is installed "immediately adjacent" to the power disconnect—so it is clear to maintenance people that *both* disconnects must be opened to kill *all* energized circuits within the starter. Control circuits operating contactor coils, etc., within controllers present a shock hazard if they are allowed to remain energized when the disconnect is in the OFF position. Therefore, the control circuit either must be designed in such a way that it is disconnected from the source of supply by the controller disconnecting means or must be equipped with a separate disconnect immediately adjacent to the controller disconnect for opening of both disconnects.

[For grounding of the control transformer secondary in Fig. 430-46, refer to Sec. 250-5(b) Exception No. 3.]

Exception No. 1 of part **(a)** is aimed at industrial-type motor control hookups which involve extensive interlocking of control circuits for multimotor process operations or machine sequences. In recognition of the unusual and complex control conditions that exist in many industrial applications—particularly process industries and manufacturing facilities—Exception No. 1 alters the basic rule that disconnecting means for control circuits must be located immediately adjacent one to each other (Fig. 430-47). When a piece of motor control equipment has more than

Fig. 430-47. Industrial control layouts with more than 12 control-circuit conductors for interlocking of controllers and operating stations (arrow) do not require control disconnects to be "immediately adjacent" to power disconnects. (Sec. 430-74.)

12 motor control conductors associated with it, remote locating of the disconnect means is permitted under the conditions given in Exception No. 1. As shown in Fig. 430-48, this permission is applicable only where qualified persons have access to the live parts and sufficient warning signs are used on the equipment to locate and identify the various disconnects associated with the control circuit conductors.

Where an assembly of motor control equipment or a machine or process layout has **more than 12** control conductors coming into it and requiring disconnect means . . .

. . . the disconnect devices required by Section 430-74(a) for the control conductors may be remote from, instead of adjacent to, the disconnects for the power circuits to the motor controllers.

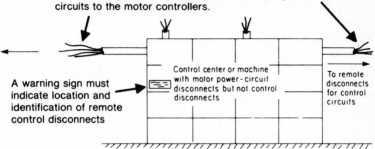

A warning sign must indicate location and identification of remote control disconnects

Control center or machine with motor power-circuit disconnects but not control disconnects

To remote disconnects for control circuits

Fig. 430-48. For extensively interlocked control circuits, control-disconnects do not have to be adjacent to power disconnects. (Sec. 430-74.)

Exception No. 2 presents another instance in which control circuit disconnects may be mounted other than immediately adjacent to each other. It notes that where the opening of one or more motor control circuit disconnects might result in hazard to personnel or property, remote mounting may be used where the conditions specified in Exception No. 1 exist, i. e., that access is limited to qualified persons and that a warning sign is located on the outside of the equipment to indicate the location and the identification of each remote control circuit disconnect.

The requirement of part **(b)** of this section is shown in Fig. 430-49. When a control transformer is in the starter enclosure, the power disconnect means is on the line side and can de-energize the transformer control circuit. Grounding of the control circuit is not always necessary, as noted in Exception No. 3 of Sec. 250-5(b). Overcurrent protection must be provided for the control circuit when a control circuit transformer is used, as covered in Sec. 430-72(b). Such protection may be on the primary or secondary side of the transformer, as described. In Sec. 450-1, Exception No. 2 notes that the rules of Art. 450 do not apply to "dry-type transformers that constitute a component part of other apparatus. . . ." A control transformer supplied as a factory-installed component in a starter would therefore be exempt from the rules of Sec. 450-3(b), covering overcurrent protection for transformers.

430-81. General (Motor Controllers). As used in Art. 430, the term "controller" includes any switch or device normally used to start and stop a motor, in addition to motor starters and controllers as such. As noted, the

Control transformer in starter does
not require overcurrent protection

Overcurrent protection for
control circuit

Disconnect switch or
circuit breaker kills
power circuit and control
circuit as required by
Section 430-74

Transformer
secondary grounded
as required by
Section 250-5

3-phase 440V

Stop

Start

Operating coil

Ground fault
could short out
OL relays without
stopping motor

Motor

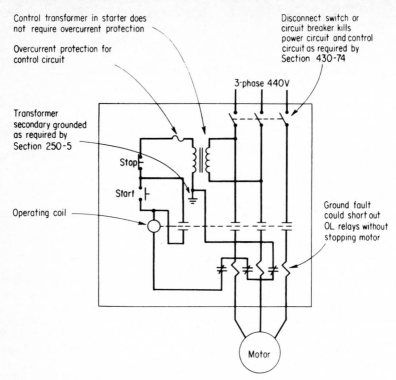

Fig. 430-49. Control transformer in starter must be on load-side of disconnect. (Sec. 430-74.)

branch-circuit fuse or CBs are considered an acceptable control device for stationary motors not over $\frac{1}{8}$ hp where the motor has sufficient winding impedance to prevent damage to the motor with its rotor continuously at standstill. And a plug and receptacle connection may serve as the controller for portable motors up to $\frac{1}{3}$ hp.

430-82. Controller Design. Every controller must be capable of starting and stopping the motor which it controls, must be able to interrupt the stalled-rotor current of the motor, and must have a horsepower rating not lower than the rating of the motor, except as permitted by Sec. 430-83.

430-83. Rating. Figure 430-50 shows the basic requirements on rating of a controller. Although the basic rule calls for a horsepower-rated switch or a horsepower-rated motor starter, there are exceptions as noted in Sec. 430-81 and as follows:

THIS IS THE BASIC RULE

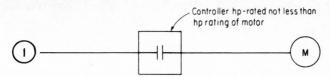

Controller hp-rated not less than
hp rating of motor

THESE ARE EXCEPTIONS TO THE BASIC RULE

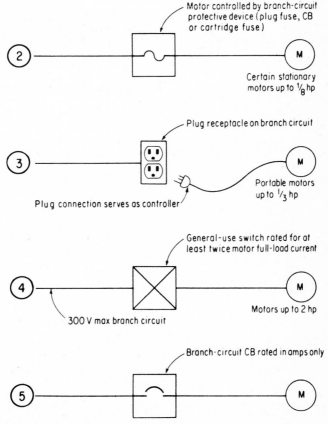

Motor controlled by branch-circuit
protective device (plug fuse, CB
or cartridge fuse)

Certain stationary
motors up to ⅛ hp

Plug receptacle on branch circuit

Portable motors
up to ⅓ hp

Plug connection serves as controller

General-use switch rated for at
least twice motor full-load current

Motors up to 2 hp

300 V max branch circuit

Branch-circuit CB rated in amps only

Fig. 430-50. Controller must be a hp-rated switch or CB—but other devices may satisfy. (Sec. 430-83.)

- A general-use switch rated at not less than twice the full-load motor current may be used as the controller for stationary motors up to 2 hp, rated 300 V or less. On AC circuits, a general-use snap switch suitable only for use on AC may be used to control a motor having a full-load current rating not over 80 percent of the ampere rating of the switch.
- A branch-circuit CB, rated in amperes only, may be used as a controller. If the same CB is used as controller and to provide overload protection for the motor circuit, it must be rated in accordance with Sec. 430-32.

In the UL's *Electrical Construction Materials Directory,* data are presented on use of switches in motor circuits, as follows:

1. Enclosed switches with horsepower ratings in addition to current ratings may be used for motor circuits as well as for general-purpose circuits. Enclosed switches with ampere-only ratings are intended for general use but may also be used for motor circuits (as controllers and/or disconnects) as permitted by NE Code Sec. 430-83 (Exception No. 1), Sec. 430-109 (Exceptions No. 2, 3, and 4), and Sec. 430-111.

2. A switch that is marked "MOTOR CIRCUIT SWITCH" is intended for use *only* in motor circuits.

3. For switches with dual-horsepower ratings, the higher horsepower rating is based on the use of time-delay fuses in the switch fuseholders to hold-in on the inrush current of the higher-horsepower-rated motor.

4. Although Sec. 430-83 permits use of horsepower-rated switches as controllers and UL lists horsepower-rated switches up to 500 hp, UL does state in its "green book" that "enclosed switches rated higher than 100 hp are restricted to use as motor disconnect means and are not for use as motor controllers." But a horsepower-rated switch up to 100 hp may be used as both a controller and disconnect if it breaks all ungrounded legs to the motor, as covered in Sec. 430-111.

Figure 430-51 covers two of those points.

For selection of a controller for a sealed (hermetic-type) refrigeration compressor motor, refer to Sec. 440-41.

430-84. Need Not Open All Conductors.   It is interesting to note that the NE Code says that a controller need not open all conductors to a motor, except when the controller serves also as the required disconnecting means. For instance, a two-pole starter of correct horsepower rating could be used for a 3-phase motor if running overload protection is provided in all three circuit legs by devices separate from the starter, such as by dual-element, time-delay fuses which are sized to provide running overload protection as well as short-circuit protection for the motor branch circuit. The controller must interrupt only enough conductors to be able to start and stop the motor.

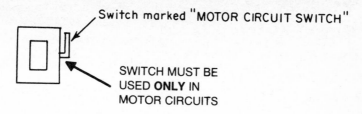

Switch marked "MOTOR CIRCUIT SWITCH"

SWITCH MUST BE
USED **ONLY** IN
MOTOR CIRCUITS

SINGLE HP-RATED SWITCH MAY SERVE
AS BOTH CONTROLLER AND DISCON-
NECT UP TO 100 HP

Motor branch circuit
fuses or CB

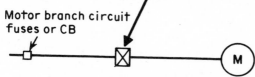

M

Fig. 430-51. UL rules limit Code applications. (Sec. 430-83.)

However, when the controller is a manual (nonmagnetic) starter or is a manually operated switch or CB (as permitted by the **Code**), the controller itself also may serve as the disconnect means if it opens all ungrounded conductors to the motor, as covered in Sec. 430-111. This eliminates the need for another switch or CB to serve as the disconnecting means. But, it should be noted that only a manually operated switch or CB may serve such a dual function. A magnetic starter cannot also serve as the disconnecting means even if it does open all ungrounded conductors to the motor.

Figure 430-52 shows typical applications in which the controller does not have to open all conductors but separate disconnect switch or CB is required ahead of the controller. In the sketch, the word "ungrounded" refers to the condition that none of the circuit conductors is grounded. These may be the ungrounded conductors of grounded systems.

Generally, one conductor of a 115-V circuit is grounded, and on such a circuit a single-pole controller may be used connected in the ungrounded conductor, or a two-pole controller is permitted if both poles are opened together. In a 230-V circuit there is usually no grounded conductor, but if one conductor is grounded, Sec. 430-85 permits a two-pole controller.

430-85. In Grounded Conductors. This rule permits a three-pole switch, CB, or motor starter to be used in a 3-phase motor circuit derived from a

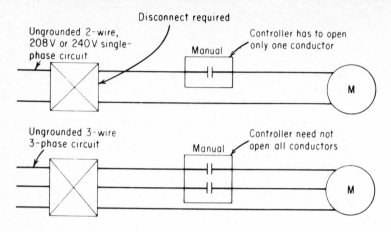

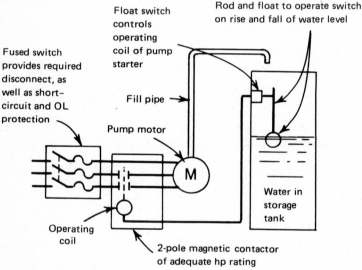

Fig. 430-52. "Controller" does not have to break *all* legs of motor supply circuit. (Sec. 430-84.)

3-phase, 3-wire, cornergrounded delta system—with the grounded phase leg switched along with the hot legs, as in Sec. 430-36.

430-86. Motor Not in Sight from Controller. Basically, the effect of this Code rule is to require that the motor and its driven machinery be within sight from the controller for the motor. When the controller is out of sight (and the Code considers a distance of 50 ft or more to be equivalent to "out of sight," even though the motor and its load might actually be visible from the controller location), the controller must comply with one of the following conditions:

1. The controller disconnecting means must be capable of being locked in the open position.
2. A manually operable switch, which will provide disconnection of the motor from its power supply conductors, must be placed within sight from the motor location. And this switch *may not* be a switch in the control circuit of a magnetic starter. (The NE Code at one time permitted a controller to be installed out of sight of the motor and its load if a switch in the coil circuit of the starter was installed within sight of the motor. Such a condition is NOT acceptable to the present Code. One of the two provisions shown in Fig. 430-54 must be made.)

These requirements are shown in Fig. 430-53. Specific layouts of the two exceptions are shown in Fig. 430-54. (*Note:* Code provisions shown in these sketches are minimum safety requirements. Additional use of disconnects, with and without lock-open means, may be made necessary or desirable by job conditions.)

The intent in paragraph (a) of this section is to permit workers to lock the disconnecting means in the open position and keep the key in their possession so that the circuit cannot be energized while they are working on it. This does not mean that a cabinet enclosing several switches could be locked to accomplish this purpose, because the other switches would be rendered inaccessible. Also it does not mean that removing a "pull out" type switch serves the purpose, because a "spare" could be inserted in the opening.

The push-button station in Fig. 430-54, Exception A, operates only the holding coil in the magnetic starter. The magnetic starter "controls" the current to the motor; for example, the control wires to a push-button station could become shorted after the motor is in operation and pushing the stop button would not release the holding coil in the magnetic starter and the motor would continue to run. This is the reason that a disconnecting means is required to be within sight from the controller. In this case operating the disconnecting means will open the supply to the controller and shut off the motor.

430-87. Number of Motors Served by Each Controller. Generally, an individual motor controller is required for each motor. However, for motors rated not over 600 V, a single controller rated at not less than the sum of the horsepower ratings of all the motors of the group may be used with a group of motors if any *one* of the conditions specified is met. Where a single controller is used for more than one motor connected on a single branch circuit as permitted under condition *b*, it should be noted that the reference is to part (a) of Sec. 430-53. That use of single controller applies only to cases involving motors of 1 hp or less and does not apply for several motors used on a single branch circuit in accordance

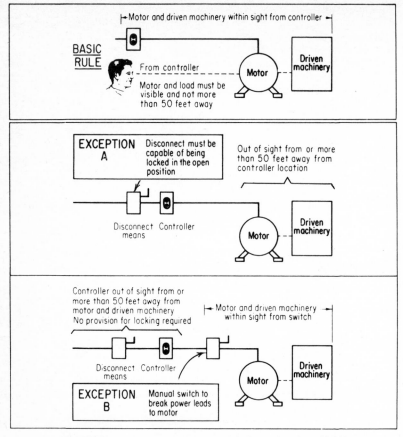

Fig. 430-53. Controller location must satisfy these rules. (Sec. 430-86.)

with parts **(b)** and **(c)** of Sec. 430-53—unless the several motors satisfy conditions *a* or *c* of this section.

See Sec. 430-112, where the same conditions are set for a single disconnect means to serve a group of motors.

430-88. Adjustable-Speed Motors.   Field weakening is quite commonly used as a method of controlling the speed of DC motors. If such a motor were started under a weakened field, the starting current would be excessive unless the motor is specially designed for starting in this manner.

430-89. Speed Limitation.   A common example of a separately excited DC motor is found in a typical speed control system that is widely used for electric elevators, hoists, and other applications where smooth control

EXCEPTION A

Combination fused-switch magnetic starter unit
in control center has **lock-open provision** on
switch.

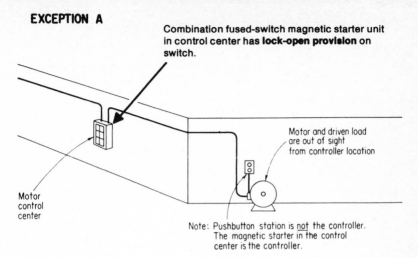

Motor and driven load
are out of sight
from controller location

Motor
control
center

Note: Pushbutton station is not the controller.
The magnetic starter in the control
center is the controller.

EXCEPTION B

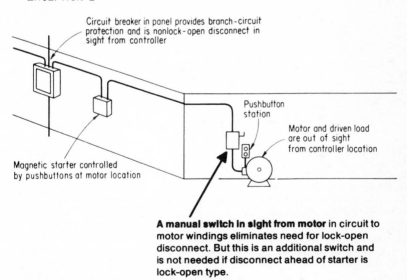

Circuit breaker in panel provides branch-circuit
protection and is nonlock-open disconnect in
sight from controller

Pushbutton
station

Motor and driven load
are out of sight
from controller location

Magnetic starter controlled
by pushbuttons at motor location

A manual switch in sight from motor in circuit to
motor windings eliminates need for lock-open
disconnect. But this is an additional switch and
is not needed if disconnect ahead of starter is
lock-open type.

Fig. 430-54. These conditions permit motor to be out-of-sight from controller. (Sec. 430-86.)

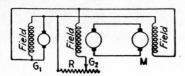

Fig. 430-55. Typical speed-control hookup involving the rule of Sec. 430-89. (Sec. 430-89.)

of speed from standstill to full speed is necessary. In Fig. 430-55, G_1 and G_2 are two generators having their armatures mounted on a shaft which is driven by a motor, not shown in the diagram. M is a motor driving the elevator drum or other machine. The fields of generator G_1 and motor M are excited by G_1. By adjusting the rheostat R, the voltage generated by G_2 is varied, and this in turn varies the speed of motor M. It is evident that if the field circuit of motor M should be accidentally opened while the motor is lightly loaded, the motor would reach an excessive speed. In many applications of this system the motor is always loaded and no speed-limiting device is required.

The speed of a series motor depends upon its load and will become excessive at no load or very light loads. Traction motors are commonly series motors, but such a motor is geared to the drive wheels of the car or locomotive and hence is always loaded.

Where a motor generator, consisting of a motor driving a compound-wound DC generator, is operated in parallel with a similar machine or is used to charge a storage battery, if the motor circuit is accidentally opened while the generator is still connected to the DC buses or battery, the generator will be driven as a motor and its speed may become dangerously high. A synchronous converter operating under similar conditions may also reach an excessive speed if the AC supply is accidentally cut off.

A safeguard against overspeed is provided by a centrifugal device on the shaft of the machine, arranged to close (or open) a contact at a predetermined speed, thus tripping a CB which cuts the machine off from the current supply.

430-90. Combination Fuseholder and Switch as Controller. The use of a fusible switch as a motor controller with fuses as motor-running protective devices is practicable when time-delay types of fuses are used. The rating of the fuses must not exceed 125 percent, or in some cases 115 percent, of the full-load motor current, and nontime-delay fuses of this rating would, in most cases, be blown by the starting current drawn by the motor, particularly where the motor turns on and off frequently. (See Sec. 430-35). The reference to "Part C" in this Code section should be to "Part D."

It may be found that a switch having the required horsepower rating is not provided with fuse terminals of the size required to accommodate the branch-circuit fuses. For example, assume a $7\frac{1}{2}$-hp 230-V 3-phase motor started at full-line voltage. A switch used as the disconnecting means for this motor must be rated at not less than 7½ hp, but this would probably be a 60-A switch and therefore, if fusible, would be equipped with terminals to receive 35- to 60-A fuses. Section 430-90 provides that fuse terminals must be installed that will receive fuses of 70-A rating. In such case a switch of the next higher rating must be provided, unless time-delay fuses are used.

430-102. In Sight From Controller Location.   Along with Sec. 430-101, this section specifically requires that a disconnecting means—basically, a motor-circuit switch rated in horsepower, or a CB—be provided in each motor circuit. Figure 430-56 shows the basic rule on "in-sight" location of the disconnect means. This applies always for all motor circuits rated up to 600 V—even if an "out-of-sight" disconnect can be locked in the open position.

There are two exceptions to this basic Code rule requiring a disconnect switch or CB to be located in sight from the controller:

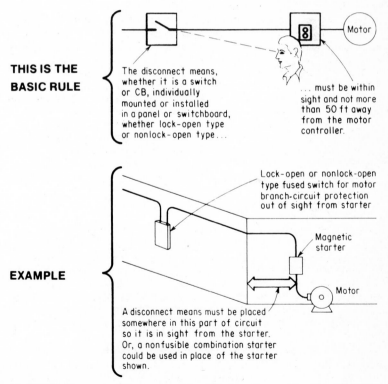

THIS IS THE BASIC RULE

The disconnect means, whether it is a switch or CB, individually mounted or installed in a panel or switchboard, whether lock-open type or nonlock-open type...

... must be within sight and not more than 50 ft away from the motor controller.

Lock-open or nonlock-open type fused switch for motor branch-circuit protection out of sight from starter

Magnetic starter

Motor

EXAMPLE

A disconnect means must be placed somewhere in this part of circuit so it is in sight from the starter. Or, a nonfusible combination starter could be used in place of the starter shown.

Fig. 430-56. The required disconnect must be visible from the controller. (Sec. 430-102.)

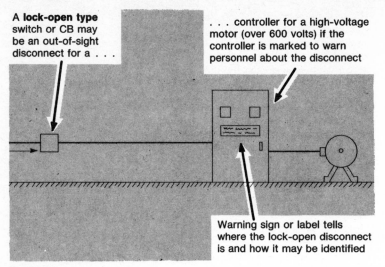

A **lock-open type** switch or CB may be an out-of-sight disconnect for a . . .

. . . controller for a high-voltage motor (over 600 volts) if the controller is marked to warn personnel about the disconnect

Warning sign or label tells where the lock-open disconnect is and how it may be identified

Fig. 430-57. An out-of-sight disconnect may be used for a high-voltage motor. (Sec. 430-102.)

Exception No. 1 permits the disconnect for a high-voltage (over 600 V) motor to be out of sight from the controller location, as shown in Fig. 430-57. But, the use of a lock-open type switch as an out-of-sight disconnect for a motor circuit rated 600 V or less is a clear Code violation.

Exception No. 2 is aimed at permitting practical, realistic disconnect means for industrial applications of large and complex machinery utilizing a number of motors to power the various interrelated parts of the machine. The Exception recognizes that a single common disconnect for a number of controllers (as permitted by part *a* of the Exception of Sec. 430-112) is often impossible to be installed "within sight" of all the controllers even though the controllers are "adjacent one to each other." On much industrial process equipment, the components of the overall structure obstruct the view of many controllers. Exception No. 2 permits the single disconnect to be technically out of sight from some or even all the controllers if the disconnect is simply "adjacent" to them—i.e., nearby on the equipment structure, as shown in Fig. 430-58.

430-103. To Disconnect Both Motor and Controller. This rule actually defines the meaning of the term *disconnecting means.*

In order that necessary periodic inspection and servicing of motors and their controllers may be done with safety, the Code requires that a switch, CB, or other device shall be provided for this purpose. Because the disconnecting means must disconnect the controller as well as the motor, it must be a separate device and cannot be a part of the controller,

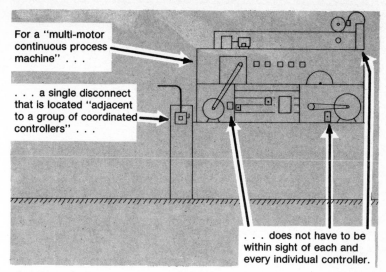

For a "multi-motor continuous process machine" . . .

. . . a single disconnect that is located "adjacent to a group of coordinated controllers" . . .

. . . does not have to be within sight of each and every individual controller.

Fig. 430-58. For multimotor machines, the disconnect may be "adjacent" to controller. (Sec. 430-102.)

though it could be mounted on the same panel or enclosed in the same box with the controller. The disconnect must be installed ahead of the controller. And note that the disconnect must open only the "ungrounded" conductors of a motor circuit.

In case the motor controller fails to open the circuit if the motor is stalled, or under other conditions of heavy overload, the disconnecting means can be used to open the circuit. It is therefore required that a switch used as the disconnecting means shall be capable of interrupting very heavy current.

430-105. Grounded Conductors.   Although Sec. 430-103 requires a disconnect means only for the ungrounded conductors of a motor circuit, if a motor circuit includes a grounded conductor, one pole of the disconnect *may* switch the grounded conductor provided all poles of the disconnect operate together—as in a multipole switch or CB. For instance, a 120-V, 2-wire circuit with one of its conductors grounded only requires a single-pole disconnect switch, but a two-pole switch *could* be used, with one pole switching the grounded leg.

430-107. Readily Accessible.   Although a motor circuit may be provided with more than one disconnect means in series ahead of the controller—such as one at the panel where the motor circuit originates and one at the controller location—*only one* of the disconnects is required to be "readily accessible" (see definition)—i.e., only one has to be easily and quickly reached for operation and any other disconnect may be high-mounted or otherwise located so a ladder must be used to reach it or a locked enclosure or room must be opened.

430-109. Type.   In a motor branch circuit, every switch in the circuit, from where the circuit is tapped from the feeder to the motor itself, must satisfy the requirements on type and rating of disconnect means. Figure 430-59 covers the basic rules on types of disconnect means.

For a motor larger than 2 hp, not larger than 100 hp, and not portable,

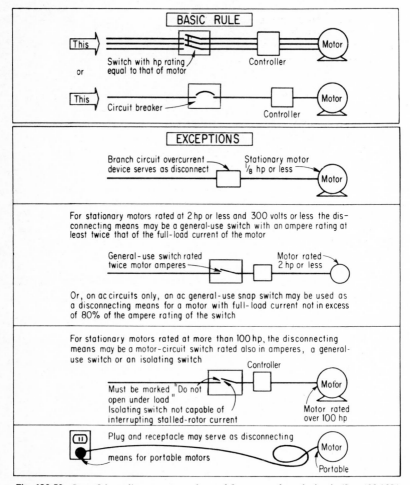

Fig. 430-59. One of these disconnects must be used for a motor branch circuit. (Sec. 430-109.)

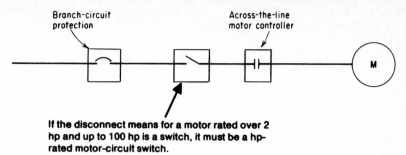

If the disconnect means for a motor rated over 2
hp and up to 100 hp is a switch, it must be a hp-
rated motor-circuit switch.

Fig. 430-60. From 2 to 100 hp, a disconnect *switch* must be horsepower-rated. (Sec. 430-109.)

a motor-circuit switch or a CB must be used as the disconnecting means
(Fig. 430-60).

A motor-circuit switch is a horsepower-rated switch. If in addition to
the disconnecting means there is any other switch in the motor circuit
and it is at all likely that this switch might be opened in case of trouble,
this switch must have the interrupting capacity required for a switch
intended for use as the disconnecting means.

Exception No. 4 to Sec. 430-109 sets the maximum horsepower rating
required for motor-circuit switches at 100 hp. Higher-rated switches are
now available and will provide additional safety. The first sentence of this
section makes a basic requirement that the disconnecting means for a
motor and its controller be a motor-circuit switch rated in horsepower.
For motors rated up to 500 hp, this is readily complied with, inasmuch as
the UL lists motor-circuit switches up to 500 hp and the manufacturers
mark switches to conform. But for motors rated over 100 hp, the Code
does not require that the disconnect have a horsepower rating. It makes
an exception to the basic rule and permits the use of ampere-rated switch
or isolation switches, provided the switch has a carrying capacity of at
least 115 percent of the nameplate current rating of the motor [Sec. 430-
110(a)]. And UL notes that horsepower-rated switches over 100 hp *must
not* be used as motor controllers. And Exception No. 4 notes that isolation
switches for motors over 100 hp must be plainly marked "Do not operate
under load," if the switch is not rated for safely interrupting the locked-
rotor current of the motor. Figure 430-61 shows an example of disconnect switch application for a motor rated over 100 hp.

Example: Provide a disconnect for a 125-hp, 3-phase, 460-V motor. Use a
nonfusible switch, inasmuch as short-circuit protection is provided at the supply
end of the branch circuit.

The full-load running current of the motor is 156 A, from NEC Table 430-150.
A suitable disconnect must have a continuous carrying capacity of 156 × 1.15 or
179 A, as required by Sec. 430-110(a).

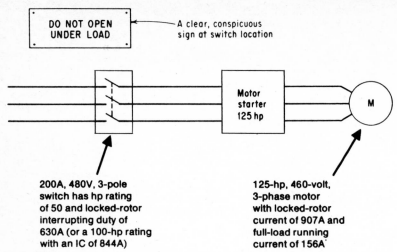

Fig. 430-61. Above 100 hp, a switch does not have to be horsepower-rated. (Sec. 430-109.)

This calls for a 200-A, three-pole switch rated for 480 V. The switch may be a general-use switch, a current-and-horsepower marked motor-circuit switch, or an isolation switch. A 200-A, three-pole, 480-V motor-circuit switch would be marked with a rating of 50 hp, but the horsepower rating is of no concern in this application because the switch does not have to be horsepower-rated for motors larger than 100 hp.

If the 50-hp switch were of the heavy-duty type, it would have an interrupting rating of 10 × 65 A (the full-load current of a 460-V, 50-hp motor) or 650 A. But the locked-rotor current of the 125-hp motor might run over 900 A. In such a case, the switch is required by Exception No. 4 to be marked "Do not operate under load."

If a fusible switch had to be provided for the above motor to provide both disconnect and short-circuit protection, the size of the switch would be determined by the size and type of fuses used. Using a fuse rating of 250 percent of motor current (which does not exceed the 300 percent maximum in Table 430-152) for standard fuses, the application would call for 400-A fuses in a 400-A switch. This switch would certainly qualify as the motor disconnect. However, if time-delay fuses are used, a 200-A switch would be large enough to take the time-delay fuses and could be used as the disconnect (because it is rated at 115 percent of motor current).

In the foregoing, the 400-A switch might have an interrupting rating high enough to handle the locked-rotor current of the motor. Or the 200-A switch might be of the CB-mechanism type or some other heavy current construction that has an interrupting rating up to 12 times the rated load current of the switch itself. In either of these cases, there would be no need for marking "Do not operate under load."

Up to 100 hp, a switch which satisfies the Code on rating for use as a motor controller may also provide the required disconnect means—the two functions being performed by the one switch—provided it opens all ungrounded conductors to the motor, is protected by an overcurrent device (which may be the branch-circuit protection or may be fuses in the switch itself), and is a manually operated air-break switch or an oil switch not rated over 600 V or 100 A—as permitted by Sec. 430-111.

430-110. Ampere Rating and Interrupting Capacity. An ampere-rated switch or a CB must be rated at least equal to 115 percent of a motor's full-load current if the switch or CB is the disconnect means for the motor.

When two or more motors are served by a single disconnect means, as permitted by Sec. 430-112, or where one or more motors plus a nonmotor load (such as electric heater load) make use of a single common disconnect, part **(c)** must be used in sizing the disconnect.

430-111. Switch or Circuit Breaker As Both Controller and Disconnecting Means. As described under Sec. 430-84, a manual switch—capable of starting and stopping a given motor, capable of interrupting the stalled-rotor current of the motor, and having the same horsepower rating as the motor—may serve the functions of controller and disconnecting means in many motor circuits, if the switch opens all ungrounded conductors to the motor. That is also true of a manual motor starter. A single manually operated CB may also serve as controller and disconnect (Figs. 430-62 and 430-63). However, in the case of an autotransformer type of controller, the controller itself, even if manual, may not also serve as the disconnecting means. Such controllers must be provided with a separate means for disconnecting controller and the motor.

Although this Code section permits a single horsepower-rated switch to be used as both the controller and the disconnect means of a motor circuit, UL rules note that "enclosed switches rated higher than 100 hp are restricted to use as motor disconnecting means and are not for use as motor controllers."

The acceptability of a single switch for both the controller and the disconnecting means is based on the single switch satisfying the Code requirements for a controller and for a disconnect. It finds application where general-use switches or horsepower-rated switches are used, as permitted by the Code, in conjunction with time-delay fuses which are rated low enough to provide both running overload protection and branch-circuit (short-circuit) protection. In such cases, a single fused switch may serve a total of four functions: (1) controller, (2) disconnect, (3) branch-circuit protection, and (4) running overload protection. And it is possible for a single CB to also serve these four functions.

For sealed refrigeration compressors, Sec. 440-12 gives the procedure for determining the disconnect rating, based on nameplate rated-load current or branch-circuit selection current, whichever is greater, and locked-rotor current of the motor-compressor.

SINGLE DEVICE FOR CONTROL AND DISCONNECT

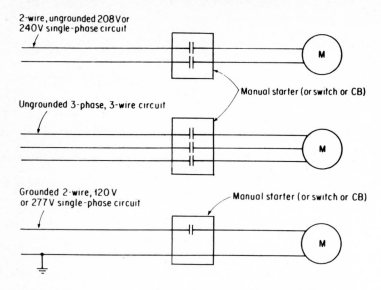

BUT MAGNETIC STARTER REQUIRES SEPARATE DISCONNECT

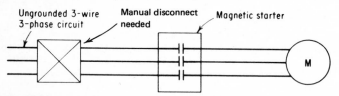

Fig. 430-62. A manual switch or CB may serve as both controller and disconnect means. (Sec. 430-111.)

430-112. Motors Served by Single Disconnecting Means. In general, each individual motor must be provided with a separate disconnecting means. However, a single disconnect sometimes may serve a group of motors under the conditions specified, which are the same as in Sec. 430-87. Such a disconnect must have a rating sufficient to handle a single load equal to the sum of the horsepower ratings or current ratings.

Exception *a*

In Sec. 610-31 it is required that the main collector wires of a traveling crane shall be controlled by a switch located within sight of the wires and

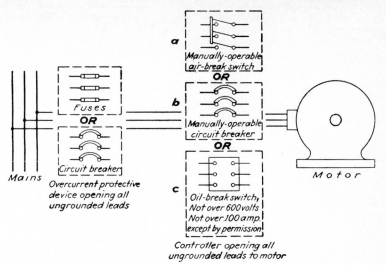

Fig. 430-63. Use of a single controller-disconnect is limited. (Sec. 430-111.)

readily operable from the floor or ground. This switch would serve as the disconnecting means for the motors on the crane. When repair or maintenance work is to be done on the electrical equipment of the crane, it is safer to cut off the current from all this equipment by opening one switch, rather than to use a separate switch for each motor. Also, in the case of a machine tool driven by two or more motors, a single disconnecting means for the group of motors is more serviceable than an individual switch for each motor, because repair and maintenance work can be done with greater safety when the entire electrical equipment is "dead."

Exception *b*

Such groups may consist of motors having full-load currents not exceeding 6 A each, with circuit fuses not exceeding 20 A at 125 V or less, or 15 A at 600 V or less. Because the expense of providing an individual disconnecting means for each motor is not always warranted for motors of such small size, and also because the entire group of small motors could probably be shut down for servicing without causing inconvenience, a single disconnecting means for the entire group is permitted.

Exception *c*

"Within sight" should be interpreted as meaning so located that there will always be an unobstructed view of the disconnecting switch from the

motor, and Sec. 430-4 limits the distance in this case between the disconnecting means and any motor to a maximum of 50 ft.

These conditions are the same as those under which the use of a single
controller is permitted for a group of motors. (See Sec. 430-87.) The use
of a single disconnecting means for two or more motors is quite common,
but in the majority of cases the most practicable arrangement is to
provide an individual controller for each motor.

If a switch is used as the disconnecting means, it must be of the type
and rating required by Sec. 430-109 for a single motor having a horsepower rating equal to the sum of the horsepower ratings of all the motors
it controls. Thus, for six 5-hp motors the disconnecting means should be
a motor-circuit switch rated at not less than 30 hp. If the total of the
horsepower ratings is over 2 hp, a horsepower-rated switch must be used.

430-113. Energy From More Than One Source.   The basic rule of this
section, which is similar to that of Sec. 430-74, requires a disconnecting
means to be provided from each source of electrical energy input to
equipment with more than one circuit supplying power to it, such as the
hookup shown in Fig. 430-64, where two switches or a single five-pole

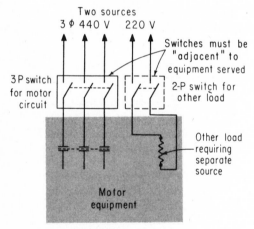

Fig. 430-64. A disconnect must be used for each power
input to motorized equipment. (Sec. 430-113.)

switch could be used. And each source is permitted to have a separate
disconnecting means. This **Code** rule is aimed at the need for adequate
disconnects for safety in complex industrial layouts. But an exception to
the **Code** rule states that where a motor receives electrical energy from
more than one source (such as a synchronous motor receiving both
alternating current and direct current energy input), the disconnecting
means for the main power supply to the motor shall *not* be required to be
immediately adjacent to the motor—provided that the controller discon-

necting means, which is the disconnect ahead of the motor starter in the main power circuit, is capable of being locked in the open position. If, for instance, the motor control disconnect can be locked in the open position, it may be remote; but the disconnect for the other energy input circuit would have to be adjacent to the machine itself, as indicated in Fig. 430-65.

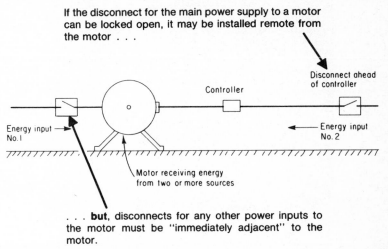

Fig. 430-65. An exception is made for disconnects for multiple power sources. (Sec. 430-113.)

430-124. Size of Conductors.   For motors rated over 600 V, the circuit conductors to the motor are selected to have a current rating equal to or greater than the trip setting of the running overload protective device for the motor.

430-125. Motor Circuit Overcurrent Protection. Overload protection must protect the motor and other circuit components against overload currents up to and including locked-rotor current of the motor. A CB or fuses must be used for protection against ground faults or short circuits in the motor circuit.

430-142. Stationary Motors.   Usually stationary motors are supplied by wiring in metal raceway or metal-clad cable. The motor frames of such motors must be grounded, the raceway or cable armor being attached to the frame and serving as the grounding conductor [See Sec. 250-91(b).]

Any motor in a wet location constitutes a serious hazard to persons and should be grounded unless it is so located or guarded that it is out of reach.

430-145. Method of Grounding.   Good practice requires in nearly all cases that the wiring to motors which are not portable shall, at the motor, be installed in rigid or flexible metal conduit, electrical metallic tubing, or

Fig. 430-66. Liquidtight flex provides flexible connection from rigid conduit supply to motor terminals but does require a separate equipment grounding conductor run within the flex with the circuit conductors or a separate external bonding jumper from the rigid metal conduit to the metal terminal box for each of the two runs. (Sec. 430-145.)

metal-clad cable and that such motors should be equipped with terminal housings. The method of connecting the conduit to the motor where some flexibility is necessary is shown in Fig. 430-66. The motor circuit is installed in rigid conduit and a short length of liquidtight flexible metal conduit is provided between the end of the rigid conduit and the terminal housing on the motor. But because the size of flex is over 1¼-in. size, a separate equipment grounding conductor (or bonding jumper) must be used within or outside the flex as noted in Sec. 351-9 and 250-91(b), Exception No. 2.

This section permits the use of fixed motors without terminal housings. If a motor has no terminal housing, the branch-circuit conductors must be brought to a junction box not over 6 ft from the motor. Between the junction box and the motor, the specified provisions apply.

According to Sec. 300-16, the conduit, tubing, or metal-clad cable must terminate close to the motor in a fitting having a separable bushed hole for each wire. The method of making the connection to the motor is not specified; presumably, it is the intention that the wire brought out from the terminal fitting shall be connected to binding posts on the motor or spliced to the motor leads. The conduit, tubing, or cable must be rigidly secured to the frame of the motor.

ARTICLE 440. AIR-CONDITIONING AND REFRIGERATING EQUIPMENT

440-2. Other Articles. Article 440 is patterned after Art. 430, and many of its rules, such as on disconnecting means, controllers, conductor sizes, and group installations, are identical or quite similar to those in Art. 430. This article contains provisions for such motor-driven equipment and for branch circuits and controllers for the equipment, taking into account the special considerations involved with sealed (hermetic-type) motor-compressors, in which the motor operates under the cooling effect of the refrigeration.

It must be noted that the rules of Art. 440 are *in addition to* or are *amendments* to the rules given in Art. 430 for motors in general. The basic rules of Art. 430 also apply to A/C (air-conditioning) and refrigerating equipment unless exceptions are indicated in Art. 440.

Article 440 further clarifies the application of **NE Code** rules to air-conditioning equipment and refrigeration equipment as follows:

1. A/C and refrigerating equipment which does not incorporate a sealed (hermetic-type) motor-compressor must satisfy the rules of Art. 422 (Appliances), Art. 424 (Space Heating Equipment), or Art. 430 (Conventional Motors)—whichever apply. For instance, where refrigeration compressors are driven by conventional motors, the motors and controls are subject to Art. 430, not Art. 440. Furnaces with air-conditioning evaporator coils installed must satisfy Art. 424. Other equipment in which the motor is not a sealed compressor and which must be covered by Arts. 422, 424, or 430 includes fan-coil units, remote forced air-cooled condensers, remote commercial refrigerators, and similar equipment.

2. Room air conditioners are covered in part G of Art. 440 (Secs. 440-60 through 440-64), but must also comply with the rules of Art. 422.

3. Household refrigerators and freezers, drinking-water coolers, and beverage dispensers are considered by the **Code** to be appliances, and their application must comply with Art. 422 and must also satisfy Art. 440, because such devices contain sealed motor-compressors.

Air-conditioning equipment (other than small room units and large custom installations) is manufactured in the form of packaged units having all necessary components mounted in one or more enclosures designed for floor mounting, for recessing into walls, for mounting in attics or ceiling plenums, for locating outdoors, etc. Figure 440-1 shows

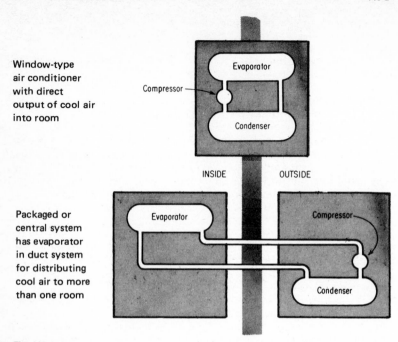

Window-type
air conditioner
with direct
output of cool air
into room

Packaged or
central system
has evaporator
in duct system
for distributing
cool air to more
than one room

Fig. 440-1. Code rules differentiate between unit room conditioners and central systems. (Sec. 440-2.)

the difference between room A/C units (such as window units) and the larger so-called "packaged units" or central air conditioners. Room units consist of a complete refrigeration system in a unit enclosure intended for mounting in windows or in the wall of the building, with ratings up to 250 V, single phase. Unitary assemblies may be console type for individual room use rated up to 250 V single phase or central cooling units rated up to 600 V for commercial or domestic applications. This type may consist of one or more factory-made sections. If it is made up of two or more sections, each section is designed for field interconnection with one or more matched sections to make the complete assembly. Dual-section systems consist of separate packaged sections installed remote from each other and interconnected by refrigerant tubing, either with the compressor within the outdoor section or within the indoor section.

Electrical wiring in and to units varies with the manufacturer, and the extent to which the electrical contractor need be concerned with fuse and CB calculations depends upon the manner in which the units' motors are fed and the type of distribution system to which they are to be connected. A packaged unit is treated as a group of motors. This is different from the approach used with a plug-in room air conditioner, which is treated as an individual single-motor load of amp rating as marked on the nameplate.

440-3. Marking on Hermetic Refrigerant Motor-Compressors and Equipment. Important in the application of hermetic refrigerant motor-compressors are the terms "rated-load current" and "branch-circuit selection current." Definitions of these terms are in notes following Secs. 440-3(a) and (c). When the equipment is marked with the branch-circuit selection current, this greatly simplifies the sizing of motor branch-circuit conductors, disconnecting means, controllers, and overcurrent devices for circuit conductors and motors.

440-4. Marking on Controllers. Note that a controller may be marked with "full-load and locked-rotor current (or horsepower) rating." That possibility of two methods of marking requires careful application of the rules in Sec. 440-41 on selecting the correct rating of controller for motor-compressors.

440-5. Ampacity and Rating. Selection of the rating of branch-circuit conductors, controller, disconnect means, short-circuit (and ground-fault) protection, and running overload protection as hermetic motor-compressors as for general-purpose motors. In sizing those components, the "rated-load current" marked on the equipment and/or the compressor must be used in the calculations covered in other rules of this article. That value of current must always be used, instead of full-load currents from Code Tables 430-148 to 430-150, which are used for sizing circuit elements for nonhermetic motors. And if a "branch-circuit selection current" is marked on equipment, that value must be used instead of rated-load current.

440-12. Rating and Interrupting Capacity (Disconnect). Note that the rules here are qualifications that apply to the rules of Secs. 430-109 and 430-110 on disconnects for general-purpose motors.

A disconnecting means for a hermetic motor, as covered in part **(a)(2)**, must be a motor-circuit switch rated in horsepower or a CB—as required by Sec. 430-109.

If a CB is used, it must have an amp rating not less than 115 percent of the nameplate "rated-load current" or the "branch-circuit selection current"—whichever is greater.

But, if a horsepower-rated switch is to be selected, the process is slightly involved for hermetic motors marked with locked-rotor current and rated-load current or rated-load current plus branch-circuit selection current—but *not* marked with horsepower. In such a case, determination of the equivalent horsepower rating of the hermetic motor must be made using the locked-rotor current and either the rated-load current or the branch-circuit selection current—whichever is greater—based on Code Tables 430-148, 149, or 150 for rated-load current or branch-circuit selection current and Table 430-151 for locked-rotor current, as follows:

For example, a 3-phase, 460-V hermetic motor rated at 11-A branch-circuit selection and 60-A locked-rotor is to be supplied with a disconnect switch rated in horsepower. The first step in determining the equivalent horsepower rating of that motor is to refer to Code Table 430-150. This table lists 7½ hp as the required size for a 460-V, 11-A motor. To ensure adequate interrupting capacity, Code Table 430-151 is used. For a 60-A locked-rotor current, this table also shows 7½ hp as the equivalent horsepower rating for any locked-rotor current over 45 A to 66 A for a 400-V motor. Use of both tables in this manner thus establishes a 7½ hp disconnect as adequate for the given motor in both respects. Had the two ratings as obtained from the two tables been different, the higher rating would have been chosen.

Figure 440-2 shows an example of disconnect sizing for a horsepower-

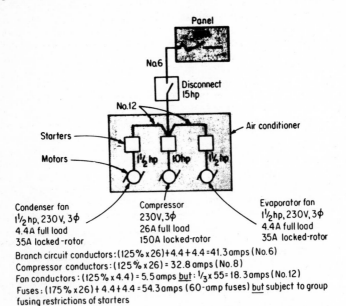

Fig. 440-2. Disconnect for multiple motors is sized from rated-load or branch-circuit selection currents and locked-rotor currents. (Sec. 440-12.)

rated switch when a hermetic motor is used, in accordance with Sec. 430-53(c), along with fan motors on a single circuit, as covered in part **(b)** and in Sec. 440-33. Fan motors are usually wired to start slightly ahead of the compressor-motor through use of interlock contacts or a time-delay relay. In some units, however, all motors start simultaneously and that is covered by part **(b)** of this section in sizing the horsepower-rated disconnect switch. Where this is the case, the starting load will be treated like a single motor to the disconnect switch, and the sum of the locked-rotor currents of all motors should be used with Code Table 430-151 to determine the horsepower rating of the disconnect. The disconnect normally must handle the sum of the rated-load or branch-circuit selection currents; hence the rating as checked against Code Table 430-150 will be on the basis of the sum of the higher of those currents for all the motors. Code Table 430-150, using the full-load total of 34.8 A (4.4 A + 26 A + 4.4 A) in this example, indicates a 15-hp disconnect. Code Table 430-151, assuming simultaneous starting of all three motors and using the total locked-rotor current of 220 A (35 A + 150 A + 35 A) also shows 15 hp as the required size.

If motors do not start simultaneously, the compressor locked-rotor current (150 A) used with Code Table 430-151 gives a 10-hp rating. However, the higher of the two horsepower ratings must be used; hence the running currents impose the more severe requirements and dictate use of a 15-hp switch. See data under Sec. 440-22.

440-14. Location.   Section 440-13 recognizes use of a cord-plug and receptacle as the disconnect for such cord-connected equipment as a room or window air conditioner. But this section applies to fixed-wired equipment—such as central systems or units with fixed circuit connection. For conditioners with fixed wiring connection to their supply circuits, the rule poses a problem. If the branch-circuit breaker or switch which is to provide disconnect means is located in a panel that is out of sight (or more than 50 ft away) from the unit conditioner, another breaker or switch must be provided at the equipment. If the panel breaker or switch does not satisfy the rule here, a separate disconnect means would have to be added in sight from the conditioner as shown in Fig. 440-3. This is also true if the service switch is installed as shown in Fig. 440-4.

440-22. Application and Selection.   Part (a) of this section is illustrated in Fig. 440-5, where a separate circuit is run to the compressor and to each fan motor of a packaged assembly, containing a compressor with 26-A rated-load current and fan motors rated at 4.4 A full-load each. The compressor protection is sized at 1.75 × 26 A (175 percent of rated-load current), or 45.5 A—calling for 45-A or 50-A fuses.

Sizing of branch-circuit protection for a single branch circuit to the same three motors is permitted by Sec. 430-53(c) as well as by Sec. 440-22(b) and is shown in Fig. 440-12. That layout is a specific example of the general rules covered in Sec. 440-22(b) (1), which ties the rules of Sec. 430-53(c) and (d) into the rules of Sec. 440-22(b), as shown in Fig. 440-6. Such application is based on certain factors, as covered in the UL *Electrical Appliance and Utilization Directory,* listed under "Air Conditioners, Central Cooling," as follows:

The proper method of electrical installation (number of branch circuits, discon-

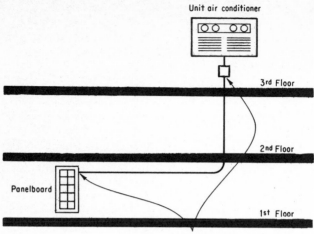

Because the air conditioner unit is not within sight from the panelboard, a suitable switch must be installed at the location of the air conditioner unit.

Fig. 440-3. For any fixed-wired A/C equipment, disconnect must be "within sight." (Sec. 440-14.)

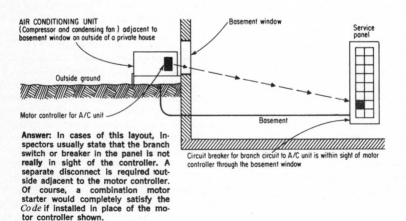

Answer: In cases of this layout, inspectors usually state that the branch switch or breaker in the panel is not really in sight of the controller. A separate disconnect is required outside adjacent to the motor controller. Of course, a combination motor starter would completely satisfy the *Code* if installed in place of the motor controller shown.

Circuit breaker for branch circuit to A/C unit is within sight of motor controller through the basement window

Fig. 440-4. "Within sight" disconnect must also be "readily accessible" at the equipment. (Sec. 440-14.)

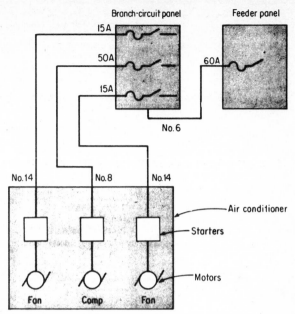

Fig. 440-5. A separate circuit may be run to each motor of A/C assembly. (Sec. 440-22.)

nects, etc.) is shown on the wiring diagram and/or marking required to be attached to the air conditioner.

In air conditioners employing two or more motors or a motor(s) and other loads operating from a single supply circuit, the motor running overcurrent protective devices (including thermal protectors for motors) and other factory-installed motor circuit components and wiring are investigated on the basis of compliance with the motor-branch-circuit short circuit and ground fault protection requirements of Sec. 430-53(c) of the 1968 Edition of the **National Electrical Code**. Such multimotor and combination load equipment is to be connected only to a circuit protected by fuses or a circuit breaker with a rating which does not exceed the value marked on the data plate. This marked protective device rating is the maximum for which the equipment has been investigated and found acceptable. Where the marking specifies fuses, the equipment is intended to be protected by fuses only.

The electrical contractor and inspector charged with wiring and approving such an installation can be sure that **Code** requirements have been met—provided that the branch-circuit protection as specified on the unit is not exceeded and the wiring and equipment is as indicated on the wiring diagram. Provision is made in such a unit for direct connection to the branch-circuit conductors; motors are wired internally by the manufacturer.

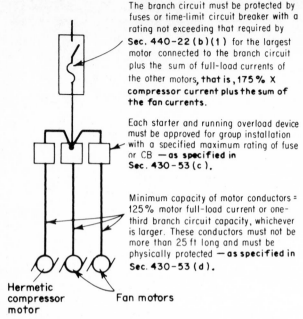

The branch circuit must be protected by fuses or time-limit circuit breaker with a rating not exceeding that required by **Sec. 440-22(b)(1)** for the largest motor connected to the branch circuit plus the sum of full-load currents of the other motors, **that is, 175% X compressor current plus the sum of the fan currents.**

Each starter and running overload device must be approved for group installation with a specified maximum rating of fuse or CB — **as specified in Sec. 430-53(c).**

Minimum capacity of motor conductors = 125% motor full-load current or one-third branch circuit capacity, whichever is larger. These conductors must not be more than 25 ft long and must be physically protected — **as specified in Sec. 430-53(d).**

Hermetic compressor motor   Fan motors

Fig. 440-6. Single multimotor branch circuit must conform to several rules. (Sec. 440-22.)

Units are sometimes encountered in which the manufacturer has wired separate fuse cutouts for the fan motors inside the enclosure to avoid meeting the requirements of Sec. 430-53(c) for group fusing as shown in Fig. 440-7. The cutouts are normally fed from the line terminals of the compressor starter.

Starter and disconnect sizes are the same as in Fig. 440-2, but starters and their overcurrent protection no longer need be approved for group fusing, and wiring inside the unit need not conform to Sec. 430-53(c). Fan motors may now be wired with No. 14 wire and protected with 15-A fuses. The supply circuit, feeding the same motors, will again be No. 6.

Since the fan motors are not subject to group fusing requirements, they will not restrict the maximum value of the main fuses. However, these fuses provide the only short-circuit protection for the compressor starter and conductors. Unless the compressor starter is approved for group fusing at a higher fuse rating, the fuses must not exceed 175 percent of the compressor full-load rating, or 45.5 A, calling for 50-A fuses. If needed to permit effective starting of all the motors, the fuses at the panel could be increased to 225 percent or 60-A fuses.

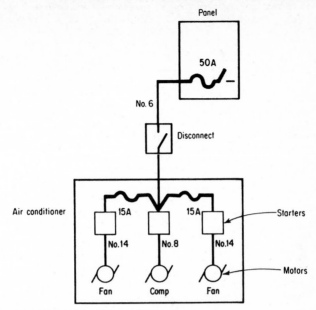

Main fuses: (175% X 26) = 45.5 amps (50-amp fuses)
Fan fuses: (300% X 4.4) =13.2 amps (15-amp fuses)
Fan conductors: (125% X 4.4) = 5.5 amps (No.14)

Fig. 440-7. Fan circuits are sometimes fused in multimotor assemblies. (Sec. 440-22.)

Figure 440-8 shows still another hookup for supplying a multimotor assembly. Units are wired with fuse blocks for all motors, as shown. The compressor motor would be fused at 50 A, with remaining fuses and conductors as above.

Main fuses no longer are subject to restriction by motor starters and are sized as feeder protection per Sec. 440-33 as shown by the diagram. This results in 60-A fuses, the differential between the two being too small. The need for time-delay fuses is indicated, using perhaps 30-A fuses for the compressor and 50-A fuses for the main.

The foregoing examples refer exclusively to fused disconnects and fused switches to maintain the continuity of calculations. However, Sec. 430-109 also recognizes the CB as a disconnecting means.

Figure 440-9 shows an arrangement which includes, in addition to the branch-circuit panel, a feeder panel for distribution to other units. The breakers in the branch-circuit panel serve as branch-circuit protection as well as the disconnecting means, and their ratings are computed from

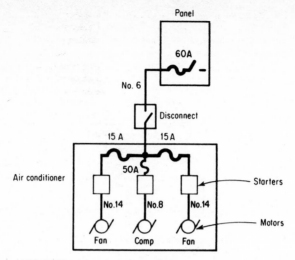

Main fuses: (175% X 26) + 4.4 + 4.4 = 54.3 amps (60-amp fuses)

Compressor fuses:175% X 26 = 45.5 amps (45-amp or 50-amp fuses)

Fig. 440-8. Each motor may have individual short-circuit protection. (Sec. 440-22.)

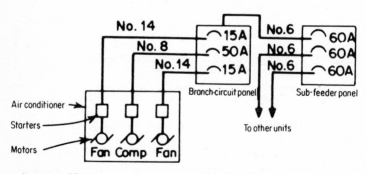

Compressor CB: Subfeeder conductors:
175% x 26 = 45.5amps (50-amp CB)   (125% x 26)+ 4.4+ 4.4 = 41.3 amps (No. 6)

Fan CBs: Subfeeder CB:
250% x 4.4 = 11.2 amps (15-amp CB)   (175% x 26)+ 4.4 + 4.4 = 54.3 amps (60a CB)

Fig. 440-9. Circuit breakers may be used for multimotor A/C assemblies. (Sec. 440-22.)

Secs. 430-52 and 440-22. Code Tables 430-150 and 430-151 would not be involved, since breakers are not rated in horsepower. Ratings of CBs in the branch-circuit panel are computed at 175 percent of motor current for the hermetic motor and at 250 percent of full-load current for the fan motors, to satisfy Table 430-152. Breakers in subfeeder panel are rated using Secs. 430-62 and 440-33.

Part **(c)** points out that data on a manufacturer's heater table take precedence over the maximum ratings set by Sec. 440-22(a) or (b).

440-32. Single Motor-Compressor. Branch-circuit conductors supplying a motor in a packaged unit are not sized in the same manner as other motor loads (Sec. 430-24). Instead of using the full-load current from Code Tables 430-148 to 430-150, the *marked* rated-load current or the *marked* branch-circuit selection current must be used in determining minimum required conductor ampacity. Note that branch-circuit selection current must be used where it is given.

Examples are shown in the typical circuits shown in Figs. 440-2 and 440-6.

440-33. Motor-Compressor(s)   With   or   Without   Additional   Motor Loads. Where more than one motor is connected to the same feeder or branch circuit, calculation of conductor sizes must provide ampere capacity at least equal to the sum of the nameplate rated-load currents or branch-circuit selection currents (using the higher of those values in all cases) plus 25 percent of the current (either rated-load or branch-circuit selection current for a hermetic motor or NEC table current for standard motor) of the largest motor of the group. Examples are shown in Figs. 440-2 and 440-6.

In Fig. 440-6, the question arises as to whether the No. 6 conductors feeding the unit may be decreased to No. 8 inside the unit to feed the compressor motor in the absence of fuses for this motor at the point of reduction. The status of the main feed to the unit—whether it should be considered a feeder or a branch circuit—is in doubt, since it is a branch circuit as far as the compressor motor is concerned and a feeder in that it also supplied the two fused fan circuits.

Considered solely as a branch circuit to the compressor, these conductors normally would be No. 8 to handle the 26-A compressor motor full-load current, protected at not more than 175 percent or 50-A fuses. Therefore, since 50-A fuses (or less) will actually be used for the main feed, they constitute proper protection for No. 8 conductors and their use should be permitted. The existence of No. 6 conductors over part of the circuit adds to its capacity and safety rather than detracting from it.

It is particularly important to keep in mind when selecting conductor sizes that the nameplate current ratings of air-conditioning motors are not constant maximum values during operation. Ratings are established and tested under standard conditions of temperature and humidity. Operation under weather conditions more severe than those at which the ratings are established will result in a greater running current, which can approach the maximum value permitted by the overcurrent device. Operating voltage less than the limits specified on the motor nameplate also contributes to higher full-load current values, even under standard conditions. Conductor capacity should be sufficient to handle these higher currents. Motor feeders are sized according to Sec. 440-33. Since overload protection may permit motors to run continuously overloaded (up to 140 percent full load), feeders must be sized to handle such overload. By basing calculations on the largest motor of the group, the extra capacity thus provided will normally be enough to handle any unforseen overload on the smaller motors involved with enough diversity existing in any normal group of motors to make consistent overloads on all motors at one time unlikely. However, a group of air-conditioning compressor motors all of the same size on a single feeder have a common function—reducing the ambient temperature. Except for slight possible variations, weather conditions affect each conditioner to the same degree and at the same time. Therefore, if one unit is operating at an overload, it is likely that the rest are also.

440-35. Multimotor and Combination-Load Equipment.   This rule ties into the data required by UL to be marked on such equipment. Refer to the UL data quoted in Sec. 440-22.

440-41. Rating (Controller).   The basic rule calls for a compressor controller to have a full-load current rating and a locked-rotor current rating not less than the compressor nameplate rated-load current or branch-circuit selection current (whichever is greater) and locked-rotor current. But, as noted for the disconnect under Sec. 440-12, for sealed (hermetic-type) refrigeration compressor motors, selection of the size of controller is slightly more involved than it is for standard applications. Because of their low-temperature operating conditions, hermetic motors can handle heavier loads than general-purpose motors of equivalent size and rotor-stator construction. And because the capabilities of such motors cannot be accurately defined in terms of horsepower, they are rated in terms of full-load current and locked-rotor current for polyphase motors and larger single-phase motors. Accordingly, selection of controller size is different than in the case of a general-purpose motor where horsepower ratings must be matched, because controllers marked in horsepower only must be carefully related to hermetic motors that are *not* marked in horsepower.

For controllers rated in horsepower, selection of the size required for a particular hermetic motor can be made after the nameplate rated-load current, or branch-circuit selection current, whichever is greater, and locked-rotor current of the motor have been converted to an equivalent horsepower rating. To get this equivalent horsepower rating, which is the required size of controller, the tables in Art. 430 must be used. First, the nameplate full-load current at the operating voltage of the motor is located in **Code** Tables 430-148, 149, or 150 and the horsepower rating which corresponds to it is noted. Then the nameplate locked-rotor current of the motor is found in Code Table 430-151, and again the corresponding horsepower is noted. In all tables, if the exact value of current is not listed, the next higher value should be used to obtain an equivalent horsepower, by reading horizontally to the horsepower column at the left side of those tables. If the two horsepower ratings obtained in this way are not the same, the larger value is taken as the required size of controller.

A typical example follows:

Given: A 230-V, 3-phase, squirrel-cage induction motor in a compressor has a nameplate rated-load current of 25.8 A and a nameplate locked-rotor current of 90 A.

Procedure: From Code Table 430-150, 28 A is the next higher current to the nameplate current of 25.8 under the column for 230-V motors and the corresponding horsepower rating for such a motor is 10 hp.

From Code Table 430-151, Art. 430, a locked-rotor current rating of 90 A for a 230-V, 3-phase motor requires a controller rated at 5 hp. The two values of horsepower obtained are not the same, so the higher rating is selected as the acceptable unit for the conditions. A 10-hp motor controller must be used.

Some controllers may be rated not in horsepower but in full-load current and locked-rotor current. For use with a hermetic motor, such a controller must simply have current ratings equal to or greater than the nameplate rated-load current and locked-rotor current of the motor.

440-52. Application and Selection.   The basic rule of part **(a)** calls for a running overload relay set to trip at not more than 140 percent of the rated-load current of a motor-compressor. If a fuse or time-delay CB is used to provide overload protection, it must be rated not over 125 percent of the compressor rated-load current. Note that those are absolute maximum values of overload protection and no permission is given to go to "the next higher standard rating"of protection where 1.4 or 1.25 times motor current does not yield an amp value that exactly corresponds to a standard rating of a relay or of a fuse or CB.

Running overload protective devices for a motor are necessary to protect the motor, its associated controls, and the branch-circuit conductors against heat damage due to excessive motor currents. High currents may be caused by the motor being overloaded for a considerable period of time, by consistently low or unbalanced line voltage, by single-phasing of a polyphase motor, or by the motor stalling or failing to start.

Damage may occur more quickly to a hermetic motor which stalls or fails to start than to a conventional open-type motor. Due to the presence of the cool refrigerant atmosphere under normal conditions, a hermetic motor is permitted to operate at a rated current which is closer to the locked-rotor current than is the same rated current of an open-type motor of the same nominal horsepower rating. The curves of Fig. 440-10

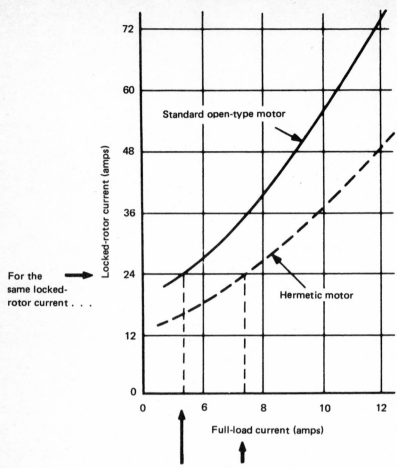

For the same locked-rotor current . . .

. . . a hermetic motor operates at a higher load current than a standard motor

Fig. 440-10. Hermetic motors operate at full-load currents closer to locked-rotor currents. (Sec. 440-52.)

show the typical relation between locked-rotor and full-loaded currents of small open-type and hermetic motors. Because a hermetic motor operates within the refrigerant atmosphere, it is constantly cooled by that atmosphere. As a result, a given size of motor may be operated at a higher current than it could be if it were used as an open, general-purpose motor without the refrigerant cycle to remove heat from the windings. In effect, a hermetic motor is operated overloaded because the cooling cycle prevents overheating. For instance, a 5-hp open motor can be loaded as if it were a 7½-hp motor when it is cooled by the refrigerant. The full-load operating current of such a motor is higher than the normal current drawn by a 5-hp load and is, therefore, closer to the value of locked-rotor current, which is the same no matter how the motor is used.

When the rotor of a hermetic motor is slowed down because of overload or is at a standstill, there is not sufficient circulation of the refrigerant to carry away the heat; and heat builds up in the windings. Special quick-acting thermal and hydraulic-magnetic devices have been developed to reduce the time required to disconnect the hermetic motor from the line before damage occurs when an overload condition develops.

Room air conditioners and packaged unit compressors are normally required to incorporate running overload protection which will restrict the heat rise to definite maximum safe temperatures in case of locked-rotor conditions. Room conditioners normally use inherent protectors built into the compressor housing which respond to the temperature of the housing. Larger units also often use inherent protection in addition to quick-acting overload heaters installed in the motor starter, which respond only to current. These protective methods are covered in paragraphs **(2)** and **(4)** of Sec. 440-52(a).

The electrical installer will normally be concerned with the running overcurrent protection of a hermetic motor only when it becomes necessary to replace the existing devices supplied with the equipment. For this purpose, compressor manufacturers' warranties explicitly specify catalog numbers of replacements which are to be used to ensure proper operation of the equipment.

440-60. General (Room Air Conditioners). These rules on room air-conditioning units recognize that such units are basically appliances, are low-capacity electrical loads, and may be supplied either by an individual branch circuit to a unit conditioner or by connection to a branch circuit that also supplies lighting and/or other appliances. For all Code discussion purposes, an air-conditioning unit of the window, console, or through-the-wall type is classified as a "fixed appliance"—which is described in Art. 100 as "fastened or otherwise secured at a specific location." Such an appliance may be cord-connected or it may be fixed-wired (so-called "permanently connected").

Section 210-23 of Art. 210 on "Branch Circuits" must also be applied in cases where a unit room air conditioner is connected to a branch circuit supplying lighting or other appliance load.

When a unit air conditioner is connected to a circuit supplying lighting and/or one or more appliances that are not motor loads, the rules of Art. 210 must be observed:

1. Section 210-22(a) says that "where a circuit supplies only air-conditioning and/or refrigerating equipment, Article 440 shall apply."

2. For plug connection of the A/C unit, Sec. 210-7(a) says that receptacles installed on 15- and 20-A branch circuits must be of the grounding type and must have their grounding terminal effectively connected to a grounding conductor or grounded raceway or metal cable armor.

3. On 15- and 20-A branch circuits the total rating of a unit air conditioner must not exceed 50 percent of the branch-circuit rating when lighting units or portable appliances are also supplied [Sec. 210-23(a)]. It was on the basis of that rule that the 7½-A air conditioner was developed. Being 50 percent of a 15-A branch circuit, such units are acceptable for connection to a receptacle on a 15-A or 20-A circuit that supplies lighting and receptacle outlets.

4. A branch circuit larger than 20 A may *not* be used to supply a unit conditioner plus a lighting load. Circuits rated 25, 30, 40, or 50 A may be used to supply fixed lighting or appliances—but not both types of loads.

440-61. Grounding. Air-conditioner units that are connected by permanent wiring must be grounded in accordance with the basic rules of Sec. 250-42 covering equipment that is "fastened in place or connected by permanent wiring." Section 250-45 covers grounding of cord- and plug-connected air conditioners by means of an equipment grounding conductor run within the supply cord for each such unit.

The nameplate marking of a room air conditioner shall be used in determining the branch-circuit requirements, and each unit shall be considered as a single motor unless the nameplate is otherwise marked. If the nameplate is marked to indicate two or more motors, Secs. 430-53 and 440-22(b) (1) must be satisfied, covering the use of several motors on one branch circuit.

440-62. Branch-Circuit Requirements. Even though a room air conditioner contains more than one motor (usually the hermetic compressor motor and the fan motor), this rule notes that for a cord- and plug-connected air conditioner the entire unit assembly may be treated as a single-motor load under the conditions given.

Examples of the rule of part **(b)** are shown in Fig. 440-11. The total marked rating of any cord- and plug-connected air-conditioning unit must *not* exceed 80 percent of the rating of a branch circuit which does not supply lighting units or other appliances, for units rated up to 40 A, 250 V, single phase.

As noted under Sec. 440-60, Sec. 210-22(a) seems to say that only Art. 440 and not Art. 210 applies when the circuit supplies only a motor-operated load. But, since Arts. 430 and 440 do not "rate" branch circuits—either on the basis of the size of the short-circuit protective device or the size of the conductors—a question arises about the meaning of the phrase "80 percent of the rating of a branch circuit." Does that mean 80

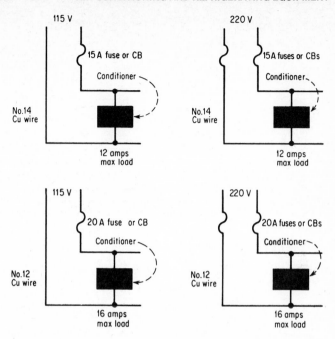

NOTE: 30-A circuits with No. 10 wire may supply units rated 17 to 24 A; 40- A circuits with No. 8 wire may supply units rated 25 to 32 A; and 50- A circuits with No. 6 wire may supply units rated 33 to 40-A.

Fig. 440-11. Room air conditioners must not load an individual branch circuit over 80 percent of rating. (Sec. 440-62.)

percent of the rating of the fuse or CB? The answer is: It means 80 percent of the rating of the protective device, which rating is not more than the amp rating of the circuit wire. The circuit as described here is taken to be a circuit with "rating" as given in Art. 210 and covered by part **(4)** of Sec. 440-62(a).

As part **(c)** of this section notes, the total marked rating of air-conditioning equipment must *not* exceed 50 percent of the rating of a branch circuit which *also* supplies lighting or other appliances. And Sec. 210-22(a) and Sec. 210-23 must be observed. From the rule, we can see that the **Code** permits air-conditioning units to be plugged into existing circuits which supply lighting loads or other appliances. By the provisions of this section, such a conditioner must not draw more than 7½ A full load (nameplate rating) when connected to a 15-A circuit; not more than 10 A when connected to a 20-A circuit. In addition, Sec. 210-22(a) requires that the branch-circuit capacity must not be less than 125 percent of the air-conditioner load plus the sum of the other loads. The existing load on the circuit (lights or other appliances) must be low enough so that the total load on the circuit after the addition of 125 percent of the ampere load of the air conditioner is not greater than 15 A in the case of the 15-A circuit, nor greater than 20 A on a 20-A circuit. This is in accordance with Sec. 210-22(a) which restricts the total loading on such a circuit.

Assuming that a 7½-A conditioner is connected to such a 15-A existing circuit, it would mean that the circuit before the addition of the air-conditioner load of 7.5 × 1.25, or 10 A, could have been loaded to no more than 5 A, as shown in Fig. 440-12.

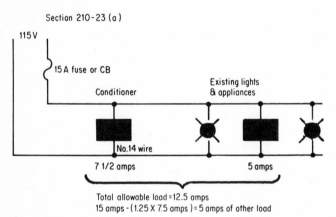

Fig. 440-12. Room air conditioner must not exceed 50 percent of circuit rating if other loads are supplied. (Sec. 440-62.)

A problem exists in connecting two or more conditioners to the same circuit. Compressor and fan motors and their controls, when installed in the same enclosure and fed by one circuit, are approved by UL for group installation when tested as a unit appliance. However, an air conditioner's component parts carry no general group-fusing approval which would permit the several separate conditioners to operate on the same circuit in accordance with Sec. 430-53(c). To connect more than one conditioner to the same branch circuit, the provisions of either Secs. 430-53(a) or 430-53(b) must be fulfilled, treating each cord-connected conditioner as a single-motor load.

According to Sec. 430-53(a), which applies only to motors rated not over 6 A, two 115-V, 6-A conditioners could be used on a 15-A circuit; three 5-A conditioners could be used on a 20-A circuit which supplies no other load; and two 220-V, 6-A units could be operated on a 15-A circuit as shown in Fig. 440-13. But it could be argued that the maximum load in

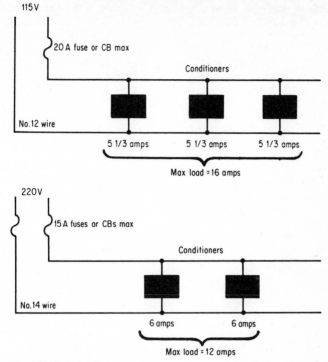

Fig. 440-13. Rules limit use of two or more room conditioners on single circuit. (Sec. 440-62.)

any such application may be calculated at 125 percent times current of largest air conditioner plus the sum of load currents of the additional air conditioners, with that total current being permitted right up to the rating of the circuit.

However, most conditioners sold today exceed 6-A full-load current. As a result, the application of two or more units as permitted by Sec. 430-53(a) is limited. But Sec. 430-53(b) does offer considerable opportunity for using more than one air conditioner on a single circuit. Figure 440-14 shows two examples of such application, which can be used if the branch-circuit protective device will not open under the most severe normal conditions which might be encountered. Although that usage is a complex connection among several Code rules and requires clearance with inspection authorities, it can provide very substantial economies.

Many local codes avoid the complications of connecting conditioners to existing circuits and connecting more than one conditioner to the same circuit by requiring a separate branch circuit for each conditioner. Multiple installations involving many room conditioners such as are frequently

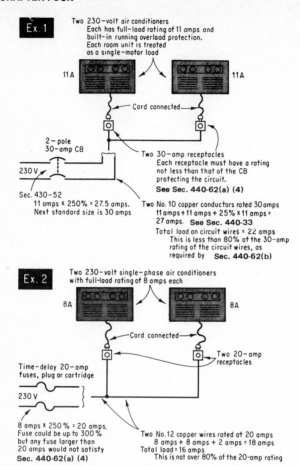

Ex. 1

Two 230−volt air conditioners
Each has full-load rating of 11 amps and
built-in running overload protection.
Each room unit is treated
as a single−motor load

11 A   11A

Cord connected

2 − pole
30−amp CB

Two 30−amp receptacles
Each receptacle must have a rating
not less than that of the CB
protecting the circuit.
See Sec. 440-62(a) (4)

230 V

Sec. 430−52
11 amps x 250% = 27.5 amps.
Next standard size is 30 amps

Two No. 10 copper conductors rated 30 amps
11 amps + 11 amps + 25% x 11 amps =
27 amps. **See Sec. 440-33**
Total load on circuit wires = 22 amps
This is less than 80% of the 30−amp
rating of the circuit wires, as
required by **Sec. 440-62(b)**

Ex. 2

Two 230−volt single−phase air conditioners
with full-load rating of 8 amps each

8A   8A

Cord connected

Two 20−amp
receptacles

Time−delay 20−amp
fuses, plug or cartridge

230 V

8 amps x 250% = 20 amps.
Fuse could be up to 300%
but any fuse larger than
20 amps would not satisfy
Sec. 440-62(a) (4)

Two No.12 copper wires rated at 20 amps
8 amps + 8 amps + 2 amps = 18 amps
Total load = 16 amps
This is not over 80% of the 20−amp rating

NOTE: Fuse or CB sizing may be required to conform to Sec.
440-22 (b), with a maximum rating of 175% times load current
of one conditioner plus the current of the other conditioner.
Or the 175% value itself may be held as the maximum rating
of branch-current protection.

Fig. 440-14. These hookups have been accepted as conforming to
rules of Arts. 440 and 430. (Sec. 440-62.)

encountered in hotels, offices, etc., require careful planning to meet Code requirements and yet minimize expensive branch-circuit lengths.

WATCH OUT! The NE Code refers to motor-operated appliances and/or to room air conditioners in Arts. 210, 422, and 440. Great care must be exercised in correlating the various Code rules in these different articles to assure effective compliance with the letter and spirit of Code meaning. There is much crossover in terminology and references making it difficult to tell whether a room air conditioner should be treated as an appliance circuit load or a motor load. However, a step-by-step approach to the problem which keeps in mind the intent of these provisions can resolve confusing points. Since the manufacturer is required to supply the motor-running overcurrent protection, no problems should arise concerning these devices. For larger units connected permanently to the distribution system, these can be treated directly as hermetic motor loads, using the provisions of Art. 440.

It may be assumed that a window or through-the-wall unit will operate satisfactorily on a standard fuse of the same rating as its attachment plug cap if there is no marking to the contrary on the unit. In any event, a time-delay fuse of the same or smaller rating could be substituted. If CBs are used for branch-circuit protection, a 15-A breaker will normally hold the starting current if a standard 15-A fuse will, since such breakers have inherent time delay. If the unit is marked to require a 15-A time-delay fuse and a 15-A breaker will not hold the starting current, few inspectors will object to the use of a 20-A breaker, since Art. 430 permits such a procedure for motor loads.

Normally, starting problems are not severe with these units, since the low inertia of present-day motor-compressor combinations permits them to reach full speed within a few cycles. Such a rapid drop in starting current is usually well within the time permitted by the trip or rupture characteristics of the breaker or fuse.

Similarly, the question of wire size may be resolved by application of either Arts. 210, 422, or 440. Rarely do room conditioners even as large as 2 tons take more than 13-A running current; hence No. 12 copper or No. 10 aluminum conductors are more than sufficient. In addition, many local codes prohibit use of conductors smaller than No. 12. In localities where No. 14 wire may be used, provisions of Sec. 440-62(b), restricting the loading to 80 percent of the circuit rating, must determine the wire size, where "rating" is interpreted as referring to the conductor carrying capacity. If Art. 440 is used to determine the wire size, the 125 percent requirement of Sec. 440-32 gives the same result.

Figure 440-15 shows one feeder of an installation involving many room conditioners which practically eliminates branch-circuit wiring and will serve to illustrate the complications of circuit calculations for a multiple-unit installation. Total running current of each unit is 12 A as shown; hence No. 14 copper wire could be used for branch-circuit conductors, protected by a 15-A fuse—either standard or time-delay. However, if the

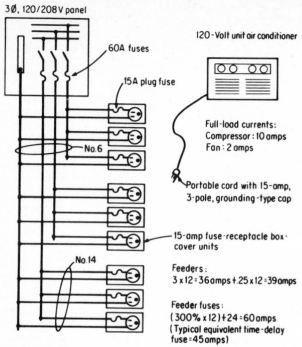

Fig. 440-15. This type of circuiting was used for air conditioners in a hotel modernization project. (Sec. 440-62.)

appropriate conductors of a 4-wire, 3-phase feeder were routed to the location of each conditioner and a combination fuseholder and receptacle installed as shown, the only existing branch-circuit conductors would be the jumpers between the feeder, the fuseholder, and the receptacles. These jumpers, then, could be No. 14 wire. Assuming that the fuse-receptacle unit is mounted directly on or in close proximity with the junction box in which the tap to the feeder is made, the No. 14 wire is justified from the fuse to the feeder since it is not over 10 ft long and is sufficient for the load supplied (Sec. 240-21, Exception No. 2). Since both motors usually start simultaneously, the total unit current is used to compute feeder conductor size and protection. 125 percent times 12 plus 24 is 39 A, permitting No. 8 conductors. However, this is practically the limit of the circuit's capacity; there is no provision for overload, and voltage drop is very likely to be a factor at the end of the feeder. Therefore No. 6 conductors should be used.

Feeder protection is calculated on the basis of 300 percent times 12 plus 24 or 60-A fuses. Substitution of time-delay fuses for this 39-A feeder load would likely permit 45-A fuses.

Important: The rules of Sec. 440-62 apply only to cord- and plug-connected room air conditioners. A unit room air conditioner that has a *fixed* (not cord and plug) connection to its supply must be treated as a group of several individual motors and protected in accordance with Secs. 430-53 and 440-22(b), covering several motors on one branch.

440-63. Disconnecting Means. A disconnect is required for every unit air conditioner. An attachment plug and receptacle or a separable connector may serve as the disconnecting means (Fig. 440-16).

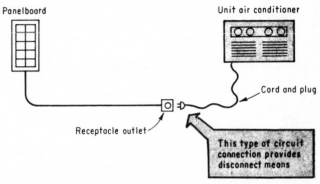

Fig. 440-16. Plug-and-receptacle serves as required disconnect means. (Sec. 440-63.)

If a fixed connection is made to an A/C unit from the branch-circuit wiring system (i.e., not a plug-in connection to a receptacle), consideration must be given to a means of disconnect, as required in Secs. 422-21 and 422-24 for appliances:

- For unit air conditioners in any type of occupancy, the branch-circuit switch or CB may, where readily accessible to the user of the appliance, serve as the disconnecting means. Figure 440-17 shows this, but the switch or CB is permitted to be out of sight by the Exception to Sec. 422-26 when the A/C unit has an internal OFF switch—which all units do have. And Sec. 422-26 requires the disconnect means for a motor-driven appliance to be within sight from the air-conditioner unit.

   Because air conditioners have unit switches within them, the disconnect provisions of Sec. 422-24 may be applied. The internal unit switch with a marked OFF position that opens all ungrounded conductors may serve as the disconnect and is considered within sight as required by Sec. 422-26 in any case where there is another disconnect means as follows:

- In multifamily (more than two) dwellings, the other disconnect means must be within the apartment where the conditioner is installed or on the same floor as the apartment.

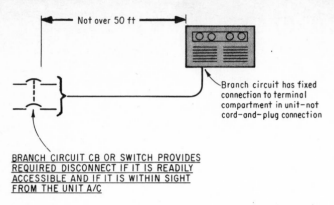

Not over 50 ft

Branch circuit has fixed
connection to terminal
compartment in unit—not
cord—and—plug connection

BRANCH CIRCUIT CB OR SWITCH PROVIDES
REQUIRED DISCONNECT IF IT IS READILY
ACCESSIBLE AND IF IT IS WITHIN SIGHT
FROM THE UNIT A/C

NOTE: Because A/C units have the "unit switch" described in Sec.
422-24, the exception to Sec. 422-26 voids the necessity for the
branch-circuit CB or switch to be within sight from the A/C unit.

Fig. 440-17. Branch circuit CB or switch may serve as disconnect. (Sec. 440-63.)

- In two-family dwellings, the other disconnect may be outside the apartment in which the appliance is installed. It may be the service disconnect.
- In single-family dwellings, the service disconnect may serve as the other disconnect means—whether the branch circuit to the conditioner is fed from plug fuses or from a breaker or switch (Fig. 440-18).

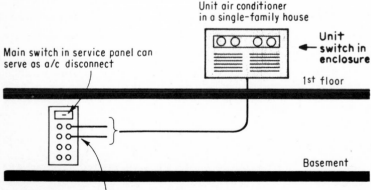

Unit air conditioner
in a single-family house

Main switch in service panel can
serve as a/c disconnect

Unit
switch in
enclosure

1st floor

Basement

Plug fuses in panel provide branch circuit protection
for a/c circuit **but cannot** provide disconnect means

Fig. 440-18. Service disconnect may be the "other disconnect" for A/C unit in private house. (Sec. 440-63.)

ARTICLE 445. GENERATORS

445-4. Overcurrent Protection.   Alternating-current generators can be so designed that on excessive overload the voltage falls off sufficiently to limit the current and power output to values that will not damage the generator during a short period of time. Whether or not automatic overcurrent protection of a generator should be omitted in any particular case is a question that can best be answered by the manufacturer of the generator. It is common practice to operate an exciter without overcurrent protection, rather than risk the shutdown of the main generator due to accidental opening of the exciter fuse or CB.

Figure 445-1 shows the connections of a 2-wire DC generator with a

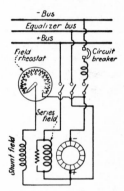

Fig. 445-1. With this connection, a single-pole CB can protect a 2-wire DC generator. (Sec. 445-4.)

single-pole protective device. If the machine is operated in multiple with one or more other generators, and so has an equalizer lead connected to the positive terminal, the current may divide at the positive terminal, part passing through the series field and positive lead and part passing through the equalizer lead. The entire current generated passes through the negative lead; therefore the fuse or CB, or at least the operating coil of a CB, must be placed in the negative lead. The protective device should not open the shunt-field circuit, because if this circuit were opened with the field at full strength, a very high voltage would be induced which might break down the insulation of the field winding.

Paragraph **(c)** is intended to apply particularly to generators used in electrolytic work. Where such a generator forms part of a motor-generator set, no fuse or CB is necessary in the generator leads if the motor-running protective device will open when the generator delivers 150 percent of its rated full-load current.

In paragraph **(d)**, use of a balancer set to obtain a 3-wire system from a 2-wire main generator is covered, as shown in Fig. 445-2. Each of the two generators used as a balancer set carries approximately one-half the unbalanced load; hence these two machines are always much smaller than the main generator. In case of an excessive unbalance of the load,

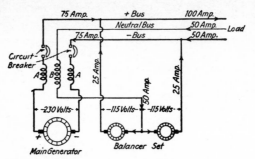

Fig. 445-2. A balancer set supplies the unbalanced neutral current of a 3-wire system, with each generator carrying 25 of the 50-A unbalance. (Sec. 445-4.)

the balancer set might be overloaded while there is no overload on the main generator. This condition may be guarded against by installing a double-pole CB with one pole connected in each lead of the main generator and with the operating coil properly designed to be connected in the neutral of the 3-wire system. In Fig. 445-2, the CB is arranged so as to be operated by either one of the coils A in the leads from the main generator or by coil B in the neutral lead from the balancer set.

445-6. Protection of Live Parts. As a general rule, no generator should be "accessible to unqualified persons." If necessary to place a generator operating at over 150 V to ground in a location where it is so exposed, the commutator or collector rings, brushes, and any exposed terminals should be provided with guards which will prevent any accidental contact with these live parts.

ARTICLE 450. TRANSFORMERS AND TRANSFORMER VAULTS

450-1. Scope. The Exceptions indicate those transformer applications that are not subject to the rules of Art. 450. The Exceptions shown in Fig. 450-1 are as follows:

Exception No. 2 excludes any dry-type transformer that is a component part of manufactured equipment, provided that the transformer complies with the requirements for such equipment. Those requirements include UL standards on the construction of the particular equipment. This exclusion applies, for instance, to control transformers within a motor starter or within a motor control center. However, although such transformers do not have to be protected in accordance with Sec. 450-3(b), such control transformer circuits must have their control conductors protected as described under Sec. 430-72(b). But a separate control

Exception No. 2

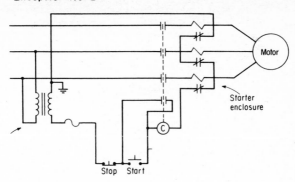

Exception No. 6

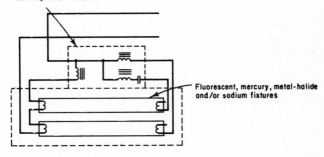

Fluorescent, mercury, metal-halide and/or sodium fixtures

Exception No. 8

If a transformer is used for research, development or testing . . .

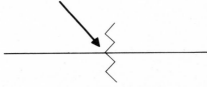

. . . it is exempt from the rules of Article 450—provided unqualified personnel are protected from energized parts.

Fig. 450-1. These transformer applications are exempt from the rules of Art. 450. (Sec. 450-1.)

transformer—one that is external to other equipment and is not an integral part of any other piece of equipment—must conform to the protection rules of Sec. 450-3 and other rules in Art. 450.

Exception No. 6 points out that ballasts for electric-discharge lighting (although they *are* transformers—either autotransformers or separate-winding, magnetically coupled types) are treated as lighting accessories rather than transformers.

Exception No. 8 notes that liquid-filled or dry-type transformers used for research, development, or testing are exempt from the requirements of Art. 450 provided that effective arrangements are made to safeguard any unqualified persons from contacting high-voltage terminals or energized conductors. Again, in the interest of the unusual conditions that frequently prevail in industrial occupancy, this rule recognizes that transformers used for research, development, or testing are commonly under the sole control of entirely competent individuals and exempts such special applications from the normal rules that apply to general-purpose transformers used for distribution within buildings and for energy supply to utilization equipment, controls, signals, communications, and the like. See Fig. 450-2.

UL listing The *Electrical Construction Materials Directory* of the UL lists "Transformers—Power." To satisfy **NE Code** and OSHA regulations, as

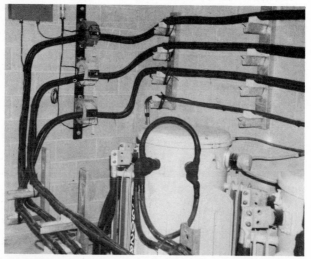

Fig. 450-2. Transformers that are set up in a laboratory to derive power for purposes of testing other equipment or powering an experiment are exempt from the rules of Art. 450 provided care is taken to protect personnel from any hazards due to exposed energized parts. (Sec. 450-1.)

well as local code rules on acceptability of equipment, any transformers of the types and sizes covered by UL listing must be so listed. Use of an unlisted transformer of a type and size covered by UL listing would certainly be considered a violation of the spirit of NE Code Sec. 110-2.

UL listing covers "air-cooled" types rated up to 333 kVA for single-phase transformers and up to 1,000 kVA for 3-phase units (all up to 600-V rating).

450-2. Location. Accessibility is an important location feature of transformer installation. The NE Code generally requires a transformer (whether liquid-filled or dry-type) to be readily accessible to qualified personnel for inspection and maintenance (Fig. 450-3). That is, it must be capable of being reached quickly for operation, repair, or inspection

Fig. 450-3. Basic rule calls for every transformer to have ready, easy, direct access for inspection or maintenance. (Sec. 450-2.)

without requiring use of a portable ladder to get at it, and it must not be necessary to climb over or remove obstacles to reach it. A transformer may be mounted on a platform or balcony, but there must be fixed stairs or a fixed ladder for access to the transformer (Fig. 450-4). But Exceptions are made:

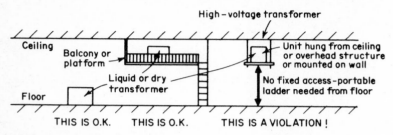

Fig. 450-4. Transformers must be "readily accessible" without need for portable ladder to reach them. (Sec. 450-2.)

Exception No. 1 permits dry-type transformers rated 600 V or less to be located "in the *open* on walls, columns, or structures"—without the need to be readily accessible. A transformer suspended from the ceiling or hung on a wall—in which cases a ladder would be required to reach them because they are over 6½ ft above the floor (see Sec. 380-8)—would be O.K., as shown in Fig. 450-5. And Exception No. 2 permits dry-type transformers up to 600 V, 50 kVA, to be installed in fire-resistant hollow spaces of buildings not permanently closed in by structure, provided the transformer is designed to have adequate ventilation for such installation. See Fig. 450-6.

Note in Exception No. 1 that a transformer *may* be *not* readily accessible only if it is located in the *open*. The words "in the open" do not readily and surely relate to such words as "concealed" or "exposed." But it is reasonable to conclude that "in the *open*" would be difficult to equate with "above a suspended ceiling." The latter location is in a generally smaller, confined space in which the transformer is not visible. Because the basic rule of Sec. 450-2 is that all transformers must be readily accessible, Exception No. 1 must be taken as a condition in which a transformer does *not* have to be readily accessible—i.e., that it may be mounted up high where a portable ladder would be needed to get at it. But the words "in the open" could logically be taken to prohibit use of the transformer above a suspended ceiling (Fig. 450-7).

It should be noted that the Exception No. 1 to this rule, which permits

Fig. 450-5. Transformer mounted on wall (or suspended from ceiling) would be considered *not* readily accessible because a ladder would be needed to reach it. But, because it is "in the open," such use conforms to Exception No. 1. (Sec. 450-2.)

high mounting that makes transformers *not* "readily accessible" applies to "dry-type transformers" only. As a result, high mounting of oil-filled transformers—as shown in Fig. 450-8—is not covered by that Exception and could be considered a violation of the *basic* rule of this section. However, Sec. 450-26 on oil-filled transformers installed outdoors actually contains an exception to the rule of Sec. 450-2. The last sentence of Sec. 450-26 requires outdoor oil-filled units to comply with the National Electrical Safety Code (*not* the NE Code). That code covers use of such transformers as shown in Fig. 450-8.

450-3. Overcurrent Protection. This section covers overcurrent protection in great detail, and other Code rules (Secs. 240-21, 240-40, and 384-16 in particular) usually get involved in transformer applications. Although there is no rule on disconnects, use of required overcurrent

Fig. 450-6. Recessed mounting of dry-type transformers is permitted within "fire-resistant hollow spaces," as in hospitals, schools, and other commercial or institutional buildings. (Sec. 450-2.)

protection results in the presence of a fused switch or CB that may serve as disconnecting means.

It should be understood that the overcurrent protection required by this section is for transformers *only*. Such overcurrent protection will not necessarily protect the primary or secondary conductors or equipment connected on the secondary side of the transformer. Using overcurrent protection to the maximum values permitted by these rules would require much larger conductors than the full-load current rating of the transformer (other than permitted in the 25-ft tap rule in Sec. 240-21,

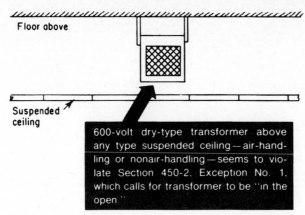

Floor above

Suspended
ceiling

600-volt dry-type transformer above
any type suspended ceiling — air-handling or nonair-handling — seems to violate Section 450-2, Exception No. 1,
which calls for transformer to be ''in the
open.''

Fig. 450-7. Watch out for transformers above suspended ceilings. (Sec.
450-2.)

Exception No. 8). Accordingly, to avoid using oversized conductors,
overcurrent devices should be selected at about 110 to 125 percent of the
transformer full-load current rating. And when using such smaller overcurrent protection, devices should be of the time-delay type (on the
primary side) to compensate for inrush currents which reach 8 to 10
times the full-load primary current of the transformer for about $^1/_{10}$ sec
when energized initially.

In approaching a transformer installation it is best to use a one-line
diagram, such as shown in the accompanying sketches. Then by applying
the tap rules in Sec. 240-21 proper protection of the conductors and
equipment, which are part of the system, will be achieved. See comments
following Sec. 240-21.

Section 230-207 and Sec. 240-3, Exception No. 5, are the only Code
rules that consider properly sized primary overcurrent devices to protect
the secondary conductors without secondary protection and no limit to
the length of secondary conductors. The strict requirements in Sec. 230-
207 apply where the transformers are in a *vault*, the primary load-
interrupter switch is manually operable from outside the vault, and large
secondary conductors are provided to achieve reflected protection
through the transformer to the primary overcurrent protection. *It is
important to note that primary circuit protection for transformer protection is not
acceptable as suitable protection for the secondary circuit conductors*—even if the
secondary conductors have an ampacity equal to the ampacity of the
primary conductors times the primary/secondary voltage ratio. See Sec.
240-3, Exception No. 5.

On 3- and 4-wire transformer secondaries, it is possible that an unbal-

Fig. 450-8. High mounting of oil-filled transformers would require use of a portable ladder for access to the units. But Sec. 450-26 covers such units installed on poles or structures. (Sec. 450-2.)

anced load may greatly exceed the secondary conductor ampacity, which was selected assuming balanced conditions. Because of this, the NE Code does not permit the protection of secondary conductors by overcurrent devices operating through a transformer from the primary of a transformer having a 3-wire or 4-wire secondary. For other than 2-wire to 2-wire transformers, protection of secondary conductors has to be provided completely separately from any primary-side protection. Section 384-16(d) states that required main protection for a lighting panel on the secondary side of a transformer must be located on the secondary side.

However, Sec. 240-3, Exception No. 5, recognizes such primary protection of the secondary of single-phase, 2-wire to 2-wire transformers if the primary OC protection complies with Sec. 450-3 and does not exceed the value determined by multiplying the secondary conductor ampacity by the secondary-to-primary transformer voltage ratio. The lengths of the primary or secondary conductors are not limited by this Exception.

In designing transformer circuits, the rules of Sec. 450-3 can be coordinated with Sec. 240-21, Exception No. 8, which provides special rules for tap conductors used with transformers. This Exception would be used mainly where the primary OC devices are rated according to Sec. 450-3(b) (2), or where the combined primary and secondary feeder lengths from the primary OC device to the secondary tap exceed 10 ft.

Where secondary feeder taps do *not* exceed 10 ft in length, the requirements of Sec. 240-21, Exception No. 2, could apply as in the case of any other feeder tap with no restriction on the size of the feeder overcurrent device ahead of the tap. In applying the tap rules in Exception Nos. 2 and 8, the requirements of Sec. 450-3 on transformer overcurrent protection must always be satisfied.

Part **(a)** of this section sets rules for overcurrent protection of any transformer (dry-type or liquid-filled) rated over 600 V. Protection may be provided either by a protective device of specified rating on the transformer primary or by a combination of protective devices of specified ratings on both the primary and secondary. Figure 450-9 shows the basic rules of such overcurrent protection. The fact that E-rated fuses used for high-voltage circuits are given melting times at 200 percent of their continuous current rating explains why this Code rule sets 150 percent of primary current as the maximum fuse rating but permits CBs up to 300 percent. In effect, the 150 percent for fuses times 2 (200 percent) becomes 300 percent—the maximum value allowed for a CB.

Part **(b)** of this section covers all transformers—oil-filled, high-fire-point liquid-insulated, and dry-type—rated up to 600 V. The step-by-step approach to such protection is as follows:

1. For any transformer rated 600 V or less (i.e., the rating of neither the primary nor the secondary winding is over 600 V), the basic overcurrent protection may be provided just on the primary side [Sec. 450-3(b) (1)] or may be a combination of protection on *both* the primary and secondary sides [Sec. 450-3(b) (2)].

    If a transformer is to be protected by means of a CB or set of fuses only on the primary side of the transformer, the basic arrangement is as shown in Fig. 450-10.

    In that layout, a CB or a set of fuses rated not over 125 percent of the transformer rated primary full-load current provides all the overcurrent protection required by the NE Code for the transformer. This overcurrent protection is in the feeder circuit to the transformer and is logically placed at the supply end of the feeder so the same overcurrent device may also provide the overcurrent

On the primary side, either at the transformer or at the supply end of the primary circuit, by fuses rated at not more than 150% of rated primary current

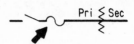

NOTE: Where 150% of primary current does not correspond to a standard fuse rating, the next higher size is permitted.

On the primary side, either at the transformer or at the supply end of the primary circuit, by a circuit breaker rated at not more than 300% of rated primary current

NOTE: Where 300% of primary current does not correspond to a standard CB trip setting, the next lower trip must be used.

On the primary side by a feeder overcurrent device sized from Table 450-3(a)(2), provided that the transformer is equipped with a coordinated thermal overload protection or has a secondary overcurrent device sized from Table 450-3(a)(2).

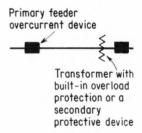

Fig. 450-9. High-voltage transformers (rated over 600 V, dry or oil- or askarel-filled) must be protected in one of these ways. (Sec. 450-3.)

protection required for the primary feeder conductors. There is no limit on the distance between primary protection and the transformer. When the correct maximum rating for transformer protection is selected and installed at any point on the supply side of the transformer (either near or far from the transformer), then feeder circuit conductors must be sized so that the CB or fuses selected will provide the proper protection as required for the conductors. The ampacity of the feeder conductors must be at least equal to the amp rating of the CB or fuses unless Sec. 240-3, Exception No. 1, is

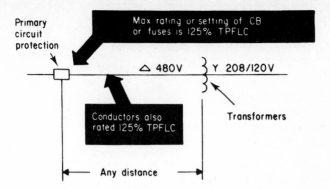

Primary circuit protection

Max rating or setting of CB or fuses is 125% TPFLC

△ 480V } Y 208/120V

Conductors also rated 125% TPFLC

Transformers

|← Any distance →|

TPFLC = transformer primary full-load current (nameplate rating)

Fig. 450-10. This is the basic rule on primary-side transformer protection. (Sec. 450-3.)

satisfied. That is, when the rating of the overcurrent protection selected is not more than 125 percent of rated primary current, the primary feeder conductor may have an ampacity such that the overcurrent device is the next higher standard rating.

The rules set down for protection of a 600-V transformer by a CB or set of fuses in its primary circuit are given in Fig. 450-11 for transformers with rated primary current of 9 A or more. Note that "the next higher standard" rating of protection may be used, if needed. Figure 450-12 shows the *absolute* maximum values of protection for smaller transformers. When using the 1.67 or 3 times factor, if the resultant current value is not exactly equal to a standard rating of fuse or CB, then the next *lower* standard rated fuse or CB must be used.

When the rules of Sec. 450-3(b) (1) are observed, the transformer itself is properly protected and the primary feeder conductors, if sized to correspond, may be provided with the protection required by Sec. 240-3. But all considerations on the secondary side of the transformer then have to be separately and independently evaluated. When a transformer is provided with primary-side overcurrent protection, a whole range of design and installation possibilities are available for secondary arrangement that satisfies the Code. The basic approach is to provide required overcurrent protection for the secondary circuit conductors right at the transformer—such as by a fused switch or CB attached to the transformer enclosure, as shown in Fig. 450-13. Or 10-ft or 25-ft taps may be made, as covered in Sec. 240-21.

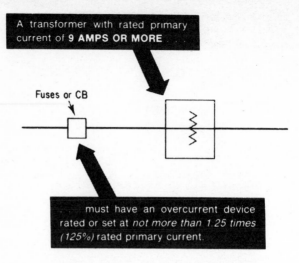

NOTE: Where 1.25 times primary current does not correspond to a standard rating of protective device, the next higher standard rating from Section 240-6 is permitted.

Fig. 450-11. Protection sizing for larger transformers is 125 percent of primary current. (Sec. 450-3.)

2. Another acceptable way to protect a 600-V transformer is described in Sec. 450-3(b) (2). In this method, the transformer primary may be fed from a circuit which has overcurrent protection (and circuit conductors) rated up to 250 percent (instead of 125 percent, as above) of rated primary current—*but,* in such cases, there must be a protective device on the secondary side of the transformer, and that device must be rated or set at not more than 125 percent of the transformer's rated secondary current (Fig. 450-14). This secondary protective device must be located right at the transformer secondary terminals or not more than the length of a 10-ft or 25-ft tap away from the transformer, and the rules of Sec. 240-21 on tap conductors must be fully satisfied.

The secondary protective device covered by Sec. 450-3(b) (2) may readily be incorporated as part of other required provisions on the secondary side of the transformer, such as protection for a secondary feeder from the transformer to a panel or switchboard or motor control center fed from the switchboard. And a single secondary protective

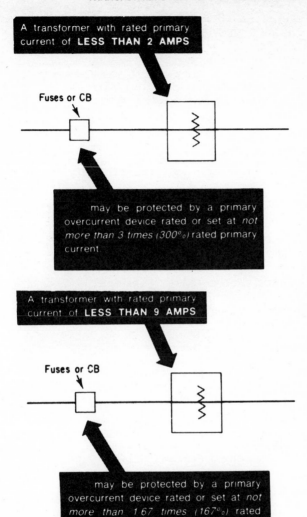

Fig. 450-12. Higher-percent protection is permitted for smaller transformers. (Sec. 450-3.)

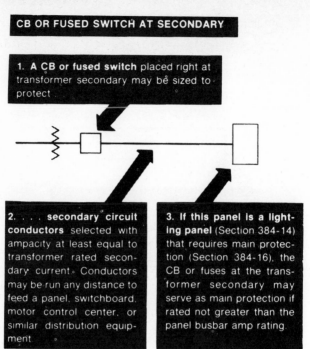

CB OR FUSED SWITCH AT SECONDARY

1. **A CB or fused switch** placed right at transformer secondary may be sized to protect

2. . . . **secondary circuit conductors** selected with ampacity at least equal to transformer rated secondary current. Conductors may be run any distance to feed a panel, switchboard, motor control center, or similar distribution equipment

3. **If this panel is a lighting panel** (Section 384-14) that requires main protection (Section 384-16), the CB or fuses at the transformer secondary may serve as main protection if rated not greater than the panel busbar amp rating.

Fig. 450-13. Protection of secondary circuit must be independent of primary-side transformer protection. (Sec. 450-3.)

device rated not over 125 percent of secondary current may serve as a required panelboard main as well as the required transformer secondary protection as shown at the bottom of Fig. 450-15.

The use of a transformer circuit with primary protection rated up to 250 percent of rated primary current offers an opportunity to avoid situations where a particular set of primary fuses or CB rated at only 125 percent would cause nuisance tripping or opening of the circuit on transformer inrush current. But the use of a 250 percent rated primary protection has a more common and widely applicable advantage in making it possible to feed two or more transformers from the same primary feeder. The number of transformers that might be used in any case would depend on the amount of continuous load on all the transformers. But in all such cases, the primary protection must be rated not more than 250 percent of any one transformer, if they are all the same size, or 250 percent of the smallest transformer, if they are of different

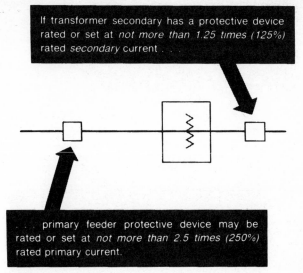

If transformer secondary has a protective device rated or set at *not more than 1.25 times (125%)* rated *secondary* current . . .

. . . primary feeder protective device may be rated or set at *not more than 2.5 times (250%)* rated primary current.

Fig. 450-14. Secondary protection permits higher-rated primary protective device. (Sec. 450-3.)

sizes. And for each transformer fed, there must be a set of fuses or CB on the secondary side rated at not more than 125 percent of rated secondary current, as shown in Fig. 450-16.

Figure 450-17 shows an example of application of 250 percent primary protection to a feeder supplying three transformers (such as at the bottom of Fig. 450-16). The example shows how the rules of Sec. 450-3(b) must be carefully related to Sec. 240-21 and other **Code** rules:

Exception No. 8 of Sec. 240-21 of the **NE Code** is a rule that covers use of a 25-ft *unprotected* tap from feeder conductors, with a transformer inserted in the 25-ft tap. This rule does not eliminate the need for secondary protection—it makes a special condition for placement of the secondary protective device. It is a restatement of Exception No. 3 as applied to a tap containing a transformer and applies to both single-phase and 3-phase transformer feeder taps.

Figure 450-17 shows a feeder supplying three 45-kVA transformers, each transformer being fed as part of a 25-ft feeder tap that conforms to Exception No. 8 of Sec. 240-21.

Although each transformer has a rated primary current of 54 A at full load, the demand load on each transformer primary was calculated to be 42 A, based on secondary loading. No. 1 THW copper feeder conductors were considered adequate for the total noncontinuous demand load of 3

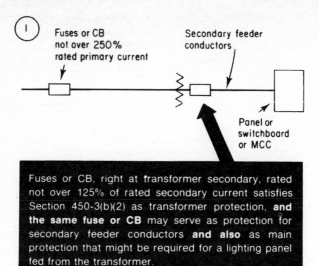

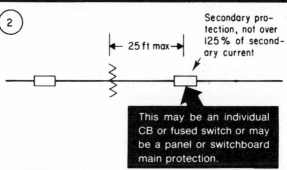

NOTE: In both cases, primary and secondary feeder conductors must be sized to be properly protected by the fuses or CB in both the primary and secondary circuit, which will give them more than adequate ampacity for the transformer full-load current.

Fig. 450-15. With 250 percent primary protection, secondary protection may be located like this. (Sec. 450-3.)

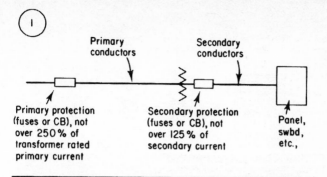

Primary
conductors

Secondary
conductors

Primary protection
(fuses or CB), not
over 250% of
transformer rated
primary current

Secondary protection
(fuses or CB), not
over 125% of
secondary current

Panel,
swbd,
etc.,

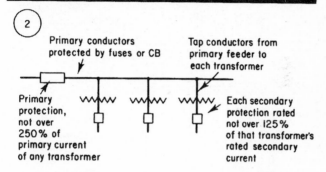

Primary conductors
protected by fuses or CB

Tap conductors from
primary feeder to
each transformer

Primary
protection,
not over
250% of
primary current
of any transformer

Each secondary
protection rated
not over 125%
of that transformer's
rated secondary
current

NOTE: Each set of tap conductors from primary
feeder to each transformer may be same size as
primary feeder conductors **OR** may be smaller than
primary conductors if sized in accordance with
Section 240-21, Exception No. 8—which permits a
25-ft tap from a primary feeder to be made up of both
primary and secondary tap conductors. The 25-ft tap
may have any part of its length on the primary or
secondary but must not be longer than 25 ft and must
terminate in a single CB or set of fuses.

Fig. 450-16. With primary 250 percent protection, primary circuit may vary.
(Sec. 450-3.)

× 42 A or 126 A. A step-by-step analysis of this system follows. Refer to
circled letters on sketch:

   A. The primary circuit conductors are No. 6 TW rated at 55 A, which
      gives them "an ampacity at least ⅓ that of the *conductors or overcur-*
      rent protection from which they are tapped . . . ," because these con-

THIS LAYOUT—

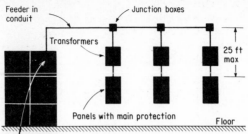

—IS HOOKED UP LIKE THIS:

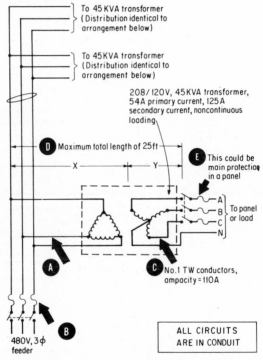

Fig. 450-17. Code rules must be tied together. (Sec. 450-3.)

ductors are tapped from the feeder conductors protected at 125 A. No. 6 TW is O.K. for the 42-A primary current.

B. The 125-A fuses in the feeder switch properly protect the No. 1 THW feeder conductors, which are rated at 130 A.

C. The conductors supplied by the transformer secondary must have "an ampacity that, when multiplied by the ratio of the secondary-to-primary voltage, is at least $\frac{1}{3}$ the ampacity of the conductors *or* overcurrent protection from which the primary conductors are tapped . . ." The ratio of secondary-to-primary voltage of the transformer is

$$\frac{208 \text{ V}}{480 \text{ V}} = 0.433$$

Note that phase-to-phase voltage must be used to determine this ratio.

Then, for the secondary conductors, Sec. 240-21, Exception No. 8(b), says that

$$\text{Minimum conductor ampacity} \times 0.433 = \frac{1}{3} \times 125 \text{ A}$$
$$\frac{1}{3} \times 125 = 41.67$$

Then, minimum conductor ampacity equals

$$\frac{41.67}{0.433} = 96 \text{ A}$$

The No. 1 TW secondary conductors, rated at 110 A, are above the 96-A minimum and are, therefore, satisfactory.

D. The total length of the unprotected 25-ft tap—i.e., the primary conductor length *plus* the secondary conductor length $(x + y)$ for any circuit leg—must not be greater than 25 ft.

E. The secondary tap conductors from the transformer must terminate in a single CB or set of fuses that will limit the load on those conductors to their rated ampacity from Table 310-16. Note that there is no exception given to that requirement and the "next higher standard device rating" may not be used if the conductor ampacity does not correspond to the rating of a standard device.

The overcurrent protection required at E, at the load end of the 25-ft tap conductors, must not be rated more than the ampacity of the No. 1 TW conductors.

Max. rating of fuses or CB at E = 110 A

But a 100-A main would satisfy the 96-A secondary load. *(Note: The overcurrent protective device required at E could be the main protective device required for a lighting and appliance panel fed from the transformer.)*

WATCH OUT FOR THIS TRAP!!

Although the foregoing calculation shows how unprotected taps may be made from feeder conductors by satisfying the rules of Sec. 240-21,

Exception No. 8, the rules of Sec. 240-21 are all concerned with PRO-TECTION OF CONDUCTORS ONLY. Consideration must now be made of *transformer* protection, as follows:

1. Note that Sec. 240-21 makes no reference to *transformer* protection. But Sec. 450-3 calls for protection of transformers, and there is no exception made for the conditions of Exception No. 8 to Sec. 240-21.

2. It is clear from Sec. 450-3(b) (1) that the transformer shown in Fig. 450-17 is *not* protected by a primary-side overcurrent device rated not more than 125 percent of primary current (54 A), because 1.25 × 54 A = 68 A, maximum.

3. But Sec. 450-3(b) (2) does offer a way to provide required protection. The 110-A protection at E *is* secondary protection *rated not over* 125 percent of rated secondary current (1.25 × 125 A secondary current = 156 A). With that secondary protection, a primary feeder overcurrent device rated not more than 250 percent of rated primary current will satisfy Sec. 450-3(b) (2). That would call for fuses in the feeder switch (or a CB) (at B in the diagram) rated not over

$$250 \text{ percent} \times 54 \text{ A primary current} = 135 \text{ A}$$

But, the fuses in the feeder switch are rated at 125 A—which are not in excess of 250 percent of transformer primary current and, therefore, satisfy Sec. 450-3(b) (2).

In addition to the two basic methods described above for protecting transformers, Sec. 450-3(b) (2) also provides for protection with a built-in thermal overload protection, as shown in Fig. 450-18.

450-4. Grounding Autotransformers.   An existing, ungrounded, 480-V system derived from a delta transformer hookup can be converted to grounded operation in two basic ways:

First, one of the three phase legs of the 480-V delta can be intentionally connected to a grounding electrode conductor that is then run to a suitable grounding electrode. Such grounding would give the two ungrounded phases (A and B) a voltage of 480 V to ground. The system would then operate as a grounded system, so that a ground fault (phase-to-conduit or other enclosure) on the secondary can cause fault-current flow that opens a circuit protective device to clear the faulted circuit.

But corner grounding of a delta system does not give the lowest possible phase-to-ground voltage. In fact, the voltage to ground of a corner-grounded delta system is the same as it is for an ungrounded delta system because voltage to ground for ungrounded circuits is defined as the greatest voltage between the given conductor and any other conductor of the circuit. Thus, the voltage to ground for an ungrounded delta system is the maximum voltage between any two conductors, on the assumption that an accidental ground on any one phase puts the other two phases at full line-to-line voltage aboveground.

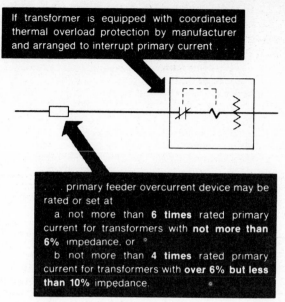

If transformer is equipped with coordinated thermal overload protection by manufacturer and arranged to interrupt primary current . . .

. . . primary feeder overcurrent device may be rated or set at
    a. not more than **6 times** rated primary current for transformers with **not more than 6%** impedance, or [a]
    b. not more than **4 times** rated primary current for transformers with **over 6% but less than 10%** impedance. [a]

Fig. 450-18. Built-in protection is another technique for transformers. (Sec. 450-3.)

In recognition of increasing emphasis on the safety of grounded systems over ungrounded systems, Sec. 450-4 covers the use of zig-zag grounding autotransformers to convert 3-phase, 3-wire, ungrounded delta systems to grounded wye systems. Such grounding of a 480-V delta system, therefore, lowers the voltage to ground from 480 V (when ungrounded) to 277 V (the phase-to-grounded-neutral voltage) when converted to a wye system (Fig. 450-19).

A zig-zag grounding autotransformer gets its name from the angular phase differences among the six windings that are divided among the three legs of the transformer's laminated magnetic core assembly. The actual hookup of the six windings is an interconnection of two wye configurations, with specific polarities and locations for each winding. Just as a wye or delta transformer hookup has a graphic representation that looks like the letter "Y" or the Greek letter "delta," so a zig-zag grounding autotransformer is represented as two wye hookups with pairs of windings in series but phase-displaced, as in Fig. 450-20.

With no ground fault on any leg of the 3-phase system, current flow in the transformer windings is balanced, because equal impedances are connected across each pair of phase legs. The net impedance of the transformer under balanced conditions is very high, so that only a low

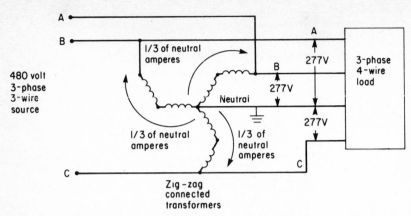

Fig. 450-19. Zig-zag transformer changes voltage to ground from 480 to 277 V. (Sec. 450-4.)

level of magnetizing current flows through the windings. But when a ground fault develops on one leg of the 3-phase system, the transformer windings become a very low impedance in the fault path, permitting a large value of fault current to flow and operate the circuit protective device—just as it would on a conventional grounded-neutral wye system, as shown in Fig. 450-21.

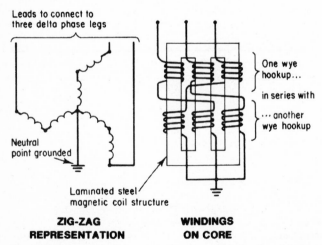

Fig. 450-20. Windings of zig-zag transformer provide for flow of fault or neutral current. (Sec. 450-4.)

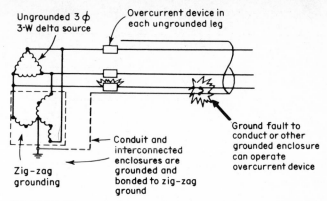

Ungrounded 3 ϕ 3-W delta source

Overcurrent device in each ungrounded leg

Ground fault to conduct or other grounded enclosure can operate overcurrent device

Conduit and interconnected enclosures are grounded and bonded to zig-zag ground

Zig-zag grounding

Fig. 450-21. Zig-zag transformer converts ungrounded system to grounded operation. (Sec. 450-4.)

Because the kilovoltampere rating of a grounding autotransformer is based on short-time fault current, selection of such transformers is much different from sizing a conventional 2-winding transformer for supplying a load. Careful consultation with a manufacturer's sales engineer should precede any decisions about the use of these transformers.

Section 450-4 of the NE Code points out that a grounding autotransformer may be used to provide a neutral reference for grounding purposes *or* for the purpose of converting a 3-phase, 3-wire delta system into a 3-phase, 4-wire grounded wye system. In the latter case, a neutral conductor can be taken from the transformer to supply loads connected phase-to-neutral—such as 277-V loads on a 48-V delta system that is converted to a 480Y/277-V system.

Section 450-4 requires such transformers to have a continuous rating and a continuous neutral current rating. The phase current in a grounding autotransformer is one-third the neutral current, as shown in Fig. 450-19.

Part **(a) (2)** of this section requires use of a three-pole CB, rated at 125 percent of the transformer phase current. The requirement for "common-trip" in the overcurrent device excludes conventional use of fuses in a switch as the required overcurrent protection. A three-pole CB prevents single-phase opening of the circuit.

450-5. Secondary Ties. In industrial plants having very heavy power loads it is usually economical to install a number of large transformers at various locations within each building, the transformers being supplied by primary feeders operating at voltages up to 13,800 V. One of the secondary systems that may be used in such cases is the network system.

The term *network system* as commonly used is applied to any secondary distribution system in which the secondaries of two or more transformers

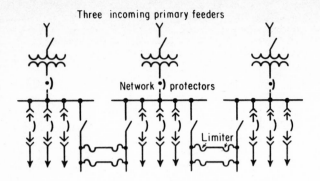

Three incoming primary feeders

Network protectors

Limiter

GENERAL NETWORK

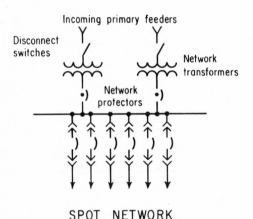

Incoming primary feeders

Disconnect switches

Network transformers

Network protectors

SPOT NETWORK

Fig. 450-22. These are the two basic types of "network" systems. (Sec. 450-5.)

at different locations are connected together by secondary ties. Two network layouts of unit subs are shown in Fig. 450-22. In the spot network, two or three transformers in one location or "spot" are connected to a common secondary bus and divide the load. Upon primary or transformer fault, the secondary is isolated from the faulted section by automatic operation of the network protector, providing a high order of supply continuity in the event of faults. The general form of the network system is similar except that widely separated individual substations are used with associated network protectors and tie circuits run between the secondary bus sections. System provides for interchange of power to accommodate unequal loading on the transformers. Limiters protect the ties. The purpose of the system is to equalize the loading of the transformers, to reduce voltage drop, and to ensure continuity of service. The use of this system introduces certain complications, and, to ensure successful operation, the system must be designed by an experienced electrical engineer.

The provisions of Sec. 450-3 govern the protection in the primary. Referring to Fig. 450-23, the network protector consists of a CB and a

Fig. 450-23. A "limiter" is a cable connection device containing a fusible element. (Sec. 450-5.)

reverse-power relay. The protector is necessary because without this device, if a fault develops in the transformer, or, in some cases, in the primary feeder, power will be fed back to the fault from the other transformers through the secondary ties. The relay is set to trip the breaker on a reverse-power current not greater than the rated secondary current of the transformer. This breaker is not arranged to be tripped by an overload on the secondary of the transformer.

Section 450-5(a) (3) provides that:

1. Where two or more conductors are installed in parallel, an individual protective device is provided at each end of each conductor.
2. The protective device (fusible link or CB) does not provide overload protection, but provides short-circuit protection only.

In case of a short circuit, the protective device must open the circuit before the conductor reaches a temperature that would injure its insulation. The principles involved are that the entire system is so designed that the tie conductors will never be continuously overloaded in normal operation—hence protection against overloads of less severity than short circuits is not necessary—and that the protective devices should not open the circuit and thus cause an interruption of service on load peaks of such short duration that the conductors do not become overheated.

A limiter is a special type of fuse having a very high interrupting capacity. Figure 450-23 is a cross-sectional view of one type of limiter. The cable lug, the fusible section, and the extension for connection to the bus are all made in one piece from a length of copper tubing, and the enclosing case is also copper. A typical device of this type is rated to interrupt a current of 50,000 A without perceptible noise and without the escape of flame or gases from the case.

Figure 450-24 is a single-line diagram of a simple 3-phase industrial-plant network system. The primary feeders may operate at any standard

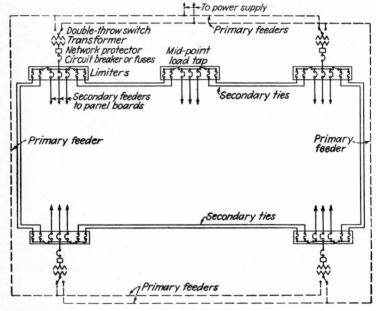

Fig. 450-24. This is a typical industrial plant network distribution system. (Sec. 450-5.)

voltage up to 13,800 V, and the secondary voltage would commonly be 480 V. The rating of the transformers used in such a system would usually be within the range of 300 to 1,000 kVA. The diagram shows two primary feeders, both of which are carried to each transformer so that by means of a double-throw switch each transformer can be connected to either feeder. Each feeder would be large enough to carry the entire load. It is assumed that the feeders are protected in accordance with Sec. 450-(b) (2) so that no primary overcurrent devices are required at the transformers. The secondary ties consist of two conductors in multiple per phase and it will be noted that these conductors form a closed loop. Switches are provided so that any section of the loop, including the limiters protecting that section, can be isolated in case repairs or replacements should be necessary.

450-6. Parallel Operation.   To operate satisfactorily in parallel, transformers should have the same percentage impedance and the same ratio of reactance to resistance. Information on these characteristics should be obtained from the manufacturer of the transformers.

450-7. Guarding.   Figure 450-25 summarizes these rules. Refer to Sec. 110-17 on guarding of live parts. Safety to personnel is always important,

1. Transformers must be protected against physical damage.

2. Exposed live parts must be protected against accidental contact by putting the transformer in a room or place accessible only to qualified personnel **or** by keeping live parts above the floor in accordance with Table 110-34(e).

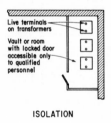

ISOLATION

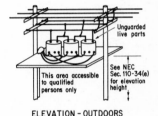

ELEVATION – OUTDOORS

3. Signs or other visible markings must be used on equipment or structure to indicate the operating voltage of exposed live parts

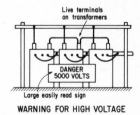

WARNING FOR HIGH VOLTAGE

Fig. 450-25. Transformer installations must be effectively guarded. (Sec. 450-7.)

particularly where a transformer is to operate with live parts. To protect against accidental contact with such components, isolate the unit or units in a room or place accessible only to qualified personnel and guard live parts, such as with a railing. When elevation is used for safeguarding live parts, consult Secs. 110-34(e) and 110-17.

450-21. Dry-Type Transformers Installed Indoors.   This rule differentiates between dry-type transformers on two considerations: (1) whether the transformer is rated up to $112\frac{1}{2}$ kVA or rated over that value, and (2) whether the transformer is a high-voltage unit (over 600 V) or rated up to 600 V. Note that high-voltage units under 112½ kVA rating must have the 12-in separation or fire barrier. For units rated over 112½ kVA, the rules are the same for high-voltage transformers and those up to 600 V. Figure 450-26 shows the rules of this section. Related application recommendations are as follows:

- Select a place that has the driest and cleanest air possible for installation of open-ventilated units. Avoid exposure to dripping or splashing water or other wet conditions. Outdoor application requires a suitable housing. Try to find locations where transformers will not be damaged by floodwater in case of a storm, a plugged drain, or a backed-up sewer.

- Temperature in the installation area must be normal, or the transformer may have to be derated. Modern standard, ventilated, dry-type transformers are designed to provide rated kilovoltampere output at rated voltage when the maximum ambient temperature of the cooling air is 40°C and the average ambient temperature of the cooling air over any 24-hr period does not exceed 30°C. At higher or lower ambients, transformer loading can be adjusted by the following relationships.

1. For each degree Celsius that average ambient temperature exceeds 30°C, the maximum load on the transformer must be reduced by 1 percent of rated kilovoltamperes.

2. For each degree Celsius that average ambient temperature is less than 30°C, the maximum load on the transformer may be increased by 0.67 percent of rated kilovoltamperes.

Depending on the type of insulation used, transformer insulation life will be cut approximately in half for every 10°C that the ambient temperature exceeds the normal rated value—or doubled for every 10°C below rated levels. Estimates assume continuous operation at full load. With modern insulations this rule is actually conservative for ambient temperature below normal operating temperatures and optimistic above it.

For proper cooling, dry-type transformers depend upon circulation of clean air—free from dust, dirt, or corrosive elements. Filtered air is preferable and may be mandatory in some cases of extreme air pollution. In any case, it can reduce maintenance.

In restricted spaces—small basement mechanical rooms, etc.—ventilation must be carefully checked to assure proper transformer operating temperature. The usual requirement is for 100 cfm of air movement for each kilowatt of transformer loss. Areas of inlet and outlet vent openings should be at least 1 net sq ft per 100 kVA of rated transformer capacity.

Height of vault, location of openings, and transformer loading affect ventilation. One manufacturer calls for the areas of the inlet and outlet openings to be not less than 60 sq ft per 1,000 kVa when the transformer is operating under full load and is located in a restricted space. And a

TRANSFORMERS RATED 112½ KVA OR LESS

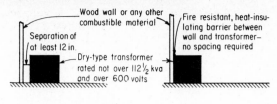

Wood wall or any other combustible material

Separation of at least 12 in.

Dry-type transformer rated not over 112½ kva and over 600 volts

Fire resistant, heat-insulating barrier between wall and transformer— no spacing required

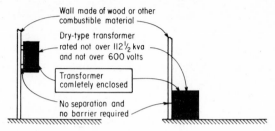

Wall made of wood or other combustible material

Dry-type transformer rated not over 112½ kva and not over 600 volts

Transformer comletely enclosed

No separation and no barrier required

TRANSFORMERS RATED OVER 112½ KVA

Completely enclosed and ventilated unit with 80°C rise or higher insulation...

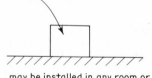

... may be installed in any room or area (need not be fire–resistant)

Clearances from combustible materials in any room or area (not fire–resistant)

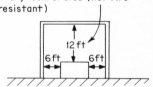

12 ft

6 ft   6 ft

Dry–type transformer with 80°C rise or higher insulation but not enclosed and ventilated

Room of fire–resistant construction to house transformer

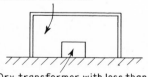

Dry transformer with less than 80°C rise insulation

Dry transformer rated over 35 KV...

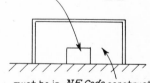

...must be in *NE Code* constructed transformer vault (Part C, Art. 450)

Fig. 450-26. Construction of dry-type transformer affects indoor installation rules. (Sec. 450-21.)

distance of 1 ft should be provided on all sides of dry-type transformers as well as between adjacent units.

Freestanding, floor-mounted units with metal grilles at the bottom must be set up off the floor a sufficient distance to provide the intended ventilation draft up through their housings.

The installation location must not expose the transformer housing to damage by normal movement of persons, trucks, or equipment. Ventilation openings should not be exposed to vandalism or accidental or mischievous poking of rubbish, sticks, or rods into the windings. Adequate protection must be provided against possible entry of small birds or animals.

450-23. High Fire Point Liquid-Insulated Transformers.   Section 450-23 covers the liquid-filled transformers designed to replace askarel-insulated transformers. Because oil-filled transformers used indoors require a transformer vault, the high fire point insulated transformer offers an alternative to the oil-filled transformers, without the need for a vault. This Code section simply permits installation of these "high fire point liquid-insulated" transformers indoors or outdoors. Over 35 kV, such a transformer must be in a vault.

Although askarel-filled transformers up to 35 kV were used for many years for indoor applications because they do not require a transformer vault, there has been a sharp, abrupt discontinuance of their use over recent years. Growth in the ratings, characteristics, and availability of dry-type high-voltage transformers has accounted for a major part in the reduction of askarel units. But another factor that led to rejection of askarel transformers in recent years is the environmental objections to the askarel liquid itself.

A major component of any askarel fluid is polychlorinated biphenyl (PCB), a chemical compound designated as a harmful environmental pollutant because it is nonbiodegradable and cannot be readily disposed of. Thus, although the askarels are excellent coolants where freedom from flammability is important, environmental objections to the sale, use, and disposal of PCBs have eliminated new applications of askarel transformers and stimulated a search for a nontoxic, environmentally acceptable substitute.

Proper handling and disposal of askarel is important for units still in use. A regulation of the EPA (Environmental Protection Agency), No. 311, required that all PCB spills of 1 lb or more must be reported. Failure to report a spill is a criminal offense punishable by a $10,000 fine and/or one-year imprisonment. Both the EPA and OSHA have objected to use of askarels. A manufacturer of askarel has established a program for disposal of spent or contaminated PCB fluid using an incinerator that completely destroys the fluid by burning it at over 2,000°F.

Non-PCB dielectric coolant fluids for use in small- and medium-sized power transformers as a safe alternate to askarels are available and transformers using these new high fire point dielectric coolants have been widely used.

Extensive data from tests on available askarel substitutes show that they provide a high degree of safety. Such fluids do have **NE Code** and OSHA recognition. Responsibility for proper clearances with insurance underwriters, government regulating agencies, and local code authorities rests with the user or purchaser of the fluid in new or refilled transformers. Underwriters Laboratories does not test or list liquid-filled equipment. Both UL and Factory Mutual Research Laboratory have been involved in providing a classification service of flammability. The silicone fluid for use in transformers has been evaluated by UL and has received a flammability classification between 4 and 5. The index puts water at zero and ether at 100. Askarels are rated at 2 to 3 and mineral oil (though not listed) would likely fall between 10 and 20. The EPA has commented favorably on such high fire point fluids.

Few physical changes to transformers are necessary when using the new fluid dielectrics. However, load ratings on existing units may be reduced about 10 percent because of the difference in fluid viscosity and heat conductivity compared with askarel. The high fire point fluids cost about twice as much as askarel. Purchase price of a new transformer filled with the fluid (such as a typical 1,000-kVA loadcenter unit) is about 10 to 15 percent more than an askarel-filled unit. But the economics vary for different fluids and must be carefully evaluated.

High fire point liquid-insulated transformers require no special maintenance procedures. The liquids exhibit good dielectric properties over a wide range of temperatures and voltage stress levels, and they have acceptable arc-quenching capabilities. They have a high degree of thermal stability and a high resistance to thermal oxidation that enables them to maintain their insulating and other functional properties for extended periods of time at high temperatures.

Since silicone liquids will ignite at 750°F (350°C), they are not classed as fire-resistant. However, if the heat source is removed or fluid temperature drops below 750°F, burning will stop. The silicone fluids are thus self-extinguishing.

450-24. Askarel-Insulated Transformers Installed Indoors. Although askarel transformers are being phased out, the Code rule says such transformers installed indoors must conform to the following:

1. Units rated over 25 kVA must be equipped with a pressure-relief vent.

2. Where installed in a poorly ventilated place, they must be furnished with a means for absorbing any gases generated by arcing inside the case, or the pressure-relief vent must be connected to a chimney or flue which will carry such gases outside the building.

3. Units rated over 35,000 V must be installed in a vault. See Fig. 450-27.

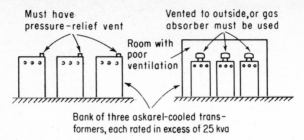

Bank of three askarel-cooled transformers, each rated in excess of 25 kva

UNITS RATED OVER 35,000 VOLTS MUST BE USED IN A VAULT

Fig. 450-27. Code rules still cover askarel transformers. (Sec. 450-24.)

450-25. Oil-Insulated Transformers Installed Indoors. The basic rule is illustrated in Fig. 450-28. Oil-insulated transformers installed indoors must be installed in a vault constructed according to Code specs, but the exceptions note general and specific conditions under which a vault is not necessary. The most commonly applied exceptions are as follows:

1. A hookup of one or more units rated not over 112½ kVA may be used in a vault constructed of reinforced concrete not less than 4 in. thick.
2. Units installed in detached buildings used only for providing electric service do not require a Code-constructed vault if no fire hazard is created and the interior is accessible only to qualified persons.

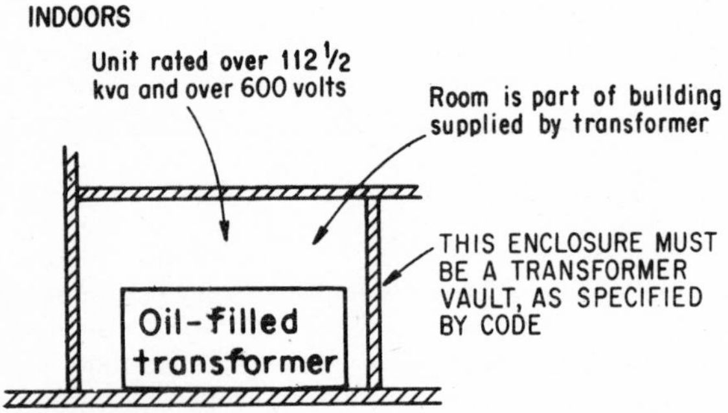

INDOORS

Unit rated over 112 ½ kva and over 600 volts

Room is part of building supplied by transformer

Oil-filled transformer

THIS ENCLOSURE MUST BE A TRANSFORMER VAULT, AS SPECIFIED BY CODE

Fig. 450-28. Oil-filled transformers generally require installation in a "vault." (Sec. 450-25.)

450-26. Oil-Insulated Transformers Installed Outdoors. Figure 450-29 shows how physical locations of building openings must be evaluated with respect to potential fire hazard from leaking transformer oil.

450-41. Location (Transformer Vaults). Ideally, a transformer vault should have direct ventilating openings (grills or louvers through the

OUTDOORS

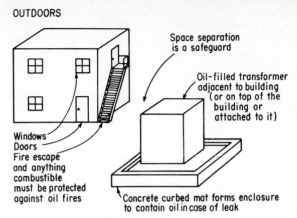

Fig. 450-29. Precautions must be taken for outdoor oil transformers. (Sec. 450-26.)

walls) to outdoor space. Use of ducts or flues for ventilating is not necessarily a **Code** violation, but they should be avoided wherever possible.

450-42. Walls, Roof, and Floor. Basic mandatory construction details are established for an **NEC**-type transformer vault, as required for oil-filled transformers and for all transformers operating at over 35,000 V. The purpose of a transformer vault is to isolate the transformers and other apparatus and to confine any fire that might be caused by the failure of any of the apparatus. It is important that the door as well as the remainder of the enclosure be of proper construction and that a substantial lock be provided. Details required for any vault are shown in Fig. 450-30 and include the following details:

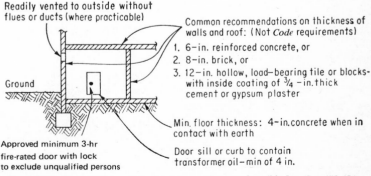

Fig. 450-30. Transformer vault must assure containment of possible fire. (Sec. 450-42.)

1. Walls and roofs of vaults shall be constructed of reinforced concrete, brick, load-bearing tile, concrete block, or other fire-resistive constructions with adequate strength and a fire resistance of 3 hr according to ASTM Standard E119-75.

2. A vault must have a concrete floor not less than 4 in. thick when in contact with the earth. When the vault is constructed with space below it, the floor must have adequate structural strength and a minimum fire resistance of 3 hr. Six-in.-thick reinforced concrete is a typical 3-hr-rated construction.

3. Building walls and floors that meet the above requirements may serve for the floor, roof, and/or walls of the vault.

An exception to the basic regulations establishing the construction standards for transformer fireproof vaults notes that the transformer-vault fire rating may be reduced where the transformers are protected with automatic sprinkler, water spray, or carbon dioxide. The usual construction standards for transformer vaults (such as 6-in.-thick reinforced concrete) provide a minimum fire-resistance rating of 3 hr. Where automatic sprinkler, water spray, or carbon dioxide is used, a construction rating of only 1 hr will be permitted.

450-43. Doorways.   Each doorway must be of 3-hr fire rating as defined in the *Standard for the Installation of Fire Doors and Windows* (NFPA No. 80-1977). The **Code**-enforcing authority may also require such a door for doorways leading from the vault to the outdoors, in addition to any doorways into adjoining space in the building.

450-45. Ventilation Openings.   This rule sets the size and arrangement of vent openings in a vault where such ventilation is required by ANSI C57.12.00-1973—"General Requirements for Distribution, Power, and Regulating Transformers," as noted in Sec. 450-8. Figure 450-31 shows the openings as regulated by part **(c)** of this section. One or more openings may be used, but if a single vent opening is used, it must be in or near the roof of the vault—and not near the floor.

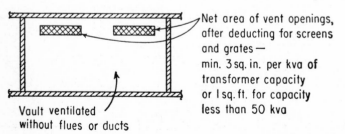

Net area of vent openings, after deducting for screens and grates —
min. 3 sq. in. per kva of transformer capacity or 1 sq. ft. for capacity less than 50 kva

Vault ventilated without flues or ducts

Fig. 450-31. Vault vent opening(s) may be in or near the roof—or near floor level also, if one is at or near roof level.

ARTICLE 460. CAPACITORS

460-1. Scope. The sections in this article apply chiefly to capacitors used for the power-factor correction of electric-power installations in industrial plants and for correcting the power factors of individual motors (Fig. 460-1). These provisions apply only to capacitors used for surge protection where such capacitors are not component parts of other apparatus.

Fig. 460-1. A typical power-factor correction capacitor bank is this 300-kvar bank of twelve 25-kvar, 480-V capacitor units installed in a steel enclosure in an outdoor industrial substation. (Sec. 460-1.)

In an industrial plant using induction motors, the power factor may be considerably less than 100 percent, particularly when all or part of the motors operate most of the time at much less than their full load. The lagging current can be counteracted and the power factor improved by installing capacitors across the line. By raising the power factor, for the same actual power delivered the current is decreased in the generator, transformers, and lines, up to the point where the capacitor is connected.

Figure 460-2 shows a capacitor assembly connection to the main power circuit of a small industrial plant, consisting of capacitors connected in a

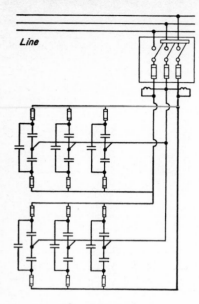

Fig. 460-2. Six internally delta-connected capacitors form a 3-phase capacitor bank. (Sec. 460-1.)

3-phase hookup and rated at 90 kVA for a 460-V system. An externally operable switch mounted on the wall is used as the disconnecting means and the discharge device required by Sec. 460-6 consists of two high-impedance coils inside the switch enclosure which consume only a small amount of power, but, having a comparatively low DC resistance, permit the charge to drain off rapidly after the capacitor assembly has been disconnected from the line.

460-6. Drainage of Stored Charge. If no means were provided for draining off the charge stored in a capacitor after it is disconnected from the line, a severe shock might be received by a person servicing the equipment or the equipment might be damaged by a short circuit. If a capacitor is permanently connected to the windings of a motor, as in Fig. 460-3, the stored charge will drain off rapidly through the windings when the circuit is opened. Reactors or resistors used as discharge devices must either be permanently connected across the terminals of the capacitor (such as within the capacitor housing) or a device must be provided that will automatically connect the discharge devices when the capacitor is disconnected from the source of supply. Most available types of capacitors have discharge resistors built into their cases. When capacitors are not equipped with discharge resistors, a discharge circuit must be provided.

Figure 460-3 shows a capacitor used to correct the power factor of a single motor. The capacitor may be connected to the motor circuit

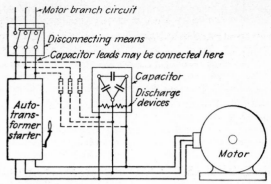

Fig. 460-3. Capacitor voltage must be discharged when circuit is opened. (Sec. 460-6.)

between the starter and the motor or may be connected between the disconnecting means and the starter, as indicated by the dotted lines in the diagram. If connected as shown by the dotted lines, an overcurrent device must be provided in these leads, as required by Sec. 460-8(b). The capacitor is shown as having discharge devices consisting of resistors.

460-7. Power Factor Correlation—Motor Circuit. Power capacitors, in most applications, are installed to raise system power factor, which results in increased circuit or system current-carrying capacity, reduced power losses, and lower reactive power charges (most utility companies include a power-factor penalty clause in their industrial billing). Also, additional benefits derived as a result of a power capacitor installation are reduced voltage drop and increased voltage stability. Figure 460-4 presents basic data on calculating size of capacitors for power-factor correction. However, manufacturers provide various tables and graphs to facilitate selection of the capacitor needed for a given motor load.

The rule of this Code section limits power-factor correction to unity (100 percent or 1.0) when there is no load on the motor. That will result in a power factor of 95 percent or better when the motor is fully loaded.

The no-load power factor of a motor is a design constant of the motor and may be obtained from the manufacturer of the motor—or it may be measured or calculated. In Fig. 460-4, using the known no-load PF (power factor) of a motor, the kilowatts can be calculated from $kW = PF \times kVA_1$. Then $kvar_1$ (the required rating of PF capacity to raise the no-load value of PF to 100 percent) equals the square root of $(kVA_1)^2 - (kW)^2$, where kVA_1 is calculated from circuit voltage and current measured with a clamp-on ammeter.

A handy rule-of-thumb method for determining the kilovar rating of a capacitor required to provide optimum power-factor correction for a given motor is as follows:

Power-factor capacitors can be connected across electric lines to neutralize the effect of lagging power-factor loads, thereby reducing the current drawn for a given kilowatt load. In a distribution system, small capacitor units may be connected at the individual loads or the total capacitor kilovolt-amperes may be grouped at one point and connected to the main. Although the total kvar of capacitors is the same, the use of small capacitors at the individual loads reduces current all the way from the loads back to the source and thereby has greater PF corrective effect than the one big unit on the main, which reduces current only from its point of installation back to the source.

Calculating Size of Capacitor:

Assume it is desired to improve the power factor a given amount by the addition of capacitors to the circuit.

Then $kvar_R = kw \times (\tan \theta_1 - \tan \theta_2)$

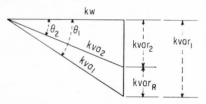

where $kvar_R$ = rating of required capacitor
$kvar_1$ = reactive kilovolt-amperes at original PF
$kvar_2$ = reactive kilovolt-amperes at improved PF
θ_1 = original phase angle
θ_2 = phase angle at improved PF
kw = load at which original PF was determined.

NOTE: The phase angles θ_1 and θ_2 can be determined from a table of trigonometric functions using the following relationships:
θ_1 = The angle which has its cosine equal to the decimal value of the original power factor (e.g., 0.70 for 70% PF; 0.65 for 65%; etc.)
θ_2 = The angle which has its cosine equal to the decimal value of the improved power factor.

Fig. 460-4. Capacitors reduce circuit current by supplying the magnetizing current to motors. (Sec. 460-7.)

1. With no load on the motor, measure the no-load kilovoltampere. That can be determined by using a clamp-on ammeter to measure the amount of current drawn by the motor under no-load condition and then using a voltmeter to get the phase-to-phase voltage of the motor circuit. Then, for a 3-phase motor, the kilovoltampere input to the motor is derived from the formula:

Input kVA = [Phase-to-phase voltage
× line current × 1.732] + 1,000

2. Because the power factor of an unloaded motor is very low—say, about 10 percent—the kilovoltampere vector for the original PF

condition as shown in Fig. 460-4 is lagging the kilowatt vector by an angle that is approaching 90°. That results from the working current being small (only the resistance of the windings) while the reactive (magnetizing) current is at its normal and very much larger value. In that condition, the reactive current causes the kilovar vector to be almost the same length as the kilovoltampere vector—so close in fact that it is generally safe to take the kilovoltampere input value as the required kilovar rating of capacitor needed to correct to 100 percent PF at no-load, which will result in a 95 to 98 percent PF at full load.

3. Then select a capacitor assembly that has a kilovar rating as close to—but *not* in excess of—the calculated value of input kilovoltampere of the motor. This method may be used on rewound motors or on other motors where it is not possible to make a better determination of needed capacitor kilovar.

Capacitors of the type to which Sec. 460-7 applies are commonly rated in kilovoltamperes, or the rating may be in "kilovars," meaning "reactive kilovoltamperes," abbreviated kvar. The capacitors are usually designed for connection to a 3-phase system and constructed as a unit with three leads brought out.

Corrective measures for improving power factor may be designed into motor branch circuits. Generally, the most effective location for installation of individual power-factor-correction capacitors is as close to the inductive load as possible. This provides maximum correction from the capacitor back to the source of power. At individual motor locations, power-factor-correcting capacitors offer improved voltage regulations. As shown in Fig. 460-5, power-factor capacitors installed at terminals of motors provide maximum relief from reactive currents, reducing the required current-carrying capacities of conductors from their point of application all the way back to the supply system. Figure 460-6 shows a typical example. Such application also eliminates extra switching devices, since each capacitor can be switched with the motor it serves.

Capacitors also may be installed as a group or bank at some central point, such as a switchboard, loadcenter, busway, or outdoor substation. Usually this method serves only to reduce the utility company penalty charges; however, in many instances, installation costs also will be lower.

When motors are small, numerous, and operated intermittently, it is often economically more desirable to install required capacitor kvar at the motor control center.

Capacitor installations may consist of an individual unit connected as close as possible to the inductive load (at the terminals of a motor, etc.) or of a bank of many units connected in multiple across a main feeder. Units are available in specific kvar and voltage ratings. Standard low-voltage capacitor units are rated from about 0.5 kvar to 25 kvar at voltages from 216 to 600 V. For high-voltage applications, standard ratings are 15, 25, 50, and 100 kvar. Available in single-, 2-, or 3-phase configurations,

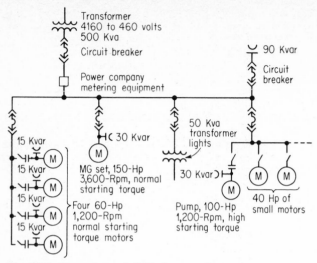

Fig. 460-5. PF capacitors at individual motors offer maximum corrective advantages. (Sec. 460-7.)

power capacitors may be supplied either unfused or equipped with current-limiting or high-capacity fuses (single-phase units are furnished with one fuse; 3-phase capacitors usually have two fuses). On low-voltage units, fuses may be mounted on the capacitor bushings inside the terminal compartment.

The Exception to this Code rule was added to cover cases where the advantage of higher full-load power factor can be safely sustained. Commentary on the addition of this Exception was noted by H. B. Love, Consultant, Tarnow Electric Supply Co., Detroit, MI, in the proposed amendments to the 1978 NE Code and included the following:

SUPPORTING COMMENT: This exception will liberate the engineer from the oversimplified rule that protects against damage in a relatively few applications at the expense of uneconomical usage of capacitors in a great many cases.

The majority of induction motors, used with simple start-and-stop cycles, can safely have their power factors improved to unity or even more if the plant conditions make it desirable. This is proved by many such installations in a good number of plants.

The engineer would still be required to limit the capacitor as stated in the present rule, in those cases where there is a hazard.

The purpose of this rule is to avoid the ill effects of over-voltage caused by induction-generator action when the motor-capacitor combination is deenergized.

In modern motors, the value is so limited by magnetic saturation that it may be questioned whether it is a sufficient hazard to be even considered by the Code.

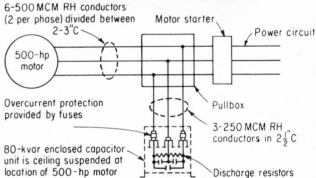

Fig. 460-6. Typical capacitor installation connected on load side of motor starter for a 500-hp motor consists of ceiling-suspended enclosed capacitors (arrow) that are rated at 80 kvar, connected through the pull box to the circuit conductors for the motor. Diagram shows how conductors were added to the equipment shown in the photo. (Sec. 460-7.)

The real potential for mechanical (and possibly electrical) damage remains to be dealt with. If the motor-capacitor combination should be reconnected to the line when its generated voltage E_G is not synchronized with line voltage E_L, shafts can be snapped.

There are two particular circumstances when the hazard arises:

(a) motor is reconnected to the line soon after being taken off, as in two-speed motor changes;

(b) motor driving high-inertia load is reconnected while speed is still great enough so E_G may be large, out of phase, and at different frequency from E_L.

The "no-load" rule does exert a desirable restraining effect on capacitor sizing, but a little consideration demonstrates that it does not completely protect the motor, nor, therefore, the people that are the real concern of the Code.

The reason is that even small amounts of capacitance have the effect of extending the residual magnetism of a motor, so that E_G can exist for considerable time even under the present capacitor-sizing rule. Therefore in case (a) above, motors can still be damaged.

Carrying the literal purpose of 460-7 to its logical end of preventing all possible damage, would therefore require that only nominal amounts of capacitors, or none at all, be applied to motors. This is of course absurd. The point is that the incomplete theory has been overridden by experience.

The second shortcoming is that the rule depends for its application on information that is not generally available. No-load current or kVA do not appear on motor nameplates. As a result, motor manufacturers have issued tables of maximum capacitor that are so extensive (due to differences in motor designs) and so different between makers, that compendiums have been published that naturally tend toward listing the lowest value "permitted" by any motor manufacturer. These are generally used for convenience, sometime modified by users for reasons of their own.

This puts an unwarranted expense on power-factor improvement . . . an unnecessary restriction on measures that would improve the economy and efficiency of the electrical system without really increasing its safety.

460-8. Conductors.   Part **(a)** of this section covers sizing of circuit conductors. The current corresponding to the kilovoltampere rating of a capacitor is computed in the same manner as for a motor or other load having the same rating in kilovoltamperes. If a capacitor assembly used at 460 V has a rating of 90 kVA, the current rating is 90,000/(460 × 1.73) = 113 A. The minimum required ampacity of the conductors would be 1.35 × 113 A, or 153 A.

The manufacturing standards for capacitors for power-factor correction call for a rating tolerance of "−0, +15 percent," meaning that the actual rating in kilovoltamperes is never below the nominal rating and may be as much as 15 percent higher. Thus, a capacitor having a nameplate rating of 100 kVA might actually draw a current corresponding to 115 kVA. The current drawn by a capacitor varies directly with the line voltage, so that, if the line voltage is higher than the rated voltage, the current will be correspondingly increased. Also, any variation of the line voltage from a pure sine wave form will cause a capacitor to draw an increased current. It is for these reasons that the conductors leading to a capacitor are required to have an ampacity not less than 135 percent of the rated current of the capacitor.

example: Given the kvar rating of capacitors to be installed for a motor, determining the correct capacitor conductor size is relatively simple. The rule here requires that the ampacity of the capacitor conductors be not less than ⅓ the ampacity of the motor circuit conductors and not less than 135 percent of the capacitor rated current. The capacitor nameplate will give rated kvar, voltage, and current. It is then a simple matter of multiplying rated current by 1.35 to obtain the ampacity value of the conductor to be installed and selecting the size of conductor required to carry that value of current, from Table 310-16. Then check that the ampacity is not less than ⅓ the ampacity of the motor circuit conductors.

For a motor rated 100 hp, 460 V, 121 A full-load current, a 25-kvar capacitor would correct power factor to between 0.95 and 0.98 at full load. The nameplate on the capacitor indicates that the capacitor is rated 460 V, 31 A. Then 31 × 1.35 = 42 A. From **Code** Table 310-16, a No. 6 TW or THW conductor rated to carry 55 A would do the job. (No. 8 THW rated at 45 A would most likely be considered not acceptable because UL generally calls for use of 60°C wires in circuits up to 100 A.) The motor circuit conductors are found to be 2/0 THW, with an ampacity of 175 A. Since ⅓ × 175 = 58 A, the No. 6 THW, with an ampacity of 65 A, should be used.

If these conductors are connected to the load terminals of the motor controller, the overload protection heaters may have to be changed (or if the OL is adjustable, its setting may have to be reduced), because the capacitor will cause a reduction in line current and adjustment of relay setting is required by Sec. 460-9.

Although part **(b)** of the rule requires overcurrent protection (fuses or a CB) in each ungrounded conductor connecting a capacitor assembly to a circuit, the Exception considers the motor-running overload relay in a starter to be adequate protection for the conductors when they are connected to the motor circuit on the load side of the starter. Where separate overcurrent protection is provided, as required for line-side connection, the device must simply be rated "as low as practicable." When a capacitor is thrown on the line, it may momentarily draw an excess current. A rating or setting of 250 percent of the capacitor current rating will provide short-circuit protection. Being a fixed load, a capacitor does not need overload protection such as is necessary for a motor.

Most power capacitors are factory equipped with fuses which provide protection in case of an internal short circuit. These fuses are usually rated from 165 percent to 250 percent of the rated kilovar current to allow for maximum operating conditions and momentary current surges. When installed on the load side of a motor starter, as noted above, capacitors do not require additional fusing. However, for bank installations, separate fuses are required.

Part **(c)** of the rule requires a disconnecting means for all the ungrounded conductors connecting a capacitor assembly to the circuit— but a disconnect is not needed when the capacitor is connected on the

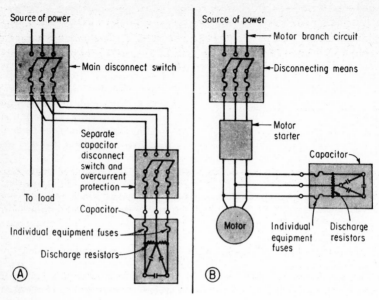

Fig. 460-7. PF capacitor assembly may be connected on the line or load side of a starter. (Sec. 460-8.)

load side of a starter with overload protection. The disconnect must be rated at least equal to 1.35 times the rated current of the capacitor.

Two accepted methods of wiring capacitors are illustrated in Fig. 460-7. Diagram A shows method of connection at a central location, such as at a power center or on busway feeder. In such an installation, the Code rule requires an overcurrent device in each ungrounded conductor, a separate disconnecting means, and discharge resistor (usually furnished with capacitors). Current rating of both the capacitor disconnect switch and the conductors supplying the capacitor must be not less than 135 percent of the rated current of the capacitor. In B, the capacitor is connected directly to motor terminals. Installation on load side of motor starter eliminates need for separate overcurrent protection and separate disconnecting means. However, motor-running overcurrent protection must take into account lower running current of motor, as required by Sec. 460-9.

460-9. Rating or Setting of Motor-Running Overcurrent Device. When a power-factor capacitor is connected to a motor circuit at the motor—i.e., on the load or motor side of the motor controller—the reactive current drawn by the motor is provided by the capacitor and, as a result, the total current flowing in the motor circuit up to the capacitor is reduced to a value below the normal full-load current of the motor. With that hookup, the total motor full-load current flows only over the conductors from the capacitor connection to the motor and the entire motor circuit up to that connection carries only the so-called "working current" or "resistive current." That is shown in the top part of Fig. 460-8.

Under the condition shown, it is obvious that setting the overload relay in the starter for 125 percent of the motor nameplate full-load current (as

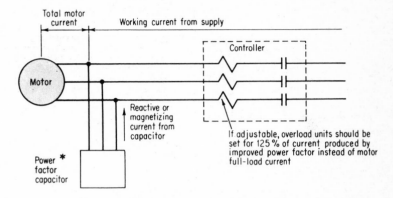

TOTAL MOTOR CURRENT = VECTOR SUM OF REACTIVE AND WORKING CURRENTS

EXAMPLE: Motor with 70% power factor has full-load current of 143 amps. Capacitor corrects to 100% PF.

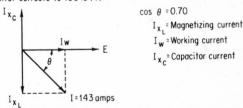

$\cos \theta = 0.70$

I_{x_L} = Magnetizing current

I_w = Working current

I_{x_C} = Capacitor current

I_{x_C} cancels I_{x_L} leaving only working current to be supplied from circuit. Working current = 143 x $\cos \theta$ = 143 x 0.70 = 100

OVERLOAD RELAYS SHOULD BE SET FOR 125% OF 100 AMPS

* The rating of such capacitors should not exceed the value required to raise the no-load power factor of the motor to unity. Capacitors of these maximum ratings usually result in a full-load power factor of 95 to 98 percent.

Fig. 460-8. Motor overload protection must be sized for the current at improved PF. (Sec. 460-8.)

required by Sec. 430-32) would actually be an excessive setting for real protection of the motor, because considerably less than full-load current is flowing through the starter. The Code rule of this section includes the Exception, which calls for 125 percent (or other percent from Sec. 430-32) to be applied to the circuit current produced by the improved power factor—as shown in Fig. 460-8.

The 25-kvar capacitor used on the 100-hp, 460-V motor in the example in Sec. 460-8 will reduce the motor line current by about 9 percent. Section 430-32(a) (also Secs. 430-34 and 460-9) requires that the running overload protection be sized not more than 125 percent of motor full-load current produced with the capacitor. If the OL protection heaters were originally sized at 125 percent of the motor full-load current (1.25 × 121), they would have been sized at 151 A. With the motor current reduced by 9 percent (0.09 × 121, or 11 A), the motor full-load current with the capacitor installed would be 121 − 11 or 110 A. Since 125 percent of 110 A is 132 A, the heaters must be changed to a size not larger than 132 A.

If the capacitor conductors could be connected on the line side of the heaters, the heaters would not have to be reduced in size, since the reduction of line current occurs only from the source back to the point of the capacitor connection. Conductor connections at this location are extremely difficult to make because of the lack of space and the large size of the connecting lugs. Controller load terminals are furnished with connectors that will accept an additional conductor, or they can be easily modified to permit a dependable connection.

460-10. Grounding.   The metal case of a capacitor is suitably grounded by locknut and bushing connections of grounded metal nipples or raceways carrying the conductors connecting the capacitor into a motor circuit or feeder.

ARTICLE 470. RESISTORS AND REACTORS

470-1. Scope.   Except when installed in connection with switchboards or control panels that are so located that they are suitably guarded from physical damage and accidental contact with live parts, resistors should always be completely enclosed in properly ventilated metal boxes.

Large reactors are commonly connected in series with the main leads of large generators or the supply conductors from high-capacity network systems to assist in limiting the current delivered on short circuit. Small reactors are used with lightning arresters, the object here being to offer a high impedance to the passage of a high-frequency lightning discharge and so to aid in directing the discharge to ground. Another type of reactor, having an iron core and closely resembling a transformer, is used as a remote-control dimmer for stage lighting. Reactors as well as resistors are sources of heat and should therefore be mounted in the same manner as resistors.

ARTICLE 480. STORAGE BATTERIES

480-1. Scope. Storage cells are of two general types: the so-called lead-acid type, in which the positive plates consist of lead grids having openings filled with a semisolid component, commonly lead peroxide, and the negative plates are covered with sponge lead, the plates being immersed in dilute sulfuric acid; and the alkali type, in which the active materials are nickel peroxide for the positive plate and iron oxide for the negative plate, and the electrolyte is chiefly potassium hydroxide (Fig. 480-1).

Fig. 480-1. Article 480 applies only to "stationary installations of storage batteries"—whether they are used for supply to lighting, generator cranking, switchgear control, or in UPS (*U*ninter-ruptible *P*ower *S*upply) systems. (Sec. 480-1.)

480-2. Definitions. "Stationary installations of storage batteries" provide an independent source of power for emergency lighting, switchgear control, engine-generator set starting, signal and communications systems, laboratory power, and similar applications. They are an essential component of UPS systems. This Code article does not cover batteries used to supply the motive power for electric vehicles.

The most commonly used battery is the lead-acid type—either lead-antimony or lead-calcium. Nickel-cadmium batteries offer a variety of special features that, in many instances, offset their higher initial cost. Other types include silver-zinc, silver-cadmium, and mercury batteries.

The lead-antimony battery is readily available at a moderate price, has a high efficiency (85 percent to 90 percent), is comparatively small, and has a relatively long life if operated and maintained properly under normal conditions. Voltage output is about 2 V per cell; ratings range to about 1,000 amp-hr (based on an 8-hr discharge rate).

Lead-calcium batteries offer features similar to the lead-antimony type, and they require less maintenance. They do not require an "equalizing" charge (application of an overvoltage for a period of time to assure that all cells in a battery bank will produce the same voltage). For this reason, they are often selected for use in UPS systems.

This type of cell can usually be operated for a year or more without needing water, depending on the frequency and degree of discharge. Sealed or maintenance-free batteries of this type never need water. Voltage output is 2 V per cell, with ratings up to about 200 amp-hr (8-hr rate).

Nickel-cadmium batteries are particularly useful for application in temperature extremes. They are reputed to have been successfully operated at temperatures from −40°F to +163°F. They have a very high short-time current capability and are well suited to such applications as engine starting and UPS operation. Initial cost is higher than lead-acid types; however, they offer long life (25 to 30 years), reliability, and small size per unit. Voltage is about 1.2 V per cell.

480-3. Wiring and Equipment Supplied from Batteries.   As indicated in Fig. 480-2, whatever kinds of circuits and loads a battery bank serves, all rules of the NE Code covering operation at that voltage must be applied to the wiring and equipment.

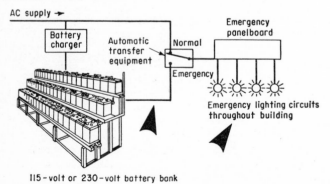

115−volt or 230−volt battery bank

Fig. 480-2. Applicable Code rules must be observed for load circuits fed by batteries. (Sec. 480-3.)

480-8. Battery Locations. Although specific "battery rooms" or enclosures are no longer required for installation of any batteries (not since the 1971 NE Code), part **(a)** does require ventilation at battery locations. A specific "battery room" was previously required for open-tank or open-jar batteries, but such units are no longer made or in use.

The overcharging of a battery can result in the breaking down of the electrolyte into gases that, if permitted to accumulate in the room, may result in an explosive mixture. Overcharging indicates problems with the charging equipment requiring correction. Proper ventilation will resolve this explosive mixture, assuring that the location is not a hazardous location subject to Art. 501.

Because the fumes given off by a storage battery are very corrosive, the type of wiring must be such that it will withstand the corrosive action, and special precautions are necessary as to the type of insulation used, as well as protection of all metalwork. It is stated by the respective manufacturers that conduit made of aluminum or Everdur (silicon-bronze) is well suited to withstand the corrosive effects of the fumes in battery rooms. If steel conduit is used, it is recommended that the conduit be zinc-coated and that it be kept well painted with asphaltum paint.

Batteries of the lead-acid type sometimes throw off a fine spray of the dilute acid which fills the air around the cells; hence steel conduit or tubing should not be brought close to any cell.

There are no special requirements on the type of fixtures or other electrical equipment used in the battery room. Proper ventilation of the room will prevent explosions. See Secs. 300-6 and 410-4(b).

Chapter Five

ARTICLE 500. HAZARDOUS (CLASSIFIED) LOCATIONS

500-1. Scope—Articles 500 Through 503. In the heading of this article, the word "classified" makes clear that hazardous locations are those which have been "classified" as hazardous by the inspection authority. Hazardous locations in plants and other industrial complexes are involved with a wide variety of flammable gases and vapors and ignitible dusts—all of which have widely different flash points, ignition temperatures, and flammable limits. And these explosive or flammable substances are processed and handled under a wide range of operating conditions. In such places, fire or explosion could result in loss of lives, facilities, and/or production.

Classification of hazardous areas must be approached very carefully, based on experience and a detailed understanding of electrical usage in the various kinds of locations. After study and analysis—and consultation with inspection authorities or other experts in such work—hazardous areas may be identified and delineated diagrammatically by defining the limits and degree of the hazards involved. In all cases, classification must be carefully based on the type of gas involved, whether the vapors are heavier or lighter than air, and similar factors peculiar to the particular hazardous substance.

Classification takes into account that all sources of hazards—gas, vapor, dust, fibers—have different ignition temperatures and produce different pressures when exploding. Electrical equipment must, therefore, be constructed and installed in such a way as to be safe when used in the presence of particular explosive mixtures. The source of hazard must be evaluated in terms of those characteristics that are involved with explosion or fire, as follows:

Flash point of a liquid is the minimum temperature at which the liquid will give off sufficient vapor to form an ignitible mixture with air near the surface of the liquid or within the vessel used. (This characteristic is not applicable to gases.)

Ignition temperature of a substance is the lowest temperature which will initiate explosion or cause self-sustained combustion of the substance.

Explosive limits: When flammable gases or vapors mix with air or oxygen, there is a minimum concentration of the gas or vapor below which propagation of flame does not occur upon contact with a source of ignition. There is also a maximum concentration above which propagation does not occur. These boundary-line mixtures are known as the lower and upper explosive (or flammable) limits and usually are expressed in terms of the percentage of gas or vapor in air, by volume. (See NFPA Bulletin No. 325M.)

Vapor density is the weight of a volume of pure vapor or gas (with no air present) compared to the weight of an equal volume of dry air at the same temperature and pressure.

NFPA No. 70C, *Hazardous Locations Classification,* was developed to supplement the **NEC**. This manual contains information on classifying locations for the purpose of determining the types of wiring systems and electrical equipment to be used. Material from 47 NFPA and ANSI standards are contained in this document.

Section 500-1 recognizes use of "intrinsically safe" equipment in hazardous locations and exempts such equipment from the rules of Arts. 500 through 517. Intrinsic safety is obtained by restricting the energy available in an electrical system to much less than that required for the ignition of flammable atmospheres such as gases and vapors that exist in processing industries. Intrinsically safe systems operate at low voltage (e.g., 24 V) and are designed safe, regardless of short circuits, grounding, overvoltage, equipment damage, or component failure. But such equipment must be "approved," which requires careful attention to UL listing and application data from the *Hazardous Location Equipment Directory* of UL.

Intrinsically safe circuits and equipment for use in Division 1 locations must be carefully applied. It is up to the designer and/or the installer to be sure that the energy level available in such equipment is below the level that could ignite the particular hazardous atmosphere. That must be assured for both normal and abnormal conditions of the equipment. Testing of an intrinsically safe system by UL is based on a maximum distance of 5,000 ft between the equipment installed in the nonhazardous or Division 2 location and the equipment installed in the Division 1 location. As noted in Sec. 500-1, a valuable guide to the use of such equipment is the NFPA (National Fire Protection Association) publication No. 493-1975, entitled *Intrinsically Safe Process Control Equipment for Use in Class I Hazardous Locations.*

Wiring of intrinsically safe circuits must be run in separate raceways or otherwise separated from circuits for all other equipment to prevent imposing excessive current or voltage on the intrinsically safe circuits because of fault contact with the other circuits.

A note in this section: Maximum effort should be made to keep as much electrical equipment as possible out of the hazardous areas—particularly minimizing installation of arcing, sparking, and high-temperature devices in hazardous locations. It is generally economically and operationally better to keep certain electrical equipment out of hazardous area. Figure 500-1 shows an example. There the drive shaft of the motor

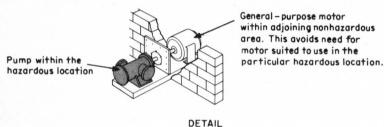

Pump within the hazardous location

General – purpose motor within adjoining nonhazardous area. This avoids need for motor suited to use in the particular hazardous location.

DETAIL

Fig. 500-1. Keeping electrical equipment in nonhazardous area eliminates costly hazardous types. (Sec. 500-1.)

is extended through a packing gland in one of the enclosing walls. To prevent the accumulation of flammable vapors or gas within the motor room, it should be ventilated effectively by clean air or kept under a slight positive air pressure. A gas detector giving a visual and/or audible alarm would be an additional desirable safety feature.

Positive-pressure ventilation is also cited as a means of reducing the level of hazard in areas where explosive or flammable substances are or might be present. Air-pressurized building interiors can provide safe operation without explosion-proof equipment. When explosion-proof equipment is not justified financially, pressurized building interiors can alter the need. For example, if a motor control center is to be located in a building in a Class I hazardous location, the entire room may be pressurized. But construction must comply with certain specific requirements:

1. The building area or room must be kept as airtight as possible.
2. The interior space must be kept under slight overpressure by adequate positive-pressure ventilation from a source of clean air.
3. The pressurizing fans should be connected to an emergency supply circuit.
4. Ventilating louvers must be located near ground level to achieve effective air flow within the pressurized room.
5. Safeguards against ventilation failure must be provided.

Fig. 500-2. A seal fitting (upper arrow) is used for equipment enclosure. But nitrogen purging of the conduit system was also applied at this installation at a space-rocket launch-pad. Equipment was specified to be listed for Class I, Division 1, Group B where exposed to hydrogen and for Group D where the equipment was in a rocket-fuel atmosphere. Where motors, panelboards, enclosures, etc., were not available in the proper Group rating, nitrogen purging and pressurization were used in addition to sealing, to add another measure of safety. The valve (lower arrow) was used in the cover of each conduit body to provide continuous bleedoff of the nitrogen to maintain a pressure (2-in. of water) within the conduit, enabling the steady flow of nitrogen to keep the conduit free of any explosive mixture. (Sec. 500-1.)

Purging of electrical raceways and enclosures is another means of reducing the degree of hazard (Fig. 500-2). But that requires both the manufacturer and the user of purged equipment to ensure the integrity of the system. Prepackaged purge controls for both Division 1 and Division 2 locations are on the market.

The purging medium—such as inert gas, like nitrogen, or clean air—must be essentially free from dust and liquids. The normal ambient air of an industrial interior is usually not satisfactory. And because the purge supply can contain only trace amounts of flammable vapors or gases, the compressor intake must be in a nonhazardous area. The compressor intake line should not pass through a hazardous atmosphere. If it does, it must be made of a noncombustible material, be protected from damage and corrosion, and must prevent hazardous vapors from being drawn into the compressor.

500-2. Special Precaution. Because of the inherently higher level of danger, design and installation of electrical circuits and systems in hazardous locations must be done in particularly strict compliance with the instructions given in product standards. Although **NE Code** Sec. 110-3(b) requires all product applications to conform to the conditions and limitations specified in the directories issued by third-party testing labs (UL, Factory Mutual, ETL, etc.), the correlation of hazardous location electrical equipment is much more thoroughly dictated than that in nonhazardous areas.

1. Section 500-2 requires that construction and installation of equipment in all hazardous areas "will ensure safe performance under conditions of proper use and maintenance." A note then urges designers, installers, inspectors, and maintenance personnel to "exercise more than ordinary care" for hazardous location work.

2. Paragraph **(a)** of this section requires that all equipment in hazardous locations be approved not only for the class of location (such as Class I, Class II, or Class III) but also for the particular type of hazardous atmosphere (such as Group A, B, C, or D for locations involving gases or vapors, or Group E, F, or G if the atmosphere involves combustible or flammable dusts). The **Code** section describes the specific atmospheres that correspond to those letter designations.

   An important regulation is given in the last paragraph of Sec. 500-2(a), which permits use of "general-purpose equipment" or "equipment in general-purpose enclosures" in Division 2 conditions of Class I, Class II, or Class III locations. That rule permits equipment that is *not* listed for hazardous locations but is listed for general use—BUT such use is acceptable only where a **Code** rule specifically mentions such application. For instance, Sec. 501-4(b) does say that boxes and fittings in Class I, Division 2 locations do *not* have to be explosion-proof type; i.e., sheet-metal boxes could be used. But controversy arises over that last paragraph of Sec. 500-2(a) because general-use enclosures are permitted only where the equipment does not pose a threat of ignition "under *normal* operating conditions." Division 2 locations, however, *are* those where the hazardous atmosphere is not present under normal operating conditions. So the last phrase of the **Code** rule seems to be superfluous, unless the "normal operating conditions" is meant to apply to the equipment itself instead of the surrounding atmosphere. Equipment that is operating normally might not pose a threat of ignition, but a ground fault or short in the equipment—which is *not* a "normal operating condition"—could ignite a combustible atmosphere that might exist at a Division 2 location. The **Code** rule here is obscure.

3. In addition to being "approved" for the class and group of the hazardous area where it is installed, equipment is required by paragraph **(b)** of Sec. 500-2 to be "marked" with that data, along

with its operating temperature when used in an ambient not over 40°C. Table 500-2(b) gives identification numbers that are used on equipment nameplates to show the operating temperature for which the equipment is approved.

Position of OSHA

With hazardous location equipment, as with all electrical equipment for nonhazardous areas, great care must be taken to assure compliance with OSHA regulations. OSHA's position has been that all new hazardous location electrical work must fully comply with all rules of the **1971 NE Code**, with all installations subject to inspection by OSHA compliance officers—and subject to fines or worse for violations. (Note that OSHA enforced the 1971 **NE Code** and *not* the 1975 code. OSHA's shift to enforcement of the 1978 **NE Code** must be observed when it is made.) And OSHA has made the basic **NE Code** sections on hazardous locations retroactive. That is, Secs. 500, 501, 502, and 503 in the 1971 **Code** have, for a long time, formed the standard of acceptability for existing hazardous location electrical installations. All such existing systems have been required to be made to conform to the 1971 **Code**—regardless of when the installation was originally made and no matter what **Code** was followed when the work was put in. Still another factor is **NE Code** Sec. 500-3, which could be interpreted to require that all of Arts. 510 through 517 are also retroactive.

A clear effect of OSHA regulations is to require "listed," "labeled," "accepted," and/or "certified" equipment to be used whenever available. If any electrical system component is "of a kind" that *any* nationally recognized testing lab "accepts, certifies, lists, labels or determines to be safe," then that component *must* be so designated in order to be acceptable for use under OSHA regulations. Every electrical designer and installer must exercise great care in evaluating any and all equipment and products used in hazardous electrical work to assure compliance with OSHA rules requiring certification by a nationally recognized testing lab.

In UL's *Hazardous Location Equipment Directory* (red book), limitations and application conditions are first set down for all equipment in general, as follows:

1. When equipment is listed and marked to show that it has been tested and is recognized for use in one or more of the **Code**-designated groups of hazardous locations, such marking indicates that such equipment is suitable for use in *either* Division 1 or Division 2 location of the particular class of hazardous location, even though no reference is made to the "division." Such equipment is, of course, also acceptable if used in a nonhazardous location. Figure 500-3 shows a typical nameplate used on such equipment, as required by parts **(a)** and **(b)** of Sec. 500-2, showing suitability as "explosion-proof" (Class I) and "dust-tight" (Class II).

2. BUT, equipment that is marked "Division 2" or "Div. 2" is suitable

Fig. 500-3. Typical UL part of equipment nameplate describes "Approval for Class and Properties." (Sec. 500-2.)

only for use in such a division and may *not* be used in a Division 1 location. However, a piece of equipment may have other marking to indicate its acceptability for other specific uses. Figure 500-4 shows a nameplate that is an addition to the nameplate in Fig. 500-2, noting that the same fixture is "Suitable for Wet Locations." Section 410-4 of the **NE Code** requires such marking on "all fixtures installed in wet locations. . . ." Care must be taken to distinguish between differ-

Fig. 500-4. Additional data on a nameplate may show other acceptability—as for "wet locations." (Sec. 500-2.)

ent parts of nameplates to precisely determine what is third-party certification.

3. Equipment that is listed and marked for "Class I" locations (explosion-proof) may be used for "Class II" locations if it is dust-tight to exclude combustible dusts and if its external operating temperature is not at or above the ignition level of the particular dust that might accumulate on it. Obviously, these characteristics must be carefully established before Class I equipment is used in a Class II location.

4. Equipment listed for Class II, Group G (for flour, starch, or grain dust)—as used in a grain elevator—is also generally suitable for use in Class III locations, where combustible lint or flyings are present. The exception noted is for fan-cooled type motors which might have their air passages choked or clogged by large amounts of the lint or flyings.

5. Because hazardous location equipment is critically dependent upon proper operating temperature, a UL note warns that the ampere or wattage marking on power-consuming equipment is based on the equipment being supplied with voltage exactly equal to the rated voltage value. Voltage higher or lower than the rated value will produce other than rated amps or watts, with the possibility that heating effect of the current within the equipment will be greater than normal. Higher than normal current will be produced by overvoltage to resistive loads and by undervoltage to induction motors. Because of this, actual circuit voltage, rather than the nameplate value, must be used when calculating the required ampacity of branch-circuit conductors, rating or setting of overcurrent protection, rating of disconnect, etc.—all to assure adequate sizing and avoid overheating.

6. Hazardous location equipment is tested and listed for use at normal atmospheric pressure in an ambient temperature not over 40°C (104°F), unless indicated otherwise. Use of equipment under higher-than-normal pressure, in oxygen-enriched atmospheres or at higher ambient temperatures can be dangerous. Such abnormal conditions may increase the chance of igniting the hazardous atmosphere and may increase the pressure of explosion within equipment.

7. Openings or modifications must not be made in explosion-proof or dust-ignition-proof equipment, because any such field alterations would void the integrity and tested safety of the equipment. Field alteration of listed products for nonhazardous application is also generally prohibited.

8. All bolts as well as all threaded parts of enclosures must be tightly made up.

9. Indoor hazardous location equipment that is exposed to severe corrosive conditions must be listed as suitable for those conditions as well as for the hazardous conditions.

The requirements of Sec. 500-2 and **Code** Tables 500-2 and 500-2(b) provide the means of properly identifying and classifying equipment for use in hazardous locations. The identification numbers in **Code** Table 500-2(b) pertain to temperature-range classifications as used by Underwriters Laboratories Inc., in UL *Hazardous Location Standards.*

While the **Code** rules for Class I locations do not differ for different kinds of gas or vapor contained in the atmosphere, it is to be noted that it is necessary to select equipment designed for use in the particular atmospheric group to be encountered. This is necessary for the reason that explosive mixtures of the different groups have different flash points and explosion pressures; also, because the ignition temperatures vary with the groups.

Underwriters Laboratories Inc. lists fittings and equipment as suitable for use in all groups of Class I, although the listings for Groups A and B are not as complete as those for Groups C and D.

In Class II locations the **Code**, in a few cases, differentiates between the different kinds of dust, particularly dusts which are electrically conductive and those which are not conductive. Here again, as in Class I locations, care must be used to determine that the equipment selected is suitable for use where a particular kind of dust is present.

In addition to the use of more than ordinary care in selecting equipment for use in hazardous locations, special attention should be given to installation and maintenance details in order that the installations will be permanently free from electrical hazards. In making subsequent additions or changes, the high standards of the original installation must be maintained.

For a more thorough knowledge of specific hazardous areas and equipment selection and location it is essential to obtain copies of the various NFPA and ANSI standards referenced in Arts. 500 through 517.

500-3. Specific Occupancies. Articles 500 through 517 of the **National Electrical Code** refer to various NFPA and ANSI standards. Because these references are broad in nature, specific extracted material has been placed in a single document to provide a much greater convenience to users of the **National Electrical Code**. NFPA No. 70C is that source. This composite document will be updated when changes are made to existing NFPA or ANSI standards, or when new standards are developed.

Copies of this manual may be obtained from the Publications Department of the National Fire Protection Association, 470 Atlantic Ave., Boston, MA 02210.

500-4. Class I Locations. In each of the three classes of hazardous locations discussed in Secs. 500-4, 500-5, and 500-6, the **Code** recognizes varying degrees of hazard; hence under each class two divisions are defined. In the installation rules that follow, the requirements for Division 1 of each class are more rigid than the requirements for Division 2.

Briefly, the hazards in the three classes of locations are due to the following causes:

Class I, highly flammable gases or vapors
Class II, combustible dust
Class III, combustible fibers or flyings

The classifications are easily understood, and, if a given location is to be classed as hazardous, it should not be difficult to determine in which of the three classes it belongs. However, it is obviously impossible to make rules that will in every case determine positively whether the location is or is not hazardous. Considerable common sense and good judgment must be exercised in determining whether the location under consideration should be considered as hazardous or likely to become hazardous because of a change in the processes carried on, and if so, what portion of the premises should be classed as coming under Division I and what part may safely be considered as being in Division 2.

ARTICLE 501. CLASS I LOCATIONS

501-1. General. The more common Class I locations are those where some process is carried on involving the use of a highly volatile and flammable liquid, such as gasoline, petroleum naphtha, benzene, diethyl ether, or acetone, or flammable gases.

In any Class I location, an explosive mixture of air and flammable gas or vapor may be present which can be caused to explode by an arc or spark. To avoid the danger of explosions all electrical apparatus which may create arcs or sparks should if possible be kept out of the rooms where the hazardous atmosphere exists, or, if this is not possible, such apparatus must be "of types approved for use in explosive atmospheres."

All equipment such as switches, CBs, or motors must have some movable operating part projecting through the enclosing case, and any such part, for example the operating lever of a switch or the shaft of a motor, must have sufficient clearance so that it will work freely; hence the equipment cannot be hermetically sealed. Also, the necessity for subsequent opening of the enclosures for servicing makes hermetic sealing impracticable. Furthermore, the enclosure of the equipment must be entered by a run of conduit, and it is practically impossible to make conduit joints absolutely air- and gastight. Due to slight changes in temperature, the conduit system and the apparatus enclosures "breathe"; that is, any flammable gas in the room may gradually find its way inside the conduit and enclosures and form an explosive mixture with air. Under this condition, when an arc occurs inside the enclosure an explosion may take place.

When the gas and air mixture explodes inside the enclosing case, the burning mixture must be confined entirely within the enclosure, so as to prevent the ignition of flammable gases in the room. In the first place it is necessary that the enclosing case be so constructed that it will have sufficient strength to withstand the high pressure generated by an internal explosion. The pressure in pounds per square inch produced by the explosion of a given gas-and-air mixture has been quite definitely determined, and the enclosure can be designed accordingly.

Since the enclosures for apparatus cannot be made absolutely tight, when an internal explosion occurs some of the burning gas will be forced out through any openings that exist. It has been found that the flame will not be carried out through an opening that is quite long in proportion to its width. This principle is applied in the design of so-called explosion-proof enclosures for apparatus by providing a wide flange at the joint between the body of the enclosure and grinding these flanges to a definitely determined fit. In this case the flanges are so ground that when the cover is in place the clearance between the two surfaces will at no point exceed 0.0015 in. Thus, if an explosion occurs within the enclosure, in order to escape from the enclosure the burning gas must travel a considerable distance through an opening not more than 0.0015 in. wide.

The basic construction characteristics of equipment for Class I hazardous locations are detailed in various sections of this article and in standards of testing laboratories. Application of the products hinges on understanding those details:

An explosion-proof enclosure for Class I locations is capable of withstanding an explosion of a specified gas or vapor which may occur within it and of preventing the ignition of the specified gas or vapor surrounding the enclosure by sparks, flashes, or explosions of the gas or vapor within. Explosion-proof equipment must provide three things: (1) strength, (2) joints which will not permit flame or hot gases to escape, and (3) cool operation, to prevent ignition of surrounding atmosphere.

UL requires that explosion-proof enclosures must withstand a hydrostatic test of four times the maximum explosion pressure developed inside the enclosure. Explosion-proof enclosures are not vapor- or gas-tight and it is simply assumed that any hazardous gases in the ambient atmosphere will enter them either through normal breathing or when maintenance is performed on the enclosed equipment.

When an explosion occurs inside a rectangular explosion-proof enclosure, the resulting force exerts pressure in all directions. The enclosure must be designed with sufficient strength to withstand these forces and avoid rupture (Fig. 501-1).

The energy generated by an explosion within an enclosure must be permitted to dissipate through the joints of the enclosure under controlled conditions. There are two generally recognized joint designs intended to provide this control—threaded and flat:

1. Threaded construction of covers and other removable parts that have five full threads engaged produces a safe, flame-arresting, pressure-relieving joint. When an explosion occurs within a threaded enclosure, the flame and hot gases create an internal

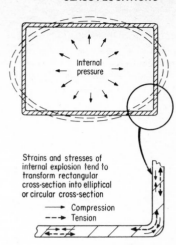

Fig. 501-1. An explosion creates strains and stresses in cross section of enclosure walls. (Sec. 501-1.)

pressure against the cover, thus locking the threads and forcing the gases out through the path between the threaded surfaces. When the gases reach the outside hazardous atmosphere, they have been cooled by the heat-sink effect of the mass of metal, down to a point below the ignition temperature of the outside atmosphere, as shown in Fig. 501-2.

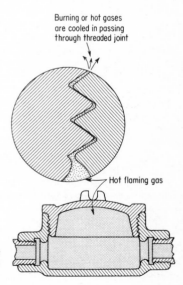

Fig. 501-2. Threaded joints cool the heated gas as it escapes from enclosure under pressure. (Sec. 501-1.)

2. A flat joint is constructed by accurate grinding or machining of the mating surfaces of the cover and the body. This flat joint works in a manner similar to the threaded joint. The two surfaces are bolted closely together, and as flame and hot gases are forced through the narrow opening, they are cooled by the mass of the metal enclosure, so that only cool gas enters the hazardous atmosphere. Figure 501-3

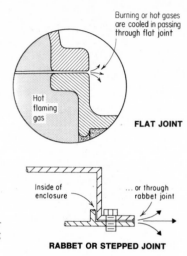

Burning or hot gases are cooled in passing through flat joint

Hot flaming gas

FLAT JOINT

Inside of enclosure

... or through rabbet joint

RABBET OR STEPPED JOINT

Fig. 501-3. Ground surfaces of flat or rabbet joint provide release and cooling of internal gases. (Sec. 501-1.)

shows the flat joint and a variation on it called a "rabbet" joint. Care must be taken to assure that all cover screws are tight and that no particles of dirt or other foreign matter get in between the cover and the body. Even a small particle could prevent tight closing and might allow the joint to pass flame.

UL standards on explosion-proof enclosures contain rules on "Grease for Joint Surfaces": "Paint or a sealing material shall not be applied to the contacting surfaces of a joint. A suitable corrosion inhibitor (grease) such as petrolatum, soap-thickened mineral oils, or nondrying slushing compound may be applied to the metal joint surfaces before assembly. The grease shall be of a type that does not harden because of aging, does not contain an evaporating solvent, and does not cause corrosion of the joint surfaces."

501-4. Wiring Methods.   Threaded steel intermediate metal conduit has been added to the wiring methods suitable for use in Class I, Division 1 locations. This permission, plus recognition by other sections of the Code, gives IMC full recognition as a general-purpose raceway equivalent in application to rigid metal conduit. Type MI cable is the only cable assembly that is permitted in Class I, Division 1 locations (Fig. 501-4).

Fig. 501-4. Type MI cable is recognized for use in Class I, Division 1 locations, provided that the termination fittings (arrow) are listed as suitable for hazardous location use. (Sec. 501-4.)

The term "approved for the location" in paragraph **(a)** means that approval is to be based on the performance of a fitting or equipment when subjected to a specific atmosphere. As applied to rigid metal conduit, to be explosion-proof, threaded joints must be used at couplings and for connection to fittings, the threads must be cleanly cut, five full threads must be engaged, and each joint must be made up tight. Conduit elbows and short-radius capped elbows provide for 90° bends in conduit but only where wires may be guided when being pulled into the conduit, to prevent damaging the conductors by pulling them around the sharp turn in the elbow. Figure 501-5 shows two types of fittings used in hazardous locations to facilitate pull-in of conductors that have stiff or heavy-wall insulation. The capped elbow is especially suited to use in tight quarters.

All fittings, such as outlet boxes, junction boxes, and switch boxes, also all enclosures for apparatus, should have threaded hubs to receive the conduit and must be explosion-proof. Explosion-proof junction boxes are available in a wide variety of types (Fig. 501-6). Box covers may have

Fig. 501-5. Conduit elbows and similar fittings may be used where wires may be guided into conduit. (Sec. 501-4.)

threaded connections with the boxes, or the cover may be attached with machine screws, in which case a carefully ground flanged joint is required.

A flexible, explosion-proof fitting, suitable for use in Class I hazardous locations, is shown in Fig. 501-7. The flexible portion consists of a tube of bronze having deeply corrugated walls and reinforced by a braid of fine bronze wires. A heavy threaded fitting is securely joined to each end of the flexible tube, and a fibrous tubular lining, similar to "circular loom," is provided in order to prevent abrasion of the enclosed conductors that might result from long-continued vibration. The complete assembly is obtainable in various lengths up to a maximum of 3 ft.

Flexible connection fittings that are recognized by **NE Code** Sec. 501-4(a) for use in Class I, Division 1 locations are intended by UL and the **NE**

Fig. 501-6. A wide assortment of boxes, conduit bodies, fittings, and other enclosures are made in explosionproof designs listed for use in Class I locations. (Sec. 501-4.)

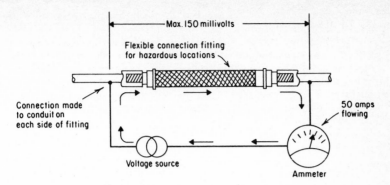

Voltage drop across fitting must not exceed 150 millivolts, measured between points on conduit ⅛ in. from each end of the fitting.

Fig. 501-7. Conductivity of flexible fitting is evaluated by voltage-drop test. (Sec. 501-4.)

Code to be used where it is necessary to provide flexible connections in threaded rigid conduit systems—as at motor terminals. Use of such flexible fittings must observe the minimum inside radius of bend for which the fitting has been tested. Those data are provided with the fitting.

Note: The UL warns that acceptability of the use of flexible connection fittings must be cleared with local inspection authorities. In general, use of such flexible fittings should be avoided wherever possible and should be limited to situations where use of threaded rigid conduit is completely ruled out by the needs or conditions of the application.

Where flexible connection fittings *are* used, the corrugated metal inner wall and the metal braid construction of the fitting provide equipment grounding continuity between the end connectors and the fitting. The UL test for conductivity through a flexible fitting is shown in Fig. 501-7. Although Sec. 501-16(b) requires either an internal or external bonding jumper to be used with standard flexible metal conduit in Class I, Division 2 locations, that rule does not apply to listed flexible fittings.

In Class I, Division 2 locations explosion-proof outlet boxes are not required at lighting outlets nor at junction boxes containing no arcing device. However, where conduit is used, it should enter the box through threaded openings as shown in Fig. 501-6, or if locknut-bushing attachment is used, a bonding jumper and/or fittings must be provided between the box and conduits, as required in Sec. 501-16(b).

As noted in part **(b)** of this section, flexible connections permitted in Class I, Division 2 locations may consist of flexible conduit (Greenfield) with approved fittings, and such fittings are not required to be specifically approved for Class I locations. It should be noted that a separate grounding conductor is necessary to bond across such flexible connections, as required in Sec. 501-16(b).

Ordinary knockout-type boxes may be installed in such locations, but Sec. 501-16(b) rules out the use of locknuts and bushings for bonding purposes, and the requirement specifies either bonding jumpers or other approved means (such as bonding locknuts on knockouts without any concentric or eccentric rings left in the wall of the enclosure) to assure adequate grounding from the hazardous area to the point of grounding at the services.

Cord connectors for connecting extra-hard-service type of flexible cord to devices in hazardous locations must be carefully applied. Section 501-4(b) permits extra-hard-usage flexible cord in Division 2 locations. But Sec. 502-4 permits its use in Division 1 and Division 2 areas of Class II locations. Section 503-3(a) (2) permits cords in Class III, Division 1 and Division 2 locations. Listed cord connectors are recognized for use in Class I, Groups A, B, C, and D or Class II, Group G locations—using Types S, SO, ST, or STO multiconductor, extra-hard-usage cord *with* a grounding conductor.

IMPORTANT! Section 501-4(b) adds power-limited tray cable (Type PLTC) to the list of wiring methods permitted in Class I, Division 2 locations, in accordance with the provisions of Art. 725 covering remote-control, signaling, and low-energy circuits. And, the last paragraph of Sec. 501-4(b) makes clear that high-voltage circuits (i.e., circuits over 600 V) may employ the wiring methods covered in the first part of Sec. 501-4(b) and, where protected from physical damage, may be made up using metallic-shielded, high-voltage cable in cable trays when installed in accordance with Art. 318. And Art. 326 dictates that such cable must be Type MV cable.

Figure 501-8 shows some applications of wiring methods that are covered by the rules of Sec. 501-4. At top, use of standard flex (Greenfield) in a Division 1 area violates part **(a)** of this section. At center, use of aluminum-sheathed cable (Type ALS) is OK in a Division 2 area. Even though Type ALS is no longer mentioned in part **(b)**, that type of cable is now covered by Art. 334 and is considered as one form of Type MC cable, which is mentioned in part **(b)** as acceptable in Division 2 areas. At bottom, use of Type MC is OK in a Division 2 location.

501-5. Sealing and Drainage. The proper sealing of conduits in Class I locations is an important matter. In Class I, Division 2 locations, each piece of apparatus that produces arcs or sparks, such as a motor controller, switch, or receptacle, should be isolated from all other apparatus by sealing within the conduit so that an explosion in one enclosure cannot be communicated through the conduit to any other enclosure. Whether used in an enclosure or in conduit, seals are necessary to prevent gases, vapors, or flames from being propagated into an enclosure or conduit run and to confine an explosion that might occur within an enclosure. When an explosion takes place within an enclosure because of arc ignition of gas or vapor that has entered the enclosure, flames and hot gases

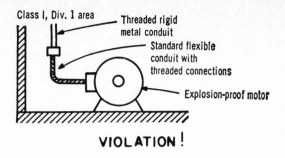

VIOLATION !

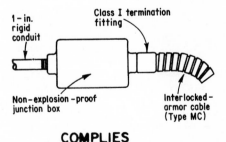

COMPLIES

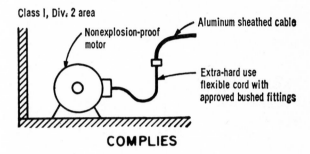

COMPLIES

Fig. 501-8. Wiring methods in Class I locations are clearly regulated.
(Sec. 501-4.)

could travel rapidly through unsealed conduits, and the resultant buildup of pressure could exceed the strength of conduit, wireways, or enclosures, causing explosive rupture.

Pressure piling is the name given to the action that takes place when an explosion occurs inside an enclosure because of flammable gas within the enclosure being ignited by a spark or overheated wiring. When this happens, and there are no seals in the conduits connecting to the enclosure, exploding gas will compress the entire atmosphere within the conduit system and flames or heat will ignite compressed gas some distance down the conduit and cause another, more-powerful explosion. The pressure and succeeding explosions are repeated through the system of raceways and enclosures, with each succeeding explosion increasing in intensity. To prevent such occurrences, it is mandatory that seal-off fittings be used in certain enclosures or conduit runs to block and confine potentially hazardous vapors.

The necessary sealing may be accomplished by inserting in the conduit runs special sealing fittings, as shown in Fig. 501-9, or provision may be

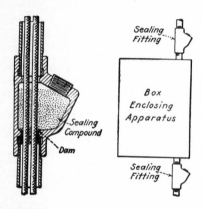

Fig. 501-9. Seal fitting is filled with compound to prevent passage of flame or vapor through the conduit. (Sec. 501-5.)

made for sealing in the enclosure for the apparatus. An explosionproof motor is made with the leads sealed where they pass from the terminal housing to the interior of the motor, and no other seal is needed where a conduit terminates at the motor, except that if the conduit is 2 in. or larger in size, a seal must be provided not more than 18 in. from the motor terminal housing.

Class I, Division 1

Part **(a)** of this section covers mandatory use of seals in Class I, Division 1 locations:

1. A seal is required in each and every conduit (regardless of the size of the conduit) entering (or leaving) an enclosure that contains one or more switches, CBs, fuses, relays, resistors, or any other device that is capable of producing an arc or spark that could cause ignition of gas or vapor within the enclosure or any device that might operate hot enough to cause ignition. In each such conduit, a seal fitting must be placed as close as is practicable but never more than 18 in. from such enclosure. As shown in Fig. 501-10, a conduit

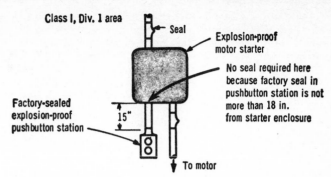

Class I, Div. 1 area

Seal

Explosion-proof
motor starter

No seal required here
because factory seal in
pushbutton station is not
more than 18 in.
from starter enclosure

Factory-sealed
explosion-proof
pushbutton station

15"

To motor

Fig. 501-10. Seal should be as close as "practicable" to the sealed enclosure. (Sec. 501-5.)

seal fitting is installed in the top conduit and one of the bottom conduits—as close as possible to the enclosure of the arcing device. But a seal is not used in the conduit to the push-button because that is a factory-sealed device and that seal is not over 18 in. from the starter. That complies with the intent of the **Code** rule, as well as the rule of Sec. 501-5(c) which recognizes "approved integral means for sealing"—as in the pushbutton. Figure 501-11 shows a seal fitting as close as possible to a box housing a receptacle.

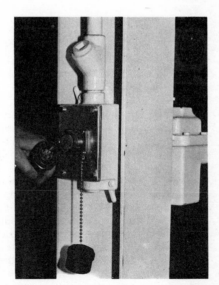

Fig. 501-11. Seal fitting is as close as possible to enclosure, providing maximum effectiveness. (Sec. 501-5.)

But questions have always risen about the acceptability of boxes or fittings between the sealing fittings and the enclosure being sealed. This section identifies the devices that may be used between the seal and the enclosure. Explosion-proof unions, couplings, elbows, capped elbows, and conduit bodies similar to L, T, and cross type shall be the only enclosures or fittings permitted between the sealing fittings and the enclosure. The rule goes on to note that any conduit body used in that position must be of a size not larger than the trade size of the conduit with which it is used. This clearly rules out the use of a box or any similar large-volume enclosure between the seal fitting and the enclosure being sealed, as shown in Fig. 501-12.

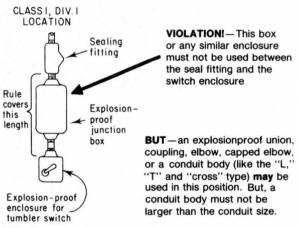

CLASS I, DIV. I LOCATION

Sealing fitting

Rule covers this length

Explosion-proof junction box

Explosion-proof enclosure for tumbler switch

VIOLATION!—This box or any similar enclosure must not be used between the seal fitting and the switch enclosure

BUT—an explosionproof union, coupling, elbow, capped elbow, or a conduit body (like the "L," "T" and "cross" type) **may** be used in this position. But, a conduit body must not be larger than the conduit size.

Fig. 501-12. Any type of junction "box" may not be used between seal and enclosure. (Sec. 501-5.)

The fittings listed as acceptable for use between the seal and the enclosure were selected on the basis that their internal volume was sufficiently small as to prevent the accumulation of any dangerous volume of gas or vapor. Acceptability was based on limiting the volume of gas or vapor that may accumulate between the seal and the enclosure being sealed. It was on this basis also that conduit bodies are prohibited from being of a larger size than the conduit with which they are used. If they were permitted, they would present the opportunity for accumulation of a larger volume of gas or vapor, which is considered objectionable.

Figure 501-13 shows an interesting variation on the above concern for use of a box between a seal and an enclosure. *No splices are permitted within seal-off fittings,* according to the UL *Hazardous Location Equipment Directory.* The illustration shows a round-box type of

Fig. 501-13. Seal fitting of the round box type is used to seal conduit run into bottom of explosionproof starter enclosure, with flexible fitting connection to the Class I, Division 1, Group D motor below and a watertight Class I cord connector control cable. (Sec. 501-5.)

seal fitting that is used for pulling power and control wires. Such a fitting takes a large, round, threaded cover equipped with a pouring spout. The cover, shown removed, is readily unscrewed to provide maximum unobstructed access to the fitting interior, which facilitates damming either one or both conduit hubs. When the cover is replaced, it can be rotated so the spout points up to permit compound fill. This fitting can be used to seal conduit regardless of its direction or run.

2. A seal is required in any conduit run of 2-in. size or larger, where such a conduit enters an "enclosure or fitting" that is required to be explosion-proof and houses terminals, splices, or taps, as shown in Fig. 501-14. Note in such cases, however, the rule does not call for

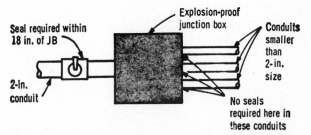

Fig. 501-14. Seals for conduits to junction boxes or fittings are required only for conduits of 2-in. size and larger. (Sec. 501-5.)

the seal to be "as close as practicable" to the enclosure or fitting, as required for a housing of an arcing or sparking device. Here, it simply requires that the seal be not over 18 in. away from the enclosure.

Another example of seal application in accordance with parts (1) and (2) of Sec. 501-5(a) is shown in Fig. 501-15.

Fig. 501-15. Seal fittings are very close to points where conduits enter the motor starter enclosures. Seals are not required for the conduits entering the junction box (arrow) because they are not 2-in. or larger size—although seals may be used there. (Sec. 501-5.)

The third part of Sec. 501-5(a) covers use of a single seal to provide the required seal for a conduit connecting two enclosures. Where two such pieces of apparatus are connected by a run of conduit not over 3 ft long, a single seal in this run is considered satisfactory if located at the center of the run. Figure 501-16 shows this rule. Although the wording is not detailed, the reference to "not more than 18 inches from either enclosure" must be understood to be 18 in. measured along the conduit, to avoid the misapplication of the rule shown in Fig. 501-17. The single seal at A is not over 18 in. from the CB enclosure and is literally not over 18 in. from the starter (it is 10 in. from the starter). But that use of a single seal for the two enclosures violates the Code intent that the 18 in. in each case *must* be measured along the conduit.

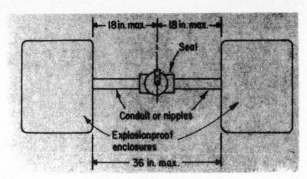

Fig. 501-16. A single seal serves two conduit entries into separate enclosures. (Sec. 501-5.)

Part **(4)** requires a seal in each and every conduit that leaves the Class I, Division 1 location—whether it passes into a Division 2 location or into a nonhazardous location. This required seal may be installed on either side of the boundary (Fig. 501-18). There must be no union, coupling, box, or fitting between the sealing fitting and the point where the conduit leaves the hazardous location. The rule does not specify a maximum distance that must be observed between the sealing fitting and the boundary. The purpose of this sealing is twofold: (1) The conduit usually terminates in some enclosure in the Division 2 or nonhazardous area containing an arc-producing device, such as a switch or fuse. If not sealed, the conduit and apparatus enclosure are likely to become filled with an explosive mixture and the ignition of this mixture may cause local damage in the Division 2 or nonhazardous location. (2) An explosion or ignition of the mixture in the conduit in the nonhazardous area would probably travel back

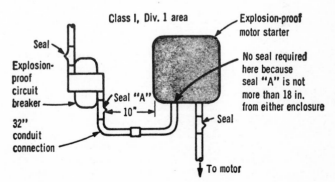

Fig. 501-17. Although this complies with the rule literally, it is a violation of the intent. (Sec. 501-5.)

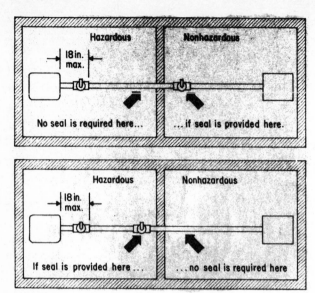

Fig. 501-18. Conduit must be provided with seal fitting where it crosses boundary. (Sec. 501-5.)

through the conduit to the hazardous area and might cause an explosion there if because of some defective fitting or poor workmanship the installation is not completely explosion-proof. If the conduit is unbroken (no union, coupling, etc.) between an enclosure seal and the point where the conduit leaves the hazardous area, an additional seal is not required at the boundary. Figure 501-19 shows two violations where conduit leaves the hazardous area.

The Exception to Sec. 501-5(a) (4) covers the case where a metal conduit system passes from a nonhazardous area, runs through a Class I, Division 1 hazardous area, and then returns to a nonhazardous area. Such a run is permitted to pass through the hazardous area without the need for a seal fitting at either of the boundaries where it enters and leaves the hazardous area. But, the wording of this Exception requires that such conduits, in order to be acceptable, must contain no union, coupling, box, or fitting in any part of the conduit run extending 12 in. into each of the nonhazardous areas involved (Fig. 501-20).

In the 1975 NE Code, the exception merely referred to "unbroken rigid-metal conduits" that pass through the hazardous area. The effect of the change is to clarify the meaning of the word "unbroken."

It is important that a similar exception to Sec. 501-5(b) (2) covers the use of an "unbroken metal conduit" passing through a Class I, Division 2

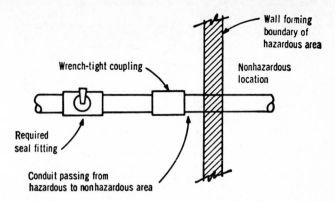

VIOLATION ! — Coupling not permitted between seal and the boundary

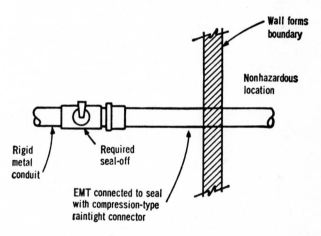

VIOLATION! — EMT not permitted in Class I location

Fig. 501-19. These violate rules on seal fittings where conduit crosses boundary. (Sec. 501-5.)

location. It does not have the same statement prohibiting unions, couplings, boxes, or fittings that are spelled out in the Exception after Sec. 501-5(a) (4). The difference in wording between the two exceptions appears to indicate that in a Class I, Division 2 location, the same prohibition against union, couplings, etc., is not applicable.

For some installations of conduits crossing boundaries, straightforward

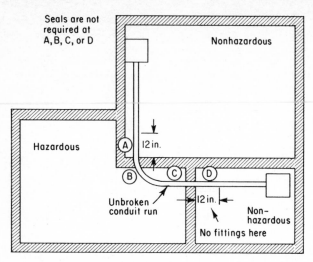

Seals are not
required at
A, B, C, or D

Nonhazardous

Hazardous

Ⓐ 12 in.

Ⓑ   Ⓒ   Ⓓ

Unbroken
conduit run

12 in.

Non-
hazardous

No fittings here

Conduit length in hazardous area must not contain any
union, coupling, box, or other fitting within the hazardous
area and for 12 in. beyond each boundary.

Fig. 501-20. Seals may be eliminated for conduit passing "completely
through" hazardous area. (Sec. 501-5.)

application of **NE Code** rules on conduit sealing is difficult. Most of these
cases involve determination as to what constitutes the boundaries of a
hazardous area; the **Code** provides no definition. The inspection authority should be consulted in cases not specifically covered by the **Code**
Because there are no provisions in the **Code** that *prohibit* the use of seals,
"*if in doubt, seal*" would be a safe practice to follow.

At the top of Fig. 501-21, the conduit run is sealed within 18 in. of an
explosion-proof enclosure, as shown below, and extends into a concrete
floor slab, emerging in a nonhazardous area. It is not clear what constitutes the boundary of the Class I, Division 1 area. Must a seal be placed at
A or might it instead be placed at B in the nonhazardous area? An **NE
Code** Official Intepretation, pertaining to a hospital operating room,
ruled that the entire concrete slab through which the conduit traveled
constituted the boundary of the hazardous area, and that the seal could
be placed either at A, where the conduit leaves the hazardous area, or at
B, where it enters the nonhazardous area. But some authorities may
require seals at A and B. With a seal at A and not at B, a heavier-than-air
gas or liquid (like gasoline) might penetrate a crack in the floor, enter the
conduit through a coupling, and pass into the enclosure in the nonhazardous area. Or, a seal at B but not at A might not prevent vapor in the

conduit from entering the nonhazardous area through a coupling in the concrete and then through a crack in that floor. That kind of gas passage has occurred.

At the bottom of Fig. 501-21, the conduit run is not in the floor slab, but in the ground below the slab. Now what constitutes the boundary? Can the seal still be placed either at point A or at point B? Code rules applying to gasoline stations and aircraft hangars may be used as a guide. The real question is whether the ground beneath the slab is hazardous or nonhazardous location. Section 514-2(d) defines dispensing and service-station wiring and equipment, any portion of which is below the surface of a hazardous area, as a Class I, Division 1 location. Also, Sec. 513-3 requires that the sealing rules of Sec. 501-5(a) (4) and 501-5(b) (2) be applied to horizontal as well as vertical boundaries of defined hazardous areas in aircraft hangars. And the last sentence of Sec. 513-7 says that raceways in or beneath a floor slab are considered as being in the hazardous location above the floor. This is also stated in Sec. 511-3.

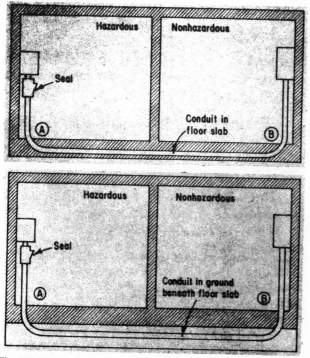

Fig. 501-21. Conduit in floor-slab boundary may require seals at both "A" and "B." (Sec. 501-5.)

A safe conclusion is that, unless specifically defined to the contrary, the ground beneath a hazardous area is an extension of that hazardous area. Or like the concrete floor in the example, the concrete *and* the ground beneath the hazardous area through which the conduit passes can be considered to be the "boundary" when there is any question of boundary. And the boundary itself is considered part of the hazardous location. That means that the conduit does not leave the hazardous area until it emerges at B. The seal should be placed there and an argument can be made that use of two seals—at A and B—would be better practice in both sketches in Fig. 501-21.

It should also be noted that Sec. 514-2(d) states that the underground Class I, Division 1 location beneath a pump island of a gas station extends at least to the point where underground conduit emerges from the ground. That concept can be logically applied to the sketches in Fig. 501-21.

Figure 501-22 is a wiring layout for a Class I, Division 1 location. The

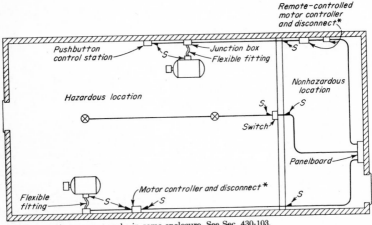

* Disconnecting means may be in same enclosure. See Sec. 430-103.

Fig. 501-22. Required seals are shown in points marked "S." (Sec. 501-5.)

wiring is all rigid metal conduit with threaded joints. All fittings and equipment are explosionproof; this includes the motors, the motor controller for motor No. 1 (lower part of drawing), the pushbutton control station for motor No. 2 (upper part of drawing), and all outlet and junction boxes. The panelboard and controller for motor No. 2 are placed outside the hazardous area and hence need not be explosionproof.

Each of the three runs of conduit from the panelboard is sealed just outside the hazardous area. A sealing fitting is provided in the conduit each side of the controller for motor No. 1 (lower part of drawing). The leads are sealed where they pass through the frame of the motor into the terminal housing, and no other seal is needed at this point provided that the conduit and flexible fitting enclosing the leads to the motor are smaller than 2 in. The pushbutton control station for motor No. 2 (upper part of drawing) is considered an arc-producing device, even though the contacts may be oil-immersed, and hence the conduit is sealed where it terminates at this device.

A seal is provided on each side of the switch controlling the lighting fixture. One of these seals is in the nonhazardous room and that single seal serves as both the seal for the arcing device and the seal for conduit crossing the boundary. The lighting fixtures are hung on rigid conduit stems threaded to the covers of explosionproof boxes on the ceiling.

About seal fittings   In using seal fittings in conduits in hazardous locations, application data of the UL must be observed, as follows:

- Conduit seal-off fittings to comply with NE Code Sec. 501-5 or 502-5 must be used *only* with the sealing compound that is supplied with the fitting and specified by the fitting manufacturer in the instructions furnished with the fitting.
- Seal-off fittings are listed for sealing listed conductors in conduit, where the conductors are thermoplastic insulated, rubber-covered, or lead-covered.
- Any instructions supplied with a seal-off fitting must be carefully observed with respect to limitation on the mounting position (e.g., vertical only) or location (e.g., elbow seal). Figure 501-23 shows a

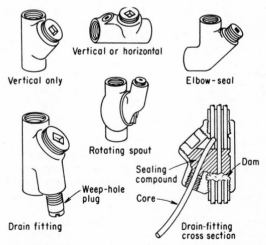

Vertical or horizontal

Vertical only

Elbow-seal

Rotating spout

Sealing compound

Dam

Weep-hole plug

Core

Drain fitting

Drain-fitting cross section

Fig. 501-23. A variety of seal fittings are suited to different applications. (Sec. 501-5.)

variety of available seal fittings. Sealing fittings are designed for vertical orientation only, for optional vertical or horizontal positioning, or as combination elbow seals. Others are compatible with conduits installed at any angle, since covers can be rotated until sealing spouts point upward.

Because conduits are installed vertically, horizontally, and at angles and require ells, tees, and offsets, the fittings used for sealing differ in construction features, orientation, and method of sealing.

Sealing fittings intended solely for vertical orientation have threaded, upward-slanting ports slightly larger than conduit hub openings to permit asbestos-fiber dams to be tamped into fitting bases. The dam prevents the fluid-sealing compound from running down into the conduit before the seal has solidified.

A second type of fitting is designed either for vertical or horizontal positioning. These units are identified by two seal-chamber plugs that can be removed to facilitate tamping dam fibers into both conduit hubs when the device is aligned horizontally. The compound is poured into the chamber through the larger of the two ports. The ports are then replugged, and the plugs tightened flush with their collars. When these fittings are oriented vertically, however, only lower conduit hubs need be dammed.

A third type of seal which can be oriented in any position is shown in the center of Fig. 501-23 and is described in Fig. 501-13. That same fitting may be used as a drain-type seal when its spout is turned down.

Elbow seals (as at upper right of Fig. 501-21) are double-duty devices that are practical either when horizontal conduits must elbow-down to connect with an enclosure's top (as indicated), or when vertical conduits must turn to enter explosionproof enclosures horizontally. In either case, sealant application openings must slant upward.

Another fitting, designed for drainage purposes, is installed only in vertical runs of conduits. Where conduit is run overhead and is brought down vertically to an enclosure for apparatus, any condensation of moisture in the vertical run would be trapped by the seal above the apparatus enclosure. The lower right of Fig. 501-21 shows a sealing fitting designed to provide drainage for a vertical conduit run. Any water coming down from above runs over the surface of the sealing compound and down to an explosionproof drain, through which the water is automatically drained off. These fittings permit passage of condensation while also blocking the passage of explosive pressures or flames. They are equipped with plugs containing minute weep-holes that can either be opened and closed periodically as need develops or allow continuous drainage.

Drain-type seal fittings must be oriented so that compound-application ports remain above the lower downward-slanting drainage plugs. To install seal and drain, both ports are unplugged and the lower conduit hub is dammed. The drainage plug-hole is then closed temporarily by a washer through which a rubber core is inserted. This core protrudes up into the upper part of the sealing chamber, although it must be guided so as not to remain in contact with any of the conductors. Sealing compound then is poured into the chamber through the upper access port, which is replugged and screwed tight.

After the compound has initially set (but has not yet had time to permanently harden), the washer is removed and the rubber core pulled down and out. This creates a clear drainage canal which extends from above the seal down into the drainage weep-hole. A drainage plug is then screwed into the threaded hole, with not less than five full threads engaged to fulfill the requirement for an explosionproof joint.

Class I, Division 2

Because Division 2 locations are of a lower degree of hazard than Division 1, the requirements for sealing are somewhat less demanding, as follows:

1. Where the rules of other sections in Art. 501 require an explosion-proof enclosure for equipment in a Division 2 location, all conduits connecting to any such enclosure must be sealed exactly the same as if it were in a Division 1 enclosure. And the conduit, nipple, or any fitting between the seal and the enclosure being sealed must be approved for use in Class I, Division 1 locations—as specified in Sec. 501-4(a).

   As shown in Fig. 501-24, where a nonexplosion-proof enclosure is permitted by other sections to be used in a Division 2 location, a seal is *not* required in any size of conduit. Note that in Division 2 locations, there is *not* always the need to seal conduits 2 in. and larger, as required in Division 1 locations, by Sec. 501-5(a) (2).

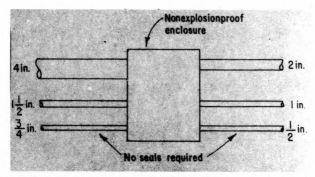

Fig. 501-24. Seals are not required for conduits connected to nonexplosionproof enclosures that are permitted in Division 2 locations. (Sec. 501-5.)

2. Any and every conduit run passing from a Class I, Division 2 area into a nonhazardous area must be sealed in the same manner as described above for conduit passing from a Division 1 area into a Division 2 or nonhazardous area (Fig. 501-25). Rigid metal conduit or IMC must be used between the seal and the point where the conduit passes through the boundary.

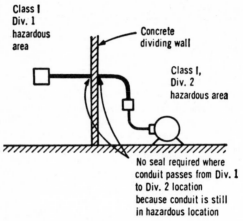

Fig. 501-25. This is a violation; a seal *is* required. (Sec. 501-5.)

The Exception to part **(b)(2)** is worded differently from a similar Exception in part **(a)(3)** for Class I, Division 1 locations. The Exception covers the case where a metal conduit system passes from a nonhazardous area, runs through a Class I, Division 2 hazardous area, and then returns to a nonhazardous area. Such a run is permitted to pass through the hazardous area without the need for a seal fitting at either of the boundaries where it enters and leaves the hazardous area. That Exception, however, does not have the same statement prohibiting unions, couplings, boxes, or fittings that are spelled out in the Exception after Sec. 501-5(a) (4). The difference in wording between the two exceptions appears to indicate that in a Class I, Division 2 location, the same prohibition against union, couplings, etc., is not applicable, and the method in Fig. 501-26 seems acceptable. That is, a seal would not be needed at A, B, C, or D, because the conduit passes "unbroken" through the Class I, Division 2 location. The use of couplings in the conduit run is not prohibited here, as it is in the Exception of Sec. 501-5(a) (4). The difference between the two exceptions seems significant, but the inspection authority should be consulted to eliminate any objections.

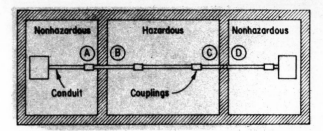

Fig. 501-26. Couplings in conduit through Division 2 location do *not* "break" conduit? (Sec. 501-5.)

Part **(c)** of Sec. 501-5 sets regulations about the kind of seals that must be used where seals are required by foregoing rules. Part **(1)** calls for an integral seal within the enclosure itself or use of a separate seal fitting in each conduit connecting to the enclosure, as described above. The use of factory-sealed devices eliminates the need for field sealing and generally is less expensive to install. In fittings of this type, the arcing device is enclosed in a chamber, with the leads or connections brought out to a splicing chamber. No external sealing fitting is required (Fig. 501-27).

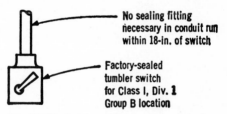

Fig. 501-27. Seal in conduit is not needed where enclosure has built-in seal. (Sec. 501-5.)

Where a seal fitting is used in the conduit, it must be *explosionproof.* The sealing compound must develop enough mechanical strength as it hardens to withstand the forces of explosions. Seals used only to prevent condensation accumulation do not have to be explosionproof; a vaportight seal is sufficient for that purpose.

A seal must be *vaportight* to stop gases and vapors. To do that, the sealing compound must adhere to the fitting and to the conductors. It must expand as it hardens to close all voids without producing objectionable mechanical stresses in the fitting.

Liquid or condensed vapor may present a problem in Class I locations. Where such is the case, joints and conduit systems must be arranged to minimize entrance of liquid. Periodic draining may be necessary, which necessitates the inclusion of means for draining in the original design of the motor (Sec. 501-5).

Installation instructions furnished by the manufacturer must be carefully followed. The seal fitting must be carefully packed with fibrous damming material, which packs more tightly and effectively around conductors when it is dampened, and then filled with the compound supplied with the fitting to a depth at least equal to the inside diameter of the conduit and never less than $\frac{5}{8}$ in. deep, as required in part **(3)** and in the UL standard on seal fittings.

Part **(2)** of Sec. 501-5(c) covers the compound used in seals (Fig. 501-28). The sealing compound used must be one which has a melting point

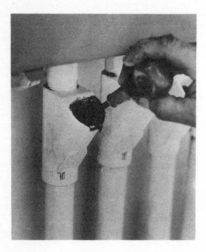

Fig. 501-28. Conduit seal fitting must be carefully packed with fibrous damming material, which packs more tightly and effectively around conductors when it is dampened and then filled with the compound supplied with the fitting to a depth at least equal to the inside diameter of the conduit and never less than $\frac{5}{8}$ in. deep (UL standard). This type of seal is for vertical mounting only. (Sec. 501-5.)

of not less than 200°F and is not affected by the liquid or gas which causes the location to be hazardous. Most of the insulating compounds commonly used in cable splices and potheads are soluble in gasoline and lacquer solvents and hence are unsuitable for sealing conduits in locations where these liquids are used. A mixture of litharge and glycerin is insoluble in nearly all liquids and gases found in Class I locations and meets all other requirements, though this mixture is open to the objection that it becomes very hard and is difficult to remove if the wires must be pulled out. No sealing compounds are listed by Underwriters Laboratories Inc. as suitable for this use except in connection with the explosion-proof fittings of specific manufacturers.

Part **(4)** prohibits splices or taps in seal fittings.

Part **(5)** recognizes use of listed Class I assemblies that have a built-in seal between a compartment housing devices that may cause arcs or sparks and a separate compartment for splicing or taps. Conduit connection to the splice or tap compartment requires a seal fitting only in conduit of 2-in. size or larger, as specified for junction boxes in Sec. 501-5(a) (2).

Part **(d)** covers seals for cables in conduit and for Type MI cable—the only cable permitted by Sec. 501-4(a) to be used in Class I, Division 1 locations. Part **(e)** covers sealing of any of the cables permitted by Sec. 501-4(b).

501-6. Switches, Circuit Breakers, Motor Controllers, and Fuses. Part **(a)** requires explosionproof enclosures (listed for Class I locations, which means suitable for use in Division 1 areas), although purged enclosures are not ruled out. Explosionproof equipment is required in Class I areas only. In addition, the equipment must operate at a temperature low enough that it will not ignite the atmosphere around it.

Division 1 Electrical equipment described must be explosionproof and specifically designed for the specific class and group.

Division 2 Equipment selected must be explosionproof only in certain cases. Purged and pressurized enclosures are recognized as an alternative to explosionproof type, as noted in Sec. 501-3(a). General-purpose enclosures may be used only if all arcing parts are immersed under oil or enclosed within a chamber that is hermetically sealed against the entrance of gases or vapors. In addition, the surface temperature of the apparatus in the general-purpose enclosure should not exceed 80 percent of the ignition temperature of the hazardous substances involved. If those conditions are not satisfied, the enclosure must be explosionproof.

Important: UL standards on explosionproof enclosures contain rules on "Grease for Joint Surfaces": "Paint or a sealing material shall not be applied to the contacting surfaces of a joint. A suitable corrosion inhibitor (grease) such as petrolatum, soap-thickened mineral oils, or nondrying slushing compound may be applied to the metal joint surfaces before assembly. The grease shall be of a type that does not harden because of aging, does not contain an evaporating solvent, and does not cause corrosion of the joint surfaces."

Figure 501-29 shows two explosionproof panelboards. Each panelboard consists of an assembly of branch-circuit CBs, each pair of CBs being enclosed in a cast-metal explosion-proof housing. Access to the CBs and to the wiring compartment is through handholes with threaded covers, and threaded hubs are provided for the conduits. Individual CBs and motor starters are also shown. "Panelboards" for light and power are limited in the UL red book. Listed panelboards for Class I and Class II hazardous locations are for "lighting and *low-capacity* power distribution." *High-capacity* panelboards (like 1,200-A floor-standing panels) and switchboards must be kept out of hazardous locations wherever possible. Enclosure requirements and details are generally the same as those described under "General rules" and for CBs and boxes. Typical hazardous-location panelboards are shown at the right in Fig. 501-30.

Fig. 501-29. Explosionproof panelboards (arrows) are assemblies made up of circuit-breaker housings coupled to wiring enclosures. Large explosionproof CB enclosure at center feeds the panelboards. Explosionproof motor controllers are at lower left. (Sec. 501-6.)

"Industrial control equipment" is a broad category in the UL Red Book, covering "control panels and assemblies" and "motor controllers." Control panels and assemblies include both enclosures and the components within them—such as motor controllers, pushbuttons, pilot lights, receptacles (Fig. 501-31). Either a single enclosure or a group of interconnected enclosures may be used for mounting the components. Where a number of interconnected enclosures are included in an assembly, it is called a "modular assembly" and may be assembled either at the factory or in the field. An example of that is shown in Fig. 501-30.

Components are provided with the enclosures, to be installed either at the factory or in the plant. Wiring between components of modular assemblies is to be field installed. Conduit seal-off fittings must be used in accordance with Sec. 501-5.

A snap switch in an explosionproof enclosure is shown in Fig. 501-32. If a snap switch has an internal factory seal between the switch contacts and its supply wiring connection in its enclosure, it will be so identified by a marking on it. Such switches do not require a seal fitting in a conduit

Fig. 501-30. Explosionproof panelboards (at right) are combined with separate enclosures for motor starters on a rack, to make up a "modular assembly" which is listed by UL under "Industrial control equipment"—which may be assembled either at the factory or in the field. (Sec. 501-6.)

entering the enclosure. The integral seal satisfies Secs. 501-5(a) (1) and 501-5(c) (1).

With reference to subparagraph **(b)(4),** it is assumed that fuses will very seldom blow, or CBs will very seldom open, when used to protect feeders or branch circuits that supply only lamps in fixed positions. In Division 2 locations the conditions are not normally hazardous but may sometimes become so. There is very little probability that one of the overcurrent devices will operate at the same time that the hazardous conditions exist; hence it is not considered necessary to require that these overcurrent devices be in explosionproof enclosures.

UL Red Book Data

As described under general regulations in the UL's *Electrical Construction Materials Directory* (Green Book) and repeated in the Red Book of UL for individual types of switching and control devices, the wiring space and current-carrying capacity of CBs and other equipment used in hazardous locations are based on the use of 60°C wire connected to the breaker terminals for circuits rated 100 A or less and on the use of 75°C wire connected to the terminals for circuits rated over 100 A.

Fig. 501-31. Combination motor starter is typical explosionproof control unit for Class I locations. Note the drain-type seal fittings that provide for draining the conduits of any accumulated condensation or other water. (Sec. 501-6.)

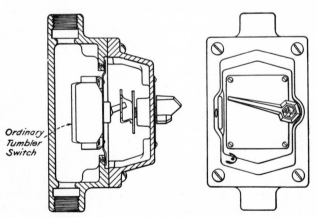

Ordinary
Tumbler
Switch

Fig. 501-32. Explosionproof enclosure suits snap switch to use in hazardous location. (Sec. 501-6.)

Although the reference clearly bases listing on wires of those maximum-temperature ratings, wires of higher-temperature ratings may be used to take advantage of the smaller conduit sizes needed for thin-wall-insulated wires (such as 90°C THHN and XHHW), along with the greater ampacities of higher-temperature wires, which offer an advantage when conductors are derated. *But,* the load on any such wire must not exceed the ampacity of the same size of 60°C- or 75°C-rated wire. The same rules also apply to switches used in hazardous locations.

Terminal lugs on switches, CBs, etc., are suitable for use with copper conductors, as noted in the UL Red Book. Lugs on equipment are commonly marked "AL-CU" or "CU-AL," indicating that the terminal is suitable for use with either copper or aluminum conductors. But, such marking on the lug itself is not sufficient evidence of suitability for use with aluminum conductors. UL requires that equipment found to be suitable for use with either copper or aluminum conductors must be marked to indicate such use on the label or wiring diagram of the equipment—completely independent of a marking, like "AL-CU," on the lugs themselves. A typical CB, for instance, would have lugs marked "AL-CU" but also must have a notation on the label or nameplate to specify "Lugs suitable for copper or aluminum conductors"—if aluminum conductors are to be used with the breaker.

A hazardous-location *enclosure* for equipment that is to be fed by aluminum conductors must have a marking on it to indicate that it is permissible to use aluminum conductors with the switch or CB that is to be mounted within the enclosure. All enclosures for CBs are marked to indicate what labeled CBs are acceptable for use within the enclosures. Only the breakers specified may be used in an enclosure.

501-7. Control Transformers and Resistors.   The term *control transformer* is commonly applied to a small dry-type transformer used to supply the control circuits of one or more motors, stepping down the voltage of a 480-V power circuit to 120 V.

Part **(a)** requires either explosionproof or purged and pressurized enclosures for Division 1 locations—the same as required for meters and instruments in Sec. 501-3(a).

501-8. Motors and Generators.   Four different types of motor applications are recognized for use in a Class I, Division 1 location. The first is a motor approved for Class I, Division 1 locations—such as an explosion-proof motor. The totally enclosed, fan-cooled motor (referred to as a "TEFC" motor) is recognized and listed by UL for use in explosive atmospheres. A motor of a type approved for use in explosive atmospheres is shown in Fig. 501-33 of the totally enclosed, fan-cooled type. The main frame and end housings are made with sufficient strength to withstand internal pressures due to ignition of a combustible mixture inside the motor. Wide metal-to-metal joints are provided between the frame and housings. Circulation of the air is maintained inside the inner enclosure by fan blades on each end of the rotor. At the left side of the sectional view a fan is shown in the space between the inner and outer

Fig. 501-33. A motor approved for use in the explosive atmosphere of a Class I, Division 1 location is the basic one of the four types recognized for such locations. (Sec. 501-8.)

housings. This fan draws in air through a screen and drives it across the surface of the stator punchings and out through openings at the drive end of the motor. The motors described in **(2)** and **(3)** of part **(a)** of this section are the only ones available for Class I, Groups A and B locations and for medium-voltage, high-horsepower applications. Cost of ducts and ventilating systems limits their application in other areas.

The UL Red Book lists motors for Class I, Groups C and D locations. To date, UL lists no motors for Groups A and B; therefore, where such

conditions are encountered, motors must be located outside the hazardous area or must conform to the alternate arrangements and conditions
of Sec. 501-8(a). Air or inert-gas purging are recognized as alternate
methods. Motors suitable for Groups C and D, Class I locations are
designated as explosion-proof.

In part **(b)**, the rule relaxes the requirements for Division 2 areas
somewhat. In Class I, Divison 2 locations open or nonexplosionproof
enclosed motors may be used if they have no brushes, switching mechanisms, or integral resistance devices. However, motors with any sparking
or high-temperature devices must be approved for Class I, Division 1
areas—as described above.

"Motors and Generators, Rebuilt" May Be Listed

A procedure has been established to provide third-party certification of
rewound or rebuilt motors in hazardous locations. Refer to the UL Red
Book on hazardous-location equipment for motor-repair centers authorized to provide certified repairs.

501-9. Lighting Fixtures. Class I, Division 1 Locations.   In these locations,
part **(a)** requires that each fixture be *approved* for the Class I, Division 1
location and marked to show the maximum wattage permitted for the
lamps in the fixture (Fig. 501-34). Reference to the listings in the UL Red

Fig. 501-34. Fluorescent luminaire, fed by Type MI cable, is
listed and marked as an explosionproof unit for use in a Class I,
Division 1 location. (Sec. 501-9.)

Book shows many manufacturers listed for Class I fixtures for use in various Groups of atmospheres. Listings range from "Class I, Group C" to "Class I, Groups A, B, C, and D." For application of a lighting fixture in a particular Group, it is simply a matter of assuring that a manufacturer's fixture is listed for Class I and the Group. The designation "Class I" indicates the fixture is suitable for Division 1, except where the listing contains the phrase "Division 2 only" following the "Class I" reference or following the "Class I" plus Group references.

But in a Class I, Division 1 location, all fixtures must be listed and marked for such use by UL or other national product testing lab. That is necessary to satisfy OSHA's definition of the word "approved" as it appears in Sec. 501-9(a) (1). And electrical inspectors invariably give the same meaning to the word "approved"—if a test-lab-listed product of the same generic type is a violation of Sec. 110-2.

Part **(a)(3)** permits support of a suspended fixture on rigid metal conduit, IMC, or an explosionproof flexible connection fitting.

Lighting Fixtures Require Careful Application

The UL data on hazardous-location lighting fixtures are given under the heading "Fixtures and Fittings" in the Red Book of UL. A lighting fixture recognized for use in Division 1 hazardous locations will be marked "Electric Lighting Fixture for Hazardous Locations" and will show the one or more Groups of hazardous atmospheres for which it is suited. If a fixture is not recognized for Division 1 locations but is limited to Division 2 installations, it will be marked "Electric Lighting Fixture for Division 2 Hazardous Locations." Other UL data are as follows:

- Class I, Division 1 fixtures with *external* surface temperatures over 100°C will have the operating temperature marked on the fixture.
- Fixtures for Class I, Division 1 and Division 2 locations are designed to operate without igniting the atmosphere of the one or more Groups for which the fixture is listed. A Class I, Division 1 fixture (explosionproof) has its lamp chamber sealed-off from the terminal compartment for the supply conductors. All modern explosionproof lighting fixtures are designed by the manufacturer to be factory-sealed, eliminating the need for seal fittings immediately adjacent to the fixtures.
- Any fixture subject to breakage must be equipped with a guard.
- A fixture with one or more germicidal lamps must have a warning to assure that its method of installation does not present a chance of injurious radiation to any person.
- Fixtures for wet locations and those suitable for use where residue of combustible paint will accumulate on them are marked to indicate such recognition.

Class I, Division 2 locations   In these locations, the selection of a suitable fixture becomes a little more involved and has caused problems in the field. Correlation between the requirements of Sec. 501-9 and the application data and listings of the UL must be carefully established.

Watch Out! Controversy!

Section 501-9(b) (2) does *not* say that a fixture in a Division 2 location must "be approved for the Class I, Division 2 location"—unlike Sec. 501-9(a) (1), which requires a fixture "approved" for the specific location. Instead, Sec. 501-9(b) (2) gives a description of the type of fixture that would be acceptable, citing a number of requirements:

1. The fixture must be protected from physical damage by suitable guards or "by location"—which can be taken to mean that mounting it high or otherwise out of the way of any object that might strike or hit it elimimates the need for a guard.

2. If falling sparks or hot metal from the fixture could possibly ignite local accumulation of the hazardous atmosphere, then an enclosure or other protective means must be used to eliminate that hazard.

3. Where lamps used with the fixture may, under normal conditions, reach surface temperature above 80 percent of the atmosphere's ignition temperature, then either of two conditions must be satisfied—(a) A fixture approved for Class I, Division 1 location must be used, or (b) the fixture must be of a type that "has been tested and found incapable of igniting the gas or vapor if the ignition temperature is not exceeded."

Figure 501-35 shows a Class I, Division 1 fixture that could be used in a

Fig. 501-35. In a Class I, Division 2 location, a lighting fixture listed for Class I, Division 1 would satisfy—such as this factory-sealed mercury-vapor luminaire in a Class I, Group D location. Otherwise, a fixture listed for Class I, Division 2 must be used. (Sec. 501-9.)

Division 2 location. But it is not necessary to use a Division 1 fixture and then questions develop.

For many years, in Class I, Division 2 locations simply an enclosed- and gasketed-type fixture was the usual choice. The fixture does not need to be explosion-proof but must have a gasketed globe. The primary requirement is that any surface, including the lamp, must operate at less than 80 percent of the ignition temperature of the gas or vapor that may be present. The effect of Sec. 501-9(b) (2) is to recognize the use of general-purpose lighting fixtures if the conditions of fixture-operating temperature and atmosphere-ignition temperature are correlated as required or if the fixture has been "tested" to verify its safety. At best, the described task of determining the suitability of a general-purpose fixture for use in the hazardous location by relating its lamp-operating temperature to 80 percent of the atmosphere-ignition temperature could be difficult for any electrical designer and/or installer. It also seems highly unlikely that any of them would have the facilities or the experience to perform the testing described in the last part of the **Code** rule and make a sound judgment on the suitability, even though the manufacturer provides the necessary temperature data on the fixture. It was the intention of the authors of that last part of the **Code** rule that the testing mentioned be done by a "qualified testing agency" (such as UL, Factory Mutual, ETL). And as a result of such testing, fixtures for Class I, Divison 2 locations would be approved and listed on the same basis that fixtures are certified for Class I, Division 1 locations.

Class I, Division 2 fixtures are listed in two ways in the Red Book. Some are listed as "Class I, Division 2 only," without reference to Group or Groups. Others are listed with an indication of the Groups for which they are listed—for instance, "Class I, Groups A, B, C, and D, Division 2 only." Great care must be used in evaluating the detail of these listing designations. If such a fixture is not marked otherwise, the temperature of the fixture is lower than the ignition temperature of any of the atmospheres for which it is listed. Where a Class I Group designation is not mentioned, the fixture must not be used where its marked operating temperature is above the ignition temperature of the hazardous atmosphere. Class I, Division 2 fixtures with *internal* parts operating over 100°C will be marked to show the actual operating temperature of internal parts.

Based on the foregoing, precise enforcement of the **NE Code** and OSHA insistence on the maximum use of third-party certified products would seem to suggest the following approach:

1. In Class I, Division 1 locations, only fixtures listed by a nationally recognized test lab may be used.

2. And because fixtures are listed for Class I, Division 2 locations (in the UL Red Book), any fixture in a Class I, Division 2 location *must be listed* for that application (or, of course, a Class I, Division 1 fixture could be used). Consistent with OSHA's rationale on the matter of listing, if a third-party certified product is available (that

is, Class I, Division 2 fixtures), then use of a nonlisted fixture in a Class I, Division 2 location would be a clear violation. Based on that analysis, it seems that the Code-rule certification of a general-purpose fixture with lamp-temperature-not-over-80-percent-of-ignition-temperature would be abrogated.

Recessed Fixtures

Recessed fixtures of both incandescent and electric-discharge lamp types are listed in the UL Red Book and are suitable only for dry locations—unless marked "SUITABLE FOR DAMP LOCATIONS" or "SUITABLE FOR WET LOCATIONS." Other rules are:

- Each fixture is marked to show the minimum temperature rating of conductors used to supply the fixture. Care must be taken to observe all such markings on these fixtures with respect to the number, size, and temperature rating of wires permitted in junction boxes or splice compartments that are part of such fixtures. Generally, no allowance is made in such boxes or compartments for heat produced by current to other loads that may be fed by taps or splices in the fixture supply wires within the JB or splice compartment. Allowance is made only for the I^2R heat input of the current to the fixture itself. If the fixture is recognized for carrying through other conductors to other loads, the fixture will be marked to cover the permitted conditions of wiring.
- Fixtures are listed to assure safe application in both Class I, Division 1 and Class I, Division 2 locations.
- In every Class I, Division 1 fixture, the wiring compartment for supply circuit connections is internally sealed from the lamp chambers.
- Fixtures that may be used as raceways for carrying through circuit conductors other than those supplying the fixtures are marked "Suitable for use as Raceway" and show the number, size, and type of wires permitted.
- Fixtures are marked to show suitability for installation in concrete and some may be used *only* in concrete.
- Fixtures are marked when they may be used *only* with fire-resistive building construction.
- Some fixtures are marked to show acceptable use *only* in Class I, Division 2 locations.

501-10. Utilization Equipment. This section covers devices that utilize electrical energy—other than lighting fixtures and motors or motor-operated equipment. Electric heaters in Class I, Division 1 locations must be listed for such application. The UL Red Book lists convection-type heaters under "Heaters," for Groups C and D. Industrial and laboratory heaters are also listed—heat tracing systems, hot plates, paint heaters, and steam-heated ovens.

501-11. Flexible Cords, Class I, Divisions 1 and 2. Although Sec. 501-4(a) does not mention flexible cord as an approved method of wiring in Division 1 locations, this rule does permit such cord for connection of portable equipment. The Exception, however, refers back to Sec. 501-3(b) (6), which permits cord and plug connection of process control instruments in Division 2 locations—to facilitate replacement of such units, which are not portable equipment. And Sec. 501-4(b) covers use of cord in Division 2 locations.

An explosionproof handlamp, listed for use in Class I locations, is an example of portable equipment covered by this rule, which requires that a three-conductor cord be used and that the device be provided with a terminal for the third, or grounding conductor, which serves to ground the exposed metal parts. Such handlamps are listed under "Portable Lighting Units" in the UL Red Book, which notes that flexible cords should be used only where absolutely necessary as an alternative to threaded rigid conduit hookups. Cords, plugs, and receptacles must be protected from moisture, dirt, and foreign materials. Frequent inspection and maintenance are critically important. Consultation with inspection authorities is always recommended where plug and receptacle applications are considered.

501-12. Receptacles and Attachment Plugs, Class I, Divisions 1 and 2. The basic rule calls for receptacles and plug caps to be approved for Class I locations, which suits them to use in either Division 1 or Division 2 locations. The Exception notes that cord connection of process control instruments in Class I, Division 2 locations does not require devices approved for Class I locations. General-purpose receptacles may be used as outlined in Sec. 501-3(b) (6).

Figure 501-36 shows a three-pole 30-A receptacle and the attachment plug which is so designed as to seal the arc when the circuit is broken, and therefore is suitable for use without a switch. The circuit conductors are brought into the base or body through rigid conduit screwed into a tapped opening and are spliced to pigtail leads from the receptacle. The receptacle housing is then attached to the base, the joint being made at wide flanges ground to a suitable fit. All necessary sealing is provided in the device itself, and no additional sealing is required when it is installed. The plug is designed to receive a three-conductor cord for a 2-wire circuit or a four-conductor cord for a 3-wire, 3-phase circuit, and is provided with a clamping device to relieve the terminals from any strain. The extra conductor is used to ground the equipment supplied.

UL data are as follows:

- Class I receptacles for Division 1 or Division 2 locations are equipped with boxes for threaded metal conduit connection, and a factory seal is provided between the receptacle and its box.
- Receptacles for Class I, Division 2 only may be used with general-purpose enclosures for supply connections, with factory sealing of

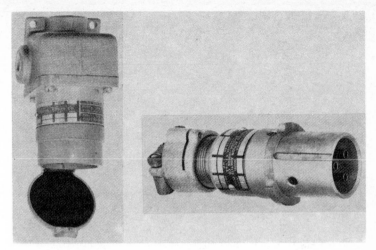

Fig. 501-36. Receptacle and plug must generally be explosionproof type for Divisions 1 and 2. (Sec. 501-12.)

conductors in the receptacle. The plugs for such receptacles are suitable for Class I, Division 1 locations.

- Frequent inspection is recommended for flexible cords, receptacles, and plugs, with replacement whenever necessary.
- For Class I, interlocked CBs and plugs are made for receptacles so that the plug cannot be removed from the receptacle when the CB is closed and the CB cannot be closed when the plug is not in the receptacle (Fig. 501-37).

Mechanical-interlock construction requires that the plug be fully inserted into the receptacle and rotated to operate an enclosed switch or CB that energizes the receptacle. The plug cannot be withdrawn until the switch or breaker has first de-energized the circuit.

The delayed-action type of plug and receptacle has a mechanism within the receptacle that prevents complete withdrawal of the plug until after electrical connection has been broken, permitting any arcs or sparks to be quenched inside the arcing chamber. And insertion of the plug seals the arcing chamber before electrical connection is made. Threaded conduit connection to the CB compartment is provided. The plug is for Type S flexible cord with an equipment grounding conductor.

501-13. Conductor Insulation, Class I, Divisions 1 and 2. Because of economics and greater ease in handling, nylon-jacketed Type THHN-THWN wire, suitable for use where exposed to gasoline, has in most cases replaced lead-covered conductors.

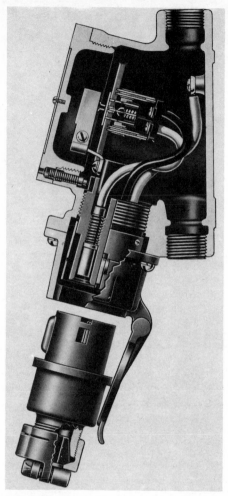

Fig. 501-37. A receptable with a plug interlocked with a circuit breaker is an explosionproof assembly with operating safety features. (Sec. 501-12.)

An excerpt from Underwriters Laboratories Inc. *Electrical Construction Materials Directory* states as follows:

Wires, Thermoplastic.

Gasoline Resistant TW—Indicates a TW conductor with a jacket of extruded nylon suitable for use in wet locations, and for exposure to mineral oil, and to

liquid gasoline and gasoline vapors at ordinary ambient temperature. It is identified by tag marking and by printing on the insulation or nylon jacket with the
designation "Type TW Gasoline and Oil Resistant I."

Also listed for the above use is "Gasoline Resistant THWN" with the
designation "Type THWN Gasoline and Oil Resistant II."

It should be noted that other thermoplastic wires may be suitable for
exposure to mineral oil; but with the exception of those marked "Gasoline and Oil Resistant," reference to mineral oil does not include gasoline
or similar light-petroleum solvents.

The conductor itself must bear the marking legend designating its use
as suitable for gasoline exposure; such designation on the tag alone is not
sufficient.

**501-14. Signaling, Alarm, Remote-Control, and Communication Sys-
tems.** Nearly all signaling, remote-control, and communication equipment involves make-or-break contacts; hence in Division 1 locations all
devices must be explosionproof, and the wiring must comply with the
requirements for light and power wiring in such locations, including
seals.

Figure 501-38 shows a telephone having the operating mechanism
mounted in an explosionproof housing. Similar equipment may be
obtained for operating horns or sirens. Figure 501-39 shows fire-alarm
hookups at a distillery. Alcohol is generally categorized as creating a Class
I, Group G location by Code Table 500-2. A vapor-laden atmosphere

Fig. 501-38. Explosionproof telephones are made and listed
for Class I, Groups B, C, and D, and must be connected with
the necessary seal fittings required in conduits to enclosures
housing arcing or sparking devices. [Sec. 501-14(b) (4).]

Fig. 501-39. Fire-alarm and control equipment at outdoor tank car delivery and pumping station of a distillery is housed and connected to comply with conduit and seal rules for a Class I, Division 1, Group D location. (Sec. 501-14.)

with an alcoholic content ranging from 3.5 to 19 percent could become flammable or explode at an ignition temperature of approximately 80°F under certain conditions of air pressure and humidity.

Referring to subparagraph **(1)**, covering Division 2 locations, it would usually be the more simple method to use explosionproof devices, rather than devices having contacts immersed in oil or devices in hermetically sealed enclosures, though mercury switches, which are hermetically sealed, may be used for some purposes. Of course, reference to Sec. 501-3(a) recognizes the use of purged enclosures as an alternative method.

The UL Red Book lists "Telephones" as follows:

- Telephones, sound-powered telephones, and communications equipment and systems are listed for Class I and Class II use in Division 1 locations and are explosionproof equipment. Such equipment complies with Secs. 501-14(a) and (b).
- Intrinsically safe sound-powered telephones are also listed for Class I, Division 1, Group D and may be used in both Divisions 1 and 2 locations in accordance with Secs. 501-14(a) and (b).

The Red Book also lists "Thermostats," "Signal Appliances" (which include fire alarms, fire detectors), "Solenoids," and "Sound Recording and Reproducing Equipment."

501-16. Grounding, Class I, Divisions 1 and 2.   Special care in the grounding of all equipment is necessary in order to prevent the possibility of arcs or sparks when any grounded metal comes in contact with the frame or case of the equipment. All connections of conduit to boxes, cabinets, enclosures for apparatus, and motor frames must be so made as to secure permanent and effective electrical connections. To be effective, this form of construction is not only necessary in the spaces that are classed as hazardous, but should also be carried out back to the point where the connection for grounding the conduit is made to the grounding electrode system serving the premises. Outside the space where the hazardous conditions exist, threaded connections should be used for conduit, unless bonding techniques are used for connections to knockouts in sheet-metal enclosures. Any conduit emerging from a Division 1 or Division 2 location must have a bonded path of equipment grounding from the hazardous location back to the bonded service equipment or to the bonded secondary of a transformer that supplies the circuit into the hazardous location, and then back to the service.

The net effect of the wording in part **(b)** of this section is to require use of "service bonding" techniques (Sec. 250-72) throughout the length of a continuous path from raceway and equipment in a hazardous location all the way back to the service or transformer grounding electrode conductor (Fig. 501-40). That means that every raceway termination in the ground return path to the service or transformer secondary must be threaded metal conduit connection to a threaded hub or boss on a fitting or enclosure or any connection to a sheet-metal KO must use one of the following methods:

1. A locknut outside with a bonding locknut inside where connection is made to a clean KO—that is, a KO cut on the job or a KO from which all concentric or eccentric rings (so-called "Donuts") have been removed.
2. A bonding bushing with a bonding jumper to a grounding terminal within the enclosure, on a KO that is clean or has rings left in the enclosure wall.
3. A bonding bushing that does not require a jumper when used on a clean KO (as at bottom right of Fig. 250-57). The various techniques

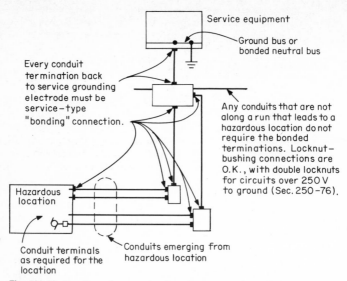

Service equipment

Ground bus or bonded neutral bus

Every conduit termination back to service grounding electrode must be service–type "bonding" connection.

Any conduits that are not along a run that leads to a hazardous location do not require the bonded terminations. Locknut– bushing connections are O.K., with double locknuts for circuits over 250 V to ground (Sec. 250 –76).

Hazardous location

Conduit terminals as required for the location

Conduits emerging from hazardous location

Fig. 501-40. Bonding of raceways and equipment must be made back to service ground. (Sec. 501-16.)

that must be used instead of locknut and bushing or double-locknut-and-bushing are described in Figs. 250-56 and 250-57.

At top, Fig. 501-41 shows a violation of part **(b)**. Although Sec. 501-4(b) permits a sheet-metal junction box (nonexplosionproof) in a Division 2 location, bonding through that enclosure (and all the way back to the service) may not be done simply by locknuts and bushings—not even the double-locknut type. At the bottom, the bonding jumpers satisfy the rule here. From Table 250-95, a No. 8 copper bonding jumper is the minimum acceptable size to be used with a 100-A rated protective device, for connecting each bushing to the box.

Lightning arresters are spark-producing devices and should be installed outside the building. For services less than 1,000 V the arresters must have grounding connections as provided in Sec. 250-131, and in addition, the grounding connection must be bonded to the service-entrance conduit. See discussion under Sec. 502-3.

Part **(d)** of this rule is an emphatic restatement of the rule of Secs. 250-50(a) and 250-53.

Part **(e)** is a repetition of the rule of Sec. 250-23(b) and is illustrated in that section. Connection from the transformer neutral into the service enclosure and to the equipment ground will help to provide proper operation of overcurrent protective devices.

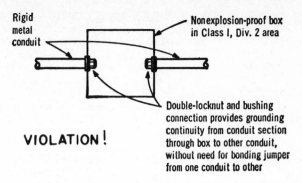

Rigid metal conduit

Nonexplosion-proof box in Class I, Div. 2 area

Double-locknut and bushing connection provides grounding continuity from conduit section through box to other conduit, without need for bonding jumper from one conduit to other

VIOLATION!

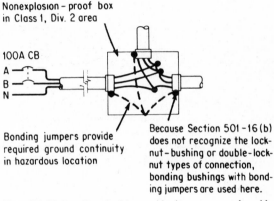

Nonexplosion - proof box in Class 1, Div. 2 area

100A CB

A
B
N

Bonding jumpers provide required ground continuity in hazardous location

Because Section 501 –16 (b) does not recognize the lock-nut–bushing or double-lock-nut types of connection, bonding bushings with bond-ing jumpers are used here.

Fig. 501-41. Bonding bushings with jumpers comply with grounding rule. (Sec. 501-16.)

ARTICLE 502. CLASS II LOCATIONS

502-1. General.   Referring to Sec. 500-5, the hazards in Class II locations are due to the presence of combustible dust. These locations are subdivided into three groups, as follows:

- Group E, atmospheres containing metal dust
- Group F, atmospheres containing carbon black, coal dust, or coke dust
- Group G, atmospheres containing grain dust, such as in grain elevators

It is important to note that some equipment that is suitable for Class II, Group G, is not suitable for Class II, Groups E and F.

Any one of four hazards, or a combination of two or more, may exist in a Class II location: (1) an explosive mixture of air and dust, (2) the collection of conductive dust on and around live parts, (3) overheating of equipment because deposits of dust interfere with the normal radiation of heat, and (4) the possible ignition of deposits of dust by arcs or sparks.

A large number of processes which may produce combustible dusts are listed in Sec. 500-5. Most of the equipment listed as suitable for Class I locations is also dusttight, but it should not be taken for granted that all explosionproof equipment is suitable for use in Class II locations. Some explosionproof equipment may reach too high a temperature if blanketed by a heavy deposit of dust. Grain dust will ignite at a temperature below that of many of the flammable vapors.

Location of service equipment, switchboards, and panelboards in a separate room away from the dusty atmosphere is always preferable.

In Class II locations, with the presence of combustible dust, UL standards call for a type of construction designed to preclude dust and to operate at specified limited temperatures. Dust-ignition-proof equipment is generally more economical to use in Class II areas; however, explosionproof devices are often used if they are approved for Class II areas and the particular Group involved.

Dust-ignition-proof equipment is enclosed in a manner so as to exclude ignitible amounts of dusts or amounts which might affect equipment performance or rating and which will not permit arcs, sparks, or heat inside the enclosure to cause ignition of exterior accumulations or atmospheric suspensions of a specified dust on or in the vicinity of the enclosure. Any assemblies that generate heat, such as lighting fixtures and motors, are tested with a dust blanket to simulate the operation of the device in a Class II location.

502-2. Transformers and Capacitors.   Part **(a)** requires use of a Code-constructed transformer vault for a transformer or capacitor that contains oil or other liquid dielectric that will burn—when used in a Class II, Division 1 location.

The UL Red Book does not list transformers or capacitors for hazardous locations. So far as can be learned, no liquid-insulated or dry-type transformers can be obtained which are dust-tight. Capacitors of the type used for the correction of the power factor of individual motors are of sealed construction, but must be provided with dust-tight terminal enclosures if installed in these locations.

Dry-type transformers must either be approved as a complete assembly for Class II, Division 1 use (none are UL-listed) or they must be used in a vault. But transformers can be kept out of the hazardous areas, and part **(a)(3)** *prohibits* any use of a transformer or capacitor in a Class II, Division 1, Group E (metal dust) location.

Part **(b)** requires a vault for any oil-filled or high fire point liquid-insulated transformer or capacitor in a Division 1 area. A dry-type unit in a Division 2 area may be used either in a vault or without a vault if the unit is enclosed within a tight metal housing without any openings *and* only if it operates at 600 V or less. There are no special requirements for capacitors in Division 2 locations, except that they must not contain oil or any other "liquid that will burn" if they are not within a vault.

502-3. Surge Protection, Class II, Divisions 1 and 2.   A common application of this requirement is found in grain-handling facilities (grain elevators) in localities where severe lightning storms are prevalent. Assuming a building supplied through a bank of transformers located a short distance from the building, the recommendations are, in general, as shown in the single-line diagram in Fig. 502-1. The surge-protective equipment

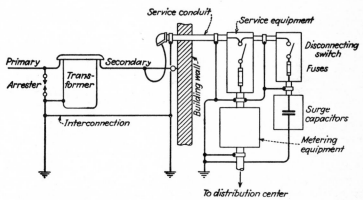

Fig. 502-1. Surge protection is required to protect Class II systems against lightning. (Sec. 502-3.)

consists of primary lightning arresters at the transformers and surge-protective capacitors connected to the supply side of the service equipment. The lightning arrester ground and the secondary system ground should be solidly connected together. All grounds should be bonded together and to the service conduit and to all boxes enclosing the service equipment, metering equipment, and capacitors.

Complete information on methods of providing surge protection may be obtained from the Mill Mutual Fire Prevention Bureau, 2 North Riverside Plaza, Chicago, IL 60606.

502-4. Wiring Methods.   Part **(a)** covers Division 1 locations. The wiring methods are essentially the same for Class II, Division 1 as they are for Class I, Division 1. Conduit connections to fittings and boxes must be made to threaded bosses. For fittings and boxes, only those used for taps, splices, or terminals in locations of electrically conductive dusts (metal, carbon, etc.) must be approved for Class II locations (i.e., listed by UL).

As covered in **(a)(2)**, where a flexible connection is necessary, it would usually be preferable to use a dust-tight flexible fitting. Standard flexible conduit may not be used but liquidtight flex may, with a bonding jumper as required by Sec. 502-16(b). The use of a hard-service cord having one conductor serving as a grounding conductor is permitted.

In Division 2 locations, in order to provide adequate bonding, threaded fittings should be used with IMC or rigid metal conduit, but EMT may also be used (Fig. 502-2). The requirement for close-fitting

CLASS II, DIV. 2 LOCATION

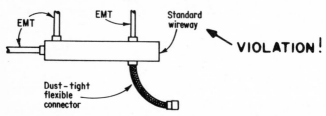

Fig. 502-2. EMT is O.K., but wireway *must* be dusttight. (Sec. 502-4.)

covers could best be taken care of by using dust-tight equipment. The standard type of pressed steel box cannot be used in any case where the box contains taps or splices. Where no taps, splices, or terminals are used in a box, a sheet-metal box may be used, but all conduit connections to boxes that do not have threaded hubs or bosses must be of the bonded type, as required by Sec. 502-16(b) and described with illustrations under Sec. 501-16(b).

Flexible connections in Division 2 locations must observe the rules given above in part **(a)(2)**.

502-5. Sealing, Class II, Divisions 1 and 2.   Note that sealing or other isolation is required only for conduits entering a dust-ignition-proof enclosure that connects to an enclosure that is not dust-ignition-proof. Seals are not generally required in Class II areas; however, where raceway connects an enclosure *required to be* dust-ignition-proof and one that is not, means must be provided to prevent dust from entering the dust-ignition-proof enclosure through the raceway. A seal in the conduit is one acceptable way of doing this, with the seal any distance from the enclosure (Fig. 502-3). However, if the connecting raceway is horizontal and at least 10 ft long, or if it is vertical, extending down from the dust-ignition-proof enclosure and at least 5 ft long, no sealing is necessary anywhere in the conduit. The distance between and orientation of the enclosures is considered adequate protection against dust passage. And that applies in Division 1 and Division 2 locations wherever the "dust-ignition-proof" is specifically required to be used by one of the sections of this article.

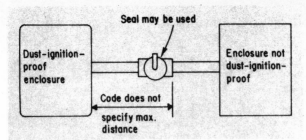

Fig. 502-3. A seal fitting must be used in short (less than 10 ft) connections like this. (Sec. 502-5.)

502-6. Switches, Circuit Breakers, Motor Controllers, and Fuses. Note that part **(a)(1)** calls for "dust-ignition-proof" enclosures—which might involve the sealing called for in Sec. 502-5.

Most of the enclosed switches and circuit breakers approved for Class I, Division 1 locations are also approved for use in Class II locations.

Switches conforming with the definition of the term *isolating switch* would seldom be used in any hazardous location. Such switches are permitted for use as the disconnecting means for motors larger than 100 hp.

502-8. Motors and Generators. In Class II, Division 1 locations, motors must be dust-ignition-proof (approved for Class II, Division 1) or totally enclosed with positive-pressure ventilation. The same motors may be used also in Class II, Division 2 areas; however, if dust accumulation is very slight, either a standard, open-type motor (without arcing or sparking parts), a self-cleaning textile motor, or a squirrel-cage motor may be used.

Part **(a)(2)** refers to a totally enclosed pipe-ventilated motor. A motor of this type is cooled by clean air forced through a pipe by a fan or blower. Such a motor has an intake opening, where air is delivered to the motor through the pipe from the blower. The exhaust opening is on the opposite side, and this should be connected to a pipe terminating outside the building, so that dust will not collect inside the motor while it is not running.

Motors of the common totally enclosed type without special provision for cooling may be used in Division 2 locations, but to deliver the same horsepower, a plain totally enclosed motor must be considerably larger and heavier than a motor of the open type or an enclosed fan-cooled or pipe-ventilated motor.

The UL Red Book lists motors for Class II, Divisions 1 and 2, Groups E, F, and G locations.

502-9. Ventilating Piping. In locations where dust or flying material will collect on or in motors to such an extent as to interfere with their ventilation or cooling, enclosed motors which will not overheat under the prevailing conditions must be used. It may be necessary to require the use of an enclosed pipe-ventilated motor or to locate the motor in a separate dust-tight room, properly ventilated with clean air (Sec. 430-16).

The reference to ventilation is clarified in this section. Vent pipes for rotating electrical machinery must be of metal not lighter than No. 24 MSG gauge, or equally substantial. They must lead to a source of clean air outside of buildings, be screened to prevent entry of small animals or birds, and be protected against damage and corrosion.

In Class II, Division 1 locations, vent pipes must be dust-tight. In Division 2 locations, they must be tight to prevent entrance of appreciable quantities of dust and to prevent escape of sparks, flame, or burning material.

Typical conditions where these requirements may apply include processing machinery or enclosed conveyors where dust may escape only under abnormal conditions, or storage areas where handling of bags or sacks may result in small quantities of dust in the air.

502-11. Lighting Fixtures.   Fixtures used in Class II, Division 1 areas must prevent the entry of the hazardous dust and should prevent the accumulation of dust on the fixture body. In Division 1 locations, all fixtures must be approved for that location. Where metal dusts are present, lighting fixtures must be specifically approved for use in Group E atmospheres. Fixtures are listed by Underwriters Laboratories Inc. as suitable for use in all three of the locations classed as Groups E, F, and G, for Divisions 1 and 2.

The purpose of the latter part of subparagraph **(a)(3)** is to specify the type of cord to be used for wiring a chain-suspended fixture. It is not the intention to permit a fixture to be suspended by means of a cord pendant or drop cord.

The only special requirements for lighting fixtures in Class II, Division 2 locations are that the lamp must be enclosed in a suitable glass globe and that a guard must be provided unless the fixture is so located that it will not be exposed to physical damage. The enclosing globe should be tight enough so that it will practically exclude dust, though dusttight construction is not called for. For Class II, Group G, Division 2 areas, fixtures normally are the enclosed and gasketed type. However, in addition, such fixtures must not have an exposed surface temperature exceeding 165°C.

There are portable handlamps approved for use in any Class II, Group G location, i.e., where the hazards are due to grain dust.

The UL Red Book notes that a Class II fixture for Divisions 1 and 2 is tested for dust tightness and safe operation in the dust atmosphere for which it is listed. A note points out the importance of effective maintenance—regular cleaning—to prevent buildup of combustible dust on such equipment.

Fig. 502-4. Flexible cords and listed connectors are used in a grain elevator that handles combustible grain dust. (Sec. 502-12.)

502-12. Flexible Cords, Class II, Divisions 1 and 2.   Figure 502-4 shows flexible cord used in a Division 2 area of a grain elevator (Class II, Group G).

Section 502-4 permits its use in Division 1 and Division 2 areas of Class II locations. Listed cord connectors are recognized for use in Class II, Group G locations—using Types S, SO, ST, or STO multiconductor, extra-hard-usage cord *with* a grounding conductor. Cord connectors for connecting extra-hard-service type of flexible cord to devices in hazardous locations must be carefully applied.

The UL Red Book notes, under "Receptacles with Plugs," that Type S flexible cord should be frequently inspected and replaced when necessary.

502-13. Receptacles and Attachment Plugs.   Class II receptacles listed as approved for Division 1 locations are equipped with boxes for threaded metal conduit connection, and a factory seal is provided between the receptacle and its box. Only receptacles and plugs listed for Class II locations are permitted in Division 1 areas.

Receptacles for Class II, Division 2 locations do not have to be approved for Class II but must satisfy the connection method described.

Frequent inspection is recommended for flexible cords, receptacles, and plugs, with replacement whenever necessary.

As shown in Sec. 501-12 for Class I locations, for Class II locations, interlocked CBs and plugs are made for receptacles so that the plug cannot be removed from the receptacle when the CB is closed and the CB cannot be closed when the plug is not in the receptacle.

502-16. Grounding, Class II, Divisions 1 and 2.   The requirements of this section are essentially the same as those of Sec. 501-16. Refer to the discussion and illustrations in that section.

ARTICLE 503. CLASS III LOCATIONS

503-1. General.   The small fibers of cotton that are carried everywhere by air currents in some parts of cotton mills and the wood shavings and sawdust that collect around planers in woodworking plants are common examples of the combustible flyings or fibers that cause the hazards in Class III, Division 1 locations. A cotton warehouse is a common example of a Class III, Division 2 location.

503-3. Wiring Methods.   Type MC (metal-clad cable) is added to those methods permitted for Class I and Class II, Division 1 locations. Type MC (Art. 334) includes interlocked armor cable, corrugated metal armor, smooth aluminum-sheathed cable (Type ALS), and smooth copper-sheathed cable (Type CS).

Fittings and boxes must have the specified construction features. Flexible connections in Class III are regulated the same as for Class II, Sec. 502-4 (a) (2).

Part (**b**) requires the same wiring methods for Division 2 as for Division 1. As indicated in Fig. 503-1, there are no seal requirements in Class III locations.

503-4. Switches, Circuit Breakers, Motor Controllers, and Fuses, Class III, Divisions 1 and 2.   Equipment suitable for Class III locations must function at full rating without developing surface temperatures high enough to cause excessive dehydration or gradual carbonization of accumulated

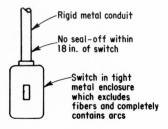

Fig. 503-1. Seals are not required in Class III enclosures or conduit. (Sec. 503-3.)

fibers or flyings. These devices have the same surface temperature limitations as Class II equipment, and construction is similar.

Enclosures for equipment in a Class III location must be provided with telescoping or close-fitting covers or other effective means which prevent the escape of sparks or burning material and have no openings through which sparks or burning material might escape, or through which adjacent combustible material might be ignited.

503-6. Motors and Generators. UL lists no Class III motors as such; however, totally enclosed nonventilated motors and the so-called lint-free or self-cleaning textile squirrel-cage motors are commonly used. The latter may be acceptable to the local inspection authority if only moderate amounts of flyings are likely to accumulate on or near the motor, which must be readily accessible for routine cleaning and maintenance. Or the motor may be a squirrel-cage motor, or a standard open-type machine having any arcing or heating devices enclosed within a tight metal housing without ventilating or other openings.

As noted in part **(c)**, motors of the partially enclosed or splashproof type may not be used in any Class III location.

503-9. Lighting Fixtures, Class III, Divisions 1 and 2. In Class III, Divisions 1 and 2 areas, lighting fixtures must minimize the entrance of fibers and flyings and prevent the escape of sparks or hot metal. And again, the surface temperature of the unit must be limited to 165°C. Available fixtures are third-party certified (by a national test lab) for Class III locations, Divisions 1 and 2. In the past, enclosed and gasketed types of fixtures, of the type that was used in Class I, Division 2 areas, have been acceptable as suitable for use in this application. But because there are listed Class III fixtures available, inspection agencies and OSHA might insist on use of *only* listed fixtures in such applications—to be consistent with the trend to third-party certification.

503-13. Electric Cranes, Hoists, and Similar Equipment, Class III, Divisions 1 and 2. A crane operating in a Class III location and having rolling or sliding collectors making contact with bare conductors introduces two hazards:

1. Any arcing between a collector and a conductor rail or wire may ignite flyings of combustible fibers that have collected on or near to the bare conductor. This danger may be guarded against by proper alignment of the bare conductor and by using a collector of such form that contact is always maintained, and by the use of guards or barriers which will confine the hot particles of metal that may be thrown off when an arc is formed.

2. Dust and flyings collecting on the insulating supports of the bare conductors may form a conducting path between the conductors or from one conductor to ground and permit enough current to flow to ignite the fibers. This condition is much more likely to exist if moisture is present. Operation on a system having no grounded

conductor makes it somewhat less likely that a fire will be started by a current flowing to ground. A recording ground detector will show when the insulation resistance is being lowered by an accumulation of dust and flyings on the insulators, and a relay actuated by excessively low insulation resistance and arranged to trip a CB provides automatic disconnection of the bare conductors when the conditions become dangerous.

ARTICLE 511. COMMERCIAL GARAGES, REPAIR AND STORAGE

511-1. Scope. At one time (1971 NEC), this section considered parking garages as hazardous locations. Now, the rule no longer requires that this article apply to locations in which more than three cars, trucks, or other gas vehicles are or may be stored. Specifically, parking garages used simply for parking or storage of gasoline-powered vehicles are *not* classified as hazardous areas, no matter how many vehicles are present. But, such parking areas in enclosed buildings must be adequately ventilated.

Below-grade areas occupied for repairing, or communicating areas located below a repair garage, shall be continuously ventilated by a mechanical ventilating system having positive means for exhausting indoor air at a rate of not less than 0.75 cfm/sq ft of floor area. An approved means shall be provided for introducing an equal amount of outdoor air.

Operations involving open flame or electric arcs, including fusion, gas, and electric welding, shall be restricted to areas specifically provided for such purposes.

All enclosed, basement, and underground parking structures shall be continuously ventilated by a mechanical system capable of providing a minimum of six air changes per hour.

Heating equipment may be installed in motor vehicle repair or parking areas where there is no dispensing or transferring of Class I or II flammable liquids (as defined in the Flammable and Combustible Liquids Code, NFPA 30-1973) or liquified petroleum gas, provided the bottom of the combustion chamber is not less than 18 in. above the floor, the heating equipment is protected from physical damage by vehicles, and continuous mechanical ventilation is provided at the rate of 0 .75 cfm/sq ft of floor area. The heating system and the ventilation system shall be suitably interlocked to ensure operation of the ventilation system when the heating system is in operation.

Approved suspended unit heaters may be used provided they are located not less than 8 ft above the floor and are installed in accordance with the conditions of their approval.

The question often arises, Does diesel fuel come within the classification of volatile flammable liquids, thereby requiring application of Art. 511 to places used exclusively for repair of diesel-powered vehicles? The third paragraph under Sec. 514-1 reads: "Where the authority having jurisdiction can satisfactorily determine that flammable liquids having a flash point below 100°F, such as gasoline, will not be handled, he may classify such a location as nonhazardous."

The NFPA Inspection Manual, under identification of flammable liquids, says, "Minimum flash points for fuel oils of various grades are: No. 1 and No. 2, 100°F; No. 4, 110; No. 5, over 130; No. 6, 150 or higher. Actual flash points are commonly higher and are required to be higher by some state laws. No. 1 fuel is often sold as kerosene, range oil or coal oil."

Diesel fuel is a Class 3 flammable liquid, having flash points above 70°F. One listing of flash points of flammable liquids showed no diesel fuel below 120°F. Therefore, a diesel-fuel installation may be classified as a nonhazardous area and wired as such, unless it can be firmly established that the particular fuel has a flash point under 100°F. But, of course, the authority enforcing the **Code** is the one responsible for classifying such areas as nonhazardous.

511-2. Hazardous Areas.   In part **(a),** the wording (which was significantly revised from the 1971 to the 1975 **NEC**) considers any floor area to be a Class I, Division 2 hazardous location up to 18 in. above the floor. It should be noted that the rule no longer says that "each floor at or above grade" in a commercial garage is considered to be a Class I, Division 2 location up to 18 in. above floor level. The rule no longer refers to "grade" and may be taken to simply apply to any floor whether it is *above* or below grade level. Any wiring within this space must be suitable for Class I, Division 2 locations.

Figure 511-1 shows the basic rule of part **(a)** and part **(b)**. Note that part **(b)** no longer refers to "floor below *grade*," but simply covers "pit or depression below *floor* level." Previous wording of these two parts resulted in the classification as Class I, Division 2 of the total shaded areas in Fig. 511-2, where vehicular servicing is done on the below-grade floor, the first floor, and the second floor. For each floor at or above grade, part **(a)** used to define the entire area up to a level of 18 in. above the floor as a Class I, Division 2 location. And part **(b)** stated that below-grade areas up to a level of 18 in. above the bottom of outside doors or other openings that are at or above grade level must be considered Class I, Division 2 locations, which is the lower shaded area in Fig. 511-2. Now part **(b)** simply requires any pit or depression below floor level to be considered as Class I, Division 2 area.

Under the new wording, for floors below grade, such as the basement in the sketch, the enforcing authority may judge that the hazardous location extends up to a level of only 18 in. above the floor. And that means that any wiring and equipment installed in any of these defined hazardous areas must be approved for Class I, Division 2 locations. Above these hazardous areas, Sec. 511-5 applies.

Part **(d)** allows the authority having jurisdiction to classify areas adjacent to hazardous locations as nonhazardous if proper ventilation, air pressure differentials, or physical separation are provided in a specific garage installation.

Equipment located in a suitable room or enclosure provided for the

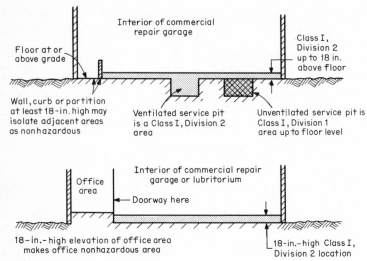

Fig. 511-1. Hazardous areas must be carefully established. (Sec. 511-2.)

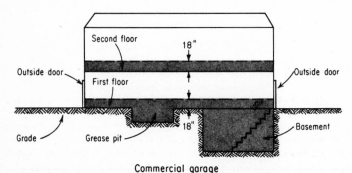

Commercial garage

Fig. 511-2. Previous wording of Code rule identified shaded areas as Class I, Division 2 locations. (Sec. 511-2.)

purpose or in a showroom separated from the garage proper by a partition which is reasonably tight up to 18 in. above the floor need not conform to the requirements of this section.

In all garages within the scope of this chapter, because of the possible presence of gasoline vapor near the floor, any equipment which in its normal operation may cause arcs or sparks, if less than 18 in. above the floor, is considered as in a hazardous location. It is seldom necessary to make use of devices having exposed live parts, but where this is unavoidable, even though the device is 18 in. above the floor, any such device should be well guarded.

511-5. Wiring in Spaces Above Hazardous Areas. The rules here apply to the lubritorium areas in service stations and *any* other space above the defined hazardous locations.

511-6. Equipment Above Hazardous Locations. Part **(a)** notes that equipment that may produce arcs or sparks and is within 12 ft of the floor above hazardous areas must be enclosed or provided with guards to prevent hot particles from falling into the hazardous area, but lamps, lampholders, and receptacles are excluded. Standard receptacles are O.K. Lighting fixtures that are within 12 ft of the floor over hazardous areas, over traffic lanes, or otherwise exposed to physical damage, must be totally enclosed, as required in part **(b)**.

511-8. Electric Vehicle Charging. The requirements for battery-charging cables and connectors are similar to the requirements for outlets for the connection of portable appliances, except that when hanging free the battery-charging cables and connectors may hang within 6 in. from the floor. The common form is a plug which is inserted into a receptacle on the vehicle, and, since the prongs are "alive," they must be covered by a protecting hood.

Note: Article 512, "Residential Storage Garages," was eliminated from the Code in the 1975 edition. As a result, such garages where the lowest floor is below adjacent grade are no longer classified as Class I, Division 2 areas. Now residential storage garages, like commercial storage garages, are *not* hazardous locations.

ARTICLE 513. AIRCRAFT HANGARS

513-2. Classification of Locations. Figure 513-1 shows the details of hangar classifications. The entire floor area up to 18 in. above the floor, and adjacent areas not suitably cut off from the hazardous area or not elevated at least 18 in. above it, are classified as Class I, Division 2 locations. Pits below the hangar floor are classified as Class I, Division 1. Within 5 ft horizontally from aircraft power plants, fuel tanks, or structures containing fuel, the Class I, Division 2 location extends to a level that is 5 ft above the upper surface of wings and engine enclosures.

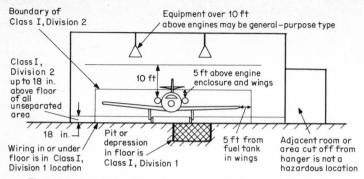

Fig. 513-1. Boundaries of hazardous areas are clearly defined. (Sec. 513-2.)

513-5. Equipment Not Within Hazardous Locations. Fixtures and other equipment that produce arcs or sparks may not be general-use types but are required to be totally enclosed or constructed to prevent escape of sparks or hot metal particles if less than 10 ft above aircraft wings and engine enclosures, as indicated in Fig. 513-1.

ARTICLE 514. GASOLINE DISPENSING AND SERVICE STATIONS

514-1. Definition. As noted under Sec. 511-1, there is a question about application of the rules of Arts. 511 and 514 to areas used for service of vehicles using diesel fuel and to dispensing pumps and areas for diesel fuel. Fuel with a flash point above 100°F may be ruled to b e *not* "a volatile flammable liquid" to which the regulations of Arts. 511 and 514 are addressed.

Note that vehicle repair rooms or areas and lubritoriums at gas stations must comply with Art. 511.

514-2. Hazardous Locations. Part **(a)** describes the hazardous area around a dispensing pump for gasoline. Obviously, the most hazardous area at a gas station is around the pump islands where gasoline is transferred to cars. The entire island area, underground and to a distance 4 ft above the driveway level, is designated as Class I, Division 1 and must be wired in an explosionproof manner (Fig. 514-1).

Part **(b)** sets the boundary of the Class I, Division 2 location around dispensing pumps, as shown in Fig. 514-2. Outdoor areas within 20 ft of a pump are considered a Class I, Division 2 location and must be wired accordingly. Such a hazardous area extends 18 in. above grade. If a building with a below-grade basement is within this hazardous area, gasoline fumes could enter the building if there were any windows within the 18-in.-high classified space, thereby making the basement a Class I, Division 2 area. This condition could be eliminated by "suitably cutting off the building from the hazardous area" by installing an 18-in.-high concrete curb between the service station and the residential property or enclosing the window openings up to that height.

Part **(c)** sets a 20-ft diameter, 18-in.-high Division 2 area around each fill-pipe for the underground gasoline tanks at a gas station—as shown in Fig. 514-2.

Part **(d)** is covered in the note below the diagram of Fig. 514-2. Any wiring or equipment that is installed beneath any part of a Class I, Division 1 or Division 2 location is classified as being within a Class I, Division 1 location to the point where the wiring method is brought up out of the ground. That means the Division 1 area may extend far beyond the limits of the 20-ft perimeter around the dispensing pumps. The Division 1 area extends to the point where the conduit comes up to the supply panelboard or runs up to a lighting standard or a sign, as shown under Sec. 514-6.

As covered in **(e)** where the dispensing unit and/or its hose and nozzle is suspended from overhead, the space within the dispenser enclosure and the area within 18 in. in all directions from the enclosure that is not suitably cut off by a ceiling or wall is classified as a Class I, Division 1 area.

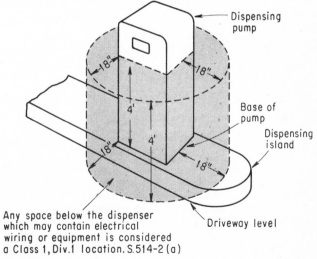

Fig. 514-1. The shaded space is a Class I, Division 1 hazardous location. (Sec. 514-2.)

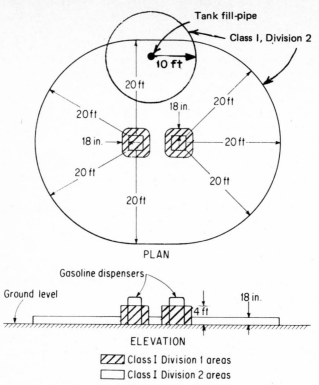

Fig. 514-2. Class I, Division 2 area extends around pumps and tank fill-pipes. (Sec. 514-2.)

The area within 2 ft in all directions from the Class I, Division 1 area and extending down to grade level is classified as a Class I, Division 2 area. The horizontal area, for 18 in. above grade and extending 20 ft measured from those points vertically below the outer edges of an overhead dispenser enclosure, is also classified as a Class I, Division 2 area. All equipment integral with an overhead dispensing hose or nozzle must be suitable for a Class I, Division 1 hazardous area.

Part **(f)** notes the hazardous space around any vent-pipe at a gas station is simply a *sphere* (a ball-like volume) around the top opening of a pipe that discharges upward, but the hazardous space around a pipe opening that does not discharge up includes the sphere described *plus* a cylinder of space from that sphere down to the ground. The space beyond the 5-ft radius from tank vents that discharge upward and spaces beyond unpierced walls and areas below grade that lie beneath tank vents are not classified as hazardous.

Part **(g)** flatly designates a pit or depression below grade in a lubritorium as a Class I, Division 1 location and does not allow for the possibility of classification as Division 2, as permitted in Sec. 511-2(b) for a pit in a repair garage. Refer to Fig. 511-1 on classification of repair area.

514-5. Circuit Disconnects.   When the electrical equipment of a pump is being serviced or repaired, it is very important that there be no "hot" wire or wires inside the pump. Since it is always possible that the polarity of the circuit wires may have been accidentally reversed at the panelboard, control switches or CBs must open all conductors.

To satisfy this Code rule, a special panel application is commonly used in gas stations. Figure 514-3 shows how the hookup is accomplished using a gas-station-type panelboard, which has its bussing arranged to permit hookup of standard solid-neutral circuits in addition to the switch-neutral circuits required. Another way of supplying such switched-neutral cir-

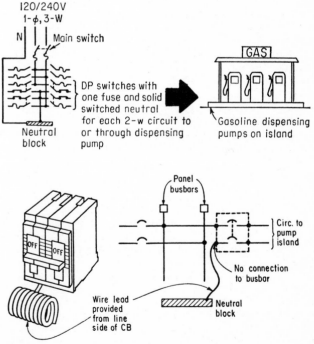

Fig. 514-3. "Gas-station" switches or CBs provide neutral disconnect. (Sec. 514-5.)

cuits is with CB-type panelboards for which there are standard accessory breaker units, which have a trip element in the ungrounded conductor and only a switching mechanism in the other pole of the common-trip breaker, as shown. Either two- or three-pole units may be used for 2-wire or 3-wire circuits, rated 15, 20, or 30 A. No electrical connection is made to the panel busbar by the plug-in grip on the neutral breaker unit. A wire lead connects line side of neutral breaker to neutral block in panel, or two clamp terminals are used for neutral.

514-6. Sealing.   Every conduit connecting to a dispenser pump must have a seal in it, as shown in Fig. 514-4. Conduits connecting to gas pumps are commonly connected through an explosion-proof junction box that is set in the pump island, as shown in Fig. 514-5. This box is approved as raintight and provided with integral sealing wells. All the conduits connecting to the box are sealed without need for separate individual sealing fittings. Additional individual seals are required where the conduits enter the pump cavity as shown. And, of course, a seal must be used in each conduit that leaves the hazardous area—such as in the conduit that feeds each lighting standard, with no fitting or coupling between the seal in the base of each standard and the boundary at the 18-in. height where the circuit crosses into nonhazardous areas. And the conduit at bottom right, which extends back to the panelboard, must also be sealed where it comes up out of the earth at the panelboard location.

The lighting fixtures in Fig. 514-5 must satisfy Sec. 511-6(b), which refers to "fixed lighting" that may be exposed to physical damage—such

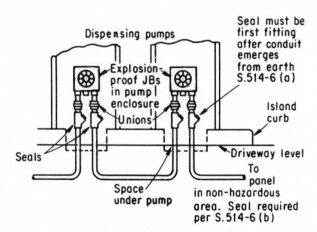

Fig. 514-4.   Seal fitting must be used for every conduit at dispenser. (Sec. 514-6.)

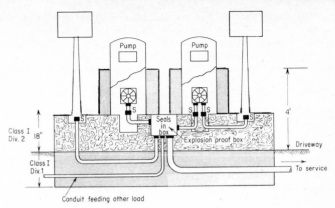

Fig. 514-5. Seals are required in conduits to pumps and to lighting fixtures or signs at points marked "S." (Sec. 514-6.)

as impact by a vehicle. If the fixtures are not at least 12 ft above the ground, they must be totally enclosed or constructed to prevent escape of sparks or hot metal. Section 514-4 specifies that.

In Fig. 514-6, four seals are shown. Normally panelboards are located in a nonhazardous location so that a seal is shown where the conduit is emerging from underground, which Sec. 514-2(d) identifies as the point where the conduit is leaving the hazardous location.

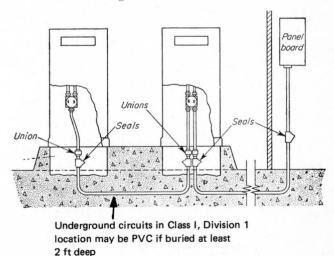

Underground circuits in Class I, Division 1 location may be PVC if buried at least 2 ft deep

Fig. 514-6. Conduit from pump island must be sealed at panelboard location. (Sec. 514-6.)

514-7. Grounding.   Because of the danger at gas stations, grounding is very important and the rule here calls for thorough grounding.

514-8. Underground Wiring.   Note that this rule permits rigid nonmetallic conduit for circuits buried at least 2 ft deep in the earth, even though the conduit in the earth may be in a Class I, Division 1 under a Division 2 area, as noted in Sec. 514-2(d). Section 347-3(a) normally excludes rigid nonmetallic conduit from hazardous locations but specifically cites Sec. 514-8 as an exception, as shown at the bottom of Fig. 514-6.

ARTICLE 515. BULK-STORAGE PLANTS

515-1. Definition.   A flammable liquid is said to become volatile when the ambient temperature is equal to, or greater than, its flash point. Typical flash points: gasoline, −45°F; kerosene, 100°F; diesel oil, 100°F. Thus, the status of gasoline is definitely established as a volatile flammable liquid regardless of geographical location of the storage facility. Other liquids may change from one state to another depending upon the relation of the ambient temperature to their respective flash points. (See "Fire Hazard Properties of Flammable Liquids, Gases and Volatile Solids," NFPA No. 325M.)

515-2. Hazardous Locations.   Figure 515-1 shows the rule of parts **(a)(1)** and **(a)(2)**.

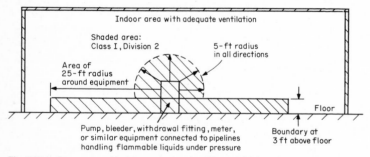

Fig. 515-1. Space around indoor equipment is a Class I, Division 2 location if adequately ventilated; or a Class I, Division 1 location, if not. (Sec. 515-2.)

For outdoor use of the same kinds of equipment the 5-ft radius is reduced to 3 ft, the 25-ft radius is reduced to 10 ft, and the 3-ft-high level is reduced to 18 in.—as covered in part **(a)(3)**. And where *transfer* of gasoline or similar liquid is done outdoors or in a ventilated indoor place, the space around the vent or fill opening becomes a Class I, Division 1 location for 3 ft in all directions from the opening and a Division 2 location out to 5 ft from the opening.

The hazardous area around a volatile flammable liquid outdoor storage tank extends 10 ft horizontally beyond the periphery of the tank (Fig. 515-2). Code designation is Class I, Division 2, and wiring installations within this range must conform to Code rules for this category. Space around the vent is a Division 1 location.

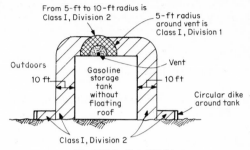

From 5-ft to 10-ft radius is Class I, Division 2

5-ft radius around vent is Class I, Division 1

Outdoors

10 ft

Gasoline storage tank without floating roof

Vent

10 ft

Circular dike around tank

Class I, Division 2

Fig. 515-2. (Sec. 515-2.)

515-5. Underground Wiring.   This rule is somewhat similar to that of Sec. 514-8. However, in this article no underground space is designated as a Class I, Division 1 location—as it is in Sec. 514-2(d). Therefore, use of nonmetallic conduit or approved cable buried at least 2 ft underground is *not* made in a hazardous location as it is under Sec. 514-2. But the reference that is made to Sec. 515-5 in Sec. 347-3(a) implies that underground wiring at a bulk-storage plant may be in a hazardous location.

ARTICLE 516. FINISHING PROCESSES

516-1. Definition.   Note that this article applies to "locations" used for finishing processes—which means open spraying areas as well as enclosed or semi-enclosed "booths."

The safety of life and property from fire or explosion in the spray application of flammable paints and finishes depends upon the extent, arrangement, maintenance, and operation of the process.

An analysis of actual experience in industry demonstrates that largest fire losses and fire frequency have occurred where good practice standards were not observed.

516-2. Hazardous Locations.   Two different types of hazardous conditions are present in a paint-spraying operation: the spray and its vapor which creates explosive mixtures in the air; and the combustible residue of paints or finishes. And each must be treated separately.

In part **(a)**, the interior of every spray booth **(1)** and some-area spraying **(2)** are Class I, Division 1 locations, When spray operations are not contained within a booth, there is greatly reduced control of flammable vapors and the area of hazard is increased considerably. This is shown in Fig. 516-1, which is a typical specific application of the concept shown in Code Fig. 1 of Sec. 516-2(b) (1). A Class I, Division 1 area exists at the actual spraying operation plus a Division 2 area extending 20 ft horizontally in any direction from the actual spraying area and for 10 ft up. Although only one corner of the room is used for spraying, the entire room area inside the 20-ft line around the spraying is classified as Class I, Division 2 and must be wired accordingly. And the Division 2 area extends 10 ft above the spray operation.

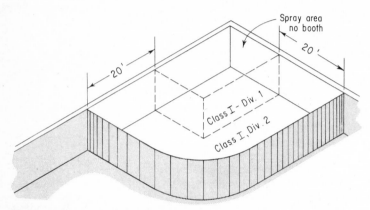

Fig. 516-1. Open spraying involves Division 1 and Division 2 Class I locations. (Sec. 516-2.)

The NFPA "Standard for Spray Finishing" (No. 33) notes that the inspection department having jurisdiction may, for any specific installation, determine the extent of the hazardous "spraying area."

516-3. Wiring and Equipment in Hazardous Locations.   In part **(a)**, spray operations that constitute a hazardous location solely on the basis of the presence of flammable vapors (and no paint or finish residues) may contain wiring and equipment for Class I locations, as specified in Art. 501.

Part **(b)** places tighter restrictions on spray booths or areas where readily ignitible deposits are present in addition to flammable vapors. In general, electrical equipment is not permitted inside any spray booth, in the exhaust duct from a spray booth, in the entrained air of an exhaust system from a spraying operation, or in the direct path of spray, unless such equipment is specifically approved for both readily ignitible deposits and flammable vapor. Electric motors driving exhaust fans are specifically prohibited inside spray booths and exhaust ducts.

Only rigid metal conduit and Type MI cable and threaded boxes or fittings containing no taps, splices, or terminal connections may be installed in such locations.

However, for that part of the hazardous area where the fixtures or equipment may not be subject to readily ignitible deposits or residues, fixtures and equipment approved for Class I, Division 1 locations may be installed. The authority having jurisdiction may decide that because of adequate positive-pressure ventilation the possibility of the hazard referred to in paragraph **(b)** has been eliminated.

Sufficient lighting for operations, booth cleaning, and repair should be provided at the time of equipment installation in order to avoid the unjustified use of "temporary" or "emergency" electric lamps connected to ordinary extension cords. A satisfactory and practical method of lighting is the use of ¼-in.-thick wired or tempered glass panel in the top or sides of spray booths with electrical light fixtures outside the booth, not in the direct path of the spray. Part **(c)** covers lighting fixtures that illuminate the spray operation through "windows" in the top or walls of a spray booth. Any such fixture used on the outside of the booth must be approved for a Class I, Division 2 location when used in any part of the top or sides of a booth that is within the Division 2 locations as shown in Figs. 2 and 3 in Sec. 516-2 of the **Code**. In the past, it was acceptable for fixtures in the Division 2 area to be enclosed to prevent hot particles falling on freshly painted stock or other readily ignitible material and if subject to physical damage had to be properly guarded.

Automobile undercoating spray operations in garages, conducted in areas having adequate natural or mechnical ventilation, may be exempt from the requirements pertaining to spray-finishing operations, when using undercoating materials not more hazardous than kerosene (as listed by Underwriters Laboratories in respect to fire hazard rating 30–40) or undercoating materials using only solvents listed as having a flash point in excess of 100°F. There should be no open flames or other sources of ignition within 20 ft while such operations are conducted.

ARTICLE 517. HEALTH CARE FACILITIES

517-1. Scope. It should be noted that the provisions of this article apply to hospitals, nursing homes, residential custodial care facilities, and other health care facilities serving patients who are unable to provide for their own safety. They also apply to the medical wiring and equipment wiring systems in mobile health care units and doctors' and dentists' offices.

Part **(c)** notes that any specific type of health care location—such as a dental office—must comply with **Code** rules whether the location is a sole occupancy itself or is part of a larger facility, like a hospital, that contains other types of health care locations.

517-2. Definitions.

Anesthetizing-Location Receptacle

Devices of the pin-and-sleeve style and also the parallel "U" blade style, both listed for Class I, Group C locations, have become a standard with many hospitals. The definition in this article permits the use of any device which is listed for use in such locations.

Patient Vicinity

This term provides a definite value for limiting the area—horizontally and vertically—in which special grounding requirements are to be observed in patient care areas.

517-11. Grounding. This rule requires the use of a separate, insulated equipment grounding conductor run with the branch-circuit conductors from a panelboard to any receptacle or metal surface of fixed electrical equipment operating over 100 V. But a separate grounding conductor is not required in a feeder conduit to such a panel. For feeders, the metal conduit is a satisfactory grounding conductor, as recognized generally in Sec. 250-91(b). But for all branch circuits to "receptacles and all . . ." in "areas used for patient care," neither the conduit, nor the use of jumpers with box clips (G-clips), nor the use of a receptacle with self-grounding screw terminals (Sec. 250-74, Exception No. 2) may be used by themselves without the grounding wire run with the branch-circuit wires (Fig. 517-1).

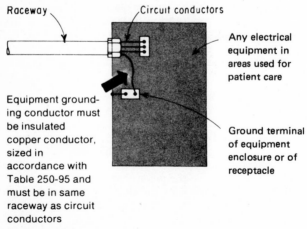

Raceway

Circuit conductors

Any electrical equipment in areas used for patient care

Equipment grounding conductor must be insulated copper conductor, sized in accordance with Table 250-95 and must be in same raceway as circuit conductors

Ground terminal of equipment enclosure or of receptacle

Fig. 517-1. Grounding conductor run with branch circuit must ground receptacles and equipment. (Sec. 517-11.)

Revision of the wording in this rule says that it applies to "areas used for patient care"—which covers patient bedrooms and any other rooms, corridors, or areas where patients are treated, like therapy areas or EKG areas. But the wording excludes waiting rooms, admitting rooms, solariums, recreation areas, as well as business offices and other places used solely by hospital personnel or where a patient might be present but would not be treated.

The Exception to part **(a)** makes clear that metal plates on wall toggle switches do not have to be connected to an equipment grounding conductor, and such a conductor is not required in conduit runs to switch boxes.

Part **(b)** notes that such assessible items as television sets, clocks, floor and table lamps, and the like, when used in such areas, must be equipped with a power supply cord having an equipment grounding conductor grounded to all noncurrent-carrying conductive surfaces of the device. Unless specifically approved for insulating purposes, paints or anodizing and similar finishes do not render the device insulated in the sense of the Exception to part **(b)**.

517-13. Ground-Fault Protection. At least one additional level of ground-fault protection is required for health care facilities where ground-fault protection is used on service equipment (see Sec. 230-95). Where the installation of ground-fault protection is made on the normal service disconnecting means, then each feeder must be provided with similar protective means. This requirement is intended to prevent a catastrophic outage. By applying appropriate selectivity at each level, the ground fault can be limited to a single feeder, and thereby service may be maintained to the balance of the health care facility.

As shown in Fig. 517-2, with a GFP (ground-fault protection) hookup on the service, a GFP hookup must be put on each feeder derived from the service. And part **(b)** requires that selection of the tripping time of the main GFP be such that each feeder GFP will operate to open a ground

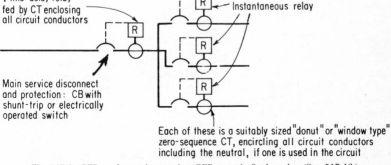

Time-delay relay fed by CT enclosing all circuit conductors

Instantaneous relay

Main service disconnect and protection: CB with shunt-trip or electrically operated switch

Each of these is a suitably sized "donut" or "window type" zero-sequence CT, encircling all circuit conductors including the neutral, if one is used in the circuit

Fig. 517-2. GFP on the service requires GFP on main feeders also. (Sec. 517-13.)

fault on the feeder, without opening the service GFP. And a time interval of not less than 0.1 sec (i.e., the time of 6 cycles) must be provided between the feeder GFP trip and the service GFP trip. As shown, if the feeder GFP relays are set for instantaneous operation, the relay on the service GFP must have at least a 0.1-sec time delay. A zone-selective GFP system with a feedback lock-out signal to an instantaneous relay on the service could satisfy the rule for selectivity.

517-30. General.   This applies the general rules on wiring systems to the specific rooms and facilities mentioned—nursing homes, etc.

517-44. Emergency System.   In part **(c)**, a single transfer switch may be used for the entire essential electrical system instead of using a separate transfer switch for each branch, as shown in **Code** diagrams 517-42. Separate transfer switches are required only if dictated by load considerations. For small facilities, the emergency electrical system generally consists of the life safety branch and the critical branch. For larger systems the critical branch is divided into three separate branches for patients, heating, and sump pumps and alarms. **Code** diagrams 517-42(1) and 517-42(2) illustrate typical installations.

517-45. Life Safety Branch.   Part **(b)** describes the switching arrangements for night transfer of corridor lighting. The rule is intended to assure that some lighting will always be provided in the corridor regardless of the mode of operation.

517-46. Critical Branch.   This section details the required loads requiring transfer from normal source to the alternate power source.

517-47. Inpatient Hospital Care Facilities.   If a nursing home provides hospital care to patients, all the **Code** rules in part **E** on hospitals must be satisfied.

517-60. General (Hospitals).   This section makes clear that essential electrical systems are to be installed in all hospitals as well as all nursing homes and similar facilities. It should be pointed out that essential electrical systems in hospitals are subdivided into the emergency system (consisting of the life safety and critical branches) and the equipment system, whereas essential electrical systems for nursing homes and the like are the branches shown in **Code** diagrams 517-42(1) and (2) for the emergency system. It should be noted that the critical branch in hospitals comprises different equipment and connections than does the critical system in nursing homes.

517-61. Emergency System—Hospitals.   Code diagrams 517-60(1) and (2) in the **Code** book clarify interconnections and transfer switches required. Handbook Table 517-1 summarizes the loads supplied by the hospital emergency system, which must restore electrical supply to the loads within 10 sec of loss of normal supply.

517-66. Switching and Overcurrent Protection.   The last sentence of part **(b)** is a mandatory requirement for a time-delay feature with a 15-min minimum setting to avoid short-time reestablishment of the normal source. That is the same as required by Sec. 700-6(b) (1).

Table 517-1. A hospital emergency system must serve these loads. (Sec. 517-61.)

Life Safety Branch	Critical Branch

Lighting and receptacles for:
—Means of egress illumination
—Exit and directional signs
—Alarm systems
  •Manual fire stations
  •Sprinklers
  •Fire & smoke detection
—Alarms for nonflammable medical gas
—Communications for emergency use
—Generator—set location
	—Isolating transformers in anesthe-
	tizing locations
	—Task illumination and selected
	receptacles in:
	  •Nurseries
	  •Medication preparation
	  •Pharmacy
	  •Acute nursing
	  •Psychiatric beds (no receptacles)
	  •Nurses stations
	  •Ward treatment rooms
	  •Surgery and obstetrics
	  •Angiographic labs
	  •Cardiac catheter labs
	  •Coronary care
	  •Delivery
	  •Dialysis
	  •Emergency
	  •Human physiology labs
	  •Intensive care
	  •Operating rooms
	  •Post-operative
	  •Recovery rooms

517-80. General (Patient Care Areas). This section deals with patient care areas in general rather than the electrically susceptible patient himself. It reserves the designation of the various types of areas to the governing body of the health care facility. The Code recognizes responsibility for evaluation of patient medical conditions, and the consequent placement of patients within specific areas is reserved to the medical staff and governing body of that health care facility. On the other hand, it now provides specific electrical rules for systems and areas which are the proper concern of architects, engineers, and maintenance staff.

The general care area would include all areas in most cases. Occasional exposure to such items as an electrocardiograph, portable x-ray, a nebulizer, and the like would not warrant exceptional electrical precautions. Basically, any electrodes applied to the patient in a general care area should be of short duration and should be noninvasive.

517-81. Grounding Performance. Initial studies of the problem which has come to be categorized as "microshock" indicated that current values as low as 20 microamperes applied directly to the interior surfaces of the heart produce ventricular fibrillation. These studies utilized dogs as their subjects, and by comparison with human data it was determined that 10 microamperes should be the maximum allowable current leakage in critical care areas. More recent studies actually utilizing human subjects now indicate that there is a wider margin between dogs and humans than was initially anticipated. The new values for permissible potential differences within patient care areas now reflect studies which have been performed both in the United States and abroad on this subject.

In most cases, it will be found that the limits for potential differences permitted in general care areas and critical care areas can be maintained using only the grounding requirements which are set forth in this article. In the 1975 **NE Code**, uncontrolled critical care areas had to have a maximum of 100 mV potential difference maintained under conditions of line-to-ground fault as well as normal operations, and the use of an isolated power system or some equivalent means was necessary to limit the rise of potential difference under fault conditions. Because there is no longer reference to "conditions of line-to-ground fault," there is no need to use an isolated power supply in critical care areas, because under normal operation the rule can readily be satisfied without an isolated power supply. That intent is supported by the elimination of the exception for permanently installed x-ray equipment—which exception was in the 1975 **NEC** because the high power needs of such x-ray could not be handled by isolated power supplies.

517-82.   This is an important addition to Art. 517, exempting certain furniture fixtures and accessories from the need to be grounded. Wording of previous **Code** editions could be interpreted to require grounding of bedpans and the other items now exempted.

517-84. Critical Care Areas.   Patient bed locations in general care areas (Sec. 517-83) must be supplied by four single or two duplex receptacles, whereas critical care area patient beds must be supplied by six single or three duplex receptacles. In both cases, at least two branch circuits must supply these receptacles. In the case of general care areas, additional receptacles serving other patient locations may be served by these branch circuits, but in the case of critical care areas at least one of these branch circuits is required to be an individual branch having no other receptacles on it except those of a single bed location. Normal and essential electrical system panelboards serving either type of patient locations must have their equipment grounding terminal bars bonded together with an insulated, continuous copper bonding jumper not smaller than No. 10 AWG (Fig. 517-3).

Regardless of what additional methods are employed, in order to keep potential differences within the required limits, equipotential grounding is essential to the electrical safety of critical care areas. Some of the earliest equipotential grounding installations consisted of copper busbars run around the walls of patient rooms to which furniture and equipment were attached by means of grounding jumpers. Based on experience obtained through these early installations as well as the refinements produced by the NFPA Committee on Hospitals, the **National Electrical Code** now contains the requirements which correlate with the pertinent NFPA standards on the subject. At the same time these new requirements

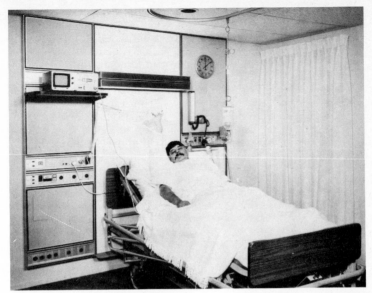

Fig. 517-3. Multipurpose patient-care modules may incorporate a variety of the circuit, receptacle, and grounding requirements for patient-care areas. In addition to patient grounding point and room bonding point, such a preassembled unit might include facilities for communications, patient monitoring, lighting, and lines for air, water, and medical gas. (Sec. 517-84.)

also permit the achievement of the desired end with a minimum of expenditure in labor and materials.

Each patient bed location is to be served by only one reference grounding point; however, one reference grounding point can serve more than one patient bed location. This reference grounding point is an extension of the grounding terminal bus in either of the two previously mentioned panelboards. The reference grounding point is connected to the panelboard by means of an equipment grounding conductor not smaller than No. 10 AWG. The reference grounding point then serves two additional points at the patient location. The first point is the patient grounding point, which contains one or more jacks which are intended to facilitate the grounding of all nonelectric portable equipment in the patient vicinity. This would include such things as nonelectric beds and bedside tables, but would not include metal chairs, over-bed tables, bedpans, and the like.

The second type of point which is to be served by the reference grounding point is the room bonding point. From the room bonding points, grounding connections are made to all exposed conductive surfaces in the patient vicinity which are a part of the building structure and the like. Such surfaces would include window frames, door frames, permanently installed metal shelving, metal sinks and plumbing, and oxygen and vacuum outlets. Either these connections can be run from the room bonding point to each individual item as individual conductors, or the conductor may be looped from item to item, whichever may be more practical.

All these points, the reference grounding point, the patient grounding point, and the room bonding point, may be combined into one point, and indeed this is most desirable when the room layout is small enough to permit it. None of the grounding connections to the building structure need to be run in conduit; however, all grounding connections made within the room must conform to the provisions of Sec. 250-113. Figure 517-4 shows how these grounding details were covered in the 1975 NEC and how the 1978 NEC has changed some of the specific techniques.

Note that there are two acceptable techniques for grounding the

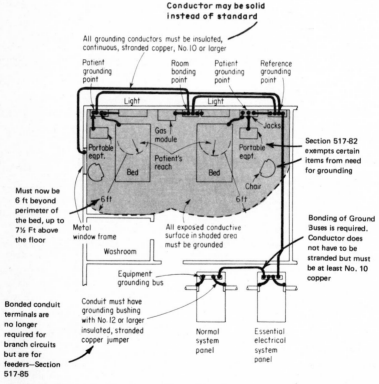

Fig. 517-4. Changes in rules on grounding and bonding were made from those on layout. (Sec. 517-84.)

"patient grounding point," as described in part (c). And part (f) permits exposed conductive surfaces in a patient vicinity to be connected to conductive building structural members having conductivity at least equal to that of AWG No. 10 copper wire. Otherwise, they must be connected to the room bonding point or reference grounding point. The permission to connect to conductive building structural members eliminates the need to install the great total length of green ground wires to bond exposed conductive surfaces to ground when totally acceptable grounding may be made to the structural steel. Small wall-mounted conductive surfaces such as soap dispensers and mirrors are excluded from the grounding requirement.

517-85. A bonding-type connection is required for *feeder* conduit terminations in critical care areas—using a bonding bushing plus a *copper* bonding jumper from a lug on the bushing to the ground bus in the panelboard fed by the conduit (see illustrations in Sec. 250-72). This is required for feeder conduits but not branch-circuit conduits. And it seems clear that bonded terminals are required at both ends of each and every feeder to a panelboard that serves the critical care area.

517-90. Additional Protective Techniques. Isolated Power Systems. Revision of these rules makes use of an isolated power system for ungrounded circuits a completely optional technique, simply noting that such systems are "permitted" to be used if the design engineer or the hospital-client wants it. That approach ties in with the deletion, in Sec. 517-81, of the maximum potential difference of 100 mV "under conditions of line-to-ground fault" in a critical care area—which previously made the isolated power system mandatory.

517-92. Wet Locations. Locations intended for ground-fault protection under this section are limited to patient care areas. So, even though the governing body of the hospital may wish to extend this form of protection to such areas as laundries, boiler rooms, and kitchens, the fact that these are not considered patient care areas does not make GFCI (ground-fault circuit interrupter) protection mandatory in such locations. The designer and/or hospital authorities must designate such "wet locations." Locations which are intended for protection would include hydrotherapy, dialysis facilities, selected wet laboratories, and special-purpose rooms where wet conditions prevail.

517-100. Anesthetizing Location Classification. Figure 517-5 shows the classified hazardous locations of part (a).

Note that part (b) requires a written designation by the hospital administration that a particular location (operating room, anesthesia room, etc.) is nonhazardous and *"prohibiting"* use of flammable anesthetics.

Hazardous locations rules are separated from those for other-than-hazardous locations. A third category is also designated—that of "above-hazardous locations." The Code covers wiring and equipment in three relations to anesthetizing locations: Sec. 517-101 (within-hazardous), Sec. 517-102 (above-hazardous), and Sec. 517-103 (other-than-hazardous) locations.

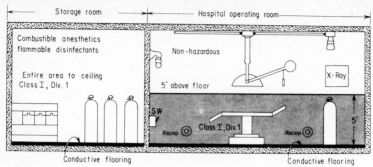

Fig. 517-5. Two types of hazardous locations must be identified. (Sec. 517-100.)

517-101. Wiring and Equipment Within Hazardous Anesthetizing Locations. Part **(a)** calls for explosionproof wiring methods, in general, for such locations.

Part **(b)** notes an extension of the hazardous boundary. Section 517-100(a)(1) defines the area of a flammable anesthetizing location as a Class I, Division 1 location from the floor to a point 5 ft above the floor. The question then arises, is the seal required in the upper conduit entering the switch box shown on the wall of a hospital operating room, as shown in Fig. 517-6? The box is partly below and partly above the 5-ft level.

Part **(b)** states that if a box or fitting is partially, but not entirely, beneath the 5-ft level, the boundary of the Class I, Division 1 area is considered to extend to the *top* of the box or fitting. Therefore, the box or fitting is entirely within the hazardous area, and a seal is required in conduit entering the enclosure from either above or below, as shown in Fig. 517-6.

If the box or fitting is entirely *above* the 5-ft level, a seal would not be required at the box or fitting, but conduit running to the box from the hazardous area would have to be sealed at the boundary, on the hazardous-location side of the box. If the box shown were recessed in the wall instead of surface-mounted, some means would have to be provided to make the seals accessible [Sec. 501-5(c)(1)], such as removable blank covers at the locations of the seals.

Part **(d)** calls for explosionproof receptacles and plugs within hazardous locations described in Sec. 517-100(a).

517-102. Wiring and Equipment Located Above Hazardous Anesthetizing Locations. Electrical metallic tubing (EMT) and intermediate metal conduit (IMC) are permitted in "above-hazardous anesthetizing locations"; but in "other-than-hazardous anesthetizing locations" (Sec. 517-103), the phrase "rigid raceways" must be taken to include EMT, IMC, and other raceways (wireways, etc.) that are "rigid," not flexible. Many of the requirements for safety in the above-hazardous anesthetizing loca-

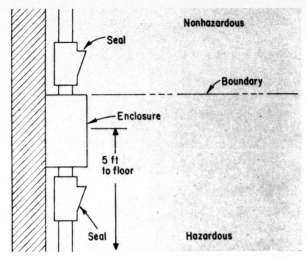

Fig. 517-6. Boundary of Class I, Division 1 location may be extended. (Sec. 517-101.)

tions are not included for other-than-hazardous locations. The rules of parts **(b)**, **(c)**, and **(d)** of this section are not included in Sec. 517-103.

Hospital-Grade Receptacles

The **NE Code** does not contain a "general" requirement that "hospital-grade" receptacles (the UL-listed "Green-dot" wiring devices) must be used in health care facilities. However, it should be noted that Sec. 517-102(e) and 517-103(b) do require use of "receptacles and attachment plugs" that are "listed for hospital use" *above* "hazardous" anesthetizing locations and *in* "other-than-hazardous" anesthetizing locations. As described, those rules require that all "2-pole, 3-wire grounding type" receptacles and plugs "for single-phase 125- or 250-volt, AC service" must be marked "Hospital Only" or "Hospital Grade," with a green dot on the face of each receptacle (Fig. 517-7). The relation between the phrase "listed for hospital use" and the phrase "Hospital Grade" is explained in the UL *Electrical Construction Materials Directory* (the UL Green Book), under the heading "Attachment Plug Receptacles and Plugs." It says:

Receptacles listed for hospital use in other than hazardous locations in accordance with Article 517 of the National Electrical Code are identified (1) by the marking "Hospital Only" or (2) by the marking "Hospital Grade" and a green dot on the receptacle. The green dot is on the face of the receptacle where visible after installation.

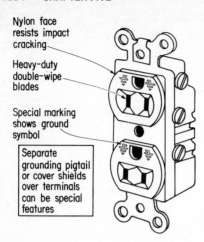

Nylon face
resists impact
cracking

Heavy-duty
double-wipe
blades

Special marking
shows ground
symbol

Separate
grounding pigtail
or cover shields
over terminals
can be special
features

Fig. 517-7. Hospital-grade plugs and receptacles are required *only* for anesthetizing locations. (Sec. 517-102.)

But it should be noted that the *requirement* for hospital-grade wiring devices applies only with respect to anesthetizing locations. It does not apply to patient care areas or other areas. And it does not apply to nursing homes, clinics, or medical offices (Fig. 517-8).

Of course, in the defined hazardous areas of flammable anesthetizing locations (Sec. 517-100 and Sec. 517-101), receptacles must be explosion-proof type, listed for Class I, Division 1 areas.

Underwriters Laboratories Inc. devised a special series of tests for wiring devices intended for hospital use. These tests are substantially more abusive than those performed on general-purpose devices and are designed to ensure the reliability of the grounding connection in particular, when used in the hospital environment. Hospital-grade receptacles have stability and construction in excess of standard specifications and can stand up to abuse and hard usage. Devices which pass this test are listed as "Hospital Grade" and are identified with these words and a green dot, both of which are visible after installation. UL listings include 15- and 20-A 125-V grounding, nonlocking-type plugs, receptacles, and connectors. This class of device is acceptable for use in any nonhazardous anesthetizing location. Their use might not be acceptable above hazardous anesthetizing areas if they are not totally enclosed and permit the escape of sparks or hot metal particles which could fall into the hazardous area, as prohibited by part **(b)** of this section. Although part **(e)** does require hospital-grade receptacles above hazardous anesthetizing locations, the rule of part **(b)** must be observed.

517-104. Circuits in Anesthetizing Locations. Figure 517-9 shows the application of a completely packaged transformer loadcenter to provide power for the ungrounded, isolated circuits required in hospital operating suites. Factors involved in such installations are as follows:

Fig. 517-8. Although the NE Code requires use of hospital-grade receptacles *only* in "anesthetizing" locations, the ruggedness and high degree of connection reliability strongly recommends their use for such critical applications as plug-connection of "iron lungs" and other respiratory or life-sustaining equipment. (Sec. 517-102.)

1. Any electrical circuit within or partially within an anesthetizing location must be supplied from an isolated ungrounded distribution system. An anesthetizing location is any area in a hospital in which flammable or nonflammable anesthetics are or may be administered to patients—operating rooms, delivery rooms, anesthesia rooms, and any corridors, utility rooms, or other areas used for administering anesthetics [part (**a**)].

2. Any transformer used to obtain the ungrounded circuits must have its primary rated for not more than 300 V between conductors and must have proper overcurrent protection. Figure 517-10 shows the circuit makeup used in a hospital to derive the 120-V ungrounded circuits, with transformation down from 480 to 240 and then to 120 V [part (**b**)]. The ungrounded secondary system must be equipped with an approved ground contact indicator—to give a visual and audible warning if a ground fault develops in the ungrounded system [part (**e**)].

3. Isolating transformers must be installed out of the hazardous area.

Supply cannot be made directly from two phase legs of 480/277-v system. On such systems, two stages of transformation are needed

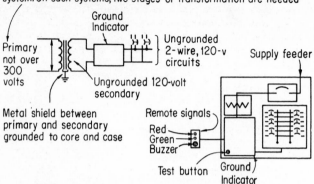

COMPLETE PACKAGED UNGROUNDED DISTRIBUTION CENTER FOR HOSPITAL OPERATING ROOM: Main CB, isolating transformer, ground indicator and CB panel for ungrounded circuits. For in-wall or floor mounting close to operating suite.

Fig. 517-9. Isolated power supply is required for circuits in anesthetizing locations. (Sec. 517-104.)

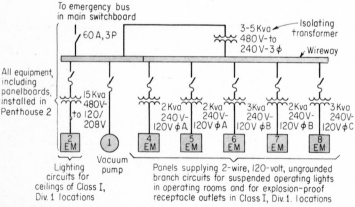

Fig. 517-10. Two-stage transformation is often needed for isolated circuits. (Sec. 517-104.)

The ground indicator and its signals must also be installed out of the hazardous area [part **(c)** and **(g)**]. In an anesthetizing location, the hazardous area extends to a height of 5 ft above the floor.

4. Fixed lighting fixtures above the hazardous area in an anesthetizing location, other than the surgical luminaire, and certain x-ray equipment may be supplied by conventional grounded branch circuits [part **(f)**].

Part **(d)(2)** requires isolated circuit conductors to be identified by brown and orange colors.

Part **(e)** details a line isolation monitor and clarifies line isolation monitor alarm values, specifying 1.7 mA as the lower limit of alarm for total hazard current. Figure 517-11 shows the basic concept behind detection and signal of a ground fault. The diagram shows major circuit components of a typical ground detector/alarm system. Partial ground energizes current-relay A, opening contact A2 (energizing red light and warning buzzer). Pressing the momentary-contact silencer switch energizes coil C, opening contact C1 (disconnecting buzzer), and closing holding contact C2. When ground is cleared, contacts resume position shown in drawing.

The purpose of such a ground indicator is to provide warning of the danger of shock hazard and the possibility of a fault in the system due to

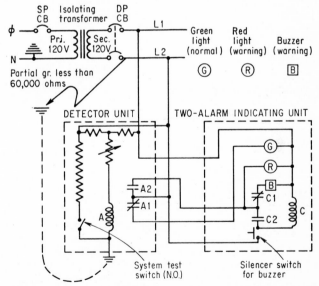

Fig. 517-11. Detection and alarm on ground fault is required for isolated power systems. (Sec. 517-104.)

accidental grounding of more than one conductor. If one conductor of an isolated system becomes grounded at one point, normal protective devices (fuses or CBs) will not operate because there is no return path and, therefore, no flow of short-circuit fault current. However, if an accidental ground subsequently develops on the other conductor, a short circuit will occur with possible disastrous consequences, such as ignition of ether vapors by arc or a lethal shock to personnel.

Part **(f)(1)** calls for a general purpose lighting circuit, fed from the normal grounded service, to be installed in each operating room. And the Exception recognizes feed from an emergency generator or other emergency service that is separate from the source of the hospital's "Emergency System," as defined in Sec. 517-2. Figure 517-12 shows a

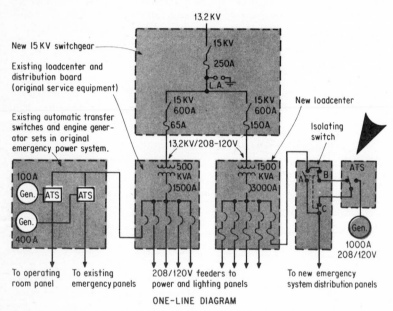

Fig. 517-12. General-purpose lighting circuit must be fed from normal service or separate alternate source. (Sec. 517-104.)

layout where such an emergency supply (at lower right) may be the source of supply to the general purpose lighting circuit in the operating room because it is a separate supply from that to the Emergency System (at left).

517-105. Low-Voltage Equipment and Instruments. Specific details are given for use of low-voltage equipment in an anesthetizing location.

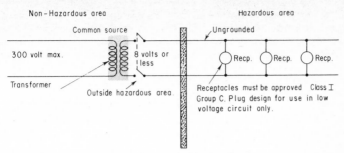

Fig. 517-13. Low-voltage circuits in anesthetizing locations must operate at 8 V *or* be otherwise approved. (Sec. 517-105.)

Figure 517-13 shows some of the rules. Section 517-104(b) limits isolating transformers to operation with primary at not over 300 V.

517-132. Enclosure (For Therapeutic Equipment). This section is intended to include all generating equipment except rotating machines, as such machines are normally enclosed according to existing motor-generator set standards. The enclosure referred to is expected to enclose the generating apparatus to protect operating personnel from the high voltages encountered in this type of equipment. The enclosure need not comply with Art. 100 where the word "cabinet" is defined.

517-140. Permanently Installed X-ray Equipment. A separate grounding and bonding conductor is required for the frame of the patient support and the stationary portion of the system for permanently installed x-ray equipment.

517-141 and 517-142. These rules tie into those of Secs. 660-4(b) and 660-6.

ARTICLE 518. PLACES OF ASSEMBLY

518-1. Scope. This article covers places of assembly which used to be covered along with theaters in Art. 520. This article does not apply to occupancies like theaters. Instead, it covers all buildings or parts of buildings or structures designed or intended for use by 100 or more persons for assembly purposes. That includes dining rooms, meeting rooms, entertainment areas (other than with a stage or platform or projection booth), lecture halls, bowling alleys, places of worship, dance halls, exhibition halls, museums, gymnasiums, armories, group rooms, mortuaries, skating rinks, pool rooms, transportation terminals, court rooms, sports arenas, and stadiums.

The clear differentiation given in this section points out that any such building or structure or part of a building that contains a projection booth or stage platform or even just an area that may, on occasion, be used for presenting theatrical or musical productions—whether the stage or platform is fixed or portable—must comply with the rules of Art. 520, as if it were a theater, and not Art. 518. A restaurant, say, that has a piano player for entertainment on Saturday night, could readily be classed as a theater and subject to Art. 520.

The question often arises, Does Art. 518 apply to supermarkets and department-store types of occupancies because such places are regularly crowded with far more than 100 persons? Although occupancies of those types have capacity to hold more than 100 persons at any given time. Art. 518 is not generally applicable.

Article 518 directs attention "to a building or part of a building" that would be used for the purposes outlined; therefore, you would have to determine how the occupancy is used.

A supermarket generally would not have a public assembly area. However, a department store could incorporate a community room for shows and similar audience functions. This room would be subject to Art. 518. The main areas of supermarkets and department stores, unlike theaters and assembly halls, have many aisles and exits that could be used in case of emergency evacuation of the building. It is these characteristics that permit conventional wiring methods to be accepted.

A proposal was once made to include supermarkets and department stores as "places of assembly," but it was rejected.

Note that places of assembly covered by this article must be for 100 or more people. No rules are given for determining the number of people, but a note refers questions of population to local building codes or to the NFPA Life Safety Code. Of course, number of seats is an index of capacity, and other reasonable indications must be observed.

The following information is found in NFPA No. 101, Life Safety Code, for determining occupant load in places of assembly.

Occupant Load. The occupant load permitted in any assembly building, structure, or portion thereof shall be determined by dividing the net floor area or space assigned to that use by the square feet per occupant as follows:

(a) An assembly area of concentrated use without fixed seats such as an auditorium, church, chapel, dance floor, and lodge room—7 square feet per person.

(b) An assembly area of less concentrated use such as a conference room, dining room, drinking establishment, exhibit room, gymnasium, or lounge—15 square feet per person.

(c) Standing room or waiting room—3 square feet per person.

The occupant load of an area having fixed seats shall be determined by the number of fixed seats installed. Required aisle space serving the fixed seats shall not be used to increase the occupant load.

The occupant load permitted in a building or portion thereof may be increased above the specified in "Occupant Load" if the necessary aisles and exits are provided subject to the approval of the authority having jurisdiction. An approved aisle, exit and/or seating diagram may be required by the authority having jurisdiction to substantiate an increase in occupant load.

518-3. Wiring Methods. The basic rule says that fixed wiring must be in metal raceway, nonmetallic raceways encased in *not less than 2 in. of concrete,* Type ALS cable, Type MI cable, or Type MC cable. The first exception says that nonmetallic-sheathed cable, BX, and rigid nonmetallic conduit may be used in building areas that are *not* required by the local building code to be of fire-rated construction. Note that use of those methods no longer relates to the number of persons that the place holds, which was once in this rule. Another exception permits the use of other wiring methods for sound systems, communication circuits, Class 2 and 3 remote-control and signal circuits, and fire-alarm circuits.

ARTICLE 520. THEATERS AND SIMILAR LOCATIONS

520-1. Scope. Where only a part of a building is used as a theater or similar location, these special requirements apply only to that part and do not necessarily apply to the entire building. A common example is a school building in which there is an auditorium used for dramatic or other performances. All special requirements of this chapter would apply to the auditorium, stage, dressing rooms, and main corridors leading to the auditorium but not to other parts of the building that do not pertain to the use of the auditorium for performances or entertainment.

520-4. Wiring Methods. Building laws usually require theaters and motion picture houses to be of fireproof construction; hence practical considerations limit the types of concealed wiring for light and power chiefly to raceway. Only Type MI or Type MC cables may be used. Cables were long ago found unsuitable for circuits in theaters because they do not readily offer increase in the size of conductors for load growth. Many instances of overfusing dictated the value of raceways, which do permit replacement of larger conductors for safely handling load growth.

Much of the stage lighting in a modern theater is provided by floodlights and projectors mounted in the ceiling or on the balcony front. In order that the projectors may be adjustable in position, they may be connected by plugs and short cords to suitable receptacles or "pockets."

520-23. Control and Overcurrent Protection of Receptacle Circuits. The term *gallery receptacles* should be understood as including all receptacles, wherever they may be located, that are intended for the connection of stage lighting equipment. Circuits to such receptacles must of necessity be controlled at the same location as other stage lighting circuits.

520-24. Metal Hood.   Because of the large amount of flammable material always present on a stage, and because of the crowded space, a stage switchboard must have no live parts on the front, and the back must be so guarded as to keep unauthorized persons away from the space in back of the board and the wall, with a door at one end of the enclosure.

The more important stage switchboards are commonly of the remote-control type. Pilot switches mounted on the stage board control the operation of contactors installed in any convenient location where space is available, usually below the stage. The contactors in turn control the lighting circuits.

The stage switchboard is usually built into a recess in the proscenium wall, as shown in the plan view, Fig. 520-1. After passing through the switches and dimmers, many of the main circuits must be subdivided into branch circuits so that no branch circuit will be loaded to more than 20 A.

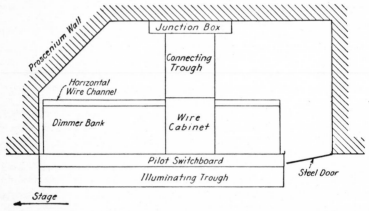

Fig. 520-1. Stage switchboards must be circuited to provide highly flexible usage. (Sec. 520-24.)

Where the board is of the remote-control type, the branch-circuit fuses are often mounted on the same panels as the contactors. Where a direct-control type of board is used, and sometimes where the board is remotely controlled, the branch-circuit fuses are mounted on special panelboards known as *magazine panels,* which are installed in the space back of the switchboard, usually in the location of the junction box shown in Fig. 520-24.

520-25. Dimmers.   Figure 520-2 shows typical connections of two branch circuits arranged for control by one switch and one dimmer plate or section. The single-pole switch on the stage switchboard is connected to one of the outside buses, and from this switch a wire runs to a short bus

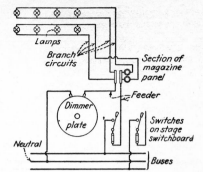

Fig. 520-2. Branch circuits of lighting may be controlled by single dimmer in grounded or ungrounded conductor. (Sec. 520-25.)

on the magazine panel. The magazine panel is similar to an ordinary panelboard, except that it contains no switches and the circuits are divided into many sections, each section having its own separate buses. One terminal of the dimmer plate, or variable resistor, is connected to the neutral bus at the switchboard, and from the other terminal of the dimmer a wire runs to the neutral bus on the magazine panel. This neutral bus must be well insulated from ground and must be separate from other neutral buses on the panel; otherwise the dimmer would be shunted and would fail to control the brightness of the lamps.

While the dimmer is permanently connected to the neutral of the wiring system, this neutral is presumed to be thoroughly grounded and hence the dimmer is dead. A dimmer is the grounded neutral does not require overcurrent protection, as noted in part **(a)**.

Figure 520-3 shows an autotransformer used as a dimmer. By changing the position of the movable contact, any desired voltage may be supplied to the lamps, from full-line voltage to a voltage so low that the lamps are "black out." As compared with a resistance-type dimmer, a dimmer of this type has the advantages that it operates at a much higher efficency, generates very little heat, and, within its maximum rating, the dimming effect is not dependent upon the wattage of the load it controls.

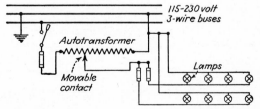

Fig. 520-3. Autotransformer dimmer must have grounded leg common to primary and secondary. (Sec. 520-25.)

520-43. Footlights. A footlight of the disappearing type might produce so high a temperature as to be a serious fire hazard if the lamps should be left burning after the footlight is closed. Part **(b)** calls for automatic disconnect when the lights disappear.

There is no restriction on the number of lamps that may be supplied by one brance circuit. The lamp wattage supplied by one circuit should be such that the current will be slightly less than 20 A.

Individual outlets as described in part **(b)** are seldom used for footlights, as such construction would be much more expensive than the standard trough type.

A modern type of footlight is shown in Fig 520-4. The wiring is carried in a sheet-iron wire channel in the face of which lamp receptacles are mounted. Each lamp is provided with an individual reflector and glass color screen or "roundel." The circuit wires are usually brought to the wire channel in rigid conduit. In the other type of footlight, still used to some extent, the lamps are placed vertically or nearly so, and an extension of one side of the wire channel is shaped so as to form a reflector to direct the light toward the stage.

520-44. Borders and Proscenium Sidelights. Figure 520-5 is a cross section showing the construction of a border light over the stage. This

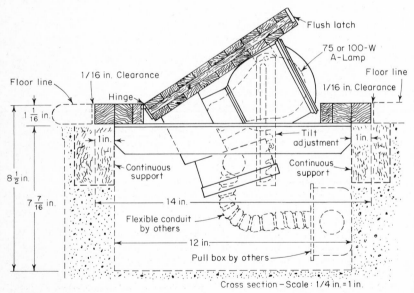

Fig. 520-4. Footlights must be automatically de-energized when the flush latch is closed down. (Sec. 520-43.)

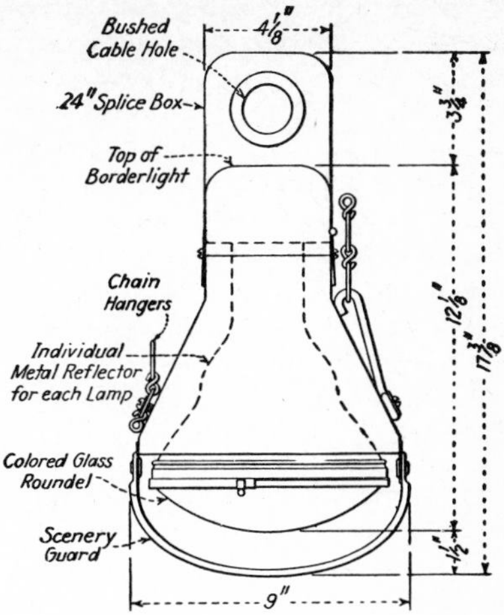

Fig. 520-5. Border lights must comply with NEC construction rules. (Sec. 520-44.)

particular type is intended for the use of 200-W lamps. An individual reflector is provided for each lamp so as to secure the highest possible efficiency of light utilization. A glass roundel is fitted to each reflector; these may be obtained in any desired color, commonly white, red, and blue for three-color equipment and white, red, blue, and amber for four-color equipment. A splice box is provided on top of the housing for enclosing the connections between the border-light cable and the wiring of the border. From this splice box, the wires are carried to the lamp sockets in a trough extending the entire length of the border.

Border lights are usually hung on steel cables so that their height may be adjusted and so that they may be lowered to the stage for cleaning and replacing lamps and color screens; hence the circuit conductors supplying the lamps must be carried to the border through a flexible cable. The individual conductors of the cable may be of No. 14, though No. 12 is more commonly used.

520-49. Flue Damper Control. A normally-closed-circuit device has the inherent safety feature that in case the control circuit is accidentally opened by the blowing of a fuse, or in any other way, the device immediately operates to open the flue dampers.

520-65. Festoons. "Lanterns of similar devices" are very likely to be made of paper or other flammable material, and the lamps should be prevented from coming in contact with such material.

520-72. Lamp Guards. Lamps in dressing rooms should be provided with guards that cannot easily be removed to prevent them from coming in contact with flammable material.

ARTICLE 530. MOTION PICTURE AND TELEVISION STUDIOS AND SIMILAR LOCATIONS

530-1. Scope. Article 520 covers theaters used for TV, motion picture, or live presentations where the building or part of a building includes an assembly area for the audience. Article 530, however, applies to TV or motion picture studios where film or TV cameras are used to record programs and to the other areas of similar application—but where the facility does not include an audience area.

The term *motion picture studio* is commonly used as meaning a large space, sometimes 100 acres or more in extent, enclosed by walls or fences within which are several "stages," a number of spaces for outdoor setups, warehouses, storage sheds, separate buildings used as dressing rooms, a large substation, a restaurant, and other necessary buildings. The so-called "stages" are large buildings containing numerous temporary and semipermanent setups for both indoor and outdoor views.

The Code rules for motion picture studios are intended to apply only to those locations where special hazards exist. Such special hazards are confined to the buildings in which films are handled or stored, the stages, and the outdoor spaces where flammable temporary structures and equipment are used. Some of these special hazards are due to the presence of a considerable quantity of highly flammable film; otherwise, the conditions are much the same as on a theater stage and, in general, the same rules should be observed as in the case of theater stages.

530-11. Permanent Wiring. The 1975 NEC used the word "metal"— between "approved" and "raceways," in the first sentence. Because the word "metal" no longer appears in the rule, rigid nonmetallic conduit is, therefore, acceptable for use in motion picture and TV studios.

ARTICLE 540. MOTION PICTURE PROJECTORS

540-1. Scope. According to the definition of hazardous locations in Art. 500, a motion picture booth is not classed as a hazardous location, even though the film is highly flammable. The film is not volatile at ordinary temperatures and hence no flammable gases are present, and the wiring installation need not be explosionproof but should be made with special care to guard against fire hazards.

540-2. Professional Projector—Definition. Figure 540-1 shows a professional movie projector, which is subject to lengthier and stricter requirements than those of nonprofessional projectors.

540-10. Enclosure. Professional projectors must be installed in a projector booth, which does not have to be treated like a hazardous location.

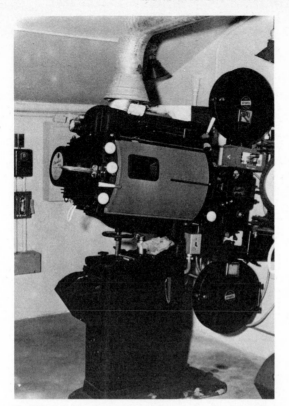

Fig. 540-1. Professional projector. But note that Art. 540 applies to *both* professional and nonprofessional movie projectors. The article is divided into part **C** on professional equipment and part **D** on nonprofessional units. (Sec. 540-2.)

Figure 540-2 shows the arrangement of the apparatus and wiring in the projection room of a large modern motion picture theater. This room, or booth, contains three motion picture projectors P, one stereopticon or "effect machine" L, and two spot machines S.

The light source in each of the six machines is an arc lamp operated on DC. The DC supply is obtained from two motor-generator sets which are installed in the basement in order to avoid any possible interference with the sound-reproducing apparatus. The two motor generators are remotely controlled from the generator panel in the projection room. From each generator a feeder consisting of two 500,000-CM cables is carried to the DC panelboard in the projection room.

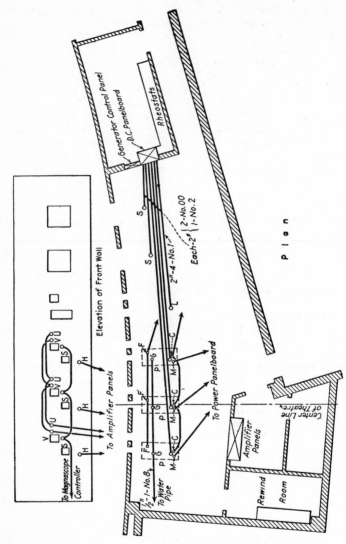

Fig. 540-2. Code rules cover many electrical details in a motion-picture projection room (or "booth"). (Sec. 540-10.)

From the DC panelboard to each picture machine and to each of the two spot machines a branch circuit is provided consisting of two No. 00 cables. One of these conductors leads directly to the machine; the other side of the circuit is led through the auxiliary gutter to the bank of resistors in the rheostat room and from its rheostat to the machine. The resistors are provided with short-circuiting switches so that the total resistance in series with each arc may be preadjusted to any desired value.

Two circuits consisting of No. 1 conductors are carried to the stereopticon or "effect machine," since this machine contains two arc lamps.

The conduit leading to each machine is brought up through the floor.

It is provided in Sec. 540-13 that the wires to the projector outlet shall not be smaller than No. 8, but in every case the maximum current drawn by the lamp should be ascertained and conductors should be installed of sufficient size to carry this current. In this case, when suitably adjusted for the large pictures, the arc in each projector takes a current of nearly 150 A.

In addition to the main outlet for supplying the arc, four other outlets are installed at each projector machine location for auxiliary circuits.

Outlets F are for foot switches which control the shutters in front of the lenses for changeover from one projector to another.

Outlets G are for a No. 8 grounding conductor which is connected to the frame of each projector and to the water-piping system.

From outlets C a circuit is brought up to each machine for a small incandescent lamp inside the lamp house and a lamp to illuminate the turntable. Outlets M are for power circuits to the motors used to operate the projector machines.

Ventilation is provided by two exhaust fans and two duct systems, one exhausting from the ceiling of the projection room and one connected to the arc-lamp housing of each machine. See Fig. 540-1.

A separate room is provided for rewinding films, but as this room opens only into the projection room, it may be considered that the rewinding is performed in the projection room.

540-11. Associated Electrical Equipment. All necessary equipment *may* be located in a projector booth, but equipment which is not necessary in the normal operation of the motion picture projectors, stage-lighting projectors, and control of the auditorium lighting and stage curtain *must* be located elsewhere. Equipment such as service equipment and panelboards for the control and projection of circuits for signs, outside lighting, and lighting in the lobby and box office must not be located in the booth.

ARTICLE 545. MANUFACTURED BUILDING

545-1. Scope. Prefab buildings—residential, commercial, and even industrial types—have gained wide acceptance over recent years and the factory-installed and job-installed electrical circuits and equipment of such buildings must comply with this article. Such buildings are commonly assembled on their site, by erecting and attaching preconstructed walls, floors, ceilings, roof, and similar subparts of a total building. Diners are very frequently preconstructed at a factory with all wiring installed and covered by walls and other finishes, requiring only construction and connection of the service-entrance layout at the job site.

545-13. Component Interconnections. A variety of available UL-listed devices and components are intended to be used to meet the requirements for component interconnections at the time of on-site assembly. Typical devices eliminate the chance for do-it-yourself wire installers to incorrectly wire component parts. Connectors, once mated, cannot be disconnected. Standard plug-and-cap connections do not satisfy the requirements of this section.

ARTICLE 547. AGRICULTURAL BUILDINGS

547-1. Scope. This is a Code article covering the types of farm buildings described.

547-3. Wiring Methods. The wording leaves much of the determination of acceptability up to the inspection authority. But Type NMC cable (nonmetallic, corrosion-resistant—so-called "barn wiring cable") is specifically recognized for these buildings. PVC conduit and other nonmetallic or protected products would be suitable for the wet and corrosive conditions that prevail. The rule accepts wiring for Class II hazardous locations, as well as open wiring on insulators (Art. 320).

Note that boxes and fittings must be both dust-tight and water-tight. Flexible connections must use dust-tight flex, liquid-tight flex or cord.

547-4. Switches, Circuit Breakers, Motor Controllers, and Fuses. In part **(a)**, the description of the type of enclosure required corresponds to the following NEMA designations on enclosures:

Type 4. Watertight and dust-tight. For use indoors and outdoors. Protect against splashing water, seepage of water, falling or hose-directed water, and severe external condensation. Are sleet-resistant but not sleet-(ice) proof.

Type 4X. Watertight, dust-tight and corrosion-resistant Have same provisions as Type 4 enclosures, but in addition are corrosion-resistant.

The rule of this section seems to clearly call for NEMA 4X enclosures (Fig. 547-1).

Stainless steel NEMA Type 4X enclosures are used in areas which may be regularly hosed down or are otherwise very wet, and where serious corrosion problems exist. Typical enclosures are made from 14-gauge stainless steel, with an oil-resistant neoprene door gasket.

Epoxy powdered resin coated NEMA Type 4X enclosures are designed to house electrical controls, terminals, and instruments in areas

Fig. 547-1. The Code rule seems to make use of this type of enclosure mandatory in agricultural buildings. (Sec. 547-4.)

NEMA Type 4X

which may be regularly hosed down or are otherwise very wet. These enclosures are also designed for use in areas where serious corrosion problems exist. They are suitable for use outdoors, or in dairies, packing plants, and similar installations. These enclosures are made from 14-gauge steel. All seams are continuously welded with no holes or knock-outs. A rolled lip is provided around all sides of the enclosure opening. This lip increases strength and keeps dirt and liquids from dropping into the enclosure while the door is open.

ARTICLE 550. MOBILE HOMES AND MOBILE HOME PARKS

550-1. Scope. Part **(a)** notes that the provisions of this article cover the electric conductors and equipment installed within or on mobile homes, and also the conductors that connect mobile homes to a supply of electricity. But the service equipment which is located "adjacent" to the mobile home is not covered in Art. 550, and all applicable Code rules on such service equipment—as in Art. 230 and 250—must be observed.

The electrical requirements presented here and in Art. 551 are included in the NEC to provide better means of enforcement by local inspection bureaus. As will be noted in Arts. 550 and 551, the provisions cover many items that will be incorporated at the factory where travel trailers and mobile homes are manufactured. The inclusion of such construction specifications permits testing laboratories, such as UL, to establish standards for these mobile units. As a result, the articles should encourage better and more uniform wiring than has been possible in the past where wiring in mobile homes and trailers presented a serious problem to electrical inspectors.

Several states have laws that require factory inspection of mobile homes by state inspectors, and some states require that mobile homes be inspected by a nationally recognized independent testing laboratory.

Underwriters Laboratories now lists a number of mobile home manufacturers, and such listings are acceptable in many areas of the country.

In setting up any factory inspection program it is in the interest of public safety to adopt the latest edition of NFPA No. 5018—Standard for Mobile Homes. This standard contains electrical requirements identical to those in Art. 550, and in addition, contains requirements on body and frame design, construction, exits, interior-finish flame spread, and installation of plumbing and heating systems. Inspection of only the wiring will not ensure complete protection for purchases or users of mobile homes.

Some inpsection authorities treat a mobile home on a private lot differently than they do a mobile home at a mobile home park. At an individual lot for a private installation, the inspector knows what is going in; but on a mobile home court, spaces for mobile homes are rented on a transient basis, and load connections for supply to individual mobile homes may vary widely.

Many so-called mobile homes do not have their main service-entrance equipment located *adjacent* to the mobile home, as required by Sec. 550-3. In some, the service equipment is mounted on the outside of the mobile home, and in others it is mounted inside. That is commonly the case with mobile homes that have had the wheels removed and are on permanent foundations. Some such mobile homes are used as living units, some as business offices, coin-operated laundries, and for many other purposes.

When a mobile home is altered by removing its wheels and installing a permanent foundation, it is no longer mobile and does not satisfy the definition of "mobile home," given in Sec. 550-2. Many inspection authorities treat such installation as a prefabricated building or structure and apply the rules of Art. 545 instead of Art. 550. The requirement for a prefabricated structure is that such buildings must satsify Code requirements the same as a building being built on the site. As with any constructed-on-site building, a prefabricated building can have the service equipment inside or outside.

550-2. Definitions.   A "double-wide mobile home" is manufactured in two sections, each being approximately 12 by 60 ft. Each section is mounted on a chassis, with one side in each section open. The sections are moved to location and joined together to make a 24- by 60-ft complete unit. Because the double-wide will most likely be placed on a foundation, the enforcing authority will usually classify it as a prefabricated structure, because it does not meet the definition of "mobile home." Article 545 would apply.

550-3. Power Supply.   Part **(a)** requires that the mobile home service equipment be located adjacent to the mobile home and not mounted in or on the mobile home. It further specifies that the power supply to the mobile home shall be a feeder circuit consisting of not more than *one* 50-A rated approved mobile home supply cord, or that feeder circuit could be a permanently installed circuit of fixed wiring.

Fig. 550-1. Service equipment for a mobile home lot consists of disconnect, overcurrent protection, and receptacle for connecting *one* 50-A (or 40-A) power supply cord from a mobile home parked "adjacent" to the service equipment. (Sec. 550-3.)

IMPORTANT: Note that the rule of part **(a)** of this section no longer permits up to three cords as feeders from the service equipment to a mobile home (as was permitted in the 1975 **NEC**) (Fig. 550-1). And the word "approved" must be taken as "listed by UL."

Part **(b)** covers use of a cord instead of permanent wiring. The power-supply cord to a mobile home is actually a feeder, and must be treated as such in applying **Code** rules. The service equipment must be located adjacent to the mobile home and could be either a fused or breaker type in an appropriate enclosure or enclosures, with not over 50-A overcurrent protection for the supply cord (or 40 A, as in the Exception). The equipment must be approved service-entrance equipment with an appropriate receptacle for the supply cord, installed to meet **Code** rules the same as any installation of service equipment. The panel or panels in the home are feeder panels and are *never* to be used as service-entrance equipment according to Secs. 550-3 and 550-4(a). This means that the neutral is isolated from the enclosure and the equipment grounding goes to a separate bus for the purpose only. As a result, there must be an equipment grounding conductor run from the service-entrance equipment to the panel or panels in the home. This is true whether there is cord connection or permanent wiring.

In the 1975 **NEC**, part **(j)** required special permission to permit two or three 50-A power-supply cords to a mobile home. Most mobile homes parks were not equipped to handle more than one such power-supply cord for each mobile home lot. But in this **Code** edition, Sec. 550-3(a) does *not* permit mobile home parks to be wired with more than one 50-A receptacle at each mobile home lot.

In some areas mobile homes are permanently connected as permitted in paragraph (l). Accordingly, local requirements must be checked in regard to the approved method of installing feeder assemblies where a mobile home has a calculated load over 50 A. In many such cases, a raceway is stubbed to the underside of a mobile home from the distribution panelboard. It is optional as to whether the feeder conductors are installed in the raceway by the mobile home manufacturer or by field installers. When installed, four continuous, insulated, color-coded conductors, as indicated, are required. The feeder conductors may be spliced in a suitable junction box, but in no case within the raceway proper.

550-4. Disconnecting Means and Branch-Circuit Protective Equipment. As shown in Fig. 550-2, the required disconnect for a mobile home may be the main in the panelboard supplying the branch circuits for the unit. Details of this section must be observed by the mobile home builder.

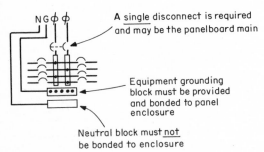

Fig. 550-2. A "distribution panelboard," not "service panelboard" may be used *in* mobile home. (Sec. 550-4.)

550-5. Branch Circuits. The manufacturer of the mobile home must assure this minimum circuiting.

550-8. Wiring Methods and Materials. In part **(j)**, the smaller-dimensional box mentioned in this rule would usually be a box designed for a special switch or receptacle, or a combination box and wiring device. Such combinations can be properly evaluated and tested with a limited number of conductors and connections and a specific lay of conductors to ensure adequate wiring space in the spirit of the first paragraph in Sec. 370-6.

550-9. Grounding. The white (neutral) conductor is required to be run from the "insulated busbar" in the mobile home panel to the service-entrance equipment, where it is connected to the terminal at the point of connection to the grounding electrode conductor.

The green-colored conductor is required to be run from the "panel grounding bus" in the mobile home to the service-entrance equipment, where it is connected to the neutral conductor at the point of connection to the grounding electrode conductor.

The requirements provide that the grounded (white) conductor and the grounding (green) conductor be kept separate within the mobile home structure in order to secure the maximum protection against electric-shock hazard if the supply neutral conductor should become open.

A common point of discussion among electrical authorities and electricians is whether or not the green-colored grounding conductor in the supply cord should be connected to the grounded circuit conductor (neutral) outside the mobile home, say at the location of the service equipment. The grounding conductor in the supply cord or the grounding conductor in the power supply to a mobile home is always required to be connected to the grounded circuit conductor (neutral) outside the mobile home on the supply side of the service disconnecting means, but *not* in a junction box under the mobile home or at any other point on the *load side* of the service equipment (pedestal).

550-21. Distribution System.   The mobile home park supply is limited to nominal 115/230-V, single-phase, 3-wire to accommodate appliances rated at nominal 230 V or a combination nominal voltage of 115/230 V. Accordingly, a 3-wire 120/208-V supply, derived from a 4-wire 208Y/120-V supply, would not be acceptable.

While the demand factor for a single mobile home lot is computed at 16,000 W, it should be noted that Sec. 550-22(c) requires the feeder circuit conductors extending to each mobile home lot to be not less than 100 A.

ARTICLE 551. RECREATIONAL VEHICLES AND
RECREATIONAL VEHICLE PARKS

551-1. Scope.   Some states have laws that require factory inspection of recreational vehicles by state inspectors. Such laws closely follow NFPA No. 501C, Standard for Recreational Vehicles. This standard contains electrical requirements in accordance with part **A** of Art. 551. It also contains requirements for plumbing and heating systems.

551-3. Low-Voltage Systems.   Sections 551-3, 551-4, and 551-5 concern 12-V systems for running and signal lights similar to those in conventional automobile systems. Also, many rereational vehicles use 12-V systems for interior lighting or other small loads. The 12-V system is derived from an on-board battery or through a transfer switch from a 120/12-V transformer often equipped with a full-wave rectifier.

ARTICLE 555. MARINAS AND BOATYARDS

555-3. Receptacles.   Figure 555-1 shows typical configurations of lock-ing- and grounding-type receptacles and attachment plugs used in mari-nas and boatyards. A complete chart of these devices can be obtained from the National Electrical Manufacturers Association or various wir-ing-device manufacturers. Locking-type receptacles and caps are required to provide proper contact and assurance that attachment plugs will not fall out easily and disconnect on-board equipment such as bilge pumps or refrigerators.

555-4. Branch Circuits.   Each single receptacle must be installed on an individual branch circuit, with only the one receptacle on the circuit.

555-7. Grounding.   The purpose is to require an insulated equipment grounding wire that will ensure a grounding circuit of high integrity. Because of the corrosive influences around marinas and boatyards, metal raceways and boxes are not permitted to serve as equipment grounding conductors.

555-8. Wiring Over and Under Navigable Water.   There are some federal and local agencies that have specific control over navigable waterways. Accordingly, any proposed installations over or under such waterways should be cleared with the appropriate authorities.

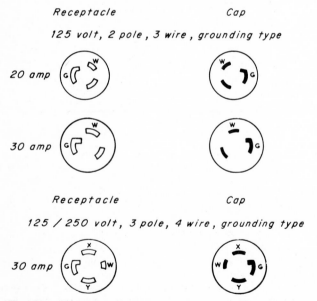

Fig. 555-1. These types of connections provide shore power for boats. (Sec. 555-3.)

Chapter Six

ARTICLE 600. ELECTRIC SIGNS AND OUTLINE LIGHTING

600-1. Scope. In the case of signs that are constructed at a shop or factory and sent out complete and ready for erection, the inspection department must require listing and installation in conformance with the listing. In the case of outline lighting and signs that are constructed at the location where they are installed, the inspection department must make a detailed inspection to make sure that all requirements of this article are complied with. In some cities, inspection departments inspect signs in local shops.

600-2. Disconnect Required. Figure 600-1 depicts the disconnecting means that shall be within sight of the sign, outline lighting, or remote controller. However, the term "within sight" is not clearly defined. It has been well understood that the term "in sight from" specifies that it shall be visible and not more than 50 ft distant from the other as indicated in Sec. 430-4.

Figure 600-2 illustrates the conditions recognized by the Exception—which allows the disconnecting means to be located within sight of the controller where the signs are operated by electronic or electromechanical controllers located external to the sign.

With respect to part **(b)**, any switching device controlling the primary of a transformer that supplies a luminous gas tube operates under unusually severe conditions. In order to avoid rapid deterioration of the switch or flasher due to arcing at the contacts, the device must be a

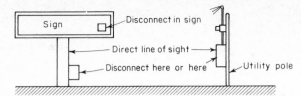

Fig. 600-1. An "in-sight" disconnect may be *in* the sign or visible from the sign. (Sec. 600-2.)

general-use AC snap switch or have a current rating of at least twice the current rating of the transformer it controls.

600-6. Branch Circuits. In part **(a)**, no limit is placed on the number of outlets that may be connected on one circuit on a sign or for outline lighting, except that the total load shall not exceed the rating of the circuit. Where in normal operation the load will continue for 3 hr or more, the load shall not exceed 80 percent of the branch-circuit rating. See Sec. 210-22(c).

Part **(b)** makes a requirement that is similar to that of Sec. 210-25(d). That rule requires installation of show window receptacles at the time of construction and a sign circuit is of equal importance. Figure 600-3 shows that a sign outlet must be installed for every ground-level store—even if an outdoor electric sign is not actually installed or planned. That also applies to a whole commercial building.

600-21. Installation of Conductors. Part **(b)** permits conductors smaller than No. 14 for portable signs. Portable signs are nearly always small and may be considered as in the same class as portable lighting equipment, and hence No. 16 or 18 wire may be used inside the sign enclosure, provided that the size used shall always have sufficient ampacity for the load.

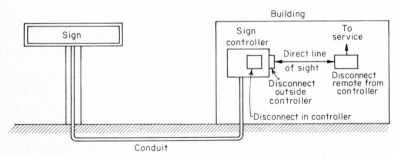

Fig. 600-2. Controller disconnect location may vary but disconnect must be lock-open type. (Sec. 600-2.)

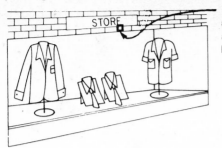

Every store with ground-floor access to customers must have at least one sign outlet fed by a separate 20-A circuit

Fig. 600-3. Commercial buildings must have outdoor sign outlet. (Sec. 600-6.)

600-32. Transformers. The transformers used to supply luminous gas tubes are, in general, constant-current devices and, up to a certain limit, the voltage delivered by the transformer increases as the impedance of the load increases. The impedance of the tube increases as the length increases and is higher for a tube of small diameter than for one of larger diameter. Hence a transformer should be selected which is designed to deliver the proper current and voltage for the tube. If the tube is too long or of too small a diameter, the voltage of the transformer may rise to too high a value.

600-34. Terminals and Electrode Receptacles for Electric-Discharge Tubing. The component parts of a gas-tube sign or lighting system are:

1. A transformer having a 115- or 230-V primary and a high-voltage secondary. Most primaries are 115 V.
2. High-voltage leads from the transformer to the tube.
3. The tube terminals, by means of which the leads are connected to the electrodes at the ends of the tube.
4. The tube itself.

Aside from the high-voltage leads and the tube terminals, the tube of a gas-tube system involves little accident hazard except that with high voltages a discharge may take place from the tube to conductive objects. The tube should be kept away from flammable material since such material might be slightly conductive, and the tube should not be located where it is likely to be broken.

In outdoor signs the tube terminals usually project within the sign enclosure. They may, however, be contained in separate enclosures of sheet metal or insulating material or may be without any enclosure if kept away from combustible material and inaccessible to unauthorized persons.

For exposed signs in show windows, the tube terminals must be enclosed in sleeves of insulating material and the high-voltage leads may consist of conductors insulated for the operating voltage and hanging free in air, if kept away from combustible or conductive material and not subject to physical damage.

ARTICLE 610. CRANES AND HOISTS

610-11. Wiring Method. In general, the wiring on a crane or a hoist should be rigid-conduit work or electrical metallic tubing. Short lengths of flexible conduit or metal-clad cable may be used for connections to motors, brake magnets, or other devices where a rigid connection is impracticable because the devices are subject to some movement with respect to the bases to which they are attached. In outdoor or wet locations liquidtight flexible metal conduit should be used for flexible connections.

610-21. Installation of Contact Conductors. Part **(f)** permits use of the track as one of the circuit conductors. In some cases, particularly where a monorail crane or conveyor is used for handling light loads, for the sake of convenience and simplicity it may be desirable to use the track as one conductor of a 3-phase system. Where this arrangement is used the power must be supplied through a transformer or bank of transformers so that there will be no electrical connection between the primary power supply and the crane circuit, as in Fig. 610-1. The secondary voltage

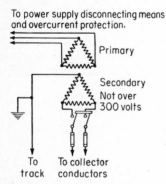

To power supply disconnecting means
and overcurrent protection.

Primary

Secondary
Not over
300 volts

To   To collector
track   conductors

Fig. 610-1. Isolating transformer is used to power track of crane or conveyor. (Sec. 610-21.)

would usually be 220 V, and the primary of the transformer would usually be connected to the power-distribution system of the building or plant. The leg connected to the track must be grounded at the transformer only, except as permitted in Sec. 610-21(f) (4).

610-32. Disconnecting Means for Cranes and Monorail Hoists. This disconnect is an emergency device provided for use in case trouble develops in any of the electrical equipment on the crane or monorail hoist, or to permit maintenance work to be done safely.

610-33. Rating of Disconnecting Means. It is possible that all the motors on a crane might be in operation at one time, but this condition would continue for only a very short while. A switch or CB having a current rating not less than 50 percent of the sum of full-load current rating of all the motors will have ample capacity.

ARTICLE 620. ELEVATORS, DUMBWAITERS, ESCALATORS, AND MOVING WALKS

620-1. Scope. These provisions may also be considered as applying to console lifts, equipment for raising and lowering or rotating portions of theater stages, and all similar equipment.

620-11. Insulation of Conductors. A distinction is made here between the conductors carrying the power current and the smaller wires of operating circuits, such as wires connected to the magnet coils of contactors. The operating current passing through the magnet coils may be quite small, and a small current leaking through damp slow-burning insulation where two insulated wires are in contact might be sufficient to operate a contactor.

620-12. Minimum Size of Conductors. Code Tables 310-16 to 310-19 do not include the ampacity for No. 20 AWG copper conductors. However, it is generally considered that the ampacity for No. 20 conductors up to two conductors in cable or cord may safely carry 3 A.

The development of elevator control equipment, which has been taking place for many years, has resulted in the design and use of equipment including electronic unit contactors requiring very much smaller currents (milliamperes) for their operation.

620-36. Different Systems in One Raceway or Traveling Cable. It would be difficult, if not practically impossible, to keep the wires of each system completely isolated from the wires of every other system in the case of elevator control and signal circuits. Hence such wires may be run in the same conduits and cables if all wires are insulated for the highest voltage used and if all live parts of apparatus are insulated from ground for the highest voltage, provided that the signal system is an integral part of the elevator wiring system.

620-53. Phase Protection. If the connections of any two leads of a 3-phase motor are interchanged, or if the connections of the two leads of one phase of a 2-phase motor are interchanged, the direction of rotation of the motor will be reversed. This phase reversal is sometimes made unintentionally when repair work is being done on the motor or wiring system and, of course, has the effect of reversing the direction of travel of the car. The reverse-phase relay makes it impossible to operate the controller and start the motor under these conditions.

If one of the leads to the motor is disconnected leaving the other leads connected, the motor winding that remains connected will draw an excessive current and a burnout will probably result unless the motor is completley disconnected at once.

ARTICLE 630. ELECTRIC WELDERS

630-1. Scope. There are two general types of electric welding: arc welding and resistance welding. In arc welding, an arc is drawn between the metal parts to be joined together and a metal electrode (a wire or rod), and metal from the electrode is deposited on the joint. In resistance welding, the metal parts to be joined are pressed tightly together between the two electrodes, and a heavy current is passed through the electrodes and the plates or other parts to be welded. The electrodes make contact on a small area—thus the current passes through a small cross section of metal having a high resistance—and sufficient heat is generated to raise the parts to be welded to a welding temperature.

In arc welding with AC, an individual transformer is used for each operator; i.e., a transformer supplies current for one arc only. When DC is used, there is usually an individual generator for each operator, though there are also "mulitoperator" arc-welding generators.

630-11. Ampacity of Supply Conductors.   The term *transformer arc welder* is commonly used in the trade and hence is used in the Code, though the equipment might more properly be described as an *arc-welding transformer*. Reference should be made here to Sec. 630-31 where the term *duty cycle* is explained.

It is evident that the load on each transformer is intermittent. Where several transformers are supplied by one feeder, the intermittent loading will cause much less heating of the feeder conductors than would result from a continuous load equal to the sum of the full-load current ratings of all the transformers. The ampacity of the feeder conductors may therefore be reduced if the feeder supplies three or more transformers.

630-12. Overcurrent Protection. Arc-welding transformers are so designed that as the secondary current increases, the secondary voltage decreases. This characteristic of the transformer greatly reduces the fluctuation of the load on the transformer as the length of the arc, and consequently the secondary current, is varied by the operator.

The rating or setting of the overcurrent devices specified in this section provides short-circuit protection. It has been stated that with the electrode "frozen" to the work the primary current will in most cases rise to about 170 percent of the current rating of the transformer. This condition represents the heaviest overload that can occur, and of course this condition would never be allowed to continue for more than a very short time.

630-31. Ampacity of Supply Conductors. Subparagraph **(a)(1)** applies where a resistance welder is intended for a variety of different operations, such as for welding plates of different thicknesses or for welding different metals. In this case the branch-circuit conductors must have an ampacity sufficient for the heaviest demand that may be made upon them. Because the loading is intermittent, the ampacity need not be as high as the rated primary current. A value of 70 percent is specified for any type of welding machine which is fed automatically. For a manually operated welder, the duty cycle will always be lower and a conductor ampacity of 50 percent of the rated primary current is considered sufficient.

example 1:   A spot welder supplied by a 60-Hz system makes 400 welds per hour, and in making each weld, current flows during 15 cycles.

The number of cycles per hour is $60 \times 60 = 216,000$ cycles.

During 1 hr, the time during which the welder is loaded, measured in cycles, is $400 \times 15 = 6,000$ cycles.

The duty cycle is therefore $(6,000/216,000) \times 100 = 2.8$ percent.

example 2:   A seam welder operates 2 cycles "on" and 2 cycles "off" or in every 4 cycles the welder is loaded during 2 cycles.

The duty cycle is therefore $\frac{2}{4} \times 100 = 50$ percent.

Transformers for resistance welders are commonly provided with taps by means of which the secondary voltage, and consequently the secondary current, can be adjusted. The rated primary current is the current in the primary when the taps are adjusted for maximum secondary current.

When a resistance welder is set up for a specific operation, the transformer taps are adjusted to provide the exact heat desired for the weld; then in order to apply subparagraph **(a)(2)** the actual primary current must be measured. A special type of ammeter is required for this measurement because the current impulses are of very short duration, often a small fraction of a second. The duty cycle is controlled by the adjustment of the controller for the welder.

The procedure in determining conductor sizes for an installation consisting of a feeder and two or more branch circuits to supply resistance welders is first to compute the required ampacity for each branch circuit. Then the required feeder ampacity is 100 percent of the highest ampacity required for any one of the branch circuits, plus 60 percent of the sum of the ampacities of all the other branch circuits.

Some resistance welders are rated as high as 1,000 kVA and may momentarily draw loads of 2,000 kVA or even more. Voltage drop must be held within rather close limits to ensure satisfactory operation.

630-32. Overcurrent Protection. In this case, as in the case of the overcurrent protection of arc-welding transformers (Sec. 630-12), the conductors are protected against short circuits. The conductors of motor branch circuits are protected against short circuits by the branch-circuit overcurrent devices and depend upon the motor-running protective devices for overload protection. Although the resistance welder is not equipped with any device similar to the motor-running protective device, satisfactory operation of the welder is a safeguard against overloading of the conductors. Overheating of the circuit could result only from so operating the welder that either the welds would be imperfect, or parts of the control equipment would be damaged, or both.

ARTICLE 640. SOUND-RECORDING AND SIMILAR EQUIPMENT

640-1. Scope. Centralized distribution systems consist of one or more disc or tape recorders and/or radio receivers, the audio-frequency output of which is distributed to a number of reproducers or loudspeakers.

A public-address system includes one or more microphones, an amplifier, and any desired number of reproducers or speakers. A common use of such a system is to render the voice of a speaker clearly audible in all parts of a large assembly room.

640-2. Application of Other Articles. In general, the power-supply wiring from the building light or power service to the special equipment named in Sec. 640-1, and between any parts of this equipment, should be installed as required for light and power systems of the same voltage. Certain variations from the standard requirements are permitted by the following sections. For radio and television receiving equipment, the requirements of Art. 810 apply except as otherwise permitted here.

Part **(b)** covers wiring to loudspeakers and microphones and signal wires between equipment components—tape recorder or record player to amplifier, etc. As shown in Fig. 640-1, amplifier output wiring to loudspeakers handles energy limited by the power (wattage) of the amplifier

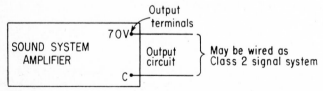

Fig. 640-1. Sound-system speaker wiring may be either Class 2 or Class 3 signal system. (Sec. 640-2.)

and must conform to the rules of Art. 725. As shown in Code Table 725-31(a), the voltage and current rating of a signal circuit will establish it as either Class 2 or Class 3 signal circuit. Amplifier output circuits rated not over 70 V, with open-circuit voltage not over 100 V, may use Class 3 wiring as set forth in Code Table 725-31(a) of Art. 725.

Article 725 of the Code covers, among other things, signal circuits. A signal circuit is defined as any electrical circuit which supplies energy to a device—like a loudspeaker or an amplifier—that gives a recognizable signal.

640-4. Wireways and Auxiliary Gutters.   Wireways and auxiliary gutters may be used with conductor occupancy up to 75 percent of cross-section area (instead of 20 percent as for power and light wires) and may be used in concealed places where run in straight lines between wiring boxes (Fig. 640-2).

Wireway for sound system

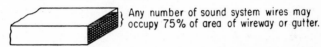

Any number of sound system wires may occupy 75% of area of wireway or gutter.

Fig. 640-2.   Signal-circuit wires may fill wireway more fully than power wires. (Sec. 640-2.)

640-6. Grouping of Conductors.   In this class of work, the wires of different systems are in many cases closely associated in the apparatus itself; therefore little could be gained by separating them elsewhere.

The input leads to a motor-generator set or to a rotary converter would commonly be 115- or 230-V power circuits. These wires are not a part of the sound-recording or reproducing system and should be kept entirely separate from all wires of the sound system.

640-10. Circuit Overcurrent Protection.   Although use of solid-state electronic equipment has been steadily replacing vacuum-tube constructions, these rules apply to tube-type components. The overcurrent protection described here is actually involved with the internal circuiting of electronic-tube equipment. Other protection for external signal circuits must comply with Secs. 725-35 and 725-36 on protection of Class 2 and Class 3 circuits.

As mentioned in part **(a)**, a 20 amp-hr battery is capable of delivering a heavy enough current to heat a No. 14 or smaller wire to a dangerously high temperature, and overcurrent protection is therefore quite necessary. A storage B battery might be capable of delivering enough current to overheat some part of the equipment. Several different positive connections may be made to the battery in order to obtain different voltages, and each such lead must be provided with overcurrent protection.

ARTICLE 645. DATA PROCESSING SYSTEMS

645-2. Supply Circuits and Interconnecting Cables. Part **(a)** limits every branch circuit supplying data processing units to a maximum load of not over 80 percent of the conductor ampacity (which is an ampacity of 1.25 times the total connected load).

Part **(b)** covers use of computer cables and flexible cords. As shown in Fig. 645-2 (under a raised floor), only flexible connections that are "approved as a part" of the system may be used.

Part **(c)** permits a variety of wiring methods under a raised floor serving a data processing system: Metal surface raceway with metal cover (as shown in Fig. 645-1), liquidtight flexible conduit, rigid metal conduit, EMT, flexible metal conduit, IMC, Type MI cable, and Type MC cable (Fig. 645-2).

Fig. 645-1. Connection of data-processing units to their supply circuits and interconnection between units (power supply, memory storage, etc.) may be made only with cables or cordsets specifically approved as parts of the data processing system. (Sec. 645-2.)

Although Sec. 352-1 prohibits use of metal surface raceway where it would be concealed, Exception No. 2 of that rule recognizes its use under raised flooring for data processing by referencing Sec. 645-2(c)(2). It should be noted that although metal surface raceway may be used under a raised floor, as shown, Sec. 645-2(c) (2) does not recognize use of "wireway" under raised floors. Section 362-2 accepts wireway "*only* for exposed work," but it may be used above suspended ceilings of lift-out tiles because of the definition of exposed. However, Sec. 300-22(c) does not recognize wireway above a suspended ceiling if the space is used for air-handling purposes.

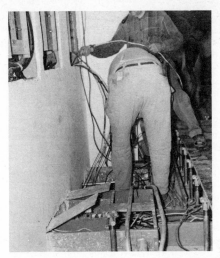

Fig. 645-2. Branch circuits from a panelboard to data processing receptacle outlets must be in a metal-clad raceway system or use either Type MI or Type MC cable. (Sec. 645-2.)

645-3. Disconnecting Means.   As shown in Fig. 645-3, a master means of disconnect (which could be one or more switches or breakers) must provide disconnect for all computer equipment, ventilation in the data processing room, and all other electrical equipment in the room except lighting.

Where computer units are installed in a general building area, a disconnect means must open the supply to all the interconnected computer units or assemblies.

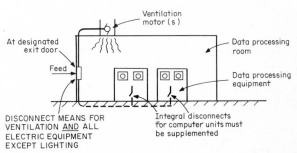

Fig. 645-3. Data processing room must have the arrangements shown above. (Sec. 645-3.)

ARTICLE 650. ORGANS

650-3. Insulation—Grounding. Organ control systems are usually supplied from a motor-generator set consisting of a 115- or 230-V motor driving a generator that operates at about 10 V. Neither the generator windings nor the control wires are necessarily insulated for the motor voltage. Assume that the frames of the two machines are electrically connected together by being mounted on the same base and that the frames are not grounded. If a wire of the motor winding becomes grounded to the frame of the motor, the frames of both machines may be raised to a potential of 115 or 230 V aboveground, and this voltage may break down the insulation of the generator winding or of the circuit wiring. If the generator is insulated from the motor, or if both frames are well grounded, this trouble cannot occur.

650-4. Conductors. In part **(d)**, the wires of the cable are normally all of the same polarity and hence need not be heavily insulated from one another. The full voltage of the control system exists between the wires in the cable and the common return wire; therefore the common wire must be reasonably well insulated from the cable wires.

650-5. Installation of Conductors. A 15-V system involves very little fire hazard, and the cable may be run in any manner desired; but for protection against injury and convenience in making repairs, the cable should preferably be installed in a metal raceway.

650-6. Overcurrent Protection. The "main supply conductors" extend from the generator to a convenient point at which one conductor is connected through 15-A fuses to as many circuits as may be necessary, while the other main conductor is connected to the common return.

ARTICLE 660. X-RAY EQUIPMENT

660-1. Scope. An X-ray tube of the hot-cathode type, as now commonly used, is a two-element vacuum tube in which a tungsten filament serves as the cathode. Current is supplied to the filament at low voltage. In most cases unidirectional pulsating voltage is applied between the cathode and the anode. The applied voltage is measured or described in terms of the peak voltage, which may be anywhere within the range of 10,000 to 1,000,000 V, or even more. The current flowing in the high-voltage circuit may be as low as 5 mA or may be as much as 1A, depending upon the desired intensity of radiation. The high voltage is obtained by means of a transformer, usually operating at 230-V primary, and usually is made unidirectional by means of two-element rectifying vacuum tubes, though in some cases an alternating current is applied to the X-ray tube. The X-rays are radiations of an extremely high frequency (or short wavelength) which are the strongest in a plane at right angles to the electron stream passing between the cathode and the anode in the tube.

As used by physicians and dentists, X-rays have three applications: *fluoroscopy,* where a picture or shadow is thrown upon a screen of specially prepared glass by rays passing through some part of the patient's body; *radiography,* which is similar to fluoroscopy except that the picture is thrown upon a photographic film instead of a screen; and *therapy,* in which use is made of the effects of the rays upon the tissues of the human body.

660-24. Independent Control.   In radiography it is important that the exposure be accurately timed, and for this purpose a switch is used which can be set to open the circuit automatically in any desired time after the circuit has been closed.

660-35. General (Transformers and Capacitors).   A power transformer supplying electrical systems is usually supplied at a high primary voltage; hence in case of a breakdown of the insulation on the primary winding, a large amount of energy can be delivered to the transformer. An askarel-filled X-ray transformer involves much less fire hazard because the primary voltage is low, and it is therefore not required that such transformers be placed in vaults of fire-resistant construction.

660-47. General (Guarding and Grounding).   This section definitely requires that all new X-ray equipment shall be so constructed that all high-voltage parts, except leads to the X-ray tube, are in grounded metal enclosures, unless the equipment is in a separate room or enclosure and the circuit to the primary of the transformer is automatically opened by unlocking the door to the enclosure. Conductors leading to the X-ray tube are heavily insulated.

ARTICLE 665. INDUCTION AND DIELECTRIC HEATING EQUIPMENT

665-1. Scope.   Induction and dielectric heating are systems wherein a workpiece is heated by means of a rapidly alternating magnetic or electric field.

665-2. Definitions

Induction Heating

Induction heating is used to heat materials that are good electrical conductors, for such purposes as soldering, brazing, hardening, and annealing. Induction heating, in general, involves frequencies ranging from 3 to about 500 kHz, and power outputs from a few hundred watts to several thousand kilowatts. In general, motor-generator sets are used for frequencies up to about 30 kHz; spark-gap converters, from 20 to 400 kHz; and vacuum-tube generators, from 100 to 500 kHz. Isolated special jobs may use frequencies as high as 60 to 80 MHz. Motor-generator sets normally supply power for heating large masses for melting, forging, deep hardening, and the joining of heavy pieces, whereas spark-gap and vacuum-tube generators find their best applications in the joining of smaller pieces and shallow case hardening, with vacuum-tube generators also being used where special high heat concentrations are required.

To heat a workpiece by induction heating, it is placed in a work coil consisting of one or more turns, which is the output circuit of the generator (Fig. 665-1). The high-frequency current which flows through this coil sets up a rapidly alternating magnetic field within it. By inducing a voltage in the workpiece, this field causes a current flow in the piece to be heated. As the current flows through the resistance of the workpiece, it generates heat (I^2R loss) in the piece itself. It is this heat that is utilized in induction heating.

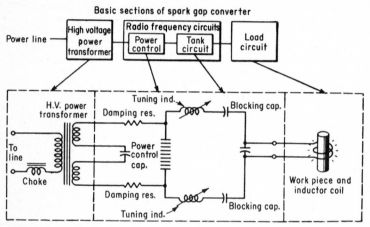

Fig. 665-1. A "generator" circuit supplies the "work coil" of an induction heater. (Sec. 665-2.)

Dielectric Heating

In contrast, dielectric heating is used to heat materials that are nonconductors, such as wood, plastic, textiles, rubber, etc., for such purposes as drying, gluing, curing, and baking. It uses frequencies from 1 to 200 MHz, especially those from 1 to 50 MHz. Vacuum-tube generators are used exclusively to supply dielectric heating power, with outputs ranging from a few hundred watts to several hundred kilowatts.

Whereas induction heating uses a varying magnetic field, dielectric heating employs a varying electric field. This is done by placing the material to be heated between a pair of metal plates, called electrodes, in the output circuit of the generator. When high-frequency voltage is applied to the electrodes, a rapidly alternating electric field is set up between them, passing through the material to be heated. Because of the electrical charges within the molecules of this material, the field causes the molecules to vibrate in proportion to its frequency. This internal molecular action generates the beat used for dielectric heating.

Generators

In general, both spark-gap and vacuum-tube generators consist of a power-supply circuit, a voltage and/or frequency conversion circuit, a control circuit, and an output circuit. In the spark-gap converter (Fig. 665-1), tank capacitors are alternately charged and discharged, to produce high-frequency oscillations in the output circuit. In vacuum-tube generators, these oscillations are produced by a vacuum-tube oscillator, which is fed by DC power from a high-voltage power supply. The induction heating generator and the dielectric heating generator differ chiefly in their output circuits.

Actual workloads are disconnected from the output circuit, emphasizing the fact that external auxiliary equipment is often needed to ensure the most efficient transfer of power from generator to load.

Except in the case of motor-generator sets, low-power generators will probably contain enough control and cooling apparatus for normal operation. However, on installations of over 50 kW, external switchgear and cooling systems are usually required. Such equipment should comply with the appropriate articles of the Code.

665-22. Access to Internal Equipment.   This section allows the manufacturer the option of using interlocked doors or detachable panels. Where panels are used and are not intended as normal access points, they shall be fastened with bolts or screws of sufficient number to discourage removal. They should not be held in place with any type of speed fastener.

665-25. Work Applicator Shielding.   See discussion under Sec. 665-44. This section is intended primarily to apply to dielectric heating installations where it is absolutely essential that the electrodes and associated tuning or matching devices are properly shielded.

665-26. Grounding and Bonding.

Bonding

At radio frequencies, and especially at dielectric-heating frequencies (1 to 200 MHz), it is very possible for differences in radio-frequency potential to exist between the equipment proper and other surrounding metal objects or other units of the complete installation. These potentials exist because of stray currents flowing between units of the equipment or to ground. Bonding is therefore essential, and such bonding must take the form of very wide copper or aluminum straps between units and to other surrounding metal objects such as conveyors, presses, etc. The most satisfactory bond is provided by placing all units of the equipment on a flooring or base consisting of copper or aluminum sheet, thoroughly joined where necessary by soldering, welding, or adequate bolting. Such bonding reduces the radio-frequency resistance and reactance between units to a minimum, and any stray circulating currents flowing through this bonding will not cause sufficient voltage drop to become dangerous.

Shielding

Shielding at dielectric-heating frequencies is a necessity to provide operator protection from the high radio-frequency potentials involved, and also to prevent possible interference with radio communication systems. Shielding is accomplished by totally enclosing all work circuit components with copper sheet, copper screening, or aluminum sheet.

665-44. Output Circuit.

RF Lines

When it is necessary to transmit the high-frequency output of a generator any distance to the work applicator, a radio-frequency line is generally used. This usually consists of a conductor totally enclosed in a grounded metal housing. This central conductor is commonly supported by insulators, mounted in the grounded housing and periodically spaced along its length. Such a line, rectangular in cross section, may even be used to connect two induction generators to the load.

While contact with high-voltage radio frequencies may cause severe burns, contact with high-voltage DC could be fatal. Therefore, it is imperative that generator output (directly, capacitively, or inductively coupled) be effectively grounded with respect to DC so that, should generator failure place high-voltage DC in the tank oscillating circuit, there will still be no danger to the operator. This grounding is generally internal in vacuum-tube generators. In all types of induction generators, one side of the work coil should usually be externally grounded.

In general, all high-voltage connections to the primary of a current transformer should be enclosed. The primary concern is the operator's safety. Examples would be interlocked cages around small dielectric electrodes, and interlocking safety doors.

On induction heating jobs, it is not always practical to completely house the work coil and obtain efficient production operation. In these cases, precautions should be taken to minimize the chance of operator contact with the coil.

665-61. Ampacity of Supply Conductors. Quite often where several equipments are operated in a single plant it is possible to conserve on power-line requirements by taking into account the load or use factor of each equipment. The time cycles of operation on various machines may be staggered to allow a minimum of current to be taken from the line. In such cases the Code requires sufficient capacity to carry all full-load cur-

rents from those machines which will operate simultaneously, plus the
stand-by requirements of all other units.

665-67. Keying.   Radio-frequency generators are often turned on and
off by applying a blocking bias to the grid circuit of the oscillator tube,
for the purpose of obtaining fast, accurate control of power. If this keying circuit does not completely block the tube oscillations, high-frequency
power will appear at the work applicator, even though the operator
thinks it has been turned off. However, if this residual output voltage is
limited to a value of 100-V peak, the operator will be protected from any
serious burns.

665-68. Remote Control.   In part **(a)**, if interlocking were not provided,
there would be a definite danger to an operator at the remote-control
station. It might then be possible, if the operator had turned off the
power and was doing some work in contact with a work coil, for someone
else to apply power from another point, seriously injuring the operator.

ARTICLE 668. ELECTROLYTIC CELLS

668-1. Scope.   This is a new article in the 1978 NE Code and was added
to provide effective coverage of basic electrical safety in electrolytic cell
rooms.

The presentation of these requirements in the "Proposed Amendments for the 1978 National Electrical Code" was accompanied by a commentary from the technical subcommittee that developed them. Significant background information from that commentary is as follows:

In the operation and maintenance of electrolytic cell lines, however, workmen
may be involved in situations requiring safeguards not provided by existing articles
of the NEC. For example, it is sometimes found that in the matter of exposed
conductors or surfaces it is the man or his workplace which has to be insulated
rather than the conductor. Work practices and rules such as are included in IEEE
Trial Use Standard 463-1974 pertinent to such specific situations have been developed which offer the same degree of safety provided by the traditional philosophy
of the NEC.

As a corollary to this concept, overheating of conductors, overloading of motors,
leakage currents and the like may be required in cell lines to maintain process
safety and continuity.

Proposed Article 668 introduces such concepts as these as have been proven in
practice for electrolytic cell operation.

668-2. Definitions.   The subcommittee noted:

An electrolyic cell line and its DC process power supply circuit, both within a
cell line working zone, comprise a single functional unit and as such can be treated
in an analogous fashion to any other individual machine supplied from a single
source. Although such an installation may cover acres of floor space, may have a
load current in excess of 400,000 amperes DC or a circuit voltage in excess of
1,000 volts DC, it is operated as a single unit. At this point, the traditional NEC
concepts of branch circuits, feeders, services, overload, grounding, disconnecting

means are meaningless, even as such terms lose their identity on the load side of a large motor terminal fitting or on the load side of the terminals of a commercial refrigerator.

It is important to understand that the cell line process current passes through each cell in a series connection and that the load current in each cell is not capable of being sub-divided in the same fashion as is required, for example, in the heating circuit of a resistance-type electric furnace by Section 424-72(a).

668-3. Other Articles.   Electrical equipment and applications that are not within the space envelope of the "cell line working zone," as dimensioned in Sec. 668-10, must comply with all the other regulations of the NEC covering such work.

668-13. Disconnecting Means.   As shown in Fig. 668-1, each DC power supply to a single cell line must be capable of being disconnected. And the disconnecting means may be a removable link in the busbars of the cell line.

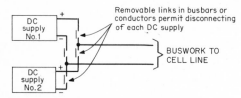

Fig. 668-1. Removal of busbar sections may provide disconnect of each supply. (Sec. 668-13.)

668-20. Portable Electrical Equipment.   This section and the rules of Secs. 668-21, 668-30, 668-31, and 668-32 cover installation and operating requirements for cells with exposed live conductors or surfaces. These rules are necessary for the conditions as noted by the subcommittee:

In some electrolytic cell systems, the terminal voltage of the cell line process power supply can be appreciable. The voltage to ground of exposed live parts from one end of a cell line to the other is variable between the limits of the terminal voltage. Hence, operating and maintenance personnel and their tools are required to be insulated from ground.

ARTICLE 670.   METALWORKING MACHINE
TOOLS

670-2. Definition: Metalworking Machine Tool.   It should be noted that these provisions do not apply to woodworking machines or to any other type of motor-driven machine which is not included in this definition of machine tools. The provisions do not apply to any machine or tool which is not normally used in a fixed location and can be carried from place to place by hand.

670-4. General.   For the disconnect required by part **(b)**, NFPA No. 79 states: "The center of the grip of the operating handle of the disconnecting means when in its highest position, shall not be more than 6½ feet above the floor. The operating handle shall be so arranged that it may be locked in the 'Off' position."

ARTICLE 680. SWIMMING POOLS, FOUNTAINS, AND SIMILAR INSTALLATIONS

680-1. Scope.   Electrification of swimming, wading, therapeutic, and decorative pools has been the subject of extensive design and Code development over recent years. Details on circuit design and equipment layout are covered in NE Code Art. 680. Careful reference to this article should be made in connection with any design work on pools and fountains, which are covered in part **D** of this article.

Research work conducted by Underwriters Laboratories Inc. and others indicated that an electric shock could be received in two different ways. One of these involved the existence in the water of an electrical potential with respect to ground, and the other involved the existence of a potential gradient in the water itself.

A person standing in the pool and touching the energized enclosure of faulty equipment located at poolside would be subject to a severe electrical shock because of the good ground which his body would establish through the water and pool to earth. Accordingly, the provisions of this article specify construction and installation that can minimize hazards in and adjacent to pools and fountains.

680-4. Definitions.   These definitions are important to correct, effective application of Code rules of Art. 680. Figure 680-1 shows a typical dry-

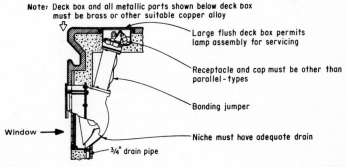

Note? Deck box and all metallic parts shown below deck box must be brass or other suitable copper alloy

Large flush deck box permits lamp assembly for servicing

Receptacle and cap must be other than parallel - types

Bonding jumper

Window

Niche must have adequate drain

¾" drain pipe

Fig. 680-1. Dry-niche fixture lights underwater area through glass "window." (Sec. 680-4.)

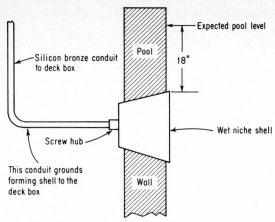

Fig. 680-2. Forming shell is a support for the lamp assembly of a wet-niche fixture. (Sec. 680-4.)

Fig. 680-3. Wet-niche lighting fixture consists of forming shell set in pool wall with cord-connected lamp-and-lens assembly that attaches to the forming shell, with cord coiled within the shell housing. (Sec. 680-4.)

niche swimming pool lighting fixture. Figure 680-2 shows a forming shell for a wet-niche lighting fixture.

Because there are differences in the requirements for "permanently installed" pools and "storable" pools, there has been some confusion in the past as to just what a "storable" pool is. The 1975 **Code** defined a "storable swimming or wading pool" as follows:

One that is so constructed that it may be readily disassembled for storage and reassembled to its original integrity.

Disagreement over the word "readily" resulted in rather large above-ground pools that were capable of being disassembled being classed as "storable" pools. The definition of "storable swimming or wading pool" was changed in the **Code** to the present wording which defines such a pool by dimensions—one with wall height not over 3 ft and no dimension over 15 ft. The introduction of the limiting dimensions now serves to differentiate storable pools from permanently installed pools.

Figure 680-3 shows a wet-niche lighting fixture.

680-5. Transformers and Ground-Fault Circuit-Interrupters. A swimming pool transformer must be in a weatherproof enclosure to suit it to outdoor use, and a grounded metallic shielding between the primary and secondary winding prevents a primary to secondary short that would connect primary voltage (120 V) to the 12-V secondary circuit—thereby creating a hazardous condition (Fig. 680-4).

Fig. 680-4. Transformers for low-voltage swimming pool lighting are listed by UL under "Swimming Pool Transformers" and such listing is used by inspectors as evidence that the unit is "approved for the purpose." (Sec. 680-5.)

Part **(b)** describes general rules on ground-fault circuit-interrupters (GFCI) that are required to be used by other rules of this article. Additional protection may be accomplished, even where not required, by the use of a GFCI. Since the ground-fault interrupter operates on the principle of line-to-ground leaks or breakdowns, it senses, at low levels of magnitude and duration, any fault currents to ground caused by accidental contact with energized parts of electrical equipment. Because the ground-fault interrupter operates at a fraction of the current required to trip 15-A CB, its presence is mandatory under following **Code** rules and is generally very desirable.

Part **(c)** calls for keeping wires on the load side of a ground-fault interrupter independent of other wiring. Figure 680-5 shows a hookup that might be considered a violation because of the presence of "other conductors"—the wires in the JB that taps to the floodlight JB. But Exception No. 1 qualifies that rule, to permit GFCI-protected conductors to be used in a panelboard enclosure with conductors not protected by GFCI. In the 1975 **Code**, when a GFCI was used in a panelboard to supply swimming pool circuits, it was necessary to use supplementary insulation (such as nonmetallic sleeving or tubing) on the GFCI conductors in the panelboard gutter to protect these conductors against excessive leakage because of capacitive coupling to the other conductors in the gutter. Excessive leakage was considered a problem because it could cause unwanted circuit opening due to the sensitivity of GFCI, especially when used in the highly conductive conditions that exist at wet locations, in such applications as swimming pools.

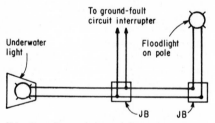

Note: Grounding conductors not shown.

Fig. 680-5. GFCI conductors are in junction box with other than conductors for underwater light. (Sec. 680-5.)

Exception No. 1 no longer specifies a need for insulating sleeving on the GFCI circuit conductors in panelboard gutters. It was concluded that such insulation did not offer sufficient protection against the problem of leakage (Fig. 680-6).

680-6. Receptacles, Lighting Fixtures and Lighting Outlets. The basic rule here prohibits receptacles within 10 ft from the pool edge and calls

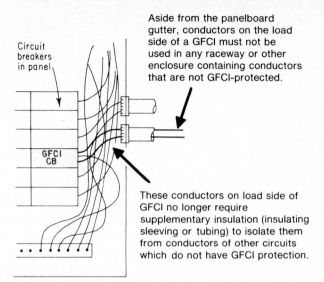

Circuit breakers in panel

Aside from the panelboard gutter, conductors on the load side of a GFCI must not be used in any raceway or other enclosure containing conductors that are not GFCI-protected.

GFCI CB

These conductors on load side of GFCI no longer require supplementary insulation (insulating sleeving or tubing) to isolate them from conductors of other circuits which do not have GFCI protection.

Fig. 680-6. GFCI conductors must be protected against leakage from capacitive coupling to other conductors. (Sec. 680-5.)

for GFCIs to protect all receptacles located between 10 and 15 ft of the inside walls of indoor and outdoor pools. But the Exception to this general rule permits the installation of a receptacle for a swimming pool recirculating pump less than 10 ft but not closer than 5 ft from the inside wall of the pool. Normally, receptacles are prohibited from installation anywhere within the 10-ft boundary around the edge of the pool. However, because swimming pool pump motors are commonly cord-connected to permit their removal during cold weather in areas where freezing may damage it, this change was made to allow provision for a receptacle for the pump motor. Such a receptacle, though, must be a single receptacle of the locking and grounding type. Of course, on a residential property, all outdoor receptacles beyond the 15-ft band around the pool must also have GFCI protection, as required by Sec. 210-8(a) (2). But for any property that does not conform to the definition of "dwelling unit" (Art. 100), GFCI protection is not required for outdoor receptacles more than 15 ft away from the pool's edge.

Another requirement in part **(a)** calls for *at least* one receptacle to be installed not less than 10 ft and not more than 15 ft from the edge of a swimming pool for those cases where a swimming pool is installed at an *existing* dwelling. This rule was added to assure that a receptacle will be available at the pool location to provide for use of cord-connected equipment. It was found that absence of such a requirement resulted in excessive use of long extension cords to make power available for appliances and devices used at pool areas. Note, however, that although the receptacle is required in the 10- to 15-ft band for a pool that is being installed at an "existing dwelling," there is no rule requiring any receptacles in the 10- to 15-ft band around a pool that is being constructed along with a dwelling—that is, where there is *no* "existing dwelling." The best interpretation that might be put on that rule is to always require at least one receptacle in the 10- to 15-ft band around every pool—regardless of whether or not the pool is at an "existing dwelling."

Figure 680-7 summarizes the rules with respect to receptacles. Note that the Code wording does not distinguish between "indoor" or "out-

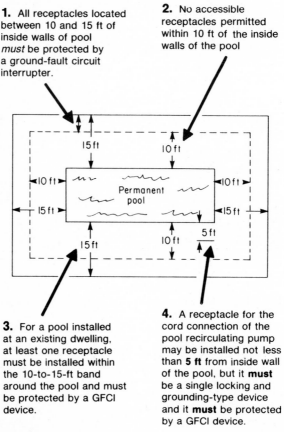

1. All receptacles located between 10 and 15 ft of inside walls of pool *must* be protected by a ground-fault circuit interrupter.

2. No accessible receptacles permitted within 10 ft of the inside walls of the pool

3. For a pool installed at an existing dwelling, at least one receptacle must be installed within the 10-to-15-ft band around the pool and must be protected by a GFCI device.

4. A receptacle for the cord connection of the pool recirculating pump may be installed not less than **5 ft** from inside wall of the pool, but it **must** be a single locking and grounding-type device and it **must** be protected by a GFCI device.

Fig. 680-7. Rules cover all receptacles within 15 ft of the pool's edge. (Sec. 680-6.)

door" receptacles—as it did in the 1971 **NEC**. The present wording appears to apply to all pools and refers simply to "receptacles on the *property....*"

Figure 680-8 summarizes graphically the rules set forth in part **(b)** of this section.

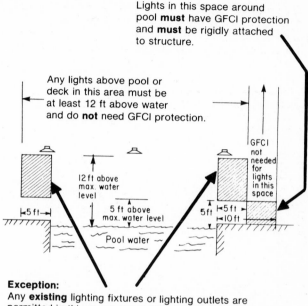

Lights in this space around pool **must** have GFCI protection and **must** be rigidly attached to structure.

Any lights above pool or deck in this area must be at least 12 ft above water and do **not** need GFCI protection.

12 ft above max. water level

5 ft above max. water level

Pool water

GFCI not needed for lights in this space

5 ft

5 ft

10 ft

Exception:
Any **existing** lighting fixtures or lighting outlets are permitted in this space around the pool if rigidly attached to the **existing** structure and protected by a GFCI in the branch circuit supplying the fixtures. But new (not "existing") lights are not permitted in this space around a pool.

Fig. 680-8. Lighting locations are governed by space bands around pool perimeter. (Sec. 680-6.)

The reference to "existing lighting fixtures" in the Exception to part **(b)(1)** must be understood to refer to lighting fixtures that are already in place on a building or structure or pole at the time construction of the pool begins. Where a pool is installed close to, say, a home or country club building, lighting fixtures attached to the already existing structure may fall within the shaded area for a band of space 5 ft wide, extending from 5 ft above the water level to 12 ft above water level all around the perimeter of the pool. Any such existing fixtures must have GFCI protection added to their one or more supply circuits—such as by use of

GFCI circuit breaker where each circuit originates in the panelboard. However, new lighting fixtures may not be installed in that space band.

Figure 680-9 applies the foregoing rules to lighting at an enclosed pool.

Fig. 680-9. The lighting fixtures over the pool and for 5 ft back from edge must be at least 12 ft above the maximum water level, without requiring GFCI protection. The fixtures at right side do not require GFCI protection because they are over 5 ft back from pool edge and are over 5 ft above the water level. Refer to Fig. 680-8. (Sec. 680-6.)

680-7. Cord- and Plug-Connected Equipment. The 3-ft cord limitation mentioned in this rule would not apply to swimming pool filter pumps used with storable pools under part **C** of Art. 680, because these pumps are considered as portable instead of *fixed or stationary*. See comments following Sec. 680-30.

680-8. Overhead Conductor Clearances. The general rule states that service drops and open overhead wiring must not be installed above a swimming pool or surrounding area extending 10 ft horizontally from the pool edge, or diving structure, observation stands, towers, or platforms But, the Exception exempts only utility company lines from the rule provided the designated clearances are satisfied.

680-20. Underwater Lighting Fixtures. In part **(a)** of this section, the wording must be followed carefully to avoid confusion on the intent.

Part **(1)** starts by requiring that any underwater lighting fixture must be of such design as to assure freedom from electric shock hazard when it is in use and must provide that protection without a GFCI. *But,* a GFCI *is* required for all line-voltage fixtures (any operating over 15 V, such as a 120-V fixture) to provide protection against shock hazard during relamping. A GFCI is not required for low-voltage swimming pool lights (12-V units) (Fig. 680-10).

**Underwater lighting fixtures
operating at more than 15 volts · · ·**

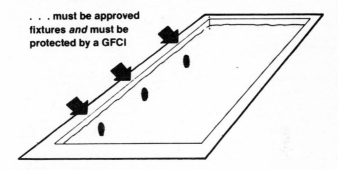

**. . . must be approved
fixtures *and* must be
protected by a GFCI**

NOTE: 12-volt fixtures do not require a GFCI.

Fig. 680-10. A GFCI must be used in the circuit to any line-voltage (120-V) fixtures. (Sec. 680-20.)

In the 1971 **NE Code**, the rule recognized the use of line-voltage, self-grounding fixtures (listed for use in pools) to prevent shock hazard—without need for a GFCI. But, although such fixtures satisfy the **Code** as safe in operation, the rule now calls for safety during relamping and requires that a GFCI must be installed in the circuit to any fixture operating at more than 15 V to prevent shock hazard during relamping.

The UL presents certain essential data on use of GFCI devices, which must be factored into application of such devices—as follows:

A ground-fault circuit-interrupter is a device whose function is to interrupt the electric circuit to the load when a fault current to ground exceeds some pre-determined value that is less than that required to operate the overcurrent protective device of the circuit.

A ground-fault circuit-interrupter is intended to be used only in a circuit that has a solidly grounded conductor.

A Class A ground-fault circuit-interrupter trips when the current to ground has a value in the range of 4 through 6 milliamperes. A Class A ground-fault circuit-interrupter is suitable for use in branch and feeder circuits, including swimming pool circuits. However, swimming pool circuits installed before local adoption of ANSI C1-1965 **National Electrical Code** may include sufficient leakage current to cause a Class A ground-fault circuit-interrupter to trip.

A Class B ground-fault circuit-interrupter trips when the current to ground exceeds 20 milliamperes. This product is suitable for use with underwater swimming pool lighting fixtures only.

A ground-fault circuit-interrupter of the enclosed type that has not been found suitable for use where it will be exposed to rain, is so marked.

The last sentence of part **(a)(1)** requires that *only* an "approved" lighting fixture be used—which means only a fixture listed by UL or other test lab. UL data on listed fixtures must be carefully observed:

These fixtures are for installation in or on the walls of swimming pools not less than 18 in. below the normal water level as measured to the top of the lens opening.

"Wet-Niche" fixtures are intended for installation in a metallic fixture housing (forming shell) mounted in or on the side of a swimming pool wall where the fixture will be completely surrounded by pool water. Such fixtures are provided with a factory-installed, permanently-attached flexible cord that extends at least 12 ft outside the fixture enclosure to permit the fixture to be removed from the forming shell and lifted to the pool deck for servicing without lowering the pool water level or disconnecting the fixture from the branch circuit wiring. Fixtures with longer cords are available for installations in which the junction box or splice enclosure is so located that a 12-foot-long cord will not permit its removal from the forming shell and placement on the pool deck for servicing. To avoid possible cord damage, cord length in excess of that necessary for servicing should be trimmed rather than stored in the forming shell. The trimming must be at the supply end. Each fixture is marked to indicate the proper housing or housings with which it is to be used, and the fixture housing is marked to indicate the fixture or fixtures with which it is to be used.

"Dry-Niche" fixtures are intended for permanent installation in the wall of the pool, having provisions for threaded conduit entries, being designed for servicing from the rear in a passageway or tunnel behind the pool wall, or from the deck surrounding the pool.

Fixtures which are suitable for use only in fresh water pools are marked "Fresh Water Only." Fixtures which are suitable for use in either fresh or salt water pools are marked "Salt Water" or "Salt or Fresh Water."

Fixtures which have been investigated for operation only in contact with water are marked "Submerse Before Lighting," or the equivalent, and such marking is visible after installation of the fixtures.

Part **(2)** sets 150 V as the maximum permitted for a pool lighting fixture—which means that the usual 120-V listed fixtures are acceptable.

Part **(3)** repeats the UL limitation on mounting distance of a fixture below water level. When installed, the top edge of the fixture must be at least 18 in. below the *normal* level of the pool water (Fig. 680-11). This 18-in. rule was adopted to keep the fixture away from a person's "chest area," because this is the vital area of the body concerning electric shocks in swimming pools. Keeping the top of the fixture 18 in. below the normal water level avoids a swimmer's chest area when he is hanging on to the edge of the pool while in the water.

Part **(4)** presents an interesting requirement on the use of wet-niche lighting fixtures. The rule here requires that some type of low-water cutoff or other approved means be provided to protect wet-niche fixtures against overheating when such fixtures depend on submersion in water.

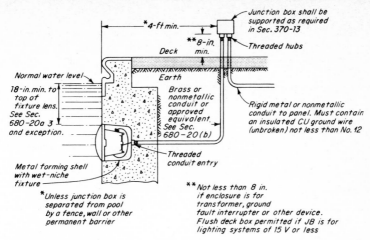

Fig. 680-11. Mounting of lighting fixture and circuit components must observe specific dimensions. (Sec. 680-20.)

for their safe operation. Note that UL rules quoted above require some fixtures to be marked "Submerse Before Lighting." The question arises—is it necessary to use a float switch or some similar liquid-level indicator to control the energy input to the light fixture? Or may a temperature-actuated device be used to signal a relay to open the supply circuit if the fixture overheats? Manufacturers of such fixtures should incorporate this protection—such as in the form of a bi-metal switch similar to those used in motor end-bells for motor overload protection.

Part **(b)** details the use of wet-niche fixtures. A wet-niche underwater lighting assembly consists of two parts—a forming shell, which is a metal structure designed to support a wet-niche fixture in the pool wall, and a lighting fixture, which usually consists of a lamp within a housing furnished with a waterproof flexible cord and a sealed lens that is removable for relamping.

Part **(b)(1)** requires that the conduit between the forming shell and junction box or transformer enclosure must be: (1) rigid metal conduit or IMC and made of brass or other approved corrosion-resistant metal, or (2) rigid nonmetallic conduit with a No. 8 *insulated,* solid copper conductor installed in the conduit and connected to the junction box or transformer enclosure and to the forming shell enclosures. Each enclosure—the forming shell as well as the box—must contain approved grounding terminals.

Figure 680-12 shows a typical connection from a forming shell to a transformer enclosure supplying the 12-V lamp in the fixture. If a 120-V fixture is used, the conduit from the shell terminates in a junction box,

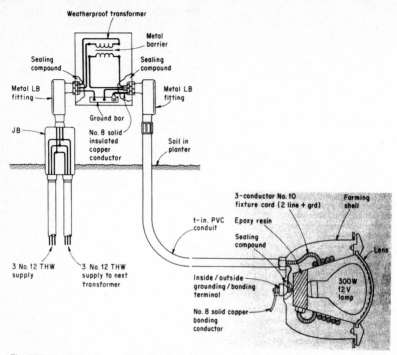

Fig. 680-12. Grounding and bonding is required in a typical hookup of low-voltage wet-niche fixture with PVC conduit. (Sec. 680-20.)

as shown in Fig. 680-11. In the sketch of Fig. 680-12, from the forming shell, a length of 1-in. PVC conduit extends directly to a 120/12-V transformer mounted on the back wall of a planter adjoining the pool [observing the 4-ft back and 8-in.-high provisions of Sec. 680-21(b) (4).]. Where the nonmetallic conduit stubs up out of the planter soil, a metallic LB connects the conduit to the transformer. The required No. 8 conductor in the PVC conduit is terminated at the grounding bar in the transformer enclosure and on the *inside* terminal of an inside/outside grounding/bonding terminal on the forming shell. The external bonding lug provides for connecting the forming shell to the common bonding grid, as required by Sec. 680-22(a) and (b). The No. 8 in the PVC conduit bonds the forming shell up to the transformer enclosure. Note that this No. 8 conductor is not needed if metal conduit connects the shell to the transformer enclosure. One of the No. 12 conductors in the supply circuit is an equipment grounding conductor that runs back to the panelboard grounding block and thereby grounds the No. 8 and the metal fittings and transformer enclosure.

Part **(b)(1)** also requires that the inside forming shell termination of the No. 8 be covered with, or encapsulated in, a suitable potting compound. Experience has shown that corrosion occurs when connections are exposed to pool water. Epoxies are available to achieve this protection; however, some inspection agencies do accept a waterproof, permanently pliable silicone caulk compound.

Note that the illustrated assembly includes three noncurrent-carrying conductors: (1) a No. 8 *bonding* conductor connecting the forming shell to the bonding grid; (2) a No. 8 insulated conductor in PVC conduit between the forming shell and the transformer enclosure; and (3) a *grounding* conductor in the fixture flexible supply cord.

Part **(b)(2)** requires sealing of the fixture cord end and terminals within the wet-niche to prevent water from entering the fixture. And grounding terminations must also be protected by potting compounds.

Part **(b)(3)** states that an underwater lighting fixture must be secured and grounded to the forming shell by a positive locking device which will assure a low-resistance contact and which will require a tool to remove the fixture from the forming shell. This provides added assurance that fixtures will remain grounded because, in the case of wet-niche fixtures, the metal forming shell provides a bond between the raceway (or No. 8 conductor in PVC) connected to the forming shell and the noncurrent-carrying metal parts of the fixture.

Part **(c)** permits use of an approved dry-niche lighting fixture that may be installed outside the walls of the pool in closed recesses which are adequately drained and accessible for maintenance. For a dry-niche fixture, a "deck box"—set in the concrete deck around the pool—may be used and fed by metal (rigid or IMC) or nonmetallic conduit from the service equipment or from a panelboard. And such a deck box does not have to be 8 in. up and 4 ft back from the pool edge, as required for a junction box for a wet-niche fixture. See Fig. 680-1.

Some approved dry-niche fixtures are provided with an integral flush deck box used to change lamps. Such fixtures have a drain connection at the bottom of the fixture to prevent accumulation of water or moisture.

680-21. Junction Boxes and Enclosures for Transformers or Ground-Fault Circuit-Interrupters. Part **(a)** covers junction boxes that *connect to a conduit that extends directly to a pool-lighting forming shell,* such as shown in Fig. 680-11. The junction box must be of corrosion-resistant material provided with threaded hubs for the connections of conduit.

For line-voltage (120 V) pool fixtures the so-called "deck box" (set in the concrete deck around the pool) is no longer permissible (except where approved dry-niche fixtures include flush boxes as part of an approved assembly), because the deck box, which was installed flush in the concrete adjacent to the pool, was the major source of failure of branch-circuit, grounding, and fixture conductors due to water accumulation within them. The rule of part **(4)** states that these junction boxes must be located not less than 8 in. aboveground, pool deck, or maximum pool water level (whichever provides the greatest elevation), and not less than 4 ft back from the pool perimeter.

The wording of part **(4)** does make clear that the elevated junction box could be less than 4 ft from the pool's edge if a fence or wall is constructed around the pool, with the box on the side of the wall away from the pool, isolating the box from contact by a person in the pool. Or the box could be within 4 ft of the edge if the box is in a permanent nonconductive barrier.

Important: The Exception to part **(a)** permits flush deck boxes where underwater lighting systems are 15 V or less if approved potting compound is used in the deck boxes and the deck boxes are located 4 ft from the edge of the pool. In Fig. 680-13, a deck box for a 12-V fixture could be used in the deck but the use of the box less than 4 ft from the pool's edge might be considered a violation of *b* of the Exception, which does not recognize the fence along the pool in the same way as in part **(a)(4)**. That is, the fence is not mentioned in the Exception as sufficient isolation of the box from the pool—although the installation certainly does comply with the basic concept in part **(a)(4)**.

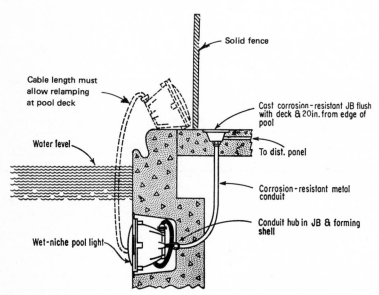

Fig. 680-13. The fence here permits the box to be closer than 4 ft from pool's edge. (Sec. 680-21.)

Part **(b)** covers installation of enclosures for 12-V lighting transformers and for GFCIs that are required for line-voltage fixtures. Such enclosures may be installed indoors or at the pool location. If a ground-fault interrupter is utilized at a pool, its enclosure must be located not less than 4 ft from the perimeter of the pool, unless separated by a permanent means and must be elevated not less than 8 in., measured from the inside bottom of the box down to the pool deck or maximum water level, whichever provides higher mounting. These rules cover installation of transformer or GFCI enclosures that connect to a conduit that "extends directly" to a forming shell.

Part **(b)(1)** requires any such enclosure connected to a conduit that extends directly to an underwater pool-light forming shell to have provisions for threaded conduit entries. The phrase, "provisions for threaded conduit entries" has caused controversy and may be interpreted differently. Some inspection authorities interpret this to mean that an enclosure with provisions for threaded conduit entries must be of cast construction with raised, threaded hubs or with threaded openings in the enclosure wall. Others believe that, since approved swimming pool transformers are available *only* in sheet-metal enclosures with knockouts, some type of threaded hub fitting must be provided in the field and connected to the knockout. Actually, a knockout itself is a "provision for threaded conduit" entry. The intent of this rule on threaded conduit entries is to provide a high degree of bonding and grounding of the underwater fixture.

Connection to a transformer enclosure has been accepted by inspectors when made up with locknuts. The intent of the section could be considered satisfied because the transformer enclosure can be well grounded and bonded by connections at the grounding bar within the enclosure. In most instances, the grounding bar must be added by the contractor.

Part **(b)** also requires that transformer or GFCI enclosures must be provided with an approved seal (such as duct seal) at conduit connections to prevent circulation of air between the conduit and the enclosure; must have electrical continuity between every connected metal conduit and the grounding terminals by means of copper, brass, or other approved corrosion-resistant metal that is integral with the enclosures; must be located not less than 4 ft from the inside walls of the pool (unless separated by a solid fence, wall, or other permanent barrier); and must be located not less than 8 in. from the ground level, pool deck, or maximum pool water level, whichever provides the greatest elevation. This distance is measured from the inside bottom of the enclosure. See Fig. 680-12.

Note that part **(b)(3)** intends to assure a grounding path *from the enclosure and its grounding terminals* to any metal conduit. The section specifically states "metal conduit." Where PVC conduit is used, the provision is not applicable, and the No. 8 ground wire in the PVC bonds to the forming shell. However, the section requires electrical continuity between an enclosure and "*every* connected metal conduit." The conduit feeding the transformer primary does not seem to be involved with that rule because the concern is with the grounding path between the transformer or GFCI enclosure and the forming shell and because the No. 12 equipment grounding conductor in the primary supply will carry any current from a fault originating within the transformer enclosure. Local code authorities should be consulted on the point.

The phrase "integral with the enclosures" is meant to cover a situation where the enclosure is nonmetallic. In this case, electrical continuity between the metal conduits and the grounding terminals must be provided by one of the metals specified, and this "jumper" must be permanently attached to the nonmetallic box so that it is "integral."

In Fig. 680-12, the transformer enclosure is being used as a junction box to an underwater light, with the equipment grounding conductors terminated at the grounding bar and carried through. However, the primary purpose of this enclosure is to house the transformer. Thus parts **(b)**, **(c)**, and **(d)** of Sec. 680-21 would apply. Section 680-21(a) would apply to boxes connected directly to underwater lights and is intended to cover situations where splices, terminations, or pulling of conductors might be required.

Figure 680-12 also involves Sec. 680-21(b) (1), which requires that the enclosure be equipped with provisions for threaded conduit entries; and Sec. 680-21(b) (3), which requires that the enclosure be provided with electrical continuity between every connected metal conduit and the grounding terminals by means of copper, brass, or other approved corrosion-resistant metal that is integral with the enclosures. The intent of those rules is to assure maximum safety with a high degree of bonding and grounding. An enclosure housing a transformer with conduit connection directly to an underwater light could be equipped with raised hubs for conduit connections, be watertight, and if nonmetallic, be provided with a permanently attached bonding jumper between all metal conduits to provide the required electrical continuity.

Part **(c)** of this section warns against creating a tripping hazard or exposing enclosures to damage where they are elevated as required. It is also important to remember that these junction boxes must be afforded additional protection against damage if located on the walkway around the pool. For protection against impact, they may be installed under a diving board or adjacent to a permanent structure such as a lamp post or service pole.

Part **(d)** must be carefully satisfied and part **(e)** calls for strain relief to be added to the flexible cord of a wet-niche lighting fixture at the termination of the cord within a junction box, transformer enclosure, or a GFCI. If this device is not supplied with the fixture, the contractor must provide it.

680-22. Bonding.   Part **(a)** spells out in detail the pool components that must be bonded together. In general, all metal parts that are within 5 ft of the inside walls of the pool and are not separated by a permanent barrier and all metal parts of electrical equipment associated with the pool water circulating system must be bonded together. That usually includes forming shells of underwater lights, ladders, rails, fill spouts, drains, reinforcing bars, transformer enclosures supplying underwater

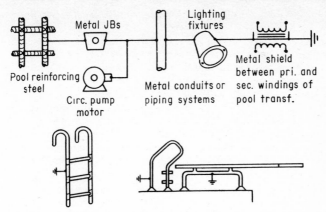

Fig. 680-14. All of these metallic, non-current-carrying parts of a pool installation must be "bonded together." (Sec. 680-22.)

lights, and equipment in the pump room (Fig. 680-14). The objective of "bonding" all metal together and then "grounding" the interconnected metal components is to bring everything within touch to the same electrical potential—earth potential. This eliminates shock hazard from any stray currents that may be induced in or conducted to the metal from outside the pool environment or from faults in any of the pool electrical equipment that, for one reason or another, are not cleared by the circuit protective devices.

In addition to specifying that underwater lighting fixtures and lighting fixture housings shall be grounded, the rule also requires that all metallic conduit and piping, reinforcing steel and other noncurrent-carrying metal components, located in or within 5 ft of a pool, must likewise be bonded together and grounded (Fig. 680-15).

These references are all-inclusive. For example, conduit and piping may relate to power circuitry, intercom or telephone wiring, supply and return water, or to gas lines serving nonelectric heaters. Reinforcing steel refers to that which is installed in deckslabs and walkways, as well as to pool structures which are poured in place, cast in forms, or "gunnited." Similarly, the phrase "other noncurrent-carrying components" includes metal parts of ladders, diving boards, platforms and supports, scuppers, strainers, filters, pump and transformer housings, etc. All these items must be bonded together with an insulated or bare solid copper conductor not smaller than No. 8 and connected to a common electrode.

Exception No. 1 recognizes that the usual steel tie wires provide suitable bonding for the individual bars of the reinforcing steel and no special type of clamps or welding is required. The structural reinforcing steel may be used as a common bonding grid [part **(b)** of this section] where

Fig. 680-15. No. 8 insulated bonding conductor connects to clamps on both sides of coupling in brass conduit from forming shell to transformer housing. Section 680-22(a) (5) requires bonding of all "metal conduit" within 5 ft of pool edge. This bonding connection, although literally required, is not always required by inspection authorities because the conduit connects to bonded enclosures at both ends. (Sec. 680-22.)

connections of the No. 8 bonding conductors are made to the steel rods by suitable clamps. Such connections must be used to bond metal parts to the reinforcing steel grid. Usually, the center-line rebars are bonded together and bonded to the No. 8 bonding conductor at several points.

The **Code** does not require each individual reinforcing bar to be bonded. It recognizes that the steel tie wires used to secure the rebars together where they cross each other provide the required bonding of the individual rods. Tests conducted over a period of several years by the **NE Code** Technical Subcommittee on Swimming Pools have shown the resistance of the path from one end to the other through the structural steel to remain at less than 0.001 ohm. The **Code** thus states in Exception No. 1 that clamping or welding these rods at their intersection will not be required.

If the pool is of metal construction and suitably welded or bolted together, only one bonding connection need be made to the pool.

The rule does not require individual sections of such pools to be bonded. However, the overlapping ends of each section to be bolted must not be painted. If they are, the paint must be removed completely to restore conductivity. In addition, resistance tests should be made across each bolted section after assembly to assure low resistance. These sections normally are fastened together by corrosion-resistant bolts at least ⅜ in. in diameter, and such an installation satisfies the bonding objectives (Fig. 680-16). But, electrical parts of such a pool must be tied into that common bonding grid by No. 8 bonding conductors.

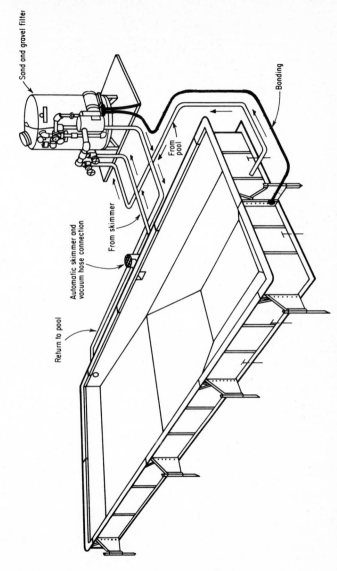

Sand and gravel filter

Bonding

From pool

From skimmer

Automatic skimmer and vacuum hose connection

Return to pool

Fig. 680-16. Walls of bolted or welded metal pool may be common bonding grid for *nonelectrical* parts only. (Sec. 680-22.)

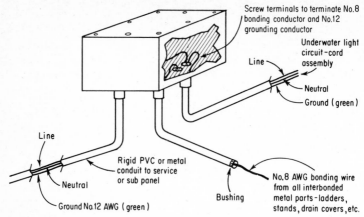

Screw terminals to terminate No.8
bonding conductor and No.12
grounding conductor

Underwater light
circuit-cord
assembly

Line

Neutral

Ground (green)

Line

Rigid PVC or metal
conduit to service
or sub panel

Neutral

Ground No.12 AWG (green)

Bushing

No.8 AWG bonding wire
from all interbonded
metal parts-ladders,
stands, drain covers, etc.

Fig. 680-17. Elevated metal junction box within 5 ft of pool edge must be bonded. (Sec. 680-22.)

Figure 680-17 shows how a metal junction box is bonded into the required bonding grid by No. 8 conductor run in conduit to reinforcing steel. This bonding of metal enclosures within 5 ft of pool edge is required by part **(a)(6)**. When the conduit to the forming shell is PVC, the No. 8 bonding wire required in the PVC by Sec. 680-20(b) (1) bonds the junction box to the forming shell, which is bonded to the rebars. In such cases, some inspectors would not require the No. 8 shown at the bottom of the box.

Important: Exception No. 3 should be carefully noted. It excludes relatively small parts—like bolts, clamps braces, etc.—from the need to be bonded.

Part **(b)** of Sec. 680-22 describes how the bonding must be achieved. Part **(b)** requires all the parts specified in part **(a)** to be connected by means of a No. 8 solid copper conductor (insulated, covered or bare) to a *common bonding grid.* This grid could be pool structural reinforcing steel, a metal pool wall, or a solid copper conductor not smaller than No. 8. The idea of connecting all parts to a common grid accomplishes more reliably the objective of equipotential interconnection. Loosening of a connection at one of the parts would not disconnect the bonded parts into two unconnected groups. But it should be noted that the rule does *not* require the common bonding grid to be *continuous,* although the word "grid" does convey the idea of a loop, as in Fig. 680-18.

Figure 680-19 shows how the reinforcing steel of a concrete pool is used as a common grid for connecting all parts together. In that sketch, the steel reinforcing rods, tied together with steel tie wires at intersections, are used as a common bonding grid to bond together pool equipment. Equipment shown here is required to be bonded. In addition, any metal parts (lighting standards, pipes, etc.) within 5 ft of the inside walls of the pool and not separated from the pool by a permanent barrier must be bonded. All connections made must be in accordance with Sec. 250-113, that is, with proper connectors, lugs, etc.

As shown in Fig. 680-19, when all the required bonding connections are made, the entire interconnected hookup will be grounded by the "equipment grounding conductor" that is required to be run to the filter pump and to the lighting junction boxes and is connected to the No. 8 bonding conductor at the pump and in the boxes. In a pool without underwater lighting, the equipment grounding conductor run with the pump-motor circuit will be the sole grounding connection for the bonded parts—and that is all that is required.

NOTE: THE NO. 8 BONDING CONDUCTOR DOES *NOT* HAVE TO BE RUN TO A PANELBOARD OR SERVICE EQUIPMENT GROUND BLOCK. Because water-circulating equipment is always used and such equipment is required to be both bonded and grounded, the enclosure of the motor terminal connections provides for bringing the bonding and grounding conductors together. The Code does not contain a specific provision requiring the bonding network to be grounded. Where wet-niche underwater fixtures are used, the metal conduit between the *bonded* forming shell and the *grounded and bonded* junction box accomplishes another connection between the No. 8 bonded hookup and the equipment grounding conductor. Or the No. 8 wire with the PVC conduit to the forming shell will make the connection.

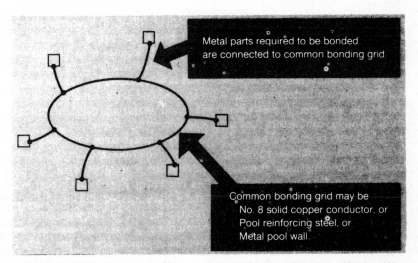

Fig. 680-18. All designated parts must be connected to a "common bonding grid." (Sec. 680-22.)

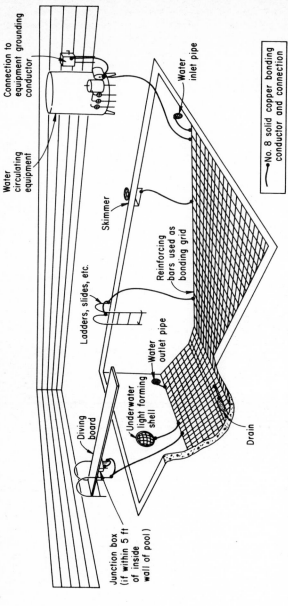

Fig. 680-19. A No. 8 bonding jumper ties each of the indicated parts to the rebar grid, completing the bonding. (Sec. 680-22.)

In part **(b)**, the rule requires that the bonding conductor be of *solid copper* not smaller than No. 8 AWG. It is not required to be insulated. If it is insulated, inspectors might require green color coding at any permanently exposed termination, if a rigid interpretation is put on Sec. 250-57(b), Exception No. 1 and if the "bonding" conductor is considered to be an "equipment grounding" conductor. Section 250-79 on "bonding jumpers" does not specify color of insulation or covering. Because the Code rules do not cover the matter of color of bonding jumpers, inspectors commonly do not require green color, permitting black or other colors. The bonding conductor is usually installed underground and under the pool deck, except where it extends into the pump room. At all visible termination points, the conductor can be wrapped with green tape for identification, similar to the permission in *c* of Exception No. 1 of Sec. 250-57(b) which applies to equipment grounding conductors larger than No. 6 (Fig. 680-20).

Fig. 680-20. Water-fill pipe and metal housings associated with the water-circulation system are "bonded" with an insulated No. 8 solid copper conductor, as required. (Sec. 680-22.)

Conflict has arisen in the past over use of this No. 8 bonding conductor because Sec. 310-3 requires No. 8 and larger conductors to be *stranded* where installed in raceways. That rule had the effect of limiting use of *solid* No. 8 conductors, and their manufacture seemed to be curtailed. Section 310-3 has Exception No. 2 which references Sec. 680-22(b) and exempts the swimming pool No. 8 bonding conductor from the need to be stranded. If solid No. 8 copper cannot be obtained, the local inspection agency must be consulted.

To comply with the requirement that all the bonded parts "shall" be connected to "a common bonding grid", it is common practice to connect metal parts of diving boards, slides, and ladders as well as the drain cover, skimmers, and water-circulating equipment to steel reinforcing in the concrete bottom or walls of the pool. These connections are made and inspected prior to the pouring of concrete, of course. The No. 8 copper bonding conductor may, in some instances, have to be connected to aluminum ladders, rails, or junction boxes (Fig. 680-21). Care must be taken to use a connector suitable for copper to aluminum connections. On some jobs, the ladders, spouts, and forming shells are made of stainless steel, and drains are cast bronze. High-quality, red brass compression connectors can be used, and connections at the iron rebars made with silicon bronze ground clamps.

Fig. 680-21. Fittings for pool ladders have bonding strips attached to them for connection of the No. 8 bonding conductor. When the supports are set in the concrete deck, the bonding connections tie them all together. The No. 8 bonding connections are shown (arrow) and a protective coating is painted on the connectors to protect against corrosion. (Sec. 680-22.)

Part **(c)** points out that water heaters rated over 50 A must have parts of the unit bonded to the other bonded metal parts by a No. 8 conductor and other parts grounded by connection to the equipment grounding conductor of the circuit supplying the heater. And the parts to be grounded or bonded will be designated by instructions with the heater.

680-23. Underwater Audio Equipment.   This section treats connection of loudspeakers for underwater audio output in the same way as a wet-niche pool lighting fixture. Wording and rules are almost identical to that in Sec. 680-20(b). Connection from the speaker forming shell is made to a junction box installed as set forth in Sec. 680-21(a) for a lighting fixture.

680-24. Grounding.   This section lists equipment that must be grounded: wet-niche and dry-niche underwater lighting fixtures, all electric equipment within 5 ft of inside walls of the pool, all electric equipment associated with the recirculating system of the pool, junction boxes and transformer enclosures, GFCIs, and panelboards supplying any electric equipment associated with the pool.

After metal parts have been properly "bonded" to comply with the rules of Sec. 680-22, then "grounding" must be provided to satisfy the many specific rules of Sec. 680-25.

The prime objective of grounding is to provide both connection to the grounding electrode at the service and also to assure a low-impedance path for fault currents to flow back to the grounded neutral to permit proper operation of overcurrent devices. Grounding brings all metallic parts to ground potential, reducing shock hazard.

680-25. Methods of Grounding.   The basic difference between *bonding* and *grounding* becomes evident when the provisions of this section are considered. Essentially, this section calls for grounding with an equipment grounding conductor run in conduit along with the supply conductors. The bonding conductor required by Sec. 680-22 does not have to be in conduit. Also, all equipment grounding conductors must terminate at an *equipment grounding terminal*. Bonding conductors may be connected directly to enclosures.

This section provides rules on methods of grounding metal junction boxes and transformer enclosures, panelboards, underwater lighting fixtures, cord-connected equipment, and other equipment. In general, metal raceways are not depended upon to provide the grounding path for swimming pool electrical systems. This is to make sure that the grounding path is maintained even though the conduit metallic current path might open because of corrosion. This can be a problem in pump houses, for example, where the conduit may be exposed to chlorine or acids. For the same reason, the equipment grounding conductor is required to be insulated. The basic intent is to require a copper, insulated equipment grounding conductor, sized in accordance with Table 250-95, but not smaller than No. 12 AWG, and run back to the bonded and grounded neutral bus in service equipment.

Part **(a)(1)** details grounding technique for each wet-niche lighting fixture, with an equipment grounding conductor in the cord from the forming shell to the junction box, as described in the right-hand text in Fig. 680-22.

The rule of part **(a)(2)** on grounding of the junction box for the light-

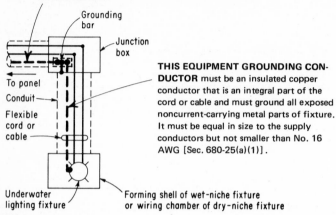

THIS EQUIPMENT GROUNDING CONDUCTOR must be without joint or splice [Sec. 680-25(a)(2)] and must be installed in IMC or rigid metal or rigid nonmetallic conduit with circuit conductors. It must be sized per Table 250-95 but not smaller than No. 12 AWG. It must be an insulated, copper conductor [Sec.680-25(d)].

Grounding bar

Junction box

THIS EQUIPMENT GROUNDING CONDUCTOR must be an insulated copper conductor that is an integral part of the cord or cable and must ground all exposed noncurrent-carrying metal parts of fixture. It must be equal in size to the supply conductors but not smaller than No. 16 AWG [Sec. 680-25(a)(1)].

To panel

Conduit

Flexible cord or cable

Underwater lighting fixture

Forming shell of wet-niche fixture or wiring chamber of dry-niche fixture

Fig. 680-22. Wet-niche fixture must be grounded back to its supply panelboard. (Sec. 680-25.)

ing fixture is also described at the top left of Fig. 680-22. Note that the size of this equipment grounding conductor must be based on the rating of the overcurrent protection for the circuit to the lighting fixture—using Table 250-95, but not smaller than No. 12 [as specified in part **(d)** of this section]. No. 12 would be required for a 15-A or 20-A branch circuit.

Exception No. 1 of part **(a)(2)** is shown in Fig. 680-23, where connection of the equipment grounding conductor to the terminal blocks is an *acceptable* joint in the conductor as an exception to the last sentence of part **(a)(2)**, which calls for the conductor to be "without joint or splice."

Exception No. 2 is illustrated in Fig. 680-24, showing that the grounding conductor requires joints when a circuit from a panelboard to the lighting fixture(s) feeds through an enclosure for a low-voltage transformer, a GFCI, or a time switch.

Part **(b)** requires an equipment grounding conductor to be run from "other equipment" [other than the types of equipment described in part **(a)**] to the "equipment grounding terminal" of the panelboard in which the supply circuit to the equipment originates. What constitutes "other equipment" has created controversy. But reason dictates that the term includes pump motors, controllers, disconnects, chlorinators, wireway, receptacles, etc., related to the swimming pool. As a result, an equipment grounding conductor for a pool filter pump or any of the other compo-

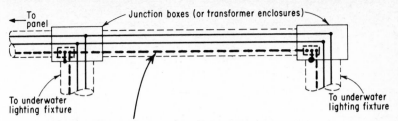

THIS EQUIPMENT GROUNDING CONDUCTOR must be terminated on approved grounding terminals in both enclosures. It must be copper, insulated, sized per Table 250-95, but not smaller than No. 12 AWG. It must be installed with the circuit conductors in IMC or rigid metal or rigid nonmetallic conduit [Sec. 680-25(a)(2) Ex. No. 2 and Sec. 680-25(d)].

Fig. 680-23. Grounding conductor between JBs may have terminal "joints" where same circuit supplies more than one pool light. (Sec. 680-25.)

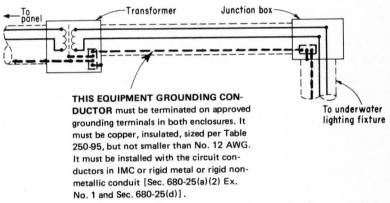

THIS EQUIPMENT GROUNDING CONDUCTOR must be terminated on approved grounding terminals in both enclosures. It must be copper, insulated, sized per Table 250-95, but not smaller than No. 12 AWG. It must be installed with the circuit conductors in IMC or rigid metal or rigid nonmetallic conduit [Sec. 680-25(a)(2) Ex. No. 1 and Sec. 680-25(d)].

Fig. 680-24. Proper terminals must be used where grounding conductor runs through enclosures. (Sec. 680-25.)

nents must be installed with the circuit wires and would seem to be subject to the rule of part (d) of this section—which calls for such a circuit to be run in rigid metal conduit, intermediate metal conduit (IMC), or rigid nonmetallic conduit (Fig. 680-25).

NOTE: THAT INTERPRETATION REQUIRES ONE OF THE THREE RACEWAYS TO FEED A FILTER PUMP AND DOES NOT PERMIT USE OF TYPE UF OR TYPE USE CABLE OR EMT FOR THE PUMP CIRCUIT.

The persuasive argument is made that Sec. 680-24 requires the same type of grounding for "electric equipment associated with the recirculat-

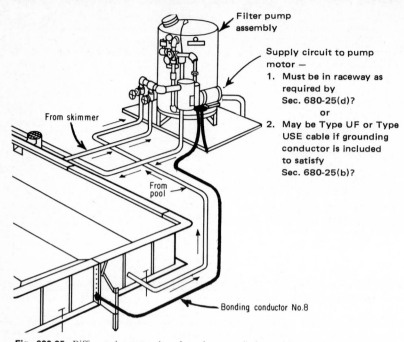

Filter pump assembly

Supply circuit to pump motor —
1. Must be in raceway as required by Sec. 680-25(d)?
   or
2. May be Type UF or Type USE cable if grounding conductor is included to satisfy Sec. 680-25(b)?

From skimmer

From pool

Bonding conductor No.8

Fig. 680-25. Different interpretations have been applied to wiring method required for pump. (Sec. 680-25.)

ing system of the pool" (the pump) as it does for wet-niche lighting fixtures and the other parts listed in Sec. 680-24. Therefore, the argument goes, part **(b)** and part **(d)** of Sec. 680-25 apply to the wiring method used to supply the pump. But some inspectors have interpreted part **(b)** loosely and have permitted use of Type UF or Type USE cable to supply the filter pump, provided an equipment grounding conductor was included in the cable to make the grounding connection required by part **(b)** (Fig. 680-25).

CONTROVERSY: Because part **(b)** of this section does not specifically require use of an "equipment grounding conductor" but simply requires such "other electric equipment" to be "grounded," it may be argued that metal conduit to a pump or other equipment is adequate. Because Sec. 250-91(b) recognizes rigid metal conduit and IMC as equipment grounding conductors, some inspectors might not require the pump and its electrical equipment to be grounded by an equipment grounding conductor, feeling that the metallic raceway could be depended on to provide a ground if a grounding bushing is added in the panel and connected to the panel grounding bus by a jumper.

It should be further noted that part **(a)** of this section, covering underwater lighting fixtures, junction boxes, and enclosures, specifically requires an equipment grounding conductor. It is argued that since it is *not* mentioned in part **(b)**, it was not intended to be required. A 1968 **NE Code** requirement that was deleted in subsequent **Codes** [Sec. 680-7(c)] said that "metallic raceways shall not be depended upon for grounding." Deletion of that statement tends to support the acceptability of metal raceway, without need for an equipment grounding conductor.

An equipment grounding conductor is required by many inspectors because of the possibility of loss of grounding continuity in the metal raceways and enclosures due to possible corrosive conditions in areas housing pumps and watertreatment equipment.

In part **(b)**, the phrase *grounding terminals* refers to the approved terminal bar for equipment grounding conductors required by Sec. 384-27.

Part **(c)** requires an equipment grounding conductor between the service equipment and a panelboard that supplies circuits to pool electrical equipment, as shown in Fig. 680-26.

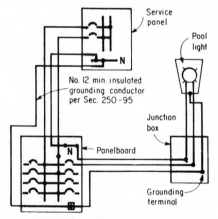

Fig. 680-26. Grounding conductor must connect subpanel ground block to grounded neutral of service equipment. (Sec. 680-25.)

Part **(d)** specifies that the equipment grounding conductor referred to in parts **(a)(2)**, **(b)**, and **(c)** must be an insulated copper conductor installed along with the circuit conductors in rigid metal conduit, intermediate metal conduit, or rigid nonmetallic conduit. AND ALL OF THESE GROUNDING CONDUCTORS *MUST* BE GREEN IN COLOR FOR THEIR ENTIRE LENGTHS IF THEY ARE UP TO NO. 6 IN SIZE. LARGER THAN NO. 6 MAY BE OF OTHER COLOR IF MARKED GREEN AT TERMINALS [see Sec. 250-57(b)].

The equipment grounding conductor required by parts **(a)**, **(b)**, and **(c)** of this section must be sized from Code Table 250-95 in accordance with the rating of the protective device for the circuit that is involved—*but* No. 12 copper is the minimum size. From Code Table 250-95, a 15-A or 20-A fuse or CB protecting a branch circuit to pool lighting, as in part **(a)**, or to some "other equipment," as in **(b)**, would require a No. 12 grounding wire with the circuit. But if 40-A fuses or a 40-A CB protected a feeder from the service equipment to a subpanel serving the pool, then Code Table 250-95 would require a No. 10 size of copper conductor for the grounding, as required by part **(e)** of this section.

Exception No. 1 points out that the use of a No. 14 or No. 16 grounding conductor, which would satisfy part **(a)(1)** for the cord of a wet-niche fixture, is not in violation of the basic rule of part **(d)**, which calls for a No. 12 minimum.

Exception No. 2 requires careful sizing of an equipment grounding conductor on the secondary side of a low-voltage transformer for 12-V pool lights. That conductor *must* be sized from Code Table 250-95 on the basis of the overcurrent-device-rating of the circuit supplying the primary of the transformer. It is not necessary to use a larger grounding conductor on the secondary even though the secondary circuit conductors are larger than the primary conductors because of the 10-to-1 current step-up (120 ÷ 12 V) (Fig. 680-27). A 300-W, 12-V fixture would require No. 10 copper secondary supply conductors (300 W ÷ 12 V = 25 A), but only needs a No. 12 copper grounding conductor.

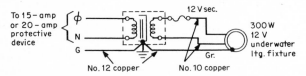

Fig. 680-27. Equipment grounding conductor does not have to be larger on transformer secondary side. (Sec. 680-25.)

Exception No. 3 is shown in Fig. 680-28. A typical arrangement that utilizes this exception is shown in Fig. 680-29. As indicated, the conduit between panels A and B must contain, in addition to feeder conductors, an extra insulated copper conductor for grounding of pool lights and equipment, sized per Sec. 250-95, but not smaller than No. 12. When either a metallic or nonmetallic cable assembly is used between panels A and B, a No. 12 or larger insulated copper conductor must be available only for grounding pool and lighting equipment. Circuit between panel B and deck boxes for lights must be in conduit. In the sketch, a nonmetallic 4-wire cable may be used between the two panelboards. Two conductors can be used for the hot leg conductors, the third used for the neutral, and the last insulated conductor used for the grounding of pool

THIS EQUIPMENT GROUNDING CONDUCTOR must be sized per Table 250-95 [Sec. 680-25(e)]. It must be copper, insulated, not smaller than No. 12 AWG, and installed with circuit conductors in IMC or rigid metal or rigid nonmetallic conduit [Sec. 680-25(d)].

EXCEPTION: If pool equipment is fed from an existing remote panel, the feeder to the remote panel may be a cable; but the equipment grounding conductor must be copper, must be sized per Table 250-95 but not smaller than No. 12 AWG, and must be insulated or covered.

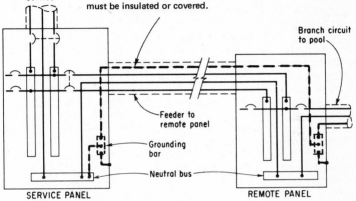

Fig. 680-28. Equipment grounding conductor may be in cable between panelboards. (Sec. 680-25.)

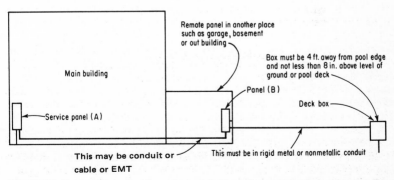

Fig. 680-29. Subpanel is commonly used to supply circuits for pool electrical equipment. (Sec. 680-25.)

equipment. The grounding conductor in the cable assembly may be either "insulated or covered." If it is covered or insulated, it must be finished in green color or green with a yellow stripe [Sec. 250-57(b)].

Note: Exception No. 3 is applicable *only* where the subpanel, as shown in Fig. 680-29, is an "existing" panel. With that wording, if a new subpanel was installed in the garage or at the pool location, it would have to be fed from the service equipment by a feeder in rigid metal conduit, IMC, or rigid nonmetallic conduit—with a separate grounding conductor in whatever type of conduit is used. In Exception No. 3, a "remote panel" is one which is "not part of the service equipment."

The integrity of this ground-return path is all the more important now that ground-fault circuit protection is required for outdoor residential outlets, and for circuits supplying electrical equipment used with storable pools. Special attention should be paid to avoiding any connection between grounding terminals and the neutral (except at the service entrance). The grounding terminal block *must* be connected to the neutral bus in the *service panel* but *not in any remote panel* unless the provisions of Sec. 250-24 are carefully considered and GFCI breakers are not used in the service panel to feed any remote panel. Bonding the neutral to ground in a subpanel can make ground-fault protection in the service panel inoperative.

Exception No. 4 permits use of flexible metal conduit where needed in any circuits involved with the rules of Sec. 680-25. *Important:* When this exception was added to the NEC, the supporting comment said:

Section 680-24 requires grounding electrical equipment such as a filter pump. Section 680-25(d) requires the equipment grounding conductor for grounding this equipment to be installed with the circuit conductors in an approved rigid metal conduit or rigid nonmetallic conduit. As written, the Code would require the rigid conduit to be run directly to the filter pump with flexible metal conduit not permitted, even if the pump and circuit to it were inside a building such as a residence garage or basement. This proposal would permit the use of flexible metal conduit where necessary to employ flexible connections.

NOTE: THAT COMMENT, WHICH WAS ACCEPTED BY THE CODE-MAKING PANEL, CLEARLY SUPPORTS THE INTERPRETATION OF PART **(b)** OF SEC. 680-25 THAT *REQUIRES* RIGID METAL CONDUIT, INTERMEDIATE METAL CONDUIT, OR RIGID NONMETALLIC CONDUIT FOR A CIRCUIT TO A POOL FILTER PUMP.

Exception No. 5 permits use of EMT for the circuits covered by Sec. 680-25 where such circuits are under the better protected conditions when installed on or inside buildings.

Part **(e)** gives the same general rule as part **(d)** on sizing a grounding conductor between a remote subpanel and the service equipment from which the subpanel is fed. This is shown in the data on Fig. 680-28, where the amp rating of the two-pole CB in the service panel must be used to select the minimum size of grounding conductor from Code Table 250-

95. If that CB was a 60-A device, Code Table 250-95 would call for a minimum No. 10 copper conductor.

680-30. Pumps (Storable Pools).   There are portable filter pumps listed by Underwriters Laboratories Inc. and they comply with Sec. 680-30.

680-31. Ground-Fault Circuit-Interrupters Required.   Ground-fault circuit-interrupters must be installed so that all wiring used with storable pools will be protected. For GFCIs see comments following Sec. 210-8.

Chapter Seven

ARTICLE 700. EMERGENCY SYSTEMS

700-1. Scope. Note that all the regulations of this article apply to the designated "circuits, systems, and equipment"—ONLY WHEN THE SYSTEMS OR CIRCUITS ARE *REQUIRED BY LAW* AND CLASSI-FIED AS EMERGENCY PROVISIONS BY FEDERAL, STATE, MUNICIPAL, OR OTHER CODE OR BY A GOVERNMENTAL AUTHORITY. THE NE CODE, ITSELF, DOES *NOT* REQUIRE EMERGENCY LIGHT, POWER, OR EXIT SIGNS.

The effect of the first paragraph of this section is to exclude from all these rules any emergency circuits, systems, or equipment that are installed on a premises but are not legally mandated for the premises. Of course, any emergency provisions that are provided at the option of the designer (or the client) must necessarily conform to all other NE Code regulations that apply to the work.

The placement or location of exit lights is not a function of the National Electrical Code but is covered in the Life Safety Code, NFPA No. 101 (formerly Building Exits Code). But, where exit lights are required by law, the NEC considers them to be parts of the emergency system. The NEC indicates how the installation will be made, not where the emergency lighting is required, except as specified in part C of Art. 517 for essential electrical systems in health care facilities.

OSHA regulations on exit signs are presented in Subpart E of the *Occupational Safety and Health Standards* (Part 1910). These requirements on location and lighting of exit signs apply to all places of employment in all new buildings and also in all existing buildings.

Prior to OSHA, there was no universal requirement that all buildings or all places of employment have exit signs. The National Electrical Code does not require them. And although the NFPA Life Safety Code does cover rules on emergency lighting and exit signs, that code was enforced where state or local government bodies required it—that is, in some areas and for specific types of occupancies. As a result, there are existing occupancies which do not have the exit signs now required by federal law.

Section 1910.35 of OSHA makes clear that every building must have a means of egress—a continuous, unobstructed way for occupants to get out of a building in case of fire or other emergency, consisting of horizontal and vertical ways, as required. Egress from all parts of a building or structure must be provided at all times the building is occupied. The law says:

Every exit shall be clearly visible or the route to reach it shall be conspicuously indicated in such a manner that every occupant of every building or structure who is physically and mentally capable will readily know the direction of escape from any point, and each path of escape, in its entirety, shall be so arranged or marked that the way to a place of safety outside is unmistakable.

Then it says:

Exit marking. (1) Exits shall be marked by a readily visible sign. Access to exits shall be marked by readily visible signs in all cases where the exit or way to reach it is not immediately visible to the occupants.

(2) Any door, passage, or stairway which is neither an exit nor a way of exit access, and which is so located or arranged as to be likely to be mistaken for an exit, shall be identified by a sign reading "Not An Exit" or similar designation, or shall be identified by a sign indicating its actual character, such as "To Basement," "Storeroom," "Linen Closet," or the like.

(3) Every required sign designating an exit or way of exit access shall be so located and of such size, color, and design as to be readily visible.

Note that marking must be supplied for the way to the exit as well as for the exit itself. Further,

(5) A sign reading "Exit," or similar designation, with an arrow indicating the direction, shall be placed in every location where the direction of travel to reach the nearest exit is not immediately apparent.

(6) Every exit sign shall be suitably illuminated by a reliable light source giving a value of not less than 5 footcandles on the illuminated surface.

A lot of discussion has been generated by that last rule. Note that an exit sign does not have to be internally illuminated, although it may be. And this lighting is required on "every exit sign" which means signs over exit doors and exit signs indicating direction of travel.

The phrase "reliable light source" raises questions as to its meaning. Just what it reliable? Does this mean that the light source must operate if the utility supply to a building fails? And is there a difference in required application in new buildings versus existing buildings?

Because the OSHA regulations on exit signs do not require emergency power for lighting of such signs, the light units that illuminate exit signs may be supplied from regular (nonemergency) circuits. OSHA does not make it mandatory to supply such circuits from a tap ahead of the service main or from batteries or an emergency generator. And this applies to new buildings as well as existing buildings. As far as OSHA is concerned, Art. 700 of the NE Code on emergency systems does not apply to circuits for exit sign lighting. Of course, OSHA does not object to the extra reliability such arrangements give. But the NEC does classify exit lights as emergency equipment (Fig. 700-1).

Fig. 700-1. Exit lights and wall-hanging battery-pack emergency lighting units are covered by Art. 700 whenever such equipment or provisions for emergency application are legally required by governmental authorities. (Sec. 700-1).

An emergency lighting system in a theater or other place of public assemblage includes exit signs, the chief purpose of which is to indicate the location of the exits, and lighting equipment commonly called "emergency lights," the purpose of which is to provide sufficient illumination in the auditorium, corridors, lobbies, passageways, stairways, and fire escapes to enable persons to leave the building safely.

These details, as well as the various classes of buildings in which emergency lighting is required, are left to be determined by state or municipal codes, and where such codes are in effect, the following provisions apply.

700-3. Equipment Approval.   This rule has the effect of requiring use of only emergency equipment that is listed for such application by UL or another testing laboratory.

Under the heading of "Emergency Lighting and Power Equipment," the UL's *Electrical Construction Materials Directory* states:

This listing covers battery-powered emergency lighting and power equipment, for use in ordinary indoor locations in accordance with Article 700 of the **National Electrical Code.** The lighting circuit ratings do not exceed 250 volts for tungsten lamps or 227 volts ac for electric discharge lamps. Other ratings may be included (motor loads, inductive loads, resistance loads, etc.) to 600 volts. This listing covers unit equipment, automatic battery charging and control equipment, inverters, central station battery systems, distribution panels, exit lights, and remote lamp assemblies, but not lighting fixtures. The investigation of emergency equipment includes the determination of their suitability of transferring operation from normal supply circuit to an immediately available emergency supply circuit.

700-5. Capacity.   It is extremely important that the supply source be of adequate capacity. There are two main reasons for adequate capacity:

  1. It is important that power be available for the necessary supply to exit lights, emergency and egress lighting, as well as to operate such equipment as required for elevators and other equipment connected to the emergency system.

  2. In such occupancies as hospitals, there may be a need for an emergency supply for lighting in hospital operating rooms, and also for such equipment as inhalators, iron lungs, incubators, and the like. See part **C** of Art. 517 for requirements in health care facilities.

700-6. Systems.   Note that the rule calls for emergency supply to lighting and/or power to be "immediately available." Because that wording implies no delay in the transfer from "normal" to "emergency" source, it has been interpreted as requiring use of an "automatic" transfer switch and making a manual transfer switch unacceptable for emergency use. A manual switch, however, would be acceptable for transfer from a normal source to a "standby" source, as covered in Art. 750 on "Stand-by Power Generation Systems."

This section then lists and describes the types of emergency supply systems that are acceptable—with one or more of such systems required where emergency supply is mandated by law.

Part **(a)** recognizes storage batteries for emergency source, as shown in Fig. 700-2.

Part **(b)** covers use of engine-generator sets for emergency supply as an alternate to utility supply. Engine-driven generators (diesel, gasoline, or gas) are commonly used to provide an alternate source of emergency or standby power when normal utility power fails. Gas-turbine generators also are used.

The first step in selecting an on-site generator is to consider applicable requirements of the **National Electrical Code,** which differ depending on whether the generating set is to function as an emergency system, a stand-by power system, or as a power source in a health care facility, such as a hospital.

For example, an *internal-combustion* type engine-generator set selected

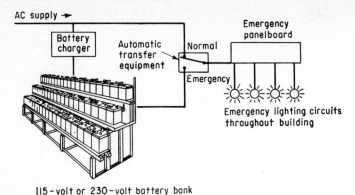

AC supply →

Battery charger

Automatic transfer equipment

Normal

Emergency

Emergency panelboard

Emergency lighting circuits throughout building

115-volt or 230-volt battery bank

Fig. 700-2. Battery bank of 1½-hr capacity may back up a standard utility service. (Sec. 700-6.)

for use under Art. 700 must be provided with *automatic starting and automatic load transfer,* with enough on-site fuel to power the full demand load for at least 2 hr (Fig. 700-3). Article 750 makes no such requirement; however, if a stand-by power system selected under the regulations of Art. 750 ls *legally* required, it must be provided with enough on-site fuel to power the full demand operation of the load for *not less than 2 hr.*

As recognized by part **(c)**, two separate services brought to different locations in the building are always preferable, and these services should

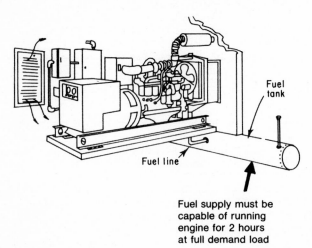

Fuel tank

Fuel line

Fuel supply must be capable of running engine for 2 hours at full demand load

Fig. 700-3. Generator must have automatic start and adequate fuel supply. (Sec. 700-6.)

at least receive their supply from separate transformers where this is practicable. In some localities, municipal ordinances require either two services from independent sources of supply, or auxiliary supply for emergency lighting from a storage battery, or a generator driven by a steam turbine, internal-combustion engine, or other prime mover. Figure 700-4 shows two different forms of the separate-service type of emergency supply. The method at bottom makes use of two sources of emergency input.

Separate Emergency Service

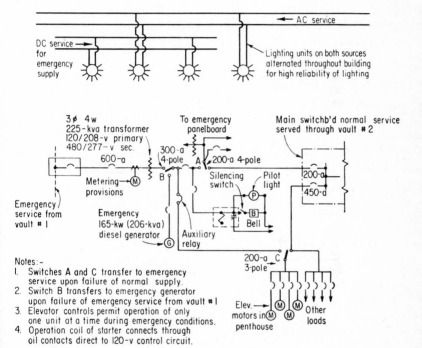

Fig. 700-4. Dual-service emergency provisions can take many different forms. (Sec. 700-6.)

Part **(d)** covers the method shown in Fig. 700-5. In that diagram, the tap ahead of the main could supply the emergency panel directly, without need for the transfer switch.

Part **(e)** covers typical wall-hanging battery-pack emergency lighting units, as shown in Fig. 700-6. The 1971 **NEC** accepted only connection of emergency light units by means of fixed wiring. Part **(e)** now recog-

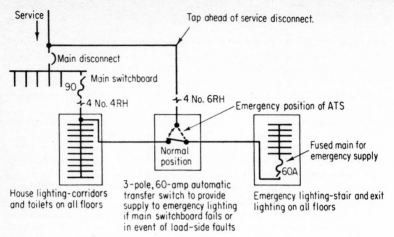

Service

Tap ahead of service disconnect.

Main disconnect

Main switchboard

90

4 No. 4RH

4 No. 6RH

Emergency position of ATS

Normal position

Fused main for emergency supply

60A

House lighting-corridors and toilets on all floors

3-pole, 60-amp automatic transfer switch to provide supply to emergency lighting if main switchboard fails or in event of load-side faults

Emergency lighting-stair and exit lighting on all floors

Fig. 700-5. A tap ahead of the service main protects only against internal failures. (Sec. 700-6.)

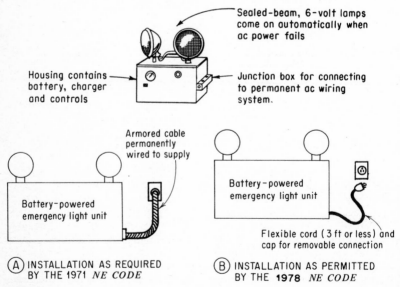

Sealed-beam, 6-volt lamps come on automatically when ac power fails

Housing contains battery, charger and controls

Junction box for connecting to permanent ac wiring system.

Armored cable permanently wired to supply

Battery-powered emergency light unit

Battery-powered emergency light unit

Flexible cord (3 ft or less) and cap for removable connection

(A) INSTALLATION AS REQUIRED BY THE 1971 *NE CODE*

(B) INSTALLATION AS PERMITTED BY THE **1978** *NE CODE*

Fig. 700-6. Unit emergency lights may serve as required source of emergency supply. (Sec. 700-6.)

nizes permanent wiring connection *or* cord-and-plug connection to a receptacle.

Even though the unit equipment is allowed to be hooked up with flexible cord-and-plug connections, it is still necessary that the unit equipment be permanently fixed in place.

Individual unit equipment provides emergency illumination only for the area in which it is installed; therefore, it is not necessary to carry a circuit back to the service equipment to feed the unit. This section clearly indicates that the branch circuit feeding the normal lighting in the area to be served is the same circuit that should supply the unit equipment.

In part **(e)** the intent of the 87½ percent value is to assure proper *lighting output* from lamps supplied by unit equipment. It is generally considered acceptable to design equipment that will produce acceptable lighting levels for the required 1½ hours, even though the 87½ percent rating of the battery would not be maintained during this period. The objective is adequate light output to permit safe egress from buildings in emergencies. Hence, the unit equipment shall supply and maintain not less than 60 percent of the initial emergency illumination for a period of at least 1½ hours.

As shown in Fig. 700-7, a battery-pack emergency unit must not be connected on the load side of a local wall switch that controls the supply to the unit or the receptacle into which the emergency unit is plugged. Such an arrangement exposes the emergency unit to accidental energization of the lamps and draining of the battery supply.

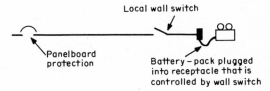

Fig. 700-7. This is a violation! (Sec. 700-6.)

700-12. Signals.   In order to be effective, the signal devices should be located in some room where an attendant is on duty. Lamps may readily be used as signals to indicate the position of an automatic switching device. An audible signal in any place of public assemblage should not be so located or of such a character that it will cause a general alarm.

The standard signal equipment furnished by a typical battery manufacturer with their 60-cell battery for emergency lighting includes an indicating lamp which is lighted when the charger is operating at the high rate, and a voltmeter marked in three colored sections indicates (1) that the battery is not being charged, or is discharging into the emergency system, (2) that the battery is being trickle charged, or (3) that the battery is being charged at the high rate. This last indication duplicates the indication given by the lamp.

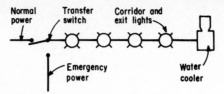

Fig. 700-8. The water cooler may not be on an emergency circuit. (Sec. 700-13.)

700-13. Loads on Emergency Branch Circuits. Figure 700-8 shows a clear violation of this rule, because appliances are excluded from emergency circuits.

700-14. Emergency Illumination. Note that all exit lights are designated as part of the emergency lighting, and, as such, their circuiting must conform to Sec. 700-15.

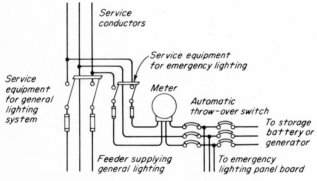

Fig. 700-9. Emergency lighting is automatically switched from normal service to the battery or generator. (Sec. 700-15.)

700-15. Circuits for Emergency Lighting. Figure 700-9 shows the basic rule of part **(1)** on transfer of emergency lighting from the normal source to the emergency source. If a single emergency system is intalled, a transfer switch shall be provided which, in case of failure of the source of supply on which the system is operating, will automatically transfer the emergency system to the other source. Where the two sources of supply are two services, the single emergency system may normally operate on either source, as in Fig. 700-10. Where the two sources of supply are one service and a storage battery, or one service and a generator set, as in Fig. 700-9, the single emergency system would, as a general rule, be operated normally on the service, using the battery or generator only as a reserve in case of failure of the service. Figure 700-11 shows an emergency

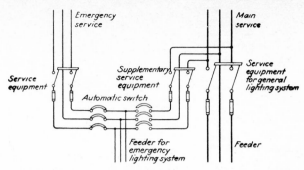

Fig. 700-10. Emergency lighting may be supplied from an emergency service. (Sec. 700-15.)

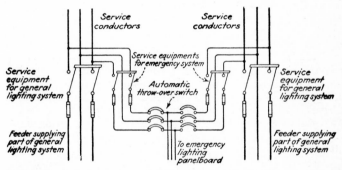

Fig. 700-11. A single emergency lighting system may be fed from two services. (Sec. 700-15.)

hookup that has two separate supplies tied into the emergency lighting system.

Part **(2)** of this section provides for use of two or more "separate and complete" emergency systems. If two emergency lighting systems are installed, each system shall operate on a separate source of supply, as where each emergency disconnect in Fig. 700-10 feeds a separate, independent emergency lighting system. Either both systems shall be kept in operation, or switches shall be provided which will automatically place either system in operation upon failure of the other system.

700-17. Independent Wiring. Figure 700-12 shows a clear violation of this rule because the wiring to the emergency light (or to an exit light, which is classed as an emergency light) is run in the same raceway and boxes.

This section requires that the wiring for emergency systems be kept entirely independent of the regular wiring used for lighting and that it thus needs to be in separate raceways, cables, and boxes. This require-

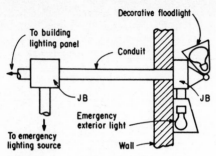

Fig. 700-12. Emergency wiring may not be run in enclosures with wiring for non-emergency circuits. (Sec. 700-17.)

ment is to ensure that where faults may occur on the regular wiring, they will not affect the emergency system wiring, as it will be in a separate enclosure.

Exception No. 1 for transfer switches is intended to permit normal supply conductors to be brought into the transfer-switch enclosure and that these conductors would be the only ones within the transfer-switch enclosure which were not part of the emergency system. Exception Nos. 2 and 3 permit two sources supplying emergency or exit lighting to enter the fixture and its common junction box.

700-18. Switch Requirements. Figure 700-13 shows a violation of the last sentence of this rule, where use of three- and four-way switches are prohibited.

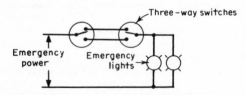

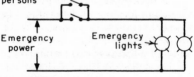

Fig. 700-13. Watch out for switches in emergency lighting circuits. (Sec. 700-18.)

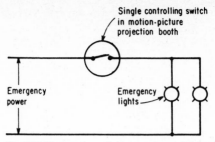

Fig. 700-14. Location of this emergency lighting switch is a violation. (Sec. 700-19.)

700-19. Switch Location. Figure 700-14 shows a violation of part **(b)** if the switch shown is the only switch in the emergency circuit.

ARTICLE 710. OVER 600 VOLTS, NOMINAL

710-1. Scope. An important consideration in selection and application of conductors for systems operating over 600 V is careful correlation of NE Code regulations and the data made available by third-party testing laboratories. Underwriters Laboratories and Electrical Testing Labs have been deeply involved in listing cables for use in high-voltage systems. The expanded testing and listing of high-voltage conductors and cable assemblies have increased the need for the electrical designer and installer to be particularly thorough and careful in establishing full and effective compliance with all applicable codes and standards.

The term *high voltage* is commonly used to refer to any circuit operating at voltage above 600 V, phase to phase. It should be noted, however, that circuits from 601 V up to 35 kV are frequently called "medium-voltage" circuits and the term "high voltage" also is used for circuits operating above 15 kV.

The NE Code contains very extensive rules on all aspects of high-voltage work. These rules must be evaluated and studied carefully. Check all questions about interpretations of Code rules with the authority having jurisdiction for Code enforcement.

710-2. Other Articles. Article 710 covers general requirements on all circuits operating at more than 600 V between conductors. Specific requirements on high-voltage application are covered within other Code articles on services, motors and controllers, transformers, capacitors, outside wiring, and other specific categories of equipment.

710-3. Wiring Methods. High-voltage circuits used for commercial and industrial feeders, both outdoors and indoors, most commonly operate at voltages up to 15,000 V (15 kV). But there is a trend to even higher voltages (26 kV, 35 kV) for extremely large installations. Typical circuits today operate at 4,160/2,400 V and 13,200/7,600 V—both 3-phase, 4-wire wye hookups.

Modern high-voltage circuits for buildings include: overhead bare or covered conductors, installed with space between the conductors which are supported by insulators at the top of wood poles or metal tower structures; overhead aerial cable assemblies of insulated conductors entwined together, supported on building walls or on poles or metal structures; insulated conductors installed in metal or nonmetallic conduits or ducts run underground, either directly buried in the earth or encased in a concrete envelope under the ground; insulated conductors in conduit run within buildings; multiple-conductor cable assemblies (such as nonmetallic jacketed cables, lead-sheathed cable, or interlocked armor cable), installed in conduit or on cable racks or trays or other types of supports. Another wiring method gaining wide acceptance consists of plastic conduit containing factory-installed conductors, affording a readily used direct-earth-burial cable assembly for underground circuits but still permitting removal of the cable for repair or replacement.

(a) Conductors aboveground must be in rigid metal conduit, in intermediate metal conduit (IMC), in cable trays, in cablebus, in other suitable raceways (check inspector for suitability of EMT), or as open runs of metal-armored cable suitable for the use and purpose. The **NE Code** now equates IMC to rigid metal conduit for indoor and outdoor (including underground) applications for high-voltage circuits.

The phrase "other suitable raceway", as used in part **(a)**, is not clear, because there is no **Code** definition of "suitable." If it is meant to accept all raceways covered under the **NE Code** definition for "raceway," then it includes EMT, flexible metal conduit, wireways, and rigid nonmetallic conduit (Fig. 710-1).

When rigid nonmetallic conduit is used in high-voltage circuits aboveground (indoors or outdoors), Sec. 347-2(b) requires that the conduit must be encased in not less than 2 in. of concrete. But, note that the rule of Sec. 347-2(b) requiring concrete encasement of PVC conduit (the only nonmetallic conduit approved by Art. 347 and UL for use aboveground) applies *only* to circuits run aboveground. The wording of that rule has proved troublesome because it does not specify that it applies *only* to use aboveground. But, directly buried nonmetallic conduit carrying high-voltage conductors does not have to be concrete-encased if it is a type approved for use without concrete encasement. If concrete encasement is required, it will be indicated on the UL label and in the listing. Sections 347-2(c) and 710-3(b) permit direct burial rigid nonmetallic conduit (without concrete encasement) for high-voltage circuits.

In locations accessible to qualified persons only, open runs of nonmetallic sheathed cable, bare conductors and busbars may be used (Secs.

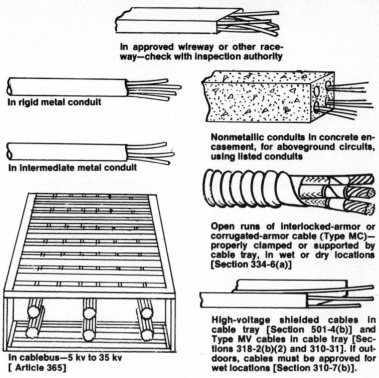

In approved wireway or other raceway—check with inspection authority

In rigid metal conduit

In intermediate metal conduit

Nonmetallic conduits in concrete encasement, for aboveground circuits,
using listed conduits

Open runs of interlocked-armor or
corrugated-armor cable (Type MC)—
properly clamped or supported by
cable tray, in wet or dry locations
[Section 334-6(a)]

High-voltage shielded cables in
cable tray [Section 501-4(b)] and
Type MV cables in cable tray [Sec-
tions 318-2(b)(2) and 310-31]. If outdoors, cables must be approved for
wet locations [Section 310-7(b)].

In cablebus—5 kv to 35 kv
[Article 365]

Fig. 710-1. A variety of wiring methods may be used for aboveground high-voltage circuits.
(Sec. 710-3.)

710-32 and 710-33). In locations accessible to qualified persons only there
are no restrictions on the types of wiring that may be used. The types
more commonly employed are open wiring on insulators with conductors
either bare or insulated, and rigid metal conduit or nonmetallic rigid
conduit containing lead-covered cable.

(b) Underground conductors may be installed in "raceways approved
for the purpose" or in approved direct burial cable assemblies.

Table 710-3(b) makes clear that underground circuits may be installed
in rigid metal conduit, in intermediate metal conduit, or in rigid nonmetallic conduit. Rigid metal conduit or IMC does not have to be concrete-encased, but it may be, of course. Direct burial nonmetallic conduit
must be an approved (UL listed and labeled) type, specifically recognized
for use without concrete encasement. If rigid nonmetallic conduit is

approved for use only with concrete encasement, at least 2 in. of concrete must enclose the conduit. All applications of the various types of non-metallic conduit must conform to the data made available by UL in the *Electrical Construction Materials Directory.*

Figure 710-2 covers the basic rules of Table 710-3(b), subject to the considerations noted in the rules and Exceptions, as follows:

1. Burial depths shown in diagrams may be reduced 6 in. for each 2 in. of concrete or equivalent above the conductors.
2. Areas of heavy traffic (public roads, commercial parking areas, etc.) must have minimum burial depth of 24 in. for any wiring method.
3. Lesser depths are permitted where wiring rises for termination.
4. Airport runways may have cables buried not less than 18 in. deep, without raceway or concrete encasement.
5. Conduits installed in solid rock may be buried at lesser depths than shown in diagrams when covered by at least 2 in. of concrete that extends to the rock surface.

Direct burial cables must have a construction in which the energized conductors are surrounded by effectively grounded, multiple concentric conductors, closely and evenly spaced, or conducting sheath of equivalent ampacity to meet requirements of Sec. 250-51. That means that only metal-tape-shielded, concentric-neutral, or drain-wire-shielded cables may be directly buried.

Part **(b)** also notes that unshielded cable (i.e., cable without electrostatic shielding on the insulation) must be installed in rigid metal conduit, in IMC, or in rigid nonmetallic conduit encased in not less than 3 in. of concrete. The effect of this rule is that unshielded, or nonshielded, cables may not be used directly buried in the earth, which is really a follow-up to the above-noted requirement that *only* concentric shielded cables may be directly buried. And any unshielded cable *must* be "listed by a nation-ally recognized testing laboratory"—as required by the Exception of Sec. 310-61 for conductors rated over 2,000 V.

Figure 710-3 demonstrates uses of direct burial high-voltage cables in relation to the **Code** rules. Figure 710-4 covers underground high-volt-age circuits in raceways.

As noted in part **(b)(2)** splices or taps are permitted in trench without a box—but only if approved methods and materials are used. Taps and splices must be watertight and protected from mechanical injury. For shielded cables, the shielding must be continuous across the splice or tap.

Figure 710-5 shows a permanent straight splice for joining one end of cable off a reel to the start of cable off another reel, or for repairing cable that is cut through accidentally by a back-hoe or other tool digging into the ground. "T" and "Y" splices are made with similar techniques. Dis-connectable splice devices provide watertight plug-and-receptacle assem-bly for all types of shielded cables and are fully submersible.

Figure 710-6 covers the rules of parts **(b)(3)** and **(b)(4)**. Figure 710-7 covers part **(b)(1)**.

DIRECT-BURIED CABLES

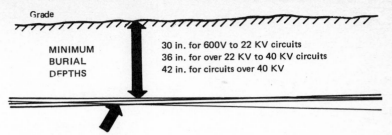

Grade

MINIMUM
BURIAL
DEPTHS

30 in. for 600V to 22 KV circuits
36 in. for over 22 KV to 40 KV circuits
42 in. for circuits over 40 KV

Direct-buried cables must be
concentric-neutral or drain-wire
shielded type or with a conducting
sheath of equivalent ampacity

**NOTE: Unshielded cables are not
acceptable directly buried!**

IN RIGID METAL CONDUIT
OR INTERMEDIATE METAL CONDUIT (IMC)

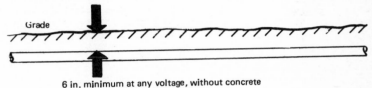

Grade

6 in. minimum at any voltage, without concrete
encasement. See Note 2 below.

IN RIGID NONMETALLIC CONDUIT

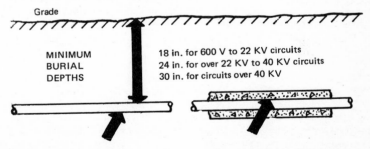

Grade

MINIMUM
BURIAL
DEPTHS

18 in. for 600 V to 22 KV circuits
24 in. for over 22 KV to 40 KV circuits
30 in. for circuits over 40 KV

Rigid nonmetallic conduit approved
for direct burial—i.e., listed by
UL or other nationally recognized
testing agency

Rigid nonmetallic conduit requiring
concrete encasement must have
at least 2 in. of concrete (or equivalent)
above conduit, and the conduit itself
must be at the depths shown.

Fig. 710-2. Underground high-voltage circuits must observe burial depths. (Sec. 710-3.)

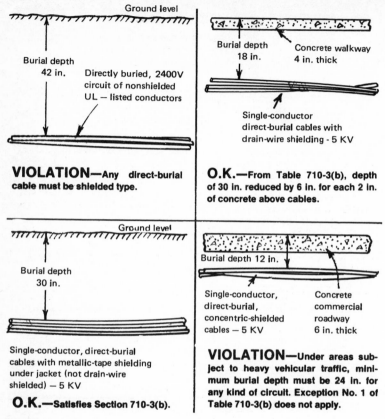

Fig. 710-3. Direct-burial high-voltage cables must be of correct type, at specified depth. (Sec. 710-3.)

710-6. Insulation Shielding. One of the basic decisions to make in selecting high-voltage conductors is whether or not electrostatic insulation shielding is required on the cable. In the 1971 *NE Code* (and previous editions), Table 710-5 set forth an elaborate variety of conditions under which solid dielectric insulated conductors had to be shielded or were permitted to be unshielded. That table set the same basic shielding requirements as recommended by the IPCEA. BUT, the *NE Code* *no longer contains* that table and now takes a different approach to mandatory shielding. The basic requirements on electrostatic shielding of high-voltage conductors are presented in Sec. 310-61 and are explained there.

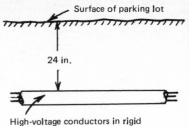

High-voltage conductors in rigid metal conduit or intermediate metal conduit laid in ground — 15 KV circuit

O.K.—Minimum 24-in. depth is required under areas of heavy traffic (even if conduit is concrete-encased).

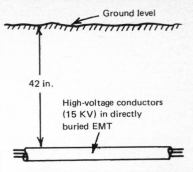

High-voltage conductors (15 KV) in directly buried EMT

?   **EMT is O.K. for direct earth burial and may satisfy Section 710-3(b) as a "raceway approved for the purpose." But Table 710-3(b) does not mention use of EMT.**

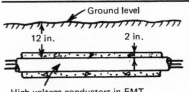

High-voltage conductors in EMT encased in 2 in. of concrete — 15 KW circuit

?   **This is O.K. if rigid nonmetallic conduit is used in the concrete and the 18-in. burial depth from Table 710-3(b) may be reduced to 12 in. because of the 2 in. of concrete above the conduit. BUT—use of EMT in the concrete in this manner is not covered by the** *NE Code*

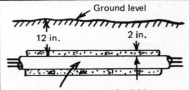

High-voltage conductors in rigid nonmetallic conduit encased in 2 in. of concrete — 26 KW circuit

VIOLATION—At this voltage, minimum burial depth for nonmetallic conduit must be 18 in. [24 in. from Table 710-3(b) minus 6 in. for 2 in. of concrete above conduit].

Concrete walkway in shopping center mall 2 in. thick

High-voltage conductors in rigid metal conduit laid on grade and covered with 2 in. of concrete

O.K.—Although Table 710-3(b) calls for a minimum 6-in. burial depth for rigid metal conduit, the 2 in. of concrete permit a burial depth reduction of 6 in.

Fig. 710-4. Underground raceway circuits may vary widely in acceptable conditions of use. (Sec. 710-3.)

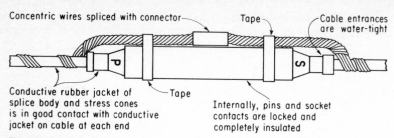

Concentric wires spliced with connector — — — Tape — — — Cable entrances are water-tight

Conductive rubber jacket of
splice body and stress cones
is in good contact with conductive
jacket on cable at each end — — Tape

Internally, pins and socket
contacts are locked and
completely insulated

Fig. 710-5. Splice may be made in direct-burial cable if suitable materials are used. (Sec. 710-3.)

BACKFILL MUST NOT DAMAGE DUCTS, CABLES OR RACEWAYS

Backfill of heavy rocks or sharp or corrosive materials must
not be used if it may cause damage or prevent adequate
compaction of ground.

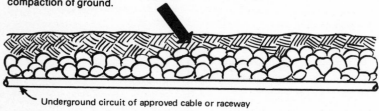

Underground circuit of approved cable or raceway

RACEWAYS MUST BE SEALED

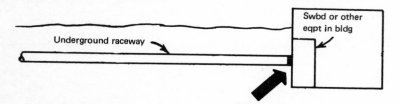

Swbd or other
eqpt in bldg

Underground raceway

Where raceway enters from an underground system, the end
in the building must be sealed with suitable compound to
prevent entry of moisture or gases; or it must be arranged to
prevent moisture from contacting live parts.

Fig. 710-6. Circuits must be protected and sealed where they enter equipment. (Sec. 710-3.)

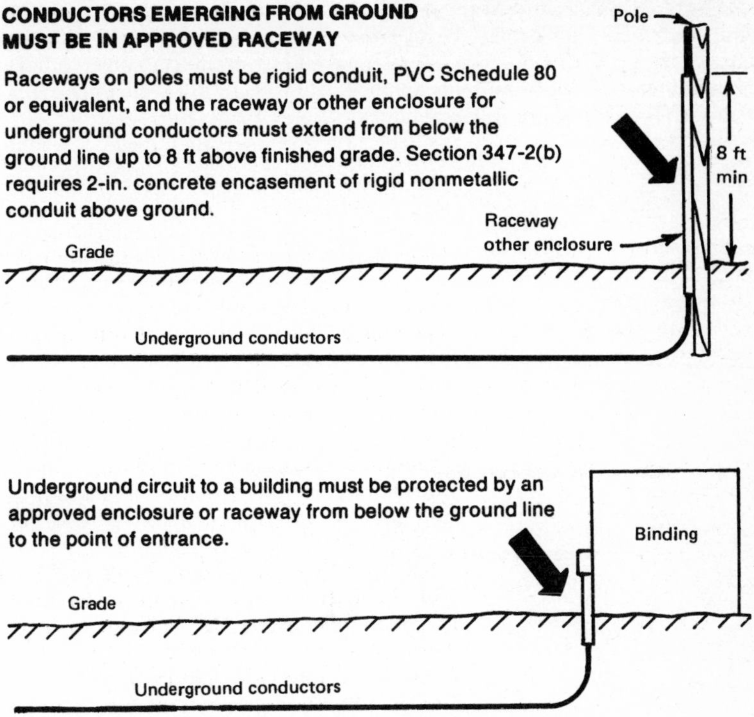

CONDUCTORS EMERGING FROM GROUND MUST BE IN APPROVED RACEWAY

Pole

Raceways on poles must be rigid conduit, PVC Schedule 80 or equivalent, and the raceway or other enclosure for underground conductors must extend from below the ground line up to 8 ft above finished grade. Section 347-2(b) requires 2-in. concrete encasement of rigid nonmetallic conduit above ground.

8 ft min

Raceway other enclosure

Grade

Underground conductors

Underground circuit to a building must be protected by an approved enclosure or raceway from below the ground line to the point of entrance.

Binding

Grade

Underground conductors

Fig. 710-7. Direct burial cables must be protected aboveground. (Sec. 710-3.)

This section sets forth very general rules on terminating shielded high-voltage conductors. The metallic shielding or any other conducting or semiconducting static shielding components on shielded cable must be stripped back to a safe distance according to the circuit voltage—at all terminations of the shielding. At such points, stress reduction must be provided by such methods as the use of potheads, terminators, stress cones, or similar devices.

The wording of this regulation makes clear that the need for shield termination using stress cones or similar terminating devices applies to semiconducting insulation shielding as well as to metallic-wire insulation shielding systems.

A stress cone is a field-installed device or a field-assembled buildup of insulating tape and shielding braid which must be made at a terminal of high-voltage shielded cable, whether a pothead is used or not. A stress-relief cone is required to relieve the electrical stress concentration in cable insulation directly under the end of cable shielding. Some cable constructions contain stress-control components that afford the cable sufficient stress relief without the need for stress-relief cones. If a cable contains inherent stress-relief components in its construction, that would satisfy Sec. 710-6 as doing the work of a stress cone. As a result, separate stress cones would not have to be installed at the ends of such cable. Or, heat-shrinkable-tubing terminations may be used with stress-control material that provides the needed relief of electrostatic stress.

At a cable terminal, the shielding must be cut back some distance from the end of the conductor to prevent any arcing-over from the hot conductor to the grounded shield. When the shield is cut back, a stress is produced in the insulation. By providing a flare out of the shield, i.e., by extending the shield a short distance in the shape of a cone, the stress is relieved, as shown in Fig. 710-8.

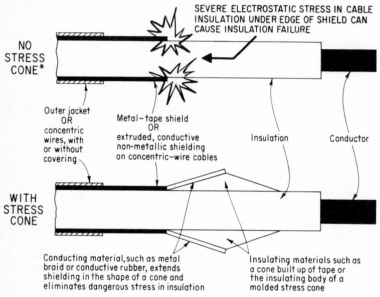

Fig. 710-8.   Here is how a stress cone protects insulation at cable ends. (Sec. 710-6.)

Stress cones provide that protection against insulation failure at the terminals of shielded high-voltage cables. Manufacturers provide special preformed stress cones (Fig. 710-9) and kits for preparing cable terminals with stress cones for cables operating at specified levels of high voltage (Fig. 710-10). A wide assortment of stress-relief terminators are made for all the high-voltage cable assemblies used today.

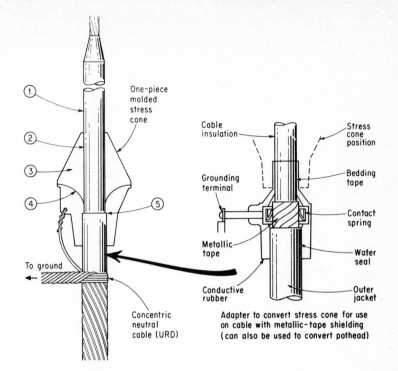

Fig. 710-9. Typical preformed stress cone is readily applied on cables up to 35-kV indoors. (Sec. 710-6.)

APPLICATION:
Cable shield is cut back about 12 in. Then, using silicone lubricant, the cable insulation surface and the inner bore of the stress cone are lubricated. The stress cone is simply pushed down over the cable end until it bottoms on the cable shield. After cable is prepared, termination takes about 30 seconds.

REFER TO DIAGRAM:
1. Cable insulation with shielding cut back
2. Tight fit between insulation and bore of stress cone
3. Insulating rubber
4. Stress relief provided by conductive rubber flaring away from insulation along bond between insulating rubber and conductive rubber
5. Conductive rubber of cone tightly fit to conductive cable shield

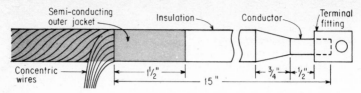

THIS IS CABLE PREPARED FOR PENNANT STRESS CONE

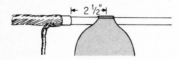

STEP 1—Wrap the cone build-up around
the insulation at a given place

STEP 2— Cone assembly with preshaped
wrap finished

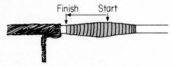

STEP 3—Semi-conducting tape contacts
semi-conducting cable jacket
and extends up to peak of cone

STEP 4—Entire stress-cone assembly
is then wrapped with insulating
tape

STEP 5— Insulate terminal fitting area at end of cable and (for outdoor use) cover entire
assembly with silicone tape or use potheads.

Fig. 710-10. "Pennant" method is one of a variety of job-site termination buildups. (Sec.
710-6.)

Metallic shielding tape must be grounded, as required by Sec. 710-6
and 300-5(b), which refers to "metallic shielding"—as in Fig. 710-11. The
shield on shielded cables must be grounded at one end at least. It is better
to ground the shield at two or more points. Grounding of the shield at
all terminals and splices will keep the entire length of the shield at about
ground potential for the safest, most effective operation of the cable.
Cable with improperly or ineffectively grounded shielding can present
more hazards than unshielded cable.

710-8. Moisture or Mechanical Protection for Metal-Sheathed Cables.   A
"pothead" is one specific form of stress-reduction means referred to in
Sec. 710-6 and has long been a common means of protecting insulation
against moisture or mechanical injury where conductors emerge from a
metal sheath (Fig. 710-12). Such protection for metal-sheathed cables
(such as lead-covered, paper-insulated cables) is required by this section.
A pothead is a cable terminal which provides sealing to the sheath of the

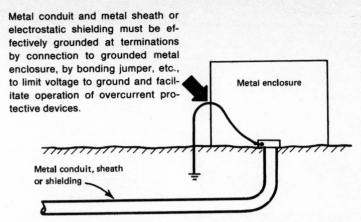

Metal conduit and metal sheath or electrostatic shielding must be effectively grounded at terminations by connection to grounded metal enclosure, by bonding jumper, etc., to limit voltage to ground and facilitate operation of overcurrent protective devices.

Metal enclosure

Metal conduit, sheath or shielding

Fig. 710-11. Metallic shielding must be grounded for all high-voltage conductors—under- or aboveground. (Sec. 710-6.)

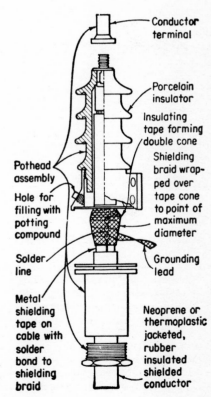

Conductor terminal

Porcelain insulator

Insulating tape forming double cone

Shielding braid wrapped over tape cone to point of maximum diameter

Grounding lead

Neoprene or thermoplastic jacketed, rubber insulated shielded conductor

Pothead assembly

Hole for filling with potting compound

Solder line

Metal shielding tape on cable with solder bond to shielding braid

Fig. 710-12. Typical single-conductor pothead protects metallic- or nonmetallic-jacketed cable. (Sec. 710-8.)

cable for making a moisture-proof connection between the wires within the cable and those outside.

When metal-jacketed high-voltage cables are terminated outdoors exposed to the weather, a pothead is commonly used to protect the insulation of conductors against moisture or mechanical injury where conductors emerge from a metal sheath, as shown in Fig. 710-13.

Fig. 710-13. A pothead is used on the end of each paper-insulated, lead-covered cable to protect against entry of moisture, with a wiped lead joint at the terminal. (Sec. 710-8.)

On use of potheads:
1. Paper-insulated cables must be terminated in potheads. This requirement also extends to such cables operated at under 600 V.
2. Varnished-cambric-insulated cables should be terminated in potheads but may be terminated with taped connections in dry locations.
3. Rubber-insulated cables are commonly terminated in potheads in locations where moisture protection is critical but may be terminated without potheads in accordance with manufacturer's instructions.
4. Although many modern high-voltage cables can be terminated without potheads, many engineers consider potheads the best terminations for high-voltage cable.

5. The use of potheads offers a number of advantages:
   a. Seals cable ends against moisture that would damage the insulation.
   b. Provides a compartment for surrounding the termination with insulating compound to increase strength of electrical insulation.
   c. Seals cable ends against loss of insulating oils.
   d. Provides engineered support of connections.

710-20. Overcurrent Protection. Figure 710-14 shows the basic rule for high-voltage circuit protection. Refer to Sec. 230-208 for high-voltage service conductors, to Sec. 240-100 on feeders, and Sec. 240-101 on branch circuits. The specified ratings of protection for high-voltage conductors are presented in those sections.

OVERCURRENT DEVICE FOR EACH UNGROUNDED CONDUCTOR . . .

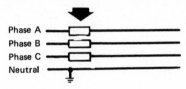

. . . must be either . . .

a **CIRCUIT BREAKER** with three overcurrent relays operated from three current transformers [see Exceptions in Section 710-20(a)]

OR

a FUSE connected in series with each ungrounded conductor.

Fig. 710-14. Basic rule calls for overcurrent protection. (Sec. 710-20.)

710-21. Circuit-Interrupting Devices. High-voltage power CBs provide load switching, short-circuit protection, electrical operation, adjustable time delays of trip characteristics for selectively coordinated protection schemes, quick reclosing after tripping, and various protective hookups such as differential relay protection of transformers. There are oil-type, oil-less (or air-magnetic), and vacuum-break CBs. The air-magnetic CB is the common type for indoor applications in systems up to 15 kV and higher. Oil CBs are sometimes used for indoor and outdoor high-voltage service equipment where they provide economical disconnect and protection on the primary of a transformer.

Modern high-voltage CB equipment meets all the needs of control and protection for electrical systems from the simplest to the most complex and sophisticated. In particular, its use for selectively coordinated protection of services, feeders, and branch circuits is unique. In current ratings up to 3,000 A, CB gear has the very high interrupting ratings required for today's high-capacity systems. Available in "metal-clad" assemblies, all live parts are completely enclosed within grounded metal enclosures for maximum safety. For applications exposed to lightning strikes or other transient overcurrents, CB equipment offers quick reclosing after operation. Drawout construction of the CB units provides ease of maintenance and ready testing of breakers. CB gear offers unlimited arrangements of source and load circuits and is suited to a variety of AC or DC control power sources. Accessory devices are available for special functions.

Figure 710-15 covers the basic rules of this section on use of CBs.

A. Indoor installations of circuit breakers must consist of metal-enclosed units or fire-resistant, cell-mounted units, except that open-mounted CBs may be used in places accessible to qualified persons only.

B. All CBs must be rated for short-circuit duty at point of application.

C. Circuit breakers controlling oil-filled transformers *must* either be located outside the transformer vault *or* be capable of being operated from outside the vault.

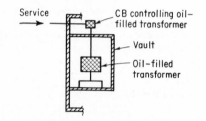

D. Oil CBs must be arranged or located so that adjacent readily combustible structures or materials are safeguarded in an approved manner. Adequate space separation, fire-resistant barriers or enclosures, trenches containing sufficient coarse crushed stone, and properly drained oil enclosures such as dikes or basins are recognized as suitable safeguards.

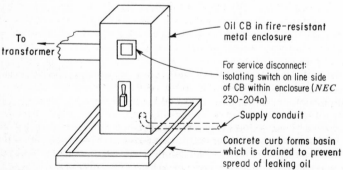

Fig. 710-15. Detailed rules regulate use of high-voltage circuit breakers. (Sec. 710-21.)

Fig. 710-16. Oil circuit breaker for high-voltage application has a disconnecting switch on its supply side to isolate the line terminals of the breaker. (Sec. 710-21.)

Figure 710-16 shows an oil CB, with the line-side isolating switch required by Sec. 230-204(a).

Part **(b)** covers power fuses, which are available in current-limiting and noncurrent-limiting types. (See Fig. 710-17 for an example of the uses to which power fuses may be put.) The current-limiting types offer reduction of thermal and magnetic stresses on fault by reducing the energy let-through. They are constructed with a silver-sand internal element, similar to 600-V current-limiting fuses. Such fuses generally have higher interrupting ratings at some voltages, but their continuous current-carrying ratings are limited.

Noncurrent-limiting types of power fuses are made in two types of operating characteristics: expulsion type and nonexpulsion type. The expulsion fuse gets its name from the fact that it expels hot gases when it operates. Such fuses should not be used indoors without a "snuffer" or other protector to contain the exhaust, because there is a hazard presented by the expelled gases. Part **(b)(5)** of this section requires that fuses

Fig. 710-17. Typical power fuses are used in load-interrupter switchgear, which is an alternative to circuit-breaker gear for control and protection in indoor high-voltage systems. (Sec. 710-21.)

expelling flame in operation must be designed or arranged to prevent hazard to persons or property. The boric-acid fuse with a condenser or other protection against arcing and gas expulsion is a typical nonexpulsion, noncurrent-limiting fuse (Fig. 710-18).

Parts **(b)(6)** and **(b)(7)** cover very important safeguards for the use of fuses and fuseholders:

In coordinating power fuses, care must be taken to account for ambient temperature adjustment factors, because time-current curves are based on an ambient of 25°C. Adjustment also must be made for preheating of fuses due to load current to assure effective coordination of fuses with each other and/or with CBs. Manufacturer's curves of adjustment factors for ambient temperature and fuse preloading are available.

Figure 710-19 shows the time-current characteristic for an R-rated, current-limiting (silver-sand) fuse designed for 2,400-V and 4,800-V motor applications. Such fuses must be selected to coordinate with the motor controller overload protection, with the controller clearing overloads up to 10 times motor current and the fuse taking over for faster

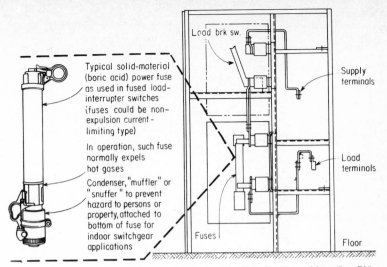

Fig. 710-18. Boric-acid fuse uses a device to protect against flame expulsion. (Sec. 710-21.)

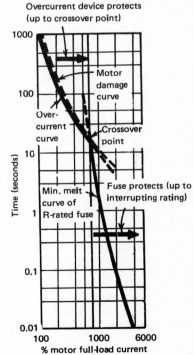

Fig. 710-19. "R-rated" fuses are used in motor starters for 2400- and 4800-V motors. (Sec. 710-21.)

opening of higher currents up to the interrupting rating of the fuse. The amp rating of R-rated fuses is given in values such as 2R or 12R or 24R. If the number preceding the "R" is multiplied by 100, the value obtained is the ampere level at which the fuse will blow in 20 sec. Thus, the rating designation is *not* continuous current but is based on the operating characteristics of the R-rated fuse. Continuous current rating of such fuses is given by the manufacturer at some value of ambient temperature.

Fused cutouts for high-voltage circuits, as shown in Fig. 710-20, are available for both indoor and outdoor application, as regulated by part **(c)** of this section. Pull-type fuse cutouts are used outdoors on pole-line

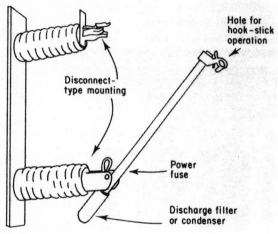

Fig. 710-20. Expanded rules cover use of distribution cutouts. (Sec. 710-21.)

crossarms or indoors in electric rooms where accessible only to qualified persons, as shown in Fig. 710-21. Such fused cutouts are acceptable for use as an isolating switch, as permitted by Sec. 710-23.

Part **(d)** of this section covers oil-filled cutouts. In addition to air CBs, oil CBs, and fused load-interrupter switches, another device frequently used for control of high-voltage circuits is the oil-filled cutout. Compared to breakers and fused switchgear, oil-filled cutouts are inexpensive devices that provide economical switching and, where desired, overload and short-circuit protection for primary voltage circuits.

The oil-filled cutout is a completely enclosed, single-pole assembly with a fusible or nonfusible element immersed in the oil-filled tank that makes up the major part of the unit, and with two terminals on the outside of the housing. Figure 710-22 shows the basic construction of a typical cutout with a listing of available entrance fittings for the terminals to suit them to various cable and job requirements. The circuit is broken or

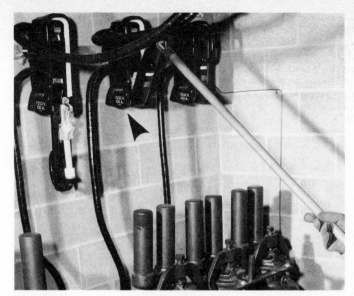

Fig. 710-21. Distribution cutouts are single-pole, fused protective, and disconnect devices that are hook-stock operable. Note voltage and current rating on case of each cutout (arrow), as required by part **(c)(5)** of Sec. 710-21. (Sec. 710-21.)

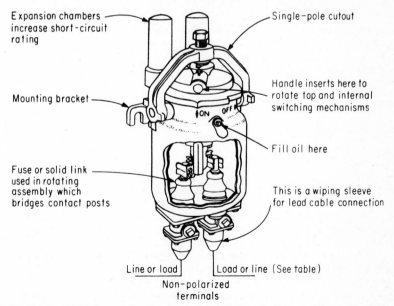

Expansion chambers increase short-circuit rating

Single-pole cutout

Mounting bracket

Handle inserts here to rotate top and internal switching mechanisms

Fill oil here

Fuse or solid link used in rotating assembly which bridges contact posts

This is a wiping sleeve for lead cable connection

Line or load

Load or line (See table)

Non-polarized terminals

Fig. 710-22. Oil-filled cutout is a fused or unfused, single-pole disconnect device. (Sec. 710-21.)

closed safely and rapidly by the internal switching mechanism. The switch mechanism is made up of a rotating element that, in the closed position, bridges two internal contacts—each contact connecting to one of the outside terminals. The rotating element is completely insulated from the external case and from the external handle that operates the element. The rotating element may be simply a shorting blade when the cutout is used as an unfused switch. When the cutout is to be used as a fused switching unit, the rotating bridging element is fitted with a fuse. Operation of an oil-filled cutout is controlled at the top end of the shaft extending out through the top of the housing.

As a single-pole switching device, the oil-filled cutout is not polarized— i.e., either terminal may be a line or load terminal. This is a result of the symmetrical construction of the switching element and suits the device to use in circuit sectionalizing or as a tie device in layouts involving two or more primary supply circuits. Note that these Code rules on oil-filled cutouts are different from those in part (c) on distribution cutouts.

With an oil-filled cutout, the switching of load current or the breaking of fault current is confined within a sturdy metal housing. Operation is made safe and quiet by confining arcs and current rupture forces within the enclosure. This operating characteristic of the cutouts especially suits them to use where there are explosive gases or flammable dusts, where complete submersion is possible, where severe atmospheric conditions exist, or where exposure of live electrical parts might be hazardous.

Oil-filled (sometimes called "oil-fuse") cutouts are made in three sizes based on continuous current—100, 200, and 300 A, up to 15 kV. In one line there are three basic types. *Pole-type cutouts* are equipped with rub-ber-covered leads from the terminals for use in open wiring. Pothead-type cutouts have a cable lead from one terminal for open wiring and a sleeve on the other for connecting a lead or rubber-covered cable from an underground circuit. *Subway-type cutouts* are for underground vaults and manholes, particularly where submersion might occur, and are equipped with a sleeve on each terminal for rubber- or lead-sheathed cable. Figure 710-23 lists the various types of terminal connections that are available on oil-filled cutouts.

For multiphase circuits, two or three single-phase cutout units can be group-mounted with a gang-operating mechanism for simultaneous operation. Figure 710-24 shows 3-gang assemblies. For pole mounting, linkage and long handle are available for operating cutouts from the ground. Or cutouts can be flange-mounted on a terminal box, as shown in Fig. 710-25, where the 3-gang assembly was added to a high-voltage switchgear on a modernization job.

Because oil-filled cutouts provide load-break capability and overcur-rent protection, they may be used for industrial and commercial service equipment, for switching outdoor lighting of sports fields and shopping centers, for transformer load centers, for primary-voltage motor circuits, or for use in vaults and manholes of underground systems.

Application	Cable cover	No. of conduits	Entrance type	Method of sealing
Indoor	Rubber or neoprene	Single	Porcelain	Tape Always tape this connection!
		Multiple	Stud bushing	
Indoor or outdoor	Rubber, lead or neoprene	Single	Stuffing box	Compression fittings
	Polyethylene	Single		Compression fittings and tube seal
	Lead	Single	Wiping sleeve	Solder wipe

Fig. 710-23. Terminals on oil-filled cutouts must be matched to application and cable type. (Sec. 710-21.)

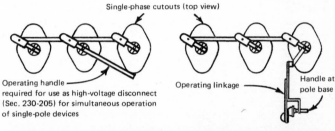

Single-phase cutouts (top view)

Operating handle required for use as high-voltage disconnect (Sec. 230-205) for simultaneous operation of single-pole devices

Operating linkage

Handle at pole base

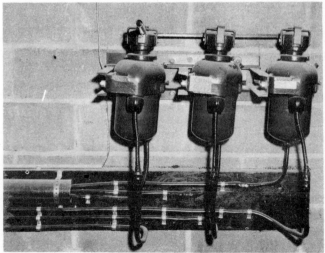

Fig. 710-24. Oil-filled cutouts can be assembled as a 3-pole device for 3-phase circuits. (Sec. 710-21.)

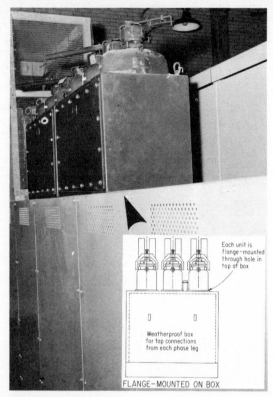

Fig. 710-25. Gang-operated 3-pole assembly of oil-filled cutouts provided addition of a new high-voltage circuit on a modernization project, but location of the units was questioned because part **(d)(7)** imposes a 5-ft maximum mounting height. (Sec. 710-21.)

In 100- and 200-A ratings, oil-filled cutouts are available in combination with current-limiting power fuses in double-compartment indoor or outdoor enclosures. These fused oil interrupter switches provide moderate load-break and high fault-current interrupting capability in an economical package.

Part **(e)** of this section is a very general recognition of use of so-called "load-interrupter" switches used in high-voltage systems. Switching for modern high-voltage electrical systems can be provided by a number of different equipment installations. For any particular case, the best arrangement depends on several factors: the point of application—either for outside or inside distribution or as service equipment; the voltage;

the type of distribution system—radial, loop, selective, network; conditions—accessibility, type of actual layout of the equipment; job atmosphere; use; future system expansion; and economic considerations.

Types of switches used in high-voltage applications include:

1. Enclosed air-break load-interrupter switchgear with or without power fuses
2. Oil-filled cutouts (fused or unfused)
3. Oil-immersed-type disconnect switches

Modern load-interrupter switchgear in metal safety enclosures finds wide application in high-voltage distribution systems, in combination with

Fig. 710-26. Load-interrupter switchgear is generally used with fuses to provide protection as well as load-break switching for high-voltage circuits. The fuses must be rated to provide complete protection for the load interrupter on closing, carrying, or interrupting current—up to the assigned maximum short-circuit rating. (Sec. 710-21.)

modern power fuses (Fig. 710-26). Section 230-208 of the NE Code covers use of air load-interrupter switches, with fuses, for disconnect and overcurrent protection of high-voltage service-entrance conductors. Part **(e)** of Sec. 710-21 covers use of fused air load-interrupter switches for high-voltage feeder in distribution systems.

Metal-enclosed fused load interrupters offer a fully effective alternative to use of power CBs, with substantial economies, in 5- and 15-kV distribution systems for commercial, institutional, and industrial buildings. Typical applications for such switchgear parallel those of power CBs and include the following:

1. *In switching centers*—Switchgear is set up for control and protection of individual primary feeders to transformer loadcenters.

2. *In substation primaries*—Load-interrupter switchgear is used for transformer switching and protection in the primary sides of substations.

3. *In substation secondaries*—Here the switchgear is used as a switching center closely coupled to a high-voltage transformer secondary.

4. *In service entrances*—This is a single-unit application of a switchgear bay for service-entrance disconnect and protection in a primary supply line.

Fused load-interrupter switchgear, typically rated up to 1,200 A, can match the ratings and required performance capabilities of power CBs for a large percentage of applications in which either might be used.

Fuse-interrupter switches for high-voltage circuits are available with manual or power operation—including types with spring-powered, over-center mechanisms for manual operation or motor-driven, stored-energy operators. Available in indoor and outdoor housings, assemblies can be equipped with a variety of accessory devices, including key-interlocks for coordinating switch operation with remote devices such as transformer secondary breakers.

Vacuum switchgear, with their contacts operating in a vacuum "bottle" that is enclosed in a compact cylindrical assembly, has gained wide acceptance as load interrupters for high-voltage switching and sectionalizing. Available in 200-A and 600-A ratings for use at 15.5, 27, and 38 kV, this switching equipment is suited to full-load interruption and is rated for 15,000-A or 20,000-A short-circuit current under momentary and make and latch operations. BIL ratings are 95, 125, or 150 kV.

Vacuum switch assemblies, with a variety of accessories, including stored-energy operators and electric motor operator for remote control, are suited to all indoor and outdoor switching operations—including submersible operation for underground systems. The units offer fireproof and explosionproof operation, with virtually maintenance-free life for its rated 5,000 load interruptions. Units are available in standard 2-way, 3-way, and 4-way configurations, along with automatic transfer options. Accessory CTs and relays can be used with stored-energy operators to apply vacuum switches for fault-interrupting duty.

710-22. Isolating Means.   Air-break or oil-immersed switches of any type may be used to provide the isolating functions described in this section. Distribution cutouts or oil-filled cutouts are also used as isolating switches.

Oil-immersed disconnect switches are used for load control and for sectionalizing of primary-voltage underground-distribution systems for large commercial and industrial layouts (Fig. 710-27). Designed for high-power handling—such as 400 A up to 34 kV—this type of switch can be located at transformer loadcenter primaries or at other strategic points

Fig. 710-27. Oil switches are commonly used for isolating equipment and circuits for sectionalizing and for transfer from preferred to emergency supply. (Sec. 710-27.)

in high-voltage circuits to provide a wide variety of sectionalizing arrangements to provide alternate feeds for essential load circuits.

Oil-immersed disconnect switches are available for as many as five switch positions and ground positions to ground the feeder or test-ground positions for grounding or testing. Ground positions are used in such switches to connect circuits to ground while they are being worked on to assure safety to personnel.

Oil switches for load-break applications up to 15 kV are available for either manual or electrically powered switching for all types of circuits. When electrical operation is used, the switch functions as a high-voltage magnetic contactor.

Switches intended only for isolating duty must be interlocked with other devices to prevent opening of the isolating switch under load, or the isolating switch must be provided with an obvious sign warning against opening the switch under load.

710-24. Metal-Enclosed Power Switchgear and Industrial Control Assemblies.   Where the previous sections presented regulations on the individual switching and protective devices, this section covers enclosure and interconnection of such unit devices into overall assemblies. Basically, the rules of this section are aimed at the manufacturers and assemblers of such equipment.

Use of all high-voltage switching and control equipment must be carefully checked against information given with certification of the equipment by a test laboratory—such as data given by UL in their Green Book. Typical data are as follows:

Unit substations listed by UL have the secondary neutral bonded to the enclosure and have provision on the neutral for connection of a grounding conductor. A terminal is also provided on the enclosure near the line terminals for use with an equipment grounding conductor run from the enclosure of primary equipment feeding the unit sub to the enclosure of the unit sub. Connection of such an equipment grounding conductor provides proper bonding together of equipment enclosures where the primary feed to the unit sub is direct-buried underground or is run in nonmetallic conduit without a metal conduit connection in the primary feed (Fig. 710-28.).

The rule of part **(o)** is particularly aimed at the designers and installers of equipment, rather than at the manufacturer. Part **(o)(2)** emphasizes

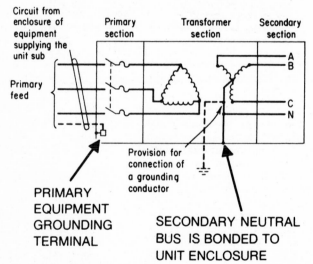

Fig. 710-28. NEC rules on equipment construction are supported by UL data. (Sec. 710–24.)

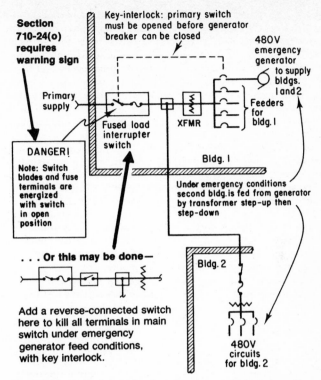

Fig. 710-29. Feedback in high-voltage hookups can be hazardous. (Sec. 710-24.)

that careful layout and application of switching components of all types is important. Figure 710-29 shows the kind of condition that can be extremely hazardous in high-voltage layouts where there is the chance of a secondary to primary feedback—such as the intentional one shown to provide emergency power to essential circuits in Building 2. Under emergency conditions, the main fused interrupter is opened and the secondary CB for the generator is closed, feeding power to the 480-V switchboard in Building 1 and then feeding through two transformers to supply power to the 480-V circuits in Building 2. This hookup makes the load side of the main interrupter switch alive, presenting the hazard of electrocution to any personnel who might go into the switch thinking that it is dead because it is open. A second switch can eliminate this difficulty, if applied with interlocks.

ARTICLE 720. CIRCUITS AND EQUIPMENT OPERATING AT LESS THAN 50 VOLTS

720-1. Scope. This article covers low-voltage applications that are not power-limited circuits as defined in Sec. 725-3 and are not remote-control or signal circuits. Determination that Art. 720 applies to any circuit or equipment must be carefully made on the basis of the particular load being supplied and circuit conditions. This article covers circuits operating at more than 30 Volts but not over 50 V—such as 32-V circuiting.

720-4. Conductors. The minimum No. 12 conductor size, rather than No. 14 as permitted for standard power and light wiring, is aimed at the higher current required for a given wattage load at low voltage. For instance, at 32 V, the current corresponding to a given wattage is 3.6 times the current for the same wattage at 115 V. It should also be noted that for a given load in watts and a given size of wire and circuit length, the voltage drop in percentage is about 13 times as great at 32 V as at 115 V.

720-5. Lampholders. Where medium-base sockets are used, there is no good reason for using any but those having a 660-W rating. The ampere ratings of candelabra and intermediate base sockets would permit the use of 25-W lamps at 32 V, but it is not considered safe to allow the installation of these low-wattage sockets on circuits operating at 50 V or less.

Fixtures, regardless of supply voltage, would need to meet the requirements given in Art. 410. If for outdoor use, they would need to comply with Sec. 410-4.

720-10. Grounding. If any circuit connected to the system is carried overhead from one building to another, a system ground must be installed. The grounding conductor should be connected to one of the buses at the switchboard or generator and battery control panel. The requirements of Art. 250 should be followed in general. If water piping connected to a fairly extensive system of street mains is not available, a local water-piping system may be used as the grounding electrode; but unless the piping system is carried for some distance at a depth where it will always be in moist earth, supplementary driven rod or pipe electrodes should also be employed. Refer to Sec. 250-81.

ARTICLE 725. CLASS 1, CLASS 2, AND CLASS 3 REMOTE-CONTROL, SIGNALING, AND POWER-LIMITED CIRCUITS

725-1. Scope. Article 725 of the Code covers power-limited circuits and remote-control and signal circuits. A signal circuit is defined as any electrical circuit which supplies energy to an appliance or device that gives a visual and/or audible signal. Such circuits include those for doorbells, buzzers, code-calling systems, signal lights, annunciators, fire or smoke detection, fire or burglar alarm, and other detection indication or alarm devices.

A "remote-control" circuit is any circuit which has as its load device the operating coil of a magnetic motor starter, a magnetic contactor, or a relay. Strictly speaking, it is a circuit which exercises control over one or more other circuits. And these other circuits controlled by the control circuit may themselves be control circuits or they may be "load" circuits—carrying utilization current to a lighting, heating, power, or signal device. Figure 725-1 clarifies the distinction between control circuits and load circuits.

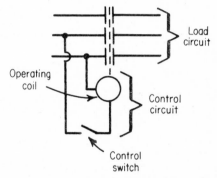

Fig. 725-1. A control circuit governs the operating coil or some other element, to switch the load circuit. (Sec. 725-1.)

The elements of a control circuit include all the equipment and devices concerned with the function of the circuit: conductors, raceway, contactor operating coil, source of energy supply to the circuit, overcurrent protective devices, and all switching devices which govern energization of the operating coil. Typical control circuits include the operating-coil circuit of magnetic motor starters (**NEC** Secs. 430-71 and 430-72), magnetic contactors (as used for switching lighting, heating, and power loads), and relays. Control circuits include wiring between solid-state control devices as well as between magnetically actuated components. Low-voltage relay switching of lighting and power loads is also classified as remote-control wiring (Fig. 725-2).

Power-limited circuits are circuits used for functions other than signaling or remote-control—but in which the source of the energy supply is limited in its power (volts times amps) to specified maximum levels. Low-

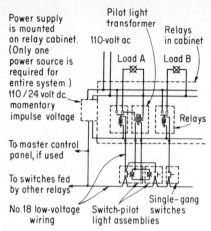

Power supply is mounted on relay cabinet. (Only one power source is required for entire system.) 110 / 24 volt dc. momentary impulse voltage

Pilot light transformer
110-volt ac

Relays in cabinet

Load A   Load B

Relays

To master control panel, if used

To switches fed by other relays

No.18 low-voltage wiring

Switch-pilot light assemblies

Single-gang switches

Fig. 725-2. Low-voltage switching involves typical "remote-control circuits." (Sec. 725-1.)

voltage lighting, using 12-V lamps in fixtures fed from 120/12-V transformers, is a typical "power-limited circuit" application.

725-2. Locations and Other Articles. All the applications under this article must observe the specified sections that also rule on use of general power and light wiring.

Part **(a)** prohibits any installation of remote-control, signaling, or power-limited wiring in such a way that there is an appreciable reduction in the fire rating of floors, walls, or ceilings.

Part **(b)** requires that circuits covered by this article must be run in metal raceway or metal cable assembly when used in an air handling ceiling—as required by Sec. 300-22. The Exception permits Class 2 and/or Class 3 circuits (as defined in Sec. 725-3) to be used without metal raceway or metal cable cover in ducts, plenums, or ceiling spaces used for environmental air PROVIDED THAT THE CONDUCTORS ARE "LISTED" AS "FIRE-RESISTANT AND LOW-SMOKE PRODUCING." Because of the definition of the word "listed" (see Art. 100, "Definitions"), this rule would require that any such nonmetallic assembly of conductors for those circuits must be specifically listed in the UL's *Electrical Construction Materials Directory* (or with similar third-party certification) as having the specified characteristics for use without metal raceway or covering in ducts, plenums, and air handling ceilings.

Note: For any such application, check that the conductors of the circuit are definitely listed by UL or others.

725-3. Classifications. The provisions of this section divide all signaling and remote-control systems into three classes.

Class 1 includes all signaling and remote-control systems which do not have the special current limitations of Class 2 and Class 3 systems.

Class 2 and Class 3 systems are those systems in which the current is limited to certain specified low values by fuses or CBs, and by supply through transformers which will deliver only very small currents on short circuit, or by other means which are considered satisfactory. The current values depend upon the voltage at which the system operates and range from 5 mA up, as shown in Table 725-31. All Class 2 and Class 3 circuits must have a power source with the power-limiting characteristics assigned in the tables in addition to the overcurrent device.

725-4. Safety Control Equipment.   The application of this rule is illustrated by Fig. 725-3, which is a simplified diagram of a common type of automatic control for a domestic oil burner. Assuming a steam boiler, the safety control is a switch that opens automatically when the steam pressure reaches a predetermined value and, preferably, also opens if the water level is allowed to fall too low. The master control includes a transformer of the current-limiting type which supplies the thermostat circuit at a voltage of 24 V. When the thermostat contacts close, a relay closes the circuits to the motor and to the ignition transformer.

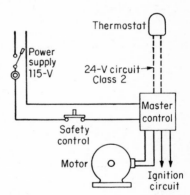

Fig.   725-3. Remote-control   circuit *must* be Class 1 if failure would create a hazard. (Sec. 725-4.)

Failure of the safety control or ignition to operate would introduce a direct hazard; hence, the circuits to this equipment are Class 1. The thermostat circuit fulfills all requirements of a Class 2 circuit and can be short-circuited or broken without introducing any hazard. The wiring of this circuit can therefore be done with any type of wire or cable that is sufficiently protected from physical damage to ensure serviceability.

725-11. Power Limitation for Class 1 Circuits.   Class 1 systems may operate at any voltage not exceeding 600 V. They are, in many cases, merely extensions of light and power systems, and, with a few exceptions, are subject to all the installation rules for light and power systems.

Part **(a)** requires that Class 1 power-limited circuits must have energy limitation on the power source that supplies them. And such circuits may be supplied from either a transformer or another type of power supply— such as a generator, batteries, or manufactured power supply. Note that a Class 1 power-limited circuit must be supplied at NOT OVER 30 V, 1,000 VA.

Part **(b)**, however, permits Class 1 remote-control or signaling circuits to operate at up to 600 V, and no limitation is placed on the power rating of the source to such circuits (Fig. 725-4).

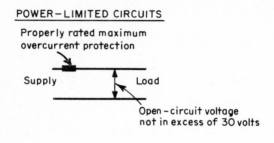

POWER–LIMITED CIRCUITS

Properly rated maximum
overcurrent protection

Supply   Load

Open–circuit voltage
not in excess of 30 volts

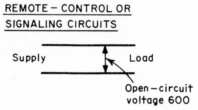

REMOTE– CONTROL OR
SIGNALING CIRCUITS

Supply   Load

Open–circuit
voltage 600

Fig. 725-4. Class 1 circuits are divided into two maximum voltages. (Sec. 725-11.)

The most common example of a Class 1 remote-control system is the circuit wiring and devices used for the operation of a magnetically operated motor controller. The term *remote-control switch* is used in various **Code** references to designate a switch or contactor used for the remote control of a feeder or branch circuit, with the operating-coil circuit as a Class 1 remote-control circuit.

The signaling systems which are included in Class 1 operate at 115 V with 20-A overcurrent protection, though they are not necessarily limited to this voltage and current. Some of the signaling systems which may be so operated include electric clocks, bank alarm systems, and factory call systems. An example of a lower voltage Class 1 signaling system is a nurses' call system, as used in hospitals. Such systems commonly operate at not over 25 V.

The vast majority of control circuits for magnetic starters and contactors could not qualify as Class 2 or Class 3 circuits because of the relatively high energy required for operating coils. And any control circuit rated over 150 V (such as 220- or 440-V coil circuits) can never qualify, regardless of energy.

Class 1 control circuits include all operating-coil circuits for magnetic starters or contactors which do not meet the requirements for Class 2 or Class 3 circuits (Fig. 725-5). Class 1 circuits must be wired in accordance with Secs. 725-11 to 725-20.

Fig. 725-5. Control wiring for automatic transfer switches, motor starters, and magnetic contactors are Class 1 remote-control circuits. (Sec. 725-11.)

725-12. Overcurrent Protection.   Part **(a)** sets the basic rule. In general, conductors for any Class 1 remote-control, signaling, or power-limited circuit must be protected against overcurrent. No. 12 and larger wires must generally be protected at their ampacities from Table 310-16. But No. 18, No. 16, or No. 14 wire is considered adequately protected by either 15-A or 20-A protection. Section 240-3 Exception No. 4 states that remote-control conductors other than those for motor-control circuits can be satisfactorily protected by overcurrent devices which are rated at not more than 300 percent of the carrying capacity of the control-circuit conductors. That applies to control wires for magnetic contactors used for control of lighting or heating loads, but not motor loads. Section 430-72 covers this requirement for motor-control circuits.

In Fig. 725-6, covering use of a magnetic contactor, the remote-control conductors may be properly protected by the feeder or branch-circuit overcurrent devices if the devices are rated or set at not more than 300 percent of (three times) the current rating of the control conductors. If the branch-circuit overcurrent devices were rated or set at more than 300 percent of the rating of the control conductors, the control conductors

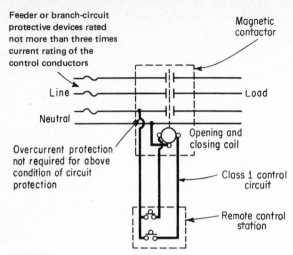

Feeder or branch-circuit
protective devices rated
not more than three times
current rating of the
control conductors

Magnetic
contactor

Line

Load

Neutral

Overcurrent protection
not required for above
condition of circuit
protection

Opening and
closing coil

Class 1 control
circuit

Remote control
station

Fig. 725-6. Protection of coil circuit of a magnetic contactor is similar to that of a starter. (Sec. 725-12.)

would have to be protected by separate protective devices located within the contactor enclosure at the point where the conductor to be protected receives its supply. It should be noted that the overcurrent protection is required for the control conductors and not for the operating coil. Because of this, the size of control conductors can be selected to allow application without separate overcurrent protection. When overcurrent protection is added in the enclosure, its rating must be such that it conforms to parts **(a)** and **(b)** of this rule.

As indicated in Fig. 725-6, protection of contactor remote-control conductors must follow either Sec. 725-13 or Sec. 240-3, Exception No. 4. As shown, separate protection of the control conductors is not required under the given conditions. If the stated requirements were not satisfied, a fuse or CB would have to be inserted in the control-circuit tap from the operating coil to the hot-line conductor. And if the control circuit were energized from two hot conductors, some inspectors would require that both taps be protected. Of course, the control circuit could have been derived from a separate source instead of the line side of the remote-control switch.

725-14. Wiring Method   In general, wiring of Class 1 signal systems must be the same as power and light wiring, using any of the cable or raceway wiring methods that are Code-recognized for general-purpose wiring. The two exceptions refer to the details of wiring permitted by Secs. 725-15, 725-16, and 725-17.

725-15. Conductors of Different Circuits in Same Enclosure, Cable, or Raceway.   Any number and any type of Class 1 circuit conductors—for remote-control, for signaling, and/or for power-limited circuits—may be installed in the same conduit, raceway, box, or other enclosure—*if* all conductors are insulated for the maximum voltage at which any of the conductors operates.

Class 1 circuit wires (starter coil-circuit wires, signal wires, power-limited circuits) may be run in raceways by themselves in accordance with the first sentence of this section. A given conduit, for instance, may carry one or several sets of Class 1 circuit wires. And Sec. 725-14 says use of Class 1 wires must conform to the same basic rules from **NE Code** Chap. 3 that apply to standard power and light wiring.

But, it should be noted that two specific sections of the **NE Code** cover the use of Class 1 circuit conductors in the same raceway, cable, or enclosure containing circuit wires carrying power to a lighting load, a heating load, or to a motor load (Fig. 725-7). Section 300-3 covers the general use of "conductors of different systems" in raceways as well as in cable assemblies and in equipment wiring enclosures (i.e., cabinets, housings, starter enclosures, junction boxes, etc.). But Class 1 circuit wires are also regulated by this section, which strictly limits use of Class 1 wires in the same box and/or raceway with power wires. Figure 725-8 shows a clear violation, if the annunciator has no relationship to the motor load.

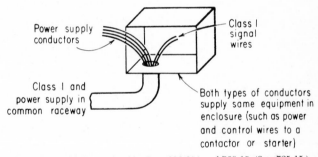

Fig. 725-7. This is permitted by Secs. 300-3(a) and 725-15. (Sec. 725-15.)

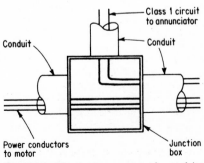

Fig. 725-8. Class 1 wires must *not* be used in raceways with "unrelated" wires. (Sec. 725-15.)

Note that this section permits Class 1 circuit wires to be installed in the same raceway or enclosure as "power supply" conductors *only* if the Class 1 wires and the power wires are "functionally associated" with each other. That would be the case where the power conductors to a motor are run in the same conduit along with the Class 1 circuit wires of the magnetic motor starter used to control or to start or stop the motor. Refer to the commentary in Sec. 300-3.

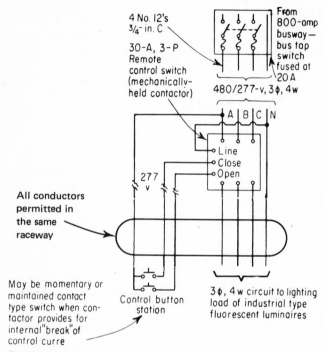

Fig. 725-9. Class 1 wires and power wires may be used in same raceway for "functionally associated" equipment. (Sec. 725-15.)

The same permission would apply to the hookup of a magnetic contactor controlling a lighting or heating load, as shown in Fig. 725-9. There, the circuit wires for the Class 1 remote-control run to the pushbutton station may be run in the same conduit carrying the wires supplying the lighting fixtures. A typical application would have the magnetic contactor adjacent to a panelboard, with the control and power wires run in the same raceway to a box at some point where it is convenient to bring the control wires down to the control switch and carry the power wires to the lighting fixtures being controlled. The contactor can be located at the approximate center of its lighting load to keep circuit wiring as short as possible for minimum voltage drop and the control wires are then carried to one or more control points. In such a layout, the control wires and power wires are definitely "functionally associated" because the control wires provide the ON-OFF function for the lighting. BUT, other control or power wires are prohibited from being in the same conduit, boxes, or enclosures with the single set of associated Class 1 and power wires.

725-16. Conductors.   Figure 725-10 shows this basic rule, which accepts use of building wire to a minimum No. 14 size. BUT, No. 16 or No. 18 fixture wires of the types specified in part **(b)** *may* be used for running starter coil circuits, signal circuits, and any other Class 1 circuits. Of course, use of No. 16 or No. 18 fixture wire for Class 1 circuits depends

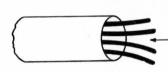

Conductors generally limited to minimum of No. 14 size, but No. 18 or No. 16 may be used if installed in raceway or approved cable or flexible cord and protected at not more than 20 amps

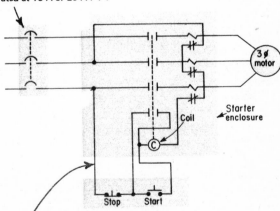

EXAMPLE :

If branch-circuit protection is rated at 15 A or 20 A . . .

. . . the Class 1 remote-control wires may be No. 18 or No. 16 fixture wire or No. 14 building wire, depending upon the ampere load of the starter coil.

Fig. 725-10. No. 16 or No. 18 fixture wire may be used for Class 1 circuits. (Sec. 725-16.)

upon such conductors having sufficient ampacity for the current drawn by the contactor or relay operating coil or by whatever control device is involved. Wires larger than No. 16 must be building types (TW, THW, THHN, etc.). Class 1 circuits may not use fixture wires larger than No. 16. And ampacity of any Class 1 circuit wires larger than No. 16 must have that value shown in Table 310-16.

Note: Section 402-5 shows that the ampacity of any No. 18 fixture wire is 6 A and the ampacity of any No. 16 fixture wire is 8 A. Any No. 18 or No. 16 fixture wire or No. 14 building wire used for a Class 1 circuit is considered adequately protected by a fuse or CB rated not over 20 A. See Secs. 725-12 and 240-4.

725-17. Number of Conductors in Raceways, Cable Trays, and Cables, and Derating.   The number of Class 1 remote-control, signal, and/or power-limited circuit conductors in a conduit must be determined from Tables 1 through 5 in Chap. 9 of the **NE Code**. There is a definite **Code** limit on the number of Class 1 wires permitted in a raceway and if these wires carry continuous loads, the derating factors of Note 8 to Tables 310-16 through 310-19 must be applied to their current ratings. If the load is noncontinuous, no derating is required for more than three wires in a raceway. When more than three wires are installed in a raceway, the derating factors of Note 8 must be applied *only* if the conductors carry continuous loads (i.e., carry their load current continuously for 3 hr or more).

When power conductors and Class 1 circuit conductors are used in a single conduit or EMT run (as permitted by Sec. 725-15), the derating factors of Note 8 must be applied as follows:

1. Note 8 must be applied to all conductors in the conduit when the remote-control conductors carry continuous loads and the total number of conductors (remote-control and power wires) is more than three. For example, in Fig. 725-11, the conduit size must be selected according to the number and sizes of the wires. Because two of the control wires to the pushbutton and the power wires to

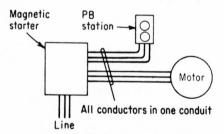

Fig. 725-11. Derating of conductor ampacity is required for this circuit makeup. (Sec. 725-17.)

the motor will carry a continuous load, a derating factor of 80 percent (from Note 8) must be applied to all the wires in the conduit.

2. Note 8 must be applied only to the power wires when the remote-control wires do not carry continuous load and when the number of power wires is more than three. In Fig. 725-12, no derating at all is applied because the control wires do not carry continuous current (only for the instant of switching operation), and there are only three power wires.

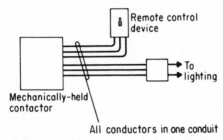

Fig. 725-12. Derating is not required here if Class 1 conductors do not carry continuous load. (Sec. 725-17.)

Those rules of part **(b)** have created controversy. It usually starts with the question, If a conduit from a starter carries the three power wires of a motor circuit and also contains three control wires run from the starter to a pushbutton station, is it necessary to derate any of the conductor ampacities?

Answer: Section 725-17(b) covers this. (Read that rule several times.) If the starter is the usual magnetically held type of contactor, the two control wires to the STOP button at the pushbutton station will carry the holding current to the coil as long as the starter is closed. Section 725-17(b) (1) says that all conductors in the raceway must be derated in ampacity if the total number of conductors (power wires plus control wires) is more than three—*but only if the Class 1 circuit conductors carry continuous loads.*

The **Code** definition for *continuous load* is: "A load where the maximum current is expected to continue for three hours or more." On that basis, derating of all the conductors (power and control wires) would be required if the starter is left closed for 3 hr or more. It may be argued, however, that because the holding current of the coil is so low (only an amp or less in most cases), the load on the control wires (for instance, No. 14) is nowhere near the ampacity of those wires and does not constitute a "maximum current" in the meaning of the definition for continuous load; therefore, derating is not required for any of the conductors—as noted in Sec. 725-17(b) (2). But it may also be argued that because the three power wires in the conduit are rated at 125 percent of motor current and protected at that value by the OL relays, such conductors could be continuously subjected to maximum operating temperature by motor overload. Under such a condition, any additional current—even 1 A in the control wires—could produce heat that would push the temperature over the limit for the particular insulation.

Because motors are not generally even fully loaded and because continuous operation of motors at 25 percent overload is extremely unlikely, it would seem unreasonable to require derating of conductors for the usual conduit with three power wires and three control wires from a magnetic starter.

Conflict: All this consideration is further confused by a conflict between part **(b)(1)** of Sec. 725-17 and Exception No. 1 to Note 8 of Table 310-16/19, which states that derating factors apply *only* to the number of "power and lighting conductors." Part **(b)(1)** says derating applies to "all conductors"—Class 1 wires as well as the power and light wires.

The certain answer to the puzzle is this: Evaluate each installation on its own conditions and circumstances. Table 310-16 gives maximum continuous current ratings with not more than three conductors in a conduit. If for any control circuit layout, there is indication that the condition of maximum temperature is likely for the power wires, then all the wires must be derated if control wires in the same conduit would be adding any heat at all—even the I^2R of very low coil current.

We should always keep in mind:

The **Code** *is a guide to safe electrical practice; it is not a design specification. Its rules must be analyzed and applied with knowledge, care, and precision.*

725-18. Physical Protection.   This rule aims at providing high reliability and protection for those remote-control circuits where damage to the circuit might cause interruption or malfunction and thereby produce some type of hazard resulting from the controlled load.

725-31. Power Limitations of Class 2 and Class 3 Circuits.   Tables 725-31(a) and (b) set the current and voltage values that define Class 2 and Class 3 remote-control, signaling, or power-limited circuits. Class 2 and Class 3 signaling, remote-control, and power-limited systems are used where the current and voltage requirements are such that it is not necessary to comply with the general requirements for light and power systems.

Current supply from primary batteries is considered as providing satisfactory current limitation as indicated by Note 2 to Table 725-31(a). Where batteries are employed to supply small bell, buzzer, or annunciator systems, it is the usual practice to use several No. 6 dry cells in series. One of these cells will deliver 25 to 30 A on short circuit but the current falls off very rapidly. It would be possible to provide a dry-cell battery that would deliver a fairly heavy current for several hours; however, such batteries are not needed for these systems, and it is therefore safe to assume that they will not be installed and that, in any practical case, supply of the system from a primary battery will provide sufficient current limitation.

Wherever AC service is available, current limitation can be provided by using so-called "current-limiting" transformers. These are transformers having so high a secondary impedance that, even on short circuit, they cannot deliver a current higher than a certain maximum. A doorbell type of transformer will provide the required current limitation for a Class 2 system. In the NEMA Specialty Transformer Standards it is stated that the open-circuit secondary voltage for a doorbell transformer shall not exceed 25 V and that the maximum input with the secondary short-circuited shall be 50 W.

The NEMA Standards include the following data applying to the type known as signaling transformers.

Output ratings: 50 and 100 VA.

Secondary open-circuit voltages for either rating: 4.4, 8.8, 13.2, 17.6, 22.0, and 26.4 volts.

Secondary short-circuit current at maximum voltage: 50-VA rating, 2.1 amp, 100-VA rating, 4.2 amp. The secondary short-circuit current at any lower voltage is proportional to the voltage.

The great majority of small bell, buzzer, and annunciator systems come under Class 2 classification, 0 to 20 V, 5 A. This will also include small intercommunicating telephone systems in which the talking circuit is supplied by a primary battery and the ringing circuit by a transformer.

The Class 2 circuit category is considered to be safe from both a fire and shock standpoint. And, generally speaking, currents of 5 mA or less represent a negligible shock hazard. The maximum power of this 150-V circuit would be approximately 0.75 W.

When the **NE Code** divided low-power control, signal, and power-limited circuits into Class 2 and Class 3, the "Preprint of the Proposed Amendments for the 1974 **National Electrical Code**" presented valuable commentary on the reasons behind the revision. The comments also assist in application of the rules. Excerpts are as follows:

725-31 defines the power limitations and overcurrent protection for Class 2 and Class 3 circuits in table form. The separation of existing Class 2 circuits reflect what is now a practical reality since UL does not, in general, list Class 2 power supplies above 30 volts ac because of shock hazard even though the **NEC** permits them. This change together with the installation requirements will allow approved Class 3 systems at voltages above 30 volts ac. The new classifications recognize the acceptability of Class 2 circuits from both a shock and fire standpoint as evidenced by experience and recognizes that Class 3 circuits control fire hazard only and thus require additional safeguards. Also it is recognized that dc is less hazardous than ac from both let-go and fibrillation effects and the classifications reflect this to include the highly desirable 48-volt dc system under Class 2.

Note 5 reflects that the historical acceptance of 30 volts was never intended for use in wet locations or where direct current was interrupted at a low frequency rate. Research work . . . supports the need for the lesser voltage limits established where wet contact is likely to occur.

The limitations permit the full 100 VA rating for power supplies irrespective of voltage as opposed to the present unnecessary restriction which permits maximum power only at the upper end of each voltage band. The maximum currents and VA outputs for ac circuits reflect the currently acceptable UL limits on presently listed Class 2 power supplies. The other limits for nontransformer supplies are considered reasonable to limit power to the same degree. It will be noted that the power limits are less restrictive where fuses are used. It will also be noted that the previous permission to derive a Class 2 circuit only from a fuse has been deleted. It was felt that a Class 2 system supplied from a source of unlimited energy and limited only by a fuse (as presently permitted, but probably rarely done in practice) should not be permitted, thus the Vmax Imax and (VA) max restrictions in Table 725-31.

With regard to overcurrent protection, where adjustable or settable it can be based on 100 VA/V rated but not to exceed 5 amperes (last column). It is not the intent to create a new line of noninterchangeable fuses: the industry standard ratings should still be used.

Important: As Table 725-31 indicates, any remote-control, signaling, or power-limited circuit operating at *less* than 30 V may only be a Class 2 circuit. All Class 3 circuits operate between 30 and 150 V.

725-34. Marking.   The UL presents data on its certification of transformer power supply units, as follows:

These transformers are intended for use in Class 2 remote control and signal circuits in accordance with the **National Electrical Code.**

The secondary open circuit voltage rating is 30 v or less.

The transformers are of two types:

Energy limiting transformer—The design is such that the short circuit current does not exceed 8 amp.

Nonenergy limiting transformer—The design includes an over-current protective device complying with the Class 2 system voltage and current limits specified in the **National Electrical Code.** The rating is 100 va or less.

The Listing Mark of Underwriters Laboratories Inc. on the product is the only method provided by UL to identify products manufactured under its Listing and Follow-Up Service. The Listing Mark for these products includes the name and/or symbol of Underwriters Laboratories Inc. (as illustrated in the Introduction of this Directory) together with the word "Listed," a control number, and the following product name: "Class 2 Transformer."

725-37. Wiring Methods on Supply Side.   Conductors and equipment on the line side of devices supplying Class 2 systems must conform to rules for general power and light wiring.

725-38. Wiring Methods on Load Side.   The present wording of this rule and its exceptions clarifies many past misunderstandings about the intent of the rule. Previous **Code** editions only mentioned raceways, porcelain tubes, or "loom" as a means of separating Class 2 circuits, such as "bell wiring," from conductors of light and power systems where such systems were closer than 2 in. And on that basis, some inspectors required such bell wiring or similar Class 2 wires to have a 2-in. clearance from any type of cable (NM, UF, AC, etc.) that contained conductors for power or lighting circuits. The old rule was also commonly applied to prohibit bell wires and NM cables in the same bored holes through studs, etc. With the present wording the 2-in. clearance from Class wiring applies only to "open" light, power, and Class 1 circuit conductors. Power and light circuits or Class 1 circuits that are in raceway or cable do not require 2-in separation from Class 2 and/or Class 3 circuits (Fig. 725-13).

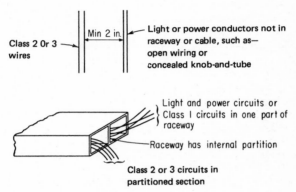

Fig. 725-13. Class 2 or Class 3 wiring must be separated from open-wiring for power and light. (Sec. 725-38.)

Class 2 or Class 3 conductors must be insulated and must be separated at least 2 in. from open power and light conductors, unless the Class 2 or Class 3 conductors are enclosed in a continuous and firmly fixed nonconductor.

Part **(a)(2)** says that Class 2 or Class 3 conductors must not be used in any raceway, compartment, outlet box, or similar fitting with light and power conductors or with Class 1 signal or control conductors, unless the conductors of the different systems are separated by a partition. But this does not apply to wires in outlet boxes or similar fittings or devices, where power-supply conductors have to be brought into supply power to the signal equipment to which the other conductors in the enclosure are connected.

In shafts, Class 2 or Class 3 conductors must be separated at least 2 in. from open power and light conductors or the conductors of either system must be encased in noncombustible tubing.

In hoistways, conductors must be installed in rigid conduit IMC or EMT, except as provided for elevators in Art. 620.

Conductors run vertically in a shaft or partition must prevent carrying of fire from floor to floor except where conductors are encased in noncombustible material or located in a fireproof shaft.

725-39. Conductors of Different Class 2 and Class 3 Circuits in Same Cable, Enclosure, or Raceway.   This rule requires separation of Class 2 and Class 3 circuits, *UNLESS* the Class 2 wires have insulation that is at least equivalent to that required for Class 3 wires.

725-40. Conductors.   Here, distinction must be made between Class 2 wiring and Class 3 wiring. Although any type of insulation is permitted for the conductors of Class 2 systems, in order to ensure continuity of service, a type of insulation should be selected which is suitable for the conditions, such as the voltage to be employed and possible exposure to moisture.

There is a marked distinction between power-limited circuits supplied by limited power sources with overcurrent protection and those without; but within the same source category, little difference exists in the power limitation.

The significant distinction between Class 2 circuits and Class 3 circuits is the character and magnitude of the voltages. The classifications of Class 2 circuits recognize their acceptability from both fire and shock hazard. Class 3 circuits recognize fire hazard only; hence the reason for more restrictive conductor and insulation requirements.

Low-voltage relay switching is a common application of Class 2 remote-control circuits regulated by Art. 725. Low-voltage relay switching is commonly used where remote control or control from a number of spread-out points is required for each of a number of small 120- or 277-V lighting or heating loads. In this type of control, contacts operated by low-voltage relay coils are used to open and close the hot conductor supplying the one or more luminaires or load devices controlled by the relay. The relay is generally a 3-wire, mechanically held, ON-OFF type, energized from a step-down control transformer.

In some cases, all the relays may be mounted in an enclosure near the panelboard supplying the branch circuits which the relays switch, with a single transformer mounted there to supply the low voltage. Where a single panelboard serves a large number of lighting branch circuits over a very large area—such as large office areas in commercial buildings—a number of relays associated with each section of the overall area may be group-mounted in an enclosure in that area.

Figure 725-14 shows 24-V control of 277-V fixtures, with constantly illuminated switchplates alongside doorways to define interior exit routes and practical hollow-partition clip-in switch boxes in interior labs of a medical research center. Control relays are in compact boxes atop luminaires. Relays are connected to switches and to 50-VA continuous-duty 120/24-V transformers by Class 2 remote-control circuits routed through overhead non-air-handling ceiling plenums and supported by insulator rings attached to fixture hangers by spring clips. Wiring of the Class 2

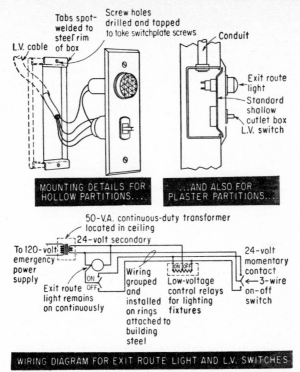

Fig. 725-14. Low-voltage relay switching is a typical application of Class 2 conductors. (Sec. 725-40.)

circuits may be done with multiwire low-voltage cable, such as 3-conductor or 4-conductor thermostat cable. Interior-area route-indicating lights and general lighting switches are mounted together in thin boxes set in partitions.

Low-voltage lighting—using recessed and/or surface-mounted fixtures containing 12-V, 20-W incandescent reflector lamps—is another application of Class 2 wiring for the power-limited circuits supplying the lamps from a transformer. In such lighting systems, which have gained popularity for interior decorative and architectural purposes, the supply transformers are available in three ratings—20 VA for one lamp, 60 VA for three lamps, and 180 VA for nine lamps. Note that the 180-VA transformer exceeds the voltampere rating of "$5.0 \times V_{max}$" for a Class 2 circuit up to 20 V. At the specified maximum voltampere rating, the 60-VA transformer (5.0×12 V) is the maximum size that complies with Table 725-31(a).

ARTICLE 750. STAND-BY POWER GENERATION SYSTEMS

750-1. Scope. It is essential to distinguish carefully between "stand-by" power sources and systems and "emergency" power sources and systems, which are covered in Art. 700. A "stand-by" source is one that supplies loads *other* than those specified in Sec. 700-1 as "systems or circuits" that are "classed as emergency" by governmental authorities that legally require provision of emergency supply. Any equipment and loads that are designated as required emergency loads *must* be supplied from one of the emergency power sources described in Sec. 700-6. And Sec. 725-13 through 725-17 must be fully satisfied. None of the equipment, circuits, or loads is permitted to be part of a "stand-by" system.

This article covers other-than-emergency alternate power systems for applications such as heating and refrigeration or communications systems where interruption of normal power would cause discomfort or damage to the product. These systems may or may not be legally required, but if they are legally required as "emergency" provisions, then Art. 700 and not Art. 750 would apply.

Because of the constant expansion in electrical applications in all kinds of buildings, the use of stand-by power sources is growing at a constantly accelerating rate. Continuity of service has become increasingly important with the widespread development of computers and intricate, automatic production processes. More thought is being given to and more money is being spent on the provision of on-site power sources to back up or supplement purchased utility power to ensure the needed continuity as well as provide for public safety in the event of utility failure.

The intent of Art. 750 is to recognize and regulate use of any permanently installed stand-by system that is not considered to be an "Emergency System" as covered in Arts. 517 or 700 of the **National Electrical Code**, or "Essential Electrical Systems for Health Care Facilities" as covered in NFPA Pamphlet No. 76A.

The most fundamental application of stand-by power is the portable alternator used for residential stand-by power where electric utility supply is not sufficiently reliable or is subject to frequent outages (Fig. 750-1). Note that a "stand-by" power load may be manually or automatically transferred from the normal supply to the "stand-by" generator. Any generator used as an "emergency" source must always have provision for automatic transfer of the load from "normal" supply to the emergency generator. But automatic transfer must be used if a stand-by power system is required by law to be installed (Sec. 750-10).

750-6. Capacity of the System. Any stand-by power source and system must be capable of fully serving its demand load. This can generally be satisfied relatively easily for generator loads. But the task can be complex for UPS systems. The uninterruptible power supply (UPS) is an all-solid-state power conversion system designed to protect computers and other

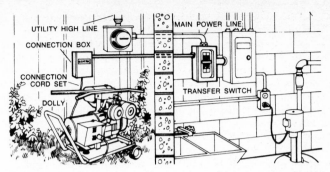

Fig. 750-1. Standby generator with manual transfer is common residential application. (Sec. 750-1.)

critical loads from blackouts, brownouts, and transients. It is usually connected in the feeder supplying the load, with bypass provisions to permit the load to be fed directly. Figure 750-2 shows a typical basic layout for a UPS system. Such a system utilizes a variety of power sources to assure continuous power. Circuits are shown for normal power operation. If normal power fails, the static switch transfers the load to the inverter

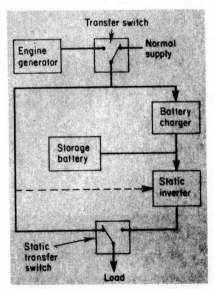

Fig. 750-2. UPS system is a common standby power system. (Sec. 750-2.)

with ¼ cycle. The battery is the power source while the engine-generator is being started. When the generator is running properly, it is brought onto the line through its transfer switch, and the static switch transfers the load to the generator supply. Dashed line indicates synchronizing signal, which maintains phase and frequency of inverter output.

Calculation of the required capacity of a UPS system must be carefully made. Data processing installations normally require medium-to-large 3-phase UPS systems ranging from 37.5 to over 2,000 kVA. Some of the typical ratings available from UPS manufacturers are 37.5 kVA/30 kW, 75 kVA/67.5 kW, 125 kVA/112.5 kW, 200 kVA/180 kW, 300 kVA/270 kW, 400 kVA/360 kW, and 500 kVA/450 kW. Larger systems are configured by paralleling two or more of these standard size single modules. Paralleling is covered below.

The necessary rating is chosen based on the size of the critical load. If a power profile itemizing the power requirements is not available from the computer manufacturer, the load may be measured using a kilowatt meter and a power-factor meter. Since UPS modules are both kVA- (apparent power) and kW- (real power) limited, a system should be specified with both a kVA and kW rating. The required kVA rating is obtained by dividing the actual load kW by the actual load power factor. For example, an actual 170-kW load with an actual 0.85 power factor would require a 200-kVA-rated UPS. The system should be specified as 200 kVA/170 kW, and the standard 200 kVA/180 kW UPS module should be selected for the application.

750-10. Legally Required Stand-by Power Generation Systems.   This rule requires determination of any building code rule or other statute that mandates use of a stand-by power system. In such cases, provisions similar to those in emergency systems must be made.

ARTICLE 760. FIRE PROTECTIVE SIGNALING SYSTEMS

760-1. Scope.   NFPA No. 71, Central Station Signaling Systems, pertains to fire protective signaling alarm services which are transmitted to a privately owned central station building from whence the fire department is notified or other action is taken as deemed adequate. The types of services provided include manual fire alarm service, guard tour supervisory service, automatic fire detection and alarm service, sprinkler system waterflow alarm, and supervisory signal service.

NFPA No. 72A, Local Protective Signaling Systems, covers provisions for supervised systems providing fire alarm or supervisory signals within the protected premises. These systems are primarily for the protection of life by indicating the necessity for evacuation of the building and secondarily for the protection of the property. The systems may provide for (1) manual fire alarm service; (2) automatic fire alarm service; (3) automatic detection of alarm or abnormal conditions in extinguishing systems, such as sprinkler and carbon dioxide; (4) watchmen's supervisory service; and (5) automatic detection of abnormal conditions in industrial processes which could result in a fire or explosion hazard affecting safety to life.

NFPA No. 72B, Auxiliary Protective Signaling Systems, provides protection to an individual occupancy or building or to a group of buildings of a single occupancy and utilizes the municipal fire alarm facilities to transmit an alarm to the fire department. An auxiliary alarm system deals with equipment and circuits in the protected property and is connected to a municipal fire alarm system to summon the fire department.

There are three types of auxiliary alarm systems, which include (1) local energy type, which provides its own power supply and is electrically isolated from the municipal alarm systems; (2) shunt type, which is electrically connected to and is an integral part of the municipal alarm system; and (3) a direct circuit, in which the alarms are transmitted over a circuit directly connected to the annunciating switchboard at the fire department headquarters.

Proprietary and local systems may be auxiliarized, in which case NFPA No. 72B would apply to the circuitry between the proprietary or local system and the transmitting device.

NFPA No. 72C, Remote Station Protective Signaling Systems, pertains to a system of electrically supervised circuits employing a direct circuit connection between signaling devices at the protected premises and signal receiving equipment at a remote station, such as a municipal fire alarm headquarters, a fire station, or another location acceptable to the authority having jurisdiction. The type of signaling services include (1) automatic fire detection and alarm service; (2) sprinkler system waterflow alarm and supervisory signal service; (3) manual fire alarm service; and (4) automatic smoke alarm service.

NFPA No. 72D, Proprietary Protective Signaling Systems, deals with electrically operated circuits designed to transmit alarms and supervisory and trouble signals for the protection of life and property to a central supervising station at the property to be protected. This system shall be maintained and tested by owner personnel or an organization satisfactory to the authority having jurisdiction.

NFPA No. 73, Public Fire Service Communications, covers the municipal fire alarm system, telephone facilities, and fire department radio facilities, all of which fulfill two principal functions; that of receiving fire alarms or other emergency calls from the public and that of retransmitting these alarms and emergency calls to fire companies and other interested agencies.

Fire alarm systems on private premises from which signals are received directly or indirectly by the communications center are covered by other NFPA standards.

NFPA No. 74, Household Fire Warning Equipment, covers the proper selection, installation, operation, and maintenance of fire warning equipment. The primary intent of this standard is to alert occupants for protection of life. This consists of a system or device which produces an audible alarm indicating the need to evacuate the premises. The types of detection devices used to sense fires are heat detectors and smoke detectors. Heat detectors should never be used by themselves, but must be used in conjunction with smoke detectors.

Many building codes and others (such as NFPA No. 501B, Mobile Homes) require at least one smoke detector located between the sleeping areas and other parts of the residence. Obviously a full-protection system, consisting of heat detectors and/or smoke detectors in each major area of the home, will give the best protection; however, one or more smoke detectors will provide a degree of protection. NFPA No. 74 should be consulted for placement and number of detection devices to be used; in addition, local building codes may require the use of full systems or individual smoke detectors.

760-4. Location and Other Articles.   The Exception to part **(d)** involves use of plastic-jacketed cables in air-handling ceilings. The same considerations are involved here as described under Sec. 725-2.

Chapter Eight

ARTICLE 800. COMMUNICATION CIRCUITS

800-1. Scope. The sections of this chapter apply basically to those systems which are connected to a central station and operate as parts of a central-station system.

The paragraph titled "Code Arrangement" of the "Introduction to the Code" states that Chap. 8, which includes Art. 800, "Communication Systems," is independent of the preceding chapters except as they are specifically referred to.

800-3. Installation of Conductors. It should be noted that the addition to "products of combustion" in part **(c)** and the requirements of the Exception to part **(d)** give authorities enforcing the Code the tools whereby they can judge whether the types of cables used in communication circuits substantially contribute to the hazards during fire conditions where fire fighters must of necessity be subjected to these products of combustion. Statistics show that most people die from smoke and products of combustion and not from the heat of fires. Because of this fact it is imperative that electrical materials which contribute products of combustion be held to a minimum. The requirements give electrical inspectors and fire marshals criteria whereby they can judge the hazards which conductors contribute to fire problems.

See discussion of the Exception to Sec. 725-2(b).

ARTICLE 810.   RADIO AND TELEVISION
EQUIPMENT

810-13. Avoidance of Contacts with Conductors of Other Systems.   For service drops and conductors on the exteriors of buildings, the requirements for insulating covering and methods of installation depend upon the likelihood of crosses occurring between signal conductors and light or power conductors. Where communication wires are run on poles in streets, it is assumed that they are exposed to contact with other wires, and in Sec. 800-11, 30-mil insulation is required. But where the overhead wires are run in an alley or from building to building and kept away from streets, lighter insulation is permitted.

Where a communication system is connected to a distribution system that is entirely underground except within the block in which the building is located, and any overhead wires in alleys or attached to buildings are not likely to become crossed with light or power wires, nearly all restrictions as to insulating covering and methods of installation are eliminated. The minimum thickness of insulation called for in Sec. 800-21 and the bushings specified in Sec. 800-11 are not required under these conditions.

810-14. Splices.   The antenna may unavoidably be so located that in case of a break in the wire it may come in contact with electric light or power wires. For this reason, the wire should be of sufficient size to have considerable mechanical strength, and the joints should be as reliable as the wire. Joints will have sufficient mechanical strength if properly made with the standard double-tube connectors used in telephone and telegraph work.

810-19. Electric Supply Circuits Used in Lieu of Antenna—Receiving Stations.   The device referred to usually consists of a small fixed capacitor connected between one wire of the lighting circuit and the antenna terminal of the receiving set. As most receiving sets are arranged, a breakdown in this capacitor would result in a short circuit to ground through the antenna coil of the set, and the capacitor should therefore be one that is designed for operation at 300 V or higher in which mica is used as the dielectric so that it will have a high factor of safety.

810-20. Antenna Discharge Units—Receiving Stations.   Where the lead-in is enclosed in a continuous metallic shield, i.e., is run in rigid conduit or electrical metallic tubing, or consists of a lead-covered conductor or pair of conductors, and the metallic enclosure is well grounded, a lightning discharge will usually jump from the lead-in conductor to the metallic shield, because this path to ground offers a much lower impedance than the path through the antenna coil of the receiving set. A lightning arrester is therefore not required where the lead-in is so shielded.

810-21. Grounding Conductors—Receiving Stations.   In order to avoid potential differences between various masses of metal, in or on buildings, and lead-in conductors, the metal portions of antenna masts should never be grounded to soil pipes, soil vent pipes, metal gutters, downspouts, etc. In other words, grounding must be done in accordance with Art. 250, and it is required to use the same grounding electrode for the grounding of masts as for the electrical system in the building.

810-54. Clearance on Building.   The creepage distance is the distance from the conductor to the building measured on the surface of the supporting insulator. The air gap is the distance measured straight across from the conductor to the building.

810-57. Antenna Discharge Units—Transmitting Stations.   A transmitting station should be protected against lightning, either by an arrester or by a switch that connects the lead-in to ground and is kept closed at all times when the station is not in operation.

Chapter Nine

A. TABLES

Tables 1, 3A, 3B, and 3C do not apply where short conduit sleeves are used to protect various types of cables from physical damage.

While Note 2 mentions bare (as well as insulated) equipment grounding conductors, Note 4 to **Code** Table 1 applies to all forms of *bare* conductors (equipment grounding conductors and neutral or grounded conductors). Where any bare conductors are used in conduit or tubing, the dimensions given in Table 8 may be used. Since *all* wires utilize space in raceways, they must be counted in calculating raceway sizes whether the conductors are insulated or bare. The only exception to this is in the footnote to Table 350-3 for short lengths of $3/8$-in. flexible metal conduit.

In regard to Note 4 there are conductors (particularly high-voltage types) that do not have dimensions listed in Chap. 9. Conduit sizes for such conductors may be determined by computing the cross-sectional area of each conductor as follows:

$$D^2 \times 0.7854 = \text{cross-sectional area}$$

where D = outside diameter of conductor, including insulation. Then the proper conduit size can be determined by applying Tables 1 and 4 for the appropriate number of conductors.

example: Three single-conductor 5-kV cables are to be installed in conduit. The outside diameter (D) of each conductor is 0.750 in. Then $0.750^2 \times 0.7854 \times 3 = 1.3253$ sq in. From Tables 1 and 4 (40 percent fill) a 2-in. conduit would be required. Code Tables 3A, 3B, and 3C are based on Table 1 allowable percentage fills, and have been provided for the sake of convenience. In any calculation, however, Table 1 is the table to be used where any conflict may occur in Tables 3A, 3B, or 3C.

Table 1 is also used for computing conduit sizes where various sizes of conductors or conductor types are to be used in the same conduit. Tables 1, 3A, 3B, and 3C apply to new work or rewiring, exposed or concealed.

An example of Note 3 would be to determine how many No. 14 Type TW conductors would be permitted in a ½-in. conduit. For three or more such conductors, Table 1 permits a 40 percent fill. From Table 4, 40 percent of the internal cross-sectional area of a ½-in. conduit is 0.12 sq in. From Table 5 (column 5) the cross-sectional area of a No. 14 type TW conductor is 0.0135 sq in. Thus 0.12/0.0135 = 8.8, or 9 such conductors would be permitted in a ½-in. conduit. Where the decimal is less than 0.8 (such as 0.7), the decimal would be dropped and the whole number would be the maximum number of equally sized conductors permitted; e.g., 8.7 would be 8 conductors.

The following is an example for computing a conduit size for various conductor sizes:

Number	Wire Size and Type	Table 5 Cross-sectional Area (ea.)	Subtotal Cross-sectional Area
3	No. 10 TW	0.0224	0.0672
3	No. 12 TW	0.0172	0.0516
3	No. 6 TW	0.0819	0.2457
		Total cross-sectional area	0.3645

Table 1 permits a 40 percent fill for three or more conductors. Following the 40 percent column in Table 4, 1¼-in. conduit or tubing would be required for these nine conductors, which have a combined cross-sectional area of 0.3645 sq in.

B. EXAMPLES

In Chap. 9, part **B**, the NE Code offers sample calculations using Code rules to determine load currents for several types of occupancies. It has been our experience that much confusion and many questions arise in applying the provisions of Arts. 220 and 230 to computing branch-circuit, feeder, and service loads in single-family residences. Accordingly, we shall devote the remainder of this article to exploring in detail NE Code examples of sizing the services and circuits for single-family dwellings (including individual apartments in multifamily dwellings), with and without air-conditioning units and including the optional calculations permitted by part **C** of Art. 220.

Two general procedures spelled out at the beginning of part **B**, Chap. 9, involve voltage values to be used and the method of handling fractions of an ampere in the calculations.

Voltage designations vary throughout the **NE Code**—systems may be designated as 230/115 V, 240/120 V, etc. To standardize calculations, however, part **B** of Chap. 9 specifies that nominal voltages of 230 and 115 V are to be used in computing the ampere load on a conductor. [Dividing these voltages into the watts load will produce higher current values than would 240 and 120 V, thus resulting in larger (safer) conductor sizes.]

Where a particular calculation produces a current value involving a fraction of an ampere, the fraction may be dropped if it is 0.5 or less. Presumably, a value such as 20.7 A should be continued to be used as 20.7. We have chosen here to round off such values as the next higher whole number, in this case 21 A. Again, this is on the safe side. There are occasions, however, when current values must be added together. In such cases, it is on the safe side to retain fractions less than 0.5, since several fractions added together can result in the next whole ampere.

It is assumed that the loads in the following examples are properly balanced on the system. If they are not properly balanced on the system, additional feeder capacity may be required.

Now, into the calculations.

Example No. 1. Single-Family Dwelling.   The basic dwelling we will consider here is assumed to have a total usable floor area of 1,500 sq ft. As indicated in Sec. 220-2(b), when load is determined on a watts/square feet basis, those areas not used as normal living quarters are excluded from the area calculation. Open porches, garages, unfinished basements and attics, and unused areas are not counted as part of the house area. Area calculation is made using the *outside* dimensions of the "building, apartment, or other area involved."

example: A two-story dwelling 30 by 25 ft. First and second floors 30 by 25 ft by 2 = 1,500 sq ft. The "floor" area is computed from the "outside" dimension of the building and multiplied by the number of floors. [Section 220-2(b).]

Cooking will be done using a 12-kW electric range.

The steps taken in arriving at the branch-circuit and feeder loads follow.

General Lighting Circuits

Because lighting usage in dwelling occupancies is a random, noncontinuous application—with no control over sizes and types of light bulbs—

the **Code** simply requires that a minimum amount of branch-circuit capacity be provided. Based on experience, the minimum required branch-circuit capacity will accommodate a fairly heavy and extensive use of general-purpose lighting fixtures in a home. Of course, if a given dwelling is provided with an unusually heavy amount of built-in indoor and outdoor lighting, then the provision of specific branch circuits for the loads is the best design approach.

Calculation of the **Code** minimum required branch-circuit capacity for general lighting is done also to determine the required capacity in feeders and service-entrance conductors.

In Sec. 220-2(b), the **NE Code** requires a minimum unit load in watts/ square feet for general lighting in the various types of occupancies listed in Table 220-2(b). For a dwelling occupancy (other than a hotel), circuit capacity for general lighting must be not less than 3 W/sq ft times the square-foot area of usable living space. For the dwelling in this example, *minimum capacity for general lighting* would be

$$1,500 \text{ sq ft} \times 3 \text{ W/sq ft or } 4,500 \text{ W}$$

When the total load capacity of branch circuits for general lighting is known, it is a simple matter to determine how many lighting circuits are needed. By dividing the total load by 115 V, the total current capacity of circuits is determined:

$$\frac{4,500 \text{ W}}{115 \text{ V}} = 39.1 \text{ A}$$

Then, using either 15-A or 20-A, 2-wire, 115-V circuits (and dropping the fraction of an ampere),

$$\frac{39 \text{ A}}{15 \text{ A}} = 2.6$$

which means three 15-A circuits.

$$-\text{OR}-$$
$$\frac{39 \text{ A}}{20 \text{ A}} = 1.95$$

which means two 20-A circuits.

Small-Appliance Circuits

The next step is to provide for 20-A, 2-wire circuits to supply *only* receptacle outlets in the kitchen, pantry, breakfast room, dining room, and family room. Section 220-3(b) requires a minimum of *two* such small-appliance circuits.

In addition, Sec. 220-3(c) requires at least one 20-A, 2-wire appliance circuit for the receptacle outlet required by Sec. 210-25(b) at the laundry location.

Range Circuit

A branch circuit for the 12-kW range is selected in accordance with Note 4 of Table 220-19, which says that the branch circuit load for a range may be selected from the table itself. Under the heading "Number of Appliances," read across from 1. The maximum demand to be used in sizing the range circuit for a 12-kW range is shown under the heading "Maximum Demand" to be not less than 8 kW. The minimum rating of the range-circuit ungrounded conductors will thus be

$$\frac{8,000 \text{ W}}{230 \text{ V}} = 34.78 \text{ or } 35 \text{ A}$$

Table 310-16 shows that the minimum size of copper conductors that may be used is No. 8 (TW—40 A, THW—45 A, XHHW or THHN—50 A). No. 8 is also designated in Sec. 210-19(b) as the minimum size of conductor for any range rated 8¾ kW or more. And the UL regulation calls for 60°C circuit conductors up to 100 A—or use of 75°C or 90°C conductors at the ampacity of the corresponding size of 60°C conductor.

The overload protection for this circuit of No. 8 TW conductors would be 40-A *fuses or a* 40-A *circuit breaker.* THW or THHN or XHHW conductors must be used as if they are TW (60°C) wires and should not be protected at their higher ampacities.

Although the two hot legs of the 230/115-V, 3-wire circuit must be not smaller than No. 8, Exception No. 1 of Sec. 210-19(b) permits the neutral conductor to be smaller, but it specifies that it must have an ampacity not less than 70 percent of the ampacity of the hot (ungrounded) legs and may never be smaller than No. 10.

For the range circuit in this example, the neutral may be rated

$$70 \text{ percent} \times 40 \text{ A (TW is used)} = 28 \text{ A}$$

This calls for a *No. 10 neutral.*

If THHN or XHHW conductors are used for the hot legs, they must be used as 40-A wires, which calls for the No. 10 neutral. The No. 10 neutral would be acceptable for *any* of the conductor insulations (Fig. 1).

Service Conductors

After calculating the required circuits for all the loads in the dwelling, the next step is to determine the minimum required size of service-entrance conductors to supply the entire connected load.

The **NE Code** procedure is the same as sizing feeder conductors for the entire load—as set forth in Sec. 220-10. Basically, the service "feeder"

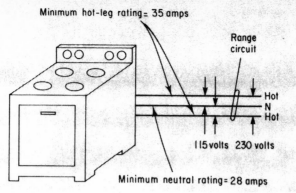

Fig. 1. Neutral for range is only 70 percent of ampacity of hot legs. (Chap. 9.)

capacity must be not less than the sum of the loads on the branch circuits for the different applications.

The *general lighting load* is subject to demand factors from Table 220-11, which takes into account the fact that simultaneous operation of all branch-circuit loads, or even a large part of them, is highly unlikely. Thus, feeder capacity does not have to equal the connected load.

Sections 220-16(a) and (b) permit the *small appliance loads* to be added to the general lighting load before applying the demand factor from Table 220-11.

General lighting	
[Three 15-A or two 20-A circuits]	4,500 W
Kitchen appliance load (two circuits)	
[1,500 W/circuit, Sec. 220-16(a)]	3,000 W
Laundry load	
[One circuit, Sec. 220-16(b)]	1,500 W
Total	9,000 W

Then the demand factors are applied:

3,000 W at 100 percent	3,000 W
900–3,000 W at 35 percent	2,100 W
Basic feeder load	5,100 W

The feeder demand load for the 12-kW range must be added to the 5,100 W. As stated in Sec. 220-19, the range feeder demand load is selected from Code Table 220-19. In this case, it is 8 kW (column A, one appliance).

Basic load	5,100 W
Range feeder capacity	8,000 W
Total feeder load	13,100 W

The minimum required ampacity of the ungrounded service-entrance conductors of a 230/115-V, 3-wire, single-phase service is readily found by dividing the *total feeder load* by 230 V:

$$\frac{13,100 \text{ W}}{230 \text{ V}} = 56.96 \text{ or } 57 \text{ A}$$

Although a load current of that rating could be readily supplied by No. 4 copper TW, THW, THHN, or XHHW conductors, there is an important provision of Sec. 230-41(b) (2) that comes into play here. Where the initial computed total feeder load is 10 kW or more for a single-family dwelling, the ungrounded conductors of a service feeder must be rated at least 100 A; i.e., **the minimum capacity of the service-entrance hot legs = 100 A** (Fig. 2).

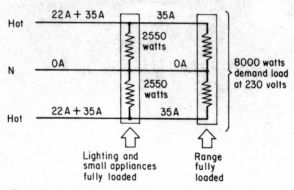

Fig. 2. Service hot legs are based on total demand load. (Chap. 9.)

That would call for a minimum of one of the following:
- No. 1 TW copper conductors (110 A)
- No. 1 THW copper conductors (130 A)
- No. 1 THHN copper conductors (140 A)
- No. 1 XHHW copper conductors (140 A)
- No. 1/0 TW, THW, THHN, or XHHW aluminum conductors (100 to 125 A)

IMPORTANT NOTE: It is a basic UL requirement that switches, CBs, and panelboards be listed *only* with 60°C conductors in ratings up to 100 A, unless any such piece of equipment is marked to indicate its use with conductors of higher temperature rating. The terminals on switches and breakers used as service equipment require the use of TW wire, in this case; or if higher temperature wires are used (THW, THHN, XHHW), they must be used at the ampacity of the corresponding size of TW wire. It would violate that UL rule to use No. 2 or No. 3 copper THW wire at its 115-A or 110-A rating for the service conductors, because TW wire in those sizes does not have a 100-A rating and would operate too hot with a 100-A load on it. Of course, in the example here, the calculated demand load current is only 57 A, and the 100-A rating of service-entrance conductors is dictated by the **Code** on the basis of experience with load additions over the life of the system. But when and if demand load does come up to 100 A, effective operation of a 100-A service CB or fused switch or panelboard would then require that the thermal condition at terminals not exceed that produced when the 100-A demand load is supplied by TW (60°C) conductors rated 100 A. In any situations that pose difficulty in correlating **NE Code** rules and UL limiting conditions, it is in the best interests of real, long-time economy and reliable life of equipment to resolve all choices of conductor selection in favor of larger size and greater adequacy. Certainly, experience indicates that far too many services have to be increased in capacity shortly after installation simply because initial design was skimpy or based on squeezing as much as possible out of "apparent" ratings of equipment.

Service Neutral

Because a neutral conductor of a 3-wire, single-phase service carries only the unbalance (or difference in) current of the two hot legs, the **NE Code** does permit the very realistic reduction of neutral conductor size from the size of the service hot legs.

Section 220-22, which covers sizing of any feeder neutral, also applies to the neutral of a service. The neutral must have an ampacity at least equal to the maximum unbalance of loads connected from the two hot legs to the neutral. This load is taken to be "the maximum connected load between the neutral and any one ungrounded conductor" (hot leg). On a service of the type considered here, it is assumed that all the 115-V loads will be divided between the two hot legs, with one half connected from one hot leg to neutral and the other half connected from the other hot leg to neutral. Section 220-3(d) requires loads to be evenly proportioned among the branch circuits to assure optimum sharing of load by the hot legs of the service (Fig. 3). Thus, in the example here, half of the 5,100-W basic demand load for the 115-V loads can be considered connected from either hot leg to neutral and that would require ampacity in the neutral of

$$\frac{5,100 \text{ W}}{2} \div 115 \text{ V} = 22.17 \text{ A}$$

Then, in addition, the neutral must have capacity for some unbalance in the 3-wire, 230/115-V circuit to the 12-kW range. Section 220-22 notes that the feeder neutral load (i.e., the required ampere capacity in the neutral service-entrance conductor) may be taken to be "70 percent of the load on the ungrounded conductors." This recognizes that use of a

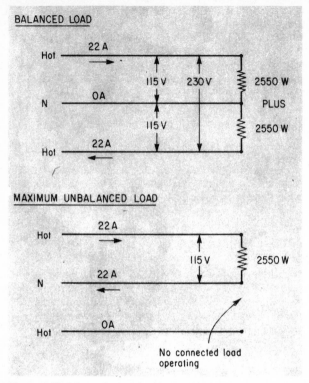

BALANCED LOAD

Hot — 22 A →

115 V   230 V   2550 W

N — 0 A — PLUS

115 V   2550 W

Hot — 22 A ←

MAXIMUM UNBALANCED LOAD

Hot — 22 A →

115 V   2550 W

N — 22 A ←

Hot — 0 A

No connected load operating

Fig. 3. Half of the total 115-V load is considered to be from hot leg to neutral. (Chap. 9.)

range usually has some load connected from each hot leg to neutral, requiring the neutral to carry *only* the unbalance. From the above calculation of the current load on the hot legs of the range branch circuit (using an 8,000-W demand load), it was found that the load was 35 (actually 34.78) A. Then, as shown in Fig. 4 the feeder neutral ampacity for the range load must be not less than

$$70 \text{ percent} \times 34.78 \text{ A} = 24.35 \text{ A}$$

Adding the two values of minimum neutral conductor ampacity for the two different loads, the total minimum required neutral conductor ampacity is determined:

Neutral load, lights and appliances .... 22.17 A

Neutral load, range circuit .... 24.35 A

Total neutral load .... 46.52 A

Since 0.52 is greater than 0.5, the total neutral load should be rounded off to 47 A. From the above, it is evident that some judgment must be exercised in dropping fractions. If the two contributions to the neutral load had been rounded off to 22 and 24 A, respectively, the total would have been 46 instead of 47. We chose to stay with the larger value since, if it ultimately makes any difference at all, it will be in the safe direction.

Of course, as with so many other calculations, there is more than one way to arrive at the same result. For instance, the total lighting and appliance load can be added to the total range demand load modified by its 70 percent neutral demand factor, and the grand total divided by 230 V to get the required amp capacity of the service neutral:

Lighting and small appliance load . . . .   5,100 W
Range load (8,000 W × 70 percent) . . . .   5,600 W

Total . . . . .10,700 W

Then, since that is the total load that forms the basis for feeder unbalance to determine the required neutral capacity, there are two ways to determine the neutral load.

1. Under conditions of maximum possible unbalance, half of that total divided by 115 V yields the result:

$$\frac{10,700 \text{ W}}{2} \div 115 \text{ V} = 46.52 \text{ or } 47 \text{ A}$$

—OR—

2. Simply take the total load and divide it by 230 V, giving the same result:

$$\frac{10,700 \text{ W}}{230 \text{ V}} = 46.52 \text{ or } 47 \text{ A}$$

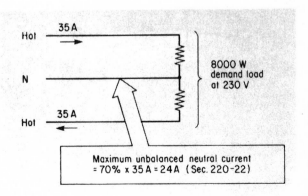

Fig. 4. Range neutral load is taken at 70 percent of hot leg current. (Chap. 9.)

Selection of the neutral conductor can then be made from Table 310-16 as required for either copper or aluminum conductor in raceway or service cable, with 60°C insulation or higher-temperature conductors of the same size as required for a 60°C conductor. The above calculations dictate the following conductor choices for this example:

Copper: Not less than No. 6 (TW, THW, THHN, XHHW)
Aluminum: Not less than No. 4 (TW, THW, THHN, XHHW)

Single-Family Dwelling with Air-Conditioning Units

Example No. 1(a) in Chap. 9 of the NE Code (page 590) deals with the same dwelling as the previous example (1,500 sq ft of living space and a 12-kW range) plus one 6-A, 230-V room air-conditioning unit and three 12-A, 115-V room air-conditioning units. The approach to the calculations is the same as the preceding example, with simple addition of the extra loads. The amp loadings on the two hot legs and the neutral break down as shown in handbook Table 1.

Table 1

Line A (One Hot Leg), amps	Neutral Leg, amps	Line B (Other Hot Leg), amps	Load
57	47	57	From first example
6	—	6	One 230-V A/C
12	12	12	Two 115-V A/C
—	12	12	Third 115-V A/C
3	3	3	25% largest motor load
78	74	90	Totals

Because the unit air conditioners are all cord-and-plug-connected units, each may be treated as a single motor load of the A/C unit's nameplate rating. Room air conditioners are considered to be fixed appliances and must be added into required service-entrance conductor capacity as required by Sec. 220-17. As indicated in the listing above, the 6-A, 230-V A/C unit places a 6-A load on each service hot leg but has no effect on neutral capacity because it has no neutral supply conductor. The three 115-V units are divided as shown on the two service hot legs—one 115-V unit connected from Line A to neutral and two 115-V units connected from Line B to neutral. Because maximum unbalance of those loads would exist when the two units on Line B are running and the one unit on Line A is off, the current drawn by the neutral under that condition would be 24 A to match the 24 A (12 + 12) drawn by the two units on Line B. Thus, 24 A of load capacity must be added to the 46-A neutral load originally calculated.

Section 430-24, on sizing of conductors supplying several motors, requires that such conductors have an ampacity equal to the sum of the full-load current ratings of all the motors plus 25 percent of the highest-rated motor in the group. In the listing above, the nameplate current values for the A/C units are shown added to each hot leg (18 A on Line A and 30 A on Line B). Then, because the 12-A-rated 115-V units have the highest current rating of the motors, a value of 3 A (25 percent × 12 A) is added to each hot leg. A load of 3 A is also added to the neutral because the 12-A motor load is connected hot-leg-to-neutral, and the neutral is part of the motor circuit and thus is a conductor "supplying several motors."

Note that the calculated demand load here (78 A for Line A and 90 A for Line B) is within the minimum 100-A required rating of service conductors from Sec. 230-41(b) (2). The service hot-leg conductors will be the same minimum size and type as indicated for the previous example (No. 1 TW copper or No. 1/0 TW aluminum).

The neutral conductor for the service conductors to this house will have to be rated for not less than 73 A. Such a neutral conductor would be:

No. 3 copper TW, THW, THHN or XHHW; or
No. 2 aluminum TW, THW, THHN, or XHHW.

INDEX

Numbers in boldface refer to article numbers; all other numbers refer to pages.

1

**Numbers in boldface refer to article numbers; all other numbers
refer to pages.**

**Numbers in boldface refer to article numbers; all other numbers
refer to pages.**

**Numbers in boldface refer to article numbers; all other numbers
refer to pages.**

**Numbers in boldface refer to article numbers; all other numbers
refer to pages.**

**Numbers in boldface refer to article numbers; all other numbers
refer to pages.**

**Numbers in boldface refer to article numbers; all other numbers
refer to pages.**

**Numbers in boldface refer to article numbers; all other numbers
refer to pages.**

**Numbers in boldface refer to article numbers; all other numbers
refer to pages.**

Numbers in boldface refer to article numbers; all other numbers refer to pages.

Numbers in boldface refer to article numbers; all other numbers refer to pages.

Numbers in boldface refer to article numbers; all other numbers refer to pages.

Numbers in boldface refer to article numbers; all other numbers refer to pages.

Numbers in boldface refer to article numbers; all other numbers refer to pages.

Numbers in boldface refer to article numbers; all other numbers refer to pages.

Numbers in boldface refer to article numbers; all other numbers refer to pages.

Numbers in boldface refer to article numbers; all other numbers refer to pages.

**Numbers in boldface refer to article numbers; all other numbers
refer to pages.**

**Numbers in boldface refer to article numbers; all other numbers
refer to pages.**

**Numbers in boldface refer to article numbers; all other numbers
refer to pages.**

Numbers in boldface refer to article numbers; all other numbers refer to pages.

**Numbers in boldface refer to article numbers; all other numbers
refer to pages.**

**Numbers in boldface refer to article numbers; all other numbers
refer to pages.**

**Numbers in boldface refer to article numbers; all other numbers
refer to pages.**

**Numbers in boldface refer to article numbers; all other numbers
refer to pages.**

Numbers in boldface refer to article numbers; all other numbers refer to pages.

Numbers in boldface refer to article numbers; all other numbers refer to pages.

**Numbers in boldface refer to article numbers; all other numbers
refer to pages.**

Numbers in boldface refer to article numbers; all other numbers refer to pages.

Numbers in boldface refer to article numbers; all other numbers refer to pages.

Numbers in boldface refer to article numbers; all other numbers refer to pages.

**Numbers in boldface refer to article numbers; all other numbers
refer to pages.**

**Numbers in boldface refer to article numbers; all other numbers
refer to pages.**

Numbers in boldface refer to article numbers; all other numbers refer to pages.

Numbers in boldface refer to article numbers; all other numbers refer to pages.

**Numbers in boldface refer to article numbers; all other numbers
refer to pages.**

Numbers in boldface refer to article numbers; all other numbers refer to pages.

**Numbers in boldface refer to article numbers; all other numbers
refer to pages.**

**Numbers in boldface refer to article numbers; all other numbers
refer to pages.**

Numbers in boldface refer to article numbers; all other numbers refer to pages.

Numbers in boldface refer to article numbers; all other numbers refer to pages.

**Numbers in boldface refer to article numbers; all other numbers
refer to pages.**

**Numbers in boldface refer to article numbers; all other numbers
refer to pages.**

Numbers in boldface refer to article numbers; all other numbers refer to pages.

Numbers in boldface refer to article numbers; all other numbers refer to pages.

**Numbers in boldface refer to article numbers; all other numbers
refer to pages.**

Numbers in boldface refer to article numbers; all other numbers refer to pages.

Numbers in boldface refer to article numbers; all other numbers refer to pages.